GREEK
ISLAND
HOPPING
2012

Frewin Poffley

GREEK
ISLAND
HOPPING
.COM

Text & Artwork: © 2012 Frewin Poffley

Printed and distributed through Thomas Cook Publishing,
The Thomas Cook Business Park,
Coningsby Road, Peterborough, PE3 8SB, United Kingdom

E-mail: books@thomascook.com
Advertising sales: 01733 (+44 1733) 416477

Distributed in the USA by The Globe Pequot Press
PO Box 480, Guilford, Connecticut 06437

ISBN   978-1-84848-552-5

Published annually
ISSN   1362-0002

Whilst every care has been taken in compiling this publication using
the most up-to-date information available at the time of going to press,
neither the author nor Thomas Cook can accept any liability arising
from errors or omissions in the text or maps, however caused. Readers
should note especially that timings and fares of many Mediterranean
ferry services are fixed only shortly before the beginning of the season
and are often subject to change without notice. It is therefore strongly
advised that all such information should be checked before beginning
any journey on one of the services listed in this publication. The views
and opinions expressed in this book are not necessarily those of
Thomas Cook Publishing or those of Thomas Cook Group plc.

Printed and bound by Nutech Print Services, India.

Drawn & typeset by Frewin Poffley/Thingumajigolo Productions

Contents

How to Use this Book

While everybody has heard of Greek island hopping, if you have yet to try it, the notion of booking a flight to Greece and then wandering between islands you have only vaguely heard of (complete with funny names written in an even more unintelligible looking alphabet) can seem a rather daunting prospect. In fact, once you understand how the Greek ferry system works and how respective islands are linked together, you will find that it is remarkably easy.

That said, those who go Greek island hopping (be they novice or a seasoned veteran) can never be said to be lacking a challenge. For Greece is a country apart. Thanks to good international ferry links and a very competitive domestic ferry system (to say nothing of small intimate islands touched by 4,000 years of history and populated with friendly islanders long used to speaking English), it offers the best island hopping in the Mediterranean. But there are problems, not least of which is Greece's inability to publish ferry timetables despite having a large fleet that carries 10 million passengers each year. Protected by cabotage laws that prevented foreign competition until late 2002 (the first foreign operator only appeared in 2005 and few

have followed since), ferry companies chop and change boats and services seemingly at random (though in fact most boats use similar routes each summer). As a result, that the majority of tourists stick to a few well-trodden routes, while guidebooks to the Greek islands concentrate on the islands themselves while glossing over the means of travelling between them.

This book attempts to address this imbalance and give you the facts you need to move around with ease. In addition to the usual sightseeing information, it contains a synopsis of the ferry network around the Greek islands (as well as other international services in the Mediterranean). It is therefore oriented towards showing you *how* to get around, as well as telling you what you will find when you get there. It has been designed to answer the questions:

'Where can I go to?'

'How can I get there?'

'What will I find there?'

'Where can I hop to from there?'

In this guide chapters are determined by the main ferry routes. These are followed by a **Port Table** section showing typical High Season departures from the Islands and Mainland Ports covered in the book. At the back of the guide is a **Reference** section containing ferry company information (including a ferry colour key), a **Useful Greek** section and the **Index.**

For ease of use chapters are divided into three sections:

1

**Overview
& Itinerary**

The initial — 'Where can I go to?' — section of each chapter is intended to give you a clear idea of the geographical area covered by the chapter and the best means of tackling the islands and ports within it. On the title page itself you will find a map showing the main ferry route linking the islands, along with approximate sailing times between them (using regular ferries) and the island name in Greek (in the form — usually the accusative case — that you are most likely to encounter it on ship destination boards and ticket agency timetables). This is followed by a brief description of the characteristics of the group, a map of the area covered, and a model itinerary showing a practical way of tackling the islands in the chain. The itinerary also identifies the best home or 'base' port in the group should you wish to use one island as a springboard to viewing the rest.

2

**Ferry
Services**

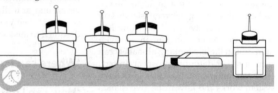

The second — 'How can I get there?' — section is devoted to the ferries that link the islands within each group. (Where a ferry's itinerary includes islands and ports split between several lines-cum-chapters it is described in the chapter in which it plays the most important role.) Each boat's previous High Season route is mapped, and the accompanying text lists the owning company, year of build (and rebuild, if any), and gross registered tonnage (GRT). In addition, there are comments on each ferry's history, reliability and likely changes in 2012. This will give you the means to interpret local advertising and assess the merits or otherwise of the individual boats.

You should find that all ferries are covered bar the four or five last-minute arrivals that turn up out of the blue each summer. Usually these new arrivals are not too much of a problem since they tend to either line up in competition with an existing service or simply replace it.

More of a handicap are the periodic fleet reshuffles which can result in up to four or five boats swapping (and adapting) itineraries and giving the appearance of far more substantive change than there really is.

3
Islands & Ports

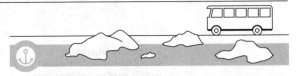

The third — 'What will I find there?' — section consists of a mini A–Z of the Islands and Ports found within the chapter area. All islands, mainland ports and the major sights are briefly described. The 60-odd islands large enough to warrant a ferry link also have an accompanying map showing typical High Season *weekday* bus and beach boat services, along with town maps identifying the important landmarks and places to stay.

Port Tables

The greatest difficulty in moving around the Greek islands is not knowing the frequency of connections between specific ports. This section of the guide is designed to clue you in on the 'hopping' potential of each port and the ships sailing from them. The Port Tables show *typical* High Season ferry departure times as well as offering **Connections Maps** showing High Season frequency of service to other ports of call.

Working within the constraints imposed by much last-minute summer scheduling by Greek ferry operators, this Port Table section of the book is *not* intended to be a timetable, but a guide that you can usefully employ to hop freely between islands and ports or to adjacent islands from your holiday base. The tables — showing services operating in 2011 (updated with the latest information where available) — are intended to give you the means of determining what is happening and the likely options available when you arrive at any port during 2012, and (given the constraints outlined on p. 32) through to 2013.

Planning an Itinerary

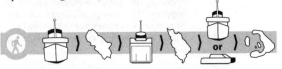

Flexibility is the key to a successful island hopping holiday. Publilius Syrus' natty apophthegm *'It is a bad plan that admits of no modification'* was surely stylused with Greek island hopping in mind. Pre-planning an itinerary around the islands is perfectly practical, provided a number of points are borne in mind:

**Decide where you
would like to go, but leave
the details until you get to Greece**

Armed with a book like this in the pre-holiday enthusiasm it is very easy to over-plan. It is far better to make a hit list of the four or five islands you simply must get to and then a list of those you would also like to see, and thereafter keep your plans reasonably fluid; you can add precise boats and times when you get to your first port of call and establish which are running.

Build a two-week itinerary along the lines of 'on Tuesday we'll arrive at the port at 14.20, giving us a free 20 minutes to sup a pint of ouzo before catching the 14.45 boat', and the chances are you will come unstuck sooner rather than later. You would also end up extremely drunk. Greece is a casual country so an 'on the Tuesday afternoon or evening we'll catch a ferry' approach will be far more successful.

**Build itineraries
using 'Daily' connections**

When pre-planning, use the Port Table Connections maps (in the timetable section at the back of this book) and try to keep as many *6–7 days per week* links in your itinerary as possible, even if this means deviating from your preferred route.

Example: Rhodes to Nissiros. The Rhodes Connections map below shows that a link exists 2–3 days a week. Closer examination of the Port Table and Ferry description reveals that the primary boat operating this route has broken down in the past. The wise island hopper will note the possibility of using this service if it happens to be running when they get to Rhodes, but when pre-planning will reckon on travelling via Kos — which has a daily link with both

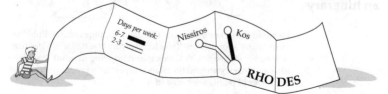

Days per week:
6–7
2–3

Nissiros   Kos

RHODES

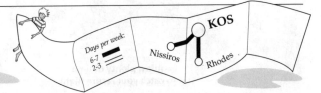

Rhodes and Nissiros (see above). The rule of thumb therefore is that *2–3 days per week* links should always be treated with suspicion: don't build an itinerary that *depends* on them — unless that link comes early enough in your holiday to make alternative plans. Similarly, if the Port Tables show that a route exists courtesy of a single boat, it pays to be aware of the vulnerability of the link to change.

**Always arrive at a
port with an Alternative Plan**

At some point in the average two-week island hopping holiday you will find yourself left high and dry on a quay waiting for a boat that for some reason or other fails to turn up. Life is far more relaxed if you have already pre-planned for such an eventuality and can blithely shrug your shoulders and say 'okay we'll do this instead…' The 'this' options usually come down to a later alternative boat, a change of route, and/or the afternoon on the nearest decent beach.

**Build in a 2-day
'delay' into your itinerary**

One of the great attractions of island hopping is that every island is different and sooner or later you will be washed up on the shores of the one the Gods made for you, tempting you to linger longer than intended. Build this into your calculations: it will also provide you with an extra safety net should weather, a fully booked ferry or lightning strike disrupt your plans.

**Allow plenty of time
to catch your return flight**

Always arrange an easily accessible final/return port of call and *allow at least one clear day spare* to ensure that you don't miss your return ferry or flight away from civilization. This is something that cannot be emphasized enough. If you are starting from a poorly connected airport give yourself two clear days: in short, always play safe — there is usually somewhere to play near your starting point so this needn't damage your holiday. If you are moving between chains (e.g. starting from the Dodecanese and moving into one of the Cycladic Lines) save the visits to islands near your return destination for the end of your holiday so that your final hops are both short and easy.

When you've used this book ...

... help us update

Greek Island Hopping is field-researched each year before being updated. Nevertheless, there will always be instances where up-to-date information was not obtainable at the time of research, and we welcome reports and comments from guide users.

Similarly, we aim to make the guide as practical and useful as possible to island hoppers and are grateful for any comments, criticisms and suggestions for improving future editions.

A free copy of the next edition of the guide, or of any other Thomas Cook publication, will be sent to all readers whose information or ideas are incorporated in future editions. Please address all contributions to:

FrewinPoffley@greekislandhopping.com
or
The Editor, Greek Island Hopping,
Thomas Cook Publishing,
PO Box 227, Peterborough, PE3 8SB, United Kingdom.

Or fax us on: 01733 416688
International: +44 1733 416688
E-mail: books@thomascook.com

ⓘ Symbols, Maps & Tables

Symbols — see front cover flap

Times — see back cover flap

Street Maps

The majority of Greek island towns do not have street names (buildings are numbered instead). The best way of using the maps in this book is to navigate via landmarks (e.g. churches & hotels)

Scale

The maps in this book use the metric system used in Greece. To convert to yards and miles:
1 metre = 1.09 yards
1 kilometre = 0.62 miles

Map Legend

┣┼┼┼┼┤	Railway			Cliff / Steep Slope
⊢▢⊢	Railway Station			Map Cross-Section
─◯─	Metro Station			Waterlogged Land
═══	Street / Path			Pedestrianized Street
▭▭▭	Staircase / Muletrack			Bridge
┄┄┄	Dirt Road			City / Castle Wall
�	Building			Ruins
	Archway			Ruins (roofed over)
▢	Park / Woodland			Line of Lost Walls
	Beach			Cemetery
	Rocks			Windmills
▯▯▯	Sports Field / Playground			
◉	Fountain / Pool			

Ferry Route Maps

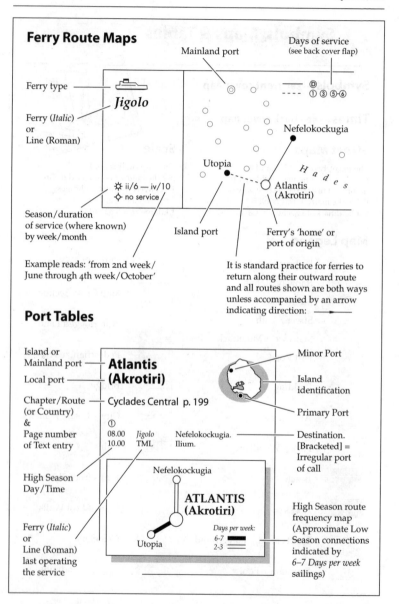

Ferry type

Jigolo

Ferry (*Italic*)
or
Line (Roman)

☀ ii/6 — iv/10
◇ no service

Season/duration
of service (where known)
by week/month

Example reads: 'from 2nd week/
June through 4th week/October'

Mainland port

Days of service
(see back cover flap)

———— Ⓓ
- - - - ① ③ ⑤-⑥

Nefelokockugia

Utopia

H a d e s

Atlantis
(Akrotiri)

Island port

Ferry's 'home' or
port of origin

It is standard practice for ferries to
return along their outward route
and all routes shown are both ways
unless accompanied by an arrow
indicating direction: ——➤

Port Tables

Island or
Mainland port

Local port

Chapter/Route
(or Country)
&
Page number
of Text entry

High Season
Day/Time

Ferry (*Italic*)
or
Line (Roman)
last operating
the service

**Atlantis
(Akrotiri)**

Cyclades Central p. 199

①
08.00 *Jigolo* Nefelokockugia.
10.00 TML   Ilium.

Nefelokockugia

**ATLANTIS
(Akrotiri)**

Days per week:
6-7 ▬▬▬
2-3 ═══

Utopia

Minor Port

Island
identification

Primary Port

Destination.
[Bracketed] =
Irregular port
of call

High Season route
frequency map
(Approximate Low
Season connections
indicated by
6–7 Days per week
sailings)

Island Bus & Beach Boat Maps

Island name/s (former name shown in light face).

ATLANTIS / KALLISTE

Symbols (from L to R):

International Ferry Connection

Base Port

Camping

Rooms available

Air, Rail, Bus connecting service

0　　km　　5

Town, Village or Hamlet (Importance indicated by the size of the text)

Upland Areas

Bus Station/s on accompanying Town Street Map

→ Athens ⓓ x 3
→ Rhodes ⓓ x 1

Domestic Flights

ⓓ 10.00

ⓓ x 6
ⓓ x 4
ⓓ x 2
▲ⓓ x 3

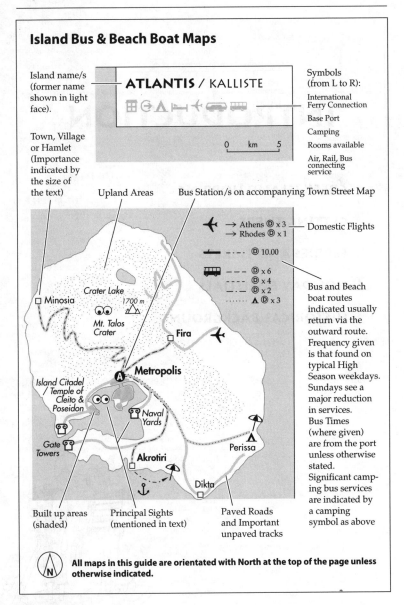

Crater Lake

Minosia

1700 m

Mt. Talos Crater

Fira

Metropolis

Island Citadel / Temple of Cleito & Poseidon

Naval Yards

Gate Towers

Akrotiri

Perissa

Dikta

Bus and Beach boat routes indicated usually return via the outward route. Frequency given is that found on typical High Season weekdays. Sundays see a major reduction in services. Bus Times (where given) are from the port unless otherwise stated. Significant camping bus services are indicated by a camping symbol as above

Built up areas (shaded)

Principal Sights (mentioned in text)

Paved Roads and Important unpaved tracks

All maps in this guide are orientated with North at the top of the page unless otherwise indicated.

INTRODUCTION

- [ ] **GREEK ISLAND HOPPING**
- [ ] **GETTING THERE**
- [ ] **FERRIES AND TICKETS**
- [ ] **HOLIDAY ESSENTIALS**
- [ ] **HISTORICAL BACKGROUND**

SIGHTSEEING ISLES

CYCLADES NORTH	DELOS
CYCLADES CENTRAL	SANTORINI NAXOS ANTIPAROS
CRETE	IRAKLION
DODEC-ANESE	RHODES KOS PATMOS
ARGO-SARONIC	AEGINA
NORTH AEGEAN	THESSALONIKA KAVALA CHIOS SAMOS SAMOTHRACE
EASTERN LINES	CHIOS SAMOS (PITHAGORIO)
IONIAN	CORFU

NIGHTLIFE ISLES

CYCLADES NORTH	MYKONOS
CYCLADES CENTRAL	IOS SANTORINI PAROS
CYCLADES WEST	SIFNOS
NORTH AEGEAN	SKIATHOS THASSOS
IONIAN	CORFU LEFKADA ZAKINTHOS
DODEC-ANESE	KOS RHODES
EASTERN LINES	SAMOS (PITHAGORIO)
ARGO-SARONIC	SPETSES

BEACH ISLANDS

CYCLADES NORTH	MYKONOS ANDROS
CYCLADES CENTRAL	IOS NAXOS PAROS SANTORINI
CYCLADES EAST	KOUFONISSIA
NORTH AEGEAN	SKIATHOS SKYROS THASSOS
IONIAN	CORFU ZAKINTHOS LEFKADA
DODEC-ANESE	KOS KARPATHOS RHODES LIPSI PATMOS
EASTERN LINES	LESBOS
ARGO-SARONIC	AEGINA
CYCLADES WEST	SERIFOS SIFNOS

WINDMILL ISLES

CYCLADES NORTH	MYKONOS
CYCLADES CENTRAL	IOS SANTORINI ANTIPAROS PAROS
CYCLADES WEST	SERIFOS KIMOLOS
EASTERN CYCLADES	ASTIPALEA

PICTURESQUE 'CHORA' ISLANDS

CYCLADES NORTH	MYKONOS	NORTH AEGEAN	SKYROS
CYCLADES CENTRAL	IOS SANTORINI PAROS	CYCLADES WEST	SERIFOS SIKINOS FOLEGANDROS
EASTERN LINES	LESBOS	EASTERN CYCLADES	ASTIPALEA AMORGOS ANAFI

QUIET ISLANDS

CYCLADES WEST	FOLEGANDROS SERIFOS SIFNOS
CYCLADES NORTH	KEA ANDROS KYTHNOS
CYCLADES CENTRAL	ANTIPAROS
NORTH AEGEAN	LIMNOS SKYROS SAMOTHRACE ALONISSOS
DODEC-ANESE	NISSIROS TILOS
IONIAN	ITHACA MEGANISI
CYCLADES EAST	ALL OF THEM !

IDEAL ISLANDS
FOR MAROONING YOUR PARTNER ON WHEN THEY ARE BEING PARTICULARLY IRRITATING

CYCLADES CENTRAL	ANAFI
NORTH AEGEAN	AGIOS EFSTRATIOS
CRETE & EASTERN CYCLADES	GAVDOS
ARGO-SARONIC	ANTIKITHERA

Greek Island Hopping

Guidebooks to Greece are apt to intimidate any would-be island hopper by observing that the country has some 1,425 islands, of which 166 are inhabited. In practice, life is much simpler: Greece has **78 islands** connected by regular ferry or hydrofoil, with another 40-odd islets visited by tour or beach boats (the remaining 48 'inhabited' islands being occupied by odd monks, goat herds and the occasional shipping billionaire). You can therefore get to some 120 islands using commercial boats.

Of course, apart from the growing number of island hopping fans devoting holidays towards the goal of doing them all, in the eyes of most tourists not all these islands are *worth* a visit; but which you add to, or cross off, your list rather depends on your vision of the ideal Greek island. Herein lies the fascination of the islands, for the mix of history and geography is different on every one. It is almost as if the Olympian Gods had taken turns at trying their hands at different combinations and then laid the results down side by side to compare each in turn. Any temptation to linger is tempered by curiosity as to what one is likely to find at the next island down the line.

The Greek islands fall into six named groups. The most popular are the **Cyclades**. With 26 ferry-linked small islands, this is the group that naturally comes to mind when thinking of island hopping. Following close on behind are the 17 **Dodecanese** islands running down the Turkish coast. The other groups have less mass appeal and fewer islands, but are growing in popularity. The most frequently visited are the closely bunched Saronic Gulf islands (running south of Athens) as all can be 'done' by day trippers from the capital, while the widely scattered Eastern and Northern Aegean islands have much to offer if you have more than a fortnight at your disposal. The Ionian islands, distinguished by being the only group to lie outside the Aegean, are poorly connected with the rest of the ferry system but also have their fans.

If you are new to island hopping the first — and most important — thing that you need to appreciate is that **the Greek ferry system** is not actually geared to moving tourists between islands within any one group, but primarily exists to ferry local Greeks between the islands and Athens (over a third of the population of Greece lives in Athens and many are economic migrants from the islands, returning periodically to their family homes). This is why there is so little timetable information in the islands — the locals are not interested in moving to other islands on the line.

The ferry network that has developed as a result is best imagined as a wheel, with the 'hub' being Athens (via its ports of Piraeus and Rafina), from which radiate ten 'spokes' or chains of islands, along which ferries regularly steam up and down — usually running 24- or 48-hour return trips from Piraeus. **Cross-chain services** that enable you to jump between islands on different chains without returning to Athens also exist, but are far fewer in number. It is therefore easy to island hop between the islands along a particular chain or line, but hopping over to an island on another can, on occasions, be quite difficult.

The **frequency of boats** down each line is very tourist-dependent. The standard Low Season daily sailing between the popular islands and the capital can mushroom up to six or more once the summer crowds start arriving. The smaller, less touristed, islands tend to retain an annual twice-weekly subsidized lifeline ferry link with the capital regardless of season, with a smaller rise in the numbers of visiting summer boats.

The first decision that any island hopper therefore needs to make is which 'spoke' or chain of islands they wish to visit. This is an important decision as the islands collected in each chain combine to offer very different experiences (individual chains also vary greatly in the opportunities on offer to cross over to another chain). This guide attempts to make this task easier by grouping the Greek islands into chapters according to their regular ferry-linked chain or line (rather than the formal group to which they belong).

The chapter summaries on the next three pages and the chain/chapter map on p. 19 should help you quickly sort out which is the best chain for you. Brief descriptions of the general characteristics of each chain are followed by short sections giving:

1. The Main Islands
These are listed in their normal order of call when sailing from Piraeus.

2. High Season Cross Lines
Crossing between 'spokes' or chains can be difficult at times (though the degree of difficulty varies with the seasons). This section seeks to highlight those islands most likely to be offering the best chance to cross over to another chain. Note: other islands will also offer irregular cross-line connections via ferries, catamarans or tourist boats.

3. Computer Ticket Traps
With the exception of a few small local ferries, anyone taking to sea in Greece has tickets generated by a centralized computer booking system. This occasionally results in some island hoppers finding that they can't travel for a day or two because of fully booked ferries. This list tries to identify those islands and times when high demand for tickets is likely to cause problems in High Season (though it would be unwise to assume that it is infallible!). Apart from the Easter holiday and the last weekend in July (when many Greeks attempt to return to their home island), you shouldn't encounter more than occasional delays.

2.
Cyclades Central .... p. 128

Easily the most popular line in Greece (regularly attracting over 40% of island hopping tourists), the Cyclades Central links four very popular islands that offer everything from nightlife to nudist beaches. The chain is characterized by being overcrowded in High Season. Out of the High Season peak period of mid-July to mid-August it remains busy, but not oppressively so.

Main Islands
Paros, Naxos, Ios, Santorini.

High Season Cross Lines
Paros — Mykonos (Cyclades North)
Paros — Syros (Cyclades North)
Paros — Sifnos (Cyclades West)
Paros — Kos, Rhodes (Dodecanese)
Paros — Samos (Eastern Lines)
Naxos — Mykonos (Cyclades North)
Naxos — Amorgos (Cyclades East)
Naxos — Syros (Cyclades North)
Ios — Sikinos, Folegandros (Cyclades West)
Santorini — Sikinos, Folegandros
                                                    (Cyclades West)
Santorini — Iraklion, Sitia (Crete),
                                Kassos, Karpathos (Dodecanese)
Santorini — Kos, Rhodes (Dodecanese)

Computer Ticket Traps
Frequency of boats should ensure that missing one shouldn't delay you too much. Weekend boats from and to Athens fill up fast in August, so you should obtain tickets for these as soon as you know when you are travelling.

3.
Cyclades North .... p. 204

A much visited group thanks to over-popular Mykonos, which shares the same characteristics as the islands on the Cyclades Central Line. The other islands are relatively quiet, most visitors being Greeks. Another feature common to the islands in this chain in High Season is the very strong *meltemi* wind that rushes south down the Aegean; this chain acts as something of a wind break for the rest of the Cyclades. Daily ferries run to these islands from both Piraeus and Rafina.

Main Islands
Syros, Tinos, Mykonos, Andros.

High Season Cross Lines
Mykonos — Paros, Naxos, Ios, Santorini
(Cyclades Central)
Mykonos — Ikaria, Samos (Eastern Lines)
Mykonos — Amorgos (Cyclades East)
Syros — Kea, Kythnos (Cyclades West)
Syros — Kos, Rhodes (Dodecanese)

Computer Ticket Traps
The holy island of Tinos is subjected to an invasion of Greeks in the week of the 15th of August, when ferries are booked solid. Ferries to Tinos on Saturdays and from Tinos on Sundays are also sure to be full. Mykonos is the only other island where you could have problems; links to Paros and Athens can fill to capacity in High Season.

A collection of relatively quiet islands increasing in popularity. Most have some nightlife and at least one good beach. Ferry links with other lines are relatively poor, but catamarans have opened up extra connections in the last couple of years.

Main Islands
Kea, Kythnos, Serifos, Sifnos, Kimolos, Milos, Folegandros, Sikinos.

High Season Cross Lines
Serifos — Paros (Cyclades Central)
Folegandros — Ios, Santorini
(Cyclades Central)
Sikinos — Ios, Santorini (Cyclades Central)
Milos — Sitia (Crete)

Computer Ticket Traps
Kea, Kythnos and Serifos are so close to Athens that they see large numbers of Greek visitors at weekends. Ferries to all are likely to be heavily booked Friday evenings to Sundays.

The quietest of the Cyclades lines, and also a sub-line running out of Naxos. The islands are the least spoilt in the Cyclades, but ferry links are erratic, hampering easy hopping.

Main Islands
Amorgos, Iraklia, Schinoussa, Koufonissia, Astipalea, Anafi.

High Season Cross Lines
Amorgos — Naxos, Paros (Cyclades Central)
Amorgos — Mykonos (Cyclades North)
Astipalea — Kalimnos (Dodecanese)
Anafi — Santorini (Cyclades Central)

Computer Ticket Traps
Space limitations on the small, local ferry running from Amorgos to Mykonos could result in High Season ticket rationing.

A popular starting point for island hopping holidays, Crete sees daily overnight non-stop ferries from Piraeus (making it an 'empty' — i.e. island-free — spoke from Athens). Crete is also the termination point for a number of ferries running down other lines. The island has something to suit all tastes, with a highly developed resort-packed north coast and a scenic hinterland and south coast.

High Season Cross Lines
Iraklion — Santorini, Paros (Cyclades Central)
Iraklion — Mykonos (Cyclades North)
Iraklion — Rhodes (Dodecanese)
Iraklion — Ios (Cyclades Central)
Sitia — Santorini (Cyclades Central)
Sitia — Milos (Cyclades West)
Sitia — Kassos, Karpathos (Dodecanese)

Computer Ticket Traps
Santorini-bound catamarans often fill up to capacity in High Season thanks to day trippers holidaying in Iraklion.

Attracting 25% of island hoppers, the Dodecanese islands offer a popular contrast with the Cyclades. They feel slightly less Greek, but have much more variety and sightseeing, with some of the best nightlife and beaches. The longest chain in the Greek islands, links are reasonable, though links with other chains are limited. The islands south of Rhodes are poorly connected to the rest of the group.

Main Islands
Patmos, Leros, Kalimnos, Kos, Nissiros, Tilos, Symi, Rhodes, Kastelorizo, Chalki, Karpathos, Kassos.

High Season Cross Lines
Rhodes — Sitia, Iraklion (Crete)
Rhodes — Paros, Santorini (Cyclades Central)
Kos — Paros (Cyclades Central)
Kos — Samos (Eastern Lines)
Kalimnos — Astipalea (Cyclades East)
Patmos — Samos (Eastern Lines)

Computer Ticket Traps
Midday ferries running either way between Athens and Rhodes tend to be filled to bursting in High Season and should be booked as soon as possible.

8.

Eastern Lines .... p. 442

A quiet line: most visitors tend to be one-stop visitors as the islands are too large and out of the way to be popular with island hoppers. Piraeus ferries run to Ikaria and Samos or to Chios and Lesbos, with small ferries connecting the two sections of the chain.

Main Islands
(a) Ikaria, Samos. (b) Chios, Lesbos.

High Season Cross Lines
Lesbos — Limnos, Kavala, Alexandroupolis
                              (Northern Aegean)
Samos — Paros (Cyclades Central)
Samos — Patmos, Kalimnos (Dodecanese)
Ikaria — Paros (Cyclades Central)
Ikaria — Mykonos (Cyclades North)

Computer Ticket Traps
None known.

9.

Northern Aegean .... p. 480

A quiet and very poorly linked line, the small Sporades sub-chain (Skiathos, Skopelos and Alonissos) sees more island hoppers than the rest of the group put together although access to them is via Athens' bus or rail links. The North Aegean islands rely heavily on thrice-weekly subsidized lifeline services.

Main Islands
Skiathos, Skopelos, Alonissos, Skyros, Limnos, Thassos, Samothrace.

High Season Cross Lines
Limnos — Lesbos, Chios (Eastern Lines)
Volos — Lesbos (Eastern Lines)
Limnos — Samos (Eastern Lines)
Limnos — Kos, Rhodes (Dodecanese)

Computer Ticket Traps
Limnos—Athens ferries fill up very early: in early August you can get trapped on Limnos for several days if you are not careful.

10.

Argo-Saronic Lines .... p. 526

A group of largely small wooded islands close to Athens and the Peloponnese. The chain is best tackled day-tripping from Athens.

Main Islands
Aegina, Angistri, Poros, Hydra, Spetses, Kithera.

High Season Cross Lines
None. You will have to return to Athens or continue south to Crete.

Computer Ticket Traps
Weekend evening departures to Piraeus.

11.

Ionian Lines .... p. 564

Despite being a chain of large wooded islands with good beaches, this is the least popular group with island hoppers as links are poor (usually requiring a hop to the mainland).

Main Islands
Corfu/Kerkyra, Paxi/Paxos, Lefkada/Lefkas, Ithaca, Kefalonia, Zakinthos/Zante.

High Season Cross Lines
None. Buses to Athens from most islands.

Computer Ticket Traps
None known.

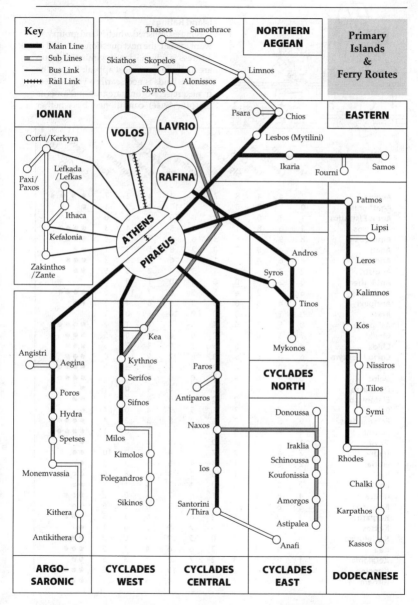

Island Ratings

Having established which island group you want to visit, the next question you need to address is which islands within the group are likely to have most appeal. Rating the Greek islands is necessarily a very subjective exercise. Not only are an island's merits (or otherwise) conditioned by whether

ISLAND RATINGS

	Main Town	Landscape	Tree Cover	Sightseeing	Nightlife	Eating	Peace & Quiet	Beaches	Nudism	Tourism Level	Summary (out of 5)
Aegina	7	4	4	8	7	7	4	4	2	7	●●●●
Agathonisi	0	1	0	0	0	2	10	0	0	1	●
Agios Efstratios	1	3	0	0	0	0	10	4	6	0	
Alonissos	3	6	8	1	2	5	5	5	4	3	●●●●
Amorgos	8	9	3	6	3	6	8	5	5	4	●●●●●
Anafi	4	4	0	2	0	2	8	5	3	1	●●
Andros	4	6	4	1	1	5	6	6	3	3	●●●
Angistri	2	3	7	0	1	3	4	2	0	5	●●
Antikithera	0	2	3	0	0	0	10	1	0	0	
Antiparos	6	4	2	4	5	5	6	7	10	6	●●●●
Antipaxi	2	4	4	0	0	3	6	6	4	3	●●
Arki	0	2	1	0	0	0	10	3	0	1	
Astipalea	8	5	2	6	4	5	7	4	1	2	●●●●●
Chalki	7	3	0	1	2	6	6	3	0	5	●●●
Chios	4	7	6	5	3	7	5	3	2	3	●●●
Corfu / Kerkyra	6	6	6	8	10	6	2	9	4	10	●●●
Crete	5	10	6	10	9	7	8	8	5	9	●●●●
Delos	0	4	0	9	0	0	6	1	0	5	●●●●
Donoussa	2	5	2	0	0	3	8	4	0	2	●
Elafonissos	6	5	1	0	0	6	10	7	5	2	●●
Evia	1	7	5	3	1	5	7	4	0	4	●
Folegandros	9	5	1	2	1	7	8	3	2	4	●●●●●
Fourni	4	4	1	0	0	6	10	5	0	1	●●●●
Gavdos	1	5	2	1	0	0	10	3	0	0	●
Hydra	7	4	0	2	7	7	4	1	0	10	●●
Ikaria	2	9	4	1	3	4	6	5	3	3	●
Ios	7	5	1	1	10	2	3	9	8	10	●●●●
Iraklia	2	3	2	0	0	4	7	4	1	2	●●
Ithaca	4	8	4	2	1	6	7	2	0	2	●●●
Kalimnos	3	6	3	3	4	5	3	6	2	6	●●
Karpathos	4	9	3	5	2	6	6	6	3	3	●●●
Kassos	2	4	0	1	0	2	9	3	0	1	●
Kastelorizo	6	5	3	4	0	5	9	0	0	2	●●●●
Kea	5	4	3	6	2	6	6	4	1	5	●●●
Kefalonia	1	8	5	3	2	7	6	7	3	5	●●
Kimolos	5	5	1	2	2	5	10	5	2	2	●●●●
Kithera	6	7	3	3	2	6	9	6	1	1	●●●●

your priorities are beaches and nightlife or peace and quiet, but many islands are apt to leave very different impressions at different times of the year. Ios is a classic example of this: quiet and dreamy in the Low Season, it becomes *the* party island in August, usually attracting very negative reviews in consequence.

Nevertheless, it is possible to give some indication of an island's likely appeal, and the table below should help in this respect. Ratings are given out of ten (*the* place to go if you want this), with zero representing 'forget it'. Summaries are given out of five. Those islands rating less than one are better avoided.

THE TOP 14	Main Town	Landscape	Tree Cover	Sightseeing	Nightlife	Eating	Peace & Quiet	Beaches	Nudism	Tourism Level	Summary (out of 5)
Kos	6	3	2	8	10	3	1	8	4	10	●●●
Koufonissia	3	4	0	1	1	6	10	6	0	2	●●●
Kythnos	2	3	1	1	0	1	8	4	0	1	●
Lefkada / Lefkas	7	7	4	4	5	4	4	6	2	6	●●●
Leros	5	5	2	1	2	5	6	4	0	3	●●●
Lesbos	5	7	3	4	3	7	6	7	3	3	●●
Limnos	6	6	2	6	3	4	8	7	2	1	●●●●
Lipsi	4	2	1	1	0	5	9	5	3	3	●●
Milos	6	8	2	6	3	6	7	6	1	4	●●●●●
Mykonos	10	4	0	6	10	8	2	10	10	8	●●●●●●
Naxos	10	8	6	6	7	7	5	10	9	10	●●●●●●
Nissiros	6	9	4	6	1	4	8	2	0	3	●●●
Oinousses	1	2	3	0	0	2	9	4	0	1	●
Paros	6	5	3	4	9	4	2	8	6	10	●●●
Patmos	8	6	1	6	4	5	7	5	2	7	●●●●●
Paxi / Paxos	5	6	5	2	6	5	6	2	0	8	●●●
Poros	4	4	5	2	6	5	3	2	0	8	●
Psara	3	5	0	1	0	4	10	4	0	1	●
Rhodes	8	7	4	10	10	6	1	8	3	10	●●●●●
Salamina / Salamis	0	2	0	1	0	0	2	0	0	0	
Samos	3	7	7	6	4	5	5	8	2	6	●●●●
Samothrace	4	8	5	4	0	6	9	3	1	2	●●
Santorini / Thira	10	10	0	10	8	5	2	4	1	10	●●●●●
Schinoussa	1	3	1	0	1	5	9	5	0	2	●
Serifos	6	6	1	1	2	5	6	7	2	4	●●●
Sifnos	7	7	3	5	5	7	6	6	0	6	●●●
Sikinos	5	4	2	2	0	3	10	3	0	1	●●●
Skiathos	7	6	8	5	8	6	3	9	10	9	●●●●
Skopelos	7	7	7	3	5	5	3	5	8	6	●●●
Skyros	8	5	5	2	1	4	9	4	3	3	●●●●
Spetses	3	4	6	1	7	4	4	3	0	8	●●
Symi	8	5	3	4	5	6	5	4	1	6	●●●●
Syros	5	1	2	2	3	4	4	3	0	4	●●
Thassos	8	9	8	7	6	7	7	10	7	5	●●●●●
Tilos	4	7	2	3	3	5	9	5	4	2	●●●
Tinos	6	7	4	5	3	4	4	3	0	8	●●●
Zakinthos / Zante	3	8	7	3	10	5	3	9	3	8	●●●

Getting There

Part of the key to a successful holiday is getting your documentation, money supply, and entry to and exit from Greece right. Attention to these details will help acquire the peace of mind needed for carefree island hopping. This can be also encouraged by taking further precautions: i.e. leave someone an idea of your likely itinerary (along with photocopies of all documents), and start out with a clear idea of what you would do if you are one of the unlucky few to hit trouble.

Passports & Visas

Personal documentation is a subject easily dealt with as no visa is required for EU nationals or nationals of Australia, Canada, New Zealand and the USA for visits to most of the countries on the shores of the Eastern Mediterranean for up to three months, though some countries (such as

Embassies and Consulates in Athens

				Opening Hours:
Australia	1–3 Kifissias Ave.	☎ (210)	870 4000	①–⑤ 09.00–13.00
Austria	26 L. Alexandras		821 1036	
Belgium	3 Sekeri		361 7886–7	
Canada	4 Ioannou Gennadiou		727 3400	①–⑤ 09.00–13.00
Cyprus	16 Herodotou		723 2727	
Czech Republic	6 G. Seferis		671 3755	
Denmark	10 Mourouzi St., Kolonaki		725 6440	
Finland	5 Chatziyianni Mexi		725 5860	
France	7 Vassilissis Sofias		339 1000	①–⑤ 09.00–11.00
Germany	3 Loukianou St., Kolonaki		728 5111	
Hungary	25 Karneadou St., Kolonaki		725 6800	
Ireland	7 Leoforos Vasileos		723 2771–2	
Israel	1 Marathonodromou		671 9530–1	
Italy	2 Sekeri		361 7260	①–⑤ 09.00–11.00
Japan	46 Ethnikis Antistaseos		670 9900	
Netherlands	57 L. Vas. Konstantinou		725 4900	
New Zealand	268 Kifissias Halandri		687 4700	①–⑤ 09.00–13.00
Norway	7 L. Vas. Konstantinou		724 6173–4	
South Africa	60 Kifissias Maroussi		610 6645	
Spain	21 Dionissiou Areopagitou		921 3123	
Sweden	7 L. Vas. Konstantinou		726 6100	
Switzerland	2 Iassiou		723 0364–6	
UK	1 Ploutarchou		727 2600	①–⑤ 08.00–13.30
USA	91 Vassilissis Sofias		721 2951–9	①–⑤ 08.30–17.00

Thessalonika Consulates

UK	8 Venizelou, Eleftheria Sq.	☎ (2310) 278 006	①–⑤ 09.00–14.00
USA	59 Nikis St.	☎ (2310) 266 121	①–⑤ 09.00–12.00

Other UK Consulates

Corfu	2 Alexandras	☎ (26610) 30055, 37995
Rhodes	23 25th Martiou	☎ (22410) 27247, 27306

Turkey) have a small visa/entry charge. Since 1993 EU nationals with ID cards have not been required to carry passports within the EU. As the UK has no ID card scheme, UK nationals must continue to travel with a passport. All nationals are recommended to carry passports as they are often required when cashing traveller's cheques or exchanging money in Greece. Passports are always required when taking day excursions to Turkey.

National Tourist Organisation of Greece

One valuable source of information worth tapping before you go to Greece is the Greek tourist service (⊕ www.gnto.gr). Usually known by the initials NTOG (or GNTO) outside the country and EOT within Greece, their offices provide advice and information on all aspects of the country. Within Greece there are branches in most of the large tourist towns (see the town maps in this book) and at larger airports. Overseas there are branches in most major countries, including:

UK

4 Conduit Street, London, W1R 0DJ
☎ 020 7734 5997

USA

645 Fifth Ave, New York, NY 10022
☎ (212) 421 5777

168 North Michigan Ave, Chicago, IL
☎ (312) 782 1084

611 West 6th St, Los Angeles, CA
☎ (213) 626 6696

Australia

51 Pitt Street, Sydney, NSW2000
☎ (02) 241 1663

Canada

1300 Bay Street, Main Level, Toronto
☎ (416) 968 2220

Money

While it is desirable to have some hard cash always to hand, the safest way of hanging onto your money is to take the bulk in traveller's cheques (*Thomas Cook* Traveller's

Cheque 24-hour UK emergency number: ☎ +44 1733 502 995). *American Express* (emergency number: ☎ 00 800 44 127 569) are also well represented in the islands, with a Travel

Centre in central Athens (see p. 94–95). Traveller's cheques are accepted by all banks in Greece.

Outside banking hours, currency and cheques can be exchanged at ticket agencies (albeit at a worse rate of exchange). Every year tourists arrive armed with cash cards only to discover that ATMs won't accept their cards, or — though this is now quite rare — aren't around at all. You should therefore ensure that you have access to some cash via other means. However you choose to take your funds, don't keep them all in one place (this way, if you are robbed you will still have something to fall back on).

Prepaid money cards (denominated in euros) are also growing in popularity as they enable quick ATM access to cash with a predetermined exchange rate. However, you can lose any cash left on them if they expire before you renew or replace them.

In 2002 Greece replaced the drachma with the euro. At the time of going to press the tourist exchange rate of the euro to the UK pound sterling was €1.14, to the US dollar, €0.69.

Travelling to Greece

How you get to Greece is going to be largely determined by the nature of your holiday. If you want to maximize your time in the islands the best way is to fly (see overleaf), possibly plugging into the Greek domestic air system (see p. 27). If you are doing the European tour then rail (see p. 29) or a combination of train and ferry (the whole of Chapter 13 is devoted to international ferry services) is the most popular route. International bus services have also been popular in the past. Having declined with the Balkan wars, they are beginning to make a comeback.

Flights to Greece

The great majority of visitors to Greece now choose to arrive and depart by air; the market is dominated by a mix of short-haul charter flights (most from Europe) and long-haul regular services focusing on countries with significant ethnic Greek immigrant populations (the two largest being the USA and Australia).

European Charter Flights

Cheap charter flights from Europe are the most popular (and cheapest) way for island hoppers to get to Greece. Because they are 'piggy-backing' on holiday flights, travellers opting to fly this way have to accept certain limitations. The most important of these are that once booked, these flights cannot be changed, and most require you to return a fortnight later (though with a bit of effort you can find operators who will offer you a 28-day return flight only ticket). Once you are in Greece there is a further dangerous potential pitfall: because charter tickets are cheap concessionary tickets aimed at encouraging tourism to Greece, it is a usual condition of issue that you do not stay overnight out of the country. This is particularly relevant should you be tempted to take one of the day-tripper boats or ferries to Turkey. You are likely to be denied your flight home should you — for any reason — be forced to stay overnight there.

Despite recent cutbacks in the number of charter holidays on offer, even in High Season it is possible to visit a Thomas Cook Flight Centre or other travel agent and pick up a last-minute return charter flight ticket from around UK£280/US$460. At other times of the year you can do even better, with some tickets costing under UK£100/US$160.

Apart from flights to Athens, there are UK and European connections to 17 Greek airports. However, most are of very limited use to the would-be ferry user. On an island hopping holiday the arrival/departure point is an important consideration, since you will have to plan your movements with a view to getting back there.

Of the various destinations available, **Athens** remains the safest in this respect, since its port of Piraeus is accessible on a daily basis from most islands in the Aegean. Naturally, the Cycladic islands of **Mykonos** and **Santorini** are also good starting points (though flights to both are apt to be more expensive than elsewhere) and Crete has a useful and popular airport at **Iraklion** (and to a lesser extent **Chania**) as well. Other regional airports tend to restrict the wider island hopping options available, though the Dodecanese island chain is well served with frequent flights to **Kos** and **Rhodes** — both islands with regular connections with the Cyclades (albeit with long 12-hour sailing times).

Other destinations are often better avoided if you are only in Greece for a fortnight as they do not connect as well into the ferry system and you could end up spending half your holiday worrying about getting back in time for your return flight. **Samos** and **Skiathos** are the best placed of these and worth considering if you are not planning to venture too far, but **Kavala (Keramoti)** and **Thessalonika** can be hard to return to quickly and shouldn't be considered unless you are planning to pick up a return flight elsewhere.

The isolated Ionian group is better served by aircraft than ferries, with charter flights to **Corfu, Kefalonia, Lefkada (Preveza)** and **Zante**, the first two of which offer starting points for viable small-scale island hopping holidays. Finally, a small number of charter flights also operate to **Patras (Araxos)** and poorly connected **Karpathos** and **Limnos**, but these are not served by all tour operators.

One-way Student/Youth Charter Flights also operate from the UK and other European destinations. These offer the possibility of staying in Greece over the one-month regular charter flight limit, since

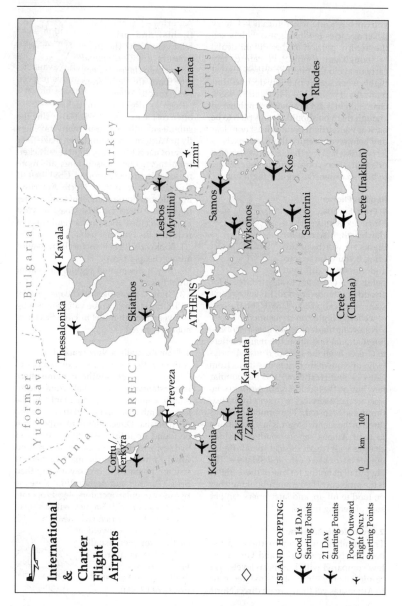

International & Charter Flight Airports

◇

ISLAND HOPPING:

Good 14 Day Starting Points

21 Day Starting Points

Poor/Outward Flight ONLY Starting Points

you can buy a one-way return ticket (ferry ticket agencies in Greece also widely sell the 'return' portion of these flight deals) — though you should take care to buy early or avoid the popular end-of-August flights when seat availability declines dramatically. If you are holidaying on a 2-week charter flight ticket it cannot be emphasized enough that you should always plan to be back at your arrival point at least one clear day before your return flight, otherwise a ferry strike, bad weather, or an overbooked or missing ferry could result in your having to buy an expensive regular flight home.

Regular Flights
1. From Europe:
More expensive than charter flights, regular flights are worth considering if you want to start and finish at different points or if you want to stay in Greece for an odd or extended period. In such circumstances the extra £100/US$160 on the cost of a charter flight can be justified.

Following the demise of *Olympic Airways'* international operation the main carriers to Greece from the UK are *British Airways* (who operate daily flights to Athens from Gatwick and Heathrow) and the popular new boy on the block, *Aegean Airlines* (who operate daily services to Athens from Heathrow and Stansted). The number of flights direct to the islands are growing. In addition to their Athens service, budget (hidden charges aside) carrier *easyJet* operate flights out of Gatwick to Corfu and Skiathos. The big pitfall in opting for one of these flights is the problem of last-minute booking; they do tend to fill up, and latecomers can't be sure of getting tickets.

2. From North America:
The numbers wishing to travel direct between North America and Greece are low compared with European levels: as a result the only direct flights to Greece are to Athens (as yet there are no direct North America—Greek island flights) and prices are relatively high. The main carriers are *Continental Airways* and *United Airlines,* who both fly daily from New York to Athens.

Regular flight return tickets often cost in excess of US$1,600 during the summer months; as a result many travellers fly to Western Europe and then make their way to Greece (via a local flight or rail ticket) from there. Low Season fares are more reasonable (usually around US$1,200). If Greece is your desired North American flight destination (a number of carriers offer flights to Athens via East Coast or West European cities) there are several ways of reducing the financial pain:

1. Book early (tickets sold well in advance attract cheaper fares).

2. Buy a discounted regular or charter flight ticket.

3. Under-24s can pick up cheaper special APEX tickets that can be valid for as long as a year, though travel in High Season is not encouraged.

3. From Australia & New Zealand:
Although the total number of visitors to Greece from the southern hemisphere is substantially lower than from North America, there is demand thanks to the large number of Greek expatriates living in Australia. Direct flights to Athens can be found from Brisbane, Melbourne and Sydney, with *Emirates, Qatar Airways* and *Ethad Airways* being the main carriers. If you are prepared to break your trip then *British Airways* and *Aegean Airlines* are the two most popular operators. *Aegean* operate in conjunction with *Emirates* with a stop in Dubai. *British Airways* (who team up with *Qantas*) are less convenient as the stopover usually is London Heathrow. Fares are inevitably quite high (in August in excess of £2,500).

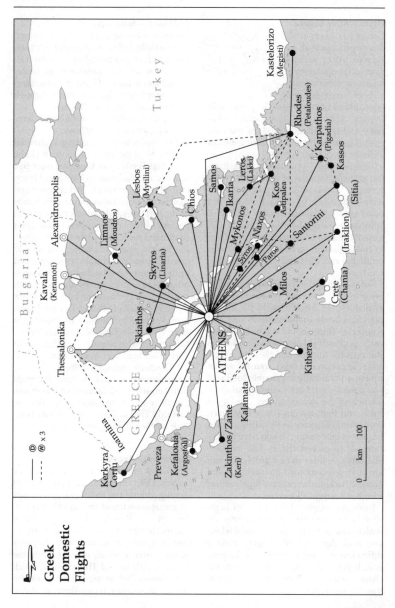

Greek Domestic Flights

Flights Within Greece

Greece has a very well-developed internal air service. After several years of deregulation in which a number of small airlines have come and gone, island links are now the preserve of *Olympic Airways* (and its associated company *Olympic Aviation*) and its growing rival *Aegean Airlines*. Both have websites with details of their services.

Competition — including that from the growing number of high-speed ferry services — ensured in the past that fares were kept down to tolerable levels, but ticket prices have been rising rapidly of late thanks to a combination of higher tolls levied by the new Athens airport, the drive to make the state-owned *Olympic Airways* profitable and the steady rise in aviation fuel costs.

Sadly, ticket price rises haven't helped resolve the traditional problem of poor availability of aircraft seats for all the popular islands (particularly in July and August) — these should still be booked as early as possible. Last-minute booking is still possible though, and these flights do offer the option of a quick transfer, and of course a potentially invaluable lifeline if you need to rush back to the capital.

Much of the domestic fleet consists of small and light aircraft (there have even been several seaplane services in the Ionian Islands in past years), so you have to take care not to exceed the 15 kilo baggage allowance — this can be a problem if you are buying a combined international and domestic ticket: international flights attract a higher baggage allowance.

Fares are roughly 150% those of high-speed catamaran fares on most routes. As with international flights, when and where you book domestic tickets does make a difference on what you will pay for your seat. If you wait until the last minute the chances are you will be paying 50% more than the minimum.

Rail Links — International

Thanks to the many sightseeing options and its geographical position, Greece is a natural objective for many trans-Europe rail travellers. There are two traditional rail routes from Europe: the first (and most popular) is via ferry from Italy, the second is through Eastern Europe and the Balkans.

1: London—Milan—Ancona or Bari: ferry to Patras, and train to Athens.

Offers the option of visiting additional islands by stopping in the Ionian chain. Superfast Ferries and Blue Star offer free basic accommodation to Eurail and Inter-Rail (all-zones or zone G) ticket holders on their ferries from Ancona and Bari to Patras (note: port taxes and fuel surcharge are still payable). Many rail travellers opt to take a chance and just turn up at the boat; but given the limited space available, you should arrive *very* early. If you are not constrained by the desire to take the cheapest route, then other more scenic options are well worth considering. Perhaps the best of these is the combination of a Patras/Corfu—Venice ferry followed by the daily afternoon train from Venice — across the Austrian Alps — to Munich and its regular connections with Paris, Hamburg and Amsterdam.

2: London overland to Athens.

This involves several changes: the most direct goes through Munich and Belgrade, but there are many alternatives. See the monthly *Thomas Cook European Rail Timetable* for the full range of options.

Rail Links — Aegean

The Greek railway system (known by the initials OSE) offers the cheapest way of getting around the mainland. After years of under-investment the rapidly improving network is at last becoming a viable adjunct to ferry services. Perhaps the most useful development for island hoppers is the partial electrification of main line between Athens and Thessalonika which has already led to significant improvements in journey times (thus enabling

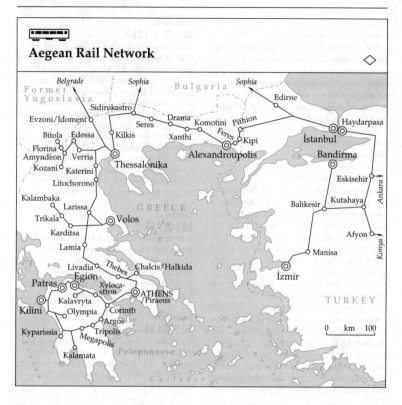

Aegean Rail Network

Belgrade *Sophia* Bulgaria *Sophia*
Former
Yugoslavia
Sidirokastro Edirne
Evzoni/Idomeni Seres Drama Komotini Pithion Haydarpasa
Bitola Edessa Kilkis Xanthi Feres Kipi İstanbul
Florina Verria Alexandroupolis Bandirma
Amyndeon
Kozani Katerini Thessalonika Eskisehir
Litochorono
Kalambaka Balikesir Kutahaya
Larissa
Trikala Volos Afyon
Karditsa
Lamia Manisa
Livadia Thebes Chalcis/Halkida
Egion İzmir
Patras Xyloca-
stron
Kalavryta ATHENS TURKEY
Kilini Olympia Corinth /Piraeus
Argos
Kyparissia Tripolis
Megapolis 0 km 100
Kalamata Peloponnese
Cyclades
GREECE
Ankara
Konya

island hopping itineraries connecting the two cities to be considered). There is also a new night train between Thessalonika and Istanbul consisting entirely of modern air-conditioned sleeping cars offering single or double berths. The two sets of coaches, one Greek and one Turkish, provide a service every night, taking 11–12 hours.

Although most fares are inexpensive, supplements for travelling on the fastest Icity (Intercity) and IcityE (Intercity Express) trains can be high. Beyond the express routes most of the system is single track; so trains have to keep stopping to allow oncoming trains to clear the line, seriously slowing things down.

In an effort to drum up more tourist custom the OSE have introduced several rail passes. The most useful is the *Vergina Flexipass*. This is for periods of 3, 5 or 10 days' travel, and the pass includes other features to increase its appeal (these include accommodation, and a city tour of Athens and a one-day cruise to Aegina, Poros and Hydra). Also available is the *Greek Flexipass*. This offers 1st class rail travel for 3 or 5 days. Another pass worth looking out for is the *Greek Flexipass Rail'n' Fly* which offers a combination of rail travel and coupons for *Olympic Airways* domestic flights. There is also a Multiple Journey Card giving unlimited second class travel for 10, 20 or 30 days, but supplements for the faster trains have to be paid in full.

If you are on a wide-ranging island hopping holiday then these passes are worth considering. In any event the rail system is useful and provides an invaluable back-up to missing ferries when travelling in the Northern Aegean, or in moving between ports on the Peloponnese. Likewise, the Turkish rail link from İzmir up to İstanbul offers a back-up option to the weekly ferry that makes the journey.

One Stop Island Hopping

The appeal of travelling across Europe and hopping on to a Greek island is seemingly very great if the numbers of InterRail and Eurail card users doing this is anything to go by. However, time is a problem since days spent island hopping are wasted rail ticket days. The ideal island is therefore one with good connections to the mainland. Many mainland holidaymakers have a similar desire to 'do' a Greek island.

Unfortunately, both groups tend to fall foul of the easy quick-to-get-to option by heading for islands close to Athens, e.g. Aegina, Hydra and Poros, that are largely devoid of the Greek island atmosphere. If you are prepared to spend a night on the island of your choice a more attractive range of possibilities are open to you:

Option 1
1) 2 +) 4 ?

Rail travellers arriving in Greece via Eastern Europe tend to head straight for Athens and then worry about finding a boat once there. Escape the crowds by abandoning your train corridor at Larissa. Frequent connections to Volos will see you a mere three hours from Skiathos — one of the most attractive Greek islands. Daily sea links with Thessalonika mean that you can jump from there as well or return to Eastern Europe without retracing your rail journey. Day trips from Athens are another way to visit; but the island deserves more time than this. Save a day for hops to neighbouring Skopelos and Alonissos.

Option 2
3) 5) 7

As everybody stops off at Athens it is inevitable that most island hoppers tend to start from Piraeus and that means a wide choice of possible destinations. Paros is the easiest island to get to. A second day can be spent on Santorini before hopping back to Piraeus.

Option 3
5) 6) 7

For those in a real hurry: Athens then on to Patras stopping over on Corfu for a day before heading on to Italy. Again a popular stopping point with travellers in either direction.

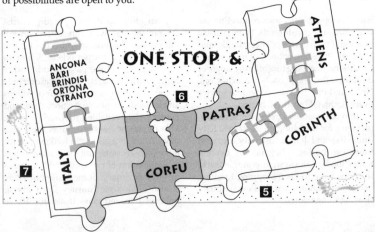

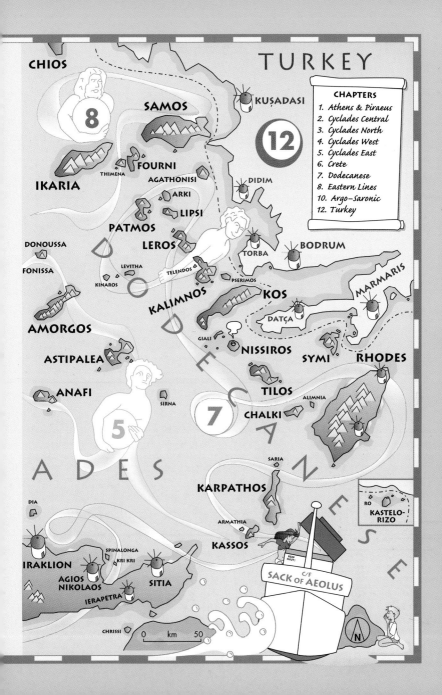

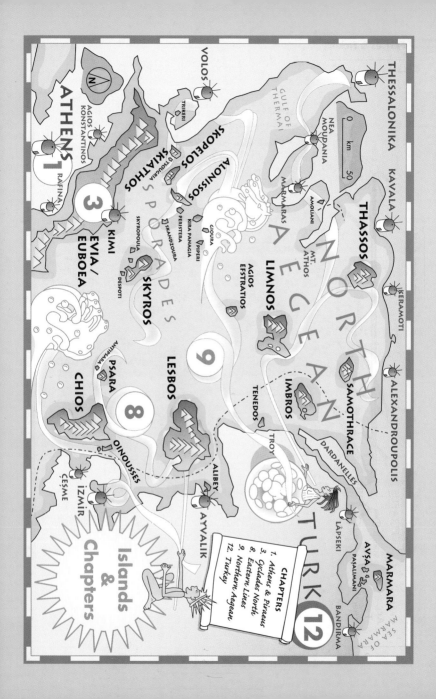

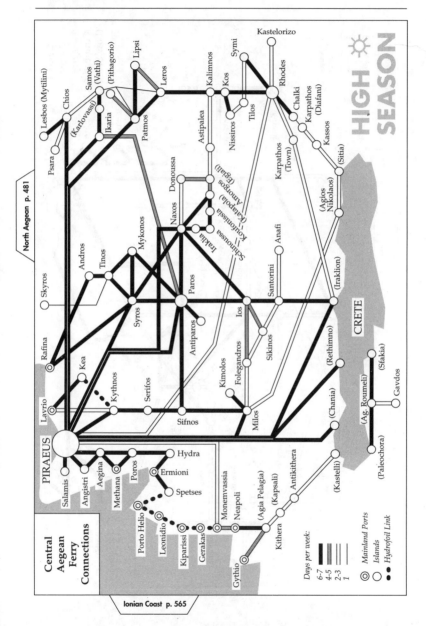

HIGH SEASON

CRETE

North Aegean p. 481

Ionian Coast p. 565

Central Aegean Ferry Connections

Kastelorizo

Lesbos (Mytilini)
Chios
Psara
Samos (Vathi)
Samos (Karlovassi)
Ikaria
Patmos
Lipsi
Leros
Kalimnos
Kos
Symi
Rhodes
Chalki
Karpathos (Diafani)
Astipalea
Nissiros
Tilos
Kassos
Karpathos (Town)
Karpathos (Town)
(Sitia)
(Agios Nikolaos)
(Iraklion)
Donoussa
Amorgos (Egeali)
Amorgos (Katapola)
Koufonissia
Schinoussa
Iraklia
Naxos
Santorini
Anafi
Mykonos
Andros
Tinos
Skyros
Paros
Syros
Antiparos
Ios
Sikinos
(Rethimno)
Rafina
Kea
Kythnos
Serifos
Kimolos
Folegandros
(Chania)
(Sfakia)
(Ag. Roumeli)
Gavdos
Lavrio
Sifnos
Milos
(Paleochora)
PIRAEUS
Salamis
Angistri
Aegina
Methana
Poros
Hydra
Ermioni
Spetses
Monemvassia
Neapoli
(Agia Pelagia)
(Kapsali)
Antikithera
(Kastelli)
Porto Helio
Leonidio
Kiparissi
Gerakas
Gythio
Kithera
Ionian Coast p. 565

Days per week:
6-7
4-5
2-3
1

◎ Mainland Ports
○ Islands
•••• Hydrofoil Link

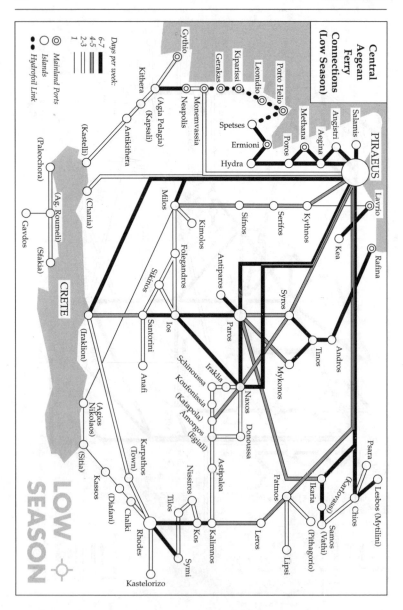

Car Ferries

Of the 60 large ferries licensed to operate in Greek waters, some 20 are engaged on international routes, with the rest operating to the islands. International ferries are on a par with those operating UK cross-Channel services and are significantly better than most of their domestic counterparts. Accommodation options range from cabins, lounges with aircraft-style seats (Pullman class) to basic deck-class facilities (i.e. saloons and open decks).

Most of the large Greek domestic ferries operate out of Piraeus, either providing a daily service, or (if venturing further afield) running a thrice-weekly overnight round trip. These services tend to be reliable (this means to within 1–2 hours of their scheduled arrival time), the most likely cause of disruption coming from odd one-day strikes. Even so, these are normally confined to Piraeus departures/arrivals rather than ferries already at sea. Normally there are a few days' warning of a strike, though unless you hear of it on the grapevine the chances are that you will only find out when you go to buy your ticket.

Conditions on domestic ships vary widely, and the gap between the best and the worst is growing. At the top end are brand-new high-speed ferries which charge double the regular ferry fare, but which get you to your destination in half the time and in some style. Regular ferries are often over 25 years old and showing it.

The ferry scene is dominated by a few companies, though this isn't apparent thanks to the larger number of company names and logos on boats. The practice of dividing fleets into separate lines and owning shares in others makes it difficult to be sure who is controlling what. A good example of this is the Minoan operation. International and Crete-bound boats run under the *Minoan High Speed* banner,

shorter-range domestic vessels sail as *Hellenic Seaways* boats, and the company also owns the popular *Highspeed* and *Flying Cat* catamarans.

All ferries have their name in English on the bow and in Greek on the stern. Class distinctions are somewhat arbitrary, with facilities classed as 'deck' on the better ships classified as 2nd or 'tourist' on the less good. Classes are segregated strictly on most vessels. Sadly, there is rarely similar distinction made between smoking and non-smoking areas. On most high-speed ferries you are expected to sit at the seat numbered on your ticket. Regular ferries allow you to sit where you will (hence the rush for saloon seats on overnight trips).

With a 'deck' ticket you can expect the seating to be divided between interior saloons (complete with TVs) and the outside upper decks (where plastic-moulded bench-style seats welded to the deck are the norm). Those travelling 2nd class will find cabin accommodation is also on offer. Food and drink facilities vary from tired cafeterias to franchise-operated sandwich and burger bars. All drinks and foodstuffs are expensive: you should reckon on paying double the shore price for most items.

Landing-Craft Ferries

In sheltered waters where car ferries are needed on short haul routes (usually mainland to island links) small 'Landing-Craft' type vessels predominate. The large ferry operators don't have an interest in these local craft, which can carry anything from four to forty vehicles. Passengers are accommodated in the cabin decks at the stern of the ship. These vessels only offer deck-class seats. The bigger boats have a bar. Usually running all year round, High Season sees occasional problems over the limited space available. In many cases, passenger tickets are normally bought on board, on or after departure.

Catamarans

The last decade has seen over a dozen of these vessels arrive in the Aegean, several with car-carrying facilities: most are classed as 'High Speed' vessels. Offering a fast, air-conditioned ride in flat seas and — with the smaller boats — a slow, stomach-churning roll in anything else, they remain summer boats, with few running during the winter months. In the past they have not been viewed with favour by the Greek government as they were seen to siphon off ferry profits in the High Season, but now their numbers are growing steadily, and they are steadily replacing many conventional ferries. Fares are normally close to double regular ferry prices (this makes these craft comparatively expensive on longer runs: e.g. Piraeus to Paros), but their speed ensures their popularity, and in High Season you often have to book ahead.

Hydrofoils

Known throughout Greece as *'Delphini'* (i.e. Dolphins), there are fewer than a dozen of these craft now operating in Greek waters. Travelling at twice the speed of the average ferry, they each carry around 140 passengers. Very much fair-weather craft, they require reasonably calm sea conditions and so tend to confine visits to islands in more sheltered waters. Consequently services are greatly reduced out of High Season. Rarely operating in the winter or out of daylight hours (their hulls are not strong enough to cope with chance collisions with large pieces of flotsam), they are a fast — if noisy — way of rattling around the Aegean.

All these boats are fitted out with aircraft-style seats divided between bow, central and rear cabins. The rear cabins (complete with WCs) sometimes have a bar where the crew socialize. As a rule, the further back you go the less bumpy the ride: an important consideration given that these boats often bring out the worst among those inclined to seasickness. Between the central and small rear cabins there is usually a tiny open deck area over the engine. Here you can stand and admire the view — provided you can cope with the noise, the petrol fumes and (when under way) the 'riding a kicking mule' sensation and occasional cascades of surf. Easily the best seats on a hydrofoil lie at the stern: here there is a small open deck complete with a popular seat offering the smoothest ride and panoramic views.

With tickets costing the equivalent of a 2nd class ferry ticket, it is rare for hydrofoil companies to compete against each other: the market just isn't strong enough. As a result, the standard of service is rather patchy. Most of the boats are of communist Russian origin and are showing their age. Almost every year brings a report of a major breakdown or engine fire (though fortunately casualties are rare).

Most hydrofoils are 'mainland coastline and their nearest islands huggers'. The few that operate in less hospitable areas tend to be far less consistent, with timetables that are only available for the month in hand, if at all, and major variations in their itineraries and schedules each year. In short, you can assume that Saronic Gulf and Dodecanese hydrofoils will be operating, but the Port Table entries for other regions are best treated as 'optimistic' projections of what might be around.

Passenger Boats

Increasingly operated as purely tourist excursion boats, these craft range from small-car-ferry-sized vessels to converted fishing boats known as caïques. Less strike-prone than the large ferries, their main bane are the seas whipped up by the *meltemi* wind in the summer months and the generally more volatile conditions during the rest of the year. They do, however, provide a useful adjunct to the larger boats, though you will encounter wide disparities in fares depending on their 'ferry' or 'tourist boat' status (the latter can be used for one-way island hopping if you are prepared to pay for a return ticket). Some larger 'passenger' boats can also accommodate 2 or 3 cars, or more commonly, motorbikes.

Ticket Agents

In the absence of any central ferry ticket-issuing or information authority, ticket agents are to be found at every port, usually occupying offices in buildings near the quay or along the sea front; they also frequently offer exchange facilities (albeit at a higher rate of commission), room finding services, and, occasionally, unsecured luggage deposit facilities to ticket purchasers. Hours are variable (an attractive feature if you need to change money or cheques out of banking hours) and are often determined by the arrival times of the boats. In Greece most agencies will open up for a short time to sell tickets during the night if a boat is due; however, you cannot count on this, and with the advent of computer ticketing (taking away the option of being able to buy tickets on board ferries) the wisest course of action is to make a habit of buying your ticket from an agent during office hours.

Ticket agents are the only people who seem to thrive on the apparent chaos of the ferry system. Many would argue that they are largely responsible for it. Inevitably they are very keen to relieve you of your money and you should enter an agency with eyes open. The vast majority of passengers do, however, use them without any difficulty. When dealing with an agent bear in mind that:

1. It is rare for a ticket agent to sell tickets for all the vessels calling at a port. The schedules they advertise are therefore incomplete and many will lie blatantly in order to get custom by telling you that their boat is the fastest, next or only one available, and they won't refund a ticket when you find out otherwise.

2. Outright attempts to sell tourists something they don't want are rare, but do occur, either by selling a higher class ticket than the basic 'deck' fare, or selling the customer a return ticket without saying so.

You can prevent most of these problems by checking that the class, ferry's name and departure time are on the ticket. Of course, the easiest way of avoiding problems is to establish which ferry you want before you approach the agent and then simply ask for a ticket for that boat.

International Tickets

International ferry travel in the Eastern Mediterranean (when it is possible) is comparatively expensive. This is due to the longer distances involved, the much higher port taxes international boats attract, and partly because in some instances you are obliged to buy a bunk or aircraft-type seating as a minimum rather than a deck ticket. Various discounts are available, depending on the operator. These range from a Student discount (20%), Return ticket discount (5%) to Group concessions (usually 15% for nine or more), as well as reduced Low Season fares. In addition, a number of lines operating to Greece in the past have offered 'Stop-over' tickets allowing you to break the journey along the way (during the High Season re-embarkation on a particular boat cannot be guaranteed). However, it is rare for you to be able to travel between two ports in the same country using international boats except as a designated 'stop over' on an international ticket. Fares also tend to be structured on a country-to-country basis so, for example, if you travel from Greece to Cyprus, the ticket will usually cost the same if you start from Piraeus or a port en route such as Rhodes.

Greek Domestic Tickets
1. Tickets

In times past it was possible to buy tickets from ticket agents, quayside vendors or on the ferry itself (hence the carefree 'just jump on the boat' image island-hopping has long enjoyed). The downside was that this led to safety problems as there was no check on the numbers boarding a ferry. Ferry operators were happy to turn a blind eye to this as the odd thousand passengers over official capacity didn't hurt revenues, besides sparing them the expense of buying additional vessels to cover the shortfall in capacity during the brief High Season period.

Things changed after a couple of highly publicized incidents of chronic overloading: first, when the C/F *Marina*'s captain received a five-month prison sentence for sailing during the Easter rush with 2,700 passengers aboard (her licensed capacity is 1,447); second, when the C/F *Express Olympia* (licensed capacity 1,200) had her captain arrested at Piraeus for trying to sail with 2,725 passengers on board.

These incidents called into question ferry safety standards in Greece besides attracting damaging international publicity, with the result that the current computer ticket system was introduced. As a result:

1. Passengers can no longer board a ferry without a valid ticket. You should therefore buy a ticket before you arrive at the quay (though at bigger ports there are often ticket kiosks on the quay).

2. At the height of the High Season travellers can no longer expect to be able to just jump on the next boat to their desired destination: advertised boats can be full. This opens up the possibility that some island hoppers could face delays (and possibly miss flights home) as a result. In High Season it is therefore highly advisable to buy the ticket for both the next stage and the final stage of your journey as soon as you have decided what they will be (particularly if your hop would be via a catamaran or involve a weekend journey to or from Piraeus). This will also give you the maximum available time to consider your other options should your chosen ferry be full.

2. Ticket Types & Fares

As the Greek ferry scene becomes increasingly deregulated the old rigid structure of fares and boat types is breaking down. In the past the Greek government set a port-to-port fare for each of the three different standards of ferry (based on vessel age and speed). There are thus three basic fare price points for each route (deregulation is unlikely to impact on this much):

1. Regular Ferry — now the preserve of the old slow boats. This is the cheapest option (typical fares are listed opposite).

2. Fast Ferries — invariably new, and some 20% faster than old regular ferries.

3. High Speed Vessels — primarily catamarans and hydrofoils, but this category also includes a number of 'High Speed' ferries that travel at speeds of over 30 knots.

Where regulation is still in place 'Deck' fares are set by the government, but operators can charge what they like for higher classes.

Domestic Tickets

With the exception of a few landing-craft type ferries and tourist excursion boats, all ferries, catamarans and hydrofoils now use a standardized computer ticket that carries a passenger name. The only differences between tickets are the use of company logos. On some islands a harbour tax slip (usually amounting to around €0.50) is also stapled to the ticket.

Between the ticket agent and the destination a passenger's ticket gets ever smaller as various sections are torn off. Keep the final section to hand for on-board inspections.

Typical Domestic Inter-Island 'Deck' Fares (Euros)

12.70	17.20	17.50	20.50	24.20	31.00	26.20	28.30	35.00	•	**Rhodes**
Kos	5.30	7.60	10.40	15.00	16.10	18.50	21.20	27.00	•	**Kos**
	Kalimnos	7.00	9.40	14.20	13.50	17.90	21.50	25.80	•	**Kalimnos**
		Leros	5.90	12.80	•	17.50	19.50	26.60	•	**Leros**
			Patmos	10.60	14.20	15.70	18.00	27.20	•	**Patmos**
	Thessalonika		**Samos**	15.30	10.90	15.20	24.60	•		**Samos**
Skiathos	16.00	**Skiathos**		**Paros**	•	•	•	•		**Paros**
Amorgos	•	•	**Amorgos**		**Chios**	12.10	19.60	27.30		**Chios**
Tinos	33.00	20.40	11.60	**Tinos**		**Lesbos**	16.20	23.60		**Lesbos**
Mykonos	35.00	21.00	11.30	4.40	**Mykonos**		**Limnos**	13.70		**Limnos**
Syros	30.70	19.60	12.80	4.00	5.50	**Syros**		**Kavala**		
Naxos	32.50	24.40	8.80	6.90	6.60	7.70	**Naxos**			
Paros	33.30	23.10	10.10	6.80	6.50	7.00	6.50	**Paros**		
Ios	34.70	26.50	15.90	12.00	11.80	13.70	7.70	8.70	**Ios**	
Santorini /Thira	35.80	30.00	16.50	14.90	12.70	14.80	10.70	10.80	6.60	**Thira**
Crete (Iraklion)	44.20	36.10	•	22.90	21.50	20.20	18.60	17.70	15.60	13.20

Typical Piraeus–Island Fares (Euros)

(Including port taxes and 8% VAT)

PIRAEUS to:	Deck	C/M or H/F
Aegina	7.50	11.00
Amorgos	26.60	•
Anafi	34.00	•
Angistri	8.10	12.50
Astipalea	34.80	•
Chalki	44.00	•
Chios	32.00	•
Crete (Chania)	34.00	•
Crete (Iraklion)	41.25	•
Crete (Rethimno)	34.50	•
Crete (Sitia)	38.00	•
Donoussa	26.50	•
Epidavros	9.00	16.00
Folegandros	25.50	•
Fourni	29.70	•
Hydra	12.00	21.00
Ikaria	28.00	•
Ios	35.00	•
Iraklia	24.50	•
Kalimnos	36.00	•
Karpathos	40.00	•
Kassos	39.90	•
Kastelorizo	48.80	•
Kea	•	23.50
Kimolos	23.00	40.40
Kithera	27.00	47.00
Kos	38.70	•
Koufonissia	24.00	•
Kythnos	15.50	26.00
Leros	33.00	•
Lesbos (Mytilini)	36.30	•
Milos	25.50	43.00
Monemvassia	•	41.50
Mykonos	26.50	44.70
Naxos	29.30	34.10
Neapoli	•	49.80
Nissiros	38.50	•
Paros	29.00	47.50
Patmos	31.70	•
Poros	10.90	18.50
Rhodes	46.00	•
Samos (Vathi)	33.50	•
Santorini / Thira	38.50	55.50
Schinoussa	25.50	•
Serifos	22.80	33.50
Sifnos	22.20	37.70
Sikinos	29.90	•
Spetses	21.00	28.90
Symi	39.00	•
Syros	23.00	37.90
Tilos	39.50	•
Tinos	24.00	38.20

Tickets for regular ferries remain the most cost-effective travel option. There are three classes on larger vessels: 1st (Luxury), 2nd (Tourist), and 3rd (Deck or Economy). Most of the newer boats and catamarans lose the tourist class and have only 1st and Economy classes. Deck tickets are the norm and unless you state otherwise you can expect to be sold one — this is usually indicated with the word 'OIK' on your ticket! On the older boats **Class numbers** are indicated on ship signs using a letter and apostrophe numbering system derived from the Classical Greek alphabet. The 'class' (ΘΕΣΙΣ / ΘΕΣΗ) is thus written accordingly: Α'= 1st, Β'= 2nd, and Γ'= 3rd.

It is standard practice to issue one-way rather than return tickets, though the latter are available (at a saving of 10–15% of the cost of two single fares) provided you don't mind the inconvenience of being locked into using the same line's boats for your return. Groups of 10 or more can also get discounted tickets, and students can occasionally get discounts by waving their student cards at agents.

The average regular ferry 'Deck' fare, when hopping to the next island down the line, is about €8; children between 4 and 10 travel half-fare. Car rates average 4 or 6 times the cost of a deck ticket, depending on whether the length of the vehicle exceeds 4.5 m. Motorcycle rates also go according to size. For a sub-250cc machine the fare is similar to a deck ticket; larger machines are up to double that. However, bicycles are usually allowed free passage, regardless of the type of vessel.

Fast ferries command a higher 'Deck' fare. Economy tickets for *Blue Star Ferries* carry this premium (the legitimate justification being that their boats are 20% faster than regular ferries). The price differential between the two is sufficiently low that it is worth paying the extra few Euros to travel on these faster and more comfortable boats. Ticket agents seem to be in two minds as to how to class these intermediate boats: some consider them to be just more pricey regular ferries, others call them high speed boats.

Tickets for high-speed ferries and cata-marans are slightly different — though with computerized ticketing they look the same. Fares are usually double the regular ferry fare on all routes (this can make these tickets very expensive on longer outings such as Piraeus to Rhodes). Your seat number is also far more important: with 'deck' tickets on regular ferries the number doesn't entitle you to sit in a specific seat, but on the high-speed boats it does, and you will normally be expected to find and sit in your numbered seat. This practice tends to be enforced far more rigorously when the boat is full. At other times some passengers opt to disregard the seat numbers (they will be the ones having arguments with boarding passengers waving tickets in their hands, and insisting on sitting in their numbered seat).

In the past it has not been the practice to buy ferry tickets for journeys unrelated to your starting point (e.g. one couldn't buy a ticket for travel from Paros to Naxos from an agent on Santorini); this was largely because agents on one island haven't had sufficient information about sailing times from other islands. This has now changed with the advent of computer ticketing, and it is worth booking ahead with these popular high-speed boats in High Season. During the rest of the year they can be a great way to travel — and sometimes not overly expensive, with occasional 50% discounts on certain tickets.

Excursion boats are not bound by government price regulation and usually charge about twice the regular ferry fare, often because you are buying a round trip (you don't have to use the return leg of your ticket if you use them for island hopping).

Greek Island Ferry Passes are the subject of regular e-mail enquiries to this book's website. Sadly, there are now no passes available in Greece: so there is no option but to buy tickets as you go. This isn't that much of a big deal as ticket prices are low com-

pared to those in other European countries. In past years (and we are now talking the best part of a decade ago) there was a ferry pass on sale in Athens, but the scheme didn't save you much and was confined to a single company's boats. The pass was only ever bought by impoverished backpackers, and one suspects that as the above companies now have a near monopoly on the cheaper, slower, regular ferries on many routes, they have concluded that they would get these customers anyway.

Paying for tickets can be interesting. In Greece it is still expected that you will pay for passenger ferry tickets in cash: credit cards are often only accepted when buying international tickets. The tickets are not transferable to other lines and are only refundable if a ferry fails to arrive (delays of a few hours are never considered refund worthy). In such instances, standing inside the office of the agent who sold you the ticket until they refund your money is the most effective way of getting it back.

Sources of Ferry Information

Current information on international services can be gleaned from the *Thomas Cook European Rail Timetable* (published monthly). A few international operators also have their timetables on websites (see p. 710).

Greece is an awkward country when it comes to obtaining timetables on the ground. In order to get the maximum information you will need to consult several sources:

(1). **The National Tourist Organisation of Greece** (addresses on p. 23). In past years overseas branches gave out domestic ferry timetables in the form of the booklet *Greek Travel Routes* (a summer timetable compiled each May) or photocopies of the timetables published in a monthly Greek trade-only publication: *Greek Travel Pages*. Neither was available last year, and it is unclear if *Greek*

Travel Routes will be available in the summer of 2012 (it isn't looking likely).

(2). **Online Sources** of information are increasingly the better bet. Most ferry lines now have timetables on websites (check out the relevant links page on this book's site). There is also a timetable of sorts at the *Greek Travel Pages* site (⊕ www.gtpnet. com) that gives point-to-point timetables that are updated on a weekly basis. Unfortunately this doesn't help you to work out ferry routes. For this the best resource is a *University of the Aegean* site (⊕ www. marinetraffic.com/ais/). This uses satellite signals to track in real time most ferry movements in Greece.

(3). **In Greece** you will find most ticket agents only display information for their port or island, along with occasional ferry company timetables. However, they will have a copy of the *Greek Travel Pages* that you can ask to see. Many also have a second — though less comprehensive — timetable called *Hellenic Travelling*. In rare instances you might also come across a timetable variant on sale: called *Hellenic Travelling Domestic Sea Lines* (€6): this booklet is a ferry timetable arranged by island, published monthly from June to September. Finally, an English-language newspaper called *Athens Plus* (€2), published on Fridays, lists weekly departures from Piraeus and Rafina.

(4). **In Athens** there are additional sources of information. Foremost among these are the National Tourist Organisation of Greece (known locally as the EOT) ferry departure sheets — available from the central Athens (see p. 92–3) and airport tourist information centres on request. These contain a list (in English) of the domestic ferry departures from Piraeus (excluding hydrofoils and Saronic Gulf boats). As these are added to on a daily basis, the EOT officer will ask you which day you are travelling and just give you that sheet (so you have to ask for a full week's worth if you are trying to get an overall picture of things). Rafina ferry departures for the week are listed on a separate sheet.

If you don't want to venture into Athens or want information on other mainland port departures you can always resort to the city newspapers. The best of these are the English language *Athens News* (€1.80) and a Greek business daily:

Η ΝΑΥΤΕΜΠΟΡΙΚΗ

which has Piraeus departures for the following week as well as limited information about departures from other mainland ports. If you are prepared to struggle with the Greek alphabet, it is worth the €1 price, and is on sale at most newspaper kiosks.

(5). **On the islands** available information is usually confined to departure times for the island you are on. Sometimes company timetables are available, and EOT offices (see individual island entries) also distribute lists of local ferry times. Some agents provide photocopy timetables, to augment the billboards to be found outside all agencies advertising boats and times (these are usually in both English and Greek capitals). In the last resort you can always try the Port Police, who are guaranteed to have a complete list of the day's sailings as well as someone who can't speak English.

Ferry Safety

The Greek island world suffered a severe shock on the night of 26 September 2000 when the C/F *Express Samina* (formerly the *Golden Vergina*), an old, decrepit ferry just months away from compulsory retirement, hit a well-known rocky islet — topped with a navigation light that is visible 12 km away — while approaching Paros, and sank with the loss of 80 lives. The captain and several of the crew were arrested and charged with manslaughter amid allegations that at the time of the collision they were watching a soccer match on TV instead of manning their positions on the ship's bridge.

Many of the 450 survivors complained of the failure of the crew to help passengers find life jackets and evacuate the ship, and reported that vital safety equipment wasn't working.

After years of deference towards the powerful ferry-operator lobby, the Greek government was stung into action by public anger. Within a week of the disaster it suspended the licences of almost half the large domestic ferries for failing safety inspections. Operators were given 20 days to sort out the problems or face losing their licences permanently.

Unfortunately, while this initial response looked impressive, it failed to address the fundamental problems of the domestic ferry fleet, as the suspended ferries failed fire safety-checks (fire wasn't an issue in the *Express Samina* tragedy). The Greek government has since brought in various measures in an effort to improve safety standards, and the number of boats over 25 years old is declining — in part thanks to the policy of allowing new faster boats to charge higher ticket prices.

Most of the safety problems — usually engine-room fires — that occur with island ferries are age-related. Greece has a concession which allows it to operate ferries until they are 34 years old, while the rest of the EU retires them at 27 (and even this isn't enforced in the current straitened economic climate). This state of affairs ensures that older boats in the domestic fleet have often been sold on to local operators because they can't be operated elsewhere in Europe. As island hoppers often depend on these vessels, some comments on the safety record of Greek ferries are worth making.

The most encouraging thing one can say is that Greece has the largest ferry fleet in Europe (over 40% of the EU total) and, until the *Express Samina,* had a good safety record. Moreover, the arrival of some 20 new ferries over the last few years has seen the poorer boats disappear from the most popular routes. If you are concerned about safety then stick to these newer — usually high-speed — boats and avoid travelling on old boats to remoter islands.

Statistically, the chances of being involved in an incident are minuscule. Without going over the top about safety, on boarding a ferry it is always worthwhile taking a couple of minutes to consider what you would do if you have to leave in a hurry. Look around for the life jackets, and, if you are inside, establish the location of the nearest exit points (if they are doors then check that they are unlocked). If you are travelling at night, have a torch handy.

On a day-to-day level, more mundane dangers pose the greater threat:

1. In order to facilitate rapid ferry turn-around, passenger embarkation/disembarkation is normally via the stern car door. Passengers are often 'invited' down on to the car deck before the ferry has docked, and are usually left standing among the vehicles while the mooring lines are secured. Vehicles are rarely lashed to the car deck — if the ferry was to collide with the quay or another boat, things could get very unpleasant.

2. Once mooring ropes are secured, and the stern door lowered, ferries keep their vulnerable stern away from the quay by maintaining 'slow forward' propulsion to keep their mooring ropes taut. The door is apt to slide along the quay while passengers are stepping on or off — occasionally trapping feet in the process. When you are caught in a pushing crowd of locals, moving vehicles and backpackers this can become a major hazard.

3. The lowering/raising cables on the doors of older ferries should also be treated with caution. Get a backpack snagged on one of those and as likely as not you'll end up in the water next to those turning propellers.

4. On small ferries it is not uncommon to find that you can get into areas to which one would not expect to have access: e.g. the bow deck (complete with capstans, winches etc.). Anyone travelling with children should check that areas containing kiddie-crushing kit are inaccessible before they are allowed to run free.

Holiday Essentials

Accommodation

Arguably the most challenging part of island hopping is finding accommodation once you arrive. But then this is part of the challenge of this sort of independent holiday. Generalizations on bed availability and price are difficult to make since much depends on when and where you arrive. But in High Season, whatever you are planning to do, it doesn't hurt to take a sleeping bag along so you can decamp to the local campsite should your luck be really out. That said, it is *very* rare to find island hoppers *forced* to resort to roughing it on one of the local beaches.

All types of accommodation are graded by the Greek government (via the NTOG / EOT). Unfortunately, an increasing number of establishments are operating without a licence, or doing their best to evade regulation by understating the number of rooms on offer, or proclaiming themselves to have a higher grade listing than their official one (thus enabling them to charge higher prices). A survey of 25 hotels on Santorini a few years ago showed that all had unlisted rooms and three no operating licence. Other islands produced similar statistics. As a result, some of the hotels mapped in this guide are shown without a class rating, and all those that are shown are given their listed class.

Prices also vary greatly between accommodation in the same class group, a reflection of the hoteliers' ability to levy additional charges and supplements (e.g. if you stay under three nights you can be charged an extra 10%). Breakfast sometimes must be paid for whether wanted or not. Regardless of where you stay, you should therefore try to ascertain exactly what your total bill will be when you check in. It also never hurts to ask to see a room before you agree to take it. If you encounter any problems don't hesitate to call in the tourist police (usually the threat is enough to resolve disputes!). It is standard practice for all types of accommodation to hold onto your passport while you are in residence (see 'Scams', p. 56).

The accommodation options in Greece are divided between hotels, pensions, rooms in private houses, the odd youth hostel and numerous campsites.

1. Hotels:

These are categorized by the Greek government into six classes, ranging from 'L' (Luxury), followed by 'A' through to 'E'. Prices are very good value by West European standards. Island hoppers usually find that most A to C category hotels are booked en bloc by package tour operators (though if you go in and ask they often have booked, but unoccupied, rooms available). D and E category hotels rely much more on independent clientele.

A-Class:

Singles: €90–250
Doubles: €130–300

Top quality rooms with prices to match. You can be virtually certain of finding air-conditioning, en suite bathrooms with unlimited hot water, TVs in all rooms and full restaurant facilities within the building. On the downside, A-class hotels are comparatively rare on all but the major tourist islands and are usually inconveniently placed well out of town so that they can take advantage of a nearby beach.

B-Class:

Singles: €65–135
Doubles: €90–170

Basically cut-down A-class hotels, B-class establishments are more common on the islands. They usually have en suite bathrooms and hot water, but TVs and air-conditioning are less common. Prices are often as high as A-class hotels. Former government-run quality hotels known as 'Xenias' usually fall into this category.

C-Class:

Singles: €45–100
Doubles: €60–135
Mid-range hotels offering reasonable rooms. Common all over Greece, they are often the top dollar hotels of twenty years ago. En suite bathrooms and air-conditioning are now standard, but few have restaurant facilities.

D-Class:

Singles: €30–55
Doubles: €40–65
Once you reach this level then shared bathrooms become the norm (most bedrooms have a sink — minus plug, of course). Buildings tend to be much older; usually being converted turn-of-the-century mansions. Popular with backpackers and local Greeks, they offer good basic accommodation, usually close to town centres and ports.

E-Class:

Singles: €20–45
Doubles: €25–50
Bottom of the range and very variable. At their best E-class hotels are excellent family-run establishments offering attractive clean rooms; at their very worst you will find saucers of rat poison on the landings. Hot water is rare and WCs are usually of the hole-in-the-floor type. Room keys will usually open half the doors in the building. In popular locations hoteliers offer backpackers roof space for a small sum.

Pensions:

Now the popular choice with island hoppers, pensions offer quality rooms at a reasonable price. Like hotels they are graded, but confusingly the grades are A to C and are rated one grade lower than the hotel equivalent (i.e. a B-class pension offers comparable rooms to a C-class hotel).

Clean rooms, usually sharing a bathroom, and with a refrigerator thrown in. Hot water is usually solar-generated, so is only available in the evenings. Pension owners usually live in the building.

2. Rooms (Domatia):

Mainly on offer in High Season, rooms in private houses sup up the thousands of independent travellers who haven't hotel accommodation and who don't want to camp. Morning ferries at most islands will be met by eager householders thrusting placards at you as you disembark, adorned with photographs of the room on offer and a price that makes a good starting point for negotiation. Other establishments simply have signs up advertising rooms and await the masses to come knocking on their door (the rooms marked on the town maps in this guide usually display a sign of some kind).

Conditions vary despite government regulation. Officially checked out *domatia* are slightly more expensive and have an EOT plaque on the door:
This is a fair guarantee of quality, as are the rooms advertised as 'Apartments', which in the main are simply pricier rooms with an en suite bathroom and a refrigerator (though at the upper end of the scale you will find cooking and laundry facilities as well).

If you opt to take advantage of a quayside offer of a room establish exactly what you are getting while haggling over the price: e.g. Where *exactly* is it? (ask them to show you on the map). Is the price for one or two people? (get them to write it down to avoid future arguments). Has the room a private bathroom, shower, hot water?

Many ticket agencies also have lists of rooms and hotels and will push you in the direction of a bed. As with hotel accommodation, room availability does tend to dry up during the day at the height of the High Season and evening arrivals could have problems.

3. Youth Hostels:

Facilities are basic (i.e. grimy) but usually adequate for the needs of the night. Unlike the rest of Europe, Youth Hostels are something of a rarity in Greece outside the big mainland cities. YHA cards are rarely necessary, but are worth taking if you already have one to hand (though few youth hostels in Greece are recognized as the genuine article by official YHAs elsewhere in Europe). Only three islands have hostels: Crete (7), Santorini (4) and Corfu (2). All offer the cheapest, and therefore popular, 'roofed' option.

4. Campsites:

Almost all Cycladic islands have at least one site; elsewhere camping is in decline. Even so, it remains popular with island hoppers as it not only offers the cheapest

accommodation option, but a guaranteed place to stay in High Season. Competition between sites is intense and most have mini-buses that meet arriving ferries. As with hotels, prices are regulated. Sites are divided up into A, B and C classes. As a rough rule of thumb, trailer-park-type sites are usually A-class, while the silent majority are B-class; it is only with the former that the price differential is apparent (most charge around €6 per person and €4 per tent in High Season).

Of more relevance are the differing High and Low Season rates: sites are apt to change these without informing campers of the transition (bar a notice advertising rates at reception). As a result, every July some get caught out by the size of their bill. There is no recognized High Season start date, so sites up prices when they can. A limited number of island sites are signatories to *Camping Club* schemes, which offer 10%+ discounts to campers visiting other sites in each scheme (see individual site entries).

Site conditions vary according to the proximity to the port (the nearer, the poorer) and the amount of competition. The time of year can also make a vast difference. Most sites have some tree cover, a mini-market selling basics, and toilet and shower blocks (be prepared for shower doors that don't lock, and salt water at some sites). Where competition is particularly fierce, sites often offer discos and swimming pools as well.

Other characteristics shared by all sites are the bone-hard ground (short, strong tent pegs are strongly recommended) and bamboo roofed areas for the large number of 'sleeping bag Sloanes'. Laundry and cooking areas (though the latter activity is rare), safety deposit facilities for valuables, and notice-boards for campers' messages are also common to all.

Outside the main sites there is a fair amount of freelance camping — though this is technically illegal in Greece and has been diminishing in popularity of late. Islands without official sites take a relaxed view of freelancers, and usually have a quiet beach where freelance camping is tolerated.

5. Sleeping on Ferries:

A good way of maximizing your island hopping opportunities, as well as saving on your accommodation bill, is to take overnight ferries wherever possible. All large ferries offer cabin facilities, though on the popular routes and at the peak season period early pre-booking is a necessity, as cabins are very popular with travelling Greeks. The price of a night in a cabin obviously varies according to the length of your journey. In most cases a ticket will cost just under double the price of a deck ticket.

Travelling on a deck ticket is also very popular despite the sometimes uncomfortable conditions. In High Season sun decks

and lounges become impromptu dormitories, though you can get quite wet on the former or, inside, over-stiff sleeping on uncomfortable chairs.

Banks & Post Offices

Greek **banks** are open 08.00–13.00 Mondays to Fridays. On some of the small islands the bank doubles up with the post office, though banking hours remain the same. Through-the-wall cash machines are now arriving in Greece in numbers and all the major islands have at least two. However, if you are relying on cash cards you are likely to encounter problems on the very small islands as ATMs are uncommon.

Most islands now have banks — usually a branch of the main bank: the National Bank of Greece. Other banks are rarer, the Agricultural Bank and the Ionian Bank being the most common. Regardless of name, the banks usually offer significantly better rates of exchange than you will find at ticket agents (who also almost always offer money-changing facilities).

Post Offices (easily identified by their yellow signs showing a horn) are unlike banks in one important respect — there is sure to be one on every island. Regular hours are 07.30–13.30 Mondays to Fridays (though local times vary). Post offices also serve a residual banking role on smaller islands. As a rule, traveller's cheques can't be cashed in post offices, but on islands too small to have a bank they usually cash them in addition to selling stamps.

Postage stamps can also be purchased from street kiosks and newsagents — with a 10% mark-up. Most post offices offer fax machines in addition to the usual *poste restante* and parcel services. It is normal in Greece to inspect the contents of parcels going abroad (though these days this usually means anywhere outside the EU) before accepting them, so don't seal them up in advance.

Beaches

One of the great attractions of the Greek islands is the abundance of excellent beaches, many conveniently placed near the main towns and ports. Most islands can boast at least one sand beach, and many are blessed with many — the best usually lying on the more protected south or west coasts (the marjority of north coast beaches are pebble). A large number of Greek beaches enjoy Blue Flag status (a widely recognized endorsement of cleanliness), though this is no guarantee that they are as clean as they should be: abuse has occurred — notably at Lindos on Rhodes (see p. 428).

Although for the most part free and easy (going topless is the norm unless the beach is right in the centre of town), on several islands, where the town strand is the only good beach within easy distance, the EOT have turned them into pay beaches (entry usually costs around €2). They are always crowded, but are kept clean and have showers.

Nudism is very popular in Greece even though it is technically illegal except on very rare licensed beaches. In an attempt to keep popular beaches clothed many islands designate one beach for nudists — these are marked 'FKK' (for 'Freikörperkultur') in this guide — though this isn't going to be much of a legal defence if the police feel like having a crackdown. This happened a few years ago on Anafi, when the island policeman received considerable publicity after he took to disappearing behind a bush on the camping beach. This in itself was harmless enough (most people disappear behind a bush at some point in their lives), but in this case he did it in order to jump out and arrest young female nudists. The Greek press called him a 'hero', though there are other, less flattering, nouns that come to mind. Rare incidents like this aside, in practice, provided you are discreet, you are unlikely to be troubled by gawpers or the police. To some extent where you can go nude depends on the time of year: in High Season you usually have to venture further afield as the more accessible beaches get crowded out with beachwear fans.

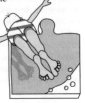

Bus Services

Greek bus services fall into two types: intercity and local. Intercity buses usually require you to buy a ticket in advance from the bus station. This will have a time and seat number on it and you will be expected to travel on the particular bus departing at that time and to start the journey in the appropriate seat (the number is on the back of your seat). Timetables are strictly adhered to. Prices are rising (reckon on paying €0.60 per km on journeys over 10 km, €0.90 per km on shorter rides), and the system is extensive, taking in all the major towns around the country. Buses on intercity routes (e.g. Thessalonika—Athens) can get booked solid on weekends and holidays, but by and large you can expect to catch your desired bus. On journeys over two hours the bus will make a 10 minute pit stop (invariably at a restaurant or shop owned by a relative of the driver).

Local, and most island, buses are very different affairs, since you normally pay on the bus and most are so crowded that you are usually doing well to find a seat at all. The majority of island buses are operated as one-vehicle family businesses. Dad will drive while one of the kids weaves their way through the masses collecting the fares. Timetables are usually fairly strictly adhered to, though this isn't quite as good as it sounds as they change much more frequently. It is also very unwise to expect to find bus services operating on Sundays outside tourist areas.

Further problems are posed by the local nature of island buses: they are geared to moving the islanders — not tourists — around. Parties of tourists all settling a €1.40 fare with a €50 note are almost made to feel unwelcome. Services tend to finish at the end of the working day and this is often not compatible with the tourist who likes his or her nightlife. Re-routing is also a problem; it is a sad fact of life that given the choice between driving down a road and an earth track, island bus drivers are irresistibly drawn to the latter. Out of High Season school days add another imponderable to timetables, as buses tour the remoter villages twice a day collecting and delivering the kids.

Electricity

Greece's electrical system runs at 220 volts, with most sockets taking standard two-pin continental style plugs (most UK and US devices will  require adaptors). Each Greek island has its own generation plant (usually whining away on the next bay but one from the main town).

Employment Opportunities

In normal economic conditions there are a number of employment options open at the student end of the market if you are looking to finance an island hopping holiday with casual work, including — most famously — the donkey-dropping collectors on Hydra and the disco dancers employed on Ios to make the outfits seem busy. Most opportunities, however, are more mundane: i.e. cleaning and bar work. However, in the current economic climate many locals have rediscovered the joys of working in the tourist industry, so it would be very unwise to bank on finding work in Greece this summer.

Rates of pay are lousy. These start at €20 per night for bar work, and, if you are lucky, up to €40 per day for a supermarket job. Payment in kind is also sometimes offered: free camping is given by some sites in exchange for a few hours on the quay pulling campers as they come off the ferries.

Campsite notice boards occasionally carry advertisements for girls wanted to work in Athens during the winter. What they have to do, and with whom, is never made clear.

Environment

The development of mass tourism has had a major environmental impact on the Greek islands over the last 20 years. Add to this the wider problems faced by the almost landlocked Mediterranean, and you have undeniable problems. The only solace is that, as yet, the islands have exhibited a surprising resilience; most beaches are cleaner than their counterparts in the Western Med (three-quarters of Mediterranean pollution comes from France, Spain and Italy), and the marine damage is, for the most part, indiscernible to the tourist — barring the damage to a small number of species (see p. 63).

Of course, there are spots where things are very bad. Athens is the main casualty, with serious air and marine pollution. The waters close by are badly damaged and have seen a fall in the number of species of marine fauna from 170 in 1960 to 30 in 1994. Near Piraeus the sea is almost dead: no health-minded Athenian will swim within 5 km of the port (fortunately beaches are few and far between anyway). There are similarly compromised waters elsewhere. İzmir is another example of note, while the northern Adriatic sees large blooms of algae along its coast. A feature common to these locations is the lack of a strong sea current to clear pollutants away. The situation can only deteriorate: problems aren't being addressed and the renewal of water in the Mediterranean by exchange with the Atlantic takes some 150 years.

The European Union has also been responsible for major terrestrial changes. Most islands have been eligible for grants to improve their previously scenic dirt road and donkey path networks. A secondary consequence of EU membership has been the relaxing of the restrictions on the ownership of holiday homes by non-Greek nationals in the islands. As the barriers come down so many new buildings are going up.

Food & Drink

Greek cuisine enjoys a rather chequered reputation. At its best it can be very enjoyable and healthy (there are notably low rates of heart disease in this part of the world), but there is no disguising the fact that many Greek restaurants fail to do more than provide an acceptable minimum, with a selection of dishes that can only be described as limited (chicken, grilled steak and fish dishes predominating). The general standard of Greek cuisine hasn't been helped by the regular practice of cooking the meal well before eating, the theory being that lukewarm food is better for the digestion. Large quantities of olive oil are also added to 'lube the tubes'. Sadly, the invention of the microwave has only served to further encourage this practice.

All this said, there is plenty of good food around; the trick in finding it is to look for the tavernas and restaurants that are attracting a local clientele: Greeks enjoy good food as much as anyone else, and their patronage is a fair indication that this is *the* place to eat hereabouts. In many cases these aren't the most glamorous-looking establishments in town, which are often the sole preserve of the tourist (not to mention seasonal staff: this is apt to make restaurant recommendations very unreliable at times).

This doesn't necessarily mean that they are bad. Thanks to the large number of expatriate Greeks returning from the USA and Australia to set up catering establishments in Greece, the number of foreign food outlets is steadily rising on the popular islands. US-style pizzerias are now opening on some of the most unlikely islands (one of the latest is at Katapola on Amorgos), and increasingly exotic eating places are adding further culinary colour to the scene.

Paros and Ios now have Chinese restaurants, Mykonos a Thai (all looking rather incongruous amidst their whitewashed chora surroundings). At the worst end of the scale, package-tour-dominated Kos even has a Mexican restaurant that requires its customers to wear sombreros. **Fast Food** burger chains are to be found on all the more heavily touristed islands, the best being a local operation called *Goody's*. Branches of *McDonald's* are confined to the cities and major package tour islands such as Corfu, Kos and Skiathos.

While Greek food is relatively cheap (you can get a reasonable meal and beer in a restaurant for around €15), those on a tight budget doing the islands on the cheap will find they can economize by living out of supermarkets. A local grocery store is a standard feature of all island settlements. Except on the islands that see very few tourists, most sell all the essentials. Common to all islands is the much underrated local fast food. Sold from small shops and bars it consists of an Arabic bread-style roll (**Pita**) filled either with **Gyros** (spit-cooked layers of meat—usually pork) or **Souvlaki** (kebab), with tomatoes, onions and yoghurt. For a hungry island hopper a plateful of Souvlaki Pita can be a fast-track stairway to heaven, but as with tavernas and restaurants, it pays to look to see where the locals are congregating for they are the ones who really know where to go for the real thing; poor tourist outlets are apt to add handfuls of french fries to the mélange (thus saving on the amount of meat in the pita).

The other great mainstay of the island culinary scene is the ubiquitous **Greek salad**. Known as *choriatiki*, it is made up of sliced tomatoes, onions, peppers and cucumbers, topped with *feta* (goat's cheese) and the odd decorative olive. It is often produced as a side dish to the main course in tavernas. **Main courses** tend to be uninspiring. The most common offerings are spiced meat-balls (*keftedes*), mousaka, and roast chicken.

Seafood is regularly on offer in the islands, though it is now quite expensive as a result of over-fishing; the strings of *chtapodi* (octopus) hung out to dry outside tavernas have traditionally been one of the more photogenic culinary sights. Somewhat less attractive is the sight of the little critters being clobbered until their pips squeak in order to soften them up to the point of being nicely chewy. If this doesn't appeal, you can always eat tender-fried baby squid (*kalamarakia*) instead. **Shellfish** is also very popular. Crayfish (*astakos*) and lobster (*kalogeros*) are commonly found on menus. Of the fish proper, the most sought-after dishes are grilled mullet (*bouni/barbounia*) and bream (*lithrini*). The small fish of the day's catch are often baked in tomato sauce — a dish known as *bourthéto*.

Vegetarians will find that the Greek practice of ordering vegetable dishes for both first and main courses ensures that most restaurants will be able to serve up something vaguely palatable. As dairy products are not widely used in Greek cooking it is also perfectly possible to follow a vegan diet in the islands.

Many islands now have patisseries offering fancy cakes and pastries. These include traditional Greek fare, notably **cheese pies** (*tiropitta*) served piping hot. Island bakeries also sell these and breakfast **doughnuts**, alongside freshly baked bread in the tourist season. Many also now stock soft canned drinks, ice cream and refrigerated chocolate bars (forget about buying chocolate that isn't) as well.

The usual brands of **soft drinks** are all widely available, though shop prices are half what you are charged elsewhere. **Mineral water** is the staple backpacker's day-time drink. On many of the islands it is claimed that you can drink the tap water, but this isn't to be recommended given that summer shortages often result in supplies being heavily adulterated with sea water. Many islands also produce wines, with heavy reds predominating, along with another speciality: *retsina* — a dubious pine-barrel 'wine' that doubles up wondrously as turpentine in a pinch.

Greek

One of the most immediate (and often intimidating) problems new visitors to Greece expect to encounter is the apparently strange Greek language with its alien-looking alphabet. Such worries are all but groundless these days. Greece has been on the tourist map for so long that Greek phrase books are now to be numbered among the 'non-essential' items (though they are widely on sale in Greece).

In fact, you can be sure of finding someone who can speak English in all the tourist facilities, if only because the language is compulsory in schools, and each summer the country is full of Greek-expatriate families from the USA, Canada and Australia (it isn't usually even necessary to ask the locals if they can speak English). Reading the Greek alphabet on signs and maps is a different matter. Fortunately most road and other tourist-related signs are in both Greek and English, as are most ferry timetables outside ticket agencies. The only exceptions to this are the less touristed islands of the Northern Aegean and the Turkish coast, where German is now the de facto lingua franca (reflecting the nationality of the majority of visitors). Even though you don't need any Greek, any efforts to speak it are appreciated. A few basic phrases, along with a summary of the letters and their English equivalents, are given on p. 712–713.

Precise transliteration between Greek and English letter forms is difficult, as in some instances equivalents are lacking. For example: the Greek for 'Saint', Agiou, can be variously transcribed as Agiou, Ag., Ayios or Aghios. It is also not uncommon to find non-Greek names used alongside their older Greek counterparts. Hence the Cretan town of Agios Nikolaos is known by island bus drivers as 'San' Nikolaos (a hangover from the days of Venetian control of the island). 'Santorini' is another example of a later Venetian name coexisting with an earlier one: 'Thira'. Both are commonly used but refer to the same island. Just to

make life really interesting 'Thira' can also be transcribed as 'Phira' or even 'Fira', and like a lot of Greek islands both the island and its principal town have the same name. This all sounds horribly confusing but it isn't really a major problem provided you look at any unfamiliar name with an eye to the possibility that it could be a variation on the name you are looking for. Thus: Cos = Kos, Lesbos = Lesvos, Siros = Syros, etc. Where an island is commonly known by two names or by a name in a form which does not correspond particularly closely to the form used in Greece (e.g. Rhodes is always referred to locally as 'Rodos', Crete = 'Kriti'), both names are given on island maps.

To aid recognition on each chapter title page you will find the names of the major ports covered by the chapter in Greek. For the most part they are shown in the accusative form as they appear on ticket agency timetables and ship destination boards: e.g. Paros = ΠΑΡΟΣ (nominative) is shown in its more commonly encountered accusative form: ΠΑΡΟ.

As a further aid to the language you will find below an old school rhyme (even though it doesn't) used to drum the Greek alphabet into the minds of countless poor kids:

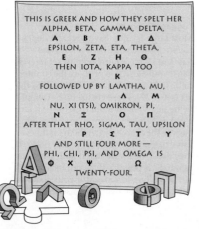

THIS IS GREEK AND HOW THEY SPELT HER
ALPHA, BETA, GAMMA, DELTA,
A   B   Γ   Δ
EPSILON, ZETA, ETA, THETA,
E   Z   H   Θ
THEN IOTA, KAPPA TOO
I   K
FOLLOWED UP BY LAMTHA, MU,
Λ   M
NU, XI (TSI), OMIKRON, PI,
N   Ξ   O   Π
AFTER THAT RHO, SIGMA, TAU, UPSILON
P   Σ   T   Y
AND STILL FOUR MORE —
PHI, CHI, PSI, AND OMEGA IS
Φ   X   Ψ   Ω
TWENTY-FOUR.

Health & Insurance

The countries along the northern shore of the Mediterranean have reasonable levels of sanitation and no inoculations are mandatory. However, vaccination against tetanus, typhoid, hepatitis A and polio is a good idea. Minor ailments are often treated by pharmacists, who have a wider remit than in many other countries. All the large islands have 'cottage' hospitals, though most are primitive by West European standards. These are backed up by at least one doctor on all the islands served by regular ferry and an emergency air ambulance service.

Reciprocal arrangements for UK NHS patients exist with most countries, but you will need to take a European Health Insurance Card (EHIC) to take advantage of these. Note: the EHIC has replaced the old E111 form. You can get an application form for an EHIC from any UK post office. Full medical insurance is very strongly recommended even with an EHIC (which does NOT cover essentials such as cover for the cost of an emergency flight home if needed). Look for a package that offers comprehensive medical insurance (including the all-important cover for accidents on mopeds). Also take care to obtain extra insurance if you are contemplating high-risk activities such as bungee jumping, diving or windsurfing, as standard policies do not usually include automatic cover.

Luggage Deposits

Most large islands have luggage deposit facilities that charge between €3 and €6 a day and staple a numbered ticket to each bag (to redeem it you produce the counterfoil). Ticket agents have also got into the act (see p. 37). These are useful but should be treated with caution: look to see if any check is being made on who is removing bags as they rarely ticket them (and never leave passports or money in your pack). If they don't, be aware that if your bag goes missing it is possible that your insurer will not be willing to recognize your claim as your bag will be deemed 'unsecured'.

Maps & Guides

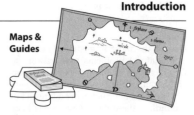

Greece has attracted guide-writers since Pausanias put inky quill to scroll in Roman times — so much so, that most guidebook series include the country. If you want to take an additional volume along you will be spoilt for choice. However, most are re-researched every third year. This tends to be a weakness as the Greek islands are changing rapidly: it pays to look at the publication date and reckon that the contents date from a year earlier. Inside Greece it is hard to find big name guides outside Athens, and those that are on sale have a hefty price mark-up. Locally produced island guides (in a form of English) are on sale on most islands.

The Greek islands also have a place in the history of cartography, featuring in one of the earliest printed atlases: the *Isolario* of Benedetto Bordone. Published in 1528, it carried woodcut maps based on old books of sailing directions known as 'island books'. The example above is of Mykonos (orientated with Jerusalem at the top).

Almost all the islands have modern maps on sale — most are about €6. To date, their quality has not been high (e.g. minor tracks often end up depicted as major highways). Salvation is now at hand, however, with the arrival of a new series — the *ROAD EDITIONS*. Sporting dark blue covers, they are easily the best road and island walking maps around. Unfortunately only 46 of the islands had been published by 2011 — though more will be in print in 2012. The lack of good town street maps has prompted the publication of many of the maps in this book. Locally, the most interesting on sale are the colourful 3D-view *Sky Maps* (though these can be deceptive, as they show only those businesses that pay to advertise in them).

Moped & Car Hire

Moped hire is very popular in Greece (reckon on €25 per day rental for a low powered machine). Unfortunately, mopeds are responsible for a large number of tourist deaths and injuries. The former are running at over a hundred a year. Many of these are the result of inexperienced and ill-equipped riders attempting too much on poor roads using poorly maintained bikes. Before succumbing to the temptation to go roaring off into a sunset that could be more final than picturesque you should take note of the following:

First, insurance: does your holiday insurance cover all the potential risks you run riding a moped or motorbike without a helmet (these can't always be hired along with the moped)? Secondly, before handing over your money and your passport (a guarantee that you will bring the machine back) you should: (1) check the condition of the machine, (2) ascertain who is liable for what if it breaks down, (3) check how much fuel you are getting (reputable outlets can often be distinguished by fuel in the tank). Once you have your machine, accept its limitations; most are not powerful enough to negotiate steeper hills.

Most of the above points also apply to car hire. Several years ago a UK TV show tested cars from nine hire outlets on Rhodes; only two of those examined by an AA mechanic met the road-worthiness standard required for UK cars. Always look closely at tyres and lights (take a second person with you to check on rear brake lights), and if possible test drive it for a block to give brakes and gearbox a trial. Car hire can be expensive if you pay by the day, but longer deals are good value: typically €200 per week (€140 for 3 days), including tax and insurance, for a jeep or buggy. You will obviously need your driving licence. A Green Card insurance warranty is also recommended.

Newspapers & Books

Most major European papers are available on all but the remotest of the islands — usually via a stationery shop or street kiosk. On the majority of islands they appear a day after publication. In central Athens they are available on the evening of the day they are published. In High Season it pays to arrive early if you want the more popular titles. The difficulty is determining when 'early' is, for it varies according to an island's links with Athens or the nearest island with a direct airport link to Western Europe. On Paros, for example, it is early afternoon as the newspapers are carried on the morning ferries from Piraeus.

Prices are high: expect to pay double the home country published price. Most newsagents also have a pricey supply of pulp fiction, as well as locally produced maps and guides.

Nightlife

One of the most charming aspects of Greek island life is the traditional evening promenade around the centre of town. Nights in Greece are the time for the locals to bask in the cooler temperatures and catch up with the gossip. As a result, even the most uninspiring of towns exude an air of companionable bustle that lasts from dusk to 10 or 11 pm. Tavernas take in the lingerers who want to chat (those near the ports also serve as a temporary home for those waiting for late ferries).

Most islands also boast at least one disco where you can touch a few more hands in the dance of life. Discos and bars usually stay open until 3 am. Thereafter the streets are often filled with slowly dispersing crowds of the slightly inebriated. This can be a problem time in some parts as a lack of manpower means that there is little of a police presence to curb the excesses of the more exuberant revellers.

Photography

Popular makes of camera card and film are available on all but the smallest Greek islands. However, if your requirements are in any way exotic you can be pretty certain of encountering considerable difficulty replenishing supplies. Costs of all media (generally around 25% more than UK prices) also vary wildly. If you want to view the results of your endeavours you will find that all the popular islands now have at least one instant processing outlet in the centre of town, so printing from media card or film is rarely a problem. However, in the case of all small islands it is best to assume that their photographic facilities will be on a par with somewhere in deepest Mongolia and plan accordingly.

If you want something more than the usual holiday snaps then you should consider using a polarizing filter to combat the brilliant sunlight that bathes the islands. A second constraint on a photographer's prowess are signs prohibiting photography in military areas. This is particularly true on parts of Kos (and other islands and ports along the Turkish coast) and Crete (home to a major NATO base). Given local sensibilities it is best working practice to avoid pointing cameras at naval craft or personnel no matter where you are.

Police

Greece has three types of police in addition to the usual customs and traffic officials: the regular Police, the Tourist Police and the Port Police / Coastguard. The islands have a varying number of each depending on their population size. Small or very popular islands have extra officials drafted in to help cope with the tourist season. Islands with a population of under 400 usually have one permanent official who wears all three hats.

The **Police** (identified by a regular police-style blue uniform and peaked cap) have a station on most islands. For the greater part of the year they don't have a lot to do given the very low crime rate among islanders (it is difficult to get away with crime on an island where everyone knows everyone else). For this reason they are relatively few in number and have little opportunity to practise and develop such detection skills as they may possess. Things of course change in the summer when they are faced with a procession of foreigners who have had a couple of dozen beers too many, their possessions stolen (usually by other holidaymakers), or worse (see p. 64). Sadly, the reaction to a procession of tourists beating at their doors is often one of polite indifference. If you are reporting a crime, the chances are it will be solely for insurance purposes; the probability of the police recovering lost items is very low. It therefore pays to be extra vigilant when it comes to looking after your property. If you are one of the very few who hit serious trouble, then it is advisable to contact your nearest consulate before the police, if practicable.

The **Tourist Police** are not to be confused with the regular police (despite having an all but identical uniform: this makes it easier for small island officials to do a quick change act). As their name implies, their function is to look after tourists and ensure that outlets serving them (i.e. hotels, pensions, restaurants, shops, taxis, etc.) are conforming to official regulations. In common with the NTOG/EOT and occasional island tourist offices they also provide maps, island information, travel and accommodation details. If you ever have difficulty finding a bed or end up embroiled in an argument with a local over a bill, then the Tourist Police should be your first port of call (often the mere threat of bringing them in is enough to resolve arguments): they are generally very helpful, can speak some English (of sorts) and are disposed to be on the tourist's 'side' if there is a just cause for complaint. They can also perform a valuable liaison role if you need to visit the regular police (their offices are often to be found in the same building); so much so, that it is worth taking most problems to them first. Unfortunately, they generally only have officials on islands with a large summer tourist population. Some of these islands (e.g. Santorini) also use summer volunteers as tourist wardens. Armed with a khaki uniform and a smile, they point the masses in which ever direction they are seeking to go.

The third — and most visible — police are the **Port Police / Coastguard**. The Port Police are decked out in a natty all-white naval-officer-like uniform, and their sole responsibility is the supervision of the island and mainland ports. Armed with whistles (which are blown constantly) they attempt to keep tourists and locals alike from boarding ferries before those passengers that wish to disembark have done so, as well as keeping both out of the road of cars and lorries attempting to use the same exit/boarding door.

On the busier islands quayside passenger sheds have been installed to make the Port Police's job easier, as they enable foot passengers to be corralled behind a locked gate at the end of the shed until the Port Police deign to release them with a key. On smaller islands they don't bother resorting to such stratagems and just roll up (often on a moped) 20 minutes or so before the ferry turns up; armed with ship-to-shore radios, they *know* exactly when a ferry is going to arrive. If you have been waiting several hours for an overdue ferry, a port policeman is always a very welcome sight.

Port Police officers are not in the least bit interested in helping you to find a room, or anything else for that matter, so don't waste your time asking (many officers in the islands are imported just for the High Season and might not know the information anyway) — though they are approachable enough if you want regular ferry information. Much depends on the size of the island (the smaller the better). Partly because of the large number of illegal immigrants now trying to get into the EU via the Greek islands, Coastguard officers (wearing military combat fatigues) have taken over the role of the Port Police on many islands.

Public Holidays

As a rule, public holidays tend to have more impact on bus rather than ferry services in Greece. Plans to travel on religious holidays should allow for the possibility that services will be reduced or suspended. The Greek Orthodox church still exerts a powerful influence, and ferries are sometimes diverted to carry pilgrims to the shrine of the moment (Tinos on August 15 being a good example of this). If you are planning an Easter break in the islands, you should expect to find ferries very busy. In Greece, Easter is the most important holiday of the year, and a great many islanders working in Athens or elsewhere on the mainland try to get back to their island homes to spend the holiday period with their families.

Public holidays in 2012:

January 1	New Year's Day
January 6	Epiphany
February 27	Shrove Monday
March 25	Independence Day
April 13	Good Friday
April 16	Easter Monday
May 1	Labour Day
June 4	Feast of the Holy Spirit
August 15	Feast of the Assumption
October 28	Ohi Day
December 25, 26	Christmas

Religion

Thanks to the Greek Orthodox church religion continues to play an important part in Greek society. The result is a profusion of churches and a veneration of things religious no longer seen in Western Europe. This even extends to little old ladies giving up their bus seats to priests just out of theological college, something which might not seem so surprising until you try to get on a ferry alongside them, for the little old ladies in black — the notorious black widows — are the original Hell's Grannies of Monty Python fame, kicking and shoving their way aboard with grim determination that refuses to admit defeat. Much of their anger can be put down to the convention that requires them to wear black for years on end. Widowers in Greece get off more lightly, wearing a black armband for a year.

Given this strict observance of the traditional dress code, it isn't perhaps too surprising to find that islanders get very upset when tourists attempt to enter churches in shorts or beachwear. Properly dressed (i.e. with torso and legs covered) tourists are made to feel very welcome.

Thanks to a tradition which expects every family to build its own chapel, small room-sized chapels abound on the Greek Islands. Roman Catholic communities are also to be found on some — a remnant from the days of Venetian or Italian rule. Thanks to the population exchanges that followed the Helleno-Turkish war of 1919–22, Islam has all but disappeared from the islands.

Athens and a number of island towns still contain mosques sporting increasingly dilapidated minarets, but without exception they have been taken out of use as places of worship and converted into museums or warehouses. This process has 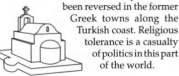 been reversed in the former Greek towns along the Turkish coast. Religious tolerance is a casualty of politics in this part of the world.

Scams

The large number of tourists (particularly in Athens) has, sad to say it, produced some sharp practices by an unscrupulous few. These are the most common scams:

1. Short-changing

The examples here normally only apply to those deemed to come from destinations outside the euro zone who are unfamiliar with the banknotes.

Version 1: the tourist pays a taxi-driver (airport taxis love this one) or waiter with a large-value banknote and by a sleight of hand it is handed back with the protest that it is only a small note. *Always* check the size of notes when paying a bill. You can avoid the problem arising by holding the note up before handing it over and saying 'I only have an xxx euro note.'

Version 2: the tourist hands over a large banknote and is given change for a smaller one. In both cases, if you do get done, vigorously stand your ground and suggest a visit to the police: this response is usually sufficient to remedy the situation.

2. The Passport Trick

Some hotel and room owners charge tourists who have checked in, found the room unsatisfactory and checked out again a fee for the return of their passport. You can avoid this by keeping your passport until you have checked the room. If you do get caught don't hand over any cash: instead call in the tourist police.

3. Bar Tricks

Two bar tricks are common enough to be worth mentioning. The first is the adding of meths or some other tasteless additive to spirits in resort bars (with dire consequences for the drinker a few hours later). The second is the occasional habit of charging bar/disco entrance fees which can be offset against your first drink. It is only when you get inside that you discover that prices are much higher than elsewhere. Ask about bar prices when buying your ticket.

Seasickness

If you fall victim to seasickness it is more likely than not that it will be thanks to the vessel you are on rather than changes in sea conditions. The Mediterranean is calm compared to the English Channel. Obviously it can get rough — particularly in the Aegean when the *meltemi* wind rushes down from the north — but as a rule on most ferries you are hard put to distinguish any sea movement. Catamarans and hydrofoils can be a different matter.

Seasickness is caused by the inability of the brain to correlate conflicting information from the eye and ear. The eye perceives the vessel as being a static object while the balance mechanism of the ear is telling the brain that the body is travelling up, down, and all over the place. The easiest way of resolving this cerebral conflict is to: (1) go up on deck where you can keep the horizon, rather than the ship, as the visual static point of reference, thus allowing the brain to accurately interpret the balance information being received from the ear; (2) take up a position in the centre of the vessel about two-thirds the length of the ship from the bow. This will be the optimum point of least vertical and horizontal movement (ferries are designed stern-heavy to ensure that their screws and rudder remain in the water) and is akin to being at the top — rather than the bottom — of a pendulum; (3) eat before you sail and keep nibbling during the journey to keep the stomach occupied.

A number of over-the-counter anti-seasickness drugs can be obtained locally in Greece. *Dramamine* is the most widely available but like many of these drugs it is apt to cause drowsiness; for this reason alone it is better to get motion sickness drugs before you travel so that you can be advised as to possible reactions. Alternatives such as adhesive patches, Ginger Root Capsules (the herbal remedy) and Sea Bands (wristbands that rely on Nei-Kuan acupressure point techniques) aren't usually available in Greece.

Shopping

Regular shopping hours in Greece are 08.00–13.30/15.00 Monday to Saturday and 17.30–20.30 on Tuesday, Thursday and Friday. In lucrative tourist towns an open-all-hours (even Sundays) regime is adopted in High Season, but city centre shopping closes down. Pharmacies in the towns open in the evenings on a rota basis: a sign in Greek on the door will tell you which one if you can read it. Street kiosks are usually open from 08.00–23.00 — so liquid refreshments, snacks and English-language newspapers (one day late) are always readily available.

Each island chain has its own specialities (the Cyclades have reproduction Cycladic idols, the Dodecanese duty-free liquor). Leather goods, reproduction statuary, bronzes and ceramics by the score and sponges are common to all. Other islands are noted for individual goods: e.g. the pistachio nuts of Aegina. Popular islands are 'blessed' with pricey gold and clothing boutiques. An incongruous (given the temperatures) and less attractive feature of the more up-market islands are the fur shops now driven to extinction elsewhere.

Sightseeing

Most archaeological sites and museums in Greece are regulated by the EOT (the local branch of the Greek National Tourist Board). Opening hours for sites vary, but most operate something akin to a 08.30–15.00 timetable, Tuesdays to Sundays, and are closed on Mondays. Major archaeological sites in Athens and elsewhere usually stay open until at least 18.00 in High Season. You can expect to pay to enter archaeological sites and museums in Greece. Ticket prices are around €3–5 to enter a museum, €6 for any of the major sites. ISIC-carrying students usually get a 50% discount, and in some instances

gain free admission. In past years Sundays have seen free entry for all visitors to sites, but many (including the popular sites in Athens) are now charging between 1 April and 31 October.

On archaeological sites, tourists are increasingly prohibited from entering individual buildings, or standing on mosaics (to prevent wear and tear): each usually has strategically sited wardens armed with forbidding whistles, to bring those who step beyond the boundary ropes back into line; as a result a visit to the Athenian Acropolis or Olympia is apt to sound like a school sports day. Site guides are usually on sale at ticket kiosks. Ruins and exhibits are usually labelled in Greek and English, but this can vary if other countries have been extensively involved with a site's excavation (e.g. signs on Delos are in French).

Taxis

Island taxis perform a valuable back-up role to the buses; on some islands (e.g. Leros) they have all but replaced them. All are metered, but it is common for the driver to forget to switch the meter on. Other common practices are similarly weighted against the passenger: it is normal for each passenger to pay the full fare and individual items of baggage also usually attract a small charge. In view of this, you should always endeavour to establish how much the journey will cost before you get going. Finally, don't be too surprised to find locals (who don't pay) grabbing a lift if they know your driver.

Telephones

The Greek telephone system has seen a radical change over the last few years thanks to the widespread introduction of telephone cards. **Phonecards** are the easy way to make both domestic and international calls. They are on sale from street kiosks and the communal telephone offices to be found in every port and town. Easily spotted by the grey satellite dish that adorns the roof, they are advertised by the initials OTE (ask for the

'Otay'). Most are open from 07.00 to 13.00.

Phonecard prices in 2011 were €4, €10 and €18 — depending on the number of units (high-value cards are only available from OTEs). The cost of making calls in Greece is quite low, and even the €4 card is good for a couple of international calls.

Phonecards aside, the Greek telephone land line system is pretty antiquated. Connections are often hard to make within Greece as most go via undersea cable and you can spend a happy twenty minutes redialling. International calls (via satellite) are less of a problem (if you need the International operator dial 161).

Mobile Phone use in Greece is very high. The Greeks have long been enthusiastic early adopters of the latest technologies thanks to the ludicrous time it takes to have land lines installed (this can be numbered in years rather than weeks). All the major European mobile phone operators are represented, and the tariffs conform to EU-wide regulations. If you are bringing in a mobile phone from outside the EU you should check with your operator that you have a compatible handset (Greek systems use GSM 900/1800 and 3G standards).

International Dialing Codes: when phoning from Greece, Cyprus and Italy prefix your home number (after removing any initial '0' in the area code) with:

Australia	0061
Belgium	0032
Canada	001
Denmark	0045
France	0033
Germany	0049
Ireland	00353
Italy	0039
Netherlands	0031
New Zealand	0064
Spain	0034
Switzerland	0041
UK	0044
USA	001

Time

Greece and the Eastern Mediterranean countries are — apart from a few days during the change-over period to and from summer time in March and October — 1 hour ahead of most European countries, 2 hours ahead of UK GMT/Summer Time, 7 hours ahead of North America Eastern Standard Time, and 10 hours ahead of Pacific Standard Time.

Walking in the Islands

The Greek islands offer some very attractive hiking territory, and a fair few island hoppers choose to hop between islands and then walk the rest of the way. The combination of a wide variety of spectacular Aegean scenery and convenient size (many islands are ideal for day-trip walking excursions) can be irresistible. The fact that walking an island is an excellent way to get to know it — while avoiding any evidence of mass tourism — also often comes into play.

The best time for hiking is between Easter and October, though this period encompasses a wide variety of conditions. The early spring is arguably the most attractive, as one is walking through hillsides dotted with wild flowers. The downside is that one can never be terribly sure about the weather, and the sea is far too cold for comfortable swimming.

May and June see the end of the flower season and are the most popular months for serious hiking, as the sea temperatures are rising and the air temperatures aren't too excessive. September and October are similarly blessed, but the autumnal end-of-tourist-season atmosphere in the towns can be a problem.

High Season tends to be far too hot for comfortable long-distance walking: unless you can be cooled by the strong *meltemi* winds, you will find it very hard going from 11.00 to 17.00 — given the lack of shade on most islands. If you want to do some serious walking at this time of the year then you should seriously consider visiting islands north of the Cyclades and Dodecanese which tend to have plenty of tree cover.

Hiking is not a pastime that appeals to Greeks: the notion of walking anywhere in the sun if you can avoid it is a bizarre concept to people living hereabouts. You should therefore assume that you will have to bring all equipment with you, as you are unlikely to find it on sale locally. It doesn't need to be very specialized: the standard items are a day-pack, good walking shoes, a whistle and water bottle. Long trousers can be helpful if the paths you are negotiating meander through scrubby vegetation. The final prerequisite is a sunhat capable of remaining on one's head in the windy conditions that are normal in this part of the world.

Conventional hiking maps don't really exist for the islands (though some, e.g. the Northern Sporades, do have excellent maps aimed at walkers). The new *ROAD EDITIONS* maps (see p. 52) are also very good as they have most paths marked. Unfortunately the ready availability of EU road-building grants means that many of the old donkey trails ('*monopatia*') are now being bulldozed into roads, and cartographers are struggling vainly to keep up with the changes.

Given the growing popularity of the islands as a walking holiday destination, it is surprising that stand-alone guidebooks on this subject are rarely to be found outside Greece. Fortunately volumes from the best series by far are on sale in the islands. Penned by Dieter Graf, the *Graf Editions* series now has six volumes with well over a hundred walks between them. Individual volumes usually cost around the €15 mark. An increasing number of islands also have on sale locally authored guides (see the 'Walking' page on this book's website). These vary considerably in style and form, but the writers in most cases are well versed in their subject and can be relied on.

Watersports

The remorseless rise in the popularity of activity holidays has had an impact in the Greek islands in the last few years. In consequence the watersports scene has grown considerably, with the result that holidaymakers seeking activities more taxing than a day on a taverna-backed beach have a growing number of options via a wide variety of outlets offering a range of activities. Most cater for beginners and offer introductory courses that include equipment and tuition. Tempting though these sometimes are, it can't be emphasised enough that your first question should not be 'How much?', but rather: 'Does my travel insurance cover me if I'm injured doing this?' In many cases it will not, so if the watersport idea appeals, check this aspect of your policy out before you go on holiday, and if needs be take out additional cover. A second sensible precaution is to stick to larger islands with airports when attempting watersports: most islands have populations too small to enjoy substantial medical facilities, so if you do hit trouble, an airlift to Athens is likely to be a strong possibility.

Windsurfing is certainly the most visible watersport, though it is restricted to half a dozen Aegean islands. During the summer the famous *meltemi* wind (see p. 62) roars south, sometimes causing the cancellation of beginner's courses, which are better suited to conditions outside the summer. The straits separating Paros and Naxos are the centre of this activity. There is also some windsurfing on the southern coast of Kos, Rhodes and Kalimnos, though not of the same calibre. Visitors to Paros will find a free 'Paros Windsurfing Guide' available at the quayside tourist information kiosk that is produced in conjunction with the Greek National Tourist Organisation. The sport is less well developed on Naxos, but is still widespread along the sandy coastal strip south of the main town. If you want to try your hand at windsurfing in July and August then a good option is to head for the sheltered and shallow bay just south of Agios Georgios beach: this is a relatively safe spot for older teenagers to first come to grips with board and sail. Smaller children need smaller boards and sails, and require you to visit one of the bigger clubs. Prices vary between clubs and at different times of the year. You can expect to pay €45 per day for board rental. An introductory course consisting of 4 hours' personal tuition and 2 days' board rental costs around €160.

Other boarding activities are far less visible; the largest — **kiteboarding** — is starting to make an appearance, but the strong summer winds are often prohibitive. **Diving** is far less dependent on local weather conditions, and diving schools are scattered much more widely around the Aegean. Given the potentially dangerous nature of the activity, there is a lot to be said for signing up with one of the larger concerns as they are likely to have better equipment, and a wider range of diving courses aimed at different experience levels. Of course, an important part of the diving experience is what you get to dive on. Unfortunately you can banish visions of swimming between barnacle-encrusted columns of sunken temples: the Greek government isn't keen on any diving near archaeological sites, so most activity seems to centre on fish-filled rocky outcrops and 20th-century wrecks for want of other options. Prices vary considerably: at the low end of the range are beginners' sessions starting at €15, but these can rise as high as €200 for wreck diving. Check when booking exactly what you are paying for: equipment and rescue diver support can sometimes result in hefty increases on the headline charges.

Other watersport activities — **waterskiing**, banana boats and tubes — tend to be more about water than sport. They can be found on the main tourist beaches on all the islands with large package-tourist contingents — usually with inflated prices to match.

What to take

When Phileas Fogg went around the world in 79 days he packed only 2 shirts and 3 pairs of stockings. Admittedly this was backed up with a manservant complete with a carpet bag containing £20,000, but this minor item aside, you could do worse than follow his example and pack as little as you can get away with: the big disadvantage of island hopping is that you have to carry all your luggage with you — so it pays to pack the absolute minimum.

Luckily, Greece in the summer is warm and dry enough for most people to comfortably get by with their beachwear and a couple of changes of clothes (girls in sarongs are becoming a common sight). Add to this sundry items determined by your interests in life (those keen on monasteries or churches tend to take more formal clothing, while most young male Italians go for designer sunglasses and five bottles of aftershave lotion), and this is quite enough to be going on with. Some other ideas that are worth considering (in no particular order):

A good **novel**: all island-hopping holidays involve a certain amount of guaranteed waiting around on harbour quays for boats — a novel will do a lot to reduce any tedium. **Backgammon** is also a popular ferry-waiting pastime. Card games, however, tend to be far less successful thanks to the strong summer winds.

A **pullover** and **windcheater**: ferries are a good way of keeping cool during the day, but a very poor way of keeping warm at night. Deck-class passengers travelling on outside decks (or waiting on quaysides) will soon regret not having some kind of wind-proof clothing.

Sleeping bags are also commonly seen accoutrements, and a good insurance policy in High Season should you not be able to find a room (as you can make tracks for the nearest campsite). The nights ashore

are so mild that it is often only the more amorous (and moany) campers who bother bringing a tent.

Foam mats and **airbeds** are also very popular with deck-class passengers wanting to sleep or lie out on deck. If you are overnighting on a ferry deck they are invaluable, as decks get too wet to place sleeping bags on them unprotected. Both mats and airbeds are available in Greece at a price, along with the cheap straw roll-up beach mats used by almost everyone.

A second useful accoutrement for heavy travellers is an **inflatable neck-pillow**. Those with more cash to hand can buy these as part of an 'Airline comfort kit' (these usually include a lightweight blanket, and sometimes an inflatable back-pillow as well). **Earplugs** are occasionally desirable on some campsites, and if you want to stand on the noisy outside decks of hydrofoils. A **can opener** is invaluable if you are eating out of local supermarkets (even small grocery shops carry odd tins from the Heinz range, and Kellogg's cereals).

Student cards: if you have one, make sure that you take it, as it will get you significant discounts on tours and site entry charges. At some archaeological sites they can even get you free entry. Luxury items are better brought with you than purchased in Greece. Cosmetics, contact lens solutions (the choice is limited outside Athens) and medicines are all notably more expensive than in the UK or US.

Camera cards are common, but unusual makes of regular **film** should be brought with you. Regular film is often more expensive. Laptop and iPod/iPad-related kit can be very hard to find outside Athens.

Turning to the cheaper end of the spectrum, you should assume that you will need to carry **lavatory paper**, **mosquito repellent** (there are more mossies than tourists in Greece — take care to look out for a repellent with a high DEET content) and a **sink plug** wherever you go. Finally, if you want to avoid backpack check-in hassle at Athens airport, a rucksack bag is a must.

When to go

The Eastern Mediterranean has a similar climate to Southern California: hot dry summers, warm wet winters and around 3,250 hours of sunshine a year. Within the Aegean there are also significant climatic variations, with the north — not surprisingly — being a couple of degrees cooler than average, Rhodes and Crete a degree above the average, and the centre and west being appreciably drier than the east. This latter feature is in part due to the Cyclades, which form a rain 'shadow', thanks to a ring of hilly islands (notably Kea, Kythnos, Serifos, Santorini, Ios, Sikinos, Folegandros, Anafi and Amorgos) obscuring rain-bearing clouds. Though there has been little apparent change in climate since prehistoric times, extensive deforestation on the islands has also contributed to the dryness of the region.

Although most island hoppers visit during July and August, the nicest time to visit Greece is in April and May when the wild flowers are out, but the weather can't always be guaranteed. September and October also have their fans, but at some point the first autumn storms arrive, and when the weather first breaks these can be positively vicious. It also rains roughly one day per month between early June and mid-September in the Northern Aegean and the Ionian islands, but rarely in July and August south of Athens.

August is the hottest month of the year, with average daytime temperatures around 26°C. July follows a degree behind but boasts a higher sea temperature. How hot you end up will depend largely on where you are: Athens in August is pretty terrible, along with much of the mainland. Fortunately, the majority of the islands (the main exceptions are the Ionian and Saronic Gulf groups) are spared over-high temperatures thanks to the summer *meltemi* wind and sea breezes.

The *meltemi* (a cooling north wind caused by summer low pressure over Asia) normally starts up in mid-morning and blows into the evening. It can be a surprise if you are not prepared for it: the central Aegean from mid-June to October is *very* windy (see overleaf). This is great for windsurfers (of whom there are many), but can leave beach lovers in sandblasted shock. Tinos, Mykonos and Paros regularly 'enjoy' over 20 days in July and August with winds over 4 on the Beaufort Scale, and 12 days when winds go over 6. (The Beaufort Scale is used to categorize wind speeds and their influence on the sea: 4 is a point where paper gets blown around and waves have small white caps; 6 is the point where telephone wires whistle, umbrellas blow inside out and large waves form, preventing smaller boats and hydrofoils from operating.) The Dodecanese, Eastern Aegean and Saronic Gulf islands escape this phenomenon and tend to be much more steamy and humid in consequence.

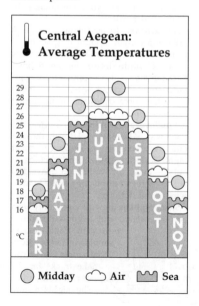

Central Aegean: Average Temperatures

○ Midday   ⌒ Air   〰 Sea

☾ Central Aegean: Wind Averages

Days:	Calm	Breezy	Windy
APR	12	11	7
MAY	14	11	6
JUN	11	10	9
JUL	9	10	12
AUG	7	12	12
SEP	9	12	9
OCT	9	14	8
Beaufort Scale	0 – 4	4 – 6	6 +

Wildlife

Sad to say it, the most visible wildlife to be found in Greece these days is human rather than animal (though most animals are pretty wild by the end of the tourist season), for the country is remarkably free of potential pests to tourists. Greece is lucky in having few life-threatening species.

Insects are likely to pose the biggest problem for tourists, particularly the large mosquito population that feed along every island promenade. Other terrestrial threats are something of a non-event. A small **scorpion** exists, but possesses a very indifferent sting.

Snakes play an important part in many island traditions, but are uncommon, and are only mildly poisonous (the only poisonous snake native to Greece is the common European adder/viper). If you are bitten you should always seek medical help. In the case of small children an anti-venom serum is usually administered. Note: this could necessitate an emergency medical flight to the mainland: bites are so rare that few islands seem to carry stocks of the anti-venom serum. Likewise, bites from

dogs should also be checked out, as rabies is also known in this part of the world.

Marine wildlife is responsible for many of the more painful encounters with nature. The rockier island coasts are home to some painful **Sea Urchins** and **Conger Eels** that regularly inflict minor damage. A more serious threat is posed by the **Dragon Fish** (or 'Drakena'), which has poisonous spikes on its spine and gills. It is to be found hidden just off sandy beaches where it burrows under the surface awaiting its prey. Most injuries are incurred while paddling. The symptoms are sharp pain followed by numbness: local doctors are equipped with a serum that will counter the crippling swelling that will otherwise occur over the following days: don't be deceived into believing that the numbness is the extent of the problem — if you are unlucky enough to step on one, seek medical attention.

Greece is also home to a number of attractive species now in decline. Most notable of these is the small colony of **Monk Seals**. Now reckoned to be one of the twelve most endangered species in the world (estimates as to its numbers range from 750 to 300), this poor creature hangs on in its reduced breeding grounds around the small islets east of Alonissos island. **Loggerhead Turtles** on Zakinthos are rapidly going the same way thanks to tourism (see p. 600) and government neglect.

In a more enlightened action the Greek government has moved to protect the magnificently horned **Kri-kri** mountain goats of Crete. Sanctuaries have been established on a number of deserted islets around Crete (notably on the island of Dia just north of Iraklion). **Dolphins** also inhabit Greek waters. If half the passengers on a ferry sun deck suddenly rush over to one side of the ship as sure as eggs is eggs the cause will be a dolphin or a school of dolphins swimming alongside.

Women Travellers

There is an old Chinese saying that runs something like 'Ying chu you yong chee choo yee' which roughly translated means 'the difference between a dream and a nightmare is no more than the thickness of the wing of a butterfly'. The Greek islands are often deemed dream country, thanks to their all-pervasive, laid-back atmosphere. However, this appealing feature is a disadvantage when it encourages one to drop one's guard too much. Greece has long taken pride in its well-merited reputation as a 'safe' destination for women travellers, and solo women island hoppers are not uncommon. However, there appears to be a small but growing problem of assaults.

Over the last decade several of the very popular islands have suffered the unfortunate experience of seeing a spate of attacks over a summer directed specifically at English-speaking girls. In these instances a multiple rapist has managed to evade the law by blending in with the large number of partying tourists. Putting this into context it has to be noted that over two million Brits visit Greece each year, so the numbers are small, but they are still worrying, given that many assaults undoubtedly go unreported.

Part of the trouble is that the treatment of rape victims by Greek police officers has left a lot to be desired. Even the UK Foreign Office has been moved to complain that victims have been treated unsympathetically. This is not because officials are indifferent, but more the result of a lack of language, training and experience in dealing with victims, combined with a conservative outlook that leads them to regard scantily clad young women who party day and night with crowds of young men, both downing alcohol as fast as they can open the bottles, as asking for trouble. It is noticeable that young Greek women have yet to gain a similar degree of freedom (or at least they feel the need to exercise a higher degree of restraint). A further unpalatable fact that local officials are loath to recognize is that a large proportion of reported attacks are by Greek youths or men. This doesn't fit readily with the undoubted fact that, once tourists are taken out of the equation, most islands are crime-free zones.

The problem is, of course, the old Mediterranean male one of seeing Western girls as (1) loose, and (2) available. Add to this the chaste nature of most of the local girls, and it is inevitable that the unattached Greek male is going to turn the charm on when holidaying alongside zillions of foreign tourists. With a new lot of victims arriving every week, they have plenty of opportunity to practise their lines.

In view of all this, the best advice must be to enjoy yourself but take care to avoid potentially dangerous situations. Most attacks appear to take place at the big resorts and party islands. Women walking home alone in the early hours or accepting lifts from locals are particularly vulnerable. Obviously, on holiday one wants a night or two on the town; on these occasions splash out on a hotel bed near the centre, don't hang around until closing time when the streets are suddenly awash with inebriated men looking for a good time, and travel home with someone you know.

If you are attacked there are a number of things you can subsequently do:

1. Get medical help or, if that isn't available, seek help from women locally, who may lend emotional support.

2. Inform your embassy or consulate (both are very sympathetic) before you talk to the police as they can liaise on your behalf.

3. If you can't be represented by an embassy or consular official, try to go to the police with a companion — preferably someone who can speak Greek.

4. Don't be afraid to curtail your holiday; embassy officials or tour reps can arrange your early return.

5. If you haven't felt up to reporting the attack in Greece, do so when you get back home; inquiries can still be pursued.

Athens

Parthenon
(East Façade)

Mosque of the Bazaar
(with the Acropolis in
the background)

WELCOME TO THE ATHENS
FLEA MARKET
OPEN THROUGHOUT THE WEEK

ΚΑΛΩΣ ΗΛΘΑΤΕ
ΣΤΟ ΔΗΜΟΠΡΑΤΗΡΙΟ
ΣΩΜΑΤΕΙΟ ΠΑΛΑΙΟ...ΩΛΩΝ
"ΑΓΙΟΙ ΑΠΟΣ...

OLD SIGN
2000
DRACHMA

Monastiraki Square
(the only good bits)

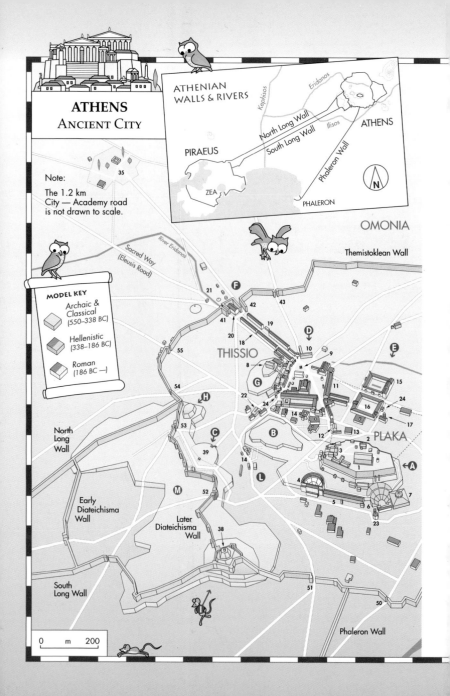

ATHENS
ANCIENT CITY

ATHENIAN WALLS & RIVERS

Eridanos

Kephisos

North Long Wall

South Long Wall

Ilisos

ATHENS

PIRAEUS

Phaleron Wall

ZEA

PHALERON

N

Note:

The 1.2 km
City — Academy road
is not drawn to scale.

35

OMONIA

Themistoklean Wall

River Eridanos

Sacred Way
(Eleusis Road)

MODEL KEY

Archaic &
Classical
(550–338 BC)

Hellenistic
(338–186 BC)

Roman
(186 BC —)

21

F

42   43

41

19

20   18

D

THISSIO

10

55

9

8

E

15

54

11

H

22   16   24

24   17

53

G   14   12   13

PLAKA

C

B   3

A

39   14

1

North
Long
Wall

L

4

7

M   52

5   6

23

Early
Diateichisma
Wall

Later
Diateichisma
Wall

38

51

South
Long
Wall

50

Phaleron Wall

0   m   200

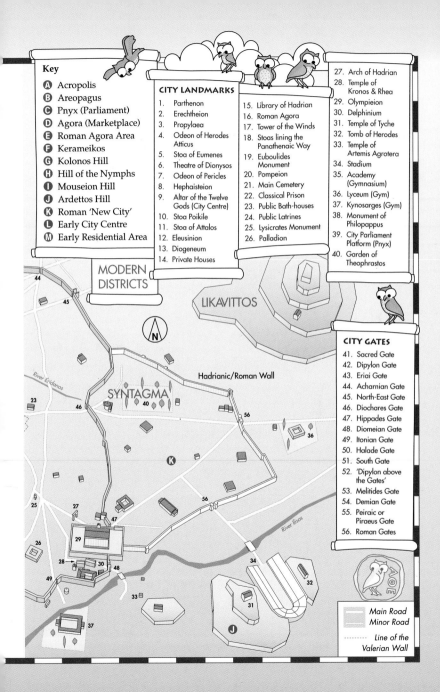

Key

Ⓐ Acropolis
Ⓑ Areopagus
Ⓒ Pnyx (Parliament)
Ⓓ Agora (Marketplace)
Ⓔ Roman Agora Area
Ⓕ Kerameikos
Ⓖ Kolonos Hill
Ⓗ Hill of the Nymphs
Ⓘ Mouseion Hill
Ⓙ Ardettos Hill
Ⓚ Roman 'New City'
Ⓛ Early City Centre
Ⓜ Early Residential Area

CITY LANDMARKS

1. Parthenon
2. Erechtheion
3. Propylaea
4. Odeon of Herodes Atticus
5. Stoa of Eumenes
6. Theatre of Dionysos
7. Odeon of Pericles
8. Hephaisteion
9. Altar of the Twelve Gods (City Centre)
10. Stoa Poikile
11. Stoa of Attalos
12. Eleusinion
13. Diogeneum
14. Private Houses
15. Library of Hadrian
16. Roman Agora
17. Tower of the Winds
18. Stoas lining the Panathenaic Way
19. Euboulides Monument
20. Pompeion
21. Main Cemetery
22. Classical Prison
23. Public Bath-houses
24. Public Latrines
25. Lysicrates Monument
26. Palladion
27. Arch of Hadrian
28. Temple of Kronos & Rhea
29. Olympieion
30. Delphinium
31. Temple of Tyche
32. Tomb of Herodes
33. Temple of Artemis Agrotera
34. Stadium
35. Academy (Gymnasium)
36. Lyceum (Gym)
37. Kynosarges (Gym)
38. Monument of Philopappus
39. City Parliament Platform (Pnyx)
40. Garden of Theophrastos

MODERN DISTRICTS

LIKAVITTOS

N

River Eridanos

SYNTAGMA

Hadrianic/Roman Wall

CITY GATES

41. Sacred Gate
42. Dipylon Gate
43. Eriai Gate
44. Acharnian Gate
45. North-East Gate
46. Diochares Gate
47. Hippades Gate
48. Diomeian Gate
49. Itonian Gate
50. Halade Gate
51. South Gate
52. 'Dipylon above the Gates'
53. Melitides Gate
54. Demian Gate
55. Peiraic or Piraeus Gate
56. Roman Gates

River Ilisos

Main Road
Minor Road
.... Line of the
Valerian Wall

Waterfront Fishmonger
RAFINA

Main Ticket Agency Block
PIRAEUS

Quayside
Breadseller

Piraeus

Historical Background

Scattered like confetti on Homer's 'wine dark' Aegean Sea, the Greek islands lie on one of the crossroads of world culture. Almost every Mediterranean civilization has left some mark, resulting in plenty of sightseeing and adding a fascinating dimension to an island hopping holiday. The islands have naturally been influenced by the major periods of Greek history, but being islands they were able to 'enjoy' a greater degree of individual historical variation, and this has added greatly to their separate identities.

Early Cycladic
4500–2000 BC

4500–3200 BC   Early Period
3200–2700 BC   Grotta–Pelos Culture
2700–2300 BC   Keros–Syros Culture
2300–2000 BC   Phylakopi I Culture

The first evidence of human activity in Greece dates from around 8500 BC. The islands appear to have been quickly populated thereafter. Most being wooded, within sight of each other, and of an ideal size for easy defence by small fishing and agrarian communities, they were natural centres of population. The Cyclades in particular flourished during the latter part of this period (3200 – 2000 BC). Removed from the outside influences of mainland cultures, they developed a distinct and unique subculture of their own.

Now known mainly through small figurines, this prehistoric Cycladic culture remains tantalizingly elusive. Even the idols carved out of white marble remain a mystery, as their function is far from clear (in this respect, echoes with the massive Easter Island figures extend beyond looks). Most have been recovered from graves (though they have also been found in settlements) and depict naked women — usually in a highly stylized form — standing with arms folded (left above right) and sometimes pregnant.

Their 'modernist' appearance has also made them very popular around the world,

with high prices and a large number of fakes typifying the market today. All this is a long way removed from the culture that created them. In the absence of evidence of political or military facets to this society, in retrospect, it looks to have existed in something like the garden of Eden. But clearly it was not all apples and Eves if the depressed, introspective posture of the occasional carved Adam is anything to go by.

Minoan
2000–1500 BC

c. 2000 BC	First sailing ships appear in the Aegean
c. 1900 BC	Palaces built on Crete
c. 1700 BC	Palaces rebuilt after earthquakes
c. 1640 BC	Santorini eruption fatally disrupts Minoan economy
c. 1450 BC	Knossos Palace destroyed

Around 2000 BC the first major power emerged in the Aegean. Named after a king whose name passed down through legend, the non-Greek Minoans were only rediscovered in the early years of the last century thanks to archaeology. Based on a commercial hegemony, the Minoan civilization, with its huge palaces, brilliant frescoes, intricate jewellery, baths, drainage systems, and above all the first writing, marked a cultural high point that was not to be regained for over a thousand years. Known only through their artifacts, the Minoans never recovered from the economically destructive volcanic eruption of Santorini c. 1640 BC. Taken over by the first Greeks, they disappeared and were forgotten even by the ancient Greeks themselves. They hovered on the edge of memory in dark legends of the sea-king Minos and his labyrinth palace, built to house his half-man, half-bull son (the Minotaur) who lived on a diet of Athenian youths, and the story of Atlantis — an island of bull-worshipping, affluent people who angered their god, who then sank their island into the sea by way of retribution.

Mycenaean & Dark Ages
1500–776 BC

c. 1500 BC	Mycenaeans conquer Minoan Crete
c. 1400 BC	Date of the Trojan War?
1200–1100 BC	Mycenaeans superseded by invading Dorian Greeks
1100–750 BC	Dark Ages
900 BC	State of Sparta founded
800 BC	Date of Homer?
	Greeks adopt Phoenician script
776 BC	First Olympic Games

The successors to the Minoans were the Mycenaeans. Already established on mainland Greece, they were able to rapidly take over the remnants of Minoan power when it collapsed. They also inherited the Minoans' Linear alphabet, but wrote in their own language — Greek. Much more militaristic, these Ionian Greeks rapidly built a trading empire across the Eastern Mediterranean (the odd little 10-year local difficulty over Troy aside). In later Archaic times this period was mythologized into the 'heroic' age given life by the Homeric poems, but latterly the clumsy fortified town walls surviving from this period have been dubbed 'Cyclopic', as they look to have been built by the one-eyed giants who the ancients believed lived on the earth before mankind arrived.

Mycenaean power diminished with the arrival of invading Dorian Greeks (c. 1100 BC): trade and communications fell away, leaving the islands in the thrall of a mini dark age. Painting and writing were forgotten, and communities reorganized themselves on a city state basis. This, combined with the arrival of the Phoenicians reopening the trade routes, proved to be the catalyst for change that led to a resurgence in Greek culture.

Only the cities such as Athens and Corinth had held out against the worst of the cultural decline. By the end of the period they were large enough to expand, establishing colony cities as far afield as France, while painting and writing (this time using a variation of the

Phoenician alphabet) reappeared. In 776 BC the Olympic Games were established, an event now seen as marking Greece's coming of age.

Archaic
776–490 BC

650 BC	First tyrants take power in Greece
621 BC	Draco takes power in Athens
594 BC	Solon takes power in Athens and overhauls political system
546 BC	Tyrant Pisistratus rules Athens
530 BC	Start of Persian Wars
508 BC	Cleisthenes takes power in Athens and introduces democratic reforms
490 BC	Persians invade Greek mainland and are defeated at Marathon

During the Archaic period Greek art and architecture developed from Egyptian models of heavy pillared buildings and votive statues into the more elegant Greek forms that we know today. Very much an age of transition, these early examples of Archaic painting and statuary — with limbs and features all misproportioned — look to the modern eye like something 'done' by an exhibitor at the Royal Academy's summer exhibition, but the artists of this period increasingly acquired a mastery of technique and moved steadily towards a more realistic rendering of their subject matter. The islands were particularly prominent during this period, as their easily defended boundaries produced a number of powerful island states, with the result that from Aegina to Samos the remains of Archaic structures and statuary can be found. This greater artistic and cultural cohesion was bolstered by a succession of invasions by the dominant East Mediterranean power of the time — Persia. The first of these attacks came against the Cyclades in 499 and 490 BC. However, the victory by the Athenian-led Greek army at Marathon and then the Athenian naval victory over the Persians at Salamis saw the emergence of regional Greek political supremacy, and this brought with it a renewed political and artistic confidence that became the hallmark of the 'Classical' era.

Classical & Hellenistic
490–180 BC

480 BC	2nd Persian invasion: Battles of Thermopylae and Salamis
478 BC	Delian League established
460–457 BC	Athenian Long Walls and Acropolis rebuilding begins

443–429 BC	Pericles rules Athens
430 BC	Plague hits Athens
431–404 BC	The Peloponnesian War
404 BC	Athens defeated by Sparta
399 BC	Socrates executed
359 BC	Philip II becomes king of Macedonia
338 BC	Philip II conquers Greece
333–327 BC	Alexander conquers Persia
323 BC	Alexander dies at Babylon
322 BC	Wars of succession
215–197 BC	Romo–Macedonian wars

The great winner in the Persian Wars was the leading Greek participant, Athens. The Aegean islands, weakened by the Persian invasion, agreed to contribute to a fund to maintain a fleet under Athenian leadership to protect them from further aggression. Known as the Delian League, this alliance was used by Athens to exert de facto political control over the islands and prompted leading Greek city states (principally Sparta and Corinth) to fight the Peloponnesian War to prevent Athens emerging as the master of Greece. The islands were reduced to minor players in the scene with local art and architecture being neglected in consequence, while becoming more important as sources of revenue and marble than centres in their own right. Islands that dared to oppose Athens (notably Aegina and Milos) also suffered greatly.

Athens, meantime, having been sacked during the Persian invasion, was ripe for redevelopment and under the leadership of Pericles spent (without consent) much of the Delian League contributions on rebuilding the temples on the Acropolis. Accompanied by a spectacular literary, theatrical and philosophical cultural explosion, this was the golden age of Greek civilization.

However, Sparta's eventual defeat of Athens prevented Greek domination by one city, and the states (none of whom was powerful enough to take overall control) bickered on until Philip II gained the throne of Macedonia. This event marked the transition from the Classical to the Hellenistic periods, for he unified Greece, and his son, Alexander the Great, started off a wave of conquest that was to extend to the borders of India. After the death of Alexander, the empire collapsed and the weakened city states and the islands reasserted

their independence in the wars of succession that followed.

The Hellenistic period also left a major mark on Greek culture, though this was more of a natural progression from the symmetry of the Classical period than a radical or sudden change. Buildings and artwork became much more decorative and ornamental, while literature and schools of learning grew from the Classical foundations. Some of the islands benefited greatly from this, with Rhodes, Kos and Samos exerting greater influence in part as a result of their emergence as major centres of learning.

Roman
180 BC–395 AD

171–168 BC	Third Macedonian War
147–146 BC	Romans impose direct rule on Greece
48–31 BC	Roman civil war
120–150 AD	Period of Roman patronage in Athens under Hadrian
170 AD	Pausanias writes guide to Greece
200–300 AD	Rise of Christianity
395 AD	Alaric the Goth sacks Athens

As Greek power waned, Rome gradually came to exercise influence over the divided city states and islands, initially as an arbiter in intercity disputes, but then as a force in her own right. Having

entered Greece in response to an attack by King Mithridates in 88 BC, she never really managed to leave and by 31 BC the whole of Greece had been incorporated into the Roman Empire: the islands divided between five provinces (the Adriatic islands were part of Epirus, the Dodecanese and Eastern Line islands were in Asia, Thassos was in Macedonia, Crete was joined with Libya in Cyrenica–Creta, and the remainder formed Achaea along with the Peloponnese, Evia, and the Greek mainland north of the Gulf of Corinth).

Despite the four centuries of stability that followed, the islands went into a slow but marked decline. Reduced to the edges of even provincial centres of power, they saw comparatively little new monumental building (a feature of Roman rule in other parts of the empire) and were increasingly prone to pirate attack. Athens and the islands also saw their first tourists during this period — notably the writer Pausanias (fl. c. 150 AD), who wrote an important guide (beloved by archaeologists wanting to know what specific buildings were called and looked like, and where they stood) to Greece describing the cities and their monuments.

Other tourists were more mercenary, and the Roman epoch also saw denudation in local art as many ancient treasures were carted off to embellish the cities and villas of Italy (the occasional shipwrecks that turn up filled with bronze statues are a legacy of this trade). The Greek cities suffered in another important respect; subsumed into Rome's urban culture, they were never able to emerge as major centres of political or cultural power again.

Byzantine
395–1453

527–567	Reign of Emperor Justinian
1050–1200	Sicilian Normans invade Venetians annex islands
1204	Sack of Constantinople
1207–1262	Latin dukedoms established in Greece
1309	Knights of St. John capture Dodecanese islands
1355–1400	Turks conquer Greece
1453	Turks capture Constantinople

By 395 the Roman Empire had grown so large that it became unmanageable: the practically minded Emperor Constantine divided it into two. Greece came under the control of the Eastern empire and was ruled from Byzantium (later renamed Constantinople and İstanbul), a city still viewed by many Greeks as a capital under occupation. The islands began the descent from a period of slow decline to one of total anarchy, suffering considerably in the Slavic and Saracen invasions of the 7th and 9th centuries before becoming embroiled in the general stagnation of the Byzantine Empire. Depopulation followed the destruction wrought by the 1204 crusade which saw the sacking of Constantinople instead of the retaking of Jerusalem. The islands were part of the spoils divided among the plunderers, with members of

Venetian and Genoese families taking control of many of them, setting themselves up in a feudal dukedom (see p. 161). Thus when Constantinople fell to the Turks in 1453 many of the islands remained in Christian hands, with widespread castle building going on — courtesy of much ancient temple demolition.

Venetian & Ottoman
1453–1830

1453–1469	Turks conquer Aegean islands
1687	Venetians capture Athens
1814	Beginnings of Greek independence movement
1815	Ionian Islands come under British rule
1821–1825	Greek War of Independence
1827	Aegina becomes capital of Greece
1830	Frontiers of new Greek state established

During the succeeding centuries the Aegean islands gradually fell to Ottoman Turk rule. Some — such as Rhodes — were lost early (1522) but others under Venetian control held out until the last (Tinos) went in 1715. For the most part Turkish rule was benign. The new landlords were content to appoint governors and collect taxes. But even as the Turks were completing their conquest of the Aegean their power had begun to wane. The islands became famous either for being the victims of pirates or for becoming their haunts; for they were natural strongholds from which they could attack other islands and the increasing trade between Europe and the Levant.

The years between 1450 and 1750 marked the nadir of the islands' fortunes, with many being abandoned altogether after their populations were massacred or sold into slavery. With Christian, Turkish, Barbary Coast, and local pirates all preying on the islands, the roll call of horrors is a long one. The 1500s saw the worst of it, with Ios being devastated in 1528, and the notorious Barbarossa starting his many depredations in the Aegean by attacking Aegina in 1537, killing all the men and taking 6,000 women and children into slavery. In 1570 the Barbary pirate Kemal Reis went on a little slave-gathering expedition and removed the

populations of Kithera, Skiathos and Skopelos to North Africa.

In the face of these attacks island communities did their best to protect themselves by abandoning coastal settlements in favour of defendable villages (or choras) inland. On a number of Cycladic islands these were built as stockade-like 'kastros' with the houses built on the inside of a defensive wall (these still survive on Folegandros, Kimolos and Antiparos — though in the case of the latter, it didn't prevent the islanders being massacred in 1794). Gradually, however, the more successful 'pirate' islands began to gain a degree of control via their fleets which also took advantage of the growing trade opportunities to enhance their status still further by building impressively mansioned towns (e.g. Hydra, Spetses and Chios).

The arrival of foreign powers (notably the Russians who held control over a dozen islands during the 1770–74 Turkish War) also helped to stabilize the region. By the 19th century Greek nationalism was becoming a potent force, the islands coming to the fore as natural bastions from which insurgents could operate against weak Turkish rule. Less powerful islands demonstrated defiance of Turkish rule by the painting of island houses (heretofore kept an inconspicuous mud-brick brown) in the Greek national colours of white and blue (now the hallmark of the typical Cycladic town), while the more powerful islands, via their fleets, gained a notable place in Greek history in the independence struggle, being more than a match for the Turks. This, however, led to reprisals (notably the massacre of 25,000 on Chios in 1822).

Modern
1830–

1833	Prince Otto becomes King
1864	Britain cedes Ionian Islands
1913	George I assassinated
1914–1918	WW1: under Prime Minister Venizelos Greece joins Allies
1920–1923	Turkish War
1940	Greece enters WW2, joining the Allies following Metaxas's 'No!' ('Ohi') to Mussolini's demand for right of access
1941	Germans conquer Greece
1945–1949	Greek Civil War
1967–1974	Military rule of the Colonels
1974	Restoration of democracy

Independence in 1832 did not see all of modern Greece gain its freedom. The Cyclades aside, the islands remained in foreign hands, only gradually being gathered into the protective arms of the Greek state. Corfu and the Ionian Islands were transferred from British control in 1864. WW1 saw the islands of the Northern Aegean come under Greek rule, while the Italians took the Dodecanese from Turkey and attempted an unsuccessful Italianization programme, only to see the islands handed over to Greece at the end of WW2.

Since independence Greece has been engaged in sporadic conflicts with Turkey, notably the war of 1920–23, when she attempted to gain control of the ancient Greek cities on Turkey's Aegean seaboard, as well as the former capital of the Byzantine empire — Constantinople (now İstanbul). The war ended disastrously for Greece, culminating with the sack of Smyrna (now İzmir) and a territorial settlement that resulted in 1½ million ethnic Greeks leaving Turkey for Greece, and some 400,000 ethnic Turks (mainly from the islands) going the other way.

Relations between the two countries remain tense. Turkey has failed to recognize Greek sovereignty over the Aegean sea-bed (with its oil deposits) and the Turkish invasion of Cyprus in 1974 has done nothing to heal old wounds. But as both are members of NATO and have economies dependent on tourism they have an interest in avoiding outright hostilities. Greece's position has been bolstered by its emergence as a democracy and membership of the EU (European Union): you can expect to see EU flags everywhere.

Politically, Greece is now relatively stable after a torrid post-WW2 period which saw a civil war (1945–49) between the government and communist forces, the military dictatorship of the Colonels (1967–74) and the abolition of the monarchy (1975) — an institution only acquired by modern Greece after the Great Powers (Britain, France and Russia), who had championed her independence, installed Prince Otto of Bavaria as King in 1833 following the assassination of the country's first president.

1
ATHENS & PIRAEUS

ATHENS · PIRAEUS (GREAT HARBOUR) · (ZEA)
LAVRIO · RAFINA · SALAMIS

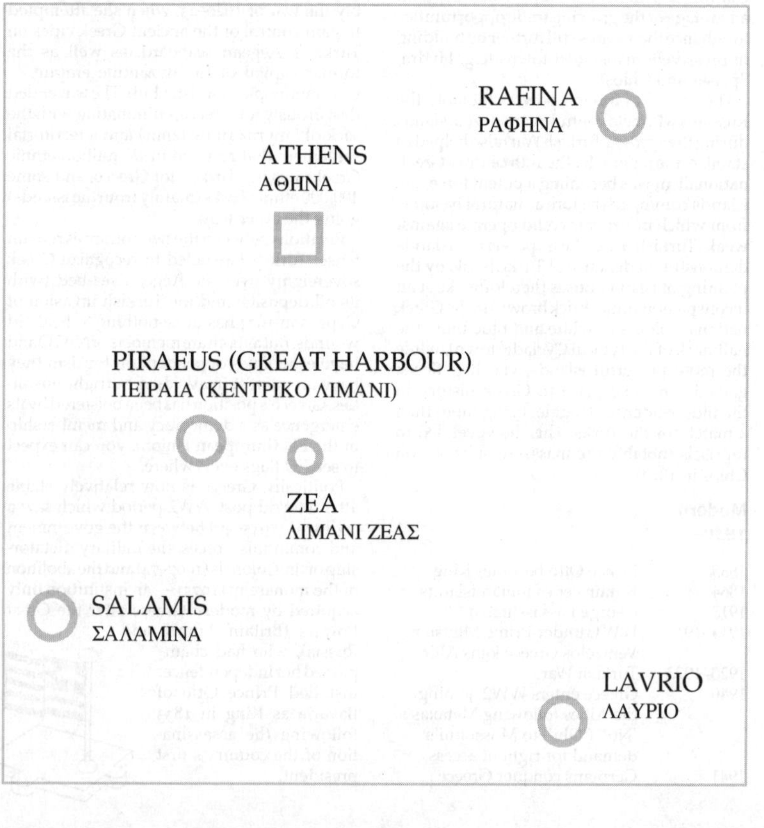

RAFINA
ΡΑΦΗΝΑ ○

ATHENS
ΑΘΗΝΑ
□

PIRAEUS (GREAT HARBOUR)
ΠΕΙΡΑΙΑ (ΚΕΝΤΡΙΚΟ ΛΙΜΑΝΙ)
○   ○

ZEA
ΛΙΜΑΝΙ ΖΕΑΣ

SALAMIS
○ ΣΑΛΑΜΙΝΑ

LAVRIO
ΛΑΥΡΙΟ ○

General Features

Lying at the centre of the Eastern Mediterranean ferry web, and still the most popular charter flight entry point into Greece, Athens sees more tourists passing through than any other port of call. Unfortunately, the rise in the city's population from 12,000 in 1820 to over 4 million today has done nothing for one of the greatest cities in the world. The atmospheric and photogenic ancient heart is now surrounded by concrete urban sprawl. Significant improvements to the 'Athens experience' have come thanks to the Olympics, but a large amount of extra concrete has been added too.

Consequently, most visitors profitably fill a couple of days doing the Acropolis and centre sights and then move on fast. This chapter can thus be said to cover the 'damaged' area of Greece. Like most tourists, its gaze is firmly directed on the ancient city centre and the ports of Piraeus, Rafina and Lavrio, as well as mentioning in passing the unattractive suburb island of Salamis.

If sightseeing is not your thing (or if you want to retain the relaxed frame of mind that idling around the islands has wrought), a final day or two in or around Athens waiting for your flight home can come as something of a shock to the system, and it is worthwhile considering the alternative of flying to one of the island airports and then island hopping to the city for a long weekend from there.

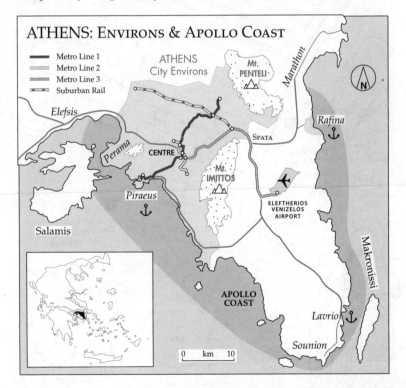

ATHENS: ENVIRONS & APOLLO COAST

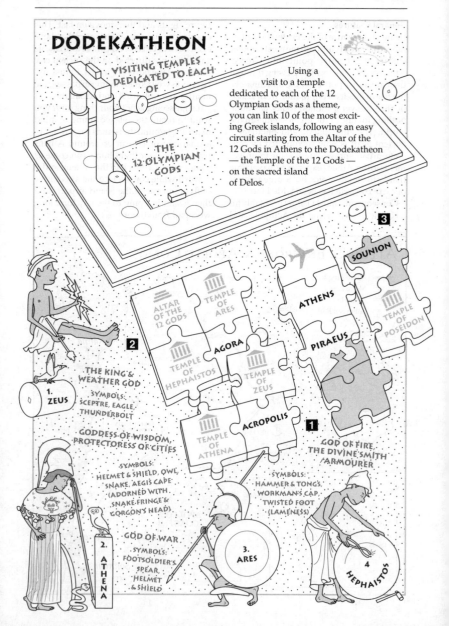

DODEKATHEON

VISITING TEMPLES DEDICATED TO EACH OF

THE 12 OLYMPIAN GODS

Using a visit to a temple dedicated to each of the 12 Olympian Gods as a theme, you can link 10 of the most exciting Greek islands, following an easy circuit starting from the Altar of the 12 Gods in Athens to the Dodekatheon — the Temple of the 12 Gods — on the sacred island of Delos.

THE KING & WEATHER GOD

1. ZEUS

SYMBOLS: SCEPTRE, EAGLE, THUNDERBOLT

GODDESS OF WISDOM, PROTECTORESS OF CITIES

SYMBOLS: HELMET & SHIELD, OWL, SNAKE, AEGIS CAPE (ADORNED WITH SNAKE-FRINGE & GORGON'S HEAD).

2. ATHENA

GOD OF WAR

SYMBOLS: FOOTSOLDIER'S SPEAR, HELMET & SHIELD

3. ARES

GOD OF FIRE, THE DIVINE SMITH ARMOURER

SYMBOLS: HAMMER & TONGS, WORKMAN'S CAP, TWISTED FOOT (LAMENESS)

4 HEPHAISTOS

ALTAR OF THE 12 GODS · TEMPLE OF ARES · AGORA · TEMPLE OF HEPHAISTOS · TEMPLE OF ZEUS · ACROPOLIS · TEMPLE OF ATHENA · ATHENS · PIRAEUS · SOUNION · TEMPLE OF POSEIDON

PARIS 2060 KM

QUEEN GODDESS / GODDESS OF MOTHERHOOD (WIFE OF ZEUS).

SYMBOLS: DIADEM / SCEPTRE

6. HERMES

7. HERA

8. ARTEMIS

THE MESSENGER GOD, BRINGER OF LUCK, CONDUCTOR OF SOULS

SYMBOLS: WINGED BOOTS, HERALD'S STAFF, WIDE BRIMMED HAT, CHLAMYS CLOAK

GODDESS OF VIRTUE & THE HUNT (TWIN SISTER OF APOLLO)

SYMBOLS: BOW & ARROWS / LONG HUNTING BOOTS

4

TEMPLE OF HERMES

TEMPLE OF HERA

5

SAMOS

EPHESUS

PATMOS

TEMPLE OF ARTEMIS

GODDESS OF LOVE

KOS

6

9. APHRODITE

CRETE IRAKLION

RHODES

TEMPLE OF APHRODITE

GOD OF THE SEA, EARTHQUAKES & HORSES

SYMBOLS: DOVE / CUPID SON EROS

SYMBOLS: TRIDENT / DOLPHIN

7

GOD OF WINE & PLEASURE

SYMBOLS: IVY-GROWN / BRANCH, THYRSOS, DRINKING CUP, DRUNKEN SATYRS & MAENADS PANTHER

5. POSEIDON

10. DIONYSOS

The Dodekatheon
Example Itinerary [3 Weeks]

In the Greco-Roman world many deities were worshipped but only the 12 gods with thrones in the palace above Mt. Olympus (and therefore known as the 'Olympians') had temples built to them on a wide scale. They were the national gods, transcending the political boundaries of the city states. The later Romans (whose capacity for original ideas didn't extend much beyond roads, concrete and killing people in circuses) adopted the Olympians wholesale, contenting themselves with giving them new names (with the exception of Apollo). Widely depicted in all forms of ancient art, each of the 12 Olympians had their own symbol/s to aid recognition (a fortunate circumstance as 'god spotting' will enliven many a vase-filled museum visit today). The remains of their temples also offer a light-hearted excuse for some good island hopping. The itinerary here offers an easy circuit around the islands seeking out the ghosts of the gods.

Arrival/Departure Point
Athens is the best starting point because you will encounter the only weak link in the itinerary (Samos to Patmos) early in the loop. But you can also join the circuit at Kos, Rhodes, Crete (Iraklion), Santorini or Mykonos should you so choose.

Season
This itinerary can be successfully executed at any time from June to September as it runs down the two most popular lines in the Greek ferry system — the Dodecanese and Cyclades Central lines.

1 Athens: The Acropolis
The centre of Athens offers an easy way to notch up a handful of the twelve temples without difficulty. If you join the circuit at the Thissio metro station and walk to the north entrance of the Agora you will pass the site of the **Altar of the Twelve Gods**. It is now not clear if these included all the Olympians but

the altar served as the *omphalos* (navel) of the city. The milestone for measuring distances throughout Attica, it is the logical starting point for the itinerary. Walking east around the Acropolis you will come to the largest temple ever built in Greece, the Olympieion or **Temple of Zeus**.

Zeus (Roman **Jupiter**), the king of the Olympian gods, was also the god of the sky, or weather god. He walked around with a handful of thunderbolts and was wont to give any passing nymphs a quick flash if his wife Hera was out of sight. He passed the rest of his time upon a throne of black marble set upon a pedestal of the seven rainbow colour steps, keeping a moody eye on the affairs of gods and men.

Turning west, a walk along the south side of the Acropolis will bring you to the western entrance. The Acropolis has the Parthenon as its main **Temple of Athena**.

Athena (Roman **Minerva**), the goddess of wisdom, was the most popular of the goddesses (thanks to her role as the protectress of cities). She also enjoyed a secondary role as a patroness of the feminine arts and crafts — notably spinning and weaving. She frequently appears in ancient art, usually wearing the Aegis cape (made out of snake's scales, fringed with snake's heads and sporting a Gorgon's head) showing her association with the hero Perseus, who killed the Gorgon Medusa with the goddess's help.

2 Athens: The Agora
Assuming you haven't broken your leg on the slippery marble of the Acropolis then you next head for the nearby south-east entrance of the Agora site. Walking across the Agora to the northern entrance, turn west to the mound that is all that remains of the **Temple of Ares**. Believed to be almost identical to the nearby complete temple of Hephaistos, it originally stood elsewhere only to be re-erected here during the Roman infilling of the Agora.

Ares (Roman **Mars**) was the god of war and thus not the most popular of deities. Feared rather than revered, worshippers sacrificed dogs to him. Nauseatingly handsome and usually naked, he was the paramour of Aphrodite, possibly siring her son Eros.

On the hill to the west is the **Temple of Hephaistos**. Once surrounded by artisan and craftsmen's workshops it is the most complete temple surviving in Greece.

Hephaistos (Roman **Vulcan**), the workman's god, was arguably the unhappiest deity. Not only was he once thrown (literally) out of Olympus by Hera (laming himself when he landed on the island of Limnos), he was also married to Aphrodite and thus forever hopping mad with her hopping into bed with just about everybody and then coming up with all sorts of lame excuses. He is easily identified by his tools and is often riding a mule.

3 Sounion

Athens sightseeing can be wound up with a day trip to Cape **Sounion** and the impressive **Temple of Poseidon** on the hillside overlooking the Aegean Sea. **Poseidon** (Roman **Neptune**) was another moody god, swimming around with a chip on his shoulder because he lost out to his younger brother Zeus when the three brothers divided the universe between them by lot — after defeating their father **Kronos** (Roman **Saturn**). Poseidon won the sea, Zeus the heavens, and poor old Pluto the underworld (they shared the earth). The god of the sea, earthquakes and horses, Poseidon is often only distinguishable from Zeus by his trademark trident and dolphin.

4 Piraeus to Samos

Returning to Athens, head on to Piraeus and your first island hop to the ugliest island port on the itinerary — Samos (Vathi). Buses here will take you on to Samos (Pithagorio) and the nearby Heraion — the largest Greek-built temple in Greece. Just to the east of it lie the foundations of two tiny **Temples of Hermes. Hermes** (Roman **Mercury**) always managed to come in as 12th man when listing the Olympians in order of importance. His natty winged boots and traveller's hat hardly encouraged respect. Temples to him were thus thin on the ground, and although he was revered as the conductor of souls to the underworld, his reputation as a trickster and cheat confined his following to the ranks of merchants, traders and thieves. Easily identified by his herald's staff he is frequently pictured taking Hera, Athena and Aphrodite to the first ever Miss Universe contest, the judgement of Paris.

The **Temple of Hera**, although only one column remains standing, is a much more substantial affair, being one of the major shrines to the goddess in Greece.

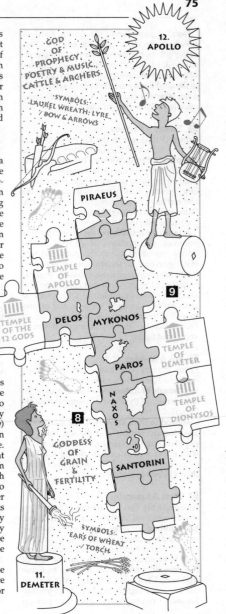

GOD OF PROPHECY, POETRY & MUSIC, CATTLE & ARCHERS.

SYMBOLS: LAUREL WREATH: LYRE, BOW & ARROWS

12. APOLLO

PIRAEUS

TEMPLE OF APOLLO

TEMPLE OF THE 12 GODS

DELOS

MYKONOS

9

PAROS

TEMPLE OF DEMETER

TEMPLE OF DIONYSOS

N A X O S

8

GODDESS OF GRAIN & FERTILITY

SANTORINI

SYMBOLS: EARS OF WHEAT, TORCH

11. DEMETER

Hera (Roman **Juno**), the queen goddess, was both the sister and wife of Zeus. They never got on, thanks to his constant attempts to ravish passing nymphs. Their life together was a litany of attempts by Hera to catch him in the act. This thwarted voyeur's symbol was a heifer but she is usually depicted with Zeus, adorned with a diadem and sceptre.

5 Turkey & Patmos

Samos (Vathi) is also the jumping-off point for day trips to Ephesus in Turkey and its **Temple of Artemis**. With one column standing it looks pretty similar to the Heraion and was built on the same massive scale. If you don't fancy visiting Turkey then pick up one of the few ferries or a tourist boat and hop down to Patmos. The monastery here was also built on the site of a temple to the goddess.

Artemis (Roman **Diana**), the beautiful virgin huntress, was goddess of all wild places, with a secondary role as the moon goddess. Having no time for the opposite sex she spent her hours protecting female chastity — along with mopping up when that failed (she was also the goddess of childbirth). Often pictured with Apollo, she used her bow and arrows to put suffering animals painlessly out of their misery — thereby acting as a sort of anti-cupid figure.

6 Kos & Rhodes

From Patmos you have very easy hops down to Kos and Rhodes. Both were home to a **Temple of Aphrodite** — though only the foundations of the Rhodes Town example are identifiable today.

Aphrodite (Roman **Venus**), the goddess of love, beauty, fertility and the sea, was very popular for obvious reasons. Usually depicted with either a dove or her winged son Eros (often depicted as a fully grown man rather than a baby-blobs style cupid).

7 Crete & Santorini

Alongside the Rhodian Temple of Aphrodite stood a temple of Dionysos. However, little of this building survives. For a better example of a temple to this god you have to do some serious island hopping on to Naxos. Easiest way is to bounce off Crete, taking one of the regular ferries from Rhodes to Crete (Iraklion). Crete was the birthplace of Zeus so there is some logic in the hop. After touring Knossos, from Iraklion you can then pick up

a Cyclades Central Line ferry stopping off at Santorini for more sightseeing before hopping on to Naxos.

8 Naxos & Paros

Naxos is home to a large Archaic temple on the small islet of Palatia just north of the ferry port. Thought to have been dedicated to either Apollo or Dionysos, visit it on the possibility that it is a **Temple of Dionysos**, since Naxos was this god's island and where he married the abandoned Ariadne.

Dionysos (Roman **Bacchus**) was the god of fun, inventing wine and orgies. Often shown accompanied by satyrs (naked bald men with horse's tails and large what-nots), nymphs or maenads (frenzied women dressed in fawn and panther skins), he started out as the god of the fruit of the trees. He was not originally one of the Olympians but gained admission when **Hestia** (Roman **Vesta**) — the old maid goddess of the hearth — stepped down in his favour.

From Naxos you have an easy hop on to Paros: the Venetian Kastro at Parikia was built on the site of a **Temple of Demeter**, its surviving wall is made up of stones from the building. **Demeter** (Roman **Ceres**) was famous for not smiling. The goddess of fertility, she was particularly associated with the crops of the soil such as grain and corn. She is often depicted holding the torch carried when she went down into the underworld (Hades) to recover her daughter Persephone, whom Zeus had ordered to be married to their brother Pluto.

9 Mykonos & Delos

From Paros you have another easy hop on to Mykonos: the starting point for excursion boats to the island of Delos — home to the foundations of an important **Temple of Apollo**. **Apollo**, the god of poetry, music and prophecy, was the most popular of the Olympian gods. He was also thought by some to be the sun god Helios. His popularity ensured that plenty of temples were erected in his name. He is often pictured as a naked and beardless youth holding a lyre.

Delos is also home to smaller temples to Aphrodite, Artemis, Demeter, and Hera, as well as the **Dodekatheon** itself. Having visited Delos and returned to Mykonos you can complete the island circuit by taking a ferry back to Piraeus for your flight home.

Athens—Mainland Port Bus Links

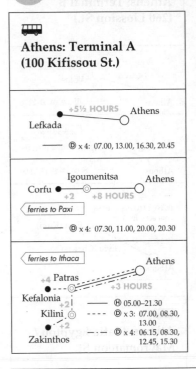

🚌

Athens: Terminal A
(100 Kifissou St.)

Lefkada ●————○ Athens
+5½ HOURS

——— Ⓓ x 4: 07.00, 13.00, 16.30, 20.45

Corfu ●——○————○ Athens
Igoumenitsa +2 +8 HOURS

⟨ ferries to Paxi ⟩

——— Ⓓ x 4: 07.30, 11.00, 20.00, 20.30

⟨ ferries to Ithaca ⟩
                                Athens
+4 Patras
●- - -○- - - - - -○
Kefalonia   +3 HOURS
+2
Kilini ◌   ——— Ⓗ 05.00–21.30
● +2   - - - Ⓓ x 3: 07.00, 08.30,
Zakinthos   13.00
               —·— Ⓓ x 4: 06.15, 08.30,
                           12.45, 15.30

Lying at the centre of the Greek bus system, Athens has a number of wider-ranging bus services of value to the island hopper. These bus routes link the capital with ports not served by Piraeus or Rafina-based ferries but which have ferry links of their own to adjacent islands. For the most part important centres in their own right, these ports have bus links from Athens timed to connect with ferries, so that buses can take passengers on to island capitals (you buy a ferry ticket along with your bus ticket). Some ferry companies also run private Athens—mainland port buses for the benefit of their passengers.

The largest bus station in Athens (Terminal A), at 100 Kifissou St., lies an inconvenient 4 km from the centre of the city, buried behind a block of semi-derelict buildings on the east side of one of the city's freeways (home to innumerable run-down scrapyards and warehouses). From the road it would be impossible to spot were it not for the constant procession of buses mysteriously disappearing down adjacent side-streets. The terminal is in fact a warehouse-like building filled with numbered bus bays and lined with confectionery stalls. Only the ticket hall

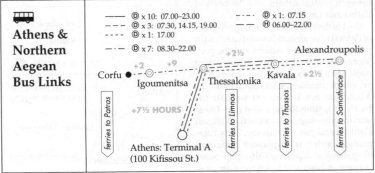

🚌

**Athens &
Northern
Aegean
Bus Links**

——— Ⓓ x 10: 07.00–23.00   —·— Ⓓ x 1: 07.15
– – – Ⓓ x 3: 07.30, 14.15, 19.00   —— Ⓗ 06.00–22.00
- - - Ⓓ x 1: 17.00
—·— Ⓓ x 7: 08.30–22.00   Alexandroupolis

Corfu ●–·–○———○- - - -○- - - - - - -○
          Igoumenitsa   Thessalonika   Kavala +2½
     +2   +9

⟨ ferries to Patras ⟩   +7½ HOURS   ⟨ ferries to Limnos ⟩   ⟨ ferries to Thassos ⟩   ⟨ ferries to Samothrace ⟩

Athens: Terminal A
(100 Kifissou St.)

is new, contrasting vividly with the surrounding decrepitude. The terminal serves most intercity buses (including buses to Thessalonika) as well as the west coast ports (Patras and Igoumenitsa), the Ionian islands and the Peloponnese.

Terminal B at 260 Liossion St. is a much smaller and altogether friendlier affair 800 m north-west of Ag. Nikolaos metro station. A similar distance out from the centre as Terminal A, it is equally badly signposted; both are best reached via taxi. Connections from Terminal B are much more limited with port/island links confined to Evia and the Sporades. Buses from both these stations usually stop in one or two of the larger towns en route but are otherwise difficult to board from the roadside (the notable exception being the popular Patras buses — which are flagged down just north of the Corinth Canal bridge as they do not enter Corinth itself). All bus times are listed on NTOG/EOT bus information sheets and in the *Greek Travel Pages* (see p. 42). (see p. 42)

The third terminus of note in Athens is near Areos Park north of the National Archaeological Museum at the junction of Platia Egyptou and Mavromateon St. (running down the west side of the park). There is no terminal building here, just a small bus parking area, along with a manned kiosk listing times and the bus stops. Buses departing from here are orange suburban variety. These provide a frequent service between central Athens and the ports of Rafina and Lavrio.

Most of the companies running boats out of Patras lay on air-conditioned coaches for passengers between Athens and the port. More expensive than regular buses (you book when buying your ferry ticket), they are worth considering since you make the 3-hour journey in comfort without the hassle of getting to the bus station (most start from Syntagma Square or the National Gardens and run via Piraeus). Ferry companies serving the Sporades (Skiathos, Skopelos and Alonissos) also offer buses between Athens and Agios Konstantinos.

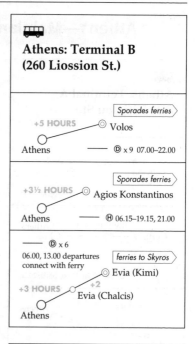

🚌 Athens: Terminal B (260 Liossion St.)

Sporades ferries
+5 HOURS ⊚ Volos
Athens   — ⓓ x 9 07.00–22.00

Sporades ferries
+3½ HOURS ⊚ Agios Konstantinos
Athens   — ⓗ 06.15–19.15, 21.00

— ⓓ x 6
06.00, 13.00 departures connect with ferry   *ferries to Skyros*
                                   ⊚ Evia (Kimi)
+3 HOURS   +2
                Evia (Chalcis)
Athens

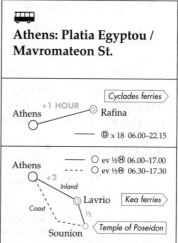

🚌 Athens: Platia Egyptou / Mavromateon St.

Cyclades ferries
+1 HOUR ⊚ Rafina
Athens
                — ⓓ x 18 06.00–22.15

Athens   — ○ ev ½ⓗ 06.00–17.00
       +2   ---- ○ ev ½ⓗ 06.30–17.30
            Inland
                ⊚ Lavrio   *Kea ferries*
Coast   ½
                ○ *Temple of Poseidon*
       Sounion

Athens: City Links

Getting Around

Athens has a large public transport system made up of buses, trolley-buses, a growing metro and tram network and a thousand of the most uncooperative taxi drivers in Europe. It can all seem pretty intimidating, but moving around is fairly easy.

The metro offers the most effective and quickest means of doing so, followed by expensive taxis and the often confusing great Athenian bus system. If you are spending more than a day or two then a visit to the **NTOG/EOT Tourist Information Office** in the city centre (opposite the Acropolis Museum; ①–⑤ 09.00–13.00) or their **Airport Information Desk** is worth the effort as they provide bus timetables and route summary sheets on request.

Like most cities Athens has various travel cards that allow unlimited use on the metro, tram and bus network (though all exclude travel to and from the airport — see overleaf). Unless you are confining travel to a couple of rides they are worth considering. In 2011 there were two on offer: a €4 day ticket and a €14 weekly ticket. The best places

to buy them are metro stations and main bus stop ticket kiosks. Both types must be validated (date and time stamped) at metro stations or via the machines on buses when you make your first journey. Thereafter you are free to enjoy the three metro lines along with the buses and tram service. Buses come in two colours: Blue (running from the centre to the suburbs) and Orange (going further afield within the province of Attica: these are NOT covered by the travel cards).

Single tickets between most metro and bus destinations are standard (in 2011 the fare was €1.40). No matter how you travel take care to validate your ticket — failure to do so can result in a heavy fine. Taxi fares are supposed to be regulated, but in practice drivers regularly overcharge. The only certainty is that between midnight and 05.00 fares are doubled.

Athens Airport

If you are arriving in Athens by air your first encounter with the city transport system is going to be the trip from the airport to the centre or port. Athens *Eleftherios Venizelos* airport lies 20 km outside the city at Spata (see map on p. 71). The airport has one

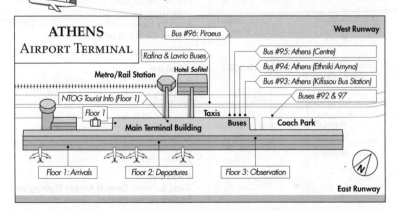

terminal building and a satellite boarding terminal (reached via an underground passage — some 20 minutes' walk away). All the usual facilities are on offer (including a branch of *McDonald's*) alongside some irritating features that defy common sense. Not least of these are baggage check-in 'travelators' that can't accommodate backpacks. Backpacks have to go to a special 'oversize' check-in point. The only way around this is to use a specialist pack travel bag.

Travelling to and from the Airport

Thanks to the **metro** link, moving between the city and the airport is a painless task. However, you do have to be careful that you buy the special airport ticket: metro officials seem to have worked out that the fine system is a good revenue generator (particularly as there is ostensibly nothing to stop you travelling from the city centre

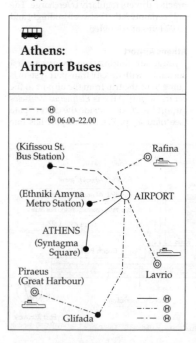

Athens: Airport Buses

– – – Ⓗ
- - - - Ⓗ 06.00–22.00

(Kifissou St. Bus Station)

Rafina

(Ethniki Amyna Metro Station)

AIRPORT

ATHENS (Syntagma Square)

Piraeus (Great Harbour)

Lavrio

Glifada

—— Ⓗ
–·–·– Ⓗ
– – – Ⓗ

to the airport using a regular metro ticket). Fares — to any destination on the system — are: €8 single, €14 return. Group tickets: 2 Person Ticket €14 single; 3 Person Ticket €18 single. Over 65s and Under 18s singles are €4. The trip to the city centre takes about 40 minutes, with services running every half hour between 05.30 and 23.00. You will need to change lines at Monastiraki if your destination is Piraeus.

Taxis from Syntagma Square cost a theoretical €14 during the day and €20 between 24.00 and 05.00. The driver will no doubt try to double this, and then sting you for the toll charged at the entry to the highway, and whatever else he thinks he can get away with (dress poor, negotiate tough and make a point of being seen to carefully check the value of your banknotes before handing them over).

At night (when the metro is closed) the airport is reached via 24-hour **bus** connections: these are popular — partly because ticket prices are lower than the metro (€5 for all destinations in 2011). The journey time to the city centre is roughly 60 minutes. Those travelling direct between the airport and Piraeus will find the bus service remains the easier option, and if you are on a flight that arrives in the small hours it is usually possible to grab the next bus to Piraeus and be on an early morning ferry out to the islands. Bus tickets are bought from the kiosk by the airport bus stops (when open) and on the bus at other times.

The four most useful services are:

● X96 Bus

Runs to/from **Piraeus**, avoiding the city centre by travelling via the coastal suburb of Glifada.
Operates: 24 hours
Frequency: 05.00–19.00 every 20 minutes.
19.00–20.30 every 30 minutes.
20.30–05.00 every 40 minutes.
Journey time: 1 hour in reasonable traffic.

● X95 Bus

Runs to/from **Central Athens (Syntagma Square metro station)**. This is the bus of choice for most tourists as it takes you right into the heart of Athens: it is the only public transport option if you are travelling between 01.00 and 05.00.

Operates: 24 hours
Frequency: 06.00–21.20 every 25 minutes.
21.20–23.35 every 30 minutes.
23.35–01.30 every 15/20 minutes.
01.30–06.30 every 30/35 minutes.
Journey time: 08.00–12.00, 15.00–19.00: 75 minutes; 12.00–15.00, 19.00–08.00: 55 minutes.

● X94 Bus

Runs to/from **Athens (Ethniki Amyna metro station)**. Tickets cost the same price as the more useful X95 Bus. Tourists find this service something of a trap as the bus sign says 'Athens', but it doesn't run into the centre, but only to the end of the metro line.
Operates: 06.00–23.20
Frequency: 06.00–20.30 every 15 minutes.
20.30–23.20 every 25/30 minutes.
Journey time: 35–45 minutes.

● X93 Bus

Runs to/from **Athens (Kifissou / Kifisos Bus Station)**. Useful if you want to connect with buses travelling to/from the Ionian islands and other long-distance bus routes.
Operates: 06.00–23.30
Frequency: 06.00–20.30 every 30 minutes.
20.30–23.20 every 25/30 minutes.

Rafina & Lavrio Buses (no number) are orange and cream-coloured KTEL Attica services. They display a destination board in the front window, and also have signs on their sides marking them as airport buses. One-way tickets are only sold on the bus. At the airport the bus stop is near the *Hotel Sofitel*. It is marked by an orange sign.
Operates: 06.00–22.00 hours
Frequency: every hour.
Journey time: 35–40 minutes to Rafina, 1 hour to Lavrio.

Buses to Intercity Bus Stations

City buses run from the centre of Athens to the two main bus stations:
● **024**: Runs between the Intercity Bus Station serving Evia and Northern Greece (**Terminal B**) at Liossion St. and Amalias Ave. (entrance to the National Gardens).
● **051**: Runs between the Intercity Bus Station serving Patras and the Peloponnese (**Terminal A**) at 100 Kifissou Street and Omonia Square.

Athens Metro

The metro system has been significantly upgraded recently with the building of two new lines and some impressive new stations. However, the new lines, with the exception of a few city-centre stops and the airport link, are of limited use to tourists as they are geared to local commuters and don't connect with major tourist transportation hubs, hotel areas or sightseeing destinations.

The original line (**Line 1**) is the most valuable: running from the city centre to Piraeus, it is largely above ground. The service is efficient, if crowded in the rush hours. The majority of the elderly stations are open to the sky and had a major facelift in the run-up to the 2004 Olympics.

Lines 2 & 3 are still being extended, but the open sections are very impressive. Line 3 shares part of its track with the new Suburban Railway in order to provide a City Centre—Airport service. Syntagma, Panepistimio and Acropoli stations are now attractions in their own right, as they have display cases with ancient artifacts discovered while boring the tunnels. Syntagma also has a glass wall cross-section through the levels of excavation, complete with an embedded skeleton.

Metro tickets are obtained from manned kiosks or ticket machines (these require you to select the ticket you need before the coin slot opens). Instructions in English are always provided. Like bus tickets, metro tickets must be validated before you are entitled to travel. NB: if you are arriving at Piraeus on an evening ferry, it is worth noting that the last train leaves promptly at midnight and calls at Omonia only, travelling there at a blistering pace (the drivers obviously have very comfortable beds and don't seem keen on hanging around).

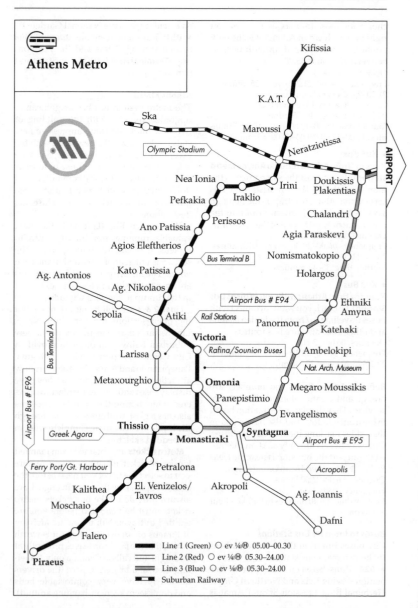

Athens Metro

Kifissia

K.A.T.

Ska

Maroussi

Neratziotissa

AIRPORT

Nea Ionia

Irini

Doukissis
Plakentias

Pefkakia

Iraklio

Chalandri

Ano Patissia

Perissos

Agia Paraskevi

Agios Eleftherios

Bus Terminal B

Nomismatokopio

Kato Patissia

Holargos

Ag. Antonios

Ag. Nikolaos

Airport Bus # E94

Ethniki
Amyna

Sepolia

Atiki

Rail Stations

Panormou

Katehaki

Victoria

Larissa

Rafina/Sounion Buses

Ambelokipi

Metaxourghio

Nat. Arch. Museum

Omonia

Megaro Moussikis

Panepistimio

Evangelismos

Thissio

Monastiraki

Syntagma

Airport Bus # E95

Greek Agora

Petralona

Acropolis

Kalithea

El. Venizelos/
Tavros

Akropoli

Ag. Ioannis

Moschaio

Dafni

Ferry Port/Gt. Harbour

Bus Terminal A

Airport Bus # E96

Falero

Piraeus

	Line 1 (Green)	○ ev ¼ᴴ⊕ 05.00–00.30
	Line 2 (Red)	○ ev ¼ᴴ⊕ 05.30–24.00
	Line 3 (Blue)	○ ev ¼ᴴ⊕ 05.30–24.00
	Suburban Railway	

⚓ Athens: Centre

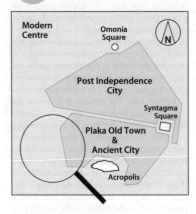

Athens

AΘHNA; pop. 4,000,001.

CODE ☎ 210
NTOG INFORMATION DESK ☎ 322 2545
TOURIST POLICE ☎ 171
POLICE ☎ 100
FIRST AID ☎ 166

Given her fantastic historical pedigree and worldwide reputation as a premier sightseeing destination, Athens is apt to inspire mixed reactions. The transition from quaint Turkish town to a city housing a quarter of Greece's population has been a very uncomfortable one, producing a glorious (if very touristy) city centre surrounded by a sea of concrete.

The Athenian conurbation is home to half of Greece's cars and 90% of the country's industry, and while the beauty of the Acropolis buildings can go to your head, so do the smog clouds (the *nephos*) that periodically force the government to ban motorists from the streets. In High Season Athens is hot and steamy, protected by the surrounding hills from the cooling summer winds that bathe the islands. However, for all this, the city offers a couple of days of

excellent sightseeing, and has good links with the islands via the ports of Piraeus and Rafina.

When visiting Athens, priority should be given to an early visit to an EOT tourist information office. This excellent service provides free city street maps along with information sheets on hotels, buses and ferry departure times for the city ports at Piraeus and Rafina. There are several offices in the city. The easiest to find are at the airport terminal building and the office below the Acropolis (see p. 93). Others are located at the Kifissou St. long-distance bus station, and the main railway station.

Modern Centre

The centre of Athens lies some 6 km from the coast, thanks to the Acropolis. This landmark stands at the heart of the city as it has always done. The modern centre, however, is made up of three distinct districts. First is the Ancient City, now slowly making a reappearance, with a growing number of archaeological sites gradually being restored and opened to the public. The best are now united into one pedestrianized 'archaeological park' which greatly improves the sightseeing experience.

The second section of the modern centre lies to the north of the Acropolis, and comprises the remaining buildings and narrow winding streets of the Ottoman city (now known as Old Town or simply the 'Plaka' district). To the north of Plaka, and the part of town most visitors first encounter via the rail, bus and metro links, is the post-1832 Greek independence new centre (largely constructed in the century before 1940). When Athens was chosen — for largely sentimental reasons — as the capital of the newly independent Greece, it was little more than a minor garrison town (thanks to the heavily fortified Acropolis) with a few thousand inhabitants.

The new Bavarian-born king of Greece took advantage of the opportunity to construct a fitting West European-style capital of wide boulevards outside the old city (which was intended to be demolished, excavated, and preserved as a vast archaeological park). All went well with this scheme until the disastrous Helleno-Turkish war of 1920–22, which resulted in a flood of refugees into Athens, overwhelming the planners with their impromptu building.

As a result, the post-independence city has a centre (roughly bounded by Syntagma Square to the east, Omonia Square to the north, and Plaka to the south) which exhibits wide boulevards graced with blocks up to a dozen storeys high, while around it, defiantly ignoring the hilly terrain, chaos reigns — in the form of the encircling kilometres of concrete suburbs bisected by traffic-choked freeways.

The Post-Independence City

Often similarly jammed with traffic (thanks to the four-times-daily rush hour in Athens), the post-independence city isn't the perfect tourist destination, and has little appeal beyond the large numbers of hotels, the National Archaeological Museum and the pleasant National Gardens to the east. Its saving grace is that the grid-iron street system makes it easy to walk between the major points via the main streets without getting too lost. The most important of these streets are **Athinas**, **Stadiou** and **Ermou** (the latter two are now home to the big city stores), which run between the three main squares.

Syntagma (Constitution) Square — the tourist 'hub' of the city and home to the Greek Parliament (complete with its famous soldier guards wearing their traditional skirts and pom-pom shoes) — is the most important and attractive of these. While it is a place tourists pass through rather than visit, it is an easy point of reference, with some greenery enlivening its otherwise empty central area. Most of the commercial activity is located on the west (Plaka) side,

where there are various food outlets and several international press stalls.

Omonia, the second largest of the big three squares, has been transformed from a very grimy traffic roundabout into something equally unappealing — thanks to a pedestrianization scheme gone wrong that has divided the traffic and connected blocks on opposite sides of the square. Sadly the improved access has simply encouraged the congregation of the worst elements of Athenian life. The square is a haven for druggies and people of the night (largely invisible), to say nothing of ever growing numbers of — seemingly unemployed — immigrant men who idle away the evenings here. In the past the atmosphere hasn't been particularly threatening, though sad to say this is beginning to change. As a result you might want to avoid the hotels (most at the poorer end of the scale) in the streets that radiate web-like from the square.

Monastiraki is the smallest of the three squares, with a cute little red-brick Byzantine church in its centre. Recently refurbished, it is the most human and on a more cosy scale than the other two, with a showcase metro station, scenic views of the Acropolis, and an archaeological viewing well offering a glimpse of the ancient river Eridanos which still flows beneath the modern city. Monastiraki also has the merit of possessing restaurants and a number of street vendors selling fresh produce, as well as access to the old town streets of the Plaka district on one side and the Athens flea market on the other.

The warren of shop-filled streets between the main squares is becoming increasingly palatable thanks to an ongoing **pedestrianization** scheme. Quite why this particular area has been so designated is more of a mystery. Admittedly, there are a large number of stores, but this isn't a noted hotel district, and overall a mild state of grime is the order of the day (though buskers do their best to cheer things up a bit). To date this attempt to give Athens a more cosmopolitan café society feel has only been partially successful, but it is undoubtedly a considerable improvement on what went before.

One major benefit of the pedestrianization of so many city centre streets is that it is now much easier for tourists to explore the capital — such as the greener parts of the city. These include the shady **National Gardens** and the more energy-sapping **Likavittos** and Filopapou (alias Mouseion) hills with their views across the city. Likavittos is reached via a cable car, while Filopapou is in the centre of a pine-wood park to the south-west of the Acropolis.

Although Athens is a relatively safe capital city even by European standards, visiting parks and wooded areas can still be dangerous at night. In the crowd-free Low Season tourists have even been mugged at midday on Filopapou, so take care. Athenians tend to put the rise in crime levels of recent years down to the influx of illegal immigrants and refugees.

Most visitors negotiate Athens without problems, but the impact of 4 million tourists a year has also had an unfortunate effect on a minority of the locals. There have always been two types of Athenian: the hospitable and charming individuals on a par with most of the Greek islanders, and the other kind — who in days past ordered the death of Socrates, amongst others. Sadly, most of the descendants of the latter class have become waiters or taxi drivers. In Athens many of the taxi drivers are something else — it pays to get into a taxi before stating your desired destination: most drivers have their own patch and aren't interested in going anywhere else ('anywhere else' usually being where you want to go). Requests for the airport or Piraeus are seen as a licence to overcharge to excess. All in all, when in Athens it is wise to keep your eyes open (see also: 'Scams', p. 56).

Plaka District / Old Town

Plaka is the last remnant of pre-Greek-independence Turkish Athens, and the only part of the city with great appeal. A warren of 17th and 18th c. red-tiled town buildings mixed with earlier small Byzantine churches, small leafy squares and excavated archaeological sites, it roughly occupies the large north-east quarter of the ancient city, and is bounded by the Acropolis and Olympieion to the south and the Agora to the west. Originally, the old town extended over the Acropolis and the Agora areas as well, but the buildings were demolished between the first half of the 19th century and the 1930s.

In fact the entire Plaka district lies directly over the ancient city. There are undoubtedly important ancient sites obscured under the photogenic Plaka buildings, but their merit is recognized, and renovation mixed with piecemeal excavation (when opportunities present themselves) is now the order of the day.

The bulk of the old town — although throbbing with souvenir shops (selling items that are available at a much better price on the islands), restaurants, hotels and everything else — has a lot going for it in spite of the overblown tourist trappings. It is quite possible to forget the horror of concrete Athens while you explore the warren of streets. In addition to housing the best of the sightseeing, Plaka is also the main eating area in the city, with the bulk of the tavernas and restaurants lining or near **Adrianou** and **Kidathineon** streets. Most are on the expensive side; however, you at least have the consolation that the views are worth the added costs of a meal.

Towering over all is the Acropolis, which, floodlit at night, casts a golden glow over the crowds that safely wander in numbers into the small hours (note: single women should still be on their guard — particularly on Sundays when the whole city shuts down). Fortunately, all the principal sights are within easy walking distance of each other, and the Acropolis provides a ready point of reference should you lose your way; the streets nearest the rock rise steeply into its shadow. Syntagma Square is another ready point of reference.

The only area of the Plaka now scheduled for demolition is the thin finger of buildings that lie to the north of the Agora. Now rather dilapidated, this area (unlike the rest of Plaka) is most definitely much better avoided at night. During the day it is home to the city's flea market (on Ifestou St.). For the most part it sells the worst sort of rubbish, but amid the imitation brand-name clothing outlets are a couple of antique shops selling detritus from scrapped ships, and an outlet offering a million different types of beads.

If you are in Athens for any length of time, you may wish to buy a definitive street map — though the free one offered by information offices of the EOT is more than fit for most purposes. Easily the best of the commerical maps are the new 'Road Editions' *Athens, Piraeus & Southern Suburbs* and — the far less relevant — *Athens: Northern & Western Suburbs* (both cost €7.50).

It is not much of an exaggeration to say that every street in central Athens boasts a hotel. A bed is not hard to find — even at the height of the season. However, you will find that room quality is significantly lower, and prices are normally higher, than with a comparable class of hotel in the islands. There also seems to be a higher degree of variation in room quality in some hotels (several are not recommended here because you can't be sure of getting one of the better rooms). It is also worth noting that many D- and E-class hotels don't take credit cards, so check on this before you book in. All this said, the recent problems in Greece, and Athens in particular, has led to a drop in hotel prices in the capital thanks to tourists staying away, so there are bargains to be had if you ask for a 'cheap' room!

Some accommodation suggestions — working out from the centre (note: map references refer to the 4-section city centre map — see the 'Locating Hotels' section on p. 91):

Plaka & Syntagma

In the perfect world the visitor to Athens should seek to stay in or near the Plaka district. Even though this is a very noisy part of town, most people don't stay in Athens long, and it is conveniently close to all the sights — so much so that you may consider it worth booking ahead to secure a room. The antiquated nature of many of the buildings means that hotels tend to be small, and therefore are more likely to be full come the evening.

Top End:

• *Grand Bretagne* (☎ 333 0000) A-class, [map 4; 21-55]. The oldest hotel in Athens. Built in 1842, it is one of the poshest places in town with prices (and phone number!) to match.

• *Electra Palace* (☎ 337 0000) A-class, [map 4; 19-60]. One of the few top-end hotels in Plaka, the big plus on offer is a roof-top swimming pool with views across to the Acropolis.

• *Plaka* (☎ 322 2096) B-class, [map 3; 17-57]. One of the cheapest of the expensive hotels in a newish building.

Mid-range:

• *Acropolis House* (☎ 322 2344) C-class, [map 4; 20-62]. Also listed as a B-class pension, this is an attractive Plaka option — though facilities are at the lower end of the C-class scale.

• *Amazon* (☎ 323 4002) C-class, [map 4; 19-58]. Formerly listed as a B-class hotel, though rooms are typical Athens C-class standard.

• *Hermes* (☎ 323 5514) C-class, [map 4; 19-59]. Up-market C-class with refurbished rooms.

• *Aphrodite* (☎ 323 4357) C-class, [map 3; 18-59]. A quieter backstreet hotel.

• *Cecil* (☎ 321 7079) C-class, [map 3; 15-50]. A small, old-fashioned 19 c. building. Atmospheric rooms are well maintained.

• *Attalos* (☎ 321 2801) C-class, [map 3; 14-51]. Although this hotel is not on the most attractive street in town, its rooms are clean: a few offer views of the Acropolis.

• *Pella Inn* (☎ 321 2229) D-class, [map 3; 12-55]. One for the desperate: poorly sited in the more dangerous, run-down part of Plaka. Worth considering if you can't find a central room elsewhere.

• *Erechthion* (☎ 345 9606) C-class, [map 3; 8-60]. An interesting option: one of the few reasonably priced hotels west of the Acropolis. Tends to fill up very quickly in High Season.

Budget:

• *Tembi* (☎ 321 3175) D-class, [map 3; 16-55]. A bit down at heel, but popular, thanks to impressive views of the Acropolis.

• *John's Place* (☎ 322 9719) E-class, [map 4; 19-59]. An option if you are really keen to be in Plaka and save money at the same time. Ask to see the room before you sign on.

Omonia & Metaxourghio

The district between Omonia Square and Karaiskaki Square is packed with hotels, most in the mid-range category. The weary traveller can simply exit at either Omonia or Metaxourghio metro stations and be sure of being only a block or two away from a bed. The only area that is a bit suspect is the block on the north side of Omonia: the hotels here tend to be pretty ropy, and contrast greatly with the large number of excellent mid-range hotels that line the streets to the north-west.

Top End:

• *Stanley* (☎ 524 1611) A-class, [map 1; 10-42]. One of the few top end hotels in this area of Athens with a prime location on Karaiskaki Square.

• *Minoa* (☎ 523 4622) B-class, [map 1; 12-42]. A good solid city-centre hotel. Well maintained and not over-priced for its category.

• *King Jason* (☎ 523 4721) B-class, [map 1; 10-46]. Reasonable, but can be hard to find.

• *Pythagorion* (☎ 524 2811) B-class, [map 1; 13-44]. Formerly listed as C-class, this hotel's rooms fall between the two.

Mid-range:

• *Theoxenia* (☎ 380 0250) C-class, [map 1; 18-44]. A very attractive option, tucked quietly away with all facilities (internet café, bar and bakery) right outside the front door.

• *Museum* (☎ 380 5611) C-class, [map 2; 20-38]. Slightly off the beaten trail, this is another one worth considering as it is reasonably quiet yet not too far from the centre of things.

• *Exarchion* (☎ 380 0731) C-class, [map 2; 20-41]. Reasonably modern, but charges extra for air-conditioned rooms.

• *Dryades* (☎ 330 2387) C-class, [map 2; 23-39]. A hotel in the student part of town. Access via a steep hillside to put older tourists off.

• *Euripides* (☎ 321 2301) C-class, [map 1; 12-49]. A large modern hotel, reasonably well placed. It lacks character but does have all the essentials.

Budget:

• *Youth Hostel* (☎ 524 1708), [map 1; 13-42]. The only official youth hostel in Athens.

• *Eva* (☎ 522 3079) D-class, [map 1; 11-41]. One of the better budget options.

• *Annabel* (☎ 524 5834) D-class, [map 1; 14-42]. A hotel that also styles itself as a youth hostel. Some dormitory accommodation.

• *Pindaros* (☎ 524 4229) D-class, [map 1; 15-48]. One of several closely grouped budget hotels, all of similar quality.

• *Elikon* E-class, [map 1; 17-44]. Very primitive hotel patronised by locals on a budget. A better than nothing option — just.

Larissa Rail Station

The rail station area has several good hotels within easy reach if you prefer a rather quieter part of town (buildings here are mostly residential). This accounts for the disproportionately high number of more expensive hotels located here.

Top End:

• *Oscar Inn* (☎ 881 3211) B-class, [map 1; 10-36]. Good up-market option close to the station.

• *Balaska* (☎ 883 5211) B-class, [map 1; 12-36]. Middle-aged rooms, but not too expensive.

Mid-range:

• *Mystras* (☎ 522 7737) C-class, [map 1; 8-40]. Conveniently close to the station. A bit down at heel, with prices to match, so will appeal to budget travellers.

• *Filoxenia* (☎ 882 8611) C-class, [map 1; 15-36]. A reasonable hotel, if a bit out of the way.

Budget:

• *Rio* (☎ 522 7075) D-class, [map 1; 8-43]. A popular and cheap backpacker option.

• *San Remo* (☎ 523 3245) E-class, [map 1; 9-38]. The cheapest option close to the station.

Δ

Athens has several poor trailer sites in the outer environs that are better avoided: camping in Athens tends to be more trouble than it is worth. The best sites are a longish bus ride away along the Apollo coast near Cape Sounion, including the over-popular *Camping Bacchus* (☎ 229 203 9571) and less appealing *Camping Varkiza* (☎ 210 897 3615).

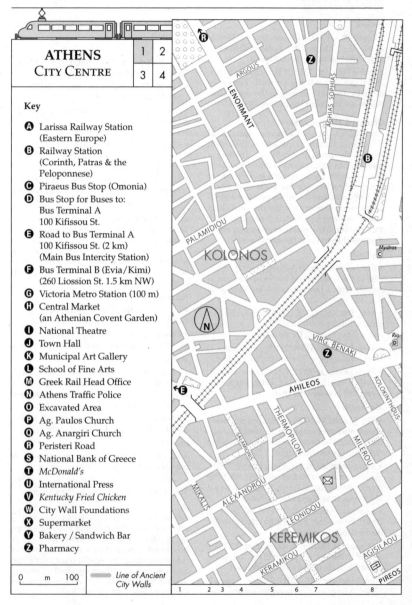

ATHENS
CITY CENTRE

| 1 | 2 |
| 3 | 4 |

Key

A Larissa Railway Station
(Eastern Europe)

B Railway Station
(Corinth, Patras & the
Peloponnese)

C Piraeus Bus Stop (Omonia)

D Bus Stop for Buses to:
Bus Terminal A
100 Kifissou St.

E Road to Bus Terminal A
100 Kifissou St. (2 km)
(Main Bus Intercity Station)

F Bus Terminal B (Evia/Kimi)
(260 Liossion St. 1.5 km NW)

G Victoria Metro Station (100 m)

H Central Market
(an Athenian Covent Garden)

I National Theatre

J Town Hall

K Municipal Art Gallery

L School of Fine Arts

M Greek Rail Head Office

N Athens Traffic Police

O Excavated Area

P Ag. Paulos Church

Q Ag. Anargiri Church

R Peristeri Road

S National Bank of Greece

T *McDonald's*

U International Press

V *Kentucky Fried Chicken*

W City Wall Foundations

X Supermarket

Y Bakery / Sandwich Bar

Z Pharmacy

0   m   100   *Line of Ancient
City Walls*

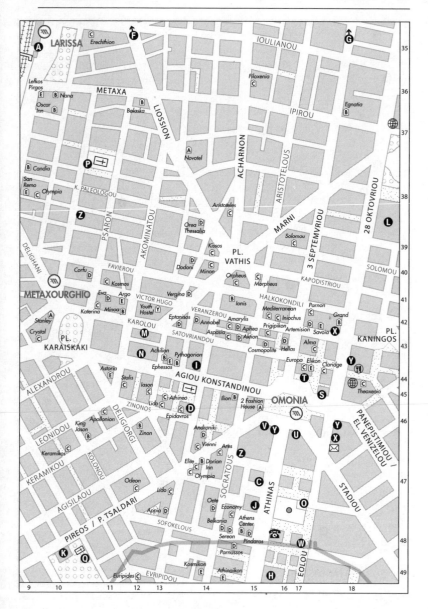

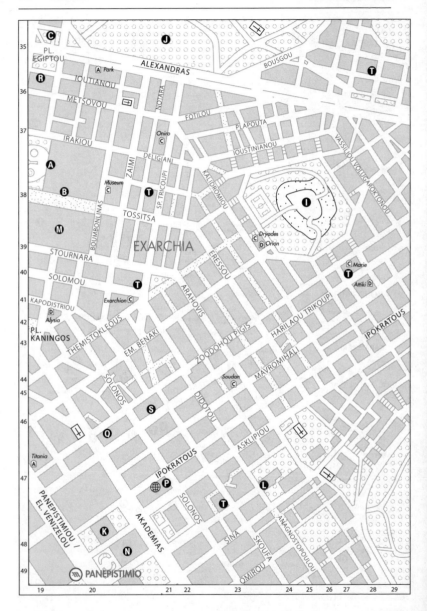

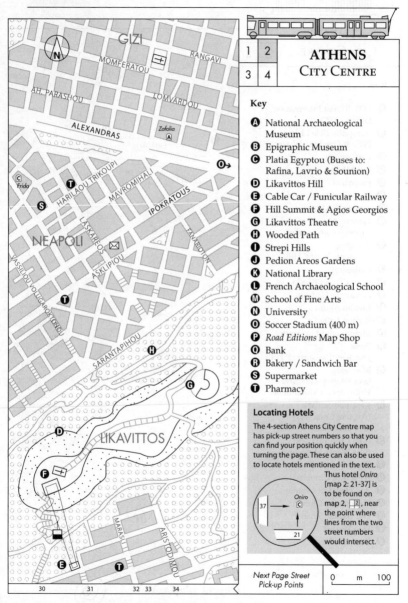

ATHENS
CITY CENTRE

Key

Ⓐ National Archaeological Museum
Ⓑ Epigraphic Museum
Ⓒ Platia Egyptou (Buses to: Rafina, Lavrio & Sounion)
Ⓓ Likavittos Hill
Ⓔ Cable Car / Funicular Railway
Ⓕ Hill Summit & Agios Georgios
Ⓖ Likavittos Theatre
Ⓗ Wooded Path
Ⓘ Strepi Hills
Ⓙ Pedion Areos Gardens
Ⓚ National Library
Ⓛ French Archaeological School
Ⓜ School of Fine Arts
Ⓝ University
Ⓞ Soccer Stadium (400 m)
Ⓟ *Road Editions* Map Shop
Ⓠ Bank
Ⓡ Bakery / Sandwich Bar
Ⓢ Supermarket
Ⓣ Pharmacy

Locating Hotels

The 4-section Athens City Centre map has pick-up street numbers so that you can find your position quickly when turning the page. These can also be used to locate hotels mentioned in the text.

Thus hotel *Oniro* [map 2: 21-37] is to be found on map 2, ▢2, near the point where lines from the two street numbers would intersect.

Next Page Street Pick-up Points

0   m   100

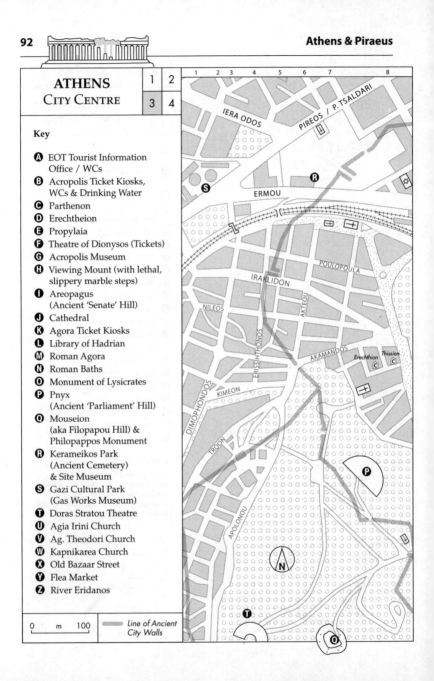

ATHENS
CITY CENTRE

| 1 | 2 |
| 3 | 4 |

Key

A EOT Tourist Information Office / WCs

B Acropolis Ticket Kiosks, WCs & Drinking Water

C Parthenon

D Erechtheion

E Propylaia

F Theatre of Dionysos (Tickets)

G Acropolis Museum

H Viewing Mount (with lethal, slippery marble steps)

I Areopagus (Ancient 'Senate' Hill)

J Cathedral

K Agora Ticket Kiosks

L Library of Hadrian

M Roman Agora

N Roman Baths

O Monument of Lysicrates

P Pnyx (Ancient 'Parliament' Hill)

Q Mouseion (aka Filopapou Hill) & Philopappos Monument

R Kerameikos Park (Ancient Cemetery) & Site Museum

S Gazi Cultural Park (Gas Works Museum)

T Doras Stratou Theatre

U Agia Irini Church

V Ag. Theodori Church

W Kapnikarea Church

X Old Bazaar Street

Y Flea Market

Z River Eridanos

| 0 | m | 100 | ▨ | Line of Ancient City Walls |

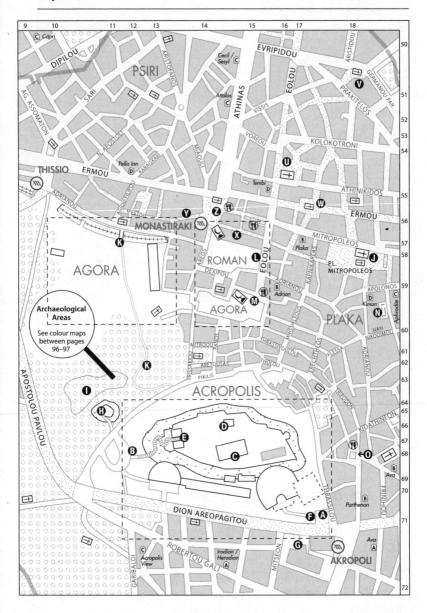

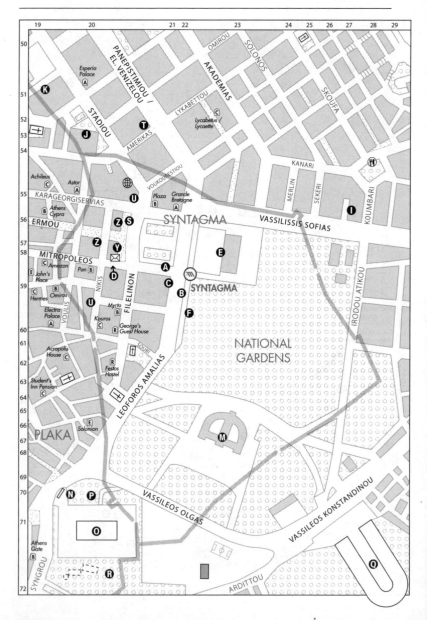

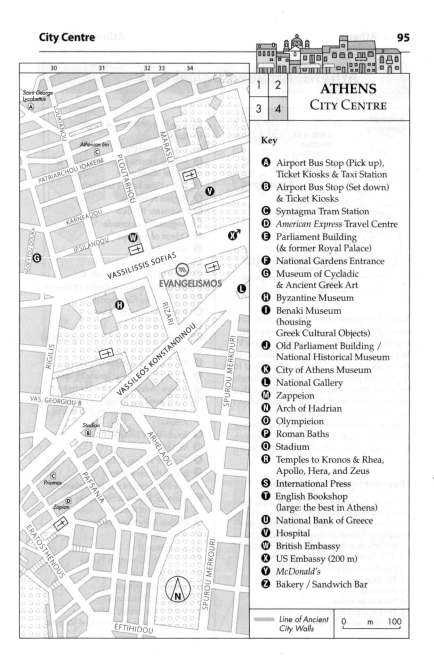

Key

Ⓐ Airport Bus Stop (Pick up),
   Ticket Kiosks & Taxi Station

Ⓑ Airport Bus Stop (Set down)
   & Ticket Kiosks

Ⓒ Syntagma Tram Station

Ⓓ *American Express* Travel Centre

Ⓔ Parliament Building
   (& former Royal Palace)

Ⓕ National Gardens Entrance

Ⓖ Museum of Cycladic
   & Ancient Greek Art

Ⓗ Byzantine Museum

Ⓘ Benaki Museum
   (housing
   Greek Cultural Objects)

Ⓙ Old Parliament Building /
   National Historical Museum

Ⓚ City of Athens Museum

Ⓛ National Gallery

Ⓜ Zappeion

Ⓝ Arch of Hadrian

Ⓞ Olympieion

Ⓟ Roman Baths

Ⓠ Stadium

Ⓡ Temples to Kronos & Rhea,
   Apollo, Hera, and Zeus

Ⓢ International Press

Ⓣ English Bookshop
   (large: the best in Athens)

Ⓤ National Bank of Greece

Ⓥ Hospital

Ⓦ British Embassy

Ⓧ US Embassy (200 m)

Ⓨ *McDonald's*

Ⓩ Bakery / Sandwich Bar

Line of Ancient
City Walls

0   m   100

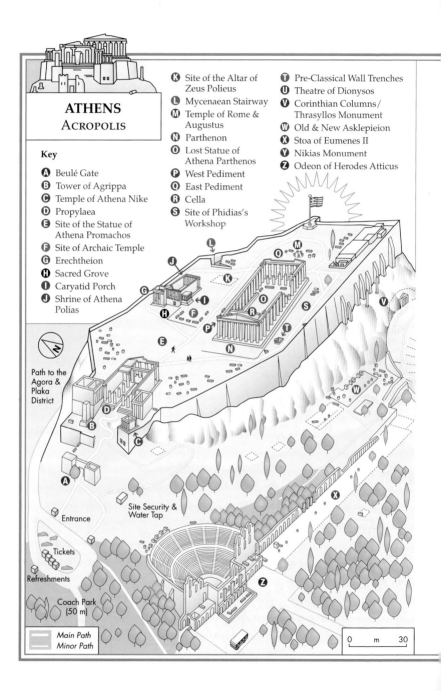

ATHENS
ACROPOLIS

Key

Ⓐ Beulé Gate
Ⓑ Tower of Agrippa
Ⓒ Temple of Athena Nike
Ⓓ Propylaea
Ⓔ Site of the Statue of Athena Promachos
Ⓕ Site of Archaic Temple
Ⓖ Erechtheion
Ⓗ Sacred Grove
Ⓘ Caryatid Porch
Ⓙ Shrine of Athena Polias

Ⓚ Site of the Altar of Zeus Polieus
Ⓛ Mycenaean Stairway
Ⓜ Temple of Rome & Augustus
Ⓝ Parthenon
Ⓞ Lost Statue of Athena Parthenos
Ⓟ West Pediment
Ⓠ East Pediment
Ⓡ Cella
Ⓢ Site of Phidias's Workshop

Ⓣ Pre-Classical Wall Trenches
Ⓤ Theatre of Dionysos
Ⓥ Corinthian Columns/ Thrasyllos Monument
Ⓦ Old & New Asklepieion
Ⓧ Stoa of Eumenes II
Ⓨ Nikias Monument
Ⓩ Odeon of Herodes Atticus

Path to the Agora & Plaka District

Site Security & Water Tap

Entrance

Tickets

Refreshments

Coach Park (50 m)

Main Path
Minor Path

0   m   30

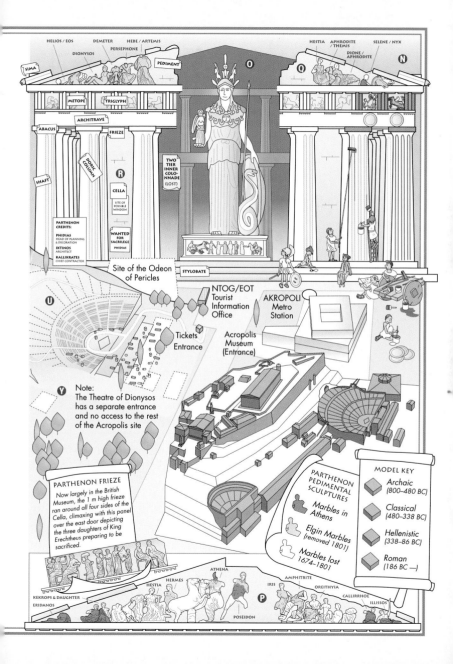

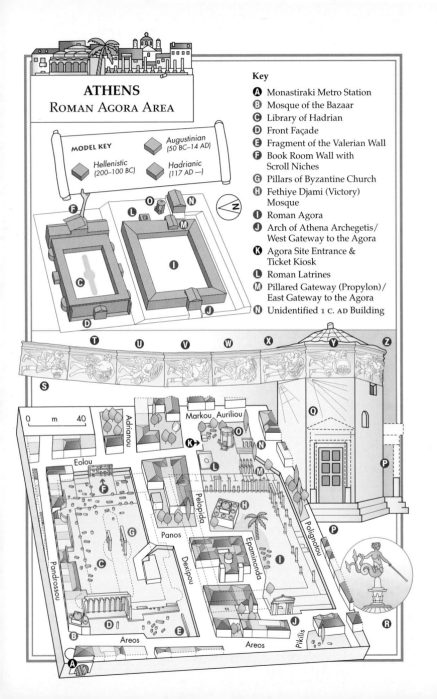

ATHENS
ROMAN AGORA AREA

MODEL KEY

Hellenistic (200–100 BC)

Augustinian (50 BC–14 AD)

Hadrianic (117 AD —)

Key

- **A** Monastiraki Metro Station
- **B** Mosque of the Bazaar
- **C** Library of Hadrian
- **D** Front Façade
- **E** Fragment of the Valerian Wall
- **F** Book Room Wall with Scroll Niches
- **G** Pillars of Byzantine Church
- **H** Fethiye Djami (Victory) Mosque
- **I** Roman Agora
- **J** Arch of Athena Archegetis/ West Gateway to the Agora
- **K** Agora Site Entrance & Ticket Kiosk
- **L** Roman Latrines
- **M** Pillared Gateway (Propylon)/ East Gateway to the Agora
- **N** Unidentified 1 C. AD Building

0 m 40

Adrianou

Markou Auriliou

Eolou

Pelopida

Panos

Dexipou

Epaminonda

Pandrossou

Areos

Areos

Pikilis

Polignotou

of the rock is now free of traffic and one can take in the view without danger to life and limb. Traffic fans can, however, still get some excitement out of the revamped 'park' as both the Olympieion and the Kerameikos Cemetery still require you to cross very busy roads.

All this is a long way from the original park concept. This involved demolishing all buildings that stood around the ancient remains and then constructing modern Athens beyond the ancient city wall line. This was partially implemented in the first half of the 19th century when the Acropolis, Agora and Roman Agora sites were systematically cleared of the houses built amidst the ruins during the three centuries of Ottoman rule. But after the initial enthusiastic demolition, further work stopped as the business of reconstruction and preservation sapped resources. Today there are no plans for further demolition (apart from a few houses north of the Agora's disfiguring metro line).

If you plan to make full use of your ticket and visit all the sites then you should set aside a couple of days for the task. During the summer months the shade-lacking Acropolis and Olympieion are best tackled either very early or late in the day.

○ The Tower of the Winds (also called the Horologion of Andronikos Cyrrhestes)

℗ Entrance Portico

○ Sundial Lines

℞ The Lost Triton Weathervane

The Winds:

🅢 NW: **Skiron** (holds charcoal cauldron)

🆃 W: **Zephyros** (showers lap of flowers)

🆄 SW: **Lips** (holds stern of trireme-like ship)

🆅 S: **Notos** (emptying an urn of raindrops)

🆆 SE: **Euros** (mantled, with arm cloaked)

🆇 E: **Apeliotes** (showers lap of fruit)

🆈 NE: **Kaikias** (holds shield of hailstones)

🆉 N: **Boreas** (mantled, and holding a conch)

☻

An appreciation of the historical background to Athens is helpful when viewing the extant remains. The jumble of ruins from different periods (particularly in the Agora areas) doesn't lend itself to easy visualization of past appearance. Sites such as the Acropolis itself and the Olympieion, which were built at one time, are much more coherent.

Athens was once the most powerful of all the Greek city states. It is best known for the work of a mere three generations in the 5 C. BC when it first stood alone as a bulwark against the massed forces of the Persian Empire (its citizens playing a crucial part in the battles of Marathon in 490 BC and Salamis in 480 BC), and then, under the leadership of Pericles and his successors, became the fountainhead of European civilization, playing host to the sudden flowering of the Greek genius that gave the western world its first theatre, greatest art and architecture, and first true history and philosophy. However, the dynamic that had set the city apart soon faded, and Athens had to settle for becoming a major centre of learning during the Hellenistic and Roman periods, then a minor town under the Turks, before emerging as the capital of Greece in the 19th century.

Thanks to the protection offered by the Acropolis, Athens has been occupied since Neolithic times. During the Mycenaean period the Acropolis was fortified, and this served the city well during the dark ages that followed, as it was able to repulse the waves of Doric Greeks pouring into Greece. By the 8 C. BC Athens had gained control of the surrounding province of Attica and emerged as one of the major art centres in Greece. This developed into a leading cultural role in the 6 C. BC under the patronage of Pisistratus, who initiated the Great Dionysia (a semi-religious eisteddfod) as part of the annual Panathenaic festival. This gave the world the first established texts of Homer, and later produced the birth of drama; most of the great plays of Greek tragedy and comedy were conceived and first performed in the city on the site of the Theatre of Dionysos.

A succession of leaders — Draco, Solon and Cleisthenes — also instituted constitutional reforms that led to Athens emerging as a champion of democracy. Rule by orators in turn prompted debate, and enquiry into words and their meanings, which in turn extended the debate to wider ideas and concepts of morality. As a result, Athens developed as a centre for the great philosophers — Socrates, Plato and Aristotle among them. Athens also emerged as a major economic power — thanks to the profits derived from the substantial silver mines at nearby Lavrio.

Athenian victories over the Persians gave the city the role of leading protector of the Greeks and, on this basis, the islands contributed funds for the maintenance of the Athenian trireme fleet. Unfortunately Athens rapidly turned these contributions into a tribute, and the islands into a de facto empire, and used the excess monies to build the Acropolis temples. Fearful of Athenian domination, the cities of Sparta and Corinth were soon embroiled in the Peloponnesian War, which Athens lost after 30 years of struggle.

Never regaining her military pre-eminence, Athens fell to Philip of Macedon in 338 BC and came under Roman control in the 2 C. BC. The city was sacked by Sulla in 86 BC, saw a brief renaissance (thanks to the patronage of Hadrian), and finally faded from the scene when it was sacked by the Herulian Goths in 267 AD. Reduced to cowering behind the small Valerian wall, Athens was a minor town in the Byzantine Empire. It was ruled by the Franks and the Venetians before the Ottoman Turks gave it three quiet centuries (their rule being briefly interrupted by the disastrous Venetian conquest of the city in 1687) prior to Greek independence in 1832.

The Ancient City & Archaeological Park Area

Considering how great a cultural and military powerhouse Athens was, the size of the ancient city comes as a surprise, for it is very small by modern standards (see map between pages 64–65). It has been calculated that the walls contained 6,000 houses for an estimated population of some 36,000. However, this figure is misleading, as a good half of the population of 'Athens' lived and worked at the Athenian port of Piraeus.

Piraeus soon developed as a city in its own right, and by the Classical period people were openly talking about the 'upper' and 'lower' cities (Athens being the former). The historian Thucydides wrote that the Athenian leader 'Themistokles thought Piraeus more useful than the upper city', and this comment reflected Piraeus's growing role as the military, business and commercial base — Athens itself

being viewed as more of the political, religious and cultural centre. This was natural enough given that Athens — represented on coins by her symbol, the owl of wisdom — was home to the traditional sites for worship (the Acropolis), law (the courts near the Agora) and learning (the three Gymnasia, including the Academy, beloved by Plato, and the recently discovered Lyceum, founded by Aristotle).

Defending this odd urban structure took some doing, particularly as Athens was primarily a maritime power (the Peloponnesian War lasted 30 years simply because Athens was dominant at sea while Sparta and her allies controlled the mainland). After the Persian sack of Athens in 480 BC, Themistokles rebuilt the city walls protecting Athens and Piraeus. Moreover, the two were connected by two walls running parallel to each other several hundred metres apart: known as the 'Long Walls', they — along with the short-lived outer Phaleron Wall — added up to a formidable defensive system that from the air would have looked like a giant dumbbell. Following the Athenian defeat in the Peloponnesian War in 404 BC, the Long Walls were demolished, only to be later rebuilt. By the Roman era they had gone, Piraeus was in decline, and the focus of Athens moved north and east, with the building of the Roman Agora and the Hadrianic Wall.

The surviving remains of the ancient city — largely within the Archaeological Park sites — are substantial, but not very representative. The Athenians built their houses and the greater part of the city walls out of adobe bricks, and over the millennia these have reverted to mud.

The park area embraces the main religious, administrative and commercial areas of the pre-Roman city, where most of the building was in stone and on an impressive scale. The reason that many of the walls and columns survive in situ is that they were sufficiently robust to form the base for medieval and later buildings. Of course while the marble stones have survived, there is little on show to give an impression of their original appearance; you would never guess that all the stonework was once painted. As for the 3,000 bronze statues observed by Roman writers: well, the National Archaeological Museum is home to the surviving odd finger or two.

The Acropolis

The greatest attraction in Athens is the Acropolis (see map between pages 96–97). The name means 'the city on the rock'. Standing some 90 m above the surrounding plain, the rock proved easily defensible, later becoming the focus of religious activity, before its defensive value again came to the fore. The buildings on the rock add up to one of the most important archaeological sites in the world. Even in their ruined state, the Parthenon and the Erechtheion remain architectural wonders, forming the nucleus of an ensemble of buildings that led the Roman writer Plutarch to say of them that 'they were created in a short time for all time … a perpetual newness blooms upon them untouched by the years, as if they held within them some everlasting breath of life and an ageless spirit intermingled in their composition'. These days this effect is diminished by the presence of three million visitors a year, but if you arrive early, you can avoid the worst of the crowds. The site is open ℗ 08.00–18.30. Coach tour guides have the right to push to the head of the ticket-kiosk queues. Tourists are not allowed to venture inside the Acropolis buildings.

The Acropolis has evidence of occupation dating back to Neolithic times, though later building has destroyed most traces. It is known that in the Mycenaean period it had a palace and saw its first major fortifications. In the Archaic period the Acropolis emerged as the religious centre of the city, with a succession of temples erected on the rock before the Persians fired them in their invasion of Greece in 480 BC. Calamitous at the time, this event cleared the way for the rebuilding programme inspired by the Athenian leader Pericles some 30 years later — just as Greek culture was bursting into full bloom; it is the ruins of these buildings that remain today.

Through the Hellenistic and Roman periods the Acropolis saw little further building, and it was only from the 7 C. AD on that the area around the temples was in-filled with other buildings, as the rock was again used as a fortress. This state of affairs continued through the period of Turkish rule (one of the early European visitors describing the Acropolis mentions that there were two streets of whitewashed houses

between the Parthenon and the Erechtheion).

Once Athens became the capital of an independent Greek state, the Acropolis was rapidly converted from a fortress-town to a museum. In 1833 work began in stripping away the detritus of 2,000 years (this included the removal of all houses and a 30 m tower built atop the Propylaea) to reveal the ancient buildings in all their ruined glory. However, restoration of the Classical buildings resulted in unwitting damage due to poor techniques. The worst of these was the use of iron staples in rebuilding that rusted and caused many marble blocks to split (the ancients coated the original staples with lead to prevent this process occurring). This has resulted in all the buildings requiring major attention in the last few years, and quite a lot of controversial new 'white' marble is visible. The nature of this restoration is a subject of much argument. Current rebuilding is limited to work needed to ensure the structural integrity of the monuments and all new blocks are dated to ensure there is never confusion between old and new material. All the additions are also reversible. Previous restoration has been more substantial, notably the rebuilding of the centre columns on the north façade of the Parthenon in 1933. It has been suggested that the south side be similarly 'repaired', but this is a contentious idea and has been shelved while other worries — notably the threat of acid rain damage — are discussed.

Acropolis Entrance / West Side

Modern visitors approach the Acropolis from the same side as the ancients, though the first building encountered is a late construction: **A** the **Beulé Gate** (named after its excavator) formed part of the defensive wall constructed in the 3 C. AD. It replaced a large processional stairway constructed by the Emperor Claudius in 52 AD. Today the path winds up to the Acropolis much as it did in Classical times. After the Beulé Gate you are confronted by two bastions projecting out from the Acropolis proper. On the northern one is **B** the distinctive **'Tower' of Agrippa** (c. 178 BC). A Hellenistic plinth 8.8 m high, it bore a succession of bronze statues (including a chariot carrying Antony and Cleopatra), and takes its name from a statue of Marcus Agrippa erected on it in 27 BC.

The south bastion is more appealing, being home to **C** the lovely small **Athena Nike**

Temple (427–424 BC). Designed by Kallikrates, it was dismantled in 1686 by the Turks so that the bastion could be used to house cannon. Fortunately, all the stones were preserved on site and it was re-erected in 1836–42. The building has a frieze running right around it, and contained a statue of Athena with Nike (Victory). Unfortunately, the lack of tourist-retaining walls on the bastion means that it is fenced off: the steps to the Acropolis offer the best view you can get of it. Like all the Acropolis buildings, it is built of Pentelic marble. Thanks to small deposits of iron in the marble, the colour has gradually mellowed from white to a creamy yellow as the iron has gradually oxidized over the millennia.

Extending out onto the bastions are the wings of **O** the **Propylaea** (438–432 BC): the ceremonial gateway to the Acropolis. Deemed to be the best of its kind by the ancients, it was never fully completed. The outbreak of the Peloponnesian War and Athenian defeat ensured that its decoration was never finished. Designed by Mnesikles, the building was famous for its five massive doors and painted ceiling.

The north wing was also a noted picture gallery. The building was used as a bishop's palace in the 13 C., and in the 17 C. became a magazine for the Turkish garrison, suffering severe damage when a passing lightning bolt struck. The Venetian bombardment of 1687 finished the job of demolition by putting paid to the famous ceiling. South-east of the Propylaea are the scanty foundations of a double-winged stoa, a votive shrine to **Artemis Brauronia** (the bear goddess), and nearer the Parthenon, the **Chalkotheke** or **Magazine of the Bronzes**.

The North Side

Surprisingly, the magnificent Parthenon temple was not the holy of holies on the Acropolis. It was more of a glorious ante-chamber to the true religious centre — the Erechtheion — which stands on the probable site of the Mycenaean palace. This building was guarded by a large bronze statue that stood at **O** facing the Propylaea. Known as the **Athena Promachos**, this famous figure is long lost, but part of the stone base has been identified. The path takes you past the site where it stood, and then divides. One branch takes you along the north side of the Parthenon (the traditional approach route to this temple); the other runs

northward past foundations at **O**. This is the site of a **Temple of Athena Polias**. Built c. 530 BC, it stood alongside another limestone temple — the melodiously named **Hekatompedon**, meaning 'one hundred footer' (c. 566 BC), which stood on the Parthenon site. Some time around 508 BC this building was demolished. Its incomplete successor — the **Pre-Parthenon** — was destroyed by the Persians. Its column drums were later used to close off the other entrances to the Acropolis and are still visible in the north wall when viewed from street level. After the Persian sacking, the Athenians swore never to rebuild the temples. They later got around this vow by levelling the Athena Polias temple site, and having made a gesture in this direction, proceeded to rebuild the other buildings.

Not least among these was the **Erechtheion** (c. 421–405 BC). This complex of shrines is a four-chambered building **O** that conformed to an ancient and irregular plan. It was home to several ancient and venerated wooden figures — notably a statue of Athena Polias — that were removed (along with the population of Athens) to the island of Salamis during the Persian sacking. The path approaches the building running past **O** the site of the **Sacred Grove** (which was home to the olive tree offered by Athena, when winning her contest for the patronage of the city with Poseidon) and then turns east at the **North Portico** (a shrine to Poseidon). Designed by Kallikrates, the Erechtheion is graced with delicate Ionic columns. It became a church in the 6 C. and later the harem for the Turkish commander — an idea no doubt inspired by **O**, the **Caryatids**, the famous maiden-column porch. All the figures now on site are copies: the originals are housed in the New Acropolis Museum (barring one in the British Museum removed by Lord Elgin). The east portico fronted the main shrine to Athena Polias and now has a **Restored Column O** at the north end. Added in 1981 (most postcard photos are still without it), it has attracted criticism thanks to its 'fake' weathered finish. In fact, it is an accurate copy of the original — now in the British Museum.

To the south-east of the Erechtheion stood a large stepped altar at **O** dedicated to **Zeus Polieus**, of which little remains. Instead, the path runs east of the site past a deep well in the floor of the rock at **O**. Known as the **Mycenaean Stairway**, it was one of two up the north side of the rock that were closed off in the Classical period (the Persians attacked the Acropolis via a second, to the north of the Erechtheion). From here the path then runs east to the flag bastion. On its way it passes the scanty remains of  the tiny, round tholos **Temple of Rome and Augustus**; a late, clumsy addition (27 BC) to the Acropolis monuments, all but ignored by ancient writers.

The Parthenon

The main temple-cum-city treasury dedicated to Athena Parthenos (the Virgin Athena), the Parthenon **⓪** dom-inates the Acropolis. Built between 447–432 BC, the building is remarkable for not having a straight line in it. The platform is deliberately convex to allow rainwater to drain off. The columns are also convex — a feature designed by the building's architects Iktinos and Kallikrates to correct the optical illusion that makes straight columns appear thinner in the middle. The simple Doric columns also lean in slightly — were they tall enough, their centres would meet at a point some 2.5 km above the building — as well as being abnormally tall and placed closer together than was traditional.

Tradition was also defied in the size of the building; most temples were built 6 columns wide — the Parthenon has 8. Its length was determined by a standard formula (2 x the number of width columns + 1), producing 17 columns down the sides, thus retaining regular proportions yet making it appear unusually long. The result is a building that makes all other Greek temples look small and clumsy by comparison.

Intact for over 2,000 years, the Parthenon has had a chequered history. Highlights include a couple of passing rulers using it to put a finger up (among other things) at the city population by using it as a brothel. In the 6 c. it was converted into the church of St. Sophia: a change which inflicted major structural damage as the orientation of the building had to be turned 180 degrees (the main entrance was originally on the east side to allow the rising sun to shine in upon the statue of the goddess), and an apse was added to the east end.

In the Ottoman period the Parthenon became a mosque, with a minaret poking through the roof on the south-west corner. It met its end

in 1687, when a Venetian army besieged the city. On hearing that the Turks were using the Parthenon as a hiding place for their arsenal (they assumed their attackers would never bombard a former church) the Venetian commander Morosini did just that. A shell landed on the building, blowing it apart, and leaving fragments of the roof, cella and the 300 women and children sheltering inside all over the Acropolis.

In its ruined state, the Parthenon continued to suffer. Reduced to two unconnected gable ends, it was used as a quarry for a mosque that was built in the shell (described by one visitor as looking like 'an ugly cork in a beautiful bottle'). Its remaining sculptures were removed by Lord Elgin (see p. 103), and poor restoration and pollution have taken their toll since. The Parthenon is currently undergoing extensive restoration work, but this is not enough for some, who have called for the re-roofing of the building to save the foundations (protected until 1687) from increasing rainwater damage.

In its prime the Parthenon was ornately decorated, with sculpture and other decorative features brightly painted in gaudy 'Mickey Mouse' colours. As much a statement of civic pride as a temple, it housed a treasury in the room in its west end, but its main function was to house the chryselephantine (gold and ivory) statue of **Athena Parthenos ⓪**. This remarkable figure cost more than the Parthenon itself, and its designer, Phidias, his reputation and almost his life. Known now through small copies bought by ancient tourists, it stood 12 m high and represented the goddess holding a shield in her left hand and a man-sized, winged Victory in her right. Her helmet was topped by a sphinx and two griffins, and her shield was decorated with scenes from the mythical battle between the Athenians and the Amazon women.

It was this shield that brought about Phidias's downfall. His pre-eminent position as the supervisor of the Acropolis rebuilding programme brought him enemies, who took advantage of a perceived likeness in the faces of two of the figures on Athena's shield to himself and his mentor, Pericles, to have him charged with sacrilege. Forced to flee the city, he took sanctuary at Olympia and there created one of the seven wonders of the world — his chryselephantine statue of Zeus. The Athena was deemed to be the inferior of the two, though she was impressive enough, with clothing made of sheets of gold tacked onto a wooden frame. Her flesh was sculpted ivory, and her eyes, precious gems. The figure stood, facing east, before a pool of sea water (to reflect light from the door) at the back of the Parthenon's main room. In its prime it must have been overwhelming; it must have seemed as if the goddess herself was standing in the chamber. The figure survived until c. 400 AD when it was removed to Constantinople and later destroyed by fire.

The Parthenon also boasted other major art treasures that survive in part. The **Pediment Sculptures** are the most obvious of these. Now reduced to fragments in museums (those now on the building are copies), by great luck they were drawn in 1674 by Jacques Carrey, a French painter, a few years before they were damaged. The **West Pediment ❼** was the best preserved until 1687. Its theme was the contest between Athena and Poseidon for the patronage of the city. Sadly, when the Venetians captured Athens, Morosini decided to remove the figures as war trophies, but they were smashed in the attempt to take them down. The central **East Pediment ❽** figures were lost in the 4 C. AD when the Parthenon was turned into a church. According to Pausanias the theme was the birth of Athena, but he gives no details. A 1–2 C. AD altar in Spain, thought to be based on this pediment, has Athena and Zeus standing in a similar pose to the main figures on the west pediment.

The other great Parthenon art treasure is the **Frieze**. Over 159 m long, it ran around the outer wall of ❾ the **Cella** (the 'building' inside the ring of columns). Long thought to depict the Panathenaic procession to the Acropolis in honour of the goddess, it is now believed by some scholars to be a representation of a myth, the sacrifice of the daughters of Erechtheus (a king of Athens). Just over half of the panels were recovered by Elgin and are in the British Museum. Along with the majority of the surviving pedimental figures, they are the most important of the 'Elgin Marbles'.

The South Side

The area to the south of the Parthenon contains a couple of oddities. Now unmarked is the site of ❺ **Phidias's Workshop**, used for the construction of the gold and ivory statue. Fragments of these materials have been found in this area. Walking along to the west end of the Parthenon you will come to ❶ the **Pre-Classical Wall Trenches**. These pits are natural fissures in the rock inside the Acropolis walls. In the Classical period they were used as 'graves' for the damaged sculptures from the temples destroyed by the Persians (now in the Acropolis Museum). Left open, with low skirting walls, they form a minor hazard. The Acropolis wall is also dangerously low, but looking over it you are able to take in the layout of the buildings lining the southern slope better than you can at street level.

Looking down from left to right, the first and largest of the south slope structures is ❿ the **Theatre of Dionysos** (c. 330 BC). Marking the spot where most of the great plays of Greek tragedy and comedy were first performed in annual competitions, the site has a separate entrance on the south-east corner of the Acropolis (◎ 08.00–18.30; tickets €2, free entry with Acropolis ticket). In the Classical period the theatre stage and seating occupied the lower tiers and were made of wood. With the rebuilding, the seating was extended right up the slope.

Above the theatre and close under the walls stand ⓥ two **Corinthian Columns** (320–310 BC). These were erected by sponsors of winning dramatic performances — the west one is known as the **Thrasyllos Monument**. Cut into the rock below is a small shrine — now the chapel of Panagia Spiliotissa. To the left of the theatre stood a major Classical hall-like building known as the **Odeon of Pericles** (little survives), while to the right are the foundations of two healing sanctuaries: ⓦ the **Old Asklepieion** (c. 420 BC) and the **New Asklepieion** (c. 300 BC).

A number of minor shrines lay between these buildings and the west Acropolis slope. Running east of the theatre is ❽ the **Stoa of Eumenes II** (c. 197–159 BC), the back wall of which has survived as part of the later city wall. At its eastern end lie the foundations of ❾ the **Nikias Monument** (320–319 BC), which was demolished to build the Beulé Gate. Finally, ❷ the **Odeon of Herodes Atticus** is the best preserved building on the Acropolis slopes. Built in 160–174 AD, the inner section of its façade survived by being incorporated into the later city wall that ran around the Acropolis. The interior seating was lost, but has since been replaced to allow performances. The rooms behind the stage have also been rebuilt from the foundations.

The Elgin (aka Parthenon) Marbles

The best Parthenon temple sculptures (including almost all the surviving pedimental figures and the greater part of the frieze), along with fragments from other Acropolis buildings, are now in the British Museum thanks largely to Lord Elgin, whose agent removed them in 1801–4. The Greek government has long sought their return without success via an on-going high-profile campaign, the latest stage of which is the building of the new Acropolis Museum (see p. 105). Various tactics have been tried over the years: the latest is to seek the return of sculptures just from the Parthenon building, accepting that material removed by Lord Elgin from other Acropolis buildings stays in London (this, and the fact that the British Museum holds other fragments of the Parthenon donated by other collectors, is why the campaign is for the return of the 'Parthenon' rather than 'Elgin' Marbles).

However, in Greece Elgin remains the villain of the piece, and you will find that he is vilified in most local guides and — taking their lead from these — not a few international ones. Over-the-top phrases like 'looter Elgin' abound, but are hardly appropriate given the facts.

Lord Elgin was one of a number of individuals (inspired by the revival of interest in the Classical tradition in Europe in the 18 c. and early 19 c.) who entered the then mysterious Ottoman Empire in search of the past. Partly inspired by a desire to raise the standards of art and architecture in Britain (though also with the less idealistic ambition of decorating a stately home he was having constructed), he secured the job of British Ambassador to the Ottoman court, taking with him a retinue of artists, architects and plaster moulders.

Once in the Aegean Elgin found that travellers' tales of collapsing temples thanks to neglect by the 'infidel Turk' were all too true. It was common to find the ancient marble temples being used as a convenient source of lime to make mortar, or being demolished to recover the iron and lead from the pins that held the marble blocks together. Confronted with reports of a rapidly deteriorating Parthenon, Elgin's ambitions grew to the point where he instructed his agent to salvage what he could (he was not the only one doing this: almost all important sculpture and artifacts discovered in Greece prior to the 20 c. are now in west European museums as a result). Elgin secured a written firman directing the Ottoman

authorities who had been ruling Athens for 350 years to allow his agents to remove 'inscriptions and sculptures' from the derelict Acropolis buildings. He only narrowly beat his French Ambassador counterpart to the marbles. The Greeks have never accepted the legitimacy of Ottoman rule, and perceive such agreements as being akin to one thief passing on stolen goods to another.

Given the uniqueness of the Parthenon and its universal recognition as the symbol of Greece, a very strong case can be made for the return of the marbles (it is difficult to view them in London and not feel considerable qualms on this score). However, Elgin-bashers hardly help their cause by failing to acknowledge that his motives, although clearly mixed, were hardly on a par with a looter's: instead they seem to have been an odd combination of very primitive rescue archaeology coupled with a collector's ambition. The highlighting of the damaging removal techniques employed, without also recognizing that plaster casts made by his workmen of sculptures he didn't remove show that they deteriorated significantly before their importance was recognized, is also very unbalanced. In this respect, Elgin's claim that he was 'saving' the marbles was borne out by events (though the 1998 revelation that many of the marbles had been 'skinned' thanks to over zealous 1930s cleaning by poorly supervised British Museum staff — using a practice also employed by the Greeks when cleaning the Hephaisteion in the late 19 c. — has somewhat eroded this).

The impact the sculptures had in London is also not readily acknowledged (beyond the fact that they bankrupted Elgin — he spent £74,240 recovering them). Widely admired (the poet Keats gazed at them for hours at a time like a 'sick eagle looking at the sky'), they have been very influential, occasionally in quite bizarre ways. Most important was their contribution to the pro-Greek romanticism sweeping Europe that led to the Great Powers supporting Greek nationalism and the foundation of the Greek state. At the other end of the scale, London dandies made total fools of themselves adopting a posture (known as the 'Grecian bend') supposedly based on the figures. However, the most delightful fall out from Elgin's acquisitions came with the horse's head removed from the north corner of the Parthenon's east pediment. Used as the model for the standard Staunton pattern chess-set knight, it has surely acquired an unassailable status as the most copied piece of sculpture in history.

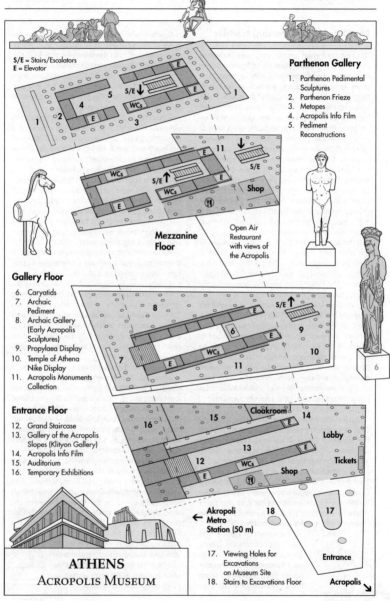

S/E = Stairs/Escalators
E = Elevator

Parthenon Gallery

1. Parthenon Pedimental Sculptures
2. Parthenon Frieze
3. Metopes
4. Acropolis Info Film
5. Pediment Reconstructions

Mezzanine Floor

Open Air Restaurant with views of the Acropolis

Gallery Floor

6. Caryatids
7. Archaic Pediment
8. Archaic Gallery (Early Acropolis Sculptures)
9. Propylaea Display
10. Temple of Athena Nike Display
11. Acropolis Monuments Collection

Entrance Floor

12. Grand Staircase
13. Gallery of the Acropolis Slopes (Klityon Gallery)
14. Acropolis Info Film
15. Auditorium
16. Temporary Exhibitions

Cloakroom

Lobby

Tickets

Shop

← Akropoli Metro Station (50 m)

17. Viewing Holes for Excavations on Museum Site
18. Stairs to Excavations Floor

Entrance

Acropolis ↘

ATHENS
ACROPOLIS MUSEUM

The Acropolis Museum

For many years the large collection of material recovered during Acropolis excavations and conservation work was poorly exhibited in a tiny museum at the back of the rock in a burrowed-out depression behind the Parthenon. This has now changed with the opening of the new Acropolis Museum below the rock itself. Located by Acropoli Metro Station (see the colour Acropolis centrefold map between p. 96–97), it is open ②–⑦ 08.00–20.00 (tickets: €5). The five-level building is home to all the artefacts now in Athens from the Acropolis complex. It is designed to have good views up to the Parthenon and to mimic parts of that building.

This new state-of-the-art museum has been many years in the planning. It was originally slated to open as part of the 2004 Athens Olympic Games celebrations, but construction was delayed by arguments (it finally opened its doors in 2009). The controversial design proved to be the first stumbling block: unashamedly modernist (some find the contrast between the grey concrete museum walls and the golden marble contents too jarring for comfort), and large relative to the size of the collection it houses, it is sited in a very prominent place in the heart of the archaeological park. The second major cause of delay centred around accusations that there was a failure to study and adequately protect the important archaeology uncovered at this site, so close to the base of the Acropolis. The matter went to the Greek courts, which ordered the suspension of building work for a time.

Views remain mixed over the design and scale of the museum, but the issues surrounding the archaeology apparently have been addressed (the foundations of buildings uncovered here now form the lower floor exhibit that is occasionally accessible via an outside staircase).

Acropolis Museum Layout

Visitors to the museum enter on the second level on the Acropolis side of the building. The **Entrance Floor** is home to the ticket desk, one of two museum shops and a cloakroom which should be the first port of call if you have a bag of any size with you (it is worth noting that many of the exhibits are vulnerable to unintentional 'bag damage'). Built around a central Parthenon-shaped core that rises to the top of the building, the largely invisible features of the Entrance Floor level are a gallery devoted to temporary exhibitions and a lecture auditorium. However, most visitors make do with watching a video presentation about the Acropolis and gingerly walking over glass panels in the floor that reveal the complex museum site excavations that make up the lower **Excavations Floor** (this part of Athens is one of the longest continuously inhabited urban areas in Europe, and the confusing jumble of remains reflects this).

The Entrance Floor also has access to the imaginatively designed sloping **Gallery of the Acropolis Slopes**. This rises to the next floor of the museum and is decorated with finds from buildings around the sides of the Acropolis.. At its far end are stairs that take you to the main display area: the **Gallery Floor** is home to the bulk of the Acropolis material, starting with the **Archaic Gallery**, which houses the remains of the decorative statues that adorned the Archaic temples that were destroyed in the Persian sack of the Acropolis in 480 BC. Fortunately they were ceremonially buried by the Athenians when they set about rebuilding. Thus protected, they exhibit traces of original paint rarely seen on ancient statuary today. The gallery is very striking as the statues are spread around the floor allowing visitors to walk amongst them, but the downside to this ambitious display is that they are scattered in no coherent order, making it difficult to appreciate any relationships between them. Somewhat lost in the crowd are the torso of the oldest European equestrian statue and the famous **Mourning Athena**, C. 460 BC.

Beyond the Archaic Gallery are smaller areas devoted to material removed from the Classical Acropolis buildings — the most notable being the heavily weathered **Temple of Athena Nike Frieze**, and the arresting display of the **Caryatids** on a balcony overlooking the Gallery of the Acropolis Slopes. Five of the six maidens-cum-pillars can be walked around here (the sixth is in the British Museum). Finally, on the Acropolis side of this floor is a gallery devoted to the rather bland monuments found around the ancient buildings.

The level above — the **Mezzanine Floor** — runs around only two sides of the museum's central core and contains no exhibits. This fourth level is home to a second shop and a restaurant that runs outside, over the museum's wedge-shaped entrance portico roof, allowing tourists to sup (surprisingly reasonably priced) beverages while looking up at the Parthenon rising above the Acropolis walls. Visitors with cameras can have fun with the mirror glass portico windows and photograph the reflection of themselves standing in front of the Acropolis.

The top floor **Parthenon Gallery** is devoted to the sculptures and reliefs that decorated the Parthenon building. The gallery is an impressive glass box that sits at an odd angle to the rest of the building, overhanging the edges at a couple of points (this is because it is sized and orientated to the same angle as the adjacent Parthenon). This is where the museum starts to get seriously controversial and overtly political. The ambition is to reunite all the panels of the famous Parthenon frieze and display the metopes and pediment sculptures in their relative positions around the inner gallery wall that replicates the upper part of the Parthenon building. Of course this great idea only works if the sculptures are in Athens. Sadly, most of them are not. Over half the frieze and most of the pedimental sculptures are in the British Museum, where they form the bulk of the Elgin Marbles collection. Other fragments are in the Louvre and Vatican museums.

As with all fragmented works of great art, a rational case exists for putting the surviving bits back together so that one can gain maximum appreciation of the whole. This museum is well equipped to display the frieze (which is very poorly arranged in the British Museum: it ran around an outside wall of the Parthenon but in London it is displayed 'inverted' around inside gallery walls). Having parts of statues and panels divided between museums also makes little sense. However, at the moment the Acropolis Museum has to make do with washed-out plaster copies of the missing stones. These fill the huge gaps in a visual protest at the current owners' failure to accede to requests for their return. Sadly, it is a tactic that backfires badly, as the display simply ends up illustrating in glorious clarity how much better preserved the material removed by Lord Elgin is compared to the badly eroded original fragments on show that were removed from the Parthenon by archaeologists 150 years later. This said, the gallery has enough original material to fully justify a visit. Prime exhibits are a few of the **Pedimental Figures** (notably the god Ilissos and the moon goddess Selene), and a reasonable number of slabs from the **Parthenon Frieze**.

The Agora
(See map facing p. 96.) Within easy walking distance of the Acropolis lie a number of notable archaeological sites. The most important of these is the **Agora**, the ancient marketplace, to the north-west (⊙ 08.00–18.30; tickets €4, free entry with Acropolis ticket). An open square during Classical times, bounded by all the major administrative buildings in the city, it was infilled with buildings in the Hellenistic and Roman periods. Add to this 3,000 years of continuous occupation and the result is the confused jumble of foundations that one sees today. The Roman travel writer Pausanias described all the major buildings, so most of those unearthed have been identified. Problems, however, do remain. The north side of the Agora still lies under the modern city (the buildings here are dilapidated, with the sword of demolition hanging over them), hindering a comprehensive assessment of the site's history. Moreover, two important buildings — the **Theseion**, the major shrine of the city's founder, and the **Stoa of Herms** — are known to have been in the vicinity of the Agora, but remain undiscovered.

The area so far exposed has been excavated since the 1930s when the Turkish buildings covering the Agora were demolished. The metro line cutting off the northern third of the site is a legacy of the last century (1891) when its importance was unrecognized. Today the Agora is heavily planted with trees, offering a shady retreat from the hot city streets.

The North and East Sides
There are two entrances to the Agora; one on the Acropolis side, and the main entrance, sited on a bridge over the metro line. The street leading to the latter (Adrianou) offers you a glimpse of several inaccessible buildings. Most notable of these is the corner of **Ⓐ**, the **Painted Stoa** or **Stoa Poikile** (c. 460 BC), currently being excavated by students from the American School of Archaeology. Once the most famous secular building in Athens, it was a natural meeting-place for the city intelligentsia. Its reputation was based on the paintings that adorned its walls (it was the Louvre of the ancient city) and the bronze shields hung about it (captured from the Spartans at the battle of Sphakteria in 425

BC — one is now in the museum). As a result of the chattering crowds that gathered here, it became the only building to give its name to a school of philosophy, as those that followed the philosopher Zeno regularly met in the building and thus became known as 'Stoics'.

Turning to the other side of the road, you can look down on the foundations of the small, winged **Royal Stoa** (c. 500 BC) at **❸**, where the city magistrates took their oath of office. Hereafter, the road runs to the railway bridge. From the ticket kiosk on the bridge, the main path descends onto **❹** the **Panathenaic Way**. Running south-east to the Acropolis, this was the most important road in the city. It was the ceremonial route for the annual procession depicted on the Parthenon frieze. Nowadays, it runs to the south end of **❺** the **Stoa of Attalos**. Rebuilt in 1953–56 by the American excavators, it is now the **Agora Museum**. The original was a gift from the king of Pergamum c. 145 BC. It replaced an earlier row of shops and is a typical example of this type of building, with two storeys and 21 square rooms at the back that functioned as shops. A pillar with a statue of Attalos in a chariot stood in front of the stoa, with **❺** a **Bema** (a speaker's platform) directly in front of that. Nearby are the circular remains of **❻** a **Roman Fountain**. To the north stood the classical law courts, but the surviving foundations (straddled by the railway line) are of a later **Hadrianic Basilica** **❼** with an **Augustan Colonnade** **❽** running west from it.

The Central Area

The centre of the Agora was an open square during the Classical period. Now it is dominated by **❶**, the **Odeon of Agrippa**, c. 15 BC. Repaired several times (largely thanks to a massive vaulted roof that collapsed now and again) it was later rebuilt as a vast gymnasium c. 400 AD. The most prominent feature today is the three colossal statues of tritons and giants that formed part of the entrance of the original building. The triton heads are of particular significance, as ancient sources say that they were modelled on the (now lost) pedimental sculpture of Poseidon on the Parthenon.

Just to the north of the Odeon lie the scanty remains of **❶** the **Altar of Ares** (c. 420 BC). It was here that dogs were sacrificed in honour of the god. To the west was **❸** the **Temple of Ares**, (c. 435 BC). Now no more than a low mound, it was originally very similar in design to the Hephaisteion on the hill to the west (it is thought to possibly be the work of the same architect). The building wasn't originally located here: all the surviving stones are numbered (indicating it was moved from a different site); the foundations are Roman, and some of the guttering seems to have come from the Temple of Poseidon at Sounion. The original site of the temple isn't known (suggestions range from the Roman Agora to Acharnai, outside the city), but this sort of movement wasn't uncommon in the Roman period, when many outlying shrines were abandoned because of urbanization.

North of the Temple of Ares, and now tucked against the metro line wall, lies a corner of the boundary wall that surrounded the small **❶** **Altar of the Twelve Gods** (6 c. BC). Now all but lost under the track, this was one of the most important monuments in Athens. The altar was not only venerated as a place of sanctuary (particularly for the destitute) but also served as the *Omphalos* or navel of the city and the province of Attica. As such, it was the official starting point from which all distances were measured.

The West Side

Travelling west, the path then emerges at **❿**, the **Stoa of Zeus Eleutherios**, c. 430 BC, which was an early (and therefore small) stoa with projecting wings. Ornately decorated, it was the base for the official in charge of religious ceremonies and trials for murder or impiety. It is better known in literature as the favourite stoa of the philosopher Socrates. It was in this building that he was wont to argue with his fellows, taking the line that he knew nothing and then proceeding to demonstrate that those who claimed to know something 'didn't know nuffin' either. Showing up large numbers of people who thought that they were intelligent didn't exactly endear Socrates to those in power, and he was tried and executed on trumped-up sacrilege charges in 399 BC.

South of the stoa of Zeus lie the foundations of **⓫** the **Temple of Apollo Patroös** (4 c. BC). One of the oldest temples in Athens, it was destroyed and rebuilt several times. The colossal statue of Apollo (now in the Agora Museum) once stood in it. On the other side of the path, and to the south, stands a replica of the torso of a **Statue of Hadrian** **⓬**, notable for the breast-plate adorned with the delightful mix of Athena (accompanied by a snake and owl) standing on the back of a wolf suckling Romulus and Remus.

Behind the buildings on the west side of the Agora and overlooking all is ❼ the **Hephaisteion** (449–444 BC). The best-preserved temple in Greece, it is the only example to retain its roof substructure substantially intact (the inner cella now has a medieval roof over it). Built just before the Parthenon (but not with money raised by the islands for the Delian League: this temple hadn't a predecessor to be destroyed by the Persians), for many years it was thought to be another important temple — the Theseion (hence the metro station of that name nearby) — but this notion has now been discredited. Inside it still contains the bronze cult statues of Hephaistos and Athena. Around it are trees planted in their classical positions; the original pots were unearthed when the site was excavated. This excavation also revealed that to the north of the Hephaisteion stood ❽ the **Arsenal** of ancient Athens, now known only through post holes.

The steps leading up to the Hephaisteion also marked the boundary between the religious and secular buildings on this side of the Agora. To the south stood ❾, the **Metroön** (430 BC); theoretically a temple dedicated to the mother of the gods, it became the repository for the government archives. It was built on the original site of ❿, the **Bouleuterion** (5 C. BC). This was the council chamber for the city senate house, and was rebuilt a number of times during its working life, gradually increasing in size, and each time further back from the main line of buildings. This allowed the Metroön to be expanded south to ⓫ the circular **Tholos** (c. 470 BC). One of the most important buildings in Athens (being the headquarters for those charged with the running of the city) it was manned 24 hours a day (and had its own kitchen). It is a controversial structure, with widely differing reconstructions being put forward (in part this is because it was rebuilt several times). In its last incarnation, it had a conical roof with diamond-shaped tiles. Opposite this collection of buildings was ⓬, the long narrow monument of the **Eponymous Heroes**. Adorned with the statues of the founders of the political tribes of Athens, it was used to display public notices.

The South Side

The southern boundary of the Agora was dominated by a series of stoas that gradually encroached north to the point where they added to the in-filling of the Classical Agora square. Temples were also added at this later stage. They included the small **South-West Temple** at ⓭, with an altar (of Zeus Agoraios) 30 m to the north, and a small stoa-like building to the south that was known to have been used by the Athenian civil service. Behind these lie the foundations of ⓮ the **Middle Stoa** (2 C. BC). The largest stoa to be built in Athens, it took the form of a double-aisled hall open on both sides. It was later incorporated into the 4 C. AD gymnasium along with the nearby Odeon. Abutting it to the west was ⓯: a block of **Small Buildings** that included a cobbler's shop and a latrine, and ⓰ the **Strategion**.

Only tentatively identified, the Strategion was probably the Pentagon of ancient Athens, and used as both the military headquarters and home of the supreme commander. Conveniently located near the city prison, its incumbents tended to move from one to the other with alarming regularity — particularly during the Peloponnesian War when the 30-year stalemate between Athens and Sparta led the frustrated population exercising their democratic right to order the execution of a succession of commanders for failing to win the war (an example of Athenian democratic short-termism that was a major contributory factor in the city's defeat). The classical **Prison** ⓱, just outside the Agora, was where Socrates was executed following another bad day for Athenian democracy in action (a clay miniature of the philosopher was found on site).

South of the Middle Stoa lie the foundations of the Classical south Agora buildings. These include ⓲ the **Heliaia** (c. 470 BC), the original city courthouse, and ⓳ the **South Stoa I** (5 c. BC). Now overlain by ⓴ the **South Stoa II** (2 c. BC), the former is of greater interest as the surviving fragment contains the foundations of the small dining rooms (the walls being no more than a dining couch and a doorway wide) that stood at the back of this stoa.

Beyond this the remains are largely Roman, consisting of: ㉑ the **South-East Fountain House** (c. 470 BC), now partly overlain by a Byzantine church. The back walls also survive from ㉒ the **Athens Mint** (c. 400 BC) where the famous owl coins were struck. To the east lies ㉓ the **South-East Temple** (1 c. BC). This was another Roman import, the materials being taken from a small Classical temple of Aphrodite at Sounion.

The other side of the Panathenaic Way was also considerably embellished in the Roman period with ✪ the **Library of Pantainos** (102 AD) and ⑩ the **South-East Stoa** (1 C. AD): yet another shopping mall on the path to the later **Wall of Valerian**. This was a rather sad structure (its location and composition reflecting the massive decline in the fortunes and size of the city) which was constructed out of the remains of demolished Agora buildings following the disastrous Herulian sack of the city in 269 AD.

The Roman Agora

Sandwiched between 18 C. mansions in the Plaka district are the remains of several important ancient structures: notably the **Roman Agora**, the adjacent **Library of Hadrian** and the Hellenistic **Tower of the Winds** (⊗ 08.00–18.30; tickets €2, free entry with Acropolis ticket). Unfortunately, an unsympathetic medieval street plan makes interpretation of the remains difficult, running as it does across the lines of the ancient ground plan.

The impressive columned façade of the **Library of Hadrian** (2 C. AD) is usually the first building encountered in this part of Athens thanks to the nearby Monastiraki metro station. Open ⊗ 08.00–18.30 (tickets €2: free entry with Acropolis ticket), this site has only been accessible since 2006. The most prominent feature of the extant remains is the north side of the front façade. This is built abnormally high, to counter the fact that the library is lower down the Acropolis slope than the adjacent market: the library was therefore made to appear the same height. The façade is dominated by 7 columns, each of which would have been surmounted with a statue.

The main peristyle court behind was, according to the Roman-era travel writer Pausanias, graced with a 'hundred splendid columns' — none of which have survived. The quad had an ornamental pool in the centre (later replaced with a 6 C. basilica, several columns from which still stand) with lecture rooms down the sides. Books took up a relatively small part of the library's space and were housed in a scroll room at the back of the building; by lucky chance, the surviving wall has the storage niches extant.

The **Roman Agora** (1 C. BC) is known to stand on the site of the Classical commercial market, but of earlier structures there is no trace. In the Roman period, it was linked to the Classical Agora via a couple of stoas running east behind the Stoa of Attalos. The surviving remains are as diverse as those of the library, in this case consisting of a reasonable number of columns arranged as picturesquely as possible around the two surviving sides of the peristyle court. Behind them lie the foundations of a number of stoa-style shops. The gateways have survived; the main entrance is reduced to an arch standing in glorious isolation (now fenced off; access to the site is from the rear). The rear gate today only exists as a series of square columns bounded by a drain on the outer side.

As you enter the Roman Agora site you are confronted by two contrasting structures. On your right are the remains of a 1 C. AD **Roman Latrine**; built to seat the masses in comfort, it offered a secluded spot to sit and chat while getting on with the business of the day. To the east stands the wonderfully preserved 2 C. BC **Tower of the Winds**. A remarkable building, cute and approachable in size, it has survived against all the odds in various guises (not least as a dervish clubhouse during the years of Turkish rule).

A marble octagon, the tower was a water-clock, sundial, and weather-vane combined, and possibly also the city planetarium. On the north-west and north-east sides were porticoed doors, while up the south side climb the remains of the clock mechanism in the form of a semicircular turret. Quite how this worked is still not really understood. Given that the ancients measured time by dividing the daylight hours into 12 (so an 'hour' was never the same length on any consecutive day) it, presumably, caused its designers a headache and a half too. The 8 cardinal winds are aligned to their respective points of the compass. Favourable winds are shown as youths; hostile winds as bearded, older figures. Each holds an appropriate object. Most are self-explanatory, with the exception of Lips (responsible for blowing an enemy fleet ashore: hence the ship's stern), and Skiron (the charcoal cauldron symbolized drought). The Roman writer Vitruvius records that the tower was topped with a bronze Triton weather-vane, holding a wand which pointed to the prevailing wind.

Other Athenian Sites

In addition to the prominent and crowded Acropolis and Agora sites, there are plenty of others that justify a visit. Close by the Acropolis is the small circular **Monument of Lysicrates** (335 BC). Three metres in diameter, it was erected to display the bronze tripod won at the Dionysia festival of that year by Lysicrates. A glorified pot-stand, it is a rare survival, and the Corinthian columns that adorn it are the oldest examples in Athens. The skimpy **Arch of Hadrian** (2 C. AD) stands nearby, though its location abutting a busy road (complete with new overhead tram lines) limits one's ability to appreciate it in the way that it deserves. Built to mark off the old city from Hadrian's Roman additions, it is adorned with inscriptions. On the Acropolis side: 'This is Athens, ancient city of Theseus'; on the reverse: 'The city of Hadrian and not of Theseus'. Constructed of Pentelic marble, it provides a gateway to the largest temple built in Greece.

The massive **Olympieion** (515 BC–132 AD) — the Temple of Olympian Zeus — took just under 650 years to build. Replacing an earlier temple built near the site of the fabled plug-hole that Zeus opened in the earth to abate Deukalion's (the Greek Noah) flood, it is a powerful reminder that Athens looked to the other Greek gods as well as her namesake. But Athens being Athens, the locals weren't afraid to make fun of strongly held beliefs. Several early Christian commentators make caustic mention of one of the (now lost) plays of the comic playwright Aristophanes, called *Flood*. Performed within shouting distance of the massive temple built over the world's plug-hole, it poked fun at the whole story by casting Deukalion as an idiot who puts only one of each animal in his ark — the bulk of the play being a discussion between the animals, after the waters have subsided, as to who should try to mate with whom and what the possible results might look like (the play apparently ended with the clouds lifting to reveal the animals' other halves stranded on a nearby mountain top).

The temple, meantime, is a less-than-half-standing monument to the more serious side of this story. It was started by the tyrant Pisistratus in 515 BC but abandoned after his overthrow. Work resumed in 174 BC, when Antiochos IV of Syria commissioned the Roman architect Cossutius to begin on a modified design (the columns now on the site date from this revised building). Unfortunately Antiochos died before work was finished, and the temple added to its record as the longest building-site in history. It even saw some of its columns removed to Rome by the general Sulla. Hadrian completed the building, adding a gold and ivory statue of himself and Zeus for good measure. Of the original 104 columns, 15 remain standing. The fallen 16th collapsed during a storm in 1852, and a 17th was demolished in 1760 by order of the Turkish governor and burnt to make lime for the construction of a mosque. It is thought that the other 4 of the 21 columns recorded standing in 1450 suffered a similar fate. The Olympieion is open ⊕ 08.00–18.30; tickets €2, free entry with Acropolis tickets.

To the east of the Olympieion lies the **Stadium** (143 AD): rebuilt in 1870 for the first modern Olympiad in 1896, it hosted the archery competition during the 2004 games. With seating for 70,000 spectators, it takes advantage of the slopes of two hills to avoid the need for expensive earth banking. It is thought that the site (initially using just the bare hillsides) was used as the stadium from the 4 C. BC.

The **Hills of Athens** played a very important part in city life. Apart from the Acropolis there are two lesser hills of note. The nearby **Areopagus** was the hill of justice. Here the supreme court of the city had its home. In addition, it was reputedly used by the Amazon women, the Persians, and St. Paul during their attacks on Athens. Today, very slippery steps take you up to a good view over the Agora. A better viewing point is the **Mouseion** (alias Filopapou Hill). The spot on which the cannon that blew up the Parthenon stood (this is where the best postcard shots are taken as well), it does not have a rodent problem as its name implies. In fact, 'the hill of the Muses' (for this is what Mouseion means) was quite a mystical spot. Today, it is home to the ugly funerary **Monument of Philopappos** (114 AD), and some foundations of the **City Wall**. These run down past another hilltop viewing-point to the oddly named **Pnyx**. This was an artificial platform, built out of the side of the hill, where the Athenian democracy held its citizens' meetings. Today it plays host to *son et lumière* shows. The final hill of note lies at **Likavittos**. The highest hill in Athens, it is blessed with good views of the Acropolis, and is accessed by cable car (€5).

The final major archaeological site, **Kerameikos** (the 'potter's district'), the cemetery of Ancient Athens, is now a replica-tomb-filled park, complete with bubbling brook full of turtles and frogs (⊕ 08.00–18.30; tickets €2, free entry with Acropolis ticket). Little visited — in part because of its location — it also has the remains of two of the city gates (the **Sacred Gate** and the **Dipylon**) and the **Pompeion**, the building from where the great Panathenaic processions to the Acropolis started.

Outside Athens is one major site within easy reach. Few regret taking the 2-hour bus ride to **Sounion**, the cape on the southern tip of Attica that is home to the photogenic **Temple of Poseidon**. Built in 444–440 BC, it functioned as a landmark, guiding sailors towards Athens. It lies about 90 minutes' sailing from Piraeus: you should be able to spot its surviving columns on the skyline when taking ferries in or out of Piraeus.

National Archaeological Museum

One of the great cultural treasure-houses of the world, this is one attraction that should figure prominently on the itinerary of every visitor to Athens. This said, the museum hit problems in early 2011 when many galleries were closed because of a lack of staff. Low Season visitors could thus find some galleries closed.

Among the principal exhibits are the **Minoan Frescoes** from the excavations on Santorini, the **Mask of Agamemnon** and other gold work uncovered by Schliemann at Mycenae, and **Sculpture** from all the important sites in Greece. Supposedly open ① 12.30–19.00, ②–③ 08.00–19.00, ⑥ ⑦ 08.30–15.00 (tickets €6: free entry on ⑦), times do vary a bit, depending on the number of attendants who turn up (no room is left without a guard). Some rooms are occasionally closed off for an hour or two if they can't be manned. If you really want to get the most out of a visit you should consider buying a copy of the museum guide (these are on sale in **Room 3**, which contains the ticket kiosk, sales desk and cloakroom, where bags must be deposited).

Room 4 is the first visitors enter, and one of the most dramatic in the museum. Known as the **Mycenaean Hall**, it contains the magnificent **Mask of Agamemnon** among its impressive gold collection culled from the graves at the palace of Mycenae in the Peloponnese.

Room 5 contains Neolithic and Pre-Mycenaean artefacts, though island hoppers will find **Room 6** of more interest — known as the **Cycladic Room** as all the exhibits have been recovered from the Cyclades. The haul adds up to a pretty disparate collection. At the main entrance end are the Early Cycladic figures — including the largest figurine yet discovered (see p. 304) and the better known **Harpist** (see p. 324) and **Flautist** (illustrated overleaf). At the other end of the gallery you will find the **Flying-Fish Fresco** fragments recovered from Milos — though the described 'blue cloth' on the display label is now thought to be a net.

Rooms 7–8 and **11–12** are devoted to **Archaic Sculpture** (**Rooms 9–10** being devoted to smaller works). Room 9 has a number of pieces from Delos and a very Egyptianesque-looking kouros from Milos. **Room 13** contains more such figures, including the **Aristodikos** figure that gives the room its name. Used to mark graves, it is logical to find next door, in **Room 14**, a collection of **Early Classical Gravestones**.

Room 15 is known as the **Poseidon Room**, thanks to the large bronze of the God that dominates it. Some believe the figure to be the god Zeus, but without knowing what he held in his right hand (it could have been either a trident or a thunderbolt depending on the god), we will never be sure. The figure lacks its eyeballs but otherwise has all its attributes. For this reason it is usually surrounded by packs of French schoolgirls gazing intently at the god's tackle (a pretty convincing argument for the pro-Poseidon lobby). This is one of many similar hazards you will encounter if you visit this museum with children; for not only does the National Archaeological Museum not have the Elgin Marbles, it doesn't have a 'willie' or 'pecker' box either (all the statues in the British Museum were defaced by a Victorian curator worried about visiting young ladies' morals; the results are now hidden away in a large cardboard box).

Rooms 16 and **18** are devoted to **Classical Gravestones**, and **Room 17** to **Classical Votive Reliefs**. **Rooms 19–20** display **Small Classical Works**. The most interesting exhibit in Room 20 is the best-preserved miniature of the famous figure of **Athena Parthenos** that stood inside the Parthenon. Hardly of great artistic merit in itself (the figure is leaning slightly to one side and the fine detail is very crudely reproduced), it has nonetheless been of great value in determining the form of the original statue. A doorway from Room 20 leads to a staircase descending to the **Atrium**, adorned with marbles recovered from a wreck off Antikithera — especially a young athlete, half-corroded by the sea, half-preserved by the mud.

On the far side of the Atrium is the museum's new up-market shop (the full-size replica of the famous bronze Zeus/Poseidon is a snip at €3,000). **Room 21** has one of the most impressive of the museum's exhibits, the bronze **Horse and Jockey of Artemision**. Fished out of the sea off the north coast of Evia, it captures the movement of boy and horse wonderfully.

Room 22 is devoted to sculpture from the sanctuary at **Epidavros**. **Rooms 23–24** and **28** contain 4 c. BC gravestones (including, in Room 28, the Youth from Antikithera); **Rooms 25–27** hold Votive Reliefs. **Room 29** is known as the Themis Room thanks to a statue of the goddess. **Room 30** contains further **Hellenistic Sculpture**, including the large **Poseidon of Milos** and an ugly cloaked child, known as the 'little refugee', recovered from Turkey. More fun is a Delian statue of Aphrodite, poised in the act of spanking a cupid with a slipper. **Rooms 31–33** contain yet more Hellenistic Sculpture, and **Room 34** remnants of an Altar, and reliefs and sculptures from other sanctuaries.

Room 36 is the first housing the museum's impressive collection of bronzes. Devoted to the smaller items, it includes a well-endowed dwarf and a grizzly collection of dismembered fingers and thumbs, and a collection of tiny animals (from Deukalion's ark?). **Rooms 37–39** contain a mix of bronze figures, including some early figurines from the Acropolis, and a collection of bronze mirrors. The most notable exhibit is the famous **Antikithera Mechanism** (a multi-cogged navigation instrument) in **Room 38**, which has invited years of speculation on what it was and how it worked (now explained via X-ray photos of its interior).

What you will find in the remaining ground-floor rooms (best described as temporary exhibition spaces) is less certain as they seem to be in a state of constant 'renovation'.

The upper floor occupies only a fraction of the ground-floor area, yet it includes a room that is the highlight of the museum: **Room 48**, home of the **Santorini/Thira Frescoes** (see p. 193), has the more famous ones lining the walls of mock-up houses. These include the **Boxing Children**, the **Fisherboys** and the

---

Rooms & Exhibits

1. Entrance Lobby
2. Northern Stoa
2A. Casts Room
3. Entrance Hall / Tickets / Baggage Store
4. Mycenaean Hall
5. Neolithic and Pre-Mycenaean Room
6. Cycladic Room
7. Archaic Sculpture 1
8. Archaic Sculpture 2
9. Small Archaic Room 1
10. Small Archaic Room 2
11. Archaic Sculpture 3
12. Archaic Sculpture 4
13. Room of Aristodikos
14. Early Classical Gravestones
15. Room of Poseidon
16. Classical Gravestones 1
17. Classical Votive Reliefs
18. Classical Gravestones 2
19. Classical Works 1
20. Classical Works 2
21. Room of Diadoumenos
22. Room of Epidauros
23. Room 1 of 4 c. BC Gravestones
24. Room 2 of 4 c. BC Gravestones
25. Decree and Votive Reliefs
26. Votive Reliefs 2
27. Votive Reliefs 3
28. Room of the Youth from Antikithera
29. Room of Themis
30. Room of Hellenistic Sculpture
31. Sculpture 1
32. Sculpture 2
33. Sculpture 3
34. Room of the Altar
35. Staircase to the First Floor
36. Karapanos Collection of Bronzes
37. Bronze Room 1
38. Bronze Room 2
39. Bronze Room 3
40. Stathatos Collection of Gold Objects
41. Collection of Clay Figurines
42. Temporary Exhibition Room 1
43. Temporary Exhibition Room 2
44. Temporary Exhibition Room 3
45. Temporary Exhibition Room 4

First Floor:

48. Thira / Santorini Frescoes
49. Geometric Vases
50. Geometric Vases from Different Workshops
51. Room of Vari Vases
52. Room of Heraeum of Argos and Sophilos
53. Room of Black Figure Vases
54. Room of Black Figure and Red Figure Vases
55. Red Figure Vases and White-ground Lekythoi
56. Room of Vases of the 4 c. BC

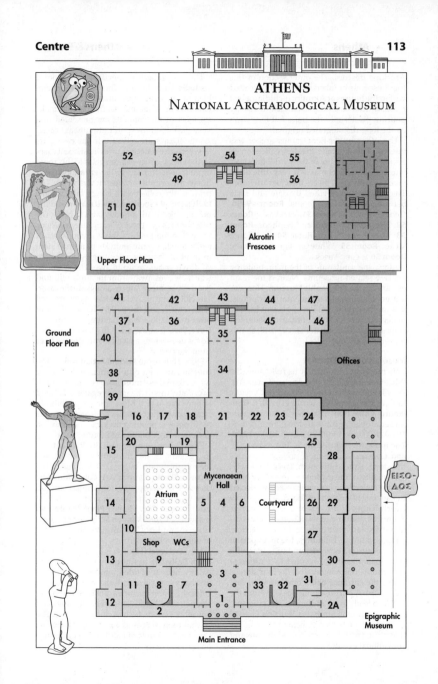

ATHENS
NATIONAL ARCHAEOLOGICAL MUSEUM

Upper Floor Plan

52 53 54 55
49 56
51 50
48 Akrotiri Frescoes

Ground Floor Plan

41 42 43 44 47
37 36 45 46
40 35
38 34 Offices
39
16 17 18 21 22 23 24
20 19 25
15 28
14 Atrium Mycenaean Hall Courtyard 26 29
10 5 4 6 27
Shop WCs
13 9 30
11 8 7 33 32 31
12 2 2A
1

ΕΙΣΟ-ΔΟΣ

Epigraphic Museum

Main Entrance

Antelope frescoes. The outer section of this room also has a number of artefacts discovered within the houses at Akrotiri, including a bed reconstructed from a plaster cast, made by pouring plaster into the holes left in the ash by the long-disintegrated original.

The other upper-floor rooms are of less interest. Home to the greatest collection of ancient Greek pottery in the world, the sheer number of artefacts makes it very difficult to give the individual pieces their just attention. The collection is divided by date and style between the various rooms: **Room 49–50**: Geometric Vases; **Room 51**: Vari Vases; **Room 52**: Heraeum of Argos and Sophilos; **Room 53**: Black-figure Vases; **Room 54**: Red-figure Vases; **Room 55**: White Background Vases; **Room 56**: 4 c. BC Vases.

Along the south side of the main building are two related museums. Nearest the main entrance is the **Epigraphic Museum**. Home to a large collection of monumental inscriptions, it is an important archive of ancient literary material. Unfortunately, unreadable letters on stones don't have much mass appeal, so this museum is always quiet.

Museum of Cycladic Art

This museum — to give it its full name: the 'Museum of Cycladic and Ancient Greek Art' — is home to the best collection of Cycladic idols anywhere in the world (The **N. P. Goulandris Collection**). Because it is a private museum opening times are irregular: ① ③ ⑤ ⑥ 10.00–17.00, ④ 10.00–20.00, ⑦ 10.00–17.00. The museum is closed on ②. Tickets cost €7, and €3.5 on ①. Like most private museums this one is small, but resemblances end here. The quality of the exhibits is unusually high; almost everything is a choice piece. Collected by several enthusiastic millionaires who have clearly haunted the sale rooms of the world for a considerable time, most exhibits would command display space in the national collection.

Housed in two buildings, the main part of the museum is a new custom-built affair with small galleries (each devoted to a different collection) occupying each of the four storeys above the entrance hall (complete with café and shop). A purpose-built passage from the hall also leads to an addition to the museum: the restored 1895 **Stathatos Mansion** (a good example of a late 19 c. Athenian town house that is used mainly for special exhibitions and educational events).

The star gallery is inevitably the Floor 1 **Cycladic Art** collection. This has been assembled in one of the best museum displays in Greece. The white marble figures that make up most of the contents are presented in a very dark room in spotlit illuminated cases. As the figures are reflected in the case glass — which also reflects figures in adjacent cases — the effect, when you can get into this room on your own (come early!) is very atmospheric in a weird, primitive cave-cult sort of way. The pride of the collection is a very tall **Cycladic Idol** (1.4 m) of superb quality. It is an incredibly potent object with a good claim to being the most impressive piece of sculpture in Athens (given the competition, this is saying a lot). In a nice touch, the museum keeps a small stool in front of the case, encouraging visitors to sit down and gaze up in awe. Those able to tear their eyes away from the idols will find good explanatory notices alongside the cases. The full range of Cycladic idol styles are well represented, and the gallery has its share of other marble objects such as the large tray-like **Dove Vase** (named after the row of carved doves in its bowl), as well as rare **Bronze Axes** from the period.

Floor 2 houses an **Ancient Art** collection. The contents are a bit of a mixture, but in many ways this makes it more interesting and digestible. Better this than a massive gallery devoted to one type of pot! Most notable exhibits are a case containing a series of **Bronze Helmets** (with notes explaining the variation in styles) and some high-quality red figure vases.

Floor 3 has been the visually least satisfying gallery in the museum (it was closed for refurbishment in 2011). It is home to the **Thanos Zintilis Cypriot Art Collection**. The display embraces pieces from the early Bronze Age through to the Roman period. The best exhibits are oddly shaped **Plank Figures**, an intriguing **Cypro-Minoan Script Stone**, some better examples of Roman glass, and a display of gold jewellery.

The final level (Floor 4) is home to a **Scenes From Daily Life in Antiquity** exhibition. The gallery here is divided into two rooms: the first has a series of murals showing artefacts in context. Exhibits include a rare **Strigil** (a bronze scraper used by athletes when bathing) and household goods such as children's toys. The second room serves as a film room were one can watch a couple of mildly dreary offerings on classical daily life and death.

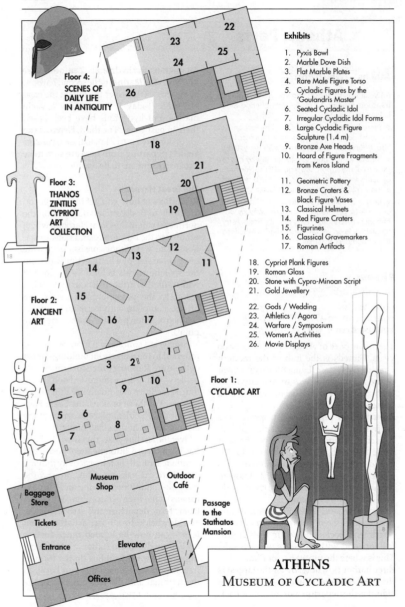

Floor 4:
SCENES OF
DAILY LIFE
IN ANTIQUITY

Floor 3:
THANOS
ZINTILIS
CYPRIOT
ART
COLLECTION

Floor 2:
ANCIENT
ART

Floor 1:
CYCLADIC ART

Exhibits

1. Pyxis Bowl
2. Marble Dove Dish
3. Flat Marble Plates
4. Rare Male Figure Torso
5. Cycladic Figures by the 'Goulandris Master'
6. Seated Cycladic Idol
7. Irregular Cycladic Idol Forms
8. Large Cycladic Figure Sculpture (1.4 m)
9. Bronze Axe Heads
10. Hoard of Figure Fragments from Keros Island

11. Geometric Pottery
12. Bronze Craters & Black Figure Vases
13. Classical Helmets
14. Red Figure Craters
15. Figurines
16. Classical Gravemarkers
17. Roman Artifacts

18. Cypriot Plank Figures
19. Roman Glass
20. Stone with Cypro-Minoan Script
21. Gold Jewellery

22. Gods / Wedding
23. Athletics / Agora
24. Warfare / Symposium
25. Women's Activities
26. Movie Displays

Museum Shop

Outdoor Café

Baggage Store

Tickets

Passage to the Stathatos Mansion

Entrance

Elevator

Offices

ATHENS
MUSEUM OF CYCLADIC ART

⚓ Athens: Ports

Athens — Which Port?

Arrive at Athens airport and you will find public transport heading to three ports offering ferry links to the islands:

• **Piraeus** is home to 80% of the ferry fleet and is the most popular starting point for tourists (it is also the only one connected to the Metro system).

• **Rafina**, a small port, lies 40 minutes by bus to the east of the airport and is good if the Northern Cyclades are your destination (you can trim about an hour off ferry journey times by starting here).

• **Lavrio**, a small town on the south-eastern side of the Attic peninsula, is an hour away by bus but offers even shorter ferry journey times. Ferry timetables, however, are hard to find in Athens so tourist numbers are small.

Piraeus
ΠΕΙΡΑΙΑΣ

CODE ☎ 210
PORT POLICE ☎ 4511 311, 4172 657
TOURIST OFFICE ☎ 4135 716

The main port of Athens for some 2,800 years, Piraeus is the hub of the modern Greek ferry system. Lying 8 km south-west of the Acropolis, it was once a city in its own right, but in the years since Greek independence it has been reduced to a suburb by the capital's urban sprawl, and is a frenetic, less than pleasant place at that. In fact, it is difficult to conceive of a spot more removed from the dreamy idyllic island most tourists are in search of. This is one port of call where it pays to know in advance roughly what you are trying to do and where you are going.

Once an island itself, Piraeus is a hilly peninsula decked with anonymous, tall apartment blocks laid out in a strict grid fashion, and with harbours on each side. This is where the fun starts: for Piraeus has three harbours of note. By far the largest is the **Great Harbour**: situated on the western side, it is the departure point for all ferries,

catamarans and hydrofoils. **Zea** (otherwise known as **Zea Marina**) is the second harbour at Piraeus (500 m over the hill on the eastern side). Today it is primarily a yacht marina, but hydrofoils have been based there in past years. The third, **Flisvos**, is an excursion-boat port 7 km to the east of Zea: vessels departing from here are sure to be expensive and are to be avoided.

The Great Harbour
Regardless of how you get to Piraeus you are likely to find yourself dumped on the north-east side of the Great Harbour, which is home to the bus, metro and railway stations. The waterfront consists of a wide quay, separated by a hedge-cum-wall from the six-lane streets behind — so clogged with traffic that in the rush hour motorbikes resort to the pavements (a pedestrian bridge, complete with escalators, outside the metro station provides the best crossing point).

Piraeus is a commercial town and this is reflected in the waterfront buildings; most of these are shipping offices or branches of banks with maritime interests. Food shops, tourist facilities and hotels are thin on the ground. For these reasons, the Great Harbour is not the ideal place to arrive at the last minute or in the small hours.

Over the last few years the Great Harbour has been turned into one huge passenger terminal, with all container activity moving elsewhere. At various points around the quay air-conditioned seating areas (under canvas) have been set up, along with electronic ferry departure and arrival boards. The downside to all this activity is that ferries can now be located much further away from the metro station, and even the improved transit facilities (in the form of free airport-style buses that run between the terminal and the western side of the harbour) don't really make up for this.

The focal point for most ferry travellers is the square housing the bus station just south of the railway and metro stations (Platia Karaiskaki). In the billboard-encrusted block next to the Port Police building (which has a full ferry departure list posted up by the front entrance) you will find the nucleus of the **ticket agents**. Step within hailing distance of an agency door and you'll get hassle. A chorus of 'Where are you going?' rings out from the moment the agencies open at 05.00. So it helps to be both prepared (the EOT ferry information sheets are invaluable in this respect) and not over-trusting.

Likewise, you should note that although ticket agents in the islands can be very useful for changing money out of banking hours, if you use the Piraeus agencies you can be sure of paying significantly over the odds. The last-minute snack shops on the waterfront should also be treated with considerable caution; budget-conscious food-hunters are better off heading for the produce stalls and the small supermarket that look onto the small square behind *McDonald's*.

Ferries are grouped according to destination (now usually identified by the nearest harbour gate number), and most have a regular berth — though these aren't individually marked. To be on the safe side you should allow yourself a good 45 minutes to find and board a ferry. The easiest way of doing this is to find the appropriate gate and then look for the funnel or hull logo. It also pays to be aware that ferries might not arrive back from their previous excursion much before their listed Piraeus departure time. Distant berths usually have ticket kiosks (complete with computer ticket-issuing facilities) somewhere nearby on the quayside.

If you do buy from one of the agents in the central ticket block (and most tourists happily do), ensure that the ferry is as direct as possible: in High Season rooms on the popular islands can disappear fast, and arriving an hour ahead of the other boats

often makes a significant difference to what's on offer and how much you'll have to pay.

International tickets should be bought early, and ferries (when they deign to run at all) dock on the south-east side of the Great Harbour. All customs buildings are sited in this area, the poor Quay 9 shed being the most used.

⊨

Few tourists attempt to stay in Piraeus as the available accommodation is either downright horrible or inconveniently located (Piraeus isn't noted for its evening feeding or nightlife). The metro also ensures that you can still stay in Athens and catch the earliest boats.

The most obvious clutch of hotels is in the backstreets south of the metro station. They tend to be noisy, some don't take credit cards, and the occasional red light is to be seen. The best of them is arguably the *Elektra* (☎ 417 7057), just off Gouniari Street. Those who are prepared to walk will find better beds elsewhere; plush establishments shun the Great Harbour, and lie on the up-market waterfront to the east of Zea Marina. These include the expensive *Kastella* (☎ 411 4735), *Cote D'Oro* (☎ 411 3744), and *Mistral* (☎ 411 7094).

Baggage Storage

If you are only in Athens for a day or so, or are taking time out while waiting for a boat, then Piraeus is arguably the best place to store baggage (**Central Athens** isn't noted for a profusion of baggage storage options, and the **Airport** houses an expensive facility that is best considered for long duration storage).

At **Piraeus** you have two storage options: the first is to use the **ticket agent** from whom you buy your ferry ticket. An increasing number of them offer free (unsecured) baggage storage facilities once you have paid up. These are usually fairly safe, but it almost goes without saying that you don't leave anything you can't afford to lose (as travel insurers aren't likely to view claims for lost baggage sympathetically if it was lost while stored in this way).

Secure luggage storage is available via a regular luggage deposit in the passenger terminal building. Costs are fixed by the number of bags and the length of time you want to store them. These are typically an expensive €4 for 5 hours.

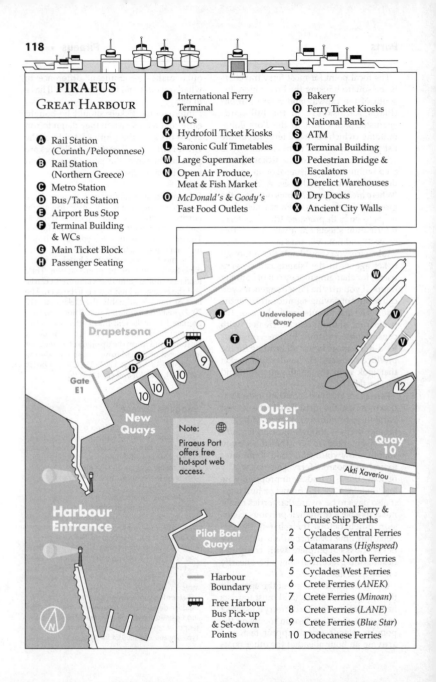

PIRAEUS
GREAT HARBOUR

- **A** Rail Station (Corinth/Peloponnese)
- **B** Rail Station (Northern Greece)
- **C** Metro Station
- **D** Bus/Taxi Station
- **E** Airport Bus Stop
- **F** Terminal Building & WCs
- **G** Main Ticket Block
- **H** Passenger Seating

- **I** International Ferry Terminal
- **J** WCs
- **K** Hydrofoil Ticket Kiosks
- **L** Saronic Gulf Timetables
- **M** Large Supermarket
- **N** Open Air Produce, Meat & Fish Market
- **O** *McDonald's* & *Goody's* Fast Food Outlets

- **P** Bakery
- **Q** Ferry Ticket Kiosks
- **R** National Bank
- **S** ATM
- **T** Terminal Building
- **U** Pedestrian Bridge & Escalators
- **V** Derelict Warehouses
- **W** Dry Docks
- **X** Ancient City Walls

Drapetsona

Undeveloped Quay

Gate E1

Note: Piraeus Port offers free hot-spot web access.

New Quays

Outer Basin

Quay 10

Akti Xaveriou

Harbour Entrance

Pilot Boat Quays

— Harbour Boundary

Free Harbour Bus Pick-up & Set-down Points

1 International Ferry & Cruise Ship Berths
2 Cyclades Central Ferries
3 Catamarans (*Highspeed*)
4 Cyclades North Ferries
5 Cyclades West Ferries
6 Crete Ferries (*ANEK*)
7 Crete Ferries (*Minoan*)
8 Crete Ferries (*LANE*)
9 Crete Ferries (*Blue Star*)
10 Dodecanese Ferries

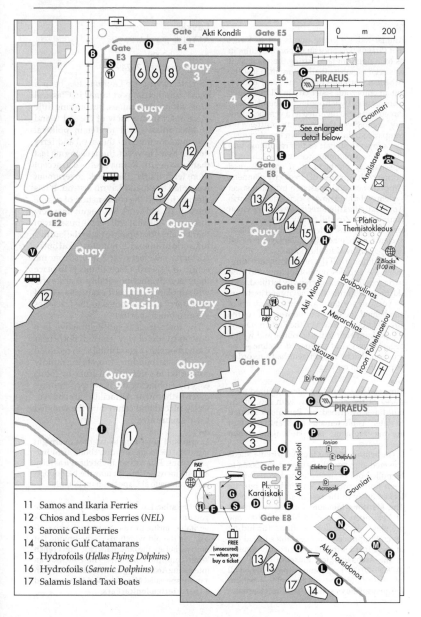

11 Samos and Ikaria Ferries
12 Chios and Lesbos Ferries (*NEL*)
13 Saronic Gulf Ferries
14 Saronic Gulf Catamarans
15 Hydrofoils (*Hellas Flying Dolphins*)
16 Hydrofoils (*Saronic Dolphins*)
17 Salamis Island Taxi Boats

😵

Amidst today's grime one is apt to forget that Piraeus was once an important centre in its own right. In fact, during the 5–4 c. BC it was seen as substantially more than just the Athenian harbour-cum-naval base, becoming an embryonic sister city in all but name. Unbelievably (when one looks around today), Piraeus was also regarded as a very beautiful city — and given the proximity of Athens for comparison, the modern town has obviously lost a great deal. Part of this reputation was due to town planning, for, unlike Athens, it was entirely pre-planned. It was designed by one of the greatest of Greek city planners, Hippodamos, and boasted a grid-like street system of the kind now associated with North American cities (the streets between the Great Harbour and Zea still follow the ancient pattern). This was considered highly desirable in ancient Greece where irregular layouts based on topography were the norm.

In addition to all the regular city accoutrements (i.e. temples, public buildings and even two agoras) Piraeus was heavily fortified, with skirting walls protecting the city and harbours — you can see the fragmentary remains of one behind the quay on the west side of the Great Harbour. However, the Roman era saw a significant shift in trade routes, and with it began a period of prolonged decline — so much so, that by 1833 Piraeus had a recorded population of only 22.

👓

Time and 19 c. building have obscured most traces of the ancient city, with few of the buildings described by Pausanias located to date. Visible remains are scanty: the best are the fragments of a Hellenistic **Odeon** west of Zea.

The remains of the famous trireme sheds (covered slipways that allowed the boats to be pulled out of the water and stored) have been found ringing Zea Harbour, but are locked away in the basements of buildings. The **Maritime Museum** (on the waterfront of Zea: open ② to ⑥ 08.30–12.30) has one on view. Archaeological finds (including several impressive bronze statues fished out of the Great Harbour) are currently housed in the **Archaeological Museum** (open ② to ⑦ 08.30–20.00). Fragments of the western wall are also visible — but not accessible — behind the quay on the west side of the Great Harbour.

Lavrio

ΛΑΥΡΙΟ; pop. 10,700.

CODE ☎ 22920
PORT POLICE ☎ 25249

To date Lavrio (or Lavrion) has been a small, commercial port famed in Classical times for its silver mines, but offering little more apart from a view of the sad island of **Makronissi** (used to detain political prisoners for much of the 20 c.) and ferry links to Kea. However, this is changing fast thanks to nearby Rafina's refusal to accept more ferry traffic. The Greek government has opted to expand Lavrio instead. It has already funded the construction of a large ferry quay, and work has begun on a new motorway link that will enable buses from the new airport at Spata to make the journey to Lavrio in around 20 minutes (local buses currently take just over 2 hours from the centre of Athens). Once all this is in place there is a distinct possibility that Lavrio will supplant Rafina as the capital's second port (ferry journey times to the Cyclades are also much shorter).

The town itself is quite attractive in a downbeat sort of way. The old centre near the harbour has a good number of red-tiled neo-classical buildings (now being rapidly converted to cafés and tavernas by locals eagerly embracing the new opportunities given to the town). All facilities are conveniently placed and centred on the wooded town square area.

🛏

Lavrio isn't geared up to cater for overnight visitors at the moment so don't build a stay into your plans. This will no doubt change as ferry activity increases, but for now the best option is the campsite at Cape Sounion (8 km).

👓

Unlike Rafina, Lavrio offers plenty to see while you are waiting for your ferry. The town is a veritable shrine to 19 c. industrial archaeology via the old warehouses, the unique flat ore washeries, the landmark cast-iron **French Wharf**, and the museums. These include an interesting **Archaeological Museum** along with a more specialist **Mineralogical Museum** and a (19 c.) **Technological Park**.

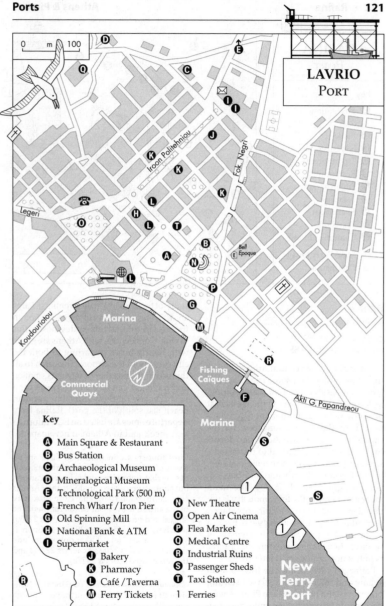

LAVRIO
PORT

Iroon Politehniou

Fok. Negri

Legeri

Bell
Epoque

Koudouriotou

Marina

Commercial
Quays

Fishing
Caïques

Marina

Akti G. Papandreou

New
Ferry
Port

Key

A Main Square & Restaurant
B Bus Station
C Archaeological Museum
D Mineralogical Museum
E Technological Park (500 m)
F French Wharf / Iron Pier
G Old Spinning Mill
H National Bank & ATM
I Supermarket
J Bakery
K Pharmacy
L Café / Taverna
M Ferry Tickets
N New Theatre
O Open Air Cinema
P Flea Market
Q Medical Centre
R Industrial Ruins
S Passenger Sheds
T Taxi Station
1 Ferries

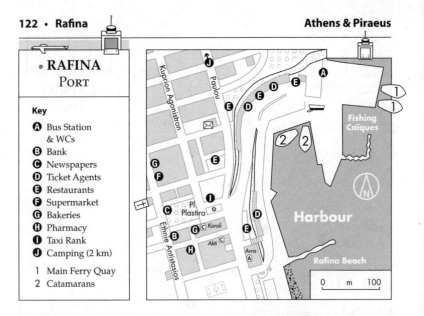

· RAFINA
PORT

Key

Ⓐ Bus Station
  & WCs
Ⓑ Bank
Ⓒ Newspapers
Ⓓ Ticket Agents
Ⓔ Restaurants
Ⓕ Supermarket
Ⓖ Bakeries
Ⓗ Pharmacy
Ⓘ Taxi Rank
Ⓙ Camping (2 km)

1 Main Ferry Quay
2 Catamarans

Rafina
ΡΑΦΗΝΑ

CODE ☎ 22940
PORT POLICE ☎ 28888

Located 27 km from central Athens, Rafina (listed as 'Athens' on some island agency ferry schedules) is a pleasant, if uninspiring, leafy small suburb town on the west coast of Attica, with a reputation for fish restaurants (it is the main fishing port for the capital). The port is also the second departure point from the capital to the islands, with regular morning and evening services to the Cyclades North line and beyond. Surprisingly, given that it is the main income generator, the ferry industry is not popular; in fact the town authority staged a one-day ferry strike a few years back in protest at the prospect of an increase of services (hence the development of ferry facilities now going on at Lavrio).

Rafina port lies below the town's main square and offers a more relaxed starting point for island hopping than Piraeus, with passengers buying tickets amid fresh fish stalls (at their busiest in the evenings). Fares are 10% cheaper than at Piraeus, although the bus fare into Athens erodes most of this saving. Connections with Athens are good, with hourly buses departing to both the city centre and the airport. The catch to all this is that the number of ferries is smaller, and travellers can face a longer wait for a boat (usually on the scruffy, but popular, beach just south of the port). Rafina ferry departure times are listed on EOT information sheets and in Athenian newspapers.

Most tourists are in transit, so there are no locals offering rooms. There are three hotels of note that almost invariably have vacancies, but all are expensive compared to their Athens city centre counterparts (the close proximity of the airport is the justification for this). The largest and best is the A-class *Avra* (☎ 22780) which will take at least €120 off you (more if you want a sea view). Other options include the main square C-class *Korali* (☎ 22477) and the rather tired *Akti* (☎ 24776).

Ⓐ
Camping Kokkino Limanaki (☎ 31603): a well-signed beach site 2 km north of the port (though the walk seems longer). Good facilities.

Salamina / Salamis
ΣΑΛΑΜΙΝΑ; 93.5 km²; pop. 23,000.

CODE ☎ 24670

Cowering behind the shipyards and rows of rusting ships anchored west of Piraeus lies the famous, but little touristed, island of Salamis (known these days as Salamina). Its great claim to fame comes via the battle between the Greek and Persian trireme fleets in 480 BC which took place in the narrow straits between the north-east side of the island and the mainland. Unfortunately, Salamis has been in decline from this high point ever since, and after 2,500 years this means that things are pretty bad in parts. Even in ancient times the close proximity of Athens resulted in it becoming little more than a suburb of the capital, and it remains in its neighbour's shadow.

Salamis is actually quite an attractive spot in places in an understated sort of way, but the bulk of the island looks not dissimilar to the outskirts of Athens: consisting of totally bare, sun-bleached hillsides, with ribbons of modern buildings (many three or four stories high) running around coastlines and along major roads. The tourist industry has barely developed at all. This is in part because nothing on Salamis can compare with the sights of Athens, but also because the island's traditional sources of income have always been relatively good and still are.

The biggest employer by far is Greece's premier naval dockyard just north of Paloukia (note: don't even *think* about pointing a camera in its direction!), and there are shipyards in the bay at Ambelakia. At first sight the island appears to have a number of viable beaches, but the locals are conspicuous by their absence. Again the close proximity of Athens does Salamis down: this is one of the few places in the Aegean

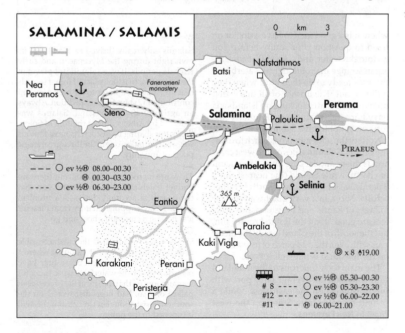

SALAMINA / SALAMIS

Nea Peramos
Steno
Batsi
Nafstathmos
Faneromeni monastery
Salamina
Paloukia
Perama
PIRAEUS

○ ev ½⊕ 08.00–00.30
  ⊕ 00.30–03.30
○ ev ½⊕ 06.30–23.00

Ambelakia
Selinia
365 m
Eantio
Paralia
Kaki Vigla
Karakiani
Perani
Peristeria

Ⓓ x 8 ₰19.00

🚌	── ○ ev ½⊕	05.30–00.30
# 8	---- ○ ev ½⊕	05.30–23.30
#12	--·-- ○ ev ½⊕	06.00–22.00
#11	--- ⊕	06.00–21.00

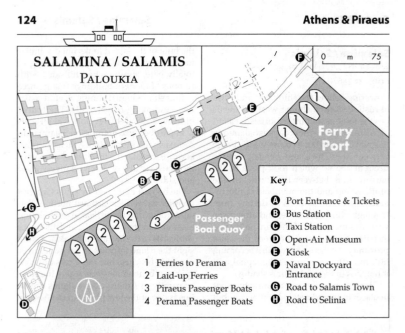

SALAMINA / SALAMIS
PALOUKIA

0   m   75

Ferry Port

Passenger Boat Quay

Key

A Port Entrance & Tickets
B Bus Station
C Taxi Station
D Open-Air Museum
E Kiosk
F Naval Dockyard Entrance
G Road to Salamis Town
H Road to Selinia

1 Ferries to Perama
2 Laid-up Ferries
3 Piraeus Passenger Boats
4 Perama Passenger Boats

where it is a good idea to have a doctor on hand to question your sanity before you go into the water, and a specialist consultant in strange microbiological waterborne diseases ready to do their stuff when they pull you out. The upshot of all this is that unless tourists are clocking up islands and ferry hops, or are students of military history, most opt to give Salamis a miss.

None of the settlements has much to offer; the capital, **Salamina**, lies on the west coast and is dusty and lacking even a modicum of charm, while Selinia (the nearest thing Salamis has on offer to a 'resort') is rather scruffy. Nicer, in a very quiet way, are the villages of Eantio and Peristeria. Bus services are good along the limited routes run, but the south of the island (easily the nicest part with even the odd patch of forest cover on the hillsides) is not well served.

The main ferry link runs to the mainland from **Paloukia** (an average ferry port with pretty fringes) on the east coast, while a second operates from **Steno** on the west coast to **Nea Peramos**.

🐍

Salamis only really thrived as a centre in its own right during the Mycenaean and early Archaic periods. It was a significant player in the Trojan War (if it took place); Homer records that the island was home to the hero Ajax and contributed 12 ships to the expedition. Always an agriculturally poor island, Salamis was annexed by Athens during the rule of Solon, thereafter sharing its history. Its most famous son was Euripides, one of the three great tragic poets of antiquity.

🛏

There are no rooms on Salamis, but there are budget hotels at Selinia and Eantio. Not that the dearth of accommodation is a problem — this is day-tripping territory from Piraeus: just hop on a commuter boat and go.

👓

Sightseeing is very limited: the most accessible is the open-air museum at Paloukia where a few rusting bits of nautical bric-a-brac have been dumped in the waterfront park. In 2006 it was announced that the site of the Mycenaean palace of Ajax had been discovered on the southern coast, though it isn't clear if this will be opened to the public.

The Battle of Salamis

The encounter between the Greek and Persian fleets in the straits between Salamis and Piraeus in 480 BC is regularly described as the most important naval battle in the whole of antiquity. All battles can be said to change the course of history, but Salamis is different because it can truly be said to have changed the whole direction of western culture. A small Greek fleet inflicted a decisive defeat on a much more powerful enemy, and effectively put paid to the Persian effort to conquer Greece. Had the Persians won there would have been no flowering of Greek democracy, theatre or philosophy in the century that followed. The far-reaching echoes of Salamis are thus apparent in all our lives today.

Background

Ten years after the Athenians had destroyed a Persian force at the Battle of Marathon in 490 BC, the Persian King Xerxes set out to conquer Greece. The invading army marched around the rim of the Aegean, supported by a fleet of 1,327 warships. At the end of August 480 BC they arrived at the narrow pass at Thermopylae, where their progress south was delayed by the '300 Spartans' (of Hollywood film fame). While the Spartans, and their king Leonidas, were heroically dying, the population of Athens — unable to defend their city against the advancing enemy — decamped to neighbouring Salamis, relying on their fleet for protection. This set the scene for the battle that followed.

As befits the greatest sea battle in antiquity, the statistics for Salamis are spectacular. Standing on the mainland shoreline, with the burning Acropolis temples behind them, were 20,000–50,000 men of the Persian army. Behind them King Xerxes set up a golden throne on the slopes of Mt. Aegaleos in order to watch the drama unfold, while 100,000 Athenians looked on from the slopes of Salamis. If the audience was big it was nothing to the numbers of combatants: 200,000 men fought, of whom an estimated 20,000 — mostly Persians — died.

Added drama was provided by political divisions. Both fleets suffered from divided command. On the Greek side were 368 ships (180 supplied by Athens) that made up the 'Hellenic League'. The main contributors (Athens, Aegina and Corinth) were not natural allies. In fact the Corinthians were all for the fleet retreating south to Corinth. The Athenian leader Themistocles only avoided this happening by using a spy to warn the Persians that the Greek fleet was preparing to escape, thus precipitating an attack before it could do so.

If anything, things were worse on the Persian side. Their fleet numbered 800–1000 ships, but they were all provided by vassal states from Egypt to the Eastern Aegean islands (there were as many Greek ships in the Persian fleet as in the Greek). Using crews of dubious loyalty, Xerxes loaded them with extra Persian soldiers to guard against treachery — with dire results. Unlike the Greek crews, few of these soldiers could swim and they drowned when ships were lost. Ship losses at Salamis were said to be 40 on the Greek side against over 200 on the Persian (hence the high Persian death toll).

Trireme Wars

An appreciation of the battle of Salamis is impossible without some understanding of the ships used. The premier warships of the ancient world at the time were highly manoeuvrable rowing boats, light enough to be beached ashore at night, and armed with murderous bronze rams. Roughly 40 m long, and manned with three banks of oarsmen, the trireme (known in Greece as the 'Trieres' or 'three-rower') was a remarkably sophisticated piece of weaponry that required an incredibly high degree of coordination on the part of the crew.

The typical trireme had a crew of 200, consisting of 170 paid oarsmen, a commander — the 'Trierarchos' (who sat on a throne at the rear of the narrow central deck, and who was often an individual of importance), a helmsman, a lookout, a flutesman (to enable the oarsmen to row in time) and ten sailors. The only armed men aboard were 10 hoplites with spears and 4 archers, and their function was to defend the ship in the event of a trireme struggling to break free of her rammed victim.

To modern eyes triremes are bizarre weapons of war: they were in effect nautical dodgem cars, with fierce painted eyes on their bows. The idea was to row past an enemy ship, rapidly turn and ram him below the water line, then quickly disengage before anyone could ram you. A second tactic was to close in on an enemy ship at speed, and just before passing, quickly ship in your oars — so that the hull of your trireme would smash the oars of the enemy as it shot past.

Thanks to the successful reconstruction of a trireme in 1986 (named *Olympias* and now part of the Hellenic Navy), understanding and appreciation of these beautiful, strange vessels has grown enormously. Their manoeuvrability and ability to pick up

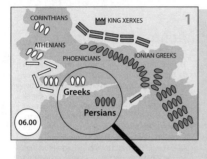

speed quickly (they can go from a standing start to 10 knots in under a minute) have occasioned much surprise. If you want to have a look at the **replica trireme** then it is possible to do so: the *Olympias* is on display in a covered dry dock at Faliron, Athens. It is close to another vessel of note, the world's only surviving pre-WW1 heavy armoured cruiser, *Georgios Averof*. Both are part of the new **Hellenic Navy Museum**. If you want to visit from Piraeus take the metro to Nea Falero, and then six stops on the coast tram to **Trocantero**. Alternatively, you can take a tram from Syntagma Square (🄲 on p. 94). An original bronze trireme ram is also on display in the Pireaus Archaeological Museum.

The Battle

Accounts of the battle are provided by the poet Aeschylus (who took part, and uses it in his play *The Persians*), and the first historian, Herodotus, who visited Athens c. 430 BC to get eyewitness reports for his *History*. In spite of this, details remain unclear, in part because the competing allies tended to amplify their own role, while disparaging others. Athens and Aegina are still arguing over which city's ship was the first to engage the enemy. Some place names are also now obscure, and the topography has changed because sea levels have risen by 2 m.

06.00: (the 25th?) of September, 480 BC.

Athenians wake to find that the Persian fleet has spent a tiring night rowing from Phaleron Bay (E of Piraeus) into the straits, blocking off exit routes.

07.00: The Greek crews man their triremes and move towards the crack enemy Phoenician ships, inviting battle. Then they back water, reversing towards the Salamis coast. The Persian fleet is drawn forward; the Greeks maintain their line until one captain spots a gap in the enemy line, advances quickly through it, and rams a vessel. However, he has difficulty withdrawing his ram, forcing other Greek triremes to come to his aid and initiating full battle. The Persians — in an action that tires their weary crews further — repeatedly charge and retreat from the Greek ships, hoping to entice further triremes out of their line (which holds).

10.00: The 'Aura' sea breeze gets going, causing the lighter Persian triremes to fall out of line, and allowing the heavier Greek triremes to move in and attack. In one of the multiple ship-to-ship engagements the admiral of the Persian fleet, Ariabignes, half-brother of Xerxes, is killed. The Persian fleet — with its tired crews and wind-tossed boats, and shorn of its commander — gradually loses its cohesion as its line collapses.

12.00: The remaining ships from the leading Persian squadrons retreat, but are unable to get clear because other squadrons from their fleet are still seeking to enter the strait and join battle. Discipline goes in the Persian fleet: the female commander Queen Artemisia of Halicarnassos (Bodrum) deliberately rams and sinks one of her own side as a means of deceiving a pursing Greek trireme.

14.00: The battle has disintegrated into a series of individual duels, with Persian ships seeking safety: the difficulty in escaping the straits prolongs the battle and adds to their casualty list.

18.00: Athenian ships launch an attack on the 400 Persian troops holding the islet of Psitalia. They take the island by nightfall, killing all the defenders.

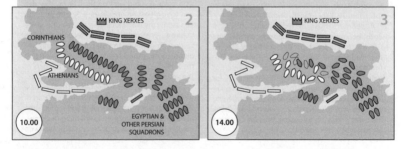

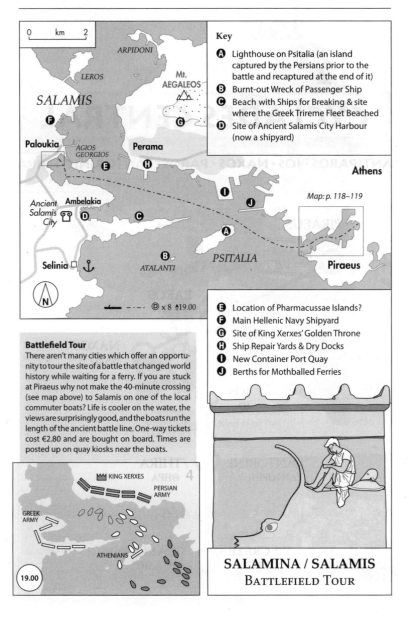

Key

A Lighthouse on Psitalia (an island captured by the Persians prior to the battle and recaptured at the end of it)

B Burnt-out Wreck of Passenger Ship

C Beach with Ships for Breaking & site where the Greek Trireme Fleet Beached

D Site of Ancient Salamis City Harbour (now a shipyard)

Map: p. 118–119

E Location of Pharmacussae Islands?

F Main Hellenic Navy Shipyard

G Site of King Xerxes' Golden Throne

H Ship Repair Yards & Dry Docks

I New Container Port Quay

J Berths for Mothballed Ferries

0   km   2

ARPIDONI

LEROS

SALAMIS

Mt. AEGALEOS

Paloukia

AGIOS GEORGIOS

Perama

Athens

Ancient Salamis City

Ambelakia

Selinia

ATALANTI

PSITALIA

Piraeus

N

(D) x 8 19.00

Battlefield Tour

There aren't many cities which offer an opportunity to tour the site of a battle that changed world history while waiting for a ferry. If you are stuck at Piraeus why not make the 40-minute crossing (see map above) to Salamis on one of the local commuter boats? Life is cooler on the water, the views are surprisingly good, and the boats run the length of the ancient battle line. One-way tickets cost €2.80 and are bought on board. Times are posted up on quay kiosks near the boats.

KING XERXES

PERSIAN ARMY

GREEK ARMY

ATHENIANS

19.00

SALAMINA / SALAMIS
BATTLEFIELD TOUR

ANTIPAROS
Main Street & Kastro

PAROS
Morning Ferries Arrive at Paros (viewed from Parikia Beach)

Sightseeing on Parikia Beach

How to make mad, passionate, erotic love on the back of a Great Striped Man–Seating Whale …

Parikia Town: Temple
Site Kastro Church

TEMPLE OF ATHENA

Down the Marble Mine:
The Crack of Doom

Visitors foolishly
attempting to
enter the Marble
Mine via the
very steep
Cave Slope Shaft

PAROS
Marble Quarries

Cyclades Central

GALERIE D'ART

JEWELLERY
GOLD & SILVER

DIMITROULA

Naxian Ferry Ticket
Agency

A small inter-island ferry
arrives at Naxos

ΝΑΟΣ ΔΗΜΗΤΡΑΣ

DIMITRA'S TEMPLE

NAXOS

Town/Chora

General Features

The Cyclades derive their name from being said to 'circle' the island of Delos — birthplace of the god Apollo. In practice, they lie in a semicircle south of a line running from the north-west to the south-east drawn just north of Delos.

Within the Cyclades the islands fall neatly into four subgroups, with Paros and the Cyclades Central line islands now forming the true centre of the group. The Central Cyclades consist of a number of islands that are known by name to most visitors to Greece. Among these, the photogenic volcanic island of Santorini is deservedly popular, being identified with the legend of Atlantis; disco-laden Ios is known by repute to every student under the sun; Paros has a happy mix of almost everything; and Naxos has an excellent blend of atmosphere and golden beaches.

However, unspoilt islands these are not. Given that most new island hoppers make for an island that they've at least heard of, it is inevitable that this group should have become the main artery in the ferry system, seeing more visitors than the rest of the Cyclades put together. Out of High Season they are fine, but in summer these islands can seem very crowded.

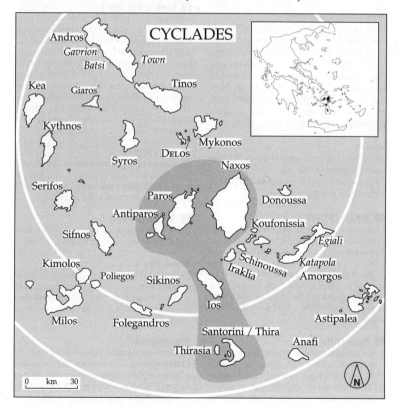

Example Itinerary [2 Weeks]

This justifiably popular group of islands forms the backbone of the Greek ferry system. High Season connections are so good that they make for extremely relaxed island hopping. With ferries almost as frequent as red buses down Oxford Street, even the most timid of travellers can wander without fear. The main islands can be done in any order since there are boats all times of the day. You won't be short on company either. Even so, with a little effort, you can escape the worst of the crowds almost whenever you choose.

Arrival/Departure Point

With good ferry links to Athens/Piraeus, Santorini, Mykonos and Crete (Iraklion) — all ports with charter flight connections — you are spoilt for choice. Athens and Santorini remain the safest options should you find yourself in a rush to get back for your return flight. Crete and Mykonos are a little less easy, since you are often dependent on a single boat each day.

Season

Daily boats operate up and down the line through most of the year, though out of High Season it will be just the one boat rather than the daily dozen.

1 Athens [1 Day]

Unless you are really unlucky with your flight arrival time, you should be able to ship out of Piraeus the day you fly in. With boats to the Cyclades Central line mornings and evenings in the High Season, you are not going to be obliged to spend a night in the capital. Once in Athens grab a handful of Euros, a meal and, of course, the NTOG / EOT ferry departure sheets and go.

2 Paros [3 Days]

Paros is a genial stopping point for your first few days, as you wind down and acclimatize. Plenty of beaches, nightlife and that all important Greek island atmosphere, and, when you want to avoid the worst of the sun, the cave on Antiparos makes an interesting excursion easily to hand.

3 Naxos [2 Days]

More relaxing than Paros, Naxos is the next stop down the line. If you don't want to stay you can always visit on a day trip from Paros; a morning boat will set you down in time for lunch and you can then pick up a Paros-bound evening Santorini—Piraeus boat. They are sufficiently frequent in both directions that you don't have to worry about not being able to complete the return trip. The probability is, however, that you will want to stay, and longer than a mere two days.

4 Santorini [4 Days]

Although Ios is the next in the chain, time spent there is unlikely to leave you in a fit state to explore Santorini. Pick up one of the ferries running down the line in the early hours when heading on to Santorini (this way you don't waste a day of your holiday looking for a room). You can always make up lost sleep on the nearest black sand beach. This is one island that shouldn't be missed. Realistically, you will need three days to explore the sights.

5 Ios [2 Nights]

Ios doesn't wake up much before 23.00 hours. The mixture of sun, 'slammers' and sand is so over the top that most island hoppers can't stand it for more than a day or two.

1 Athens [2 Days]

Get a boat back to Athens and spend your flight 'safety' day in hand touring the city.

Alternative 1

Rather than spend two days enjoying the delights of Naxos, advance your schedule and return to Piraeus via Paros and **Mykonos**. You can glean the latest Paros departure times on your way south.

Alternative 2

Another option is to head further south to **Crete (Iraklion)** and take in the Minoan palace at Knossos. Ferry links are more tenuous this far south, so allow 3 days to do the round trip and book tickets in advance if possible.

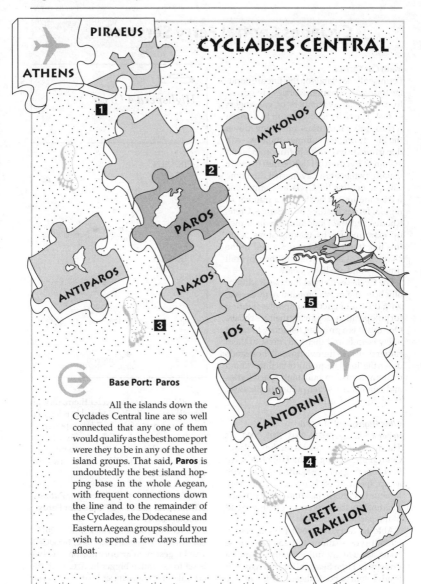

CYCLADES CENTRAL

ATHENS · PIRAEUS

1

MYKONOS

2

PAROS

ANTIPAROS

NAXOS

3

5

IOS

Base Port: Paros

All the islands down the Cyclades Central line are so well connected that any one of them would qualify as the best home port were they to be in any of the other island groups. That said, **Paros** is undoubtedly the best island hopping base in the whole Aegean, with frequent connections down the line and to the remainder of the Cyclades, the Dodecanese and Eastern Aegean groups should you wish to spend a few days further afloat.

SANTORINI

4

CRETE IRAKLION

Cyclades Central Ferry Services

Main Car Ferries

Because all the islands on this line are popular tourist destinations, ferries are geared to moving large numbers of passengers — fast. The rich pickings result in a dozen ferries and catamarans operating down the line during the summer months, with departures from Piraeus both mornings and evenings. Even out of High Season there are usually two boats a day in each direction. Complementing the Cyclades Central line ferries are tourist boats and a number of regular ferries heading on to Samos, Crete, Rhodes and the Dodecanese, which pick up extra income by making stops along this line (these boats are described in the chapter most appropriate to their overall itinerary and are listed below).

The Cyclades Central line has traditionally been the most competitive in Greece, with the leading ferry companies fighting for pole position, deploying their best boats. One result is a growing tendency to target a few islands and then sail direct to them rather than take time visiting all the islands down the line. The quality of facilities found on the new custom-built high-speed ferries and catamarans is even pulling traffic away from domestic airlines.

C/Ms *Highspeed 4/5/6*
Hellenic Seaways / HFD; 2004, 2005, 2000.
The most popular vessels on the Cyclades Central line belong to the HFD *Highspeed* fleet. Offering very fast journey times, with a top speed of 38 knots, they run from Piraeus to Paros in just under three hours. This enables them to cream off the top end of the passenger market.

Able to carry over 600 passengers (in aircraft-type seating) and 150 cars, these boats are usually full on journeys out of Piraeus in High Season (for this reason it is advisable to book ahead). This can be a problem as locals tend to fill them up at peak

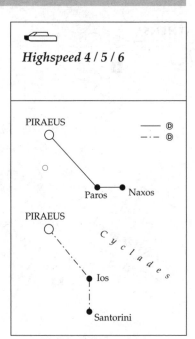

periods. Tourists also prefer them, though there is no sun deck, so travel is relegated from being part of the 'holiday experience' to a chore. On all the *Highspeed* vessels you are expected to sit in the numbered seat indicated on your ticket. Itineraries are well established.

C/F *Blue Star Delos* – C/F *Blue Star Patmos*
C/F *Blue Star Naxos* – C/F *Blue Star Paros*
Blue Star Ferries
Blue Star Delos/Blue Star Patmos; 2011, 2012.
Blue Star Naxos/Blue Star Paros; 2002, 16500 GRT.
The biggest regular operator on this line is set to get much bigger in 2012 with the arrival of two new super boats — the *Blue Star Delos* and the *Blue Star Patmos* — which

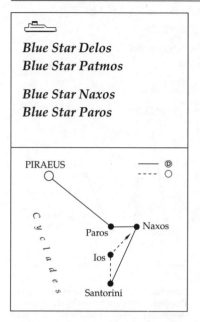

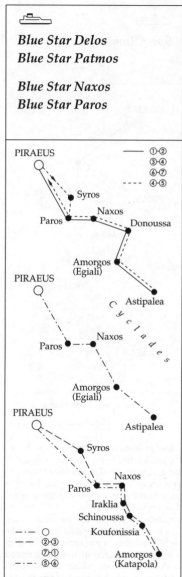

are slated to take over from the *Blue Star Naxos* and *Blue Star Paros*, who have dominated services since their arrival in 2002. All are Korean-built ferries built specifically for the Greek market. The two boats that will be on the route will run a morning and evening departure from both ends of the line (and, if past experience is anything to go by, they sometimes swap itineraries, so don't be surprised by this). Fares are 20% higher than regular ferries because these newer boats are 20% faster (Piraeus to Paros in 4 hours instead of 5+).

The arrival of the two new boats is to be welcomed as they will increase capacity from 1500 to 2400 passengers on a line where boats can be booked solid in High Season. The only possible problems are calls to the Little Cyclades islands, as the new boats may be too large to dock at a couple of them. This could result in one of the older boats continuing to do these itineraries. One

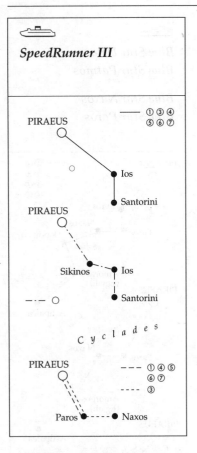

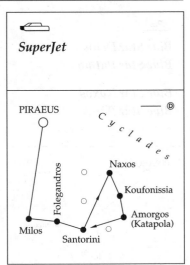

branch of *Goody's*—a popular Greek chain). Passenger luggage is usually deposited in designated storage areas. Finally, the island of Ios is rarely visited by these boats, but when they do call it is usually only on the return leg. On these occasions you can end up buying an expensive ticket from Piraeus only to arrive later than if you had taken a slower boat.

C/F *SpeedRunner III*
Aegean Speed Lines; 1999; 4463 GRT.
Slightly larger than the *SpeedRunner II*, this boat has become a useful link over the last two summers to the popular islands of Paros and Naxos, with a service six days a week. Hopefully she will be back on the route this year, but boats running a direct service to just these two islands have changed frequently in past years, and she will face increased competition from the new Blue Star boats.

C/M *SuperJet*
SeaJets
The former *SeaJet 1*, this small catamaran

minor problem with all the Blue Star boats is the limited amount of sun-deck space, and the arrangement of chairs inside seems to encourage 'empty seat hogging' by other passengers: if you are travelling at night it is advisable to pay an extra €3 and get a numbered seat. Otherwise facilities are first rate, with shiny escalators (only on the right-hand side as you approach the ship) whisking passengers up to well-equipped deck-class saloons which are complete with an on-board burger-bar franchise (a

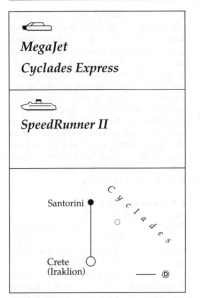

MegaJet

Cyclades Express

SpeedRunner II

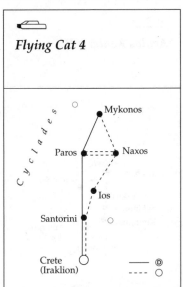

Flying Cat 4

has run a series of wide-ranging schedules since 2006. Unfortunately there is little consistency from year to year — Crete (Iraklion) was her base until 2010, when she started her current ambitious itinerary out of Piraeus which has several useful connecting links. Having operated this service for the last two summers, it is reasonable to hope she will be going again in 2012. Sadly, this is not a boat to totally rely on as she is apt to stay in port in poor weather conditions.

C/M *MegaJet*
SeaJets; 1995; 3989 GRT.
The largest boat in the SeaJets fleet, this catamaran has confined her runs to day-tripper trips between Crete (Iraklion) and Santorini. Not visible in 2011.

C/M *Cyclades Express*
NEL Lines; 1991; 3003 GRT.
This small catamaran was a new addition to the NEL fleet in 2010. She spent her first

summer in the Aegean running a day-tripper service between Crete (Iraklion) and Santorini and was not operating in 2011.

C/F *SpeedRunner II*
Aegean Speed Lines; 1996; 3971 GRT.
A less than flamboyant boat that has been around since 2008, the *SpeedRunner II* moved from the Cyclades West line to provide competition on the service to Ios and Santorini, before being advertised as running between Iraklion and Santorini in 2011. In the event she didn't show up at all, so it is anyone's guess where she will be in 2012. She probably could make a go of it if she appears on this route this year given the number of boats advertised on the route who fail to operate.

C/M *Flying Cat 4*
Hellas Flying Dolphins; 1996.
Given the absence of the competition above, this small, but attractive, catamaran provides a very useful connecting service from

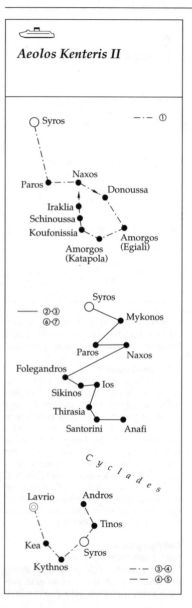

Aeolos Kenteris II

Crete to the Cyclades Central and Cyclades North lines (schedules have changed little in the last few summers — the only one of note came when Naxos was dropped from her itinerary). Her size can be a problem as services are apt to be disrupted once the *meltemi* winds blow: don't rely on this vessel if she is on the route again in 2012 and you are returning to Crete to collect a flight home. Picking her up at the last moment at Iraklion can also be difficult as she is increasingly used as a day-tripper boat. In fact in High Season there is very little chance of getting a seat unless you book 48-hours in advance.

C/F *Aeolos Kenteris II*
NEL Lines; 2001; 6000 GRT.

This speedy ferry (ironically named after the disgraced Greek sprinter who failed to turn up for a drug test at the start of the Athens Olympics) has had problems due to ever rising fuel prices that have made it uneconomic to run her at full throttle (as a result she now sails at regular ferry speeds). She has run out of Syros around the Cyclades for the last two summers with few changes to schedules — which augurs well for this summer. Facilities are on a par with the *Highspeed* catamarans. This boat is popular when operating, although her lightweight construction means that she does rock and roll more than most boats you are likely to sail on.

	See also:	
•	C/F *Blue Star Ithaki*	p. 209
•	C/F *Express Skopelitis*	p. 302
•	C/F *Aqua Jewel*	p. 258
•	C/F *Diagoras*	p. 367
•	C/F *Blue Star 1/2*	p. 366
•	C/F *Prevelis*	p. 259
•	C/M *Highspeed 2*	p. 213
•	C/M *SeaJet 2*	p. 212
•	C/M *Nissos Mykonos*	p. 446
•	C/M *Adamantis Korais*	p. 257

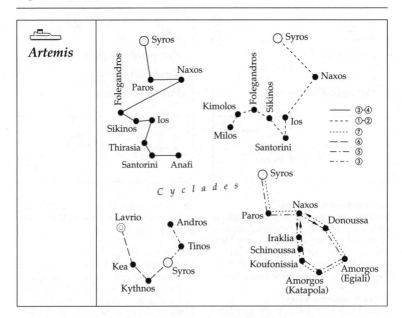

C/F Artemis
Hellenic Seaways / HFD; 1997; 1612 GRT.

One of the concessions to the summer tourist influx is the regular appearance of a small ferry running out of Syros to the Cycladic islands. For the last three years the modern *Artemis* (whose previous regular haunt was the Saronic Gulf) has provided the service, running the same set of itineraries both summers — though the days they were undertaken were changed. Despite her small size she is a good boat for irregular hops, though there are problems: her timetable continues to be very poorly advertised and some of her ticket agents aren't up to much. Note: her ticket agent on Anafi is usually closed, so it is worth buying return tickets elsewhere before arriving.

C/F Arsinoe – C/F Nissos Thira
Local

For the last few years Santorini has been the base for a small ferry that provides Anafi with its main link with the outside world, though in the summer of 2011 regular ferries called sufficiently frequently to make this link unnecessary. If either of these boats are running this year, expect minimal facilities. The *Nissos Thira* is the smaller of the two, though there isn't much between them.

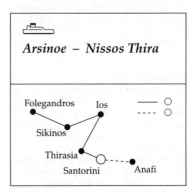

Aristeides
Leukas
Panagia Faneromene

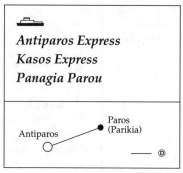

Antiparos Express
Kasos Express
Panagia Parou

Antiparos—Punta Ferries

Several small ferries provide a vehicle link across the straits between Antiparos Town and the quay at Paros (Punta). Their big plus is their reliability as they do run when winds prevent the Parakia tour boats. Regular buses complete the connection.

Paros—Antiparos Boats

Three small boats roll between Paros and Antiparos, providing an hourly 40-minute 'tourist' link. Don't be surprised if you have to take one of the Punta ferries back, because of over-choppy afternoon seas. The three boats attempted to combine forces one summer, enabling tourists to buy open-dated return tickets. However, it is now back to throat-cutting normal and you now buy single tickets (€5) on the vessel you travel on (no computer ticketing with these boats). One, usually the *Antiparos Express*, has been known to run a Paros—Sifnos (Faros) service in High Season.

C/F *Nissos Thirassia*

One landing-craft ferry operates a 'lifeline' service to Thirasia disguised as a Santorini caldera tour. Actually, stopping off at the hot springs to allow tourists a quick bathe is quite an enterprising way of subsidizing a ferry link. In High Season the *Nissos Thirassia* runs a twice-weekly day-return service (usually departing around 07.45 from Fira Old Port) that offers a much

cheaper way (€5.50 Rtn.) of spending five hours on uncrowded Thirasia than taking a caldera tour.

Tour Boats

Lightweight tourist boats also operate in the Central Cyclades. Not for sea-sickies, and expensive, they offer extra hopping options: in 2011 these included Paros to Delos (€35), Paros to Serifos (€35), and Ios to Sikinos (€30). These boats really come into their own if you want to have a quick look at the Little Cyclades, as they run good-value day trips that enable you to get a look at Iraklia and Koufonissia (€35).

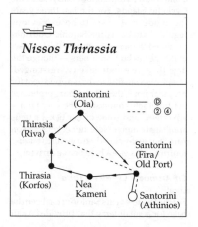

Nissos Thirassia

Cyclades Central Islands & Ports

ANTIPAROS

Official Nudist Beach

KAVOURAS

DIPLO

Camping Beach

Sunset Beach

Antiparos Town

FKK

Town

0   km   4

Glyfa

299 m.

Cave

Apandima

KRIMITRI

Agiós Georgios

Soros

DESPOTIKO

Ⓓ x 10
Ⓓ x 2

Antiparos

ΑΝΤΙΠΑΡΟΣ; 55 km²; pop. 820.

CODE ☎ 22840
POLICE ☎ 61202
FIRST AID ☎ 61219

If your idea of the perfect island includes excellent sand beaches, a cosy atmosphere, a picturesque port filled with prune-faced fishermen mending their nets, a spot of nudism, and plenty of discreet nightlife then the small island of Antiparos is it. Only accessible via neighbouring Paros, this place is a gem. Be warned; the chances are that if you visit it once, you will want to come back again: the number of devoted returnees grows every year. The island is also an excellent day-trip destination and sees many day-trippers from Paros who brave the half-hour crossing to visit the famous cave, or to explore the town and then head for a beach.

In many ways Antiparos is a strange place, having been severed from Paros as the result of an earthquake around 550 BC. The straits between it and Paros are very shallow (which is why all ferries are obliged to sail around the top of Paros when heading for Santorini) and narrow, with the fields on the western side of the island rolling into the sea. The only settlement, **Antiparos Town** — straddling the flat northern tip of the island and with a fortress at its centre — forms the focus of island life. Enough of the old town survives to give plenty of atmosphere, though the environs are dominated by establishments offering accommodation. On the south side of town is a salt flat that dries white every summer; it is separated from the sea by a tree-fringed beach.

Apart from the tavernas and boutiques lining the winding main street, the town's great attraction lies in its beaches. Within easy walking distance there is one guaranteed to suit most tastes. Families (of which there are a good many, for Antiparos is a good destination if you are holidaying with younger children) head for the shallow and sheltered beach to the north of the port, while the sand beach opposite **Diplo** islet (reached via the track to the campsite and then a 100 m path to the right) is the preserve of windsurfers (boards can be hired) and nudists (this is one of only three official nudist beaches in Greece). Diplo islet itself is accessible — it is possible to wade across from the nudist beach. More hardy types in search of solitude either head here or for

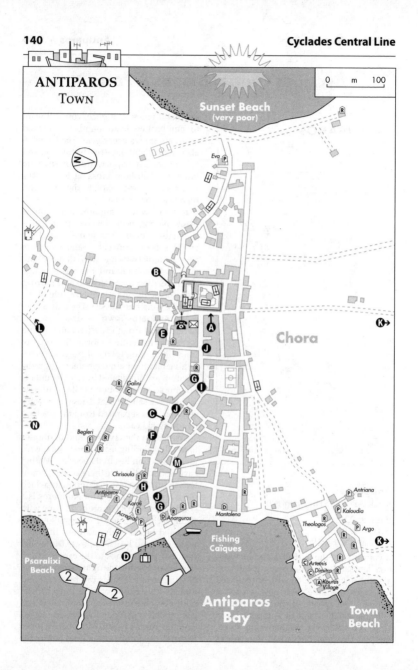

ANTIPAROS
TOWN

0　　m　　100

Sunset Beach
(very poor)

Eva

N

B

Chora

E

A

J

R

G

Galini

I

C

N

C

J

R

Begleri

F

E

R

M

Chrisoula

E R

H

Antiparos

E

Koroli

J

Antriana

E

G

R

R

P

Acregioli

E

D

Anarguros

D

Kaloudia

P

D

Mantalena

R

P Argo

Theologos

R

K→

R

Psaralixi
Beach

2

2

D

Fishing
Caïques

1

C Artemis

C Dimitra

R

A Kouros
Village

Antiparos
Bay

Town
Beach

L

K→

Sunset Beach behind the town; windswept and with an abandoned air, it is the place for contemplating the meaning of life (and what one is doing with it) and for quietly drowning oneself if one isn't happy with the conclusions.

Drowning one's sorrows back in town is even easier as bars aplenty cluster around the fortress and trickle down the main street. The town also has several discos (notably establishments in the inland town windmill and near the *Galini* hotel).

The rest of the island is relatively undeveloped; a decent road has only recently been completed, allowing buses to run south to the cave, and occasionally to Agios Georgios on the south-west coast. There is a comfortable scatter of holiday homes along the coast road, as well as taverna-backed sand beaches at **Glyfa** and at **Apandima** (the mooring point for boats bringing visitors to the cave).

The beach at **Agios Georgios** is remote, but worth the effort of getting to, though there is some development here: a system of roads has been laid out in a grid behind the beach, anticipating the building of a major holiday home development. This is another symptom of the popularity of Antiparos — the holiday home business is big on the island, though if you are tempted you would be wise to choose either your

building site or house with care: most of Antiparos Town is less than 10 m above sea level. The predicted rises in sea levels thanks to global warming suggest that buying property here is a high risk option.

The hills that dominate the centre and west of Antiparos offer some low-key hill walking out of the High Season. They were once home to several major early Cycladic settlements—the most important being the site above Agios Georgios beach. The first to have ever been systematically explored, it yielded up a large number of 3000–2500 BC Cycladic figures (see p. 321) that now form the nucleus of the British Museum's impressive collection. This site (along with a number of others on Antiparos and Paros) was excavated by another of those 19 C. gentleman travellers, an Englishman by the name of **James Theodore Bent** (see p. 145). Bent not only introduced the world to the art of the early Bronze Age Cycladic culture, but also penned one of the most famous — and readable — of 19 C. travel books describing his tour.

In ancient times Antiparos was known as 'Oliaros'. It has always been too small to be a significant historical force in its own right, being dependent to a greater or lesser extent on Paros. Like Paros it was a subject of Athens, following Parian support for the losing Persians at Salamis (480 BC). Thereafter not much is known as the island was too small to feature in historical accounts, and too small to defend in the late Byzantine era when pirate raids became a feature of life in the Aegean.

Uninhabited for periods, Antiparos first acquired its current name in the 13 C. when it was resettled following a succession of pirate raids. In the hands of the Dukes of Naxos it briefly flourished and was known to be well populated by 1400, but was abandoned again soon after. In 1440 it was given by the Duke of Naxos to the Venetian Loredano family as part of a marriage dowry. This prompted the resettlement of the island with imported farmers and the building of the protective castle.

A brief period of stability came to an end in 1537: Antiparos fell to the Turks when Khayr al-Din Barbarossa paid a very destructive visit.

Key

Ⓐ	Kastro	**Ⓚ**	Camping Antiparos & Nudist Beach (800 m)
Ⓑ	Main Town Square		
Ⓒ	High Street	**Ⓛ**	Cave Road
Ⓓ	Bus Stop	**Ⓜ**	Open-Air Cinema
Ⓔ	Medical Centre		
Ⓕ	National Bank & ATM	**Ⓝ**	Salt Flats
Ⓖ	Supermarkets		
Ⓗ	Bookshop	1	Tourist Boats
Ⓘ	Newspapers	2	Punta Ferry Quay
Ⓙ	Bakery		

This initiated a period of regular attacks by pirates (mostly Christian adventurers who felt free to attack any vulnerable point in the Ottoman Empire). The worst incident occurred in 1675 when a French pirate, Daniel, Knight of St. John of Malta, sought refuge on Antiparos after being defeated by several Turkish ships in a confrontation off Despotiko. Having been offered a substantial bounty if they hid him and his crew, the locals opted to take the cash and then hand him over to the Turks. When this story got out, Daniel's fellow captains (with the picturesque names of Orange, Honorat and Hugo de Crevellier) turned up after the Turkish ships had departed, sacking the Kastro and town, and massacring the inhabitants.

Repopulated yet again, Antiparos was the victim of further devastating attacks, most notably in 1794 when some passing Kefalonian pirates sacked the island, killing all the inhabitants, including the French vice-consul's daughter. With a history like this it is not surprising that incomers quickly signed up for the Greek independence struggle, joining the new Greek state in 1830. After independence Antiparos began to prosper. The mainstay of the economy prior to WW2 was mining (though there is little evidence of this today, the exception being a small railway wharf on Soros beach that was used to load ships with ore deposits). Between 1873 and 1956 Antiparos was mined for zinc, iron and lead.

There is plenty of accommodation in Town, though it is pricey. Top of the range is the A-class *Kouros Village* (☎ 61084) and the C-class *Artemis* (☎ 61460), both with good views over the harbour. Equally good, but less well-placed, is the inland *Galini* (☎ 61420). The remainder of the hotel accommodation is cheaper. This includes the waterfront D-class *Mantalena* (☎ 61206), and several E-class establishments in the streets behind the waterfront buildings — the *Korali* (☎ 61236), *Antiparos* (☎ 61358), *Chrisoula* (☎ 61224) and the popular *Argo* (☎ 61419/61186). Budget travellers should note that the E-class *Begleri* (☎ 61378) is more expensive than the C-class establishments! Room availability is good, but many bookings are on a long-stay basis, so arrive early in High Season.

Λ

Camping Antiparos (☎ 61410): 1 km along a dirt track north of the town. Tents are pitched in bamboo compounds. Mini-bus meets boats.

👓

Antiparos has two sights of note — the Kastro and the Cave: both can be done in the course of a day trip, but it is best to do the cave first as it closes at 15.00.

The Kastro

On most Greek islands you will find a small castle or 'kastro' dating from the pirate-plagued late medieval period either close by or in the heart of the main town. They are usually sited on an ancient acropolis or cliff top, surrounded by houses that are built together to form a defensive outer wall. The kastro at Antiparos, although it embraces the same basic concept, is a very different sort of structure. It is unique in being located not on a defendable inland or hill site, but on a flat plain in full view of the sea. It is also unique in being the earliest known example of 15 c. urban planning in the Cyclades, and it was clearly used as a model for more elaborate later examples (most notably on Kimolos a century or so later — see p. 271).

Built on the orders of the Venetian Leonardo Loredano c. 1440 to house and protect a community of farmers shipped in to repopulate and farm the island, the kastro is a rectangular structure that in its heyday looked akin to a three-storeyed Alamo-like stockade, with a single Gothic-style gateway on its south side and rooms accessed by staircases lining the inside walls. In the centre, sited on a small low mound (which presumably dictated the building's precise location on the flat farmland plain that makes up northern Antiparos), was a large circular tower.

Originally designed to be seen and to intimidate potential attackers, the kastro was a very distinctive building that quickly became a local landmark. At a time when the representation of towns and buildings on maps was very casual, it was even recognizably drawn by the first Greek island cartographer — the Venetian sailor Bartolomeo dalli Sonetti — in his *Insolario* published in 1485.

However, the limitations of the kastro were soon apparent. The first problem was size: with only 72 single-room apartments in its walls accommodation was limited to around 300 people. As a result, within 100 years of its construction the original structure — known as the Pirgo ('tower') — acquired a second square of buildings built onto its front end (the arched main door became an inner gate). Known as

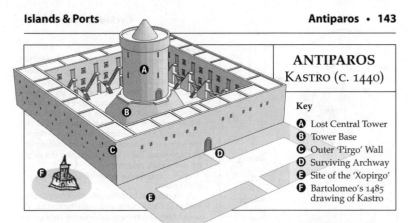

ANTIPAROS
KASTRO (C. 1440)

Key

Ⓐ Lost Central Tower
Ⓑ Tower Base
Ⓒ Outer 'Pirgo' Wall
Ⓓ Surviving Archway
Ⓔ Site of the 'Xopirgo'
Ⓕ Bartolomeo's 1485 drawing of Kastro

the Xopirgo ('out of the tower'), this addition doubled the living space, but has not survived in the modern street plan (though the churches later built within it are extant and have carved on their door lintels the dates 1660 and 1703).

The second problem — and this was the biggy — is that when it came to the crunch the kastro just wasn't defendable. It was the castle equivalent of a DeLorean car—it looked really cool, but was always breaking down. The building was all about psychology rather than real security. It made the inhabitants feel safe as it appeared suitably intimidating, but it was only good for defence against day-tripping pirates; those prepared to stay overnight or who brought with them a serious force could soon break in. On three known occasions (1537, 1675 and 1794) the kastro fell and the inhabitants massacred. The destruction wrought on the structure necessitated repeated rebuilding. Somewhere down the line the central tower was destroyed (most probably in the 1537 sacking by Barbarossa) and the Xopirgo was not rebuilt, leaving just the original core rectangle visible today.

Today you can walk around Antiparos Town and miss the kastro completely: in fact, until one is inside it, one is hard put to recognize it at all. With the top storey gone on two sides, and windows, doors and WCs built into the outside walls, the exterior looks pretty much like any typical white cubist Cycladic row of buildings. All is revealed when you come to a small unpainted Gothic archway — the original single doorway in the wall. Even today it is the only way you can gain access to the courtyard of the kastro without going through

one of the houses. This ensures that much of the original enclosed atmosphere remains.

Although the central tower has long gone, its base does survive: stairs directly facing the entrance arch run up to a central 'hump' that is now home to a large water tank, several washing lines and the tiny one-room **Antiparos Folklore Museum**. Free, and open at irregular hours during the week, this 3 m sq. cell has nothing on display apart from some photos of an archaeological dig on neighbouring Despotiko island, several reproduction Cycladic idols donated by the Museum of Cycladic Art in Athens, and a tatty model of the Antiparos cave entrance, made c. 1970. All in all it is a big disappointment, though you have to give the curator points for friendly enthusiasm.

The tower base, however, offers good views over the building, which is harder to appreciate at ground level as there has been some infilling: the area around the tower base is now home to three small churches and the odd house. The inner court ground level has also risen with the rubble of the years so that many of the original ground-storey rooms are now half below street level. Even with all this the kastro still impresses: it still has original Venetian marble doorframes and lintels in some doorways, and the odd dated coat of arms (from later rebuilds) scattered around. It doesn't require much imagination to hear the far off echoes of the pirate Daniel being brought inside in chains demanding his money back, or the screams of the inhabitants during one of the massacres, or the silences that followed, broken only by the 'drip, drip, drip' of blood running down the many staircases: all good, cheerful stuff!

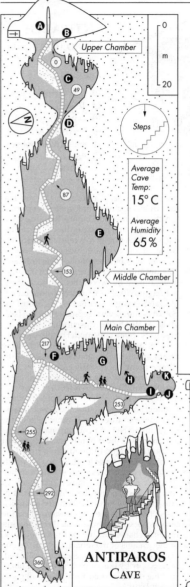

0
m
20

Upper Chamber

0

49

N

Steps

Average
Cave
Temp:
15° C

Average
Humidity
65%

87

Middle Chamber

153

Main Chamber

217

253

255

292

360

The Antiparos Cave

The best sight on Antiparos is undoubtedly the cave. A couple of centuries ago this cave was one of the most famous in the world, so much so that it inspired many by its reputation alone. Not least among these was Johann Wyss (the author of *Swiss Family Robinson*) who — picking up on the juxtaposition of an island and a cave — appears to have derived the idea for the Rock House from reading of the Antiparos cave, acknowledging the debt by having the narrator say:

'I had … read the description of the famous grotto of Antiparos.'

After this build-up the cave itself inevitably suffers in comparison with both the myth and some other caverns accessible today. However, even allowing that discriminating troglodytes are likely to be disappointed, for most the cave is a gentle and rewarding introduction to the underworld. Certainly there are enough buses hell-bent on getting you there (and making an equally big hole in your pocket). For this reason you should exercise caution; if you are not careful the cave is not the only pitfall that you could encounter. You should be aware of the following:

(1). The round tour bus-trip is €5. One-way tickets, €2.50. Several agency buses and the regular bus (a mere €2) run to the cave but tickets are not interchangeable; it pays to buy single tickets so that you can return on the first bus back.

Key

Ⓐ Entrance Cavern
Ⓑ Refreshments
Ⓒ Antechamber
Ⓓ Cave Entrance
Ⓔ Dripping Cavern
Ⓕ Path Junction
Ⓖ Royal Cavern
Ⓗ Large Stalactite
Ⓘ Sanctuary Cavern
Ⓙ Altar Table
Ⓚ Black Stalactite
Ⓛ Lower Chamber
Ⓜ Cave Floor

ANTIPAROS
CAVE

(2). Tours and bus tickets do not include the cave ticket price of €3.50.

(3). Buses decant passengers on a bend of a road halfway up a mountain side, just below the cave. There is no bus stop, so check return times if travelling by regular bus. There are also no refreshments on site, so bring drinks with you.

(4). Low Season sees buses reduced to a trickle, so expect delays when both departing and returning. In addition, the cave is often locked, prompting further delays.

Once inside Mt. Agios Gianni you will find yourself in a cave that has been on the tourist map almost as long as the Parthenon, and unfortunately it is as badly damaged. Many of the stalagmites and stalactites (sexist mnemonic: tights come down) are broken. In times past the cave's fame ensured that stalagmites were carried off by the Russian navy to the Kremlin. More recent damage was inflicted during WW2 when German soldiers used the stalactites for rifle shooting practice.

The walls are also covered with graffiti dating back 300 years, the more notable vandals including King Otho of Greece (in 1840) and Lord Byron. Tales persist of a stalactite inscribed by some failed assassins of Alexander the Great hiding in the cave. Graffiti is less of a problem today as movement in the cave is restricted to a narrow stairway barely wide enough for two people to pass (in High Season rotund visitors have been known to commit mass murder simply trying to pass by on the other side). The current staircase (a new construction with spotlights in the steps) is a substantial affair and takes some of the excitement out of the tour as — unlike with the previous staircase — it is difficult to appreciate that in some parts it is built onto stalagmites. The cave is floodlit, but it might be worthwhile bringing a torch as power cuts are not unknown in this part of the world.

Pottery has been found in the cave indicating occupation back to archaic times, though the nearest it has ever come to fame was in 1673 when a potty French Ambassador to Constantinople (one Marquis de Nointel) organized a Christmas Day mass (complete with fireworks) in the main chamber — the congregation being 500 of the bemused population of Paros (who were paid to indulge this exhibition of antiquarian eccentricity). In 1774 the locals built the chapel at the cave entrance to prevent anything like this happening again.

James Theodore Bent — Author of *The Cyclades*

The Greek Islands have inspired many visitors to write about them, but one man — James Theodore Bent — penned a work that stands head and shoulders above the rest. His book, *The Cyclades or Life Among the Insular Greeks*, published in 1885, has stood the test of time as one of the great travel books, and no dedicated island-hopper should miss out on reading it. Rightly described as 'the classic of Aegean travel', the tome's stature rests both on the calibre of its prose (it is very readable, with a very pithy turn of phrase), and the nature of the content. Bent was happy to entertain his readers with quaint and bizarre stories culled from the islands, but his descriptions of his wanderings have in themselves become increasingly exotic as the years have passed.

Bent describes the islands at a time when they were in a state barely changed from the late 18 c. — when there were few ferries and fewer hotels (in his day there were only two in the whole of the Cyclades: both on Syros, and rarely full). Island hopping in the 1880s was as popular as snowboarding is in darkest Azerbaijan today, if not quite as dangerous. The contrasts between Bent's Aegean and its modern counterpart are often dramatic indeed.

The Author

James Theodore Bent (1852–1897) was the Oxford-educated son of a wealthy Yorkshire family. His affluent background enabled him to turn full-time freelance traveller, self-taught archaeologist and writer in turn. He visited the Cyclades islands with his young Irish wife — Mabel Hall-Dare — between November 1883 and April 1884, dividing their time between a series of island-hopping itineraries and conducting archaeological excavations of Early Cycladic culture sites on Antiparos and its neighbour Despotiko. On their return to London he published an account of Easter celebrations on Amorgos, and its success led him to expand on this and write a full description of the Cycladic islands. His archaeological work and collection of Cycladic Idols (see p. 321) also enabled him to contribute articles to the *Journal of Hellenic Studies*.

After the success of his Cycladic islands venture, Bent and his wife — an inseparable couple from first to last — ventured into ever more remote parts of the world, pursuing a lifestyle that is pure Indiana Jones. Between 1885–1888 they travelled through southern Turkey in search of the ruined Hellenic cities. In 1889 they went to Bahrain looking for the original home of the Phoenicians. Between 1890–1891 they explored the Great Zimbabwe ruins in southern Africa. Then in 1893 they were off to Eritrea in search of the sacred city of Aksum. Bent's final years were spent exploring Arabia and the Red Sea coast. Between 1895–1896 Bent explored the Sudan coast, returning to Arabia in 1897. There he contracted malaria and was sent back to England, dying a few days after his arrival, aged 45.

Bent's legacy doesn't just rest on his book. Along with his more famous contemporaries, Heinrich Schliemann and Sir Arthur Evans, he played an important role in developing the understanding of Aegean archaeology. Although he didn't discover another Troy or Knossos, in many respects his work was just as important. Bent was the first archaeologist to take an interest in the Aegean's early prehistoric period, and his work enabled him to draw up the basic prehistoric Cycladic culture phase framework and the scheme of idol types that — with minor changes — is still in use today. Almost all his finds are now in the British Museum, making up the core of their impressive collection of Early Cycladic culture material.

The Book

Although *The Cyclades* has been published in a number of editions over the years, it can still be hard work finding a copy — it certainly isn't on sale in the islands. Problems

don't end when you do track an edition down: some of Bent's place-name spellings are positively archaic, and can on occasions be so bizarre as to leave even experienced island-hoppers scratching their heads with bafflement. Fortunately, *The Cyclades* is now out of copyright, so it has been possible to put the entire text on this book's website. In order to make life as easy as possible, it has been modified so that all place-name spellings are standardized with those used on maps in this guidebook.

Bent's Island Hopping Itinerary

Attempts to retrace Bent's rather convoluted wanderings around the Cyclades are complicated by three things. First, he made two trips to the Aegean, with an initial reconnoitre in March 1883 (when — from clear references in his book — he must have visited both Syros and Tinos), followed by his main tour between November 1883 and April 1884. (It is clear that like all 'posh' — port out, starboard home — Victorians he clearly took pains to avoid the sun whenever possible.) Second, Greece had yet to move to the modern calendar, so dating references in his text can be a rather dangerous game — particularly when he starts referring to religious festivals or the 'new year'. Finally, Bent's journey is not narrated in chronological order — island descriptions are often given out of sequence to the order in which they were visited.

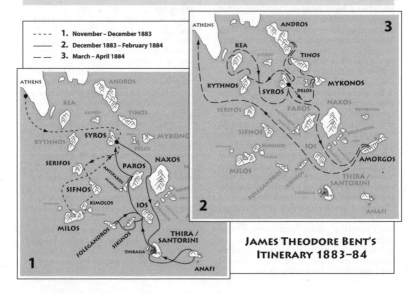

- - - - **1.** November – December 1883
———— **2.** December 1883 – February 1884
— — **3.** March – April 1884

JAMES THEODORE BENT'S ITINERARY 1883–84

From references in the text, Bent's wanderings appear to have taken the form of a series of extended island hopping excursions out of Syros (at this time Syros, rather than Paros, was the hub of the local ferry system, thanks to its role as the major coaling station in the Cyclades). Each of the main 19 islands visited was described in a chapter devoted to it. In total Bent visited 22 of the Cyclades (three of the minor islands were described within other island chapters).

Trip 1. November to December 1883
Bent's first leg commenced with a steamer from Piraeus to Syros before taking fishing boats down the islands of the Cyclades West line. In his book he later grouped Syros with his descriptions of the Northern Cyclades islands, though it is clear that it was his first port of call. Bent's itinerary was thus:
Piraeus—Syros—Serifos—Sifnos—Kimolos—Milos—Syros.

Trip 2. December 1883 to February 1884
Bent's second leg took in the islands of the Cyclades Central line and the smaller southern Cycladic islands. The islands don't seem to have been visited in any particular order, though his account — at the end of his Folegandros chapter — of an abortive attempt to visit Amorgos shows that his objective was to explore all the main southern islands during this trip — though he doesn't seem to have considered the Lesser Cyclades (Iraklia, Koufonissia, Schinoussa and Donoussa) to be worth the trouble.

Several smaller islands were visited as excursions from neighbouring islands (Anafi was visited midway through the exploration of Santorini, and Antiparos and Despotiko provided an extended interlude — for archaeological excavations — in Bent's wanderings around Paros). His itinerary was thus:
Syros—Naxos—Santorini—Volcano—Santorini—Anafi—Thirasia—Ios—Sikinos—Folegandros—Ios—Paros—Antiparos—Paros—Syros.

Trip 3. March to April 1884
Bent's final series of hops are rather more chaotic and reflect the fact that he needed to take in islands on three different lines in order to fully explore the Cyclades. This leg starts with the islands on the Cyclades North line, with a probable hop back to Syros to get connections to the northern islands on the Cyclades West line. His final hop was by steamer to distant Amorgos, the island that he'd missed on the second stage of his itinerary. This final stage was thus:
Syros—Mykonos—Delos—Mykonos—Tinos—Andros—Kythnos—Kea—Syros—Amorgos—Syros—Piraeus.

THE CYCLADES
OR
LIFE AMONG THE INSULAR GREEKS
JAMES THEODORE BENT - 1885

15. PAROS

ON landing at Paroikia, the chief town of Paros, you immediately come in contact with the speciality of the place: the little jetty on which you land is made of marble, marble pillars for mooring boats to are jotted here and there, and you realise before long that Paros is nothing but one huge block of marble covered with a thin coating of soil. In ages long gone by these central islands...

16. ANTIPAROS

A more wretched fever-stricken lot than the six hundred inhabitants of the one village of Antiparos I never saw; it is just one of the usual fortified Kastros of the islands, with the backs of the houses fitting close together, so as to form a circular wall. It has gates which are now never closed, and its streets, are filthily dirty; and, as it lies low, in summer time it is a hotbed of fever. The priest, whom I afterwards learnt did not bear an excellent character, and who had narrowly escaped being unfrocked for his naughty ways, is the ruling spirit of the place..... People believe that these old wizards ... make a mistake ... once the old man ... in front

ANTIPAROS CAVE

It is not the pleasantest of all sensations to be dangling in the air over an abyss, the depth of which you cannot measure by the uncertain light of your torch, and to be solely dependent on your ability in holding a rope which is tied to a stalactite for your safety. Down, down we went, descending three difficult places by ropes and two by ladders until we were safely landed in a perfect sea of stalactites and stalagmites of dazzling beauty. We had brought with us a large quantity of dried brushwood with which to kindle a light, and by this means we were able to penetrate with our eyes the labyrinth of sparkling chambers..

Bent's Full Text is now online @ greekislandhopping.com

Complete with

ITINERARY MAPS

BACKGROUND INFO

Island Hopping in the Footsteps of James Theodore Bent ...

Ios
ΙΟΣ; 108 km²; pop. 1,650.

CODE ☎ 22860
PORT POLICE ☎ 91264
POLICE ☎ 91222
HOSPITAL ☎ 91227

Ios (pronounced *EE*os) has gained a reputation and a half as *the* party island since it emerged as a popular student destination in the 60s, offering a heady cocktail of sun, sand and sex. The reality is a little more complicated, for a lot depends on when you go and which part of the island you visit. From mid-July to the end of August the crowds pour in, and Ios attempts to live up to its reputation — those looking for a traditional, unspoilt Greek island would do better to avoid it, but for the rest of the year, even if partying isn't your thing, it is worth paying a call, for Ios has a lot going for it.

In many ways Ios is an ideal holiday island; it has two of the best beaches to be found anywhere in Greece, a picturesque old chora, good connections for day trips to other islands, and — most importantly of all — a buzz about it that you just don't find anywhere else. It is difficult not to get caught up by the atmosphere, and, as you don't have to join the all-night party, it is possible to avoid the excesses of those that do (though occasional bizarre manifestations of the scene — such as tavernas advertising 'Breakfast 10.00–16.00' — are apt to catch the eye) and simply embrace those aspects of Ios that appeal to you.

In some respects the island's reputation is rather overblown, for although the days of the youthful hanger-out are not exactly over, a growth in the number of families visiting (thanks to the thirty-somethings returning to the haunts of their giddy youth) is beginning to restore the balance a bit. The telling fact that Paros and Fira Town on Santorini both now have more nightlife is also rarely acknowledged, in part because the nightspots on Ios are heavily concentrated in the centre of town

and not obscured among a plethora of competing attractions.

Not all is sweetness and light, however, and Ios does have a less appealing side that the island's more passionate fans are loath to accept. The height of the season sees it ludicrously overcrowded, with the attendant problems of noise, poor sanitation, alcohol abuse and theft — all of which are more evident than on other islands. There are also regular reports from tourists (readers of this book included) of receiving adulterated drinks, invariably with dire consequences for the drinker a few hours later. Violence is also a problem thanks to the large numbers of revellers heading home in the hours before dawn in a state of near-catatonic drunken vulnerability: the rumour mill regularly churns out rape figures running at over a dozen each summer (occasional victims being male). How much truth there is in such sobering bar talk is hard to establish, as the police are not keen on highlighting this aspect of island life.

Describing the geography of Ios is easy enough, for there are only three main points of reference, with a bare 4 km between them: the Port, the Chora set up on the hill behind (known as the Village), and the Beach (Milopotas) on the other side of the chora hill. At first sight the island seems innocuous enough, for the port of **Gialos** is quite sleepy — give or take a dozen bars. Indeed, it is positively quiet compared to its counterparts on Paros and Santorini, besides being far more attractive than either of them. For this reason it attracts those who want to be able to escape the worst excesses of the island's nightlife, and has a good supply of hotels, along with an excellent bakery and several restaurants. It is only when you step inside the supermarket and discover that the check-out racks are filled with condoms that you first get a hint that something, somewhere, could be up.

Behind the port climbs the old mule **stairway** up to the Chora. This offers an appealing alternative to the new road, but

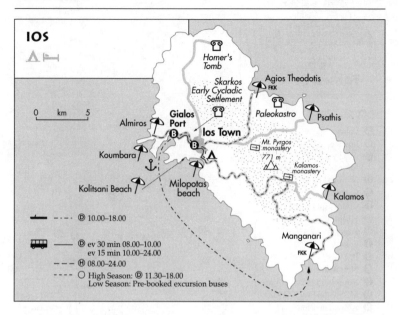

IOS

Homer's Tomb

Skarkos Early Cycladic Settlement

Agios Theodotis FKK

Paleokastro

Psathis

0   km   5

Almiros

Gialos Port Ⓑ

Ios Town

Koumbara ⚓

Mt. Pyrgos monastery
771 m

Kalamos monastery

Kolitsani Beach

Milopotas beach

Kalamos

⚓ Ⓑ

Manganari FKK

━━ --- Ⓓ 10.00–18.00

🚌 ━━ Ⓓ ev 30 min 08.00–10.00
          ev 15 min 10.00–24.00

--- Ⓗ 08.00–24.00

---- Ο High Season: Ⓓ 11.30–18.00
        Low Season: Pre-booked excursion buses

thanks to slippery, sloping steps that are awkward enough when one is sober (never mind when one is totally sozzled and in the dark), it accounts for the fact that there is always someone hopping around with a leg in plaster, and the widely advertised doctors' practices in the town. Most visitors prefer to use the island buses instead. These are more crowded than buses elsewhere — and this is really saying something. Until you have tried travelling on an Ios bus in one of the 'rush hours', you haven't fully enjoyed the Greek island experience. The sardine-tin times are between 11.00–14.00 when heading for the beach, 15.00–18.00 returning from the beach, and after 21.00 heading for the village. The buses do nothing else except run from the Port to the Chora and then down to Milopotas and Koumbara.

Ios Town (alias the Village) at the top of the muleway-cum-stairs, is a real contradiction. Built on two small hilltops, with the main square occupying the hollow between

them, it reflects the fact that the islanders having made a far better job of combining a pretty chora village with a heavy bar and disco scene than their counterparts on the other popular islands. During daylight hours see the old part of town (on the taller of the hills) retain much of its former small village atmosphere, and at first sight you would be hard put to know that it was anything more. Come dusk, the windows and doors of the lower town buildings open to reveal a profusion of bars and boutiques, with a large number of places to eat scattered in between.

After bars, beaches are the great attraction of Ios. **Milopotas Beach** is one of the best in the Aegean: a long stretch of golden sand, it is large enough to accommodate even the High Season crowds and is backed by a scatter of bars and tavernas. However, in summer it is wind-blasted by the *meltemi*. Visitors to Ios in decades past will mourn the arrival of a road running the length of the beach that has destroyed the nudism

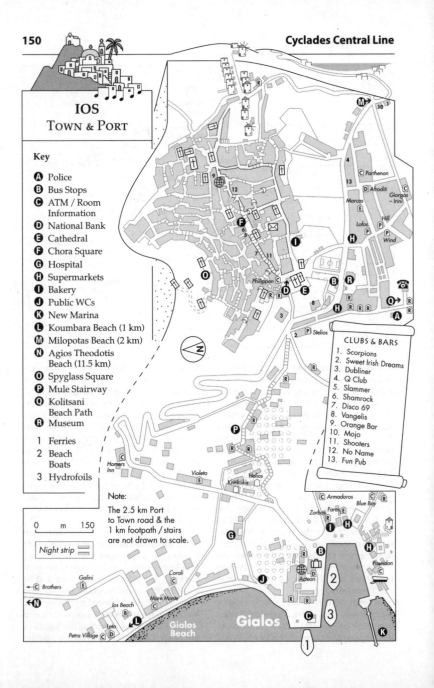

IOS
Town & Port

Key

- **Ⓐ** Police
- **Ⓑ** Bus Stops
- **Ⓒ** ATM / Room Information
- **Ⓓ** National Bank
- **Ⓔ** Cathedral
- **Ⓕ** Chora Square
- **Ⓖ** Hospital
- **Ⓗ** Supermarkets
- **Ⓘ** Bakery
- **Ⓙ** Public WCs
- **Ⓚ** New Marina
- **Ⓛ** Koumbara Beach (1 km)
- **Ⓜ** Milopotas Beach (2 km)
- **Ⓝ** Agios Theodotis Beach (11.5 km)
- **Ⓞ** Spyglass Square
- **Ⓟ** Mule Stairway
- **Ⓠ** Kolitsani Beach Path
- **Ⓡ** Museum

- **1** Ferries
- **2** Beach Boats
- **3** Hydrofoils

Note:
The 2.5 km Port to Town road & the 1 km footpath / stairs are not drawn to scale.

0   m   150

Night strip ▭

CLUBS & BARS
1. Scorpions
2. Sweet Irish Dreams
3. Dubliner
4. Q Club
5. Slammer
6. Shamrock
7. Disco 69
8. Vangelis
9. Orange Bar
10. Mojo
11. Shooters
12. No Name
13. Fun Pub

Parthenon
Afroditi
Giorgos – Irini
Marcos
Lofos
Hill
Wind
Philippon
Stelios
Horners Inn
Violeta
Krikakis
Helios
Armadoros
Blue Bay
Zorbas
Faros
Poseidon
Brothers
Galini
Corali
Mare Monte
Ios Beach
Leto
Petra Village
Acteon
Gialos Beach
Gialos

at the far end. The whole beach is now developed with the full range of water and beach sports now on offer.

The rest of the island — being arid and very hilly — is quiet, though regular buses (starting at the port) now run daily in the summer to the main beaches. The best of these is the superb stretch of sand taking in several bays at **Manganari** on the south coast. Reasonably quiet to date (only one bus a day runs from the port), this beach is set to become much busier as the dirt road used to access it is now being upgraded and metalled (summer beach boats also visit). **Agios Theodotis**, on the east coast, is even quieter and almost as good, with the skimpy ruins of a Venetian kastro in lieu of the former's disco/taverna and windsurfing school. Both have a nude end, unlike the official nude beaches at oily **Koumbara** (which is now very restrained thanks to the arrival of hotels and a regular bus service) and at **Kolitsani**. This latter beach is in a small cove (favoured by yachts as a quiet mooring point) that is best reached via the path that runs east from the town post office road.

😠

Ios, formerly known as 'Io' or 'Nio', was a much prized island in history thanks to its harbour (the Turks called it 'Little Malta'). The island was allied to Athens and shared her political fortunes through the Classical and Hellenistic periods. It was captured by the Romans in the 1 c. BC and became a place of exile. In the Byzantine period Ios was repeatedly visited by pirates. On occasions — almost certainly because of the sheltered harbour —they opted to stay, and for a time the island gained a reputation as a dangerous pirate's nest.

Between 1207–96 the island was part of the Duchy of Naxos; thereafter the Venetians ruled. Turkish pirates arrived in 1558 in 14 galleys, laying waste to the buildings and taking the population into slavery. Ios was uninhabited for 21 years before it was resettled by Albanians and the few survivors from the pirate raid. Like the rest of the Cyclades the island was briefly under Russian rule from 1770–74, before finally breaking away from Turkish rule in 1821.

🛏

Rooms are plentiful on Ios, though the usual caveat about arriving early in the day applies here as well. Start at the accommodation office on the ferry quay. If you are staying more than a fortnight (it is not unknown for people to get off a ferry and then ask in the nearest ticket agency for a three-month room!) then negotiate a reduced rate. If you are staying for several weeks you will be expected to pay your bill on a weekly basis.

The **Port** is well equipped with several good mid-range hotels (though ferry noise can be a problem). These include the C-class *Armadoros* (☎ 91201), *Blue Bay* (☎ 91533) and the *Poseidon* (☎ 91091). There is also the somewhat noisy D-class *Acteon* (☎ 91207) over the ticket agency, and the E-class *Faros* (☎ 91569). Nearby **Gialos Beach** offers some of the most relaxed rooms on Ios. These include the beach-side C-class *Corali* (☎ 91272) and *Mare Monte* (☎ 91564), the expensive *Petra Village* (☎ 91409) and B-class *Ios Beach*, and the D-class *Leto* (☎ 91279).

The **Chora** has a plentiful supply of rooms — mostly in the new part of town — and a number of reasonable hotels. Best among these are the D-class *Afroditi* (☎ 91546) and the C-class *Parthenon* (☎ 91275). The C-class *Giorgos Irini* (☎ 91527) is also popular, as is the *Philippon* (☎ 91290) near the Cathedral, and the E-class *Marcos* (☎ 91060).

The road to and behind **Milopotas Beach** also has a large number of pensions and hotels perched along it. These include the C-class *Far Out* (☎ 91446), *Delfini* (☎ 91340), and *Nissos Ios* (☎ 91306), and the E-class *Aegeon* (☎ 91392). Milopotas is also home to the expensive B-class *Ios Palace* (☎ 91269). Finally, if you are really seeking the quiet life on Ios, there are also some rooms at **Agios Theodotis Beach**.

▲

Thanks to high student numbers, Ios has traditionally been well equipped with campsites; however, their popularity is on the wane as ever more cheap rooms become available, and one long-established site (*Ios Camping* at the port) closed in 2010. Regardless of when you visit, you should take extra pains to secure all valuables as petty theft is depressingly common. Owing to the number of long-stay (i.e. a couple of months or more) visitors — many of whom are strapped to find the funds to party *and* pay their camping bills — it is all but impossible to stay a week without hearing of someone losing cash from their tent.

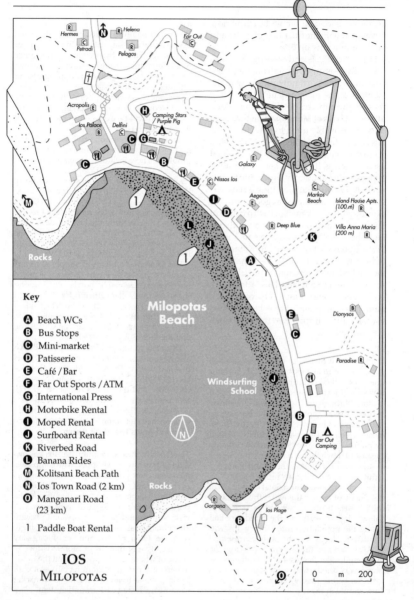

Far Out

Hermes

Helena

Petradi

Pelagos

Acropolis

Ios Palace

Delfini

Camping Stars / Purple Pig

Galaxy

Nissos Ios

Aegeon

Markos Beach

Island House Apts. (100 m)

Villa Anna Maria (200 m)

Deep Blue

Rocks

Milopotas Beach

Dionysos

Paradise

Windsurfing School

Far Out Camping

Rocks

Gorgana

Ios Plage

Key

🅐 Beach WCs
🅑 Bus Stops
🅒 Mini-market
🅓 Patisserie
🅔 Café / Bar
🅕 Far Out Sports / ATM
🅖 International Press
🅗 Motorbike Rental
🅘 Moped Rental
🅙 Surfboard Rental
🅚 Riverbed Road
🅛 Banana Rides
🅜 Kolitsani Beach Path
🅝 Ios Town Road (2 km)
🅞 Manganari Road
   (23 km)

1   Paddle Boat Rental

IOS
MILOPOTAS

0   m   200

The remaining sites on Ios both back onto Milopotas beach: *Camping Stars* (☎ 91302), nearest the village road, is a well-established if small site, recently revamped. It has plenty of tree cover, and tries to compete at the port for the party types by calling itself 'The Purple Pig'. Note: the only things partyish or purple on-site are the painted gates and lamp-posts. *Far Out Camping* (☎ 91468) is at the end of Milopotas. Its 'far out' location and amenities combine to make it a venue in its own right (don't come here if you enjoy your beauty sleep). Facilities include a pool complete with rock music and DJ. There is a pool-side ear-piercing service if the loudspeakers haven't already done the job for you.

≋✿

All the large clubs (which need more space) now lie along the road and strip of building-free ground (thanks to ownership disputes) that divide the old and new halves of the town. Things don't really get going much before 23.00 (it is a truism of Ios that the sun sets as a new day dawns), after which life gets wilder by the hour. Shutting — or rather falling — down time is 03.00–04.00. If you are young, and male, and have come to Greece looking for the girl of your dreams, you will probably find Ios disappointing; most nightspots seem to find males outnumbering females by two to one (though this improves considerably outside High Season). Nightspots catering for those with minority sexual orientations are also all but non-existent. Bars can change name and in popularity regularly, so recommendations are difficult. Getting feedback from revellers is equally hard: most end up joining the masses doing an extended bar and club crawl. The exact itinerary has never been recorded because no one who has done it has ever been in a fit state to remember anything about it the next day.

Of the bigger dance clubs (and none have particularly large dance areas), *Scorpions* seems to have had the edge of late, but the *Dubliner* and *Sweet Irish Dreams* also draw crowds. Finally, there are a good collection of quieter bars and evening eating spots in the port; these do a reasonable trade until the late boat to Piraeus departs, whereupon the action moves with a rush into the town.

◉◉

The official and oft-quoted sight is **Homer's Tomb** — or rather the alleged stones from which it was made (now topped with a modern headstone bearing the poet's name). Lying near the north coast of Ios, it is merely one of several prehistoric graves excavated by a Dutch traveller in 1770. Paasch van Krienen claimed to have found a stone in it inscribed 'Homer' (the stone next to this one — now marked 'Simpson' — is just someone repeating the joke 230 years later). These graves are all but impossible to get to and, frankly, not worth the effort of the difficult journey. As a result, most visitors justifiably prefer to get stoned in the bars and discos of Ios Town instead.

Close to the bus stop in the centre of Ios Town is a neoclassical building that houses a new and very contemporary small **Archaeological Museum**. Open ⑤ ex ① 08.00–14.30 (tickets €3), it houses a collection of average-quality local finds. The most notable exhibits are a snake-decorated stone that set a date for sacrifices, and finds from the **Early Cycladic Settlement** on Skarkos Hill. The settlement itself is sited on a low hillock at the back of the harbour bay (it is easy to spot on the left-hand side as you take the bus up to the town). The archaeological site, recently restored and landscaped, opened to the public for the first time in 2009. There has been no entry charge to date, partly because there isn't a lot to see beyond the low-hill-on-the-plain setting and a few rubble walls, but it is of interest as it is just about the only undisturbed Early Cycladic settlement that is easily accessible in the islands.

The one Ios sight not to be missed is the view from the top of the **Chora Hill**. Finding your way up through the warren of streets is, admittedly, half the fun of it (a couple of stairways that disintegrate into steep tracks on the western side of the Chora will eventually get you there), but there is usually a steady trail of sunset-watchers heading in the same direction to help you. The top, adorned with several chapels and a scree slope of pebbles, offers fantastic views of the port framed with the island of Sikinos behind in one direction, and the Chora and distant Santorini in another. The best time to visit is at sunset, when the port is bathed in a golden glow, and the wine-dark harbour sea is furrowed by a procession of ferries running up from Santorini en route to Piraeus; the combination offers one of the best panoramic views in the Greek islands.

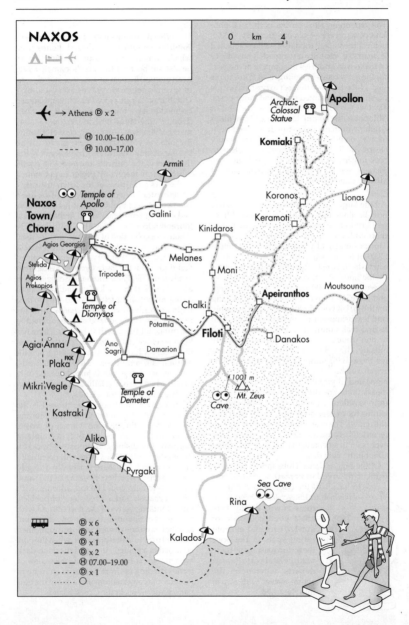

NAXOS

0   km   4

→ Athens ⓓ x 2

────── Ⓗ 10.00–16.00
- - - - - Ⓗ 10.00–17.00

Apollon

Archaic
Colossal
Statue

Komiaki

Armiti

Koronos

Lionas

Keramoti

Temple of
Apollo

Naxos
Town/
Chora

Galini

Kinidaros

Agios Georgios

Melanes

Moni

Stelida

Tripodes

Agios
Prokopios

Temple of
Dionysos

Chalki

Apeiranthos

Moutsouna

Potamia

Filoti

Danakos

Agia Anna

Ano
Sagri

Damarion

FKK
Plaka

Mikri Vegle

Temple of
Demeter

1001 m
Mt. Zeus
Cave

Kastraki

Aliko

Pyrgaki

Sea Cave

Rina

Kalados

───── ⓓ x 6
- - - - ⓓ x 4
— — ⓓ x 1
-·-·- ⓓ x 2
- - - Ⓗ 07.00–19.00
········· ⓓ x 1
········· ◯

Naxos

ΝΑΞΟΣ; 448 km²; pop. 18,000.

CODE ☎ 22850
PORT POLICE ☎ 22300
POLICE ☎ 22100
FIRST AID ☎ 23333

Naxos can lay claim to being one of the most popular Greek islands — at least with island hoppers. The numbers visiting are higher and the average length of stay is also greater than that for other popular islands. This isn't surprising given that Naxos offers an alluring mix of an attractive port town, a succession of wonderful, easily accessible sand beaches (complete with proper sand-dunes), an interior landscape of lush valleys and ruin-topped skylines, and good links with other islands. Naxos is also a popular day-trip destination, and the primary jumping-off point for the islands of Amorgos and the Little Cyclades.

Writers — ancient and modern — have regularly labelled Naxos the most beautiful of the Cyclades. Thanks to a prosperous agricultural base, the island long ignored tourism in a rather disdainful way, but this is now changing. The last decade has seen the opening of an airport, and with this has come a large increase in the number of tourists. To date the impact has been relatively benign, as the tourist strip is confined to Chora and its environs. At the moment Naxos thus enjoys just enough activity to make the 'typical' tourist feel comfortable, but not so much that the island's character is irredeemably damaged. Sadly, this could change as the ferry quay is to be doubled in length and width to accommodate large cruise liners. There could be minor disruption to ferry berthing positions if this work goes ahead this year.

Naxos Town (or **Chora**) is the arrival point for all visitors, and — thanks to the romantic skyline arch of a ruined temple on the causeway-linked islet at the edge of the town — this is one destination where it is difficult not to know that you have arrived at the right place. Most tourists are content to divide their time between Naxos Town and the miles of fine sandy beaches that run down the coast to the south. First impressions can be rather mixed, as the enchantment of the temple is somewhat offset by an increasingly glitzy waterfront dominated by tourist shops and ATMs. Most of the amenities are to be found here, including a good bookshop and a bus station complete with timetables. The municipal authorities have also woken up to the tourists' occasionally more pressing needs and have installed a WC and shower house on the main street behind the promenade. Step into the streets behind the main street and wander into the chora, and you will discover the older and more attractive face of the town. The 12 c. Latin castle, Greek chora and Venetian houses combine to make for shady and interesting wandering, and near the castle walls you will find several good restaurants to augment the collection running the length of the promenade.

The coastline south of Naxos Town is a **beach strip** without equal in the Aegean. Running for kilometres between headland and cove are a succession of excellent sand beaches. The nearest lies on the edge of town at **Agios Georgios**. This is a good family beach, even if the large numbers visiting mean that it isn't the cleanest. A small headland to the south divides it from the low 'dam' that was built (at great cost to the wildlife) to prevent the salt flats behind — now home to the island airport — from flooding. A very windy beach has grown up along the north side of the dam, which is popular with windsurfers and ignored by everyone else (note: there is an excellent windsurfing school here, offering a good opportunity to try repeatedly falling off a surfboard in shallow, sandy-bottomed waters — its location makes it ideal for teenagers wanting to try their hand at the sport). **Stelida** beach to the west is more popular with bathers and has a taverna.

South of the Stelida headland lie the bigger beaches (now sadly being marred by unsympathetic hotel and holiday home development). **Agios Prokopios** is the first of these. Home to a rather ragged collection of establishments offering beds and bars (some excellent, the more unscrupulous complete with bouncers), the only paved street in town is the main road. Be sure to take a look at the small salt lakes behind the beach to the north of this beach 'resort'; dry in summer, the beds are caked with a layer of salt: earlier in the year they are less appealing as the stagnant water evaporates.

Travelling in the opposite direction the coast road runs as far as **Agia Anna** beach. Thereafter a dusty track leads you to the quieter **Golden** and **Plaka** beaches. Very occasional beach boats also run from Agia Anna and Naxos Town to the isolated beaches of **Kalados** and **Rina** on the south coast.

In spite of its attractive main chora town, Naxos's fame has always rested on its verdant mountainous hinterland where an attractive rural Greek atmosphere pervades. You don't have to venture far to discover that farming is still a very important feature of the local economy (the island is noted for its wines and cheeses). Sadly, many of the island's roads are in a positively lethal condition in parts (this is one destination where it is better to stick to buses rather than resort to mopeds, though car hire is a popular alternative). A good general rule is that the further you are from Naxos Town the worse the roads are likely to be. In part this is due to the mountainous terrain: sections of road are regularly washed away in winter rains.

There are two ways of exploring the interior by bus. The first is to take a dedicated tour bus (€20 — tickets from most waterfront agencies in Naxos Town). This runs daily through the mountain villages north to Apollon and then back to Naxos Town via the west coast road. The second option is to take the daily morning regular bus to Apollon (€4). The journey takes around 2¾ hours and is fantastic value for

money: you will have a good three hours in Apollon before it returns.

The meandering mountain roads connect a succession of villages. Three are of particular note: the first is attractive hillside **Filoti**, which, in addition to lying at the centre of the fertile Tragaia Valley and offering a view of an appealing unspoilt Greek island community, is also the starting point for the 2-hour trek to the summit of **Mt. Zeus** (the highest peak in the Cyclades). Serious hikers will find that it is worth attempting the ascent (despite the poorly marked paths) to marvel at the view of the archipelago, and the cave halfway up, where the god was supposed to have been born.

The second village worthy of a stop is **Apeiranthos**. Arguably the most attractive on Naxos, it has several Venetian towers and streets paved with the island's famous marble. It is also home to a small Archaeological Museum housing some Early Cycladic figures. The village school also has a small Geological Museum which charts the area's 17–19 c. emery mining industry. This was responsible for the road to the former port of **Moutsouna** — now a quiet beach backed by holiday homes (the remainder of the east coast of Naxos is quiet in the extreme, with tourists something of a rarity: this is in part due to the opencast mining south of Lionas, which reduces its tourist appeal for obvious reasons).

The final mountain village that stands out is pretty **Komiaki** — the highest village on the island, and marking point for the steep descent (on very dodgy roads) to the small northern 'resort' of **Apollon**. Dramatically located at the foot of a deep ravine, it is a very small fishing village that has attempted to make it as a secluded holiday destination. However, thanks to a very wind-prone beach and little nightlife, few people opt to stay here, and as the harbour tavernas testify, Apollon largely subsists on the tour parties taking in the local sight — the giant Kouros (see p. 164) — and lunch before returning to civilization.

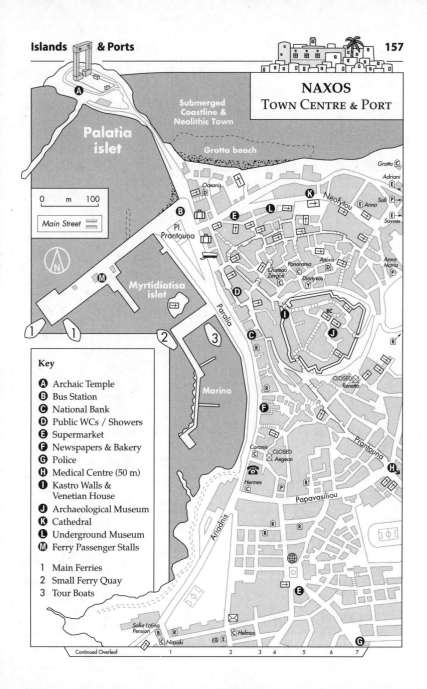

NAXOS
TOWN CENTRE & PORT

0 m 100

Main Street

N

Key

Ⓐ Archaic Temple
Ⓑ Bus Station
Ⓒ National Bank
Ⓓ Public WCs / Showers
Ⓔ Supermarket
Ⓕ Newspapers & Bakery
Ⓖ Police
Ⓗ Medical Centre (50 m)
Ⓘ Kastro Walls &
    Venetian House
Ⓙ Archaeological Museum
Ⓚ Cathedral
Ⓛ Underground Museum
Ⓜ Ferry Passenger Stalls

1 Main Ferries
2 Small Ferry Quay
3 Tour Boats

Palatia
islet

Submerged
Coastline &
Neolithic Town

Grotta beach

Myrtidiotisa
islet

Pl.
Prantouna

Marina

Paralia

Ariadnis

Papavasiliou

Prantouna

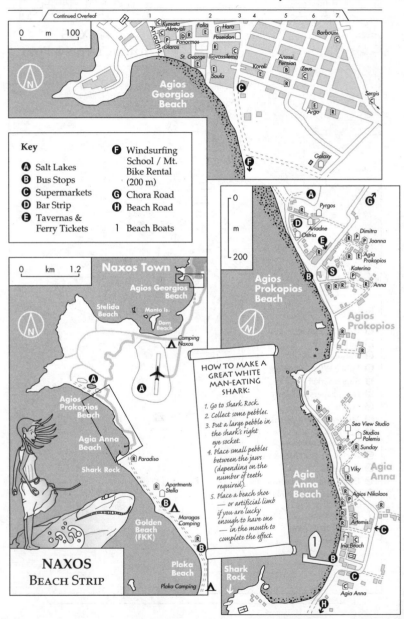

Continued Overleaf

0   m   100

Ariadnis

C Kymata
Akrovali
C Folia
E Hara
Poseidon
C Glaros
Panormos
St. George Iliovassilema
E Soula

Barbouni C

Anessi
Pension B
Korali
E Zeus C
E
Argo R

Sergis C

Galaxy

**Agios
Georgios
Beach**

F

Key

Ⓐ Salt Lakes
Ⓑ Bus Stops
Ⓒ Supermarkets
Ⓓ Bar Strip
Ⓔ Tavernas &
   Ferry Tickets

Ⓕ Windsurfing
   School / Mt.
   Bike Rental
   (200 m)
Ⓖ Chora Road
Ⓗ Beach Road

1 Beach Boats

0   m   200

Ⓐ
Pyrgos
G
Ⓓ Ariadne
Ostria
Ⓔ
Dimitra
R P Joanna
R
Agia
Prokopios
Katerina
S
R R R
Anna R

**Agios
Prokopios
Beach**

Ⓑ

**Agios
Prokopios**

0   km   1.2

Naxos Town

Agios Georgios Beach

Stelida
Beach
Manto Is.
Dam
Beach

Camping
Naxos

Ⓐ

Ⓐ

**Agios
Prokopios
Beach**

**Agia Anna
Beach**

Shark Rock

R Paradiso

Apartments
Stella

Ⓑ

**Golden
Beach
(FKK)**

Maragas
Camping

Ⓑ

Ⓑ

**Plaka
Beach**

Plaka Camping

NAXOS
Beach Strip

R
R
Sea View Studio
Studios
Polemis
R Sunday

Viky R

**Agia
Anna**

R Agios Nikolaos

R R
Ⓒ Artemis
 Ⓒ→
R
Ⓒ
Ina Beach
Ⓑ

1

**Agia
Anna
Beach**

**Shark
Rock**
↓

Ⓒ
Agia Anna

Ⓗ

HOW TO MAKE A
GREAT WHITE
MAN-EATING
SHARK:

1. Go to Shark Rock.
2. Collect some pebbles.
3. Put a large pebble in
   the shark's right
   eye socket.
4. Place small pebbles
   between the jaws
   (depending on the
   number of teeth
   required).
5. Place a beach shoe
   — or artificial limb
   if you are lucky
   enough to have one
   — in the mouth to
   complete the effect.

😓

According to Herodotus, the inhabitants of Naxos were Ionians of Athenian origin. The island was sacked by a Persian expedition in 490 BC. The islanders responded by sending four ships to fight at Salamis, thereafter joining the Delian League and the control of Athens. In the Hellenistic and Byzantine periods the island drifted in quiet obscurity. The change came in 1207 when the island was captured by Marco Sanudo who founded the Venetian Duchy of Naxos. His family and its successor the Crispo ruled over most of the Cyclades until the Turkish conquest in 1566. In 1770–74 the island was briefly held by the Russians, gaining its freedom from the Turks in 1821.

🛏

The various ticket and travel agencies on the waterfront road are a good starting point when bed hunting (assuming you escape the room owners besieging the ferries). **Naxos Town** is home to the bulk of the island accommodation, with an easily located batch of hotels in the northern town. Nearest the ferry quay is the D-class *Oceanis* (☎ 22436), with the E-class *Anna* (☎ 22475) and *Savvas* (☎ 22213) down the street behind. There is also a nice hotel in the C-class *Grotta* (☎ 22215).

In addition to several places offering rooms, the promenade has a cluster of C-class hotels at its southern end, including the *Hermes* (☎ 22220) and the *Coronis* (☎ 22626). The warren of streets around the castle is also home to a number of hotels, while the maze of streets to the north contains the *Panorama* (☎ 22330) and the pricey *Chateau Zevgoli* (☎ 22993), along with the D-class *Anixis* (☎ 22112) and a pension, the *Dionysos* (☎ 22331), all conveniently placed for the town nightspots.

The **Agios Georgios Beach** area is also well endowed with hotels and pensions, including the E-class *Soula* (☎ 23637) and less good *St. George* (☎ 23162). On the town road to the beach stands the C-class *Helmos* (☎ 22455) and the E-class *Folia* (☎ 22210) to the south. Two other hotels of note are the E-class *Korali* (☎ 23092) behind the beach supermarket and, three blocks behind, the C-class *Zeus* (☎ 22912).

The beach strip is gradually being developed; at **Agios Prokopios** there are a scatter of pensions and the E-class *Agia Prokopios*. **Agia Anna** is more up-market with three C-class hotels near the beach: the *Iria Beach* (☎ 24178), the *Agia Anna* and the *Artemis* (☎ 24880).

Λ

There is fierce competition between the three sites that lie on the beach road running south of Naxos Town. The sites are very different, so it is worthwhile deciding what your priorities are before choosing between them:

Naxos Camping (☎ 23500) is the nearest site to Naxos Town (2 km), and is open from late June to the end of August. The site is large, with plenty of shade, clean (if aging) facilities and a roadside pool. Agios Georgios beach is a 1 km walk up the road.

Maragas Camping (☎ 24552) is 7 km from the town. It is a typical (if large) beach site. The absence of anywhere else to go ensures that the beach-fronting bar is well patronized. The site is ever popular with the younger beach-loving crowd. Echoes of hippydom pervade.

Plaka Camping (☎ 42700) is the newest site on Naxos. If your idea of perfect camping is a good beach and immaculate facilities provided by friendly owners then it is a very good bet. However, its isolated position means that if you want anything more you are dependent on hourly buses or your own wheels.

⇛✿

Naxos Town and its beach strip to the south play host to most of the island's nightlife. This is surprisingly tame given the popularity of Naxos, which has thrived regardless on a diet of good beaches peopled by holidaying couples wallowing in dreamy romance. The brasher singles scene is only now emerging (though so far its impact on the town is minimal), with more bars and clubs arriving each year. Recent arrivals include the *Ocean Club Disco* behind the National Bank and the nearby *Musique Café*, the *Caesar's Club* and the *Super Island*, all on the promenade. Two other nearby bars can get very lively — *Mike's Bar* and *The Jam* (tucked away behind the OTE).

A popular collection of nightspots lies along the main port—Grotta road just off the ferry quay, the best being the *Empire*, *Seven* and the *Loft Bar* near the cathedral. Turning south, the promenade is home to the imaginatively named *Greek Bar*. Agios Georgios beach also has a number of discos attached to the hotels and other bars in the nearby streets.

👓

Naxos Town offers easy sightseeing thanks to two premier Greek island attractions:
1. **The Archaic Temple of Apollo**
2. **The Castle of the Dukes.**

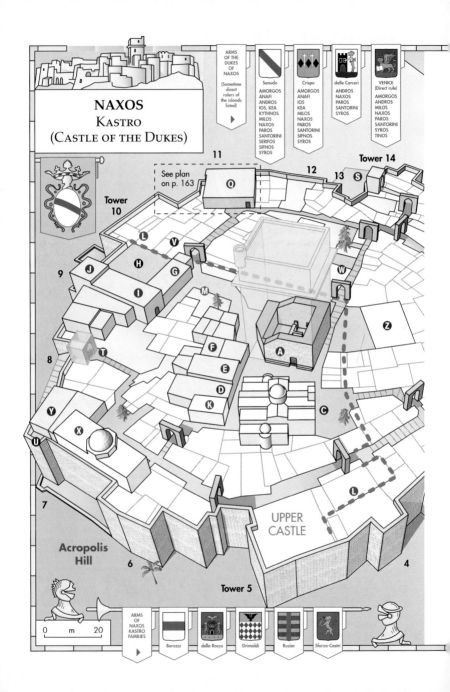

NAXOS

KASTRO

(CASTLE OF THE DUKES)

ARMS OF THE DUKES OF NAXOS

(Sometime direct rulers of the islands listed) ▶

Sanudo
AMORGOS
ANAFI
ANDROS
IOS, KEA
KYTHNOS
MILOS
NAXOS
PAROS
SANTORINI
SERIFOS
SIFNOS
SYROS

Crispo
AMORGOS
ANAFI
IOS
KEA
MILOS
NAXOS
PAROS
SANTORINI
SIFNOS
SYROS

dalle Carceri
ANDROS
NAXOS
PAROS
SANTORINI
SYROS

VENICE
(Direct rule)
AMORGOS
ANDROS
MILOS
NAXOS
PAROS
SANTORINI
SYROS
TINOS

See plan on p. 163

Tower 10

Tower 14

11

12

13

9

8

7

Acropolis Hill

6

UPPER CASTLE

Tower 5

4

ARMS OF NAXOS KASTRO FAMILIES ▶

Barozzi

della Rocca

Grimaldi

Ruzier

Sforza-Castri

0   m   20

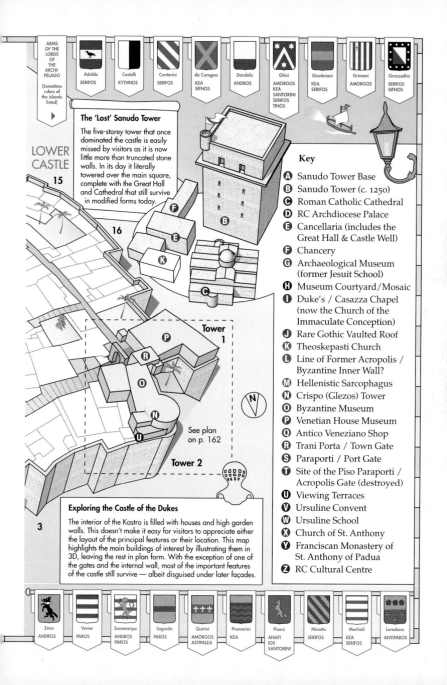

ARMS OF THE LORDS OF THE ARCHIPELAGO
(Sometime rulers of the islands listed)

Adoldo — SERIFOS
Castelli — KYTHNOS
Contarini — SERIFOS
da Corogna — KEA SIFNOS
Dandolo — ANDROS
Ghisi — AMORGOS KEA SANTORINI SERIFOS TINOS
Giustiniani — KEA SERIFOS
Grimani — AMORGOS
Grozzadini — SERIFOS SIFNOS

Zeno — ANDROS
Venier — PAROS
Sommaripa — ANDROS PAROS
Sagredo — PAROS
Quirini — AMORGOS ASTIPALEA
Premarini — KEA
Pisani — ANAFI IOS SANTORINI
Minotto — SERIFOS
Mechieli — KEA SERIFOS
Loredano — ANTIPAROS

The 'Lost' Sanudo Tower

The five-storey tower that once dominated the castle is easily missed by visitors as it is now little more than truncated stone walls. In its day it literally towered over the main square, complete with the Great Hall and Cathedral that still survive in modified forms today.

LOWER CASTLE
15
16

Tower 1

See plan on p. 162

Tower 2

Key

Ⓐ Sanudo Tower Base
Ⓑ Sanudo Tower (c. 1250)
Ⓒ Roman Catholic Cathedral
Ⓓ RC Archdiocese Palace
Ⓔ Cancellaria (includes the Great Hall & Castle Well)
Ⓕ Chancery
Ⓖ Archaeological Museum (former Jesuit School)
Ⓗ Museum Courtyard/Mosaic
Ⓘ Duke's / Casazza Chapel (now the Church of the Immaculate Conception)
Ⓙ Rare Gothic Vaulted Roof
Ⓚ Theoskepasti Church
Ⓛ Line of Former Acropolis / Byzantine Inner Wall?
Ⓜ Hellenistic Sarcophagus
Ⓝ Crispo (Glezos) Tower
Ⓞ Byzantine Museum
Ⓟ Venetian House Museum
Ⓠ Antico Veneziano Shop
Ⓡ Trani Porta / Town Gate
Ⓢ Paraporti / Port Gate
Ⓣ Site of the Piso Paraporti / Acropolis Gate (destroyed)
Ⓤ Viewing Terraces
Ⓥ Ursuline Convent
Ⓦ Ursuline School
Ⓧ Church of St. Anthony
Ⓨ Franciscan Monastery of St. Anthony of Padua
Ⓩ RC Cultural Centre

Exploring the Castle of the Dukes

The interior of the Kastro is filled with houses and high garden walls. This doesn't make it easy for visitors to appreciate either the layout of the principal features or their location. This map highlights the main buildings of interest by illustrating them in 3D, leaving the rest in plan form. With the exception of one of the gates and the internal wall, most of the important features of the castle still survive — albeit disguised under later façades.

3

The Base of the Sanudo Tower

Naxos Causeway & Chora

Cyclades Central

The Doorway of Ariadne's Palace often prompts speculation over the size of her lover — the god Dionysos …

Temple of Apollo / Ariadne's Arch
NAXOS

The Castle of the Dukes

The Kastro of Naxos (see the centrefold map in the colour section opposite) was built soon after 1207 by the Venetian Marco Sanudo when he set up shop as the Duke of Naxos, and for over four centuries it was the seat of military power in the Cyclades. Built around the site of the ancient city acropolis on a 30 m high harbour-side hill, the castle consisted of a curtain wall made up of houses, that formed a rough pentagon with towers on the corners. Three stairways from the harbour and north gate sides led up to an upper castle on the landward side, on the site of the old acropolis. This was topped with a tall imposing central keep (known as the Sanudo Tower), a great hall and ducal palace complex, and the Roman Catholic cathedral. Later house building gradually filled in the remainder of the interior.

Although the Kastro is reasonably well preserved, it is greatly diminished from its original splendour. It is a bit like a cake with all the icing stripped off. Of the ancient and Byzantine buildings little remains (bar the 9 c. Church of Theoskepasti). An internal dividing wall shown in early map sketches that separated the lower and upper wards of the castle (possibly an original Byzantine castle wall) has long gone too. Studies of the curtain wall suggest it originally had 16 towers, but apart from the circular Crispo tower these are hard to spot today — though most are still there if you look hard enough. One forms the northern part of the Venetian House Museum, while others are partly obscured by later houses built against the outer side of the curtain wall.

As for the central keep (known from a 1750 engraving), it is now reduced to a two-storey-high stump, with one of its corners chopped off to create a street linking the small squares on either side. It is not clear when it disappeared: most likely it was deliberately demolished in the early 19 c. following Greek independence. The locals would have been all too keen to remove such a sinister symbol of tyranny from their town skyline: the destroyed acropolis gate probably came down at the same time.

The islanders have not managed to shake off their ambivalent feelings toward the Kastro — hence the very antiseptic streets (no shops or tavernas to be found here). Most of the buildings remain official Roman Catholic property or private houses, but tucked away there is enough sightseeing to fill a busy morning. The five attractions of note are:

The Dukes of Naxos

Following the sacking of Constantinople in 1204 by the loot-obsessed 4th Crusaders, Venice exploited the demise of Byzantine power by attempting to take control of the Aegean. Sons of leading Venetians were encouraged to follow Marco Sanudo (a nephew of the Doge) and set themselves up under him as rulers of individual Greek islands. Sanudo seized Naxos after a five-week siege in 1207, whereupon he promptly rejected Venetian overlordship and became the first of the 22 Dukes of Naxos. This ushered in a period of erratic Latin rule that only drew to a close with the Ottoman conquest 362 years later.

However, unlike the Hospitaller Knights of St. John based on Rhodes, Crete and Kos, who were respected for regularly fighting the Turks even if they weren't exactly popular as alien overlords, the Latin families who controlled the Cyclades had few redeeming qualities. Constant inter-family feuding for power produced centuries of chronic instability. Moreover, they regarded the local Greeks as vassals and treated them accordingly, with inevitable results. The Naxos Kastro is a good example of this. Its primary function was to house and protect the Latin newcomers from the local population, a situation analogous to that in England in the aftermath of the Norman conquest. Unfortunately in Greece the two communities never assimilated (in part due to religious differences). On Naxos the enmity carried on long after the Turks brought an end to Latin rule. The Roman Catholic Latin population on Naxos (which was rarely more than 600 strong) even tacitly sided with the Turks during the Greek independence struggle, and most visiting writers before 1890 comment on the deep-rooted apathy between the two sides.

The Original 'Archipelago'

One singular by-product of this period of Latin rule has been the adoption of the word 'archipelago' into the English language. Today a noun applied to any constellation of islands, 'Archipelago' was originally the early medieval local name for the Aegean Sea (literally 'chief sea' — from the Greek for chief, 'archi', and sea, 'pelagos'). The Latin dukes gave the name a wider currency by formally adopting the grandiose title 'Duke of Archipelago' (though 'Duke of Naxos' was more often used, particularly as their influence waned and rule was reduced to the vicinity of Naxos itself). Even so, the result was 400-odd years of map production in Europe with the mystic word 'Archipelago' inscribed between the drawn islands, and from these origins it was but a short journey to the modern usage.

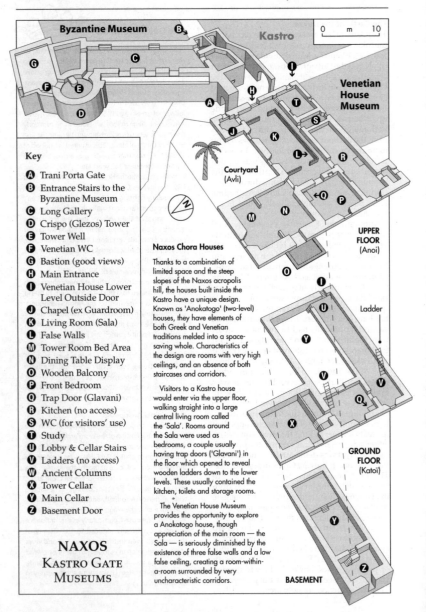

Byzantine Museum

Kastro

0   m   10

Venetian House Museum

Courtyard (Avli)

Naxos Chora Houses

Thanks to a combination of limited space and the steep slopes of the Naxos acropolis hill, the houses built inside the Kastro have a unique design. Known as 'Anokatogo' (two-level) houses, they have elements of both Greek and Venetian traditions melded into a space-saving whole. Characteristics of the design are rooms with very high ceilings, and an absence of both staircases and corridors.

Visitors to a Kastro house would enter via the upper floor, walking straight into a large central living room called the 'Sala'. Rooms around the Sala were used as bedrooms, a couple usually having trap doors ('Glavani') in the floor which opened to reveal wooden ladders down to the lower levels. These usually contained the kitchen, toilets and storage rooms.

The Venetian House Museum provides the opportunity to explore a Anokatogo house, though appreciation of the main room — the Sala — is seriously diminished by the existence of three false walls and a low false ceiling, creating a room-within-a-room surrounded by very uncharacteristic corridors.

UPPER FLOOR (Anoi)

Ladder

GROUND FLOOR (Katoï)

BASEMENT

Key

- **A** Trani Porta Gate
- **B** Entrance Stairs to the Byzantine Museum
- **C** Long Gallery
- **D** Crispo (Glezos) Tower
- **E** Tower Well
- **F** Venetian WC
- **G** Bastion (good views)
- **H** Main Entrance
- **I** Venetian House Lower Level Outside Door
- **J** Chapel (ex Guardroom)
- **K** Living Room (Sala)
- **L** False Walls
- **M** Tower Room Bed Area
- **N** Dining Table Display
- **O** Wooden Balcony
- **P** Front Bedroom
- **Q** Trap Door (Glavani)
- **R** Kitchen (no access)
- **S** WC (for visitors' use)
- **T** Study
- **U** Lobby & Cellar Stairs
- **V** Ladders (no access)
- **W** Ancient Columns
- **X** Tower Cellar
- **Y** Main Cellar
- **Z** Basement Door

**NAXOS
KASTRO GATE
MUSEUMS**

1. The Archaeological Museum

The majority of the visitors to the Kastro come in search of the **Archaeological Museum** (⑩ ex ① 08.00–14.30; tickets €3). Guarded by the south walls of the Kastro, this is home to the world's largest public display of the Early Cycladic marble figurines so sought after by art thieves. There are fragments of over 120, including 8 of the very rare seated variety. The rest of the exhibits are inevitably an anticlimax, but include fragments of sculpture, Roman glassware, and some quaint terracotta birds and miniature bootees. An outside courtyard is home to a large mosaic and sculpted coats of arms salvaged from Kastro buildings.

2. The Byzantine Museum

A free museum (⑩ ex ① 08.00–14.30) with so little in it that most visitors are still tempted to ask for their money back, the reason to visit is the chance to see more of the Kastro interior. The museum consists of a long gallery with photo displays of art and inscriptions found in the islands. This leads to the only surviving circular tower (the **Crispi Tower**), with a well, and a terrace looking over the windswept northern shoreline of Chora, known as **Grotta** — site of an Early Cycladic settlement.

3. The Venetian House Museum

Just inside the surviving main door of the Kastro is the **Venetian House Museum** (⑩ 08.00–15.00; tickets cost €5 and include a guided tour). This is a small private museum run by the descendants of its original owners. It is worth the cost of admission just to explore the interior of a Kastro house (note: access to the lower levels is via the street door rather than the ladders). The contents are another matter. A mass of 19 c. junk (e.g. the orphaned violin bow decorating the sitting room wall) make this more of an exhibition than an accurate representation of a Venetian house interior. There are some nice pieces in the half-dozen rooms, but too many of them could be found in a typical English house-clearance shop.

4. The Antico Veneziano Shop

Follow the Kastro street from the two gate museums and you come to an antique shop housed in another Venetian house. Only one level is accessible, but this is more than made up for by the existence of four ancient pillars used to support beams — wonderfully atmospheric. As this is a shop access is free, but the owners should really be charging for this, so buy a postcard and help keep it open.

Antico Veneziano Shop

5. The Cathedral Tour

On one side of the central Roman Catholic cathedral's locked main door is a fading notice advertising a daily church tour starting there at 17.00 (if it isn't visible ask inside). This usually attracts a dozen or so tourists who find that they have stumbled upon one of the best-value tours going in the islands. You might find it useful to get hold of a copy of the cathedral guide first (from the Casazza Chapel), as the tours are conducted by a few of the Roman Catholic women living on Naxos: explanations are usually in a garbled version of the majority language of the tourists present (French being the preferred option).

The tour starts with the **Cathedral** itself. Sadly, this isn't the high point that it could be thanks to extensive refurbishment in the last century. This included refacing the exterior walls with marble, adding a bell tower, and raising the floor of the interior by 1 m (giving all the reused ancient pillars a stubby, truncated look). The highlights are a unique double-sided full-length icon, and some amusing hidden stairs up to the bell tower.

From the cathedral the tour moves to the former private chapel of the Dukes of Naxos. The **Casazza Chapel**, now more usually known as the **Church of the Immaculate Conception**, boasts a Gothic vaulted roof unique in the Cyclades. It also has a couple of anterooms filled with modern artwork.

Next on the tour hit list is the **Palace of the Dukes**, now the Palace of the Roman Catholic Archdiocese of Naxos & Tinos. A mix of monument and working palace, the ground floor is being restored to its Venetian form. Visitors enter by the Great Hall and then explore the side rooms that were once the private quarters of the Dukes (hence the barred doors, arrow slits and doorways to the keep). One room is

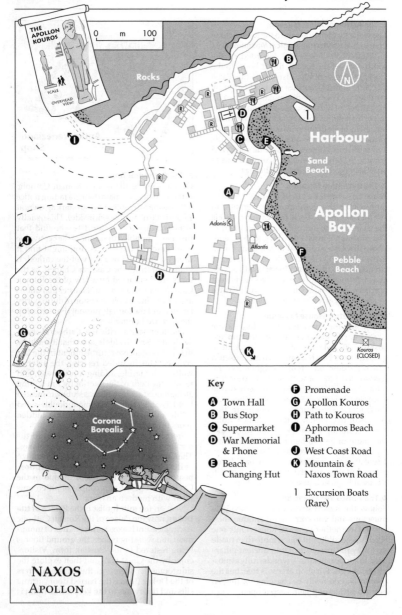

THE APOLLON KOUROS

SCALE
OVERHEAD VIEW!

0   m   100

Rocks

Harbour

Sand Beach

Apollon Bay

Pebble Beach

Adonis ⒸC

Atlantis

Kouros
(CLOSED)

Corona Borealis

Key

Ⓐ Town Hall
Ⓑ Bus Stop
Ⓒ Supermarket
Ⓓ War Memorial & Phone
Ⓔ Beach Changing Hut

Ⓕ Promenade
Ⓖ Apollon Kouros
Ⓗ Path to Kouros
Ⓘ Aphormos Beach Path
Ⓙ West Coast Road
Ⓚ Mountain & Naxos Town Road

1 Excursion Boats (Rare)

NAXOS
APOLLON

full of various church objects that should be in museum cases, but aren't because of a lack of funding. The upper floors contain the bishop's private quarters: you get to visit, but it's a case of old vests rather than vestments.

The final part of the tour takes in the **Church of St. Anthony of Padua** (complete with a very attractive painted pulpit), and its Franciscan monastery. Closed in the 1950s, the monastery hasn't been touched since: visitors get to see everything from the infirmary to the rusting kitchen toast rack. Once out of the monastery the guide (sans voice by this stage) holds out a hand for a spot of financial appreciation. The going rate is €4 per person, but €5 is surely the minimum for the effort involved — on a garrulous day the complete 'Cathedral' tour can last close on 2 hours!

Outside the castle, the **Old Town** (another product of the period of Venetian rule) runs around the northern and western walls and is filled with a lovely warren of little streets to get lost in. The best of these lie on the north, in the former main shopping area. The atmosphere today still offers a good impression of how the Naxians (banned from living in the castle) adapted to the arrival of the Dukes. This part of town is also home to the small and disappointing **Underground Museum**. Little more than a roofed area of excavation, it will only appeal to real die-hard archaeology fans.

Sights Around Naxos

Around Naxos are a number of archaeological sites of varying merit. The most visited of these are the ancient marble quarries at **Melanes** and **Apollon**, where there are the partially carved remains of large male statues known as **Kouroi**. These are stylized figures which were abandoned half-completed due to faults in the stone. The colossal bearded **Apollon Kouros** (7 c. BC) is easily the best of the three; 10.5 m tall (making the figure five times life-size), it is a giant rough sketch in stone of a god — probably Dionysos — and was almost certainly abandoned because of flaws in the marble. Thanks to the numbers of tourists opting to be photographed sitting on it the marble is now rather slippery.

The two **Melanes Kouroi**, despite being abandoned in something nearer their intended final form, are much smaller (being only just over life-size) and of a much cruder design than the Apollon figure. Most visitors to Melanes only see the better preserved kouros: the second

figure is hidden away down an overgrown track some 300 m to the south. The remains of a finished Naxian colossal figure of similar size to the Apollon Kouros can be seen on the nearby island of Delos (see p. 222). Naxos was a major exporter of sculpture during the Archaic period (the famous lions on Delos were also carved from Naxian marble), but export — rather than local construction — was the order of the day, so Naxos itself has comparatively little Archaic material on show.

Remains of ancient structures are to be found in remoter areas. The nearest — a **Temple of Dionysos** — lies hidden in bamboo beds that lie behind the beaches just south of Naxos Town. Its remains are very fragmentary, consisting of a few foundations and the odd column fragment, augmented by a few larger reconstructed columns for show. Entrance is free, but the limited nature of the site and the noisy guard dogs do little to encourage visitors.

Naxos is also noted for its medieval **Towers** (over 30 in number, they are known as 'Pyrgi' and are the remains of fortified manor houses), **Castles**, and even the odd fortified monastery for good measure. The closest one to the tourist strip is well-preserved **Paleopirgos Castle**, one hour's walk inland via a track running from Plaka beach. Most of the Pyrgi require hard walking if you want to visit them, and Naxos is popular with walkers. Those exploring on foot should step first into a local bookshop and buy a copy of Christian Ucke's *Walking the Greek Islands: Naxos* (€16); this offers 25 suggested routes and a lot of background detail.

The highest sight on Naxos is the **Mount Zeus** and **Zeus Cave** combination. Not a trek for the faint-hearted, the walk from the hill village of Filoti to the summit takes in the cave where, tradition has it, Zeus was raised. A far less strenuous option (particularly in July and August) is to cut the walk short at the cave and then return to Filoti. If you take the 07.00 bus to Filoti from Naxos Town this makes an enjoyable morning excursion. Truth to tell, the cave isn't on a par with the larger cave on Antiparos. Relatively shallow, it is a sloping cavern 150 m deep and is home to a colony of bats and a species of large yellow cave cricket — a creepy-crawly that is often described as a spider but is two legs short of one. Few visitors — even those with torches — venture much beyond the entrance. You will find a Zeus Cave walk route map, a cave plan and photos on this book's website.

Temple of Demeter

The most noteworthy building on Naxos outside of Chora, this temple lies a 3 km walk south of the hamlet of Ano Sagri (which has regular buses to Naxos Town). Entrance is currently free (though a ticket kiosk has been built for future use, so this could well change) and opening times are flexible — no site gates!

Constructed some time around 530 BC, on a low hill sited at the head of a fertile valley that was previously home to an open-air fertility cult, the temple's importance lies in its architecture. It was built at a crucial time in the development of temple design and represents a unique intermediate form. **The Temple** was highly unusual in having a square floor plan with 5 Ionic columns on its pedimental side, and a roof made up of marble beams and thin marble tiles that allowed a diffused light into the interior. The cella was also noteworthy as all the inside wall stones were left uncut, with the result that the temple's holy of holies would have resembled a cave or grotto, illuminated by the translucent marble roof.

The building was converted into a church (**Church 1**) some time before 600 AD. This involved changing the orientation of the building from south–north to west–east. The main structural change was the bricking in of the spaces between the temple's columns on the south side (the main south-facing entrance to the temple thus became a side apse to the church). This building was not a success thanks to the internal temple column layout, and a more substantial demolition and rebuild occurred some time around 700 AD, with only one wall (the west) of the original temple remaining in situ. The new structure (**Church 2: The Basilica**) was an orthodox shaped basilica, complete with east wall apse, stone sanctuary screen, and pulpit. It survived until the 9 C. AD, when it was destroyed, probably in one of the major piratical raids that hit the islands at this time.

Fortunately, the remoteness of the site has meant that sufficient stones from the original temple (often showing signs of their reworking into the later basilica) have survived on site to enable a partial reconstruction of the building — or more accurately *buildings*. The modern taste in reconstructive archaeology is to preserve evidence of all phases on a site rather than just the most notable one, so the most obvious architectural elements of temple, first church and basilica have all been retained where possible (a hundred years ago a reconstruction would have focused on the temple at the expense of everything else). The result is 'interesting' but very odd: three different buildings made from the same stones, reassembled in a way that history would not recognize. This wouldn't be a problem if the temple plan was regular, but the fact that this was an irregular design in the first place makes working out what is going on more difficult. The one big plus is that there are plenty of explanatory notice boards.

Given that the temple is quite small, the task of sorting out the architectural puzzle is manageable and can be fun. Looking at the building face on when you climb the site hill, one is first confronted by **A** the partially restored **Temple Facade or Porch**. This consists of two reconstructed columns (during the basilica phase they were relocated inside the church). Behind these columns is a wall with two doorways (**B** is arched, **C** less complete) that would have led into the temple. On the west side of the porch is **D**, a small **Doorway** cut into the porch (pronaos) wall when it was converted into Church 1. What lies behind all this is less temple and almost all the remains of an apsed church. In addition to the Apse **E** itself, there are a couple of partial **Interior Columns F**, in their church rather than temple locations: the basilica had a central aisle with two rows of columns, the temple simply a single row of centrally placed columns running east–west. Around the building are remains from other periods: the ones you need to take most care of are the ankle-turning **Pre-Temple Level Pits G**, which, when not filled with tourists, contain fragments of the open-air site phase walls. There is also a small **Chapel H** which prior to the reconstruction stood on the temple site itself. The site also has a superb small museum. However, opening hours are very irregular: it is best to establish the closing time when you arrive.

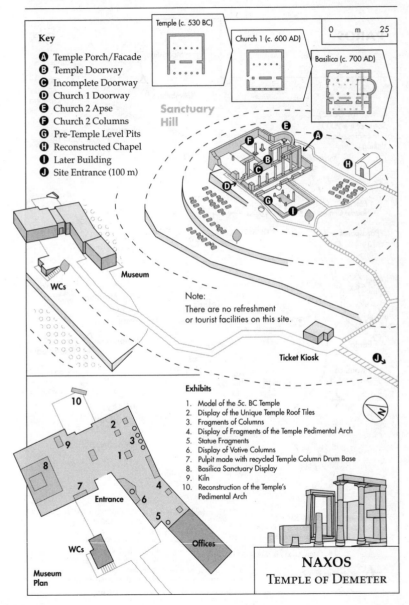

Key

- **A** Temple Porch/Facade
- **B** Temple Doorway
- **C** Incomplete Doorway
- **D** Church 1 Doorway
- **E** Church 2 Apse
- **F** Church 2 Columns
- **G** Pre-Temple Level Pits
- **H** Reconstructed Chapel
- **I** Later Building
- **J** Site Entrance (100 m)

Temple (c. 530 BC)

Church 1 (c. 600 AD)

Basilica (c. 700 AD)

0   m   25

Sanctuary Hill

Museum

WCs

Note:

There are no refreshment or tourist facilities on this site.

Ticket Kiosk

Exhibits

1. Model of the 5c. BC Temple
2. Display of the Unique Temple Roof Tiles
3. Fragments of Columns
4. Display of Fragments of the Temple Pedimental Arch
5. Statue Fragments
6. Display of Votive Columns
7. Pulpit made with recycled Temple Column Drum Base
8. Basilica Sanctuary Display
9. Kiln
10. Reconstruction of the Temple's Pedimental Arch

Entrance

WCs

Offices

Museum Plan

NAXOS
TEMPLE OF DEMETER

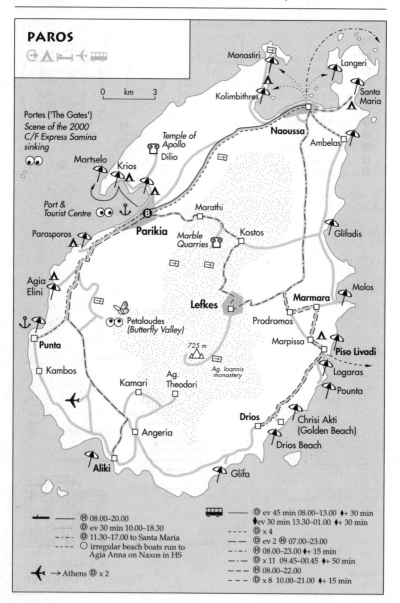

PAROS

Monastiri

Langeri

Santa Maria

Kolimbithres

Naoussa

Portes ('The Gates')
*Scene of the 2000
C/F Express Samina
sinking*

Temple of Apollo
Dilio

Ambelas

Martselo

Krios

Port &
Tourist Centre

Marathi

Parikia

*Marble
Quarries*

Kostos

Glifadis

Parasporos

Agia
Elini

Molos

Marmara

Lefkes

Prodromos

Petaloudes
(Butterfly Valley)

Marpissa

Piso Livadi

Punta

725 m

*Ag. Ioannis
monastery*

Logaras

Kambos

Pounta

Kamari

Ag.
Theodori

Drios

Chrisi Akti
(Golden Beach)

Angeria

Drios Beach

Aliki

Glifa

Ⓗ 08.00–20.00

Ⓓ ev 30 min 10.00–18.30

11.30–17.00 to Santa Maria

Ⓞ irregular beach boats run to
Agia Anna on Naxos in HS

✈ →Athens Ⓓ x 2

Ⓓ ev 45 min 08.00–13.00 ♦+ 30 min

♦ev 30 min 13.30–01.00 ♦+ 30 min

Ⓓ x 4

Ⓓ ev 2 Ⓗ 07.00–23.00

Ⓓ 08.00–23.00 ♦+ 15 min

Ⓓ x 11 09.45–00.45 ♦+ 50 min

Ⓗ 08.00–22.00

Ⓓ x 8 10.00–21.00 ♦+ 15 min

Paros
ΠΑΡΟΣ; 194 km²; pop. 7,900.

CODE ☎ 22840
PORT POLICE ☎ 21240
POLICE ☎ 21221
FIRST AID ☎ 22500

A relatively large and well-placed island, Paros has become the de facto hub of the Greek ferry system in recent years, and it is now difficult for Cycladic island hoppers to avoid calling at some point during their holiday. As a result, Paros is apt to get horribly overcrowded at the late July/early August peak of the High Season (though the rest of the year it is just pleasantly busy). In part this is due to the charms of the island itself, for it is ringed with good, accessible sandy beaches, is fertile inland (though tree cover is distinctly limited), and now has plenty of summer nightlife into the bargain.

Paros's main port and tourist centre is at **Parikia** (though you find that except on the island itself all ticket agents and schedules simply refer to it as 'Paros'). Occupying a sheltered bay on the west coast, it has been the main island centre since the Bronze Age, when an Early Cycladic village existed on the site. It briefly lost its role as the island capital during the Ottoman period, when inland Lefkes took over (being far less vulnerable to pirate attack). Today the port town has re-emerged as the undisputed centre on the island, ribboning ever further along the shore.

At its heart lies a typical Cycladic chora, complete with the odd wall of a Venetian kastro, built on the site of the ancient acropolis in 1207 from the fragments of the ancient temples that stood on the site. Neither the chora nor the kastro is the best example of its type (though Chora manages to retain a surprising amount of charm even when it is swarming with tourists), but they are suitable symbols, in their way, of Paros as a whole.

Very much tied to the shoreline, Parikia does not extend inland to any great extent,

and is neatly divided by the road running south from the recently extended ferry quay (Prombona St.). To the west lies the old part of town, to the east the modern hotel and beach strip. Between the two lies the church of Ekatontapiliani, discreetly tucked out of sight behind a park-cum-wood of pine trees.

All the essential facilities are to be found within easy distance of the quay 'square' and its distinctive windmill. The building block opposite the quay is devoted en masse to ticket agents. Behind the waterfront buildings lies the town's main square; decorated with shrubs and trees of a sort, it has more the feel of a crossroads between the various quarters of the town and the ferry quay.

The **waterfront** is the real centre of activity in Parikia. Apart from the section composed of the whitewashed kastro walls, it is lined with restaurants, bars, shops and hotels, though it has to be said that it isn't the most photogenic in the Aegean. The best thing it has going for it is its orientation — it is ideally positioned for sitting back and admiring the sunset over a drink or two. At night it is very lively: in High Season the road is closed to traffic and the tavernas are free to spill tables out to the waterfront. The promenade west of the ferry quay ends in a small headland decked with a windmill (with a couple more hidden amid the hotels on the hill behind).

East of the ferry quay things are quieter (though this is relative) and home to some of the better restaurants in town. Up one of the backstreets behind lies an open-air cinema, with current release films in English, served up with popcorn and all the trimmings, in someone's backyard. A second cinema — the *Rex* — lies on the ring road at the back of the town.

Parikia has a number of **beaches** within easy reach. The most popular is the main town beach, opposite the tourist hotel and restaurant strip east of the ferry quay (during the small hours it plays host to drunken bathers kitted out in their under-

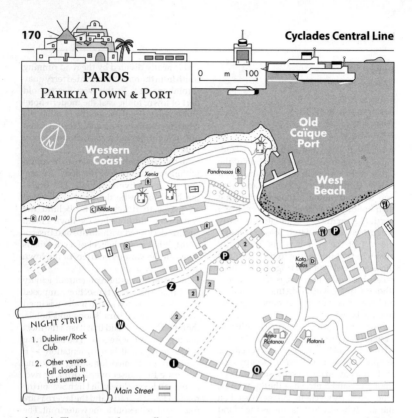

PAROS
PARIKIA TOWN & PORT

0　　m　　100

Old Caïque Port

Western Coast

Xenia

Pandrossos

West Beach

Nicolas

← ℝ (100 m)

Kato Yalos

NIGHT STRIP
1. Dubliner/Rock Club
2. Other venues (all closed in last summer).

Anna Platanou　*Platanis*

Main Street ═══

clothes). There is another — albeit more skimpy — beach on the east side of the bay that is also crowded, and a less attractive strand on the west end of the town promenade. All are adequate for the odd day of sunbathing, but are pretty inferior compared to some of the other beaches on Paros. One of these, a collection of coves a boat ride across the bay at **Martselo**, is easily accessible from Parikia, and has many fans thanks to the opportunity it offers to remove more beachwear than is acceptable nearer the town (i.e. everything).

The fenced-off ferry quay is one of the largest in the Cyclades and in High Season sees ferries queuing up to berth during the midday and midnight busy periods. Waiting ferry passengers are corralled in three quayside passenger stalls. At the ferry end of each is a gate that is unlocked when the ferry calls; it therefore pays to be in the correct stall (the port police chalk up the names of the next three boats due in on blackboards on the town side of each). When arriving at Paros you should also note that the quay exit gate is on the west/old town side of the passenger stall block (this is kept locked until the first arrivals reach it, to prevent stall-jumping by departing passengers).

The town's bus station is at the far end of the quay. Bus links are good around the island — though travelling around usually entails a return to Parikia. Paros is also unusual in offering a €6 'Daytrip' ticket which is valid on all routes.

On Paros the sheer number of tourists also makes it advisable to buy ferry tickets well

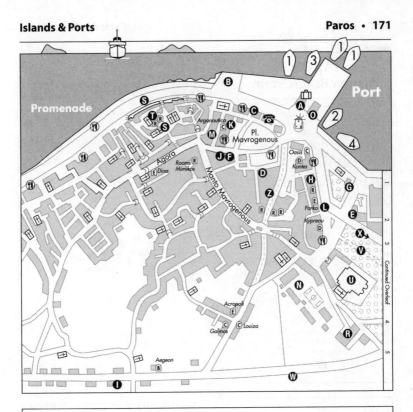

Key

- **Ⓐ** Tourist Information
- **Ⓑ** Bus Station
- **Ⓒ** Taxi Rank
- **Ⓓ** Police / Tourist Police
- **Ⓔ** Hospital / Clinic
- **Ⓕ** National Bank of Greece
- **Ⓖ** Public WCs
- **Ⓗ** Bookshop
- **Ⓘ** Supermarket
- **Ⓙ** Bakery
- **Ⓚ** Pharmacy
- **Ⓛ** International Press
- **Ⓜ** Paros Craft Shop
- **Ⓝ** School

- **Ⓞ** Ferry Passenger Stalls
- **Ⓟ** Night Strip
- **Ⓠ** Cinema Rex
- **Ⓡ** Archaeological Museum
- **Ⓢ** Frankish Kastro Walls
- **Ⓣ** Foundations of the Temple of Aphrodite
- **Ⓤ** Ekatontapiliani Cathedral & Baptistry
- **Ⓥ** Pine Wood Park
- **Ⓦ** Ring Road
- **Ⓧ** Naoussa Road
- **Ⓨ** Asklepieion (200 m) & Punta Road
- **Ⓩ** Street / River Bed

- **1** Ferries
- **2** Antiparos Town & Cave Tour Boats
- **3** Hydrofoils
- **4** Krios Beach & Camping Taxi Boats

Panagia Ekatontapiliani —
The Cathedral Church

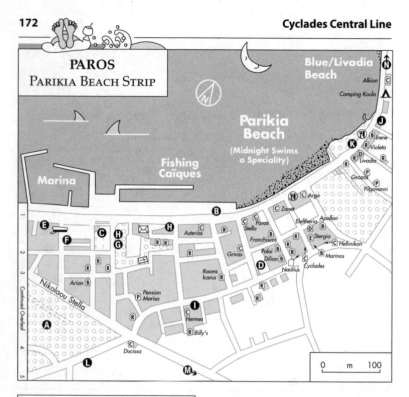

PAROS
PARIKIA BEACH STRIP

Blue/Livadia Beach

Parikia Beach
(Midnight Swims a Speciality)

Fishing Caïques

Marina

Nikolaou Stella

Key

Ⓐ Pine Wood Park

Ⓑ Car Rental

Ⓒ Excavated Classical & Hellenistic Cemetery

Ⓓ Open-Air Cinema

Ⓔ Books & International Press

Ⓕ Large Supermarket

Ⓖ Mountain Bike Rental

Ⓗ Moped Rental

Ⓘ Supermarket

Ⓙ Pizzeria

Ⓚ Bar Strip

Ⓛ Parikia Town Ring Road

Ⓜ Naoussa Road

Ⓝ Krios & Dilio Roads

in advance if you are planning to take one of the popular boats in High Season. Apart from the crowds, the only problem you are likely to encounter is the delightfully large choice of connections available. During the Low Season Paros remains the best-served Aegean island, with the number of daily departures still reaching double figures.

Around Paros there are a number of resorts and beaches that are easily accessible. Picturesque **Naoussa**, the nightlife captial of Paros, is set in a bay on the northern coast and dominated by a tall Orthodox church, has rapidly expanded to become the island's second major centre. Smaller and prettier than Parikia, it shares one thing in common, in as much as it is also bursting at the seams with tourists during the summer months. At the height of the season numbers get quite oppressive as its capacity to absorb them is not nearly so great. At the centre of town is a whitewashed chora.

Laid out in an almost grid-like pattern, Naoussa is more boutique-filled than its Parikia counterpart. In spite of this, it is the taverna-lined waterfront that is the great draw, with a charming caïque harbour backed by pretty Venetian houses (now doubling as dreamy tavernas) and protected on the seaward harbour wall side by the remains of a kastro-cum-tower — now reduced to a surf-kissed breakwater. Running through, and dominating, the centre of town is a dry (in summer) river bed that is home to the bus station.

The oldest part of town lies to the east, gradually ascending the hillside to the dominating church and a handful of derelict windmills to the north. West of the river bed Naoussa is reduced to a ribbon of houses running a mere two or three blocks deep along the coast. This coast road is home to the OTE and police station as well as the best Naoussa can offer by way of a beach; be warned, this isn't a lot. As a result, boats run from the waterfront to beaches around the bay, and round the headland to a good beach at **Santa Maria** (also reached via a daily bus from Parikia or a local bus from Naoussa). Popular with windsurfers it always has a fair bit going on.

The number three resort destination, **Piso Livadi**, is much more relaxed and low key. A quaint fishing village gathered around a cute little harbour (complete with an irregular ferry link) on the east side of the island, it is a nice place to stay if you are seeking to escape the worst of the crowds. This said, a resort is developing behind a couple of good beaches immediately to the south of the village at nearby Logaras and Pounta, and is attracting a fair number of the younger crowd.

At the top of the isolated cone-shaped hill that climbs up behind Piso Livadi is a medieval fortress. Standing within its wall are a disused monastery and the church of Agios Antonios. Access is via a small road that starts in the backstreets behind the

windmill at nearby Marpissa (which backs right onto Piso Livadi).

Piso Livadi is also conveniently close to the island's best beach — all the best beaches on Paros are to be found along this stretch of coast — at **Chrisi Akti** (Golden Beach). As the name suggests, this is an excellent stretch of sandy coast and is also popular with windsurfers. Nearby lies the village of **Drios**; now rapidly being spoilt by ugly uncontrolled hotel development, it is the destination of Parikia buses.

The fourth centre of note is at **Aliki** on the south coast. Little more than a quiet beach village filled with more than the usual number of holiday homes, it offers a peaceful and more relaxing alternative to the main resorts — though its waterfront lacks the charm of the other centres. Many will find it too quiet for comfort (except when flights are taking off or landing at the nearby airport). In High Season it also has an irregular taxi-boat service to Antiparos (sometimes continuing east to a beach on the islet of **Despotiko**).

The inland village of **Lefkes** flourished as the Parian capital during the years of Ottoman rule, when pirates ruled the seas, forcing the abandonment of the traditional centre at Parikia. Built in the shape of a vague amphitheatre in the hills, it is well worth a look and is an appealing hangover from the days before Paros was irredeemably changed by tourism. Access is easy via the frequent Parikia—Piso Livadi buses, though it is better to avoid them at peak periods when the sun-and-sand-seeking masses are either travelling to or from the east coast beaches.

Buses from Parikia also run hourly to the middle of nowhere. This is the lonely small quay at **Punta**, landing place for the regular Antiparos car ferries. Little more than a quay, a church, a taverna and a small shop, it is hardly a destination in its own right. Most tourists who visit are doing so unwillingly (usually because the seas have become too rough for the Antiparos—Parikia tourist boats).

The combination of size, fertility and marble has ensured that Paros has always been an important island. As early as the 7 c. BC it was sufficiently powerful to send a colony to Thassos (the standard procedure employed by Greek city states and islands for dealing with population overspills). In 490 BC Paros sided with the Persians at the Battle of Salamis (via one trireme), and thereafter found itself under the control of Athens. Like the other Cycladic islands, Paros drifted out of the scene in the Hellenistic and Byzantine periods, enjoying increasing pirate activity and diminishing prosperity.

In the medieval period Paros was an important component of the Duchy of Naxos until 1389. Conquered by the Turks in 1537, Paros saw the Russian fleet use it as a winter base in 1770–71, and the island remained in Russian hands until 1774 when the Turks regained control. Independence was achieved in 1821.

Paros has a good Accommodation Office on the ferry quay with staff that will phone around for you. If you walk past them you will find plentiful offers of rooms greet boats arriving before 18.00 (many by room owners offering accommodation on nearby Antiparos), but prices rise in High Season when the morning ferries from Piraeus arrive after midday. From then on you will have to be prepared to pay up or look further afield. Naoussa is the best bet, as the town is plastered with 'Rooms' signs. Piso Livadi also has a reasonable supply.

Well-endowed **Parikia** is home to the greatest number of the island's hotels. These are divided between the old part of town (mostly smaller, budget establishments) and the new, tourist-dominated suburb to the east (which is home to the bulk of the package tour hotels). Other hotels lie around the town environs — including the expensive *Xenia* (☎ 21394), located 100 m west of the town's west beach behind a couple of windmills.

Mid-range hotels mostly cater for package tourists, but they are quick to snap up island hoppers to fill any empty beds. Some even have signs outside indicating vacancies. The waterfront east of the ferry quay includes the well maintained C-class *Asterias* (☎ 21797), the smaller *Stella* (☎ 21502) and the *Argo* (☎ 21367). Quieter hotels lie in the streets behind, including the *Cyclades* (☎ 22048). If you want to splash out at the middle end of the range,

the C-class *Argonautica* (☎ 21440) is conveniently placed behind the main town square with attractive, if pricey, rooms. Near the ferry quay are a couple of reasonable D-class establishments that are easy to find: the *Kontes* (☎ 21096) and the *Kypreou* (☎ 21383). The latter is the cheaper of the two.

Another popular group of hotels lie along the river-bed-cum-road: the C-class *Galinos* (☎ 21480) and *Louiza* (☎ 22122), and E-class *Acropoli* (☎ 21521). Other E-class hotels in town include the *Dina* (☎ 21325) and the *Parko* (☎ 22213). At the budget end of the market are a number of establishments offering rooms (these are effectively backpackers' pensions), notably *Rooms Icarus* (☎ 21695) in the new strip and the better *Rooms Mimikos* (☎ 21437) in the chora part of town.

Other towns also have hotels on offer. **Naoussa** is the best equipped, though it is best to avoid establishments in the town centre as noise levels can be a problem. **Piso Livadi** has fewer rooms, but they are much quieter. One of the best is the C-class *San Antonio* overlooking the village.

A

On Paros there are a large number of sites:
Camping Koula (☎ 22081): nice olive-grove site and the nearest to the port. The site cashes in on its convenient location, though sleepers sometimes experience more disruption than most from 03.00 ferry arrivals and disco returnees. There is a strictly enforced 23.00–07.00 noise ban (lovers have to moan quietly) and free WC-rolls are issued to all. If you are visiting early in the season this is likely to be the only site open on the island.
Camping Krios (☎ 21705) is one of the newer sites on the beach opposite the port. Sadly let down in the past by a lack of regular cleaning, it seems to be better these days. The taxi-boat link to Parikia (last at 19.30) is also not conducive to nightlife or catching an early morning ferry (though there is a fair mini-bus service).
Parasporos Camping (☎ 21394) is a better site 3 km south of the town, with mini-buses that also provide campers with a free service to and from town. Good on-site facilities include a pool. Past years have seen free tents provided to campers out of High Season.

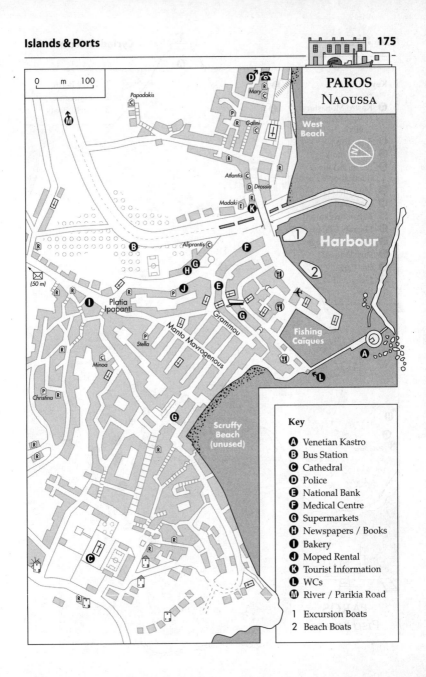

PAROS
NAOUSSA

West Beach

Harbour

1

2

Papadakis

Mary

Galini

Atlantis

Drossia

Madaki

Aliprantis

Platia Ipapanti

Stella

Minoa

Christina

Manto Mavrogenous

Grammou

Fishing Caïques

Scruffy Beach (unused)

0   m   100

(50 m)

Key

Ⓐ Venetian Kastro
Ⓑ Bus Station
Ⓒ Cathedral
Ⓓ Police
Ⓔ National Bank
Ⓕ Medical Centre
Ⓖ Supermarkets
Ⓗ Newspapers / Books
Ⓘ Bakery
Ⓙ Moped Rental
Ⓚ Tourist Information
Ⓛ WCs
Ⓜ River / Parikia Road

1 Excursion Boats
2 Beach Boats

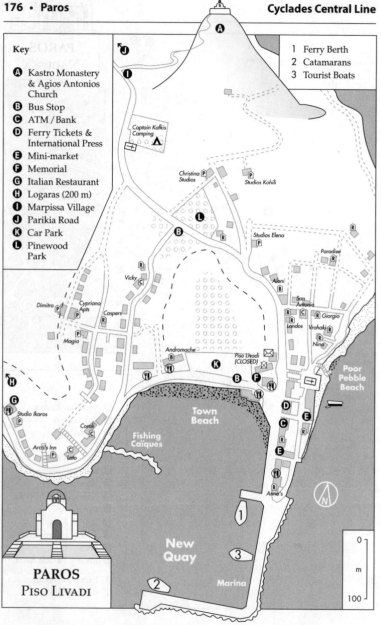

Key

Ⓐ Kastro Monastery & Agios Antonios Church
Ⓑ Bus Stop
Ⓒ ATM / Bank
Ⓓ Ferry Tickets & International Press
Ⓔ Mini-market
Ⓕ Memorial
Ⓖ Italian Restaurant
Ⓗ Logaras (200 m)
Ⓘ Marpissa Village
Ⓙ Parikia Road
Ⓚ Car Park
Ⓛ Pinewood Park

1 Ferry Berth
2 Catamarans
3 Tourist Boats

Captain Kafkis Camping

Christina Studios
Studios Kohili
Studios Elena
Paradise
Aloni
San Antonio
Vicky
Giorgio
Dimitra
Cypriana Apts
Caspers
Landos
Vrohaki
Magia
Nina
Andromache
Piso Livadi (CLOSED)
Poor Pebble Beach
Town Beach
Studio Ikaros
Corali
Fishing Caïques
Arca's Inn
Lato
Anna's

PAROS
PISO LIVADI

New Quay
Marina

0
m
100

Camping Naoussa (☎ 51398) is one of the better sites on Paros if a frenetic nightlife isn't a priority; again, mini-buses meet boats.

Camping Surfing Beach (☎ 51013), nestling in the scrub behind Santa Maria beach, is the newest site on Paros, and popular with windsurfers. Facilities are good, with a free shuttle service to and from Parikia.

Camping Agia Elini (☎ 91144) is a low-key site on one of the best island beaches.

Captain Kafkis Camping (☎ 41479), 1 km outside Piso Livadi, is for those who like a very quiet life with fair facilities. The site is usually only open during July and August.

≽✿

Nightlife on Paros has gravitated to **Naoussa** in the last few years, with several clubs to be found on the river-bed road that leads from the sea to the bus station. **Parikia** has its own club strip but this was all but closed in 2011. The only show in town was the large *Dubliner/ Paros Rock* complex. Built on two levels, this is a real hot spot, with two dance floors and a few quiet corners where you can find out the name of the person you are trying to get off with. Other clubs, when operating, have less going for them, and most years end up under new ownership and with new names into the bargain. A visit to one of the two open-air cinemas also just qualifies as nightlife (it makes a good starter to an evening of bar crawling). Don't be surprised to find the locals diving for the entrance if the national anthem is played. The Greek anthem, with its 158 verses, is the longest in the world (in most places the locals just sing the first two and then whistle the rest, but it's never wise to chance it).

◉◉

Most of the sightseeing is to be found in **Parikia**. The **Venetian Kastro** (1260 AD) in the heart of the chora was largely constructed from the remains of Archaic **Temples of Demeter & Apollo**, remnants of which can be seen in the form of the circular column drums now embedded in the kastro walls and the black marble foundations of the temple base. You do, however, have to hunt around among the later buildings to spot the ancient members.

The town has a more complete architectural monument: the 6 c. AD cathedral church of **Ekatontapiliani**. This rather odd name (thought to be a corruption of 'in the lower town') now means 'Our Lady of the 100 doors' — for the building was supposed to have had as many. Truth to tell you would be

hard put to know it today, though a number of architecture students have managed to trace a dozen on their first attempt and 99 after a few ouzos. The 100th is believed to have been carried off by the Turks (a delightful notion as it suggests in a subtle way that the old enemy is completely unhinged along with it). Tradition also claims that the church was designed by Isidore of Miletus, with the construction carried out by his pupil Ignatius. When it was completed, Isidore is said to have been so jealous of the church's beauty that he attacked his pupil on the roof with the result that both fell to their deaths. Given that Isidore was one of the architects responsible for the infinitely more wondrous Agia Sofia in İstanbul/Constantinople one suspects this is hyperbole. Much of the building is constructed from ancient building fragments anyway. A couple of floodlit excavations in the nave floor (now covered with glass) reveal the bases of a couple of columns from a Hellenistic temple. The church precincts are also home to a small museum of Byzantine religious art.

The **Archaeological Museum** (⊕ ex ① 08.00– 14.30; tickets €3) behind the church has part of the Roman pavement uncovered in the church on display amongst other island exhibits. Not least of these are architectural fragments from two small temple sites that are within easy walking distance of Parikia.

The first of these is the **Asklepieion**, which lies on a seaward-facing hill on the western edge of town. Some attempt has been made to make the site presentable, but the info centre is empty and closed, and the site little more than incoherent foundations. The most prominent feature is a neo-classical templet above the site that is, in fact, a 19 c. memorial to a local family. Its location does offer good views over the town and the procession of ferries heading into the bay.

The **second temple** (built c. 480 BC. and dedicated to Apollo & Artemis) site is on a hilltop, an hour's walk north of the ferry quay, at Dilio. Now stripped of anything recognizable (including the substantial remains of the cult statue of Artemis — now in the Archaeological Museum), it is still an enjoyable objective for those wanting a not-too-demanding walk. Once you scale the foundation walls of the precinct, the reason for its location becomes apparent: it would have been visible from both the two major settlements on Paros in ancient times (at Parikia and Naoussa).

Somewhat further afield, but regularly visited by tour groups, is the **Valley of the Butterflies** (alias tiger moths) at **Petaloudes** (from May to July). These gather before dying to mate in this quiet shady valley-cum-garden (open ℗ 09.00–20.00. Entrance fee: €3 for humans, moths free). Unfortunately, the poor creatures are now subjected to clapping and shouting exhibitions by tourists — thus alarming them into flight: the clouds of butterflies are, after all, what they have come to see. This is very debilitating for animals nearing the end of their lives and trying to conserve energy, and is producing dire consequences; as every jump means they have the energy for one less hump, their numbers are declining rapidly.

Ancient Marble Quarries

One of the great unsung tourist attractions in the Greek islands is the **Ancient Marble Quarries** located just outside Marathi, some 4 km inland from Parikia Port. The site is sadly neglected by most visitors to Paros, yet — if precautions are taken — it offers one of the most memorable sightseeing opportunities going in the Aegean.

The first thing that needs to be said is that the use of the term 'quarry' in this instance is very misleading — and one suspects rather off-putting to many (few people travel to Greece to take time out looking at large pits in the ground). However, far from being confronted by a conventional open-air quarry, visitors to the site initially struggle to see anything at all. This is because the so-called quarries (plural) consists of one mine (singular) with several obscured entrances. In mining circles the workings at Marathi would be described as a '**Slope Mine**', but as every road sign, map and guidebook under the sun refers to 'quarries' this guidebook will do so as well to avoid confusion (albeit with 'miner' reservations).

Paros has been famed for the quality of its marble since antiquity. In the ancient world it was rare for stone to be exported far — most temples were built out of local marbles — yet Paros was exporting from as early as the 6 c. BC. This was because Parian marble is more translucent than most; light penetrates further through it, giving it a sparkling white, light-absorbent appearance. Its texture also made it ideally suited for carving fine sculpture. As a result, its fame spread far and wide, and it even acquired its own name; it was known as '*Lychnites*' (from the word

'lychnos', an oil lamp) because it was mined by lamplight. This was unusual in ancient Greece where most stone was acquired from surface quarries. The good stuff on Paros required tunnelling, but it justified the effort — it was the favoured marble of almost all of the great sculptors, and not a few lesser ones with clients who wanted the Rolls-Royce touch. Famous sculptures made with it include the 'Venus de Milo' (see p. 278) and the 'Winged Victory of Samothrace' (see p. 504).

Paros had a number of mines and quarries in ancient times, but the Marathi site is the only one now accessible. Establishing when digging began is difficult as much evidence has been destroyed by later 19 c. working. However it is clear that activity was well established by the 4 c. BC as the two principal entrances were decorated with carved reliefs sometime between 350–325 BC. The date at which working stopped is also hazy, but the best guess is sometime in the 7 c. AD. Thereafter the site was abandoned until the 18 c. when the awakened interest by European travellers in ancient Greece brought the first tourists to see the entrance carvings.

The Marathi working's next claim to fame came in 1835 when it became the first recorded ancient industrial site to attract the attention of an archaeologist: Ludwig Ross took time out from his work restoring the Acropolis buildings in Athens to visit. Sadly, the site was badly damaged a few years later when Stamatis Cleanthes, the leading Athenian city planner and architect, arrived in 1857. Establishing the 'Hellenic Parian Marble Company', he reopened the workings. This venture was later expanded by the short-lived 'Franco-Belgian Company' who drove the two large slope shafts visible today into the ancient mine in 1881. The ruinous buildings at the site date from this episode, as do the ruined waterfront buildings near the Port Police office at Parikia Port (in the 19 c. the mine was connected to the coast via a narrow gauge rail link).

The Marble Quarry Site Mine

It cannot be stressed enough that this site is not a regular tourist attraction: it remains an undeveloped destination that individuals can explore at their own risk. There are no supervisors or support if you get into trouble. In the last few years the three mine entrances have been fenced off in a half-hearted way with warning notices against entry, but it is easy enough to walk around these obstacles, and the well-worn paths testify that many people do so. In fact, a lot of work was done to prepare the site for tourists — a substantial EU-funded marble path has been laid from the main road to the fringes of the quarry, and some work has been undertaken inside the mine to make it relatively 'safe'. However, development funds ran out at this point. As a result, the majority of visitors (most are groups of tourists on bus tours of Paros) just walk to the mine entrances for a quick look, while their tour guide bangs the odd rock together to show an example of Parian marble in all its pristine glory.

Travelling to the site is very easy as buses on the Parikia—Drios route drop you right at the entrance if you ask (there is a request bus stop). From the bus stop the shining marble path seemingly runs off to the middle of nowhere, but a walk down the rough track that continues on from it quickly brings you to the site entrance proper. This is marked by a low gate in a stone wall. On the other side of this is a long, low spoil heap topped with a couple of ruinous winding houses. Built on this rather unstable mound, they are collapsing as it disintegrates — though, again, some work has been undertaken to make them safe. The spoil heap hides the mine entrances that sink down from the base of a low cliff. Around the extremities of the site are the ruins of a marble cutting factory and a lime kiln.

Exploring the Mine

Once you summon up the courage to enter one of the shafts that disappear into the ground at an intimidating angle, you will find that the mine is safe enough — *provided* you come properly equipped (see p. 182) and take note of the few danger areas shown on the map overleaf. The three entrance shafts are each less than 100 m long and connect up, so you can travel down one and return up another. Doing the loop takes 30 minutes. If you are venturing into the side galleries as well, then reckon on spending around an hour underground.

Many visitors entering the mine head down the most visible of the entrances; that of the **Cave Slope Shaft** (❶ on the map overleaf). This is a mistake! Descending at an angle of 35°, this is the steepest of the shafts. Travelling down is slippery and difficult: it is much better tackled as your exit route. Instead, the best way in is via the **Doorway Slope Shaft ❻**. The entrance is in an overgrown cutting, but it

The Lost Marble Quarry Entrance & Dancing Nymph Relief

The Marble Quarries at Marathi were a popular destination for travellers visiting the Cyclades in the 18 c. and 19 c. The site was a recognised stopping point on the Grand Tour and was visited by several artists who produced engravings showing the impressive main entrance to the mine complex. The best and most detailed of these was drawn in 1776 by J. B. Hilaire who travelled around the Aegean in the employ of Le Comte de Choiseul-Gouffier, recording scenes for his famous '*Voyage Pittoresque de la Grèce*' (published in Paris in 1782). Hilaire's illustration depicts a scene that was clearly the 'standard' view at the time: it shows a large high cave-like entrance opening onto a landscape fringed with palm trees, drawn from a point some 10 m inside the cavern. Both sides of the entrance are guarded by large rectangular blocks, and the right wall (looking out) is decorated with an ancient relief sculpture depicting dancing nymphs, carved almost life size.

The only problem with this appealing vista is that it is impossible to reconcile it with anything at the marble quarry today. Thanks to 19 c. mining works virtually everything in the scene has been obliterated. It is, however, just possible to identify the two former entrance blocks now standing above the 19 c. Doorway Slope Shaft entrance. The cavern itself was presumably chopped away when the doorway was cut. It is not known what happened to the dancing nymph relief. The probability is that it was cut away and sold to a 19 c. collector or dealer and transported overseas to adorn some stately home or landscape garden folly.

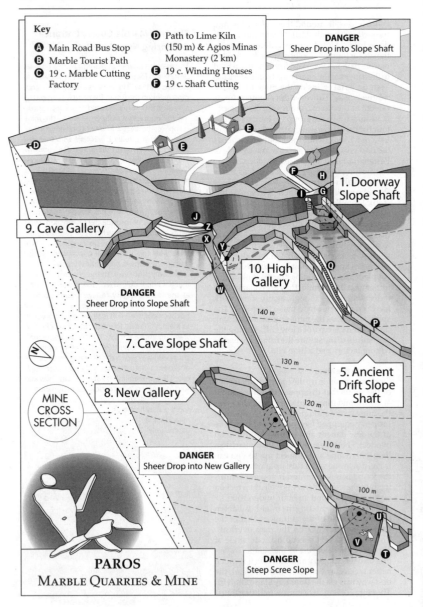

Key

Ⓐ Main Road Bus Stop
Ⓑ Marble Tourist Path
Ⓒ 19 c. Marble Cutting Factory
Ⓓ Path to Lime Kiln (150 m) & Agios Minas Monastery (2 km)
Ⓔ 19 c. Winding Houses
Ⓕ 19 c. Shaft Cutting

DANGER
Sheer Drop into Slope Shaft

1. Doorway Slope Shaft

9. Cave Gallery

10. High Gallery

DANGER
Sheer Drop into Slope Shaft

7. Cave Slope Shaft

5. Ancient Drift Slope Shaft

140 m
130 m
120 m
110 m
100 m

8. New Gallery

MINE CROSS-SECTION

DANGER
Sheer Drop into New Gallery

DANGER
Steep Scree Slope

PAROS
MARBLE QUARRIES & MINE

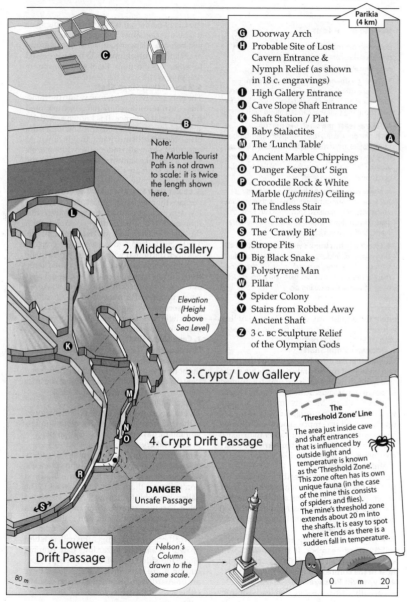

Parikia
(4 km)

G Doorway Arch
H Probable Site of Lost
   Cavern Entrance &
   Nymph Relief (as shown
   in 18 c. engravings)
I High Gallery Entrance
J Cave Slope Shaft Entrance
K Shaft Station / Plat
L Baby Stalactites
M The 'Lunch Table'
N Ancient Marble Chippings
O 'Danger Keep Out' Sign
P Crocodile Rock & White
   Marble (*Lychnites*) Ceiling
Q The Endless Stair
R The Crack of Doom
S The 'Crawly Bit'
T Strope Pits
U Big Black Snake
V Polystyrene Man
W Pillar
X Spider Colony
Y Stairs from Robbed Away
   Ancient Shaft
Z 3 c. BC Sculpture Relief
   of the Olympian Gods

Note:

The Marble Tourist
Path is not drawn
to scale: it is twice
the length shown
here.

2. Middle Gallery

*Elevation
(Height
above
Sea Level)*

3. Crypt / Low Gallery

**The
'Threshold Zone' Line**

The area just inside cave
and shaft entrances
that is influenced by
outside light and
temperature is known
as the 'Threshold Zone'.
This zone often has its own
unique fauna (in the case
of the mine this consists
of spiders and flies).
The mine's threshold zone
extends about 20 m into
the shafts. It is easy to spot
where it ends as there is a
sudden fall in temperature.

4. Crypt Drift Passage

DANGER
Unsafe Passage

**6. Lower
Drift Passage**

*Nelson's
Column
drawn to the
same scale.*

80 m

0   m   20

Marble Mine Tour

Exploring the marble mine is great fun provided due care is taken. The basic rules for staying safe are:

1. Don't go down the mine on your own.
If you are running solo — don't despair! In the summer months you won't have to wait long to find someone that you can tag along with.

2. Take at least one torch per person.
Each person *needs* a torch — given the number of obstacles underfoot in the mine. Make sure they have fresh batteries. Head torches are ideal as they leave the hands free — a boon in the occasional slippery areas.

3. Make sure someone knows your plan.
Tell your hotel or someone topsides that you are going into the mine, so that they can raise the alarm if you don't return. This sounds melodramatic, but it is a sensible precaution.

4. Check out this book's website beforehand.
Online you will find explanatory photos and video footage of the field research trips for the mine map in this book. This will give you a good idea of what you will be taking on.

---

offers the easiest way down. Because of this, it forms the starting point for the suggested plan of exploration below:

1. Doorway Slope Shaft
This shaft is the most boring part of the mine. Fortunately, it quickly takes you down to the shaft station or **plat ⓚ**, from which a number of narrow passages lead off. These can be explored in turn. Most are lined with rough walls of mined material: it was standard practice to fill up empty spaces and disused shafts with quarried debris rather than take it to the surface. The accessible corridors today are only a tiny part of the likely total.

2. Middle Gallery
Reached via a passage leading up from the plat, this is clearly an ancient working. There are chisel marks on stones and the ceiling of the vault has tiny 2,500-year-old stalactites. It is sobering to see how small they are.

3. Crypt / Low Gallery
The ancient corridor along runs down to this mildly scary chamber. It is decorated with stone shelves that look as if they should play host to the coffins of a family of vampires.

4. Crypt Drift Passage
A partially closed passage that leads off from

the Crypt Gallery, it is worth venturing in as it contains the miner's 'Lunch Table' **ⓜ** and, just before a 'Danger Keep Out' sign, a group of ancient marble chippings **ⓝ** that have fused together on the floor thanks to constantly dripping water over the centuries.

5. Ancient Drift Slope Shaft
The only surviving ancient way into the mine, this is an interesting shaft that is best explored from the plat entrance. It is known as a 'drift' shaft because the miners were following a seam of marble rather than driving straight down. At one point you walk under pure white marble **ⓟ**; it is a bit like standing under ice. Near the top of the shaft are the remains of the mine's only staircase: the 'Endless Stair' **ⓞ**.

6. Lower Drift Passage (aka 'The Crawly Bit')
Perhaps the most exciting part of the mine, this low drift passage connects the two main shafts. It boasts a very low ceiling — complete with the 'Crack of Doom' **ⓡ** and two **strope pits ⓣ**. The largest is deep, and as a warning to visitors has been decorated with a fallen figure made out of polystyrene **ⓥ**. It falls away suddenly from the passage, so — as an additional alert aid — it is guarded by a big black snake **ⓤ**. Some people with over-vivid imaginations have seen its two huge 30 cm-thick coils in the torch light and taken them for old tyres — an easy mistake to make.

7. Cave Slope Shaft
Dubbed the 'Heaven–Hell Stairway', this cavernous shaft is hell to go down, but stand at the bottom and watch others doing the ascent: they disappear into the light like a scene from the film '*Ghost*' — pure visual poetry.

8. New Gallery
A very large open gallery that clearly belongs to the 19 C. workings. It is inaccessible — unless you fall in. Take great care at this point.

9. Cave Gallery
A low cave partly filled with spoil, this gallery is home to a colony of spiders who spin webs between the rocks on the floor (provided you don't disturb them they won't attack). The gallery is notable for having the only surviving relief carving; representing the Olympian Gods, it is protected by an iron grille.

10. High Gallery
Part of the ancient workings, this gallery is best visited via a mildly hazardous path running along the side of the Doorway Slope shaft cutting. Care must be taken inside as there are unguarded drops into the two 19 C. shafts either side of the gallery.

Santorini / Thira

ΣANTOPINI / ΘHPA; 73 km²; pop. 7,100.

CODE ☎ 22860
TOURIST POLICE ☎ 22649
PORT POLICE ☎ 22239
HOSPITAL ☎ 22237

The most spectacular of all the Greek islands (and also one of the most expensive), Santorini is subject to ever-increasing waves of tourists drawn by the landscape, the archaeological discoveries at Akrotiri, and the legend of Atlantis. The island is commonly known by two names: the Venetian 'Santorini' (after the 3 C. AD St. Irene who died in exile hereabouts) or its Classical name of 'Thira' (now reinstated as its official name). 'Santorini' is more popular with tourists. Ferry operators usually prefer 'Thira' (also transcribed as 'Fira'), in the interests of brevity on ship destination boards.

The island is the largest fragment of a volcanic archipelago made up of the broken remnants of the largest caldera on earth. It is now thought by many to be the origin of the Atlantis legend, the inpouring of the sea into the caldera during a massive eruption c. 1640 BC giving early sailors the impression that the greater part of the island had sunk, taking the Minoan settlements on the island with it. Within the caldera, subsequent volcanic eruptions (the last in 1950) have spawned new islets of ominous, black, razor-sharp lava. The volcano is now quietly simmering with sulphur emissions and hot springs. If this wasn't enough by way of icing the tourist cake, the caldera rim is frosted with scenic white cubist towns that take a tumble every time an earthquake hits. Santorini also has a reputation as a home for vampires. All this ensures that the island is on the itinerary of every cruise ship, day tripper and casual tourist within range, and usually full to overflowing, regardless of the time of year (a major problem in itself, as the island has no freshwater springs; supplies are tankered in daily from the mainland).

The centre of activity on Santorini is **Fira Town** (also transcribed as 'Thira' and 'Phira'). This large island capital is perched precariously on the edge of the caldera rim, with a switchback staircase (carpeted with donkey droppings) down the crater wall, and a cable car for those who don't care for the donkey rides or the 587 awkward steps. These run to the old port of Skala Fira — and its mooring buoys for cruise ships — below the town. Now unashamedly a tourist centre, Fira has preserved enough of its charm to make a visit enjoyable. This might not seem to be the case if you arrive in the early hours when the main town square is thronged with inebriated tourists enjoying what amounts to an open-air party, but once the surprisingly efficient town street cleaners have done their dawn stuff and revealed once again the black lava stone used to cobble the streets, a vague semblance of the Greek island idyll is restored, and even enhanced by the weird nature of the place. For Fira Town rolls dramatically with the landscape, falling fast from the caldera rim to the coastal plain, with its views of neighbouring Anafi. The rim itself is by no means level, and has the buildings rolling up and down every photogenic step of the way.

The great attraction in town is the view over the caldera and the volcano (principally from Ipapantis St.). Bars clutter up the best viewing places, fronting the warren of boutique-filled backstreets behind. Hidden away in these are several museums. Along the rim you will find occasional fragments of buildings that fell into the caldera on the 9th of July 1956, during an earthquake that all but levelled the town — killing 53 people and destroying 2,400 homes (one is apt to wonder if the restaurants perched precariously on the rim are really such a good idea). If losing many of its old buildings wasn't bad enough, Fira has suffered further disfigurement thanks to the large disused pumice quarry at the southern edge of the town, a gaping hole in the caldera wall that has been excavated down to the

SANTORINI / THIRA

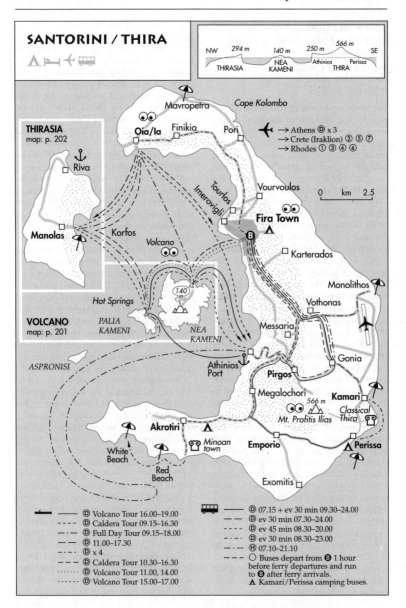

NW 294 m   140 m   250 m   566 m   SE
THIRASIA   NEA   Athinios Perissa
             KAMENI   THIRA

THIRASIA
map: p. 202

⚓
Riva

Manolas

Korfos

Mavropetra
Oia/Ia Finikia   Pori   Cape Kolombo

Tourlos
Imerovigli

Vourvoulos

→ Athens Ⓓ x 3
→ Crete (Iraklion) ② ⑤ ⑦
→ Rhodes ① ③ ④ ⑥

0   km   2.5

Fira Town Ⓑ

Karterados

Monolithos

Vothonas

Volcano

VOLCANO
map: p. 201

Hot Springs

*PALIA
KAMENI*

*NEA
KAMENI*

ASPRONISI

Messaria

Athinios
Port

Gonia

Pirgos

Megalochori

566 m
Mt. Profitis Ilias

Kamari

*Classical
Thira*

Akrotiri

*Minoan
town*

White
Beach

Red
Beach

Emporio

Perissa

Exomitis

— Ⓓ Volcano Tour 16.00–19.00
---- Ⓓ Caldera Tour 09.15–16.30
—·— Ⓓ Full Day Tour 09.15–18.00
— Ⓓ 11.00–17.30
···· Ⓓ x 4
——— Ⓓ Caldera Tour 10.30–16.30
—— Ⓓ Volcano Tour 11.00, 14.00
······ Ⓓ Volcano Tour 15.00–17.00

— Ⓓ 07.15 + ev 30 min 09.30–24.00
— — Ⓓ ev 30 min 07.30–24.00
---- Ⓓ ev 45 min 08.30–20.00
—·— Ⓓ ev 30 min 08.30–23.00
—··— Ⓗ 07.10–21.10
--- Ⓞ Buses depart from Ⓑ 1 hour
before ferry departures and run
to Ⓑ after ferry arrivals.
Ⓐ Kamari/Perissa camping buses.

pre-eruption level, revealing the stumps of petrified trees.

To get the most out of Fira you have to pick your moment. Early mornings are the best time to explore — it is cooler, the rising sun gives the buildings a lovely warming glow, ferries glide silently across the caldera over a cobalt-blue sea, and the streets are free from the camera-clutching hordes and the moped packs that cruise round looking for someone to mow down. As the sun sets the town comes into its own again as the vibrant nightlife scene takes over.

The island ferry terminus is at **Athinios**, 4 km south of Fira. Little more than a long quay at the bottom of the caldera cliff face, it is backed with ticket agencies, tavernas (to be avoided as they charge their captive market exorbitant prices) and a WC at the far end. It exists here solely because it was at this point that it was possible to cut a switchback road down the cliffside. In spite of this, access is still very limited; in High Season the number of vehicles attempting to reach the quay can result in major traffic jams, and it is not unknown for bus passengers to have to walk down the cliff to join their boats. These often hang around for a few hours: Santorini's popularity is reflected in the ferry schedules — some 9 hours' regular ferry sailing time from Piraeus, the island is an obvious terminus for boats doing a daily round trip.

The caldera rim also has other settlements clinging to it. The most important of these is the pretty small northern town of **Oia** (otherwise transcribed as 'Ia' and pronounced as 'EEa'). Also badly damaged by the 1956 earthquake, the town has been rebuilt after a fashion. Promoted as the 'Paris of the Aegean' for no apparent reason other than its photogenic nature (the best picture-postcard caldera rim views are invariably of Oia), it has fewer crowds and a nicer small-town atmosphere than Fira; this along with a reconstructed windmill and superb sunset views brings in the tour parties by the coach load. Sunsets aside, Oia is best explored during the day. Relatively

cheap buses run from Fira (though the road is a disappointment as it runs too far inland for travellers to enjoy sweeping caldera views), leaving you to explore at your own pace. When you are tired of walking you always have the option of descending one of the two cliffside stairways to the tiny port below the town. This has seen ferries decant passengers into taxi boats in past years, but now relies on fish-dish tavernas for its income. There is also a cliffside path running back into the caldera basin and ending at swimming rocks with a small — chapel-topped — lava stack 20 m offshore.

Following the rim around there are several other villages that are increasingly filled with expensive tourist accommodation, but which are still noticeably less spoilt than the main towns. The biggest of these are **Finikia**, just outside Oia, and **Tourlos** and **Imerovigli**. These last two run into the residential northern section of Fira Town (not shown on the map on p. 188).

Turning inland from the caldera rim, the bulk of the island slopes steeply away and looks rather scruffy, being dry and treeless; the land is given over to producing tomatoes and ground-crawling vines that provide the wine for which Santorini is famous. The most accessible vineyards — with imaginative names like 'Volcano' — are to be found near Kamari, and they thrive on a procession of tour coaches that bring the masses to get their tongues around labels like 'Lava'. The reds certainly live up to the billing, giving the tastebuds a big bang that rapidly dwindles to an ashy nothing.

Dotted around the grey volcanic landscape between the vines are a number of whitewashed villages, which these days serve to mop up the tourists who can't find beds elsewhere. The largest of these — such as impressive hilltop **Pirgos**, and less dramatic **Emporio** and **Gonia** — have become minor centres in their own right. The best, however, is the dusty and rather ragged-looking village of **Akrotiri** on the

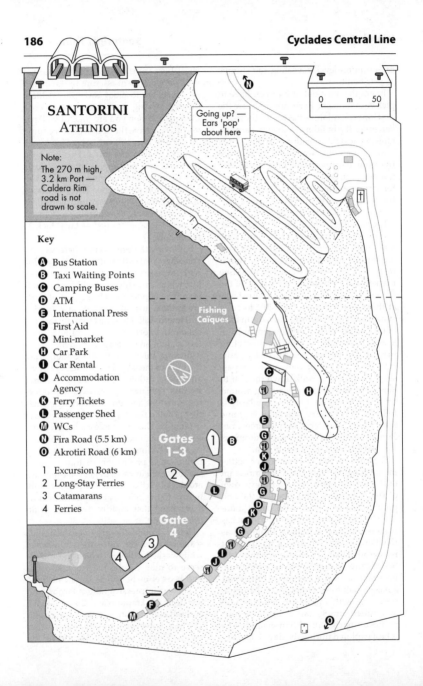

SANTORINI
ATHINIOS

Note:
The 270 m high, 3.2 km Port — Caldera Rim road is not drawn to scale.

Going up? — Ears 'pop' about here

Key

Ⓐ Bus Station
Ⓑ Taxi Waiting Points
Ⓒ Camping Buses
Ⓓ ATM
Ⓔ International Press
Ⓕ First Aid
Ⓖ Mini-market
Ⓗ Car Park
Ⓘ Car Rental
Ⓙ Accommodation Agency
Ⓚ Ferry Tickets
Ⓛ Passenger Shed
Ⓜ WCs
Ⓝ Fira Road (5.5 km)
Ⓞ Akrotiri Road (6 km)

1   Excursion Boats
2   Long-Stay Ferries
3   Catamarans
4   Ferries

0   m   50

Fishing Caïques

Gates 1-3

Gate 4

southern wing of the caldera rim. Sited on the side of a low hill, it is only now opening up to tourism. It still retains much of its traditional character, thanks to the odd windmill, though the nearby Minoan town excavation is helping to change this. The town also offers good views of the volcano set against the backdrop of the towns of Fira and Oia on the caldera rim (telescopes are provided on the headland to the west of the town). The downside to Akrotiri is the lack of a convenient nearby beach.

Volcanic islands are not generally noted for having brilliant beaches, and Santorini is no exception. Beaches there are in profusion, but most are strewn with black pebbles or pumice. However, on the south-east coast the beaches consist of wide stretches of black sand which, although it lacks sparkle and gets painfully hot (leaving sun worshippers looking like so many rows of pink sausages in a Teflon frying pan), has prompted the emergence of two large and successful beach resorts at Perissa and Kamari. Both are unashamedly tourist centres and nothing more, but they cater for very different markets.

Perissa is very much the haven of the independent and downmarket budget traveller, with a host of pensions, rooms and bars along a main road running inland from the beach (it has even acquired its own waterpark for good measure). **Kamari** is better established and more up-market, with a lot of package tour hotels and a much more sophisticated waterfront. It is also conveniently placed for the island's airport. The two resorts are separated by an iron curtain of a headland which is topped by the ruined Classical and Roman capital of the island. Access on the Perissa side is via a well-trodden, but poor, path that requires a good hour's hard walking.

On the Kamari side there is a longer switchback road (built for the coach tours) that is serviced by mini-buses. Both road and path arrive at a roundabout of sorts, usually complete with a van selling refreshments.

Other beaches on Santorini are to be found near the Minoan excavation at Akrotiri. The site — and its regular bus link to Fira — is only a short walk from the southern shore and caïques to two more of the island's beaches, Red Beach and White Beach. Both are named after the colour of their cinders-cum-sand. Oia also has an indifferent beach nearby, at Mavropetra.

☻

Santorini (originally believed to have been called 'Kalliste') has been occupied since at least 2000 BC. The island was at the extreme southern limit of the Bronze Age Cycladic culture and was later a major Minoan power base until the devastating eruption c. 1640 BC. Thereafter on the fringes of history, and somewhere along the line changing its name to 'Thira', Santorini first made an impact in the historical period when it was one of only two Cycladic islands (the other being Milos) to side with Corinth against Athens in the Peloponnesian War. For reasons that are unclear, when it inevitably fell under Athenian control Santorini escaped the fate of Milos (which saw its menfolk killed and the rest of the population carried off into slavery). Perhaps its relatively low political and economic status played a part: lacking good agricultural resources, Santorini seems to have been a very minor player throughout from the Classical to Roman periods. Its impressive harbour seems only to have acquired significance briefly during the Hellenistic period, when it was used by the Ptolemies as a naval base. For most of the time it was used as a place of exile, the most notable prisoner being St. Irene of Thessalonika who died on Thirasia in 304 AD.

Like the other islands in the Aegean, Santorini had a bad Dark and early Middle Ages. Piracy and depopulation took their inevitable toll. Some stability was restored with the arrival of Western Europeans in the wake of the crusades. From 1207 until the Turkish conquest in 1537 it was ruled first by Venetian families and then the Duchy of Naxos (when it acquired the name 'Santorini' after the long-dead saint), finally gaining its freedom in 1821. However, it was a rather peculiar form of freedom: the embryonic Greek state not only brought back 'Thira' as the island's official name, but re-established its use as a home for political prisoners, a state of affairs that lasted until WW2.

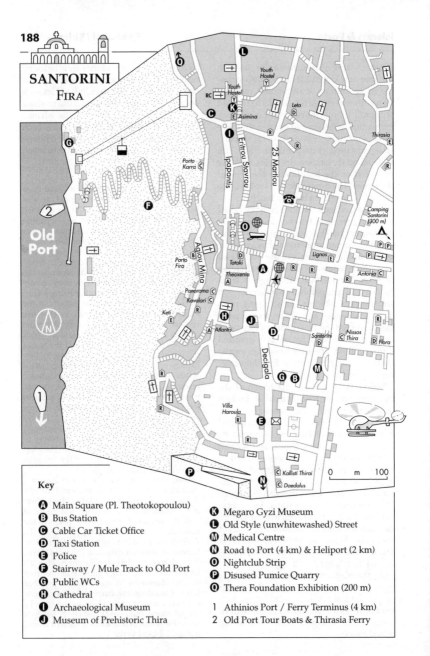

SANTORINI

FIRA

Old Port

Key

Ⓐ Main Square (Pl. Theotokopoulou)

Ⓑ Bus Station

Ⓒ Cable Car Ticket Office

Ⓓ Taxi Station

Ⓔ Police

Ⓕ Stairway / Mule Track to Old Port

Ⓖ Public WCs

Ⓗ Cathedral

Ⓘ Archaeological Museum

Ⓙ Museum of Prehistoric Thira

Ⓚ Megaro Gyzi Museum

Ⓛ Old Style (unwhitewashed) Street

Ⓜ Medical Centre

Ⓝ Road to Port (4 km) & Heliport (2 km)

Ⓞ Nightclub Strip

Ⓟ Disused Pumice Quarry

Ⓠ Thera Foundation Exhibition (200 m)

1 Athinios Port / Ferry Terminus (4 km)

2 Old Port Tour Boats & Thirasia Ferry

⊨

The supply of beds dries up early in High Season on Santorini. Even if you arrive on the first of the Piraeus morning boats (berthing around 15.00), you could have to settle for a night in a campsite or hostel before finding something more to your taste. The more expensive hotels tend to lie on the caldera rim (if you choose to stay in one, it pays to forget both your bank balance and the fact that when the last earthquake struck most of the rim-side buildings ended up a lot nearer sea level than they were before). Top of the range, and a landmark in its own right, is the chunky A-class *Atlantis* (☎ 22232) near the cathedral. Nearby lies the B-class *Porto Fira* (☎ 22849). To the north of this is the C-class *Porto Karra* (☎22 979), while two more C-class hotels lie up the slope: the *Panorama* (☎ 22481) and *Kavalari* (☎ 22455).

The east side of Fira Town offers the best prospect of finding a bed in High Season, with a number of 'cheaper' hotels. These include the C-class *Nissos Thira* (☎ 23252) and *Antonia* (☎ 22879), the D-class *Santorini* (☎ 22593) and *Flora* (☎ 81524), and the E-class *Lignos* (☎ 23 101) and *Thirasia* (☎ 22546). The road to the campsite is also worth trying, as it is lined with pensions. Other hotels lie to the south of the town, including the C-class *Kallisti Thirai* (☎ 22317) and the *Daedalus* (☎ 22834). More hotels are being built to the south, overlooking the ugly old pumice quarry — pretty desperate stuff. The cable-car area of town also has a number of cheaper establishments. These include three youth hostels — the *Youth Hostel* (☎ 22722) on Eritrou Stavrou being easiest to find — and the E-class *Asimina* (☎ 22034). Inland the D-class *Leta* (☎ 22540) stands near the main road. A final option is to head for the village of **Karterados**, which mops up the tourist overspill at the cost of a thirty-minute walk into town.

Perissa is also popular, with two large hostels on the outskirts of town. There are also plenty of pensions and small hotels offering

relatively cheap beds. These include the E-class *Meltemi* (☎ 81325), *Boubis* (☎ 81202), and *Marousiana* (☎ 81124) on the main road. Rather more up-market is the D-class *Marianna* (☎ 81286), complete with pool.

Kamari has fewer non-pre-booked beds on offer, and outlets offering rooms are decidedly thin on the ground. The better bets here are the C-class *Arkis* (☎ 31670) and *Adonis* (☎ 31956), the D-class *Blue Sea* (☎ 31481) and *Andreas* (☎ 31692), and the E-class *Dionysos* (☎ 31310). Other towns with hotels and rooms include **Oia** — complete with a good youth hostel: *Youth Hostel Oia* (☎ 71465) — and **Pirgos** on the road to the port.

Δ

There are three campsites on Santorini; most have mini-buses meeting ferries:

Camping Santorini (☎ 22944) lies down the hill from Fira Town, and is easily the most convenient if you want to be close to the island's transportation hub and nightlife. The site has a small swimming pool, a small but good mini-market — that even sells international newspapers — and reasonable tree cover. Prices are typical for Santorini (i.e. €2 more expensive than sites on Paros but still cheaper than Mykonos).

Perissa Beach Camping (☎ 81343) is an equally expensive and crowded beach site right in the centre of Perissa. The camping entrance also seems to act as a general information centre. With a fair amount of tree cover, the site is great if you want to stagger straight from bar to sea via a tent. The downside is the noise level and the salt-water showers.

Caldera View Camping (☎ 82010), outside the village of Akrotiri. The site has a swimming pool and new facilities; it also has a large number of bungalows that provide the bulk of the site's income. On the wrong side of the road to actually have a 'view' of the caldera and too far from the island's beaches or nightlife, this site is struggling to attract campers.

≋☆

Radiating out from Fira's main square are a profusion of bars and clubs that have one characteristic in common — they are all expensive. As Santorini will make a huge hole in your pocket you could do worse than dance in one; the *Tithora Club*, near the top of the port stairway, offers a dance floor in an old pumice cave and troglodyte male dancers. There are also three large discos/clubs in town: the *Dionysos*, the *Enigma* and the *Koo Club* — all are located in the nightstrip area just to the north-west of the main town square. Popular bars in Fira include the *Blue Note* (a bar turned disco also near the main square) and the very expensive *Tropical* (on the caldera rim).

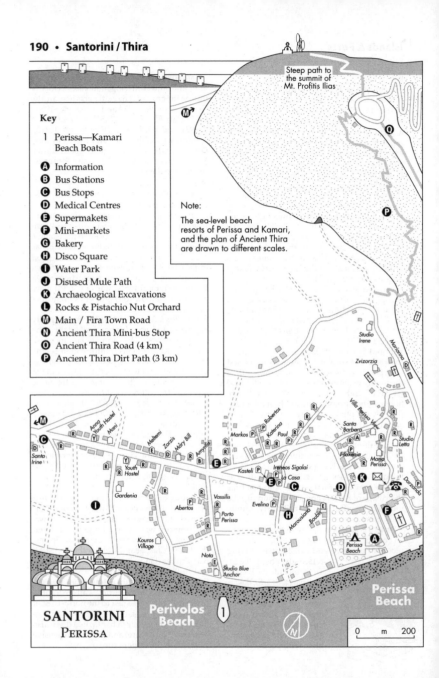

Steep path to
the summit of
Mt. Profitis Ilias

Key

1   Perissa—Kamari
     Beach Boats

A   Information
B   Bus Stations
C   Bus Stops
D   Medical Centres
E   Supermakets
F   Mini-markets
G   Bakery
H   Disco Square
I   Water Park
J   Disused Mule Path
K   Archaeological Excavations
L   Rocks & Pistachio Nut Orchard
M   Main / Fira Town Road
N   Ancient Thira Mini-bus Stop
O   Ancient Thira Road (4 km)
P   Ancient Thira Dirt Path (3 km)

Note:

The sea-level beach
resorts of Perissa and Kamari,
and the plan of Ancient Thira
are drawn to different scales.

SANTORINI
PERISSA

Perivolos
Beach

Perissa
Beach

0   m   200

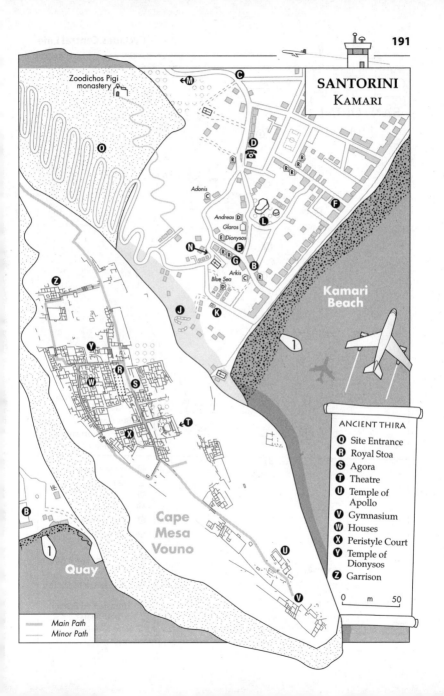

SANTORINI
KAMARI

Zoodichos Pigi
monastery

Kamari
Beach

Cape
Mesa
Vouno

Quay

Adonis C
Andreas D
Glaros E
Dionysos E
Arkis C
Blue Sea D

ANCIENT THIRA

Q Site Entrance
R Royal Stoa
S Agora
T Theatre
U Temple of
Apollo
V Gymnasium
W Houses
X Peristyle Court
Y Temple of
Dionysos
Z Garrison

0   m   50

Main Path
Minor Path

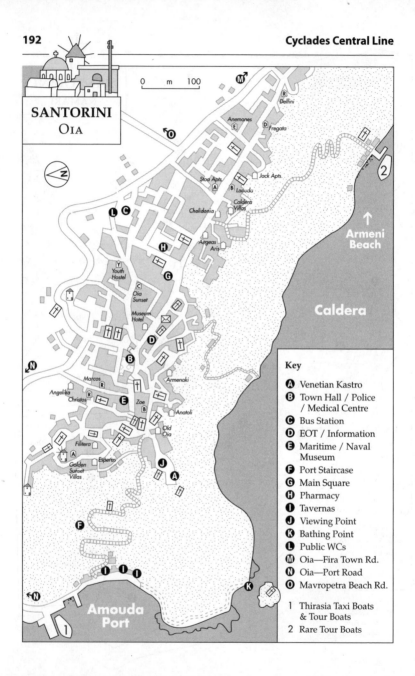

SANTORINI
OIA

0   m   100

Delfini
Anemones
Fregata
Jack Apts.
Stoa Apts.
Laouda
Chelidonia
Caldera Villas
Aegeas Aris
Youth Hostel
Oia Sunset
Museum Hotel
Marcos
Angolika
Christos
Zoe
Armenaki
Anatoli
Old Oia
Filitera
Esperas
Golden Sunset Villas

Armeni Beach

Caldera

Amouda Port

Key
- Ⓐ Venetian Kastro
- Ⓑ Town Hall / Police / Medical Centre
- Ⓒ Bus Station
- Ⓓ EOT / Information
- Ⓔ Maritime / Naval Museum
- Ⓕ Port Staircase
- Ⓖ Main Square
- Ⓗ Pharmacy
- Ⓘ Tavernas
- Ⓙ Viewing Point
- Ⓚ Bathing Point
- Ⓛ Public WCs
- Ⓜ Oia—Fira Town Rd.
- Ⓝ Oia—Port Road
- Ⓞ Mavropetra Beach Rd.

1   Thirasia Taxi Boats & Tour Boats
2   Rare Tour Boats

Santorini Taxi Boat

Caldera View from
Oia/Ia

**SANTORINI
/THIRA**

Athinios
Port

Oia/Ia Town
(with Santorini's charateristic
anti-earthquake barrel-vaulted
houses)

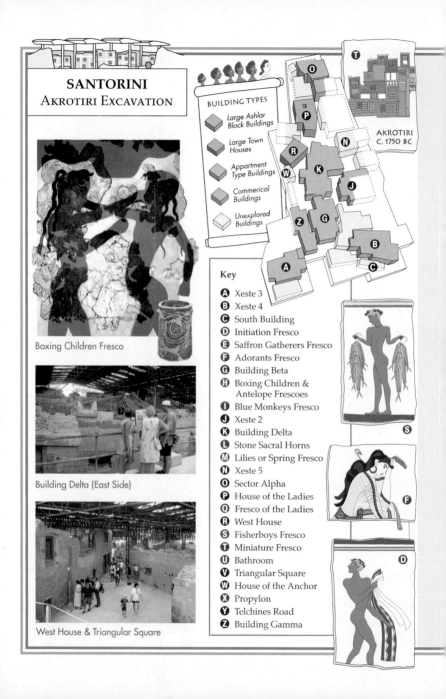

SANTORINI
AKROTIRI EXCAVATION

Boxing Children Fresco

Building Delta (East Side)

West House & Triangular Square

BUILDING TYPES

Large Ashlar Block Buildings

Large Town Houses

Appartment Type Buildings

Commerical Buildings

Unexplored Buildings

AKROTIRI C. 1750 BC

Key

- **A** Xeste 3
- **B** Xeste 4
- **C** South Building
- **D** Initiation Fresco
- **E** Saffron Gatherers Fresco
- **F** Adorants Fresco
- **G** Building Beta
- **H** Boxing Children & Antelope Frescoes
- **I** Blue Monkeys Fresco
- **J** Xeste 2
- **K** Building Delta
- **L** Stone Sacral Horns
- **M** Lilies or Spring Fresco
- **N** Xeste 5
- **O** Sector Alpha
- **P** House of the Ladies
- **Q** Fresco of the Ladies
- **R** West House
- **S** Fisherboys Fresco
- **T** Miniature Fresco
- **U** Bathroom
- **V** Triangular Square
- **W** House of the Anchor
- **X** Propylon
- **Y** Telchines Road
- **Z** Building Gamma

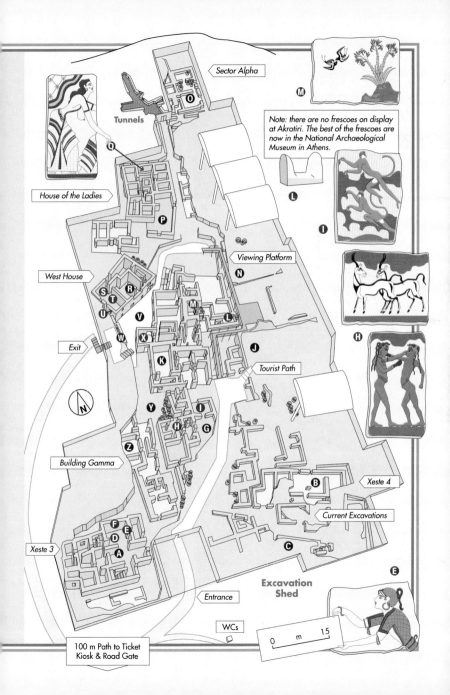

Sector Alpha

Note: there are no frescoes on display at Akrotiri. The best of the frescoes are now in the National Archaeological Museum in Athens.

Tunnels

House of the Ladies

West House

Viewing Platform

Exit

Tourist Path

Building Gamma

Xeste 4

Current Excavations

Xeste 3

Excavation Shed

Entrance

WCs

0 m 15

Panagia Evangelistra Church
TINOS

SANTORINI/THIRA
Views of the Volcano
(Kameni Islands)

SYROS
Ermoupolis

Cyclades

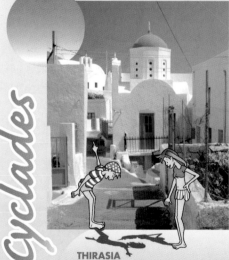

THIRASIA
Busy Main Street in August

The whole 'Thira' archipelago is one vast tourist attraction, and there is sufficient sightseeing to fill a good four days, though tour buses — all taking in the inevitable winery — manage to cram a lot into a few hours. The highlights (not necessarily in their pecking order) are:

1. Ancient Thira.

The remains of the Hellenistic capital (known as Ancient Thira) on the headland between Perissa and Kamari.

2. Museum of Prehistoric Thira (p. 194).

One of the most important museums in the Greek islands, and a good introduction to the archaeological discoveries on Santorini.

3. The Akrotiri Excavation (p. 194).

One of the most important archaeological sites in the world.

4. The Volcano / Kameni Islands (p. 200).

The most visually impressive sight in the Greek islands.

In addition to the above, there are a number of 'lesser' sights that would still merit star status were they to be located on any other Greek island. **Fira** is home to several of these. First and foremost is the **Thera Foundation Exhibition** in the Petros M. Nomikos Center (the main caldera-view street north of the cable car has a number of signs pointing the way: these take you to steps up to a large terraced building, just with the exhibition entrance tunnel located just behind). Housed in a series of whitewashed tunnel-linked galleries cut into the pumice, the Foundation has an excellent exhibition of three-dimensional life-size reproductions of **'The Wall-paintings of Thera'** (€3). At first sight a display of fresco copies wouldn't seem to be much of a draw, but the quality of the computer-derived reproduction is fantastic, with every last bump and scratch reproduced in detail. All the major frescoes reassembled to date are reproduced. Even with the opening of the Museum of Prehistoric Thira, the Foundation display remains the best place to appreciate these art works, and the only place where you can see an ensemble of all the frescoes in one location.

Fira also has two more museums: first, the old **Archaeological Museum**. This is filled with post-Minoan artifacts and is rather disappointing: the lack of star exhibits and tired displays make it no match for the state-of-the-art Museum of Prehistoric Thira. Second, there is also a privately run town museum — known as the **Megaro Gyzi** — which is a repository for

odds and ends. Its most interesting exhibits are unlabelled photos of the pre-1956 earthquake town. The northern town of **Oia** also has a good, if small, **Nautical Museum** (open ②–⑦ 12.30–16.00, 17.00–20.30), complete with a number of 19 c. ships' figureheads.

Ancient Thira

Santorini has such a wealth of volcanic and prehistorical material to look at that anything dating from the historical period is apt to be treated rather casually. In fact, the island has some of the best-preserved Archaic to Roman era remains in the Aegean.

A few centuries after the eruption that destroyed the Minoan settlement on Santorini, the fertile volcanic soils brought colonizing Doric Greeks to the island. The new centre emerged on the east coast, on the easily defendable high headland north of Perissa (see map on p. 191), and the remains of the town (dating from the Archaic to the Roman era) can be explored. The site has yet to be fully excavated; the exposed remains mainly consist of nondescript foundations and a poorly preserved theatre. As a result, ancient Thira is more of scenic than archaeological merit. Its main attractions are a number of very faint carvings of an erotic (well, okay, 'porno') nature on some of the buildings, and, on the headland, an early Archaic temple of Apollo that has a ground plan more in common with a house. There is also an agora, a stoa and the remains of several large Hellenistic houses.

The site is open ⑥ ex ① 09.00–15.00 (last admissions at 14.30). One word of warning: although the site closes at 15.00 it is advisable to depart a good 15 minutes before this, as the caretaker takes care of stray tourists by unleashing a couple of large Rottweilers. Being chased across a hilltop peninsula through the remains of a Hellenistic town by a ferocious dog is certainly a holiday experience you won't forget in a hurry, although you will certainly leave the site in one.

Expensive mini-buses run to Ancient Thira from Kamari. Given this, it isn't very surprising that the site is a popular destination for island walkers, along with nearby Mt. Profitis Ilias, which is topped by a radar station and monastery.

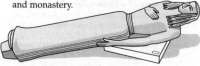

Museum of Prehistoric Thira

Standing by Fira Town taxi station, and built to house the finds from the Akrotiri excavation, this new museum joined the tourist map in 2000. Open ②–⑦ 08.30–15.00 (entrance fee is €3: tickets, from the separate building inside the museum grounds, include entry to Fira's regular Archaeological Museum), it is set to become one of the most important museums in Greece. Although it is not particularly large, the quality of the exhibits and the detailed explanatory texts is very high, and it is easy for even the uninitiated to spend the best part of an hour taking in the displays: the museum offers a superb introduction to the Akrotiri site and the pre-eruption island.

One of the few gripes one can make about the museum is its confusing entrance. Visitors are expected to turn left on entering (from a door on the caldera-rim side of the building) to read the explanatory text on the discovery of Akrotiri and then, ignoring the alluring glimpse of frescoes and gold further on, turn back and go around the galleries in an anti-clockwise direction. The first exhibits pre-date the city of Akrotiri and therefore aren't, at first sight, particularly interesting. However, there are important gems to be found here. Not least of these are the **Cycladic Idols**. The examples here are unusual in (a) being carved out of local pumice rather than marble, and (b) possessing 'male' attributes: until recently only female idols had been recovered from excavated sites. Male figures of unknown provenance had appeared via the black market, but given the large number of fake idols in circulation, it was unclear if any were genuine.

Having dispensed with pre-Minoan era culture in a few cases, the museum soon gets down to the serious business of displaying the Akrotiri artefacts. To set the scene it starts with a large **Model of the Excavations**. This leads on into a number of gallery sections devoted to various aspects of life in the town. The first of these deals with day-to-day household items. Highlights of these first display cases are the **Plaster Cast of a Three-Legged Table** (as at Pompeii, wooden artefacts from Akrotiri are 'recovered' by pouring plaster into holes that appear in the volcanic ash — the original wood having long since disintegrated) and a small

Clay Oven (both illustrated top right opposite). Nearby is a large **Bathtub** that is much more 'pot'-like than its Knossos counterpart (compare the illustration on this page with that on p. 348). This gallery leads into exhibits on writing and painting — including some of the famous **Pithoi (Jars)**. This in turn naturally leads into the frescoes. Unfortunately, only a few are on display: the best come from two rooms in the **House of the Ladies**, and include the famous **Ladies Fresco** and the less interesting **Lilies Fresco**.

Further fresco fragments (including one showing an African figure) are scattered through the rest of the museum, which hereafter focuses on pottery. Because Akrotiri was abandoned by its inhabitants prior to the eruption, smaller or valuable items (pottery excepted) are rare. A notable exception is a 10 cm long snub-nosed **Gold Ibex Figurine**: recovered from the site in December 1999, it takes pride of place as the climax to the museum display.

The Akrotiri Excavation

Nestling in an undistinguished ravine that runs down to the sea beyond Akrotiri village lies the Pompeii-like Minoan town (map between pages 192–193) that has elevated Santorini to the top of the archaeological world map. A complete town buried by the ash and pumice from the massive eruption that blew the pre-Santorini island apart, Akrotiri is a sightseeing 'must' — even though the accessible area is quite small and can be viewed in half an hour. Buses run direct to the site from Fira Town. Currently closed (see below), former opening times were: ②–⑦ 08.30–15.00; the entrance fee: €5 (reduced to €3 until the new roof work is complete).

Akrotiri Excavation Closure

On the 23rd of September 2005 a British tourist was killed, and a further five tourists were seriously injured, when part of the futuristic glass and steel 'bio-climatic shelter' being built over the Akrotiri ruins collapsed, prompting the immediate closure of the site. At the time of this book's going to press it was unclear when the site would reopen, but it could well remain closed throughout 2012. Information on the latest situation can be found on this book's website.

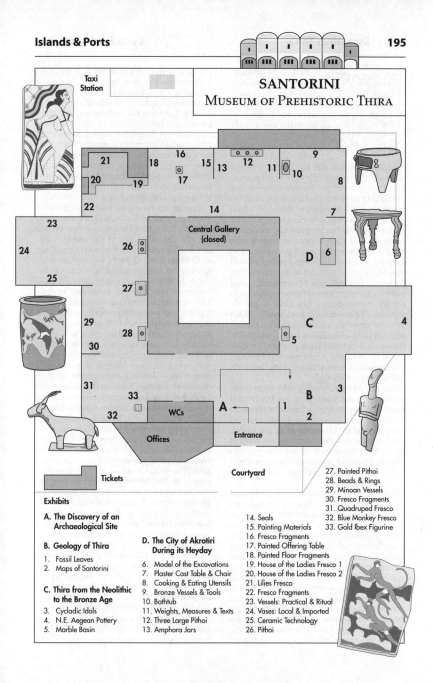

SANTORINI
MUSEUM OF PREHISTORIC THIRA

Taxi Station

Central Gallery (closed)

Entrance

Courtyard

WCs

Offices

Tickets

Exhibits

A. The Discovery of an Archaeological Site

B. Geology of Thira
1. Fossil Leaves
2. Maps of Santorini

C. Thira from the Neolithic to the Bronze Age
3. Cycladic Idols
4. N.E. Aegean Pottery
5. Marble Basin

D. The City of Akrotiri During its Heyday
6. Model of the Excavations
7. Plaster Cast Table & Chair
8. Cooking & Eating Utensils
9. Bronze Vessels & Tools
10. Bathtub
11. Weights, Measures & Texts
12. Three Large Pithoi
13. Amphora Jars

14. Seals
15. Painting Materials
16. Fresco Fragments
17. Painted Offering Table
18. Painted Floor Fragments
19. House of the Ladies Fresco 1
20. House of the Ladies Fresco 2
21. Lilies Fresco
22. Fresco Fragments
23. Vessels: Practical & Ritual
24. Vases: Local & Imported
25. Ceramic Technology
26. Pithoi

27. Painted Pithoi
28. Beads & Rings
29. Minoan Vessels
30. Fresco Fragments
31. Quadruped Fresco
32. Blue Monkey Fresco
33. Gold Ibex Figurine

Part of the pleasure of visiting Akrotiri is that the 35-century-old site is still under excavation. Archaeologists are slowly unearthing an incredible Minoan town, with all the attributes of high civilization that have come to be the hallmark of this remarkable pre-Greek people. These range from the humble street drains (that didn't appear elsewhere in the Mediterranean for a millennium) and inside WCs (that weren't a feature in European homes until a century ago) to the surprisingly modernist appearance of their houses (equipped with large windows and central light wells). Most amazing of all are the large number of wall frescoes — most reduced to fragments that have to be painstakingly reassembled — that exhibit a spontaneity and freshness that seem wholly contemporary (an illusion greatly enhanced by the boxing boys fresco, which depicts two pubescent naked youths sporting Michael Jackson lookalike hairstyles). Sadly, almost all of the better known frescoes on view are in the National Archaeological Museum in Athens, but even without them the site is still impressive enough.

Because Akrotiri is still under excavation, tourists are confined to a predetermined route that runs though a couple of streets of the town. Some 10,000 m² of the site has now been excavated. Estimates as to the town's size range from 30,000 to 200,000 m². Neither the harbour (thought to lie in a now pumice-filled inlet west of the current excavation) nor any overtly public buildings (if they exist) have been unearthed.

Discovered in 1967, the site was the reward for years of searching. Following the discovery of the Minoan civilization (with the excavation of the palaces on Crete) archaeologists were increasingly wont to ask why they were finding palaces and villas but nothing resembling towns or commercial centres. Their absence implied that they must have existed elsewhere in the Aegean and attention turned to possible sites, notably to Santorini where, in 1867, a fresco-filled house had been uncovered and subsequently lost. Akrotiri came to light thanks to its location in a ravine; the stream that formed it eroded the layers of pumice to reveal evidence of buildings beneath. Once a

prospering 16 C. BC town that — if the street plan revealed to date is typical — looked similar to Greek island choras today, it was abandoned (probably thanks to early earthquakes that were the harbinger of the main eruption) by its inhabitants a couple of decades prior to the explosion that ripped the heart out of the island. Covered by layers of volcanic ash, the quake-damaged buildings, some several storeys high, have been preserved. Frescoes aside, the houses have limited contents, as the townsfolk had time to hurriedly collect valuables when they abandoned their homes.

On entering the excavation shed, you arrive in an open area from which a path runs north along the line of the former stream that exposed the site. On either side of the entrance you can see the remains of two major buildings — **Ⓐ Xeste 3** and **Ⓑ Xeste 4** — that are often ignored by tourists heading for the ticket check. In fact, both are examples of the most important building type uncovered to date. They are large mansions with ashlar block façades, and notable for possessing removable interior wooden panel walls in the major front rooms along with 'lustral basins', which appear to have had some religious use. **Xeste 4** has only been partially excavated (work stopped in 1974, when Professor Marinatos — Akrotiri's discoverer — died in a wall collapse, has now resumed). A further house at **Ⓒ**, known as the **South Building**, has also yet to be explored. All these buildings appear to have major frescoes within them. Indeed, **Xeste 3** (the only one completely excavated to date) has provided the richest haul of frescoes recovered from one building. These include the **Monkey Musician Fresco** (depicting blue monkeys — a sacred animal in Minoan art — playing lyres and pipes), **Ⓓ The Initiation Fresco** (portraying youths preparing for a coming-of-age ritual), **Ⓔ The Saffron Gatherers Fresco** (showing young girls picking blooms) and **Ⓕ The Adorants Fresco** (which depicts a number of young women and a 'Demeter-like' mother-earth goddess).

Once you pass the ticket check you arrive at **Ⓖ Building Beta**. Badly damaged by the stream, it is an example of the second type of building uncovered, being a large structure filled with small rooms. The layout and the lack of kitchen facilities (there is usually only one per block) suggest that the inhabitants lived in a communal, rather than family, unit. These houses appear to represent the lowest housing rank. They did, however, have frescoed rooms like the other buildings, and Building Beta has provided us with several of the best known Akrotiri frescoes: the **Boxing Children and Antelope Frescoes**, and the **Blue Monkeys Fresco**. At the end of this structure the path arrives at a small square and **Xeste 2**, a third (unexplored) ashlar block mansion.

From this point, tourists have to walk along a viewing platform that runs past the central area of the excavation. This is dominated by the block at known as **Building Delta**. Easily identified by the **Stone Sacral Horns** now sitting on the wall beside the walkway (they are believed to have once adorned the top of the building), this is another of the communal-living-type buildings. Within it archaeologists discovered the almost complete **Lilies** (or **Spring**) **Fresco**, depicting a landscape of lilies and swallows. The swallows provide a poignant insight into the changed conditions on the island, for Santorini is now one of the few Aegean islands not to see swallows nesting in the summer (the dry volcanic ash isn't adhesive enough for them to build their mud nests), though they do still wistfully fly around looking for suitable sites. To the east of Building Delta are the tops of the walls of the unexplored building **Xeste 5** at .

At the end of the viewing platform the path turns west, taking you past the northern section of the site. Currently roped off, it is inaccessible to tourists beyond tiptoe views. Following the line of the former torrent bed, this open area leads to , the most northerly part of the excavation. Known as **Sector Alpha**, it is the site of a **Pithos Storehouse** several storeys high, and apparently some kind of communal food warehouse or shop. It marks the spot where digging commenced at Akrotiri in 1967, and where the first fresco fragments were found. These include a fragment showing a North African man and a palm tree, and a swallow fragment (illustrated below). Just visible at stands the **House of the Ladies**. An important town house (it is the only building so far discovered with a light well), it has yielded up the **Fresco of the Ladies** (depicting some well-endowed women robing a lost figure), and the **Papyrus Fresco** (deftly painted with yellows, blues and reds, as the painters of the Akrotiri frescoes had no green pigments at their disposal). This fresco suggests trade links with Egypt, as this plant is not native to Greece. Unfortunately, the House of the Ladies

looks a bit of a mess because, in the eruption, the ground storey collapsed, the upper floor falling on top of it.

After running past the northern façade of Building Delta (notable for having a stairwell filled with 'karate-chopped' stairs), the tourist path turns south-west, following the path of one of the ancient town's streets now known as the **Telchines Road**. On the opposite side of the path to the Building Delta stairs is a small pithos display against the wall of the **West House**. Along with the House of the Ladies, this is an example of the third type of building on the site, being a large independent town house for the middle rank of Akrotiri society (though again interpretations differ as — judging by the contents — the large upstairs window belonged to a 'weaving room'; this suggests some commercial activity was taking place in the building). Smaller than the ashlar-block mansion type, this house was nonetheless well adorned with frescoes, yielding up , the famous **Fisherboys**, and the tapestry-like river and nautical festival scenes on the **Miniature Fresco**. This narrow strip fresco is of particular importance as it appears to be a pictorial narrative of a voyage between four towns (ending at Akrotiri itself). Its information on the ships and houses of the period is invaluable and unique. Another unique feature of the West House — though it is not possible to see this wonder — is the upstairs bathroom at (complete with a latrine connected to a pipe running down inside the external wall). This led to a mains drain under the **Triangular Square**. This is the most impressive part of the site, thanks to the height of the buildings.

The tourist path formerly ended at the Triangular Square (the exit stairs ran up over the unexcavated **House of the Anchor**), but while the roof rebuilding is going on tourists get to see more of the site as they now have to follow the path through the **Propylon**, or entrance hall, of Building Delta, and then down , the Telchines Road to the so-called **Mill-House Square** (this is another of the tiny open areas that appear to have played an important part in the ancient town's life). From this square, the street narrows, running between Building Beta and a similar type of building at : **Building Gamma**. Still only partly excavated (only the street-side area has been explored), this structure has also yielded up its first fresco fragments.

the story of **Atlantis** and **Santorini?**
Listen, then, Socrates to a tale, which, though strange, is certainly true...

The Atlantis Legend

You can't travel far around Santorini without coming across claims that the island is the site of Atlantis. The problem is, almost any lost civilization — and certainly sunken city — has the same claims made for it too, with the more ardent Atlantis theorists embracing everyone from Hawaii to visiting aliens from bizarre worlds similar to their own. The trouble with the Atlantis mystery is that it is too attractive to clear up. The problem for the alien lovers is that serious scholars are increasingly inclined to stamp this particular X-file 'SOLVED'.

The Atlantis story is briefly this: There once was a mighty maritime civilization that ruled the waves and many islands as far as Egypt and Italy. Over the generations they became extremely wealthy, building the great island city of Metropolis, and hunting bulls in its temple precincts. But greed and a lust for power overtook their rulers, angering the gods, who undertook retribution by sinking both the people and city into the sea which 'disappeared in one terrible day and night'.

In fact, the Atlantis tale, although it sounds like the stuff of Greek myth, isn't Greek at all — but is an old Egyptian story. Who the old Egyptian was who told it isn't known, but the philosopher Plato says that the tale was spun to the Athenian leader Solon on a visit to Egypt c.590 BC, while he was being ribbed about the Greeks being a new people, lacking a long written historical tradition and ignorant of their ancestry. On his return, Solon is said to have repeated the tale to Plato's great-grandfather, and it was passed down thereafter as a family story. Plato used it in two of his written educational dialogues. There is a brief account in *Timaeus* (c.350 BC) and an implausibly detailed fragment in the uncompleted *Critias* (c.340 BC).

Plato's Contribution

Although Plato preserved the story, he also clearly added a number of red herrings. Not least of these is that he was using the tale to make philosophical points, almost certainly distorting details to that end. Certainly any Egyptian names have been replaced with appropriate Greek ones ('Atlantis' and 'Metropolis' cannot have been part of the original tale).

Plato's better geographical and poorer historical knowledge than the original Egyptian storytellers also appear to have created further misconceptions. Atlantis was said to lie in the 'far west'. Plato naturally placed it in the Atlantic (the western limit of his world), but the term is relative to where one is and the world one knows (hence later attempts to locate Atlantis in the Americas and beyond). It is clear from other evidence that the limit of the known world for the inward-looking and desert-locked Egyptians 1,000 years before Solon's day extended no further west than Sicily at best (they knew of the pre-Greek Minoans, and called them the people of 'Keftiu').

Plato's weaker historical knowledge also prevented him from connecting the story with the local Minoan civilization. Thanks to the Dark Ages — the 350-year period in Greek history when the art of writing was forgotten — the Classical Greeks had no knowledge of the earlier Minoans beyond the garbled oral myth of King Minos and the Minotaur. Finally Plato's sense of time and his use of numbers is seriously awry. He describes Atlantis as 'larger than Africa and Asia' (though these terms only applied to the Mediterranean coastlines of each continent), dates the events as taking place 9,000 years before Solon's day, and gives detailed measurements for Metropolis. Interestingly, the Santorini eruption was just over 900 years before Solon's visit to Egypt, and similarly knocking zeros off the Metropolis figures produces an area close to that occupied by the Santorini volcano.

The Case for Minoan Santorini

Separating fact from fiction isn't easy with a tale like this: it is always dangerous to select favourable details to one's case while ignoring others that contradict it. However, within the whole there is enough corroborating detail to suggest that the Minoan civilization and its subsequent demise, following the Santorini eruption, is the basis of the Atlantis myth:

1. Even allowing for 900 years' worth of exaggeration, the latest geological models of the pre-c.1640 BC island are uncannily close to Plato's description of Metropolis. The 'island within an island' concept is unique to both this one story and this one location.

2. The existence of a city-topped island in the pre-c.1640 BC eruption caldera is supported by

the Miniature/Flotilla Fresco discovered at Akrotiri. This appears to show a substantial settlement covering an island lying within a cliff- and hill-backed lagoon.

3. Both Minoans and Atlantians were noted for having a highly advanced civilization characterized by opulent buildings with running water and baths, wide-ranging trade, a powerful fleet and a highly unusual bull cult that involved ritual activity with loose bulls in building precincts.

4. Both Minoan and Atlantian civilizations suffered catastrophic and rapid collapse following a natural disaster that involved an island disappearing.

5. Finally, Plato says that the concentric island rings of Metropolis had walls plated respectively with tin and bronze. The tin walls of the inner island were blown sky high in the eruption, but look across the Santorini caldera at sunset today, and it is surely clear to all but the meanest doubter that the walls of plated bronze are still standing, broken in parts, but otherwise (thanks to further eruptions) taller than ever.

ATLANTIS
METROPOLIS

1. Major Land Zone
2. Minor Land Zone
3. Citadel
   (with Temple & Royal Palace)
4. Wall Plated with Tin
5. Wall Plated with Bronze
6. Great Harbour
7. Second Harbour
8. Guard Towers
9. Mercantile Quarters
10. Great South Plain
11. Mountain to the North
    Protecting the Plain
12. Hills & Forests

SANTORINI
VOLCANO
HISTORY

(Text: p. 200)

30,000 BC — Crater

1,500,000 BC
Mt. Profitis Ilias
Pre-volcanic
Island
Kristina Is.
Eruption

15,000 BC — Caldera Forms

350,000 BC

1700 BC

200,000 BC — Crater

1650 AD — Kolombo Is. Eruption

Santorini before the c. 1640 BC Eruption

Note:
The numbers on this model indicate areas of similarity between Plato's 'Metropolis' and 1700 BC Santorini.

Akrotiri

Santorini Today (from the NW)

Fira

Minoan Akrotiri

Site of Second Minoan Settlement

SANTORINI 3D

Oia/Ia

The Volcano: 1. History

Santorini is one of the most intensely studied volcanoes in the world. Quite apart from having the largest caldera on earth, it is also one of the most explosive — sea water rushing into a crater of molten magma is always apt to cause a massive bang (in Santorini's case these occur roughly every 20,000 years).

Volcanic activity in the Santorini region isn't confined to the visible eruptive matter: as the Eurasian plate buckles (see: inside back cover) the earth's crust in this area is slowly cracking in a north-easterly direction. The prehistoric eruptions began with the formation of the Kristina islets 20 km to the south-west of Santorini (now only visible as faint rocks on the horizon from ferries heading to or from Crete). At that early time Santorini was a small non-volcanic island (this original island now forms Mt. Profitis Ilias). Thereafter volcanic activity moved to Santorini and stayed there. The slow movement north began again in 1650 when there was an eruption 7 km to the north-east of Santorini. This resulted in a volcanic cone rising up out of the sea. It survived just long enough to be named Kolombo (Columbus) island before disappearing back under the waves. Kolombo is now an underwater cone, with its summit some 17 m below sea level. Volcanologists believe it will one day reappear to form a permanent island between Ios and Santorini.

One important development to emerge from new studies of Santorini is a reassessment of the volcano's appearance prior to the c. 1640 BC eruption which did so much damage to the Minoans. Until recently it had been assumed that it would have looked similar to the high mountain cone of Krakatoa — another island volcano (albeit three times smaller) — which blew itself apart in 1883 with an explosion that was heard halfway around the globe. However, close examination of the caldera wall has shown that in many places it has a thin pre-eruption soil covered with pumice — indicating it had already formed when the c. 1640 BC eruption took place, and that the 'high mountain cone' phase of Santorini's life belonged to an earlier epoch.

The Volcano: 2. Kameni Islands

Since the c. 1640 BC eruption emptied the caldera bay, new islands (the 'Burnt Islands') have again risen out of the sea in subsequent eruptions. The largest, the volcano islet of **Nea**

Kameni (New Kameni), is a popular sight on the itineraries of all boat tours, though the sun-baked 20-minute walk along a cinder track can be a bit of a strain. Most tours don't give you time to wander off: the guides lead you direct to the main crater, walking at a pace which suggests that they know the time of the next eruption and don't want to hang around.

The objective of this route march is the **Georgios Crater**. It does nothing more than give off a bad smell from a number of steaming fumeroles, and is not the idyll that it seems from Santorini (where fake postcards are on sale depicting it as a glowing inferno). This said, excursions are good value for they offer a unique opportunity to walk over the cinder-black lava of a sleeping volcano. Visitors find a daunting, frying-pan-hot landscape lacking refreshment facilities (bring water) and vegetation (the only tree is on Palia Kameni).

Tour boats also call at the hot springs for a popular swim session in a narrow cove off the small and older island of **Palia Kameni**. The hot springs (for 'hot' read 'warm') offer those prepared to swim ashore the chance to wallow in a salty mud-bath. Those left on board get to view the spectacle of several hundred people splashing in a scene that looks like a rehearsal for a shot at the end of the *Titanic* movie.

Palia Kameni was the first island to emerge, in an eruption in 196 BC. A second briefly put in an appearance in 46 AD, before Mikri Kameni emerged in 1573. Nea Kameni appeared in 1711, was enlarged in the eruption of 1866–68 when the Georgios crater appeared, and was joined with Mikri Kameni in the 1925–26 eruption. As Santorini must be due for another one soon, you should note that before the last two, the waters around the islands turned a milky colour due to underwater sulphur emissions. If this phenomenon recurs, catching the next ferry to anywhere is a very good idea.

All **tour boat itineraries** visit Nea Kameni and the hot springs. There are three basic packages on offer: the Full Day Tour (09.15–18.20) costs €35 and takes in the works, including a sail round to Cape Akrotiri. The Caldera Round Trip (09.15–16.30) excludes this run and is better value at €20, while the two half-day burnt island (alias 'Volcano') trips — the first also taking in the hot springs (15.20–19.30); the second, the town of Oia (10.30–16.30) — are a more rushed €15. Students receive a 20% discount. Also note that tour tickets can be up to €3 cheaper at the port.

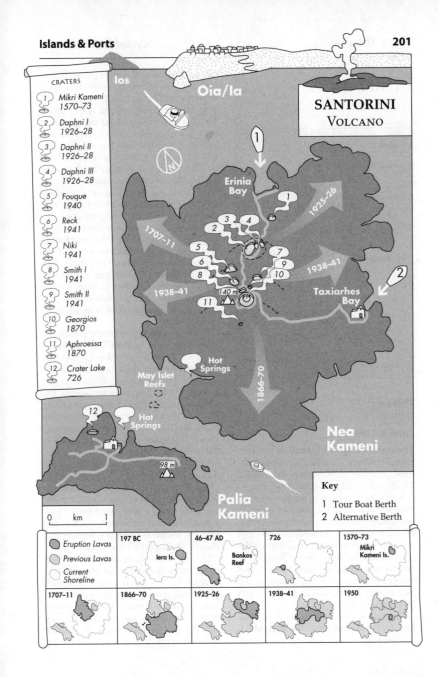

CRATERS

1. Mikri Kameni
   1570–73
2. Daphni I
   1926–28
3. Daphni II
   1926–28
4. Daphni III
   1926–28
5. Fouque
   1940
6. Reck
   1941
7. Niki
   1941
8. Smith I
   1941
9. Smith II
   1941
10. Georgios
    1870
11. Aphroessa
    1870
12. Crater Lake
    726

Ios

Oia/Ia

SANTORINI
VOLCANO

Erinia Bay

1925–26

1707–11

1938–41

1938–41

Taxiarhes Bay

140 m

Hot Springs

May Islet Reefs

1866–70

Nea Kameni

98 m

Hot Springs

Palia Kameni

Key

1 Tour Boat Berth
2 Alternative Berth

0   km   1

Eruption Lavas
Previous Lavas
Current Shoreline

197 BC — Iera Is.

46–47 AD — Bankos Reef

726

1570–73 — Mikri Kameni Is.

1707–11

1866–70

1925–26

1938–41

1950

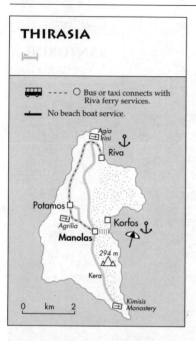

THIRASIA

🚌 ---- ○ Bus or taxi connects with Riva ferry services.

⚓ No beach boat service.

Agia Irini ⚓

Riva

Potamos

Agrilia

Manolas □ *Korfos* ⚓

294 m ⛰

Kera

Kimisis Monastery

0 — km — 2

Thirasia

ΘΗΡΑΣΙΑ; 9 km²; pop. 260.

CODE ☎ 22860

The second largest fragment of the pre-eruption island, Thirasia offers a blissfully quiet alternative to Santorini's crowds. The island — and particularly the chora — is a miniature version of Santorini before tourism swamped all. Thirasia owes its tranquillity to an earlier swamping, for the island was joined to northern Santorini until an eruption in 236 BC collapsed the land bridge between them. Without it, and lacking the good beaches that would encourage the development of the island as a tourist destination in its own right, Thirasia remains very quiet.

The only settlement of any size is perched high on the caldera rim at **Manolas**. Much smaller than Fira (of which it has views),

it is an irregular and stringy affair, ribboning along the caldera rim without a maze of backstreets behind. Its appeal lies in its size, for wandering around is to journey through an unspoilt island village rather than a tourist destination. Odd houses carved hobbit-like into the pumice cliffs and a couple of windmills simply add to its charm (Fira lost all its mills in the 1956 earthquake). Most visitors are day trippers who arrive via the caldera rim staircase (boasting the usual awkward steps and donkey transport), but beyond the existence of several tavernas in the town their impact is confined to the old port of **Korfos** tucked inside the northern wing of the caldera below Manolas. Little more than indifferent shingle beach backed by half a dozen tavernas and the odd shop, it is the usual destination for the small caldera tour boats as well as regular taxi-boats from Oia on Santorini.

Thirasia's second port is located in an isolated northern bay at **Riva**. This is the usual berth for the landing-craft ferry (that also doubles up as a caldera tour boat). Unfortunately, it isn't the most prepossessing of places with nothing on offer beyond the odd taverna, a string of houses and a dusty road; its only feature of note is a long pebble beach that is rendered all but unusable by the oil that mars it. The exposed quay is the usual home of the island bus that does little other than serve caldera tour parties during their brief sojourn on the island. Other boats are met by two 'truck-taxis' which shuttle between Riva and Manolas along the island's only paved road. Those who are hopping with empty pockets will find the walkable dirt track between the chora and the port a better option.

The rest of the island feels like the back of beyond and is scarred in places thanks to years of pumice quarrying. In fact much of Thirasia is now lining the banks of the Suez Canal, as it was a principal source of both materials and manpower. This activity also exposed some of the first 'Minoan' remains to be discovered in the archipelago (in 1869), alerting archaeologists to Santorini's potential. Unfortunately, the site has long since been lost. Tours try to make up for this by stopping at the diminutive hamlet of **Potamos** (home to an ugly multicoloured campaniled church) and at even smaller **Agrilia**.

┈

The only hotel on Thirasia, a purpose-built B-class affair complete with pool, closed for good in 2003. Clearly the lack of links between Thirasia and Santorini proved too great a handicap. As a result the only accommodation now on offer consists of High Season rooms at a couple of the town's tavernas.

⚭

Unless you stay on Thirasia you won't have time to take in more than the port and town. Those that do stay shouldn't miss the walk along the caldera rim to the southern tip and its 1851-built Kimisis monastery. Running from Manolas, the path passes through the abandoned pumice-cliff house village of **Kera**. Riva also has a 'sight': to the west of the bay is the church of **Agia Irini** — a structure of no great distinction, it is notable for giving neighbouring Santorini (literally 'Saint Irene') its Venetian name.

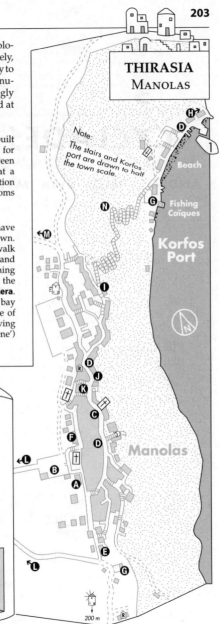

THIRASIA
MANOLAS

Note:
The stairs and Korfos port are drawn to half the town scale.

Beach

Fishing Caïques

Korfos Port

Manolas

0   m   100

Key

Ⓐ Town Hall
Ⓑ Riva Bus & Taxi Square
Ⓒ Cardphone & Medical Centre
Ⓓ Mini-market
Ⓔ Bakery & Pastry Shop
Ⓕ Pumice-Cliff Houses
Ⓖ Mule Stables
Ⓗ Tavernas
Ⓘ Restaurant Panorama
Ⓛ Nick's Restaurant
Ⓜ Candouni Restaurant
Ⓝ Manolas—Riva Road
Ⓞ Dirt Track to Riva Port
Ⓟ Stairway

1   Ferries / Tour Boats &
    Oia Taxi Boats

3
CYCLADES NORTH

ANDROS · DELOS · EVIA · MYKONOS · SYROS · TINOS

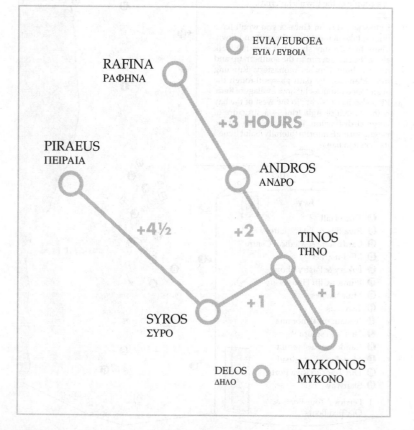

EVIA / EUBOEA
EYIA / EYBOIA

RAFINA
ΡΑΦΗΝΑ

+3 HOURS

PIRAEUS
ΠΕΙΡΑΙΑ

ANDROS
ΑΝΔΡΟ

+4½

+2

TINOS
ΤΗΝΟ

+1

SYROS
ΣΥΡΟ

+1

DELOS
ΔΗΛΟ

MYKONOS
ΜΥΚΟΝΟ

General Features

The Northern Cyclades line covers those Cycladic islands to the east of Piraeus and the 'Athenian' port of Rafina, and is served by daily boats from both. The islands lying along this line include the former Mecca of the Greek World — the tiny sacred island of Delos (birthplace of the God Apollo) — and its modern equivalent, the island of Tinos (home to the most important shrine of the Orthodox church in Greece). Delos lies, in theory if not in fact, at the centre of the Cyclades. While all the islands vary greatly in their characteristics, the one feature common to all is a tendency to be extremely windy. The *meltemi* 'hits' these Greek islands the hardest and they form something of a buffer for the rest of the Cyclades.

Cosmopolitan Mykonos and its satellite Delos remain the best-known islands on this line, the former being numbered among the most popular of all the Greek islands. Syros is often mentioned in older guidebooks as being the hub of the Cycladic ferry network, as its 19 c. commercial port of Ermoupolis is the formal capital of the group; however, the island has faded into relative obscurity and can now only boast half the number of ferry sailings of its southern neighbour Paros.

The remaining islands are very much oriented to Greek rather than international tourism. Andros and Evia (now little more than an extension of the Greek mainland) remain well off the beaten track. Tinos is less so, thanks to the constant stream of locals enjoying a spot of religious pilgrimage, and has hordes of little old ladies descending upon it to join the — mainly package — tourists at the height of the season for the feast of the Assumption of the Virgin Mary. As for Giaros, long famed as a place of exile, it has just been abandoned by the Greek military, and there are plans to open it to tourists at some point in the future.

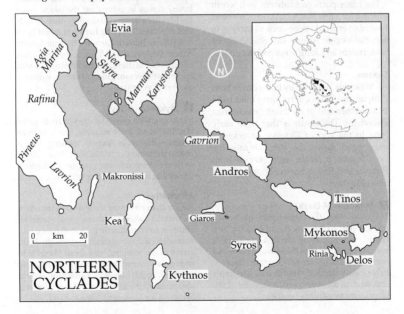

NORTHERN CYCLADES

Example Itinerary
[2 Weeks]

The two ferry routes running out of Piraeus and Rafina that meet at Mykonos combine to provide a nice island hopping circuit that is both easy and for the inexperienced reasonably safe. Boats are sufficiently frequent down both lines for you to be sure of a daily boat up and down at least one of the lines even out of High Season.

Arrival/Departure Point

There are two easy alternatives when visiting islands on this line: Athens and Mykonos. Athens is invariably the cheaper of the two, and with far more frequent flights into the bargain. You can do the loop easily from either base. Mykonos is chosen here as it offers a more relaxed start and end to a holiday and a pleasant alternative to arriving at and rushing back to Athens.

The other ports en route are well worth visiting for a few hours but you don't need to stay overnight to see such as there is to see; the loop to Athens can effectively be undertaken as a long weekend excursion.

Season

As Mykonos is served by boats out of both Piraeus and Rafina, ferry links tend to be better either end of the High Season than elsewhere. The result is that from early June to the end of October coverage is very good down the line. During the Low Season a single ferry service from Piraeus and Rafina normally operates on alternate days.

1 Mykonos [4 Days]

Mykonos offers the opportunity for a very relaxed start to a Greek island holiday. You can happily idle away the first few days of your stay with day trips to Delos and Paros and even Tinos if you want to cut corners later on. In between you can tilt at Mykonos windmills and start an all-over body tan on one of the island's many naturist beaches.

2 3 Tinos/Andros [1 Day]

If you take the daily 08.00 Mykonos—Rafina ferry to Tinos you'll arrive in time for a late breakfast. An interesting day stop, you can either stay overnight or have the option of picking up the afternoon boat to Andros (note: accommodation is thin on the ground there) or on to Rafina, where you can take an evening bus into Athens.

4 5 Rafina/Athens [4 Days]

If you are not tied to budget accommodation it will be to your advantage to pre-book your Athens hotel accommodation while on Mykonos via one of the ticket agents. It will be hard not to arrive in the capital at any other time than the evenings (hardly an ideal time to start hunting for your bed). Thereafter you will be free to explore at your own pace and adjust the length of your stay as your fancy takes you.

6 Syros [1 Day]

On the schedule of Piraeus—Mykonos ferries, Syros offers an interesting day out. The difficulty comes in getting off the island since the Mykonos link is usually only once daily. If you don't fancy staying here you might have to repair to Tinos or Paros for the night. After Athens you could find Syros something of an anticlimax; but the island does ensure that you appreciate how much nicer Mykonos is during the rest of your stay.

1 Mykonos [4 Days]

Returning with plenty of days to spare gives you the scope for a relaxing finish to your holiday (though in August 'relaxing' isn't a useful definition of Mykonos!). Not having to worry about missing your return flight is something not to be underestimated.

Alternative

Rather than returning via Syros, **Paros** offers an attractive alternative (or for that matter an addition to your itinerary). A stop here could necessitate a stay overnight — though, if you arrive in the morning, you should be able to pick up a catamaran or ferry on an evening run back to Mykonos. A Paros stop would also open up possible calls to Naxos, Ios and Santorini for those with time to hand.

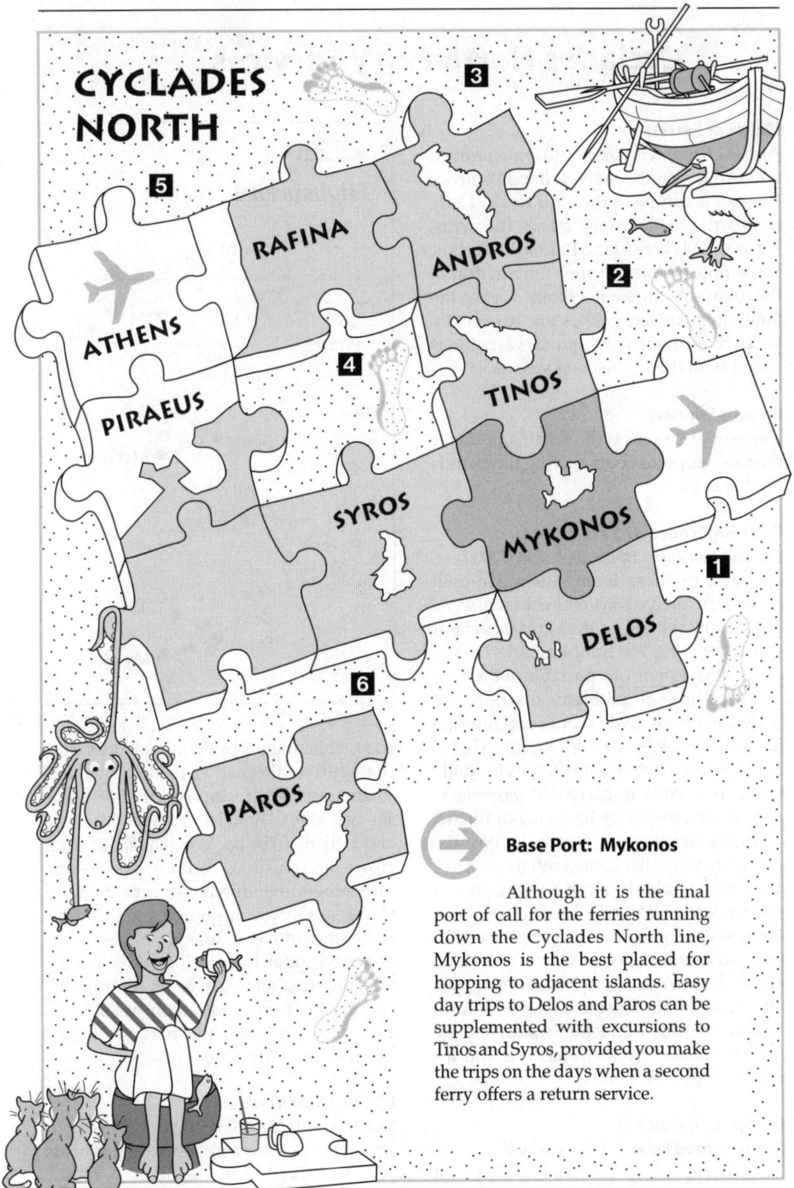

CYCLADES NORTH

5

3

RAFINA

ANDROS

2

ATHENS

PIRAEUS

4

TINOS

SYROS

MYKONOS

1

DELOS

6

PAROS

Base Port: Mykonos

Although it is the final port of call for the ferries running down the Cyclades North line, Mykonos is the best placed for hopping to adjacent islands. Easy day trips to Delos and Paros can be supplemented with excursions to Tinos and Syros, provided you make the trips on the days when a second ferry offers a return service.

Cyclades North Ferry Services

Main Car Ferries
Although the Cyclades North line is defined within this section as a single line, in practice it is not a complete through route. Daily ferries run both from Piraeus (to Syros, Tinos and Mykonos) and Rafina (to Andros, Tinos and Mykonos): the combination of the two sub-lines effectively forms the 'line'. Regular ferry times are reasonably well established; more annual variation is found with the high-speed vessels.

Piraeus Services
The port of Piraeus is the starting point for the most popular boats serving the islands on this line.

C/Ms *Highspeed 4 / 5 / 6*
Hellenic Seaways / HFD; 2004, 2005, 2000.
The first of these large Australian-built catamarans arrived on the Greek ferry scene in 2000, and initially offered great spectator sport watching the fumbling attempts to dock at Mykonos old port. Once the new port was built all problems disappeared. Now a mainstay of this route and offering fast journey times — with a top speed of 40 knots — the *Highspeed*s run a twice-daily round-trip. Able to carry 600 passengers and 70 cars, they have had a major impact as many locals seem happy to pay the premium fares that come with them. They are very popular in High Season, so it is advisable to book ahead. The *Highspeed*s are interchangeable and also operate on other lines, so it doesn't do to read too much into particular boat numbers. The morning and afternoon High Season departures from Piraeus are now well established. All three of these boats call at the port of Tourlos when visiting Mykonos.

C/F *SpeedRunner III*
Aegean Speed Lines; 1999; 4463 GRT.
One of the more low-key arrivals in

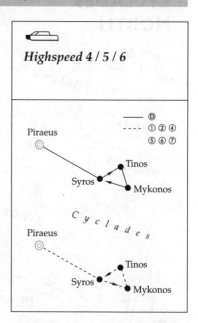

2009, this Italian-built vessel offered a competitive alternative to the *Highspeed* catamarans. With a top speed of 38 knots she was able to hold her own on this route and is likely to be back on it again in 2012. However, schedules could well see some futher bedding down, so expect minor changes. Out of High Season this boat sometimes moves onto other routes, as the preferred option for most local travellers are the *Highspeed* alternatives. A comfortable enough boat and reasonably reliable, in 2011 she was using the port of Tourlos when visiting Mykonos.

C/F *Blue Star Ithaki*
Blue Star/Strintzis; 2000; 16500 GRT.
One of the first of a new generation of boats built specifically for the Greek domestic

market, this ferry has been one of the most sought-after since her arrival in 2001. On-board facilities are first rate, with shiny escalators whisking passengers up to a well-equipped deck-class saloon, which boasts comfortable seating and a burger-bar franchise (a branch of *Goody's* — a popular local chain). Add to this the fact that the crew treat people like customers instead of unwelcome monkeys, and you have a large, smooth-sailing vessel that is one of the best domestic boats in Greece.

Her main itinerary — a morning run out of Piraeus to Syros, Tinos and Mykonos — is very well established, but during 2011 rumours emerged suggesting that she would be moved and would operate out of Rafina when the new Blue Star boats arrived on the Cyclades Central line. If she does go then you can expect one of the Blue Star boats below to take over, running much the same schedule. It operates most of the year, with just the addition of a few extra night runs to Paros in High Season. As with the other Blue Star boats, tickets cost 20% more than other (slower) regular ferries. In 2011 the *Blue Star Ithaki* was using the port of Tourlos when visiting Mykonos.

C/F *Blue Star Naxos* –
C/F *Blue Star Paros*
Blue Star/Strintzis; 2002; 16500 GRT.
Both these boats (see p. 132) are expected to move this year. There is persistent talk that one of them will take over from the *Blue Star Ithaki* above.

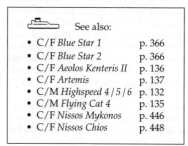

See also:

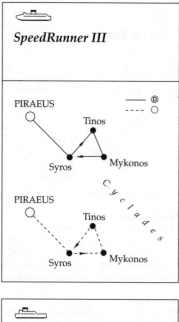

SpeedRunner III

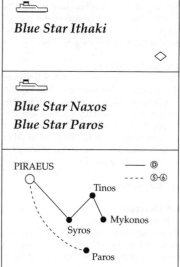

Blue Star Ithaki

Blue Star Naxos
Blue Star Paros

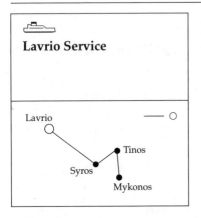

Lavrio Service

Lavrio ○

Tinos

Syros

Mykonos

Lavrio Service

There have been several attempts to run a service to the islands on this line out of the port of Lavrio over the last three years. The service wasn't operating in 2011, but it is worth a mention in case it reappears in 2012.

Rafina Services

The largest number of boats to the Cyclades North islands operate out of the port of Rafina. Customers are more likely to be locals rather than foreign tourists.

C/F *Blue Star* Service

One of the main players on this line over the last decade has been Blue Star Ferries. In anticipation of moving one of their other boats onto this route they sold the *Superferry II*, and then found themselves without a ferry running out of Rafina at all, as other boats couldn't be released because of a delay in the arrival of a new ferry elsewhere. The probability is that the *Blue Star Ithaki* will run this service in 2012.

C/F *Theologos P*
Fast Ferries; 2000; 4140 GRT.

This boat was the new arrival on the Rafina—Cyclades North route in 2007. A former Japanese ro-ro called *Ferry Kochi* (she still has some saloon and deck signs in

Japanese), she has been converted to take far more passengers and fewer vehicles. Unfortunately, the results are mixed — as is the case with all such conversions. She is certainly no match for properly designed passenger ferries when it comes to her layout and facilities, even though she is much newer than two of the boats on this line. In 2011 she docked at Tourlos when visiting Mykonos.

C/F *Superferry II*
Golden Star Ferries; 1974; 5052 GRT.

The second 'regular' ferry operating out of Rafina down the Cyclades North line is the *Superferry II*. Until last year she was a Blue Star boat, but she is now an independent. In the past this boat has been an escalator and a patisserie ahead of any of her rivals, but with the arrival of newer competitors she is suddenly looking her age. Even so, her open-deck plan is far in advance of much of the competition, and she feels ten years newer than boats such as the *Penelope A*, although she is barely two. This is a good boat, thanks to her large open-plan interior (the Rafina—Mykonos route is usually far too windy for comfortable sun-deck travel in High Season). Her change of ownership did result in itinerary variations in 2011 — most notably a very useful cross-line call at Naxos four days a week. In 2011 she docked at Tourlos when visiting Mykonos.

C/F *Penelope A*
Agoudimos Lines; 1972; 5109 GRT.

Formerly the flagship of Agoudimos Lines this boat has operated on this route since 1992, and it is difficult to see her moving elsewhere — though if a Blue Star boat appears on the line she would be the first candidate for the chop, given that the amount of competition she would face would probably be too much for her to survive. Formerly the cross-Channel *Horsa*, she is sister of the *Express Apollon* (now out of action) and the *Agios Georgios*, and, livery aside, looks identical. In 2011 she docked at Tourlos when visiting Mykonos.

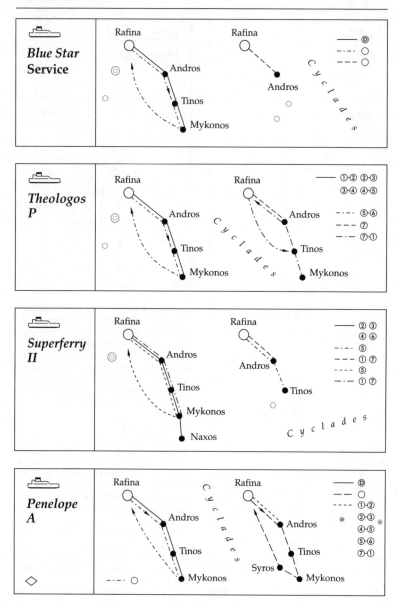

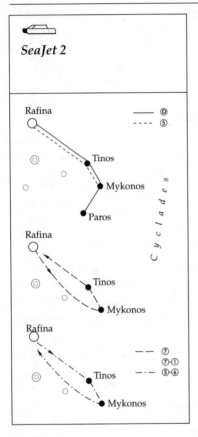

SeaJet 2

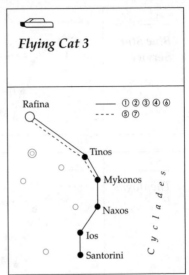

Flying Cat 3

minutes after you reach your destination). Like other small craft in this region she suffers in strong wind conditions, when she is usually confined to port. This is something of a handicap when it comes to reliability in the summer season: for this reason it is unwise to build an itinerary that *depends* on this boat turning up. It is best to buy tickets on your day of travel.

C/M *SeaJet 2*
SeaJets; 1995; 499 GRT.

The diminutive *SeaJet* 2 arrived in 1999, and has been a regular on this line ever since — though she has had occasional mishaps, most notably in 2003, when she crashed into the harbour breakwater at Tinos. This left her engine room flooded, but after a few months out of action she was back. Occasional floods of seawater aside, on-board conditions are generally good — provided you can live with the diet of TV movies (guaranteed to end 15

C/M *Flying Cat 3*
Hellenic Seaways / HFD

Moved from her traditional route between Thessalonika and Skiathos, the *Flying Cat* 3 has now spent four summers operating around the Cyclades. Initially based at Syros, she moved to Rafina last year, so further changes are possible in 2012 — particularly if one of the *Highspeed* catamarans resumes running a Rafina service. Her runs to Ios and Santorini were an innovation last year and she does curtail runs if seas are too high. Even so, as small cats go, this boat is one of the more stable, and most of the time the ride is very smooth.

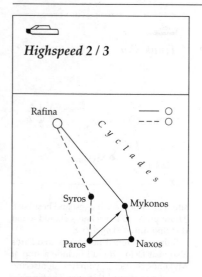

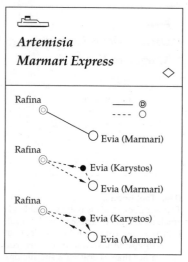

C/M *Highspeed 2 / 3*
Hellenic Seaways / HFD; 1996; 4480 GRT.
One inconsistent Hellenic Seaways cata-maran service that is worth noting is a link out of Rafina down to Mykonos and on to Paros. This used to be a regular summer service, but has disappeared during the last two years. These two *Highspeed* vessels also vanished in 2010. Still, they remain boats and a service to look out for in 2012.

C/F *Artemisia*
Local
A new arrival in 2005, this ferry is now the premier boat running between Rafina and Evia. Small by Aegean ferry standards, but her facilities are adequate for the journey.

C/F *Marmari Express*
DD Ferries
A small but useful ferry that appeared in 2000 on the Evia (Marmari): clearly a refurbished vessel, she is not in the first divi-sion, but is adequate. Evia isn't a popular island with hoppers, so most are content to view it from a distance. With the arrival of the *Artemisia* the *Marmari Express* is set to

spread her wings: expect to see her move to the Lavrio—Kythnos route during the High Season rush in 2012. Out of season she is likely to reappear here.

C/F *Evia Star*
Local
This gaudily painted orange-hulled small boat is rarely used by tourists. She used to call at the Evian port of Karystos, but now confines her itinerary to the more popular Marmari.

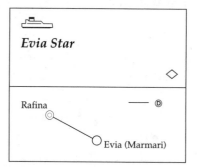

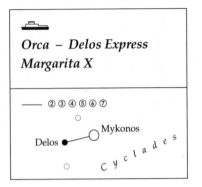

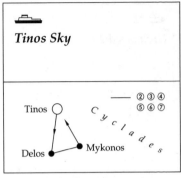

Delos Tour Boats

The island of Delos is only accessible via small tourist boats. These often don't run in heavy seas, so it pays to be flexible about plans to visit Delos. Aim to go when you can, rather than allocating a specific day (and don't forget that Delos is closed on Mondays). The boats run from Mykonos several times a day in High Season; you can pick up your boat on any of its return runs, so you can spend up to 5 hours on Delos. Return tickets cost €7 for the larger *Orca*, €6.50 for the others, and are not interchangeable. Boat tickets do not include the entrance fee for the archaeological

site. The *Orca* is the biggest and best boat. Those prone to seasickness should avoid the diminutive *Margarita X*.

Tour boats from Tinos, Naxos and Paros also visit Delos, but all include a stop at Mykonos, restricting your time sightseeing on Delos to around 1½ hours. The fares are also much higher (Naxos—Delos trips cost around €30 because you are buying a day trip to several islands). The Naxos-based *Alexander* is the best of these boats, the *Naxos Star* being on the small side. The Tinos-based *Tinos Sky* sometimes condescends to head for Delos (she has her own marked berth), but outings are increasingly rare.

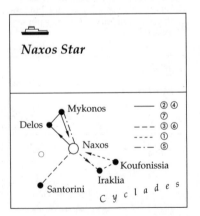

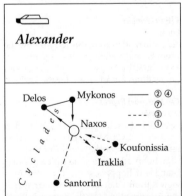

Cyclades North Islands & Ports

Andros

ΑΝΔΡΟΣ; 380 km²; pop. 9,020.

CODE ☎ 22820
GAVRION POLICE ☎ 71220
ANDROS TOWN POLICE ☎ 22300
HOSPITAL ☎ 22222

Despite being the second largest and most northerly of the Cyclades, Andros is only slowly edging its way onto the tourist map. A combination of rich vegetation and mountains has failed to bring the crowds. The only obvious reason for such a paradox is the lack of any notable population centre, for Andros really has a lot going for it if a downbeat, understated beach holiday is your kind of thing. The locals of course have long been in the know, and like Kea, Andros has been the preserve of Greek, rather than foreign, tourists, with many of the better-off Athenians having villas on this appealing island.

Despite the fact that Andros is on a major ferry route, independent island hoppers don't visit in large numbers; the great majority of foreign visitors are package tourists who spend their time on the south coast, split between the port of Gavrion and the tourist resort village of Batsi to the east. Relatively few venture across the island to the capital at Chora, a symptom of the limited bus service; Andros is another of those islands that are best explored with your own transport.

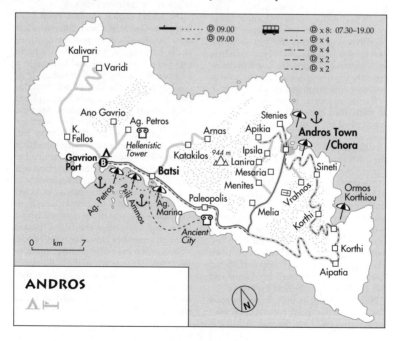

Most visitors arrive by ferry and thus find themselves deposited at the port of **Gavrion**. Set in a deep inlet, it consists of a large ferry quay, backed by a little port village strung along the waterfront behind. All the usual facilities (including an information office housed in an old dovecot) lie along the shore: Gavrion is one of those 'what you can't see isn't there' sort of places. It offers up a remarkable number of tavernas (whose clientele is almost exclusively holidaying Greeks) and a near complete lack of accommodation for foreign tourists.

Island buses (centred on Andros Town) turn around by the ferry quay before running back along the coast to the capital. More often than not they take any arriving tourists with them, as Gavrion offers little incentive to linger (writing in 1884 J. T. Bent said that 'of all places in the world Gavrion is one of the most desolate'). Things have improved considerably today, but the port beach is a sadly indifferent affair (most people who stay in town migrate to the excellent sand beaches that run down the coast towards Batsi), and the commanding hilltop church of Agios Nikolaos that dominates the town reveals itself to be too new to be interesting when you get close up to it.

The main tourist resort on Andros is at **Batsi** (in Greek 'ΜΠΑΤΣΙ', and also transcribed as 'Vatsi') some 8 km east of Gavrion. Unashamedly a tourist town, it has developed from a tiny hamlet since the last war to become the island's premier resort. Given that it is so new and lacking an atmospheric centre, the town has managed to acquire a surprising amount of character with an attractive and lively waterfront (it is easy to see why some tourists choose to return regularly). Thereafter it is divided into two halves by a tree-filled valley, with the east (and older) side of the town clambering rapidly up a staircase-cluttered hillside, while the western 'hotel strip' end lies along the plain behind the beach.

However, there is little to see beyond the sea and the usual collection of tourist tavernas and bars. Serious nightlife is

harder to find — a reflection of the fact that Batsi is very much a 'family holiday' orientated resort — and you don't have to wander around for long to come across bored-looking teenagers (dreaming wistfully of Ios Town, Faliraki on Rhodes, and Malia on Crete) who are just not quite old enough to be allowed on parent-free vacations. The limited nightspots are located on the outskirts of town.

Batsi's importance to tourists has grown of late, and it is now the base for the island's beach boats, with daily departures to a number of good sand beaches in the coves and bays either side of the town (these include a nudist beach at Delavogias on the south-east side). Most are accessible from the well-made main road, and moped or car hire fans will find themselves enjoying a major advantage over other tourists, as they can thus guarantee a stretch of sand beach all for their very own.

The island capital, **Andros Town** (also known as **Chora**), is a very different affair from the island's other port towns. Unusually for a capital, it is sited on the more exposed northern coast, and is home to a number of wealthy Greek families. This, combined with the lack of accommodation and nightlife, and poor ferry and bus links, means that many island hoppers are happy to place Andros Town on their 'island capitals we can afford to miss' list. The accommodation situation is so bad that Andros Town usually has to be explored as a day trip excursion. Sightseeing fans will find more of interest as the town is home to a couple of excellent museums. As an added bonus, the bus ride (just over an hour from Gavrion — it is one of the cheapest island tours around) across the island passes through some very attractive countryside.

Sited on a wind-buffeted, finger-narrow peninsula, the majority of the buildings in the town are typical neo-classical 19 c. red-tile roofed piles. The main street dominates the town, running its length and dotted with shops and up-market boutiques. It ends in a small square adorned with an ugly bronze

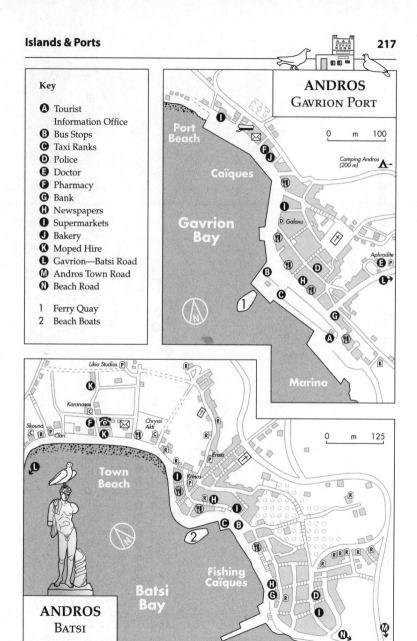

Key

- **A** Tourist Information Office
- **B** Bus Stops
- **C** Taxi Ranks
- **D** Police
- **E** Doctor
- **F** Pharmacy
- **G** Bank
- **H** Newspapers
- **I** Supermarkets
- **J** Bakery
- **K** Moped Hire
- **L** Gavrion—Batsi Road
- **M** Andros Town Road
- **N** Beach Road

1 Ferry Quay
2 Beach Boats

ANDROS
GAVRION PORT

0   m   100

Camping Andros (200 m)

Port Beach

Caïques

Gavrion Bay

Galaxu

Aphrodite

Marina

ANDROS
BATSI

Likio Studios

Karanasos

Skouna
Clari

Chryssi Akti

Erato

Krinos

Town Beach

Batsi Bay

Fishing Caïques

0   m   125

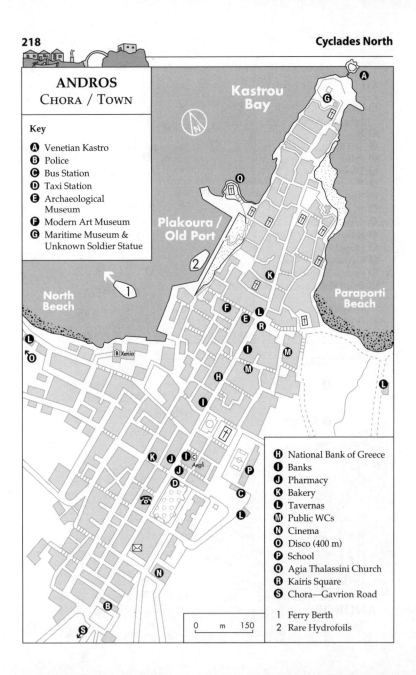

ANDROS
CHORA / TOWN

Key

- **Ⓐ** Venetian Kastro
- **Ⓑ** Police
- **Ⓒ** Bus Station
- **Ⓓ** Taxi Station
- **Ⓔ** Archaeological Museum
- **Ⓕ** Modern Art Museum
- **Ⓖ** Maritime Museum & Unknown Soldier Statue

Kastrou Bay

Plakoura / Old Port

North Beach

Paraporti Beach

Xenia

Aegli

- **Ⓗ** National Bank of Greece
- **Ⓘ** Banks
- **Ⓙ** Pharmacy
- **Ⓚ** Bakery
- **Ⓛ** Tavernas
- **Ⓜ** Public WCs
- **Ⓝ** Cinema
- **Ⓞ** Disco (400 m)
- **Ⓟ** School
- **Ⓠ** Agia Thalassini Church
- **Ⓡ** Kairis Square
- **Ⓢ** Chora—Gavrion Road

1 Ferry Berth
2 Rare Hydrofoils

0   m   150

(entitled 'The Unknown Sailor') waving out to sea, and a Maritime Museum that is usually closed. The sailor's view of the horizon is blocked by an islet topped by the remains of a long abandoned Venetian kastro. Known as the Mesa Kastro, it was built between 1207–33, and is reached via a narrow, arched bridge. The whitewashed buildings and the backstreets behind this square are the most appealing part of town, and are all that remains of the medieval capital of Kato Kastro. At the landward end of the old part of town are a notable Archaeological Museum and a Museum of Modern Art. Both have enjoyed the patronage of the wealthy Goulandri family — Andros is another of those islands that has among its sons a family of benevolent shipping millionaires.

The rest of the island remains virtually tourist free, thanks to the lack of a decent bus service and obvious sightseeing destinations: Andros is a good island to visit if unspoilt hill villages filled with dovecots (a legacy of the period of Venetian rule) appeals. The most visited inland settlement is **Mesaria** on the Andros Town road. This village retains a number of medieval buildings, including several ruined tower houses. Mesaria also has a 10 c. Byzantine church. Just up the road is the picturesque village of **Menites**, a settlement with an even greater ancestry: the main church stands on the site of a temple of Dionysos. In the mountains south of Andros Town stands the Monastery of Panachrantou. Founded in 961, it is home to St. Panteleimon's skull. Said to have healing powers, this relic packs quite a bit of pilgrim-pulling power. The monastery is just one of many possible destinations for walkers on Andros, which is another of those islands that seems to attract walking guidebook writers.

😋

Andros has always enjoyed a quiet existence on the fringes of history. Its location so close to Athens ensured that it was under the control of whichever power controlled that city. This changed in 200 BC when the Romans took control and handed over to Pergamon. Devastated in the Byzantine period by pirates, Andros fell under Venetian control from 1207, until the Turks took the island in 1556.

🛏

Accommodation is thinly spread around the island. In **Gavrion** the waterfront *Galaxu* (☎ 71228) offers very basic rooms along with the better *Gavrion Beach* (☎ 71312). **Batsi** is host to the bulk of the island's accommodation, with the *Chryssi Akti* (☎ 41236), *Skouna* (☎ 41240) and *Karanasos* (☎ 41480) — complete with restaurant — being augmented by several pensions and plenty of hillside rooms. In **Andros Town** the best bet is the C-class *Aegli* (☎ 22303). There is also an expensive *Xenia* (☎ 22270) overlooking the beach and port on the north side of the town.

A

Camping Andros (☎ 71444): a good site well hidden down winding roads behind Gavrion, it tries to make up for its location by providing a swimming pool and restaurant. Mini-bus meets some daytime ferries. Night arrivals should consider a short taxi ride to get here.

👓

Sightseeing is limited as the major archaeological sites have yet to be seriously explored. The most accessible object of interest is a 20 m high **Hellenistic Tower**: a 3 km hour-long hike inland from Gavrion. Known as the 'Tower of Agios Petros', conjecture varies wildly as to its purpose and age, with Mycenaean to Byzantine dates being suggested.

The remains of the ancient city of **Paleopolis** offer an attractive boat excursion from Batsi. Largely unexcavated, the capital (from 600 BC to 500 AD) is sited down a steep path off the town road and also under the sea (the site has one beach, where visitors are not encouraged to carry a bucket and spade). Tourists visit to enjoy the pretty valley walk between the beach and the modern village. Of ruins there are few signs; the most notable discovery is a 2 c. BC marble copy of a bronze statue of Hermes by Praxiteles. Unusually, the island has managed to retain this major piece of sculpture and it is the prize exhibit in the Andros Town **Archaeological Museum**. The **Museum of Modern Art** is also worth exploring (despite having several works by the sculptor of the Unknown Sailor), if only for the strange 'sound' exhibits that follow you around.

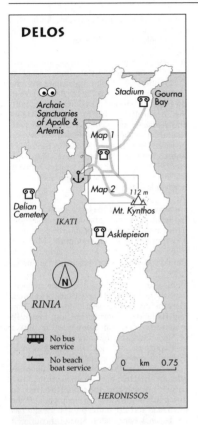

DELOS

Stadium

Gourna Bay

Archaic Sanctuaries of Apollo & Artemis

Map 1

Map 2   112 m

Delian Cemetery

IKATI

Mt. Kynthos

Asklepieion

N

RINIA

🚌 No bus service

━━ No beach boat service

0   km   0.75

HERONISSOS

Delos

ΔΗΛΟΣ; 3.6 km²; pop. 20.

Easily the smallest populated island in the Cyclades (though technically Delos isn't part of the group as it can't 'circle' itself), Delos is also one of the most famous. Home to one of the most important sanctuaries in ancient Greece, the island is now one of the great classical archaeological sites of the Mediterranean, not least because it was all but abandoned during the Roman era and thus remains unspoilt by the gradual accretion of later buildings.

💀

Tradition had it that in an effort to escape the amorous attentions of the god Zeus, a wench named Asteria ignored the maxim that no woman is an island and contrived to metamorphose into one, thereafter drifting where tide and current would take her, sometimes above the surface, other times submerged. Not unnaturally, this did nothing for ancient ferry schedules, and Poseidon finally intervened and anchored the island of 'Asteria' to the sea floor. As a result it was thereafter known as 'Delos' or 'visible'. Years passed only for another of Zeus's escaping lovers — Leto — to land on the island, disguised as a swan, and give birth to the twin deities Apollo (the most popular of all the Greek gods) and his sister, Artemis.

This set Delos up nicely: with a background of divine sex and religion it not unnaturally became a leading spiritual centre in ancient Greece. This role was bolstered by a quadrennial games festival on a par with the Olympics, and the island's emergence as the trade centre of the Aegean. In its later years, during the Hellenistic period, its trade markets came to overshadow the sanctuary, and the excavated complex of temples and markets is an impressive testament to this double life. That said, the extant structures are confined to jumbled foundations, thanks to a history of systematic demolition.

A major Mycenaean site, Delos took off as a sanctuary with the construction of a Temple of Apollo in the early 7 c. BC (largely under Naxian patronage). As the sanctuary grew in importance, it underwent various stages of ritual purification. This started in 540 BC with the removal of all graves to neighbouring Rinia island. This was followed in 426 BC with an edict making it illegal to give birth or die on Delos (this policy is maintained today via a ban on overnight stays, and if that was not discouragement enough, the only hotel has been in ruins for 1,600 years). The 426 BC edict prompted the growth of a town on neighbouring Rinia island (otherwise known as 'Larger Delos') — where one could be born or die and not get blamed for it. On the political front, such moves helped Delos emerge as a neutral non-partisan sanctuary — a sort of mini-Switzerland amid the warring Greek city states — under the control of none.

Following the seeing off of the Persian threat at Marathon (490 BC) and Salamis (480 BC),

Delos was chosen as the nominal centre of an anti-Persian alliance of Greek city states intent on ensuring that their security was never threatened again. Organized by Athens, it was to Delos that each sent contributions to a common war chest. However, the Delian League (as the alliance was known) was soon dominated by Athens, and this led to de facto political control of the island passing to the city, and the neutering of Delian influence. Thereafter, under Athenian patronage, the commercial aspect of Delos became ascendant.

After 250 BC Delos came under the control of the kings of Macedonia, and gradually emerged as the largest slave market in the Mediterranean. The geographer Strabo (64 BC – 19 AD) estimated that on a typical day 10,000 slaves would change masters. The wealth that came with this trade brought about the island's downfall. After coming under Roman control in 168 BC, it was sacked in 88 BC by Mithridates Eupator, king of Pontos, in his war with Rome. Having lost 20,000 of its population in the attack, Delos was sacked again in 69 BC by the pirates of Athenodoros, an ally of Mithridates. Delos never recovered. Abandoned by her rich patrons, and her trade functions re-centred elsewhere, she settled into a period of long slow decline that culminated with the arrival of Christianity — an event that destroyed her tarnished remaining religious role.

From the 6 c. AD Delos appears to have been abandoned: too small and agriculturally poor to be of any interest. In 1566 the Turks occupied the island, the tiny population doing a brisk trade selling much of the masonry, and burning the fine marble to make lime, before being driven away by the establishment of a pirate base on the island that survived despite periods of abandonment into the early 19 c. From the mid 18 c. the first modern tourists arrived, attracted by the island's fame. Fortunately very little was removed as most of the surviving archaeology was buried, but a number of notable pieces, including one of the famous lions and the head of the colossal statue of Apollo, did go missing.

𝕲𝕬

Visitors to Delos should bring a sunhat, good shoes and beverages (refreshments are scandalously expensive on Delos; e.g. a can of cola costing €0.60 in a supermarket will set you back €5 here). Local visitors from Mykonos also wear stout shoes for fear of deadly snakes, but this is mostly paranoia. There aren't any really deadly snakes in Greece — the nearest that comes to it is the small Melian viper, a subspecies unique to the Cyclades: it is possible that there once were some on Delos, but they are now very rare (estimated numbers are below 8,000 and 90% of these are on Milos). Step on one and the chances are the locals will be more worried about the health of the snake than they are about you.

This is not to say that you shouldn't be careful about where you walk. It is best to stick to the established paths if you don't want to be attacked, if not by snakes then the site guards. There is so much stuff just lying around on Delos that they are mildly paranoid about tourists. Attempt to pick anything up, and you will be seriously shouted at.

All tour boats arrive at a mole (complete with barrier and ticket kiosk on the island side) built out of the debris from the excavations (see the colour centrefold map between p. 224–225). In poor sea conditions boats berth on the other side of the island in Gourna Bay. There is a site entrance fee of €6 (this is included in the price of *some* agency tours — it is advisable to check when buying) which also includes the museum. Establish carefully boat return times. You will need 2–3 hours in order to visit all the major features on the site — all are marked with stones inscribed in Greek and French (a few newer signs are now in English). Unfortunately, there isn't a set route to follow when exploring Delos. Tourists peel

DELOS
SLAVE MARKET
SPECIALS!

ORGY GIRL—
10,000 TALENTS!
WITH FREE
PET HUNK
ATTACHED!

off in all directions as soon as they pass the ticket kiosk. Given the summer heat, an anti-clockwise circuit is best as you can attempt the summit of Mt. Kynthos while still fresh; this means starting with Map 2, and then taking in the sites on Map 1 and the museum as you find them.

The Sanctuary Area

The heart of ancient Delos was made up of the central Sanctuary and Sacred Lake areas. On arriving at the site most tourists head for the enormous rubble field that once was the Sanctuary Area. In its prime it was the heart of Delos, containing the shrines to Apollo and holy sites dating back to Mycenaean times.

All arrivals to Delos start from **A** the Hellenistic **Agora of the Competialists**. This was a market dividing the religious and commercial areas of Delos; it is adorned with the bases of monuments erected by guildsmen. The main path from this crossroads ran north. This was the **Sacred Way** (or **Dromos**), the processional road to the sanctuary, and bounded by **B** the **Stoa of Philip V** (c. 150 BC), named after a king of Macedon, and **C** the **South Stoa** (3 C. BC). Both were filled with shops.

The religious part of the site began with **D** the **Propylaea** (2 C. BC). This was the ceremonial gateway to the main sanctuary precinct (the **Hieron of Apollo**). It boasted three doors and four pillars (the bases of which survive, along with a statue base on the west side that has the footprints left by some long-lost bronze hero). Just inside stood one of the oldest buildings on Delos: **E** the **Oikos of the Naxians** (7 C. BC), an odd shrine with open ends and a roof supported by a row of internal pillars. Along its north wall stands **F** the **Base of the Colossal Statue of the Naxians**.

This famous sculpture (see **R**) was a 6 C. BC **Kouros** of Apollo that stood over 10 m high — i.e. more than twice the height of the Heraion Kouros now on display in the Archaeological Museum in Vathi, Samos (see p. 474). The broken base is inscribed 'I am of the same marble, both statue and base' on its east side and 'The Naxians to Apollo' on its west. The statue looked out to sea, over the monuments within **G** the L-shaped **Stoa of the Naxians** (6 C. BC). First among these was the famous **Bronze Palm Tree of Nicias** (417 BC) which was apparently lost when the Colossal Statue of the Naxians fell on it during a storm; only its base survives.

North of the Oikos lie the foundations of three Apollo temples. Delos is unusual in that later temples were built alongside (rather than replacing) earlier buildings. This had the side effect of leaving the site with a series of small temples, rather than acquiring one great temple, as other major shrines did. The focus provided by the sacred harbour also prompted another change in tradition, as all the temples have their main entrances on their west sides, instead of the usual east (it was normal building practice for the main door, opening on the statue within, to face the rising sun). The largest and newest of these temples was **H** the **Great Temple of Apollo (Temple of the Delians)**. Built on the founding of the Delian League in 478 BC, this was the only temple on Delos to have columns on all four sides. North of it lies **I** the **Temple of the Athenians** (425–417 BC). Built out of Pentelic marble by Athenian workmen, it was highly decorated with sculptures. **J** the **Porinos Naos of Apollo** (6 C. BC) was the oldest temple, with columns only across its west front.

Running in an arc north and east of the three Apollo temples are the foundations of **K** the **5 Treasuries**. All date from the 6 or 5 C. BC, and lead round to several more important sanctuary precinct buildings. First among these is **L** the 3 C. BC **Neorion** (otherwise known as the **Monument of the Bulls** because of its

decorative reliefs). This is one of the most unusual buildings known from ancient Greece. A stoa with a two-storey north end, it housed a trireme in its lower southern half. This

glorified warship shed was built by Antigonos Gonatas to commemorate a naval victory over the Ptolemies. To the east lie the remains of several buildings housing minor cults, the **Bouleuterion** (6 C. BC) and the **Prytaneion**. To the west lies **M** the **Altar of Zeus Soter & Polieus** (3 C. BC).

South of the precinct boundary lies **N** the **Agora of the Delians**. This was lined with 2 C. BC stoas on its north and east sides and a 3 C. BC stoa on its south. Behind this complex stood a late Christian **Basilica of Agios Kyrikos**, along with a series of houses, including the **House of Kerdon** (marked by a couple of columns). The precinct boundary street runs from here to **O** the **Sanctuary of Dionysos**, a popular tourist venue (thanks to the two broken giant phalli on pillars), and the nearby **Monument of Gaius Billienus** (1 C. BC), the marble torso of a Roman general. This backs onto ❼ the foundations of the massive **Stoa of Antigonos** (3 C. BC), a ceremonial building surrounded by monuments. These include ❽ the water-and-frog-filled **Minoa Fountain** (6 C. BC) on its north side and, on the south, the semicircular **Graphe** or **Oikos**, the Mycenaean tomb of Arge and Opis (the maidens who supposedly attended Leto at Apollo's birth).

Artemis was worshipped in the north-west corner of the sanctuary; ❾ the **Artemision** (C. 175 BC) was built on the site of an Archaic temple which was built over a Mycenaean shrine. It is easily located as it is now the home of the divided white marble torso of the **Colossal Statue of the Naxians** (this was cut in two and its head lost in pre-18 C. AD attempts to remove it — one of the statue's hands is in the site museum, and a foot is in the British Museum).

South of the Artemision lie the confused remains of several rather obscure and oddly named buildings: the **Keraton** (4 C. BC), a building that was used in a bizarre feathery crane-dance ritual first stepped by Theseus, the **Oikos of the Andrians & Heiropoion** (otherwise known as the **Monuments of the Hexagons**), and ❺ the **Thesmophorion**, a 4 C. BC shrine complex that included a **Temple of Demeter**.

The Sacred Lake Area

Lying north of the Apollo temples precinct and the Stoa of Antigonos is the Sacred Lake Area. The Sacred Lake (so called because it was on its banks that Apollo and Artemis were born) marked the boundary of the Archaic sanctuary. With the rise of Delos as a trading centre, the area later became an up-market mansion district.

The main street leading to the Sacred Lake runs from ❼ the **Agora of Theophrastos** (126 BC) on the north side of the Sacred Harbour. When commercial forces were in the ascendant even the Sacred Harbour was put to commercial use with the building of ⓤ the **Hypostyle Hall** or **Stoa of Poseidon** (3 C. BC), a many-pillared merchants' exchange that was open on the harbour side. Now reduced to a field of capitals and bases, it was graced by 44 Doric and Ionic pillars (their absence is a clear sign of deliberate demolition). To the east stood ⓥ the **Temple of the Dodekatheon**

The Delian Lions

One of the most iconic images of the Greek islands is that of the heavily weathered stone lions of Delos, standing defiantly in a row under a deep blue Aegean sky. Captured giving a collective roar by early Archaic sculptors, they lack the refinement, sophistication and uniformity of later Classical sculptures, but are all the better for it, having a spontaneity and vitality that make them much more plausible. Though there are contradictions: not least of these is the fact that they have been carved without manes — although all the lions are obviously male (and clearly high on Viagra into the bargain).

The lions were dedicated by the Naxians to the Sanctuary of Apollo at the end of the 7 C. BC. They stood on a natural terrace overlooking the Sacred Lake and the Sacred Palm from which Leto hung to give birth to Apollo and Artemis east towards the dawn.

Thought to have once been between 9 and 19 strong, only 5 lions survive on Delos. Most were unearthed between 1886 and 1906: their scattered locations strongly suggest that they were later used as construction material in a wall built in 67 BC to guard against pirate attacks. Repositioned on the terrace, they were moved to the museum in 1999 (their position on the terrace is now marked by plaster copies).

The body of a 6th lion does exist, but was removed in 1716 to guard the Arsenal in Venice. Unfortunately, the locals touched it up, replacing the original head with something closer to the traditional Venetian Lion (complete with mane). The result is best summed up by the creature's expression of pained surprise, a case of being not so much maned as maimed. The Greek government has requested the torso's return and it is difficult not to sympathize given the poor beast's obvious distress …

(4 C. BC); dedicated to the 12 gods (see p. 72), it replaced an earlier Archaic structure.

Around the corner lies Ⓦ the **Letoon** (or **Temple of Leto**). Built in the 6 C. BC, it honoured the mother of Apollo and Artemis, and — unusually — faced south, in order to face their temples. The surviving base of the building is easy to miss, thanks to the more impressive remains that stand either side, namely Ⓧ the **Agora of the Italians** (2 C. BC), a large two-storey peristyle building named after its excavators, and Ⓨ the **Granite Monument** (2 C. BC), a large building constructed out of granite blocks that is thought to have been a religious meeting house.

The high point of any tour of Delos is undoubtedly ❷ the **Terrace of the Lions** (7 C. BC). Although the orginals are in the museum, the on-site copies at least give an impression of the Terrace's former grandeur.

The site Ⓕ of the **Sacred Palm Tree** is probably the circular trunk-sized hole amid the foundations next to Ⓐ the **Sacred Lake**. Dry since 1925 (when it was drained for fear of malarial mosquitos), it was originally perfectly circular and graced with swans. However, during the Hellenistic period, when the mansion district was built, the secular merchants (no doubt still being broken on a wheel in Hades) had the street to the harbour widened, prompting the narrowing of the lake and leaving it with the current oval shape. When it was drained the existing wall was erected to mark its perimeters, and a commemorative palm tree planted in the centre.

North of the Sacred Lake are the remains of several 3 C. and 2 C. BC mansions. Two have yielded up statues: Ⓞ the **Koinon of the Poseidoniasts of Beirut** was built by Syrian merchants (a statue of Aphrodite whopping a hapless cupid with a slipper — now in the National Archaeological Museum in Athens — was found here); Ⓝ the **House of the Diadumenos** was named after a 2 C. BC copy of Polykleitos' Apollo. Other houses have more to see: Ⓢ the **Hillside House** has been excavated out of the hill and gives an overhead view of the typical internal layout, while Ⓤ the **House of the Comedians** has a good example of a central cistern (complete with water and Kermit-green frogs) with part of its roof-cum-floor intact. Some way north stands the **House at Scardana**. Turning east brings you to Ⓢ the **House of the Lake**, which has a pretty little peristyle court, while Ⓤ the large **Palaestra of**

Granite (2 C. BC) behind it is dominated by a large water-filled cistern divided into quarters. Ⓟ the **Palaestra of the Lake** (3 C. BC) is more nondescript, but also has a cistern.

Behind it lies the line of the **Wall of Triarius** (66 BC), built by a Roman legate to protect against pirates. The wall ran over demolished ancient buildings past Ⓞ the **Temple of Anios** (7 C. BC), a small temple dedicated to a mythical king of Delos. From here a path runs north-east, past the site of the vanished U-shaped **Hippodrome**. Built c. 200 BC, it was later demolished to build defensive walls. Its predecessors, the **Gymnasium** (3 C. BC) and **Stadium** (C. 274 BC), survive in part on the east side of Delos, but see few tourists. Beyond them are the remains of a number of houses and a large 2 C. BC **Synagogue**.

Mount Kynthos

The Mount Kynthos area (see the colour map facing p. 225) contains a diverse mix of buildings. The theatre and residential buildings are the main attractions; some of the latter are among the best preserved 3 and 2 C. BC houses in Greece. Most retain walls up to chest height (these are not shown on the map for fear of rendering it unusable) and many adorned with mosaics have undergone some rebuilding. The mosaics — many quite famous — are something of a disappointment in the bright Aegean sunlight. They really need watering to bring out their colours.

Along with visitors heading for the central sanctuary district, Ⓐ the **Agora of the Competialists** is the starting point for exploration of the Mount Kynthos district. Running down to the south is Ⓑ the **Maritime Quarter**. Little visited today, this area is made up of warehouse buildings. Most are only partly excavated, but enough has been discovered to show that this was where the slave market flourished. The tourist path, however, moves in the direction of Ⓒ the **Theatre Quarter** (the residential area near the theatre), where all the buildings have been explored.

A walk up the ancient main street will bring you to a marked side-street leading off to Ⓓ the **House of Cleopatra & Dioscurides** (137 BC); named after the statues of two wealthy Athenians to be seen within (this Cleopatra is not the queen of Egypt with the famously lovely nose: in fact, this lady hasn't even got a head), it has the remains of a typical peristyle pillared central courtyard. The statues on

MYKONOS
Town Waterfront

Mosaic & Plaster 'Pebble'
from a Delos Beach

Paraportiani Church
& Little Venice House

DELOS
Delian Lioness

Rubble Field & Mt. Kynthos

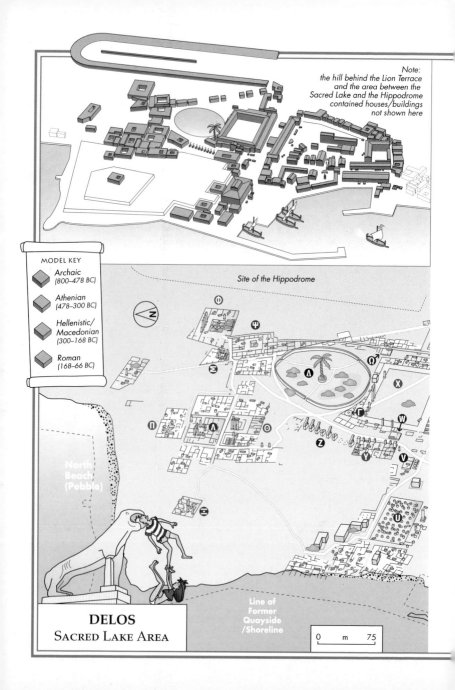

Note:
the hill behind the Lion Terrace
and the area between the
Sacred Lake and the Hippodrome
contained houses/buildings
not shown here

MODEL KEY

Archaic
(800–478 BC)

Athenian
(478–300 BC)

Hellenistic/
Macedonian
(300–168 BC)

Roman
(168–66 BC)

Site of the Hippodrome

North
Beach
(Pebble)

Line of
Former
Quayside
/Shoreline

DELOS
SACRED LAKE AREA

0   m   75

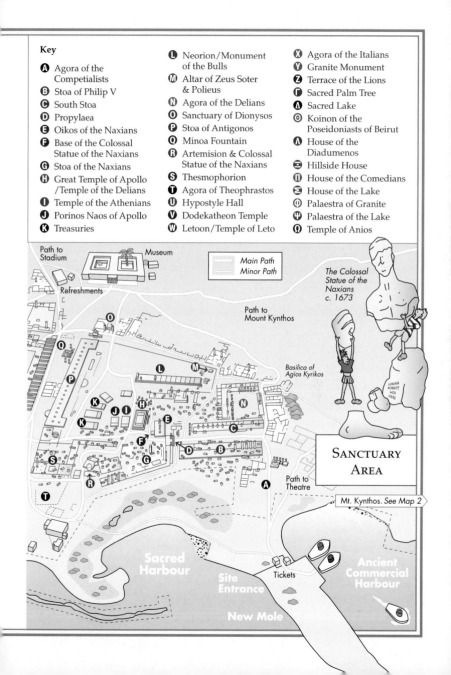

Key

- **A** Agora of the Competialists
- **B** Stoa of Philip V
- **C** South Stoa
- **D** Propylaea
- **E** Oikos of the Naxians
- **F** Base of the Colossal Statue of the Naxians
- **G** Stoa of the Naxians
- **H** Great Temple of Apollo /Temple of the Delians
- **I** Temple of the Athenians
- **J** Porinos Naos of Apollo
- **K** Treasuries
- **L** Neorion/Monument of the Bulls
- **M** Altar of Zeus Soter & Polieus
- **N** Agora of the Delians
- **O** Sanctuary of Dionysos
- **P** Stoa of Antigonos
- **Q** Minoa Fountain
- **R** Artemision & Colossal Statue of the Naxians
- **S** Thesmophorion
- **T** Agora of Theophrastos
- **U** Hypostyle Hall
- **V** Dodekatheon Temple
- **W** Letoon/Temple of Leto
- **X** Agora of the Italians
- **Y** Granite Monument
- **Z** Terrace of the Lions
- **Ｆ** Sacred Palm Tree
- **Λ** Sacred Lake
- **Ｏ** Koinon of the Poseidoniasts of Beirut
- **Λ** House of the Diadumenos
- **Ｓ** Hillside House
- **Π** House of the Comedians
- **Ξ** House of the Lake
- **Ｏ** Palaestra of Granite
- **Ψ** Palaestra of the Lake
- **Ｏ** Temple of Anios

Path to Stadium

Museum

Refreshments

Main Path
Minor Path

Path to Mount Kynthos

The Colossal Statue of the Naxians c. 1673

Basilica of Agios Kyrikos

LORENA BOBBITT WAS HERE

SANCTUARY AREA

Mt. Kynthos. *See Map 2*

Path to Theatre

Sacred Harbour

Site Entrance

Tickets

Ancient Commercial Harbour

New Mole

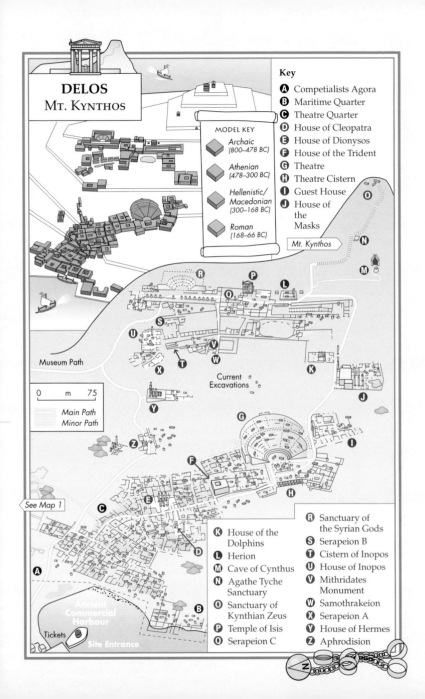

DELOS
Mt. Kynthos

Key

A Competialists Agora
B Maritime Quarter
C Theatre Quarter
D House of Cleopatra
E House of Dionysos
F House of the Trident
G Theatre
H Theatre Cistern
I Guest House
J House of the Masks

MODEL KEY

Archaic
(800–478 BC)

Athenian
(478–300 BC)

Hellenistic/
Macedonian
(300–168 BC)

Roman
(168–66 BC)

Mt. Kynthos

Museum Path

0   m   75

Main Path
Minor Path

Current Excavations

See Map 1

Ancient Commercial Harbour

Tickets

Site Entrance

K House of the Dolphins
L Herion
M Cave of Cynthus
N Agathe Tyche Sanctuary
O Sanctuary of Kynthian Zeus
P Temple of Isis
Q Serapeion C

R Sanctuary of the Syrian Gods
S Serapeion B
T Cistern of Inopos
U House of Inopos
V Mithridates Monument
W Samothrakeion
X Serapeion A
Y House of Hermes
Z Aphrodision

site are reproductions: the originals are now standing in the site museum.

Further up the main street lies ❺ the **House of Dionysos**. The first of the 'mosaic' houses, it is named after the impressive mosaic of Dionysos riding side-saddle on a panther. Similarly, ❻ the rebuilt **House of the Trident** has a trident mosaic. Both houses can be locked and are only open if sufficient site staff have turned up for guard duty.

The main residential street finally emerges at ❼ the **Theatre** (4 C. BC). Now badly preserved in detail (its seating proved too tempting to masonry thieves) it is still impressive. Climbing to the level of the higher tiers, it is easy enough to imagine it filled with a 5,500 capacity crowd. It is unique among ancient theatres in having a stage building constructed on its circular orchestra or stage: the **Skene**. Possibly three floors high (to allow the 'gods' to appear from above) it had colonnaded lower storeys. Only foundations remain, with rubble running back to ❽ the **Theatre Cistern**. This stored rainwater running off the theatre. Some 22.5 m long and 6 m wide, it is filled with water; its roof is missing, though the supporting arches remain.

The tourist path ascends the hill south of the theatre past a marble-lined doorway that marks ❾ the **Guest House**. Thought to have been an inn, it is notable for having the deepest cistern of any house on Delos. It is 8.3 m deep and guarded with protective rails. Those that don't fall in will find the path continuing up to ❿ the **House of the Masks** (named after a mosaic illustrating a series of actor's masks). A large building, it had shops along its street side. Nearby stands ⓚ the **House of the Dolphins**, a smaller, richer structure with mosaics depicting cupids riding dolphins.

Once past the House of the Dolphins the tourist path emerges at an upper sanctuary level. This area contains a number of small temples, as well as shrines devoted to eastern deities (a reflection of the island's days as an international trading centre).

The first recognizable building is ⓛ the **Herion** (c. 500 BC). A small temple dedicated to Hera, its columns survive. This temple also marks the point where the main path divides. One branch steps up to the summit of **Mt. Kynthos** (don't miss the tiny path running to the mysterious **Cave of Cynthus** or **Grotto of Hercules** at ⓜ. Dating from the 3 C. BC, it contained a statue of the hero under its roof of pitched granite slabs, and has a circular marble altar outside the door). The main path runs up past the foundations of ⓝ the **Sanctuary of Agathe Tyche** (of which little survives) before reaching the summit. Here stood ⓞ the **Sanctuary of Kynthian Zeus & Athena** (7 C. BC). Once similar in size to the Herion, the only surviving remains are a few slippery foundation stones from which you get blown into next week trying to take in the superb panoramic views.

Returning to the Herion, the path moves on to a relatively isolated area of Delos (reflecting the comparatively late date of the majority of its religious buildings). The first building of note is ⓟ the heavily restored **Temple of Isis** (3 C. BC), complete with a headless statue of Isis standing within its walls. Nearby is ⓠ **Serapeion C**, a small stoa-lined court. Further along this terrace is ⓡ the **Sanctuary of the Syrian Gods** (c. 100 BC) which included a religious amphitheatre for witnessing ceremonies.

Below this terrace is the site of a second stoa-lined court: ⓢ **Serapeion B** (2 C. BC), and below that ⓣ the **Cistern of Inopos** (3 C. BC). Still filled with green water, it was built to collect the fountainhead waters of the Inopos, the sacred river of Delos. Legend had it that its source was the Nile. Nearby is ⓤ the **House of Inopos**. South of the cistern lie the remains of ⓥ the **Monument of Mithridates Eupator** (c. 100 BC), a king of Pontos. This stood in front of ⓦ the **Samothrakeion** (4 C. BC), a temple to the Great Gods of Samothrace.

East of the cistern, in the largely unexcavated area, lie other buildings of interest, notably ⓧ **Serapeion A** (3 C. BC), a third stoa-lined court, and — accessed via a narrow path branching off the museum path — ⓨ the **House of Hermes** (4 C. BC). This two-storey house is the best-preserved peristyle court mansion on Delos, and is worth making the effort to get to even if you don't have time for the rest of the Mount Kynthos area. Further along this path lies ⓩ the **Aphrodision** (4 C. BC), a tiny temple of Aphrodite. From here the path rejoins the main sanctuary area.

Delos Archaeological Museum

Built a century ago, the yellow-ochre-painted site museum is the most imposing building on Delos. It is one of the best archaeological museums in Greece, for even though the major discoveries have inevitably found their way into the National Archaeological Museum in Athens, the finds on the island have been so plentiful that the 10 galleries are home to a good collection of sculpture, mosaics, plaster wall paintings, and household utensils. Realistically you need to allow an hour for your visit if you are to do the exhibits justice.

The museum, unusually, doesn't have a shop. Nor is there an entry charge (it is included in the Delos site ticket) — in fact the only thing it does have is one big rule that you break at your peril: no flashers or posers! The museum guards are constantly shouting 'No flashing' or 'No posing' at the bewildered masses, who are either attempting to take photos (allowed) with a flash (not allowed), or who are standing in front of open-mouthed lions with a view to being photographed being eaten alive.

Most visitors start with the sculpture galleries and on entering the museum just keep on going into **A. The Archaic Sculpture Large Gallery**, home to a varied collection of pieces. The best are a Hand of the Colossal Statue of the Naxians (hidden just inside the gallery door) and a well-preserved Sphinx. The doorway at the end of the gallery is flanked by a pair of Dove torsos (the iron supports holding each of them up looking uncannily like legs), and leads into **B. The Archaic Sculpture Small Gallery**. Too small to contain much at all, it continues the avian theme as its best exhibit is the very finely worked body of a siren.

C. The Late Archaic & Classical Sculpture Gallery is the weakest offering in the museum: the sculptural fragments are just too bashed up. Some surviving detail (particularly on a couple of equestrian exhibits) is very fine, but the room has become little more than an antechamber for the prize exhibits next door.

D. The Lion Gallery is the highlight of the museum. Home to the famous Delian Lions, it is a far from ideal display space. The museum labels this as a temporary arrangement and with good reason. The statues are just too large for the gallery: you just can't step away from them far enough to appreciate them as an ensemble. Even so, there are advantages to having the lions in the museum: when they stood on the terrace you couldn't get near

them, but now you can stand up close and walk around them. This enables one to pick up on details that weren't so obvious before (for example: two of the lions lean over to one side thanks to some dodgy carving).

After the Lions, the rest of the sculpture is inevitably something of an anticlimax. **E. The Hellenistic Sculpture 1 Gallery** does its best with a vivid statue of Artemis and some actor figures found in the theatre area. The gallery is also home to a large wall-mounted floor mosaic depicting Hermes and Athena. The gallery next door — **F. Hellenistic Sculpture 2** — is filled with carved rock of lesser merit: mostly large, overblown later work, the impression is of money rather than style. Military and Roman figures dominate. The best piece is the figures of Dioscurides & Cleopatra from the house of the same name.

Next up is **G. The Portrait Gallery**. With walls painted blood red, the room contains nameless stone heads aplenty. This gallery does have one notable exhibit: a unique stone statue base with the usual carved footprints — though in this case one bronze foot and sandal are still attached to the stone.

From here on the museum improves by leaps and bounds. **H. The Daily Life Gallery** is packed with small objects that tempt you to linger. Most of the high quality exhibits come from Delian houses, which were amongst the richest in Greece. They include a delightful terracotta doll with platform shoes, plaster paintings, and a fine leopard mosaic. More unusual is a circular marble table, and — tucked away in the gallery corner — a terracotta cooking hob.

Passing through **I. The Entrance Hall**, complete with its model of the Delos site and a tiny display showing how mosaics were made, you come to **J. The Pottery Gallery**. Packed with pots in tall display cases, this room gets passed over rather quickly by most visitors as there is too heavy a preponderance of Geometric patterned pieces. However, the final **K. Temporary Exhibition Gallery** (oddly named as the exhibits haven't changed for a number of years) more than makes up for the walk. Clearly laid out with a younger audience in mind, it is home to several small statutes of Aphrodite, and (for after she has done her stuff) a couple of delightful terracotta fish and dolphin feeding 'bottles' for babies: day-to-day objects that enable us to span the gulf with the ancient world better than any statue, no matter how impressive.

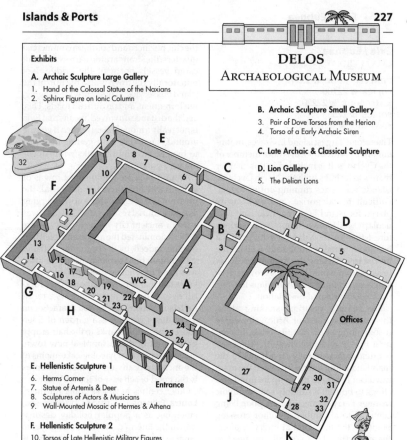

Exhibits

DELOS
ARCHAEOLOGICAL MUSEUM

A. Archaic Sculpture Large Gallery

1. Hand of the Colossal Statue of the Naxians
2. Sphinx Figure on Ionic Column

B. Archaic Sculpture Small Gallery

3. Pair of Dove Torsos from the Herion
4. Torso of a Early Archaic Siren

C. Late Archaic & Classical Sculpture

D. Lion Gallery

5. The Delian Lions

E. Hellenistic Sculpture 1

6. Herms Corner
7. Statue of Artemis & Deer
8. Sculptures of Actors & Musicians
9. Wall-Mounted Mosaic of Hermes & Athena

F. Hellenistic Sculpture 2

10. Torsos of Late Hellenistic Military Figures
11. Statues of Dioscurides & Cleopatra
12. Large Statue of Ofellius Ferus

G. Portrait Gallery

13. Roman Portrait Heads
14. Statue Base with Bronze Foot & Sandal

H. Daily Life Gallery

15. Bead Jewellery
16. Terracotta Girl with Platform Shoes
17. Red Figure Wall Plaster Paintings
18. Wall Mosaics (including a Leopard's Head)
19. Double-Winged Phallus Relief
20. Display of Household Dishes
21. Bronze Household Objects & Medical Instruments
22. Terracotta Multi-Hob Cooking Stand
23. Circular Marble Table Top

I. Entrance Hall

24. Copy of a Statue of Apollo
25. Model of Delos Site
26. Mosaic Manufacture & Rock Type Display

J. Pottery Gallery

27. Geometric Vase Display

K. Temporary Exhibition Gallery

28. Aphrodite Figurine Display
29. Steles (Gravestones) from Rinia
30. Amphora Collection
31. Dolphin & Anchor Mosaic, Anchors & Dolphin Objects
32. Terracotta Dolphin & Fish Baby Feeding Bottles
33. Display of Shellfish Shells & Dishes from Dining Areas

Entrance

WCs

Offices

Evia / Euboea
EYIA / EYBOIA; 3580 km²; pop. 165,000.

CHALCIS: CODE ☎ 22210
POLICE ☎ 22100
KIMI: CODE ☎ 22220
POLICE ☎ 22555
FIRST AID ☎ 22322

The second-largest island in Greece, mountainous Evia (or Euboea) is not a member of the Cyclades; it is included in this chapter thanks to its links with the North Cycladic islands via ferries running out of Rafina. Difficult to categorize, and awkwardly placed for island hopping, Evia isn't particularly well known (though some serious forest fires in 2007 did raise its profile a bit) and it remains stubbornly well off the tourist trail, lacking the dramatic beaches or sights that would bring the crowds. It is, however, popular with Athenians looking for a good weekend destination.

The island's position, snaking along the north-east coast of Attica, does give it something of an identity crisis. Linked by a bridge and motorway to Athens, it is often seen as merely an adjunct to the mainland it hugs so closely. Even the main town can't seem to make up its mind and clings to both in a suitably schizophrenic manner. Ferry connections are poor, being confined to a number of minor crossing points to the mainland at intervals along the coast (this tells you all you need to know about the island's roads) and the main Skyros—'mainland' link. These are all local subsidized 'lifeline' services and times vary little during the year.

The island capital is at **Chalcis**, located halfway up the west coast at the narrowest point of the Evian Strait (known as the Euripus Channel). The town was an important centre in ancient Greece, thanks to its strategic position on the straits, but is now an ugly commercial centre with only a distinctive Turkish quarter, and a popular, up-market waterfront to redeem it. The old-fashioned swing bridge that straddles the 30 m strait marks the boundary between the chic northern and southern commercial quarters; the straits are too narrow to admit cargo vessels north of the bridge. Not unnaturally the town is also the hub of the island bus services. These are wide-ranging, but infrequent, and on difficult roads. This, and the distances involved, means that Evia is not really a moped island either. If getting around is not very easy, getting overland to Evia is: bus and rail links with Athens are very good.

Around Evia are a number of towns or villages with little in common. **Eretria** is the most notable of them, and is now emerging as a poor tourist resort. Like Chalcis, it was a major ancient city in the 6 c. BC, before Athens dominated the region and it fell into decline. Indeed, by the beginning of the 19 c. the population was so small that the town was used to rehouse those inhabitants of Psara that managed to escape the 1824 Turkish devastation of that island. As a result Eretria is also known as **Nea Psara**. Set on a dry dusty plain, it is a garden of Eden short of beautiful thanks to the half-empty grid layout of the incomplete new town, but the plentiful archaeological remains of the ancient city are some compensation, as is the good beach east of the harbour.

Other centres have less going for them. **Loutra Edipsos** is Greece's premier spa, emerging as a popular holiday destination in the late 19 c. However, it has yet to emerge as a modern tourist resort and is marred by the rather dismal air of a faded watering hole. More cheerful spots are to be found elsewhere. **Limni** is a coastal village turned resort, as is **Pefki** on the northern coast, but even so, there is little disguising the fact that neither are worth flying all the way to Greece for. The latter does, however, receive occasional calls from Sporades-bound hydrofoils, and in 480 BC even had a visit from the invading Persian trireme fleet (en route to Salamis: see p. 125) — which came off the worse in a two-day sea battle with a much smaller Athenian squadron in what has become known as the Battle of Artemision.

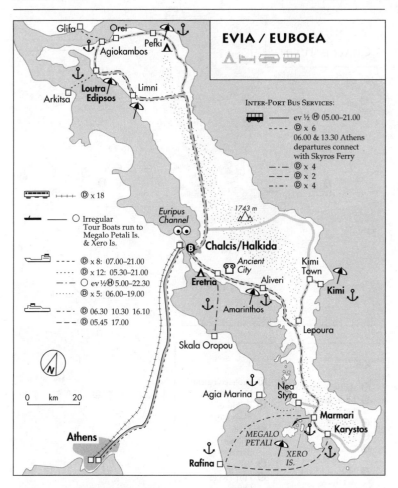

The southern half of Evia is dominated by **Karystos** and **Marmari**. Both have ferry links with Rafina and clog up with escaping Athenians during the weekends. Karystos is the nicer of the two, set in a wide bay with a Venetian-built harbour. Marmari has less charm but does offer regular boat trips to the small wooded Petali Islands (**Megalo Petali** & **Xero**) 1 km to the south.

Kimi port (as distinct from Kimi Town, a hillside village 4 km inland) is the principal jumping off point for Skyros and its links with the other Northern Aegean destinations. It is tucked beneath the mountain range that makes up the backbone of Evia, and is a very pretty little place with an excellent beach just below the harbour. Unfortunately, beds are thin on the ground.

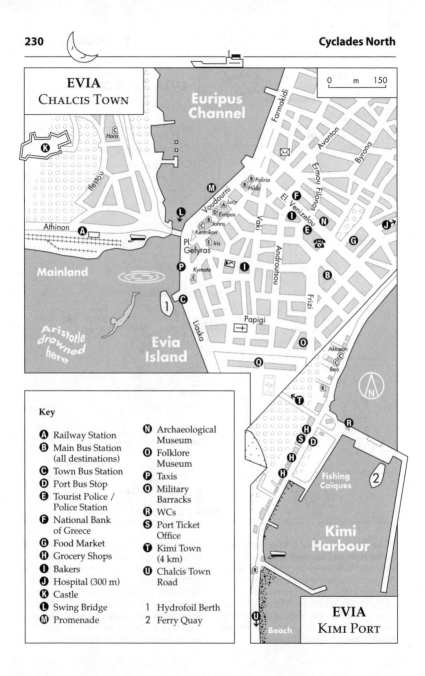

EVIA
CHALCIS TOWN

0   m   150

Euripus
Channel

Farmakidi

Avanton

Byrona

Ermou Filonos

Hara

K

Voudourni

M

L

Athinon

A

PI.
Gefyras

Mainland

P

Kymata

E

C

Liaska

Aristotle
drowned
here

Evia
Island

B Paliria
B Hilda
A Lucy
D Evripos
C Johns
Kantrikon
C
E Iris

Vaki

El Venizelou

F

I

E

N

J

G

B

Androutsou

Frizi

I

Papigi

O

Aktaeon
C
C
Beis

O

R

N

Kimi Town
(4 km)

T

R

H
S
D

H

H

H

Fishing
Caïques

2

Kimi
Harbour

R

U

Beach

EVIA
KIMI PORT

Key

Ⓐ Railway Station
Ⓑ Main Bus Station
   (all destinations)
Ⓒ Town Bus Station
Ⓓ Port Bus Stop
Ⓔ Tourist Police /
   Police Station
Ⓕ National Bank
   of Greece
Ⓖ Food Market
Ⓗ Grocery Shops
Ⓘ Bakers
Ⓙ Hospital (300 m)
Ⓚ Castle
Ⓛ Swing Bridge
Ⓜ Promenade

Ⓝ Archaeological
   Museum
Ⓞ Folklore
   Museum
Ⓟ Taxis
Ⓠ Military
   Barracks
Ⓡ WCs
Ⓢ Port Ticket
   Office
Ⓣ Kimi Town
   (4 km)
Ⓤ Chalcis Town
   Road

1 Hydrofoil Berth
2 Ferry Quay

Thanks to Evia's motorway link with Athens, Kimi is a de facto mainland port with regular buses, and most visitors pass straight through. The link with Skyros is the mainstay of ferry activity. Other departures (usually twice weekly to the Sporades in High Season) are poorly advertised, and remain easier to arrive than depart on.

😋

Evia was never a significant player in history. Normally size confers status and power on a Greek island, but Evia has always been too large to be managed by a single city state, and too close to Athens to be allowed to do so. In the Archaic period the island was home to no fewer than seven cities, the big two being Chalcis and Eretria, who indulged in regular confrontations across the rich Levantine plain which lies between them. The feud only ended with the Persian invasion of 490 BC when Eretria was sacked and its inhabitants enslaved by the invaders. It was subsequently rebuilt but never again became a political force.

Chalcis prospered only because of its location as a crossing point with the mainland — and even this was a double-edged sword: Athens moved in and took control of the island when the Persians withdrew. Evia revolted against Athenian rule in 446 and 411 BC, but was unable to regain any real independence. Its fortunes followed those of Athens until the disastrous Fourth Crusade when it was dissected between a number of Frankish nobles. Between 1209 and 1366 control of Evia gradually passed to Venice.

Under Venetian rule the island was known as 'Negroponte' (black bridge) after the mainland bridge at Chalcis, and was rather extravagantly set up as a mini-kingdom, complete with its own flag. This enabled it to get extra attention from 13 C. cartographers (who could never resist exotic-sounding locations), but did nothing to prevent the island being captured by the Turks in 1470. Apart from an abortive attempt in 1688 to retake Chalcis by Morosini (the much despised Venetian general who fired the fatal shells into the munition-filled Parthenon in Athens) obscurity set in. Though not a big player in the independence struggle, Evia became part of Greece in 1830.

🛏

Considering its size, Evia is poorly equipped with hotels, and rooms are a rarity. **Chalcis** offers the greatest choice of beds thanks to its hotel-littered waterfront. Unfortunately, the majority are pricey, top end of the market establishments. Top of the range is the A-class *Lucy* (☎ 23831). Budget hotels lie nearer the bridge. These include the *Kentrikon* (☎ 71525) and the very noisy (and primitive) *Kymata* (☎ 21317) and *Iris* (☎ 22246). Meantime, on the mainland side you will find the quieter *Hara* (☎ 25541) is very reasonable.

Eretria has several mid-range hotels including the good C-class *Xenia* (☎ 61202). As it stands alone on a causeway-linked islet on the east side of the town (recently renamed **Dream Island**) noise is not a problem. **Kimi Port** has rooms and two hotels, the best being the C-class *Beis* (☎ 22604).

A

There is camping on Evia — 19 sites in all — but they are poorly placed and totally geared up to serving motor-campers rather than backpackers. Island hoppers are likely to find that the reasonable site near **Pefki**: *Camping Pefki* (☎ 22960 41121) is of most use. There is also a fair site near **Eretria**: *Camping Milos* (☎ 22290 60420).

👀

If you discount the attractive pine-clad mountain scenery, the **Euripus Channel** in **Chalcis** is Evia's most noteworthy sight, and boasts a 2500 year pedigree as a tourist attraction thanks to the odd combination of land and currents which make the tide change eight times a day. Since the building of the first bridge over the 30 m-wide narrows in the 5 C. BC, the locals have wondered over the phenomenon. Aristotle is reputed to have drowned when he threw himself into the sea in exasperation at his inability to explain it. His successors still haven't come up with the answer but, given the murky state of the water, have generally opted for cleaner and less terminal forms of expressing their frustration.

Signs of the ancient city are as well hidden (thanks to obscuring later buildings) as the seabed, and archaeology fans will do best to head for the **Archaeological Museum**, which houses finds from all over the island. The remains of ancient **Eretria** offer better sightseeing; the great rival of **Chalcis** has a notable theatre (largely denuded of stone), several important houses and a section of city wall, complete with the best-preserved Archaic period gate in Greece.

GIAROS

🚌 No bus service

⛵ No beach boat service

N

Prison ●●

489 m ⛰⛰ □ ⚓

●●
Sea Cliffs

0   km 5

GLARONISI

Giaros
ΓΙΑΡΟΣ; 19 km²; pop. 0.

Travel on a ferry out of Piraeus to Paros and the first substantial island you steam past is Giaros (also transcribed 'Yiaros', 'Gyaros' and 'Gioura'). This is somewhat ironic, because this is the only Cycladic island which has never been accessible to the hordes that swarm across the Aegean each summer. Instead it has been home to a succession of unwilling visitors — its history being a barometer of political extremism in Greece in the last century.

Boasting a sea-cliff along its south side and a generally crinkly coastline, Giaros looks barren and inhospitable — an impression that isn't dispelled on landing. Covered with a thin scatter of thistles, rough grass and scruffy bushes, this is one island that wasn't reoccupied after pirate incursions in the early Middle Ages. However, its proximity to Athens made it an ideal location when a repressive Greek government in the 1930s was looking around for a suitable island on which to establish a detention centre for political prisoners. Briefly abandoned during WW2, it came

under military control soon after and was converted to a political prison during the 1946–50 Greek civil war (the task of the first inmates was to construct their own cells). The last prisoner was released in 1961, but the respite from misery was short-lived: the prison was again reactivated as a home for political dissidents between 1967–74, when the Colonels seized power. After the restoration of democracy the island was used as a naval base-cum-gunboat firing range.

However, things are now set to change. In 2002 Giaros was declared by a presidential decree to be a 'national monument' and released from military control. Plans were put forward to restore the prison buildings, build a new pier and turn the island into a tourist attraction. Since the announcement was made, silence has reigned, but it is just possible that tours will start up — probably from Syros. If you get the chance to go, take it, as Giaros promises to offer a Greek island experience like no other — particularly if another mooted idea comes to fruition. Given the opposition on many islands to wind farms, it has been suggested that Giaros be topped with several hundred turbines, each 70 m high: the project could generate up to a tenth of Greece's energy needs and help meet demanding EU renewable energy targets.

😲

Giaros can claim one notable footnote in history: in 37 AD it was suggested that two leading Romans — Silanus and Marsus Vibius, who attracted the wrath of the dying Emperor Tiberius — be exiled to the island after facing charges of treason and adultery. In the event the Roman Senate decided that this punishment would be inhuman and the two ended up suffering the 'torments' of banishment to Amorgos instead. As Rome's power waned, Giaros took on a new identity as a base for pirates — a role that continued into the Middle Ages. This history of operating as a prison before pirates move in is being repeated today: in 2001, as the military moved out, modern day pirates — in the form of refugee smugglers — moved in, marooning 35 illegal immigrants, after they were intercepted by the Coast Guard en route to Kythnos.

Mykonos

MYKONOΣ; 88 km²; pop. 5,700.

CODE ☎ 22890
PORT POLICE ☎ 22218
POLICE ☎ 22482
FIRST AID ☎ 23994

Now among the most heavily touristed (and expensive) of all the Greek islands and the location for the get-away-from-it-all film *Shirley Valentine*, Mykonos is one of those islands that are really superb at the quieter times of the year, but which descend into the realms of the truly awful at the peak of the High Season (with over 750,000 visitors a year some of the residents even go island hopping to get away from the chaos—especially in mid-July to mid-August).

Mykonos has been near the top of the Greek island tourist map since the mid-1960s, courtesy of one of the most scenic harbours in the Mediterranean, a profusion of good sand beaches tolerating nudism, and the nearby premier sightseeing island of Delos. Unfortunately, the prolonged exposure to heavy tourism is reflected in the terrible damage wrought on the landscape—thanks to the excessive amount of hotel and holiday-home building—and on the local tourist industry (the attitude on Mykonos to tourists is increasingly reminiscent of Athens: the old-fashioned Greek ideal that 'visitors are guests' somehow completely goes by the board in the face of the sheer numbers visiting). Sadly, you need to always check your change carefully — even on buses — and keep an eye out for double-charging in supermarkets.

Formerly a preserve of the world's jet-setters, Mykonos always has exhibited wildly inflated prices, with a town centre dominated by expensive boutiques and nightclubs where French and the party crowd thrive. A procession of cruise ships calling provides little incentive to keep prices down (you should reckon on paying a 25% premium for the pleasure of a stay on Mykonos). Notwithstanding the cost of living, backpackers also swarm over the

island each summer in large numbers, their great redeeming function being to make the island much safer for the single male who, in years past, was apt to find out what the fairer sex have to put up with — thanks to a vibrant gay scene.

Unfortunately, Mykonos also attracts a goodly number of rowdy urban Greeks, seemingly attracted by the island's reputation for loose living. At their best they clog the roads with mass moped displays; at their worst they have, in past years, included a rapist with a knife, and a mass convention of graffiti artists. All this sounds pretty dire, but if you are careful when here, and come at the right time, Mykonos is still a very rewarding place to visit — so don't be put off by the negative aspects; there are plenty of positives as well.

Mykonos — Which Port?

● When you buy a ferry ticket on Mykonos check carefully which of the island's two ports (**Old Port** or **Tourlos**) your boat or catamaran is departing from.

● If you buy a ticket for a boat departing from Mykonos on another island, be sure to check on its departure point with a local ticket agent when you get to Mykonos.

The new port at **Tourlos**, looking like a large offshore runway (linked by a bridge to the island), was built primarily to cater for cruise ships too large to enter the **Old Port**. The majority of ferries and catamarans are now using it too — but some are not. This is regularly causing confusion for island hoppers, and almost every day sees passengers caught at the wrong port when their boat turns up.

Unfortunately the distance between the ports makes it difficult to rectify the problem once a boat has docked — though those caught out often do try: the most dramatic attempt saw the world treated to the sight of a desperate running island hopper pushing her wheelchair-bound partner along the coast road in the dark, in a breathless (and futile) attempt to catch a night boat.

Mykonos Town—Agios Stephanos buses call at both ports during daylight hours, but there is no transport at Tourlos at night. There are no ticket facilities at Tourlos.

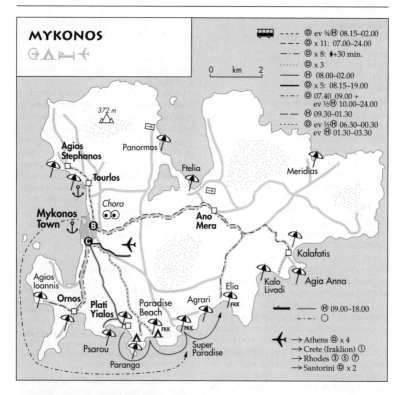

MYKONOS

The only large settlement on a small island, **Mykonos Town** is the overburdened hub of all this activity. Centred on the famous crescent-shaped harbour bay with its headland topped with windmills, it is an attractive maze of whitewashed cubic houses riddled with alleyways. A popular story hereabout is that the town layout was deliberately planned to distract both would-be pirates (to say nothing of tourists) and the *meltemi* wind that attacks Mykonos very hard each summer. In fact this isn't the case: most of Mykonos Town has been constructed since the 18 c., with only the small Little Venice/Kastro district on the harbour headland dating from the time of pirate activity. The story has none the less

gained credence because it so easily could be true. The chora street maze is one of the largest of its kind in the Cyclades and is so intricate that it happily baffles seasoned visitors. The chances are that sooner or later you will be obliged to head for either the hills and the roads that surround the town, or the chaos that is the bus square at Plati Yialos, or the harbour itself, in order to re-establish your bearings.

The harbour, naturally the focal point of the town, is stunningly attractive when viewed from the hill behind the quay. However, the heavy waterfront mix of tavernas, souvenir and (expensive) gold and silver shops, backed by bars, nightclubs and restaurants, quickly dispels any pretence that this is an unspoilt island town. This is not to say that Mykonos Town doesn't exude Greek island charm, for it does — almost to excess. But it is difficult to escape the impression that it is contrived and done purely for the tourists' benefit. This can be seen in the spate of windmill rebuilding on the hills around the town.

Fortunately, amidst the tourists and building, echoes of the old Mykonos can still be found; the locals who aren't in the tourist industry somehow manage to carry on with their daily routine, seemingly oblivious to the mayhem around them, and still walk down to the waterfront each morning to buy freshly caught fish, produce and newly laid eggs (note: the ostrich eggs on show are only for advertising purposes). Tourists also get in on the act by relieving the fishermen of any part of their catch that they can't sell, so that they can throw fish to the very photogenic pelicans that are allowed to flap the streets at will.

If the pelicans have got any sense, they keep their feathers well down at night, for Mykonos Town after dark is something else; in High Season the place literally throbs. Unfortunately, some hereabouts throb too much, particularly when confronted by an unattached female, and Mykonos has had more than its share of problems (those who find all this difficult to square with the fact that this is the *Shirley Valentine* island should note that the film was shot well out of season — in sunny November would you believe — when the pretence of a dreamy, idyllic Greek island could be maintained). Things reached a new low in the summer of 2008 when a 20-year-old Australian tourist was chased and beaten to death by four nightclub staff following an argument over a bag.

Of course you don't have to join the partying crowds following each other around in search of the latest hip bar. Provided you can live with the prices (scenic views add a serious premium to food and bar bills) you will find plenty of places to socialize over a meal. The big taverna districts are the old

The Mykonos Pelicans

The history of the Mykonos pelican (the town's famous mascot, and a beast that is snapped for every photo-orientated Greek island guidebook) is worth a mention as it provides a good insight into how the island has gone ever down.

For some strange reason only known to themselves, pelicans have a history of being attracted to Mykonos: this is an odd addiction as there is nothing obvious to draw them to the island. None the less, they have been a feature of the tourist scene for over three hundred years. The first recorded skirmish with a holidaymaker occurred in 1689 when an English savant called Bernard Randolph encountered a small colony of the birds. Like all tourists he couldn't resist the temptation to fill a pelican's enormous bill — though in his case he seems to have killed the creature first. He amused himself thereafter by pouring jugs of water into its beak pouch, recording that it took twelve quarts and still had room to spare.

Squawks of this terrible incident obviously got around, because after this pelicans gave Mykonos the bird until a reckless individual landed on the island in 1956 during a storm. The castaway rapidly emerged as a premier attraction, and the locals persuaded it to stay by clipping its wings and naming it Petros. In the event this was a slight misnomer as it was petrol that did for it: the poor thing was run over in 1985 — a victim of the island's traffic injury boom. Fortunately, its killer — a passing taxi driver — also fancied himself as a taxidermist and attempted to recover the situation by stuffing his victim. This was not an unqualified success, as the deception was noticed; the islanders thereafter decided to install Petros in the Folklore Museum and get in a couple of replacements, hoping that no one would spot the difference (they are now usually to be found near the waterfront, looking vainly for a refuge from the camera-snapping crowds).

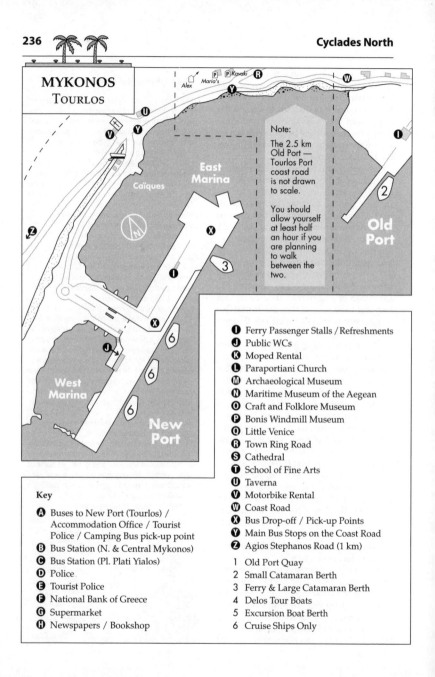

MYKONOS
TOURLOS

Note:

The 2.5 km Old Port — Tourlos Port coast road is not drawn to scale.

You should allow yourself at least half an hour if you are planning to walk between the two.

East Marina

Caïques

Old Port

West Marina

New Port

I Ferry Passenger Stalls / Refreshments
J Public WCs
K Moped Rental
L Paraportiani Church
M Archaeological Museum
N Maritime Museum of the Aegean
O Craft and Folklore Museum
P Bonis Windmill Museum
Q Little Venice
R Town Ring Road
S Cathedral
T School of Fine Arts
U Taverna
V Motorbike Rental
W Coast Road
X Bus Drop-off / Pick-up Points
Y Main Bus Stops on the Coast Road
Z Agios Stephanos Road (1 km)

1 Old Port Quay
2 Small Catamaran Berth
3 Ferry & Large Catamaran Berth
4 Delos Tour Boats
5 Excursion Boat Berth
6 Cruise Ships Only

Key

A Buses to New Port (Tourlos) / Accommodation Office / Tourist Police / Camping Bus pick-up point
B Bus Station (N. & Central Mykonos)
C Bus Station (Pl. Plati Yialos)
D Police
E Tourist Police
F National Bank of Greece
G Supermarket
H Newspapers / Bookshop

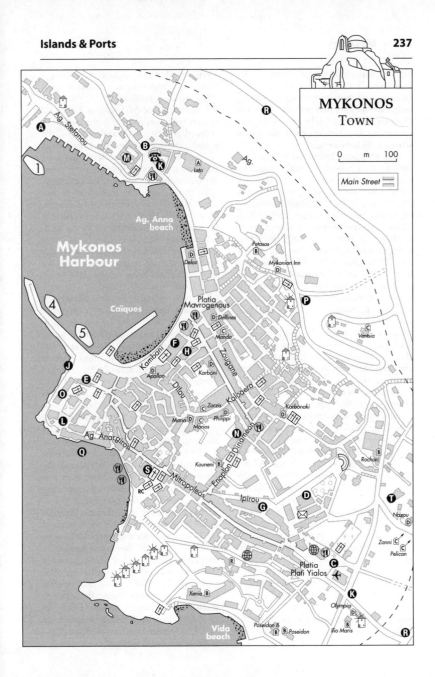

MYKONOS
Town

0 m 100

Main Street

Mykonos Harbour

Ag. Stefanou

Ag. Anna beach

Caïques

Platia Mavrogenous

Kambani

Apollon

Karboni

Ditou

Zorzis

Maria

Marios

Philippi

Ag. Anargiron

Kouneni

Mitropoleos

RC

Ipirou

Leto

Petasos

Delos

Delfines

Manda

Zougane

Kaloaera

Karbonaki

Dinameon

Enoplon

Vendsia

Rochari

Olympia

Ilio Maris

Poseidon II

Poseidon

Xenia

Vida beach

Platia Plati Yialos

Nazou

Zanni

Pelican

Mykonian Inn

harbour waterfront and the Little Venice area of the chora. As with all premier tourist areas, staff turnover is high so making recommendations that will stand the test of time are difficult: it is best to follow your eyes and make a decision after looking over what others are eating.

After Mykonos Town and its nightlife, the island's beaches are the other big draw — particularly those on the south coast, which offers an appealing mix of windy headlands and bays decorated with long strands of fine sand. These start at **Plati Yialos**, a crowded, hotel-backed beach with a small quay from which caïques shuttle along the coast to Paradise, Super Paradise and Elia beaches. All bar Plati Yialos have their nudist end. **Paradise Beach** is the most famous (and crowded), though it is somewhat overrated: the sheer numbers of people packing it out during the High Season result in it being much more of a social venue than a viable beach. Nudism is confined to a few brave women and a clutch of posing gay men on the western end. The beach bar attached to the disco-cum-campsite complex behind the beach also really goes to town when it comes to charging very high prices.

Super Paradise has traditionally been the island's gay beach, but these days it has a pretty even mix of sexes, and more nudity than Paradise. **Elia Beach** is the best of the four and is predominately nude. All are linked by a rough path which on a windy day, or out of High Season can make for pleasant, if energetic, walking (it is also worth noting that the stretch between Paradise and Super Paradise is a gay cruising ground during the summer months).

Taking the overspill from the crowded south-coast strands are the windy north-coast beaches. However, most require you to get there under your own steam as they are not served by the island buses. You have to take care where you swim as offshore currents can be dangerous in places. The best of these beaches are to be found at **Panormos** and **Ftelia**; both draw sufficient crowds to have several tavernas behind them, though Ftelia is the more popular thanks to good windsurfing conditions.

The interior of Mykonos is hilly and barren with surprisingly few villages. In marked contrast with nearby Paros, the island is made of granite rather than marble. Its starker hills have scattered outcrops of dark grey rocks that contrast more vividly with the whitewashed buildings. Like Tinos it also has more than its fair share of elaborately constructed dovecots. However, the landscape's former charm is being significantly degraded by the massive numbers of new holiday homes now under construction. Hill sky lines (which were formerly sacrosanct no-go areas for new builds) are being ruined right across the island.

The only village of any size inland is at **Ano Mera**. Developed out of a cluster of farmsteads, its limited tourist development potential has saved it from the worst excesses seen elsewhere. It is the centre of one of the few remaining unspoilt parts of the island, and actually has a larger winter population than Mykonos Town. The village is very low key, but the main street is home to one notable building — a 17 c. monastery church, **Panagia Tourliani**. Although comparatively new, it contains fragments of earlier buildings, suggesting that it replaced an earlier church on the same site (during the period of Turkish rule the inhabitants of the Greek islands were forbidden to build new churches, but replacing existing buildings was permitted).

Other centres are small; the most visited is **Agios Stephanos**, which has a substandard (for Mykonos) beach that is popular because it is easy to get to. Buses run frequently around Mykonos, particularly between the town and all the popular beaches. Unusually for a Greek island they operate into the small hours during the summer months. Ferry links are also good. Sailings to Rafina (usually labelled 'Athens') are widely advertised without mention of the stops at Tinos and Andros.

☺

Lying so close to Delos, ancient Mykonos found itself eclipsed by its more famous neighbour. Lacking notable cities or sanctuaries, it was best known — thanks largely to the writer Strabo — for being the home of an excessively large number of bald men (some things don't change). When Athens took control of Delos via the Delian League, rule over Mykonos inevitably came as part of the package, and thereafter the island's fate was tied to that city. This only changed with the collapse of the Byzantine empire. Mykonos then found itself first under the rule of the Dukes of Naxos and, once that brief dynasty foundered, under Venetian control (via Tinos). This lasted until the Ottomans took the island in 1537.

During the years of Turkish rule Mykonos quietly prospered, its shipping and trading activities developing because of its strategic position. During the 17 c. the island managed to avoid pirate attacks by setting itself up as a booty-laundering trading post. Ostensibly a centre for regular sea merchants, it turned a blind eye to any tradesmen sporting eye patches (an 'it might be going on, but we don't see any of it' attitude that continues to serve the islanders well). This trade became so developed that it was said that some of the captain's houses in the town had secret basements in which to store booty.

Thanks to its large merchant fleet, Mykonos played an important part in the War of Independence against the Turks, providing a heroine called Mando Mavrogenous. A local merchant's daughter, she led the island's uprising in 1822, and funded the arming of ships to fight for the embryonic Greek state.

⊨

Mykonos has a hotel and room information office next to the Old Port quay; this makes life easy, but not that easy as beds fill up early in High Season. Perhaps more than with any other island it pays to arrive before noon.

The town has a number of C and D 'standard' (one hesitates to say 'priced') hotels, including the waterfront *Apollon* (☎ 22223) and a varied collection on Kaloaera St., including the C-class *Zorzis* (☎ 22167) and *Marios* (☎ 22704) and the D-class *Maria* (☎ 24212) and *Philippi* (☎ 22294). The hills behind the town include the noisy *Olympia* (☎ 22964), the better-placed *Nazou* (☎ 22626) and C-class *Zanni* (☎ 22486) and *Pelican* (☎ 23454). In a pinch, both campsites offer over-priced chalets.

At the top end of the market is the A-class *Leto* (☎ 22207), which earlier in the last century played host to the King of Greece, and those similarly well-off ever since. A second bet if you want everything from satellite TV to saunas and jacuzzis is one of the three *Petasos Hotels* on Mykonos: one in the town (☎ 22608), and two at Plati Yialos (☎ 23437).

A

Mykonos has two sites an easy five minutes' walk from each other (via the coast path). Intense competition ensures a frantic grab for campers off the boats. Both sites charge the same rates and are among the most expensive in the Aegean (reckon on paying at least €3 more per day than elsewhere).

Camping Mykonos (☎ 24578) is the newer of the sites. It sits astride a headland abutting Paranga beach. Now easily the best on the island (though this is relative and, compared to sites on other islands, isn't saying a lot), its facilities include a reception internet link. The site is served by hourly buses running to Mykonos Town. It is let down by a pricey mini-market and very basic washing facilities. *Paradise Beach Camping* (☎ 22852): the older site on Mykonos, in recent years it has become more of an expensive entertainment venue rather than a serious place to stay. As a campsite it suffers thanks to the total inability of anyone staying here to get any sleep. This is because of the noise generated by the on-going non-stop beach disco (complete with fireworks and pool parties, and DJ-led dancing on bar tops from midday on). On the plus side, the site's showers and toilets have, after years of neglect, now had some attention.

≥✿

Nightlife is scattered pretty evenly around the town. The hottest venues change with each year, though there are regular favourites. These include the inevitable big *Hard Rock Café* complex on the Ano Mera road (reached via free mini-buses from the town) and a cluster of small bars near the Paraportiani church. These include the *Windmill Disco*, the *Irish Disco* and the *Scandinavian Bar*. More up-market venues are to be found behind the waterfront at Little Venice and the yacht marina near the ferry quay.

👁️👁️

Mykonos lacks archaeological or historical sites (the proximity of neighbouring Delos did little to encourage building during the Classical period), but **Mykonos Town** offers plenty by way of compensation. Although the Venetian kastro that once adorned the western promontory of the town is long gone, a row of wooden galleried houses known as **'Little Venice'** remain from the period, the multicoloured balconies hanging over the sea providing one of the town's picture-postcard views.

Close by the site of the kastro stands the **Paraportiani**, the famous group of five picturesque chapels plastered together in 'melting ice cream' fashion (four on the ground level, with one above). Usually kept locked, it is said to date back to the Byzantine era, though the earliest datable remains are from 1425, while most of the structure is a product of the 16 c. and 17 c. The church's name means 'little door' and is said to reflect the fact that it was built just outside the lost castle's postern gate.

The rest of Mykonos Town also lends itself to exploration with a clutch of five museums to visit:

The **Archaeological Museum** (open ②–⑦ 08.30–15.00; entrance fee €3) is housed in a large drab and dusty 1905-built building overlooking the old port that hasn't been touched since. Built specifically to house the finds from Delian graves on the nearby island of Rinia (when Delos was sanctified in the 5 c. BC, the new laws forbidding death and burial on the island required all existing burials to be reinterred on Rinia), it has to be said that this is probably the most boring museum in the Greek islands. The vast majority of finds from Rinia are decorated pots from the geometric period. Even ardent archaeology fans are likely to find that after the 20th display case even patterned pots begin to pall. There are a few pieces from later periods (including some red-figure ware with engaging animal illustrations — including a hare held by its ears) and some later Roman glassware. The few pieces of sculpture aren't up to much either.

In fact the only reason to visit is to see the museum's one great object: commanding pride of place in the main gallery is a 7 c. BC red terracotta pithos vase decorated with a relief showing the earliest known depiction of the wooden horse of Troy. A product from a workshop on Tinos, it was found in the kastro district of Mykonos Town.

Walk around Mykonos Town and sooner or later you will stumble upon a redundant cannon barrel lying in the street close by a low boundary wall of an old town house. This is the signpost for the **Maritime Museum of the Aegean** (open ⑨ 10.30–13.00, 18.30–21.00; entrance fee €3). Established and funded by a local shipping millionaire, the museum offers a rewarding hour's browsing. The exhibits consist of a varied collection of nautical odds and ends spread over three rooms, and a lawn garden. While there is little of serious historical interest on show, the collection — in the main of model ships — is of a quality that you would expect to find belonging to an affluent patron. The rooms are stuffed with items, making for a very colourful secret hoard-like display.

Prize exhibits include a front-room display of early Aegean coins featuring ship designs, which then follow through into model examples of ship types from triremes to Venetian galleys set out in chronological order. The larger of the two back rooms displays artefacts relating to the sea war in Greece's struggle for independence, while the smaller is devoted to maps, ship's papers and other ephemera. The garden is home to rusting anchors, reproduction ship gravestones and the impressive top 20 feet of a late 19 c. lighthouse which once stood on the north-west tip of Mykonos.

The oddball nature of some of the exhibits adds something to this museum. Any collection that can embrace a model of the *Endeavour* (the ship made famous by Captain Cook — who apparently discovered the Aegean by way of Australia) and a parasol sported by the rebel leader Mando Mavrogenous is sure to have something going for it.

Next door to the Maritime Museum is **Lena's House**, the perfectly preserved 19 c. home of a local woman. Irregular opening times, but worth a look if you want a sanitized view of a Cycladian house in J. T. Bent's time.

Finally, the tiny **Craft and Folklore Museum** on the seafront (open ⑨ 17.30–20.30) takes the form of a restored 17 c. sea captain's house. It offers a brief glimpse of pre-tourist island life and *that* over-stuffed pelican (minus any tale-telling taxi tyre tracks). A museum offshoot is the working **Bonis Windmill** (complete with various agricultural exhibits) on the hillside east of the harbour; admission is free. Even though the mill is usually locked, this is an absolute 'must visit' attraction thanks to the spectacular town and harbour views.

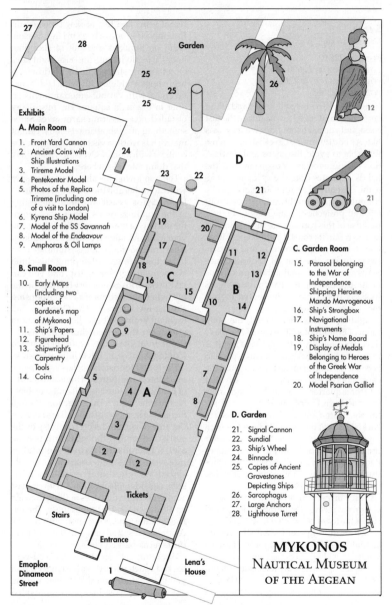

Exhibits

A. Main Room

1. Front Yard Cannon
2. Ancient Coins with Ship Illustrations
3. Trireme Model
4. Pentekontor Model
5. Photos of the Replica Trireme (including one of a visit to London)
6. Kyrena Ship Model
7. Model of the SS *Savannah*
8. Model of the *Endeavour*
9. Amphoras & Oil Lamps

B. Small Room

10. Early Maps (including two copies of Bordone's map of Mykonos)
11. Ship's Papers
12. Figurehead
13. Shipwright's Carpentry Tools
14. Coins

C. Garden Room

15. Parasol belonging to the War of Independence Shipping Heroine Mando Mavrogenous
16. Ship's Strongbox
17. Navigational Instruments
18. Ship's Name Board
19. Display of Medals Belonging to Heroes of the Greek War of Independence
20. Model Psarian Galliot

D. Garden

21. Signal Cannon
22. Sundial
23. Ship's Wheel
24. Binnacle
25. Copies of Ancient Gravestones Depicting Ships
26. Sarcophagus
27. Large Anchors
28. Lighthouse Turret

Garden

Tickets

Stairs

Entrance

Emoplon Dinameon Street

Lena's House

MYKONOS
NAUTICAL MUSEUM
OF THE AEGEAN

Syros

ΣΥΡΟΣ; 86 km²; pop. 21,000.

CODE ☎ 22810
PORT POLICE ☎ 22690
TOURIST POLICE ☎ 22620
POLICE ☎ 23555

Imagine a relatively small, arid island with a large mainland-sized town built on the east coast, and you have some idea what Syros is like. An oddity among Greek islands, Syros was able to avoid the chaos and destruction encountered by most islands at the hands of pirates from the 17 c. on, thanks to the existence of a strong Roman Catholic community that sought and got the patronage and protection of the King of France. Because of this connection, the island was able to retain its coastal settlements rather than retreat from them to inland centres. Even during the War of Independence Syros was able to maintain a precarious neutrality, making it a haven for refugees (notably from Chios) who served to give the economy a massive boost.

Building on this background, the main town of **Ermoupolis** ('The city of Hermes') developed rapidly in the 19 c. (as a result of its role as *the* mid-Aegean coaling port) to become the largest in the Cyclades and the capital of the group. The town is divided into three quarters. This might sound Greek but is perfectly logical given the geography; for the waterfront and its environs are backed by two building-clad hills — each topped with a church, one Roman Catholic, the other Orthodox. Add to this a superb natural harbour, and they combine to produce one of the most impressive approaches when viewed from a ferry.

Closer inspection reveals a rather more chequered picture, for the rapid commercial rise of the town is reflected in its buildings, which are more in keeping with the dowdy capitals of Chios and Sami rather than the white cubist buildings that are such a feature of the Cyclades. Fortunately the islanders have made a conspicuous — and largely successful — effort to improve things in recent years and the all-new polished-up Ermoupolis exudes a buzz in High Season. Dead on Sundays and out of shopping hours, it explodes into life once night falls. Quiet narrow streets filled with down-at-heel shops suddenly fill with tables and tavernas, with various entertainments on offer in the main square. The miscellany of faded neo-classical charm gives Syros something neighbouring islands cannot match: it is worth a visit just to capture the contrast with the cute Cycladic-village look that dominates elsewhere.

The two town hills also contrast greatly with each other and the lower town. Catholic **Ano Syros** is easily the more interesting as the buildings on its upper slopes form the nucleus of the original island chora. On your left-hand side as you enter the harbour, it has a meandering staircase running down to the lower town. Attempting this climb is a popular sightseeing trip, and you can take in the British Cemetery halfway up the hill (where the victims of a WW1 troopship sinking are interred). The Orthodox hill town on **Vrontado** only dates from the 19 c. and, bar the domed church that marks it out from the more kastro-like church topping Ano Syros, it has little of interest.

The recent tourist influx has yet to make much impact on the rest of the island. North of Ermoupolis, tourists will find they have become the main local attraction, though increasing numbers of hillwalkers head for the area. The main resort (courtesy of the best island beach — though this isn't saying a lot) is at scruffy **Galissas**, a 15-minute bus ride away on the west coast. Once a widely spread-out agricultural community, it has seen considerable in-filling with tourist accommodation that does nothing to create an attractive sense of community. The village is a disappointing spot, with no real centre; as a result all things radiate out from the taverna-backed bus stop.

Weekends find the tree- and reed-bed-backed beach packed with islanders, so if you like solitude you will do better going elsewhere. One possible option — provided

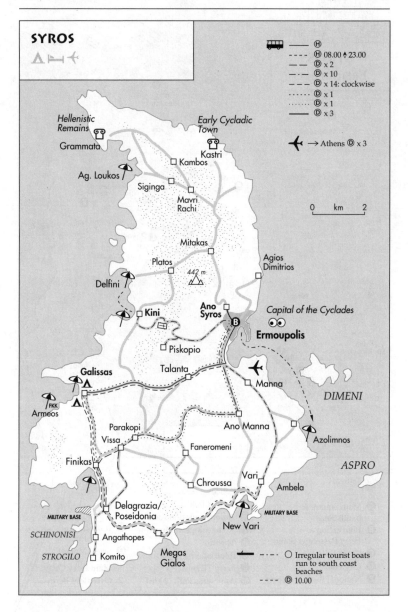

SYROS

🚌 ───	Ⓗ
----	Ⓗ 08.00 ♦ 23.00
──	Ⓓ x 2
──	Ⓓ x 10
──	Ⓓ x 14: clockwise
····	Ⓓ x 1
····	Ⓓ x 1
───	Ⓓ x 3

✈ → Athens Ⓓ x 3

Hellenistic Remains
Grammata

Early Cycladic Town
Kastri

Kambos

Ag. Loukos

Siginga

Mavri Rachi

0   km   2

Mitakas

Platos

442 m.

Agios Dimitrios

Delfini

Kini

Ano Syros
Ⓑ

Capital of the Cyclades
👁👁

Ermoupolis

Piskopio

Talanta

Manna

DIMENI

Galissas

Parakopi

Ano Manna

Vissa

Azolimnos

FKK
Armeos

Faneromeni

ASPRO

Finikas

Chroussa

Vari

Ambela

Delagrazia/
Poseidonia

MILITARY BASE

MILITARY BASE

SCHINONISI

Angathopes

New Vari

STROGILO

Komito

Megas Gialos

──·── ○ Irregular tourist boats run to south coast beaches

---- Ⓓ 10.00

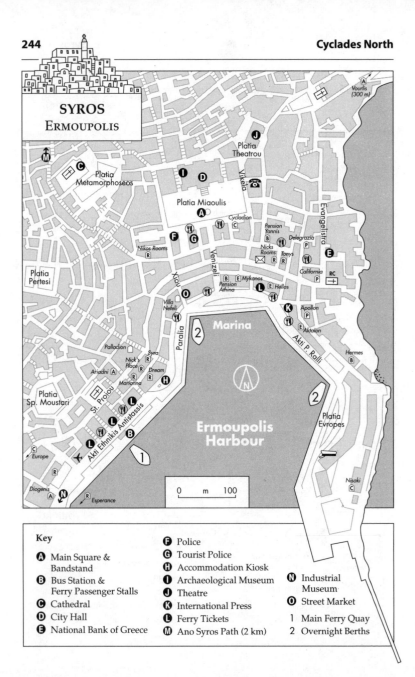

SYROS
ERMOUPOLIS

Platia
Theatrou

Vikela

Platia
Metamorphoseos

Platia Miaoulis

Cycladion

Evangelistra

Pension
Yannis

Delegrazia

Nikos Rooms

Nicks
Rooms

Tonys

California

RC

Platia
Pertesi

Xiou

Venizelou

Pension
Athina

Mykonos

Hellas

Apollon

Villa
Nefeli

Paralia

Marina

Aktaion

Palladion

Syra

Nick's
Place

Dream

Ariadni

Margarina

St. Protou

Akti P. Ralli

Hermes

Platia
Sp. Moustari

Akti Ethnikis Antistassis

Platia
Evropes

Ermoupolis
Harbour

Europe

Nisaki

Diogenis

Esperance

0   m   100

Key

A Main Square &
Bandstand

B Bus Station &
Ferry Passenger Stalls

C Cathedral

D City Hall

E National Bank of Greece

F Police

G Tourist Police

H Accommodation Kiosk

I Archaeological Museum

J Theatre

K International Press

L Ferry Tickets

M Ano Syros Path (2 km)

N Industrial
Museum

O Street Market

1 Main Ferry Quay

2 Overnight Berths

you are up to it — is to take the path over the southern headland to the island's recognized nudist beach at **Armeos** (voyeurs shouldn't get their hopes up as there are usually as few nudists as clothes on view: Syros isn't a noted naturist destination).

South of Galissas is a resort strip running from **Finikas** down to **Delagrazia** (alias **Poseidonia**). However, the beaches are even more scruffy (though less crowded), and one has to search pretty hard to justify stopping here with so many other good beach islands close to hand. The remaining southern half of Syros is, if truth be told, best seen from a bus: merely a collection of small villages scattered over low-lying countryside and lacking tourist appeal.

Ferry links with Syros, after a few years in decline, are now growing again. We are still a long way from the days when Ermoupolis was the hub of the Cycladic ferry system, but Syros is now the home port for several ferries that run around the Cyclades, providing invaluable High Season links between different island lines. Overnight they dock at points around the harbour rather than at the main ferry quay (which is easily identified by the passenger stalls and neighbouring taxi and bus stations). Frequency of buses to the main centres is good, but dominated by one-way services.

😙

In prehistoric times Syros was an important centre (though most remains lie in the less accessible north). In the Classical and Hellenistic period the main city, Syria (which until recently was still used as an alternative name for the island), stood on the site of Ermoupolis, but almost nothing survives. It was abandoned during the pirate-infested Middle Ages in favour of Ano Syros. Syros wasn't an active player in the 19 c. War of Independence, but the island was irrevocably changed by it thanks to the influx of refugees from scorched Chios and Psara. Thereafter it grew to become Greece's largest 19 c. coal bunkering port.

🛏

There are beds aplenty in **Ermoupolis**; most are at the budget end of the market, and are advertised by a forest of signs. Given the comparatively small numbers of tourists visiting

Syros, finding a bed is rarely a problem and there is now a quayside kiosk to help you. At the top end of the market are the plush A-class *Ariadni* and the quayside *Dream Rooms*. Cheaper options include *Tonys*, buried in the warren of streets behind the waterfront, the better located *Apollon* (☎ 22158) and *Athina* (☎ 23600). Mid-range hotels are not so centrally placed. Nearest is the B-class *Hermes* (☎ 28011) with its own tiny private beach. On the west side of the port is the C-class *Europe* (☎ 28771). Elsewhere on Syros beds are few except at **Galissas**, which has a supply of rooms.

Λ

The campsite on Syros is at **Galissas**. Set in a pistachio tree grove, *Two Hearts Camping* (☎ 42052) is an attractive, well-maintained site. Don't be put off by the romantic pitch to their advertising — the author of this book can testify that broken single hearts are also admitted. Mini-buses meet boats berthing at the main ferry quay only.

👓

Ermoupolis offers the main sightseeing on Syros, and unusually for a Greek island town is well endowed with street names (the west European influence coming to the fore again). Several blocks up from the waterfront are the impressive **Miaoulis Square**. Adorned with a statue of the Greek hero of the War of Independence after which it is named, and a bandstand, it is lined with bars along all but the north side. To the west side of the town hall dominating the square is a free three-room **Archaeological Museum** housing exhibits (including several Cycladic figures) from other Cycladic islands too small to possess one. Just north-east of the square you will also find a miniature version of La Scala **Opera House**: built in 1862, it has been closed almost ever since. In the industrial area south of the port is a good **Industrial Museum** — the main building (one of three) being a converted lead-shot factory.

The hills north of **Kastri** offer possibly the most intriguing and (unless you like hard hill-walking) inaccessible sites on the island. Ringing the top of one are the walls of one of the largest of the **Early Cycladic** culture villages discovered. It clearly was defensive in function (the odd horseshoe-shaped bastion aside, the surviving 'ramparts' look just like typical hill farm walls), and was accompanied by a large cemetery that has yielded up a number of important Cycladic figurines.

Tinos
ΤΗΝΟΣ; 193 km²; pop. 7,730.

CODE ☎ 22830
PORT POLICE ☎ 22348
POLICE ☎ 22100
FIRST AID ☎ 22210

The spiritual centre of modern Greece, mountainous Tinos even outshines Patmos for raw pilgrim-pulling power. Both are officially 'holy islands' but the religious element is far more pervasive here — even though Tinos is far less well known outside Greece. Billed as the Lourdes of the Aegean, Sundays and the Virgin Mary-related festivals on the 25th March (Annunciation), and particularly the 15th of August (Feast of the Assumption), see the main centre of Tinos Town jam-packed with the faithful. If you plan to stay, then you should try to avoid arriving on Tinos on Saturdays and in the week preceding these festivals.

The focus of all this activity is an icon housed in the church that dominates the town: the Panagia Evangelistria (or Megalochari, meaning 'Great Joy'). As a result of this, Tinos has thrived happily on Greek rather than foreign tourism (something all too evident in the all-Greek timetables outside ticket agencies), and it is still struggling to emerge as a significant foreign tourist destination.

Coated with a sprinkling of small villages and over 1,200 picturesque dovecots (the island speciality), Tinos is very attractive. However, it remains very much of a 'one town' island and is best explored via excursions from the port and centre of **Tinos Town**. A largely modern affair, it owes its existence solely to the church and icon; and this shows, for as you approach by ferry, the seemingly thin scatter of buildings looks to have a rather tenuous hold on the foreshore.

Once within the confines of the harbour mole the town reveals itself to be a substantial, but largely modern, settlement — no old-world chora charm here. Its most conspicuous feature is the main street that

runs up the hillside from the waterfront to the impressive walls and ornate plaster façade of the church at the back of the town. In fact, Tinos Town is dominated by three streets: the waterfront (replete with ticket agencies, restaurant, and a reasonable small supermarket south of the Port Police office), the pedestrianized Evangelistrias (lined with a number of particularly tacky souvenir shops) and Leoforos Megalocharis, the main processional road to the church. On feast days devout pilgrims process up it on their knees (a carpet is nailed to the side of the road expressly for this purpose), stopping off only to buy candles — some up to 2 m high — from shops along the way. This all sounds serious stuff, yet the town feels a very relaxed, laid-back sort of place, and is a nice base for exploration. It is even a viable base for day-tripping to Mykonos and its boats to Delos — if you don't mind starting early and paying return fares on the catamarans.

As elsewhere the waterfront is the centre of activity. The harbour road is quite busy, and the location of the bus station, at the end of the old ferry quay, hardly helps matters, but if the waterfront isn't the most idyllic in the islands, there are plenty of tavernas of the larger pilgrim catering type. The menus are exclusively Greek.

Tinos Town also has a couple of beaches reasonably close to hand. The closest — Ag. Fotias beach — is a walk away, 500 m past the town's campsite. However, the better options are at **Stavros**, and a little further on — **Kionia** (now complete with the island's only package tourist hotel and several tavernas). Frequent taxis and irregular buses run from Tinos Town, or if you are feeling energetic you can walk along the coast past the scanty remains of a temple to Poseidon and Amphitrite and the site of a stoa.

The god Poseidon was the island's favourite deity after he relieved Tinos from a plague of snakes by sending along a flock of hungry storks ('Tinos' is derived from the Phoenician word for snake: *tenok*). These days finding a snake is very difficult, but bottles for holy water and replica icons are to be found in abundance.

Tinos Town aside, the island is very quiet (apart from the incessant cooing of doves). The most prominent landmark is **Mt. Exombourgo**; its upper slopes are the site of both the Archaic and Venetian capitals of the island. In safer times — notably the Classical and Hellenistic eras, and after the late 18 c. — the port of Tinos Town took on the role. Precious little is left of the former capital. If you care to attempt the steep walk, you will find the remains of the Venetian fortress behind a monastery and part of the Archaic city wall. The summit was an important landmark in ancient times, when sailors navigated by always keeping in sight of land. Local tradition had it that, when it was obscured by cloud, it was a sure sign that unsettled weather was on the way, but you should take this with a pinch of salt as even in High Season the island peak is often hidden from view.

The villages of Tinos are, in the main, pretty mountainside affairs little visited by tourists, with the notable exception of the attractive northern centre of the island, the hill village of **Pirgos**. Since the middle of the 19 c. it has been home to a substantial artistic and sculpting community — which thrives in these parts thanks to several quarries producing high-quality green marble. It is a very attractive place in its own right, and you will find on sale works produced by students from the School of Fine Arts now established there. Most of the local marble is exported via the nearby small port village of **Panormos**, which is home to one of the island's best beaches and a few rooms. Buses run to both daily (other villages have irregular bus calls), though Sunday services are not good. One word of warning: if you are easily irritated by other people's personal habits then avoid sitting next to priests or little old ladies on the island buses. These delightful souls indulge in the practice of crossing themselves every

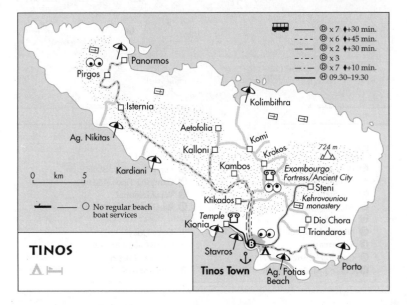

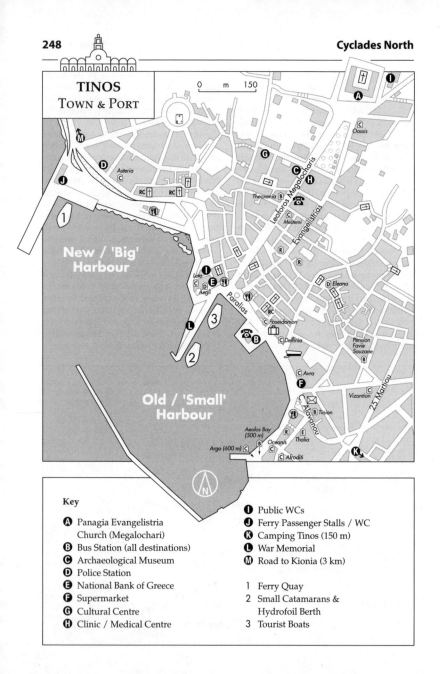

TINOS
TOWN & PORT

0   m   150

New / 'Big'
Harbour

Old / 'Small'
Harbour

New / 'Big' Harbour

1

3

2

L

Paralias

Leoforos Megalochari

Evangelistrias

25 Martiou

Alavanou

M

D

J

Asteria
C

RC

RC

G

C

H

Theoxenia
B

C
Meltemi

R

R

D Eleana

Lefo
C
D E
Aegli

I

B

C Poseidonion

C Delfinia

R

RC

Pension
Favie
Souzane

C Avra
F

Vizantion
C

B Tinion

Aeolos Bay
(500 m)

R
Oceanis
C

E
Thalia

Argo (600 m) C

C Afroditi

K

N

A

I

O

Oassis
C

Key

🅰 Panagia Evangelistria
   Church (Megalochari)
🅱 Bus Station (all destinations)
🅲 Archaeological Museum
🅳 Police Station
🅴 National Bank of Greece
🅵 Supermarket
🅶 Cultural Centre
🅷 Clinic / Medical Centre

🅘 Public WCs
🅙 Ferry Passenger Stalls / WC
🅚 Camping Tinos (150 m)
🅛 War Memorial
🅜 Road to Kionia (3 km)

1 Ferry Quay
2 Small Catamarans &
   Hydrofoil Berth
3 Tourist Boats

time they pass a chapel or roadside shrine. There are said to be 643 chapels on Tinos.

Most of the beaches on the island are a bit off the beaten track, and sadly, they get better the further you go from Tinos Town. The long sandy strand at **Kolimbithra** is arguably the island's best; it has a taverna and a few rooms, but without your own transport isn't easy to get to. The same can be said for the beaches at Ag. Nikitas and Kardiani.

⊚

In ancient times the island was known as 'Ophiousa', which like 'Tinos' is snake related. It was forced to provide ships for the invading Persians in 480 BC, but one of its triremes deserted, and gave the Athenian fleet at Salamis information on the enemy battle plan. The island subsequently joined the Delian League. During the Roman period the island became a place of exile, gradually descending into obscurity, suffering regular pirate raids during the Byzantine years. From 1207 Tinos came under Venetian control. The island's role as a focus of Greek nationalism was further advanced by its being the last of the Aegean strongholds to succumb to Turkish rule (in 1715) after 500 years as a bastion of Venetian control. The transfer of power was by treaty so the island didn't suffer from invasion.

Tinos was also the scene of a pivotal event in WW2, when the torpedoing of the visiting Greek warship *Elli* outside the town harbour, on Assumption Day 1940 by an Italian submarine (before Greece had formally joined the war on the side of the allies), served to encourage Greek resistance to the notion of capitulating to Italian demands for surrender without a fight.

╞╡

Tinos Town has plenty of hotels and some rooms. Prices are slightly higher than average, but on pilgrimless nights you can usually haggle advantageously. Arrive at festival time, however, and well … you may have heard of the 'feeding of the five thousand', but the streets of Tinos Town see an annual re-enactment of the less talked about 'sleeping of the five thousand' that came after that memorable nosh-up. Budget beds are limited to a scatter of rooms and two D-class hotels: the quayside *Aegli* (☎ 22240) and the backstreet *Eleana* (☎ 22561). The majority of hotels are

C-class, the more appealing being those along the waterfront. These include the *Oceanis* (☎ 22452), the *Avra* (☎ 22242), the *Delfinia* (☎ 22289) and the B-class *Tinion* (☎ 22261).

▲

Tinos Camping (☎ 22344): a reasonable site. Blown clean daily, it comes with some tree cover, a dovecot and tortoises wandering around (it is best to check that the rock you use to bang in your tent pegs is a rock). There is no mini-market as there is a supermarket 200 m opposite the site entrance.

◉◉

The stucco-plastered church of **Panagia Evangelistra** (complete with the icon causing all the fuss) is the main sightseeing destination on Tinos — though it doesn't do to forget this is very much a revered shrine when visiting. The lower level of the building is home to a chapel with a spring with which pilgrims fill bottles of holy water, and a shrine devoted to the warship *Elli*. The upper level houses the main church, and the **icon**, now black with age and covered in a jewel-studded silver case that hides everything but the face, is so obscured that it is impossible to get anything other than a brief impression. The overall effect is rather unsatisfactory, being reminiscent of the gaudy seaside pictures made with varnished seashells to be found in tackier resorts. With so little of it visible, it is difficult to gauge the merits of the painting itself. It is reputedly the work of St. Luke (the time involved in pursuing a second career as a painter no doubt explains why the author of the third gospel copied roughly 60% of Mark's gospel into his own), and if true shows a remarkable anticipation of later Byzantine art.

Probably from a church sacked by pirates in the 10 c., the icon is widely believed to be endowed with healing powers. It came to light in 1822 after a passing nun saw a hunky bronzed workman digging in a field and had a vision (of what, history hasn't recorded). Given instructions where to dig he unearthed the icon, miraculously unharmed — though the back of the board on which it was painted showed evidence of burning. The current church was built in 1823 on the discovery site. The icon's appearance during the birth throes of the Greek state has further enhanced its symbolic importance to the Greek people. Take care to observe the church dress code; it is very strictly enforced here.

Around the island there are several attractions worthy of consideration. Buses provide good links to another popular religious excursion destination — the 12 c. village-like convent at **Kehrovouniou**. Suitably clad visitors can enter and see the cell that belonged to the convent's most famous inhabitant, Sister Osia Pelagia, who had that all important icon vision at Tinos Town. Her story has a rather revolting twist in the tale: after her death her fellow sisters promptly chopped her head off and had it embalmed. Regarded as a holy relic (being a sort of direct telephone line to God), it is kept in a small chest by the 50-odd axe-wielding nuns now in residence, though it is difficult to believe that its owner's late body isn't left regretting that she didn't join a silent order instead.

The Venetian fortress at **Exombourgo** is another local notable that got the chop: it was demolished by the Turks after they gained control of Tinos (it had held out against them for so long, it was deemed desirable to destroy the castle rather than risk it becoming a focus for future rebellion). Today just fragmentary stretches of wall remain. Some excavation of the Archaic city has been done on the site, revealing the foundations of an 8 c. BC **Sanctuary of Demeter & Persephone** on the old acropolis.

Continuing west, **Pirgos** has a small museum devoted to the town art school's most famous sons: the leading Greek sculptor of the 19 c., Iannoulis Chalepas, and his fellow artists. All the local literature makes great play on how famous these sculptors and painters were, but unless you have a taste for minor heavy-duty Baroque, you are unlikely to have heard of any of them. While wandering around the museum looking at copies of their work, it is all too easy to imagine that if any of these sculptors had been under the tutelage of a contemporary such as August Rodin (of 'The Kiss' fame) they would have been on the receiving end of a succession of D minuses.

The Sanctuary of Poseidon & Amphitrite

Located just behind the beach and beach road at Kionia, this sanctuary site — dedicated to the god Poseidon and one of his consorts, the little-known sea nymph Amphitrite — is a testament to the canny marketing abilities of the ancient islanders in the 3 c. BC. Faced with the awesome pilgrim-pulling power of nearby Delos, they managed to cash in on

their location by providing a purification shrine where pilgrims en route could wash themselves in a sacred fountain and thus arrive on Delos suitably cleansed in body and spirit. It operated between the 4 c. BC until it was abandoned c. 250 AD — a short lifespan as ancient sanctuaries go.

The best way to appreciate the site today is to head off in a completely different direction and start by visiting the **Archaeological Museum** in Tinos Town. Home to all the finds and sculpture fragments from the sanctuary, this small museum (open ②–⑦ 08.30–15.00; entrance fee €3) is staffed by a helpful curator who is happy to answer questions. The sanctuary exhibits are mostly sculptural and housed in the museum courtyard: not surprisingly given the site's dedication, dolphins and sea monsters are the dominant themes. But there are other objects of interest, such as decorated fragments of ceilings, a group of Roman imperial statues that includes the Emperor Claudius, and a late Hellenistic — bizarrely shaped — sundial of some fame made by Andronikos of Kirrhos. Those with enquiring minds can look forward to hours of fun speculating on how it might have worked.

The range of other museum exhibits is not large: the most notable is the gallery devoted to the giant pithoi from a workshop at Exombourgo. The earliest known relief pottery in the Cyclades, they are sister vessels to the example in the museum on Mykonos with its relief depicting the Trojan horse.

The **Sanctuary** itself (open ②–⑦ 08.30–15.00; entrance free) will probably disappoint on first sight as the initial impression is of a field filled with foundation stones and nothing more. As is common with ancient shrines located close to later centres, they became a ready source of building materials, and this sanctuary was no exception. Clear evidence of deliberate stripping can be seen at the stoa, where you will find the thin fluted edge of a column lying on the ground: an unwanted fragment left over by a workman recutting a curved column drum to make a flat-sided stone. In spite of this the site is still worth a look. The 10 major buildings (including 2 temples, 3 bathing buildings and the end of the longest stoa in the Cyclades) can still be clearly discerned, and a viable impression is gained of the site. This is helped by a free explanatory leaflet handed to visitors by the curator.

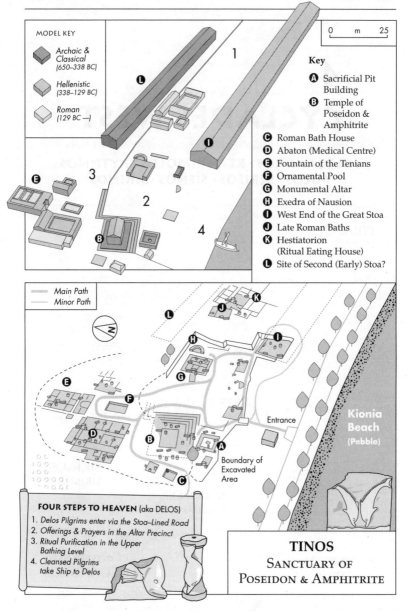

MODEL KEY

Archaic & Classical
(650–338 BC)

Hellenistic
(338–129 BC)

Roman
(129 BC —)

0   m   25

Key

A Sacrificial Pit Building
B Temple of Poseidon & Amphitrite
C Roman Bath House
D Abaton (Medical Centre)
E Fountain of the Tenians
F Ornamental Pool
G Monumental Altar
H Exedra of Nausion
I West End of the Great Stoa
J Late Roman Baths
K Hestiatorion (Ritual Eating House)
L Site of Second (Early) Stoa?

Main Path
Minor Path

Kionia Beach (Pebble)

Entrance

Boundary of Excavated Area

FOUR STEPS TO HEAVEN (aka DELOS)
1. Delos Pilgrims enter via the Stoa–Lined Road
2. Offerings & Prayers in the Altar Precinct
3. Ritual Purification in the Upper Bathing Level
4. Cleansed Pilgrims take Ship to Delos

TINOS
SANCTUARY OF
POSEIDON & AMPHITRITE

4 CYCLADES WEST

FOLEGANDROS · KEA · KIMOLOS · KYTHNOS
MILOS · SERIFOS · SIFNOS · SIKINOS

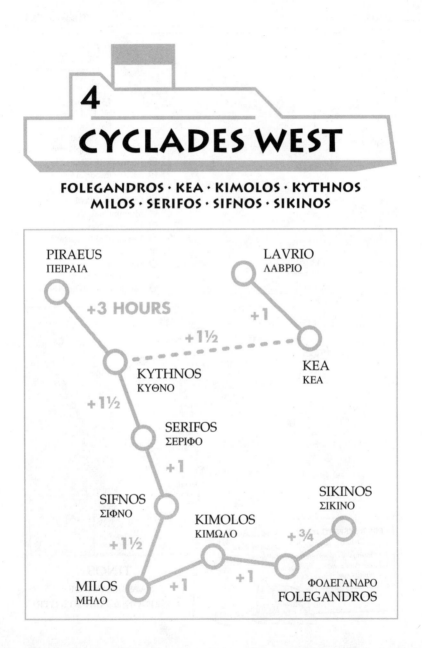

PIRAEUS
ΠΕΙΡΑΙΑ

LAVRIO
ΛΑΒΡΙΟ

+3 HOURS

+1½

+1

KYTHNOS
ΚΥΘΝΟ

KEA
KEA

+1½

SERIFOS
ΣΕΡΙΦΟ

+1

SIFNOS
ΣΙΦΝΟ

KIMOLOS
ΚΙΜΩΛΟ

SIKINOS
ΣΙΚΙΝΟ

+1½

+¾

+1

+1

MILOS
ΜΗΛΟ

ΦΟΛΕΓΑΝΔΡΟ
FOLEGANDROS

General Features

The Western Cyclades line runs in an irregular 'L'- shaped chain around the rim of the group. In past years a paucity of budget accommodation has left its mark: these islands have a history of seeing fewer backpackers and greater numbers of Greek holidaymakers than elsewhere, thus helping to keep the islands free from the worst trappings of mass tourism. In fact out of the High Season July / August peak foreign tourists are thin on the ground.

The chain is peculiar in that the nearer the island is to Athens, the fewer foreign tourists it tends to see. Northerly Kea — served by the mainland port of Lavrio — is very much of an Athenian's get-away-from-it-all weekend island, but very quiet in midweek. Kythnos and Serifos are quite off the beaten track despite the frequency of Piraeus ferries. Sifnos, on the other hand, is the only island in the group that comes close to being labelled 'touristy' and even this is mild by Central Cyclades standards. Milos — famous as the island where the Venus de Milo was discovered — attracts tourists by virtue of name recognition and is slowly emerging as a resort island in its own right.

Neighbouring Kimolos (a little known minor gem) makes an interesting day excursion, as are the two at the tail end of the line, Sikinos and Folegandros. Bridging the Central and Western lines, they do not fit comfortably into either, being serviced by boats steaming down both, but as they are more characteristic of the Western Cyclades they are covered here.

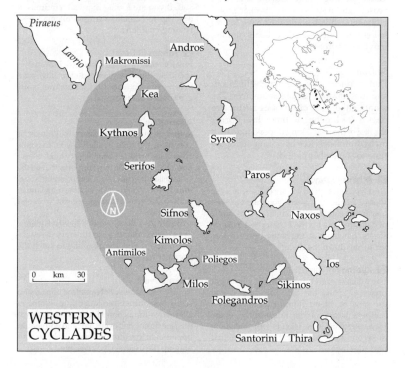

WESTERN
CYCLADES

Example Itinerary [2 Weeks]

Those looking for a fortnight's holiday that combines the sights of Athens with some relaxed island hopping without huge crowds could do worse than the Western Cyclades. An atmosphere of sleepy indifference rules. The islands are close to the capital and fairly quiet (unless you travel at the weekends), yet with enough going on so that you don't end up feeling as if you had been washed up at the back of beyond.

Arrival/Departure Point
None of the islands boast an international airport, and connections with other island groups are so poor that Athens is the only viable starting point. During the High Season Santorini becomes another possibility, though you could well have to hop to Paros for one of the daily boats running into the line from there.

Season
Daily services operate down the line from late June through to late September. The month either side of this sees ferries five days a week falling to three days during the rest of the year. Don't depend too much on hydrofoil services operating out of the June to September period.

1 Athens [2 Days]
Since you can't spend all day in the sun at the start of a holiday anyway, you might as well take in the sights of the capital over a couple of days (picking up the EOT ferry departure sheets/timetable at the same time), before venturing down the chain.

2 Kythnos [1 Day]
The quietest island in the group; you might prefer to spend the day elsewhere if you are new to island hopping. Experienced hoppers weary of the hurly-burly of the more popular Greek islands will find more to savour in the somnolent atmosphere that pervades here.

3 Serifos [2 Days]
A day is all that is needed to take in the port and dramatic Chora hanging on the hill behind. After this you can retire to the beach and wait — if needs be for an extra day — for a *morning* ferry to Sifnos; enabling you to take your pick of the accommodation on arrival there.

4 Sifnos [4 Days]
As this is the best beach island in the group (and by this stage you should be better conditioned to enjoy spending more extended time in the sun), Sifnos offers the opportunity to enjoy a few days of complete relaxation.

5 6 Milos/Kimolos [3 Days]
Milos provides the best sightseeing in the Western Cyclades. Three days can be happily spent between the catacombs, beach and, if you are feeling more adventurous, a day trip to Kimolos via the Pollonia-based landing-craft ferry.

1 Athens [2 Days]
Finally, take a boat direct to Piraeus — spending the recommended clear day spare before your return flight finishing your exploration of the capital.

Alternative 1
Rather than returning direct to Piraeus, if you have the time available, you can take advantage of the occasional ferry links to visit **Kea**. Once one of the most important of all the Greek islands, it offers some good sightseeing. Ideally, you should aim to explore the island in midweek as rooms disappear as the weekend approaches.
    You are also recommended to visit Kythnos in passing earlier in your itinerary (to establish times) if you are planning to catch the irregular ferries.

Alternative 2
In July and August **Folegandros** appears on schedules sufficiently frequently to become an alternative destination. However, ferries down this line do not visit every day, and you should be prepared to return to Piraeus via boats running up the Central Cyclades line.

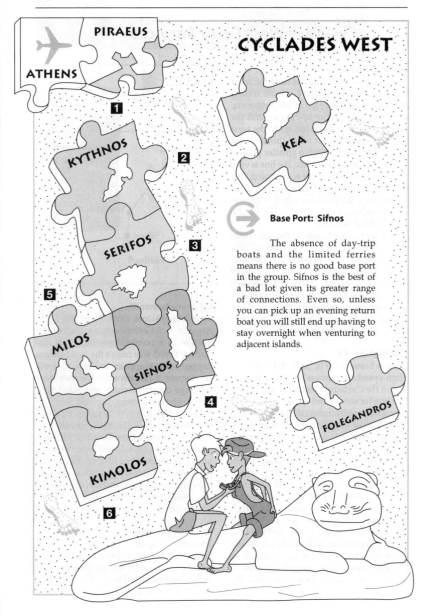

CYCLADES WEST

ATHENS

PIRAEUS

1

KYTHNOS

2

KEA

SERIFOS

3

Base Port: Sifnos

The absence of day-trip boats and the limited ferries means there is no good base port in the group. Sifnos is the best of a bad lot given its greater range of connections. Even so, unless you can pick up an evening return boat you will still end up having to stay overnight when venturing to adjacent islands.

5

MILOS

SIFNOS

4

FOLEGANDROS

KIMOLOS

6

KEA
Archaic Lion
& Tourist Circus

Cliff-top Chora Views on
Folegandros

Cyclades West

Kastro Houses & Main Square Church
FOLEGANDROS

SIFNOS
Chapel of the 7 Martyrs
at Kastro

Main Street
at Kastro

FOLEGANDROS
Shop Signs

KIMOLOS
The Kastro (South Wall Houses)

Adamas Port on Milos

The Catacombs

MILOS
Mining Museum Exhibits

Cyclades West

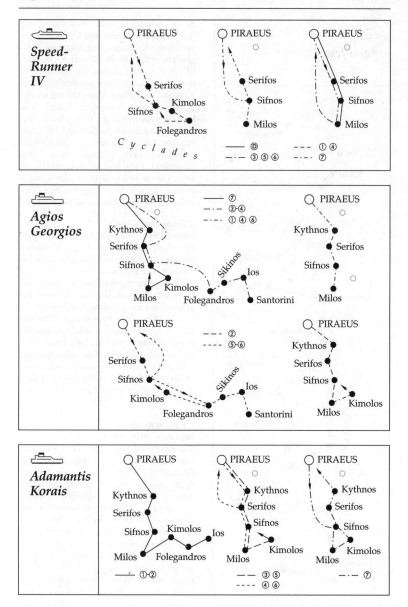

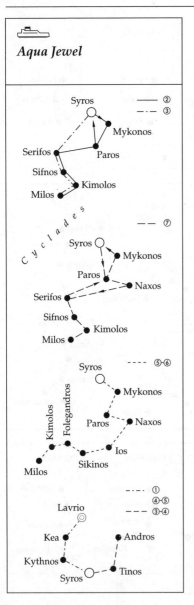

Aqua Jewel

in VSL colours (a near defunct company that in the 80s dominated Cyclades ferry services), she steams into harbours like a ghost from the past. With the disappearance of other regular ferries she has become important for the less popular island of Kythnos, providing a daily linking service in High Season. A dependable and clean boat, in appearance she is identical to her former sister ferries, the *Express Apollon* and *Penelope A*. She is steaming fast towards the retirement point for Greek ferries, so it is possible that she will be replaced during 2012. This would be a pity as she is one of the few boats of this vintage in Greece that still offer an enjoyable travel experience.

C/F *Adamantis Korais*
Zante Ferries; 1997 (rebuilt 2008); 2291 GRT.
A new arrival in 2009, this ferry seems larger than her tonnage would suggest. With her distinctive orange hull, she has become the most popular regular boat on the route, though some locals do seem to steer clear of her. This may or may not have something to do with her passenger saloon: kitted out with not very practical white chairs and boasting fluorescent strip lighting over her passageways that is continuously changing colour, this is one ferry guaranteed to give ex-hippies returning to the haunts of their giddy youth a psychedelic experience without a weed in sight.

C/F *Aqua Jewel*
NEL Lines; 2002; 3045 GRT.
The *Aqua Jewel*, after an eventful few years running down the Cyclades North line (including a little collision with another boat), moved over to replace the *Aeolos Kenteris I* on this inter-island run. Operating out of Syros, she runs to islands in the Cyclades West line, providing an invaluable cross-link service. She is a modern boat, so don't be put off by her exterior, which looks more like something designed in the 1970s. If she is moved in 2012 it is likely that a replacement will be brought in to cover as this is a set of well-established itineraries.

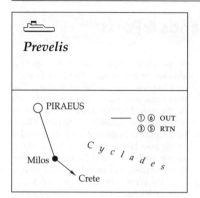

C/F *Prevelis*
ANEK Lines; 1980; 5653 GRT.
In past years a useful adjunct to regular Cyclades West ferries has been provided by the Crete-bound ANEK Lines and LANE Lines boats. These regularly stop at Milos on their outward and return runs to Crete (so much so that their midnight appearance came to mark the end of the evening promenade time at Adamas). These days this is a service in decline (the route operated only two days a week in the summer of 2011, with the *Prevelis* making all the calls). It is likely to be operating at a similar level in 2012, though days could change.

C/F *Nissos Kimolos*
Karametsos Ferry Lines
This small landing-craft ferry runs between Kimolos and Milos anything up to five times

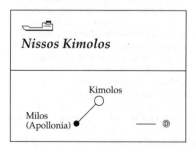

daily in High Season (depending on day-tripper coach excursions to Kimolos from Milos). If these aren't running then three round-trips daily are more usual. Changes are unlikely in 2012.

C/F *Macedon*
Goutos Lines; 1972; 1974 GRT.
Now the main companion to the *Mirina Express*, the *Macedon* is a chunky-looking ex-Japanese boat. Solid and reliable, though she is beginning to show her age, she covers the Lavrio—Kea run, with just occasional runs to Kythnos.

C/F *Mirina Express*
Goutos Lines; 1975; 1168 GRT.
This vessel has long been the mainstay of the Lavrio—Kea route (although she was absent in 2010). Greek-built, she has the traditional, but now rare, external staircases for passengers at her stern, which makes for very easy identification.

C/F *Marmari Express*
DD Ferries
This small but useful ferry moved from the Rafina—Evia (Marmari) route to cover for the missing *Mirina Express* in 2010. Clearly a refurbished vessel, she is not in the first division, but is adequate. Provided both the above boats are running, this ferry will probably be back on the Evia run in 2012.

Cyclades West Islands & Ports

Folegandros

ΦΟΛΕΓΑΝΔΡΟΣ; 32 km²; pop. 650.

CODE ☎ 22860
PORT POLICE / POLICE ☎ 41249
FIRST AID ☎ 41222

A 'romantic' island boasting one road and no large shops, Folegandros has long been known as a get-away-from-it-all sort of place. In the last few years it has attracted a select clientele of up-market island lovers drawn by the quiet, laid-back atmosphere. The islanders, eager to get the economic benefits of tourism but not over-keen on the more tacky aspects of the trade, have happily promoted this image, with the result that Folegandros has managed to retain its traditional lifestyle yet also take advantage of a relatively small number of visitors with money to spend.

If your object in island hopping is to find a port of respite from the modern world then you could do far worse than be washed up here — provided, of course, that your budget can stand it. This is not to say that those with limited funds should be put off visiting (note that the island has an ATM but no proper bank). Those that are miss a lot; you just have to work on the assumption that this is one place where you might have to splash out a bit for a day or two if you visit in High Season, when the available accommodation is hard put to keep up with demand. Much will depend on the time of year that you visit.

Out of High Season Folegandros could never be described as crowded, but during July and August the island often seems to be so, simply because the port and town are very small and have difficulty coping with those that do call. In fact, compared to any of the 'popular' islands the numbers visiting are surprisingly low.

At first sight Folegandros appears to live up to its historical role as a place of exile,

courtesy of its arid and rocky landscape, but as is so often the case with Greek islands, first impressions can be misleading. The dusty little port in Karavostasis bay doesn't do the island justice. Relatively new, it is little more than a motley collection of tourist-generated buildings trailed around a rather poor beach. Now used as the island caïque harbour, the fishermen weighing their catches and mending nets on the quay inadvertently add some colour, and with each season the port becomes a little more lively. The locals have tried to tart it up as best they can (latterly by adding an elaborate staircase down to a second, very poor, beach over the quayside headland), but it remains more of a place to pass through rather than stay in. Two roads run out of the port. The first skirts the port beach and then round the bay and over a headland before running down to Livadi beach (an indifferent strand of sand) with the campsite on the hillside behind. The second is the main island road, running up to the Chora and the settlements behind. Buses run regularly between the two (times are posted up at the 'bus station' on the ferry quay).

Chora is the only large centre and lies 4 km from the port. One of the most attractive of the traditional whitewashed cubist Cycladic villages, it is a mini Mykonos Town without the crowds, and feels like the sort of place where everybody obviously knows everybody else and everybody else's grandmother besides. Part of the secret of its appeal is its location. Set atop a 200 m cliff on the northern coast that 'living on the edge of the world' feeling common to the caldera towns on Santorini. However, unlike the latter, Chora doesn't look the dizzy views in the eye (though there are several good vantage points), but for the most part turns in on itself. The result is a cosy huddle of houses and churches centred

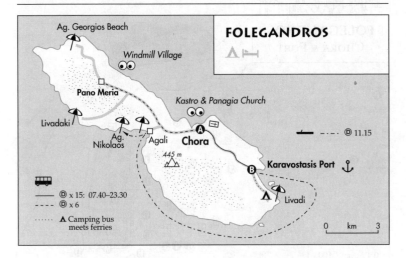

on a couple of leafy squares (thanks to a number of large plane trees) decked with pots of red geraniums and check-cloth taverna tables that leave one feeling that one is tucked away in the heart of a provincial French hill village.

Chora is a great place for romantic evening meals (to say nothing of futile cliff-edge gestures if all you end up with is a spot of unrequited love or the taverna bill). Joking aside, Folegandros has figured in occasional press reports thanks to several tourists disappearing off cliff paths without even the consolation of a broken heart to justify their fall. Visitors who manage to stay topsides will find that the old Kastro quarter is the best part of town. This neatly hides the cliff edge from view, besides offering the most attractive example of the medieval house-stockade forts built to defend Cycladic islands from pirate attacks. Its interior is a real delight, the flower-filled aisles of whitewashed houses being adorned with brightly painted balconies and ranks of external staircases (each with its own resident cat). New development in the town (largely up-market hotels and apartment blocks) is confined to strips along the access roads, the liveliest being along the Pano Meria road which has several bars and a disco en route to the Fani Vevis pension.

After passing by Chora the main road runs west along the spine of the island. Although there is a regular bus service along it, it is also a ready-made excursion if you are up to the walk; the best strategy is to take the bus to **Pano Meria** and then return to Chora. The walk isn't too stressful, and winds through a delightfully unspoilt rural island landscape, with a mix of farms, derelict windmills and churches. Pano Meria isn't much of a place, but is a useful starting point. Little more than a loose scatter of houses and farmsteads along the island spine road, it only becomes apparent that you are here when the bus goes no further.

Beach fans have to walk from the spine road down unmade tracks to the shoreline: the first beach of note is the excellent sand strand at **Agali** (also known as Vathi) complete with several tavernas and outlets offering rooms. From here a coastal path winds its way to a second good beach at **Ag. Nikolaos**. Both can be reached by a daily High Season beach caïque.

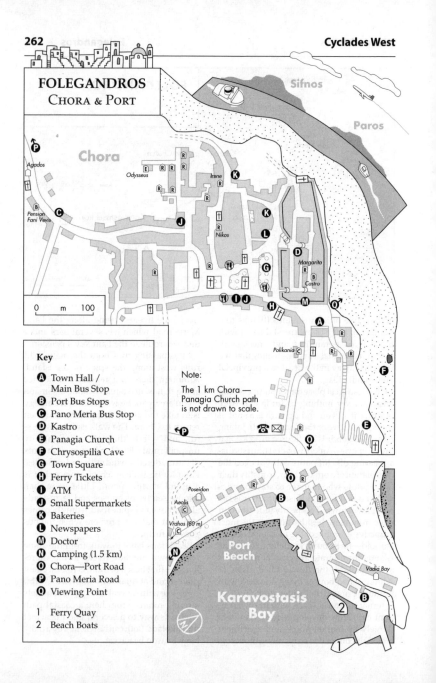

FOLEGANDROS
CHORA & PORT

Sifnos

Paros

Chora

Agados

Pension
Fani Vevis

Odysseus

Irene

Nikos

Margarita

Castro

Polikania

0   m   100

Key

Ⓐ Town Hall /
Main Bus Stop
Ⓑ Port Bus Stops
Ⓒ Pano Meria Bus Stop
Ⓓ Kastro
Ⓔ Panagia Church
Ⓕ Chrysospilia Cave
Ⓖ Town Square
Ⓗ Ferry Tickets
Ⓘ ATM
Ⓙ Small Supermarkets
Ⓚ Bakeries
Ⓛ Newspapers
Ⓜ Doctor
Ⓝ Camping (1.5 km)
Ⓞ Chora—Port Road
Ⓟ Pano Meria Road
Ⓠ Viewing Point

1   Ferry Quay
2   Beach Boats

Note:

The 1 km Chora —
Panagia Church path
is not drawn to scale.

Poseidon

Aeolis

Vrahos (80 m)

Port
Beach

Vadia Bay

Karavostasis
Bay

☻

Folegandros has enjoyed a chequered history, with periods of quiet prosperity alternating with devastation. The island's early story is not known: the first record surviving is a tax payment to Athens in 425 BC as part of her contribution to the Delian League. However, at some point in the Hellenistic period the island was abandoned — in the Macedonian era it is recorded as being uninhabited. During the Byzantine era silence reigns, though clearly settlements were established. Some time around 1212 AD — while under Venetian rule — the Kastro was built. However, an Italian monk called Boudelmonti reported in 1416 that the island was deserted thanks to raids by pirates and Turks.

Around 1577 Folegandros was resettled by inhabitants from Sifnos and Crete. The Turks took Folegandros in 1617, all but ignoring it except as a source of tax revenue. This amiable occupation lasted just under a century until 1715 when a passing Turkish admiral, Janoum Hodja, devastated the island and enslaved the surviving population — shipping them off to İstanbul. In 1718 a few survivors managed to return. After a short period of Russian rule between 1770–74, disaster followed quickly after as pirates successfully attacked the kastro in 1774. A further attack by Maniote pirates under a commander called Zacharias in 1794 marked the end of this troublesome period. Folegandros joined the Greek state in 1828. Between 1920–67 the island was used again as a place of internal exile for political prisoners.

╠═╣

Rooms are available to rent in the port, but most tourists take the bus that meets all boats to **Chora**, which is both prettier and has more options. The most appealing of these are in the old kastro: the small B-class *Castro* (☎ 41230) and the *Margarita Rooms* (☎ 41321). Rooms are scattered around the town with hotels confined to the outskirts, notably the new C-class *Polikania* (☎ 41322) on the port road. The Chora—Panagia Church path also has some plush furnished apartments along it. More down-market rooms lie on the west side of town, along with the E-class *Odysseus* (☎ 4139). The Chora—Pano Meria road has a couple of pensions, including the deceptively dour-fronted B-class *Fani Vevis* (☎ 41237). **Karavostasis Port** also has several hotels including the C-class *Aeolis* (☎ 41205).

Λ

Camping Livadi (☎ 41204): a very friendly site 2 km west of the port along the coast path. Lack of competition (and water) is all too evident with the poor washing facilities. Bring all foodstuffs with you as the campsite restaurant hasn't much and it's a longish walk to the port (a mini-bus meets ferries).

👓

The only major island sights regularly visited are the **Chora** and its **Kastro**, their photogenic appeal greatly enhanced by trees, wells and quaint hand-painted signs over shop doorways. The attractive whitewashed **Panagia Church** lies on the cliff-hill on the north-east side of the Chora, and stands on the foundations of the ancient city wall that stood on the site. Although it is quite a climb to the church, the wonderful views over the town and island are more than worth it.

Walking is a popular activity on Folegandros (thanks in part to a good map on sale locally showing all the major paths). Even the less ambitious have been known to head along the road to **Pano Meria**. Although the village is little more than a string along houses (and the odd windmill) strung along the spine of the island, the scenery is excellent. Pano Meria is also home to the only museum on Folegandros: a preserved farm-cum-**Folk Museum** which has a fair collection of rural island exhibits.

A number of islands offer **round the island boat tours**, and Folegandros has one of the best. The trip is made at least once a week during the summer, the route depending on sea and wind conditions: tickets and information can be obtained from the travel agent in the chora bus square. The boat tour gives you the only chance to get a glimpse of the island's greatest attraction — the **Chrysospilia Cave** ('Golden Cave'). Located in the cliff side directly below Chora, it looks like an unblinking dark eye some 10 m above sea level. Unfortunately it is closed to tourists pending archaeological excavation. With walls covered with over 400 male names inscribed in the 4 C. BC, and contents that include an erotically shaped stalagmite and several carved stone phalluses, it appears to have been the scene of a coming-of-age ritual. Quite what this ritual involved is anyone's guess — though the sculpture hereabouts does rather suggest that teenage youths have been religiously practising it whenever they have found themselves alone in the dark ever since.

Kea
KEA; 131 km²; pop. 1,700.

CODE ☎ 22880
PORT POLICE ☎ 21344
POLICE ☎ 21100
FIRST AID ☎ 22200

Despite being only three hours from Athens, Kea (also transcribed as 'Tzia') is one of the hidden pearls of the Aegean, retaining much of its rural charm and now popular with those who like walking holidays. This is something of an unfamiliar role for an island that was home to an important Minoan outpost and was one of the cradles of Greek civilization.

Kea has always been, and remains, an island set apart from the rest. Not only did it manage to support four city states where most islands could barely manage one, but it was also a pioneer of social change by introducing a compulsory celebratory cup of hemlock when its citizens reached retirement age at 70.

These days the locals prefer to buy holiday homes on Kea instead of fleeing when they get older. As a result, the island tends to fill up quickly on weekends with Athenians escaping the city smog: Kea is comparatively fertile for a Cycladic island and is graced with countryside that is noticably greener than neighbouring Kythnos. If you intend to stay during High Season then plan for a midweek arrival. Foreign tourists are comparatively thin on the ground, and nightlife is sparse and scattered.

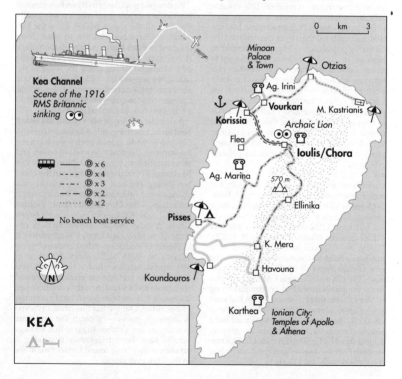

Kea Channel
Scene of the 1916
RMS Britannic
sinking

Korissia
Flea
Ag. Marina
Pisses
Koundouros

Minoan
Palace
& Town
Ag. Irini
Vourkari
Otzias
M. Kastrianis
Archaic Lion
Ioulis/Chora
570 m
Ellinika
K. Mera
Havouna
Karthea   Ionian City:
Temples of Apollo
& Athena

0   km   3

Ⓓ x 6
Ⓓ x 4
Ⓓ x 3
Ⓓ x 2
Ⓦ x 2

No beach boat service

N

KEA

All ferries and hydrofoils dock at the small port of **Korissia**, a tapering port-village that is now emerging as the island's main 'resort', sited on the west side of Agios Nikolaos bay. On the south is a long sand beach and the largest collection of accommodation on the island. However, apart from these attractions there is little incentive to linger. In truth, the waterfront lacks interest thanks in part to the bland topography of this part of the bay. The port beach also isn't the world's greatest, being quite awful at the quayside end (it improves noticeably as you progress around the bay).

Korissia is also more substantial than it looks from the sea, with more building in the valley floor behind the waterfront. This part of town is dominated by the red brick chimney of a derelict Victorian enamel and metallurgy factory. This sounds rather dour, but it doesn't impact on the touristy areas. Further evidence of late 19 C. industrial activity lies on the north side of Korissia bay: an excellent natural harbour, the bay was an important coaling station in the years leading up to WW1, and the roofless coal stores still stand at Kokka near the village of **Vourkari** — laid out like a miniature version of Korissia and now a growing up-market resort thanks to a large yachting marina located here.

Buses run from the port to Vourkari and, more frequently, to the red-tile roofed main town of **Ioulis** or **Chora**. Visible from the port, it sits in a natural amphitheatre in the hills, overlooked by a handful of ruined windmills that are all that remain of the 26 that once topped the so-called Mountain of Mills. The town is built around nine springs (now decorated with mule troughs) and clings to a couple of hillsides; the old Kastro dominates one, and the Chora the other. The streets are too narrow to admit vehicles, and this remains a very attractive working town packed with tiny houses, though most visitors simply pass through in search of the famous Kea Lion. Ioulis is also the best base for exploring the rest of the island.

The rest of Kea is an odd mix of unspoilt countryside and holiday-villa-filled villages. Best of these is the delightfully named **Pisses**. In the normal course of things one would assume that this name was just an unhappy accident, but the existence of another hamlet bearing the equally appealing name of 'Flea' suggests that the islanders have really got this place-naming thing down to a fine art. With a good sand beach backed by a prosperous market-garden valley, Pisses is served by a very inadequate once-daily bus service. The northern hamlet of **Otzias** is better served, but, filled with holiday villas, it is of little interest, as is the south-west coast 'resort' of **Koundouros**; now tarted up with pseudo-windmill homes near the tiny quay, it sees hydrofoils en route to Korissia. Walkers, meantime, will find bus-free **Flea** has more buzz as a destination than most thanks to its location in a ravine with 13 cute watermills.

💬

Known in antiquity as Keos, Kea's history began with the Minoan settlement at Ag. Irini. In the 6 C. BC the four cities were established. Kea fought with the Athenians at Salamis, and later joined the Delian League in 478 BC. During the Hellenistic period pirate attacks disrupted the local economy and by the 2 C. BC the city of Poiessa was abandoned. Others followed and by the 4 C. AD only Ioulis was still inhabited. Kea suffered more pirate raids, followed by capture by the Venetians in 1207. The Turks held the island between 1537–1821.

🛏

Rooms are on offer in Korissia and the Chora. Hotel and pension options are thin on the ground, though this shouldn't mean difficulty in finding a bed in midweek. **Ioulis** has one superbly placed B-class pension (on top of the old kastro site), the *Ioulis* (☎ 22177) — complete with a terrace restaurant — and a small E-class hotel charmingly placed on one of the main town alleys, the *Filoxenia* (☎ 22057). **Korissia** has the C-class hotel *Karthea* (☎ 21204) on the waterfront and a B-class 'motel', the *Tzia Mas* (☎ 21305), at the better end of the beach. However, the best hotel in town lies down a dusty track behind the beach:

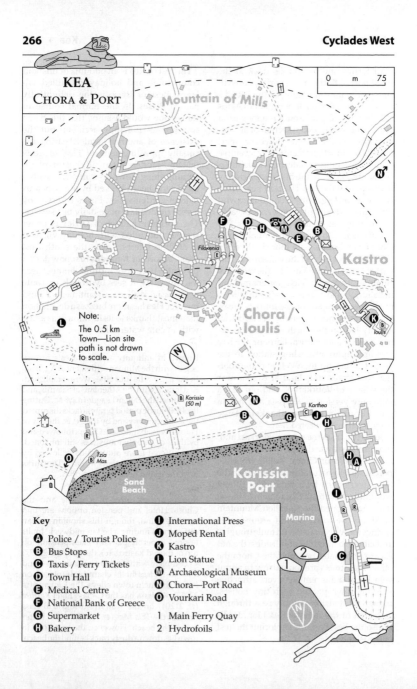

KEA
CHORA & PORT

Mountain of Mills

0   m   75

Kastro

Chora /
Ioulis

Filoxenia

Ioulis

Note:
The 0.5 km
Town—Lion site
path is not drawn
to scale.

Karthea

*Korissia
(50 m)*

*Tzia
Mas*

Sand
Beach

Korissia
Port

Marina

Key

- **A** Police / Tourist Police
- **B** Bus Stops
- **C** Taxis / Ferry Tickets
- **D** Town Hall
- **E** Medical Centre
- **F** National Bank of Greece
- **G** Supermarket
- **H** Bakery

- **I** International Press
- **J** Moped Rental
- **K** Kastro
- **L** Lion Statue
- **M** Archaeological Museum
- **N** Chora—Port Road
- **O** Vourkari Road

- **1** Main Ferry Quay
- **2** Hydrofoils

the newish B-class *Korissia* (☎ 21484, 21355). **Koundouros** also has one hotel: the pricey B-class *Kea Beach* (☎ 31230).

Λ

Camping Kea (☎ 31302): a nice site on the best island beach at Pisses 16 km from the port, it suffers from its isolated location.

👓

The oldest and most accessible of the Kea sites is on the promontory north of the port: the foundations of a **Minoan Palace** at Agia Irini. There is little here but a jumble of thick-walled foundations: the remains of half a dozen elaborate houses (with cellars complete with drains), streets with public benches, and defensive walls. The site takes its name from the red-tiled church on the promontory.

The most impressive sight on Kea — the grey granite 6 c. BC **Lion of Kea** — lies on an olive-groved hillside on the far side of Ioulis; 6 m long, it is carved sphinx-like from an out-

crop of rock and looks back across the valley towards the town wearing an enigmatic smile. This often seems to wear a little thin when the inevitable parties of tourists queue up to be photographed bestriding his head.

Of the four classical cities surprisingly little remains except at remote **Karthea** (for which you will need your own transport), where there are the dramatic cliff-side remains of a late Archaic temple of the Pythios Apollo. **Ioulis** (home of the 5 c. BC poet Simonides) has the remains of a **Venetian Kastro** built out of the ruins of a second temple to Apollo. There is also an **Archaeological Museum** housing island finds in the town. The third city (Korissia) produced a famous Kouros statue (now in Athens) but otherwise (like the fourth of Kea's cities Poiessa — near Pisses) there is little extant on the ground today. Elsewhere on Kea you will find the substantial remains of a **Hellenistic Watchtower** at **Ag. Marina** and a monastery at M. Kastrianis.

The Kea Channel

One objectless site of interest is the steamy, mirror-smooth Kea Channel. Although there is nothing to see except 'sea, sea, sea', the strait is the last resting place of the *Britannic* (sister ship of the *Titanic*). Originally laid down as the *Gigantic*, she was renamed after the *Titanic* disaster.

Launched in 1914, she struck a mine off Kea on the 21st of November 1916 — while serving as a hospital ship during the WW1 Dardanelles campaign. Fortunately she was sailing to collect casualties, so was half empty at the time. She sank in a mere 55 minutes with the loss of only 30 lives (after two of her lifeboats were sucked into her rotating propellers, as her captain vainly headed for Korissia in a last-gasp attempt to beach her). Like her sister, she was the largest vessel semi-afloat at the time of her sinking, and still holds the record as the largest liner on the seabed. Lying on her starboard side in 110 m of water, she is now attracting ever more attention. This began in 1995 when Dr. Robert

Ballard (the discoverer of the *Titanic*) explored the ship and found her excellently preserved, with even her relatively frail smokestacks extant (albeit separated from her hull). The vessel is pictured in *Lost Liners* (Hodder & Stoughton/Madison Press). Dr. Ballard has a long-term ambition to use the *Britannic* to establish 'The world's first under-sea museum', with internet tourists, though so far it has come to nought. An indifferent TV movie of the sinking also appeared in 2000.

Meantime, the wreck is now dived on regularly each summer, and is becoming an ever more popular venue thanks to its condition and shallow location (turned end up, over half the vessel would stand out of the water). However, it is not a wreck without risks: a British diver died on the site in 2009.

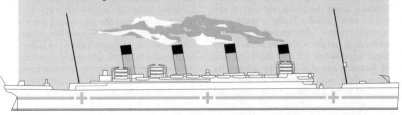

KIMOLOS

0   km   4

Prassa

397 m

Klima

Chorio

AGIOS
ANDREAS   FKK
Ancient
City   Remma

Ellinika   Aliki   Psathi

AGIOS
EFSTATHIOS

Ⓟ x 7
- - - - Ⓟ x 3

Kimolos
ΚΙΜΩΛΟΣ; 38 km²; pop. 800.

CODE ☎ 22870
PORT POLICE ☎ 22100
POLICE ☎ 51205
FIRST AID ☎ 51222

A good destination to head for if you want to escape the crowds and the more commercial trappings of tourism, the small island of Kimolos is a minor gem. Named after the 'kimolia' or chalk that was mined here in ancient times, the island's prime claim to fame has been as a source for chalk, silver, and — most recently — fuller's earth (used in the manufacture of porcelain). All this makes Kimolos easy to spot as ferries running along the north-east side of the island pass hillsides badly scarred with opencast mines. This sounds singularly uninviting, yet the sea view creates a very false impression, for the southern half of Kimolos has a nice sleepy backwater atmosphere with a number of fine sand beaches, some interesting sightseeing, and

not a mine in sight. In addition, the islanders are among the declining number that treat visitors as honorary members of their large extended family.

Volcanic in origin, the downside to the island's abundant mineral wealth is that there are no springs or wells; the locals have traditionally relied on collecting water in cisterns for all their supplies. To date the small number of tourists hasn't posed too high a demand on the available supplies, but water remains a precious commodity here. The good news for those addicted to having twice-daily showers is that Kimolos can be visited as a day-trip destination via the small ferry that makes the 20-minute run to and from Pollonia on the north coast of Milos.

All ferries arriving at Kimolos dock at the small port of **Psathi** on the south-east coast. A bar-backed quay beside a beach lined with odd trees and fishermen's houses, it is often quite lively, thanks to a couple of tavernas, and a couple of very popular beach restaurants. The air of gentle abandon is greatly enhanced by the crescent of hills behind the port, most topped with derelict windmills. This is relieved by the attractive hilltop chora that trickles down the hillside towards the port. The chora and port are linked by an easily walked 1.5 km road — islanders will often offer visitors a ride on the back of a truck if the tiny island bus isn't to be seen (Kimolos is this sort of a place).

Chorio itself is a pretty, unspoilt, working island village complete with a dominating tall 'cathedral' (a disappointing 1867-built edifice with the usual large dome and bell towers). Deftly hidden away in the ramshackle streets in its centre is another of those stockade-type kastros built to protect the townsfolk from the marauding pirates of five centuries ago. The town has grown up around this, and latterly along the valley-floor road to the north. Consisting mainly of housing, there is no obvious centre of town (most of the important services have been added on at the edges). There are small squares where the inhabitants gather, the one on the west side of the kastro being the most 'cosy'. Shops are spread equally thinly all over town (and choice of goods tends to be limited as tourism has yet to reach a point where retailers stock up with outsiders in mind). If you are staying on Kimolos then it is worth making the ascent to the top of the windmill-lined hill behind the town for the superb panoramic views of the chora, port and nearby islands (including large Poliegos opposite the port, which is used for grazing goats).

The rest of the island is quiet, though somewhat noisier than in past years thanks to another of those large EU road-building grants. This has seen Kimolos acquire the less than idyllic Tarmac roads that have scarred many of the smaller Greek islands, spoiling the place for some visitors. In this case the upgraded roads run from Chorio to the mining hamlet of **Prassa** on the north-east corner of the island, and the much more appealing beach hamlet of **Aliki** on the south coast.

😜

The history of Kimolos is very difficult to chart as there is very little information to go on. The island from its earliest years was dominated by its large neighbour Milos — so much so that it received scant mention by ancient writers. Records aren't much better from the medieval period: Kimolos was sacked a number of times with the loss of almost all documents, leaving us to piece together a story from occasional known facts and surviving monuments.

Archaeological finds suggest that Kimolos has been inhabited since Mycenaean times. Its history through the ancient period is closely tied to neighbouring Milos. The island was formerly known as Echinousa (after a sea urchin). Mining for both silver and fuller's earth started by the 4 c. BC and appears to have been the main source of income into the Byzantine period. From 1207 to 1579 the Dukes of Naxos and their Venetian successors ruled Kimolos — renaming it 'Argentiera' (silver) after the mines. Thereafter the Ottoman Turks took over nominal control, the island becoming a pirate's lair on and off. By the early 19 c. stability had returned (the French even had a

vice-consul stationed on the island — though on one occasion his daughter had to hide in a cave from pirates who apparently took the 'vice' part of her father's title too literally for comfort). Kimolos — frustrated pirates and all — joined Greece in 1821.

🛏

The lack of hotels reflects the small number of overnight visitors to Kimolos. Fortunately, accommodation isn't as thin on the ground as it looks from the map overleaf (rooms are not advertised; locals either meet boats or rely on tavernas to refer customers on).

Most rooms are in **Chorio** (or in the case of the *Meltemi Bar Rooms*, on the far side of it). The nearest the island has to a hotel is the large purpose-built rooms outlet on the port—Chorio road. Tavernas backing on to **Aliki** beach also offer beds, notably *Taverna Aliki* (☎ 51340). Freelance camping is tolerated on the remoter beaches.

👓

Sightseeing on Kimolos consists of one 'big' attraction in the form of the old Kastro (described overleaf), and a small number of less tangible sights in remoter parts of the island that offer a good excuse to explore, even if there isn't that much to see when you get to your destination.

In addition to the kastro, Chorio also has several churches dating back to the 1600s. The best of these is the lovely **Agios Ioannis** (1608) just outside the north walls of the kastro; bare of plaster, it stands in warm contrast to the surrounding whitewashed buildings. The street along the south side of the kastro (formerly the main market street in town) is now home to the island's new **Archaeological Museum**. Just completed in a refurbished house, it contains finds from the island's ancient capital.

The chora aside, the main points of interest on Kimolos are a sulphur spring at the northern hamlet of **Prassa**, a surviving **Tower** of the ubiquitous ruined Venetian kastro (built on the slopes of the island's highest mountain, Paliokastro), and the site of the island's **Ancient Capital** on the west coast; presumably once straddling a narrow isthmus between Kimolos and Agios Andreas islet (otherwise known as Daskaleio), it sank into the sea at some unknown point in late antiquity. Agios Andreas was the old acropolis, and near Kambana beach are the remains of a number of **Mycenaean Tombs**, once located outside the Kimolos side of the city.

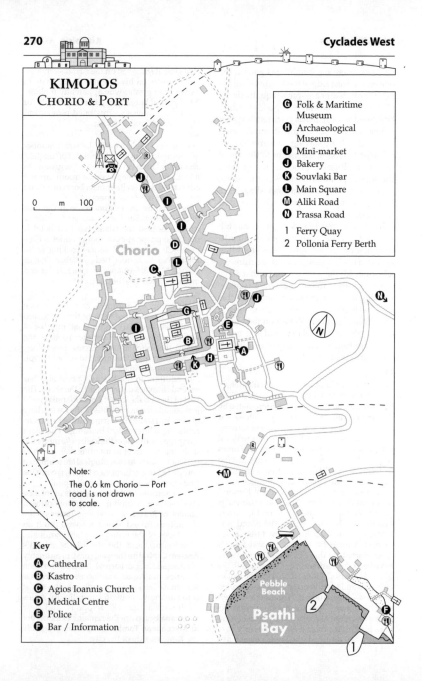

KIMOLOS
CHORIO & PORT

0 m 100

Chorio

G Folk & Maritime Museum
H Archaeological Museum
I Mini-market
J Bakery
K Souvlaki Bar
L Main Square
M Aliki Road
N Prassa Road

1 Ferry Quay
2 Pollonia Ferry Berth

Note:
The 0.6 km Chorio — Port road is not drawn to scale.

Pebble Beach

Psathi Bay

Key
A Cathedral
B Kastro
C Agios Ioannis Church
D Medical Centre
E Police
F Bar / Information

The Kastro

The Kimolos stockade-type kastro is a younger brother of the better known example on Antiparos (illustrated on p. 143). The basic concept is the same with both buildings: a strong rectangular fortification wall lined with apartments that face into a central courtyard area, each with its own external staircase.

There are, however, significant differences between the two. Instead of a large courtyard area and a central tower, the Kimolos kastro has a second — inner — ring of houses within which stands a church (complete with gateways, it is known as the inner kastro or 'Messa Kastro'). In addition the Kimolos kastro is 25% larger and had more rooms (123 in all): it also has a second gate in its outer wall, and is built on the side of a hill (so each two-storey unit is at a slightly different height to its neighbour, the flat roofs appearing from the air to ascend the slope as a series of large steps).

The construction date of the Kimolos kastro is the subject of much debate thanks to a complete lack of documentary evidence. There are dated stones over the two gateways; the main south gate (Kato Porta) has the year 1650, while the eastern gate (Pano Porta) has 1647. However, it is likely that these commemorate refurbishment or rebuilding after major pirate attacks, rather than being original construction dates (the Antiparos kastro — known to have been built in the 1440s — has a similar stone in its walls dated 1611). The best guess is that the Kimolos kastro, which is clearly modelled on the Antiparos building, was built some time between 1485 (the first Greek island cartographer, Bartolomeo dalli Sonetti, who visited the islands, does not show it on his map of Kimolos published that year) and 1537. This was the year that the Antiparos kastro fell to the Ottoman 'pirate' Barbarossa: an event that first revealed the inadequacies of this type of fortification. The latest plausible date of construction must be just prior to 1579 (when the Turks assumed full control of Kimolos): the Venetian-style kastro would have been expensive to build and could only have been funded by a powerful pre-Ottoman local overlord — possibly a member of the ruling Gozzadini family on neighbouring Sifnos.

Today the kastro is an odd mix of good preservation and total ruin. The inner castle buildings — with the exception of the church — are piles of rubble, as are both the east range and part of the north range of the outer castle. But the rest of the structure, although dilapidated, is intact. There is far more original material on show here than there is at Antiparos, though you have to look for it.

Kimolos Kastro — c. 1690 (depicted on an icon now in the Byzantine Museum in Athens).

Following Greek independence in the 1820s, doors and windows were put into the outer wall, and additional buildings were built on the outside, but even so it isn't difficult to imagine the kastro in its heyday. Crammed with upwards of 400 people relying on cistern water and with no sanitation, the kastro — rather bizarrely — acted as a magnet for pirates rather than intimidated them. A small defendable structure close to a shipping route, too small to be of military interest to the ruling powers, it made an ideal haven once captured. For significant parts of its life it appears to have been a medieval Port Royal, ringing with cries of 'yo-ho-ho and a bottle of ouzo'.

There are ambitions to renovate the kastro to a greater or lesser degree; the Greek government compulsory purchased a number of the ruined houses a few years ago, but little seems to be happening: as with the much bigger kastro at Naxos these medieval buildings get a very low priority for funding as they are still seen as objects of Greek repression constructed by invading powers. The fact that this kastro, were it to be restored in a sympathetic way, would be quickly acknowledged as one of the major tourist attractions in the Cyclades, doesn't seem to count for much.

Some people are doing their best to change this — notably the curator of the privately funded **Folk and Maritime Museum of Kimolos** (open ⊕ 11.00–13.00, 18.00–19.00; entrance fee €1) which occupies a couple of kastro houses on the north range, just inside the eastern gate. Quite simply one of the best small museums of its kind in the Greek islands, you shouldn't consider a visit to Kimolos without taking it in. Although — typically for a folk museum — it only has four rooms (you have to use an outside staircase to access the upper floor), the mix of folk and nautical exhibits, combined with the chance to examine the interiors of two kastro apartments, makes for a very rich experience. The enthusiastic conducted tour (you get a lot for your €1) makes it memorable as well.

Kythnos
ΚΥΘΝΟΣ; 86 km²; pop. 1,500.

CODE ☎ 22810
PORT POLICE ☎ 32290
POLICE / TOURIST POLICE ☎ 31201
FIRST AID ☎ 31202

A friendly, rocky little place three hours' sailing south of Athens with few tourist facilities, Kythnos (also often transcribed as 'Kithnos') is not the sort of island where the casual island hopper will be tempted to linger. The main attraction of the place is its very lack of attractions: a feature more likely to appeal to the jaded palette of the experienced island hopper than a novice. As such it is not, perhaps, the ideal first port of call for most island hoppers. None of the island centres (primarily the port, Chora and the inland hill village of Driopida) can offer excessive amounts of tourist appeal beyond the undeniable attraction of being 'unspoilt' communities, while the rest of the island is spectacularly undramatic.

The port of **Merihas** is untidily strung around three sides of a small bay on the west coast and is very slowly emerging as a resort village in lieu of better alternatives elsewhere. Truth to tell, things haven't got very far; it has a pebbly-sand beach of sorts backing onto a tree- and taverna-lined waterfront that is also home to a number of rather down-at-heel-looking small stores and not a lot else, beyond growing clusters of holiday homes and rooms on the hillsides and valley behind. This is hardly the stuff of heady romantic quayside evening strolls. However, Merihas isn't all bad; almost all the island accommodation worth knowing about is here and there are better beaches concealed beyond the two headlands to the north of the ferry quay, the best being a long tree-backed strip of sand two headlands along the Port—Chora road.

An erratic bus service links the port with the main towns (times are posted in the front windscreens). Inland there are two settlements of note: the capital at Chora, and the village of Driopida. In ancient times Kythnos was divided between them, and even today they manage to all but ignore each other (an attitude made easier by the need to take different roads from the port to each of them).

Set amid a gently undulating plain of brown stubble fields and low hills topped with windmills, **Chora** (also known as **Kythnos**), for all its lack of 'sights', offers an attractive destination, with friendly inhabitants and plenty of whitewashed charm. It more than makes up for Merihas. The island's comparative lack of popularity has ensured that it has remained unspoilt, with no tourist accommodation and only two or three souvenir shops on the main street that runs the length of the town. The side streets are also appealing, with a donkey lingering around every other corner. Fortunately, in this part of the world they earn their keep in the traditional way instead of lugging well-heeled tourists around.

Chora also does its bit for Greek island church architecture; churches here add to the variety by having their bells hung on the outside walls (usually near the door). At various points in the town you will find signs to the wind park that sits on the hills rising behind the far end of town. A destination worth attempting as it requires you to explore the length of the town, don't go expecting Disneyland. There is nought there but several modern power-generating windmills poignantly positioned alongside derelict traditional mills.

Other towns on Kythnos have less going for them. First among these (at least with the elderly Greeks who make up the bulk of the island's visitors) is the 19 c. spa resort and fishing port at **Loutra** on the north coast. Unfortunately, a thimbleful of the thermal waters has more fizz than all the tourists here put together, and if you want to be spared a depressing experience then avoid the town. The village of **Driopida** is a much more uplifting destination; located in a fertile hill valley, its houses are topped with red-tile roofs reminiscent of town houses on Kea.

The rest of Kythnos is very low-key, consisting mainly of arid treeless hills, highly terraced, and speckled with the thyme from which the rich island honey derives its distinctive flavour. Given that Kythnos barely recognizes the existence of tourists, it is almost superfluous to add that the best island beach — on the east coast at **Ag. Stefanou** — is not served by buses, and thus is inaccessible, unless you fancy the dusty walk down the hillside from Driopida. A better option is to walk up the western coast from Merihas to **Fikiado**, a golden causeway of sand that links Kythnos with the islet of Agios Loukas.

☻

Formerly known as 'Themia', Kythnos was a minor player in antiquity. The island is recorded as having supplied two triremes to fight at the Battle of Salamis, later joining the Delian League. Thereafter it was ruled from Athens. Its subsequent history mirrored that of nearby Kea, with pirate raids followed by capture by the Venetians in 1207. The Turks held Kythnos between 1537–1821.

⊫

Even in High Season you can't walk far from the ferry quay without islanders calling out 'Room?' The comparative lack of tourists all but guarantees a cheap bed on demand. Most rooms are to be found at **Merihas**, though it is worthwhile ascertaining where your bed is before accepting an offer: some are at the top of taxing hillside staircases that one wouldn't want to tackle more than once a day. If you want to phone ahead, try the rooms near the dentist — complete with early morning calls (well, screams) from 08.00 (☎ 32284, 32104) — or the second establishment offering rooms past the small chapel on the south side of the bay (☎ 32105).

Hotel accommodation in Merihas is much thinner on the ground, being confined to the mid-range *Kythnos* (☎ 32092). The island also has three C-class establishments in the spa 'resort' of **Loutra**. At the bottom end of the range is the inexpensive *Xenia Anagenissis* (☎ 31217). This is followed by the pricier *Kythnos Bay* (☎ 31218) and the *Meltemi* (☎ 31271).

◉◉

Visitors don't come to Kythnos for the sightseeing: it is pretty limited. **Chora** has some

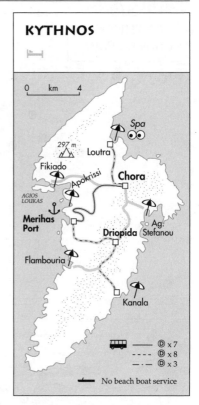

unidentifiable small fragments from ancient buildings tucked away in a 'garden' just off the main street, and Driopida lays claim to the notable **Katafiki Cave** at the head of its valley. The cave extends for over a kilometre and has several lakes. Sadly, it is closed due to the lack of funds needed to employ guides (one of the tourist shops at Merihas sells a guidebook — though as you can't get in this is as about as useful as a guidebook to Mars).

A small **Venetian Kastro** on the northern tip of the island is notoriously difficult to get to, but a much more practical walk does run between Chora and Driopida. Finally, there are many **churches** littering the hillsides, but an increasing number are locked following a series of icon thefts.

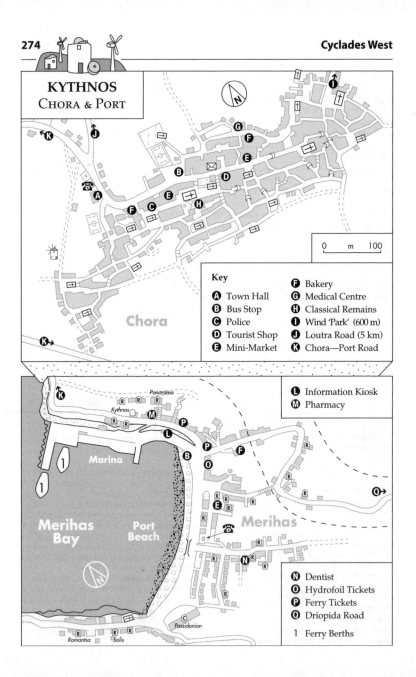

KYTHNOS
Chora & Port

Chora

0 m 100

Key

- **A** Town Hall
- **B** Bus Stop
- **C** Police
- **D** Tourist Shop
- **E** Mini-Market
- **F** Bakery
- **G** Medical Centre
- **H** Classical Remains
- **I** Wind 'Park' (600 m)
- **J** Loutra Road (5 km)
- **K** Chora—Port Road

- **L** Information Kiosk
- **M** Pharmacy

Panorama

Kythnos

Marina

Merihas Bay

Port Beach

Merihas

Possidonion

Romantsa   Solis

- **N** Dentist
- **O** Hydrofoil Tickets
- **P** Ferry Tickets
- **Q** Driopida Road

- **1** Ferry Berths

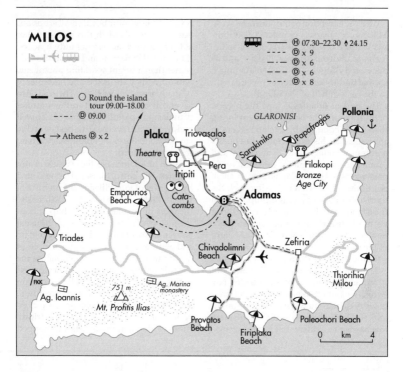

Milos

ΜΗΛΟΣ; 161 km²; pop. 4,500.

CODE ☎ 22870
PORT POLICE ☎ 22100
TOURIST OFFICE ☎ 22445
POLICE ☎ 21378

Like its more scenic neighbour Santorini, Milos is volcanic in origin, offering a vivid contrast with the islands higher up its respective ferry line. However, similarities are apt to end there for Milos is a very different sort of place, and it is worth taking some pains to pay a visit just to experience the contrasts. One of the most obvious of these is the level of tourism, for Milos has come very late onto the sightseeing scene, having traditionally relied on mining as the mainstay of the local economy. Although

mining remains a very big employer, this is now changing fast and the locals have made strenuous efforts in the last five years to develop their tourist facilities (which, to be honest, were a bit on the basic side before). With these in place now is the ideal time to pay the island a visit — before the island's charms bring in too many new visitors.

First impressions of Milos are apt to be somewhat contradictory, for the island hides many of its finer points amid a rather bizarre hilly landscape — the result of repeated ancient eruptions, mining activity and the workings of archaeologists looking vainly for the arms of the Venus de Milo (the Hellenistic statue of an overplump Aphrodite that has ensured that most people are at least familiar with the island's name).

With the exception of the north and west, Milos is very sparsely populated. Few tourists venture beyond the triangle of settlements made up of Adamas, Plaka — and its associated villages — and Pollonia (so much so, that the bus service doesn't even extend to the eastern half of the island).

The port of **Adamas** is now the biggest of the three and the best base for exploring the island. Founded by Cretan settlers in 1824, it lacks a historical centre, but boasts a recently redeveloped waterfront and promenade, and arguably the finest ferry-passenger shed in the islands (though 'shed' is still the operative term). Almost all the tourist facilities and a high proportion of the island's hotels are built here, and after years of struggling to take off the place now has quite a buzz about it at the height of the season.

Built upon a weathered plug of magma, Adamas has a town-on-the-hill look about it, and enjoys views across the central bay (which looks more like a lake as the entrance is hidden from view). Although it might look similar in shape to Santorini on a map, this bay isn't a caldera, but just the chance result of a large number of small eruptions building the island in this shape. Either side of the town are small sandy beaches: they are rather narrow and the sand is grey rather than a bright sparkling photogenic white, but they are usable and have plenty of shady trees behind them. There are also several discos in town that are the sum total of the island's nightlife. Adamas is also well endowed with tavernas (the best lie on the coast road to the east of the area shown on the map overleaf).

North of Adamas lies the classical centre of Milos. This part of the island is dominated by a cluster of four villages, the prettiest of which, **Plaka**, is the island capital. Easily the most photogenic part of Milos, it is an unspoilt whitewashed chora with the usual warren of streets to get hopelessly lost in, and with superb views and a couple of museums worth visiting. Dominating the town is another volcanic mound topped with a number of chapels, all that remain of the old Venetian castro-cum-town. The other villages in the quartet are close enough to walk to: the best is **Tripiti**, running down from a windmill-topped

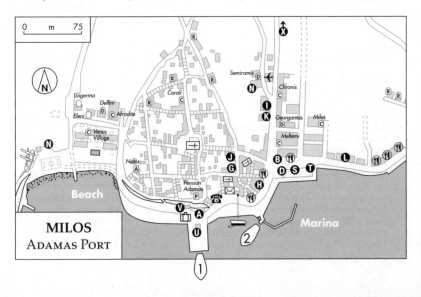

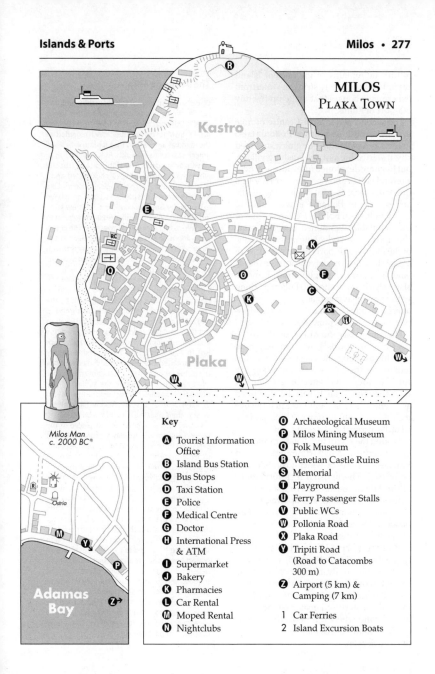

MILOS
PLAKA TOWN

*Milos Man
c. 2000 BC®*

Key

A Tourist Information Office
B Island Bus Station
C Bus Stops
D Taxi Station
E Police
F Medical Centre
G Doctor
H International Press & ATM
I Supermarket
J Bakery
K Pharmacies
L Car Rental
M Moped Rental
N Nightclubs

O Archaeological Museum
P Milos Mining Museum
Q Folk Museum
R Venetian Castle Ruins
S Memorial
T Playground
U Ferry Passenger Stalls
V Public WCs
W Pollonia Road
X Plaka Road
Y Tripiti Road (Road to Catacombs 300 m)
Z Airport (5 km) & Camping (7 km)

1 Car Ferries
2 Island Excursion Boats

hill to the remains of the ancient island capital and the lovely string of waterfront fishermen's houses that make up the tiny old port of **Klima**.

The second major tourist centre of note lies on the north-east coast at **Pollonia** (also known as Apollonia). Fringing a sheltered bay, it started life as a small fishing village, but has now developed into a low-key pension and holiday home style resort (though this latter term is a bit misleading — the atmosphere of Pollonia is more akin to Greek village on holiday). Even in spite of the inevitable abandoned opencast mine eating away an overlooking hillside, it is one of the more scenic parts of the island, with a very attractive windswept northern headland. The ferry to neighbouring Kimolos also helps bring visitors to Pollonia (along with some nice tavernas and rooms): the overall result is that most visitors to Milos pay a call at some point during their stay.

The main bay of Milos tends to be neglected by tourists, who are happy to take buses along the coast road without looking further. As a walking or jogging route it does have something going for it. Although it can hardly be described as 'scenic' there is plenty to catch the eye including a coaling quay, salt flats (and the island's airport) and a goat farm.

Around the rest of the island are a scatter of wonderfully scenic swimming spots and beaches — some of which just shouldn't be missed. The unusual rock-formations of the Milian coastline have left a sort of cliff-lined sea canal at **Papafragas** and weathered white lunar rock coves at **Firiplaka** and **Sarakiniko**. There are also more conventional beaches in abundance. The best of these served by the bus system is the pebble beach at **Paleochori**, with several buses running daily in High Season. If you have your own transport you can do better: a set of wheels gives you very easy access to the monastery and goat-inhabited west of the island where it is perfectly possible to find a sandy beach all to yourself, even in High Season.

The Venus de Milo

One of the most famous statues in the world, and now in the Louvre Museum in Paris, the Venus de Milo ('the one without the arms') was pirated away from Milos in 1820. The statue is regarded on the island as a stolen key that, if returned, would unlock vast tourism wealth. As it is, Milos has to do with offering tourists a sign indicating the site where the statue was allegedly discovered, and a plaster copy in the Archaeological Museum. Like the Elgin Marbles, this piece of sculpture has been exploited by Greek government ministers seeking a populist profile, with at least one request to the French for her return. However, unlike Elgin's acquisitions, the Venus (known on Milos as the 'Aphrodite') has come in for serious criticism, with some claiming that she is a lot more than two arms short of being a great work of art.

Discovered by a farmer digging in a field, the statue was bound for the local Ottoman administrator's collection until a warship, sent by the French ambassador to Constantinople, turned up and persuaded (via cash handouts) the locals to put the Venus on board. The skulduggery didn't end there: rumours persist that when this plumpish lady was first unearthed she was not brachially disadvantaged (the first two Frenchmen who saw the statue reported the existence of arms). Quite what happened to them is the subject of any number of tall tales, the best embracing ransom demands, with almost every islander having, if not an arm, then at least a hand in the business.

On her arrival in Paris she was placed in the Louvre Museum, which having just been denuded of Napoleon's stolen works of art, was desperate to restore its reputation by being seen to acquire a great sculptural masterpiece. In a masterly example of 19 c. hype, the statue was immediately 'identified' as a major work by Phidias or Praxiteles — the two great sculptors of Classical Greece. Clear evidence to the contrary was suppressed. Early drawings of the statue show that a broken fragment of the base (which accompanied the figure to Paris, only to go missing) bore an inscription stating that it was made by one Agesandros of Antioch, an obscure and little regarded provincial Hellenistic sculptor. The quality of the sculpting suggests this to be the case: it is very inferior to good pieces of the Classical period. More than one critic has observed that if the Venus still had her arms, or had stayed in Greece, the world would have ignored a powerful icon of both art — and the power of political spin.

Key

Ⓐ Tripiti Village Bus Stops
Ⓑ Main Path to Archaeological Site
Ⓒ Entrance to the Catacombs
Ⓓ Circular Bastion
Ⓔ Internal Defensive Wall
Ⓕ Stadium
Ⓖ Discovery site of the Venus de Milo / Gymnasium
Ⓗ Foundations of Baptistry & Early Christian Font

Ⓘ Roman Theatre
Ⓙ Site of Main City Temple?
Ⓚ Roman Baths
Ⓛ Private Houses
Ⓜ 'Hall of the Mystai' Mosaic
Ⓝ Sections of City Wall
Ⓞ Road to Triovasalos Village (1 km)
Ⓟ Road to Plaka Village (1 km)
Ⓠ Road to Adamas Port (4 km)
Ⓡ Current hiding-place of the Venus de Milo's arms

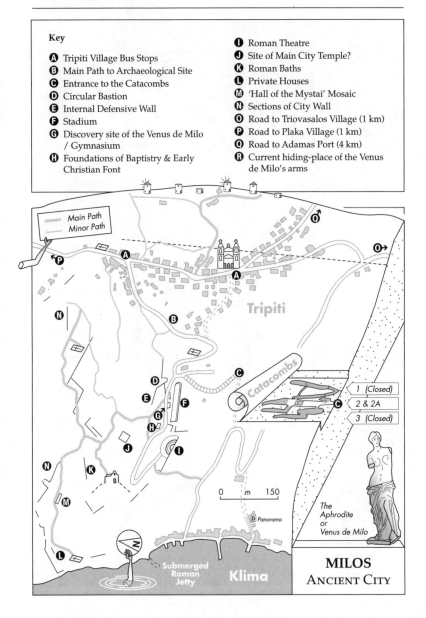

Main Path
Minor Path

Ⓟ   Ⓐ   Ⓠ
                                                              Ⓞ→

Ⓝ   Ⓐ

                    Ⓑ   Tripiti

Ⓝ
                                    Ⓒ   Catacombs

        Ⓓ   1 (Closed)
    Ⓔ   Ⓕ   Ⓒ   2 & 2A
        Ⓖ   3 (Closed)
        Ⓗ

        Ⓙ   Ⓘ

Ⓝ
    Ⓚ
                            0   m   150
    Ⓜ

                                Ⓓ Panorama   The Aphrodite or Venus de Milo

Ⓛ   **MILOS**
        N   Ancient City
            Submerged
            Roman
            Jetty   Klima

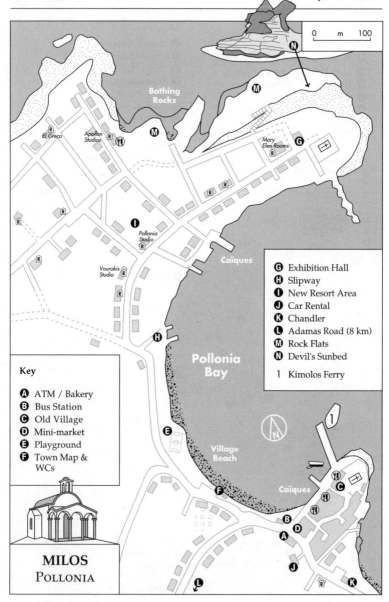

Key

Ⓐ ATM / Bakery
Ⓑ Bus Station
Ⓒ Old Village
Ⓓ Mini-market
Ⓔ Playground
Ⓕ Town Map & WCs

Ⓖ Exhibition Hall
Ⓗ Slipway
Ⓘ New Resort Area
Ⓙ Car Rental
Ⓚ Chandler
Ⓛ Adamas Road (8 km)
Ⓜ Rock Flats
Ⓝ Devil's Sunbed

1 Kimolos Ferry

MILOS
POLLONIA

Bathing Rocks

El Greco

Apollon Studios

Mary Elen Rooms

Pollonia Studio

Vourakis Studio

Caïques

Pollonia Bay

Village Beach

Caïques

☻

Thanks to its large, sheltered harbour Milos was an important island in ancient times, rivalling Naxos as a centre of pre-Hellenic civilization, with an important Minoan settlement developing on the northern coast at Filakopi. Prior to this Milos appears to have been a major trading post thanks to the availability of obsidian, a volcanic glass that could be cut to make sharp tools. Mycenaean and Archaic settlement followed apace, and by the Classical era Milos was one of the more notable of the minor players in the internecine struggles of the Greek city states.

The island's great moment in history occurred in 416 BC when Milos refused to join Athens in her war with Sparta and Corinth (an event later immortalized by the historian Thucydides via the 'Melian Dialogue' in his *History of the Peloponnesian War*). By way of a reprisal the Athenians voted for the execution of all the adult males on the island. With the women and children sold into slavery, the island was repopulated with 500 Athenians (who in turn were thrown out by the Spartans after Athens lost the Peloponnesian War). Milos—even under Venetian (1207–1566) and Turkish (1566–1821) rule — kept a very low profile from then on, apart from a short period in the 17 c. when it emerged as a notorious pirate centre, and WW1 when it was used as an Allied naval base and coaling station.

►◄

The ferry quay Information Office (☎ 22445) hands out information sheets showing the location of all hotels. Most of the hotels and pensions are in **Adamas**. These include the spiffy, pricey C-class *Venus Village* (☎ 22030) complex, complete with swimming pool and the port's best beach. Also ideally placed to take advantage of this are the C-class *Afrodite* (☎ 22020) and the D-class *Delfini* (☎ 22001).

More hotels are to be found on the east side of the port. Near the waterfront are the C-class *Meltemi* (☎ 22284) and *Milos* (☎ 22087) along with the D-class *Georgantas* (☎ 21955). On the Plaka road behind are the C-class *Chronis* (☎ 22226) and the D-class *Semiramis* (☎ 22117). The Adamas 'hill' has less accommodation, with the C-class *Corali* (☎ 22204) augmented by the B-class pension *Adamas* (☎ 22322) and a number of rooms. Around the rest of the island the only hotel of note is the friendly D-class *Panorama* (☎ 21623) at **Klima**.

▲

Camping Milos (☎ 31410), located 7 km from Adamas on the coast directly opposite the ferry quay, is a clean, well-equipped site. Sited on a headland, it has a large pool, fair canteen and a poor shop — so bring supplies with you. A camping mini-bus meets all ferries and offers occasional lifts into town (the main weakness of this site is its location: there are only a couple of regular buses a day). The journey can be made on foot in a pinch.

👓

Plaka and the surrounding villages have the main concentration of sights on Milos. There are five of particular note:
1. The Archaeological Museum.
2. The Catacombs.
3. The Ancient City.
4. The Bronze Age Town at Filakopi.
5. The Milos Mining Museum.
If you take the Bronze Age town at Filakopi (which was closed in 2007 due to site refurbishment) out of the equation the remainder can — with a little bit of planning — be explored in the course of a busy day.

The **Archaeological Museum** (open ⓓ ex ①08.00–15.30; entry fee: €3) is the best place to begin a sightseeing day on Milos. Its limited opening hours, combined with island bus times, push it to the front of the queue. Housed in an ornate neo-classical mansion, the museum is inevitably something of a disappointment, as the island's main attraction — the Venus de Milo — is represented only by a plaster replica. Even so, the juxtaposition of the replica with other statues of similar vintage does provide revealing artistic context, and makes her look to be one of a crowd rather than something special. Of far . more merit is the enjoyable collection of finds from Filakopi — these include long-horned pottery steers, some tall short-legged figures who are very obviously letting it all hang out, and a Minoan hip bath.

From the Archaeological Museum it is only a 2 km downhill walk to the **Catacombs** (open ⓓ ex ⑦ 08.00–17.00, ⑦ 08.00–13.00; entry is free — which is just as well as a visit only takes a couple of minutes). The earliest known Christian site in Greece, the catacombs are thought to date from the 1 c. AD when St. Paul was shipwrecked on Milos (an arrival that appears to have prompted the locals to dig a series of tunnels capable of hiding away the entire population). The site of burials and worship for close on 400 years, they lie just outside the East Gate of the city wall. Dug into the easily worked volcanic rock, they originally took the form of three unconnected tunnels (the longest is some 184 m) with secondary chambers leading off them. Since their discovery in 1840, connecting corridors have been dug between them, and two of the three entrances closed off. Only the central catacomb is open to the public. Once inside you will find yourself in a long, floodlit chamber with burial niches in the walls and floor, along with cavities for oil lamps. Estimates as to the numbers interred range from 2,000—8,000, but as 'dem bones' appear to have risen up and legged it during repeated pillaging in the island's piratical years, it is impossible to arrive at an accurate figure.

The **Ancient City**, which lies adjacent to the catacombs, is worth wandering around, though to call the extant remains a 'city' casts a very misleading impression — given their scanty nature (so much so that they are unfenced and have no entry fee). Built on a relatively steep hillside, the site was the home of the island capital from around 1000 BC through to the Byzantine period. The best preserved remains are parts of the city walls, a Roman theatre, and the inaccessible stadium, deftly cut out of one side of a hill. A plaque also stands on the alleged site where *the* statue was discovered (there are plans to erect a copy of the Venus here): it is thought to have originally graced a niche in a gymnasium that stood near the stadium. The lower part of the city stood behind an ancient harbour and was dominated by a small temple-topped hill (a small church now stands on the site).

The **Bronze Age Town** at **Filakopi** is the second major site from antiquity on Milos and is reached by taking the Adamas—Pollonia bus. Currently undergoing a restoration programme after years of neglect under overgrown vegetation, it offers plenty for archaeologists to ponder on, but little for the layman. The jumble of walls (extending under the sea) are not readily intelligible, but are important as one of the largest Minoan towns outside Crete and Santorini. Later a Mycenaean centre, Filakopi remained the island capital until its decline c. 1100 BC. The majority of the objects found here are in the island's Archaeological Museum, but the best —including the famous flying-fish fresco fragment (useful tip: avoid discussing this object

when you are drunk) — are in the National Archaeological Museum in Athens.

The final sightseeing objective of note is the **Milos Mining Museum** (open ◉ 09.15–13.45, 18.45–21.15: free entry). Sited on the waterfront 400 m east of the port, it is easily spotted thanks to the rusting mine-related objects (including a suitably WW1 'mine'-like ore ship's mooring bollard) adorning the entrance. The museum is a good final port of call as it — very unusually—has evening opening hours. This reflects the fact that it is a new purpose-built private institution donated by the largest mining company on Milos. The ground floor is home to an exhibition of mining artefacts and clothing, while the upper floor gallery is devoted to smaller objects (including some very Maunday money-like payment tokens) and display cases containing colourful examples of the island's geology. The museum basement houses a media centre that shows a rolling 12-minute film that includes islanders' inevitably grim recollections (with English subtitles) of working conditions in the mines in the first half of the last century. The small shop is also of minor interest — there aren't many museums in the world where you can buy collections of mineral samples. Gift boxes of rocks come at different prices depending on the number of samples contained: the 1970s 'pet rock' craze is still rocking here.

Continuing the geology and mining themes, Milos also offers a series of excursions that make a natural follow-through from a visit to the Mining Museum. These include one of the more original day excursions in the Greek islands in the form of a **Mining and Geology Tour** that starts with the above and ends at a working mine, taking in the catacombs en route. Thanks to the exotic appearance of much of Milos's volcanic coastline, the **Round-the-Island Boat Tour** (€25) also makes an interesting excursion. The regular trip takes in the volcanic Glaronisi islets, the uninhabited (rare chamois goats excepted) island of Antimilos to the north-west, colourful abandoned sulphur mines, and — too briefly to do more than explore the harbour — the island of Kimolos.

Finally, daily guided **Sea Kayak Excursions** cost a hefty €55 (all kit and lunch included) but do enable you to get up close to some of the coastal rock formations. Information on all these excursions is available from the island tourist office at the end of the ferry quay at Adamas.

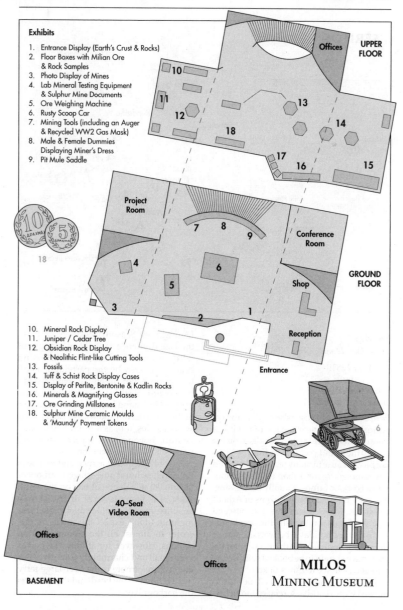

Exhibits

1. Entrance Display (Earth's Crust & Rocks)
2. Floor Boxes with Milian Ore & Rock Samples
3. Photo Display of Mines
4. Lab Mineral Testing Equipment & Sulphur Mine Documents
5. Ore Weighing Machine
6. Rusty Scoop Car
7. Mining Tools (including an Auger & Recycled WW2 Gas Mask)
8. Male & Female Dummies Displaying Miner's Dress
9. Pit Mule Saddle

10. Mineral Rock Display
11. Juniper / Cedar Tree
12. Obsidian Rock Display & Neolithic Flint-like Cutting Tools
13. Fossils
14. Tuff & Schist Rock Display Cases
15. Display of Perlite, Bentonite & Kadlin Rocks
16. Minerals & Magnifying Glasses
17. Ore Grinding Millstones
18. Sulphur Mine Ceramic Moulds & 'Maundy' Payment Tokens

UPPER FLOOR

Offices

GROUND FLOOR

Project Room

Conference Room

Shop

Reception

Entrance

40-Seat Video Room

Offices

Offices

BASEMENT

MILOS
MINING MUSEUM

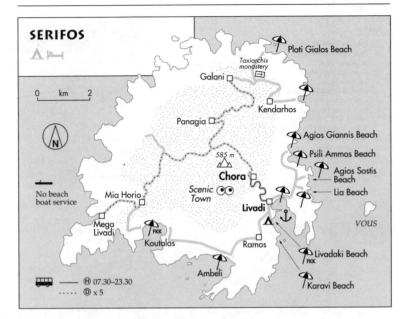

SERIFOS

Plati Gialos Beach

Taxiarchis monastery

Galani

Kendarhos

Panagia

Agios Giannis Beach

Psili Ammos Beach

585 m

Chora

Agios Sostis Beach

Scenic Town

Lia Beach

No beach boat service

Mia Horio

Livadi

VOUS

Mega Livadi

FKK

Koutalas

Ramos

Livadaki Beach

FKK

Ambeli

Karavi Beach

⊕ 07.30–23.30

Ⓓ x 5

Serifos

ΣΕΡΙΦΟΣ; 70 km²; pop. 1,100.

CODE ☎ 22810
PORT POLICE ☎ 51470
POLICE ☎ 51300
HOSPITAL ☎ 51202

Serifos is one of those islands that always seems to end up near the top of the list of 'one of those places the ferry calls at on the way to the island you are heading for'. This is a pity, because in many respects the island has more going for it than its more popular neighbour Sifnos. Equally distressing, a goodly number of the citizens of Athens are in the know about this and descend like a plague of locusts for weekends and summer holidays: be warned, ferries departing Serifos for Athens on Sundays are almost certain to be booked solid before you get a chance to buy a ticket.

Athenians aside, sun-baked Serifos is blessed with a laid-back, relaxed ambience.

During Low Season weekdays, at least, the island offers a tantalizing glimpse of what Ios might have been like if it hadn't been discovered by the partying masses; the set-up is not dissimilar, with a small port over-looked by an appealing chora, coupled by a good beach a headland away. Serifos is as barren and with as poor a road system as Ios, too; as a result few visitors venture beyond the closely connected port—chora—beach combination.

The only means of arrival and escape is the cosy beach and pine-fringed harbour of **Livadi**. Set in a deep-cut bay on the south coast, it is home to most of the island's facilities, from the bank, supermarket and nightlife (don't expect too much on this score) to almost all the accommodation options. However, for all this, the port is very small and charmingly primitive. The one feature of note is the over-large ferry quay built onto the headland that protects the harbour bay.

The bay itself is lined by hotels and houses offering rooms. These look onto a passable sand beach (though the dust thrown up by cars negotiating the port's one-way traffic system means that it pays to walk to the east of the hotel strip). A better beach lies to the west of the ferry quay at **Livadaki**. This is supposedly designated as one of the island's two nude beaches, but the crowds turn this into an all-family affair during the summer months. Those looking for the chance to reveal more to fewer people should consider taking the short path that runs from the end of Livadaki beach over the headland to **Karavi** beach.

The more energetic might also consider taking the track that runs from the far end of the harbour beach to the succession of charming beaches on the east coast. These start with **Lia** and run up to **Agios Giannis** — passing en route the island's best beach, a long stretch of sand backed by a couple of tavernas at **Psili Ammos**.

New arrivals to Serifos are confronted with a sign (now only in Greek) on the quay welcoming you 'to the island with Europe's most beautiful beach — *Sunday Times 25/5/2003*'. This is a bit disingenuous (to put it mildly) as the newspaper in question had twenty of its writers nominate their top European beach: Psili Ammos was merely one of those listed. Moreover, the recommendation doesn't call the beach beautiful, but instead dwells more on the merits of two tavernas behind it which 'make a good beach a great one' (the liquid refreshment on sale here is pretty potent stuff). About an hour's walk from the port bay, the beach can also be reached via a track running down from Chora. Beyond Psili Ammos is a longer beach at **Agios Giannis**; usually very quiet, it tends to be the sole preserve of the occasional nude hiker.

A second walking option (provided you are prepared to keep your clothes on) is the old mule path running from the road behind the port up a steep hillside to the island's only town. The path and modern road repeatedly meet and turn away all the way up the hillside — like a pair of virgin lovers' furtive glances, with mule water troughs taking the part of occasional tears along the way. Unless you attempt it during the heat of the middle of the day it is an easy and pleasant walk, though at some points where path and road meet you have to look quite hard to pick up where the path continues.

Just over 2 km long, the path finally wanders into the lower slopes of the island capital at **Chora**. Straddling the slopes of a finger of rock pointing skyward (complete with a whimsical small chapel placed deftly on the tip) Chora is not to be missed. It deserves a visit for it is one of the most photogenic choras around: a mini-Astipalea Town, complete with a ridge of windmills, and a hill topped with whitewashed chapels and the scanty remains of a kastro. The views over Chora and the port bay from the top are suitably breathtaking, and worth the effort of finding your way through the narrow warren of streets (many in a poor state of repair).

The main hill aside, Chora neatly divides into two quarters. The older section runs in an arc north along the hill spine until it reaches the windmills (most of the houses run down the east slope before farming terraces take over). The 'new' town cascades down the south slope of the Chora hill, and there is limited access between the two. Still very much a residential town with few concessions to tourism, Chora lacks landmarks (thereby guaranteeing you will get lost in it for a street or two). Fortunately, it is not so big that this is much of a problem and some relief is to be gained by the provision of working water taps at strategic points on the edge of the chora and the old road.

The rest of Serifos is not visited by the great majority of tourists. Consisting of arid, stone-littered hills ('Serifos' means 'stoney') that are relieved only by odd patches of vegetation (like equally dry Santorini, the island's principal crops are tomatoes and ground-creeping vines) and a scatter of isolated farms, it doesn't exactly invite exploration, though ambitious walkers will find plenty to please them. The dull red-brown landscape isn't really enhanced by the litter of rusting remains from the island's — now defunct — iron mining industry. This thrived a century ago but declined between the world wars: its only lasting impact was in the field of Greek industrial relations — a 1916 miners' strike saw the deaths of four strikers before workers' rule was established. More appealing are the small villages connected by poor roads. These lead variously to the island's other official nudist beach at Koutalas, and to the **Taxiarchis** monastery on the north coast.

An earlier island attraction is presumably still lying around somewhere and, if discovered, is probably better left where you find it; for Serifos was the childhood home of Perseus, the Greek hero who cut off the head of the Gorgon Medusa (a personified shriek who, if looked at directly in the eye, would turn the viewer into stone). Armed with this little trinket, Perseus went around the island flashing it at anyone who didn't take his fancy; this included the king and most of the population. This seems to have left the modern inhabitants in a quandary: on the one hand this mythological hero provides the only event in the history of Serifos worth talking about, yet he presumably did to death their ancestors. As a result Perseus, although a hero, is all but ignored here.

Elsewhere Perseus was a popular figure. Not to be confused with the god Hermes, he was armed with a mirror shield (provided by his patron Athena), a pair of winged boots, a head-satchel and cap of invisibility, and a sickle. His foe Medusa was one of the horror figures of Greek mythology. Noted for having a head of snakes instead of hair, she was made to appear infinitely more terrible by Classical artists who represented her as a beautiful maiden. Her beheading and Perseus's subsequent pursuit by her two sisters (Stheno 'the Strong' and Euryale 'the wide-leaping') was a popular theme in Ancient Greek art.

The Myth of Perseus & the Gorgons

Once upon a time Acrisius, the king of Argos, was warned by an oracle that his daughter Danaë would produce a son who would kill him. Whereupon he imprisoned her in a bronze chamber (an ancient variation on the chastity belt). Needless to say the god Zeus — disguised as a golden shower (of what it is probably politic not to ask) — visited her and nine months later Perseus appeared. Loath to kill his grandson, Acrisius promptly put him into a chest with his mother and cast it out to sea. It drifted to Serifos, where mother and son were received cordially by the local king Polydectes, who fell violently in love with Danaë, allowing both mother and son to live in his palace. Danaë, however, successfully rejected the king's advances until Perseus was fully grown. Polydectes then sought to get him off the scene while he pursued his mother by sending him off on a seemingly impossible task — to fetch the head of the Gorgon Medusa. This Perseus did with a little help from his friends, notably the goddess Athena, the god Hermes and some Gorgon-hating sea nymphs.

On returning to Serifos, Perseus turned Polydectes and his courtiers into stone by producing the head of Medusa after he discovered that the king had attempted to force his mother into marriage. After returning the gifts of Hermes and his patron Athena (who thereafter wore the Aegis cape, adorned with the Gorgon's head and fringed with snakes), Perseus and his mother decided to return to the mainland, where en route to his home he mis-threw a discus while competing in some funeral games, accidentally killing a member of the crowd — his grandfather.

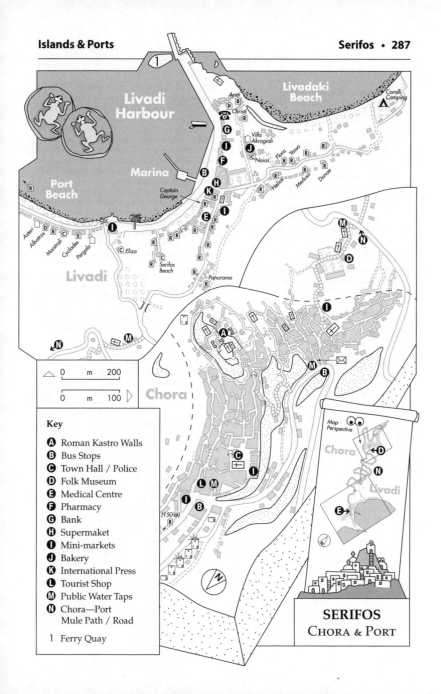

Key

- **A** Roman Kastro Walls
- **B** Bus Stops
- **C** Town Hall / Police
- **D** Folk Museum
- **E** Medical Centre
- **F** Pharmacy
- **G** Bank
- **H** Supermaket
- **I** Mini-markets
- **J** Bakery
- **K** International Press
- **L** Tourist Shop
- **M** Public Water Taps
- **N** Chora—Port
  Mule Path / Road

1 Ferry Quay

SERIFOS
CHORA & PORT

☠

Serifos has enjoyed quite a colourful history for an island of its size. Despite this, its main claim to fame for many years — thanks to a passing remark by the Roman author Livy — was as the home for a strange species of frog. The famous frogs of Serifos were said to be silent and would only croak if they were moved to another place. Who conducted this bizarre experiment (or why) isn't clear, though it is likely that the story has something to do with the Perseus myth: local worship of the hero was bound up with symbols of frogs — who even made it onto the island's coinage. In any event their descendants evidently learnt to speak, as J. T. Bent begins *The Cyclades* (see p. 145) complaining that they gaily croaked.

Moving on to historical times, Sifnos was one of the early democracies, with the first experiments coming as early as the 7 C. BC. During the Persian Wars the island first sided with the Persians, but deserted to the Greek cause. It later came under Athenian control via the Delian League, and was subsequently ruled by the Macedonians, the Ptolemies and Romans. During the later Roman years the island was used as a place of exile.

In obscurity during most of the Byzantine era, Serifos was captured by the Venetians in 1207 who promptly began the first full-scale commercial exploitation of the iron-ore reserves. Unfortunately the prosperity that followed increased the dangers from predators. The first of these turned up in 1393 when a Venetian named Adoldo hired Cretan mercenaries to capture the island's richer individuals. They were taken to the top of the chora kastro and those who failed to reveal where they kept their personal savings were thrown from the walls. An attack by the pirate Barbarossa in 1537 was of a different order: the whole island was depopulated, with full control passing to the Turks in 1566.

More trouble followed: in 1680 Serifos was hit by an outbreak of plague so devastating that the island was uninhabited for several years. Briefly under Russian control between 1770–74, Serifos joined Greece in 1821. It again saw conflict in 1916 when the island's miners began a strike for an 8-hour day that ended with the deaths of four of their number in a series of bloody struggles with the mine owners. The iron-ore reserves were depleted by heavy mining in the first half of the 20 C. — the last mine closed in the 1960s.

⊨

Most of the accommodation on Serifos is to be found in and around the port of **Livadi**. This includes the expensive B-class hotel *Areti* (☎ 51479) overlooking the beach. At the far end of the port beach stands the B-class *Asteri* (☎ 51191) and the *Maistrali* (☎ 51381). In addition there are three C-class hotels: the *Naias* (☎ 51585), the *Eliza* (☎ 51763), and the *Serifos Beach* (☎ 51209), complete with restaurant and tucked down a side alley.

At the budget end of the range is the D-class *Albatros* (☎ 51148) along with the E-class *Cyclades* (☎ 51315). A scatter of rooms — notably the faded *Captain George Rooms* (☎ 51274) near the main square — are complemented by newer establishments behind the port beach and along the campsite, and Ramos roads.

Ⓐ

Coralli Camping (☎ 51500), 400 m west of the port (mini-buses go 2 km around the port one-way system to get there), is one of the best and cleanest sites in Greece, on the beach with shady shrubs and a pool. Bungalows are also rented out. The big weak point is the site policy of dictating where you pitch your tent.

👓👓

The main sight on Serifos should have been the **Kastro** on the Chora hill. Sadly, it was reduced to walls by repeated attack. Even less is to be seen of the temple of Athena that preceded it (most of its stones are now in the walls of two nearby churches). Near the other end of history's spectrum is the Town Hall. Built in 1909, it stands resplendent in the main square, glorying in the contrast it offers with the surrounding whitewashed houses. The only other sight is a small **Archaeological Museum** by the bus station (free entry) containing a tiny collection of minor local finds.

The **Ancient Capital**, which was at Mia Horio, has left few traces on the ground today, and in lieu of anything else, the castle-like **Taxiarchis Monastery** ('Monastery of the Archangels'), built c. 1600 AD, is the main sightseeing destination. Access isn't easy (it is now inhabited by a single monk who isn't in the habit of opening up on a daily basis), and the surest way of getting there is to pack a few bottles of water and walk it: the round trip from the town takes a little over four hours. Despite being looted on occasions by pirates, it is still home to a notable collection of artefacts. Finally **Panagia** has the island's oldest church. Built c. 950 AD, it is adorned with 14 C. wall paintings.

SIFNOS
◎ Δ ⊨

0   km   3

Ancient
Gold Mines

Ag.
Marina
Kamares ⚓   ☂
                    □ ▲

                         Artemonas   Scenic
                         □ Pano   Village
                           Petali   ◉◉
Apollonia Ⓑ   **Kastro**
/Chora   ⊞
                              □ Kato
                                Petali
              Ag. Andreas
              680 m
              ΛΛ ⊞   **Faros**
                                      ⊞   ☂
Bus Routes: Taxiarchis
                       Monastery
Sifnos has a good bus system built ▲   □
of some 11 routes criss-crossing the **Vathi**   **Platis** ◉◉
island. All pass through Apollonia: **Gialos** ☂ **Chrisopigi**
                                                      Monastery

Bus frequency legend:
Ⓓ x 24 07.00–24.00
Ⓓ x 24 07.00–24.00
Ⓓ x 20 07.00–24.00
Ⓓ x 22 07.00–24.00
Ⓓ x 3
Ⓓ x 6

Sifnos has a good bus system built
of some 11 routes criss-crossing the
island. All pass through Apollonia:
their combined frequency is shown on
this map. Expect to change at Apollonia.
There are three bus stops in the town:
1. In front of the Post Office
   (for Kamares)
2. In front of the Hotel Anthoussa
   (for Platis Gialos, Faros)
3. Opposite the Hotel Anthoussa
   (for Artemonas, Kato Petali & Kastro)

Sifnos

ΣΙΦΝΟΣ; 89 km²; pop. 2,200.

CODE ☎ 22840
PORT POLICE ☎ 31617
TOURIST OFFICES ☎ 31977, 32190
FIRST AID ☎ 31315

The most touristed island in the Cyclades
West group, Sifnos (sometimes transcribed
as 'Siphnos') is still fairly quiet by Central
Cyclades line standards. Much of the
island's popularity can be attributed to
its hilly landscape, sprinkled with typical
white Cycladic villages and several good
beaches; sightseeing usually gives way
to general exploring, given the limited
number of sights of interest.

During the Archaic period Sifnos was very
prosperous, thanks to the discovery of gold
deposits. By way of a thanks offering for this
good luck the islanders were in the habit
of making an annual gift of a golden egg
to the god Apollo's shrine at Delphi (this
wasn't as odd as it sounds, for the oracle
stone at Delphi, the *Omphalos* marking the
centre of the world, was egg-shaped; it was
the point where two eagles — flying from
the opposite ends of the earth — met). The
story has it that one year they sent a gilt egg
instead and, surprise, surprise, their mines
(which by now had extended out under the
sea) were mysteriously flooded. This had a
catastrophic effect on the island's fortunes,
and by the Classical period Sifnos had

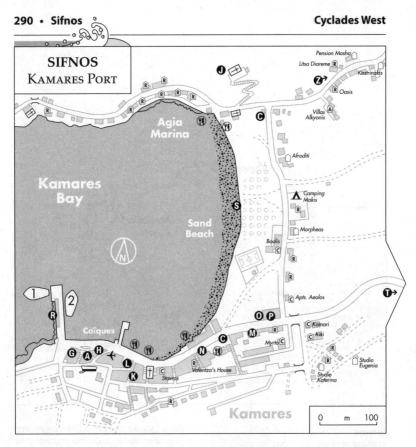

ceased to be a major player and relied on pottery production for its livelihood — the islanders presumably working on the practical notion that if you can't dig up pots of gold you can at least make the pots.

These days Sifnos is one of those leading the pack in the second eleven of Greek islands. Despite its popularity, it suffers from a shortage of accommodation. This is one of the few islands where there is a real possibility of not being able to find a High Season bed (and those that are available tend to be expensive); it pays to arrive on a morning boat if you haven't phoned ahead.

Ferries dock on the 'wrong' side of Sifnos (relative to the main settlements) where a horseshoe gorge provides a natural harbour at cheerful **Kamares**. Considering how small the port is, it is a surprisingly lively place thanks to its de facto role as the tourist centre, defying the stark hills that climb high above it, seeming to almost bundle it into the sea. Clinging to the shoreline can be found tavernas by the score, several travel agents and shops providing all the basic necessities (albeit at rather higher than normal prices). The back of the bay is adorned with a bamboo-backed sand-and-pebble beach of some length.

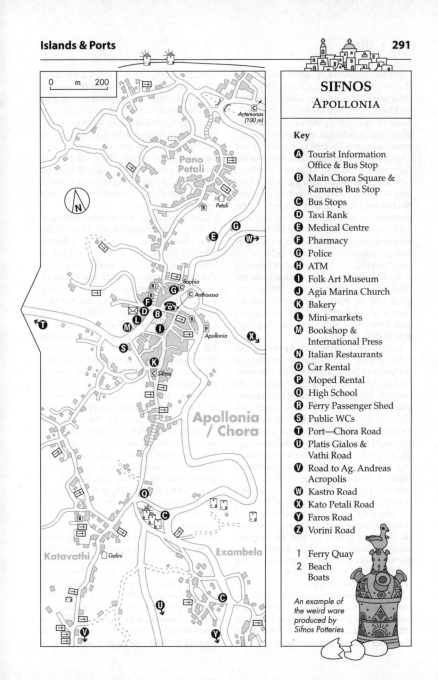

SIFNOS
APOLLONIA

Key

A Tourist Information Office & Bus Stop

B Main Chora Square & Kamares Bus Stop

C Bus Stops

D Taxi Rank

E Medical Centre

F Pharmacy

G Police

H ATM

I Folk Art Museum

J Agia Marina Church

K Bakery

L Mini-markets

M Bookshop & International Press

N Italian Restaurants

O Car Rental

P Moped Rental

Q High School

R Ferry Passenger Shed

S Public WCs

T Port—Chora Road

U Platis Gialos & Vathi Road

V Road to Ag. Andreas Acropolis

W Kastro Road

X Kato Petali Road

Y Faros Road

Z Vorini Road

1 Ferry Quay

2 Beach Boats

An example of the weird ware produced by Sifnos Potteries

Accommodation is spread evenly around the port, the quieter establishments for the most part hidden behind clumps of bamboo and trees that fringe the back of the beach. Kamares is certainly the most convenient place to stay on Sifnos, but if you do prefer to be away from the port then you will find a helpful tourist information office near the ferry quay. Frequent buses also run from here into the interior, making escape very easy — though most journeys require you to change at Apollonia if that is not your destination. All the routes run east and south as the northern third of the island is all but unpopulated, the gold mines now being inaccessible even to the archaeologically minded. The bus ride out of Kamares is itself something of a revelation as the road runs up a steep valley filled with olive and fig trees; for Sifnos is not the barren island that the sea views suggest, and agriculture still plays an important role in its economy.

The modern 'capital' of **Apollonia** lies 5 km inland, and gained its position in the years of pirate attacks in the Ottoman period. As island capitals go it is a regular oddball, being merely one of four closely placed hill villages that has grown (by virtue of its role as the island's crossroads) to become the de facto nucleus. Lacking a historical heart of note, the settlement has grown along the roads to the neighbouring villages rather than in a traditional manner, creating an unusual village-cum-suburb web of buildings. Tourist activity is centred on the bland square in the heart of this jumble; little more than a road junction fringed with houses, it doesn't do the town justice, though all essential services are conveniently to hand. In fact, the tourist-shop-cluttered street behind the square is supposed to be the true centre of the universe hereabouts.

For the Apollonia conurbation to have any appeal you have to enjoy walking; if you do so, you can be rewarded with an interesting day clambering up and down the whitewashed streets. The best views

are to be found on the windmill-topped hill above **Pano Petali** — the mills themselves being rather fun thanks to their fish-shaped weather vanes (a more interesting piece of religious symbolism than the more usual cross). The farmyard-backed backstreets behind **Exambela** are also quaint in a downbeat sort of way. Both offer excellent views of the comparatively isolated east-coast former capital of Kastro, which is within walking distance if you are not tempted by the bus.

Located on a low, free-standing hill overlooking a tiny shingle-beached bay on the west coast of Sifnos, the village of **Kastro** was the ancient and medieval capital of Sifnos and a far more worthy one than Apollonia. So much so, that the lack of space for a viable modern ferry port is the only thing that has prevented it being restored as the primary settlement. From a distance the white houses of Kastro combine to look like snow lying atop a low oblong hill. Once you get closer it soon becomes clear that they are configured in several irregular tight defensive circles around the upper slopes.

As elsewhere the former defensive outer wall of the settlement has been heavily punctured with modern windows and doorways, but three substantial gateways survive on the landward side. Once inside, Kastro presents a rather unusual face: the impression gained is of an unspoilt collection of buildings, seriously cleaned up with gallons of white paint. There are virtually no tourist shops and no tavernas (there are two in town but they are carefully sited on the outskirts, outside the former walls). Local colour is provided by a litter of fragments of ancient buildings incorporated into the houses or just lying around (three large Roman sarcophagi and a broken giant Archaic pithos being the most obvious); a series of early churches and the odd palm tree complete the collection. The site of the former acropolis at the top of the hill is the one serious non-event; little now survives beyond the odd anonymous wall.

SIFNOS
KASTRO

Chapel of
Epta Martyres
(7 Martyrs)

Kastro

Seralia

Site of the Venetian
Harbour

Poor
Pebble
Beach

0   m   50

Key

A Site of the Kastro
B Bus Stops
C Archaeological
Museum
D Hellenistic
Sarcophagi
E Line of the former
Kastro Outer Wall
F Venetian Gate
G Central Gates
H Port Gate
I Ancient Pithos
J RC Cathedral of
St. Anthony of
Padua (closed)
K Panagia Eleoussa
Cathedral
L Excavation Trenches
M Apollonia Road
(3.5 km)

The string of beaches along the south coast are the island's other great attraction. Of these, the best is at taverna-backed **Vathi** and is now visited by a new road and buses. A dirt track also runs from Vathi to the south-coast beach resort at **Platis Gialos**. A line of tavernas, rooms and the odd hotel strung along the foreshore, it is the main beach and resort on Sifnos. Its main weak point is the lack of serious shopping facilities and services. Further east lies the less popular — but more attractive — small village of **Faros**. The point of access for three small beaches, some summers it hosts a weekly small boat link with Paros.

☻

According to Herodotus the population of Sifnos were the wealthiest in the Greek islands in the pre-Classical period, thanks to the gold and silver mines. The islanders fought alongside Athens at Salamis, continuing in reasonable prosperity until the Byzantine era when pirate attacks took their toll. Sifnos was incorporated into the Duchy of Naxos in the 13 c., later coming under control of the despotic Da Coronia in 1307. In 1464 Sifnos came under the control of the Italian Gozzadini family, who used it as a power base until it fell to the Turks in 1566. Briefly under Russian control between 1770–74, Sifnos joined Greece in 1821.

ⵎ

Good tourist offices on the port waterfront and Apollonia main square are of major help finding accommodation. There are four hotels in **Apollonia**, and all are C-class. Nearest the town square is the *Anthoussa* (☎ 31431), with the *Sophia* (☎ 31238) tucked away in a nearby street. Quieter than both is the *Sifnos* (☎ 31624) away to the south. The *Artemonas* (☎ 31303), 1 km to the north-east, is nice, but inconveniently placed. There is also a pension in town — the *Apollonia* (☎ 31490).

Kamares has accommodation in the form of the C-class *Stavros* (☎ 31641), the *Myrto* (☎ 32055), *Kiki* (☎ 32329), *Boulis* (☎ 321 22), and the C-class pension *Kamari* (☎ 31710). There are also rooms — including half a dozen establishments on the north side of the bay: these will appeal to worshippers of Aphrodite as they will have to undertake romantic moonlit walks along the length of the beach when their partner needs feeding and watering.

Other settlements also have a scatter of hotels: **Faros** has the D-class *Sifneiko Archontiko* (☎ 31822) along with the expensive B-class *Blue Horizon* (☎ 31442), and **Platis Gialos** the B-class *Platys Gialos* (☎ 31324) and the D-class *Filoxenia* (☎ 322212).

Λ

Kamares has a friendly site — *Camping Makis* (☎ 32366): very small, but well maintained. Late arrivals in July/August are sometimes turned away as it fills quickly with local campers. It can also be very windy as it lies directly behind the beach. Sifnos also has a second site near the south coast: *Camping Plati Gialos* (☎ 71286) is a remote — and usually empty — site tucked 1 km behind the resort.

👓

Not only keen on pots, the locals on Sifnos have a history of being equally potty about putting churches on remote hilltops and low peninsulas. The most accessible of the hilltop variety is the site of the **Mycenaean Acropolis**, south-west of Apollonia at **Agios Andreas**. A walkable distance from the main bus stop, the 20-minute switchback ascent up the hill brings you to a modern church of no interest, and an ongoing archaeological dig that has revealed building foundations within a low Mycenaean curtain wall that runs around the hilltop. The main reason to visit are the views which are truly spectacular: the entire collection of villages on Sifnos are briefly laid out before you — before you are laid out by the seriously strong hilltop winds.

The peninsula churches are just as picturesque. The most popular is the small **Chrisopigi Monastery** sited on a small islet (now linked to Sifnos by a causeway) lying west of Faros. Equally photogenic is the small church on the seaward side of the former acropolis hill at **Kastro**. The impeccably kept village (built largely between the 14–18 c.) is home to a three-room **Archaeological Museum** (open ②–⑦ 08.30–15.00; entrance free). Easily located thanks to the large sarcophagus outside, it houses finds on Sifnos dating back to prehistory. The very mixed collection of exhibits include several figures of the goddess Artemis, a lovely 7 c. BC Proto-Corinthian cotyle bowl, and an early Hellenistic marble table leg.

Of the other villages around Apollonia, Venetian-built **Artemonas** is the most attractive, with the Kohi church built on the foundations of a Temple of Artemis.

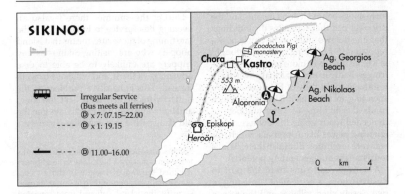

Sikinos

ΣΙΚΙΝΟΣ; 41 km²; pop. 330.

CODE ☎ 22860
POLICE ☎ 51222
FIRST AID ☎ 51211

If you want to experience an 'unspoilt' Greek island you can't do much better than pitch up on Sikinos. A small hilly gem close to Ios, it is only in recent years that a ferry quay, roads and tourist rooms have appeared to mildly change the working island atmosphere. After Anafi, Sikinos is the least touristed large island in the Cyclades, and offers a unique insight as to what Ios and other popular islands were like in pre-tourist days.

Apart from a scatter of tavernas, there are few overt concessions to tourism, and much of the island's attractiveness stems from the fact that the local donkeys are carrying water rather than tourists: the islanders' main sources of income are still fishing and agriculture (wine, olive oil, wheat and honey are the staple products). Another plus is the hospitality of the locals, who have the unusual distinction of being almost exclusively of Cretan stock (their ancestors repopulated Sikinos in the 16 c. after it had been abandoned by its previous inhabitants).

Lying between the Cyclades East and Cyclades West lines, Sikinos is visited via irregular ferries that detour from itineraries down one of these routes. If you are on a two-week holiday you therefore do need to try to plan how you intend to move on before you visit. This said, summer services are frequent enough, even if the building of the island's ferry quay in the 1990s has made the arrival here a lot less memorable than it was: prior to this visitors had to jump — or hop poetically — from a ferry's lowered back car door into a wildly bobbing fisherman's caïque. This twist to the island 'hopping' experience was great fun in the dark with a backpack on — and even more enjoyable to watch. Any undersea *Titanic*-type explorer turning cameras on the seabed hereabouts will find a debris field made up of decomposing backpacks and pairs of flip-flops (poignantly resting side by side), the only surviving markers of the poor souls who missed the boat while jumping off the backs of ferries in the dark, without a passing Leonardo DiCaprio to pull them back on board.

Ironically, the big casualty of the arrival of the ferry quay is the bay port of **Alopronia**; in times past tourists were so grateful to still be alive on landing that it seemed the most wonderful spot on earth. Nowadays, you don't need to have an overly critical eye to recognize that it is a scruffy place that doesn't do the island justice. There is a viable sand beach, but the rusting furnishings behind it don't inspire, and the dry river bed that separates the buildings that line the two sides of the bay is now a repository for building materials brought in to construct ever more rooms around its fringes. Badly in need of a makeover, it is a testament to the folly of EU-development spending in the Greek islands — which funds the building of large numbers of unneeded roads going to nowhere, while ignoring places like Alopronia which, for want of a few Euros, diminish their island's tourism-revenue-generating potential.

A narrow road runs from the port to Kastro/Chora, a settlement consisting of two closely sited villages and the reason that fully justifies a visit to Sikinos. Gently climbing up the spines of opposing hillsides on either side of a cliff-edged shoreline, they are delightful, picturesque examples of their kind. The eastern settlement of **Kastro** is the larger of the two, and its lower quarter is now the de facto centre of the combined settlement (complete with an impressive-looking 'bank' that houses nothing more than the island's ATM). There are a few basic shops — almost all that Sikinos has to offer — and a couple of those appealing tables-in-the-narrow-street tavernas, adorned with overhead garlands of flowers.

Shrunken **Chora**, on the other hand, lacks tavernas and shops, and these days merely doubles as a suburb, with a trail of ever more ruinous houses and mills climbing up the hillside behind. Running down the flank of the hill on its south side are the substantial paved remains of the old mule path that once ran down to the port. Sadly neglected these days it is just about usable.

The hollow between the two settlements is home to a large taverna with cliff-top views, and the main bus stop. The island's only bus runs between Chora and the port to meet all ferries and at irregular times during the day (timetables are posted up): the sporadic nature of the service is such that walking the 4 km road is a commonly exercised option — the lack of vehicles on Sikinos means you rarely have to dodge traffic.

During the summer there is also an evening bus service to Episkopi, but the late timing of these runs means that island hoppers who are visiting Sikinos as day trippers are unlikely to be able to take advantage of them, and will have to walk instead. This is hardly a problem as the butterfly-frequented road isn't too long, and halfway along you can always join the old mule path if you want more variety.

☺

Sikinos was once called 'Oinoe' (wine) thanks to the vines that grew here. Like its neighbours it joined the Delian League in the 4 C. BC. Never really large enough to maintain its own security, the island suffered from repeated pirate attacks until it came into the hands of the Spanish Da Coronia family in 1307. In 1467 control of Sikinos passed to the Gozzadinis, an Italian Frankish family based on Sifnos, who renamed it 'Syrandros'. The Turks captured the island in 1537, it was briefly held by the Russians (between 1771–74) and it finally joined Greece in 1829.

⊨

A reasonable supply of rooms in the port is augmented by a small number in Kastro/Chora. Few in the latter have signs: owners meet boats. The only hotel, the B-class *Porto Sikinos* (☎ 51220), rises behind the harbour.

👀

Kastro/Chora aside, the only sights on Sikinos are two unusual defunct (and locked-up) monasteries. Nearest is **Zoodochos Pigi,** overlooking the main town. Surrounded by an impressive fortified wall (backed with ruined cells on its inside), it gives Kastro its name. Those negotiating the steep path up to it are rewarded with superb views.

More ambitious sightseers can make the scenic and windswept walk across the island (via the new road) to **Episkopi**, a delightfully adapted Roman templet now masquerading as a monastery. Originally thought to be a Hellenistic temple to Hera (hence Heroön), it is now deemed more likely to have been a 3 C. AD mausoleum. It is the only surviving remnant of the ancient centre which was here rather than at Kastro. Virtually intact, it was converted into a monastery in 1673, after being damaged in an earthquake. There are the remains of a second ancient sanctuary on the north-east tip of the island.

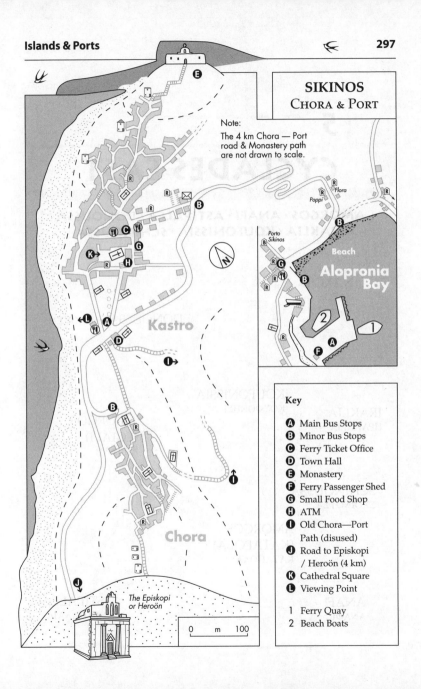

SIKINOS
CHORA & PORT

Note:
The 4 km Chora — Port
road & Monastery path
are not drawn to scale.

Flora

Poppi

Porto Sikinos

Beach

Alopronia Bay

Kastro

Chora

The Episkopi or Heroön

0   m   100

Key

- **A** Main Bus Stops
- **B** Minor Bus Stops
- **C** Ferry Ticket Office
- **D** Town Hall
- **E** Monastery
- **F** Ferry Passenger Shed
- **G** Small Food Shop
- **H** ATM
- **I** Old Chora—Port Path (disused)
- **J** Road to Episkopi / Heroön (4 km)
- **K** Cathedral Square
- **L** Viewing Point

1 Ferry Quay
2 Beach Boats

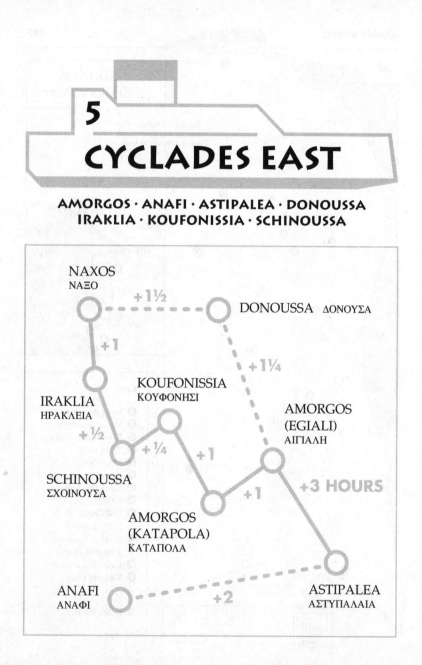

5
CYCLADES EAST

AMORGOS · ANAFI · ASTIPALEA · DONOUSSA
IRAKLIA · KOUFONISSIA · SCHINOUSSA

NAXOS
ΝΑΞΟ

+1½

DONOUSSA ΔΟΝΟΥΣΑ

+1

+1¼

KOUFONISSIA
ΚΟΥΦΟΝΗΣΙ

IRAKLIA
ΗΡΑΚΛΕΙΑ

AMORGOS
(EGIALI)
ΑΙΓΙΑΛΗ

+½

+¼

+1

SCHINOUSSA
ΣΧΟΙΝΟΥΣΑ

+1

+3 HOURS

AMORGOS
(KATAPOLA)
ΚΑΤΑΠΟΛΑ

+1

ANAFI
ΑΝΑΦΙ

+2

ASTIPALEA
ΑΣΤΥΠΑΛΑΙΑ

General Features

In the centre of the Aegean lie a number of islands that do not fall easily into chapters organized by ferry routes. Rather than distort the reader's perception of those routes by describing them elsewhere, these islands are gathered together here. All are relatively untouristed (though this is slowly changing): the last redoubt of the pre-tourist era, and all the better for it. The fact that they are untainted by mass tourism is their great charm: in many ways these are the *real* Greek islands!

The best known (and most accessible) is scenic Amorgos. It lies at the end of the line for most ferries that call — as does quiet Anafi to the south. To the east lies Astipalea, administratively one of the Dodecanese, but more characteristic in appearance of the Cyclades and usually served by ferries visiting the other islands in this chapter (hence its inclusion here).

The minor Cycladic islands running south-east of Naxos to Amorgos make up the balance of this chapter. Variously known as the 'little', 'lesser', 'minor' or 'small' Cyclades, they are all little gems. Only four are inhabited (Iraklia, Koufonissia, Schinoussa and relatively isolated Donoussa), and all are small enough to make you feel as if you really are on an island, since it is almost impossible not to lose sight of the sea. These islands are a true delight — if you can live without banks, discos and other tourist trappings. All have small, friendly populations that subsist on fishing.

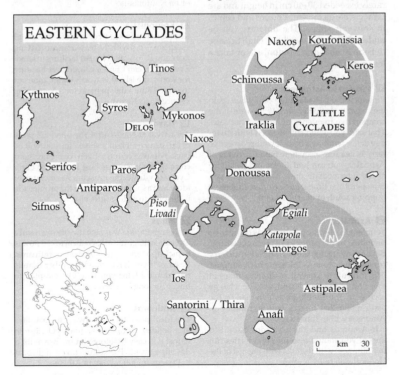

Example Itinerary [2/3 Weeks]

This chapter covers two islands — Amorgos and Astipalea — widely hailed as amongst the most attractive and unspoilt in the Aegean. Lying off the main ferry routes, they are passed over as impracticable by most island hoppers restricted to a fortnight's travelling. Yet, in fact they can easily be incorporated into a tight timetable. The trick is to tackle them as primary objectives. By visiting them first you can build them into a wider-ranging island-hopping holiday, and as Amorgos was a major centre of the Early Cycladic culture, the itinerary below takes in other islands similarly blessed. However, don't expect to find idols standing on every hilltop; they rarely exceeded 30–40 cm in height and are only visible as museum pieces and copies in souvenir shops. The itinerary can be undertaken in two weeks in High Season; outside it, abandon Koufonissia or take a leisurely three.

1 Piraeus to Astipalea

Piraeus is the best starting point when seeking to get to Astipalea simply because of the comparative frequency of ferry connections. That said, you could still be faced with a two-day delay awaiting a boat. If your prospective ferry is heading elsewhere before arriving at Astipalea, you can hop ahead and pick it up at the intermediate port. Alternatively, you can spend the time sightseeing in Athens or hopping south to nearby Aegina.

2 Astipalea

Your length of stay on Astipalea is going to be delimited by the paucity of a means of escape. Beyond saying that the overall pattern of ferry connections remains the same each summer it is difficult to generalize as ferry times at this end-of-the-line island tend to change each year. You should be able to plan on the assumption that a ferry will be running to Amorgos within three days.

If Amorgos and the Cyclades have less appeal you should also find that ferries run to Kalimnos (with its links with the rest of the Dodecanese) twice a week.

3 Amorgos (Egiali)

The great majority of visitors to Amorgos head for Katapola, but if you didn't encounter a long delay at Athens, those who like quiet island ports should find themselves with plenty of time to stop off at Egiali first. When you are ready to move on you can take either a bus or ferry on to Katapola.

4 Amorgos (Katapola)

Once at Katapola you are effectively plugged back into the ferry mainstream. With daily boats to Naxos you are within easy striking distance of the Cyclades Central line. Katapola is also the best jumping-off point for the Little Cyclades and Koufonissia, but if the *Express Skopelitis* isn't running daily, you should allow for the possibility of being stranded on the beach a day longer than intended, either here or on Koufonissia.

5 Koufonissia

Koufonissia offers a fair degree of small island escapism — but with the reassurance of having just enough by way of tourist facilities to hand. Even if you can't find a caïque-tour heading for Keros, the island is worth taking time out to visit. Allow a day in hand for a connecting service on to Naxos.

6 Naxos

An arrival at Naxos after the previous ports of call can be a bit of a shock, for you will be back in tourist country. Even so, the northern coast of the town was host to a major Early Cycladic village, the museum has a clutch of idols, and a souvenir shop near the promenade is devoted to selling little else.

7 Paros

Although Parikia was also the site of an early Cycladic village the main reason to call now is to pick up a ferry or tour boat on to Antiparos. Besides, if you have found the other islands restful and idyllic you won't be tempted to linger for long here anyway.

8 Antiparos

The ideal place to while away the last days of a holiday, Antiparos is quiet, yet close to Paros. It is easy to lounge on the beach for a day, nip across to Parikia and take a night boat to Piraeus for a final day in Athens.

EASTERN CYCLADES

Base Port: Naxos

Not the best collection of islands for springboard island hopping. **Naxos** offers the greatest number of possibilities with easy hops to Paros and Antiparos as well as tour boats to the Little Cyclades and Koufonissia. Links with Amorgos (Katapola) are daily in High Season and thrice weekly for most of the remainder of the year.

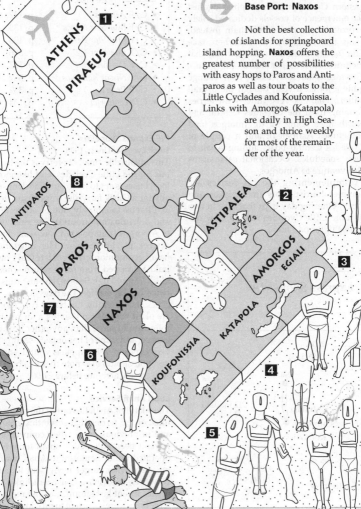

Cyclades East Ferries

Main Car Ferries

The isolated nature of the islands in the Eastern Cyclades has conspired against the emergence of vessels dedicated solely to providing services to this chain. Instead, boats that normally run elsewhere take time out to make an extended run that includes various islands in the group. This means that services and boats change quite a lot each year, though the overall pattern changes very little, with ferries running from the Cyclades Central and North lines going on to Amorgos (and sometimes Astipalea), and a couple of Cyclades Central boats adding Anafi to their schedules. Occasional catamarans also venture to Amorgos.

Complementing the car ferries are summer tourist boats from Naxos and Paros. Offering day trips that take in two or more Little Cyclades islands, they can be useful for odd hops.

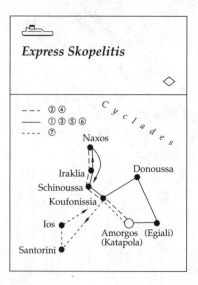

Express Skopelitis

◇

- - - ② ④
—— ① ③ ⑤ ⑥
- - - ⑦

Cyclades

Naxos
Iraklia   Donoussa
Schinoussa
Koufonissia
Ios •
        Amorgos (Egiali)
        (Katapola)
Santorini •

<table>
<tr><td>🚢</td><td>See also:</td><td></td></tr>
</table>

- C/F *Artemis*   p. 137
- C/F *Blue Star Naxos*   p. 133
- C/F *Blue Star Paros*   p. 133
- C/F *Blue Star 1/2*   p. 366
- C/F *Diagoras*   p. 367
- C/F *Nissos Kalimnos*   p. 369
- C/F *Prevelis*   p. 332
- C/M *SuperJet*   p. 134

C/F *Express Skopelitis*
Small Cyclades Lines; 1998.

This invaluable small car-ferry is the local bus for the Little Cyclades, and like most local buses is apt to fill to bursting. Unusually for a Greek ferry she was constructed at Piraeus (seemingly out of spare bits and bobs floating around). She runs out of Amorgos (Katapola) to Naxos six days a week in High Season. Her itineraries have become more erratic of late (2011 saw Iraklia dropped from some return schedules). Out of High Season, she just runs a twice-weekly service. The days do vary, so check this carefully. On-board conditions are okay, but this isn't saying a lot, as she rolls around more than any other boat in Greece, and some of her outside seating is very exposed. If Katapola is your destination you should also note that this boat is slow, rarely arriving before 21.00.

Local Anafi Service

The island of Anafi lies out of the range of most of the ferries that serve this group, and in previous years when connections haven't been adequate a small ferry has operated out of Santorini to Anafi covering days when larger ferries fail to call. However, this isn't a consistent link and it was absent last summer, as the regular ferry links were sufficient to provide cover.

Cyclades East Islands & Ports

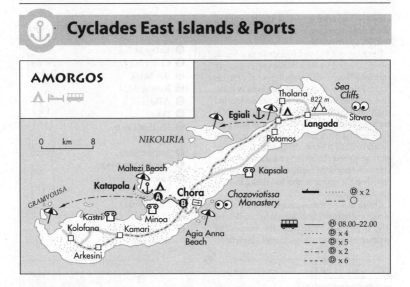

Amorgos

ΑΜΟΡΓΟΣ; 117 km²; pop. 1,720.

CODE ☎ 22850
PORT POLICE ☎ 71259
POLICE ☎ 71210
FIRST AID ☎ 71208

The most easterly of the Cyclades, Amorgos has been one of the least touristed of the large Aegean islands. This is rapidly changing as its reputation grows, for Amorgos *should* be on the itinerary of any Cycladic island hopper. It is rugged, mountainous, often battered by choppy seas, and at first sight more intimidating than many other islands. But once ashore, it turns out to be very friendly and charmingly unspoilt.

The 'Amorgos' experience is dominated by the island's mountainous terrain. One consequence of this is that the road system has been very poor, the two main settlements at each end of the island only recently being connected by a good road and regular bus. As a result, ferries call at both centres (ticket agents habitually use the port names in lieu of 'Amorgos' on

timetables), and even the islanders tend to think of their end as a separate entity to the other half.

Katapola, the principal port, lies on the more populous western half of Amorgos. Tucked into a suitably scenic and well protected bay on the north coast, it is rapidly acquiring all the trappings of a mini resort (including one of the best pizzerias in the Cyclades and a patisserie). It also offers the best facilities on the island, though this isn't saying a great deal in some respects: shopping — as elsewhere on Amorgos — is rather limited. The port beach, backed by a narrow raised promenade, is more for show than lying on (such surf as there is looks curiously soapy), and a regular taxi boat chugs across the bay to a much better beach behind the eastern headland.

Katapola is sufficiently spread out to have three centres of activity. The largest is on the ferry quay side, which contains the nucleus of tourist facilities and a waterfront lined with tavernas; the second is the hill behind the bay beach, which is dominated by a large church, with islanders' housing clustered around it; while the far side of the bay is home to a growing number of tourist apartments.

Fanning out behind Katapola is a fertile plain bisected by a road that winds steeply up the hills behind. Katapola literally means 'below the town', a name that is fully justified as the island's capital at Chora is located high on the cloud-clad hillside behind (as ferries steam toward the bay it is just possible to make out the Chora windmills and satellite dish towers on the skyline). The port acquired the name in antiquity when it was the harbour for ancient Minoa which stood on the much nearer hill rising behind the ferry quay.

Chora is a superb example of a Cycladic white-cubic town. Still geared to local island life, it has yet to acquire the bespoiling retinue of tourist shops found elsewhere.

Key

- **A** Katapola Bus Station
- **B** Chora Bus Station
- **C** Bus Stops
- **D** Bank & ATM
- **E** ATM
- **F** Police
- **G** Medical Centre
- **H** Bakery
- **I** Tourist Shop
- **J** Car & Moped Hire
- **K** Laundry
- **L** WCs
- **M** Mini-Market
- **N** Pharmacy
- **O** International Press & Bookshop

The largest Cycladic Figurine yet discovered (148 cm)

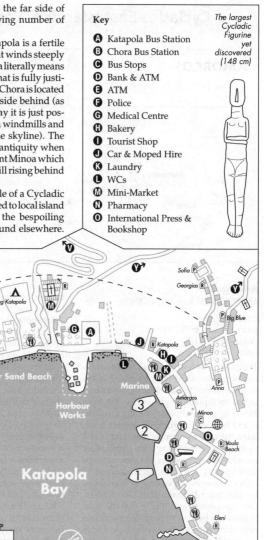

AMORGOS
KATAPOLA

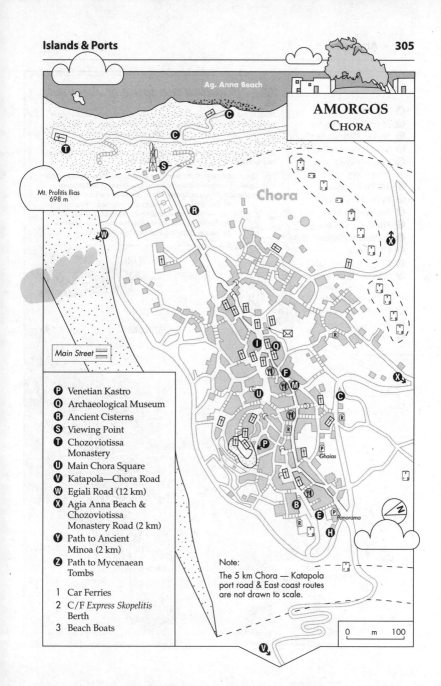

Ag. Anna Beach

AMORGOS
CHORA

Mt. Profitis Ilias
698 m

Chora

Main Street

- **P** Venetian Kastro
- **Q** Archaeological Museum
- **R** Ancient Cisterns
- **S** Viewing Point
- **T** Chozoviotissa Monastery
- **U** Main Chora Square
- **V** Katapola—Chora Road
- **W** Egiali Road (12 km)
- **X** Agia Anna Beach & Chozoviotissa Monastery Road (2 km)
- **Y** Path to Ancient Minoa (2 km)
- **Z** Path to Mycenaean Tombs

1 Car Ferries
2 C/F Express Skopelitis Berth
3 Beach Boats

Ghaias

Panorama

Note:
The 5 km Chora — Katapola
port road & East coast routes
are not drawn to scale.

0 m 100

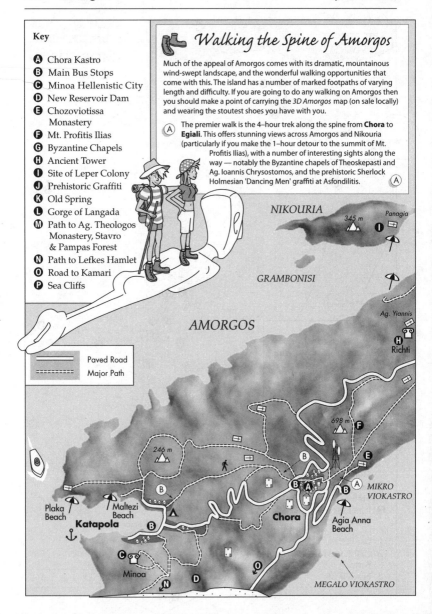

Key

Ⓐ Chora Kastro
Ⓑ Main Bus Stops
Ⓒ Minoa Hellenistic City
Ⓓ New Reservoir Dam
Ⓔ Chozoviotissa
   Monastery
Ⓕ Mt. Profitis Ilias
Ⓖ Byzantine Chapels
Ⓗ Ancient Tower
Ⓘ Site of Leper Colony
Ⓙ Prehistoric Graffiti
Ⓚ Old Spring
Ⓛ Gorge of Langada
Ⓜ Path to Ag. Theologos
   Monastery, Stavro
   & Pampas Forest
Ⓝ Path to Lefkes Hamlet
Ⓞ Road to Kamari
Ⓟ Sea Cliffs

Walking the Spine of Amorgos

Much of the appeal of Amorgos comes with its dramatic, mountainous wind-swept landscape, and the wonderful walking opportunities that come with this. The island has a number of marked footpaths of varying length and difficulty. If you are going to do any walking on Amorgos then you should make a point of carrying the *3D Amorgos* map (on sale locally) and wearing the stoutest shoes you have with you.

Ⓐ The premier walk is the 4–hour trek along the spine from **Chora** to **Egiali**. This offers stunning views across Amorgos and Nikouria (particularly if you make the 1–hour detour to the summit of Mt. Profitis Ilias), with a number of interesting sights along the way — notably the Byzantine chapels of Theoskepasti and Ag. Ioannis Chrysostomos, and the prehistoric Sherlock Holmesian 'Dancing Men' graffiti at Asfondilitis. Ⓐ

NIKOURIA

345 m   *Panagia*

Ⓘ

GRAMBONISI

Ag. Yiannis

AMORGOS

Ⓗ
Richti

—— Paved Road
- - - - Major Path

698 m   Ⓕ

246 m

Ⓑ   Ⓔ

Ⓑ   Ⓑ Ⓐ Ⓐ *MIKRO VIOKASTRO*

Plaka Beach   *Maltezi Beach*   Ⓑ   **Chora**   *Agia Anna Beach*

Katapola

Ⓒ
Minoa

Ⓝ   Ⓓ   Ⓞ

MEGALO VIOKASTRO

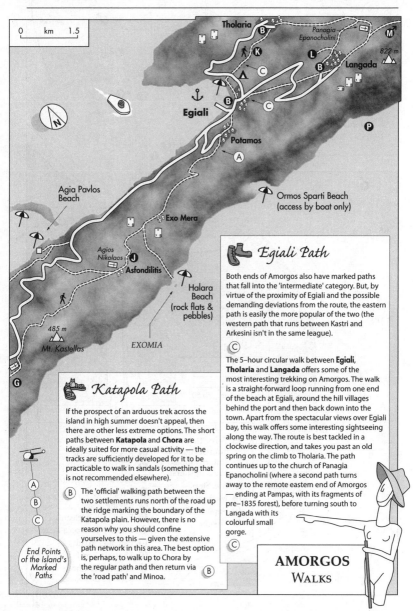

0   km   1.5

Tholaria

Panagia Epanocholini

822 m

Langada

N

Egiali

Potamos

A

Agia Pavlos Beach

Ormos Sparti Beach (access by boat only)

Exo Mera

Agios Nikolaos
Asfondilitis J

Halara Beach (rock flats & pebbles)

485 m
Mt. Kastellas

EXOMIA

🥾 Egiali Path

Both ends of Amorgos also have marked paths that fall into the 'intermediate' category. But, by virtue of the proximity of Egiali and the possible demanding deviations from the route, the eastern path is easily the more popular of the two (the western path that runs between Kastri and Arkesini isn't in the same league).

Ⓒ

The 5–hour circular walk between **Egiali**, **Tholaria** and **Langada** offers some of the most interesting trekking on Amorgos. The walk is a straight-forward loop running from one end of the beach at Egiali, around the hill villages behind the port and then back down into the town. Apart from the spectacular views over Egiali bay, this walk offers some interesting sightseeing along the way. The route is best tackled in a clockwise direction, and takes you past an old spring on the climb to Tholaria. The path continues up to the church of Panagia Epanocholini (where a second path turns away to the remote eastern end of Amorgos — ending at Pampas, with its fragments of pre–1835 forest), before turning south to Langada with its colourful small gorge.

Ⓒ

👢 Katapola Path

If the prospect of an arduous trek across the island in high summer doesn't appeal, then there are other less extreme options. The short paths between **Katapola** and **Chora** are ideally suited for more casual activity — the tracks are sufficiently developed for it to be practicable to walk in sandals (something that is not recommended elsewhere).

Ⓑ The 'official' walking path between the two settlements runs north of the road up the ridge marking the boundary of the Katapola plain. However, there is no reason why you should confine yourselves to this — given the extensive path network in this area. The best option is, perhaps, to walk up to Chora by the regular path and then return via the 'road path' and Minoa. Ⓑ

Ⓐ
Ⓑ
Ⓒ

End Points of the Island's Marked Paths

AMORGOS
WALKS

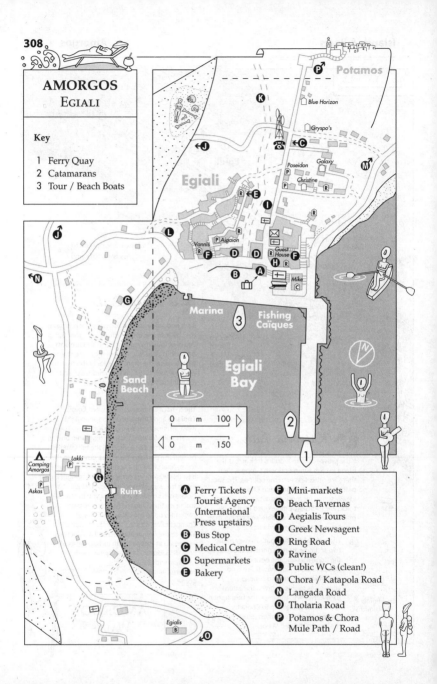

AMORGOS
EGIALI

Key

1 Ferry Quay
2 Catamarans
3 Tour / Beach Boats

Potamos

Blue Horizon

Gryspo's

Galaxy

Egiali

Poseidon

Christine

Vannis

Aigaion

Guest
House

Mike

Marina

Fishing
Caïques

Egiali
Bay

Sand
Beach

0   m   100 ▷

◁ 0   m   150

Camping
Amorgos

Lakki

Askas

Ruins

Egialis
B

A Ferry Tickets /
  Tourist Agency
  (International
  Press upstairs)
B Bus Stop
C Medical Centre
D Supermarkets
E Bakery

F Mini-markets
G Beach Tavernas
H Aegialis Tours
I Greek Newsagent
J Ring Road
K Ravine
L Public WCs (clean!)
M Chora / Katapola Road
N Langada Road
O Tholaria Road
P Potamos & Chora
  Mule Path / Road

The ruined buildings on the outskirts of the town and a skyline crowned with derelict windmills (for some unclear reason each extended family on Amorgos had to have its own mill) add greatly to the unspoilt character of the place. This is enhanced further by delightful small tree-filled squares and melting ice-cream-style churches that in turn generate a cosmopolitan touch via the odd artist sketching in dreamland.

The main street (inaccessible to vehicles) is the centre of activity and winds up the floor of the shallow valley in which the town lies, arriving at the windy top of the southern cliffs of the island. Here there is a viewing point (under one of the town's two satellite dish towers) and the top of the staircase that winds down to both the main tourist attractions on Amorgos: the monastery of Chozoviotissa and the road to the island's most popular beach — at **Agia Anna**—a tiny pebble affair known for nudism (both can also be reached by bus). To the north looms Mt. Profitis Ilias which, even in summer, is usually accompanied by a playful cloud chasing its tail around the upper slopes. This intimidating spectacle sets the tone for the island hinterland that is little frequented by tourists thanks to the paucity of bus services.

Egiali, the island's second port, is significantly smaller than Katapola, and feels much newer, with more of a quiet beach resort atmosphere. In fact the scatter of holiday apartments and hotels that make up much of the settlement running up the hill behind the ferry quay are built on the remains of an ancient city. Sadly, nothing is visible, and all later buildings went west in a massive fire in 1835, which burnt for three weeks, destroying the entire settlement and the cedar and holly-oak forests that, until then, stood behind it.

Modern Egiali is defined by an excellent family sand beach (fringed with shady trees) that runs the width of the bay and the wide, intensively farmed plain behind it. Embracing both port and plain is a ring of hills topped with attractive, unspoilt vil-

lages at **Langada, Tholaria** and **Potamos**. In past years backpackers have predominated at Egiali, but the port is cultivating a more up-market image with the first package-tour operators starting to move in, and an increasing number of beach-bound day trippers from Chora and Katapola using the island bus service (the first and last buses running the length of the island are thus rather crowded in High Season).

☠

Amorgos was a sufficiently important island in antiquity that it could boast three cities (all sited along the northern coast) at Minoa, Egiali and Arkesini (at Kastri). None, however, really made much of an impact on the course of history, and Amorgos was best known by the Roman era as one of the 'gentler' islands of exile. Amorgos was pillaged extensively from the 7 c. on by pirates, with the centres of population moving away from the coast to places such as Chora. During the 9 c. Byzantine control was re-established, and held sway until 1207 when the Venetian Ghizi family took the island, maintaining a perilous hold on power until 1446 when the ruling house on Astipalea — the Quirini family — gained control. Amorgos fell to the Turk Khayr-ad-Din Barbarossa in 1537, becoming an unstable pirate-ridden island thereafter. It broke away from Turkish rule in 1822 and joined the new Greek state shortly after.

⊨

Hotels and rooms fill fast in High Season, though the island doesn't have a reputation for being short of beds: new building is keeping up with demand. **Chora** has a limited number of establishments (often without signs) offering rooms and a couple of pensions, the *Panorama* and the larger *Ghaias* (☎ 71277), but building restrictions aimed at preserving the town have limited the options here. The vast majority of visitors stay at one of the two ports instead.

Katapola has the greater number of beds. The pensions include the *Amorgos* (☎ 71214) and the *Sophia*. In addition, the port has two notable C-class hotels: *St. George/Valsamitis* (☎ 71228), on the far side of the port bay, and the excellent C-class *Minoa* (☎ 71480), which also houses the island's internet café.

Egiali has a wider mix of accommodation that includes the B-class hotel *Egialis* (☎ 73393), with its panoramic views, and C-class *Mike* (☎

73208). The village is overlooked by the good, but pricey *Poseidon Rooms* (☎ 73452).

A

Both ports on Amorgos have sites offering plenty of shade. Because this isn't one of the really popular backpacker islands, sites tend to open late and close early: roughly mid-June to mid-September. At **Katapola** is *Camping Katapola* (☎ 71257): an inexpensive municipal site (so no one meeting boats or touting for customers), it is an easy walk away around the harbour bay. In August it is popular with French school groups and can sometimes feel like a playground during a fire drill. Washing facilities are a bit on the primitive side.

A new private site — *Camping Kastanis* (☎ 71277) — has been built several km inland from Katapola in quite the wrong place. With views of the island's cement works and power plant, and a difficult road into town, it is usually empty and not a good option. The owner meets boats and is happy not to disabuse passengers of the assumption that the site is the camping at Katapola.

Egiali has the best site on Amorgos: *Camping Amorgos* (☎ 73500) is a cheaper and much quieter site. A mini-bus sometimes meets ferries arriving at Katapola.

◐◑

The island sight on Amorgos is the spectacularly impressive cliff-hugging **Chozoviotissa Monastery** sited on the desolate south side of the island. Open ◉ 08.00–13.00, 17.00–19.00, a limited part of it is accessible to visitors, but as is usual with working religious sites, 'formal' clothing must be worn by all. In this case this means no shorts, mini-skirts or bikinis for women; no shorts for men. In the past appropriate clothing was provided to tourists if needed, but the church clothes box is now empty, so come prepared. Even with these restrictions the monastery is worth the effort of dressing up. It justifies adding Amorgos to any itinerary and is not to be missed.

Plastered into the side of a cliff 300 m above sea level, Chozoviotissa is a heavily buttressed, whitewashed building some 40 m in length and eight storeys high. Most of the narrow rooms are only 5 m wide and carved into the cliff face. If you suffer from claustrophobia you might find the labyrinth of small rooms and

narrow staircases less than appealing. There is also an appreciable cliff overhang above the building; bits do occasionally fall off — smashing rooms — so pick your visiting day with care. No photographs are allowed inside and you are not free to roam: this is a working monastery (albeit one with only four monks). Except on special feast days access is limited to rooms immediately above the entrance door and the church above them. There is no entrance charge, though donations are welcome; visitors are offered sweets and a drink.

Nominally founded in 1088 AD, the monastery appears to have earlier origins — if tradition is to be believed — as a refuge for a group of Palestinian monks from the monastery of St. George at Khozova (now Koziba near Jericho) who fled west in the 9 c. AD in a much larger exodus of Christians fleeing a wave of Arab persecution. They arrived on Amorgos by way of Cyprus with yet another miraculous icon — this time of the Blessed Virgin — and opted for the site because of its inaccessibility, living in caves carved in the cliff face. The choice of location has prompted speculation that the Palestinian refugee tradition has a basis in fact as it resembles the desert monastery at Koziba, which likewise had monks' cells and a chapel carved into a cliff face, complete with another dangerous overhang.

Most major religious centres start from humble beginnings, and Chozoviotissa, after several piratical raids, followed this tradition, emerging as a rich and powerful institution during the rule of the Latin Dukes, with a very close relationship with the monastery on Patmos. Somewhat surprisingly the monastery flourished during the centuries of Ottoman rule, enjoying tithes of produce from Amorgos, large estates on other islands, and in the case of most of the Little Cyclades direct ownership of the islands themselves. However, since Greek independence the monastery's fortunes have waned, arriving at its nadir in 1952 when it was dispossessed of its estates.

The structure that exists today is something of a historical puzzle, having clearly been extensively rebuilt on a number of occasions. The interior has doorways reflecting the different periods in the island's history, and remains pretty much as it would have been two hundred years ago — though denuded of its monks it has become a warren of empty storage rooms, monks' cells and kitchens. Plans (that never seem to materialize) include opening up more of the building to visitors: the most notable rooms are a refectory, complete with a roughly hewn long wooden table, and the sacristy, which is home to a very rarely seen display of the monastery's important collection of manuscripts and ecclesiastical treasures.

The dramatic exterior of the building has been less immune to change. For much of the monastery's history its walls would not have been whitewashed in such a conspicuous fashion, and the huge buttresses are a 19 c. addition. The main door is 17 c. and the stone stairs are even later: originally the building was accessed by a drawbridge, and then later by a wooden ladder that could be pulled up when needs be, thus discouraging visits from passing pirates, pilgrims or tourists.

Chora itself is more scenic than sight-filled: it is a place to wander around without arriving anywhere in particular. The nearest to a sight on offer is the finger of rock poking up from the whitewashed buildings: this is home to an unimpressive wall of a tiny 13 c. Venetian **Kastro**. Sadly, the archaeological museum has been closed for several years, and was too small anyway to house the major find from Amorgos — the largest **Cycladic Idol** yet discovered (it is almost life size and was said to have been unearthed at remote **Kapsala**) — is now a centrepiece of the Cycladic culture display in the National Archaeological Museum in Athens.

Minoa, the ancient city overlooking Katapola port, offers another worthy excursion. The site is predominantly on the landward side of the 290 m high hill, and is reached via an old mule path, then unmade road running up from the back of Katapola. The city took its name from a rock hole near the summit which local tradition said was the tomb of King Minos. The remains have only been partially excavated, so there isn't a vast amount to see beyond jumbled foundations. However, don't let this put you off: the site is free and has good explanatory notices at the entrance, detailing the layout (both ascertained and — in the case of the theatre — conjectured). Best of all are the stunning views of Katapola and Chora (to say nothing of the island's new reservoir): if you don't attempt any other walks on Amorgos, it is worthwhile making this short one.

In High Season regular beach boats leave for neighbouring islets, notably the good beach on the ex-leper colony islet of **Nikouria** and the beach islet of **Gramvousa**.

Anafi
ΑΝΑΦΙ; 38 km²; pop. 340.

CODE ☎ 22860
POLICE ☎ 61216
TOURIST OFFICE ☎ 61253
MEDICAL CENTRE ☎ 61215

Only one hour's sailing east of Santorini, the small island of Anafi at first sight seems something of a paradox as it has been one of the least accessible destinations in the Aegean: so much so, that 'Anafi' is the Greek equivalent of 'Timbuktu'. Fortunately this is now changing and Anafi has reasonable ferry links in High Season. Myth has it that the island sprang up out of the sea by order of Apollo when the legendary Argonauts, sailing north from Crete, were overwhelmed by a 'pall of darkness' (thought by some to be a vague folk memory of the c. 1470 BC eruption of Santorini) and found themselves in desperate need of a sanctuary. Their plight must have been pretty desperate as the island isn't furnished with a spring. As a result Anafi has never been a prosperous place.

Those washed up on Anafi's mountainous shores today will find a barren island that — approached from the south — looks like a double-humped mountain top sticking out of the sea, but for all its stark barrenness the 'living on the edge of the world' atmosphere is superb. As a result, Anafi is attracting increasing numbers of visitors drawn to the laid-back isolation and a succession of sandy, crowd-free beaches. This is one island that really is worth a visit, but medical facilities are very limited. Any serious problems require an air ambulance lift to the mainland. This resulted in the death of a patient in 2002 when the air ambulance helicopter crashed at night with a hillside shortly after taking off, killing all on board.

The only settlement on Anafi is a photogenic hilltop chora overlooking a diminutive cliff-backed port. Anafi's **Chora** can lay claim to be one of the last truly unspoilt Cycladic choras, and is a pretty place, with Santorini-style anti-earthquake barrel-

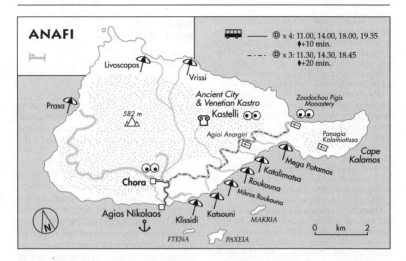

roofed houses and exterior baking ovens. The government has slapped a building restriction order on it to protect it (hence the spate of building 'extensions' now appearing), for as word has spread about the delights of Anafi, so has new construction dedicated to tourism, and this continues unabated around the chora's fringes.

This is a bit sad, for this chora is almost all fringes: although its setting is little short of majestic, it lacks an obvious foĉus; the hilltop at its heart is missing its all-important kastro (long since lost) — though it offers superb views over the town. Instead, the main centres are the bus squares at each end of the main street: the eastern sees more activity, while the western is a quiet picture-postcard affair.

There is no bank, but there are two food-cum-tourist shops, a bakery and several tavernas. EU funding has also produced several new roads: the most useful is the 4 km Chora—port link (the old 1.5 km mule track still exists for energetic traditionalists). On the other hand, the useless road to **Prasa** is a genuine 'road to nowhere'.

Somewhat better is the 9 km road that runs east of Chora some distance behind the south-coast beaches. Though it is so poorly made that there is regular subsidence (moped users will occasionally have to 'mind the gaps'). Access to the beaches requires a good walk down unmarked tracks from the roadside. The best of these long, empty strands are **Roukouna** (where there is some nudity and freelance camping) and at **Mega Potamos**. But in truth all the beaches are well worth the effort involved in getting to them, though if you opt to walk the tortuous coast path good walking shoes are essential.

The port of **Agios Nikolaos** has several tavernas and an agent that sells tickets for most boats (note: others are obtained from a Chora agent whose listed opening times are only wishful ambition: an evening visit is the best bet). A short cliffside-path walk from the port is attractive palm-tree-backed **Klissidi** beach: the most accessible strand on the island (though it still requires negotiating a very steep hill), in summer it is now quite crowded for Anafi — expect to find a good 50 people on it daily in August.

🕱

Anafi was too impoverished to ever be a major centre, and little is known of its early

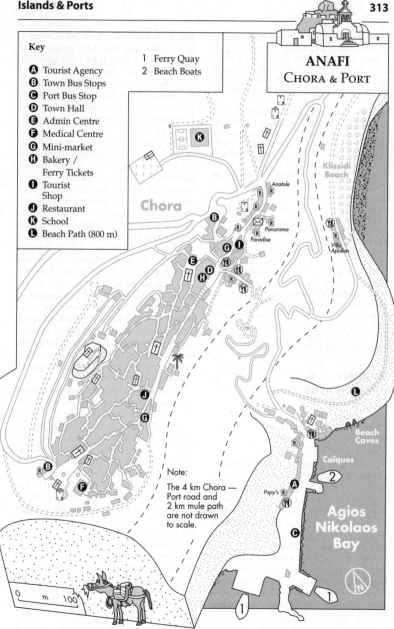

Key

- **A** Tourist Agency
- **B** Town Bus Stops
- **C** Port Bus Stop
- **D** Town Hall
- **E** Admin Centre
- **F** Medical Centre
- **G** Mini-market
- **H** Bakery / Ferry Tickets
- **I** Tourist Shop
- **J** Restaurant
- **K** School
- **L** Beach Path (800 m)

1 Ferry Quay
2 Beach Boats

ANAFI
CHORA & PORT

Chora

Anatole
Panorama
Paradise
Villa Apollon

Klissidi Beach

Beach Caves

Caïques

Agios Nikolaos Bay

Popy's

Note:
The 4 km Chora — Port road and 2 km mule path are not drawn to scale.

0   m   100

history, beyond that deduced from remains at Katalimatsa and Kastro (which suggest a small community has always lived here). Little excavation has been done, and most visible remains of note were removed to St. Petersburg by the Russians between 1770–74.

No hotels, but rooms are on offer at the Chora, port and beach. Mini-buses from the various establishments meet all boats — as does the island bus. Two good bets from the port road end of the **Chora** are *Ta Plagia* (☎ 61308) and *Panorama Rooms* (☎ 61292). If you fancy something more secluded then try *Villa Apollon* (☎ 61237) tucked behind **Klissidi Beach**.

Sightseeing on Anafi is more for the adventurous than on most islands. Masochists into very serious hill walking will find a ruined **Venetian Kastro** at Kastelli: ask the bus driver to set you down at the (barely visible) path from the road and take plenty of water. Those that stay on the bus can visit the now monkless **Zoudochou Pigis Monastery** (complete with the foundations of a **Temple of Apollo** supposedly set up by the Argonauts) behind the 450 m peak that dominates eastern Anafi. The bus route ends 300 m short of the building: don't be put off by the noisy caged guard dogs — their owner enjoys showing people around.

Astipalea
ΑΣΤΥΠΑΛΕΑ; 95 km²; pop. 1,150.

CODE ☎ 22430
PORT POLICE ☎ 61208
TOURIST OFFICE ☎ 61217
POLICE ☎ 61207
FIRST AID ☎ 61222

Administered from Kalimnos, butterfly-shaped Astipalea is technically a member of the Dodecanese group. Yet, in both appearance and frequency of ferry links, the island has far more in common with the neighbouring Eastern Cyclades, with a white-cubist-house chora (complete with windmills and castle) and typical barren, arid hillsides. Even the locals find Astipalea's membership of the Dodecanese somewhat anachronistic (the 'Dodecanese' only came into being in 1908: the term is derived from the '12 islands' under Turkish

rule that protested against the removal of special privileges held from the Sultan since the 16 c.). The story is told that when the new Greek state's borders were agreed in 1830 the map used to draw the boundary was so bad that Astipalea was mistakenly positioned on the Turkish side of the line, losing its status as member of the Cyclades in the process.

Now well on the Greek side of the line, if not back in the Cyclades, Astipalea's relative remoteness, lack of nightlife and reasonable — but not spectacular — beaches have all conspired to keep at bay the masses and tour operators requiring reliable and frequent ferry links. This in part accounts for the popularity of Astipalea with holidaying Greeks who tend to fill hotels and the campsite in August. Island hoppers are fewer in number, though this is now changing; one only has to sail between the folds of Astipalea's wings and see the castle-topped chora for a certain fascination to take hold. The end-of-the-world sense of introspection that pervades is enhanced by the combination of the island's beach-comber scruffiness (there are insufficient tourists to fund municipal cleanups here) and the picturesque litter of islets around the coastline.

Astipalea is a perfect spot to quietly unwind and soak up some Greek island atmosphere in tangibly exotic surroundings. Folks come here to clamber up the hillsides behind the town and drink in the views. Buffeted by the wind (Astipalea is very exposed, so the *meltemi* 'wind tunnel' effect is particularly noticeable here), this is an island which encourages you to feel exhilaratingly alive. Rich, blue-sea-filled vistas drenched in a dreamy bright sunlight worthy of an Alpine ski-slope and all that sort of stuff.

Coming back down to earth, the only settlement of any significance is the main **Chora** and port complex, an odd mix of staircases and new buildings running up to one of Greece's nicer old towns. Finding your way around is not particularly difficult: just

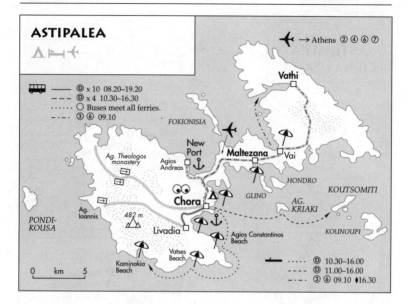

keep climbing and sooner or later you arrive at the castle entrance. It offers a shady (and wind-free) retreat in the form of a passage that burrows quaintly under one of the two surviving whitewashed interior churches to the forecourt, and spectacular views of the coastline and islets to the south.

Most tourist facilities are to be found fringing the **Chora Port** (an area made up of buildings constructed since WW2), in the saddle-top windmill square above, and strung along the stairways and roads between the two. The popular port beach is lined with tavernas, as is the breezy windmill square. Astipalea has a single bank — near the waterfront and complete with an ATM.

Buses run from both the port and chora squares. The prime destinations are **Livadia** to the west, site of the island's best beach and backed by a fertile valley that gave the island renown in Classical times as a source of market garden produce, and to the east **Maltezana** (also known as **Analipsis**).

A former pirate lair and the spot where a French commander, Captain Bissiou, died in 1827 by firing his corvette to avoid capture, Maltezana is the closest Astipalea has to a resort beach, though the nearest thing you'll see to skulls and crossbones these days are paraded by elderly nudists.

The rest of the island lacks decent roads; buses crawl to Astipalea's second port at **Vathi** only twice a week. Blessed with a good beach and set in a deep fjord-like cove, this is a scenic hamlet (in a very impoverished sort of way) with a cave. Paths lead to several hilltop monasteries and to a number of narrow tree-filled valleys.

☠

Surprisingly, given its rather remote location, Astipalea was an island of some note in antiquity. It never acquired the status of the major islands such as Kos or Rhodes, but it was a noted centre for agriculture and fishing. Its most famous son was a boxer by the name of Kleomedes. Disqualified for killing his opponent (one Ikkos of Epidavros) at the 71st

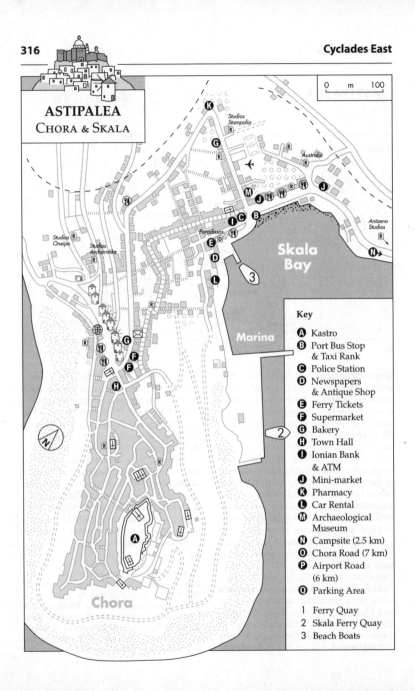

ASTIPALEA
CHORA & SKALA

Studios Stampalia

Australia

Studios
Oneipo

Studios
Archarntika

Paradissos

Antzena
Studios

**Skala
Bay**

Marina

3

2

Chora

N

Key

Ⓐ Kastro
Ⓑ Port Bus Stop
& Taxi Rank
Ⓒ Police Station
Ⓓ Newspapers
& Antique Shop
Ⓔ Ferry Tickets
Ⓕ Supermarket
Ⓖ Bakery
Ⓗ Town Hall
Ⓘ Ionian Bank
& ATM
Ⓙ Mini-market
Ⓚ Pharmacy
Ⓛ Car Rental
Ⓜ Archaeological
Museum
Ⓝ Campsite (2.5 km)
Ⓞ Chora Road (7 km)
Ⓟ Airport Road
(6 km)
Ⓠ Parking Area

1 Ferry Quay
2 Skala Ferry Quay
3 Beach Boats

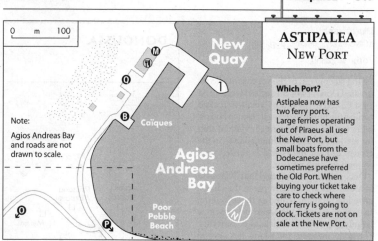

ASTIPALEA
NEW PORT

Which Port?

Astipalea now has two ferry ports. Large ferries operating out of Piraeus all use the New Port, but small boats from the Dodecanese have sometimes preferred the Old Port. When buying your ticket take care to check where your ferry is going to dock. Tickets are not on sale at the New Port.

Olympic games, he returned in disgrace and did a Samson, pulling down the pillars of the island school and killing all the children along with himself (his late opponent obviously got in at least one good head blow).

Astipalea briefly came to prominence as a base for a Roman fleet engaged in anti-piracy operations, before falling into obscurity during the Byzantine period. Its isolation served it well between 1207 and 1522 when it was ruled by the Venetian Quirini family. Thereafter it was under Turkish rule until 1919, and then Italian until joining the Greek state in 1947.

⊨

Room supply is good, with owners meeting the boats, and three inexpensive, but reasonable, hotels in the lower part of the town. The best of these — notably the clean but spartan *Paradissos* (☎ 61224) and the *Astynea* (☎ 61209) — are on the waterfront. Rooms are also available on the north side of the port bay: these include the *Antzena Studios* (☎ 61343) and have great night views of the floodlit Kastro. There are also beds available in Livadia and Maltezana.

A

Camping Astipalea (☎ 61900): a pleasant and shaded (if isolated) pebble-beach site 2.5 km east of the port. Very popular with Greeks who book it solid in August. Mini-bus meets ferries.

👓👓

Astipalea's great attraction is its imposing **Kastro**. Built on the site of the ancient acropolis,

it is a 9 c. Byzantine fortification, later rebuilt after a fashion by the Venetians. Never a traditional castle, it thereafter evolved into a medieval apartment-block of sorts during the centuries of piracy that followed.

In its prime it was home to some 4,000 people, its walls containing a labyrinth of staircases and four-storey buildings (if accounts of it are anything to go by then the island has lost an amazing tourist attraction). This was extant until the 1920s, when the development of the port shifted the axis of settlement away from the chora, prompting partial demolition. An earthquake in 1956 destroyed most of the remaining buildings, leaving the Kastro a desolate shell, with only the churches and the fragmentary remains of the houses that nestled against the window-choked walls (now a storey lower than in times past) surviving.

The only pre-medieval remains of note are at Maltezana where there are the poorly kept remains of a **Zodiac Mosaic** from a 5 c. AD **Bathhouse**.

Little of pre-medieval Astipalea survives. Odd fragments of buildings are to be found in the Kastro walls and the island has yielded up a number of important inscriptions. The most unusual remains are found at Maltezana (or to be more accurate — on the fringes of a reed bed, a couple of fields past the small Analipsis quay), where well-preserved **Zodiac Mosaics** from the 5 c. AD **Talaras Bathhouse** are on view.

Donoussa
ΔΟΝΟΥΣΣΑ; 13 km²; pop. 100.

CODE ☎ 22850

Rising steeply out of the sea east of Naxos, isolated Donoussa is the second largest and least visited of the Little Cyclades. Tucked behind the untouristed east coast of Naxos, it lies too far north to be a convenient stop for ferries serving the other islands in the group, though the island is served well enough in High Season.

Once ashore, you will find that Donoussa is a downbeat, friendly place that has a growing reputation among those looking to 'enjoy' a tranquil week or two in a largely unspoilt Greek island community. For good measure the island has several good sandy beaches on the south coast and three hamlets on the girdling coastal road. The largest settlement lies in a bay on the south-east coast at **Agios Stavros**. Although it is a very small centre, it is home to most

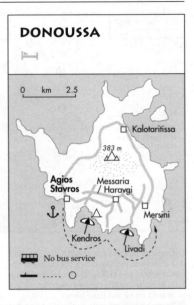

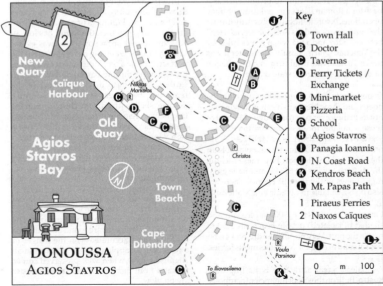

Key

- **Ⓐ** Town Hall
- **Ⓑ** Doctor
- **Ⓒ** Tavernas
- **Ⓓ** Ferry Tickets / Exchange
- **Ⓔ** Mini-market
- **Ⓕ** Pizzeria
- **Ⓖ** School
- **Ⓗ** Agios Stavros
- **Ⓘ** Panagia Ioannis
- **Ⓙ** N. Coast Road
- **Ⓚ** Kendros Beach
- **Ⓛ** Mt. Papas Path

- **1** Piraeus Ferries
- **2** Naxos Caïques

of the available tourist accommodation. However, outside the half-dozen tavernas, little English is spoken, and there is only one general store. A souvenir shop/ticket agency on the waterfront also offers exchange facilities with rates so bad that it is more advantageous to head back to Naxos for a couple of days and visit a bank there instead.

The rest of Donoussa offers rewarding walks and several excellent empty beaches at **Kendros** and **Livadi**. Both tend to suffer at the height of the summer from the miscellany of campers living free-style (this can include nudity) behind the sand — sans toilets! The island's hamlets are studies in unspoilt rural communities, **Mersini** being the most prosperous, thanks to the existence of a spring which is the island's main water supply. Isolated **Kalotaritissa** has appeal as a walking destination. In past years the coastal walk was about the only notable activity Donoussa had to offer. Unfortunately, the coast road is now partly metalled (enabling the island's two vehicles to have grand prix races), so the 16 km circumambulation isn't quite as appealing as it once was.

⊨

All the accommodation is at **Agios Stavros**. Rooms are not over-abundant (take up offers made when ferries arrive). The pension *Christos* (☎ 51555) is complemented by several establishments offering rooms. These include the waterfront *Nikitas Markolas* (☎ 51566) and the *Voula Parsinou* (☎ 61455).

Iraklia
ΗΡΑΚΛΕΙΑ; 17.5 km²; pop. 110.

CODE ☎ 22850

A hilltop sticking out of the sea that tapers away into low hills to the north, Iraklia (usually pronounced 'Heraklia', and not to be confused with Heraklion / Iraklion, the capital of Crete) is marginally the most accessible of the Little Cyclades, thanks to occasional tour-boat trips from Naxos Town. Like Donoussa, the island has a growing reputation for 'get-away-from-it-

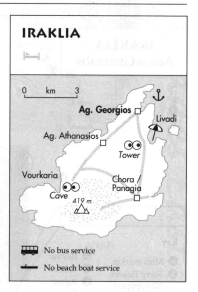

all' fans but, unlike the other Little Cyclades, it hasn't yet resorted to building extra facilities to meet growing High Season demand.

All ferries call at the north-coast port of **Agios Georgios**. Set in a deep inlet, it is a rather ramshackle affair, with two main streets of sorts, bisected by a small ravine that winds up the most fertile valley on the island. The village has all the usual lack of amenities with a scattering of tavernas and a single food shop (that sells bread and milk imported from Naxos and ferry tickets). Additional pluses are a sandy harbour beach backed by shady trees, and friendly locals who treat those staying more than a day or two as honorary villagers (though most rooms are carefully sited on the outskirts of town). This is not without advantages as most visitors find themselves nicely placed to walk to Iraklia's best sand beach at **Livadi**. This is a wide strand with views across the narrow strait to Schinoussa (10 minutes' sailing time away).

The rest of the island offers an ideal retreat for leisurely walks, though past visitors

SCHINOUSSA
Windmill & Sign

RESTAURANT

KOUFONISSIA

IRAKLIA
Quay & Village

Lifeboat
from the
original

South-East Coast Beaches

C/F Skopelitis

Cyclades East

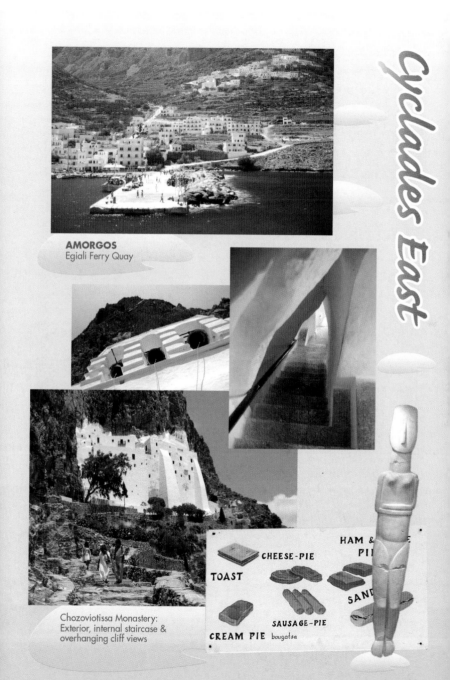

AMORGOS
Egiali Ferry Quay

Chozoviotissa Monastery:
Exterior, internal staircase &
overhanging cliff views

TOAST

CHEESE-PIE

HAM & ...
PI...

SAND...

SAUSAGE-PIE

CREAM PIE *bougatsa*

AMORGOS
Chora

Chora Bus Station
Square

Waterfront at
Katapola

Amorgos:
Conch-blowing
fishermen sell
their catch in
the streets of
Chora

ASTIPALEA
Chora Windmills
& Kastro

Cyclades East

KEROS

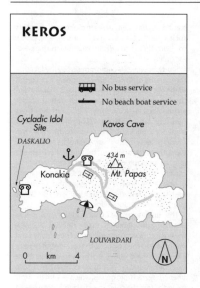

🚌 No bus service

⛵ No beach boat service

Cycladic Idol Site

DASKALIO

Kavos Cave

434 m

Konakia   ⛰ Mt. Papas

LOUVARDARI

0   km   4   Ⓝ

Keros

ΚΕΡΟΣ; 17.5 km²; pop. 0.

A large hilltop poking out of the water, Keros is easily the largest of the Little Cyclades. However, apart from the obligatory mad monk, the island is uninhabited, and used for grazing. This is a strange reversal from its historical role as the dominant member of this small group. Quite how important Keros once was is only now beginning to be appreciated. Ongoing archaeological excavations (in the Daskalio islet area) are showing that the island was a sort of spiritual 'Delos' of the Early Cycladic culture (c. 3000–2000 BC). Keros is the source for over half of the Cycladic idols discovered, including the famous harpist and flautist (both are now in the National Archaeological Museum in Athens). Access is becoming increasingly problematic as its archaeological importance grows, but it is possible to charter a caïque to take you across from Koufonissia (expect to pay at least €70 for a day round-trip).

Cycladic Idols

During the Early Bronze Age the central Aegean islands saw the flourishing of a unique local mini-civilization known as the 'Cycladic Culture' (see p. 65). Today it is known largely through the unique white marble idols that have been unearthed in their settlements and graves. Sparkling replicas now adorn every tourist souvenir shop in the Cyclades, though no one can be sure what they are actually replicas of.

The Cycladic idols were made over a 1,400-year period between 3200 and 1800 BC, and have been the cause of much head-scratching ever since the first examples were brought back to Western Europe by early 19 c. travellers as curios. Initially dismissed as primitive oddities, they were slowly elevated into objects of serious scholastic merit as a greater understanding of prehistoric Greece developed. The big surge of interest came in the 1950s and 60s when their 'modernist' look tallied closely with prevailing artistic fashion; this resulted in both massive looting of Cycladic sites as art collectors scrambled to acquire examples, and a fair bit of counterfeiting. The best displays of idols are to be found in the Museum of Cycladic Art in Athens (see p. 115), and the Archaeological Museum on Naxos.

The majority of idols are 15–40 cm tall (or, more accurately, long, because with their feet pointing down they were incapable of standing unsupported). Larger examples do exist, but are rare; the tallest — said to have been found on Amorgos — is 1.48 m, and is in the National Archaeological Museum in Athens, along with a number of the more unusual pieces. All but a handful of the idols are carved out of white marble. A few have evidence of having had painted eyes, and it is now believed that hair and clothing would have been painted on as well (the minimalist 'modern' appearance of the idols is therefore just an accidental conceit).

Most of the figures are female, though rare male examples have been found. Other very rare variants include seated harpists, flute players, and double figures with one standing on the other's shoulders. Just over 1,400 examples of the full-length figures have come to light so far, and careful comparison has enabled several artists to be identified (museum exhibits thus

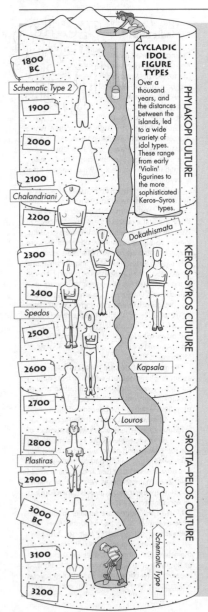

CYCLADIC IDOL FIGURE TYPES

Over a thousand years, and the distances between the islands, led to a wide variety of idol types. These range from early 'Violin' figurines to the more sophisticated Keros–Syros types.

(timeline labels, top to bottom): 1800 BC · Schematic Type 2 · 1900 · 2000 · 2100 · Chalandriani · 2200 · 2300 · 2400 · Spedos · 2500 · 2600 · 2700 · 2800 · Plastiras · 2900 · 3000 BC · 3100 · 3200

(vertical culture labels): PHYLAKOPI CULTURE · KEROS–SYROS CULTURE · GROTTA–PELOS CULTURE

(river labels): Dokathismata · Kapsala · Louros · Schematic Type 1

sometimes have tentative attributions to sculptors such as the 'Goulandris Master' or 'Steiner Master'), so clearly there was a distinct manufacturing process going on.

Study, however, is compromised by the fact that the majority of idols have just 'appeared' as a result of the looting rush in the 1960s. Less than 40% of the figures have been recovered during proper archaeological excavations. The bulk of the others have a tentative provenance, but often there is no evidence to back it up. This, coupled with the known faking of idols, has led some scholars to question the authenticity of some of the figures. For example, it is an uncomfortable fact that archaeological excavation has so far failed to find even a fragment of one of the larger idol examples (though, when seen face-to-face, their potency gives the lie to any suggestion of counterfeiting).

The function of the Cycladic idols remains very unclear. Speculation is made difficult because there are so many contradictions. They clearly were important to their owners: the fact that they were carefully carved out of marble shows that. Most examples found on islands other than Keros have been recovered from graves, which — with the arms folded across the chest in a stylized funerary pose — implies some sort of death rite, but undisturbed graves have been found without idols in them. The females are often visibly pregnant, but other elements common in fertility rites are not visible (breasts, for example, are often very understated). Interpretations have ranged widely — from the possibility that they are servants or concubines for the dead in the afterlife, to personal protective fetishes, with even children's toys being mooted as an unlikely option. The current favourite is that they are household cult figures that were buried with the head of the household or destroyed (like a papal ring) on his or her death.

The best clue to the likely purpose of the idols seems to lie with the discovery of several hoards of deliberately broken figures on Keros (one of these is on display at the Museum of Cycladic Art). The latest find was in 2005 at a site of an Early Cycladic settlement on the west coast that extends under the sea to the islet of Daskalio: the excavation is still ongoing, so sightseeing is not encouraged. The common feature to all these buried hoards is that they consist of random fragments of figures that appear to have been deliberately smashed elsewhere. It therefore looks as though an important part of idol ritual involved the bringing of broken figures to Keros for some kind of communal burial ceremony at a sacred site.

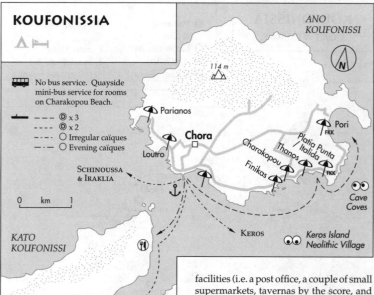

KOUFONISSIA

No bus service. Quayside mini-bus service for rooms on Charakopou Beach.

--- Ⓓ x 3
--- Ⓓ x 2
-·- ○ Irregular caïques
-·- ○ Evening caïques

0   km   1

ANO KOUFONISSI

114 m

Parianos

Pori FKK

Chora

Platia Punta / Italida

Charakopou

Thanos

Loutro

Finikas

FKK

SCHINOUSSA & IRAKLIA

Cave Coves

KATO KOUFONISSI

KEROS

Keros Island Neolithic Village

Nero Beach

Koufonissia

ΚΟΥΦΟΝΗΣΙ; 3.8 km²; pop. 280.

CODE ☎ 22850

This being Greece, it is not surprising that the smallest inhabited island in the Little Cyclades is the most heavily populated, and indeed, touristed. Koufonissia is now a very trendy place to visit, for although it can offer only the usual mix of beaches and mule tracks, the former are of a high quality and the generally cosy beach island atmosphere gives it an edge over its companions.

If you have time to visit only one of the Little Cyclades, or are a little wary of venturing too far from the tourist trail, then Koufonissia is probably the island to go for. Truth to tell, part of its attraction is that it does have at least a modicum of

facilities (i.e. a post office, a couple of small supermarkets, tavernas by the score, and an ever-growing number of new establishments offering good quality rooms), and ferry connections are as good as any in the group. In addition the island is also accessible via regular High Season day trips from Naxos. Tourist boats run excursions once a week (usually Wednesdays) that briefly visit Iraklia before giving you four or more hours on Koufonissia. A word of warning though; at the respective ends of the summer season these boats can suffer from 'mechanical failures' if the number of bookings isn't sufficient to cover costs.

'Koufonissia' is, in fact, a collective name for two low-lying islands: Ano (upper) Koufonissi and Kato (lower) Koufonissi — though these days the name is generally taken to mean the former. **Ano Koufonissi** is the main island (its companion being little more than a reef rising a few metres above sea level and used for grazing goats), and is home to the only settlement and the ferry quay. Hemmed in by Kato Koufonissi and Glaronissi, with much larger Naxos

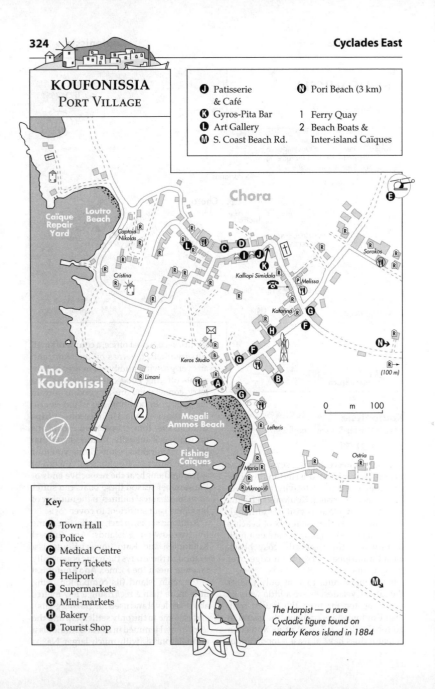

KOUFONISSIA
PORT VILLAGE

J Patisserie & Café
K Gyros-Pita Bar
L Art Gallery
M S. Coast Beach Rd.

N Pori Beach (3 km)
1 Ferry Quay
2 Beach Boats & Inter-island Caïques

Chora

Caïque Repair Yard

Loutro Beach

Captain Nikolas

Cristina

Ano Koufonissi

Limani

Keros Studio

Kalliopi Simidala

Melissa

Katarina

Sorokos

E

N→

(100 m)

0   m   100

Megali Ammos Beach

Fishing Caïques

Lefteris

Ostria

Maria

Akrogiali

M

Key

A Town Hall
B Police
C Medical Centre
D Ferry Tickets
E Heliport
F Supermarkets
G Mini-markets
H Bakery
I Tourist Shop

The Harpist — a rare Cycladic figure found on nearby Keros island in 1884

dominating the northern horizon and the much taller island of Keros close by to the south, Koufonissia has a wonderful little-kid-in-the-playground feel about it.

The island is easily identified thanks to the white-roofed windmill to the left of the quay as you view it from the ferry. In addition, it is low and flat, tapering gently down to the sea on the south side. Moreover, you will invariably find a picturesque flotilla of fishing caïques moored in the sandy bay to the east of the ferry quay.

Standing on the gentle hill behind the quay is the **Port Village**. This has all the essential facilities (with the singular exception of a bank) and is pretty enough in a ragged sort of way, but in truth it is a rather tame affair compared to most island choras, being very spread out and lacking an obvious centre. The old-style main street is too narrow to admit vehicles, which is its only great plus: the dressing-up opportunities here haven't been exploited. Most of the newer buildings in the village are holiday homes or tavernas which also connive to give the island much more of a closed-down feeling out of the summer months than you will find elsewhere.

However, no one comes to Koufonissia for much other than the beaches. Most of these are gentle crescents of golden sand gracing a series of wide coves running south from Parianos on the west coast to Pori on the east. All are accessed via dirt tracks. The beaches get progressively better the further east you go: Charakopou and Thanos are the busiest, thanks to the growing number of holiday apartments built behind them. The very limited tree-cover on Koufonissia is also at its poor best here.

Nudism is supposedly banned on the island, but the islanders seem very laid-back about this, and **Platia Punta** and **Pori** are de facto nudist affairs thanks to their comparative isolation. Both are reached by a dirt path that meanders along the edge of the low-cliffed coastline. This has been badly eroded by the sea, producing a succession of coves each with a tiny

cave under the cliff path. In August each is usually home to a latter-day troglodyte couple, whose presence can be deduced by the scent of evaporating suntan oil wafting up to the cliff path.

Increasingly popular with windsurfers, Pori is the best beach on Koufonissia and worth the effort to get there, but be warned: the coastal path walk is much longer than it looks because of the indented coastline. There is an inland mule path to Pori, but this is less picturesque thanks to the lack of turquoise seas, caves, coves and nudists.

Fortunately, beach boats run from the port to Pori and also to neighbouring **Kato Koufonissi**, where there is a quiet sand beach at Nero. The island's other great attraction is a taverna with such a high reputation that it struggles to keep up with the demand in High Season.

🛏

The port village is increasingly devoted to providing rooms for summer visitors. If you are phoning ahead there is plenty of choice. Harbour views are offered by the *Maria* (☎ 71436), the *Akrogiali* (☎ 71685) and the *Keros Studio* (☎ 71600). In the centre of town are the pension *Melissa* (☎ 71454), the *Katarina* (☎ 71455) and the *Kalliopi Simidala* (☎ 71462). Those looking for something more tucked away should try either the *Sorokos* (☎ 71453) or the *Ostria* (☎ 71671). In addition to rooms in the port village, a number of rooms are also available behind Charakopou beach: a taverna there also once offered semi-official camping, but both are now firmly closed.

👓

Koufonissia is all about beaches rather than sightseeing. The island isn't ideally placed for day tripping either. This said, caïques regularly make trips to neighbouring islands (including Volaka on Naxos) during the peak of the summer season. Very occasional boats go to the Neolithic village site on neighbouring **Keros**. However, most visitors charter a caïque to get across. If you do then take care you don't end up instead at the remains of a medieval village on the north coast. Avoid taking anything that might suggest you are going to 'idol' your day away digging: this is one beach destination where you should leave bucket and spade at home.

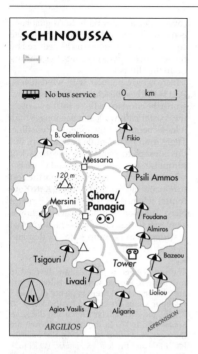

SCHINOUSSA

No bus service 0 km 1

B. Gerolimionas

Fikio

Messaria

120 m

Psili Ammos

Mersini

Chora/ Panagia

Foudana

Almiros

Tsigouri

Tower

Bazeou

Livadi

Lioliou

Agios Vasilis

Aligaria

ARGILIOS

ASPRONISION

Schinoussa

ΣΧΙΝΟΥΣΣΑ; 8.5 km²; pop. 100.

CODE ☎ 22850

Dreamy and diminutive Schinoussa (pronounced '*Skin*oussa') found itself making headlines in the world's press in 2006 after it was exposed as the secret base of a major antiquity smuggling operation. This came as something of a surprise to everyone — islanders included. Still, once the battalions of police and the ferry stuffed with crates of sculpture had departed, things soon returned to normal: Schinoussa is back to being one of those small islands where nothing much ever happens.

From the deck of a ferry Schinoussa presents a rather barren and uninviting aspect that on landing reveals a much more attractive quaint mix of hills, the odd

olive grove and scattered areas of pasture, complete with mangy cattle.

Unfortunately, the island needs hordes of guidebook readers dropping in every year like a hole in its ferry quay; its charm comes from nothing more than being so delightfully unspoilt. How long it will remain this way is another matter. To date it has been well served by its poor harbour, which for many years discouraged visitors by forcing ferries to dump passengers into taxi boats, and, even now a proper quay has been built, it still discourages casual island hoppers by looking so intimidatingly quiet (the inlet has only three buildings to its name).

The only settlement of any size is known variously as '**Chora**' or '**Panagia**'. Skilfully sited on a low ridge between the island's low hills, it commands good views without being too obvious itself — a hangover from the pirate days which saw Schinoussa depopulated several times (the current inhabitants are descendants of Amorgos stock who repopulated the island in the early 1800s). For the most part, Chora is a less than photogenic single-street affair, but despite having few older buildings, it has a very appealing atmosphere — largely thanks to the few concessions to tourism.

The main street is home to the usual litter of tavernas and occasional small shops, and finally peters out into a couple of tracks that wander down to the popular beach at Livadi and to the east coast beaches. In fact, Schinoussa is well endowed with beaches: there are a dozen in all. However, although adequate, they are made of grey, coarse sand and are not on a par with the golden strands to be found on neighbouring islands — a fact that partly explains Schinoussa's relative unpopularity.

The rest of the island can best be described as looking like a group of interconnected rock dunes. Schinoussa is made up of some nine hillocks (the northern two topped with derelict windmills, with another on the hill between Tsigouri beach and the chora). With the notable exception of the port—Chora road, all the roads on the island

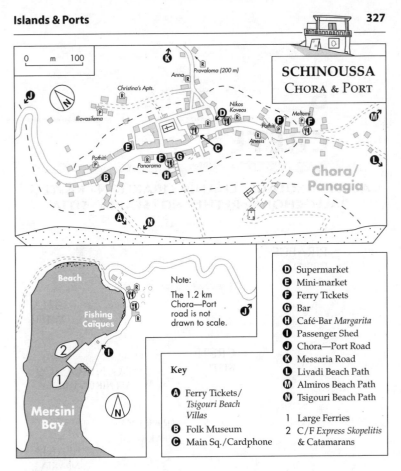

SCHINOUSSA
CHORA & PORT

Chora/
Panagia

Beach

Note:
The 1.2 km
Chora—Port
road is not
drawn to scale.

Fishing
Caïques

Mersini
Bay

D Supermarket
E Mini-market
F Ferry Tickets
G Bar
H Café-Bar *Margarita*
I Passenger Shed
J Chora—Port Road
K Messaria Road
L Livadi Beach Path
M Almiros Beach Path
N Tsigouri Beach Path

Key

A Ferry Tickets/
*Tsigouri Beach
Villas*
B Folk Museum
C Main Sq./Cardphone

1 Large Ferries
2 C/F *Express Skopelitis*
& Catamarans

---

are dirt-track affairs and the preserve of the island's mule population, which seems to outnumber the human inhabitants.

The only other settlement is the hamlet of **Messaria**, north of Chora, which is home to some 20 people. Ironically, given the comparative lack of inhabitants and visitors, Schinoussa has the best water supply of any island in the Little Cyclades, thanks to the existence of three springs. In the absence of tourists, they water the wild chewing-gum bushes (mastica) that cover the hillsides instead.

⊨

Given its size, Chora has a surprising number of rooms on offer. As with Iraklia, expect to pay €3 above other island rates. Accommodation in Chora starts with the *Pension Pothiti* (☎ 71184) and *Panorama Rooms*. At the other end of town are the *Meltemi* and the *Anesis* (☎ 71180). Other options lie on the Messaria road with the *Anna* (☎ 71161) and the solitary *Provaloma* (☎ 71185). If you want both ferry tickets and a nearby beach then *Tsigouri Beach Villas* (☎ 71930) is for you. From time to time there is also some freelance camping behind Livadi beach.

6

CRETE

**AGIOS NIKOLAOS · CHANIA · IRAKLION · KASTELI
PALEOCHORA · RETHIMNO · SFAKIA · SITIA**

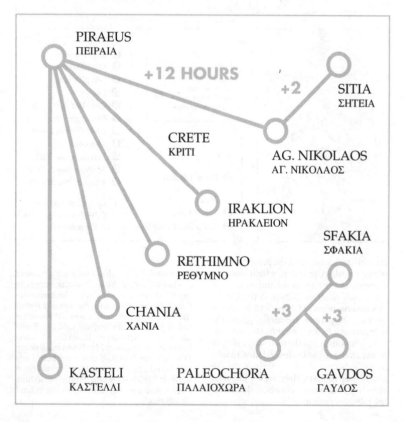

PIRAEUS
ΠΕΙΡΑΙΑ

+12 HOURS

+2

SITIA
ΣΗΤΕΙΑ

CRETE
ΚΡΙΤΙ

AG. NIKOLAOS
ΑΓ. ΝΙΚΟΛΑΟΣ

IRAKLION
ΗΡΑΚΛΕΙΟΝ

SFAKIA
ΣΦΑΚΙΑ

RETHIMNO
ΡΕΘΥΜΝΟ

CHANIA
ΧΑΝΙΑ

+3

+3

KASTELI
ΚΑΣΤΕΛΛΙ

PALEOCHORA
ΠΑΛΑΙΟΧΩΡΑ

GAVDOS
ΓΑΥΔΟΣ

General Features

Crete is such a large island that it justifies a separate volume in several popular guide series. A goodly number of island hoppers also sample the island in passing: for the most part restricting their visits to the string of port cities along the northern coast. These are worthy destinations in their own right and play such an important role in Cretan life that it is almost better to think of Crete as half a dozen 'city-states' sharing the same island. The modern capital of Iraklion (Venetian 'Candia') is the most visited thanks to its good ferry and air links, though it doesn't have half the atmosphere of the former capital of Chania or nearby Rethimno.

The remaining cities of Agios Nikolaos, Sitia and Kasteli have less going for them, but they do have important ferry links for wide-ranging island hoppers. In addition to the north-coast ports, the south-west coast has a miniature ferry system of its own that invites exploration — as does the odd collection of associated islets scattered around the Cretan coast.

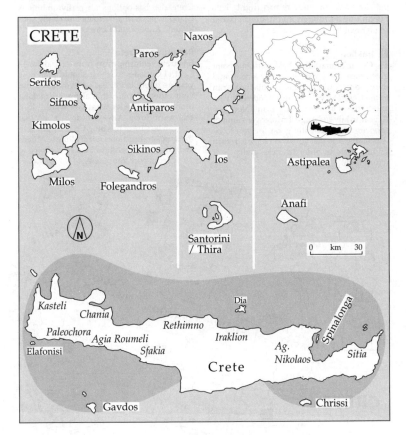

Crete-based Itineraries

Many regular island hoppers choose to avoid annual visits to Athens by flying to and from Crete. This is an attractive option (by any standards Crete is a much more appealing destination), but you do have to be careful given the limited nature of the ferry links between Crete and the islands. Not only is there the very real possibility that you will have to wait a day or two before being able to jump across, but you also have the problem of getting back for your return flight. This needn't be a problem if you are prepared to be flexible.

1 Iraklion

The Cretan capital is the obvious starting point given the close proximity of the airport and the good ferry connections. Regular boats run to the Central Cyclades and Rhodes all year and to the Northern Cyclades and Northern Aegean in July and August. Moreover, summer services are sufficiently good for you to be reasonably sure that you won't have to return unduly early in order to make your return flight.

2 Sitia & Agios Nikolaos

The east Crete town of Sitia and, to a lesser extent, Agios Nikolaos (which now has only occasional ferry services) are also worth considering as starting points, the former having annual links with the Cyclades West island of Milos and the south Dodecanese islands to Rhodes. However, services are not frequent, and change with the seasons, so it is advisable to get hold of a current timetable before heading for either destination.

3 Kasteli

The small port of Kasteli on the west side of Crete also has options for really ambitious island hoppers, thanks to its links with Antikithera, Kithera and Piraeus.

Returning to Crete

If you are venturing away from the Iraklion—Central Cyclades axis you should plan how you are going to get back as you work out your outward route. It is also worth taking time out to consider what you would do if that went down. Always bear in mind that you can be sure of reaching Crete by going in the opposite direction: i.e. travelling to Athens and taking an overnight boat to a choice of Cretan port from there.

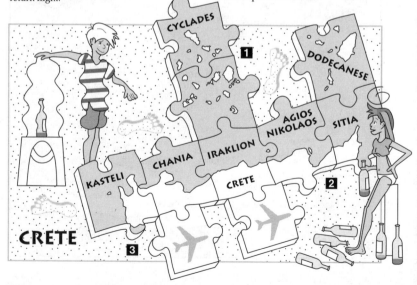

Cretan Ferries

Main Car Ferries
Crete is the sole destination for a number of dedicated boats, as well as being used as a springboard by long-haul ferries heading elsewhere. The former are reliable and can be timed to the minute. However, indirect ferries can be several hours late; Crete is often at the end of scheduled routes, and thus delays tend to be longer than elsewhere in the system. Such ferries either steam down from the Central Cyclades or ricochet off Crete en route to Rhodes.

C/F *Festos Palace* – C/F *Knossos Palace*
Minoan Lines
Festos Palace; 2000; 30000 GRT.
Knossos Palace; 2000; 30000 GRT.
These two ferries have dominated all direct services between Crete and the mainland for the best part of a decade. Minoan's high-speed ferries *Festos Palace* and *Knossos Palace* cut the travel time from 11 to 6 hours on their arrival in the Aegean and the competition have only just managed to catch up. Facilities on board are first rate: these are arguably the best domestic boats in Greece. Understandably they are very popular, and it pays to book several days ahead in High Season — otherwise you could well be disappointed. Evening departures each way throughout the year (note: departure time can shift slightly) are augmented by occasional extra midday sailings at peak periods.

C/F *Superfast XII*
Superfast Ferries; 2002; 23000 GRT.
C/F *Olympic Champion*
ANEK Lines; 2000; 32694 GRT.
Serious competition for Minoan only really got going in 2011 with the Superfast/ANEK combination provided by these two boats. They have manged to make an impact by offering similar travelling times and very slightly lower fares. There is little to choose when it comes to the facilities offered by these competing craft, though this pair are not particularly well matched. The *Superfast XII* is significantly smaller than her Minoan rivals, while the *Olympic Champion* is a tad larger. If you are looking for a reason to choose one pair over the other then one does exist thanks to some seriously daft thinking on the part of someone at Superfast/ANEK. Travel on these two boats and you are expected to put your luggage in a specially modified container lorry during the trip. This means you have to queue for up to an hour when you arrive at your destination retrieving your bags. Minoan still let you carry your bags on and off and keep them during the voyage. There is a work-around for this one: don't board until 20 minutes before departure as by this

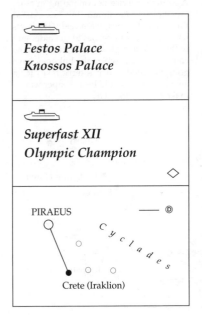

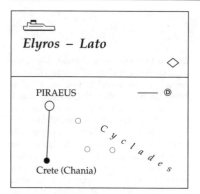

Elyros – Lato

PIRAEUS

Crete (Chania)

Cyclades

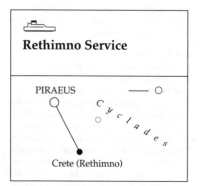

Rethimno Service

PIRAEUS

Crete (Rethimno)

Cyclades

time the luggage lorry has been loaded on board and you can hang onto your bags in the usual way.

C/F *Elyros* – C/F *Lato*
ANEK Lines
Elyros; 1998; 12325 GRT.
Lato; 1975; 15504 GRT.

For many years ANEK have found a profitable niche offering a daily service to the north-western town of Chania (via its port at Souda). The boats on the route are both okay — though no match for the fast ferries elsewhere. They compete by offering slightly cheaper tickets. The *Elyros*, a former Japanese ferry rebuilt to look like an ultra-modern fast boat, is the better of the two, the *Lato* now nearing retirement age. Previous years have seen a high-speed boat running against them, but they had the route to themselves in 2011.

C/F Rethimno Service

A summer service not operating in 2011, the Piraeus—Rethimno link has existed for eight out of the last ten years. The boats have varied, from ferries at the older end of the scale to high-speed craft. Given the competition elsewhere the link may have gone for good, but if a ferry takes it on again in 2012 it could be a cheaper way to make the hop to Crete.

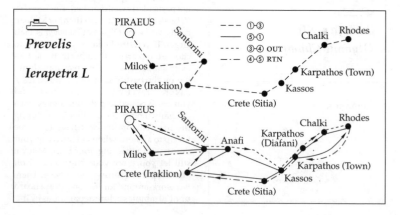

Prevelis

Ierapetra L

C/F *Prevelis*
ANEK Lines; 1980; 5653 GRT.

In past years Crete has seen several lines attempting to make a go of a link from Piraeus to Agios Nikolaos and Sitia via Milos. Unfortunately, neither Cretan port offers lucrative pickings, and Agios Nikolaos is no longer a regular port of call. The current company on the route is ANEK Lines. The *Prevelis* is one of the better smaller Greek domestic ferries. She moved onto this route in 2009 and began an unwelcome trend to exclude the Cretan ports from this itinerary during the summer: the rest of the year she does regularly call.

C/F *Ierapetra L*
LANE Lines; 1975 (rebuilt 1995); 6135 GRT.

Formerly the ANEK's *Talos*, this ferry — along with the *Vitsentzos Kornaros* — covers for the *Prevelis* (both have run the route full time in the past). On-board conditions are okay but not fantastic. The lack of competition really shows on this route, and this boat is typical: she gets you where you want to go, but the travel experience isn't the greatest going. The one plus is that these boats are rarely crowded.

Southern Crete Services
ANENDYK Ferries
Daskalogiannis; 1993; 650 GRT.
Samaria I; 1986; 445 GRT.
Sfakia I; 1991; 380 GRT.

Three interchangeable ferries (operated by one of the most awkwardly named ferry lines in Greece) run along the south-west coast of Crete from the ports of Paleochora and Sfakia/Chora Sfakion. Their primary role is ferrying tourists disgorged from the mouth of the Samarian Gorge to adjacent coastline towns, but they also offer an annual service once a week to the remote island of Gavdos to the south (the bulk of the weekday services have lately been from Paleochora, while weekend runs have been out of Sfakia). These boats are very tourist-dependent and operate between April and October. Full services only run during the July/August peak.

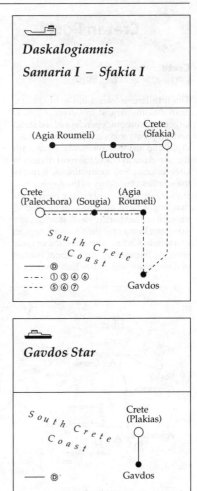

P/S *Gavdos Star*

A new arrival in 2011, this small passenger boat ran a daily service out of the otherwise unconnected town of Plakias on the south coast of Crete with Gavdos. One to look out for if you are trapped on Gavdos; otherwise the other ferries are a safer bet.

⚓ Cretan Ports

Crete

KPITI; 8259 km²; pop. 460,000.

The fifth largest island in the Mediterranean and the largest in Greece, Crete is larger than some independent island states and has plenty to occupy the visitor. Geography and history have combined to mark the island out as one of the most diverse in Greece. Long and mountainous, it marks the southern boundary of the Aegean Sea, supping up the contents of any rain clouds that might have otherwise attempted to venture further north as well as acting as a giant breakwater for the southern Aegean as a whole. Crete is also an island of great strategic importance, for without control of it no power was able to fully command the rest of the Aegean. As a result, the island is littered with the remains of all the great powers from the region, and indeed, appears to have been the power base of the earliest of them all — the Bronze Age Minoan civilization. Their palaces are among the top sightseeing destinations, though later Greek and Roman temples, Byzantine churches, Venetian fortresses, Ottoman mosques, and WW2 German battlefields also lie thick on the ground.

If this was not enough, Crete is also very fertile and, following in the tradition of its role as an important grain producing island in the ancient world, now is the major supplier of market garden produce to Greece. The self-sufficiency gained by this has given the Cretans a reputation

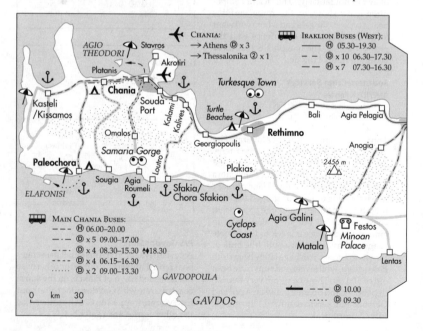

for hot-headed independence and radical politics. Tourism, although not vital to the economy, is now rampant thanks to good beaches, impressive sightseeing and a climate befitting an island lying further south than the northern coast of Tunisia. All major settlements now lie on the north coast which has developed into an English-speaking tourist strip that looks increasingly closer to Benidorm rather than the bucolic, unspoilt Greek island idyll.

Fortunately, the south coast (the resort town of Ierapetra aside) and greater part of the hinterland — rugged and mountainous, covered in pine forests and wildly beautiful — remain remarkably untainted and invite exploration, though comparatively few visitors to Crete venture beyond the spectacular walk down the longest gorge in Europe at Samaria. This winds down to the nicest part of the island — the collection of small port villages and dreamy shoreline of

the south-west coast from Matala (with its history of 1970s hippy troglodytes) to the dusty town of Paleochora and its caïques to the exquisite islet of Elafonisi with its sandy beaches and turquoise seas.

The size of Crete has resulted in ferry links with the mainland developing to six ports on the northern coast. All significant towns in their own right, they provide good bases for exploring the adjacent coastlines and hinterland. They are linked by the island's main road (which runs the length of the northern coast, with feeder roads running south from the main towns to the mountain villages and the south coast) and are served by frequent buses.

The island bus service is excellent, making travel on Crete both easy and cheap, besides providing a valuable link between ferry routes. The only minor problem of note are the distances; these are very long by Greek island standards.

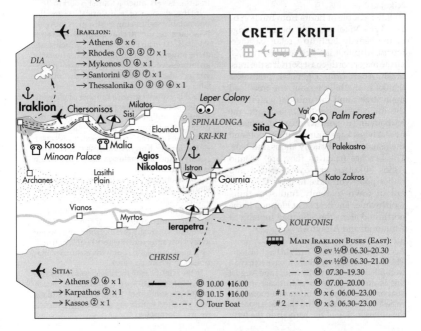

Agios Nikolaos
ΑΓΙΟΣ ΝΙΚΟΛΑΟΣ; pop. 19,000.

CODE ☎ 28410

TOURIST POLICE ☎ 22321

POLICE ☎ 22338

TOURIST INFORMATION ☎ 22357

Formerly the premier port of eastern Crete (though now neglected by ferry companies for the last three years), Agios Nikolaos is an attractive — though all too obviously tourist — town perched on a tiny headland deep within the Mirambelou Gulf. Called after the patron saint of sailors, the town's name is a common one, and not to be confused with other ports in the Gulf of Corinth or on Anafi. In fact, for most of its life it was known as 'Lato', but the Venetians chose to rename it and the modern authorities have simply opted for a Hellenized version of the name (though you will still find local bus drivers referring to the town as 'San Nikolaos').

Only a couple of hours from Iraklion by bus, Agios Nikolaos marks the eastern edge of the heavily built-up Cretan package-tourist strip that lies between the two. Of all the major north-coast ports it is the most brash. Apart from a general 'prettiness' thanks to the hilly terrain, the tree-lined main streets and the unusual waterfront, the town lacks sights. As a result, the harbour and downtown area is dominated by sickly package-tourist eating spots and the usual mix of holiday shops and bars. The beaches (such as they are) around Agios Nikolaos are overcrowded and rather poor: you have to go quite a way out of town to really find something worthwhile. The best lie at Elounda to the north, and along the Sitia road (notably at Ammoudi and Almyros).

⊨

Accommodation fills up early in High Season. This is also one town where it pays to have a well-filled wallet: certainly in July and August this is not the place to prevaricate if your boat or bus is met with offers of a room. The easiest hotels to find lie on the waterfront on the opposite side of the harbour to the ferry quay. These include the C-class *Alcestis* (☎ 22454) and (250 m north-west) the B-class *Coral* (☎ 28363) and the B-class pension *Lydia* (☎ 22130). Finally, the C-class *Mandraki* (☎ 28880) lies east of the bus station, and further up the hill is an establishment (easily identified via the green 'Rooms' sign) offering very cheap rooms at a price — the price being the minimalist facilities.

Å

The nearest site to the town, *Gournia Moon Camping* (☎ 28420 93243), is well away from the centre at Gournia, near a Minoan palace.

◎◎

The town itself has no buildings of particular merit, thanks to the Turks who demolished the Genoese fortress. Instead the heart of the town is dominated by a **lagoon**-like sea-lake inner harbour of reputedly measureless depth. The reality doesn't live up to the mystique: the 'lake' (which is some 55 m deep) was only connected to the sea in 1907 when the existing channel was dug. It is lined by expensive tavernas that provide a sobering reminder that this is very much a tourist resort town.

In the absence of a historical centre the one notable sightseeing destination in Agios Nikolaos is the **Archaeological Museum** (located 500 m up Paleologou St., which starts at the inner harbour bridge), which is home to an impressive display of artefacts (giant pithos jars included) recovered from nearby Minoan sites — including Malia.

As it is a tourist town, a number of pleasure boats operate from the port, though most of them are ludicrously expensive, given the distances involved. The most popular of these excursions is to the Cretan version of Alcatraz — the former Knights' fortress turned leper colony island of **Spinalonga** (see p. 361), which is invaded most days a week.

Taxi-boat services also operate to the resort of **Elounda** and the quiet village of **Plaka**. There are also excursions to the remains of the Roman city of **Olous** up the coast, as well as Bird and Kri-Kri (named after the local species of goat) islands. If you really feel like throwing money away you can go on a mystery boat tour (these visit the same islands but without an explanation as to where you are).

In the High Season there is a weekly bus and boat trip to **Chrissi** (see p. 359), the exotic beach island off south-east Crete. Agios Nikolaos buses connect with boats at the southern beach resort of **Ierapetra**.

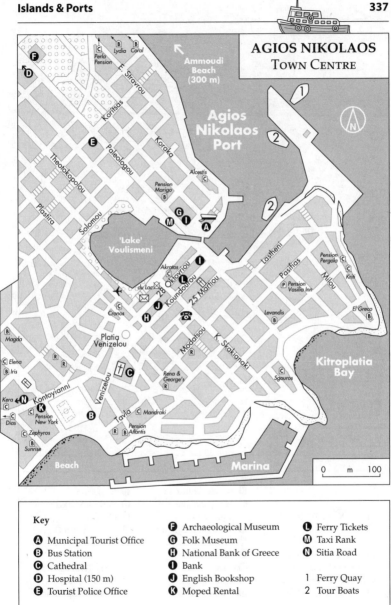

AGIOS NIKOLAOS
TOWN CENTRE

Lydia Coral

Perla Pension

Ammoudi
Beach
(300 m)

Agios
Nikolaos
Port

E. Stavrou

Koritsas

Koraka

Theotokopolou

Paleologou

Alcestis

Pension
Marigo

Plastira

Solomou

'Lake'
Voulismeni

Lastheni

Pension
Pergola

Krithi

Akratos

Oikonomou

du Lac

Koundourou

Pasifias

Milou

Pension
Vasilia Inn

28

25 Martiou

Cranos

El Greco

Levandis

Platia
Venizelou

Modatsou

K. Skakianaki

Kitroplatia
Bay

Magda

Elena

Iris

Venizelou

Rena &
George's

Sgouros

Kera

Kontoyianni

Dias

Pension
New York

Tavla

Mandraki

Pension
Altantis

Zephyros

Sunrise

Beach

Marina

0   m   100

Key

A Municipal Tourist Office
B Bus Station
C Cathedral
D Hospital (150 m)
E Tourist Police Office
F Archaeological Museum
G Folk Museum
H National Bank of Greece
I Bank
J English Bookshop
K Moped Rental
L Ferry Tickets
M Taxi Rank
N Sitia Road

1 Ferry Quay
2 Tour Boats

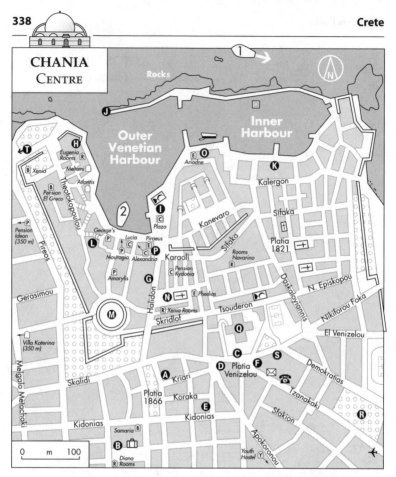

CHANIA
CENTRE

Rocks

Outer
Venetian
Harbour

Inner
Harbour

Eugenia
Rooms

Xenia   Meltemi

Atlantis

Pension
El Greco

Pension
Ideon
(350 m)

George's

Lucia   Piraeus

Mouragio   Alexandria

Amarylis

Ariadne

Plaza

Kanevaro

Sifaka

Karaoli

Pension
Kydonia

Phedias

Xenia Rooms

Kalergon

Sifaka

Platia
1821

Rooms
Navarino

N. Episkopou

Daskaloyannis

Nikiforou Foka

Skridlof

Villa Katerina
(350 m)

Skalidi

Platia
1866

Kidonias

Samaria

Diana
Rooms

Tsouderon

El Venizelou

Kriari

Koraka

Kidonias

Platia
Venizelou

Demokratias

Tzanakaki

Sfakion

Youth
Hostel

Apokoronou

Gerasimou

Pireos

Theotokopoulou

Halidon

Megalo Metachaki

0   m   100

Key

- **Ⓐ** NTOG / EOT Office
- **Ⓑ** Main Bus Station
- **Ⓒ** Souda Bus Stop
- **Ⓓ** Youth Hostel Bus Stop
- **Ⓔ** Tourist Police Office
- **Ⓕ** National Bank of Greece
- **Ⓖ** Archaeological Museum
- **Ⓗ** Nautical Museum
- **Ⓘ** Mosque of the Janissaries
- **Ⓙ** Venetian Lighthouse
- **Ⓚ** Venetian Arsenal
- **Ⓛ** Renieri Gate
- **Ⓜ** Shiavo Bastion
- **Ⓝ** Cathedral
- **Ⓞ** Police
- **Ⓟ** Bookshop
- **Ⓠ** Turkish Market
- **Ⓡ** Gardens
- **Ⓢ** ANEK Ticket Office
- **Ⓣ** Beach & Pool (200 m)

1   Ferry Terminal (6 km East at Souda)

2   Beach & Tour Boats

Chania

XANIA; pop. 50,000.

CODE ☎ 28210
TOURIST POLICE ☎ 24477
NTOG ☎ 26426
EMERGENCY ☎ 22222

The capital of Crete until 1971, Chania (pronounced 'Han*ya*') is now the number two city on the island. As such, it is the beneficiary of the second daily direct service between Crete and Piraeus. Chania boasts one of the most attractive town centres on Crete, retaining much of its Venetian/ Turkish heart and offering an attractive caïque-filled harbour lined with tavernas (complete with expensive package tourist orientated menus). Unfortunately, some of the outer suburbs are pretty ropy, and the town's modern port (thanks to the inability of the old harbour to handle large vessels) is located an inconvenient 6 km to the east of the town centre — across the Akrotiri headland at Souda.

In addition to the heavy package tourist trade, local prices are pushed up by the military personnel from the nearby Akrotiri NATO air and naval base. The military presence is strong in the area (i.e. 'photography banned' notices abound, and there are always plenty of unattached males in the local discos), but in the main it doesn't detract from the town.

Inevitably, the harbour is the main centre of activity. Used as the set for the film *Zorba the Greek*, it is easily the most attractive on Crete — even with the crowds. Taxi boats run from here (ferry fans shouldn't miss the free raft across the harbour to the Fortella restaurant) to local beaches and the small islet of **Agio Theodori**. The winding streets behind the waterfront are inevitably very boutique-laden, but also contain a fair number of easily found pensions.

All the main services are to be found in the centre — apart from the bus station, which lies outside the old city walls, some five blocks in from the waterfront. Chania is the main junction for the Eastern Crete

bus system with good links to Paleochora and the ports on the south Cretan coast, as well as the villages in the White Mountains that rise behind the town.

⊨

Rooms are in limited supply, but pricier beds are less hard to come by. The NTOG/EOT office can help you find a bed. The B-class *Samaria* (☎ 51551) is right next to the bus station and easily located; so too is the E-class *Piraeus* (☎ 54154) on the Old Port waterfront. Like all the hotels and pensions in this area it is rather noisy. Tucked behind the Nautical Museum are the much more expensive B-class *El Greco* (☎ 90432) and A-class *Palazzo* (☎ 43255). The Old Harbour and the main street (Halidon St.) between the Old Harbour and the bus station have a number of pensions in the side-streets behind them. There is also a *Youth Hostel* (☎ 53565) at 33 Drakonianou Street, south of the town centre.

▲

Camping Chania (☎ 31138). A reasonably good site 3 km beyond Chania on the road to Kasteli (take the Kasteli bus and ask for the camping).

∞

Known as the 'Venice of Greece' the town itself is the main sightseeing attraction. Needless to say, this being Greece, it is without a single canal, the city acquiring the label by virtue of its largely Venetian-built centre. Although heavily bombed during WW2, the heart of Chania is graced with a remarkable collection of Venetian buildings (now protected by government decree). First among these are the **City Walls**, built c. 1590 after the Barbary pirate Barbarossa sacked nearby Rethimno. The city fathers' fear was such that they added a 15 m deep moat to the outer side for good measure. The harbour was also fortified (the ruins of the **Arsenal** can be seen on the waterfront), and a **Nautical Museum** is now housed in the old walls.

Within the old town there are a number of 16 C. **Venetian Churches**: the one on the main street now houses the city **Archaeological Museum**, which contains material from the town's early Minoan settlement through to the classical period.

Two centuries of Turkish rule have also left their mark, most notably in the form of the lovely multi-domed waterfront **Mosque of the Janissaries** — built to mark the Ottoman conquest of the city in 1645.

Iraklion

ΗΡΑΚΛΕΙΟ; pop. 102,000.

CODE ☎ 2810
PORT POLICE ☎ 282002
TOURIST POLICE ☎ 283190
EOT / NTOG OFFICE ☎ 228203
EMERGENCY (FOR MOST OF CRETE) ☎ 100

The main port and modern capital of Crete, Iraklion (also commonly transcribed as 'Heraklion' and 'Iraklio') can make the dubious claim of being the one Greek island capital that wouldn't look out of place on the mainland. The fifth largest city in Greece, it shares the common characteristic to all of suffering from a massive amount of unsympathetic late 20th century building around a historically interesting core. As elsewhere the resulting townscape exhibits all the usual characteristics of a place suffering from the unwelcome effects of a catastrophic explosion at a local cement factory. However, in Iraklion's case, it is not all dust and grime: the mollifying existence of the well-preserved Venetian city walls, waterfront fortress and arsenal does something to redeem the ambience, and the sightseeing combination of the nearby Minoan palace at Knossos and the city's Archaeological Museum (home to the largest display of Minoan artefacts in the world) is enough to justify adding Iraklion to any itinerary.

Iraklion is a very popular starting point for Greek island hopping holidays, thanks to the international airport on the city limits that is one of the leading charter flight destinations in Greece. In fact

many regular island hoppers prefer to start from here just to avoid Athens. The city is also the hub of the island bus system and an important ferry junction. Ferry links are adequate, but hardly brilliant. In addition to daily services to Piraeus, in High Season you can also be fairly sure of at least one boat daily to Santorini (book well ahead), and a ferry twice a week to Rhodes.

Describing Iraklion is easy as most of it is very avoidable. The city divides fairly neatly into the Byzantine, Venetian and Modern sectors. The modern town, which lies outside the Venetian walls for several kilometres in all directions, has nothing to recommend it and can be safely explored via the window of the bus to Knossos Palace (which lies 1 km beyond its southern limits). The Venetian city is surprisingly bland today as it has lost most of its buildings to earthquakes and bombing in WW2. The singular exception is the north-east quarter which backs onto the old port and stands on the site of the Byzantine city. It is this part of Iraklion that is home to most of the hotels, sights and tourist facilities.

Regardless of whether you arrive by air or sea your first point of reference is likely to be the city **bus station** which lies between the old and new ports, just outside the city wall. The bus terminal building (a long single-storey affair) also has a convenient baggage store, as well as some tourist information during regular working hours and the usual watering facilities. Towering over the bus park are the impressive city walls. Built over three centuries, they are so substantial that they enabled the inhabitants of Candia (the city only acquired the decidedly less romantic name of 'Iraklion' with Cretan independence) to withstand a Turkish siege for over two decades before capitulation in 1669. Today they still serve a similar function, and finding

IMMENSELY LARGE OTTOMAN AXE
USED IN THE AXE MURDERS OF 1700 AD

HISTORICAL MUSEUM

ARCHAEOLOGICAL MUSEUM

MEDIUM SIZED MINOAN AXE
USED IN THE AXE MURDERS OF 1700 BC

your way up into the city (the old town is built up the side of a hill) is always the visitor's first task.

The simplest way into the city that enables you to keep your bearings is to walk along the waterfront past the old port until you arrive at **25 Augoustou** Street. Home to most of the ferry ticket agents and banks, this major artery climbs up to the main square — **Platia Venizelou**, the lively, not to say chaotic, hub of the old town. It is easily recognized thanks to the large working lion fountain that is one of the few surviving architectural remnants of the Venetian city. The square is home to several tavernas and a bus stop for Knossos Palace (though those in the know prefer to pick the bus up at the bus station as there is a much better chance of getting a seat), and is the starting point for another of those naff wild-west motorized package tourist 'trains' which runs tours around the city wall.

Radiating out from Platia Venizelou are a number of streets (an increasing proportion of them pedestrianized) running to all the main sights, making navigation very easy. The most important of these is the tourist-shop-lined **Dedalou St.** which heads eastwards direct to the second large square in town at **Platia Eleftherias**. Here you will find the Archaeological Museum and useful hotel and airport bus stops. Running north-west from Platia Venizelou is Kydonias St. (complete with a useful *Road Editions* map shop) which drops you on the waterfront a block east of Iraklion's second major museum — the Historical Museum of Crete.

The junction between Platia Venizelou and Odhos 1821 is also the starting point for the pedestrianized **Odhos 1866** street, which heads to a small square at Platia Kornarou containing a notable scenic Turkish fountain and several coffee shops. The north side of Platia Venizelou abuts the small **El Greco Park** which, in truth, is more garden than park, but does at least offer some shady seating. The area of town north of this is a somewhat confusing

warren of narrow streets heading down to the sea front.

Apart from a couple of days' sightseeing and ferry links, Iraklion has little more to offer, and although a large number of tourists pass through, they rarely stay long. Nightlife is poor (for foreign tourists at any rate) and as a beach destination it doesn't score highly either. If you are looking to wash off the dust, the hotel strip (starting 4 km west of the centre) bus takes you to a sandy strip of sorts. To the east, there is a fair sand beach at Amnissos (take the #1 bus), 8 km from Iraklion centre: plane spotters will love it as it is directly under the airport flight path. Like all beaches near Iraklion it is usually very windy.

☻

The hill on which Iraklion stands has been inhabited continuously since since Neolithic times. However, unlike nearby Knossos which appears to have retained its pre-Greek Minoan name, Iraklion (which served as its primary port) has had great difficulty hanging onto any name for more than a few hundred years. Its Minoan name is unknown, the Romans called it 'Heraclium', and the Saracens called it 'Rabdh el Khandak' (after they conquered the town in 824 AD, turning it into a regional slave trade centre). The Byzantines then changed the name to 'Khandakas' when they conquered Iraklion only to find the Venetians modifying the name again in 1210 AD. This time the variant was 'Candia' — a choice that proved so popular that through the medieval period the whole of the island was known by it.

The city's fame increased as it became an important bastion against the Ottoman advance west. Considerable effort went to building the walls between the 14 C.–17 C., in anticipation of the inevitable siege. The showdown began in 1648. Inevitably the city fell (in 1669 at a cost of some 30,000 Venetians and their French allies and 118,000 Turks). However, the walls, though they kept out the Turks for 21 years, were less effective in helping the city to retain its name: Candia was promptly renamed after them and 'Megalo Kastro' (the great castle) was born. This name was used until Turkish rule ended in 1898 and the current name (based on the Roman) was adopted.

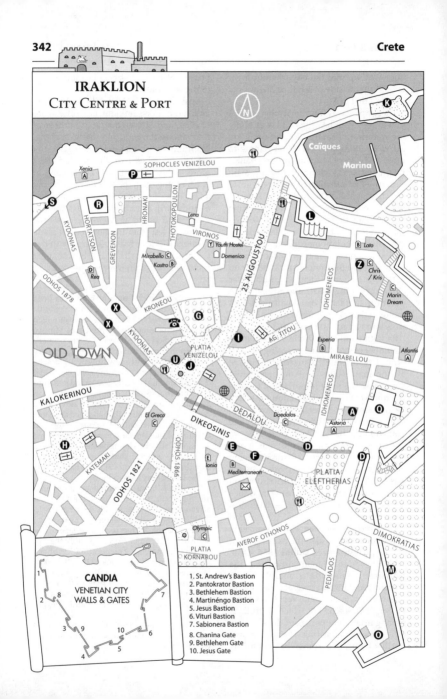

IRAKLION
CITY CENTRE & PORT

N

SOPHOCLES VENIZELOU

Xenia
A

P

Caïques

Marina

K

S

R

KYDONIAS
HORTIATSON
GREVENON
HRONAKI
THOTOKOPOULON

Lena

VIRONOS

Y *Youth Hostel*

Mirabello C
Kastro B

Domenico

25 AUGOUSTOU

L

B *Lato*

Z C

Chris / Kris

C

Marin Dream

D *Rea*

ODHOS 1878

X

X

KRONEOU

KYDONIAS

G

I

AG. TITOU

IDHOMENEOS

Esperia
B

MIRABELLOU

Atlantis
A

OLD TOWN

PLATIA
VENIZELOU

U

J

KALOKERINOU

El Greco
C

KATEMAKI

H

ODHOS 1821

ODHOS 1866

DEDALOU

Daedalos
C

DIKEOSINIS

IDHOMENEOS

A

Astoria
A

Q

D

E

F

E
Ionia

B
Mediterranean

D

PLATIA
ELEFTHERIAS

Olympic
C

PLATIA
KORNAROU

AVEROF OTHONOS

PEDIADOS

DIMOKRATIAS

M

O

CANDIA
VENETIAN CITY
WALLS & GATES

1
8
2
3
9
4
5
10
6
7

1. St. Andrew's Bastion
2. Pantokrator Bastion
3. Bethlehem Bastion
4. Martinéngo Bastion
5. Jesus Bastion
6. Vituri Bastion
7. Sabionera Bastion
8. Chanina Gate
9. Bethlehem Gate
10. Jesus Gate

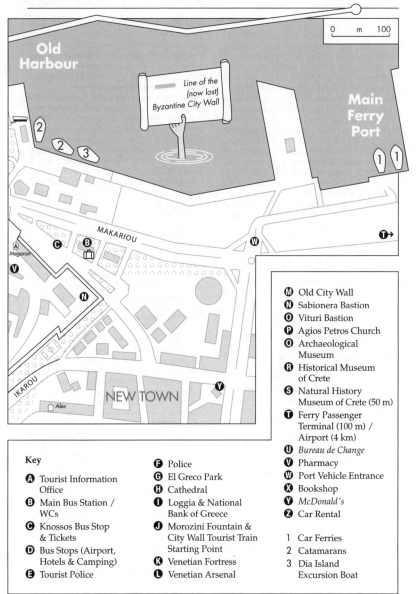

0   m   100

Old Harbour

Line of the (now lost) Byzantine City Wall

Main Ferry Port

MAKARIOU

Megaron

IKAROU

NEW TOWN

Alex

Key

A Tourist Information Office

B Main Bus Station / WCs

C Knossos Bus Stop & Tickets

D Bus Stops (Airport, Hotels & Camping)

E Tourist Police

F Police

G El Greco Park

H Cathedral

I Loggia & National Bank of Greece

J Morozini Fountain & City Wall Tourist Train Starting Point

K Venetian Fortress

L Venetian Arsenal

M Old City Wall

N Sabionera Bastion

O Vituri Bastion

P Agios Petros Church

Q Archaeological Museum

R Historical Museum of Crete

S Natural History Museum of Crete (50 m)

T Ferry Passenger Terminal (100 m) / Airport (4 km)

U *Bureau de Change*

V Pharmacy

W Port Vehicle Entrance

X Bookshop

Y *McDonald's*

Z Car Rental

1 Car Ferries

2 Catamarans

3 Dia Island Excursion Boat

⊨

Hotel accommodation is reasonably plentiful in Iraklion. Top of the range are the A-class *Xenia* (☎ 284000) on the waterfront and the *Astoria* (☎ 229002) overlooking leafy Eleftherias Square. C-class hotels lie pretty thick on the ground with relatively little to choose between them. They include the quiet *Olympic* (☎ 288861) and the noisier *Daedalos* (☎ 224391); both offer good value rooms if your budget isn't too tight. Another C-class option is the family-run *Mirabello* (☎ 285052): prices here vary as some of the (rather austere) rooms have air-conditioning and bathrooms and some don't. Those with limited funds should make for the D-class *Rea* (☎ 223638) near the Historical Museum. Finally, there is a good *Youth Hostel* (☎ 286281) at 5 Vironos/Cyronos St. complete with fairly priced rooms, a café/bar, and baggage storage facilities.

Λ

The size of Cretan towns ensures that sites are inconvenient distances from centres. Iraklion is no exception, the nearest being an excellent beach site: *Camping Creta* (☎ 28970 41400), lying 30 minutes east via a #18 bus, then a 20-minute walk.

◖◗

Iraklion boasts two attractions that draw the crowds. The **Minoan Palace** at **Knossos** (see opposite) is the big pull: 5 km from the town centre, it is an easy bus ride (a bus runs every 15 minutes from the bus station; tickets from the kiosk by the bus stop) and is the most important Minoan site on the island. The **Archaeological Museum** (closed for refurbishment in 2011; it is doubtful if it will be open this year) in Iraklion is rich in associated finds, and offers a cool retreat from the heat of the city streets. Star exhibits include spectacular large bronze axe heads, the Knossos fresco fragments, a wooden model reconstruction of the palace, and finds from the smaller Minoan palace complexes at Festos and Malia. Be warned: this museum gets very crowded in July and August — the best time to visit is either first thing or very late afternoon.

Iraklion also has a second (greatly underrated) museum that is never full: the **Historical Museum of Crete** (open ②–⑦ 08.00–19.00; entrance fee €3). Star exhibits here are the model of Venetian Candia, Byzantine icons, memorabilia of the heroes of the independence struggle, and German WW2 occupation items

(including personal effects recovered from graves of local massacre victims). The museum is also home to the only two paintings in Greece by the country's most famous painter: El Greco (alias Domenikos Theotocopoulos), who was born in Iraklion in 1541. Nearby is the good **Natural History Museum of Crete**.

Hunting **around the town**, you will find a few architectural lights amid the grey modern buildings. First and foremost is the **Rocco al Mare** — the wonderfully well-preserved Venetian 16 c. fortress that stands at the entrance to the old harbour; its front portal is still adorned with a Venetian winged lion. It is open ⑨ 08.00–15.00; entrance fee €3. Inside you will find assorted dank halls filled with cannon, a mule stairway to the upper levels and a delightful capless miniature minaret added by the Turks (tourists can ascend it).

Near the Rocco al Mare are the remains of the **Venetian Arsenal**, now reduced to a few heavily restored arches: the remains of long sea-galley sheds that once reached down to the sea. The city centre has the ornate **Morozini Fountain** (1625), a charming lion-inspired work commissioned by the nephew of the vandal who blew up the Parthenon in Athens. To the east of the fountain is a reconstructed **Venetian Loggia**, which was damaged by bombing in WW2.

Thanks to its position as the central Crete bus hub, Iraklion is a good point from which to visit the Minoan palace sites on **Malia** and **Festos** (also transcribed as 'Phestos'). Regular buses run past Malia and some five a day venture to Festos. Both sites are open ⑨ 08.00–19.00; entrance fee €5. Unlike Knossos, neither site has undergone 'reconstruction' and both are as excavated. For this reason alone, a visit to one is worthwhile as you will get a good insight into what newly excavated Knossos looked like. Malia is the better preserved and is unusual in its coastal plain location. The palace at Festos is more dramatically sited on a hilltop above the Messara plain, and has a more sophisticated theatre-cum-dancing floor than the famous example at Knossos. Iraklion buses also run across the island to the southern coast town of **Matala**. Famous in the 1960s as a hairy hippy haven (who took to getting as high as possible while living in the local beach-cliffs — these are honeycombed with caves that have been inhabited by men and Cyclops since Neolithic times), the town is now a much tamer family resort.

Knossos

The Palace of Knossos (see colour map between pages 352–353) was the centre of Minoan civilization between 3000–1400 BC. Its fame was such that faint memories of it, and its name ('Knossos' is not Greek and is thought to be close to the site's earlier Minoan name), lingered on in Greek myth long after the site of the palace and the Minoan civilization were forgotten. By the Classical period, a thousand years after its destruction, beyond the myths and a horribly pessimistic belief that a Golden age had long since given way to a more prosaic age of Iron, no local recollection of the pre-Greek Minoan culture survived. Elsewhere the Minoans were remembered — not least in Egypt, where the story of their fall possibly came to be immortalized in the Atlantis legend (see p. 198).

Incredibly, beyond the odd painted pot and some clay tablets bearing a strange script that turned up in Mycenaean palace excavations in the 19 C., the Minoans remained completely unrecognized until Sir Arthur Evans began excavating at Knossos in 1900. The site had long been seen as one of potentially great importance, but even so, his unearthing of a massive, elaborate, surprisingly modern-looking palace adorned with frescoed walls, pillared light wells and drains (a feature not found in other European civilizations for a millennium), yet lacking defensive walls (suggesting an awesome military command of the region), was equal to any other 20 C. archaeological discovery.

Evans continued to excavate at Knossos until the 1930s, and also undertook considerable rebuilding, replacing the lost wooden pillars and beams with concrete substitutes. Had his sponsors not balked at providing additional funds for concrete he would probably have rebuilt the whole complex. The result gives you plenty to see (even if this sort of 'reconstruction' is nowadays regarded as over enthusiastic) and offers a nice compromise between the impression given of the former palace as it was and the warren of foundations that recall the palace of Greek legend, the famous Labyrinth where the Athenian hero Theseus fought the dreaded Minotaur before running off with the King's daughter, Ariadne. Worth recalling, it ran something like this:

The Myth of Theseus & the Minotaur

Far away and long ago there lived a king called Minos. He presided over a powerful maritime empire. Unfortunately for Minos, his wife, Queen Pasiphae, took a fancy for the idea of a night in bed with a large white bull that the king had refused to sacrifice to Poseidon (a strange desire which rather suggests that King Minos was King Minus-an-inch-or-two when it came to the tackle department). Pasiphae sought out the chief craftsman — Daedalus — and ordered him to devise some kind of heifer-shaped sex aid that would allow her to...

Well, anyway, one hell of a night and nine months later she gave birth to the Minotaur, the monstrous creature with the body of a man and the head of a bull. King Minos then ordered Daedalus to construct the labyrinth in which the Minotaur was hidden away. Here it lived on an annual diet of 14 Athenian youths and maidens who were pushed into the entrance and never seen again. Daedalus, meantime, was imprisoned to prevent him from divulging the secret of the labyrinth (to say nothing of indulging the queen's fancies) whereupon, with his son Icarus, he made some wings out of feathers and wax and flew to Sicily by way of Ikaria (where Icarus died after flying too near the sun).

Meantime, back at the labyrinth, Theseus, the son of the king of Athens, disguised as one of the annual sacrificial youths, killed the Minotaur with the help of Ariadne, who gave him a ball of thread that enabled him to escape from the labyrinth. The couple then fled to Naxos where the highly strung Theseus unceremoniously dumped his love, returning to Athens alone.

The large palace uncovered by Sir Arthur Evans is multi-layered and complex, the structure being built around the four sides of a flattened hilltop. Originally built in the Middle Minoan period c. 1950 BC, the palace was destroyed (along with all the other early Minoan palaces) c. 1700 BC, probably as the result of a massive earthquake. Rebuilt in the opulent style reproduced by Evans, the succeeding structure boasted the staircases, light wells and plaster-coated walls that make it so distinctive, although to call it a 'palace' is rather misleading, for the building complex at Knossos appears to have not only been the focus of political and religious life, but was also the centre of judicial, administrative, commercial and industrial activity. The hectares around the site contain the remains of a number of associated Minoan villas and houses, and a small town.

The massive eruption of Santorini c. 1640 BC triggered the collapse of the Minoan civilization, with all the Cretan palaces being destroyed — Knossos among them (seemingly by fire). Partially rebuilt by alien Mycenaean Greeks, it was the only Minoan palace site that wasn't abandoned. However, it didn't survive for long, being finally abandoned — possibly as the result of a raid by invaders — c. 1400 BC. Thereafter, the palace hill (still known as 'Knossos') was home to a small undistinguished Archaic settlement that survived into the Roman era.

Visitors to the palace today no longer need a ball of string to find their way around. From the moment they arrive at Knossos, life becomes very easy: you just follow the crowds. These start at the main road (lined with tavernas and tourist shops) which runs between the palace site and the small modern village of Knossos (where a limited number of rooms are available). Iraklion buses stop near the large coach park (complete with WCs) at the site entrance.

Open ☉ 08.00–19.00, the ticket fee is €6 (students: €3. In past years ISIC-holding students have been admitted free). Now surrounded by large pine trees, the site is accessed from the west. Most visitors explore the features of Knossos in the sequence given below, but you are free to wander (though rumour has it that plans are in hand to confine access to parts of the site, as heavy tourism is wearing down the floors).

On entering the site, visitors pass along a tree-lined avenue which ends with a bust of Sir Arthur Evans. This stands on the edge of the palace **West Court** that is dominated by Ⓐ three tree-filled circular **Offering Pits** used in Minoan worship. Into these were thrown ceremonial pottery vessels (an odd habit curiously replicated by the later Greeks with their passion for smashing platters after meals).

Behind the West Court stands the reconstructed west façade of the palace. Although roped off, doorways enable you to peer into Ⓑ the **Pillar Hall**, the first of the palace's estimated thousand rooms. Next door are Ⓒ the **West Magazines**. These are long storage pits containing the large pithos jars used to store oil and wine (the palace had a secondary role as a communal warehouse for the region). Originally they were unlit rooms deep in the bowels of the building. The path brings you to the **Western Propylon** (porch) and Ⓓ the **Corridor of the Procession** (which takes its name from the fresco depicting gift-bearers and a goddess figure).

From the Western Porch the path divides: one branch dives steeply off to the site boundary fence, running around the small Ⓔ **South / High Priest's House**, outside the palace walls. This is a two storey structure with rebuilt mini-sized red-tapered Minoan pillars. Meanwhile the tourist route turns back, past Ⓕ the **South Propylon** or gatehouse (complete with a fake white tapered column). To the east of this structure stands a pair of large **Sacred Horns** (now a popular seat for tourist photos): part of the Minoan bull-cult, they were replicated many times over in a smaller form as a decorative device along the tops of the palace walls. From the back of the South Propylon run Ⓖ the **Stairs** that led into the religious wing of the palace (follow them up today and you are able to get a better view of the pithoi in the West Magazine).

A path from the South Propylon runs east to Ⓗ the **Central Court Corridor**, which now contains a reproduction of the famous **Prince of the Lilies Fresco**. One of the most famous frescoes found at Knossos (and adopted as the symbol of Minoan Lines), it shows a kilted youth wearing a crown of lilies and peacock feathers. However, the figure is made up from fragments that could belong to three different individuals, and is a good example of the high degree of 'reconstruction' undertaken by Evans.

The corridor leads to ❶ the **Central Court** — a feature common to all Minoan palaces but implemented at its best at Knossos. This formed the centre of palace life, with the various quarters of the palace opening out onto it. The court is also thought to be the place where the famous bull-leaping contests, or rites, were performed. Artwork found on the site and elsewhere suggests that young men would grab the lowered horns of a charging bull, then, as the animal attempted to free itself by rearing its head, would use the momentum of that movement to somersault over the horns, landing on their feet on the animal's back before jumping clear. This was clearly a far more sophisticated exercise than modern bull-fighting, and was probably an integral part of Minoan religious ritual.

The **West Side Buildings** adjacent to the Central Court appear to have contained the religious centre of the palace. The most famous of the remains is ❹ the **Throne Room**. Arguably the most interesting room on the site, it is viewed via a basin-filled anteroom (complete with a second dummy throne placed so tourists can photograph each other sitting on it). The throne you can't sit on was originally thought to be that of the ruler at Knossos (hence its title: 'the throne of Minos'), but is now believed to have seated a High Priest. Made of gypsum, it has gypsum benches on either side, above which are frescoes of griffins and lilies (the design dates from the Mycenaean occupation). The throne's shape is also of interest as it mimics a wooden ceremonial chair design. The Throne Room is also a good example of the degree of reconstruction undertaken by Evans: photographs of the excavation show that the throne's back   stood several feet above the height of

the surrounding walls, with only the griffin's feet surviving from the frescoes. All of this room (and the storey above) from seat height is, therefore, 'fake'. The frescoes, along with most of the others found, have been reconstructed from fragments. Applauded at the time, they have come in for criticism since, following the discovery of the better-preserved Akrotiri frescoes on Santorini. By comparison, the Knossos reconstructions (produced by a Swiss father-and-son artist combination with the name of Gillieron) look curiously lifeless, and in some instances the fragments were completely misinterpreted (in the most notorious 'reconstruction', the remains of a blue monkey ended up being rebuilt as the figure of a youth).

Directly to the south of the Throne Room are the remains of the **Central Staircase** that served the west wing of the palace. Today it ascends to the rebuilt floor level at the top of the South Propylon stairs, and then further on up to nowhere (though the views are good). Ascending to the first level, then weaving your way around the back of the staircase, you come to the small reconstructed chamber over the Throne Room. This contains the light well that descends into the room and a number of fresco fragments on its walls. The covered-over ruins to the south of the Central Staircase yielded up the famous statuettes of the topless snake-waving ladies.

Returning to the Central Court and then heading north, the path leads down past the most photographed architectural feature on the site: the rebuilt tapered columns of ❸ the **North Entrance Bastion**. The most impressive of the entrances to the palace complex (thanks in part to the steepness of the hillside corridor at this point), it is home to the reconstructed **Racing Bull Relief**. Although the notion is a bit fanciful, it has been suggested that this wall remained visible among the ruins of the palace into the Archaic period, helping to give rise to the legend of the Labyrinth and the Minotaur.

Behind it are yet more rooms and storage chambers, and ❺ the **Lustral Basin**: a small reconstructed sanctuary complete with tapering pillars.

Following the path down past the North Entrance Bastion brings you into the square-pillared chamber now known as ❿ the **North Hypostyle Entrance** or **Custom House**. It is believed that this room was an accounting point where goods (brought up

BULL LEAPING

from the harbour 5 km away) and personnel were checked into the palace. Turning west from the Custom House, the path runs on to a feature of greater fame:  the **West Court** or **Theatre**. Truth to tell, it doesn't conform much to modern ideas as to what a theatre should look like, being merely an earthquake-damaged paved area with a flight of steps and no seating. It has been identified as a 'theatre' for want of any other feature at Knossos that could serve as the 'dancing floor which Daedalus made for Ariadne in broad Knossos' described by Homer. In reality it is more of a terminus for the **Royal Road** that runs west from it. Described as the oldest paved road in Europe, the road dates from the earliest palace period. Originally, it was lined with houses and led to the **Little Palace** (a large Minoan villa that stood nearby) and the town that is thought to have built up outside the palace complex. Today, the deeply excavated path runs into the supporting wall of the site coach park, and has partially excavated buildings on its south side. Nearer the palace, excavation has opened up a path that runs back to the entrance court past the **Altars**. A second excavated Minoan road runs north of the Custom House to an inaccessible building known as the North Pillar Hall.

East of the Custom House, the site path drops away sharply (all the east-side rooms of the palace were built on the slope of the hill). The north-east corner of the palace was home to the **Servants' Quarters**: now little more than a jumble of meaningless foundations, their function has been determined by the contents when excavated. The singular exception to these incomprehensible ruins is the re-roofed room on the edge of this quarter containing the **Giant Pithoi Jars**. These stand over 2 m high, and are the largest found at Knossos. The 'room' they are in was once part of the complex of eastern storage rooms in the palace. The best means of seeing these is to take the staircase running from the central court to the **East Bastion**. The stairs divide the servants' quarters and storerooms from the **Workshops**, where the palace craftsmen did their stuff. Individual rooms (directly opposite the Giant Pithoi Jars) have been identified as potters' and stone-cutters' workshops. The craftsmen in the latter carved stone utensils out of blocks of basalt imported from the Peloponnese.

The south-east sector of the palace containing the royal quarters was the most luxurious part of the complex. Unfortunately, the reconstructed buildings on this part of the site have been closed for years while they await restoration, so they are highly unlikely to be open this year (the 1900s concrete used to replace the lost wooden pillars and beams has flaked and cracked, and proved no durable substitute for the missing originals).

When this building is closed visitors have to make do with standing at the Central Court entrance and peering down into the reconstructed **Grand Staircase**, that in its prime stood five storeys high (only the bottom two of the three rebuilt storeys contain a significant amount of original material). Built around a light well adorned with the usual colonnades of tapering pillars (originally upturned trees) and spacious verandas adorned with frescoes, the Grand Staircase is the single most impressive architectural feature of the palace, besides marking Knossos out as a royal residence above the rest (other palaces on Crete had nothing to match it). It formed a royal approach to the **Royal Quarters**, with bathrooms on each floor (off the south-west corners) and doorways leading off into shrines and private rooms. The rebuilt staircase has been used to display reconstructions of a number of frescoes found in nearby rooms, notably the Mycenaean-period figure-of-eight shields and the lovely **Dolphin Fresco**. Fortunately the original fragments of these frescoes are on display in the Iraklion Archaeological Museum, so not all is lost if the Grand Staircase is still closed when you visit.

Sadly, if the staircase remains closed you will miss out on the Royal Quarters, which are closed along with it. The nearest you will get to seeing them is to glimpse into the **Royal Apartments' Lower Entrance** (this is

GRAND STAIRCASE & QUEEN'S APARTMENTS

CLOSED for renovation

reached via the path that runs around the site or — from the Central Court — via the East Bastion steps). From here you can just make out the **Hall of the Double Axes** (now thought to be the King's Audience room as the remains of a throne — complete with a four-pillared canopy — were discovered here) and the **King's Megaron**. This private royal room had a private balcony and was the original home of the figure-of-eight shield frescoes. Evans believed the room contained another throne.

Another room leading off the Hall of the Double Axes leads to the **Queen's Megaron**. Smaller than the King's Megaron, it was also adorned with frescoes — the most famous being the Dolphin Fresco. From this room runs a gallery complete with a triple window that opens out onto a light well. On this gallery stands the **Queen's Bathroom** (complete with a small painted hip-bath) and the **Queen's Toilet Room** which served as a dressing room. It, too, had a window and door into the light well (the door provided access to another small room off the light well that served as her most private of throne rooms).

The floor of the light well is also known as the **Court of the Distaffs**, after a symbol carved on the walls. From it runs a second corridor that leads to the **Treasury Room**. In this room Sir Arthur Evans discovered a number of fragments from gold and ivory objects. These are believed to have fallen from a room immediately above. The private royal living quarters are also lost; they are thought to have been located on the upper floors of the royal quarter of the palace.

The eastern edge of the palace now sits at the base of a small pine-shaded valley formed by the excavation of the lower hill rooms. From the Royal Quarters, the path runs on to the covered-over remains of the south-east corner of the palace. These include a number of 'private' apartments now named after their excavated remains: ❶ the **House of the Fallen Blocks** (no guesses as to what you will find here), the **House of the Channel Screen**, the **House of the Sacrificed Oxen**, the **House of the Monolithic Pillars**, the **South-East House**, and west of that ❷ the **Shrine of the Double Axes**. The double-headed axe was another popular Minoan motif; known as a 'Lavrys' it is thought by some to be the origin of the word 'Labyrinth' — meaning 'palace where the Lavrys is worshipped' (though others claim this is a load of bull).

Kasteli
ΚΑΣΤΕΛΛΙ; pop. 2,800.

CODE ☎ 28220
PORT POLICE ☎ 22024

A small, rather drab town on the western edge of Crete offering all the essential facilities but no more, Kasteli is often called, by ticket agents and maps alike, by its older name of **Kissamos**. The only ferry connections are the services to Kithera, Piraeus and the southern Peloponnese, a fact reflected in the location of the ferry quay, over 2 km west of the town centre on a particularly quiet stretch of coastline.

The solitude of the surrounding countryside — particularly the Gramvoussa Peninsula to the west — is the only real attraction, given that the town (complete with an uninspiring centre and a comparatively poor beach) itself lacks zip at all times of the day. Despite being the local transportation hub, the absence of frequent buses means you will need to hire a moped or car to explore the wilds.

🛏

A plentiful supply of rooms are on offer in the town square and waterfront, even at the height of the season. There are also a number of reasonable hotels, including the C-class *Kissamos* (☎ 22086), *Castle* (☎ 22140) and the *Peli* (☎ 22343). There is also one B-class hotel/pension, the *Astrikas*, and one D-class outlet with expensive apartments, the *Mandy* (☎ 22825).

A

Camping Mythimna (☎ 31444): very quiet, 5 km east of the town centre on an excellent beach (take a Chania-bound bus and ask to be dropped at the campsite). There is also a semi-official site closer to hand — *Camping Kissamos* (☎ 23444). Complete with pool, it lies 200 m west of the town centre.

👓

Sightseeing is thin on the ground if you don't have your own wheels. The best thing on offer is the 7 km trek (buses are rare) inland to the village of **Polirinia** which has the substantial remains of an **Ancient City** (complete with an aqueduct commissioned by Hadrian) on the hillside above the current centre.

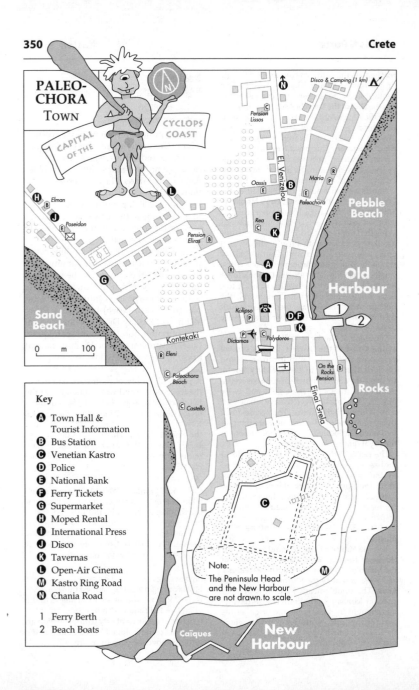

PALEO-CHORA Town

CAPITAL OF THE

CYCLOPS COAST

Disco & Camping (1 km)

Pension Lissos

El. Venizelou

Oasis

Maria

Paleochora

Pebble Beach

Elman

Poseidon

Rea

Pension Eliras

Old Harbour

Sand Beach

0   m   100

Kontekaki

Kalipso

Dictamos

Polydoros

Eleni

Paleochora Beach

Castello

On the Rocks Pension

Einai Greia

Rocks

Key

Ⓐ Town Hall & Tourist Information
Ⓑ Bus Station
Ⓒ Venetian Kastro
Ⓓ Police
Ⓔ National Bank
Ⓕ Ferry Tickets
Ⓖ Supermarket
Ⓗ Moped Rental
Ⓘ International Press
Ⓙ Disco
Ⓚ Tavernas
Ⓛ Open-Air Cinema
Ⓜ Kastro Ring Road
Ⓝ Chania Road

1 Ferry Berth
2 Beach Boats

Note:
The Peninsula Head and the New Harbour are not drawn to scale.

Caïques

New Harbour

Paleochora
ΠΑΛΑΙΟΧΩΡΑ; pop. 3,000.

CODE ☎ 28230
PORT POLICE ☎ 41214
POLICE ☎ 41111
FIRST AID ☎ 41211

The south-west coast of Crete is characterized by cliffs, ravines and a number of small, isolated settlements. The region is also famed as Cyclops country, though there is little sign of these one-eyed giants today. The main town on the coast is **Paleochora**. A dusty peninsular town that is increasingly under the sway of up-market package tour operators, it lies caught between the sea on two sides and the remains of a Venetian Kastro (constructed in 1279 and destroyed by the pirate Barbarossa), which offers some exceptional views of the neighbouring coastline, and an attractive base for a few days while one explores the region.

The town's shoreline is graced with a popular sand beach on the west side and a pebble affair on the east (its comparative lack of appeal making it popular with nudists). In addition, Paleochora is host to a usually full-to-bursting daily boat which heads for the idyllic brush-covered beach islet of **Elafonisi** to the south-west. Paleochora itself isn't the most attractive town on Crete, but it is pleasant enough, with the main streets closed to traffic during the summer evenings.

Paleochora also has a regular small ferry that runs east along the coast to a number of secondary settlements. **Sfakia** (also known as **Chora Sfakion**) is the next largest in size and lies at the other end of the line. Its main attraction is the bus service with Chania which ferries large numbers of tourists home after their walk down the Samaria Gorge.

During WW2 all the traffic was the other way, as the village was a major Allied evacuation point in the latter stages of the Battle of Crete. **Agia Roumeli**, at the mouth of the Samaria Gorge, is a tourist trap of little merit. Now living off the large number of

tourists walking the gorge, it has a passable beach but little else to recommend it. In between these three 'major' ports are two tiny fishing hamlets also served by the south coast ferry service. **Lutro** is the least developed — thanks to the lack of a beach — but can be reached via a coastal path from Sfakia. **Sougia** has a beach and growing numbers of tourists. It also lies at the mouth of a second gorge—the **Agia Irini Gorge**. Local ticket agencies offer organized tours from Paleochora.

The coastline east of Sfakia is riven with further gorges. These start with the **Kavi Ravine** 1 km to the east, the 8 km **Imbros Gorge**—accessible from the inland hill village of Imbros (which in turn is reached via a Chania bus) — and the more inaccessible **Kallikrates Ravine** and the **Aradena Gorge**, which remain the preserve of heavy-duty trekkers.

This area of coastline effectively terminates with the 'resort' at **Matala** (accessed by bus from Iraklion), home to a good beach backed by cliffs pockmarked with caves that look to have once been home to a colony of Cyclops. During the 1960s these hapless giants failed to keep a spare eye out for squatters and the hippy brigade moved in, changing all the boulders on the caves, and generally making a nuisance of themselves. Most are now company executives so things have calmed down a bit. Even so, this part of Crete is still an odd mixture of local conservatism and discreet foreign liberalism.

🛏

Rooms are available in all ferry ports, but supplies are necessarily limited. Most are to be found in Paleochora. At the budget end of the range are the E-class *Paleochora* (☎ 41023) and *Oassis* (☎ 41328), the C-class *Polydoros* (☎ 41068) and *Rea* (☎ 41307), and some pensions including the dangerously named *On the Rocks* (☎ 41713).

A

Camping Paleochora (☎ 41120) lies 2 km east of the town in an olive grove behind a pebble beach. A beach disco keeps campers awake several nights a week in summer.

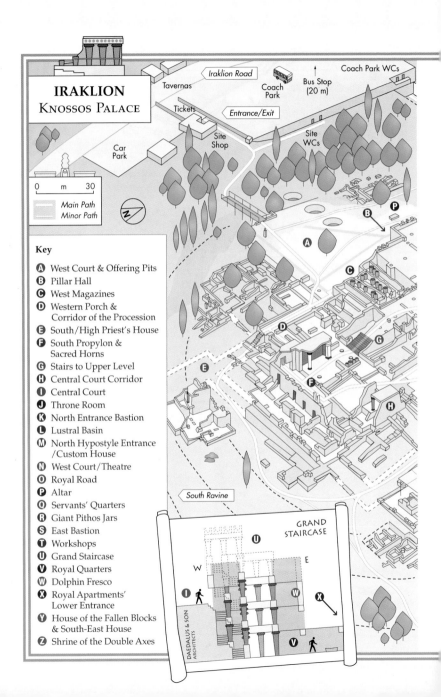

IRAKLION
KNOSSOS PALACE

Iraklion Road

Tavernas

Tickets

Coach Park

Bus Stop (20 m)

Coach Park WCs

Entrance/Exit

Site Shop

Site WCs

Car Park

0   m   30

Main Path
Minor Path

Key

ⓐ West Court & Offering Pits
ⓑ Pillar Hall
ⓒ West Magazines
ⓓ Western Porch & Corridor of the Procession
ⓔ South/High Priest's House
ⓕ South Propylon & Sacred Horns
ⓖ Stairs to Upper Level
ⓗ Central Court Corridor
ⓘ Central Court
ⓙ Throne Room
ⓚ North Entrance Bastion
ⓛ Lustral Basin
ⓜ North Hypostyle Entrance /Custom House
ⓝ West Court/Theatre
ⓞ Royal Road
ⓟ Altar
ⓠ Servants' Quarters
ⓡ Giant Pithos Jars
ⓢ East Bastion
ⓣ Workshops
ⓤ Grand Staircase
ⓥ Royal Quarters
ⓦ Dolphin Fresco
ⓧ Royal Apartments' Lower Entrance
ⓨ House of the Fallen Blocks & South-East House
ⓩ Shrine of the Double Axes

South Ravine

GRAND STAIRCASE

W

E

DAEDALUS & SON ARCHITECTS

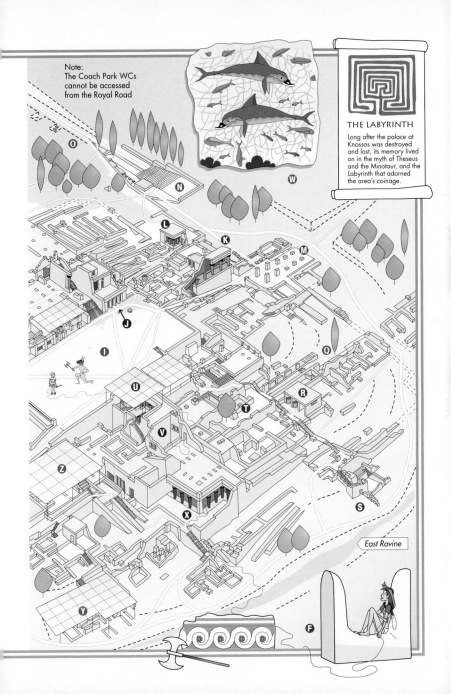

Note:
The Coach Park WCs cannot be accessed from the Royal Road

THE LABYRINTH

Long after the palace at Knossos was destroyed and lost, its memory lived on in the myth of Theseus and the Minotaur, and the Labyrinth that adorned the area's coinage.

East Ravine

Crete

The ubiquitous Greek Island Taverna

Rocca al Mere

Minoan Axes in the Archaeological Museum

IRAKLION
Morozini Fountain

∞

Chania is the best jumping-off point for the **Samaria Gorge**: 18 km long and ranging from 3.5 km down to 3 m wide, the gorge is Crete's Lilliputian Grand Canyon (and the longest canyon in Europe). It has been a national park since the 1960s. Local ecologists are becoming increasingly concerned by the numbers visiting the gorge (an average of 2,000 a day now do the walk in the summer months). Paths are being eroded, and the rare horned Cretan ibex (the kri-kri) and the golden eagles that once thrived here are departing for the less noisy hillsides of the adjacent gorges along this coast.

Walking the Gorge

The gorge is open from the 1st of May to the 31st of October (at other times of the year the rivers are high and the danger from falling rocks is too great). It is patrolled by National Forest Service staff who ensure that visitors don't come to grief, attempt to stay overnight, or enter outside the permitted hours (08.00–15.00: from 15.00 to sunset visitors are allowed to visit only the first 2 km of each end. All visitors are checked in and out).

Buses run daily to the village of **Omalos** at the northern entrance to the gorge from Iraklion (05.30: 3–4 hours), and four times daily from Chania (1 hour). The trek down the gorge takes some six hours with good shoes, and is very pretty — particularly in the spring. High Season travellers will find the walk less attractive, the numbers of trekkers turning a communion with nature into a noisy hobbit's walking party. It is best to do the walk early in the day to be sure of picking up a Sfakia ferry from **Agia Roumeli** in time for the last bus (usually 18.30).

1. Xyloskalo—Neroutsiko

[1.7 km, 45 minutes]. The gorge officially begins at Xyloskalo, at an altitude of 1200 m. The name means 'wooden staircase' after the early stairway that was built down the steep wall of the gorge. These days it has been replaced with a proper stone and pine-tree-lined path that descends steeply to the Neroutsiko spring.

2. Neroutsiko—Riza Sykias

[1 km, 20 minutes]. From Neroutsiko the path follows the bed of a small spring, descending much more gently to Riza Sykias.

3. Riza Sykias—Agios Nikolaos

[1 km, 20 minutes]. Riza Sykias is a second spring which joins the path at this point, with the gorge widening out as it approaches Agios Nikolaos.

4. Agios Nikolaos—Vryssi

[0.8 km, 15 minutes]. Agios Nikolaos is a small whitewashed chapel nestling under some large cypress trees. Site of a spring, it has had a religious function since Minoan times. The path continues under the trees to the Vryssi fountain.

5. Vryssi—Samaria

[2.9 km, 1 hour]. Crossing the river bed, the path runs past hilltops decorated with Turkish fortresses and on to the bridge that leads to Samaria, the abandoned village at the heart of the gorge. The inhabitants were forced to leave when the National Park was created. Only the churches survive intact.

6. Samaria—Perdika

[1.6 km, 20 minutes]. From Samaria the gorge passes a second abandoned village and becomes much deeper: the path runs parallel to the river bed, before arriving at the Perdika spring.

7. Perdika—Kefalovryssi

[2.3 km, 45 minutes]. From Perdika the walls of the gorge rise steeply, and for much of the time the path and river bed are indistinguishable.

8. Kefalovryssi—Christos

[1 km, 20 minutes]. At Kefalovryssi the gorge briefly opens out to reveal a spring shaded by plane trees. A little further, and the path comes to the small Church of Christ.

9. Christos—Portes

[0.6 km, 15 minutes]. The highlight of the gorge is at **Portes / Sideropontes** ('the iron gates'), where its width narrows to 3 m, while the walls rise over 300 m. Rockfalls are common in the early mornings and at nightfall — thanks to the activities of Cretan ibex and changes in rock surface temperatures.

10. Portes—Park South Entrance

[1.4 km, 30 minutes]. After the gates, the gorge quickly widens again, slowly descending to the National Park guard post.

11. Park South Entrance—Agia Roumeli

[2.4 km, 45 minutes]. From the south entrance the path runs along the right bank of the river, through a wide valley to Agia Roumeli.

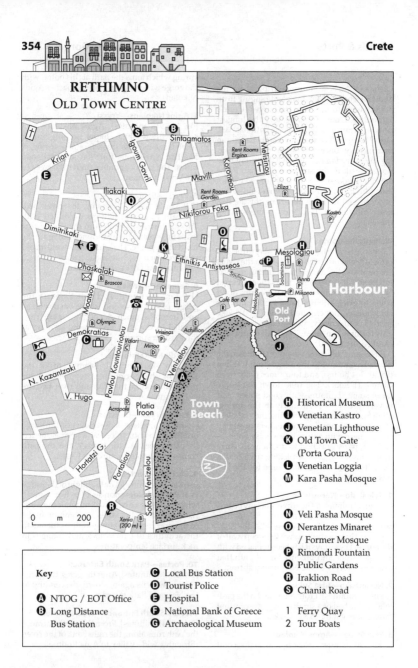

RETHIMNO
OLD TOWN CENTRE

Kriari

Igoum Gavril

Sintagmatos

Dimitrikaki

Iliakaki

Mavili

Rent Rooms
Ergina

Koroneou

Melisinou

Rent Rooms
Garden

Nikiforou Foka

Eliza

Kastro

Dhaskalaki

Moatsou

Brascos

Ethnikis Antistaseos

Mesologiou

Soutiou

Anna

Salaminos

Mikonos

Harbour

Olympic

Demokratias

Café Bar 67

Old
Port

Vrisinas

Achillion

Vurina

N. Kazantzaki

Pavlou Koutouriou

Valari

Minoa

V. Hugo

Acropole

Platia
Iroon

Town
Beach

Hortatzi G.

Pontaliou

Sofokli Venizelou

El. Venizelou

Poleologou

0　　m　　200

Xenia
(200 m)

H Historical Museum
I Venetian Kastro
J Venetian Lighthouse
K Old Town Gate
(Porta Goura)
L Venetian Loggia
M Kara Pasha Mosque

N Veli Pasha Mosque
O Nerantzes Minaret
/ Former Mosque
P Rimondi Fountain
Q Public Gardens
R Iraklion Road
S Chania Road

1 Ferry Quay
2 Tour Boats

Key

A NTOG / EOT Office
B Long Distance
Bus Station

C Local Bus Station
D Tourist Police
E Hospital
F National Bank of Greece
G Archaeological Museum

Rethimno

ΡΕΘΥΜΝΟ; pop. 20,000.

CODE ☎ 28310
TOURIST POLICE ☎ 28156
POLICE ☎ 25247
NTOG OFFICE ☎ 29148

Of the major port towns along Crete's north coast, picturesque Rethimno is the jewel in the crown. Not only can it claim to have the best preserved historical centre — German bombing in WW2 left it comparatively unscathed — packed with an interesting mix of Venetian and Ottoman buildings (the particularly rich Turkish overlay adds much to the exotic atmosphere of the town), but it is unique in having a very good town beach into the bargain.

With its very attractive enclosed harbour (complete with a very helpful tourist office on the waterfront), and the largest Venetian castle in Greece, it is not surprising that Rethimno is developing as a popular package tourist resort destination. Hotels are mushrooming up all over the place — particularly along the coast east of the town — and doing little to enhance the ugly suburbs (one of the few negative points) around the old town.

If it wasn't for the tourists the old town would offer the chance to walk back a few centuries thanks to the narrow streets lined with unspoilt buildings. Some of the Ottoman era houses have even retained their original wooden balconies, to say nothing of a couple of minarets attached to buildings that started life as Venetian churches.

In spite of its being laid out in a regular fashion it is easy to get lost in the maze of the old town (it is worth allowing for this before you start exploring); fortunately you don't have to go far in any direction before coming upon a recognizable landmark. The taverna-lined Venetian harbour in particular is a visual delight, but also the town's bane. Too small to accommodate large boats, and prone to silting up, it accounts for the town's relative obscurity in the last couple of centuries.

Ferry connections reflect this state of affairs and are scanty — consisting of boats running direct to Piraeus augmented by occasional more expensive tourist boats to Santorini.

🛏
The popularity of Rethimno leads to higher prices, so you may have to ask around, though there are rooms and pensions aplenty — most within a block of the town beach or waterfront. There is also a *Youth Hostel* (☎ 22848) at 41 Tombasi St. With some forty hotels in the town or its environs finding a bed isn't difficult. Finding a cheap bed is a bit more tricky. The best bets are the D-class *Minoa* (☎ 22508), *Kastro* (☎ 24973), *Acropole* (☎ 27470) and the E-class *Achillion* (☎ 22581). Higher up the range is the C-class *Valari* (☎ 22236) near the OTE and the B-class *Olympic* (☎ 24761) by the local bus station.

A
Camping Elisabeth (☎ 28694): a reasonable site 4 km east of the town. There is also a second site further out: *Camping Agia Galini* (☎ 91386).

👁👁
The **Venetian Kastro** is the obvious attraction in the town. Known as the **Fortezza** it was built in 1574 after repeated Barbary pirate raids. One of the best preserved Venetian castles in Greece, in its prime its walls almost held a town in themselves, but most of the interior buildings have gone now (apart from the former church that was later converted into a mosque) and you have to make do with the lovely views over the town.

Somewhat surprisingly (considering how much of the old centre has survived) the Venetian town walls have all but disappeared, the only remnant being one gate known as the **Porta Goura** (1572). Within the alleyways stands a Venetian **Loggia**. Built c. 1600, it served as a meeting place for the town's officials. Nearby flows the 17 C. **Rimondi Fountain**, a late Venetian addition to the town. The later Turkish presence offers another sightseeing option: the climb to the top of the minaret of the 18 C. **Nerandzes Mosque**, with its views over the castle and town.

Rethimno also has **Archaeological** and **Historical Museums** housing a variety of (indifferent) finds, from its Minoan origins to its later role as a haven for scholars fleeing the Turkish conquest of Constantinople.

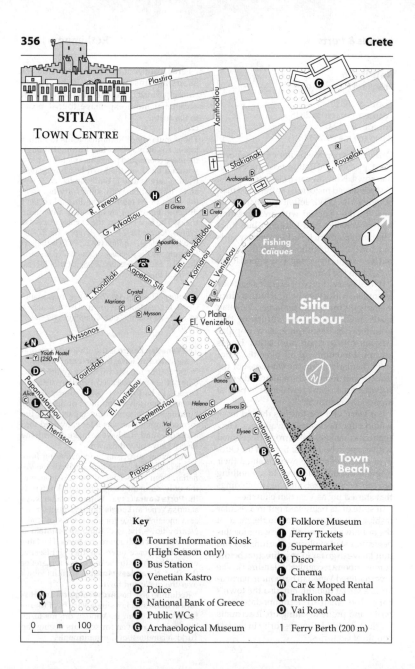

SITIA
TOWN CENTRE

Plastira

Xanthodiou

Stakianaki

Archontikon

E. Rouselaki

R. Fereou

G. Arkadiou

El Greco

Creta

Apostilos

Fishing
Caïques

Kapetan Sifi

I. Konditaki

Em. Foundalidou

V. Kamarou

El. Venizelou

**Sitia
Harbour**

Crystal

Mariana

Mysson

Denis

Platia
El. Venizelou

Myssonos

Youth Hostel
(250 m)

G. Vourlidaki

Itanos

Papanastassiou

Alice

El. Venizelou

4 Septembriou

Itanou

Helena

Flisvos

Therissou

Vai

Elysee

**Town
Beach**

Praisou

Konstantinou Karamanli

0   m   100

Key

Tourist Information Kiosk
(High Season only)

Bus Station

Venetian Kastro

Police

National Bank of Greece

Public WCs

Archaeological Museum

Folklore Museum

Ferry Tickets

Supermarket

Disco

Cinema

Car & Moped Rental

Iraklion Road

Vai Road

1   Ferry Berth (200 m)

Sitia
ΣΗΤΕΙΑ; pop. 8,000.

CODE ☎ 28430
PORT POLICE ☎ 22310
TOURIST POLICE ☎ 24200
POLICE ☎ 22266
FIRST AID ☎ 24311

The most easterly large town on Crete, scenic Sitia is the poor relation compared to the other ports along the northern coast when it comes to ferry connections, even though it is now the only one east of Iraklion with a regular ferry link at all. Set in a wide bay, the Venetian-built town (that nonetheless manages to feel more like a regular island chora, being all white houses and staircases) attracts its share of tourists in High Season, thanks in part to its lovely fishing port atmosphere and a three-day annual August wine festival (grapes and raisins are the region's principal exports).

The town, which is built like an irregular amphitheatre around the port, is also blessed with a reasonable sand beach that extends east for over a kilometre, and has a couple of days of sightseeing for those who want it. The municipal tourist information kiosk that opens every summer in the main square offers information on the sights and accommodation options.

🛏

In **Sitia** rooms are plentiful (except for the end of August Sultana Festival), with over a dozen hotels in the centre. For a reasonable bed try the B-class pension *Denis* (☎ 28356) on the waterfront. At the budget end of the range is the D-class *Archontikon* (☎ 22993). There is also a *Youth Hostel* (☎ 22693) 500 m from the town centre (towards Iraklion) at 4 Therissou Street.

👓

Thanks to a good **Archaeological Museum** (housing finds from the Minoan palace at Zakros), and a passable **Folklore Museum** in the town, there is enough to keep you occupied if you have to wait for a boat. The only building of note is the restored **Kastro** on the hill behind the town. Really a glorified fort rather than a full-blown castle, it was built in 1204 and later enlarged by the Venetians,

repelling a Barbary pirate raid in 1538 before falling to the Turks in 1651. In the absence of any significant Turkish remains (the town lay in ruins for the two centuries following its capture), popular tourist-buses also head east to the good sand beach (graced with islets offshore) at **Vai**: the beach, however, isn't the reason the tourists come, for behind the sand is the only natural **Palm Forest** in Europe. Looking like a piece of transplanted North Africa, it is now a national park.

Sitia is the north coast port for the finger of land that makes up the eastern extremity of Crete. The windmill-cluttered hinterland known as the Lasithi plain is very quiet, with poor roads: you usually have to double back to Agios Nikolaos to get to the other population centres on the south coast. Fringing the Libyan Sea, they escape the attentions of the *meltemi* wind that slams into Crete's northern coast and thus enjoy calmer seas during the summer. The only large town is at **Ierapetra**, which can be reached by regular buses from Sitia.

Ierapetra
ΙΕΡΑΠΕΤΡΑ; pop. 10,750.

CODE ☎ 28420

Built on the site of an important Minoan and later Roman town, Ierapetra (pronounced '*EE*rapetra') was very late in embracing tourism. Today the town has a small, but noisy and vibrant, tourist industry (centred heavily on the waterfront), but the main focus of economic activity still centres on market-garden agriculture. With a large fertile plain behind the town and something approaching a mild North African climate, Ierapetra is well placed and takes every advantage of its location. So much so, that a good number of the visitors are seeking casual work in the industry. The same climatic conditions make it a poor choice of destination in July and August as it can get insufferably hot.

Sadly, the town itself doesn't live up to its history. The problem is finding any, for apart from a very small old town that dates from the years of Ottoman rule, the rest of the place is post-1960 concrete. The pluses are a good (grey) sand town beach and — for

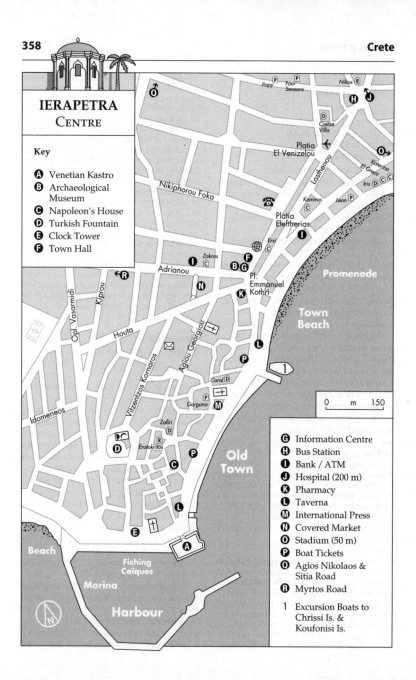

IERAPETRA
CENTRE

Key

Ⓐ Venetian Kastro
Ⓑ Archaeological Museum
Ⓒ Napoleon's House
Ⓓ Turkish Fountain
Ⓔ Clock Tower
Ⓕ Town Hall

Ⓖ Information Centre
Ⓗ Bus Station
Ⓘ Bank / ATM
Ⓙ Hospital (200 m)
Ⓚ Pharmacy
Ⓛ Taverna
Ⓜ International Press
Ⓝ Covered Market
Ⓞ Stadium (50 m)
Ⓟ Boat Tickets
Ⓠ Agios Nikolaos & Sitia Road
Ⓡ Myrtos Road

1 Excursion Boats to Chrissi Is. & Koufonisi Is.

Popy
Four Seasons
Nikos Ⓡ
Ⓗ Ⓙ
Cretan Villa
Platia El Venizelou
Lasthenou
Ⓞ
Katerina
El Greco Ⓒ Ⓒ
Iris Ⓓ Ⓒ
Nikiphorou Foka
Kamiros Ⓒ
Leon Ⓟ
Ⓘ
Platia Eleftherias
Ⓘ Zakros Ⓒ
Ⓑ Ⓖ
Ersi Ⓒ
Ⓕ
Adrianou
Pl. Emmanuel Kothri
Promenade
Ⓝ
Ⓚ
Town Beach
Ⓡ
Kiprou
Opl. Vasarmidi
Houta
Ⓛ
Ⓟ
1
Idomeneos
Vitzenizos Kornaros
Agiou Georgiou
Coral Ⓓ
Ⓟ
Gargona Ⓜ
0 m 150
Zafiri Ⓓ
Ⓓ
Erotokritos Ⓡ
Ⓒ
Ⓟ
Old Town
Beach
Ⓔ
Ⓛ
Ⓐ
Fishing Caïques
Marina
N
Harbour

island hoppers — regular caïques that run to **Chrissi** island during the summer months (see below).

📫

Ierapetra has a good amount of budget accommodation: notably, the D-class *Cretan Villa* (☎ 28522) near the bus station, the beach front D-class *Iris* (☎ 23136) and C-class *El Greco* (☎ 28471). In the centre of town are the noisier D-class *Coral* (☎ 22848) and the pension *Gorgona* (☎ 23935).

👓

There is nothing to be seen of the Minoan and Roman towns (the last remaining major building, a bathhouse, was lost two hundred years ago). The few surviving fragments are housed in a one-room **Archaeological Museum**. The other sightseeing attractions include a small **Venetian Kastro**, rebuilt in 1626 after an earthquake. The Old Town also boasts a Venetian town house where **Napoleon** stayed while returning to France from Egypt following the Battle of the Nile.

⚓ Crete: Minor Islands

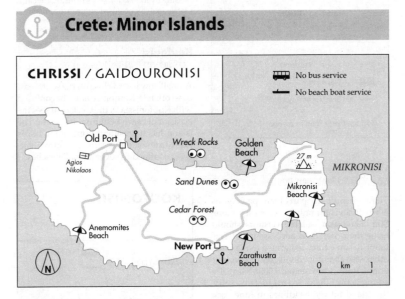

Chrissi
ΧΡΥΣΗ; 6 km²; pop. 0.

Once known as Gaidouronisi ('donkey island'), the small island of Chrissi is a nature reserve (now sans donkeys) and beach island sitting in the Libyan Sea 9 km to the south of the Cretan town of Ierapetra. Daily excursion boats (10.30 & 12.30) run from the town in High Season.

Blessed with an intriguing mix of good clean sandy beaches, backed by sand dunes and a small forest of cedar trees, Chrissi is the nearest thing in Greece to a plausible desert island. Usually uninhabited, it has a couple of tavernas (located at the new harbour) that open during the tourist season and freelance camping has been tolerated in the past. Chrissi is traversed via a dirt track that links the new harbour with its predecessor (complete with a nearby chapel and lighthouse) to the north-west and the best of the beaches — Golden Beach — to the north-east.

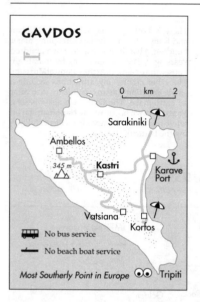

GAVDOS

0   km   2

Sarakiniki

Ambellos

345 m   **Kastri**

Karave Port

Vatsiana

Korfos

No bus service

No beach boat service

Most Southerly Point in Europe   Tripiti

Gavdos

ΓΑΥΔΟΣ; 34 km²; pop. 50.

The most southerly part of Europe, Gavdos is worth a visit if only for curiosity value. Sun-baked and isolated (visitors should bring their own food and essentials), it is home to some forty fishermen living on in otherwise abandoned villages (the former population once exceeded 8,000). Normally sitting in the Libyan Sea in quiet obscurity, the island hit the headlines in June 1996 when Turkey — in the wake of the argument over the sovereignty of Imia (see p. 376) — claimed Gavdos was 'disputed territory', a delicious piece of nonsense as Turkey is hundreds of kilometres away.

Despite its tiny population Gavdos has a post office/OTE, a doctor and — bizarrely — a policeman, all housed in the capital of Kastri. The island has quiet beaches at Korfos (at the mouth of a small fertile valley) and Sarakiniki: the only other bathers are likely to be the doctor and the policeman.

A few rooms are available in both Karave and Kastri (pre-booking is possible via travel agents in Paleochora). Freelance camping is also tolerated in season.

The nearest Greece has to a ghost-town island, Gavdos lacks sights beyond an air of wild abandon. However, it does offer some interesting walks. Those trekking to the end of Europe at Tripiti will, however, be able to enjoy the incongruous sight of oil tankers passing by like spook ships from another age. Occasional caïques also venture to uninhabited **Gavdopoula** to the north-east.

Koufonisi

ΚΟΥΦΟΝΗΣΙ; 11 km²; pop. 0.

A small, low island close off the south-east coast of Crete, Koufonisi (not to be confused with Koufonissia in the Cyclades) sees the occasional beach boat from Ierapetra. The island has no resident population, but is host to a few summer farmers. Tourist interest is confined to several small beaches.

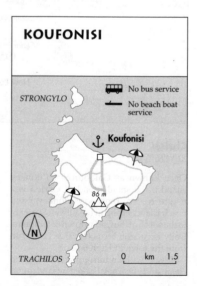

KOUFONISI

STRONGYLO

No bus service

No beach boat service

Koufonisi

86 m

TRACHILOS

0   km   1.5

Spinalonga
ΣΠΙΝΑΛΟΝΓΑ; 1 km²; pop. 0.

Spinalonga is a small islet on the north-east coast of Crete. The island is dominated by a well-preserved Venetian fortress that skirts the entire coastline. It is now billed by excursion boat operators at Agios Nikolaos as the 'island of the living dead' thanks to its history as a leper colony between 1903–55.

It is this role that takes centre stage today. For although Spinalonga was supposedly a hospital, in reality it was a dumping ground, with lepers of all ages (including children) deliberately marooned here, living in the former Turkish village built within the fortress's massive curtain walls. Guided tours (usually included in the tour boat price) are standard, as all the buildings are now derelict and most in a ruinous state of repair. Tours take in the circuit path that runs inside the enceinte, visiting all the major landmarks — these include the leper's cemetery and the battlements.

As an excursion destination Spinalonga offers good value and an interesting experience, but there is no escaping the fact that the island is a melancholy place: this isn't a daytrip for those who want to party.

☻

The Venetian fortress is so substantial that it has obliterated any evidence of earlier constructions. Built in 1579, it achieved fame across Europe as a bastion of heroic resistance for holding out against Turkish attack for thirty years after the rest of Crete had succumbed to Ottoman rule (it finally fell in 1715). Thereafter it housed a Turkish garrison and their families. By 1898, when Crete effectively joined modern Greece, the Turkish population was over 3,000. Most left, but a good number refused to leave their homes. In 1903 the Greek government decided to turn Spinalonga into a leper colony, and for some reason the remaining Turkish inhabitants opted to leave — very quickly.

The new inhabitants didn't get the same opportunities. Attempts at escape by lepers were discouraged by removing all the baths from the island (after several were used as makeshift boats), while in WW2 four escaping lepers were shot by German troops.

Although many of the lepers did their best to make the most of life on the island, their existence was very hard. All food and water had to be brought in, and supplies were very irregular. Medical necessities were also often lacking (hence the cheery tales of limb amputations without anaesthetics).

The worst horror story concerns an 18-year-old girl who was dumped on the island after being diagnosed with leprosy of the throat. Shortly after arriving she choked on an apple. The following day her body was interred in the leper cemetery. As is usual in Greece, the grave was opened four years later (by which time all soft matter has rotted away) so that the bones could be moved and the grave reused. To the horror of those who removed the stone slab covering the grave, the girl's bones were not in their laid-out position, and it was clear from their location that she must have awoken from a comatose state only to find herself entombed alive. The last lonely hours of this girl's terrible life don't bear thinking about, but in a way, do sum up the tragedy of Spinalonga.

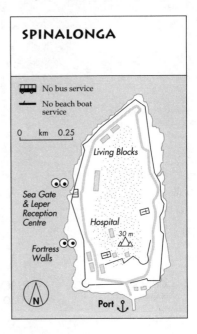

SPINALONGA

🚌 No bus service

⛱ No beach boat service

0   km   0.25

Living Blocks

Sea Gate & Leper Reception Centre

Hospital

30 m

Fortress Walls

Ⓝ

Port ⚓

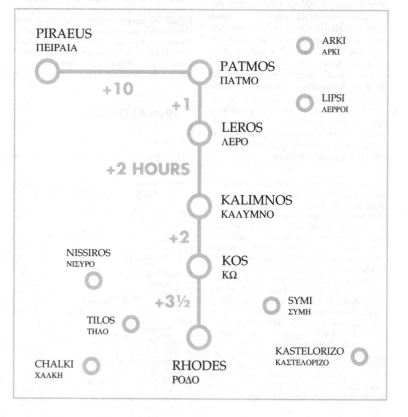

7
DODECANESE LINES

**CHALKI · KALIMNOS · KARPATHOS · KOS · LEROS
LIPSI · NISSIROS · PATMOS · RHODES · SYMI · TILOS**

PIRAEUS
ΠΕΙΡΑΙΑ

ARKI
ΑΡΚΙ

PATMOS
ΠΑΤΜΟ

+10

+1

LIPSI
ΛΕΙΨΟΙ

LEROS
ΛΕΡΟ

+2 HOURS

KALIMNOS
ΚΑΛΥΜΝΟ

NISSIROS
ΝΙΣΥΡΟ

+2

KOS
ΚΩ

+3½

SYMI
ΣΥΜΗ

TILOS
ΤΗΛΟ

KASTELORIZO
ΚΑΣΤΕΛΟΡΙΖΟ

CHALKI
ΧΑΛΚΗ

RHODES
ΡΟΔΟ

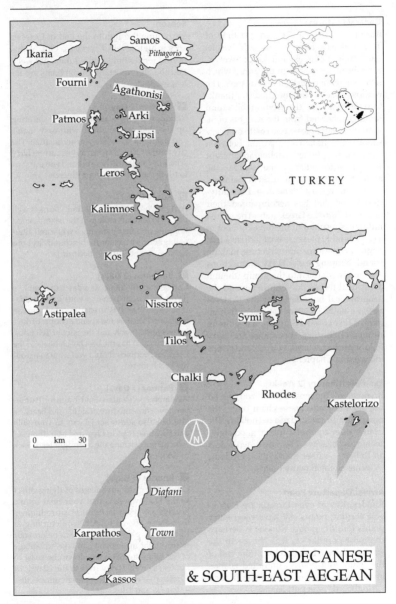

Ikaria

Samos
Pithagorio

Fourni

Agathonisi

Patmos

Arki

Lipsi

Leros

TURKEY

Kalimnos

Kos

Astipalea

Nissiros

Symi

Tilos

Chalki

Rhodes

Kastelorizo

0 km 30

N

Diafani

Karpathos

Town

Kassos

DODECANESE
& SOUTH-EAST AEGEAN

General Features

Running down the Aegean coastline of Turkey, the Dodecanese chain derives its name from the Greek 'dodeka' or 'twelve', after the major islands in the group which revolted against Turkish rule in 1908. The islands possess a unique character thanks to a combination of the strong architectural heritage inherited from the Knights of St. John (who left at least one castle on every island), the Italian occupation between 1913 and 1943 (when a deliberate attempt was made to Italianize the islands), the allure of day trips to the Turkish mainland (visible from most islands), and the duty-free status that has accompanied their late entry into the Greek state. The tourist influx has resulted in the development of a considerable pleasure boat industry that augments the ferry infrastructure, making island hopping easy. Ferry connections are mostly confined to the group (though occasional ferries do venture beyond the geographical boundaries of the Dodecanese). Finally, isolated Astipalea, though part of this post-1908 group, has more in common in history, appearance and ferry links with the Eastern Cyclades, and is thus included in Chapter 5.

Example Itinerary [2 Weeks]

If you aren't the most adventurous island hopper the Dodecanese chain offers the prospect of an easy and relaxed holiday. The islands offer a popular mix of good sight-seeing and beaches. The only down-side is an Italian — rather than typical Cycladic — atmosphere in many towns.

Arrival/Departure Point

Rhodes, Kos or even Piraeus are reasonable starting points. All have good entry points into the group. Rhodes is perhaps the most popular (so it is chosen in the example here); though lying at the end of the chain with poorly connected islands immediately north of it, it is an indifferent springboard/base port island.

Season

Early June through to the end of October sees a high level of services. Out of this period ferries only run 3–4 days per week and the all-important tourist boats are far less evident.

■ Rhodes [2 Days]

Rhodes is a good starting point if venturing up the Dodecanese chain, with easy flights and plenty to see while you acclimatize. The city tourist office also distributes current ferry schedules and with these in hand you can start to fill in the details of your itinerary.

■ Kos [4 Days]

Arriving on Kos you will find yourself well placed to take advantage of the island's good hopping options by staying a while and alternating between days on the beach and day hops to Nissiros and Turkey (Bodrum).

■ Kalimnos [2 Days]

Can be happily 'done' as a day trip from Kos if you don't want to change your accommodation. Otherwise, it is an easy hop and you can head on to Mirities and spend a couple of days between the beach and the islet of Telendos. Kalimnos also has the best beach boats to the island of Pserimos should you want to try out the beach there.

■ Patmos [3 Days]

A suitably spectacular island to aim for, Patmos has a nice lazy mixture of sights and beaches. You can also add other islands to your tally and take boat trips to Lipsi and Marathonisi/Arki before catching the overnight ferry back to Rhodes.

■ Rhodes [3 Days]

One of the great advantages of flying direct to the Dodecanese is that your final couple of days are spent in far nicer surroundings than those offered by Athens. Returning to Rhodes with plenty of time to spare before your return flight means you can take advantage of the many tourist boats down the coast to Lindos, as well as day trips to the islands of Symi and — with a little more circumspection — Chalki and Tilos.

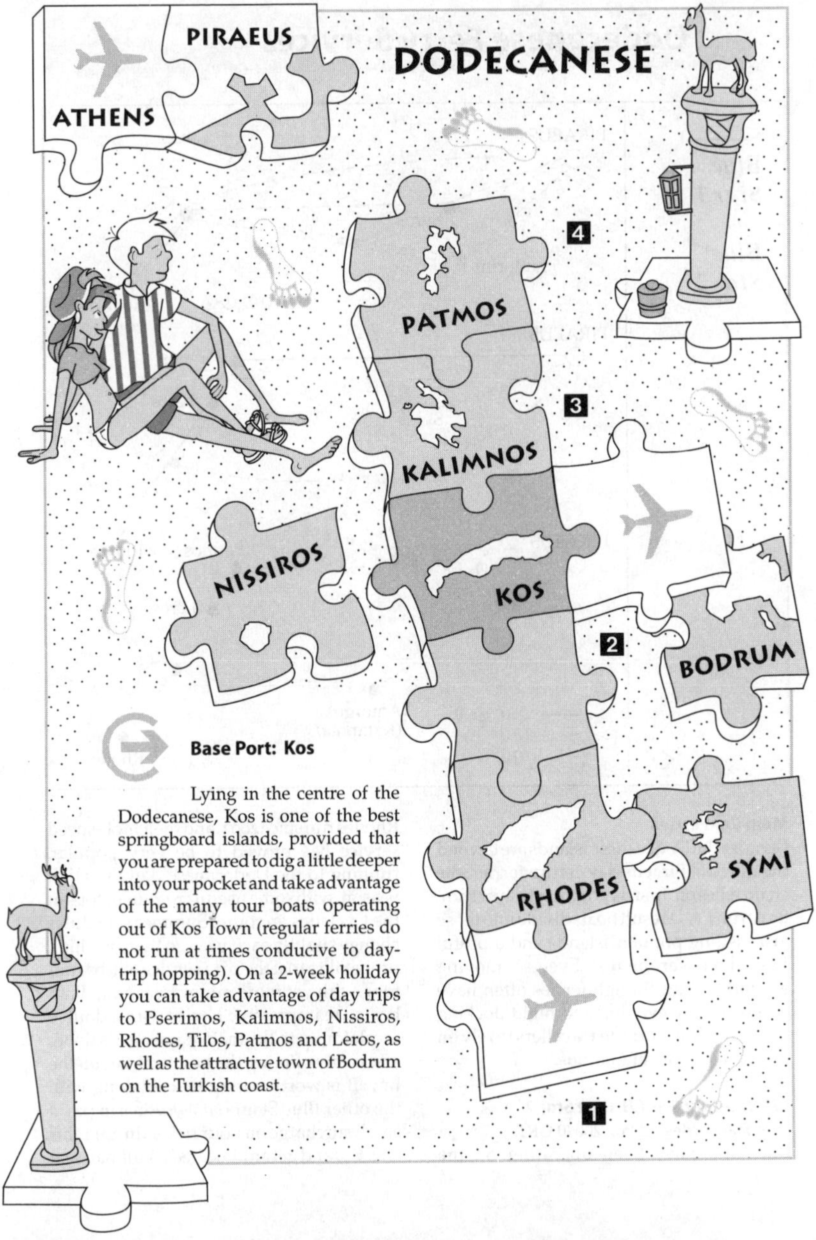

DODECANESE

ATHENS PIRAEUS

PATMOS **4**

KALIMNOS **3**

NISSIROS

KOS

2 BODRUM

RHODES SYMI

Base Port: Kos

Lying in the centre of the Dodecanese, Kos is one of the best springboard islands, provided that you are prepared to dig a little deeper into your pocket and take advantage of the many tour boats operating out of Kos Town (regular ferries do not run at times conducive to day-trip hopping). On a 2-week holiday you can take advantage of day trips to Pserimos, Kalimnos, Nissiros, Rhodes, Tilos, Patmos and Leros, as well as the attractive town of Bodrum on the Turkish coast.

1

Dodecanese Ferry Services

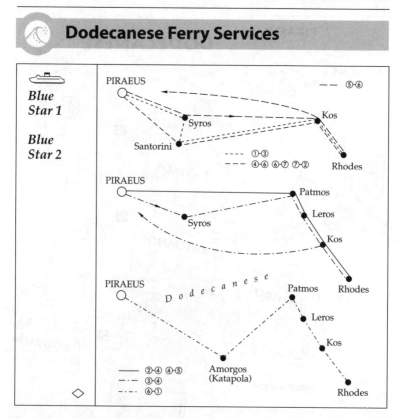

Blue Star 1

Blue Star 2

Main Car Ferries

Because the Dodecanese islands are beyond the range of Piraeus day-return ferries, the chain relies on 'first day out, next day return' ferry runs. As a result boats divide into those just visiting popular islands and a pitiful few who cover the rest. Even so, moving around is easy, though ferries often have awkward late evening and night docking times, forcing morning travellers to rely on tourist boats or catamarans.

C/F *Blue Star 1* – C/F *Blue Star 2*
Blue Star Ferries; 2000; 20000 GRT.
Blue Star have been operating on the

Rhodes run since 2003, and their high-speed service has proved to be very popular, running to the Dodecanese daily in High Season, with some useful cross-line stops in the Cyclades en route. Summer schedules change slightly each year, so there is a high probability that the 2012 service will be running with yet more minor tweaking. Both boats are impressive ferries with a double escalator up to the main passenger saloon, and easily offering the best facilities on the line. It is worth noting that — along with the other Blue Star boats — you can pay a small surcharge on your ticket (in 2011 this was €3) and get an allocated a Pullman seat

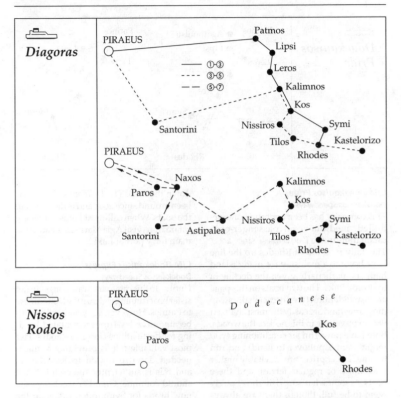

C/F *Diagoras*
Blue Star Ferries; 1990; 6939 GRT.

Formerly operated by the defunct D.A.N.E Lines, this reasonably modern ferry now runs in Blue Star colours. Initially she contributed some welcome extra top-end capacity on the route, but with the demise of other ferry operators (notably G.A. Ferries) she has taken on the role of providing the lifeline links between the smaller islands and Piraeus. This ferry is a nice boat and is certainly better than any other 'lifeline'

number. This is worth doing on overnight trips, though there will be a fair chance that you will have to argue another passenger out of your seat when you get on board.

vessel. Try to board early if you can, as the better seating tends to fill up quickly. If she follows the normal pattern of year-on-year scheduling by Blue Star, she is likely to operate much the same timetable in 2012.

C/F *Nissos Rodos*
Hellenic Seaways / HFD; 1987; 13730 GRT.

A new arrival in 2010, this boat vanished last year. Although a comparatively unimpressive large ferry she was missed in 2011 and hopefully will be back. Running thrice weekly out of Piraeus to Paros, Kos and Rhodes, she was an attraction for those seeking to travel between the Dodecanese and Paros, as she offered the only link between the two chains.

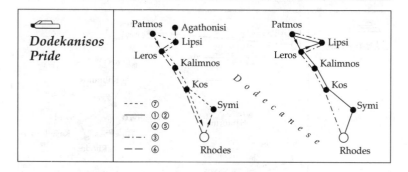

C/M *Dodekanisos Pride*
Dodekanisos Speedways

This company has been operating orange-hulled, medium-sized passenger-only catamarans in the Dodecanese since 2000. The daily runs out of Rhodes up the line have become a mainstay for many island hoppers, particuarly given the decline in hydrofoil links. The two boats on this page are near indentical (they occasionally swap itineraries) and are easily the most civilized way of travelling in this neck of the woods. Both have powerful air conditioning (you might want a pullover to hand) and run to time. Ticket prices are inevitably higher than those of regular ferries, and these boats — somewhat surprisingly — rarely seem to be full, though there are always plenty of passengers waiting to board (most are making quick hops to the next island down the line). The *Dodekanisos Pride* has been around since 2005 and is the newer of the boats. When calling at Leros both these catamarans visit Agia Marina instead of the main ferry port at Lakki.

C/M *Dodekanisos Express*
Dodekanisos Speedways

Until 2010 this catamaran ran alongside her sister boat running right up the Dodecanese to Patmos. However, last year her itinerary became more day-tripper orientated, heading for destinations closer to Rhodes. Her most valuable role is providing a much-needed day-trip option to Kastelorizo, and this is sufficiently successful that it should continue. On other weekdays she now heads for Symi (often calling at the monastery of Panormitis in addition to Gialos port) or to Datça in Turkey.

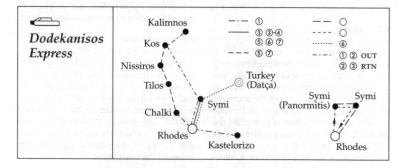

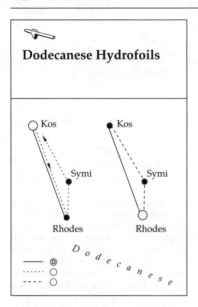

Dodecanese Hydrofoils

Dodecanese Hydrofoils

Hydrofoils have been an important option in the past when island hopping in the Dodecanese, if only because they don't require night travel (a depressing feature of many ferry departure times). However, their numbers are now dimishing and the remaing craft operating are very tourist-orientated. There are considerable fluctuations in levels of activity, with little happening

outside the June to September period. It is very much a case of looking to see what is running when you arrive. The links that you can confidently expect to find are daily Kos—Rhodes and Rhodes—Kos day-tripper runs (note: they often fill up in High Season, so it is best to buy tickets at least 24 hours before you want to travel). Other destinations are now less regularly served. It is also worth noting that hydrofoils can use different harbours or quays (Rhodes and Kos) or even ports (at Leros they call at Agia Marina) to those used by ferries, and timetables don't indicate this fact.

C/F *Nissos Kalimnos*
A. N. E. Kalimnos Sea Lines; 1988; 754 GRT.
This Greek-built vessel operates out of Kalimnos and provides an invaluable service to adjacent islands. Run by a one-boat company, she was once known for visiting most islands north of Rhodes, but she now confines her itinerary to Astipalea and sorties up to Samos. For the most part reliable, this ferry broke down in July 1992, leaving her passengers with nought to do but admire the view while listening to the soporific 'lip-lip' of the sea kissing the ship's sides. The *Nissos Kalimnos* looks set to continue running her 'lifeline' service into the future. Her somewhat quirky interior has been considerably smartened up of late, though some design oversights (such as a decent staircase between car deck and passenger saloon) remain.

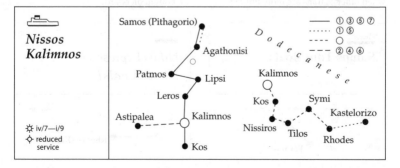

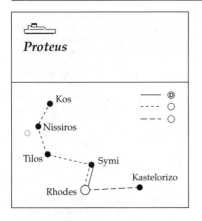

C/F *Proteus*
Local; 1973; 1160 GRT.

This small elderly ferry appeared a couple of years ago and has been chugging around out of Rhodes ever since. Her main claim for attention is that she does offer an inexpensive way of getting to the smaller islands north of Rhodes. A boat to take, but not necessarily one to enjoy.

Samos Tour Boats
The large amount of package tourists on the south coast of Samos has generated a number of small tour-boats. As a result, it is possible to island hop at least four days a week if you don't mind paying higher fares. They are particularly useful in Low Season when other options are more limited.

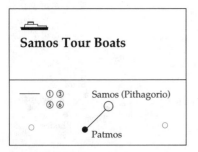

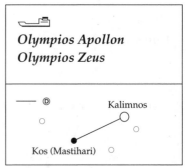

C/F *Olympios Apollon*
C/F *Olympios Zeus*
Two landing-craft ferries operate out of Kalimnos to the resort of Mastihari on Kos. Running three times daily, they exist in part to serve charter holidaymakers running to and from the airport on Kos. At the same time, these boats also provide a useful evening standby for any day-trippers who have missed their tour boat and are marooned on Kalimnos or Kos.

T/B *Nikos Express* – T/B *Nissos Chalki*
Two caïques turned tour boats provide Chalki with its main link with the wider world, running daily to Rhodes (where they connect with the daily bus service to and from Rhodes Town). The *Nikos Express* is the better of the two, though both are apt to roll for the full 90-minute crossing. Tickets are bought on board.

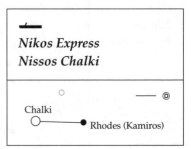

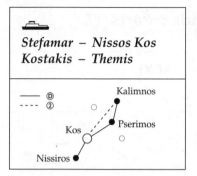

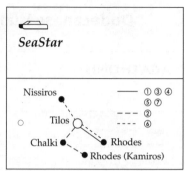

Dodecanese Tour / Island Boats

The inconvenient departure times of many ferries in the Dodecanese mean that most island hoppers resort to at least one of the tourist craft shown on this page. Although they cost a bit more, the convenience value makes them worth it, and they partly exist to provide one-way journeys for those not enamoured with day-tripping.

Kos is the main base for tour boats, with two large and comfortable vessels — the *Stefamar* and the *Nissos Kos* — augmented by smaller boats. They swap destinations several times a week, but in practice combine to run a daily service to Nissiros, Kalimnos and Pserimos; a quick wander around the town's travel agents or along the waterfront will enable you to find out which one you want. Tickets are sold on the quayside prior to departure as well as at travel agents. You can also pick these

vessels up on their return runs, if they have spare capacity (when tickets are sold on board). The same is true of the smaller boats operating out of Patmos to Lipsi, and the larger Rhodes—Symi boats.

One of the most useful is the small car-ferry *Symi I* (the former *Eftichia*). Worth looking out for as she runs an early morning Symi—Rhodes service, she returns to Symi filled with tourists. The catamaran *Symi II* runs alongside. As a means of getting to Symi in time to find accommodation she has been invaluable, but of late the operators haven't been keen on one-way backpackers; as a result you might have to buy a return ticket to use her.

Tilos is also now in on the 'get tourists to visit our island by having our own daily boat link to Rhodes' act, with its own cata-maran—the *SeaStar*—which now provides the main Rhodes link to the island.

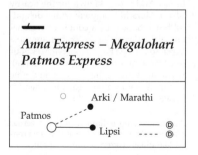

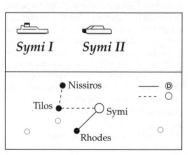

⚓ Dodecanese Islands & Ports

AGATHONISI

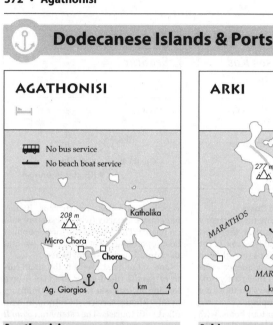

🚌 No bus service
⛵ No beach boat service

208 m
⛰

Micro Chora
Chora
Katholika

Ag. Giorgios ⚓   0   km   4

ARKI

🚌 No bus service

277 m
⛰

⛵ No beach boat service

Arki ⚓

MARATHOS

MARATHI

0   km   2

Agathonisi
ΑΓΑΘΟΝΗΣΙ; 13 km²; pop. 110.

CODE ☎ 22470
PORT / REGULAR POLICE ☎ 23770

Poorly connected Agathonisi is home to a small fishing community, six islets (all uninhabited), and a ferry quay. An uninspiring hilly island covered with thorn bushes, it remains the preserve of the odd northern European grimly determined to get away from it *all*. The best reason to visit is the sense of elation that comes on leaving it; you can guarantee that you will return from your holiday feeling you have really achieved something. Unfortunately, the sum of the parts is considerably less than the whole. The two hamlets aren't worth spending three days on the island for, and the only activity on offer is walking the donkey path to an abandoned village at Katholika.

🛏

Restricted to slowly growing number of beds at the port.

Arki
ΑΡΚΟΙ; 7 km²; pop. 50.

CODE ☎ 22470

Consisting of scrub-covered dune-hills unrelieved by anything of interest, Arki is not really on the tourist map. In the past this has been partly the result of the lack of a ferry quay, but EU funding has now sorted this problem out, and Arki should attract more get-away-from-it-all types in future. In fact Arki is best known for the nearby islet of **Marathi** (complete with a delightful beach backed by a couple of seasonal tavernas): this is the destination for most 'Arki' advertised Patmos boats (check your exact destination if taking one of these). If you are heading here you should note that there is no regular beach-boat service between Arki and Marathi.

🛏

Accommodation is limited to two tavernas offering rooms at the port. One of the tavernas on Marathi also offers rooms in summer.

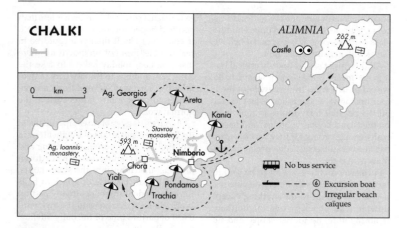

CHALKI

ALIMNIA

Castle

0   km   3

Ag. Georgios

Areta

Kania

Stavrou monastery

593 m

Ag. Ioannis monastery

Nimborio

Chora

Yiali

Pondamos

Trachia

No bus service

⑥ Excursion boat

○ Irregular beach caïques

Chalki

ΧΑΛΚΗ; 28 km²; pop. 300.

CODE ☎ 22410
PORT POLICE ☎ 45220
POLICE ☎ 45213
FIRST AID ☎ 45206

If you are seeking out that elusive Greek island that just isn't like any other Greek island then Chalki (pronounced 'Hal-key', and often transcribed as Khalki, or Halki) should be pretty high up your hit list. A small, barren, undistinguished island located just west of Rhodes, Chalki is little more than a bone-dry rock (the island takes its name from the bronze that was once mined here). Indeed, Chalki has no fresh water supply, and as a result, all produce and fresh water is tankered in from Rhodes twice a week. To help conserve stocks, tap water is heavily adulterated with sea water: drink from a tap on Chalki and you'll end up thirstier than before you started.

On top of this, a touch of early 1900s sponge-blight and a failed 1980s attempt to turn the island into a summer UNESCO youth conference centre, and circumstances were dire enough to ensure that most of the islanders (who formerly eked out a living via sponge fishing) opted to cut

their losses and move to Florida, leaving the way open for a couple of enterprising small tour operators to move in and save the day. Over the years they have contrived to make the island something pretty special: for the truth is that Chalki is really an up-market tourist resort in the middle of nowhere masquerading as an unspoilt Greek island.

At first sight everything seems pretty normal, for the island has only one settlement of note in the form of a typically picturesque, semi-dilapidated port town backed by neglected hinterland, but when you look closer it is clear that the port of **Nimborio** is by no means a typical Greek island town despite initial appearances. A trail of red tiled Venetian (or if you prefer Symi or neo-classical) style mansion houses set around a horseshoe-shaped bay, and with a skyline topped by three ruined windmills, it is quite attractive, but when you start walking the streets it quickly becomes clear that many of the properties have been converted into holiday villas.

Add to the above the diminishing number of houses still in ruins and it is doubtful if more than a third of the houses are actually occupied by islanders. This is not to say that Chalki is all about tourism, for there is a small nucleus of genuine town life adding colour to the several hundred upper-middle class Brits playing at being make-believe Greek villagers for a fortnight.

All this might sound unduly critical but it is not meant to be so: to be fair, Chalki would be in serious trouble without these tour operators, as the island is just too far off the popular ferry routes to rank high on the island hopper's hit list, and hasn't really enough going for it by way of either beaches or sightseeing to have more appeal in its own right.

Furthermore, there is a lot to be said in favour of Chalki as a holiday destination if you don't want to do anything except unwind with a book for a fortnight (there is no nightlife, no tourist shops, and no bank), or are blessed with children able to entertain themselves and want a quiet holiday where you can let them roam the streets at will without worrying about their safety (there are no watersports, and no cars or mopeds as there is nowhere to go).

Of course, as any experienced island hopper can tell you, the problem is that this just isn't normal for a Greek island. The Greek islands never were like this and none of the others are: Chalki is a glorious fake — a sort of Greek island variation on Agatha Christie's *Bertram's Hotel* (but without the excitement of having Miss Marple and an organizing crime syndicate living in). Even the island's main beach — a 15-minute walk away from the town at **Pondamos** — is now artificial (courtesy of some imported sand); the original was swept away in a bad winter storm in 1995. Worse still, the absence of a 'normal' mix of tourists contributes to a rather odd atmosphere: painted in tour brochures as the ultimate unspoilt island, in an odd sort of way Chalki ends up feeling more spoilt than many more heavily touristed islands. It is a place you will either love or hate, and this can be bad news.

The flip side to escapist islands is that they can be difficult to escape from. Most islands offer a choice of alternatives within easy reach if you find your own is less than you had hoped for: sadly, Chalki doesn't. If you don't like it then you could be in real trouble: it is not unknown for more disenchanted holidaymakers to take the daily boat and bus to Rhodes City (a two-hour trip each way) several times a week simply to enjoy a few hours back in the normal world.

Of course it is possible to escape on Chalki itself: walkers not afraid of rougher terrain will find the island offers something and the waterfront is enlivened by half a dozen tavernas that hum into the small hours. This is in part because of a lack of beds for independent travellers (many end up beating a hasty retreat) and the awkward 05.30 departure time of the daily 'lifeline' boat to Rhodes.

🛏
Unless you are travelling well out of season then you should phone ahead and book a room. The options are limited to the small *Captain's House* (☎ 45201), the B-class pension *Kleanthi* (☎ 45334), the *Argyrenia* (☎ 45205), and the C-class hotel *Manos* (☎ 45295). None have distinguishing signs on display. Villas run by independent tour operators are pre-booked well in advance but several have agents on the waterfront who will be able to advise if they have any spare rooms.

👓
Nimborio (alias Emborio) can claim to have one notable sight in the form of the tallest campanile in the Dodecanese: it dominates the town in addition to adding plenty of photogenic character. The only 'sightseeing' destination on Chalki is the former **Chora**, topped with a chapel-filled castle built by the Knights of St. John and complete with a derelict monastery nearby. Set safely inland, it is now all but abandoned, and sees almost as few tourists as it did pirates: faced with the choice between a very steep walk from the port (the road rises 300 m in 2 km) and caïques heading for tiny scraps of beaches around the island, most opt for the latter.

The main sightseeing excursion is also a caïque-ride away on the adjacent island of **Alimnia**. Blessed with some excellent beaches, an abandoned village, and a castle straddling a ridge on the south-eastern side, the island has more going for it than Chalki.

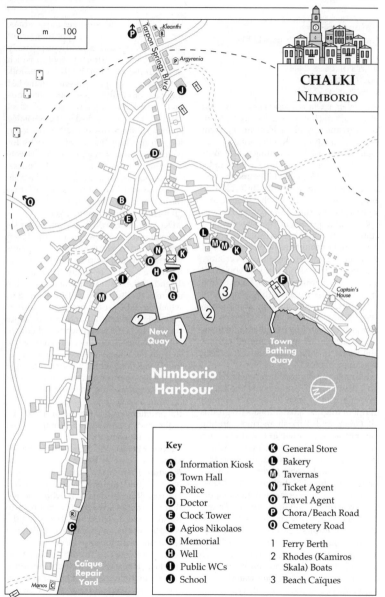

CHALKI
NIMBORIO

Key

Ⓐ Information Kiosk
Ⓑ Town Hall
Ⓒ Police
Ⓓ Doctor
Ⓔ Clock Tower
Ⓕ Agios Nikolaos
Ⓖ Memorial
Ⓗ Well
Ⓘ Public WCs
Ⓙ School

Ⓚ General Store
Ⓛ Bakery
Ⓜ Tavernas
Ⓝ Ticket Agent
Ⓞ Travel Agent
Ⓟ Chora/Beach Road
Ⓠ Cemetery Road

1 Ferry Berth
2 Rhodes (Kamiros Skala) Boats
3 Beach Caïques

Kalimnos
ΚΑΛΥΜΝΟΣ; 111 km²; pop. 14,500.

CODE ☎ 22430
PORT POLICE ☎ 24444
POLICE ☎ 22100
HOSPITAL ☎ 28851

A number of Dodecanese islands have laid claim to being the sponge-fishing centre of the Aegean — Symi not least among them — but relatively quiet Kalimnos has a better claim than most. Yet to embrace mass tourism, Kalimnos is a medium-sized chunky island north of Kos that hides understated attractions behind superficially forbidding mountains and one of the largest and most dour of 19 c. Greek island towns (population 11,000) in the Aegean. First impressions are, however, misleading, for between the mountains lie dark pockets of verdant vegetation, and there is certainly enough on the island to see if you don't mind poking around in dark holes to find it. In fact, holes are something of an island speciality. Not only are they abundant in the island's sponges, but Kalimnos has three caves visited by irregular excursions, and a whole lot more scattered around the island in which you can risk getting irrecoverably lost.

Kalimnos hit the headlines in 1996 thanks to a dispute with Turkey over the neighbouring islet of Imia. Used by Kalimnot farmers to graze goats, Imia saw groups of Greek and Turkish marines landing on the island in order to tear down each other's flags and raise their own. Add to this a couple of gunboats, and the incident threatened to become a very nasty affair until mediating US diplomats negotiated a joint stand-off. Fortunately this dispute has gone off the boil in the years since.

Gunboats notwithstanding, ferries call at the capital, **Pothia** (also known as **Kalimnos Town**), which fills the floor of a sheltered bay on the mountainous south coast. Also the object of daily excursion boats from Kos Town, the Italianesque waterfront is arguably one of the best of its type in the

Dodecanese. Lined with trees and tavernas, it manages to offset the unappealing size of the town that sprawls behind it surprisingly well, offering an attractive spot in which to watch the world go by. The townsfolk have made a conspicuous effort in the last few years to enliven the waterfront area and there is now a good scatter of street cafés and tavernas, backed by the inevitable sponge shops. Sadly, the rest of the town has too much of the world going by for comfort: the locals treat the narrow streets as if they were a motorbike rally course, and this makes exploration uncomfortable to say the least. The only consolation is that the relative lack of sights means that Pothia offers little temptation to linger.

Day trippers from Kos aside, most tourists seem to spend a day in the capital and then rapidly head on over the hills to the expanding resort/beach strip running along the north-west coast, opposite the island of Telendos (the big draw hereabouts). At the centre of the strip is the village of **Mirities**, which has little to offer besides an indifferent white-pebble beach and regular caïque services to Leros and Telendos (there are better beaches along the coast to the south). In truth the village is more of a hilly, tree-lined road along which has grown a fringe of hotels, tavernas and tourist shops. In many ways the setting is quite attractive: it is certainly a vast improvement on Pothia, but the problem again is the motorbike traffic — the shady pine-tree idyll is compromised too often for comfort.

From Mirities the hotel strip dribbles along the coast to become the resort of **Masouri**. There isn't a clear point at which one ends and the other begins, but if you are travelling by bus it is worth noting that the route used takes the hill road to Masouri and then doubles back along the coast to Mirities. The small beach village of Kantouni, with its large incomplete hotel (only the top two of five floors have been finished), is also visited by the Mirities bus.

Buses on Kalimnos are a law unto themselves: they tend to be of the shortened

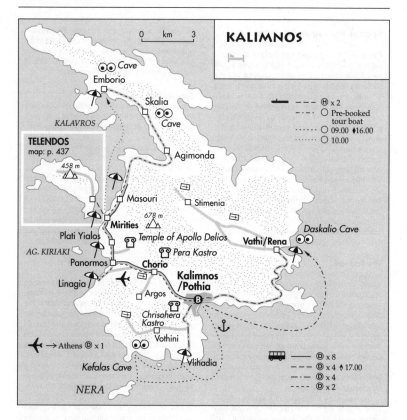

KALIMNOS

0   km   3

TELENDOS
map: p. 437

458 m

ⓗ x 2
O Pre-booked
   tour boat
O 09.00 ♦16.00
O 10.00

Cave
Emborio
Skalia
Cave
KALAVROS
Agimonda
Masouri
Stimenia
678 m
Mirities
Plati Yialos
Temple of Apollo Delios
AG. KIRIAKI
Pera Kastro
Panormos
Chorio
Linagia
Kalimnos
/Pothia
Argos
Chrisohera
Kastro
Vothini
→Athens ⓓ x 1
Vlihadia
Kefalas Cave
NERA
Vathi/Rena
Daskalio Cave

🚌   ⓓ x 8
     ⓓ x 4 ♦17.00
     ⓓ x 4
     ⓓ x 2

variety in order to cope with Pothia's narrow streets. Summer timetables are posted up regularly, but most of the drivers seem happy to keep to the winter one: as a result you can never be quite sure when they are likely to turn up, so factor this in to your travel time calculations.

Bus links as far north as Masouri are adequate, but very limited along the quiet road that takes you to the northern finger of Kalimnos. Despite this, it is worth visiting thanks to an interesting cave just outside the village of **Skalia** and the blissful isolation of the pebble beach village of **Emborio**, which is attracting growing numbers.

The rest of Kalimnos tends to be little explored. The best and most popular alternative destination is the deep inlet of **Vathi** on the east coast. Set in a citrus-filled market-garden valley, the harbour of **Rena** offers a hotel, a few rooms and a notable sea cave (visited by occasional tour boats from Pothia). If you fancy spending four hours getting to Vathi the hard way, you can always attempt the walk from Pothia over the top of the island (the old dirt track runs up from behind the museum) in the happy knowledge that there is a bus that will get you back — though this excursion is likely to be hot work in High Season.

Sponge Fishing and Kalimnos

Kalimnos is the sponge capital of the Mediterranean, and formerly of the world. The island grew very rich on the fruits of sponge fishing, but this came at a terrible price for the inhabitants. Today the industry still exists (Kalimnos is home to the only surviving sponge fishing fleet in Greece), but it is a shadow of its former self and, in reality, is little more than a convenient branding label to draw in the tourists. Once you get to Kalimnos there is surprisingly little of this industry on show. Visitors will find the inevitable sponge seller stalls near the ferry quay and a couple of small sponge 'factories' in waterfront buildings — where you can see the bleaching process under way. But that is just about it, apart from displays in museums. The small Nautical Museum in Pothia chronicles the history of sponge fishing on Kalimnos, while the Sea World Museum at Vlihadia has a good display of the different sponge types.

The Sponge

Long considered to be part of the plant kingdom, sponges have only comparatively recently been reclassified as animals (for over two thousand years the locals had been wondering why the little vegetables squeaked when they hit them). In fact sponges are the fibrous excreta of colonies of micro-organisms. They feed by drawing nutrients from sea water passed through the pores in their bodies. Under the sea, sponges are an inconspicuous black or dull grey colour: the beguiling golden yellow of the objects you see on sale is only achieved by a lot of painful labour.

The traditional processing of a sponge is briefly thus: after being cut from rocks on the seabed, it arrives on board a fishing boat exuding a nasty smell and possessing a tough surface layer. The first stage of the processing involves stamping on the poor smelly little critter to squash all the 'milk' out of it. It is then left under a sheet in the sun to warm up and kill off any organisms still alive inside. Once cooked, the sponge is strung on a line and then repeatedly washed in the sea and beaten with sticks (to break down the hard outer surface). Finally, irregular areas are trimmed off. The second stage takes place on shore in the sponge factories: the sponge is quickly dunked for a few seconds in a mix of potassium permanganate and sulphuric acid, to bleach it to the golden or light yellow colour we are so familiar with (the length of the dunking determines its shade of yellow), and then washed in fresh water.

Sponge Fishermen

If anyone is tempted to think that the sponges have had a raw deal from the sponge fishing industry, give a thought to the sponge fishermen: if anything, they had it worse.

Kalimnos has long been at the forefront of the sponge industry (other islands with notable fleets included Hydra, Poros, Spetses and Symi). At its prime the island had the largest fleet in the Aegean, with over 350 boats setting out during the summer fishing season (the waters — even in this part of the world — were too cold during the rest of the year). In the second half of the 19th century Kalimnos sponges were well known throughout Europe, but over-fishing and injury brought about a rapid decline in the industry's fortunes. After 1920 only Kalimnos, Hydra and Symi still possessed fleets, and by 1950 Kalimnos was on her own.

The Kalimnot fleet enjoyed two distinct periods of prosperity. The first was achieved by sheer numbers of boats. Each of the 350-odd vessels in the fleet carried up to a dozen divers who would make several dives a day. Without oxygen, they would free-fall naked to the seabed holding onto a large stone, hack off sponges with an axe and return to the surface (all within the space of 2–4 minutes). Despite the low returns from this method of fishing, enough sponges were recovered during a season to make it worthwhile. The limitations, however, were obvious. Divers couldn't go deeper than 30 m and stocks of sponges so near the surface were soon fished out — forcing the fleet to venture ever further afield.

The second, and more deadly, period of prosperity came with the introduction of helmeted diving suits (locally known as the 'skafandro') from 1865. These enabled the divers to go down to depths of 70 m — thanks to the use of compressed air pumped down from the surface. This greatly increased production as the fleet was able to exploit the large stocks of previously untouched sponges at these greater depths. But this did not come without cost to the divers. Many suffered from the 'bends' after second or third dives, returning to boats without any decompression facilities.

At the time the causes of the 'bends' (which occur when small bubbles of excess nitrogen enter the bloodstream and block blood-flow to limbs and

organs if a diver attempts to surface too quickly) weren't clearly understood. Nor were the dangers of making several dives a day appreciated — at least at first. The heaviness of the diving suit itself also contributed to the problem: it was so difficult to walk around in that divers took deeper breaths and so absorbed more compressed air.

The divers were only hired hands. They couldn't dictate working conditions and suffered accordingly. Between 1886 and 1910 an estimated 10,000 Aegean sponge divers died, and a further 20,000 ended up crippled with varying degrees of paralysis. The population of Kalimnos was particularly hard hit. At one point the island's boats were returning with only half the divers they set out with, and the womenfolk took to meeting them wearing black shawls. The Kalimnots even developed a macabre sponge-divers' dance (called the 'mihanikos') in which a dancing youth suddenly falls to the ground and then drags himself around on shaking legs with the aid of a stick.

There was an attempt at a revolt against using the suits. In 1882 they were banned on Kalimnos, but the economic damage inflicted by going back to the old diving technique was such that the suits were back within a couple of years (and continued in use until the aqualung arrived in the 1960s).

From the 1920s on, improved safety measures and equipment cut down the toll of death and injury in the Kalimnos fishing fleet, but a long-term decline had set in. The new diving suits resulted in massive over-fishing of sponge beds, so the island's fleet was again forced to travel ever further each year in search of viable fishing grounds (the boats operating out of Pothia today work mainly off the coast of North Africa).

Such long journey times also contributed to a collapse in the island population as sponge fishermen often opted to start working out of other ports far afield (Tarpon Springs, Florida, is home to a large community of Greek-Americans, most claiming links to Kalimnos thanks to the sponge fishing industry). Further decline came with the arrival of cheap synthetic sponges in the 1950s, and just to top things off in 1986 the Aegean sponge population was devastated by a mystery virus disease, though it is now reviving.

Buying Sponges

These days a surprising number of tourists seem to be turned off by the idea of rubbing themselves down using the body of an animal that has been stamped on, cooked alive in the sun, beaten repeatedly with sticks, and then dunked in a vat of acid for good measure. But if you are tempted to buy a body for your bath, here are some pointers to look out for:

1. Avoid sponges if they are either black, squeak when you squeeze them, or are still moving.

2. Look at the frequency and size of holes in the sponge (small, densely packed holed sponges are to be preferred and cost more).

3. Squeeze your potential purchase to check the consistency of the texture over the whole sponge.

4. Size is also an important consideration: avoid the bags on sale that contain small cut-off remnants: don't end up buying a leg for the price of a whole body.

5. Shape: different shapes attract different prices. There are a number of sponge species with oddball names (most are self explanatory) such as Elephant's Ear and Turkey Cup. In addition to the more predictable 'honeycomb' (Kapadiko) varieties.

6. Enquire about the nationality of your sponge: the majority of the sponges now on sale on Kalimnos — and in Greece for that matter — are imported from as far afield as the Caribbean and the Red Sea, rather than animals caught in the Mediterranean.

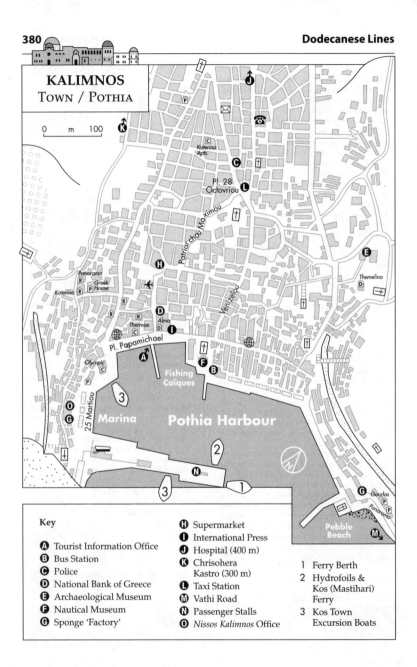

KALIMNOS
Town / Pothia

0   m   100

Katerina Apts.

Pl. 28 Octovriou

Patriarchou Maximou

Venizelou

Panorama

Katerina   Greek House

Themelina

Thermae

Alma

Pl. Papamichael

Olympic

Fishing Caïques

25 Martiou

Marina

Pothia Harbour

Pebble Beach

Gourlas

Panorama

Key

- **A** Tourist Information Office
- **B** Bus Station
- **C** Police
- **D** National Bank of Greece
- **E** Archaeological Museum
- **F** Nautical Museum
- **G** Sponge 'Factory'
- **H** Supermarket
- **I** International Press
- **J** Hospital (400 m)
- **K** Chrisohera Kastro (300 m)
- **L** Taxi Station
- **M** Vathi Road
- **N** Passenger Stalls
- **O** *Nissos Kalimnos* Office

1   Ferry Berth
2   Hydrofoils & Kos (Mastihari) Ferry
3   Kos Town Excursion Boats

⊨

Like most of the islands in the Dodecanese Kalimnos lacks a campsite. There are, however, plenty of beds available, most in Pothia and Mirities, and in the former you can easily seek help via the helpful tourist office housed in a waterfront beach hut on the opposite side of the harbour to the ferry quay.

Pothia has a pretty mixed collection, starting with the waterfront C-class *Olympic* (☎ 28801) and *Thermae* (☎ 29425), along with the D-class *Alma* (☎ 28969). A quieter D-class hotel, the largely package tour *Villa Themelina* (☎ 22682), stands near the museum. A clutch of establishments lie up in the backstreets rising behind the harbour. These include the C-class *Panorama* (☎ 23138) and *Katerina Rooms* (☎ 22532) — not to be confused with the package-tourist-dominated *Katerina Apartments* near the back of the town — along with the excellent pension *Greek House* (☎ 22559).

Mirities also has over a dozen hotels including the D-class *Myrties* (☎ 47512) and E-class *Paradise*. Finally, **Rena** has the C-class *Galini* (☎ 31241) and the pension *Manolis* (☎ 22641), and **Emborio** also has a few rooms.

◎◎

Pothia was built on the back of the sponge-fishing industry and has relatively few sights beyond an impressive new Archaeological Museum (see below). In the town the most visible things on show are a number of bronze waterfront **Statues**. These are staggeringly ugly, modern affairs: the worst is a figure of Poseidon who looks as if he has been caught sitting on a very private sort of throne. Another offering (on the far side of the harbour) is a look-a-like of Copenhagen's Little Mermaid who doesn't, thanks to lumps. Strangely, the perverse fates have since sent Kalimnos relief from this assault on artistic taste. The island is now an archaeological hot spot, with major ancient statues now turning up every other year. The best of these are now in the Archaeological Museum. Next to the museum is the mid 19 c. **Vouvalis Mansion**. It was formerly used as the museum, but amid the now empty rooms are four (including a large dining room and a fur-filled saloon) which have been preserved to show the lifestyle of a wealthy sponge-fishing family.

Pothia is also the starting point for tour boats that run to the main sea cave: **Kefalas Cave**. Famous for its stalagmites and stalactites, this cavern is said to be that in which the god Zeus hid from his immortal father before killing him (gods can do *anything*). These boats also often stop off at the islet of **Nera** to the south-west, where there is a monastery. Other tour boats irregularly visit the **Daskalio Cave** at Vathi. If you fancy venturing further afield, Pothia has also lately seen the arrival of regular day-trips to **Kos** and **Bodrum**.

Elsewhere on Kalimnos the biggest draw is the site of the **Sanctuary of Apollo Delios** near Panormos: the remains of the temple were used to build the now ruined 5 c. AD **Church of Jerusalem**. There are also two reasonable castles on the island: the **Castle of the Knights of St. John** (alias **Chrisohera Kastro**), complete with its own monastery, outside Pothia, is the better preserved, but a more rewarding excursion is to be had visiting the second, the abandoned fortress-village (with its nine preserved whitewashed chapels) of **Pera Kastro**, just outside the old capital of Chorio, thanks to its impressive views. The beach hamlet at **Vlihadia** is host to a small family-run **Sea World Museum**. Interesting exhibits include a large number of encrusted amphoras.

Archaeological Museum of Kalimnos

Open ② to ⑦ 08.30–15.00 (ticket price €3), this museum is one of the best in the Greek islands. With only three galleries it is quite small, but it is packed with an almost ridiculously high proportion of quality exhibits. If you are archaeologically minded you can spend a good hour looking them over.

There are two major collections of material. In **Room A** are displayed the remarkable finds from the Sanctuary of Apollo Delios. In 2001 an islander digging a well came across a statue burial site near the temple. Subsequent excavations revealed **35 Marble Statues**. All over 1.2 m tall and dating from the 2 c. BC, the figures were mutilated prior to burial (fortunately the damaged parts were all buried together so some repairs have been possible). They are thought to be victims of the Emperor Theodosius (378–395 AD), a fanatical Christian, who persecuted ancient Greek religion. The statues are believed to have decorated the cella of the temple. Only the best are on display in the museum, but the show is still very impressive.

Room B is a lot emptier, but the contents are equally arresting. The gallery is home to a collection of bronzes fished from the waters around Kalimnos. The first appeared

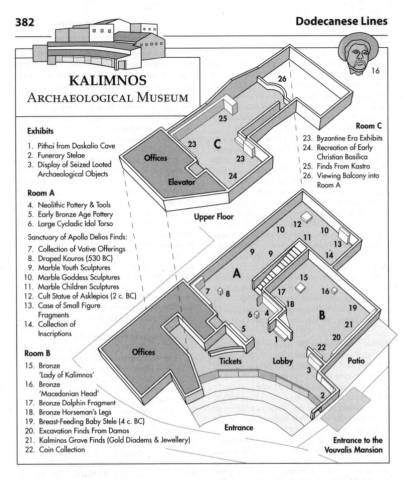

KALIMNOS
Archaeological Museum

Exhibits

1. Pithoi from Daskalio Cave
2. Funerary Stelae
3. Display of Seized Looted
   Archaeological Objects

Room A

4. Neolithic Pottery & Tools
5. Early Bronze Age Pottery
6. Large Cycladic Idol Torso

Sanctuary of Apollo Delios Finds:

7. Collection of Votive Offerings
8. Draped Kouros (530 BC)
9. Marble Youth Sculptures
10. Marble Goddess Sculptures
11. Marble Children Sculptures
12. Cult Statue of Asklepios (2 c. BC)
13. Case of Small Figure
    Fragments
14. Collection of
    Inscriptions

Room B

15. Bronze
    'Lady of Kalimnos'
16. Bronze
    'Macedonian Head'
17. Bronze Dolphin Fragment
18. Bronze Horseman's Legs
19. Breast-Feeding Baby Stele (4 c. BC)
20. Excavation Finds From Damos
21. Kalminos Grave Finds (Gold Diadems & Jewellery)
22. Coin Collection

Room C

23. Byzantine Era Exhibits
24. Recreation of Early
    Christian Basilica
25. Finds From Kastro
26. Viewing Balcony into
    Room A

Upper Floor

Offices
Elevator

C

Offices

Tickets   Lobby   Patio

Entrance

**Entrance to the
Vouvalis Mansion**

in 1995 when a fisherman netted one of the best **Hellenistic bronzes** ever discovered. Known as the **'Lady of Kalimnos'**, the 2 m high figure of a veiled woman is a late 2 c. BC copy of a work by sculptor Praxiteles. It has been described as the only example of its kind to survive from the period. A grateful government gave the fisherman a million drachmas by way of a reward for not trying to sell it on the black market.

In addition to the Lady of Kalimnos the museum also has a **Macedonian Head**, which was fished up in 1997 from the waters north of Telendos. Unusually, the glazed enamel

eyes (usually missing on recovered bronzes) are intact. Other bronze exhibits include fragments of a **Dolphin** and the gloriously detailed legs and feet from a male equestrian bronze. Ironically, it is probable that none of these figures saw Kalimnos in ancient times as they are almost certainly from ships wrecked while engaged in the lucrative antiques trade that existed during the Roman period.

The **Upper Floor** of the museum, which is given over to post-Roman exhibits, is inevitably something of an anticlimax, but a good attempt has been made to recreate details of an early **Christian Basilica**.

Karpathos
ΚΑΡΠΑΘΟΣ; 301 km²; pop. 5,400.

CODE ☎ 22450
PORT POLICE ☎ 22227
TOURIST POLICE ☎ 22218
POLICE ☎ 22222
HOSPITAL ☎ 22228

Along with Kassos to the south and Saria to the north, the island of Karpathos forms a small archipelago midway between Rhodes and eastern Crete. An appealing destination if you are looking for a quiet, relatively unspoilt Greek island, it remains a tricky spot to get to: the great majority of visitors are package tourists flying in direct from Europe. Given the low level of ferry links (the 'two boats in each direction' pattern of weekly services has been running for a good many years now), you should allow a couple of days in hand, if you visit, to make your escape.

Like Amorgos, Karpathos enjoys a history of division with the two sides of the island effectively separated by inhospitable terrain, with the result that ferries call at two island ports. The similarities end there, however, because Karpathos has higher mountains, has much more tree cover (though this has been sadly diminished by recent forest fires), is graced with some excellent beaches and — thanks to the large expatriate community (many now in the US) who send back funds — is now among the most affluent islands in the Aegean. In spite of the appearance of regular charter flights, tourism has yet to take off (and there is not much sign of it doing so), with the somewhat paradoxical effect of creating a High Season surplus of demand for what limited facilities do exist.

Buses run to the most popular island beach at Ammopi, but the service is otherwise generally very poor. Other transport options are pretty dire, the taxis being too expensive except for the shortest journeys, and car and moped hire limited by the poor quality of the road network and the lack of fuel stops outside the capital.

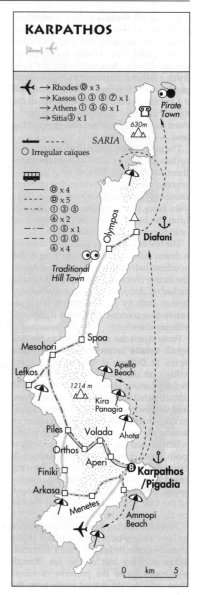

KARPATHOS

→ Rhodes ⓊⓊ x 3
→ Kassos ① ③ ⑤ ⑦ x 1
→ Athens ① ③ ⑥ x 1
→ Sitia ③ x 1

Pirate Town

630m

SARIA

○ Irregular caïques

Ⓤ x 4
Ⓤ x 5
① ③ ⑤
⑥ x 2
① ⑤ x 1
① ③ ⑤
⑥ x 4

Diafani

Olympos

Traditional Hill Town

Mesohori — Spoa

Apella Beach

Lefkos

1214 m

Kira Panagia

Piles   Volada   Ahata

Orthos

Aperi

Karpathos /Pigadia

Finiki

Arkasa

Menetes

Ammopi Beach

0   km   5

Asklepieion:
View from the
Upper Terrace

Statue Niches in the
Middle Terrace Wall

Kos Town:
Main Square Mosque

KOS Old Harbour
Waterfront

Dodecanese

Key

- **A** Entrance Stairs & Small Roman Bath
- **B** Entry Propylon
- **C** Galleries
- **D** Statue Niches & Middle Terrace Wall
- **E** Statue Torsos
- **F** Fountains
- **G** Roman Latrines (not in use)
- **H** Second Staircase
- **I** Great Altar of Asklepios
- **J** Early Temple of Asklepios
- **K** Priests' Quarters
- **L** Exedra/Public Platform
- **M** Temple of Apollo
- **N** Lesche (Conference Hall)
- **O** Upper Andria/Terrace Wall
- **P** Monumental Staircase
- **Q** Large Temple of Asklepios
- **R** Galleries
- **S** Patients' Rooms
- **T** Sacred Wood & Small Temple
- **U** Large Roman Baths

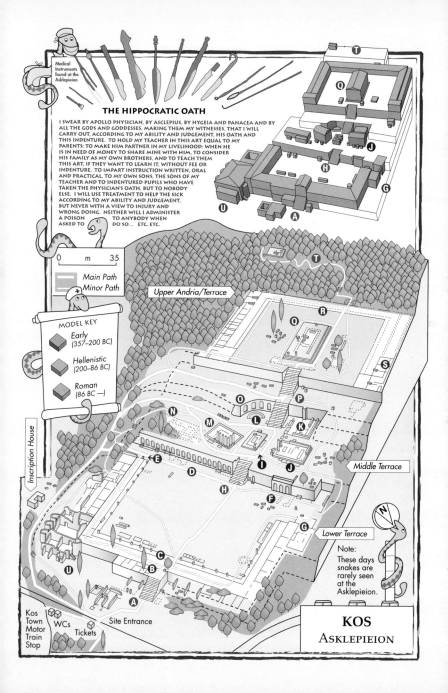

Medical
Instruments
found at the
Asklepieion

THE HIPPOCRATIC OATH

I SWEAR BY APOLLO PHYSICIAN, BY ASCLEPIUS, BY HYGEIA AND PANACEA AND BY
ALL THE GODS AND GODDESSES, MAKING THEM MY WITNESSES, THAT I WILL
CARRY OUT, ACCORDING TO MY ABILITY AND JUDGEMENT, HIS OATH AND
THIS INDENTURE. TO HOLD MY TEACHER IN THIS ART EQUAL TO MY
PARENTS: TO MAKE HIM PARTNER IN MY LIVELIHOOD: WHEN HE
IS IN NEED OF MONEY TO SHARE MINE WITH HIM, TO CONSIDER
HIS FAMILY AS MY OWN BROTHERS, AND TO TEACH THEM
THIS ART, IF THEY WANT TO LEARN IT, WITHOUT FEE OR
INDENTURE. TO IMPART INSTRUCTION WRITTEN, ORAL
AND PRACTICAL, TO MY OWN SONS, THE SONS OF MY
TEACHER AND TO INDENTURED PUPILS WHO HAVE
TAKEN THE PHYSICIAN'S OATH, BUT TO NOBODY
ELSE. I WILL USE TREATMENT TO HELP THE SICK
ACCORDING TO MY ABILITY AND JUDGEMENT,
BUT NEVER WITH A VIEW TO INJURY AND
WRONG DOING. NEITHER WILL I ADMINISTER
A POISON   TO ANYBODY WHEN
ASKED TO   DO SO... ETC. ETC.

0   m   35

Main Path
Minor Path

MODEL KEY

Early
(357–200 BC)

Hellenistic
(200–86 BC)

Roman
(86 BC —)

Upper Andria/Terrace

Inscription House

Middle Terrace

Lower Terrace

Note:
These days
snakes are
rarely seen
at the
Asklepieion.

Kos
Town
Motor
Train
Stop

WCs

Tickets

Site Entrance

N

KOS

ASKLEPIEION

RHODES
Lindos Acropolis &
Faliraki Shop Sign

EXCHANGE
RENT HERE
FANS WHEEL CHAIRS
WALKING STICKS
CRUTCHES

KASTELORIZO
Megisti at Dawn
(with mainland Turkey in the
background)

LEROS
Windmill at
Agia Marina

Dodecanese

EVENING ARGOS

**WELL-WISHERS
FLOOD
AEGEAN**

TOURISTS BLAMED
FOR LOSS OF AN
GREEK ISLANDS

DELPHI ORACLE
— LATEST —
· Glub, glub, glub,
glub, glub, glub

NISSIROS
Town Well

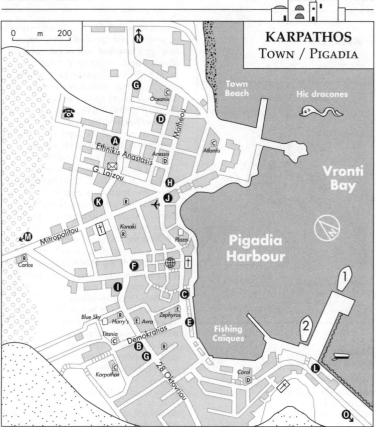

0   m   200

KARPATHOS
Town / Pigadia

Town Beach

Hic dracones

Vronti Bay

Pigadia Harbour

Fishing Caïques

Oceanis

Matheou

Ethnikis Anastasis

Ariessis

Atlantis

G. Laizou

Mitropolitou

Konaki

Plaza

Carlos

Blue Sky

Harry's

Avra

Zephyros

Titania

Demokratias

Karpathos

28 Oktovriou

Coral

1

2

Key

Ⓐ Tourist & Regular Police
Ⓑ Bus Station
Ⓒ National Bank of Greece
Ⓓ Hospital
Ⓔ Waterfront Clock Tower
Ⓕ Town Hall
Ⓖ Supermarket
Ⓗ Pharmacy
Ⓘ Bakery
Ⓙ Newspapers
Ⓚ Moped & Car Hire
Ⓛ WCs
Ⓜ Airport & Menetes Road
Ⓝ Aperi, Spoa & Diafani 'Road'
Ⓞ Ammopi Beach Road

1   Ferry Quay
2   Beach & Excursion Boats

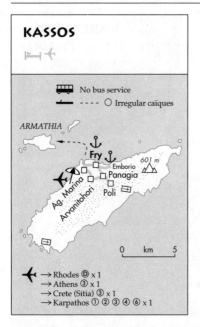

KASSOS

No bus service

---- ○ Irregular caïques

ARMATHIA

Fry

Emborio   601 m

Panagia

Ag. Marina

Arvanitohori   Poli

0   km   5

✈ → Rhodes Ⓓ x 1
    → Athens ③ x 1
    → Crete (Sitia) ③ x 1
    → Karpathos ① ② ③ ④ ⑥ x 1

Kassos

ΚΑΣΟΣ; 66 km²; pop. 1,184.

CODE ☎ 22450
PORT POLICE ☎ 41288
POLICE ☎ 41222
HOSPITAL ☎ 41333

An arid, mountainous island with more cliffs than beaches, Kassos is definitely not on the tourist map and has seen ferry services dwindle over the last decade, and its population over the last two centuries. It has an odd history, having been subjected to an attack by a band of marauding Egyptians who carried off most of the women and children in 1824 with the thanks of their Ottoman overlords (Kassos was another of those small islands with a large fleet that enthusiastically joined the 1824 bid for Greek independence, only to see savage retribution). The few male members of the population who were not killed or enslaved

were invited to Suez a few decades later on a goodwill visit (no doubt they hoped to look up a long-lost wife or two) and only allowed home when they'd dug the odd canal. Sadly, the Egyptians have not offered ferry links since, and it is best to allow three days to get away or take advantage of the lifeline flights to Rhodes and Crete.

Kassos has three harbours: the new ferry quay just north of the capital **Fry**, the old ferry port at the small taverna-backed harbour of **Emborio** 1 km round the bay from Fry, and the tiny caïque harbour known as Bouka — at Fry itself. Also transcribed as 'Phry', the capital is a peculiarly ramshackle affair, but for all that, it has a certain scruffy charm and the inhabitants are all smiles (often American).

Behind the 'town' lie four closely located villages, all exhibiting signs of gentle decay — particularly **Ag. Marina**, the old capital, and **Panagia**, which has yet more of those derelict early 19 c. mansions so typical of southern Dodecanese towns.

Lacking roads or beaches the rest of the island is little visited. **Armathia**, an islet just west of Kassos, sees caïques heading for a good sand beach when sufficient numbers can be generated; otherwise the main tourist activity is hill walking.

🛏
So few tourists call that facilities are very poor. Harbour tavernas offering rooms and two C-class hotels combine to cater for the few that do call (they can more than handle the number of visitors, even in High Season). Best is the *Anagennisis* (☎ 41323), with the poor *Anessis* (☎ 41201) limping in behind.

👓
Kassos is not noted for its sightseeing. That said, there are sights of a sort. Most notable is the **Sellai Cave** near the airfield, complete with all the usual subterranean accoutrements.

The village of **Poli** is also of some interest, being located (as its name suggests) on the site of the **Ancient City** (complete with the scanty remains of the old Acropolis). A Byzantine church now adorns the site. A second church of note stands at nearby **Arvanitohori**, which is partly carved out of the bedrock of the hillside.

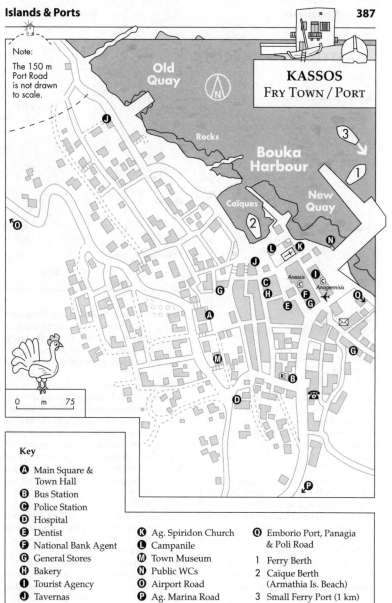

Note:
The 150 m
Port Road
is not drawn
to scale.

KASSOS
FRY TOWN / PORT

Old
Quay

Rocks

Bouka
Harbour

Caïques

New
Quay

Anessis

Anagennisis

0   m   75

Key

Ⓐ Main Square &
    Town Hall
Ⓑ Bus Station
Ⓒ Police Station
Ⓓ Hospital
Ⓔ Dentist
Ⓕ National Bank Agent
Ⓖ General Stores
Ⓗ Bakery
Ⓘ Tourist Agency
Ⓙ Tavernas

Ⓚ Ag. Spiridon Church
Ⓛ Campanile
Ⓜ Town Museum
Ⓝ Public WCs
Ⓞ Airport Road
Ⓟ Ag. Marina Road

Ⓠ Emborio Port, Panagia
    & Poli Road

1 Ferry Berth
2 Caïque Berth
   (Armathia Is. Beach)
3 Small Ferry Port (1 km)

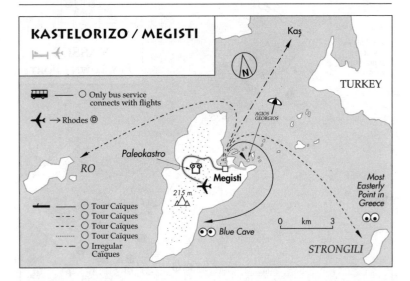

Kastelorizo

ΚΑΣΤΕΛΟΡΙΖΟ; 9 km²; pop. 210.

CODE ☎ 22410
PORT POLICE ☎ 49270
POLICE ☎ 49333
FIRST AID ☎ 49267

Six hours' steaming east of Rhodes, isolated Kastelorizo is both a Greek tragedy in island form, and an absolute must for island hoppers looking for that island that defies even the usual range of differences that are usually to be found between one island and the next.

Sometimes known as Megisti ('large'), Kastelorizo is the only large island in a small archipelago of fourteen. Endowed with the best natural harbour on the Asiatic coast between Beirut and Makri, it took full advantage of this to acquire great wealth during the 19 c. only to see almost all turn to ruin in the fighting for this strategic prize in the first half of the last century. Two world wars and the Greco-Turkish conflict have conspired to leave Kastelorizo one of history's victims, but even allowing the

fact that it is impossible to visit the island and not experience a powerful feeling of tragedy, there is plenty to quietly enjoy — in truth Kastelorizo is a real gem — even if it doesn't feel quite the done thing to 'party' here.

Union with Greece in 1947 has brought a measure of quiet stability, but lying 90 km east of Rhodes and under 3 km from Turkey, Kastelorizo — the most easterly part of Greece — is very isolated. The brutal truth is that it isn't viable without close contact with the Anatolian coast, yet to date, that hasn't really been a practical proposition — given the politics of the region and the exclusively Greek inhabitants. As a result, it floats in a limbo sea, with a tiny population encouraged to stay by a mix of subsidies and new housing provided by a government afraid that if the numbers decline much more Greek sovereignty could be called into question. A strong sense of identity felt by expatriate islanders and their descendants (who book solid all available accommodation at the height of the season) is a powerful source of sustenance.

The government is doing its best to turn things around: in 2003 an inter-governmental EU conference brought the foreign ministers of Europe to Kastelorizo. The island's location as the best place in Europe to see an eclipse also attracted a couple of thousand visitors for a day in 2006. A notable change is the arrival of a regular summer catamaran service from Rhodes that allows day trips once a week. This is an appealing way of having a look at Kastelorizo given the very limited accommodation options on offer.

☻

First the tragedy. For most of its history Kastelorizo has been a relatively insignificant island, controlled by whichever power was master of Rhodes; its significance being primarily military, courtesy of the castle that gave it its name (Kastelorizo means 'Red Castle'). However, as the Ottoman Empire opened up to European traders in the first half of the 19 c. the island economy developed quickly — thanks to its harbour and its location on the east–west trade route.

By 1850 Kastelorizo was very wealthy, with many of its population of 17,000 owning property on the island and in the adjacent mainland town of Kaş (ironically pronounced 'Cash'). Tragedy was heralded with a change in governing policy by the ruling Turks in 1908, which resulted in a local revolution in 1913 followed by an unstable period of self-rule that saw the island cut off from the Anatolian mainland and economic decline setting in. Worse was to follow with the arrival of WW1. The French occupied the island in 1915, turning it into a naval base. This prompted Turkish forces to blockade the island and shell the harbour and town in 1917.

In 1921 the French handed over Kastelorizo to the Italians under the Treaty of Sèvres that gave the Dodecanese islands to Italy, thereby condemning the island's economy to a prolonged period of decline: the lack of any contact (never mind trade) with the mainland and changes in shipping routes proved to be a fatal double blow. The Italians attempted to turn Kastelorizo into a passenger seaplane base (serving Rome—Beirut flights) but this wasn't successful. Their integration policy, which sought the Italianization of the Dodecanese islands by banning the speaking of Greek in

schools and public places, proved an even greater disaster, being fiercely resisted by the islanders. This left the Italians ill-disposed to help rebuild the town after it was badly damaged by an earthquake in 1926. As a result of all this, the town's population fell from 9,000 in 1910 to 1,400 in 1940.

In 1941 WW2 came to Kastelorizo when the British briefly captured the island only to see the Italians rapidly retake it. With the Italian surrender in 1943 the British regained control, and the heart of the old town was then subjected to dive-bomb attacks by German planes. This resulted in massive damage and the decision to evacuate the remaining island population to Cyprus. Following their departure, in 1944 a fire completed the devastation of the town, the burnt-out buildings being bulldozed by the British for safety reasons. Some islanders asserted it was to cover up looting by the garrison, a hard claim to substantiate given the years of decline that preceded the war and the bomb damage to the town during it.

The final tragedy was yet to come: in 1946 the elderly British ship *Empire Patrol* — overloaded with 500 returning islanders — sank after a fire broke out on board: 33 of them died.

Megisti or **Kastelorizo Town** has less than a third of its former buildings still standing. Old postcards and guidebooks on sale from waterfront shops reveal the pre-WW2 town to have looked very like a second Symi, with similar tiers of mansion-style buildings crowding around the magnificent, wide, U-shaped harbour bay. Only the houses behind the back of the harbour survive in any numbers, the castle hill that once formed the centre of town now being reduced to bulldozed rubble.

The waterfront — shorn of many of its buildings by German bombing — is slowly being rebuilt. New houses (presumably copies of their predecessors on the site) have appeared in the 'gap' backing onto the new ferry quay, and concrete footings for several more houses have been marked out (this is a way of registering

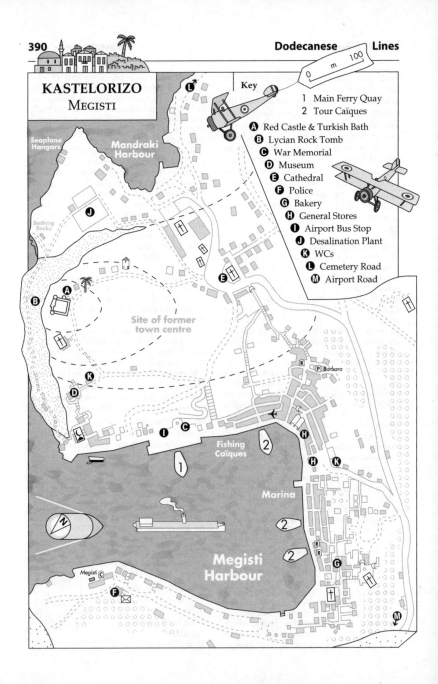

KASTELORIZO
MEGISTI

Key

1   Main Ferry Quay
2   Tour Caïques

A   Red Castle & Turkish Bath
B   Lycian Rock Tomb
C   War Memorial
D   Museum
E   Cathedral
F   Police
G   Bakery
H   General Stores
I   Airport Bus Stop
J   Desalination Plant
K   WCs
L   Cemetery Road
M   Airport Road

0   m   100

Seaplane Hangars

Mandraki Harbour

Bathing Rocks

Site of former town centre

Fishing Caïques

Marina

Megisti Harbour

Megisti

P Barbara

plots by expatriate islanders). The attractive pastel painted waterfront buildings that have survived are home to the new 'centre' of town and here you will find the bulk of the town's shops and tavernas (which happily sprawl to the edge of the harbour as the quayside street is too narrow to admit vehicles).

The backstreets are more sobering: for the most part rows of semi-derelict houses and blocked off alleyways, they have a distinct ghost-town feel to them. The only one of any length runs up the periphery of the castle hill; once a backstreet, it is now the main town artery between the waterfront and the partially rebuilt main square (now home to the cathedral, several churches, odd houses and a barracks).

Paths also lead across the hill to the former main stairway (now reduced to an impressive flight of steps ascending into demolished oblivion) and to the castle. The castle is the only significant survival from the old town centre (bar a small redundant Turkish bath and a ruined windmill), and is really little more than a glorified tower (albeit a pretty impressive one). Access is via a steep metal staircase that runs up against one of the side turrets. Walking on, the path passes a new museum and then runs down to the pitiful collection of houses around the locked mosque. On the other side of the hill is the small harbour of **Mandraki**: semi-derelict and home to a desalination plant, it is backed by hills now being developed with government-built homes. A road of sorts also leads to a headland that is home to the town cemetery.

Kastelorizo not only enjoys very high summer temperatures (without the cooling influence of the *meltemi* these are regularly over 40 °C) but also has a military presence. The main garrison lies on the airport road and does much to add to the frontier-town feel of the place. When tensions with Turkey are running very high, armed patrols parade along the waterfront and helicopters occasionally pass low overhead, in serious anticipation that Kastelorizo — an isolated

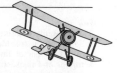

Greek thorn in the soft underbelly of the Turkish Mediterranean coast — will be the first victim of a Turkish attack on Greece.

All this sounds pretty grim, but Kastelorizo is actually a very cheerful place in High Season and is becoming a very trendy place to stay. This is largely thanks to the many Australian expatriate visitors who do much to add to the vitality of the town: 80% of those able to claim Kastelorizian ancestry are settled in Australia (in this part of Greece a man doesn't bring a phrase book; he just brings his Sheila). The only downside is that with so many expats around, others can end up feeling a bit like outsiders.

The **rest of the island** is difficult to visit unless you like hiking. Walkers will enjoy Kastelorizo thanks to an excellent walking guide, *Capture Kastelorizo* (€10), by Marina Pistisonis (who describes herself as 'A Greek Aussie but always a Kassie at heart'). Available in a waterfront shop, it is also a good introduction and guide to the island as a whole. The main destination is the ancient acropolis at **Paleokastro**.

Accommodation in August is in very short supply: if you haven't booked you are cooked. In a worst-case scenario, try the police station and ask for a spare cell! Out of High Season you can always find a bed and will be met with offers when ferries dock. The only hotel is the expensive B-class *Megisti* (☎ 49221). This is augmented by several pensions. Most easily found is the *Barbara* (☎ 29295); others are signless and include the *Kristallo* (☎ 41209) behind the main square and the *Paradisos* (☎ 49074) near the west end of the port. There are also rooms (☎ 29074) opposite the *Barbara*.

There isn't a campsite, and freelance camping isn't an option given the high military presence. Roughing it in the woodland on the outskirts of town isn't viable as their floors are littered with pine needles and spent cartridges: both are deadly, though the former are surprisingly toxic and will leave those who make an impromptu bed out of them looking like a walking example of some strange boil-producing disease a day or two later.

∽

The 1380-built **Castle** is the main sight in town, followed by the free **Museum**. It contains an odd assortment of finds from the ancient acropolis at Paleokastro, earthenware from a medieval wreck off the south-west coast, and a collection of local house artefacts and costumes. Cut out of the rock beneath the castle is the only **Lycian Tomb** to be found in Greece (though there are plenty on the coast opposite). If you feel minded to attempt the short clamber up the steep cliff-side steps you will find a tomb with a view with room for six. Finally, although the **Cathedral** only dates from the 19 c. it is also of interest as the columns in the nave were taken from the temple of Apollo at Patara in Lycia (back in mainland contact days).

Thanks to a roadless and hilly interior, sightseeing is limited to Paleokastro and boat excursions to the **Blue Cave / Fokiali Cavern** — the best sea-cave in Greece if not the Med. Tour boats run from the harbour, making irregular runs to Turkey and to the outlying islands of **Strongili** and **Ro** (which has passed into Greek nationalist folklore thanks to its last inhabitant — a little old lady — who heroically ran up the Greek flag each day until her death in 1986. Her grave is one of the first things you see on landing there).

As is the case with many Greek islands, some of the more interesting 'sights' are no longer there to see. Kastelorizo has its sightseeing ghost in the form of the aircraft carrier *Ben My Chree* (Manx for 'girl of my heart'). One of the first half-dozen carriers in the Royal Navy, she was launched in 1908, starting out as a passenger steamer running between Liverpool and Douglas. On the outbreak of WW1 she was rebuilt as a carrier, with the addition of a flight deck and a prominent stern hangar — that housed 4 Sopwith Camels and 2 Short seaplanes. In 1915–16 she served in the Dardanelles during the Gallipoli campaign, and in January 1917 she sailed to Kastelorizo to replenish the supplies of the French garrison. Forced to use the main harbour because of her size (she was 375 feet long), she was shelled by the Turkish mainland artillery batteries. Her hangar received a direct hit on the 9th of January 1917, setting it on fire. Within half an hour the ship had been abandoned and continued to blaze until she sank on the morning of the 11th. In 1919 the hulk was refloated, towed to Piraeus, and sold to a German scrap merchant.

Kos

ΚΩΣ; 290 km²; pop. 21,500.

CODE ☎ 22420
PORT POLICE ☎ 26594
TOURIST POLICE ☎ 28227
POLICE ☎ 22222
HOSPITAL ☎ 22330

Thanks to an attractive mixture of sand and sights, Kos (often transcribed as 'Cos') is a justifiably popular package tourist destination. Large for a Greek island (45 km from east to west), Kos is long and tapering, with a high spine of mountains running along its southern side. The second largest island in the Dodecanese, it lies midway down the chain, and is the de facto hub of much of the group's ferry and hydrofoil activity, with virtually every boat putting in an appearance. Kos also has an unsurpassed number of tourist craft operating to neighbouring islands and the Turkish coast, a mere 5 km away, which dominates the eastern horizon.

☻

Kos was an important centre in the ancient world, its capital being one of the major commercial ports in the Aegean. Unlike Rhodes, Kos was never large enough to be a major force in its own right, leaving it more prone than most of the larger islands to the vicissitudes of history: it variously relied on the patronage of Egypt (under the Ptolemies), Rome (from 130 BC) and Rhodes (from the 1 C. AD) for its protection. Its shaky geology has also played a major role: it was devastated by massive earthquakes on several occasions, notably in the 6 C. AD. (which totally flattened the ancient city, founded in 336 BC) and again as recently as 1933. As a result, much of its fame was derived from an odd mix of figures and famous associations rather than economic or military prowess. First among the historical figures were Hippocrates (460–357 BC) — the so-called 'Father of Medicine' — who was born and had his school here, and a famous painter contemporary of Alexander the Great named Apelles. Kos was also a noted producer of fine wine, and scandalously, in the Roman era, see-through silk garments beloved by senators' wives and the transvestite Emperor Caligula.

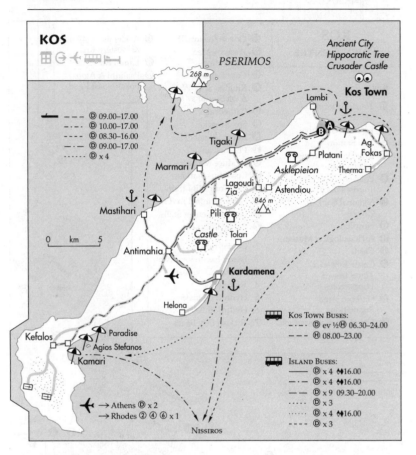

KOS

PSERIMOS

268 m

Ⓓ 09.00–17.00
Ⓓ 10.00–17.00
Ⓓ 08.30–16.00
Ⓓ 09.00–17.00
Ⓓ x 4

Ancient City
Hippocratic Tree
Crusader Castle

Kos Town

Lambi

Tigaki

Marmari

Mastihari

0   km   5

Antimahia

Helona

Kefalos   Paradise
          Agios Stefanos
          Kamari

A
B
Platani   Ag.
               Fokas
Asklepieion   Therma
Lagoudi
Zia   Asfendiou
       846 m
Pili
Castle Tolari

Kardamena

→ Athens Ⓓ x 2
→ Rhodes ② ④ ⑥ x 1

NISSIROS

Kos Town Buses:
--- Ⓓ ev ½Ⓗ 06.30–24.00
--- Ⓗ 08.00–23.00

Island Buses:
——— Ⓓ x 4 ♦♦16.00
–··– Ⓓ x 4 ♦♦16.00
——— Ⓓ x 9 09.30–20.00
····· Ⓓ x 3
····· Ⓓ x 4 ♦♦16.00
---- Ⓓ x 3

Kos Town, the main port and capital of the island, lies on the sandy east coast with views across to Turkey. It is a gentle, wide-avenued centre of flowers and trees that would be very restful if it wasn't for a spot of mass tourism. For the most part the more scenic parts of town have stood up to this remarkably well, but the streets north of the castle-dominated old harbour (and indeed, the coastline north and south) are dominated by a heavy concentration of hotels, discos and tee-shirt shops that will

either be your idea of holiday heaven or a variation of hell: this is the secret of the town's success for there is something here to appeal to most tastes — unless you like solitude, or prefer to holiday with vacationing Greeks (thanks to the heavy package tour influence, Kos is most definitely not on their list of favoured islands).

An additional handicap to attracting Greek tourists is the town centre, which has a very Italianesque feel, having been largely rebuilt during the interwar occupa-

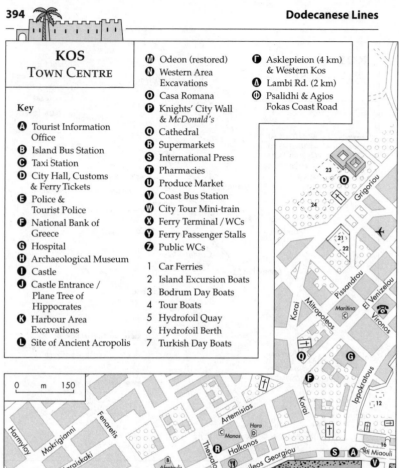

KOS
Town Centre

Key

- **A** Tourist Information Office
- **B** Island Bus Station
- **C** Taxi Station
- **D** City Hall, Customs & Ferry Tickets
- **E** Police & Tourist Police
- **F** National Bank of Greece
- **G** Hospital
- **H** Archaeological Museum
- **I** Castle
- **J** Castle Entrance / Plane Tree of Hippocrates
- **K** Harbour Area Excavations
- **L** Site of Ancient Acropolis
- **M** Odeon (restored)
- **N** Western Area Excavations
- **O** Casa Romana
- **P** Knights' City Wall & *McDonald's*
- **Q** Cathedral
- **R** Supermarkets
- **S** International Press
- **T** Pharmacies
- **U** Produce Market
- **V** Coast Bus Station
- **W** City Tour Mini-train
- **X** Ferry Terminal / WCs
- **Y** Ferry Passenger Stalls
- **Z** Public WCs

1. Car Ferries
2. Island Excursion Boats
3. Bodrum Day Boats
4. Tour Boats
5. Hydrofoil Quay
6. Hydrofoil Berth
7. Turkish Day Boats

- **F** Asklepieion (4 km) & Western Kos
- **A** Lambi Rd. (2 km)
- **O** Psalidhi & Agios Fokas Coast Road

0   m   150

ANCIENT CITY

10. Temple of Pandimos Aphrodite
11. Temple of Heracles
12. Small Temples
13. Roman Agora
14. Stoas (4 c. BC)
15. City Wall
16. Site of East Wall Gate
17. Harbour Baths
18. North Baths
19. Roman House

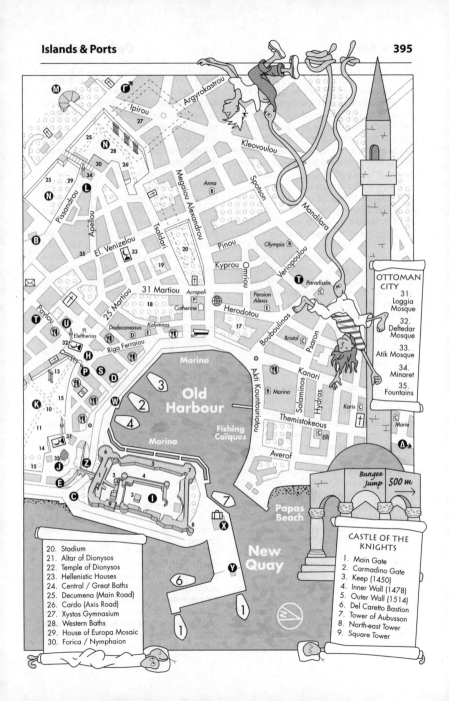

Ipirou

Argyrokastrou

Kleovoulou

Spotson

Mandilara

Megaliou Alexandrou

Tsaldari

Anna

Pinou

Olympia

Vertiopoulou

Kyprou

Omriou

Paradissos

Pissandrou

Apellou

El. Venizelou

31 Martiou

Acropoli

Catherine

Herodotou

25 Martiou

Pavliou

Pl. Eleftherias

Dodecanessus

Kalymnos

Riga Ferraiou

Pension Alexis

Bouboulinas

Psaron

Bristol

Marina

Old Harbour

Akti Koumbouriou

Kanari

Salaminos

Hydras

Karis

Marina

Marina

Fishing Caiques

Themistokeous

Elli

Averof

Papas Beach

New Quay

OTTOMAN CITY
31. Loggia Mosque
32. Deftedar Mosque
33. Atik Mosque
34. Minaret
35. Fountains

Bungee Jump **500 m**

CASTLE OF THE KNIGHTS
1. Main Gate
2. Carmadino Gate
3. Keep (1450)
4. Inner Wall (1478)
5. Outer Wall (1514)
6. Del Caretto Bastion
7. Tower of Aubusson
8. North-east Tower
9. Square Tower

20. Stadium
21. Altar of Dionysos
22. Temple of Dionysos
23. Hellenistic Houses
24. Central / Great Baths
25. Decumena (Main Road)
26. Cardo (Axis Road)
27. Xystos Gymnasium
28. Western Baths
29. House of Europa Mosaic
30. Forica / Nymphaion

N

tion years (courtesy of the massive 1933 earthquake). Some consolation for the loss of any tangible 'Greek' atmosphere is to be found in the Italian disinclination to rebuild over any archaeological remains that came to light, leaving Kos Town with wide, ruin-topped vistas along with the boulevards. To add to the appeal, much of the town centre has now been pedestrianized, with a new one-way traffic system.

Hotels are strung out along the east coast from Lambi to Ag. Fokas. This hotel-strip road is served by city buses. Note: tickets bought on the buses cost up to 20% extra. Tickets for the toy trains that run to the island's main sightseeing attraction — the Asklepieion, a healing sanctuary that became a major focus for pilgrimage thanks to the fame of **Hippocrates** — and also for the toy train Kos Town tour are also bought here.

Local guidebooks will give you a detailed biography of Hippocrates, though his story is rather elusive. The earliest advocate of a 'scientific' practice of medicine, he seems to have gained fame by travelling the Aegean, stopping plagues and other little mass infections by advocating the novel ideas of boiling drinking water and the isolation of the sick from the healthy. Thereafter, almost every medical saying and practice was ascribed to him, glorying in the association, and leaving scholars wondering if he ever said anything notable at all (the Hippocratic Oath — see the map between p. 384–385 — probably started life as something like: 'I wish this pesky snake would stop following me around'). The most recent manifestation of this hero-worship by association is the ancient tree he is supposed to have taught under, standing opposite the entrance to the castle.

Much of the appeal of Kos Town is the large number of good sand **beaches** that line the east coast either side of the town. The beach and hotel strip to the **north of the centre** is now very developed, and one is often hard put to see the sand for sun umbrellas and tourists. This is the part of town that really has suffered as a result of the package-tourist boom, and it really hasn't got much going for it now, simply because it caters primarily for the bottom end of the market.

The coast strip to the south of the castle is the more appealing (though it is slowly deteriorating), and has more variety — thanks largely to the nature of the beaches. For the first kilometre they are golden sand, but after that they progressively degenerate to scruffy pebble affairs. The boundary is marked by a substantial yachting marina that has been constructed around 1 km from the castle. None the less, the coast road (lined with palm and eucalyptus trees) sees plenty of tourists and has a popular cycle-way running on its beach side as far south as the island's former campsite.

Bicycle hire is deservedly very popular in Kos Town as the wide streets and flat layout are well suited to this mode of transport (indeed, the northern side of the island has proved so popular with cyclists that a number of roads now have designated cycle lanes running parallel to them). These often coincide with pavements, and who has right of way isn't usually made clear, so pedestrians beware.

The Rest of Kos is fertile (the island boasts the best water supply of any of the Dodecanese islands) but is rather scruffy and littered with military encampments thanks to the close proximity of Turkey — take care to avoid taking photographs of anything remotely military. It is served by very overcrowded buses (timetables from ❸) running along the one main road down the island spine, with feeder roads linking it with coastal villages. Kardamena and Mastihari are the largest of these, with regular ferry links to Nissiros and Kalimnos respectively. Both have become tourist resorts in their own right.

Kardamena is easily the biggest resort after Kos Town, managing to outdo parts of it for discos, bars and beach life (though if this mix appeals then you are likely to find Faliraki on Rhodes a larger and 'wilder'

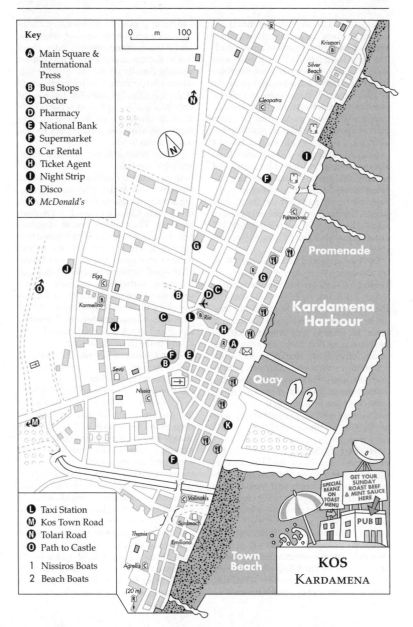

Key

A Main Square &
International
Press
B Bus Stops
C Doctor
D Pharmacy
E National Bank
F Supermarket
G Car Rental
H Ticket Agent
I Night Strip
J Disco
K *McDonald's*

L Taxi Station
M Kos Town Road
N Tolari Road
O Path to Castle

1 Nissiros Boats
2 Beach Boats

0   m   100

Krismari

Silver
Beach

Cleopatra

Panorama

Promenade

Kardamena
Harbour

Quay

1 2

Elga

Karmelina

Seva

Nissia

Rio

Valinakis

Sunbeach

Themis

Emiliana

Agrellis

Town
Beach

SPECIAL
BEANZ
ON
TOAST
MENU

GET YOUR
SUNDAY
ROAST BEEF
& MINT SAUCE
HERE

PUB

KOS
KARDAMENA

(20 m)

destination). Lacking any significant old centre, Kardamena is a mass of hotels some six blocks deep and over a kilometre long. The town has a crowded beach on its west side, a harbour filled with tourist boats (that head daily for the beaches along the south-west coast) in the centre and several small quays on the east side. As one would expect with a major package-tourist town, all the important facilities are readily available: most are in the blocks that line the promenade. There is a main waterfront square of sorts, but it is a bit bland and usually the home of touts pushing the latest bar or disco. The beaches east of the town centre are relatively narrow shabby affairs, but much quieter; the only point of interest being a couple of redundant WW2 concrete machine-gun pill boxes leaning at drunken angles in the sand.

The bus stops and taxi rank are 150 m up Kardamena's main street running up behind the ferry quay (if you are heading to Kos Town then make for the bus stop by the supermarket). Sad to say it, but they are in many ways the biggest attraction in town, for there is very little of Greece to be found here: one could just as easily be in any other down-market package-tour resort filled with beer-and-chips type Brits and Germans — the former often propping up bars showing videos of ancient UK TV comedy shows or enjoying the wet bikini and tee-shirt contests. One of the few pluses are the tour-boat links that all these tourists have generated with nearby Nissiros.

Mastihari, the largest settlement on the north coast, also has a sand beach but is much quieter than Kardamena and offers a better mix of tourism and regular town — though this is rapidly being eroded by the growing number of all-in-one resort-villages-cum-hotel complexes that are being built on this part of the Kos coast. The proximity of Mastihari makes it an ideal close destination for evening taverna meals, and this has all but killed off the fishing industry: this is a village now rebuilding itself as an out-and-out beach resort.

Built on a wide, flat promontory, Mastihari has a small harbour (that, it must be said, is regularly on the smelly side), a ferry link to Kalimnos, and a single major street running directly inland (many of the side streets have recently been pedestrianized). It also has a bus link with Kos Town — the only problem being lack of services after 18.00. If you arrive on the evening ferry from Kalimnos you should plan for the cost of a taxi (€20).

The best beach in town — and it is a very fine white sand strand — lines the wide bay to the west of the headland. It provides an attractive walk to the only close sightseeing attraction close to Mastihari, the ruins of an early Christian church 3 km from the town. The coastline east of Mastihari has less going for it and is dominated by a large A-class hotel complex. In this respect it mirrors the north coast village of **Tigaki**. This small settlement offers a popular alternative to the Kos Town beaches, via its impressively large expanse of sand that is popular with windsurfers. Like Mastihari, it consists of a promenade (complete with a disco) and a main street that runs directly inland to the main island road.

Given the size of Kos and the economic pull of its large resorts, other areas of the island are inevitably harder to get to. The bus service is by no means bad, but links to the western end of Kos are sufficiently few that excursions become de facto day trips (don't be surprised if you have to change buses at Kardamena or Mastihari: running only part of the route seems to be a favoured working practice in this neck of the woods). The primary west end destinations are the beach resort of Kamari and the village of Kefalos — which, some 45 km from Kos Town, lies at the end of the line for bus travellers.

Widely spaced out **Kamari** is the favoured destination of most venturing in this direction. This is a resort village with a lovely long sand beach that is really excellent windsurfing territory. Sadly the plaudits end there because if watersports are not

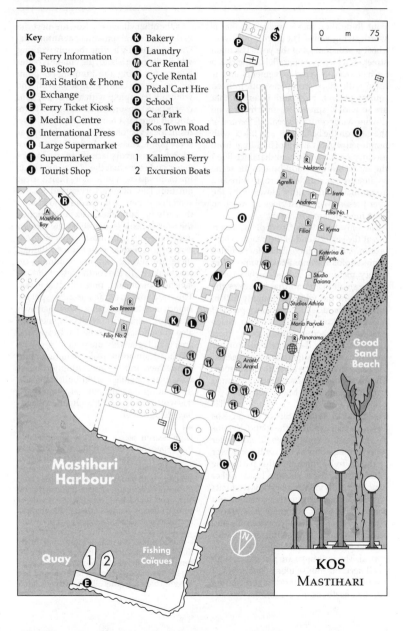

Key

- **A** Ferry Information
- **B** Bus Stop
- **C** Taxi Station & Phone
- **D** Exchange
- **E** Ferry Ticket Kiosk
- **F** Medical Centre
- **G** International Press
- **H** Large Supermarket
- **I** Supermarket
- **J** Tourist Shop
- **K** Bakery
- **L** Laundry
- **M** Car Rental
- **N** Cycle Rental
- **O** Pedal Cart Hire
- **P** School
- **Q** Car Park
- **R** Kos Town Road
- **S** Kardamena Road
- **1** Kalimnos Ferry
- **2** Excursion Boats

Mastihari Bay

Nektaria
Agrellis
Irene
Andreas
Filio No.1
Filio
Kyma
Katerina & Efi Apts.
Studio Daiana
Studios Athina
Maria Parvaki
Panorama
Sea Breeze
Filio No.2
Arant/Arand

Good Sand Beach

Mastihari Harbour

Quay

Fishing Caïques

KOS
MASTIHARI

your thing then this is one resort that is worth giving a miss. The place is positively ghost-townish most of the year. The main street — which runs parallel to the beach — has weed-covered pavements and is lined with shops (complete with inflated tourist prices), bars and tavernas that are so widely spread out that there is no downtown or centre to speak of. Several of the gaps on the beach side are 'filled' with nondescript excavations of buildings from an early 5 c. AD settlement that once lined the shore, but these add little to the scene as they are surrounded by rusty wire and accumulate tourist litter blown in by the ever-present wind that does so much to keep the windsurfers happy.

The only half-decent part of the resort lies at the eastern end of the beach, which is dominated by a large *Club Med* complex behind **Agios Stefanos Beach** (named after a very picturesque ruined early basilica on the small headland that separates the beach from the village). Roughly 100 m offshore is the attractive chapel-topped islet of Agios Nikolaos (tourists either beach boat or swim across and announce their arrival by ringing the chapel bell). Further east are a series of superb beaches reached via boats or bus stops along the main road. These include the unimaginatively named Paradise, Sunny and Magic beaches.

Sited on a hilltop 4 km beyond Kemari is the village of **Kefalos**. Site of the pre-Kos Town ancient capital of the island, Kefalos means 'head', a name that could either refer to its former status as the centre of power or the claim by some that this part of the island resembles a sheep's head. Either way, today this village is best known for its views over the surrounding coastline and across to Nissiros. Although it is graced with a couple of disused windmills and an alleged 'castle' that is little more than a ruinous walled hilltop, Kefalos struggles to appeal. The buildings are just old enough to all need out-house toilets, but aren't of a sufficient vintage where this sort of thing becomes aesthetically charming.

Of the other villages on Kos, the most visited is the central settlement at **Antimahia**. Distinguished by having the only working windmill on the island, the village is better known for being the jumping-off point for the nearby charter-flight airport. The windmill (complete with a large adjacent coach park) ensures that all island tours stop off here for a refreshment break. As a result most visitors to Kos pass through at some point. This said, Antimahia is a very anonymous sort of place: those arriving are never quite sure that they have done so as the main square is little more than a street junction. The village is very spread out and is relatively new — it was only founded in the early 19 c. after the Greek population of the nearby castle (see p. 402) were thrown out by the Turks. Its most visible building is a large US-style water tower, though there are several ruinous windmills on the outskirts. To the south-west of the village lie some notable pine woods at **Plaka**. These are now an attractive picnic spot for island coach tours and those with their own transport. Although hotel development has also encroached onto the landscape, the area is still relatively unspoilt.

Other destinations really require car hire before they can be visited. To the north-east is the unspoilt village of **Pili**: built alongside its beautiful, ruined medieval counterpart, it is worthy of a look. Other inland villages have less to offer.

⋈

High Season sees a rush for the available hotel space and rooms, and understandably so, for Kos, an island overloaded with upper and mid-range package tour hotels, is poorly supplied with budget accommodation, given the number of visitors it sees. If you arrive by ferry you won't be greeted with crowds of people offering rooms — though the chances are someone will ask you if you want one when you head into town. It thus pays to arrive on a morning boat (i.e. Rhodes hydrofoil rather than afternoon ferry). Anyone planning to camp on Kos should take note that *Kos Camping* has now closed its gates for good and has reverted back to a quiet olive grove populated by baby owls.

Up-market hotel rooms in **Kos Town** aren't hard to find (though all the inmates are likely to be of the package tourist variety): drop into the nearest ticket agent and they will work the phones for you.

The limited-budget rooms in the centre of town are divided between seven establishments. To the south of the ferry quay the D-class *Hara* (☎ 22500) lies one block behind the beach road that is home to package tour hotels for a kilometre each side of the town (if funds aren't too much of a problem then finding a bed in one of them is never very difficult). Alternatively, you can try the C-class *Maritina* (☎ 23241) near the OTE. Although it is on a busy street, it is not as noisy as the clutch of hotels overlooking the Old Harbour. These consist of the E-class *Kalymnos* (☎ 22336), and the reasonable but popular D-class *Helena* (☎ 22986), near the internet café, and the *Dodecanessus* (☎ 28460).

There is also one good pension in the centre of town — the *Acropoli* (☎ 22244). To the north lies a second, the *Alexis* (☎ 28798). Although rooms are not so plentiful as on the Cycladic islands there are a reasonable number scattered around the town: the owners, however, are in the habit of only meeting the major boats.

Each of the main tourist villages on Kos has more hotels than most islands can muster. At the budget end of the range **Mastihari** has the C-class *Kyma* (☎ 59045) and a good number of establishments offering rooms including *Maria Parvaki* (☎ 59001) and the rooms *Filio* (☎ 59278). **Kardamena** has the D-class *Paralia* (☎ 51205) and the E-class *Olympia*, and **Kefalos**, the D-class *Sidney* and E-class *Eleni* and *Maria* (☎ 71308). Rooms are also available at all the above as well as at **Tigaki** and **Kamari**.

≽✿

Nightlife in **Kos Town** often looks to be in a not dissimilar condition to Hippocrates' tree: by the early hours the town is festooned with limp limbs propped up by bars. The main nightclub area lies on the north-east boundary of the Harbour Excavation, though the northern part of town along Kanari St., home to the *Playboy Club* (famed for disco light shows) and the *Beach Boys* bar (arguably home to the best music), is also replete with bars. Other discos in town are also in the northern Kanari/Lambi district and include *Disco Heaven*, the *Kalua* (both on the beach) and the *Disco Rock Club*. There is also the inevitable outdoor cinema — in this case the *Orpheus* — on the waterfront.

Nightclubs, bars and discos are easy to find in **Kardamena**. The most visible establishments are the *Tropicana* disco in the block at the east end of the promenade, and *Disco Starlight*  on the landward side of the main road into town.

◉◉

Kos is one of the better islands when it comes to sightseeing options; the only problems are the crowds. There are three major sites (listed in order of convenience rather than merit):

1. Kos Town & Castle
The old quarter of Kos Town offers easy sightseeing thanks to the extensive archaeological remains and the picturesque old harbour castle.

2. Antimahia Castle
The massive, but comparatively little known, castle on the hilltop above Kardamena is now beginning to emerge as a worthy tourist destination.

3. The Asklepieion
One of the greatest Hellenistic shrines in Greece, the reconstructed remains of the complex are the 'must see' option on Kos.

Kos also has boat excursions aplenty, with craft running daily across the 5 km straits to **Bodrum** in Turkey and to all the adjacent islands, including the volcanic beach islet of **Pserimos**. This is a crowded beach island reserved for day-trippers seeking (in vain) to escape the crowds. Boats berth at a small quay serving the small settlement on the west coast.

Kos Town

By mixing exploration, shady trees, and the occasional drink at a passing taverna, you can spend a relaxed and interesting day's sightseeing in Kos Town. It is hard to go far without coming across areas of excavation, revealing remains of the extensive **Ancient City**. Sadly, the grand scheme of things isn't particularly clear as there isn't much on-the-ground information. The most coherent areas are larger ones.

Immediately to the west of the castle lies the largest excavated area of the ancient city.

Known as the **Harbour Area Excavation** (entry free), it also roughly corresponds with the site of the medieval town, though 'town' is something of a misnomer by modern standards given the tiny area that the walls enclosed. At various points along its boundary fragments of these survive. The bulk of the excavation consists of foundations and the inner stone cores of temples (only the long-gone exteriors were faced with marble); it is the preserve of lizards during the day and couples serenading the moon at night. Amid the rubble are the remains of a temple of Aphrodite and a couple of reconstructed columns from the Roman Forum. Sadly, the remains are very confused so it isn't easy to appreciate the overall site layout.

The **Western Excavation** area to the east of the town centre is (thanks to Italian restorers) the best of the ancient sites. A number of pillars that formed the gymnasium's peristyle court have been 'reconstructed', and the streets still bear the ruts worn into the stones by ancient carts. The site also has walls complete with original painted plaster work. The ancient Acropolis is now marked only by the mosqueless minaret on the nearby hill.

To the south of these excavations lie two other attractions heavily restored by the Italians. The first is the **Odeon**, sited at the end of a small avenue of trees. The second is a rebuilt Hellenistic and later Roman house. Known as the **Casa Romana** (entry free in 2011), it offers a mixture of pools and mosaics. Don't be put off by the ugly cement façade of the exterior — even that is semi authentic as ancient houses always were decorated with very plain outside walls, and the interior, although empty, is still very atmospheric.

The final destination relating to the ancient period is the small, centrally located **Archaeological Museum**. Open ②–⑦ 08.30–18.00, it is better described as a sculpture museum because there is little else in it. It was built in the 1930s during the period of Italian rule, and the contents reflect the tastes of the time when grandiose objects were generally favoured over small domestic or interesting curios. There are a few appealing pieces, but the place is very badly in need of a revamp and more diversity of exhibits: at the moment it doesn't do much but help to give museums in general a bad name. All in all it would make much more sense to close this museum and display the exhibits in the Casa Romana.

Kos Town Castle

The well-preserved **Castle of the Knights**, also known as the **Castle of Neratzia** (the 'castle of the citrus trees' — after the orchards that surrounded the medieval town), dominates the Kos Town waterfront and offers some excellent sightseeing, not least because you are visiting two castles for the price of one. It is open ②–⑦ 08.30–18.00; tickets €3.

Originally built on either a small peninsula or a low-lying islet, it was constructed to defend the town some fifty years after the Knights of St. John arrived on Kos. Almost all the building material was gathered from the remains of the ancient city and the Asklepieion. However, its exposed location made it rather vulnerable, and despite its impressive appearance it was dwarfed in size and importance by the Castle of Antimahia (p. 403). In its prime the garrison consisted of only 25 Knights, 10 men-at-arms, 100 infantry men, and a galley crew of 20 oarsmen.

The building visible today consists of the original castle walls now surrounded by a second stronger curtain wall or enceinte, producing the 'castle within a castle' effect. Begun c. 1391, the inner castle boasted a central keep, and a moat-cum-lagoon on the landward side. It was connected by a drawbridge and bridge to city walls built at the same time (fragments of these survive on the north side of the Harbour Area Excavation, and include a gateway and the south-west tower).

The castle fell to the Ottomans in the attack of 1457. This, and the unsuccessful Turkish assault of Kos in 1480, prompted the building of the outer wall. Work began in 1495 under the Grand Master D'Aubusson, and was completed by his successor Fabrizio Del Carretto in 1514; their coats-of-arms (see the Rhodes City map between p. 416–417) are carved on the walls at various points. The castle was handed over to the Turks in 1522 undamaged when the Knights evacuated Rhodes and Kos. Thereafter both Greeks and foreign travellers were banned from entering the building.

In these more enlightened days access is via a bridge over the former moat (now occupied by the waterfront road). Standing opposite the bridge is the impressive 14 m girthed (and now hollow) **Plane Tree of Hippocrates** — its limbs supported with a metal frame. Supposedly the one that Hippocrates taught under, it is at best about 500 years old. Once inside the castle you will find a remarkably well preserved building, though several of the towers now lean at drunken angles thanks to earthquakes. The only significant damage is the loss of part of the inner castle wall and its north-east tower in a gunpowder explosion in 1846. You are free to wander (or fall from towers or walls) where you will, so considerable care is needed, particularly if you are visiting with children. There is a display of ancient architectural fragments (though the whole building is made up of them) and WCs just inside the entrance. The road below the walls and the ferry quay are disfiguring later additions.

Antimahia Castle

Sited atop a hill north of Kardamena, the castle outside Antimahia was the primary stronghold of the Knights of St. John for most of their time ruling Kos. Strategically sited on the edge of an upland central plain, the castle enabled the Knights to keep a firm grip over the island. It exudes a suitable air of menace, and provides a stark contrast with its more picture-postcard (but less effective) counterpart at Kos Town. The castle was built some time between the capture of the island in 1337 and the death of the Grand Master Helion de Villeneuve in 1346, to an irregular design. It has an odd-ball shape (vaguely reminiscent of an open mouth with downturned corners) because its south and east sides take advantage of steep hillsides running down to the coast. On its west side a large notch has been cut out of the hillside to provide both a dry moat and building materials, while the long north side that faces the plain has a massive fortification wall—complete with a central circular bastion — that is on a par with the strongest sections of the Rhodes Old City walls.

The result proved to be a very successful fortress. It held out successfully against a number of Ottoman attacks — most notably a 23-day siege by 16,000 men in 1457 — and was never taken by force. It suffered significant damage in a major earthquake in 1493, but was repaired and further strengthened by the Grand Master D'Aubusson (the great circular bastion protecting the entrance door dates from this period). After the Turks gained control in 1522 a town of sorts was allowed to develop in its interior, but the inhabitants were forced out following the establishment of the Greek state (building the village of the same name down the road), and most of the buildings within the walls — a couple of churches aside — were

either abandoned or demolished. Some street lines and foundations are still visible.

Over the last year tourist facilities have been set up after repair work: there are no opening times and entrance is free (though a ticket kiosk is in place): a refreshment building has also been constructed in the interior. Because the castle is not yet fully on the sightseeing or island tour circuit, access can be difficult if you haven't opted for car hire. The easiest option is to take a bus to Antimahia village and then walk south to a tree-covered traffic roundabout which has the first of several signs pointing the way (note: if you come to the Antimahia windmill then you've gone north!). The castle lies at the end of a small feeder road which starts immediately behind a large army base and runs across a plain of parched stubble and grazing cattle: a journey of some 3 km from the bus stop. The alternative option is to head for Kardamena and then climb the hill via a poorly marked track which starts behind the town: there is also a road that starts 700 m east of the town boundary. Either way, this option entails a 10 km uphill walk.

The Asklepieion

(See map between p. 384–385.) The remains of one of the most imaginative and effective creations of Greek architecture lie on a hillside 4 km west of Kos Town. Overlooking both the town and the Turkish strait, the Asklepieion (open ②–⑦ 08.30–15.00; tickets €3) was the leading medical sanctuary in the ancient Greek world. Aside from walking (not recommended as the main out-of-town road is rather busy), there are two ways of getting there: expensive tour bus or mildly embarrassing fake car-train (of the variety used in theme parks, but fortunately without humans dressed in fluffy animal costumes waving to all and sundry in the back). Regular buses have been abandoned in favour of these tacky contraptions which pick up passengers from Kos Town harbour waterfront.

Dedicated to the god of healing, Asklepios (a son of Apollo, whose symbol was a snake curling up a staff), the Asklepieion was —thanks to the revenue that accompanied the pilgrims that flocked there — an architectural and cultural centre. The sanctuary was founded a century after the death of Hippocrates (357 BC) and because of his associations developed thereafter. Built on four terraces carved out of a gentle hillside adorned with a sacred wood, it was considered a masterpiece of Hellenistic architecture in its day, and boasted a series of famous paintings by Apelles to heal the spirit when they couldn't manage the body. Offices to the latter were undertaken by a priestly order supposedly descended from the god. The sanctuary also offered a much-used right of asylum.

Despite losing some of its most notable art works to Rome in its middle years, the Asklepieion thrived until the 6 C. AD, when it was reduced to rubble, either by the Anatolian attack on Kos in 554 AD or an earthquake. The ruins lay undisturbed until 1450, when the Castle of the Knights was constructed in Kos Town, the need for building blocks being sated by the readily available ancient masonry in the town and at the Asklepieion. As a result, the site was all but stripped bare of architectural members and its location passed out of memory.

Once one of the lost great shrines known only through literary sources, the search for the Asklepieion began in earnest in 1896. The probable site was eventually pinpointed by an English archaeologist, W. R. Paton, in 1902 — though it was left to a local antiquarian, G. E. Zaraphtis, and his German archaeologist sponsor, Rudolf Herzog, to crudely excavate the remains in a classic early archaeological 'grub-and-grab' dig that enabled him to walk off with the glory and his sponsor with the more attractive finds.

From 1904 on Zaraphtis began a much better and more systematic excavation that continued until his death in the great 1933 earthquake. Thereafter Italian archaeologists did as much building as excavating, rebuilding the impressive terrace walls (with rough tuff-stone blocks in lieu of smooth marble) and staircases, and adding a pillar or two for good measure. The visible remains are therefore as much of a 'fake' as the Minoan palace at Knossos on Crete, but, as in that case, the reconstruction is really inspired and of great value to those seeking an appreciation of the site's former grandeur.

Today the Asklepieion is approached via a pleasant suburb road that emerges through

an avenue of cypress trees at a large coach and bus park.

A short path takes you past a drinking-water tap to the ticket kiosk at the entrance to the site. At this point you have to choose between taking the path up the south side of the site and then walking down the terraces from the upper terrace or taking the ancient route (i.e. walking up the staircases). The description below assumes the latter, if only because it is easier to climb, rather than descend, stairways without handrails.

Directly inside the site entrance are the foundations of a small Roman bathhouse (with hypocaust floor in the hot room and a beautifully preserved plunge pool complete with steps), where pilgrims would cleanse themselves before entering the sanctuary proper. The modern path runs past this to ❶ the **Entrance Stairs**. Consisting of 24 steps they climb to the **Lower Terrace** and the site of the formal gateway to the sanctuary, ❷ the **Entry Propylon**, now marked only by a pillar base under a shady tree. The vision — on passing through it — of the wedding-cake terrace layers ascending to the main temple is now only to be dimly gleaned. So too is the enclosed 'courtyard' atmosphere of the Lower Terrace created by ❸ the **Galleries** — pillared, stoa-like buildings which once ran from either side of the gate to the middle terrace wall. Even so, the Lower Terrace retains the wide, open aspect that graced it in antiquity, and it was probably on this terrace that athletic contests associated with festivals honouring the god were held.

Unfortunately, the votive statues that were such a feature of this terrace have long gone. All that remain are ❹ the rebuilt **Statue Niches**. In one of these niches stood a very famous statue of antiquity now lost — the Aphrodite by the even more famous sculptor Praxiteles. The only figures remaining are the **Torsos** at ❺, propped against the **Middle Terrace Wall**. On the stoa side of the path at ❺ you will also find one of the few remaining statue bases (complete with the ghostly footprints of its owner) that adorned this terrace.

Walking along to the north side of the terrace wall you arrive at ❻ the **Fountains**. Fed by both sulphurous and iron-rich springs, these were revered for the supposed healing properties of the water. The later Romans debased the atmosphere by building ❼ the **Latrines** nearby (no doubt the steady tinkle of water dribbling into the sacred pool prompted too many to go in search of a sacred tree or two).

Returning back along the terrace you come to **①** the **Second Staircase**. Running up to the Middle Terrace via 30 steps, it brings you onto the real heart of the sanctuary, for directly in front of you is **①** the **Great Altar of Asklepios** (4 C. BC), the oldest building of the Asklepieion. Now reduced to its foundations, it was similar (albeit on a smaller scale) to the Great Altar at Pergamon, with a central stairway running up to the winged base. The base was also roofed, and one of the ornate roof coffers lies on the edge of the foundations.

To the north lies the oldest temple in the sanctuary: **①** the **Asklepios Early/Small Temple.** Dating from the 4 C. BC, it was built in the Ionic style (two of the columns have been restored) and functioned as the sanctuary treasury after it was replaced as the main shrine on the site. In this capacity it housed a series of wooden panel paintings by Apelles. One — the Aphrodite Anadyomene — was regarded as a masterpiece of ancient art. It was carried off to Rome by the Emperor Augustus. On the Lower Terrace side are the bases for lost votive statues, while tucked away on the Upper Terrace side is a Roman building on Greek foundations **①**, believed to have been the **Priests' Quarters**.

Opposite the Priests' Quarters are the semicircular foundations of **①** the **Exedra / Public Platform.** An odd building, with no clear function, suggestions as to its purpose have ranged from a public bench to an assembly point for priests or doctors. The terrace wall behind it has several more statue niches. To the east, the Romans infilled the terrace by building **⑩** an irregularly orientated **Temple of Apollo**, now the most visible of all the buildings on the site thanks to the seven fake columns erected by the Italians to give you something to look at. Two of them contain fluted fragments of the original drums.

To the south, now little visible and partly overgrown with trees, are the foundations of **①**, usually known as the **Lesche** or **Conference Hall** — though the precise function of the building remains unclear. Given the snake cult associated with the god Asklepios, it is somewhat surprising that the Asklepieion does not appear to have possessed a snake house (its counterpart at Epidavros had a magnificent Tholos built for this purpose), so perhaps this was it. Snake rooms were common at medical shrines, for these lovely little critters were deemed to have healing powers — given the

numbers of lame men who suddenly acquired the ability to run very fast when faced with one (to say nothing of the numerous compulsive stammerers suddenly able to say 'Asklepieion' three times in as many seconds at the first time of asking).

Behind the buildings on the Middle Terrace is **①**, the first stage of the double **Upper Terrace Wall**. In fact, the Middle Terrace can be divided into two (hence the four terraces), but as the upper part of the Terrace is too small to contain buildings, it is viewed as merely a halfway point up **①** the **Monumental Staircase**. This consists of two closely positioned flights that rise 60 steps to the **Upper Terrace** and its superb views over both the site and Kos Town.

Dominating the centre of the Upper Terrace is **①** the **Large Temple of Asklepios**. Built in the 2 C. BC, this was the main temple on the site to the god. Doric in style, it was an irregularly shaped 6 x 11 columned building, notable in its day for having the lowest of its three steps made of black marble (though you would be hard-pressed to know it now). Today only the foundations and part of the interior floor survive.

Around the side and back perimeter of the terrace ran **①** the **Galleries**, forming a peristyle backdrop to the temple, and closing in the rear of the site. At some later date, additions — in the form of cell-like cubicles — were made to the back of the side galleries: now little more than unintelligible foundations, these are thought to have been **①** **Patients' Rooms**.

From the back of the terrace a path winds into **①** the **Sacred Wood** — a delightful, shady canopy of pine trees that surrounds the site — emerging a hundred metres later in a small grove adorned with the remains of a **Small Temple** of unknown attribution (only the foundations of the base remain). Returning to the main terrace, another path runs to the southern end and joins the main path running down the south side of the site. This takes you to a disused museum (still adorned outside with blocks containing inscriptions found on the site) and the back of the **Large Roman Baths**. Dating from the 1 C. AD, this is a late but major structure with hypocaust floor pillars. The high walls have been extensively raised by the Italians (this is Roman after all!). However, one of the front rooms — at **①** — retains some original painted plaster (though there is little visible detail). From here the path returns past the small bathhouse to the site entrance.

Leros

ΛΕΡΟΣ; 53 km²; pop. 8,200.

CODE ☎ 22470
PORT POLICE ☎ 23256
POLICE ☎ 22222
HOSPITAL ☎ 23251

Leros is a real oddity among the Greek islands. Conveniently placed between the popular islands of Patmos and Kos, it is sufficiently attractive to deserve its fair share of the crowds — even despite its lack of obvious sights — and yet, although it is well served by ferries, the island remains stubbornly off the tourist trail. There is, of course, a reason, and that is its very unsavoury reputation. This is so bad that leaflets issued to tourists in past years by the Municipality of Leros were, unusually, forced to acknowledge the problem thus:

'In 1958 the Community of Psychopaths was established at Leros, which is still here today, under the name of 'State Therapeutical Hospital of Leros'. Stemming from that, by mistake or sometimes in purpose, an infamous picture of Leros has been promoted, which in no way can identify with the island and its people. Since 1989 various press reports in Greek and foreign press presented in excess the negative sides of such an establishment.'

In short, a past Greek government came up with the idea of conveniently placing all the country's lunatics and severely mentally handicapped adults in one location — Leros. The media reports in question were humiliating accounts, widely publicized across Europe, that patients in the hospital were being kept in concentration-camp-like conditions.

Happily, thanks to international pressure, a huge EU grant, and the surreptitious dumping of a number of patients to institutions arguably as bad as on other islands, things have now improved massively on Leros, though the legacy of this nasty episode lives on in the lack of visitors. Greek tourists tend to avoid the island in droves (its name has become a byword hereabouts carrying much the same resonances that

'Bedlam' has acquired in English). In many ways this is unfortunate, because Leros has a fair bit going for it in a downbeat sort of way, and you are likely to find that the islanders are both very welcoming and almost pathetically grateful that you are mad enough to have paid them a visit (note: given the circumstances, it is probably wise not to look *too* mad).

Its reputation notwithstanding, Leros is not by any means a typical Greek island. Superficially, it is not dissimilar to Patmos, being small and hilly, with a deeply indented coastline offering a number of sheltered bays complete with — predominantly pebble — beaches. Like Patmos it is all but impossible to lose sight of the sea. However, the years of Italian rule between the world wars have left a greater mark than on other islands in the chain, and it is fair to say that Leros still retains the atmosphere of an Italian island. This is largely because the crumbling plastered 1930s buildings, the harbour and military roads (lined with plane trees) are Italian built, with the tiny nucleus of the Greek chora failing to make an impact.

Most visitors to the island arrive at the port of **Lakki**, set in a deep inlet on the south-west coast. Thanks to the shelter offered by this bay, Leros was a major naval base and was occupied by the Allies at the start of WW2. The island was successfully attacked by German forces in 1943, with 5,000 casualties (war cemeteries are scattered around the island — the largest British cemetery being near Alinda). The memory of this does little to relieve the atmosphere that is set by the airfield-like lights of an abandoned mental hospital complex on the southern shore. Used to detain political prisoners by the Colonels between 1967–1974, it no doubt made the perfect asylum, as any sane person within its precincts would soon be driven mad by the sight of the means of escape constantly steaming in and out of the harbour.

The port town is a very artificial affair, revealing its Italian-planned origins. In a grandiose statement of urban planning, roads were laid out, impressive waterfront buildings were erected and then, well, not a lot really, as the local economy has never grown enough to allow a town to fully develop in the space provided. The result is a mix of odd faded buildings and clumps of trees that is a bit ghost-townish.

More positively, accommodation is easily found (even if the views are not very appealing), along with all services, and in summer the promenade has been known to play host to a circus, complete with little top. As with most Greek island towns, some attempt has been made to give the place a facelift, but in this case it consists of flying all the flags of the member states of the EU on the waterfront, which is also now adorned with the odd cannon, and a somewhat incongruous large plastic chess set (sadly, this is not useable as someone — no doubt a passing escapee, drunk and needing a ride home in the small hours — keeps riding off on one of the black knights).

The bus service on Leros is so poor that taxis thrive along the 3 km road to the chora at Platanos. Historically there is a reason for the poor bus service: visitors were usually relatives of patients who didn't want the stigma of being seen boarding a bus to an asylum — taxis offered a more discreet way of making the journey. In fact the island roads are quite walkable: like those on Kos they are lined with trees planted by the Italians.

Platanos (or Chora) is slightly more Greek in appearance than Lakki. Sited high on a saddle ridge between two bays, it still contrives to lie under the protecting walls of the imposing Kastro. This is one town where almost all roads head up or down at very steep angles. Its appearance is somewhat spoilt by indifferent buildings, a rather dingy atmosphere and the busy road running through the centre. All the main services lie on the main street that is part of the road which connects Lakki with the little port of Agia Marina.

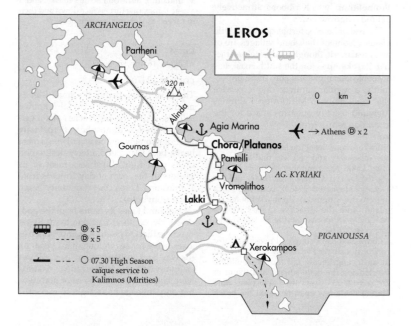

The 19 C. port at **Agia Marina** is now making something of a comeback after years on a somewhat neglected backwater. This is almost entirely because it is used as the island's main port by hydrofoils, catamarans and the island's excursion boats. Lying on the more sheltered east coast of Leros, these smaller vessels find the sea much calmer and prefer to call in here rather than venture round to Lakki. Once the island's main port, Agia Marina certainly has a more attractive waterfront than its successor, with a small quay and several tavernas. It also boasts a pebble beach complete with a distinctive sea windmill gracing a submerged mole.

However, when it comes to tourist appeal, it loses out to **Pantelli**, tucked away in a little bay to the south-east of the Chora, for this hamlet has a much better beach that is an attractive mix of pebbly sand (like the beach at the resort hamlet of **Alinda**) and the odd fishing boat besides. Other hamlets are also noted for their beaches — particularly **Vromolithos**, which ribbons attractively behind a narrow beach.

The rest of Leros is fertile, quiet and little visited. None of the island villages are of any great merit, though moderately attractive **Xerokampos**, on the south coast, has a pebble beach of sorts and, more importantly, a regular summer caïque service that runs daily to Mirities on Kalimnos (demand usually outstrips space for the afternoon return trip).

◫

Offers of rooms meet the large ferries; arrive any other way and you will find an empty quay. **Lakki** has a number of hotels including the D-class *Miramare* (☎ 22043) and the E-class *Katerina* (☎ 22460), both one block in from the waterfront. Up-market hotels lie inland, with the attractive C-class *Artemis* (☎ 22416) supported by the B-class *Agelou Xenon* (☎ 22514).

Chora also has a couple of pensions: most conspicuously the *Platanos* (☎ 22608) housed in an incongruously tall modern building overlooking the main square, and the nicer *Elefteria* (☎ 23550) on the Lakki road. **Agia Marina** has a few apartments on the beach

road but no other advertised accommodation. **Pantelli** (off the map) also has a scatter of pensions and taverna rooms, as does the package resort village at **Alinda**.

A
Camping Leros (☎ 23372): at Xerocampos. Forever listed in the official annual NTOG tourist booklet of campsites, but almost never visited. More a theoretical option than a real one.

⚭
The 12 c. **Castle** built by the Knights of St. John on the site of a Byzantine fortress is the main attraction. It contains a church and offers panoramic views of the island and islets nearby. The Chora stairway starts to the right of a small florist's just off the main square.

Leros has an **Archaeological Museum** (open ②–⑦ 08.30–15.00; entry free) housed in a rebuilt 19 c. town house. In this case the lack of an entry charge is a reflection of the limited contents: the truth is that Leros hasn't really been explored yet. The island's recent history hasn't been one in which the locals — or anybody else — have been encouraged to dig holes or tunnels. Even so, what is there is well laid out. Prize exhibits include a series of 4 C. BC miniature terracotta actor's masks, and a 3 C. BC tombstone turned face down and then re-carved as a church column base.

Lipsi
ΛΕΙΨΟΙ; 16 km²; pop. 650.

CODE ☎ 22470

The most developed of the small islands north of Patmos, quiet Lipsi (also known as Lipsos) offers good beaches and a getaway-from-it-all atmosphere. Perpetually hovering somewhere between being a mere beach-boat island and a ferry destination in its own right, Lipsi sees most of its visitors in the form of day trippers from Patmos and Leros (there are daily beach boats from both).

The island takes its name from the goddess Calypso: local tradition has it that it was here that Odysseus was imprisoned as a sex slave for seven long, hard years on his way back to Ithaca from Troy. Almost as many other Mediterranean islands have laid claim to this piece of notoriety, but only this one has sought to make the

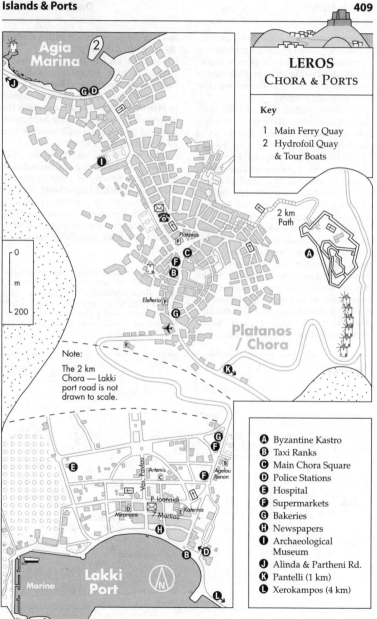

LEROS
CHORA & PORTS

Key

1 Main Ferry Quay
2 Hydrofoil Quay
   & Tour Boats

Agia Marina

2 km Path

Platanos

Elefteria

Note:
The 2 km Chora — Lakki port road is not drawn to scale.

Platanos / Chora

Artemis

Vas. Pavlou

Agelou Xenon

P. Ioannidi

Miramare

7 Martiou

Katerina

Marina

Lakki Port

N

Ⓐ Byzantine Kastro
Ⓑ Taxi Ranks
Ⓒ Main Chora Square
Ⓓ Police Stations
Ⓔ Hospital
Ⓕ Supermarkets
Ⓖ Bakeries
Ⓗ Newspapers
Ⓘ Archaeological Museum
Ⓙ Alinda & Partheni Rd.
Ⓚ Pantelli (1 km)
Ⓛ Xerokampos (4 km)

claim by virtue of its name alone, for there is absolutely nothing else here to support it. Lipsi has never been an important island: lacking defendable features it has existed as a political satellite of Patmos for most of its recorded history.

All ferries, hydrofoils and tour boats dock at the only settlement — the tiny fishing village-cum-chora that is set in the deep bay on the south coast. From a boat it looks to be a singularly uninspiring place, with a prominent blue-domed church surrounded by a small collection of whitewashed houses backed by low, arid hills. Once ashore you will find this impression is somewhat misleading, for the chora is graced with a couple of cosy squares and the islanders are very friendly. Even so, there is no disguising the fact that the village isn't the most photogenic around (in part thanks to ongoing building work): it is the succession of quiet beaches that brings visitors to Lipsi. Unfortunately, it is difficult to take these in within the time available on day trips from other islands. As it is, most visitors 'do' the town and then head for the nearest beach within walking distance (close by the port).

If you are able to stay longer, then it pays to be more adventurous and head for the coves that make up **Katsadia** beach (complete with a taverna offering rooms), or **Plati Gialos** (wide, sandy, and easily the best beach on the island) on the north coast. It is close on an hour's walk — unless you avail yourself of the island bus.

Other beaches are quieter and the objective of occasional beach boats. **Monodendri** is the most notable of them, being the island's designated nudist beach (though discreet nudism is possible on most of them). If the beaches are not to your taste, irregular caïques also run to several islets around the coast (details on the caïque quay).

🛏

Day-tripper tourism has left a dearth of budget accommodation, with the result that beyond several quayside outfits offering pricey rooms (out of High Season you will do well to hunt around for the best deal) and the D-class hotel *Calypso* (☎ 41242), there is nought but the beach to head for.

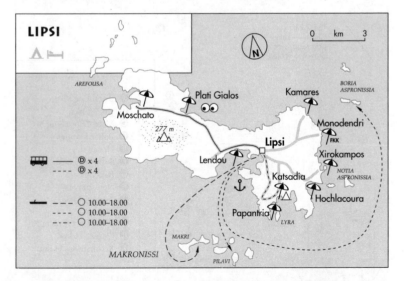

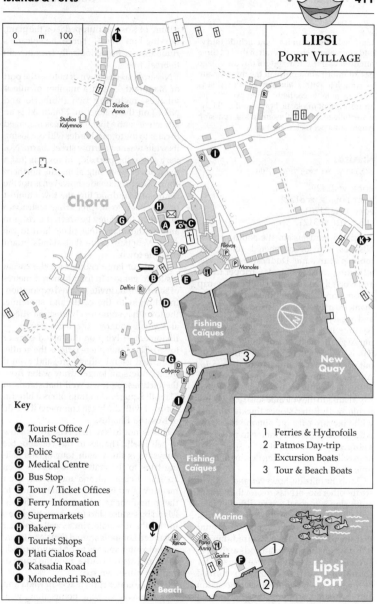

LIPSI
PORT VILLAGE

0   m   100

Studios Anna

Studios Kalymnos

Chora

Fishing Caïques

New Quay

Flisvos

Manoles

Delfini

Calypso

Fishing Caïques

Marina

Renas

Pano Anna

Galini

Beach

Lipsi Port

Key

- **A** Tourist Office / Main Square
- **B** Police
- **C** Medical Centre
- **D** Bus Stop
- **E** Tour / Ticket Offices
- **F** Ferry Information
- **G** Supermarkets
- **H** Bakery
- **I** Tourist Shops
- **J** Plati Gialos Road
- **K** Katsadia Road
- **L** Monodendri Road

1 Ferries & Hydrofoils
2 Patmos Day-trip Excursion Boats
3 Tour & Beach Boats

👓

Lipsi lacks sights (unless you include thirty-odd churches or chapels built in the last three hundred years), but in spite of this the village has an information office in the main square — complete with a **Museum** of sorts that is short of notable contents. Prize exhibits are an assortment of plastic bottles full of 'Holy' water (allegedly) and the remains of a passing American's pet rock collection.

Nissiros

ΝΙΣΥΡΟΣ; 41 km²; pop. 1,100.

CODE ☎ 22420
PORT POLICE ☎ 31222
POLICE ☎ 31201
FIRST AID ☎ 31217

A small island just to the south of Kos, Nissiros is to be numbered among the more picturesque Dodecanese islands, attracting considerable day-tripper traffic and worthily so. It is easily the best day-trip destination from Kos (Rhodes excepted), thanks to a lovely small island atmosphere and a real Jekyll and Hyde personality. For Nissiros is a volcano cone jutting out of the Aegean. In shape not unlike the Aeolian islands north of Sicily, it looks oddly out of character in this part of the world. Another feature that contrasts markedly with other southern Aegean islands is that it is (thanks to the volcanic soil) remarkably fertile, with outer slopes thickly planted with vineyards, fig and almond trees, and wild flowers. These combine to make this a gorgeous island to visit in the spring and an excellent shady walking destination any time of the year.

Climb the hillside, however, and you will see the other face of Nissiros, for the verdant outer slopes conceal a very different interior: this takes the form of a deep and barren crater caked with a yellow sulphurous mud that smells as bad as it looks. Tradition has it that when the Olympian gods arrived in Greece they had to fight a race of giants for control of the earth. Nissiros was formed as the result of a battle between Poseidon and the giant Porphyris; the god speared a lump of Kos and dumped it on the giant, burying him alive — hence the volcano's rumblings as he periodically tries in vain to break free.

Nissiros has one town of note — the port of **Mandraki** — and a number of minor villages, including two (Emborio and Nikia) on the crater rim. Mandraki is an attractive centre that to date has managed to cater to the tourist hordes without losing its whitewashed narrow street charm. Not very large, the port side of town is just a main street ribboning along the northern shore. The promenade, however, is not the centre of Mandraki life: the town almost has its back to it, preferring instead to huddle in the valley between the volcano and the headland that plays host to the small Venetian castle that stands guard over the town.

Just about large enough for the casual visitor to get lost in for a hundred metres or so, Mandraki invites relaxed exploration. In addition to the castle and shoreline, the town has some lovely unspoilt streets and small squares (the main square — Ilikiomeni — lying on the inland edge of town). The atmosphere reflects the gentle, unhurried island village life, and even if the islanders no longer draw water from the picturesque town well that stands in Piaoulli Square, Mandraki offers a blissful contrast with the brash commercial bustle of Kos and Rhodes.

This is not to say that Nissiros is slow to sell itself. Thanks to the volcano, the quayside is lined with tour agents selling trips to the crater and there is even an island-cum-volcano model for good measure. Tour buses run from the quay to the crater floor and the crater rim villages. Island buses also start from here, but go no further than the crater rim, as well as to other inhabited hot spots around the island (there are hot water springs to be found outside **Nikia** and also at **Loutra**, now the home of a rather run-down spa).

Both the crater rim villages of **Nikia** and **Emborio** have viewing points along with steps/paths down into it. Nikia is the better of the two, both as a viewing station and in the degree of inhabitation. Thanks to the building of a number of holiday homes it is quietly thriving, while Emborio is now half abandoned (the population having retreated to the small beach village of Pali).

Like Santorini, Nissiros has black or red sand beaches, but in the main these are poor affairs (people generally come to Nissiros to have a day off from burning on a beach), the best being **White beach** near **Pali** (the only white sand beach of any size on the island), followed by **Lies** beach (made up of tiny grey pebbles). The nearest beach to Mandraki (**Koklaki**) lies below the cliffs on the west side of town, and is reached by a hazardous (beware of falling rocks) path that runs around the shoreline under the kastro. The beach is made up of large blue volcanic 'pebbles' and is more scenic than comfortable. On the ferry front, connections are comparatively poor, but daily boats from Kos (Town and Kefalos) and Rhodes hydrofoils make Nissiros easily accessible.

➤

There are plenty of rooms in **Mandraki**, with some in Pali and Nikia. Hotel accommodation is adequate, even if there isn't much at the top of the range. The nearest Nissiros comes to luxury is the C-class *Porfyris* (☎ 31376). Hotels just to the left as you leave the ferry quay include the *Three Brothers* (☎ 31344) and the *Romantzo* (☎ 31340); these are on a par with the B-class pension *Haritos* (☎ 31322) on the Loutra road.

More down-market is the pension *Drossia* (☎ 31328) in the town. Out of Mandraki the only hotel of note is the C-class *White Beach* (☎ 31497/8) on the hill just before you get to Pali.

👀

Even without the volcano **Mandraki** would attract tourists to Nissiros, being a scenic whitewashed chora with two castles. Above the town stands the Venetian Knights of St. John **Castle** (1315) which contains a multi-iconed monastery within its walls, while 1 km inland stands the older **Kastro**: complete

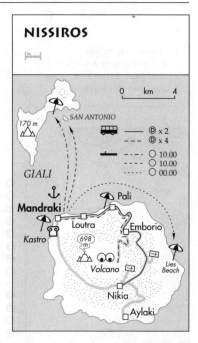

with a Cyclopian wall and gateway built out of imposing lava blocks, it marks the site of the ancient acropolis (though there is little to see within the enclosure). It can be reached via the road south of Mandraki or via a clifftop track. Occasional boat excursions are also available to **Giali** — a small double-hilled island which has a pleasant beach surprisingly unmarred by the pumice quarrying in the hillside behind it — and to a beach on the islet of **San Antonio**.

The **Volcano**, however, is the great attraction, and better done first thing if you are on a day trip. Tour buses run to the crater floor, returning 2–3 hours later. The more ambitious (armed with plenty of water and half a day) might also consider walking the path that runs from Mandraki, over the rim, past Mt. Profitis Ilias and down into the crater. As with other Greek volcanos, Nissiros is not all fountains of magma and pillars of steam, but more a lunar landscapey hole — in this case with 5 shallow craters set in the main crater floor.

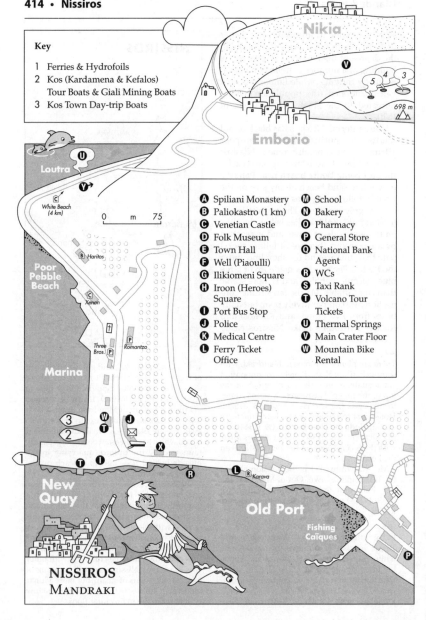

Key

1 Ferries & Hydrofoils
2 Kos (Kardamena & Kefalos)
   Tour Boats & Giali Mining Boats
3 Kos Town Day-trip Boats

Nikia

Emborio

698 m

Loutra

White Beach
(4 km)

0   m   75

Poor
Pebble
Beach

Haritos

Xenon

Three
Bros.

Romantzo

Marina

New
Quay

Old Port

Fishing
Caïques

Karava

NISSIROS
MANDRAKI

Ⓐ Spiliani Monastery
Ⓑ Paliokastro (1 km)
Ⓒ Venetian Castle
Ⓓ Folk Museum
Ⓔ Town Hall
Ⓕ Well (Piaoulli)
Ⓖ Ilikiomeni Square
Ⓗ Iroon (Heroes)
   Square
Ⓘ Port Bus Stop
Ⓙ Police
Ⓚ Medical Centre
Ⓛ Ferry Ticket
   Office

Ⓜ School
Ⓝ Bakery
Ⓞ Pharmacy
Ⓟ General Store
Ⓠ National Bank
   Agent
Ⓡ WCs
Ⓢ Taxi Rank
Ⓣ Volcano Tour
   Tickets
Ⓤ Thermal Springs
Ⓥ Main Crater Floor
Ⓦ Mountain Bike
   Rental

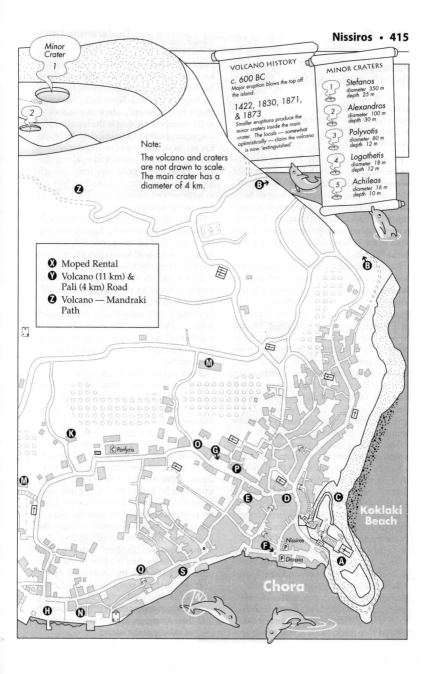

Minor
Crater
1

2

VOLCANO HISTORY

c. 600 BC
Major eruption blows the top off
the island.

**1422, 1830, 1871,
& 1873**
Smaller eruptions produce the
minor craters inside the main
crater. The locals — somewhat
optimistically — claim the volcano
is now 'extinguished'.

MINOR CRATERS

1. **Stefanos**
   diameter 350 m
   depth 25 m

2. **Alexandros**
   diameter 100 m
   depth 30 m

3. **Polyvotis**
   diameter 80 m
   depth 12 m

4. **Logothetis**
   diameter 18 m
   depth 12 m

5. **Achileas**
   diameter 16 m
   depth 10 m

Note:

The volcano and craters
are not drawn to scale.
The main crater has a
diameter of 4 km.

X Moped Rental
Y Volcano (11 km) &
    Pali (4 km) Road
Z Volcano — Mandraki
    Path

C *Porfyris*

M

K

M

O **G**
    P

E **D** **C**

F *Nissiros*
    P
    P *Drossia*

A

Q **S**

H **N**

Chora

**Koklaki
Beach**

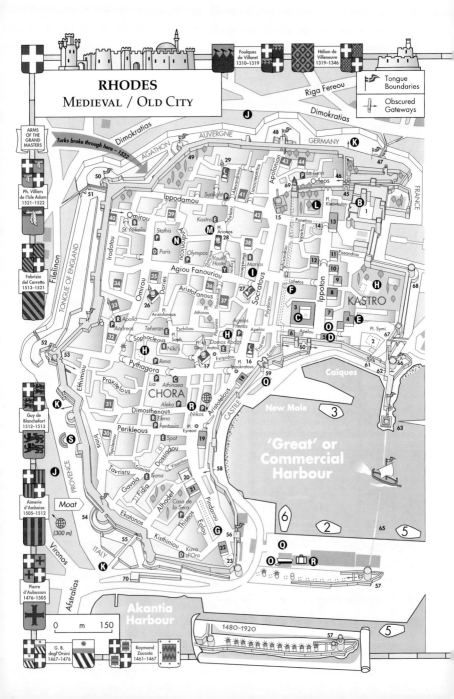

BYZANTINE CHURCHES

30. Agia Ekaterini
31. Agia Triada
32. Aghii Theodori
33. Agia Kyriaki
34. Archangelos Michaii
35. Agios Fanourios
36. Agios Spiridon
37. Archangelos Michaii
38. Agios Konstantinos
39. Agios Nikolaos
40. Agios Athanasios
41. Agia Paraskevi
42. Aghii Apostoli
43. Agios Georgios
44. Agios Marcos

OLD CITY GATES & TOWERS

45. Artillery Gate
46. St. Anthony Gate
47. Amboise Gate
48. St. George Tower
49. Tower of Spain
50. St. Mary / Virgin Tower
51. St. Athanase Gate
52. Koskinou / St. John's Gate
53. Koskinou / St. John's Tower
54. Tower of Italy / Carretto
55. Italy Gate (1924)
56. St. Catherine's / Mill Gate
57. Tower of the Mills / France

58. Port Gate (1924)
59. Marine Gate
60. Arnardo Gate
61. Arsenal Gate
62. St. Paul's Gate
63. Nailac Tower Base
64. Lost Nailac Tower
65. Harbour Chain Line
66. St. Paul's Tower
67. Liberty Gate (1924)
68. St. Peter's Tower
69. Clock Tower
70. Akantia Bastion

Key

A City Tourist Office
B Grand Masters Palace Museum
C Archaeological Mus.
D Byzantine Museum
E Folk Art Museum
F Kastro Inner Wall
G Ancient City Wall
H Classical Excavations
I Drinking Fountain
J Moatside Park
K Moat Access Points
L Turkish Library
M Turkish Baths
N Folk Dancing Theatre
O ATM / Bank
P Italian Cathedral
Q Taxi Stations
R Public WCs
S Moat Theatre

1 Ferry Quay (1 km)
2 International Boats
3 *Dodekanissos* Catamarans
4 Hydrofoils
5 Cruise-ships
6 Turkish Day Boats

Dieudonné de Gozon 1346–1353
Pierre de Corneillan 1354–1355
Roger de Pins 1355–1365
Raymond Béranger 1365–1374
Robert de Juilly 1374–1377
Ferdinand d'Hérédia 1377–1396
Philibert de Nailac 1396–1421
Antoine Fluvian 1421–1437
Jean de Lastic 1437–1454
Jacques de Milly 1454–1461

Makariou
Plessa
Platia Vas. Georgiou II
Pl. Eleftherias
24

Mandraki Harbour

Marina

Akti Boumbouli

25

64

25

The Colossus of Rhodes (attempting the pose favoured by 15 c. illustrators)

CITY LANDMARKS

1. Palace of the Grand Masters / Temple of Helios Site
2. Temple of Aphrodite
3. Hospital of the Knights
4. Inn of Auvergne
5. 'Our Lady of the Chateau' Church
6. Inn of England
7. Inn of Italy
8. Inn of France
9. 'Palace of Zizim'
10. Chapel of France
11. Inn of Provence
12. Inn of Agathon / Spain
13. Loggia
14. 'St. John of the Collachium' Site
15. Suleymaniye Cami Mosque
16. Chadrevan Mosque
17. Ibrahim Pacha Cami Mosque
18. Castellinia
19. Admiralty / Bishop's Palace
20. 'Our Lady of the City' Church
21. Hospice of St. Catherine
22. St. Pantaleon

23. 'Our Lady of Victory'
24. Site of Ancient & Medieval Dockyards
25. St. Nicholas Fortress / Site of the Colossus ?
26. Redjeb Pasha Mosque
27. Agha Mosque
28. Mastapha Mosque
29. Hamza Bey Mosque

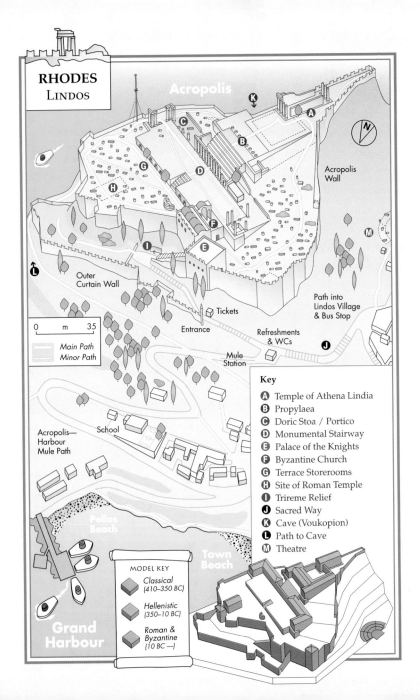

RHODES
LINDOS

Acropolis

K

A

C

B

G

D

H

F

E

I

Acropolis
Wall

M

L

Outer
Curtain Wall

Path into
Lindos Village
& Bus Stop

| 0 | m | 35 |

Main Path
Minor Path

Tickets

Entrance

Refreshments
& WCs

J

Mule
Station

Acropolis—
Harbour
Mule Path

School

**Pellas
Beach**

**Town
Beach**

**Grand
Harbour**

Key

A Temple of Athena Lindia
B Propylaea
C Doric Stoa / Portico
D Monumental Stairway
E Palace of the Knights
F Byzantine Church
G Terrace Storerooms
H Site of Roman Temple
I Trireme Relief
J Sacred Way
K Cave (Voukopion)
L Path to Cave
M Theatre

MODEL KEY

Classical
(410–350 BC)

Hellenistic
(350–10 BC)

*Roman &
Byzantine
(10 BC —)*

The rest of the island has much more going for it, being a lovely mix of bays and beaches tucked away within the folds of an intricate coastline. Beach caïques run from Skala to the best of these — **Psiliamos** to the south and the multicoloured pebble **Lampi** on the north coast, as well as to the adjacent beach islands of Lipsi and Arki (most 'Arki' taxi boats in fact go to a beach and taverna on the adjacent islet of Marathi).

The only other settlements of any size at all are at **Kambos** — which is a pleasantly unspoilt hill village complete with an attractive pebble beach — and **Grikos**, billed as a 'resort' village (though it has fewer hotels than Skala).

In addition to the beach boats, Patmos has a good bus service running between the main centres. Photocopied timetables for these and all regular ferries are available from the information office located in the quayside post office building.

⊨

Plenty of rooms are available, thanks to the island's pilgrim status. Offering hordes meet all boats. The tourist office in the block behind the ferry quay also has lists of hotels. The majority are to be found in Skala, which is also the name of the premier hostelry — the B-class hotel *Skala* (☎ 31343). At the north end of the port, it is close by other up-market establishments, including the *Patmion* (☎ 31313). Best of the mid-range hotels are the C-class *Chris* (☎ 31001) and *Hellinis* (☎ 31275). Cheaper hotels are also plentiful. Just off the quay is the D-class *Rex* (☎ 31242), and behind the town are the *Kastro* (☎ 31554), the *Plaza* (☎ 31217), and cheaper *Rodon* (☎ 31371).

Δ

Camping Stefanos alias *Patmos Flowers Camping* (☎ 31831) lies 2 km away, around the harbour and over the steep hill at Melloi. A quiet bambooed site, it is home to a on-site taverna that is popular with locals. The camping bus only ventures to the port in High Season. A pick-up truck also collects campers.

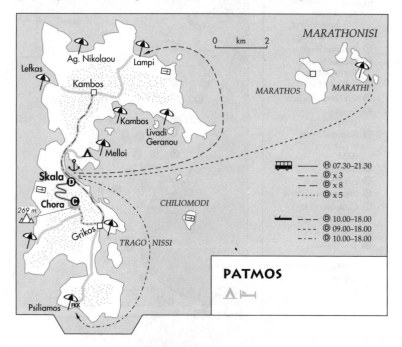

07.30–21.30
x 3
x 8
x 5

10.00–18.00
09.00–18.00
10.00–18.00

PATMOS

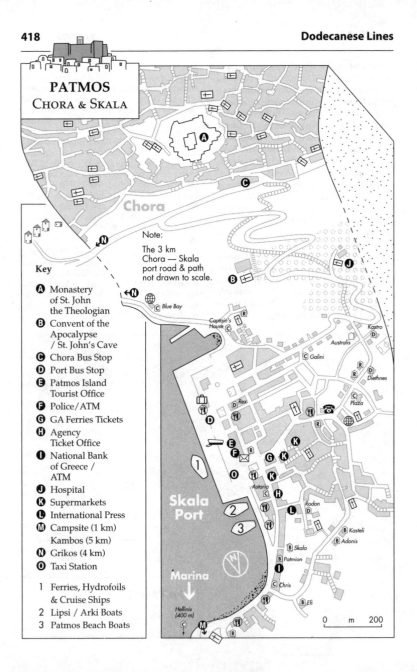

PATMOS
CHORA & SKALA

Note:

The 3 km
Chora — Skala
port road & path
not drawn to scale.

Key

Ⓐ Monastery
of St. John
the Theologian
Ⓑ Convent of the
Apocalypse
/ St. John's Cave
Ⓒ Chora Bus Stop
Ⓓ Port Bus Stop
Ⓔ Patmos Island
Tourist Office
Ⓕ Police / ATM
Ⓖ GA Ferries Tickets
Ⓗ Agency
Ticket Office
Ⓘ National Bank
of Greece /
ATM
Ⓙ Hospital
Ⓚ Supermarkets
Ⓛ International Press
Ⓜ Campsite (1 km)
Kambos (5 km)
Ⓝ Grikos (4 km)
Ⓞ Taxi Station

1 Ferries, Hydrofoils
& Cruise Ships
2 Lipsi / Arki Boats
3 Patmos Beach Boats

Chora

Blue Bay

Captain's
House

Kastro

Australis

Galini

Diethnes

Rex

Plaza

Astoria

Rodon

Kasteli

Skala

Adonis

Patmion

Chris

Efi

Skala
Port

Marina

Hellinis
(400 m)

0   m   200

☙

The main attraction is impossible to miss: the castle-like **Monastery of St. John the Theologian** standing majestically atop Mt. Kastelli. Founded in 1088, it started out as merely a hilltop monastery, but repeated pirate raids prompted its fortification. This process continued when the island fell under the rule of the Dukes of Naxos (from the 13 c. to the 16 c.) who allowed it an unusual degree of autonomy, so that when the Turks finally took control of the Aegean, Patmos — like Mt. Athos — was able to retain semi-independent status.

The present monastery-cum-castle layout is relatively recent: a damaging earthquake in 1956 that brought down a tower and several walls prompted its partial rebuilding. Open daily: precise times vary, but it is always open ⓢ 08.00–13.30, ② ④ ⑦ 16.00–18.00. Entry is free, though you must take care to be modestly dressed (no shorts, bikini tops or women wearing trousers). Surly guards do wonders for the atmosphere — successfully repelling all boarders since the monastery's foundation. As a result it is a treasure house containing over 890 early Christian manuscripts (notably an early 6 c. version of St. Mark's Gospel), a large collection of icons, and the most important display of monastic artefacts in Greece. Built on the site of the ancient acropolis, fragments of a temple of Artemis also litter the building.

Halfway up the Skala—Chora road and mule-track you will come to the second major monastery on Patmos: the **Convent of the Apocalypse** (opening times are the same as above). This foundation is built over the cave where St. John saw and dictated (to his disciple Prochoros) all. Banished to the island in 95 AD by the Emperor Dominian for winding up the population of Ephesus, he spent 15 years in a cave writing the Book of Revelation. Quite why he was disposed to conjure up such happy notions as 'And I looked, and behold a pale horse: and his name that sat on him was Death, and Hell followed with him' remains a mystery; modern Patmos encourages far happier thoughts, and the island in St. John's day (complete with a picturesque temple in place of the forbidding monastery) had even more going for it.

Finally, when you have had enough of Patmos, boat trips offer a taste of freedom. Daily tour boats head for Lipsi, hydrofoils for Samos.

Rhodes
ΡΟΔΟΣ; 1398 km²; pop. 68,000.

CODES: (TOWN) ☎ 22410
   (REST OF THE ISLAND) ☎ 22440
PORT POLICE ☎ 28888
NTOG / EOT OFFICE ☎ 23255
TOURIST POLICE ☎ 27423
POLICE ☎ 7423
HOSPITAL ☎ 22222

The largest island in the Dodecanese, Rhodes (known locally as 'Rodos'), is one of the most touristed islands in Greece thanks to an attractive mix of good beaches, plenty of sightseeing, an unspoilt interior, and a sound reputation for being the sunniest island in the Aegean (it sees over 300 days of sunshine a year). This is probably just as well, for myth has it that when Zeus divided up the world he forgot to allocate a portion to the sun god, Helios, who promptly took for his own the fertile island of Rhodes that was just then emerging from the sea.

Even allowing for repeated earthquakes and invasions, Rhodes has been pretty much sunny-side up ever since, for the island has something for just about everyone. The main tourist strip runs down the east coast: a necklace of sand beaches hung between the two sightseeing jewels of Rhodes City and the acropolis-topped town of Lindos.

Inevitably there is a significant downside to this: with package tourists descending all year round, the island has growing problems attracting those looking for traditional Greek island virtues. Rhodes also comes more expensive than many other islands, and clearly doesn't feel the need to cater for independent travellers in great numbers. On the plus side, the heavy tourist presence has encouraged a proliferation of pleasure boats augmenting the ferries that call — thanks to the island's role as a terminus on the domestic ferry network and point of call for international services to Cyprus, Israel and Egypt. The combination makes Rhodes an attractive point from which to start an island hopping holiday.

☠

Sightseeing fans will find rich pickings on Rhodes thanks to the island's colourful history. For most of the classical period Rhodes was — like most others — a bit player in the wider struggle between Greek and Persian and Athens and Sparta, swapping sides whenever it was deemed politic to do so. She first left her fingermarks on the pages of history following the death of Alexander the Great when she sided with Ptolemy in the wars between his successors, prompting one of his rivals, Demetrius Poliorcetes, to lay siege to Rhodes City in 305 BC. The siege failed in spectacular fashion (the townsfolk selling the abandoned siege engines and using the money to build the mighty Colossus). Inspired by the victory and growing success as a trading centre, Rhodes came into its own as a Hellenistic power centre, boasting an artistic school that produced works of the calibre of the famous Winged Victory of Samothrace and gave — according to Strabo — Rhodes City over 2,000 statues, and a navy that controlled the Eastern Aegean.

However, Rhodes was eclipsed by the rise of Roman power, paying the price for supporting Julius Caesar (by way of retribution she was captured in 44 BC by Cassius and stripped of her art works), and finally becoming part of the Empire in 70 AD. Further damage followed with regular earthquakes and invasions of Goths (269 AD), Persians (620), Saracens (653), and Fourth Crusaders (1204).

Stability of a sort came with the arrival of the crusading Knights of St. John in 1309, who fortified Rhodes City, establishing it as the home of the Knights Hospitallers, and the European front line against the Ottoman Turks. Besieged in 1444 and 1480, Rhodes City finally fell in 1522. Treated badly by the Turks (who stigmatized islands that had resisted them), Rhodes was occupied by the Italians between the world wars, finally joining Greece in 1947.

👓

Rhodes City

The story of Rhodes City is really the story of three cities (Ancient, Medieval and Modern). It was founded as a unifying capital in 408 BC by three ancient cities that previously had ruled the island. Lying on the northern tip of Rhodes and now home to over 60% of the population, it is a bustling centre packed with history and tourists. No matter how you

arrive, the chances are you will end up here. The main bus terminus lies on the boundary between the Modern City and the walled Medieval City. Arrive by large ferry and you will be decanted onto a huge quay 1 km from the Old City walls; catamarans, hydrofoils and tourist boats usually dock at one of three small harbours abutting the walls.

Ancient City

Unfortunately, the fact that Rhodes has been continually occupied since its foundation in 408 BC has led to the obscuring of most traces of the ancient city. In its time it was deemed beautiful and notable. Built on a greenfield site, it was the product of the famous town planner Hippodamos of Miletus, and was laid out in a grid form with distinct commercial, residential, administrative and religious quarters. Fragments of the city walls reveal that it ran east to west across the neck of the peninsula between the Great Harbour and the Upper Acropolis (which stood outside the city walls). At its centre was the Lower Acropolis, which was home to the Great Temple of Helios (now the site of the Palace of the Grand Masters).

The most notable surviving remains visible today are the foundations from a 3 C. BC **Temple of Aphrodite** just inside the Old City walls (which also contain other assorted fragments that include foundations from the city walls). The Upper Acropolis is also hidden away. Lying to the west of the current Old City, it is also known as Mt. Smith (after an English admiral who used it as a spyglass hill) and is now a park (it is open all day, all week, and entry is free). The site offers a shady view of the best-preserved **Stadium** in the Greek islands and small **Theatre**, as well as several standing columns of a **Temple of Apollo** (over-heavily restored by its Italian excava-tors). The **Archaeological Museum** (open ②–⑦ 08.30–15.00; entrance fee: €3) contains most of the surviving movable Ancient City remains. These include a notable head of Helios (see p. 423), and a famous 1 C. BC marble statuette of a bathing, nude Aphrodite drying her hair, known as the 'Aph-rodite of Rhodes'.

APHRODITE
OF
RHODES
1 C. BC

GLUE

RHODES / RODOS

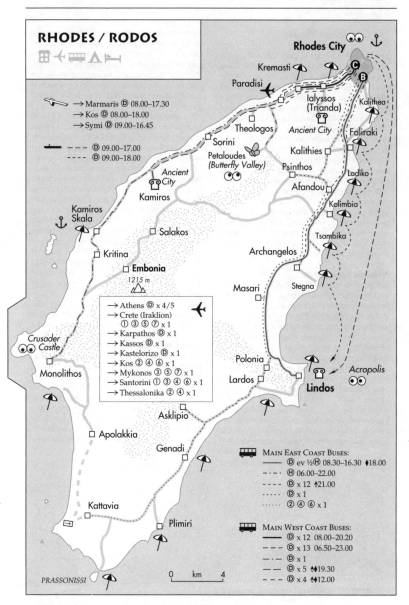

→ Marmaris ⒟ 08.00–17.30
→ Kos ⒟ 08.00–18.00
→ Symi ⒟ 09.00–16.45

--- — ⒟ 09.00–17.00
---- ⒟ 09.00–18.00

Rhodes City

Kremasti
Paradisi
Ialyssos
(Trianda)
Kalithea
Theologos
Ancient City
Faliraki
Sorini
Kalithies
Petaloudes
(Butterfly Valley)
Psinthos
Ladiko
Ancient City
Afandou
Kamiros
Kolimbia
Kamiros
Skala
Tsambika
Salakos
Archangelos
Kritina
Stegna
Embonia
1215 m
Masari

→ Athens ⒟ x 4/5
→ Crete (Iraklion)
  ① ③ ⑤ ⑦ x 1
→ Karpathos ⒟ x 1
→ Kassos ⒟ x 1
→ Kastelorizo ⒟ x 1
→ Kos ② ④ ⑥ x 1
→ Mykonos ③ ⑤ ⑦ x 1
→ Santorini ① ③ ④ ⑥ x 1
→ Thessalonika ② ④ x 1

Crusader
Castle
Polonia
Acropolis
Monolithos
Lardos
Lindos
Asklipio

Apolakkia
Genadi

Main East Coast Buses:
—— ⒟ ev ½Ⓗ 08.30–16.30 ♦18.00
-·-· Ⓗ 06.00–22.00
---- ⒟ x 12 ♦21.00
-- ⒟ x 1
···· ② ④ ⑥ x 1

Kattavia
Plimiri

Main West Coast Buses:
—— ⒟ x 12 08.00–20.20
--- ⒟ x 13 06.50–23.00
-·- ⒟ x 1
-- ⒟ x 5 ♦♦19.30
--- ⒟ x 4 ♦♦12.00

PRASSONISSI

0   km   4

The Colossus of Rhodes

Best summed up as the original Statue of Liberty, the Colossus of Rhodes was one of the Seven Wonders of the World. Built c. 290 BC with the money obtained by selling the siege engines left after the unsuccessful attempt by Demetrios to take the city in 305/4 BC, it was designed by Chares of Lindos, a pupil of the famous Lysippos (Alexander the Great's favoured sculptor). The figure took 12 years to complete and was the largest colossal statue ever made in ancient Greece and one of the most renowned in the ancient world. Made of bronze (probably on an iron and stone frame), it only stood for 63 years before it collapsed — along with most of the rest of the city — during a massive earthquake in 227/6 BC. Thereafter it lay as a wondrous ruin for over nine centuries, until it was broken up and removed in 653, after the island fell under Arab rule, exaggerating legend having it that it took nine hundred camels to transport the bronze from Aleppo to Syria.

Probable Appearance

No trace of the statue has ever been found, nor did ancient writers describe its pose. This has opened the way for a flood of theories as to where it stood and what it looked like. The most famous of these was dreamed up by Italian Renaissance artists, who opted for the compelling image of a giant figure bestriding the harbour entrance, and holding a light into the bargain. Sadly, all the evidence is against such a notion. First, the figure just wasn't tall enough to have been capable of such a feat even if its feet had been capable of sustaining it upright in such an unstable posture. Secondly, the statue fell onto land (if it had been straddling the harbour entrance it would surely have toppled into the sea). Thirdly, ancient writers comment on the figure's beauty and height (pacing out the length of the fallen Colossus was obviously a popular pastime) but make no mention of its posture. It is always dangerous to argue from silence, but the lack of comment on this score means one can say that the figure's pose was literally 'unremarkable'. This same argument also tells against the notion that the figure acted as a lighthouse (a concept that is totally alien to the tradition of colossal statues in the ancient world).

So, what did the Colossus look like? If Chares kept to the Lysippian tradition (and he is known primarily as a pupil of Lysippos) it is reasonable to assume that the Colossus had much in common with the Lysippian statues of Alexander that rapidly became the model for statues of many other heroes and gods (Apollo not least among them). This 'Alexander' pose was a derivative of the kouros form with the left foot traditionally placed slightly forward but with a much more relaxed stance and a reduction in the ratio of head to body size from the traditional 7:1 to the Lysippian 10:1 (giving the figure a hunky torso look). Using fragments of various Lysippian figures, it is possible to come up with a plausible reconstruction of the fallen Colossus as it might have looked on the day of the annual Vestal Virgin Brass-Rubbing Club outing in any of the centuries that followed.

This bit of fun is made easier thanks to the head of Helios (identifiable by the crown of holes that would have held the gold sun-rays) in the Rhodes Archaeological Museum. Dating from a hundred years of the construction of the Colossus (it could even be a copy of it), it is a variant of the Lysippian head of Alexander. A second great aid to reconstruction is the fact that the statue's height is known: it was 31 metres high (making it a metre shorter than the Statue of Liberty, measured from head to toe). A further check on its size comes from the comment of Pliny, who wrote — no doubt from personal experience — that it was only with difficulty that a man could put his arms round the figure's thumb.

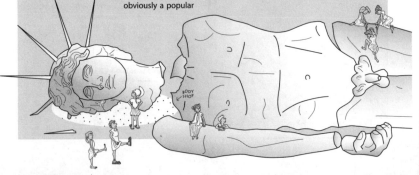

Location Sites

Where the Colossus stood is also the cause of much debate among scholars today thanks to the almost total absence of evidence, combined with the fragmentary understanding of the layout of the Ancient City. Colossal statues traditionally stood either near the temple of the god to whom they were dedicated (e.g. the statue of Apollo on Delos) or at port entrances, usually on the end of man-made moles. On Rhodes, the Temple of Helios is thought to have stood on the site now occupied by the Masters' Palace.

During the 1930s, the Italians extensively excavated before rebuilding the palace, and found nothing to suggest that the Colossus stood in this area. The port alternatives also present problems as there were five ancient harbours, and all Rhodian moles are man-made. In order to be sure of visiting the site of the Colossus, you therefore need to take in:

1. The Tower of the Mills
2. The base of the lost Nailac Tower
3. The landward entrance of Mandraki harbour
4. The circular Fort of St. Nicholas on the Mandraki harbour mole.

This last location is arguably the most likely site for the Colossus. The site's champions point to a number of curved marble blocks built into the walls of the circular central tower of the fort that appear to come from a Hellenistic structure with the same 17 m diameter, the suggestion being that the tower is built directly onto the remains of the lost base of the Colossus.

Helios: The Sun God

The deity that inspired the Colossus of Rhodes has left his mark in more tangible ways beyond the memory of his statue. Widely respected in the Eastern Mediterranean (Apollo occupied his role as the god of light in the rest of the Greek world) from the Archaic period on, Helios was particularly associated with beginnings, rebirth and light coming up out of darkness. The ancients believed that he rode a chariot of fire across the sky each day before spending the night sailing around the dark side of the world in a giant cup.

From the Hellenistic period on, his cult developed from basic superstitions (it was considered dangerous to turn one's back on the rising sun) to a point from the mid-2 c. when it became the religion of the Roman world. Even the Emperor Constantine — who made Christianity the state religion of the Empire — combined worship of the 'Unconquered Sun my companion' with his Christianity, for the first decade of his rule.

As a result, the church ended up inadvertently adopting holy days that had no biblical significance, merely because they had already become established as holy days in the Empire thanks to the brief flirtation with Helios. Not least of these was the use of Sunday as the day of worship rather than the Jewish Sabbath. Sunday — as the first day of the week — was literally 'Sun'-day: the day of the sun god. (Note: this guide adopts the European timetable convention of numbering Monday — the first working day — as ① .) Helios's birthday was also absorbed into Christianity. The 25th of December (the first day that could be shown to be getting longer after the winter equinox) was a popular feast day in the Eastern Mediterranean from the 5 c. BC on.

Not content with nabbing the sun god's birthday and day of worship, the early church made off with his symbol too. All ancient gods had an identifying symbol (see p. 72–73); Helios's was a sunburst — represented as an orb, or points of light around the head — the original halo: all of which leads one to wonder how many clergymen have looked forlornly across ranks of empty pews of a Sunday morning and mourned the fact that Helios wasn't also the god of orgies.

THE COLOSSUS OF RHODES
RECONSTRUCTED FROM THE LYSIPPIAN-STYLE HEAD OF HELIOS IN RHODES, THE TORSO OF A LYSIPPIAN BRONZE OF ALEXANDER, AND THE FEET AND GOOLIES OF A LYSIPPIAN APOLLO.

Medieval / Old City

Many Greek island towns offer a dramatic contrast between the ancient centre and modern quarters, but Rhodes City takes this to extremes with the character-packed, moated and walled medieval Old City seemingly standing apart from a quintessentially Italianesque New Town. This is not to say that the Italians didn't leave their mark on the Old City, for they did in a large way, repairing the walls and medieval buildings, and allowing the locals to tear down the forest of minarets that the Turks had added to the Byzantine city churches that had been converted into mosques. Occupying the eastern half of the ancient city, the Old City also contains reminders of its more illustrious past, including a hint of the former grid street layout that is still visible in the position of the main thoroughfares — now rather distorted by centuries of encroachment by buildings repeatedly rebuilt after earthquakes.

The Old City offers several days of sightseeing and plenty of opportunity to get lost time and time again in the warren of narrow streets. Bounded by a moated wall breached by 11 gates, the Old City was divided by an inner wall (now largely lost) into two sections, from the Byzantine period on, the smaller northern section forming the inner defensive core of the fortified city. Known as the **Kastro** or **Collachium**, it contained most of the important buildings during the 14 and 15 C., when the city housed the West European Knights of St. John; the lowly Greeks lived in the larger southern part of the city, known as the Chora. Surrounding both sections of the town are the impressive **City Walls**. Rebuilt several times by the Knights of St. John, they represent one of the best-preserved medieval fortifications in Europe. In their day they proved a formidable barrier to Turkish ambitions to take the island, protected by a deep, dry moat, and divided into defensive sections known as **Tongues** (the Knights of St. John recruited members to their order right across Europe, and they were grouped in units according to language). After several unsuccessful assaults, it finally took a 6-month siege by 200,000 Turks to capture the city, held by 290 Knights supported by 6,000 local Greek soldiers. The losses were equally impressive, with 50,000 Turks killed compared to 2,000 defenders. The high death rate among the Ottomans can in part be attributed to the arrival of the cannon into siege warfare. The

defenders' casualties were so low because, once the Turks finally breached the wall, the Knights negotiated a withdrawal in return for leaving the city intact.

Beyond exploring the gates and towers, the walls also offer various attractions. The best of these is the guided tour that allows you to walk along the walls (②, ⑥ 14.30; tickets: €6). This runs anticlockwise from the courtyard of the Palace of the Grand Masters to the stairs beyond St. John's Gate. It is also possible to walk the moat — which was always dry (there are access points at intervals in the walls). Below the north wall is a daily *son et lumière* that tells the story of the 1522 siege.

Protected by the moat against land attack, the seaward side of the city wall circuit was also formidably fortified. The walls here bounded the **Great Harbour** (now significantly diminished by the building of a seaward-side road, a new mole and the enlarged ferry quay), with the impressive **Marine Gate** providing the main entrance to the city. The ancient moles built on both sides of the harbour were also utilized, with the construction of impressive towers that guarded a massive chain that closed off the entrance. Today only one of these towers survives (the **Tower of the Mills**); its much more romantic-looking partner, the lost **Nailac Tower** (named after a Grand Master and adorning many early drawings of the city), collapsed in an earthquake in 1863. The Italians did plan to rebuild it, but WW2 put paid to that ambition, so tourists have to make do with standing on its base instead.

Within the walls, the biggest pull is **The Palace of the Grand Masters**. Sadly, it is a fake. The original — converted into a prison by the Turks — blew up in 1856 after some bright spark (no doubt a warder determined to prove that cigarettes do kill) ignited a thousand tonnes of forgotten gunpowder that the Knights had left in one of the dungeons. Rebuilt in the 1930s as a palace for Mussolini, the building (open ②–⑦ 08.30–15.00; the ticket fee is €6) is home to many Kos Town mosaics. It also contains an interesting museum that houses artefacts from all three cities.

To the south-east of the Palace stands a **Loggia** that once covered the way to the last cathedral church of the Knights. The church was also demolished in the gunpowder explosion, and the Italians built a reconstruction of sorts by modelling Evangelismos Church (at the entrance of Mandraki Harbour) on

YE TACKY OLDE CITY SOUVENIR SHOPPE

GENUINE 16 C. WIND CHIMES

MADE FROM YE CANNONS OF RHODES

This bombard is now at the *Hotel des Invalides* in Paris.

ST JEAN

LE HARDY

LE TERRIBLE

LA FRAYEUR

The practice of giving large guns nicknames goes way back...

LE FURIEUX

Kiss Me

early drawings of the original. The Loggia archway opens out into one of the best-preserved medieval streets in Europe: cobbled **Ipaton Street**, which was once the ancient processional street from the Temple of Helios to the harbour. Lined with the **Inns of the Knights** (meeting houses for each Tongue), it has been restored by the Italians, though the result is curiously lifeless. At the harbour end of the street stands the **Knights' Hospital**: the Knights of St. John were not known as the Hospitallers without reason. The hospital now houses the **Archaeological Museum**. Nearby is a **Byzantine Museum** housed in the **Our Lady of the City Church**.

A short walk south of the museum brings you into **Socratous** — the main shopping street-cum-souk that is now filled with tourist shops. At the west end is the pink **Suleymaniye Cami Mosque**, built on the site of a church by the victorious Suleiman in 1522. Now disused, older postcards show it with an impressive minaret that was recently taken down for structural reasons. The locals don't seem keen on restoring it, preferring to devote their energies to renovating the many Orthodox churches converted into mosques. Depending on their age, local guidebooks refer to these buildings by their mosque or saint names (it is only recently that their original dedications have become apparent — as covered-over frescoes and mosaics are exposed).

The last great building from the medieval period lies outside the Old City on the mole of **Mandraki Harbour** (with its two bronze deer). This is the turret fort of **St. Nicholas** (open ②–⑦ 10.00–13.00; entry is free). Now adorned with a lighthouse, this fort also housed a harbour chain.

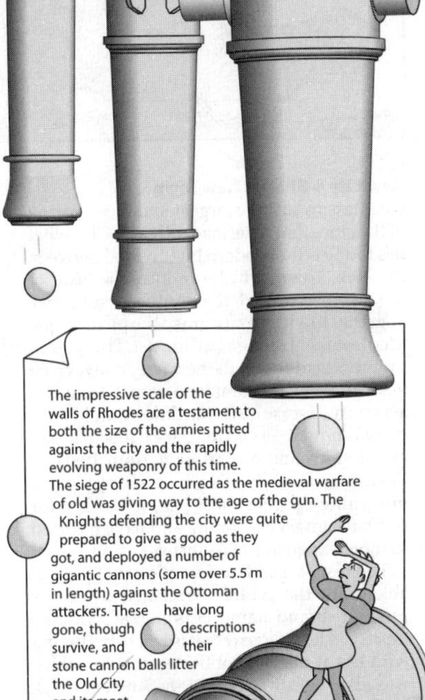

The impressive scale of the walls of Rhodes are a testament to both the size of the armies pitted against the city and the rapidly evolving weaponry of this time. The siege of 1522 occurred as the medieval warfare of old was giving way to the age of the gun. The Knights defending the city were quite prepared to give as good as they got, and deployed a number of gigantic cannons (some over 5.5 m in length) against the Ottoman attackers. These have long gone, though descriptions survive, and their stone cannon balls litter the Old City and its moat.

THE (LOST) CANNONS OF RHODES

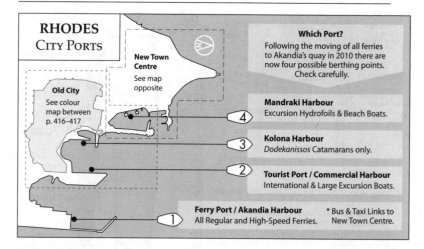

RHODES
CITY PORTS

New Town Centre
See map opposite

Old City
See colour map between p. 416–417

Which Port?
Following the moving of all ferries to Akandia's quay in 2010 there are now four possible berthing points. Check carefully.

④ **Mandraki Harbour**
Excursion Hydrofoils & Beach Boats.

③ **Kolona Harbour**
Dodekanissos Catamarans only.

② **Tourist Port / Commercial Harbour**
International & Large Excursion Boats.

① **Ferry Port / Akandia Harbour**
All Regular and High-Speed Ferries.

* Bus & Taxi Links to New Town Centre.

New City & Rhodes New Town

Needless to say, the largest and most boring of the cities that have made Rhodes City what it is today is the modern bit (divided between the New Town, which occupies the head of the peninsula, and the southern suburbs). Together town and city grasp the picturesque Medieval centre like a ball in a fist. The eastern thumb is made up by the new ferry quay which lies inconveniently removed from the centre of action, and worse has no facilities (the old ferry quay is now reserved for the exclusive use of cruise ships and day-trippers from Turkey). Buses meet boats, but they have a happy knack of turning up after most people looking for one have given up hoping and have resorted to more expensive taxis instead.

The rest of the New Town is equally missable, with the centre dominated by shops pushing brand-name clothing at package tourists. The only part that is worth bothering with lies at the head of the peninsula (which was also the site of part of the Ancient City). It takes its name from the earlier Greek settlement that emerged here during the Ottoman period (when Greeks were banned from living within the Old City). Sadly, nothing of this late medieval settlement survives beyond five windmills behind the western beach.

Following WW1, the occupying Italians embarked on an extensive rebuilding programme, adding many grandiose structures

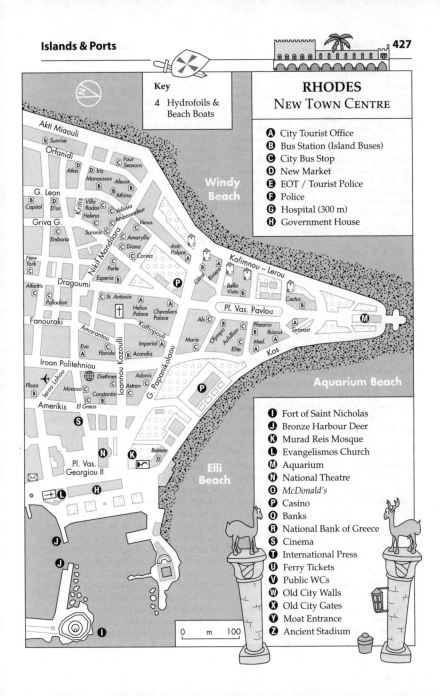

Key

4 Hydrofoils &
   Beach Boats

RHODES
NEW TOWN CENTRE

Ⓐ City Tourist Office
Ⓑ Bus Station (Island Buses)
Ⓒ City Bus Stop
Ⓓ New Market
Ⓔ EOT / Tourist Police
Ⓕ Police
Ⓖ Hospital (300 m)
Ⓗ Government House

Windy
Beach

Akti Miaouli
Ⓑ Sunrise
Orfanidi
Ⓓ Ⓓ Iris Ⓓ Four
Atlas Manoussos Seasons
Ⓑ Alexia
G. Leon Ⓒ Villa Ⓑ Athina
Ⓑ Ⓓ Rodos Ⓒ
Capitol D'or Helena Ⓒ Valissia
Ⓒ Ambassadeur
Griva G. Ⓒ
Venus
Ⓒ Saronic Ⓒ
Embona Ⓒ Amaryllis
New Ⓒ Diana Astir
York Ⓒ Carina Palace Ⓐ
Atlantis Perle Ⓐ Coral Riviera Ⓐ
Ⓒ Ⓒ Esperia Ⓑ Ⓐ Bella
Palladion Vista Ⓑ
Fanouraki Ⓐ St. Antonio Cactus
Ⓐ Chevaliers Pl. Vas. Pavlou
Amarantou Helios Palace Ⓐ
Palace Als Ⓒ Ⓑ Pheonix
Eva Ⓒ Imperial Ⓐ Marie Olympic Ⓐ Siravast Ⓐ
Ⓑ Florida Ⓐ Acandia Ⓒ Achillion Ibiscus Ⓐ
Iroon Politehniou Elite Med. Ⓐ
Diethnes Adonis Kos
Plaza Ⓒ Astron Ⓒ
Ⓑ Mimosa Ⓒ Constantin Ⓒ
Amerikis El Greco
Ⓢ

Kalimnou – Lerou

Ⓜ

Aquarium Beach

Ⓝ
Ⓚ Belman Ⓓ
Pl. Vas.
Georgiou II
Ⓗ
Elli
Ⓛ Beach

Ⓙ

Ⓙ

Ⓠ
Ⓘ

Ⓘ Fort of Saint Nicholas
Ⓙ Bronze Harbour Deer
Ⓚ Murad Reis Mosque
Ⓛ Evangelismos Church
Ⓜ Aquarium
Ⓝ National Theatre
Ⓞ *McDonald's*
Ⓟ Casino
Ⓠ Banks
Ⓡ National Bank of Greece
Ⓢ Cinema
Ⓣ International Press
Ⓤ Ferry Tickets
Ⓥ Public WCs
Ⓦ Old City Walls
Ⓧ Old City Gates
Ⓨ Moat Entrance
Ⓩ Ancient Stadium

0   m   100

in an effort to reflect the town's status as the capital of the Italian Dodecanese. Add to this thirty years of hotel construction, and it isn't much of a surprise to find that these days package-tourist accommodation and bars dominate. As a result, the New Town has little to offer, bar a bracing sunbathe on aptly named Windy Beach and a rather seedy sea-level **Aquarium**. This is filled with a mix of local marine life (alive, and not on a restaurant table for once), and rarer or almost extinct exhibits (including some intriguing moonfish and several stuffed monk seals fighting a losing battle with moths).

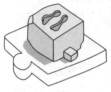

Lindos

After Rhodes City the next great centre and sightseeing attraction is the picturesque, acropolis-topped village of Lindos. Although it isn't the island capital, Lindos has a pedigree that puts most Greek island capitals to shame. Of the three early Doric Greek cities of Rhodes, it was the only one that had sufficient going for it to survive the collective decision to found a new capital at Rhodes City. This was, in large part, due to its having a major shrine that remained the premier shrine on the island even after Rhodes City was built. Indeed, the famous Temple of Athena Lindia that stood atop the dramatic coastal acropolis was famed throughout the Greek world. Gradually fortified during the Roman and Byzantine eras, the acropolis ensured that the ancient city beneath its walls remained occupied, developing in the last few centuries into a scenic whitewashed village complete with narrow cobbled streets (now protected from further development by a government decree).

Even without the acropolis, the village would be a sightseeing destination of note, and it is not surprising that Lindos has emerged as a premier day-trip destination, with a procession of tour buses and boats running down from Rhodes City and arriving at the small leafy town square

or the pitifully small harbour quay. Even with the crowds lining up to take donkey rides or paying high local refreshment prices (expect to fork out at least 20% more than you would elsewhere), Lindos defiantly manages to retain a fair measure of charm. In short, it is well worth taking time out to visit.

In addition to the acropolis and the foundations of a 4 C. BC theatre, the village also has a number of notable 17 C. mansion houses with ornately carved doorways, and a Byzantine church decorated with frescoes. Most visitors, however, seem to find the tourist shops and the sandy beaches either side of the village more interesting (this is partly because the mansions are not easily identifiable from their exteriors).

Lindos village lies in a hollow, sandwiched between the seaward acropolis and the hills that surround the village. Either side of the acropolis are beach-lined bays. The northern bay — usually known as the **Grand Harbour** — is home to the town beach, and the small quay where the day-tripper boats from Rhodes City berth. The southern bay is reputedly the point where St. Paul arrived on the island in 43 AD and is now known as St. Paul's, or the **Small Harbour**. Legend has it that the bay was formed when the rocks opened up to protect St. Paul, as his ship battled against seas that threatened to shipwreck him. This was no doubt a wonderful event for the saint, but it must have left the owners of the land pretty browned off.

Lindos also has problems beyond passing saints knocking holes in the coastline, and the price-inflating crowds. The first one is accommodation: there just isn't enough of it: if you want to stay then plan a visit out of High Season. The Grand Harbour town beach also struggles valiantly to cope with the summer crowds, and has additional problems with pollution from yachts which favour the enclosed bay as a natural anchorage, but aren't able to take advantage of any marina facilities because they are non-existent.

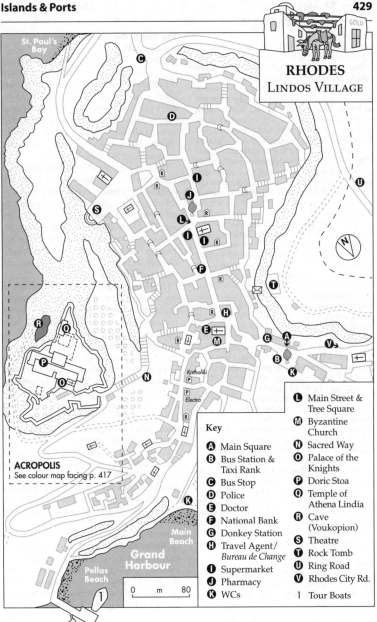

RHODES
LINDOS VILLAGE

St. Paul's Bay

ACROPOLIS
See colour map facing p. 417

Main Beach

Grand Harbour

Pellas Beach

Katholiki

Electra

Key

- **A** Main Square
- **B** Bus Station & Taxi Rank
- **C** Bus Stop
- **D** Police
- **E** Doctor
- **F** National Bank
- **G** Donkey Station
- **H** Travel Agent/ *Bureau de Change*
- **I** Supermarket
- **J** Pharmacy
- **K** WCs
- **L** Main Street & Tree Square
- **M** Byzantine Church
- **N** Sacred Way
- **O** Palace of the Knights
- **P** Doric Stoa
- **Q** Temple of Athena Lindia
- **R** Cave (Voukopion)
- **S** Theatre
- **T** Rock Tomb
- **U** Ring Road
- **V** Rhodes City Rd.
- **1** Tour Boats

0   m   80

The Acropolis

Open ②–⑦ 08.30–15.00 and ① 12.30–15.00 (the entrance fee is €6), the acropolis (see the colour map opposite p. 417) is one of the most spectacular archaeological sites in Greece; so much so, that the 116 m rock has been drawing tourists since antiquity, thanks to ❹ the **Temple of Athena Lindia**. Built in 348 BC, the surviving structure is a tiny affair with its end columns and side walls (it never had columns down its sides) partially reconstructed. It replaced earlier temples (including its immediate Classical predecessor, which burnt down) dating as far back as the 10 C. BC. As the sanctuary grew in importance other buildings were added, the most notable being ❸ the formal gateway or **Propylaea** (407 BC) to the temple precinct, and ❻ a large, 42-column, double-winged **Doric Stoa** (208 BC) that formed the entrance to ❶ a **Monumental Stairway**. The construction of this majestic Stoa heralded a phase of Hellenistic sanctuary embellishment on the grand scale, and was a precursor to the major development along similar lines of the Asklepieion on Kos. As with the Asklepieion, the Italian excavators attempted a considerable amount of reconstruction (rescuing many of the stones that were reused in later buildings on the site). Unfortunately, like that at the Rhodes City acropolis, the touch is not quite so deft, and the overall impression, although positive, is one of excess (the amount of tasteless new material is apt to leave the unfortunate impression that these remains are more akin to those of bombed-out WW2 buildings).

During the Byzantine period, the acropolis was fully fortified, a process completed with the construction work carried out by the Knights of St. John. Within the walls they also rebuilt ❸ a medieval castle on a grand scale, turning it into a fortified **Palace** (complete with the now ruined Byzantine church of Agios Ioannis). This final phase of fortification saw the best survival on the site brought within the walls: the **Trireme Relief**. Measuring 4.6 m long and 5.5 m high, it was carved by Pythocretes on the cliff wall and shows the stern and rudder of an ancient Greek warship. The relief served as the base for a statue of a priest named Hagesandros.

Finally, outside the acropolis walls on the seaward side, there is a large cave (only partly accessible). Lying directly underneath the main temple, it seems to have added to the religious significance of the site during the Dark Ages.

The Rest of the Island
1. East Coast

While Rhodes City and Lindos dominate the tourist industry on Rhodes, the rest of the island also has much to offer. The east coast sees regular boats running down each morning, stopping at resorts and sand beaches en route to Lindos. Provided you can afford them, they are preferable to taking a bus (and cooler), as the coast road does not hug the shoreline.

The first port of call is usually the faded 1920s spa town of **Kalithea**: built by the Italians, it offers a delightfully quixotic collection of pseudo-Moorish buildings set in an odd landscape of small park areas between the rocks of the seashore. These days, the world has moved on (in every sense) down the coast to the youth nightspot Mecca of Greece — the disco and bar resort of Faliraki.

Home to arguably the wildest nightlife in the whole of Greece, **Faliraki** has featured in a popular UK TV series and more than a few newspaper reports charting its wilder excesses. In many ways there is a lot to be said for having all the partying in one resort, but as with other similar destinations elsewhere in the Mediterranean you can hit trouble if you don't take care. If partying is your thing then you will probably enjoy a visit, but keep in mind that levels of all types of reported crime are higher here than elsewhere in the islands, and take the precautions necessary to stay safe.

The next major beach down the coast is rocky **Ladiko**. The place where much of *The Guns of Navarone* was filmed, it has been known as 'Antony Quinn' beach (after the late film star who played the lead), but this is now changing as too many visitors are simply asking 'Who?'

South of Ladiko come the resort beaches of **Kolimbia** and **Tsambika** (which has a monastery-topped hill behind the beach, offering good views along the coast), and the far less spoilt beach at **Stegna**. This is best reached via a track that runs down from the inland village of **Archangelos**. After

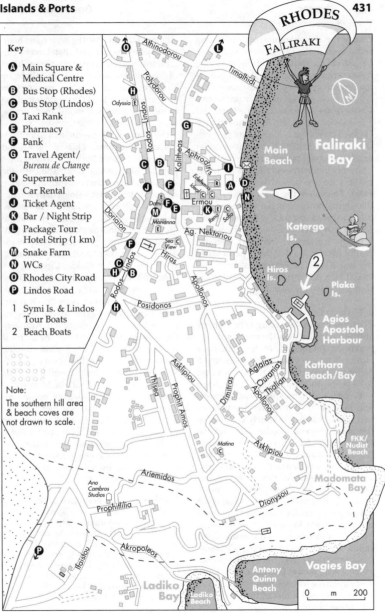

RHODES
FALIRAKI

Key

A Main Square & Medical Centre
B Bus Stop (Rhodes)
C Bus Stop (Lindos)
D Taxi Rank
E Pharmacy
F Bank
G Travel Agent/ *Bureau de Change*
H Supermarket
I Car Rental
J Ticket Agent
K Bar / Night Strip
L Package Tour Hotel Strip (1 km)
M Snake Farm
N WCs
O Rhodes City Road
P Lindos Road

1 Symi Is. & Lindos Tour Boats
2 Beach Boats

Note:
The southern hill area & beach coves are not drawn to scale.

Athinodorou
Polydorou
Odyssia
Rodou
Kalitheas
Aphroditis
Timalhidi
Doriation
Ermou
Dafni
Marianna
Ag. Nektariou
Sea View
Hiras
Lindos
Posidonos
Apollonio
Asklipiou
Thisea
Prophit Amos
Ariemidos
Prophitilia
Akropoleos
Iraklou
Ano Cambros Studios
Matina
Dimitras
Aglaias
Ouranias
Thalias
Apollonos
Asklipiou
Dionysou

Main Beach
Faliraki Bay
Katergo Is.
Hiros Is.
Plaka Is.
Agios Apostolo Harbour
Kathara Beach/Bay
FKK/ Nudist Beach
Madomata Bay
Vagies Bay
Antony Quinn Beach
Ladiko Bay
Ladiko Beach

0   m   200

Lindos, this is perhaps the most interesting settlement on the east coast (it is also the largest 'village' on the island). Set in a valley noted for its orange groves, Archangelos is made up of typical white-cubist houses, but has the added bonus of a very impressive Castle of the Knights (built in 1467) and a fresco-decorated late Byzantine church (1377). The village is also on the tour-bus circuit as it is a leading hand-woven carpet and leather boot manufacturing centre.

South of Lindos the only significant resort is the pine-tree-backed beach village at **Pefki**. Thereafter the coast is very quiet (though the beaches are good enough), with buses reduced to a trickle: **Kattavia** sees a service only three times weekly. However, if you have your own transport, then this part of Rhodes is a delight — particularly the beach islet of **Prassonissi**, which is linked by a sandy beach causeway to the southern tip of the island.

2. The West Coast

The west coast of Rhodes is greener, quieter and less popular than the east coast. The winds that hit this side of the island have blown away any chance of it becoming a major package tourist strip. Beaches tend to be pebble rather than sand, and littered with driftwood; escapist beachcombers will love them. Tourist development on this side of Rhodes is largely confined to the coast between Rhodes City and the airport at **Paradisi**. This is as developed as the top half of the east coast. Thereafter, you are into country dominated by farms and vineyards. In spite of this, many visitors to Rhodes venture down this coast during island excursions, for the coast road is the jumping-off point for a number of sightseeing destinations. Regular — but infrequent — buses also run down this coast to the sights. The best served of these is **Trianda**, the stop for the ancient city of Ialyssos and, to the south, **Mount Filerimos**. This latter destination is a low hill picturesquely clad in pine trees and a mix of Byzantine and Knights of St. John era churches.

Beyond the airport, the west coast highway is joined by the road to **Petaloudes**. This is the inland butterfly valley where millions of tiger moths are scared into flight by almost as many tourists between late June and early September. Like the similar site on Paros, the numbers of moths are declining each year, thanks to the tourists.

The next notable destination after Petaloudes is **Kamiros**. This is the second west-coast ancient city and the third most popular sightseeing destination on the island. Thereafter the road continues along an ever-quieter coast: a single daily Rhodes City bus gathers passengers at the rather sad hamlet of Kamiros Skala en route to Monolithos. **Kamiros Skala** (not to be confused with the ruined city) has a daily caïque link to Chalki (times on the ferry timetable sheet issued free in Rhodes City).

Monolithos is the most important village on the southern half of the west coast. In truth it is a rather poor beach resort redeemed by a Castle of the Knights perched on an overlooking hill. Arguably the most impressive castle on the island, it was built in the 15 C. Today it offers stunning views across the sea to the island of Chalki, and some dangerously crumbling walls on its sea-cliff side. South of Monolithos Rhodes is relatively sparsely populated. Large parts were heavily damaged by extensive forest fires in 2008, causing the evacuation of several coast hotels. Those wishing to visit the south will need a good road map and their own transport; car hire comes into its own when exploring an island of this size.

🚤

Rhodes City is the best place to stay if you don't have your own wheels, as it is at the hub of the transportation network. The city has a good supply of rooms (the tourist office also offers a room-finding service). The New Town is dominated by block-booked package tourist hotels (though they often have empty rooms). Most of the independent travellers' accommodation is to be found in the best part of town, in the Old City, but rates are at least 10% higher than on other islands.

At the bottom end of the range you will find pensions aplenty, among the best being the *Nikos* (☎ 23423) and the *Aleka* (☎ 33701) — both within easy distance of the port (look for 'CHORA' on the Old City map). A street to the north-east is home to the good *Rena* (☎ 26217), and tucked quietly away on the south side of town are two more good-value establishments: the *Andreas* (☎ 34156) and the *Apollo Rooms* (☎ 35064). Thanks to the competition, E-class hotels are all pretty reasonable. These include the *Spot* (☎ 34737), the *Domos Rodos* (☎ 25965) and the *Teheran* (☎ 27594). The cheap *Kastro* (☎ 20446) near the Turkish baths has noisy rooms overlooking a square. D-class hotels include the excellent, if out of the way, *Kava d'Oro* (☎ 36980) and *Paris* (☎ 26356).

Outside of Rhodes City there are plenty of options (though camping is not one of them — the island's only site at Faliraki closed in 2001). If you are looking for nightlife then **Faliraki** has several inexpensive, if noisy, hotels on its bar-fronted main street, including the C-class *Ideal* (☎ 85518) and *Edelweiss* (☎ 85442, 85305), and the E-class *Dafni* (☎ 85544).

Lindos has few accommodation options of note beyond a couple of expensive pensions, the *Katholiki* (☎ 31445) and the *Electra* (☎ 31266). Both need to be booked ahead by phone regardless of the season.

๛

Most visitors to Rhodes, if they are island hopping, will have their work cut out just taking in the sights in Rhodes City and Lindos without having time to venture further afield, though the island has sufficient sightseeing to fill a two–week holiday.

Top of the list are the other two pre-408 BC cities (both accessible by bus from Rhodes City). **Kamiros** is, in fact, the best preserved of the three former centres of power. Abandoned after Rhodes City was built, much of the city plan is still visible, but sightseeing suffers considerably thanks to the lack of notable major buildings.

The remains at **Ialyssos** are far more fragmentary and consist of the foundations of a 3 C. BC **Temple of Athena Polias and Zeus Polios** on the site of the ancient acropolis. Unlike Kamiros, a settlement of sorts survived at Ialyssos until comparatively recently. Its close proximity to Rhodes City ensured that it was a centre of operations for besiegers of the city: both the Knights of St. John and Suleiman used it as a base prior to their conquests of the island.

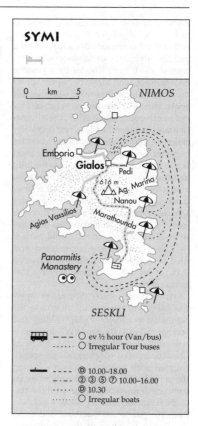

SYMI

NIMOS

0   km   5

Emborio

Gialos   Pedi

616 m   Ag. Marina

Nanou

Agios Vassilios   Marathounda

Panormitis
Monastery

SESKLI

🚌 – – – ○ ev ½ hour (Van/bus)
······ ○ Irregular Tour buses

⛴ – – – Ⓓ 10.00–18.00
– · – · ② ③ ⑤ ⑦ 10.00–16.00
······ Ⓓ 10.30
······ ○ Irregular boats

Symi
ΣΥΜΗ; 58 km²; pop. 2,500.

CODE ☎ 22410
PORT POLICE ☎ 71205
TOURIST OFFICE ☎ 71215
POLICE ☎ 71111
FIRST AID ☎ 71290

A small island half tucked within the folds of the indented Turkish coast, hilly Symi (inappropriately pronounced 'Seamy') is both a popular day-tripper destination from Rhodes, and the prized objective for an exclusive few able to find overnight accommodation. There are two stories as to how the island got its name. The first is that Symi is named after a little-known goddess daughter of Ialyssos who was carried away from Rhodes by a passing boat-builder, who thereafter upset her by doing nothing but ignore her while he built boats. This story is as boring as he was and not worth going into further. The alternative tale has it that the island was originally called 'Simia' or 'monkey island'. Besides being far more appealing, this explanation is also much more plausible given the hilly nature of the terrain (you almost need to be a monkey to get around here). Of course, day trippers from Rhodes aside, there isn't a monkey in sight: the simian bit comes from Prometheus (the man who stole fire from Zeus) who — myth would have it — was subsequently imprisoned and died here after the wrathful god zapped 1.6% of his DNA, thereby turning him into a monkey.

Symi was once one of the most prosperous islands in the Aegean, thanks to the combined industries of shipbuilding and sponge fishing. Its pre-WW2 history is not unlike nearby Kastelorizo; for Symi likewise enjoyed considerable prosperity coupled with political autonomy during the period of Ottoman rule, only to see its fortunes dramatically wane with the rise of the steamship and the island's isolation from the Anatolian mainland, following the Italian takeover of the Dodecanese after WW1.

Having cut down its trees to furnish wood for its shipbuilding industry, Symi depended on timber from mainland Turkey to maintain its output of over 500 caïques a year. Once this was lost, and the sponge fishing declined, the island fell into comparative poverty. Not even the regrowth of a good part of its forest cover was able to reverse the island's decline. Salvation of a sort came with the Turkish invasion of Cyprus in 1974, when Symi emerged as a popular Rhodes day-tripper excursion (in lieu of Turkish Marmaris, which was

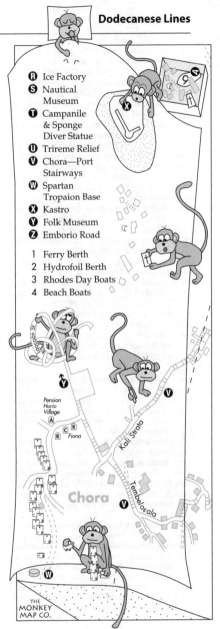

R Ice Factory
S Nautical Museum
T Campanile & Sponge Diver Statue
U Trireme Relief
V Chora—Port Stairways
W Spartan Tropaion Base
X Kastro
Y Folk Museum
Z Emborio Road

1 Ferry Berth
2 Hydrofoil Berth
3 Rhodes Day Boats
4 Beach Boats

Gocoon St.

Pension Horio Village **A**

R **C** **R**
Fiona

Kali Strata

Chora

Tembelosala

THE MONKEY MAP CO.

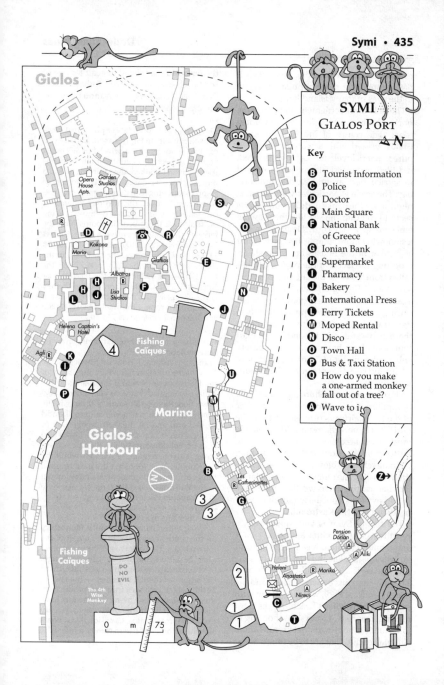

SYMI
GIALOS PORT

N

Key

- **B** Tourist Information
- **C** Police
- **D** Doctor
- **E** Main Square
- **F** National Bank of Greece
- **G** Ionian Bank
- **H** Supermarket
- **I** Pharmacy
- **J** Bakery
- **K** International Press
- **L** Ferry Tickets
- **M** Moped Rental
- **N** Disco
- **O** Town Hall
- **P** Bus & Taxi Station
- **Q** How do you make a one-armed monkey fall out of a tree?
- **A** Wave to it

Gialos

Opera House Apts.
Garden Studios
Kokona
Maria
Glafkos
Albatros
Lisa Studios
Helena   Captain's Hotel
Agli
Fishing Caïques
4
4
Marina
Gialos Harbour
Fishing Caïques
DO NO EVIL
The 4th Wise Monkey
0   m   75
3
3
2
1
1
Les Catherinettes
Pension Dorian
Aliki
Heleni
Anastasia   Marika
Nireus
Z→

necessarily out of bounds). Since then it has become ever more popular, overly so in the eyes of many island hoppers.

The only large settlement on Symi is the port—chora combination on the north coast. The centre of life is the port of **Gialos**, graced with a waterfront that is pure magic: a lovely mix of pastel painted, red-tiled, neo-classical mansions arranged in serried tiers around an amphitheatre bay. The scene is particularly attractive at night when the banks of dull orange lights seem to roll into the sea like the glowing embered lip of a lava flow. Daylight reveals a somewhat more complicated picture, for a number of the houses are mere shells, reflecting the fact that the population has fallen from 30,000 in the late 19 c. to under 3,000 today. The waterfront (complete with a campanile near the ferry quay) is crowded during the daytime, but quickly reverts to its normal sleepy self once the tour boats go; these arrive after midday and then depart four hours later, having done their best to enhance Symi's reputation as an expensive island and keep the sponge and herb shops in business.

The upper town of **Chora** retains an air of tranquillity, thanks to the need to climb one of the two stairways running up from the port. This is more than enough to dissuade most. A second disincentive is the state of the town (at the end of WW2 the departing Germans chose to blow up a couple of hundred houses). The remaining town is large, if rather scrappy, but is worth a visit to take in the bay views from the windmill-topped headland and the Kastro hill.

The rest of Symi is very quiet, with a coastline of steep cliffs and sandy bays and a hinterland that has nought but odd farmsteads, hamlets and goat-tracks galore; this makes it a good hillwalking island. The only bus runs between Gialos and the beach hamlet at **Pedi**, which — along with sandy **Agios Nikolaos** beach — sees most of Symi's tourists. Visitors not choosing to loiter among the crowds, or brave the small shingle beaches that are to be found along

the **Emborio** road, head instead for one of the beach caïques that run to bays down Symi's east coast (pebbly **Nanou** being the most popular).

🛏

The lack of accommodation puts great pressure on capacity in High Season. Usually you can find something (at a price), but in August you can expect to encounter huge problems if you haven't booked ahead or arrived on a morning boat: it is common for late arrivals to resort to roughing it on the mosquito-haunted waterfront to await the next day when they can snap up rooms vacated by those moving on. **Gialos** has the bulk of the rooms. Near the ferry berth are the expensive A-class *Aliki* (☎ 71665), *Nireus* (☎ 72400) and the *Dorian* (☎ 71181). Best bets behind the harbour are the *Albatros* (☎ 71707), the *Kokona* (☎ 71549), the tiny *Glafkos* (☎ 71358) and the *Opera House Apts* (☎ 72034). On the Chora side of the bay is the cheapish *Agli Rooms* (☎ 71665). **Chora** also has a few rooms, the hotel *Fiona* (☎ 72088) and the pension *Horio* (☎ 71800).

👁👁

Gialos has a number of sights ranging from the **Trireme Relief** on the waterfront (a 1945 replica of the ship relief at Lindos on Rhodes) to the *Les Catherinettes* taverna where the Treaty of the Dodecanese (handing the islands to the Allies) was signed that same year. There is also a two-floor **Nautical Museum** (€3); the exhibits consist of half a dozen model caïques, the odd stuffed bird and an unlabelled collection of nautical bric-a-brac (mostly brac). **Chora** also has a fair **Folk Museum** (follow the blue arrows) along with the remains of the **Kastro** built by the Knights of St. John, but the most original things in town are the majestic stairway known as the **Kali Strata**, and the large circular base of a **Tropaion** (victory monument) set up by the Spartans after a nearby naval victory over the Athenians in 411 BC.

Along with Gialos, **Panormitis Monastery** on the south coast is the prime target of the tourist boats. This palatial institution (named after the patron saint of sailors, the Archangel Michael) seems to exist for tourists. It also owns the largest of Symi's satellites — the islet of **Seskli**, which provides fruit and produce for the monastery's lone monk. Some tours have visits in their itineraries, including a weekly excursion from Gialos. Occasional taxi boats also make the short trip to **Nimos**, a hilly islet north of Gialos.

Telendos

ΤΕΛΕΝΔΟΣ; 5 km²; pop. 90.

CODE ☎ 22430

Hidden away behind Kalimnos, Telendos is a substantial hilltop, sitting like a giant boulder 700 metres offshore. The island is supposed to resemble the head of a petrified princess caught at the moment she was looking out to sea for her long lost lover. This tradition baffles most as the resemblance doesn't exactly hit you in the eye.

The nearest most visitors to the Dodecanese get to Telendos is the ferry view of the island's forbidding west side. Those in the know are more than happy to keep this arrangement, for although the mountain isn't exactly cosy, the fishing village that nestles along the coastline opposite the Kalimnos resort of Mirities is. Even the three caïques (complete with carpeted decks) that run every half-hour across the straits add to the feeling, giving an escapist edge to the place: when you are on Telendos you really do feel as if you have pulled up a drawbridge linking you to the rest of the world (which is still on view in a comfortably visible way).

The only village, backed by slopes covered with a light confetti of pine trees, is so small that the waterfront is the main street in all but name. The only facilities are a tiny mini-market and half a dozen tavernas. Telendos really does give you the chance to experience life in a working Greek island fishing village. When you want tourist facilities and shopping then a quick caïque ride to Mirities is an easy way of fulfilling the need.

One reason why Telendos hasn't come to the fore are its beaches. The most accessible — white pebble **Hohlaka** (alias 'Chochlaka') lies at the bottom of a low cliff behind the village. It is apt to be windy. The islanders have attempted to improve its appeal by adding sunbeds — as they have at the other main beach at Paradise (pebbles and dark sand) ·to the north of the village.

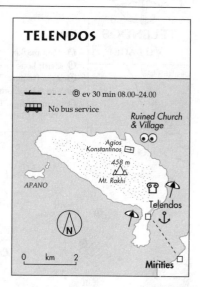

TELENDOS

◀━━ ---- Ⓓ ev 30 min 08.00–24.00

🚌 No bus service

Ruined Church & Village

Agios Konstantinos

458 m
Mt. Rakhi

APANO

Telendos

Ⓝ

Mirities

0   km   2

🛏
No hotels, but a surprising number of beds are available. Waterfront establishments offering rooms include *Studio Rita* (☎ 47914), *Rooms Fotini* (☎ 47401), *On the Rocks* (☎ 48260) and *Villa Erminia* (☎ 47446).

💬
Originally joined to Kalimnos, Telendos was merely a hill that overlooked the ancient Kalimnos capital of 'Pothia' that had been built on low land between the two. A massive earthquake in 554 AD changed all that: the ancient capital did a 'Port Royal' and sank under the modern straits, and the newly created Telendos island became a sleepy backwater.

👀
Sightseeing on Telendos is surprisingly plentiful — though most of it consists of **ruined churches**. The easiest of these to find is 6 C. AD **Agia Triada** behind the town. The remains of another three lie at the abandoned village on the north coast if you care to attempt the walk to **Agios Konstantinos**. The southern spur of the island has fragments of a **Roman bath** — the only ancient remains still extant. Of the lost city of Pothia under the sea, nothing is visible, though 'tis said that you can sometimes hear church bells tolling under the waves'.

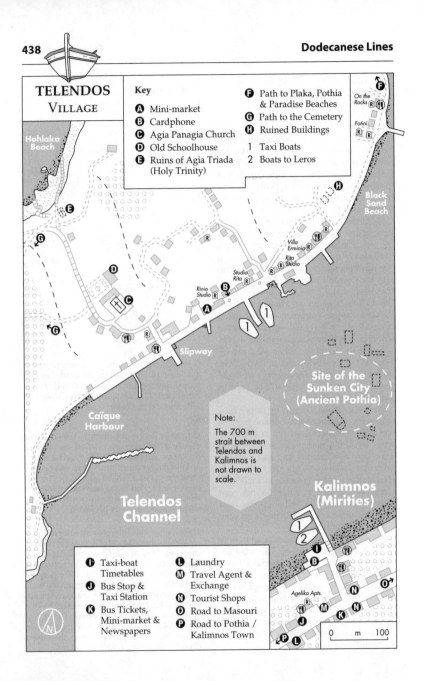

TELENDOS VILLAGE

Key

- **Ⓐ** Mini-market
- **Ⓑ** Cardphone
- **Ⓒ** Agia Panagia Church
- **Ⓓ** Old Schoolhouse
- **Ⓔ** Ruins of Agia Triada (Holy Trinity)
- **Ⓕ** Path to Plaka, Pothia & Paradise Beaches
- **Ⓖ** Path to the Cemetery
- **Ⓗ** Ruined Buildings
- **1** Taxi Boats
- **2** Boats to Leros

Hohlaka Beach

On the Rocks

Fotini

Black Sand Beach

Villa Erminia

Rita Studio

Studio Rita

Rinio Studio

Slipway

Caïque Harbour

Site of the Sunken City (Ancient Pothia)

Note:

The 700 m strait between Telendos and Kalimnos is not drawn to scale.

Telendos Channel

Kalimnos (Mirities)

Agelika Apts.

- **Ⓘ** Taxi-boat Timetables
- **Ⓙ** Bus Stop & Taxi Station
- **Ⓚ** Bus Tickets, Mini-market & Newspapers
- **Ⓛ** Laundry
- **Ⓜ** Travel Agent & Exchange
- **Ⓝ** Tourist Shops
- **Ⓞ** Road to Masouri
- **Ⓟ** Road to Pothia / Kalimnos Town

0   m   100

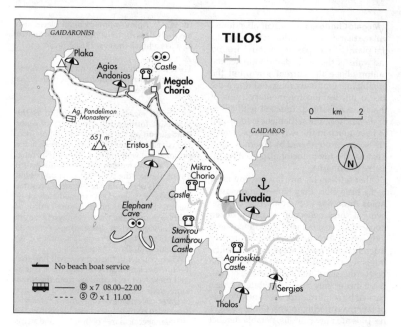

Tilos

ΤΗΛΟΣ; 63 km²; pop. 320.

CODE ☎ 22410
PORT POLICE ☎ 44350
POLICE ☎ 44222
FIRST AID ☎ 44210

A sleepy island even in High Season, tiny Tilos is an attractive and cosy place, made up of hills topped with castles, quiet orchard valleys and empty beaches. For years it has been all but ignored by tourists and locals alike, though in 2008 the mayor made the island a talking point all over Greece by conducting the first gay marriage in the country. This isn't the first time that Tilos has powered the local rumour mill; talk of internecine feuds between the islanders has gone up and down the Dodecanese for years, reflecting past antagonism between the two communities on the island. Happily today there is nothing on Tilos to support the rumours: the islanders are generally

very friendly and welcoming. Even better, unlike many small islands in the region, you can be reasonably sure of finding a room of some sort no matter when you visit.

Having abandoned several tiny hill villages, the island population is now divided between the port of Livadia and the tiny capital of Megalo Chorio, the two being linked by a recently paved road. **Livadia** is the more vibrant of the two centres with a plethora of new hotel and apartment building going on behind the old waterfront. Although tourism is the only economic god now worshipped in town, Livadia has managed to retain much of its former homely small island appeal, with a leafy central square, sleepy tavernas (which only come to life once darkness falls) and a handful of friendly shops. The port quay also gives way to a long clean beach that unfortunately is little used, as it is made up of large pebbles that are just a bit too big for comfort.

Megalo Chorio is a small, half-abandoned village that sits on a foothill at the back of a flat plain. In ages past it clustered around the walls of the castle that dominates the hilltop above the current town, but the inhabitants gradually migrated down the kastro hill leaving fragmentary ruins of their houses behind. Touched with a hint of melancholy, the settlement is too small to have much in the way of shops, which are easily outnumbered by tavernas. As at Livadia, the town doctor also doubles up as the pharmacist.

Other settlements on Tilos are tiny, most being little more than names on the map. **Agios Andonios** is the only one of note, being a sorry collection of half a dozen houses near a small jetty huddling near a long scruffy 'beach' backed by the turret of a derelict windmill. **Eristos** is even smaller, but is set to grow, thanks to its beach. The best on the island and at times over-popular, it is a mix of grey sand and white pebbles, backed by some mature trees and a couple of tavernas offering rooms. Other villages on Tilos are now ruinous, notably derelict **Mikro Chorio**, abandoned in the 1950s.

The main roads on Tilos have recently been made up with concrete, and keep to the valley floor. These are surprisingly fertile, with lovely shady, mature oak trees, fields of silage and collections of hives (the island is known for its honey). With the improved road system has also come a bus (one of the cut-down regular type). Bus times are posted up on bus stops. Services out of High Season are limited, but summer services are frequent enough.

⊨

Livadia has the bulk of the accommodation including two hotels: the C-class *Irini* (☎ 44293) (hidden away in a jungle of a garden) and the E-class *Livadia* (☎ 44266). There are also a number of apartments charging hotel rates — including the good B-class *Apollo Studios* (☎ 44379) just off the main square, and the C-class *George Apartments* — and pensions. Most island rooms are also at Livadia. **Megalo Chorio** also has establishments offering rooms, including the *Milou* (☎ 44204) and *Elecantakia*

(☎ 44213). **Agios Andonios** of all places also has the B-class *Australia* (☎ 44296), and **Eristos** also has a hotel: the new *Eristos Beach*.

Λ

There is no official campsite on Tilos: however, freelance camping is tolerated at both Plaka and Eristos beaches.

👁👁

The main sightseeing destination is the 1470-built fortified hill **Monastery of Agios Pandelimon** on the north-west side of Tilos. The island bus runs there twice a week in the summer and waits an hour before returning.

The **Castle** above **Megalo Chorio** is also worth a visit, though the path that runs up behind the town is not for the faint-hearted. At some points the way ahead isn't immediately obvious (the locals have piled up small cairns of pebbles to mark the way — though these are more obvious when descending). Allow 45 minutes to get up the path, 15 minutes to do the castle and 30 for the return.

When you get to the top you will find that the fortress isn't nearly as large, nor is it as well preserved, as it appears from the town: some walls are all but missing and a couple of water cisterns have unguarded holes that descend to god-knows-where. Views from the castle are spectacular — both of Tilos and across the straits to Nissiros, which from this vantage point really looks like a volcano.

A few years back, a small island near Siberia received considerable publicity after the discovery that it was home to a species of **Dwarf Mammoth** a couple of hundred thousand years earlier. What is less well known is the fact that they came to Tilos for their summer holidays (the fossilized bones of those killed in moped accidents litter caves on the island). The town hall at Megalo Chorio is home to a small bones **Museum**.

Finally, hillwalkers and hikers will love Tilos. Armed with a good island map (look for the good blue one on sale in Livadia), it is possible to wander at will, exploring the series of castles that run down the spine of the island, including one at **Mikro Chorio** which is worth the walk anyway.

A walk to the Agios Pandelimon monastery on the north-west coast also enables you to take in **Agios Andonios Beach**. This has a sobering reminder of the dangers of over exposure thanks to the petrified remains of three sailors who were caught napping by an eruption of Nissiros c. 600 BC.

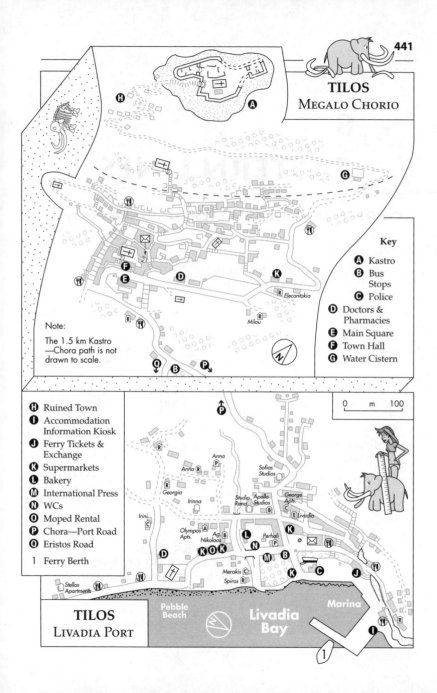

TILOS
MEGALO CHORIO

Key

- **A** Kastro
- **B** Bus Stops
- **C** Police
- **D** Doctors & Pharmacies
- **E** Main Square
- **F** Town Hall
- **G** Water Cistern

Note:

The 1.5 km Kastro
—Chora path is not
drawn to scale.

Elecantakia

Milou

N

- **H** Ruined Town
- **I** Accommodation Information Kiosk
- **J** Ferry Tickets & Exchange
- **K** Supermarkets
- **L** Bakery
- **M** International Press
- **N** WCs
- **O** Moped Rental
- **P** Chora—Port Road
- **Q** Eristos Road
- **1** Ferry Berth

0   m   100

Anna

Anna

Sofias Studios

Georgia

George Apts.

Irinna

Studia Rena

Apollo Studios

Livadia

Irini

Olympos Apts.

Ag. Nikolaos

Perhali

Merakis

Spiros

Stellas Apartments

TILOS
LIVADIA PORT

Pebble Beach

N

Livadia Bay

Marina

1

8 EASTERN LINES

CHIOS · FOURNI · IKARIA · LESBOS · PSARA · SAMOS

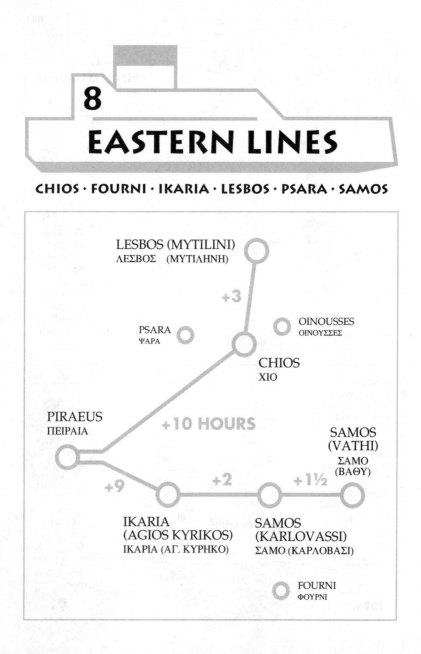

LESBOS (MYTILINI)
ΛΕΣΒΟΣ (ΜΥΤΙΛΗΝΗ)

+3

PSARA
ΨΑΡΑ

OINOUSSES
ΟΙΝΟΥΣΣΕΣ

CHIOS
ΧΙΟ

PIRAEUS
ΠΕΙΡΑΙΑ

+10 HOURS

SAMOS
(VATHI)
ΣΑΜΟ
(ΒΑΘΥ)

+9

+2

+1½

IKARIA
(AGIOS KYRIKOS)
ΙΚΑΡΙΑ (ΑΓ. ΚΥΡΗΚΟ)

SAMOS
(KARLOVASSI)
ΣΑΜΟ (ΚΑΡΛΟΒΑΣΙ)

FOURNI
ΦΟΥΡΝΙ

General Features

The Eastern Aegean line is made up of two separate routes running from Piraeus east across the Aegean to those Greek islands adjacent to the Turkish coast north of the Dodecanese. All the ferries operating Eastern line services follow the natural geographical division of the islands into the two sub-groups, either running Piraeus—Ikaria—Samos or Piraeus—Chios—Lesbos (Mytilini).

The more southerly route takes in the large and increasingly popular island of Samos as well as the less well known Ikaria. Each boasts two regular ports at which ferries can call, giving scope for alternations in schedules. The more northerly route runs across to Chios and then up the Turkish seaboard to Lesbos (Mytilini); both are large islands which have remained

economically independent of the tourist hordes but which are increasingly attracting Grecophiles jaded by the over-tourism encountered elsewhere.

Northern route sailings are almost exclusively confined to the major ports of Chios Town and Lesbos (Mytilini), but a number of ferries then continue on into the northern Aegean to varying ports of call. Both groups also include minor islands little visited by tourists: Fourni and Samiopoula off Samos, Oinousses and Psara accessible from Chios.

Links between the two lines remain poor, but are slowly improving with a connecting Chios—Samos service three days a week. Equally indifferent are connections with the Dodecanese which are so thin on the water that locals utilize Patmos-bound tourist boats.

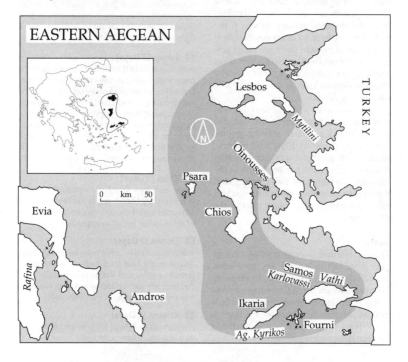

EASTERN AEGEAN

Example Itinerary [2 Weeks]

An itinerary based on the Eastern lines is for those who prefer a scattering of trees rather than High Season crowds with their Greek islands, and are happy to settle for quiet taverna eating and making their own entertainment with the locals. It is unlikely to appeal to those who like to boogie between boats. The islands en route are comparatively quiet thanks to a mix of fewer ferry connections and the need to get a bus to the nearest reasonable beach (on the popular Cycladic islands you only have to fall overboard near to port to find yourself on one). The crowds are missing more than they realise.

Arrival/Departure Point

On a fortnight's holiday there are two easy flight options: Athens and Samos (more poorly served Lesbos (Mytilini) is a third possible option). Athens is the easiest to get back to in a rush. Samos is an equally accessible point provided you travel in an anticlockwise direction (thus ensuring you can pick up one of the daily Piraeus—Samos links in the latter part of the trip if needs be).

If you have three weeks at your disposal then Mykonos, Santorini or Kos can also be considered as viable starting points. However, unlike Athens and Samos, neither will give you advance information on the 2–3 days per week link in the itinerary: the Samos—Chios crossing, and this is a disadvantage given that you will have to structure your plans around the days it runs.

Season

Travel in late June through late October and you shouldn't encounter any problems. Low Season sees difficulties in crossing between the Samos and Chios lines; ferries along both decline from the daily High Season services to the usual 3–4 days a week level, with links to the Northern Aegean disappearing altogether.

1 Athens [2 Days]

Quite apart from the city sights, Athens offers agents in Piraeus who will show you the Miniotis Ferries timetable (if they are operating) when you ask about links between Chios and Samos. With this info you can then work out how many days you have either side of this weak link and allocate nights and stops accordingly.

2 Paros [2 Days]

As there are not usually morning and evening boats out of Piraeus along the Samos line it is often more convenient to make for better connected Paros and then jump from there onto a Samos boat. It also breaks up an otherwise 12-hour voyage and offers a quick dash down to Naxos and the Cyclades Central line if you have a third week to hand.

3 Ikaria [1 Day]

An optional island (it is a good idea to build in flexibility by having one in any itinerary) you can fit (time willing) into a tight schedule.

4 Samos [3 Days]

Arriving at Vathi the number one priority is to confirm the Monday and Friday boat to Chios is running (in the unlikely event of this service not operating—and it has for the last few years—you always have the option of heading south by picking up a tourist boat from Pithagorio down to Patmos and the Dodecanese). This established, you can fill the available time on excursions to Pithagorio and Turkey.

5 Chios [2 Days]

Once on Chios you have optional hops to neighbouring Oinousses, to Turkey, and even adjacent Psara if the notion of a couple of days of untouristed isolation appeals.

6 Lesbos [2 Days]

A nice island on which to relax before catching an overnight boat back to Piraeus. Irregular ferries to Volos and Rafina (via the Northern Aegean) are also options if you don't mind a bus ride into Athens at the other end.

1 Athens [2 Days]

Arrive back in Athens with the precautionary day in hand before your flight home.

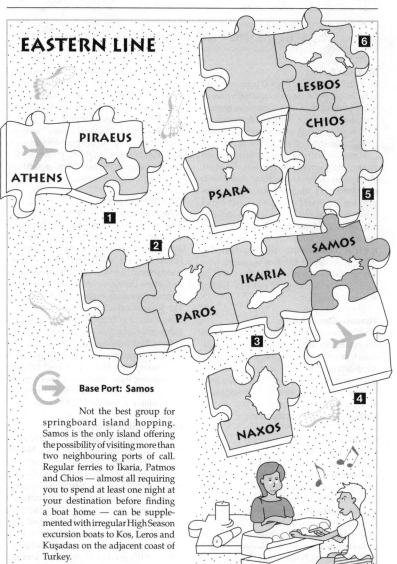

EASTERN LINE

6

LESBOS

CHIOS

PIRAEUS

ATHENS

PSARA

1

5

2

SAMOS

IKARIA

PAROS

3

Base Port: Samos

Not the best group for springboard island hopping. Samos is the only island offering the possibility of visiting more than two neighbouring ports of call. Regular ferries to Ikaria, Patmos and Chios — almost all requiring you to spend at least one night at your destination before finding a boat home — can be supplemented with irregular High Season excursion boats to Kos, Leros and Kuşadası on the adjacent coast of Turkey.

NAXOS

4

Eastern Line Ferry Services

Main Car Ferries

Ferry traffic to all the islands in this chapter is far less dependent on tourism than some other parts of the Greek system as none of the islands are big hopping destinations. This is just as well, as 2010 saw a sudden drop in the level of services as three ferry companies serving Samos either went bankrupt or opted not to trade. Even so, since then daily connections have been maintained in both directions, as the ferries provide important services to what are all fairly large islands by Greek standards. The islands of Fourni and Psara, however, are irregularly served by Piraeus ferries at the best of times, with calls often added to schedules only at the last moment. Low Season can see services fall to as few as four days a week, with links to Turkey severely curtailed.

Piraeus—Samos Ferries

The Piraeus—Ikaria—Samos route is now seeing change after a decade of little variation. Unfortunately, the comparative lack of tourists using ferries to these islands results in lower revenues than on the popular lines (hence the high toll on operators last year), so there is little incentive to put new or high-speed ferries on the route.

C/F Nissos Mykonos

Hellenic Seaways/HFD

Nissos Mykonos; 2005; 14720 GRT.

The first modern ferry to operate to Samos in years, the *Nissos Mykonos* (see p. 448) moved over from the Chios—Lesbos route in 2008, quickly becoming the most popular boat and with good reason. A large well-maintained vessel, she runs to time and is fairly speedy into the bargain. For the last two summers she has ended up being the only boat on the route, departing from Piraeus in the late afternoon and returning from Samos the following morning. There

are, however, a couple of downsides to this monopoly. First, the previously regular links with Paros and Naxos have disappeared as this boat only called at Syros and Mykonos, and second, the lack of competition has enabled Hellenic Seaways to keep fares high, so this boat offered some rather expensive island hopping. In the circumstances it is reasonable to assume she will be operating a similar service in 2012.

C/F Express Pegasus

Hellenic Seaways / HFD; 1977; 4810 GRT.

This small ferry provides an occasional alternative option to the *Nissos Mykonos* out of High Season on this route. Regular island hoppers will have almost certainly encountered this vessel as either the *Pegasus* or *Express Dionyssos* on journeys past. The *Express Pegasus* is quite a small boat, and her limited capacity is a liability on the Samos route in High Season. A converted lorry ro-ro, she has one of her car decks refurbished for passenger use, but access is more limited than with custom-built passenger boats. She was moved to cover for missing boats elsewhere after serving on this route, but could return in 2012, particularly out of the High Season.

Piraeus—Chios Ferries

Unlike the Samos route, the Piraeus to Lesbos and Chios services have a history of being dominated by one company — the Maritime Co. of Lesbos (NEL Lines) — for many years. The lack of heavy tourist traffic in the northern Aegean hasn't encouraged other operators to move in. Paradoxically this is now changing as Hellenic Seaways are making inroads into this market. Both lines achieve a commendable standard in terms of the quality of their fleet and the level of service. NEL Lines are, however, something of a timetable-compiler's bane by pooling their boats. For these reasons the

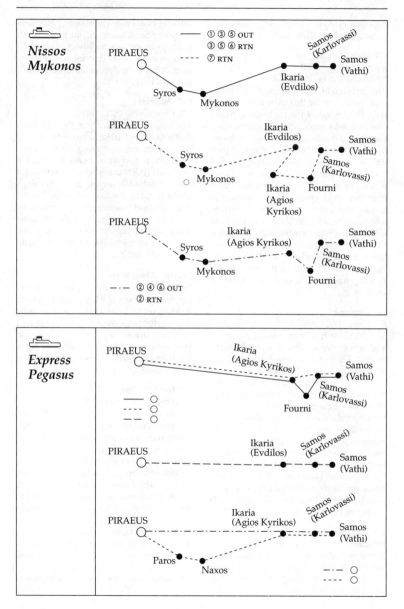

NEL services opposite are mapped together rather than by individual ferry.

C/F *Nissos Chios*
Hellenic Seaways/HFD
Nissos Chios; 2006; 14720 GRT.
The first sign of serious competition to the NEL hegemony on this route came in 2006 with the arrival of the high-speed *Nissos Mykonos* (now replaced by her sister ferry, the *Nissos Chios*). On-board conditions on both boats are excellent, and although they are not high-speed vessels, they are fast boats (on a par with the *Blue Star Paros/ Naxos*), running to Chios four hours faster than their NEL rivals. Their construction history has been very chequered: they were laid down in a Greek shipyard in 1999 as sisters to the Blue Star boats. But shipyard difficulties left their hulls rusting for years before being completed for their current owners. The schedule of the *Nissos Chios* doesn't change much, so is likely to be the same in 2012.

C/F *Mytilene*
NEL Lines; 1973; 6702 GRT.
The *Mytilene* has been around for years and is now the number two regular ferry in the NEL fleet. Her design is something of a problem given the numbers she can carry. The search for the sun deck or the WCs is apt to be hard on the feet thanks to an excess of over-long corridors, and her turnaround times are not good because of the limited entry/exit facilities. If you are safety-conscious you might want to avoid her. It is also worth noting that when picking her up at the start of her route it is wise to join her at least an hour before her departure: although the deck-class passenger lounge is large, demand for seats always exceeds supply in High Season.

C/F *European Express*
NEL Lines; 1974; 15074 GRT.
A new arrival in 2010, this ferry is anything but new herself. In fact she is very much a stop-gap option brought in so that other boats in the NEL fleet could cover for

missing boats elsewhere in the Northern Aegean. She is, however, one of the larger boats in this company's fleet, so it could well be other boats that move elsewhere in 2012. She is best summed up as reliable but very boring.

C/F *Theofilos*
NEL Lines; 1975; 19212 GRT.
The largest regular ferry in the NEL fleet, this boat arrived in the Aegean in 1995 after running as the Australian *Abel Tasman*. She came a cropper in 2008 when she ran aground off Oinousses, which put her out of action indefinitely (repairs are continuing). When running she took on all the 'heavy' peak-demand passenger runs. As with the *Mytilene*, life on board isn't exactly cosy: she is just too big for comfort. That said, she is an excellent overnight ferry with good-value cabins.

Lavrio—Chios Ferries
Last year saw the re-emergence of a link between the port of Mesta on Chios with Athens, with Lavrio as the starting point. Truth to tell links like this really are geared to local custom (e.g. the population of Psara) or commercial vehicles, as links between the port at Mesta and the rest of Chios aren't good.

C/F *Panagia Thalassini*
NEL Lines; 1996; 4934 GRT.
The sister of the *Panagia Parou* (see p. 484), this boat briefly appeared in 2010 to provide emergency cover for missing ferries elsewhere, before finding this regular service in 2011. Like her sister she rolls around a bit thanks to her lightweight construction. You can also forget her high-speed status as she never travels at full throttle due to the need to rein in her fuel consumption.

Eastern Lines Local Ferries
In addition to large ferries there are a number of small boats offering links to small islands near Samos and Chios, and occasionally connections between the big two as well. The only thing all these boats have in

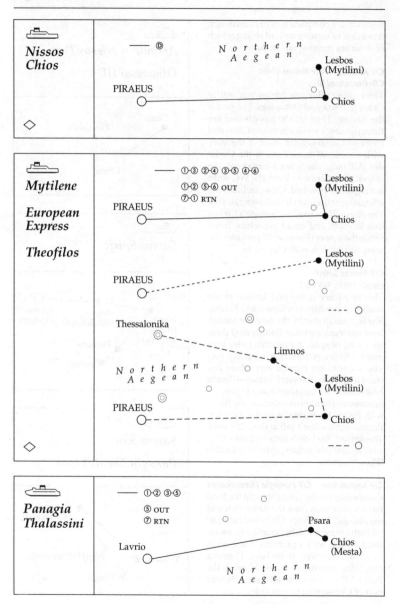

Nissos Chios

◇

Northern Aegean

— ⓓ

PIRAEUS

Lesbos (Mytilini)

Chios

Mytilene

European Express

Theofilos

◇

— ①-③ ②-④ ③-⑤ ④-⑥
①-② ⑤-⑥ OUT
⑦-① RTN

PIRAEUS

Lesbos (Mytilini)

Chios

PIRAEUS

Lesbos (Mytilini)

Thessalonika

Limnos

Lesbos (Mytilini)

Chios

Northern Aegean

PIRAEUS

---- ○

Panagia Thalassini

— ①-② ③-⑤
⑤ OUT
⑦ RTN

Lavrio

Psara

Chios (Mesta)

Northern Aegean

common is a complete lack of consistency. It is a case of turning up and seeing which of them are running on the day.

C/F *Arsinoe* – C/F *Nissos Thira* – C/F *Oinoussai III*

Three diminutive car ferries run out of Chios to Psara and Oinousses. The best is the *Arsinoe*. Thus far she has divided her time, running a service between Chios and Psara or Oinousses for most of the year, with occasional excursions to the Cyclades. Although she is not a large boat, she is well maintained — even the WC sinks are regularly polished. Other facilities are adequate for the quiet link she operates on. The *Nissos Thira* used to provide a lifeline link to Anafi and could yet return there, while the newer *Oinoussai III* provides the most regular link with Oinousses.

C/F *Samos Spirit*
Local; 1981; 363 GRT.
This tiny ferry is the best known of the boats that run between Samos and Fourni. She is so small that by the time her funnel, bow and stern are taken into account there isn't a lot of space for anything else very much. She is a picturesque lump that gets you in a not over-hurried way where you want to go. Like the small Samos—Fourni boats below, her main function is to provide a connecting link between Samos and Ikaria with Fourni on the majority of days when Piraeus ferries don't call at the latter port. The days of this boat's runs therefore vary as other timetables change: she's the flexible 'Plan B' option.

C/F *Samos Sun* – C/F *Panagia Theotokosos*
Competition to the *Samos Spirit* in the local ferry wars comes from the *Samos Sun* and the *Panagia Theotokosos*. On-board facilities on both are minimal, but journey times are short so this isn't a problem. Their main function, however, is to keep Thimena connected with the wider world, while the *Panagia Theotokosos* also added the Fourni port of Chrisomilia to schedules in 2011.

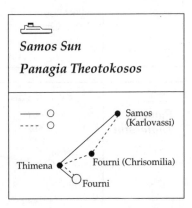

Arsinoe – Nissos Thira Oinoussai III

Psara
Oinousses
Chios
—— ○
······ ○

Samos Spirit

Ikaria (Agios Kyrikos)
Samos (Karlovassi)
Samos (Vathi)
Thimena
Fourni
—— ○

Samos Sun Panagia Theotokosos

—— ○
---- ○
Samos (Karlovassi)
Thimena
Fourni (Chrisomilia)
Fourni

Eastern Line Islands & Ports

Chios
ΧΙΟΣ; 852 km²; pop. 54,000.

CODE ☎ 22710
TOURIST OFFICE ☎ 24217
TOURIST POLICE ☎ 26555
PORT POLICE ☎ 44433
FIRST AID ☎ 23151

Relatively untouristed (thanks to an ugly main port with no good beaches close by) nor offering much in the way of photogenic sightseeing, the large island of Chios remains quiet, with its low-key attractions hidden away. It commands a special place in the Greek independence struggle: having joined the rebellion against Ottoman rule in 1822 it was suitably close to the Turkish mainland to be singled out for retribution; over 100,000 of its population were either killed or enslaved in an ethnic-cleansing type attack by the Turkish fleet.

To do Chios justice you need to take time to explore away from the capital, for the island has a merited reputation for having some of the most fertile and attractive terrain to be found in the Aegean. Indeed, in many ways the landscape is the best thing about Chios, as well as being the source of its quiet affluence, thanks to the growing of mastic (the sticky stuff used to make paint adhere to walls and chewing-gum to everything else). This resin, which oozes out of the trunk of a low bush, gave Lesbos its wealth: introduced by the Genoese, the island was the only source of commercial mastic production in the world during the late Middle Ages.

Most of Chios is mountainous, with the mastic bush crop covering much of the south, while the north of the island is forested — though major fires in 1981 and 1987 inflicted considerable damage to this region. A more recent and lucrative contribution to the local economy has come via the sea, for almost every Greek

shipping tycoon in sight seems to hail from here or the neighbouring satellite of Oinousses.

The capital, **Chios Town**, has retained its late 19 c. industrial port waterfront and this has little to recommend it. Demolished in 1881 by an earthquake, its rebuilding has left the town an inadequate harbinger to the attractiveness of the rest of the island. As one might expect on Greece's premier chewing-gum-growing island, Chios Town is home to a large expatriate North American community that returns to the island each summer. The backstreets behind the waterfront offer an incongruous mix of crumbling mansions, pool bars and New Yorker run pizza bars. The quayside is more reminiscent of a mini version of Piraeus than any other harbour in Greece.

The centre of activity lies near the north-western corner: this is where all the large ferries dock, with the most scenic part of the town behind (complete with a closed mosque and a large tree-filled square/park). In an attempt to humanize the waterfront, the western side is now pedestrianized during the evening, the local mosquitoes taking full advantage of the humans taking in the night air: this is one harbour where it can be quite potent. Commendable though this effort is, the waterfront just doesn't lend itself to romantic evening strolls (it is too smelly, for one thing), and once the crowds have departed taxis and motorbikes use it as a race track into the small hours, when they give way in turn to packs of stray dogs which chase each other along its length instead. All this is rather a pity because the town does have enough in it to justify a short visit once you get behind the grubby, down-at-heel feel of the place, thanks to a castle, a warren-streeted old quarter filled with shops that aren't stuffed with tourist souvenirs and several small museums.

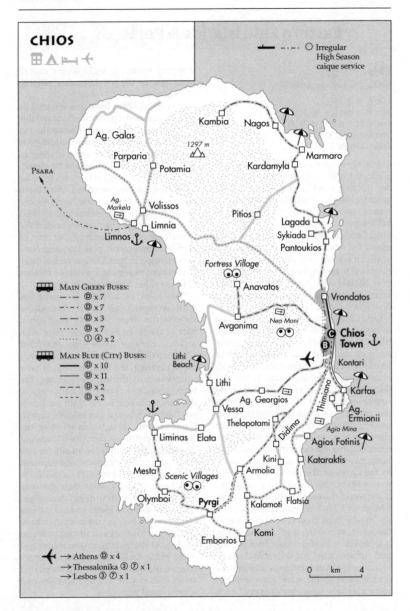

CHIOS

━ ━ ⋅ ━ ⋅ ━ ○ Irregular
                High Season
                caique service

Kambia

Nagos

Ag. Galas

Parparia

1297 m

Marmaro

Potamia

Kardamyla

PSARA

Ag.
Markela

Volissos

Pitios

Limnia

Lagada

Limnos

Sykiada

Pantoukios

Fortress Village

Main Green Buses:
— ⋅ — Ⓓ x 7
— ⋅ ⋅ Ⓓ x 7
— — Ⓓ x 3
⋅ ⋅ ⋅ ⋅ Ⓓ x 7
⋅ ⋅ ⋅ ⋅ ① ④ x 2

Anavatos

Vrondatos

Nea Moni

Avgonima

Ⓒ Chios
Town

Ⓑ

Main Blue (City) Buses:
——— Ⓓ x 10
——— Ⓓ x 11
— — Ⓓ x 2
— — — Ⓓ x 2

Lithi
Beach

Kontari

Lithi

Karfas

Ag. Georgios

Vessa

Thimiana

Ag.
Ermionii

Thelopotami

Agia Mina

Liminas

Elata

Didima

Agios Fotinis

Kini

Kataraktis

Mesta

Scenic Villages

Armolia

Olymboi

Pyrgi

Kalamoti

Flatsia

Komi

Emborios

✈ → Athens Ⓓ x 4
  → Thessalonika ③ ⑦ x 1
  → Lesbos ③ ⑦ x 1

0   km   4

Getting away is easy as most of the major villages on Chios are linked by the island bus services. Blue city buses — in their eagerness to escape the capital — run well beyond Chios town environs to cover the whole central portion of the island, while less consistent Green long-distance buses (both start from their own terminals near the town park) serve the rest. Timetables for both services — and ferries — are provided by an official NTOG / EOT office on Kanari St. (a side street off the north-east corner of the harbour).

Southern Chios has most to offer the tourist thanks to a series of scenic medieval fortress villages built in the inland mastic-growing region when the island was a Genoese dukedom. Having introduced commercial growing of the mastic crop to the island, the dukes also put in place the necessary infrastructure to cultivate and harvest it. The resulting settlements, known as the **'mastic villages'** (mastichoria), should be a must on the itinerary of anyone spending more than a day on Chios. Their numbers vary according to which local guidebook you happen to pick up, but the total is in the high teens.

Like their counterparts in the Cyclades, these fortress settlements were built to prevent the local population being massacred in pirate attacks, their common feature being a line of houses built around their perimeter that doubled up as a defensive wall. However, the Chios examples differ from their Cycladic counterparts in medieval town-planning in being much larger and altogether much more ornate in design. Protective watchtowers stand on any exposed corners along the wall, and the streets within adopt a warren pattern, deliberately designed to confuse any enemy that managed to get in. In the centre of most of the villages is a well-protected church or tower that provided a final point of refuge. Most seem to have been successful in warding off pirate attacks, but their limited defensive capabilities meant they were no match for an invading army.

Despite this, the populations of the mastic villages were the only ones to escape alive in the 1822 devastation of Chios — though, somewhat bizarrely, it was purely because the Turkish sultan wished to protect the chewing-gum supply to the wives of his hareem. **Pyrgi** is the biggest and prettiest of the mastic villages. It is noted for the whitewashed houses that adorn its streets, and a main square that is over-painted with a wide variety of geometric blue patterns that extend even to the underside of the balconies. Nearby lies the smallest of the mastichoria, **Armolia** — a noted pottery production centre.

Mesta is also worth exploration, for although not as pretty as some, it retains more of its medieval buildings (including the largest church on the island) and with it, its old-world atmosphere. **Olymboi**, on the road between Pyrgi and Mesta, is in many ways the best preserved, with little building beyond its almost rectangular walls and a well-preserved central tower. It also has a port at **Liminas**, complete with a large new quay that every other summer (the last being in 2011) sees a ferry out of Lavrio call several times a week.

To the west of Chios Town is one of the most northerly of the mastic villages in **Vessa**. Built on the side of a hill, it offers an easy half-day's excursion. Just to the south are a couple of other popular destinations: **Karfas** with its reasonable beach — now rapidly developing as the island's premier tourist resort — and the monastery of Agia Mina, site of another massacre by the Turks.

North of the town, buses run frequently to **Vrondatos** and the Daskalopetra or 'teaching rock', which tradition associates with Homer (Chios — an island without many ancient notables of its own — is yet another of those islands that claim the famed and mysterious poet as a son). North of this resort the island is a quiet, tourist-free zone. The largest village is at **Kardamyla**, though it isn't much bigger than its equally rustic and undisturbed

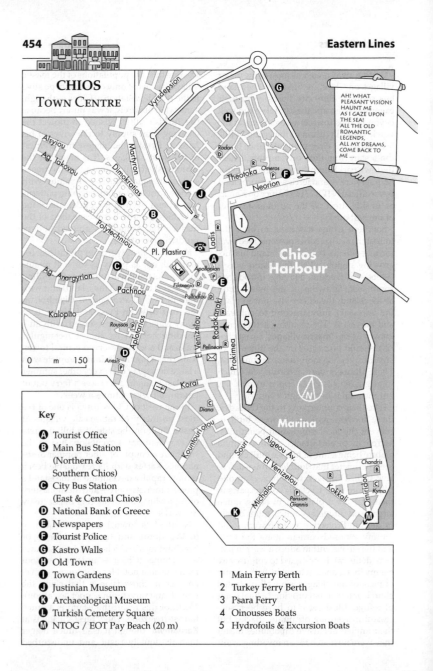

CHIOS
TOWN CENTRE

AH! WHAT PLEASANT VISIONS HAUNT ME AS I GAZE UPON THE SEA! ALL THE OLD ROMANTIC LEGENDS, ALL MY DREAMS, COME BACK TO ME ...

Chios
Harbour

Marina

Key

Ⓐ Tourist Office
Ⓑ Main Bus Station
   (Northern &
   Southern Chios)
Ⓒ City Bus Station
   (East & Central Chios)
Ⓓ National Bank of Greece
Ⓔ Newspapers
Ⓕ Tourist Police
Ⓖ Kastro Walls
Ⓗ Old Town
Ⓘ Town Gardens
Ⓙ Justinian Museum
Ⓚ Archaeological Museum
Ⓛ Turkish Cemetery Square
Ⓜ NTOG / EOT Pay Beach (20 m)

1 Main Ferry Berth
2 Turkey Ferry Berth
3 Psara Ferry
4 Oinousses Boats
5 Hydrofoils & Excursion Boats

neighbours. Whitewashed Volissos on the west coast has more to offer, with remnants of a fortress and a pretty little harbour at **Limnos** with caïques to Psara.

😺

A bastion of quiet prosperity, Chios has enjoyed a very low-key history for much of its existence. The island was a noted centre for sculpture in the 6–5 c. BC, its most famous sculptor being a character called Glaucus, who produced the first soldered figures. However, during most of antiquity its population appear to have been too busy making a mint through growing and chewing gum, viticulture and — less happily — pioneering slavery in Greece to have had time for philosophical speculation or political struggle. Its history mirrors neighbouring islands until the Venetians arrived in 1204, followed by the Genoese in 1261. When the Turks captured Chios in 1566 the island gained limited autonomy and an extended period of quiet prosperity. This changed with the 19 c. Greek independence struggle, the devastating impact of which haunts Chios still. Like many islands located close to the Turkish coast the island suffered disproportionately. Having joined the rebellion by a number of islands against Turkish rule in 1822, Chios was singled out (along with neighbouring Psara) for the most severe retribution. On the orders of the Sultan the entire island was sacked, with its buildings burnt. Over 30,000 islanders were massacred in the process and a further 70,000 (mainly women and children) were enslaved and deported. A devastating earthquake in 1881 killed 3,500 and set back the island's recovery. This is now complete, though the scars of the last two centuries are still very evident.

🛏

The lack of tourists means that accommodation options are adequate but not vast. Chios Town has the most beds, but in High Season finding an empty one come the evening can be a problem; ticket agencies will phone around for you. Best (and most expensive) hotel in town is the *Chandris* (☎ 25761), hiding in the street below the harbour. Nearby is the popular mansion *Kyma* (☎ 44500). The *Radon* (☎ 24335) in the old town also offers a quiet atmosphere and reasonable prices. Noisier, but clean, are the *Diana* (☎ 24656) and cheaper *Filoxenia* (☎ 22813). Rooms along the waterfront are popular and generally good value. Most of the towns also have hotels (Karfas being the best served, with five) along with a scatter of rooms in Pyrgi and Mesta.

👓

Lacking any notable sites from the Classical, Hellenistic or Roman periods, the main attraction on Chios is an 11 c. **Byzantine Monastery** at **Nea Mona**, 15 km west of Chios Town. Carefully tucked away in the foothills, it is founded on the spot where shadowy myth says three passing hermits discovered an icon. Quite what three hermits were doing in each other's company in the first place isn't clear, nor is the picture of how they happened upon the icon any clearer. This remains an event more weird than wonderful. Be this as it may, the monastery thrived and is now home to some of the finest Byzantine frescoes and mosaics known. Many date from the monastery's foundation in 1042, though a fair number were lost in a damaging earthquake in 1881.

The monastery's charnel house is also home to a ghoulish display of skulls, tastefully arranged in glass-fronted bookcases. Victims of the 1822 massacre (the Turks axed to death those members of the population who had sought refuge in the church, along with 600 monks), they stare at visitors in serried rows like a hungry crowd of evangelicals looking for converts. Another relic of Greek nationalism housed in the monastery is a grandfatherish clock that was carried away by the Greek inhabitants of Smyrna (modern Izmir) when they fled the city in 1923. Note: the dial is melodramatically set to Constantinople time, so it doesn't do to check your wristwatch by it. East of the monastery lies another popular sight: the abandoned cliff village of **Anavatos** whose inhabitants did a collective jump as the Turks approached (sightseeing on Chios is not for the squeamish).

Chios Town has a few sights worth hunting out, including the remains of the Genoese **Kastro** (1433) housing the **Turkish Quarter** to the north of the harbour. The only part of the town to survive the 1881 earthquake, it was badly damaged, but still boasts some impressive fortification walls and a deep moat (dry). The quarter also contains a redundant mosque and a Muslim graveyard. Less inspiring are the **Archaeological Museum** and Cathedral. The town is also home to the **Justinian Museum** (devoted to church art). Those with more cash in hand can also splash out on a day trip to Turkish **Çeşme** on the coast opposite.

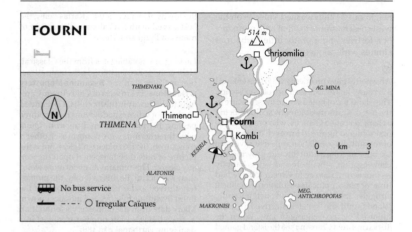

Fourni
ΦΟΥΡΝΟΙ; 37 km²; pop. 970.

CODE ☎ 22710
PORT POLICE ☎ 44433
POLICE ☎ 44427
FIRST AID ☎ 112

Fourni is the largest island in a small rocky archipelago lying between Ikaria, Samos and Patmos. If you are looking for something close to an unspoilt island, then look no further: for Fourni is one of the few genuine articles left in Greece. Formerly a noted nest for pirates during much of the Byzantine period, the island is quiet even in High Season, only recently emerging as a regular ferry destination and still lacking proper roads. Unfortunately, as word gets around, this is starting to change and Fourni now sees regular day boats from Ikaria dropping in to augment the tourists that seek it out.

The bulk of the population lives in the chora settlement of **Fourni**. Home to a large fishing fleet, Fourni is very much a working town: its waterfront is usually covered with mounds of yellow nets, and the well-supplied fish tavernas behind stand cheek by jowl with a tiny ice factory (the production lines run from late afternoon). At the end of the harbour is a usable beach, the two combining to form the centre of town life. Littered with caïques all year round, the beach becomes a playground for the local kids in summer — offering an appealing change from the usual monotonous rows of tanning tourists encountered elsewhere.

The town itself is unusual without having tangible sights on offer (beyond the inevitable derelict windmills topping the hills ringing the port). The narrow, over-straight, mulberry tree-lined main street is an odd mix of quaint provincial Greece combined with a rare — for the islands at any rate — grid layout (this pattern gives way to the usual chaotic street arrangement once the land rises behind the main square).

Most of the few facilities in town (bar the anonymous medical centre which is marked only by the presence of an ambulance parked outside) are located on either the main street or the rather bland square that lies at one end. It is also worth noting the absence of banks or traveller's cheque exchange facilities; Fourni is now one of the few islands without them (at the moment visitors have to make do with a solitary ATM near the bakery).

The locals, although very friendly, are apt to be more than a little eccentric at times.

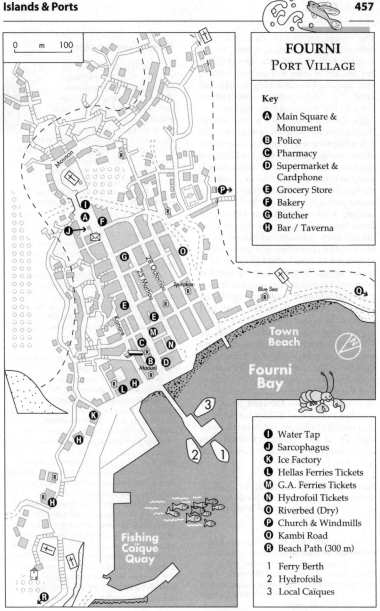

0 m 100

FOURNI
PORT VILLAGE

Key

Ⓐ Main Square & Monument
Ⓑ Police
Ⓒ Pharmacy
Ⓓ Supermarket & Cardphone
Ⓔ Grocery Store
Ⓕ Bakery
Ⓖ Butcher
Ⓗ Bar / Taverna

Mouson

28 Octovriou

25 Martiou

Kanare

Spirakos

Maouni

Blue Sea

Town Beach

Fourni Bay

Fishing Caïque Quay

Ⓘ Water Tap
Ⓙ Sarcophagus
Ⓚ Ice Factory
Ⓛ Hellas Ferries Tickets
Ⓜ G.A. Ferries Tickets
Ⓝ Hydrofoil Tickets
Ⓞ Riverbed (Dry)
Ⓟ Church & Windmills
Ⓠ Kambi Road
Ⓡ Beach Path (300 m)

1 Ferry Berth
2 Hydrofoils
3 Local Caïques

The Fourni versions of those notorious little old ladies in black have been known to jump fully clothed into the sea (black hat and all) in order to play with bathing kids (looking like something out of Roald Dahl's *The Witches* in the process). Quaint, but a bit disconcerting none the less.

It is also not uncommon to find parents feeding toddlers with bowls of runny white yuk while they walk along the town beach of an evening. If you like fish/shellfish then don't be put off by such exhibitions of madness, for fish lovers will find that Fourni is the next thing to paradise. Prices, however, are surprisingly high; with the fishing fleet sending most of its catch to Athens, the locals have come to accept city prices as normal. Even so, it is difficult to resist giving one's wallet a nip when confronted with a waterfront taverna bathed in the glow of the setting sun, its tables heaving with red lobsters (this, and the heaving toddlers on the beach, add up to a colourful spectacle).

Emptier beaches lie to the north and south of the village if you are prepared to negotiate the rough tracks that run to them. The locals aren't terribly keen on island walking and prefer to take taxi caïques to the other villages on Fourni at Chrisomilia (with its own irregular ferry link to Samos) and Kambi. The second inhabited islet in the archipelago — **Thimena** (complete with one untouristed hillside hamlet) — is also visited by caïques, but as yet there are virtually no concessions to tourism. This could change with the arrival of the first regular ferry service.

⊨

Fourni village is home to all the available accommodation. There are no hotels, but even in August you can be sure of being greeted with offers of rooms.

⌒⌒

Fourni has little sightseeing, bar the lidless **Hellenistic Sarcophagus**, which stands in the town square acting as a litter bin, and a few blocks south of the town, at **Marmari** cove, a relic from the days when Fourni was used as a marble quarry for the city of Ephesus on the adjacent Turkish coast.

Greek Island Vampires

Cosy as the Greek islands are, they have their dark side. Not least is a well-attested and widespread belief across the Aegean in vampirism. Forget Transylvania and all the associated Victorian melodrama of capes, stakes and dark brooding castles: a spot of serious necking on a sunny Greek island can be much more scary: the stark contrast between the benign homely environment and the blood-sucking dead adds an essential extra ingredient to the horror.

The Aegean and Romanian vampire myths reflect a wider regional superstitious dread of the undead. Greek culture has always placed great emphasis on the propriety of following proper burial rites, and extra precautions were often taken when particularly unwholesome islanders died if it was thought that they might start snacking on the living in the future.

Luckily Greek island vampires do have their limitations — most notably an inability to travel over water. This offers up an easy solution for dealing with potential vampires; you bury their bodies on adjacent uninhabited islands. Small islands with darker backgrounds (for example, those with a history as pirate strongholds that were at some point abandoned) are particular magnets: thus Antiparos, Fourni and Kimolos all have strong vampire superstitions.

When burial over the water wasn't an option other precautions could be taken. The excavation of a 19 c. Muslim cemetery in Mytilini on Lesbos generated space in the world's press in 1994 when a stone-lined crypt hollowed out of the city wall was found to contain a vampire's coffin. The inhabitant, a middle-aged man, had been nailed through his neck, pelvis, and ankles to the casket base in order to prevent him from rising again. A second option was to nail horseshoes to the deceased's hands and feet so that if they were to go walkies they would be heard coming.

The problem today is that the above practices have gone out of fashion, leaving island hoppers at risk. Greek vampires do have the usual dislike of garlic (this is one of the few elements of the popular image that does have a basis in reality: it is not unknown in the islands to see strings of garlic cloves on doors and gates). So by carrying garlic and checking the provenance of any love bites around your partner's neck very carefully, you can at least take some basic precautions.

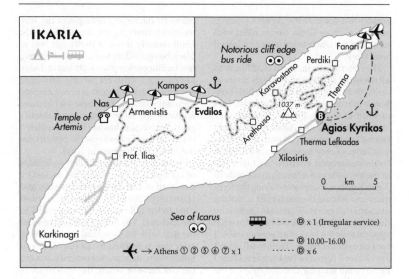

Ikaria

IKAPIA; 260 km²; pop. 9,500.

CODE ☎ 22750
TOURIST OFFICE ☎ 22222
PORT POLICE ☎ 22207
HOSPITAL ☎ 22330

Named after the unfortunate Icarus who fell and drowned (in the sea of the same name), after the wax holding the feathers to his man-made wings melted on flying too near the sun, wing-shaped Ikaria is a mountainous island with a thin covering of trees standing on the slopes like so many pins in a cushion. In fact, those who like the usual trappings of tourism will find that the view from the ferry is almost the most comfortable thing about the island.

Often used as a place of exile, Ikaria seems to lack a coherent sense of identity. With five changes of name in the last two thousand years, a three-month existence as an independent state in 1912 before union with Greece, a failed 19 c. spa resort (boasting thermal springs so radioactive that they had to be closed down), and more recently,

a freelance hippy colony on the northern coast monopolizing the best beaches, this is perhaps not too surprising. But it does leave the island with a decidedly faded air: the locals haven't got much and don't seem to expect much either. The few tourists who call are often left feeling much the same; though if you are prepared to grub around, with a bit of effort Ikaria offers an interesting and highly rewarding variation on the Greek island theme.

The main town of **Agios Kyrikos** lies on the south-east coast and the scanty remains of an ancient city. Most of the current buildings date from the 19 c. when the port expanded to serve the nearby spa resort at Therma. As a result, it hasn't developed much beyond a street or two behind the waterfront, and is filled with the cheaper and uglier type of old-style Aegean mansion house. The only quarter with any atmosphere lies north of the *Hotel Adam*: a warren of narrow streets filled with shoe shops.

On the plus side, the backstreets clambering up the hillside behind the boulder-strewn waterfront exude an air of quiet, small-town domesticity (Agios Kyrikos is another of those Greek towns filled with cats), and the whole town is well endowed with trees.

The waterfront is the focus of all life, with all the usual facilities and several tavernas doing their best to inject a (very) little bonhomie into things. This isn't due to any lack of spirit of the inhabitants, who are very friendly, it is just that Agios Kyrikos isn't geared up to any sort of tourism. Unless you have a fancy to visit nearby Therma (crammed around a narrow bay to the east of the town) there isn't much to see or do in Agios Kyrikos, except stroll along the ferry quay and admire the modernist sculpture of Icarus that greets all arrivals. Quite why the failed aviator is depicted caught in what appears to be the beak of an enormous bird isn't immediately clear. (Truth to tell, it isn't any clearer if you come back ten years later.) Perhaps the sculptor decided to spice the story up a bit by adding a mythical Halcyon bird, quietly nesting on the waves when Icarus decided to drop by.

Most tourists who visit Agios Kyrikos are doing little more, for the main attraction of the town is its role as the local transportation hub. In addition to the caïques to Fourni, it is the starting point for the island bus link: a service that is very unreliable — often terminating at Evdilos — and departing when full rather than on schedule. Buses on Ikaria are a law unto themselves (the morning Agios Kyrikos to Evdilos bus starts out at Evdilos because the driver lives there: he thus drives an empty bus to the capital before starting his working day; it doesn't seem to have occurred to anyone that he could carry passengers as well). When you can get aboard, the bus provides excellent value for money thanks to a cliff-edge ride that will leave you with a vivid insight as to what Icarus saw and felt as he fell to sea.

At the end of the mountain road lies the more appealing north side of the island (home to pine forests, vineyards and the island's best beaches). **Evdilos**, the bus's final destination, is Ikaria's second port. It offers an interesting example of the way tourism is changing the face of the islands. Until recently it was a pretty sad sort of place, being a village in decline and offering few facilities or temptations to linger. Today just enough tourists are passing through to encourage development without ruining the unspoilt cosy atmosphere, and it is now arguably the more attractive of Ikaria's ports. A new quay has just been completed that will allow lorries to use the port (ferries may start docking here in 2012).

Huddled around a small hilly bay, Evdilos offers a picturesque waterfront backed by a confetti of loosely scattered houses and churches on the green hills behind (most cling to the hill road that runs parallel to the harbour). The village has two centres: the first is on the headland near the ferry quay and is reached by an impressive, if rather steep, staircase; the second is around the old harbour where the waterfront is dominated by leafy tavernas that come into their charming own after dark.

Provided you aren't trying to exist on a backpacker's budget, then Evdilos could be a very attractive option. The two hotels seem to thrive on the sort of holidaymaker who would be comfortable on an island like Chalki, but who prefers to be surrounded by local islanders rather than fellow vacationers. In short, Evdilos is ideal for spooning lovers who want dreamy evenings in tavernas with lots of local colour. Those looking for nightlife and cheap accommodation will be disappointed.

Ferry links are surprisingly good for a second island port, and the quay is invariably lined with a fleet of taxis whenever a boat comes in. Most disembarking here are those in the know — heading for the wide sand beach at **Armenistis**, 15 km along the coast. The village on the headland beyond is now witness to the first signs of Ios-like disco and taverna development (though this is a bit misleading as the scale of the scene here is much smaller). Some 2 km further west lies the pretty hamlet of **Pappas** and the nearby archaeological site at **Nas**,

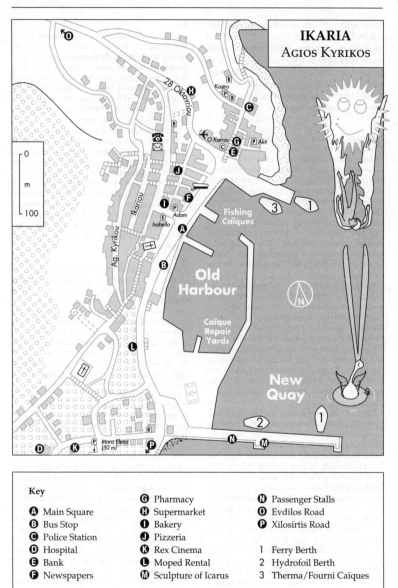

IKARIA
AGIOS KYRIKOS

Kastro

28 Oktovriou

O Karras

Adam

Isabella

Ikariou

Ag. Kyrikou

Fishing Caïques

Old Harbour

Caïque Repair Yards

New Quay

Akti

Mara Elena (50 m)

0
m
100

N

Key

A Main Square
B Bus Stop
C Police Station
D Hospital
E Bank
F Newspapers

G Pharmacy
H Supermarket
I Bakery
J Pizzeria
K Rex Cinema
L Moped Rental
M Sculpture of Icarus

N Passenger Stalls
O Evdilos Road
P Xilosirtis Road

1 Ferry Berth
2 Hydrofoil Berth
3 Therma/Fourni Caïques

after which roads degenerate into dirt tracks. From this point Ikaria is the preserve of walkers, and thus little visited. In past years rare ferries have made a taxi-boat rendezvous off the hill village of **Karkinagri**, providing a link with the outside world in lieu of a terrestrial means of access, but this service is unlikely to appear again.

☻

In antiquity Ikaria had something of an identity crisis, being variously known as Makris, Dolichi and Doligi (all names derived from its oblong shape), and Ichthyoessa (derived from the plentiful fishing to be found hereabouts). The name 'Ikaria' most likely has its origins in the Phoenician word for fish ('ikor') despite the claims of the Ikarus myth. The limited amount of archaeology to date on the island makes it uncertain when it was first settled and by whom. This does allow some fairly extreme speculation to flourish (the Ikarus story has even been cited by some as evidence of Minoan control).

Be this as it may, it is at least clear that Ikaria was home to three significant towns during most of the ancient period. The most important (and de facto capital) was at Kampos and called **Oinoi**. It lasted well into the late Byzantine period. The second city of note was just east of Therma and also grew up around hot springs. It was swept into the sea by a landslide in the 1 c. BC. Both cities sided with Athens and then Macedon in the wider power struggles in Greece, before coming under the control of the kings of Pergamum.

Decline followed and by the late Byzantine period Ikaria was used as a place of banishment for members of the imperial family. During the late Middle Ages the Genoese Arangi family ruled before the Turks took Ikaria in 1521. The island rebelled against Turkish rule in July 1912 following the Italian occupation of the Dodecanese islands. However, the Greek state, not wanting to provoke Turkey, and otherwise concerned with a failed attempt to secure the Dodecanese from Italian control, opted to leave Ikaria in limbo. The islanders, having burnt their boats, had little alternative but to declare the **'Free State of Ikaria'**: a slightly absurd one-island state — complete with its own currency and newspaper. This lasted all of four months: formal union with Greece coming on the 4th of November 1912.

🛏

On the south coast gloomy **Therma** has a monopoly on faded up-market waterfront hotels, while **Agios Kyrikos** has a motley collection of cheaper establishments, including the B-class pension *Adam* (☎ 22418), the C-class *O Karras* (☎ 22494) and E-class hotel *Isabella* (☎ 22839) — all on the waterfront. More attractive is the pension *Kastro* (☎ 22474), which offers rooms overlooking the town.

Evdilos currently has two pricey hotels which are either B-class or expensive C-class according to which source you consult. The newer and better of the two is the *Atheras* (☎ 31434), which offers attractive singles starting at €45. The more expensive *Evdoxia* (☎ 31502) has lovely views over the port, but a horrible staircase every time you want to get to it. Rooms are generally scarce elsewhere on the island — though a few exist at Evdilos (arrive early), and there are a goodly number at **Armenistis**.

👓

The only great archaeological site of interest on Ikaria is a **Temple of Artemis Tavropoleio** (or 'Patroness of Bulls': a euphemism for a fertility and end-of-the-world cult) at Nas, foundations of which survive along with remnants of an ancient city harbour. A local story has it that in the 19 c. a marble statue of the goddess Artemis was unearthed at the site, but an enlightened priest put paid to the island's chances of making it as a major sightseeing destination by burning it in a lime kiln on the grounds that it was a pagan idol.

Other archaeological sites of note are lesser affairs, the best being a two-storey high 3 c. BC **Hellenistic Tower** on a hilltop at Faros, and the remains of a **Byzantine Mansion House** at Kampos, which is also home to the ruins of Ikaria's oldest church, the 12 c. basilica of St. Irini.

Agios Kyrikos sees frequent water taxis running to the ugly spa and hotel hamlet of Therma, 4 km from the town, a fair beach at **Fanari**, and more interesting daily High Season caïques to the Fourni archipelago. Waterfront signs pointing out the town museum (150 m south of the hospital) take you on a town walk to a long abandoned building. On the west side of Agios Kyrikos lies a second, less popular spa village, at **Therma Lefkadas**, with the hamlet of **Xilosirtis** further down the road. After that the southern coast is little more than a steep mountain side falling into the sea.

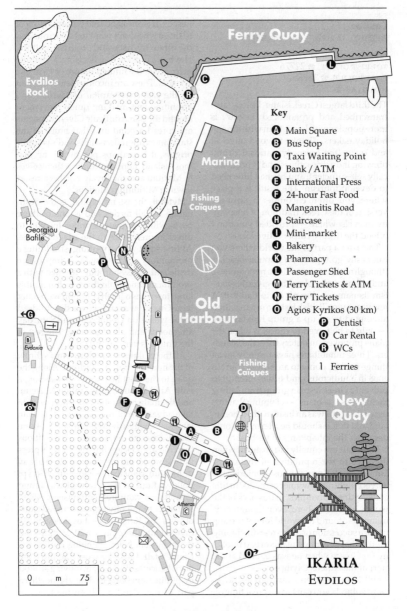

Key

- **A** Main Square
- **B** Bus Stop
- **C** Taxi Waiting Point
- **D** Bank / ATM
- **E** International Press
- **F** 24-hour Fast Food
- **G** Manganitis Road
- **H** Staircase
- **I** Mini-market
- **J** Bakery
- **K** Pharmacy
- **L** Passenger Shed
- **M** Ferry Tickets & ATM
- **N** Ferry Tickets
- **O** Agios Kyrikos (30 km)
- **P** Dentist
- **Q** Car Rental
- **R** WCs

1 Ferries

IKARIA
EVDILOS

Lesbos
ΛΕΣΒΟΣ; 1630 km²; pop. 104,600.

MYTILINI CODE ☎ 22510
TOURIST OFFICE ☎ 22776
PORT POLICE ☎ 28888
HOSPITAL ☎ 28457

The third largest Greek island, Lesbos (also transcribed and pronounced 'Les*vos*') is more popular with locals than with foreign holidaymakers. Thanks to good olive oil and ouzo (the aniseedy national drink) brewing industries, the island is economically self-sufficient, and has had little need to develop tourism. The result is a place where you often encounter a stronger version of the Greek tradition of hospitality than elsewhere — provided you don't offend the deeply conservative locals.

This isn't a part of the world where you can easily go topless on popular beaches (though nudism is possible on remote ones), and although the island has given lesbianism its name, it doesn't do to flaunt it. A few years ago a British lesbian organization attempted to set up a group holiday here — only to be forced to cancel it when the plans provoked an outcry from the islanders. Three inhabitants have recently taken things further, going to an Athens court in 2008 in a ludicrous (and futile) attempt to prevent a Greek lesbian group from calling themselves 'Lesbians' — claiming that this use of the word was an insult to their homeland and that it should be a term that only describes the inhabitants of Lesbos!

The locals are equally intransigent when it comes to the reputation of their most famous son, Konstantinos Kenteris, the 'Greece-lightning' winner of the 200 m title at the Sydney Olympics. In this neck of the woods he is still a hero, even though he is infamous around the world for not turning up for a succession of drugs tests (including the one that generated reams of bad publicity for Greece when he was banned at the start of the Athens Olympics).

Still, if you can keep away from such awkward subjects you can have a great time on Lesbos. It is an island that will appeal most to those who don't want to be surrounded by other tourists and 'tourist' culture. Having your own wheels is a definite help, given the limited nature of local bus services. These are inconveniently centred on the east-coast capital of Mytilini and are infrequent, making quick movement around the island difficult. Given that sights are spread around and that much of the stark landscape reflects the island's volcanic origins, it is perhaps not surprising that most island hoppers confine themselves to Mytilini and the lovely northern resort town of Mithimna/Molivos.

Mytilini, the island capital, is the destination for all ferries and is one of those ports which operators prefer to refer to direct in preference to the island's name. At first sight very appealing, straddling a promontory adorned with an impressive castle and a busy harbour crowned with a prominent pineapple-domed church, this large town has a lot in common with other large Greek towns and cities in that it is dead to the world on Wednesday and Saturday afternoons and all of Sunday. The rest of the time it is very stimulating.

All the facilities are within a euro's throw of the inner harbour waterfront. Along the quay to the west lie the city bus station, a Folk Art Museum, a Byzantine Museum and the main bus station. You may wish to take advantage of this sooner rather than later for although the Mytilini townsfolk are friendly enough they are more superstitious than most, and leapt into the world's press in 1994 when, during an excavation of a 19 c. Muslim cemetery, a stone-lined crypt hollowed out of the city wall was found to contain a vampire's coffin (see p. 458).

Thanks to the olive-grove-fringed gulfs of Gera and Kallonis, Lesbos is effectively divided into three parts, with Mytilini and the peninsula below hanging on like the island's tail. Links between the three are poor: hence the difficulty in moving around by public transport. To date, the northern part of the island has been the focus of

LESBOS

0   km   10

MAIN GREEN BUSES:
—— ⑩ x 4 ♦18.00
— — ⑩ x 6 ♦18.00
-·-· ⑩ x 2/3
-··- ⑩ x 2/3 ♦13.15
— —— ⑩ x 1 13.15

MAIN BLUE (CITY) BUSES:
- - - ⑪ 07.00–20.00
·· ·· ⑪ 07.00–18.00
······ ⑪ 06.30–20.00

Skala Sikamias

Castle 🏰 ⛺
Molivos/
Mithimna
Petra
Mantamados

Anaxos

Moni Perivolis
Agios
Paraskevi
Kalloni   Temple of
Aphrodite
Moni Limona

Sigri   Antissa

Petrified Trees

Eressos

Gulf of
Kallonis

Aqueduct

Lambou Mili

◉◉ Spa
Pirgi Thermis

Castle &
Theatre

Mytilini

Skala
Eressou

Agiassos
968 m   Paleokipos
Polihnitos   Skopelos
Vrissa
Temple of
Dionysos   Vatera

Gulf of
Gera

Varia

Loutra

Agios
Ermoyenis
Beach

Plomari   Ag. Isidoros
Tarti Beach

✈ → Athens ⑩ x 4
→ Thessalonika ⑩ x 1
→ Limnos ⑩ x 1
→ Chios ③ ⑦ x 1

—— -·-· ⑩ x 2
-·-· ⑩ x 2
······ ○ Irregular Service

⛴ —— ⑩ x 8

the tourist industry, owing to the attractive castle-topped northern coast town of **Molivos** (officially known by its older name of **Mithimna**). Once Mytilini's great rival for control of the island, it has benefited immeasurably from losing out and not ending up the home of innumerable grimy 19 C. mansions. Instead, cobbled streets, a pebble beach and photogenic houses are the order of the day. The village of **Petra**, 5 km to the south, is also a growing beach resort of note.

The best island beaches, however, lie elsewhere. The surprisingly quiet resort village of **Vatera** has an amazing 7 km stretch of sand and can be reached direct by bus or beach boat from the indifferent southern resort of **Plomari**. The bus route is better as it takes in the lovely old hill village of **Agiassos**, carved out of a pine forest with cobbled streets and old timber houses, and the objective for regular excursions.

The west side of Lesbos is visibly less fertile than the east and dominated by stark hills. It is comparatively quiet, with the exception of **Eressos** and its impressive beach at Skala Eressou (and site of ancient Eressos). Home to the poet Sappho (see p.

468), the long sandy beach is comparable with that at Vatera. Those seeking more seclusion should head for the pretty west-coast fishing village of **Sigri** — an ideal spot for quiet romance in an infinitely more attractive place than the capital and, in past years, home to the occasional summer ferry service.

😋

Both size and location have conspired to give Lesbos an important place in Aegean history. The island has always been a significant player in the region. Oligarchy was the preferred method of rule in antiquity, with Pittacus (one of the seven sages) numbered among its rulers. The island's proximity to Asia meant that it fell to the Persians in 527 BC, and was only freed in 479 BC, joining the Delian League. In 428 BC it attempted to break away from Athenian control, an act that only narrowly avoided a massacre by way of a reprisal. After the Peloponnesian War Lesbos changed hands regularly, being variously under Spartan and Ptolemaic control before the Romans moved in. During the Byzantine era Lesbos became a place of exile, and was later under Venetian and then Genoese control. It fell to the Turks in 1462 and joined Greece in 1912.

🛏

A Tourist Police office lies just off the ferry quay offering accommodation details. Most of it is well away from **Mytilini Town**. In town (which is where you often need to be thanks to ferry departure times that prohibit sleeping elsewhere) options are more limited. Rooms offer the best value for money, but fill quickly in the summer. Most are on or near Ermou St., though the best lie on the south side of the harbour. The hotels are a pretty diverse collection. The B-class *Blue Sea* (☎ 23994) on the waterfront behind the ferry quay offers the prospect of an easy, if pricey, bed, but they don't seem terribly keen on backpackers (even those with money!). The C-class *Sappho* (☎ 28888) is more accommodating, but very popular (phone ahead in High Season). If you can afford it, the nearby B-class *Lesvion* (☎ 22038) offers an attractive option.

In **Mithimna / Molivos** there is so much accommodation on offer that one is spoilt for choice. The tourist office near the bus stop can help find a bed, but it pays to check how far from the waterfront any bed is before

you accept it. The town has B-class hotels in abundance and little else; these include the *Poseidon* (☎ 22530 71570) by the bus stop, and the *Sea Horse* (☎ 22530 71320).

Λ

Camping Dionysos (☎ 22520 61340) is a newish site just inland from Vatera. Its remote location means it largely relies on Greek campers.

👓

Mytilini is dominated by the **Castle**, built in 1373 on the site of the old acropolis; it can be visited, but, overlooking the Turkish coast, is another of those photographically sensitive sites. Impressive views of the castle can, however, be gleaned from the hillside that is home to the bowl (sans seats) of the 3 C. BC **Hellenistic Theatre** that marked the edge of the ancient town. Mosaics found in excavations nearby are now residing in the good **Archaeological Museum** 50 m north-east of Mytilini's ferry quay. Other undoubted town sights are no longer extant, notably a canal that once separated the castle peninsula from the rest of the island (Ermou Street follows much of its former course) and the now defunct northern harbour.

Elsewhere on the island the hamlet of Moria, 4 km outside Mytilini, has the impressive remains of a 3 C. AD **Roman Aqueduct** that watered Mytilini. Odd fragments survive along its 20 km length, notably at Lambou Mili. Some way beyond are the remains of Temples of Aphrodite and Dionysos. **Mithimna / Molivos** offers some of the best sightseeing on Lesbos courtesy of the 14 C. Genoese **Kastro** built on the site of the ancient acropolis, and the almost too picturesque cobbled and stone-house town that lies below. Finds from the ancient town (including sarcophagi) are in the **Museum** in the town hall.

The west side of Lesbos has the remains of a building alleged to be **Sappho's Home** and, on the road to Antissa, the curious remains of a **Petrified Forest** dated as being from one to twenty million years old. Several of the excavated old tar-coloured tree stumps have been set up like pillars from some very early Greek temple, and there is also a useful museum attached to the site. Finally, **Sigri** on the west coast has a very atmospheric 18 C. cannon-filled **Turkish Fortress**. Similar in design to the castle at Kos Town (see p. 402), it also stands on a promontory with a picturesque town on its landward side, and a quay on the seaward.

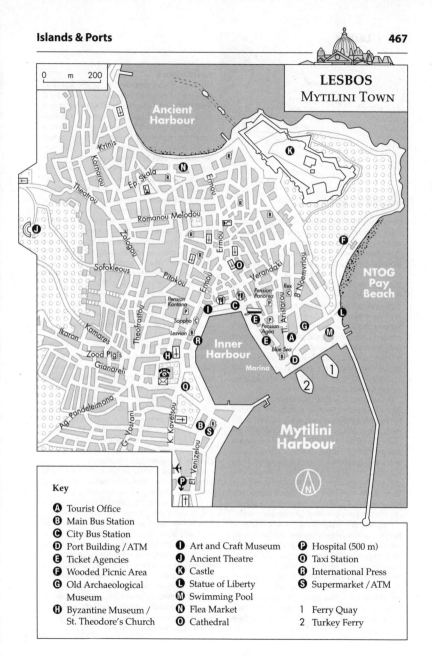

Ancient Harbour

Ep. Skala

Krinis

Konnarou

Theatrou

Zalogou

Romanou Melodou

Sofokleous

Pitakou

Ermou

Ermou

Verandaki

NTOG Pay Beach

Ag. Noemvriou

Ikaron

Kamares

Theofrastou

Zood Pigis

Gianareli

Ag. Pondeleimono

G. Yosani

K. Kavetsou

El. Venizelou

Pension Kontana

Pension Pariorea

Rex

Sappho

Lesvian

Pension Agea

Blue Sea

Inner Harbour

Marina

Mytilini Harbour

Ti Aristarou

Key

- **A** Tourist Office
- **B** Main Bus Station
- **C** City Bus Station
- **D** Port Building / ATM
- **E** Ticket Agencies
- **F** Wooded Picnic Area
- **G** Old Archaeological Museum
- **H** Byzantine Museum / St. Theodore's Church
- **I** Art and Craft Museum
- **J** Ancient Theatre
- **K** Castle
- **L** Statue of Liberty
- **M** Swimming Pool
- **N** Flea Market
- **O** Cathedral
- **P** Hospital (500 m)
- **Q** Taxi Station
- **R** International Press
- **S** Supermarket / ATM
- 1 Ferry Quay
- 2 Turkey Ferry

IT SEEMS TO ME THAT MAN IS EQUAL TO THE GODS THAT IS WHOEV SITS OPPOSITE YOU, AND, COMI NEARER, RELISHES AS YOU SPEAK THE SWEETNESS OF YOUR VOICE, AND TH THR VE SO STIRRED OF YOUR LOVE, WHICH BREAST THEN HEART IN MY OWN WHENEVER I CATC THEN MY VOICE SIGHT OF YO VE OR A MOMEN ME AND MY TONGU IS DESERT STRUCK SILENT. THE DELI TE FIRE SUDDENLY RACES BENE MY S MY EYES SEE N

Sappho of Lesbos

Described as the '10th Muse' by no lesser figure than Plato, Sappho was the most highly respected poetess in antiquity. A figure from the shadowy middle of the Archaic period in Greek history, relatively few biographical details are known. Sappho was born into an elite family on Lesbos c. 612 BC. Thereafter she spent much of her childhood exiled on Sicily (probably because her father — bearing the Asterix-type name of Scamandronymus — was embroiled in political troubles). On her return to Lesbos she appears to have become the leading light of a group of women devoted to celebrating Aphrodite and the Muses. Quite what this outfit was, or how it was structured, is now lost in the mists of time (possibilities range from a sort of glorified wives and daughters social network to something more formal, even of a religious nature).

In any event, it is clear that Sappho composed in and for a circle of woman friends. She is known to have been married to a leading member of the ruling circle on Lesbos named Cercylas, and she had a daughter called Cleis. One of her poems also mentions a brother, Charaxus. After this even ancient biographers run out of information. There is a story that she died by throwing herself off a cliff on Lefkada after suffering unrequited love for a middle-aged man called Phaon (see p. 592). However, this is probably no more than a deliberate piece of satire by a New Comedy playwright.

Sappho's work is significant because of both its personal female perspective and also the time she was composing. She was writing at the very beginning of Greek lyric poetry and is a sort of transitory figure between the oral tradition embodied by the works of Homer and later text-orientated authors. It isn't even known for sure if she physically wrote anything down. Although she is known as a poetess all her material was composed as songs and sung to music, so books of her collected poems were early compilations of song lyrics.

Surviving Work

The body of work attributed to Sappho was large by ancient standards. It is known that the library at Alexandria had 9 volumes devoted to her poems in the 3 C. BC. The books were seemingly divided between verses of different metres (for example Book 1 had poems in her unique Sapphic stanza). Unfortunately, none have survived — in part because her work became less popular in the late Roman era. All that has come down through the years are odd verses, quotes by other authors and fragments recovered from Egyptian papyrus finds. The survivors are so piecemeal that they are actually entitled by scholars 'Fragment 1, 2, 3...' etc.

The tally of Sapphic material available to us thus consists of some 200–250 fragments (including tentative attributions). These contain only one complete poem — a unique survivor thanks to its being quoted in a 1 C. BC book on poetry — and a further 3 fragments complete enough for their structure to be understood. The pitiful total is thus: only 4 readable poems, only 21 fragments with complete stanzas, only 63 fragments with complete lines. This isn't much on which to base an assessment of Sappho's output or character.

Sappho the Feminist Icon

With so little of her work extant, perspectives on Sappho are heavily influenced by others with agendas. Surviving material shows that she opted for a very personal writing approach, intimately describing her friends' fancies and feelings. In addition she wasn't afraid to explore popular tales from a female perspective (for example, reworking the story of Troy from Helen's point of view). On the back of this she became a deserved romantic feminist icon in the early 19 c. when women began to break free from social constraints.

Sappho and her female social circle have also given modern lesbianism its name, though it is impossible to say if her sexual preferences were orientated this way. The evidence from her work is ambiguous to say the least. Because she is writing for a female group with a pro-Aphrodite bias her language is inevitably full of romantic metaphor when describing relationships between them: the fact that she was a married mother who wrote celebratory songs for the weddings of members of her group suggests a more complex picture. This would be in keeping with the mores of her time anyway; the modern preference for labelling sexual orientation wasn't shared in the ancient world, where whether you were the active or passive participant generally counted for more than gender.

Oinousses

ΟΙΝΟΥΣΣΕΣ; 16 km²; pop. 420.

CODE ☎ 22720
POLICE ☎ 55222

Oinousses (also transcribed as 'Inousses') is the collective name for a group of nine tiny islands that lie off the north-east coast of Chios. The only inhabited island — the largest in the group — goes under the same name and is ignored by all regular ferry services.

Blessed with several good beaches, attractively clear seas and one large town that feels more like a city suburb on the slide than an island capital, Oinousses has the distinction of being the birthplace of several of Greece's richest shipping owners. Summers therefore see luxury yachts in the harbour, their owners visiting luxury villas tucked discreetly away in an otherwise attractive, but declining, town. The strong seafaring tradition hereabouts sees many of the menfolk working away: the result is a curious mix of affluence combined with boarded-up summer holiday homes. For this reason tourism is all but ignored as the remaining islanders (many of whom work in fishing-related industries) have enough coming in to be able to resist the temptations to turn their home into a resort island.

The most obvious consequence of all this is that tourist facilities are scarce to the point of being non-existent (beyond the normal bank-cum-post office), and the usual welcoming attitude typical of most Greek islanders is thin on the ground if you try to sleep on it (you will as likely as not be rounded up by cadets from the island's nautical school). Those that resort to the only hotel fare somewhat better.

The town harbour likewise reflects the absent nature of tourism: it is a bit bleak with only one taverna — though it has a lot of potential, with a veritable concertina of small quays and a harbour protected by three islets (one topped with a monastery and another with a church). Given the lack of accommodation, beaches and sights,

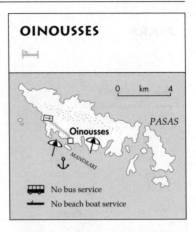

the island is best visited on a day-tripper boat basis (frequency varies according to the time of year). In addition to visiting Oinousses proper, these boats often also stop at the privately owned harbour-mouth church islet of **Mandraki**, 300 m from the town quay.

⊨

No rooms, but a nice, if pricey, C-class hotel in the town — the *Thalassoporos* (☎ 55475) — usually has rooms available.

∞

Oinousses is relatively bereft of things to see or do other than lie on the beach (the best are in quiet coves to the west of the town).

The only attraction of note in town is a surprisingly well-stocked **Maritime Museum** filled with mementos donated by local shipping millionaires. This means that most visitors are reduced to doing the coastal walk to the **Evangelismou Convent** on the western tip of the island. Home to the mummified corpse of a shipping billionaire's daughter who snuffed it shortly after becoming a nun, the monastery was rebuilt as a shrine to her memory by her father (who has now joined her in her mausoleum). The fact that her body hadn't decomposed after its traditional three-year stint underground (in Greece graves are reused, so once the flesh has rotted the bones of the deceased are usually interred elsewhere) was taken as a fortuitous (for the monastery's finances at any rate) sign of sainthood.

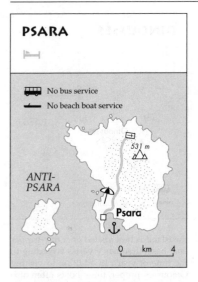

PSARA

🛏️

🚌 No bus service

⛴ No beach boat service

531 m

ANTI-PSARA

Psara

⚓

0   km   4

Psara
ΨΑΡΑ; 45 km²; pop. 460.

CODE ☎ 22740

Barren and dusty Psara rarely figures on tourist itineraries and, ignored by most ferry operators, wallows quietly in the shadows of its own grim history. An obscure island in ancient times, it came to prominence (along with the Saronic islands of Hydra and Spetses) in the early 19 c., thanks to an indigenous fleet of merchant adventurers. Psara was thus well placed to play a prominent part in the early liberation struggle of the independent Greek state, but — lying just off the Turkish mainland — very badly placed when it came to avoiding the wrath of the Turks that came after. By way of setting an example to would-be rebellious islands the Turks laid waste to the island in 1824, killing the bulk of the population (inflated by refugees from other islands) of 20,000 (3,000 escaped by boat to found a town on Evia: Nea Psara). Psara has never really recovered from the event the Greeks call the 'holocaust'.

Some survivors drifted back; the island has never prospered. Almost all live in the only town of **Psara**. Traversing a headland on the south coast, it is hardly the typical island town. Photographs suggest that it is quite developed, but the reality is rather different. With few made-up roads and not much in the way of shops, the town feels like an undeveloped version of Lipsi. Town buildings — which for the most part are gloriously undistinguished — are pretty scattered, as there is no pressure on space. Most of the town life — such as it is, for the settlement feels like one large suburb — centres on the waterfront square which is home to one bar, a couple of shady trees and a memorial adorned with miniature cannon. A gun-topped bastion of sorts has also been built on the northern headland of the caïque harbour which is also home to a couple of tavernas. On the plus side the typical 'family' small island atmosphere pervades, and there are a reasonable number of American-English speakers in the streets thanks to expatriates returning 'home' each summer.

The rest of the island is barren and has little to offer apart from walks to distant windmills or empty beaches (sadly, most are poor quality: the best lie along the road to the north-east of the town) and an 18 c. monastery on the north side of the island.

🛏️
The thin supply of beds on the island are dominated by a prison converted to a hotel by the EOT, the B-class *Miramare* on the north side of town, and the *Xenonas Pension* (☎ 612 93). There are also a few rooms.

👓
Sightseeing on Psara is thin on the ground. The Turks took a lot of trouble to ensure that there was nothing left to look at, totally demolishing the castle that stood on the headland still known as **Paleokastro**. Now topped by a couple of chapels it offers sun-baked views across to Antipsara but little more. A few ruinous pre-holocaust buildings survive, and there is a small museum on the outskirts of town that is usually closed.

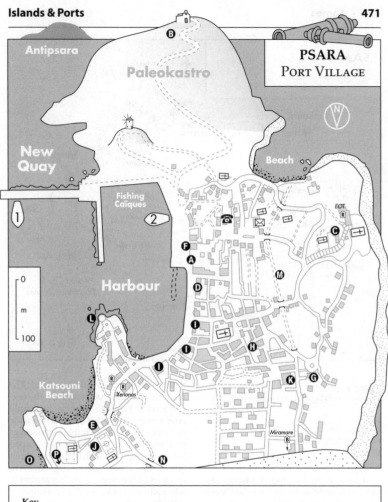

PSARA
PORT VILLAGE

Antipsara

Paleokastro

New Quay

Beach

EOT

Fishing Caïques

Harbour

Katsouni Beach

Xenonas

Miramare

Key

- **A** Town Square
- **B** Site of Venetian Kastro
- **C** Police
- **D** National Bank of Greece
- **E** Museum
- **F** Main Square Bar & Ferry Tickets
- **G** Supermarket
- **H** Bakery
- **I** Tavernas
- **J** School
- **K** Old Water Wells
- **L** Cannon Memorial
- **M** Ravine (dry in summer)
- **N** Village Ring Road
- **O** Lazoreta Beach
- **P** Dirt Track to Lakka Beach & Limnos Beach

- **1** Ferry Berth
- **2** Berth for (rare) Excursion Caïques

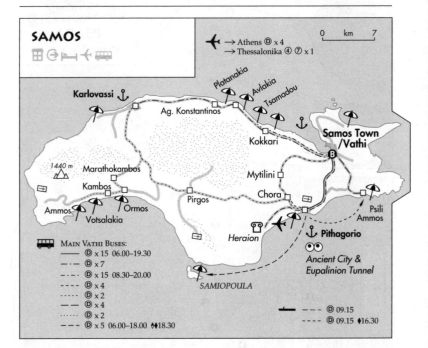

SAMOS

→ Athens ⑩ x 4
→ Thessalonika ④ ⑦ x 1

0　　km　　7

Karlovassi ⚓

Platanakia
Avlakia
Tsamadou

Ag. Konstantinos

Samos Town /Vathi
Ⓑ

Kokkari

1440 m
Marathokambos

Mytilini

Kambos

Chora

Ammos
Votsalakia
Ormos

Pirgos

Psili Ammos

Heraion

Pithagorio

🚌 MAIN VATHI BUSES:
——— ⑩ x 15　06.00–19.30
—·—· ⑩ x 7
—··—·· ⑩ x 15　08.30–20.00
– – – – ⑩ x 4
········ ⑩ x 2
——— ⑩ x 4
········ ⑩ x 2
– – – ⑩ x 5　06.00–18.00 ♦♦18.30

Ancient City & Eupalinion Tunnel

SAMIOPOULA

—— – – – ⑩ 09.15
– – – – ⑩ 09.15 ♦16.30

Samos

ΣΑΜΟΣ; 472 km²; pop. 41,500.

CODE ☎ 22730
TOURIST OFFICE ☎ 28530
PORT POLICE ☎ 27318
HOSPITAL ☎ 27407

A large island just to the north of the Dodecanese, mountainous Samos (the name is thought to derive from the Phoenician word for 'high') is known for its tree-clad slopes (though a series of devastating fires in July 2000 destroyed 50% of its tree cover), a scattering of reasonable beaches, and top end of the package tourist market. Island hoppers are not noted for visiting in large numbers.

Thanks to its large size, Samos boasts three modern centres with ferry connections. The most important of these is **Samos Town** (or **Vathi** as it appears on all timetables). The modern island capital, it is easily the biggest town on Samos (bus timetables simply refer to it as 'Samos'). It consists of a wide ribbon of houses, four or five blocks deep, that winds around a horseshoe-shaped bay, with steep, wooded hills climbing quickly up behind. Like all large towns in this part of the Aegean, the waterfront is adorned with commercial, 19 c. buildings in the neo-classical style, many topped with red-tile roofs. If you venture here by way of Pithagorio the hillside views over the town are superb, with the vivid mix of blue seas, red roofs and green hills.

This all adds up to a pretty and attractive picture, but Vathi somehow lacks charm once you descend to street level: it is too big, and once you delve beyond the waterfront the backstreets prove to be rather drab and dingy affairs. The overall feel of Vathi is much more akin to that of a mainland town, and one without much tourist activity at that. This feeling is reinforced by the fact that the whole place shuts down on Sundays and Wednesday afternoons (tourist towns on most other islands all but ignore mainland conventions such as this).

This is not to say that Vathi is a place to be avoided. The pluses certainly are there when you look for them: Vathi has a small but excellent Archaeological Museum, a diminutive shady park, and a number of good tavernas in the street one block behind the ferry side of the harbour (avoid the poor affairs on the waterfront itself). The most attractive part of Vathi climbs up the windmill-topped hill to the south of the harbour; called Old Vathi, it is the pre-19 c. heart of the town.

Vathi isn't noted for its beaches, but a number of fine pebble strands lie an easy bus ride away along the coast. The most developed of these is at **Kokkari**, which has evolved into the largest north-coast tourist resort. Further west are quieter, but attractive, options at **Tsamadou, Avlakia** and **Platanakia**; all are pebble, but are fringed with pine woods and the coast road. Though the latter feel remote, they are easily visited via the hourly Vathi—Karlovassi buses which stop at all of them.

Thanks to its role as the hub of the bus system, Vathi is the best base if you want to explore the island by public transport. It also dominates ferry activity and as a result ends up on the itineraries of most island hoppers who venture into the Eastern Aegean. It is the terminus for all Piraeus—Ikaria—Samos ferries, with invaluable linking services on to Chios. Turkey, and the well-preserved ancient Greek city of Ephesus, is also a popular hop away from here.

As usual in this part of the world political tensions are evident: the Port Police are very sensitive when Turkish boats are in, and are quick to shepherd interested spectators away from them. Sleeping on

the ferry quay is also a non-starter thanks to the attentions of mice and men (or in Vathi's case, rats and policemen).

The second of the island's ports is commercial **Karlovassi**. Only 50 minutes from Vathi by bus, it is sited on the north-west coast, an hour's steaming closer to Piraeus. This port had its heyday during the late 19 c. when boats were slower and it formed the nearest convenient link with the mainland. Even today most Vathi-bound ferries call. It might thus sound an attractive option if you don't want to spend more time than you can help on a ferry, but you are best advised to give Karlovassi a miss: tourist facilities are thin on the ground. At first sight all looks pleasant enough: the port (tucked neatly behind a wooded hillock 1 km west of the town — though this was damaged in a large forest fire in 2010) is actually quite cosy, with a couple of tavernas and several hotels, but Karlovassi proper is awful. The waterfront is all but derelict, with run-down 19 c. neo-classical warehouses giving way to a drab concrete-built town beyond. The all-important bus stop is 2 km from the port in the tiny old chora part of town.

One of Karlovassi's few pluses is that it is the jumping-off point for the south-west coast (though Vathi and Pithagorio are equally good if you don't mind longer journey times). This is in many ways the most attractive part of Samos, being an appealing mix of taverna-lined beaches and fishing villages that form a relaxed and unexploited backwater. **Votsalakia** and **Ammos** beaches are easily the best and usually quiet, even in High Season.

The third Samian port of **Pithagorio** on the south coast offers a complete contrast to the northern ports. Now the centre of the island's tourist industry, it has a very attractive atmosphere and the bulk of the island sights, but bar a few tourist boats and a daily summer hydrofoil (most heading for Patmos) it is poorly connected with the ferry network, with only a couple of regular departures each week. The modern town lies directly over the ancient capital of the

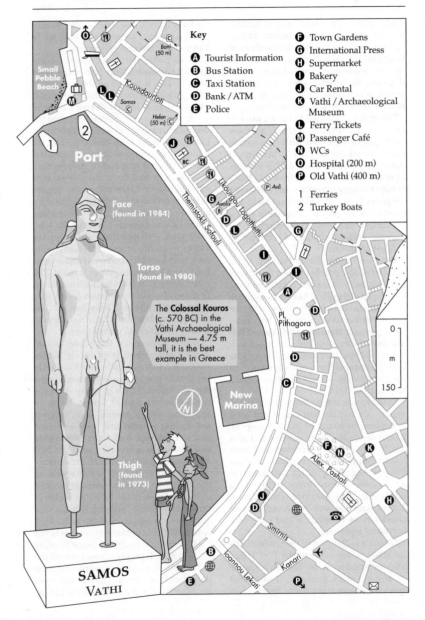

Key

- **Ⓐ** Tourist Information
- **Ⓑ** Bus Station
- **Ⓒ** Taxi Station
- **Ⓓ** Bank / ATM
- **Ⓔ** Police
- **Ⓕ** Town Gardens
- **Ⓖ** International Press
- **Ⓗ** Supermarket
- **Ⓘ** Bakery
- **Ⓙ** Car Rental
- **Ⓚ** Vathi / Archaeological Museum
- **Ⓛ** Ferry Tickets
- **Ⓜ** Passenger Café
- **Ⓝ** WCs
- **Ⓞ** Hospital (200 m)
- **Ⓟ** Old Vathi (400 m)

1. Ferries
2. Turkey Boats

Small Pebble Beach

Bani (50 m)

Koundourioti

Samos

Helen (50 m)

Port

Face (found in 1984)

Torso (found in 1980)

Themistokli Sofouli

RC

Likourgou Logotheti

Avli

Aeolis

The **Colossal Kouros** (c. 570 BC) in the Vathi Archaeological Museum — 4.75 m tall, it is the best example in Greece

Thigh (found in 1973)

Pl. Pithagora

New Marina

0 m 150

Alex. Pashali

Smirnis

Ioannou Lekati

Kanari

SAMOS VATHI

island. Known at the time as 'Samos', it is not to be confused with the modern capital with that name on the north coast. In fact, Pithagorio has changed names several times, and the current name only dates back to 1953 when the town was rechristened in honour of the island's most famous son: the mathematician Pythagoras (from the Middle Ages until 1953 the town was called Tigani).

Despite the numbers of package tourists in town (hotel development along this coast has been extensive thanks to the large number of good sand beaches), Pithagorio manages to retain a surprisingly dreamy air, with a snug taverna- and tree-lined small harbour backed by red-roofed town behind. Unfortunately, all this means that the town is expensive — a reflection of the top-island-resort status it enjoys. This is set to get worse now that a huge new yachting marina has been built in the bay just east of the town. Tourism has at least ensured the existence of regular taxi boats to Psili Ammos beach as well as to **Samiopoula** islet (visiting a north-side beach and taverna).

☠

Samos was one of the most important islands in ancient Greece, and particularly noted as a centre of learning. This reputation was derived from her most famous sons, notably Aesop (of fable fame), Pythagoras, Epicurus, Aristarchus (the astronomer who worked out that the earth revolved around the sun), and the navigator Kolaios — the Columbus of the ancient world — who dared to sail a ship through the Pillars of Hercules in 650 BC. Politically the island was rather unstable, with the ruling aristocracy producing a series of tyrants, the most famous being Polykrates, who came to power in 540 BC. Following his capture and execution by the mainland-ruling Persians the island lost effective independence. Samos fought on the Persian side at the Battle of Salamis, but changed sides soon after.

The island was later part of the Delian League and stayed loyal to Athens during the Peloponnesian War. It did, however, change hands several times, and had its entire population replaced by Athenian colonists in 365 BC (the original inhabitants returned in 321 BC). Samos was later ruled by the Ptolemies of Egypt, before coming under Roman control in 129 BC. Thereafter decline set in; the island was subject to repeated pillaging from

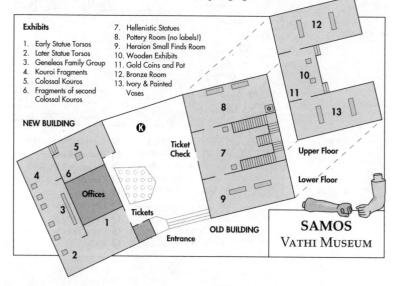

Exhibits

1. Early Statue Torsos
2. Later Statue Torsos
3. Geneleos Family Group
4. Kouroi Fragments
5. Colossal Kouros
6. Fragments of second Colossal Kouros
7. Hellenistic Statues
8. Pottery Room (no labels!)
9. Heraion Small Finds Room
10. Wooden Exhibits
11. Gold Coins and Pot
12. Bronze Room
13. Ivory & Painted Vases

NEW BUILDING

Ⓚ

Ticket Check

Offices

Tickets

Entrance

OLD BUILDING

Upper Floor

Lower Floor

SAMOS
VATHI MUSEUM

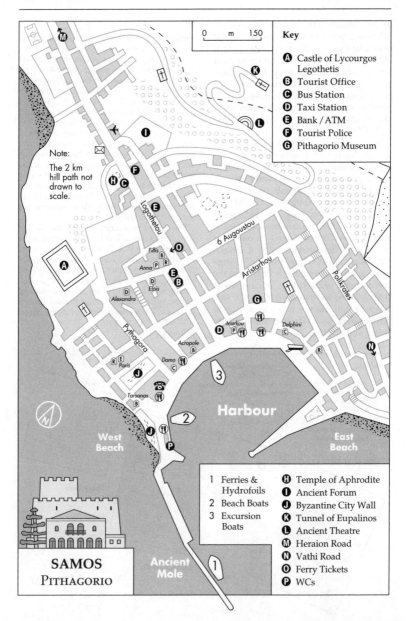

Note:
The 2 km hill path not drawn to scale.

Harbour

West Beach

East Beach

SAMOS
PITHAGORIO

Ancient Mole

Key

Ⓐ Castle of Lycourgos Legothetis
Ⓑ Tourist Office
Ⓒ Bus Station
Ⓓ Taxi Station
Ⓔ Bank / ATM
Ⓕ Tourist Police
Ⓖ Pithagorio Museum

1 Ferries & Hydrofoils
2 Beach Boats
3 Excursion Boats

Ⓗ Temple of Aphrodite
Ⓘ Ancient Forum
Ⓙ Byzantine City Wall
Ⓚ Tunnel of Eupalinos
Ⓛ Ancient Theatre
Ⓜ Heraion Road
Ⓝ Vathi Road
Ⓞ Ferry Tickets
Ⓟ WCs

82 BC on (the raiders even included Antony and Cleopatra, who stopped off in 39 BC and made off with everything of value that could be moved). During the Byzantine period Samos was in steady decline. After the island was conquered by the Turks in 1473 it was forcibly depopulated, and remained so for some two hundred years. The recolonized island finally achieved union with Greece in 1912.

◄►

Budget accommodation is thin on the ground in the popular towns, and there is no camping. As a result Samos can be a tricky island on which to find a reasonably priced bed in August: at this time of the year it pays to phone ahead. Ticket agencies have lists of accommodation, as do the Tourist Police.

Vathi has a reasonable supply of accommodation. The waterfront has a number of hotels including the well-placed *Aeolis* (☎ 28904), and the very well maintained C-class *Samos* (☎ 28377), which has pricey but good value rooms (prices are advertised on a board outside). Nearer the budget end of the range is the pension *Avli* (☎ 22939) in a former convent school when 'nun' but the cheapest will do.

Pithagorio has a tourist office/booth just off the main street with accommodation information. The quayside has a number of pricey but justifiably popular hotels hidden behind the tavernas, including the B-class hotel/pensions *Tarsanas* (☎ 61162) just off the ferry quay, and the *Acropole* (☎ 61261), along with the almost as pricey C-class *Damo* (☎ 61303) and *Delphini* (☎ 61205). The streets behind offer the prospect of better hunting. On the main street is the B-class *Fillis* (☎ 61296) and behind, the budget D-class *Alexandra* (☎ 61429) and E-class *Paris* (☎ 61513). These are augmented by several minor pensions and a limited number of rooms.

Karlovassi is such an ugly place finding a bed is rarely a problem. Cheapest option is a Youth Hostel behind the large Panagia Church, but there are hotels in town. At the bottom end are the D-class *Morpheus* (☎ 32672), the *Astir* (☎ 33150) and, outside the town, the *Aktaeon* (☎ 32356) on the port road.

∞

Given that Samos was one of the better-endowed islands with monuments in ancient times, the extant remains are something of a disappointment: much has gone and the remainder can comfortably be taken in during the course of an extended day-trip to the island.

The only sightseeing of note at Vathi is the town's **Archaeological Museum** (plan on p. 475; open ⑨ ex ① 08.30–15.00; tickets are €3). This isn't the largest museum in the islands by any means, but it is one of the most interesting as it houses all the finds from the on-going excavations at the Heraion (see overleaf). It has had an extension built to house the more recent discoveries. Not least among these is the **Colossal Kouros**, which was one of a pair that stood on the sacred way. Originally painted in gaudy colours, it is now admired for the rippling veins in its marble. Other star exhibits include the **Geneleos Family** statues, a collection of bronze griffin heads, and very rare fragments of wooden Hellenistic furniture preserved by the Heraion site's marshy soil.

Pithagorio is the sightseeing town on Samos, though at first sight this might seem rather surprising as there doesn't initially appear to be much to see beyond the exhibits in its **Archaeological Museum**. In fact during the 6 c. BC the tyrant Polykrates left a series of monumental works here. No doubt it was a considerable source of satisfaction to him when, crucified (by the Persians in 522 BC) on the Turkish coast opposite the town, he hung around and surveyed the wondrous constructions he had commissioned. All survive — in various states of repair — today. These include the **Temple of Hera** (usually known as the **Heraion** and described overleaf) and the best preserved of the Polykratic monuments, the **harbour mole** (now the ferry quay); most tourists walk its length without knowing it to be any different from quays the islands over. The quay reflects the fact that Pithagorio hides all but scant remains of the ancient city. Beyond odd collections of stones and the foundations of some Hellenistic houses behind the **Castle of Legothetis** (built in 1824 by a hero of the independence movement) only the ruinous **Theatre** and **City Walls** skirting the tops of the hills behind give a hint as to what was here before.

The oddest of the Polykratic monuments is well hidden (though signposts around the town give the game away today): the 1,034 m **Tunnel of Eupalinos** (named after its architect and completed in 524 BC), hewn through the mountain, was designed to guarantee water supplies to the city as well as offering a means of escape. The first claustrophobic 70 m is open to the public ⑨ ex ① 9.00–14.00; the entrance fee is €2.

The Heraion

Lying 9 km west of the ancient capital of Samos at Pithagorio is the massive **Temple of Hera** — more usually known as the **Heraion**. Open ②–④ 08.30–15.00; the entrance fee is €3. Although it is the main sightseeing attraction on Samos, the Heraion is more likely to appeal to archaeology fans than casual visitors, the remains consisting of foundations and a single incomplete column that is now the island's totem. All of the major finds are in the Vathi Museum as there isn't one on site.

One of the most unusual things about the Heraion is the site itself: for at first sight this major shrine is bizarrely set in an anonymous field that has nothing of the grandeur of an acropolis to enhance it (a characteristic also shared by the site of the Great Temple of Artemis on the nearby Turkish coast). This apparent whimsy on the part of the ancients becomes clear when one appreciates that temples were usually surrounded by groves of trees and gardens (a fact now lost on most modern visitors to what are usually dry, dusty, treeless excavation sites), and these factors came to the fore with the siting of the Heraion.

Placed on the banks of the Imbrasos stream in a meadow of lygos trees (a variety of willow) that was believed to be the birthplace of the queen goddess Hera, the Heraion's location so far out of town makes more sense once one remembers that ancient temples were not the equivalent of the modern church or mosque but were more akin to glorious hotels, built as a private residence for the god or goddess when they happened to be in the neighbourhood (the theory being that the better the temple, the better the chance that the patron deity would be tempted to visit and then stay). Worship took place outside at nearby altars.

Easily the most impressive feature on the site is the surviving column of **Ⓐ** the **Heraion** or **Temple of Hera**. A famous building, it had the odd distinction of being the eighth of the seven wonders of the world (getting into later lists that excluded Babylon). The structure extant today was the fourth temple on the site. Four times the size of the Parthenon in Athens, it had 3 x 8 30 m columns at its east end, 3 x 9 along the west and 24 x 2 down each side; it was begun in the 6 c. BC, but never finished, though the Romans added steps along the east front. The massive temple was really like a roofed bed of nails: a mass of columns reflecting the concreteless Archaic Greeks' inability to solve the problem of bridging large internal spaces. The three temples that preceded it stood more to the east, the first recently surrendering the claim to be the oldest known temple built with columns at each end and down its sides. Like the later second temple it was small: the third temple built in the 6 c. BC by Rhoikos was the first Great Temple on the site. Destroyed by fire c. 525 BC after standing for only 25 years, its extant successor was built by Polykrates.

Alongside the Heraion other buildings were erected, notably **Ⓑ** the **Temple of Aphrodite** or **Hermes**, and **Ⓒ** the now invisible **South Stoa**, now vaguely marked by **Ⓓ** the base of the **Ciceros Monument** (2 c. AD), home to statues of the Roman orator Cicero and his brother Quintus. To the east stands an enigmatic group of stones that are thought to be the **Kolaios Ship Base Ⓔ** on which stood the first Greek ship to sail on the Atlantic (it was viewed by the ancients with all the awe of an Apollo space capsule).

The area in front of the Heraion was the religious hot spot on the site. Originally the area was a paved square bounded by **Ⓕ** the **Rhoikos Altar** (6 c. BC) which was built on the site of an ancient **Lygos Tree Shrine**. The later Romans in-filled, adding **Ⓖ** a **Temple** (on the site of the earlier Heraion temples), **Ⓗ** the **Monopteros Altar/Temple**, **Ⓘ** a second **Temple** (2 c. AD) along with **Ⓙ** a tiny **Bathhouse**. In the early Christian era a **Basilica Ⓚ** was also constructed.

The area to the north of the Heraion has revealed traces of several structures including **Ⓛ** a **Mycenaean Tholos Tomb** and **Ⓜ** the **North Stoa**. This is the site of the earliest known example of this uniquely Greek form of architecture. Originally a wooden structure, it was replaced in stone in the Hellenistic period. A small town grew up to the east of it and several **Ⓝ** **Hellenistic Houses** have been excavated. Temples, however, lined the sanctuary precinct: the foundations of two, **Ⓞ** **Temple A** and **Ⓟ** a **Temple of Aphrodite**, are still extant. Nearby lie the foundations of an Archaic shrine with **Ⓠ** the base of the **Geneleos Statue Group**. Copies of several of the statues have been erected on the base. The originals are the only survivals from the 2000 statues that graced **Ⓡ** the **Sacred Way**, the paved road running from the Heraion to Pithagorio, and now irreparably damaged by the island's airport runway which bisects it.

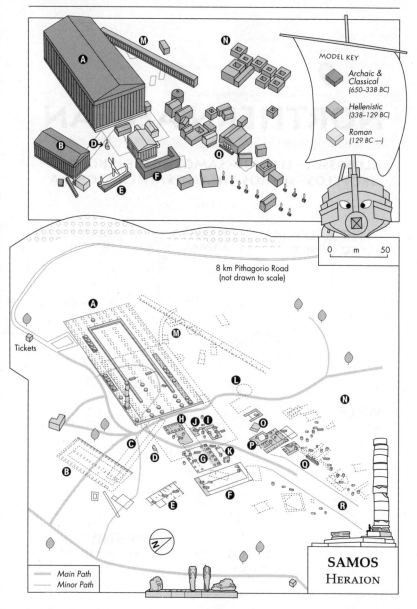

MODEL KEY

Archaic & Classical (650–338 BC)

Hellenistic (338–129 BC)

Roman (129 BC —)

0   m   50

8 km Pithagorio Road
(not drawn to scale)

Tickets

SAMOS
HERAION

Main Path
Minor Path

9

NORTHERN AEGEAN

ALONISSOS · LIMNOS · SAMOTHRACE · SKIATHOS
SKOPELOS · SKYROS · THASSOS · THESSALONIKA

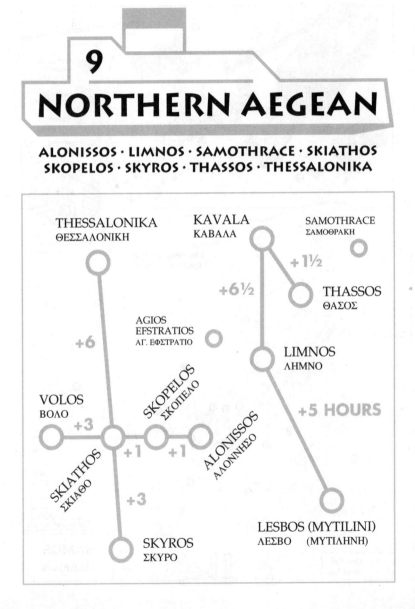

THESSALONIKA
ΘΕΣΣΑΛΟΝΙΚΗ

KAVALA
ΚΑΒΑΛΑ

SAMOTHRACE
ΣΑΜΟΘΡΑΚΗ

+1½

+6½

THASSOS
ΘΑΣΟΣ

AGIOS
EFSTRATIOS
ΑΓ. ΕΦΣΤΡΑΤΙΟ

+6

LIMNOS
ΛΗΜΝΟ

VOLOS
ΒΟΛΟ

SKOPELOS
ΣΚΟΠΕΛΟ

+5 HOURS

+3

+1 +1

SKIATHOS
ΣΚΙΑΘΟ

ALONISSOS
ΑΛΟΝΝΗΣΟ

+3

LESBOS (MYTILINI)
ΛΕΣΒΟ (ΜΥΤΙΛΗΝΗ)

SKYROS
ΣΚΥΡΟ

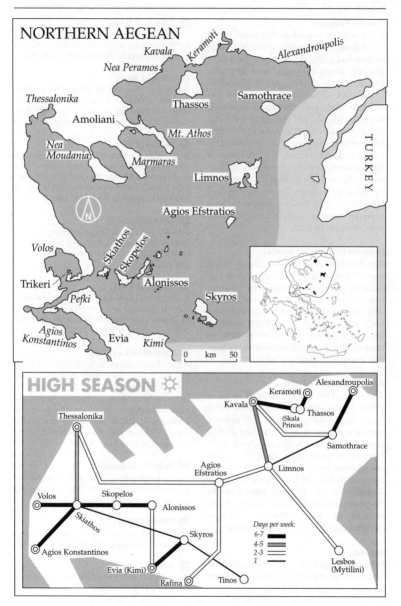

General Features

The Northern Aegean is characterized by a combination of poorly connected large islands and mainland ports, coupled with an easily accessible small Sporades chain. Travel is either very easy or extremely problematic depending upon where you are. The 'easy' part consists of the small, wooded islands off the coast of Evia: Skiathos, Skopelos, Alonissos and — to a lesser extent — Skyros. These are linked by a good hydrofoil service. The remainder of the northern network requires more time and really can only be happily negotiated by those with more than a fortnight at their disposal. In the Low Season the lack of ferries running north of Lesbos curtails non-Sporades options.

Example Itinerary [3 Weeks]

The Northern Aegean offers some of the nicest Greek island hopping, but at the price of a loss of flexibility as you are constrained by the few boats available. This itinerary has been achieved in 8 days with a lot of luck. It is more usual to encounter delays, and allowing time to explore, you should allow three rather than two weeks to complete the circuit.

Arrival/Departure Point

There are charter flight airports at three points on the circuit: Athens, Kavala and Thessalonika and you can happily operate from any of them. Athens is the best should you need to get back in a rush, with daily bus or boat connections. Similarly, as you are visiting poorly connected ports it is better to travel anticlockwise as the latter destinations all have easy ferry links to the mainland and bus links to the capital, reducing any danger of finding yourself caught out and missing a flight home.

Season

July and August only: the months either side see reduced services sinking away to all but nothing in the Low Season.

■ Athens [3 Days]

An easy starting point with access to NTOG ferry departure sheets from which you can deduce departure times further up the line.

■ Chios [2 Days]

Worth a stop-over, Chios has a lot to offer. You can establish in Athens when subsequent boats are running down the line and thus deduce the times of Chios—Lesbos ferries.

■ Lesbos [2 Days]

A nice island, which is just as well given that you will probably have to wait a day or two for a boat north. Depending on how long you have to wait you can either stay in Mytilini or head up to much prettier Mithyma.

■ Limnos [2 Days]

Unless you have to change here you can treat Limnos as an optional port of call that can be missed if your Lesbos boat north leaves you running late.

■ Kavala [4 Days]

An attractive town in which to rest up for a few days. You should take advantage of the ferries to **Thassos** and the less regular **Samothrace** boat — stamina and time permitting.

■ Thessalonika [1 Day]

Athens buses run every hour from Kavala so you can run across at your leisure and pick up either hydrofoil or ferry to Skiathos. This is one of the weak connections in the chain as weekend services out of Thessalonika can be booked solid. Should this happen you can take a train to Volos and then a Skiathos-bound hydrofoil or ferry from there.

■ Skiathos [3 Days]

Another nice resting point with good Athens links if the need arises via Volos. Even so, try to find time to continue on to Skyros.

■ Skyros [2 Days]

The final island in the loop with ferry links with Kimi and the waiting bus to Athens.

■ Athens [2 Days]

Arrive back with two days to spare if you have a flight pre-booked.

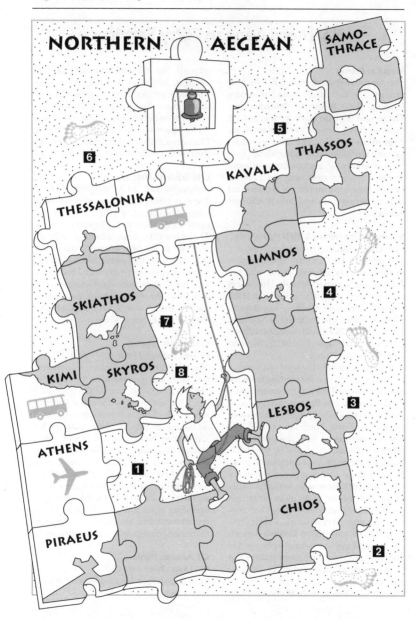

Northern Aegean Ferry Services

Main Car Ferries

The North Aegean ferries fall into four groups. The first is composed of ferries bustling along the small Sporades line. The second is made up of ferries running from northern Aegean ports to southern Aegean destinations. The third are wide-ranging ferries running to mainland ports in the Northern Aegean (the majority being summer services operating via Lesbos). Finally, there are a number of shorter-haul ferries offering mainland links to adjacent islands.

Sporades Line Ferries & HFD Hydrofoils

The Greek islands were traditionally divided into two groups: the Cyclades or those islands 'circling' Delos, and the Sporades or 'scattered' islands. Nowadays the latter term is usually applied to just the small archipelago of Skiathos, Skopelos and Alonissos (also referred to as the Northern Sporades). These small wooded islands attract considerable tourist traffic and therefore ferry activity.

In the past this has consisted of a number of small car ferries, most starting from the mainland town of Volos, but some from tiny Agios Konstantinos. But this has changed as services were slowly consolidated between three larger boats. There now is only limited competition on the route as the great majority of boats are owned by the Hellas Flying Dolphin group of companies. Links between these islands and the rest of the ferry network have also suffered badly in the last few years as more ambitious services have been withdrawn. They now exist in a little ferry network of their own.

Flying Cat and *Flying Dolphin* vessels are the most popular tourist option in the Sporades as they are frequent and regular (a large part of their custom is obtained ferrying parties of package tourists to and from Skiathos, with its charter flight

airport), but the timetable sees regular changes, and with the lack of competition some streamlining of services is now taking place. The overall package always ends up much the same. Itineraries A and E (see opposite) are the most widely run. Occasional calls at isolated ports — notably Evia (Pefki) — have occurred in past years.

C/M *Express Skiathos*
Hellenic Seaways / HFD; 1994; 5000 GRT.
The only HFD boat dedicated to an annual schedule on the route is the *Express Skiathos* (until 2005 known as the *Express Haroulla*). The largest catamaran operating in Greece and one of the best boats for deck-class passengers into the bargain, she is a vehicle-carrying, passenger-ferry-sized boat, with a modern, open deck-class lounge and a sun deck. She operates twice daily along the line from Volos. A very reliable boat; major changes are unlikely in 2012.

C/F *Express Pegasus*
Hellenic Seaways / HFD; 1977; 4810 GRT.
This small ferry (see p. 446) was moved over two years ago to cover for a missing boat and the *Express Skiathos* (in the latter case just for a few weeks while she was under repair). The *Express Pegasus* also operated on the line in 2011, running route B. This itinerary involves calls at Agnontas when visiting Skopelos. Normally only used in poor weather conditions, this quiet quay isn't the best place to end up if Skopelos is your destination. It is anyone's guess what will happen in 2012, but if this boat isn't operating again it is all but certain that a replacement will be, as this line requires more than one regular ferry in High Season.

C/F *Panagia Parou*
NEL Lines; 1996; 4934 GRT.
In addition to their large high-speed vessels, NEL Lines own a couple of good smaller

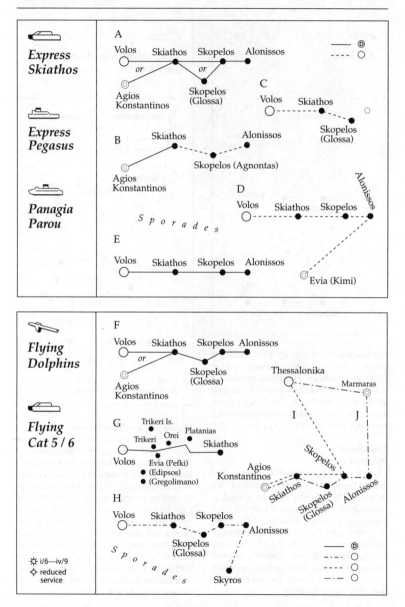

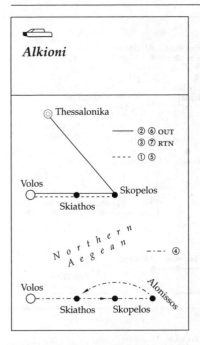

Alkioni

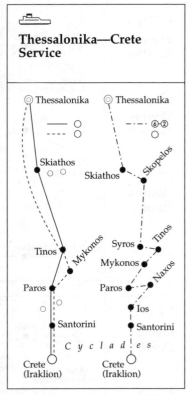

Thessalonika—Crete Service

fast boats that are equally erratic when it comes to running consistent year-on-year summer schedules. High fuel costs are a problem — as a result they now steam slow ahead most of the time. The *Panagia Parou* appeared on this line last summer operating route A out of Agios Konstantinos.

C/M *Alkioni*
NEL Lines
One regular feature of the ferry scene in this part of the world has been a summer link between Thessalonika and the Sporades. Formerly the preserve of the *Flying Cat 5* and *Flying Cat 6* (which abandoned the route in 2009 despite their obvious popularity), NEL have moved to fill the gap with a large catamaran of their own. Hopefully she will run again in 2012. Book early if travelling in High Season, as runs on this route are normally full to bursting.

Thessalonika—Crete Service
Until a few years ago at least one ferry ran an extremely useful summer thrice-weekly service between Thessalonika and Crete, linking several groups of islands en route. A return in 2012 looks unlikely. The service existed to provide the large numbers of islanders working in Thessalonika with a quick means of getting back home. Clearly there is a demand for this service, but this route does have one major problem: boats run full when heading south in the early part of the High Season, and empty when running north; in mid-to-late August this pattern of usage is reversed.

Rhodes—Alexandroupolis Link
C/F *Diagoras*
Blue Star Ferries; 1990; 6939 GRT.

Until recently the Northern Aegean played host to a third 'north coast to southern island' summer service, but unlike the other links this was very much a High Season six-week peak-period-only service, and involved one ferry running down the Greek islands along the Turkish seaboard to Rhodes from either Thessalonika or Alexandroupolis. The *Diagoras* was the last to have the job but was too busy operating links to the smaller Dodecanese islands in 2011 to have the time to make the run. Hopefully the link will be restored in 2012, but any chance of this will depend on lost ferry capacity being restored elsewhere.

C/F *Achilleas*
Skyros Shipping Co.; 1987; 13597 GRT.

A small ex-Japanese ferry provides the isolated 'lifeline' service between the ports of Evia (Kimi) and Linaria on Skyros. This little-changing link runs once a day throughout the year, with a regular second and an occasional third trip in High Season. The *Achilleas* is a conventional boat with nothing exciting about her. However, she

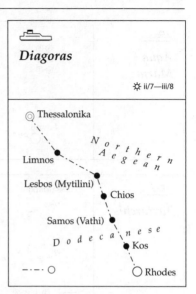

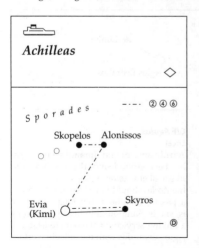

has been known to venture further afield in High Season, with occasional runs to Alonissos and Skopelos. These seem to happen on quiet days when there is less demand on her main route. Athens buses are timetabled to link up with her Evia (Kimi) sailings (see p. 78).

C/F *Aqua Maria*
NEL Lines; 1976; 2889 GRT.

This repainted ferry will be known to a few as the old *Mirtidiotissa* — a boat with an unfortunate history of failing ferry safety checks. Prior to her latest revamp she operated the lifeline service from Piraeus to Kithera until 2008, when she was taken off the route after running aground. Now in the hands of NEL Lines she is again running a lifeline service three times a week between Lavrio and Kavala. In the circumstances it is difficult to recommend this boat.

C/F *Taxiarchis*
NEL Lines; 1976; 10750 GRT.

For the last two summers this rather

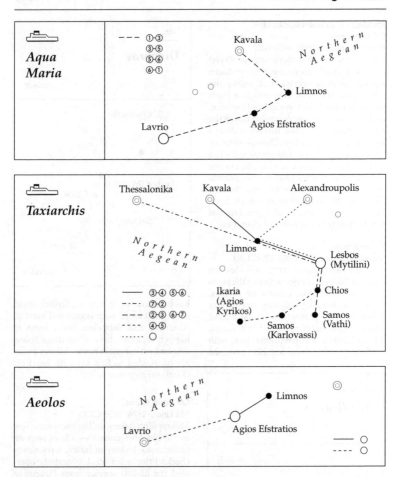

ramshackle old ferry has provided cover for the missing Saos Ferries boats. Operating out of Lesbos she traipses around the Northern Aegean providing an invaluable linking service — so much so that she is currently about the only vessel that makes island hopping in this part of the world possible. One of the smaller NEL vessels, she could well remain in this neck of the woods this summer.

C/F Aeolos
Local

A truly ancient and diminutive ferry that has been around since the Ark and looks like a steel version of the same, by rights the *Aeolos* should have been grounded on a passing mountain top long ago. As it is, she is eking out a living by providing a linking service for the remote island of Agios Efstratios with the outside world.

Thassos—Mainland Ferries

This service is provided by nine landing-craft car ferries: most are run by the local A.N.E.T. Line and are named along the lines of *Thassos I*, *Thassos II* etc. Tickets are bought from kiosks on the quayside or on board. The main service is the 70-minute crossing between Kavala and the Thassos port of Skala Prinos. A 30-minute crossing between Thassos Town and Keramoti attracts more vehicles. Reliability and frequency (every 2 hours) of these boats is good. Skala Prinos ferries also provide a four times daily (mainly commercial vehicle) service to the roadside hamlet of Nea Peramos, 20 km west of Kavala.

C/F *Saos II*
Saos Ferries

The *Saos II* is a small car ferry that has been a mainstay on the Samothrace service for many years. Operated by Saos Ferries, a company that hit financial problems in 2010, she continued to run a service even though all other Saos Ferries boats are now laid up and out of action. A second of their boats on this route — the *Nona Mairy* — wasn't operating last year. Presumably the *Saos II* survives courtesy of the 'lifeline' subsidy that this route attracts. In happier years it was also possible to use occasional hydrofoils that run to Samothrace in the summer. None were operating in 2011.

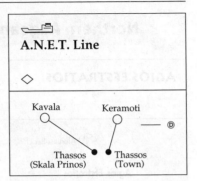

Thassos Hydrofoils

Kavala is the home of a couple of hydrofoils that combine to provide a six times daily service to Thassos Town. Popular with tourists and locals alike, they are faster than taking a ferry to Skala Prinos and then a bus on to Thassos Town. The *Thission Dolphin* is operated by A.N.E.T. Line, while the *Marina II* is owned by NEL Lines. During the summer season at least one of them will make additional morning and evening day-tripper runs to ports down the west coast of Thassos. They operate in much the same way as a bus service, with tickets for both boats usually being bought on the quayside or on board.

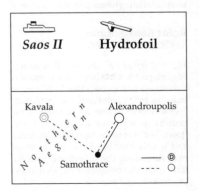

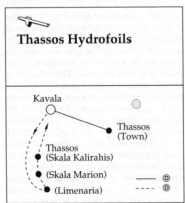

⚓ Northern Aegean Islands & Ports

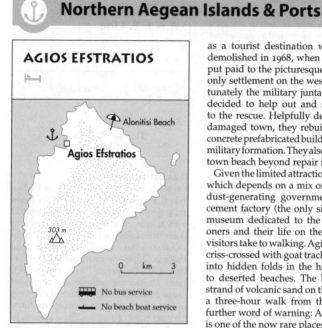

AGIOS EFSTRATIOS

🛏️

⚓ Alonitisi Beach

Agios Efstratios

303 m △

0   km   3

🚌 No bus service

⛴ No beach boat service

Agios Efstratios
ΑΓΙΟΣ ΕΥΣΤΡΑΤΙΟΣ; 43 km²; pop. 300.

A remote, sun-baked island with vegetation (mostly scrub and scattered oak trees) hidden away in the folds of the rocky hills, Agios Efstratios sits like a drowned camel's hump to the south-west of Limnos (from where it is administered). The island shot to fame in 2010 when it was held up as a prime example of Greek goverment financial excess, with reports of its having 40 full-time teachers and a child population of just 10. Rarely visited by tourists, it offers close to the ultimate in 'get-away-from-it-all' experiences (assuming you exclude schoolteachers from your list). Used as an isolation camp for some 5,000 political prisoners between 1930–62, the island has never been popular. Any chance of its emerging as a tourist destination was effectively demolished in 1968, when an earthquake put paid to the picturesque houses of the only settlement on the west coast. Unfortunately the military junta ruling Greece decided to help out and sent the army to the rescue. Helpfully demolishing the damaged town, they rebuilt it with ugly concrete prefabricated buildings laid out in military formation. They also bulldozed the town beach beyond repair in the process.

Given the limited attractions of the town, which depends on a mix of fishing and a dust-generating government sponsored cement factory (the only sightseeing is a museum dedicated to the political prisoners and their life on the island), most visitors take to walking. Agios Efstratios is criss-crossed with goat tracks that wander into hidden folds in the hills and down to deserted beaches. The best is a long strand of volcanic sand on the north coast, a three-hour walk from the chora. One further word of warning: Agios Efstratios is one of the now rare places where few of the locals speak English — a phrase book is a necessity.

🛏️

A pension (housed in one of the few pre-earthquake buildings still standing) and some tavernas offering rooms provide all the beds.

Agios Konstantinos
ΑΓΙΟΣ ΚΩΝΣΤΑΝΤΙΝΟΣ

Figuring larger on schedules than in real life, this port is something of a nonentity as a destination in its own right. Little more than a stopping point on the main intercity highway from Athens to the north of the country, there is scant reason to stay. The 'town' backs onto the mountains of Attica and is only four blocks deep. The main road runs along the waterfront, with the ferry quay an apologetic extension to the promenade, and adjacent to a leafy central

AGIOS EFSTRATIOS
CHORA VILLAGE

0   m   100

Key

Ⓐ Chora Square
Ⓑ Main Street
Ⓒ Police
Ⓓ Medical Centre
Ⓔ Shop
Ⓕ Ferry Tickets
Ⓖ Tavernas
Ⓗ Public WCs
Ⓘ New Buildings
Ⓙ Site of Old Town
Ⓚ Ruined Church
Ⓛ School (100 m) &
    Path to North Beach
Ⓜ River Bed
Ⓝ Track to Beach

1 Ferries
2 Limnos Boats

Caïques

Beach

Harbour
Bay

New
Quay

square. Most visitors are only staying until the next ferry or Athens bus leaves, and the facilities reflect this: on the plus side there are a number of reasonable tavernas, along with the inevitable ticket agencies. There is a bus station (with hourly services to Athens) several blocks from the ferry quay. If you are travelling via a Hellenic Seaways hydrofoil, you can take advantage of the pricey company buses that are laid on to meet the hydrofoils (buy your bus ticket along with the hydrofoil ticket: Athens-bound buses terminate near the ancient stadium).

Alexandroupolis
ΑΛΕΞΑΝΔΡΟΥΠΟΛΗ; pop. 34,600.

CODE ☎ 25510
TOURIST OFFICE ☎ 24998
POLICE/TOURIST POLICE ☎ 26418

A rather drab modern town on the northern Aegean coast redeemed only by a lively promenade decked with a lighthouse, Alexandroupolis is named after an obscure 19 c. king of Greece rather than Alexander the Great (who renamed half the cities of Asia after himself during his campaigns). This fact eloquently sums the place up, and not even the annual July to August wine festival can dispel the 'okay, but not a great place' impression. In truth for all its attempts to appear to be a significant city, there is a distinct frontier-town feel to Alexandroupolis. The city's location near the Turkish border makes it both difficult to get to (it's the de facto end of the line for both ferries and the coastal bus service) and a useful stepping stone for journeys into Turkey (thanks to the daily buses to İstanbul).

Sadly, there is no reason to come to the city itself and most visitors only stay long enough to catch a ferry or hydrofoil to Samothrace, or one of the seven buses a day to Kavala, or the Athens railway link.

The waterfront is naturally the centre of activity, and is dominated by a high esplanade topped with an elderly, but fully functional, lighthouse that is increasingly surrounded with (empty) taverna seating that isn't up to the grandiose scale of its surroundings. A steep descent from the waterfront street brings you to the extensive — but underutilized — port and an area of scruffy, reclaimed land that is variously used as a car park or as a fairground area whenever a small travelling circus hits town.

Key

- **A** Main Square & Lighthouse (1880)
- **B** Bus Station
- **C** Railway Station
- **D** Police / Tourist Police
- **E** National Bank of Greece
- **F** Pharmacy
- **G** Cathedral / Ecclesiastic Art Museum
- **H** WCs
- **I** Ferry & Hydrofoil Tickets
- **J** Road to Komotini & Kavala
- **K** Road to Kipi & Turkey

1 Ferry Berth
2 Hydrofoil Berths

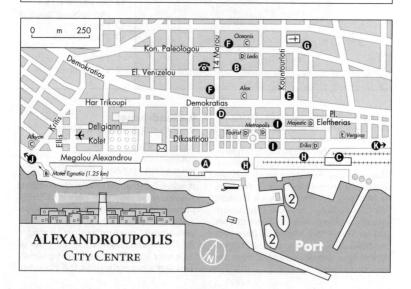

ALEXANDROUPOLIS
CITY CENTRE

The city-centre streets behind the water-front do nothing to enhance the impression of the place: for the most part they are typical of modern Greek towns, and have no noteworthy sightseeing to relieve the concrete and glass monotony. The nearest to 'character' are those abutting the port and railway station area.

⊢⊣

The wine festival produces considerable pressure on the limited accommodation available in High Season. The Tourist Office has lists of rooms in the town, but if you arrive after midday the only option likely to be open to you is an expensive waterfront B-class *Motel Egnatia* (☎ 37630), 2 km west of the ferry quay.

There are, however, a number of hotels in town worth a try first, the best bets being away from the waterfront. These include the D-class *Ledo* (☎ 28808) and *Majestic* (☎ 26444) and the C-class *Alex* (☎ 26302) and *Alkyon* (☎ 23593/5).

Alonissos

ΑΛΟΝΝΗΣΟΣ; 64 km²; pop. 1,500.

CODE ☎ 24240
PORT POLICE ☎ 65595
POLICE ☎ 65205
MEDICAL CENTRE ☎ 65208

The least populated of the larger Sporades, Alonissos is a very popular destination for daily day-tripper boats from Skiathos and Skopelos, thanks to an attractive port lined with low cliffs garnished with pine trees, a pretty hilltop chora and a nearby marine nature reserve that is one of the few remaining homes for the threatened Mediterranean monk seal. The island is also rapidly developing as a rather chic holiday destination in its own right.

The fact that Alonissos is less touristed than its neighbours makes it appealing to increasing numbers of visitors attracted by the quiet beaches (accessible only via a flotilla of caïques, thanks to the dirt track roads), the friendly islanders and the over-whelmingly cosy ambience of the place — if you want to unwind on a quiet Greek island then this is one destination that can't be beaten. Given this, it is best to allow for extended stays here when planning your holiday: seductive Alonissos is one of those places where one can't help but linger.

The largest settlement on Alonissos is now the port of **Patitiri**. Nestling in a delightfully piratesque cliff and taverna-decked cove, it has managed to acquire considerable charm despite the fact that it is a modern village from roof to cellar. The atmosphere is pleasantly low-key, with a good taverna-backed family beach (fine pebbles) that never gets too crowded. The port does get quite busy when the tour boats are in. Fortunately, they don't stay more than a few hours so the dreamy nature of the place isn't interrupted for too long.

In fact Patitiri only developed thanks to a disastrous earthquake in 1965 which left it in ruins and the hilltop capital of Chora badly damaged. Coming after extensive depopulation that followed after the island's vineyards were wiped out in 1950 by disease, the earthquake prompted the junta then ruling Greece to dictate that the remaining islanders be rehoused in the rebuilt port (the hastily erected housing is fortunately confined to an 'estate' well away from the waterfront). Other settlements on Alonissos remain tiny in comparison.

Thanks to the island's growing popularity, the sleepy, photogenic hilltop **Chora** above the port is now seeing many of its houses renovated thanks to the large number of outsiders wanting holiday homes, but the lack of a significant year-round population means that it isn't reverting to its previous significant status. Fortunately those that do live there seem content with it continuing as no more than the major sightseeing destination hereabouts.

The only other significant settlement of note is the hamlet of **Steni Vala**. Tucked neatly away in a creek halfway up the east coast, it is served by the daily taxi-boats than run out of Patitiri. Here you will find several tavernas, a single shop, and the headquarters of the Hellenic Society for the Protection of the Monk Seal.

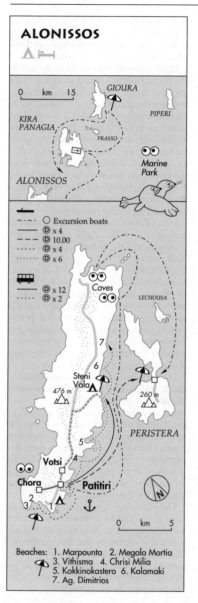

ALONISSOS

0   km   15

KIRA
PANAGIA

GIOURA

PIPERI

PRASSO

ALONISSOS

Marine
Park

— — — ○ Excursion boats
—— ⒟ x 4
— — — ⒟ 10.00
· · · · · ⒟ x 4
· · · · · · ⒟ x 6

—— ⒟ x 12
· · · · · ⒟ x 2

Caves

LECHOUSA

7

6

Steni
Vala

476 m

260 m

PERISTERA

5

Votsi   4

Chora   Patitiri

3

2   1

N

0   km   5

Beaches: 1. Marpounta   2. Megalo Mortia
3. Vithisma   4. Chrisi Milia
5. Kokkinokastero   6. Kalamaki
7. Ag. Dimitrios

🛏
Alonissos has 14 hotels divided between
Patitiri port and the suburb of **Votsi** some 20
minutes' walk to the north. Most are B and C
category establishments with prices at the top
end of the range. Among the most expensive
is the B-class *Alkyon* (☎ 65450) on the waterfront, but the east cliff-top hotels offer better
views for less, notably the E-class *Liadromia*
(☎ 65521), and the pricier B-class pension
Cavos (☎ 65216).

▲
Alonissos had two small, unofficial sites that
may (or more likely may not) be open. *Camping Rocks* lies 1.5 km from the port. An idyllic,
mature pine-forest site (albeit with rudimen-
tary facilities), it has been empty/closed for
several summers (though signs are still up).
The second site was at isolated Steni Vala.

👀
Tours on Alonissos centre on the **Marine Park**.
Boats leave daily from Patitiri to north-coast
sea caves and then on to a monastery on **Kira
Panagia** island and a beach on **Gioura** island
(which has yet another of those 1,000-stalag-
mite caves with Cyclops legends attached).
However, don't go expecting to see any seals:
the islands are home to an estimated 20 pairs
out of a world population of 800. Pessimists
predict the species will be extinct within a
decade. **Peristera**, lying across a narrow strait
off the east coast of Alonissos, is also a beach-
boat destination. There is also a small fishing
village straddling the neck of the island.

Sightseeing on Alonissos itself is more
limited — an inevitable consequence of the
island's history as a minor satellite of Skopelos.
In 2000 a privately operated **Historical and
Folklore Museum** appeared in Patitiri. Open
⒟ 09.00–21.00 (€3), it houses an impressively
large collection of traditional artefacts reflecting the island's rural and agrarian heritage.
Unfortunately the labelling is poor to non-
existent, but in most cases the displays are
reasonably self-explanatory, ranging from
the contents of a typical house to the various
tools of various professions from cobbler to
saddle-maker. An upper floor has a collection
of maps of the island, and some shells and a
mine (all of the military variety).

Finally, walkers should note that Alonissos
is a pine-clad heaven, with a number of gentle
wooded walks to beaches. You can buy locally
an excellent walking and swimming guide
called *Alonissos on Foot* (€9).

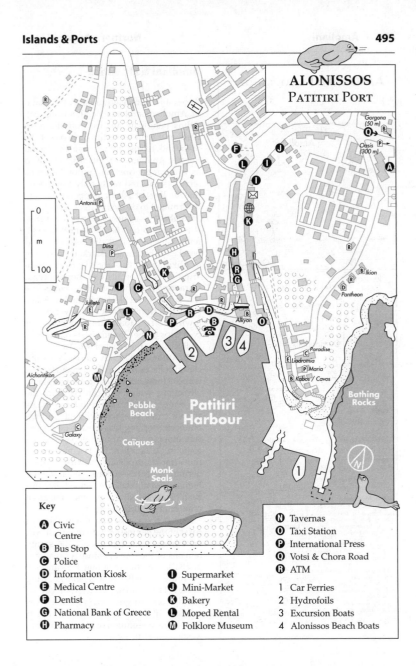

ALONISSOS
PATITIRI PORT

Gorgona
(50 m)

Oasis
(300 m)

Antonis

Dina

Julieta

Aichontikon

Galaxy

Ikion

Pantheon

Paradise
Liadromia
Maria
Kalos / Cavos

Alkyon

**Pebble
Beach**

**Patitiri
Harbour**

Caïques

**Monk
Seals**

**Bathing
Rocks**

Key

Ⓐ Civic
   Centre
Ⓑ Bus Stop
Ⓒ Police
Ⓓ Information Kiosk
Ⓔ Medical Centre
Ⓕ Dentist
Ⓖ National Bank of Greece
Ⓗ Pharmacy
Ⓘ Supermarket
Ⓙ Mini-Market
Ⓚ Bakery
Ⓛ Moped Rental
Ⓜ Folklore Museum

Ⓝ Tavernas
Ⓞ Taxi Station
Ⓟ International Press
Ⓠ Votsi & Chora Road
Ⓡ ATM

1 Car Ferries
2 Hydrofoils
3 Excursion Boats
4 Alonissos Beach Boats

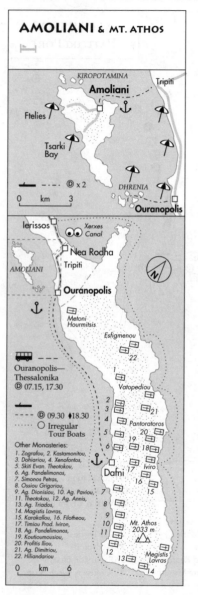

Amoliani & Mt. Athos

Accessible from Thessalonika, the island of Amoliani and the neighbouring Mt. Athos peninsula are well off the ferry lanes and tend to be the preserve of the mainland tourist rather than the island hopper. Amoliani is about as far removed as you can get from the rest of the Greek ferry system, and really only features on the hit lists of island hoppers who are determined to do every Greek island.

Amoliani is an unassuming little place. It is home to one hamlet which offers a few rooms as well as dirt roads to good beaches at Ftelies and Tsarki (also known as Alikes) bays. Passenger boats run from Tripiti, a quay on the Ouranopolis road. **Ouranopolis** is the last settlement before the 'border' that closes off the Mt. Athos peninsula from the rest of the world. The town is a bit of a tourist trap, but does offer boat trips to the Dhrenia islets offshore as well as along the coast of Mt. Athos.

Mt. Athos, a politically autonomous and closed collection of medieval monasteries, is one of those curiously Greek sightseeing attractions which you can see from the sea but can't visit. As a result, tour boats simply cruise off-shore without landing, but each morning one does a 'provision' run, stopping at various monasteries en route to Dafni where the few males with the almost impossibly hard-to-obtain permits to visit disembark. Females (both human and animal) are banned, but this hasn't stopped Mt. Athos emerging as an important wildlife sanctuary.

Tourist boats also run down the east coast of the peninsula from the small port of **Ierissos**. Near Ierissos are the scanty remains of the trans-peninsula canal dug in 480 BC for the invading Persian fleet (en route to the Battle of Salamis) of King Xerxes. His abortive invasion of 491 BC having come to grief when his fleet was wrecked off the tip of Mt. Athos, he opted for the drastic solution of digging his way west on his return visit.

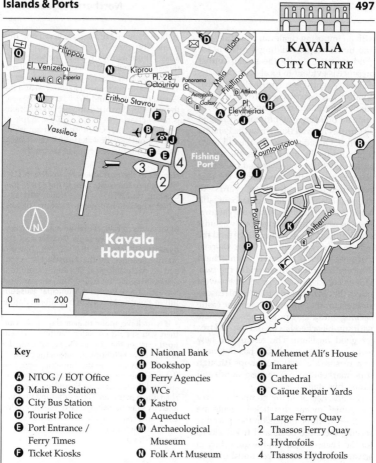

KAVALA
CITY CENTRE

Kavala
Harbour

Fishing
Port

Kavala

0   m   200

Key

A NTOG / EOT Office
B Main Bus Station
C City Bus Station
D Tourist Police
E Port Entrance /
     Ferry Times
F Ticket Kiosks

G National Bank
H Bookshop
I Ferry Agencies
J WCs
K Kastro
L Aqueduct
M Archaeological
     Museum
N Folk Art Museum

O Mehemet Ali's House
P Imaret
Q Cathedral
R Caïque Repair Yards

1 Large Ferry Quay
2 Thassos Ferry Quay
3 Hydrofoils
4 Thassos Hydrofoils

Kavala

ΚΑΒΑΛΑ; pop. 57,500.

CODE ☎ 2510
NTOG/EOT OFFICE ☎ 222425
POLICE ☎ 222905
HOSPITAL ☎ 228517

If you exclude hydrofoils from the equation, Kavala (ancient Neapolis) is easily the premier port of the Northern Aegean, with

good links to the otherwise unconnected islands of Thassos and Samothrace, and also — in High Season — the Athenian port of Rafina, the Dodecanese and Rhodes. If this wasn't reason enough to venture in this direction, the city itself is one of the nicest in Greece; set against a backdrop of rolling hills, it nestles snugly between their lower folds and the shoreline, with a picturesque Turkish quarter topped with an imposing castle, an aqueduct and traditional caïque-building thrown in for good measure. Sadly the strong tourist presence is evident in local prices.

The city centre is surprisingly compact, dividing into two quarters. To the east lies the old town dominated by the castle set upon the building-clad promontory ringed by the old city wall (known as the Panagia Quarter). Outside the walls, the old town continues to the north under the arches of the delightful aqueduct that once took water to the castle. The inlet to the east is littered with boatbuilders' yards. To the west lies the old fishing harbour, still home to a fair number of working caïques. They sit somewhat incongruously against a backdrop of 'modern' buildings (and the ugly main city square — Pl. Elevtherias) that now make up the new town behind the very busy road that divides the two. Things are a bit more relaxed on the west side of the old harbour, with several reasonable restaurants with views over the castle backing onto a long promenade, complete with sun-bleached lawns and the odd tree for good measure. The rest of the new town isn't up to much, but has the merit of a reasonable scatter of shops (though supermarkets are thin on the ground) and a busy bus station.

The absence of many competing ferry companies means that ticket agents are confined to three outlets on the quayside serving the large boats and ticket kiosks for the Thassos boats on the quay. Buy in advance if you can, but if you find the kiosks closed then tickets are bought on board after the ferry has departed. The quay has ferry times up at the entrance gate kiosk (in Greek) and a procession of large landing-craft-type car ferries and a hydrofoil heading for Thassos. The Samothrace ferry berths on the east side of the harbour under the castle walls.

⊨
A good NTOG/EOT office on the edge of Pl. Elevtherias has free city maps and will help you find where the one empty bed is to be located. Hotel accommodation is rather limited, and at the bottom end of the scale very poor; this is one city where it pays to look up-market a bit. Within an easy walk of the waterfront there are a number of C-class establishments: the *Acropolis* (☎ 223643) and *Panorama* (☎ 22 4205) — both near the old harbour — and the *Esperia* (☎ 229621) and *Nefeli* (☎ 227441) near the museum. Best of the down-market options is the D-class *Attikon* (☎ 222257) a couple of blocks behind the EOT office. If you can afford to splash out then the waterfront B-class *Galaxy* (☎ 224521) is the best hotel in the centre.

▲
Nearest to the port is a poor, treeless NTOG site 3 km to the west, 5 km to the east is *Irini Camping* (☎ 229785): a good trailer park site. A better bet is to hop over to a site on Thassos.

◎◎
Main sights in Kavala are the maze of streets that make up the **Panagia Quarter** and the **Byzantine Kastro** (℗ 10.00–17.00), the old quarter spanned by the **Aqueduct** (c. 1550) and an **Archaeological Museum** (home to a disparate collection culled from sites around Kavala). There is also a **Municipal Museum** full of the usual round of bric-a-brac dating from the early 19 c. on.

If you have more than a day in Kavala then you should consider venturing 15 km north-east of the city to the remains of the ancient city of **Philippi**: the site of the battle in which Octavian (later the Emperor Augustus) defeated the murderers of Julius Caesar, Cassius and Brutus, in 42 BC. Straddling the main road, the remains are substantial and undamaged by later building. One of the highlights is a well-preserved latrine (this is more than modern Kavala can boast). Kavala buses run every ½ hour.

Keramoti
ΚΕΡΑΜΩΤΗ

An isolated port turned growing resort, Keramoti owes its existence to the fact that it is the nearest point on the mainland to Thassos. A reasonable sand beach has enabled it to grow into a minor destination in its own right, with a reasonable number of rooms and a campsite. Package tourists often pass through via the ferries serving Thassos Town en route for Keramoti airport, some 20 km to the north-west.

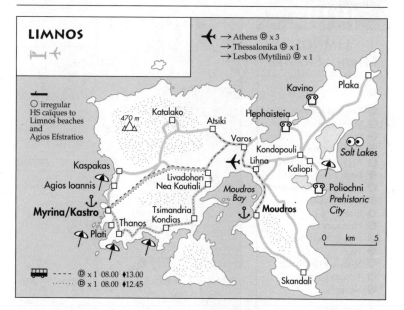

Limnos

ΛΗΜΝΟΣ; 477 km²; pop. 16,000.

CODE ☎ 22540
PORT POLICE ☎ 22225
TOURIST OFFICE ☎ 22315
POLICE ☎ 22200
HOSPITAL ☎ 22203

The home of Hephaistos, the divine smith, Limnos (also commonly transcribed as 'Lemnos') is a fertile, volcanic island opposite the entrance to the Dardanelles — a strategic location that attracts a strong military presence. An accompanying lack of tourists (who are missing a lovely island) has ensured a continuation of the traditional island culture now sadly absent elsewhere. This, coupled with good beaches, very friendly islanders and an attractive (in a weird volcanic molehill, lumpy, sort of way) main port of Myrina, are all the more reason to visit. Somewhat less appealing is the reputation of the curative properties of the local soil; indeed, Limnosian mud

pills were viewed as a sort of Viagra-like wonder drug by much of the ancient world. These days the locals seem less adept at weaving money-spinning yarns to ensnare gullible visitors.

Myrina (also known as Kastro, thanks to the floodlit castle built on the ancient acropolis) is very much the centre of island life. It is a prosperous little working town with an interesting warren of backstreets leading off the main street that snakes its way from the cute little square backing onto a small caïque harbour near the constantly enlarging ferry quay, under the castle walls and then east into the suburbs. Lined with an odd mix of hardware shops, discos and men's clothing outlets (it is difficult to forget that Limnos has a large army garrison), it is very much the focus of town life. Either side of the castle are the town's sandy beaches; the one to the north is decidedly more up-market.

Limnos is a good destination if you have your own transport, and very frustrating

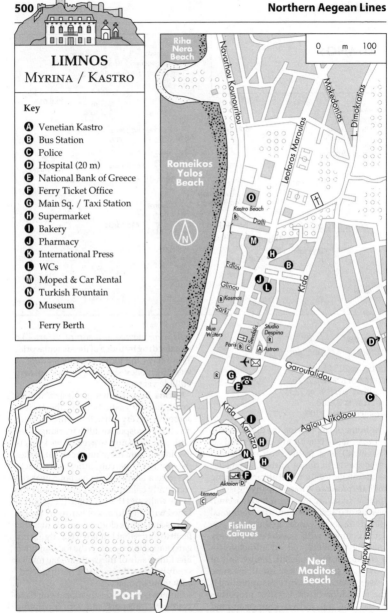

LIMNOS
Myrina / Kastro

Key

- **A** Venetian Kastro
- **B** Bus Station
- **C** Police
- **D** Hospital (20 m)
- **E** National Bank of Greece
- **F** Ferry Ticket Office
- **G** Main Sq. / Taxi Station
- **H** Supermarket
- **I** Bakery
- **J** Pharmacy
- **K** International Press
- **L** WCs
- **M** Moped & Car Rental
- **N** Turkish Fountain
- **O** Museum

1 Ferry Berth

— given the almost non-existent bus service — if you haven't. The two halves of the island contrast greatly. The east side is flat and fertile, with two lakes adding to the oddly un-Greek landscape of cornfields and grazing cattle, while the west has a starker rocky volcanic terrain and the bulk of the best beaches. Apart from Myrina the only large settlement is at **Moudros** (the forward Allied military base during the ill-fated Gallipoli campaign; thanks to the sheltered bay, it also safely housed the Allied generals).

Buses link the town with the capital, but unfortunately the service is geared to moving islanders into Myrina for work in the mornings and returning them at night. With only two services offering a same-day return to Myrina, buses are all but useless for tourism purposes. Short of hiring a moped, the best way to see the remote sites of interest on Limnos is to take the once-a-week bus excursion (unfortunately, the day varies).

ᴴ━┥

In High Season a Tourist Police office is open in Myrina's town hall which will help you find a bed. This usually means directing you to one of the **Myrina** hotels (of which there is a reasonable selection). On the waterfront the D-class *Aktaion* (☎ 22258) and the C-class *Lemnos* (☎ 22153) are easily found and reasonable. Harder to find is the C-class *Sevdalis* (☎ 22691), which lies in a side street one block beyond the OTE square on the town's main street. More up-market establishments tend to lie near the beaches. These include the B-class *Paris* (☎ 23266) and the expensive *Kastro Beach* (☎ 22148), which lies at the east end of the town's north beach.

ᴳᴼ

Limnos was an important island during the Archaic period, and the primary archaeological site — the city at **Poliochni** even predates Troy on the adjacent Turkish coast. Tours visit the rather confused archaeological remains along with those of the classical city at **Hephaisteia**. This was built on the spot where the god Hephaistos landed and lamed himself after Hera threw him from the summit of Mt. Olympus in a fit of 'peak'. The tangible remains include fragments of a temple to the god and an odeon.

Marmaras
ΜΑΡΜΑΡΑΣ

A resort on the middle fork (known as Sithonia) of the Halkidiki peninsula, Marmaras (alias Nea Marmaras) is on hydrofoil itineraries. A pricey resort with a reasonable beach, bus links to Thessalonika, and a campsite, the main incentive to visit is the boat tour along the coast offering a glimpse of the monasteries of Mt. Athos. Marmaras is the easiest departure point for island hoppers wanting a look; the daily excursion costs €30.

Nea Moudania
ΝΕΑ ΜΟΥΔΑΝΙΑ

An over-touristed small town on the Northern Aegean's west coast just north of the left-hand fork (alias Cassandra) of the Halkidiki peninsula, Nea Moudania is the weekend getaway resort for Thessalonika, and now sees a number of hydrofoils calling en route to the Sporades.

Beyond the crowded beach, some over-expensive hotels and a crowded campsite, it has very little to recommend it — unless you are in a hurry to continue on to Cassandra. Hourly buses to Thessalonika offer frequent means of escape.

Nea Peramos
ΝΕΑ ΠΕΡΑΜΟΣ

Unless you have a vehicle, this mainland port 15 km west of Kavala is not really a practical proposition given the 'inter-city' nature of local buses. However, host to several daily landing-craft ferries running to Thassos, it offers a short cut to motorists arriving from or departing to the west. Set in a cosy, open-mouthed bay, this hamlet (complete with beach, kastro and campsite) is an infinitely more relaxing jumping-off point to Thassos than Kavala. If you are prepared to stop overnight, Nea Peramos is worth considering as a quiet overnight excursion for Thassos trippers.

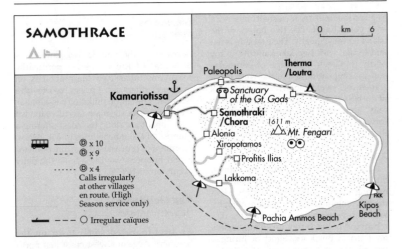

Samothrace

ΣΑΜΟΘΡΑΚΗ; 178 km²; pop. 2,800.

CODE ☎ 25510
PORT POLICE ☎ 41305
POLICE ☎ 41203
FIRST AID ☎ 41217

A dramatic, heavily wooded mountain peak rising from the sea, Samothrace was an island of spiritual pilgrimage in the ancient world; partly, one suspects, because it was as difficult to get to then as it is now. First impressions of a comparatively bleak and mountainous island are enhanced by the almost apologetic way the main island town and port of **Kamariotissa** clings to the foreshore against a backdrop of undulating hills devoid of vegetation bar the odd wind-broken tree and stubbly cornfields. A couple of horribly modern electricity-generating windmills on the long western spur do nothing to relieve the almost forbidding sense of isolation. This tends to do Samothrace something of a disservice for once ashore it is quite a friendly place.

All the nightlife and essentials are to be found in the port along with most of the accommodation. For once on a Greek island, English is little spoken as most visitors are German or Scandinavian.

Almost all tourist activity is confined to the northern coast thanks to the impressive archaeological remains of the Sanctuary of the Great Gods at Paleopolis and the spa village at Therma. Other island villages see few tourists. Buses run regularly to the whitewashed island capital at **Chora**; a jumble of whitewashed houses tucked comfortably out of sight in a fold in the foothills, it is devoid of hotels and all the other trappings of modern tourism and topped with the remains of a lovely castle. Equally attractive is the pretty hill village of **Profitis Ilias** (buses also head for here calling irregularly at other villages en route).

Buses also run direct to the campsites via **Therma** (also known as Loutra). As the name implies, this is a spa resort of sorts and now the main tourist centre on the island, though trees outnumber tourists for the greater part of the year.

Not really a beach island, Samothrace does have two excellent examples along its south coast that are sadly only accessible by dirt track or irregular caïque on the south coast at Pachia Ammos and delightfully remote Kipos.

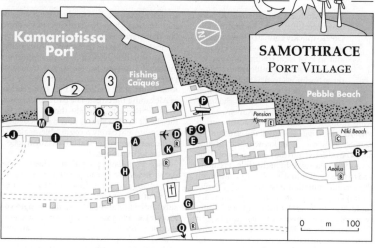

Key

A Information / Bus Office
B Bus Stop
C Police
D National Bank of Greece
E Pharmacy
F Supermarket
G Grocery Store

H Bakery
I Moped Rental
J Disco & Promontory
K Bar / Ferry Tickets
L Passenger Stalls
M WCs
N Old Lighthouse
O Waterfront Park

P Beach Square
Q Chora Road
R Therma Road

1 Ferry Berth
2 Hydrofoil Berth
3 Irregular Beach
  Caïques

🛏

Rooms and hotels are scattered thinly between the port, Paleopolis, Therma and Chora. Low numbers of visitors means low prices. At the **Port** you will find, at the northern end of the waterfront, the C-class *Niki Beach* (☎ 41561), with the pricey B-class *Aeolus* (☎ 41595) close by, along with a pension, the *Kyma* (☎ 41268). **Paleopolis** has the B-class *Xenia* (☎ 41230) and the C-class *Kastro* (☎ 41850) close to hand. **Therma** is also blessed with a couple of establishments: the B-class *Kaviros* (☎ 41577) and the C-class *Mariva* (☎ 41759).

▲

There is one north-coast High Season only site: *Camping Loutra* (☎ 41784) is 3 km east of Therma. Services are pretty basic, but the site at least has the merit of being fairly quiet.

👓

Samothrace offers two great attractions, the most obvious being **Mt. Fengari** (the 'Mountain of the Moon'). Used by Poseidon as a seat while he observed the Trojan War, mortals seeking serious hill walking (via Therma) find that when they get to the summit after a day's climb that the ground is still warm.

The **Sanctuary of the Great Gods** at Paleopolis sees far more visitors. The remains of one of Greece's premier places of pilgrimage (the first historian, Herodotus, was initiated into the rites, and Alexander the Great's parents met and fell in love here), it is sadly diminished, but is located in a marvellous woody ravine setting that more than makes up for the limited remains. The sanctuary was pre-Greek in origin, being originally dedicated to the

Great Mother Earth goddess Axieros and a fertility god, Kadmilos. The Greeks quickly conflated these figures with their own Demeter and Hermes and so kept local traditions going for the best part of a millennium. What those traditions were is still a mystery. Ancient writers were loath to mention them thanks to the belief in shadowy demon figures (known as the Kabeiroi) who were thought to harbour implacable wrath towards any that divulged the sanctuary's secrets. However, it is known that anyone could be initiated into the sanctuary's mysteries and that the torch-lit night-time ceremony had two stages (the first involving purification, the second, initiation into the rites). Despite earthquakes and pirate attacks, the sanctuary (politically independent throughout its life) was only abandoned with the adoption of Christianity by the Roman Empire, and most of the important buildings were rebuilt several times during the course of their lives.

Access to the site today is via a footpath running inland from the main coast road. Walking past the hotel and the museum along the path running parallel with the central ravine stream, on your right you will see the remains of **Ⓐ** the **Milesian Building** (so called because of an inscription associated with it), and behind it **Ⓑ** a **Byzantine Fort** built from stones from the sanctuary.

The most important buildings were all located on the 'island' of land bounded by the (usually dry) streams running down the ravines. Crossing the stream brings you to **Ⓒ** the rotund **Arsinoeion**, also an important structure though of much later date. Built c. 285 BC, it was the largest circular building ever constructed by the ancient Greeks. Commissioned by Queen Arsinoe of Thrace, it was used for public sacrifice. To the north is **Ⓓ** the **Anaktoron** (also known as the 'Hall of the Lords'); it was one of the oldest buildings on the site, being in continuous use from the 6 C. BC to the 4 C. AD. It was used for the first stage of the initiation rites. In the Roman period a robing room, **Ⓔ** the **Sacristy**, was added to the building, when it was substantially rebuilt.

Turn south of the Arsinoeion and you come to **Ⓕ** the **Temenos** (an open air precinct with a ceremonial entrance on the north-east side), and **Ⓖ** the **Hieron**. Now the most prominent building on the site, thanks to its columns, the temple was the location for the second stage of the initiation. The remains of spectator seating line the interior walls. On its west side lie the scanty foundations of **Ⓗ** the **Hall of Votive Gifts** (C. 540 BC), little evident now, but important in that it survived for close on a thousand years without rebuilding. Next door is the **Altar Court** at **Ⓘ**, dedicated by a half-brother of Alexander the Great. The path now crosses a culvert that ran under the theatre stage. **Ⓙ**, the site of the **Theatre**, is now a tree-covered depression and barely recognisable, as almost all the seats were removed for the construction of later fortifications.

Once you have passed the theatre, the paths divide. The eastern path wanders over the stream and a hill (that was home to **Ⓚ** the **South Necropolis**) before coming to the substantial foundations of **Ⓛ** the **Propylon of Ptolemy II**, a formal gateway constructed for the use of the local townspeople (the ancient capital—Paleopolis proper—stood to the east of the sanctuary). When originally built it had the stream channelled to emerge through it. On the west side of that stream are two rather obscure buildings: **Ⓜ** a **Circular Building** and **Ⓝ** a **Doric Structure** dedicated by Phillip III and Alexander IV.

The western path turns west up the hillside behind the theatre, bringing you to the foundations of **Ⓞ** the **Nike Niche**: a small building cut into the hillside that was built specifically to house **Ⓟ** the famous **Winged Nike (Victory) of Samothrace**. Made of Parian marble, this sculpture is the site's greatest archaeological find, and (bar the missing head) is now in the Louvre. It takes the form of an 'angel' standing on the prow of a ship. The Nike niche was in fact a fountain house, and the prow stood in a double-level floor basin filled with water.

The path continues up the hill to the higher level behind the theatre and **Ⓠ** a **Stoa**. Plenty of fragments lie scattered around but nobody has yet found the time to reassemble them. Between the stoa and the ravine stream at **Ⓡ** lie scanty remains of **Hellenistic Buildings** (purpose unknown).

Finally, returning to the main path you come back to the site's **Archaeological Museum**: it is well laid out and worth a visit, though — as with many 19 C. excavated sites — all the important sculptures found on the site have long since found their way into French and Austrian museums.

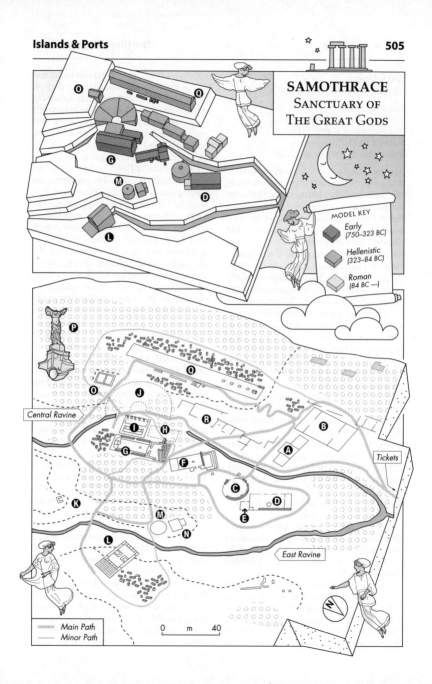

SAMOTHRACE
SANCTUARY OF THE GREAT GODS

MODEL KEY

Early (750–323 BC)

Hellenistic (323–84 BC)

Roman (84 BC —)

Central Ravine

Tickets

East Ravine

Main Path
Minor Path

0   m   40

Skiathos

ΣΚΙΑΘΟΣ; 61 km²; pop. 4,900.

CODE ☎ 24270
PORT POLICE ☎ 22017
TOURIST POLICE ☎ 21111
POLICE ☎ 23172
FIRST AID/HOSPITAL ☎ 22040

The mini-Corfu of the Aegean, Skiathos is arguably the most attractive and certainly the most touristed island in the Sporades — thanks to a combination of a delightful pine-clad landscape, excellent sand beaches, and a heavily used charter flight airport. Unfortunately, the cosy 'ideal family holiday' atmosphere is now under siege in High Season thanks to the sheer number of visitors. Skiathos is particularly popular with British package tourists and Italians of all descriptions. To these can now be added the legions of *Mamma Mia* fans as the island featured heavily in the hit movie.

In years past this has always been a rather up-market package tour destination, but things seem to be sliding downwards (fortunately taverna owners have so far resisted the temptation to play non-stop *Abba* tracks to diners) — the only exception being prices, which are comparatively high. The net result of all this is that those in the know mark Skiathos down as one of the best Greek islands going for spring/early summer visits and a spot to be avoided during the height of the season. That said, even when the huge crowds are in town it remains a very friendly place, and there are plenty of quieter spots you can escape to if you are so minded.

As with many smaller Greek islands, Skiathos has one substantial settlement and no other major centres. Considering how many tourists pass through, **Skiathos Town** weathers the storm remarkably well. Set in an islet-littered bay, it is a picturesque mix of red-tile roofs, white buildings and bell towers, set against the rich green hills.

The crowds that throng the narrow streets have had a major impact. For the most part this has taken the form of boutiques, patis-series and bars rather than neon lights and discos, but there are blots on the landscape; the worst is the main thoroughfare running in from the ferry dock — Papadiamantis St. — which has recently acquired new paving, naff street lights that wouldn't look out of place in *Disneyland*, and a branch of *McDonald's* for good measure.

The restaurant-lined waterfront is far more appealing, and adds greatly to the cosmopolitan ambience of the town. It is ideal for interesting evening promenades, taking in the beach boats tied up in the old harbour, the wooded **Bourtzi islet** (which once housed a fort but now is home to a taverna and cultural centre), and the assorted portrait painters, sponge sellers and street entertainers — to say nothing of campaigners protecting the endangered monk seals that breed in this part of the world — that appear out of nowhere once darkness falls. The town is also endowed with a yacht marina, and several flotilla sailing holiday companies are based here.

The **south coast road** (the only one made up on the island) is home to the great majority of the large package tour hotels. Strung irregularly, like so many octopuses out to dry, they hug the high ground, and the larger complexes usually have a supermarket nearby (there are well over a dozen). This isn't as depressing as it sounds, as the mix of wooded headlands and small bays — most with golden sand beaches — works very well, and the low-rise hotels are almost lost amidst this attractive jumble, apart from an area near **Troulos** which suffered a serious forest fire in the summer of 2007.

The road is very busy, particularly at rush periods, but at least it is almost impossible to get lost, and there are frequent taxis and bus stops along its length. The **bus service** is one of the more 'interesting' features of Skiathos. The bus stops have numbers as this saves tourists from having to remember the name of their cove, bay or hotel. A much bigger problem is simply getting on board: buses here would give those on Ios a run

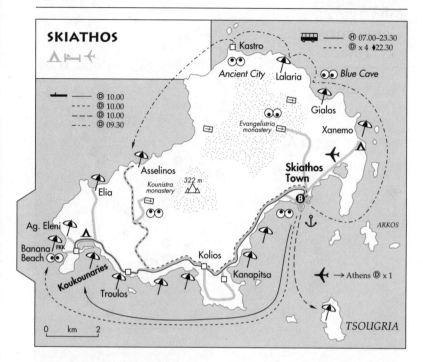

for their money in a tourist sardine contest. The trouble is that although the buses run every 15 minutes, they simply can't cater for the massive demand. The battle to get on and off also pushes up journey times.

The primary destinations lie at each end of the road; in the evenings everyone is heading for Skiathos Town, while in the mornings the big draw is **Koukounaries** beach, a long crescent-shaped stretch of sand filled with bodies of various hues, and sporting a sea-water lagoon, complete with wildlife-sustaining reed-bed backed by yet more umbrella pines. A short walk away is quieter **Banana Beach**, reputedly the best naturist beach in the Mediterranean — most of the bananas on display tend to be middle-aged and Italian.

The north coast is very quiet, without hotels or settlements of note, thanks to a lack of roads and the strong winds that turn the beaches into a beachcomber's paradise. In fact, the only easily accessible point is at **Asselinos** (reached via a dusty woodland track that runs past the odd stud farm), which is a blissfully quiet and verdant little valley only let down by a rather tatty beach. Equally underdeveloped is the wooded interior of the island which is popular with hikers.

The east coast is similarly the preserve of those looking for a quiet life, the one blot on their happiness being the noisy airport (see p. 509). There is a poor beach at **Xanemo**, and you will have to resort to beach boats if you want to do better. **Lalaria** on the north-east corner is the best bet; a very picturesque tapering pebble beach at the base of a cliff, it is more Beachy Foot than Head and is well worth the cost of a visit.

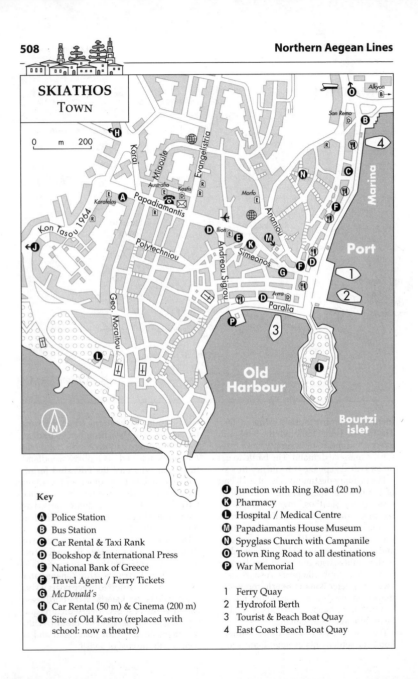

SKIATHOS TOWN

0   m   200

Korai

Miaoule

Evangelistria

Australia

Kostis

Karafelas

Papadiamantis

Kon Tasou 1064

Morfo

Polytechniou

Andreou Sigrou

Ananiou

Simeonos

Geo. Moraitou

Avra

Paralia

San Remo

Marina

Port

Old Harbour

Bourtzi islet

Alkyon

N

Key

- **A** Police Station
- **B** Bus Station
- **C** Car Rental & Taxi Rank
- **D** Bookshop & International Press
- **E** National Bank of Greece
- **F** Travel Agent / Ferry Tickets
- **G** *McDonald's*
- **H** Car Rental (50 m) & Cinema (200 m)
- **I** Site of Old Kastro (replaced with school: now a theatre)
- **J** Junction with Ring Road (20 m)
- **K** Pharmacy
- **L** Hospital / Medical Centre
- **M** Papadiamantis House Museum
- **N** Spyglass Church with Campanile
- **O** Town Ring Road to all destinations
- **P** War Memorial

1   Ferry Quay
2   Hydrofoil Berth
3   Tourist & Beach Boat Quay
4   East Coast Beach Boat Quay

⊨

Rooms can be hard to come by in High Season, though of late large ferries are met by a few townsfolk offering beds. A quayside kiosk just north of the ferry quay provides useful accommodation advice. Hotels there are aplenty on Skiathos. Most are block-booked by package-tour operators. Seeking out untaken-up rooms is an option, though you will find almost all the A to C class hotels are well out of town, bar the B-class *Alkyon* (☎ 22981) on the airport road.

Within Skiathos Town there are a number of budget establishments: the poor D-class *Avra* just off the waterfront, the *San Remo* (☎ 22078) at the other end of the harbour and the *Kostis* (☎ 22909) behind the post office. E-class hotels are to be found near Papadiamantis St. These include the *Ilion* (☎ 21193), the *Morfo* (☎ 21737), the basic *Australia* (☎ 22488) and the *Karafelas* (☎ 21236). All adequately offer the basics at a reasonable price.

▲

There are two sites on Skiathos: nearest to the port is a municipal campsite at Xanemo. Under the airport flight path, it does a roaring trade but attracts few campers: so few in fact that it is a moot point how long it will remain open. This leaves *Koukounaries Camping* (☎ 49250) as the only option worth considering. Quite apart from other considerations it is easily the best for the beach of the same name and buses to Skiathos Town, though it is relatively expensive. Summer prices are maintained throughout the year, but on the plus side the grass, flower and willow-tree filled site is very well maintained too. There is also a good supermarket 40 m west of the site entrance at Bus Stop 23.

👁👁

Skiathos Town is the island's main attraction: though it lacks tangible sights (substantial rebuilding following bombing damage in WW2 hasn't helped). The only 'sight' as such is the well-preserved late 19th century home of the writer **Alexandros Papadiamantis** (1851–1911). One of Greece's most notable literary figures, he grew up on Skiathos and returned to die. A journalist turned author, he penned over 100 novels and short stories (most based on island life) — the most famous being *The Man Who Went to Another Country, The Gypsy*, and *The Murderess*. Translations of several are on sale in the town's bookshop. Perhaps they

are losing something in translation, but his work can be a bit heavy going.

As for his house, it is a simple homestead. Unfortunately, Papadiamantis had as few possessions as his fellow islanders and the building reflects this wonderfully. Minimalists and creaky-floorboard fans will love it: most others seem to leave with the impression that the removal men have already been in and removed most of the furniture.

The southern waterfront is home to a second memorial to long-departed island sons. In this case it is a cannon- and flag-decorated **War Memorial**. Placed in honour on a quay of its own, it commemorates the unfortunate men who were summarily rounded up and executed in 1943 by the German troops — as a reprisal for local resistance to occupation. Sadly its inscription is only in Greek, so its significance isn't appreciated by most tourists. However, the event still colours many islanders' attitude to visitors — as when visiting Crete, it helps if you are a national of one of the Allied powers.

Most tourists visit Skiathos Town at least once a day if only to pick up the daily tour boats heading on to Skopelos and Alonissos, the beach boats (most heading for Koukounaries, Banana and a beach on the adjacent islet of **Tsougria**), or the anticlockwise island boat tour. The island boat tour also stops briefly at the **Blue Cave**, a sea cave on the east coast, and at **Kastro**, site of the medieval centre of the island until it was abandoned in the 19 C. after piracy was no longer a threat to the islanders' security. Set on an all but impregnable headland, it is now a picturesque ruin of houses, streets and churches.

Excursions also run to two monasteries: **Kounistra** to the west (for the view) and **Evangelistria** (a popular donkey-ride destination north of Skiathos Town, famed in Greece as the place where the Greek flag was first raised in 1807 by a group of conspiring independents).

Finally, if you want some really inspired sightseeing try the beach road running past the end of the airport runway. Supposedly closed every time a flight leaves, it made headlines in 1996 after three tourists unwittingly stood behind the engines of a departing jet. When it took off they did as well, one landing on a nearby beach, a second waist-deep in the sea and the third ending up on a mainland-bound hydrofoil with a broken jaw.

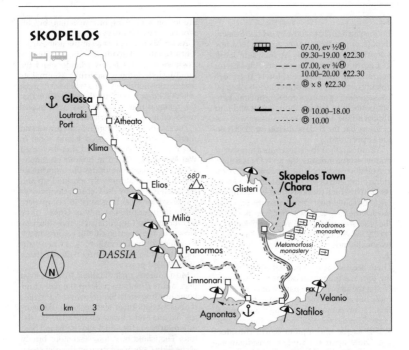

SKOPELOS

🛏 🚌

⚓ **Glossa** ☐
Loutraki
Port   ☐ Atheato

Klima ☐

☐ Elios   680 m
△△   Glisteri
⚓ **Skopelos Town**
/Chora

☐ Milia   ☐
Prodromos
monastery

DASSIA   ☐ Panormos
△   Metamorfossi
monastery

🧭 Ⓝ   Limnonari ☐
FKK
Velanio

0   km   3   Agnontas ⚓   ⚓ Stafilos

🚌 ── 07.00, ev ½Ⓗ
     09.30–19.00 ◊22.30
─ ─ 07.00, ev ¾Ⓗ
     10.00–20.00 ◊22.30
─ ·─ Ⓓ x 8 ◊22.30

⛴ ─ ─ Ⓗ 10.00–18.00
···· Ⓓ 10.00

Skopelos

ΣΚΟΠΕΛΟΣ; 96 km²; pop. 4,700.

CODE ☎ 24240
PORT POLICE ☎ 22180
POLICE ☎ 22235
FIRST AID / HOSPITAL ☎ 22220

The largest island in the Sporades group, Skopelos has less sparkle than neighbouring Skiathos but benefits equally from the *Mamma Mia* effect (scenes from the film were shot on both). Overall the beaches are not as good (mostly pebble), there is less sightseeing and the main town is quieter. Even so, it is an attractive island — covered in pine forests and agricultural land. With the easy links to the airport on Skiathos, Skopelos has seen a dramatic rise in tourism as package-tour operators have moved in, promoting the island as an ideal quiet family-holiday destination. Independent

travellers are less visible, but their numbers are on the increase as the appeal of over-touristed Skiathos wanes, and many are apt to rank it ahead of Skiathos thanks to its more relaxed, laid-back atmosphere.

The main settlement is **Skopelos Town**, tucked beneath a ring of sheltering hills in a deep bay on the northern coast. This is a disadvantage as, lying on the exposed side of the island, ferry and hydrofoil services are subject to regular disruption. On windy days these, and tourist boats, are often diverted to a small wooded inlet at **Agnontas** on the sheltered south side, where confused passengers are decanted onto an empty quay seemingly in the middle of nowhere (the three village tavernas aren't immediately obvious). When this happens free buses into town are laid on.

Skopelos Town has retained much of its whitewashed traditional appearance,

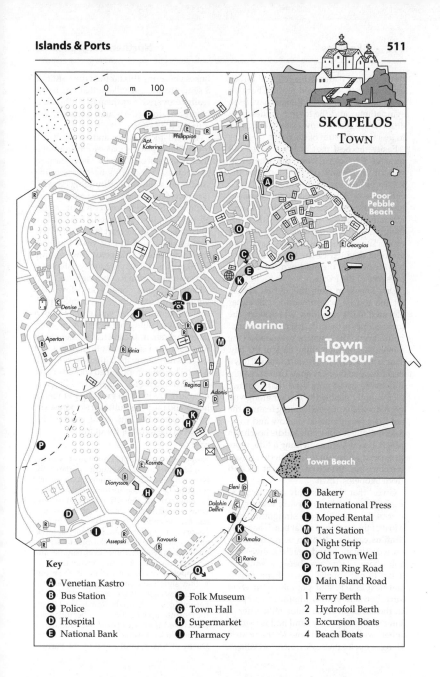

SKOPELOS
Town

Poor
Pebble
Beach

Apt.
Katerina

Phillipion

Georgios

Marina

Town
Harbour

Denise

Aperton

Ionia

Regina

Adonis

Kosmos

Dionyssos

Assepski

Kavouris

Eleni

Dolphin /
Delfini

Akti

Amalia

Rania

J Bakery
K International Press
L Moped Rental
M Taxi Station
N Night Strip
O Old Town Well
P Town Ring Road
Q Main Island Road
1 Ferry Berth
2 Hydrofoil Berth
3 Excursion Boats
4 Beach Boats

Town Beach

Key

A Venetian Kastro
B Bus Station
C Police
D Hospital
E National Bank

F Folk Museum
G Town Hall
H Supermarket
I Pharmacy

despite being badly damaged in the 1965 earthquake that put paid to the Chora on neighbouring Alonissos. Repairs have been sympathetic, and the town is undeniably attractive, but somehow the total adds up to less than the sum of the parts.

Easily the best part of town is the old quarter that rises from the tree-lined waterfront steeply up the slopes of the kastro hill on the west side of the bay: a collection of labyrinthine streets chock-a-block with steep staircases, chapels and attractive houses — many with over-hanging wooden balconies and red-tile roofs. The streets abutting the waterfront are now devoted to the tourist industry, but the heart of the old town remains the preserve of the locals.

One knock-on from this is that almost all the tourist accommodation is either elevated to the ring road, which skirts the lower slopes of the hills that make a natural boundary to the town, or relegated to the newer part of town at the back of the bay. This latter area is also home to a small town beach beyond the ferry quay. Unfortunately, it is made up of grey sand that becomes increasingly pebbly the further along you go. It does have one redeeming feature: the sea floor hereabouts is shallow and rock-free, making it a passable kiddie beach in a pinch. If you want something a little more private, caïques run to the otherwise inac-cessible, but attractive, beach at **Glisteri** from Skopelos Town.

Given that there is only one metalled road and a good bus service, visiting the rest of the island is very straightforward. Most of the bus stops are at beach hamlets. **Stafilos** can lay claim to being the over-crowded main island beach: it owes this role thanks largely to being a walkable 4 km from Skopelos Town. **Panormos** is the next beach, and popular with wind surfers (there is also unofficial camping in the coves on either side). **Milia** offers a long strand of pebbly sand and is usually quiet, while **Elios** is home to the nearest thing Skopelos possesses to a resort village.

Buses venturing this far then run to **Klima**, a semi-abandoned village that has never really recovered from the 1965 earthquake, before arriving at the island's second major settlement of Glossa.

A small picturesque and unspoilt hill town, **Glossa** perches majestically in amphi-theatre fashion on a hillside above the port of Loutraki. Despite its narrow winding streets and whitewashed buildings appeal, it attracts few visitors — most are day trip-pers from Skopelos Town on tours of the island. Despite this, three or four hydro-foils call daily at the port below the town. Ferries also called in past years (note: all timetables refer to Skopelos Town simply as 'Skopelos'; Glossa is usually listed as if it were an island in its own right).

Loutraki, lying some 4 km down the winding hill road (there is a donkey path with more appeal for walkers), is now a diminutive fishing hamlet with an over-large harbour. In ancient times, however, it was home to a significant Roman town (it takes its name from the baths that were built here). The waterfront is lined with attractive tavernas, and the few original buildings are now surrounded by a growing number of hotels and purpose-built tourist rooms. The port also boasts a large windswept pebble beach to the north of the quay.

😷

Skopelos shares a similar quiet history to her neighbours. Lacking size and arable land, the Northern Sporades were never particularly wealthy. Lying close to the mainland, they became part of the Athenian empire and were later sacked by Philip V of Macedon in 220 BC. The only really notable event in their history came just before the battle of Salamis in 480 BC when a preliminary skirmish took place off Skiathos between three Greek triremes and a Sidonian squadron of the Perisan fleet.

Skopelos was the only island in the group with a significant city. In ancient times the island was called Peparethos by the Greeks, becoming Skopelos in the Roman era. During the Byzantine period it was another unfancied island used as a place of exile. With the arrival of the Franks it came under the rule of the Duchy of Naxos, until a visit by the Barbary

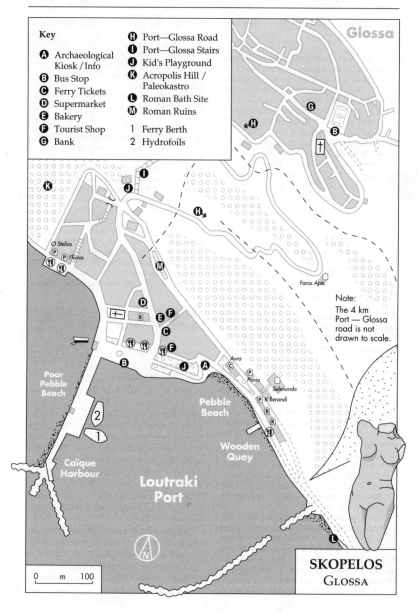

Key

ⓐ Archaeological Kiosk / Info
ⓑ Bus Stop
ⓒ Ferry Tickets
ⓓ Supermarket
ⓔ Bakery
ⓕ Tourist Shop
ⓖ Bank
ⓗ Port—Glossa Road
ⓘ Port—Glossa Stairs
ⓙ Kid's Playground
ⓚ Acropolis Hill / Paleokastro
ⓛ Roman Bath Site
ⓜ Roman Ruins

1 Ferry Berth
2 Hydrofoils

Glossa

Ó Stelios
Flisvos

Faros Apts.

Note:
The 4 km
Port — Glossa
road is not
drawn to scale.

Avra
Pavia
Selenunda
K Berandi

Poor Pebble Beach

Pebble Beach

Caïque Harbour

Wooden Quay

Loutraki Port

SKOPELOS
GLOSSA

0   m   100

pirate Barbarossa who slaughtered the entire population in 1538.

⊨

There are plenty of rooms in **Skopelos Town** (a kiosk on the ferry quay offers information). Hotel beds are also reasonably plentiful. Nearest the ferry quay is the E-class *Georgios* (☎ 22308), but like other waterfront hotels it is apt to be a bit noisy. For a quieter life try the cluster of hotels behind the town beach. These include the pricey C-class *Delfini* (☎ 23015), the D-class *Eleni* (☎ 22393), and the E-class *Rania* (☎ 22486). At the upper end of the market are the B-class *Amalia* (☎ 22688), the *Dionyssos* (☎ 23210) and, nearer the centre of town, *Ionia* (☎ 22568). Glossa's port of **Loutraki** also has several pensions with sea views on offer, as well as the largish C-class hotel *Avra* (☎ 33550).

A

There are no official sites, but freelance camping has been tolerated at Velonio (the unofficial nudist beach), and at Panormos beach — though it has been discouraged of late.

👓

The town and beaches are the main attractions; sightseeing on Skopelos tends to come in a poor third. **Skopelos Town** provides just about enough to justify a day-trip from a neighbouring island, but lacks specific sights. The **Kastro** is a serious disappointment, now being reduced to little more than a couple of walls that hardly grab the eye, though the town is interesting enough.

The only museum in town is the tiny **Folk Art Museum** hidden away in the backstreets, and largely passed by. Once you start wandering (well okay, given the number of staircases, climbing) around backstreets the churches offer the main landmarks. The town is reputedly home to some 120 of them, but it isn't clear which clubs and bars the person doing the counting frequented before embarking on his task. First among the churches is the clifftop **Panagia ston Pirgho** which overlooks the harbour entrance.

Coach trips around the island are quite popular, and usually take in at least one of the island monasteries. Three of these open their doors to visitors, **Prodromos** and **Evangelismou** (both dating from the 18 c.: now denuded of monks they are occupied by nuns) and 16 c. **Metamorfossi** (now uninhabited, so you can be a bit more uninhibited when it comes to

observing the dress code). In addition, tour boats operate daily out of Skopelos Town to Skiathos and Alonissos (including the Marine Park). If you fancy city sightseeing in the heat of the day, ticket agencies also offer day trips to Athens (via early morning hydrofoil and coach) — at a price.

With plenty of shade and scenery Skopelos is an excellent island for **walking**, even in high summer. Walkers should buy the snappily titled *Sotos Walking Guide to Local Beauty Spots & Places of Historical Interest* by Heather Parsons (€6), which is on sale in several waterfront shops.

Finally, **Loutraki** also has limited sightseeing thanks to the fragmentary remains of the ancient city of **Selinous** which once stood here. The only obvious remains are 4 whitewashed column fragments in front of the Avra hotel, but once you visit the Archaeological information kiosk nearby you will find photos of the overgrown site of the ancient **Bathhouse**, the largely inaccessible **Acropolis** Hill. Sadly, the port has no museum: the more significant finds — notably a torso of a statue of Aphrodite — are now in the Volos Archaeological Museum.

Skyros
ΣΚΥΡΟΣ; 208 km²; pop. 2,900.

CODE ☎ 22220
PORT POLICE ☎ 96475
POLICE ☎ 91274
FIRST AID ☎ 92222

A gem of an island to the east of Evia, Skyros (pronounced Sk*ee*-ros) offers an appealing mix of one of the best Cycladic-style choras and a history laced with everything from transvestism and a Greek Excalibur to pirates and poets. The weak spots that have prevented it emerging as a major tourist destination are the limited number of good beaches and the fact that it is too far from regular ferry routes (out of High Season links with other islands are non-existent).

The main settlement of **Skyros Town** lies hidden from view from the sea in the folds of a hill on the east side of the island — a 20-minute bus ride from the west-coast port hamlet of **Linaria**. This desire for seclusion was prompted by the piracy of the 16 and

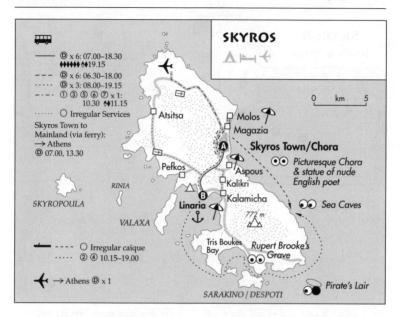

SKYROS

Skyros Town to
Mainland (via ferry):
→ Athens
Ⓓ 07.00, 13.30

— Ⓓ x 6: 07.00–18.30
✚✚✚✚ ✚✚19.15
‒ ‒ ‒ Ⓓ x 6: 06.30–18.00
· · · · Ⓓ x 3: 08.00–19.15
‒ · ‒ ① ③ ⑤ ⑥ ⑦ x 1:
10.30 ✚✚11.15
· · · · · O Irregular Services

0   km   5

Atsitsa
Molos
Magazia
Skyros Town/Chora
👁👁 *Picturesque Chora
& statue of nude
English poet*
Pefkos
Aspous
Kalikri
RINIA
Kalamicha
👁👁 *Sea Caves*
SKYROPOULA
772 m
Linaria
VALAXA
Tris Boukes
Bay
*Rupert Brooke's
Grave*
👁👁
→ ‒ ‒ ‒ O Irregular caïque
· · · · ② ④ 10.15–19.00
← → Athens Ⓓ x 1
SARAKINO / DESPOTI
👁👁 *Pirate's Lair*

17 c., but did not prevent 'Three Entrance Bay' at the southern end of the island becoming a notorious pirate lair and home to a Hellenic proto-Blackbeard.

During the Heroic Age the warrior Achilles had much the same hideaway idea with equally little success, for foreseeing his death at Troy, he hid on Skyros disguised as a girl only to let his frock slip when Odysseus (offering a particularly heroic sword for sale) discovered him and dragged him by the heel to its date with destiny (see p. 607). Surprisingly, there is nothing commemorating this event in the town. Instead, you will find a bronze of another poetic warrior who died with a sore point — Rupert Brooke, the First World War poet, who came off worse in a fight with a mosquito, dying unheroically here of his wound in 1915, en route to Gallipoli. If he sauntered around the island wearing as little as his statue it is not surprising that he was smitten and, all things considered, he was lucky not to share the fate of the third notable to come a

cropper here — the hero Theseus who was thrown over a cliff onto a nudist beach by the then king of Skyros, Lykomides. These days the towns folk are more friendly, in part because the Chora has managed to retain much of its unspoilt charm thanks to the bulk of the island accommodation being located a bus-ride away on the beach. The car-free Chora is dominated by the castle and the main street which winds up the hill towards it, and is particularly appealing in the evenings when the streets are thronged with gossiping locals. It is, however, often quite windy.

Rupert Brooke's grave aside, the rest of the island is little visited by tourists: most visitors to Skyros confine themselves to the chora and the relatively close resort villages of **Magazia** and **Molos** which are linked by a good sand beach (the island bus service isn't geared to getting tourists anywhere else). Those hiring their own transport to explore further will find the expense well worth it.

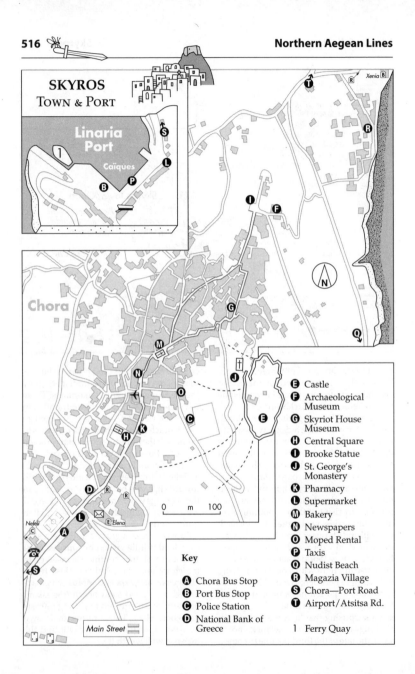

SKYROS
TOWN & PORT

Linaria
Port

Caïques

Chora

N

E Castle
F Archaeological
　Museum
G Skyriot House
　Museum
H Central Square
I Brooke Statue
J St. George's
　Monastery
K Pharmacy
L Supermarket
M Bakery
N Newspapers
O Moped Rental
P Taxis
Q Nudist Beach
R Magazia Village
S Chora—Port Road
T Airport/Atsitsa Rd.

0　m　100

Nefeli

Elena

Xenia B

Main Street

Key

A Chora Bus Stop
B Port Bus Stop
C Police Station
D National Bank of
　Greece

1　Ferry Quay

The northern half of Skyros is relatively flat and fertile, while the south is mountainous and delightfully unspoiled, being well wooded with pine trees (making this magnificent hillwalking country, even at the height of summer). The hills are also home to a rare ancient breed of horse (*Equus Caballus Skyriano*) similar to the small, heavy animals depicted on the Parthenon frieze. Now down to 104 animals living in small herds in the south-east hills, the species' future survival now rests in the hands of the newly formed 'Union of the Small-bodied Skyros Horse Breed' which helps farmers with these animals conserve them.

In addition to its poets and horses Skyros has also attracted media attention thanks to a 'holistic holiday community' established at remote **Atsitsa** on the north-west coast. Offering courses for those asking questions like 'What is stopping me from being who I really am?', the community has been accused of encouraging marital breakdown thanks to the allegedly high number of subsequent divorces by holidaymakers. This is unfair, because any partner who chooses to spend a holiday alone 'painting the soulscape' is surely in pretty serious trouble anyway. To do the holistic community justice, most who go on these courses return swearing by them, and the impact on Skyros is far less obtrusive than most tourist activities on other islands.

However, this doesn't stop some of the locals asking 'Why us?' First someone erects a bronze nude of a poet they have never heard of in the middle of town (at a time when most chaste village maidens wouldn't have known what a poet's lyric metre was, still less seen one), and now they have ranks of skinny-dipping middle-management types asking 'Where am I going?' On Skyros this question at least is easy to answer, as regular ferry connections are now confined to the link with Evia (Kimi).

⊢

There is a reasonable supply of rooms on Skyros spread between the town and the beach villages of Magazia and Molos. Hotels are thin on the ground and rather pricey, though the island is worth it. The best establishments are also in the beach villages to the north. **Molos** has the new A-class *Skyros Palace* (☎ 91994) on the beach (a large apartment complex on the beach with its own pool), the B-class *Angela* (☎ 91764), and the new C-class *Paradissos* (☎ 91220). Closer to the town lies the B-class *Xenia* (☎ 91209), a lovely hotel on the beach under the kastro at **Magazia**. Hotel options in Chora are limited, your best bets being the C-class *Nefeli* (☎ 91964) on the road just before you enter the town and the E-class *Elena* (☎ 91738) behind the Post Office. Chora also has a good supply of rooms — though these tend to be offered by owners on the ferry quay rather than bearing identifying signs in town.

Λ

There is no official camping on Skyros. However, a taverna on the beach in the bay just to the north of Linaria port has allowed unofficial camping in past years.

👓

Chora, with its traditional Skyriot houses and blue and white 'Delftware' pottery (a noted Skyriot product) is the main attraction on the island. The streets are so narrow vehicles are confined to the outskirts, and like all good choras it just invites you to get lost and then lost again. The town climbs to an impressive **Venetian Kastro** of Byzantine origin, with fantastic views over the town and island as well as housing a small **Archaeological Museum** which sadly lacks any outstanding exhibits. Below the castle walls is the **Monastery of St. George**. All three suffered minor damage in an earthquake that rocked the island on the 26th July 2001, but almost everything is now back to normal.

The chora also has a folk museum in the form of a traditional house (known as the **Faltaits Museum**) decked out with examples of the island wares (though most of the town houses retain the fittings and platters that give the museum its atmosphere).

The grave of **Rupert** ('If I should die, think only this of me: That there's some corner of a foreign field that is forever England') **Brooke** is set under a small grove of olive trees in the **Pirate Bay** on the south of Skyros, and is the premier destination of tourist caïques (which occasionally also visit the pirate base — one of the largest in the Aegean — of **Despot's Island**) and bus tours (the most accessible way of seeing Skyros). The east coast cave was also a **Pirate Grotto** in its day.

Thassos

ΘΑΣΟΣ; 398 km²; pop. 16,000.

CODE ☎ 25930
PORT POLICE ☎ 22106
POLICE / TOURIST POLICE ☎ 22500
FIRST AID ☎ 22190

A large, beautiful island tucked against the northern Aegean seaboard, Thassos is the most northerly inhabited island in Greece. Mountainous and green, with over half of its surface covered with cedar, oak and pine forests (now criss-crossed with bulldozed fire gaps to keep any forest fires under control) and fringed with good sand beaches, the island has emerged as a popular (if somewhat pricey) north European package-holiday destination, as well as attracting caravaners willing to motor through the Balkans. Fortunately, hotel development, although evident, is by no means over-conspicuous thanks to reasonable spacing around the attractive 95 km coastline, and the island is further improved by being out of the reach of the backpacking hordes that so damage the dreamy Greek island idyll elsewhere.

The main settlement at **Limenas** (also popularly known as **Thassos Town**) lies in a large bay on the north coast — offering the shortest crossing point to the mainland (12 km). A very pleasant mix of modern town and ancient city ruins, it reflects the island's history as a quietly prosperous state during the ancient period (its wealth generated by gold and silver mines and marble quarrying). With a scatter of later Turkish houses, infilled with modern (invariably tourist-related) buildings, the town is probably akin to what Kos Town would have looked like today if both Crusaders and Italians had not come a-building. Even the presence of tourist outlets and discos accompanying the holidaymakers fails to diminish the appealing relaxed atmosphere.

Activity naturally centres on the waterfront, which is surprisingly diverse with three distinct zones: the ferry quay (home to most of the services and shops), the ancient harbour (base for tour and beach boats, starting point for town tours, and offering leafy night-time waterfront promenades), and the popular town beach (backed by restaurants and tavernas). The tree-filled streets behind are thinly lined with buildings that are rarely more than one deep.

Movement around Thassos is dominated by the coast road that runs in a rough circuit around the island. Most buses travel in an anticlockwise direction to connect with the main port of **Skala Prinos** perched on an east coast spit: a tourist-dominated hamlet, but with more going for it than many Greek ports with a number of tavernas and holidaymaker-orientated shops, a goodly number of trees dividing the outlets offering accommodation and a working caïque repair yard.

South of Skala Prinos the west coast is fairly quiet with the bulk of the island's low-key agriculture and scattered beach villages until it reaches **Limenaria** on the south coast. The island's main resort (courtesy of a long, narrow sand beach) and the only other large town, it is largely a product of the mining industry in the early years of the last century, though this fact is somewhat misleading as the only dark holes these days are provided by the local discos. These exist in numbers, as if trying to compensate for the damaged landscape around the town: this southern part of the coast is the most spoilt part of Thassos thanks to extensive forest fire damage in recent years.

Those in search of scenery will do better to head on to neighbouring resort villages of **Pefkari** and **Potos** which have quieter beaches. Potos is also a convenient place to pick up buses heading inland to the island's medieval capital at **Theologos**. Now reduced to a quiet, whitewashed hill village, Theologos has only benefited from its isolation.

The attractive beach at **Makriammos** aside, the east coast of Thassos is the best on offer. More scenic (the road deviates from the coast to take in the attractive mountain villages of **Panayia** and **Potamia**; the latter is

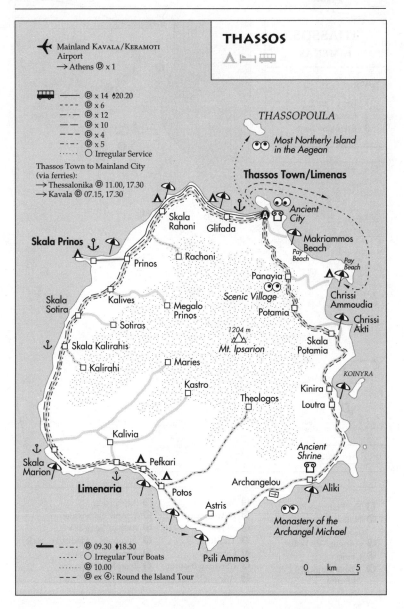

THASSOS

Mainland KAVALA/KERAMOTI Airport
→ Athens Ⓓ x 1

━━━━━ Ⓓ x 14 ⧫20.20
- - - - Ⓓ x 6
— ·— Ⓓ x 12
— — Ⓓ x 10
— - — Ⓓ x 4
- ·· - Ⓓ x 5
· · · · · ○ Irregular Service

Thassos Town to Mainland City
(via ferries):
→ Thessalonika Ⓓ 11.00, 17.30
→ Kavala Ⓓ 07.15, 17.30

Skala Prinos

Skala Rahoni
Glifada

Prinos

Rachoni

THASSOPOULA

Most Northerly Island
in the Aegean

Thassos Town/Limenas

Ancient City

Makriammos Beach
Pay Beach

Pay Beach

Chrissi Ammoudia

Chrissi Akti

Panayia
Scenic Village
Potamia

Skala Sotira

Kalives

Megalo Prinos

Sotiras

Skala Kalirahis

Kalirahi

Maries

1204 m
Mt. Ipsarion

Skala Potamia

KOINYRA

Kastro

Theologos

Kinira

Loutra

Kalivia

Ancient Shrine

Skala Marion

Limenaria

Pefkari

Potos

Astris

Archangelou

Aliki

Monastery of the
Archangel Michael

Psili Ammos

━─ - - - Ⓓ 09.30 ⧫18.30
· · · · · ○ Irregular Tour Boats
· · · · · Ⓓ 10.00
— — Ⓓ ex ④: Round the Island Tour

0   km   5

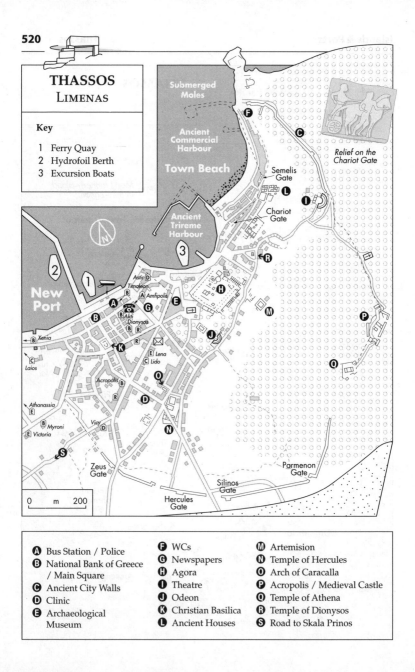

THASSOS
LIMENAS

Key

1 Ferry Quay
2 Hydrofoil Berth
3 Excursion Boats

Submerged Moles

Ancient Commercial Harbour

Town Beach

Relief on the Chariot Gate

Semelis Gate

Chariot Gate

Ancient Trireme Harbour

New Port

Astir
Timoleon
Amfipolis
Akti Dionysos
Xenia
Laios
Lena Lido
Acropolis
Athanassia
Myroni
Victoria
Vicy
Zeus Gate
Parmenon Gate
Silinos Gate
Hercules Gate
Road to Skala Prinos

0   m   200

Ⓐ Bus Station / Police
Ⓑ National Bank of Greece / Main Square
Ⓒ Ancient City Walls
Ⓓ Clinic
Ⓔ Archaeological Museum
Ⓕ WCs
Ⓖ Newspapers
Ⓗ Agora
Ⓘ Theatre
Ⓙ Odeon
Ⓚ Christian Basilica
Ⓛ Ancient Houses
Ⓜ Artemision
Ⓝ Temple of Hercules
Ⓞ Arch of Caracalla
Ⓟ Acropolis / Medieval Castle
Ⓠ Temple of Athena
Ⓡ Temple of Dionysos
Ⓢ Road to Skala Prinos

a popular tour destination in consequence), it runs down to the picture-postcard village of **Aliki** and, arguably the most attractive part of the island, the long, golden sand pine-backed beach running from **Kinira** to **Psili Ammos**.

⊨

Thassos Town is the best place to stay on the island. A few rooms are around. The wide range of hotels in Thassos Town have prices that are higher than average, and the balance of accommodation is towards the upper end of the range. At the top is the A-class *Amfipolis* (☎ 23101). B-class hotels include *Xenia* (☎ 71270) and the pensions *Acropolis* (☎ 22488), *Myroni* (☎ 23256), *Akti* (☎ 22326) and *Dionysos* (☎ 22198). C-class hotels are confined to the *Lido* (☎ 22929) and *Laios* (☎ 22309). At the bottom end of the range are the D-class *Astir* (☎ 22160) and E-class *Victoria* (☎ 22556), the justly popular *Lena* (☎ 22793) and the *Athanassia* (☎ 22545).

A

There are several sites at Skala Prinos including a pleasant NTOG/EOT site: *Camping Prinou* (☎ 71170), 700 m west of the ferry quay. Complete with its own pebble beach, it is easy to get to without your own transport, but like other sites it is geared to the trailer/camper market and full of young families in High Season.

Other sites are more isolated and invariably have a full range of facilities (including reasonable mini-markets). *Camping Perseus* (☎ 81352) at Skala Rahoni is well placed and worth considering. Even better — if you can live with the isolation — are south coast *Pefkari Camping* (☎ 51595) and east coast *Chryssi Ammoudia Camping* (☎ 61472).

👓

Thassos Town offers an easy day's sightseeing, along with a readily accessible beach. Ancient remains are scattered liberally around the town, though in almost every case nothing but foundations survive. Most obvious of these is the **Agora**, which backs onto the ancient harbour and houses the remains of a couple of Roman stoas, a tholos (a small circular temple) and several monumental altars. Nearby is a small **Archaeological Museum** (it has a notable 3 m high Archaic kouros, various pieces of sculpture, labels in French and no entry fee).

To the south lies a small **Odeon** fronted by a tiny remnant (50 m) of a paved **Hellenistic**

Street. This led to the triumphal **Arch of Caracalla**, now reduced to some impressively large foundations. Other survivals consist of temples to assorted gods along with a well-preserved **Theatre**. Hidden away in the forest, this theatre is one of the most appealing in the Greek islands. However, the number of pine trees enthusiastically growing amid the tiers of bench seats does suggest that the occasional performances put on here for the tourists' benefit are a bit on the wooden side.

Perhaps the most impressive feature of the ancient town is the well-preserved 4 C. BC **City Wall** that skirts the hills around the modern town and includes the old Acropolis. The wall fragments are in varying states of repair, along with the gates that each take their name from the Archaic reliefs carved on them. A wooded path (complete with street lamps) runs from the theatre up to the **Acropolis** — its ancient remains now incorporated into the walls of a ruined **Medieval Castle** (built in 1259). From the Acropolis the path runs on to a **Temple of Athena**. Little remains of the building, but the views over Thassos Town are worth the walk.

The buses that run around the coast road are also popular with visitors. Mornings and late afternoons they make a circuit of the island — thus offering tourists the opportunity to make 'day trips' to the destination of their choice. Most either make for the east-coast villages of **Panayia** and **Aliki** (the latter offering the remains of a small Doric shrine and ancient marble quarries), or head for the **Monastery of the Archangel Michael**, which has a gift shop staffed by some very friendly nuns and a hut full of fancy dress 'cover-ups' for the underdressed (a category which tends to include most holidaying visitors).

Thessalonika

ΘΕΣΣΑΛΟΝΙΚΗ; pop. 406,500.

CODE ☎ 2310
PORT POLICE ☎ 531504
NTOG OFFICE ☎ 263112
TOURIST POLICE ☎ 544162
POLICE ☎ 522589

The 1997 European City of Culture and the second city of Greece, Thessalonika (usually called 'Thessaloniki' and often abbreviated to plain 'Saloniki') commands attention as an important bus and railway junction, but the city has to work hard to keep the many tourists passing through. With a population approaching half a million, it can boast the crowds and concrete of the capital, Athens, but without the mitigating grace of an Acropolis complex. Despite an extensive attempt to improve the centre by pedestrianizing key streets and squares, Thessalonika has limited appeal unless you are prepared to venture well away from the waterfront, though its nightlife (if you are able to mix with the locals) is said by some to be second to none.

☺

Founded in 316 BC by the Macedonian commander Cassander (husband of Alexander the Great's half-sister), the city, unlike most other important centres in Greece, was never a major city state in its own right (hence the lack of Classical antiquities); instead, ideally placed on the trade route between the Levant and the Balkans, it has thrived as a major staging post from the Roman era (when it became the capital of the province of Macedonia) to the present day. Its history, therefore, is one of repeated changes in ruler as the warring powers in the region through the centuries have fought to secure its strategic position, leaving a legacy of impressive Byzantine churches and an even more spectacular city wall. Poets and philosophers are conspicuous by their absence: Thessalonika just wasn't their sort of town. Trade has always been the order of the day and with it came waves of immigrants (notably 1492, when 20,000 Spanish Jews settled in the city, and 1923, when Greeks emigrating from Turkey arrived in numbers).

The last hundred years have not been particularly kind to the city. Victim of a devastating fire in 1917 (which resulted in the waterfront and commercial centre being totally destroyed and then reconstructed on a grid system, with only the odd rebuilt church or ancient monument poking out incongruously amid the new buildings giving a reminder of the city of old), Thessalonika saw its commercial stuffing all but knocked out during WW2 when the occupying German forces deported the large Jewish population to the death camps. This was followed by a major earthquake in 1978 that inflicted considerable damage on the rich legacy of Byzantine churches (many only recently rebuilt after the fire).

The **city centre** offers up a very odd mix of wide, well-laid-out shopping streets that occasionally give way to ancient ruins or small churches. The pervading downtown atmosphere is one of a utilitarian, if cosmopolitan, commercialism; this is all rather a pity given that this city is often the first port of call for visitors to Greece—courtesy of its position on the main railway line to Europe. Even so, while this isn't Greece at its best, there is certainly enough sightseeing to fill a couple of leisurely days. If you are looking for something more, then you would be better advised to move on: certainly swimming is a non-starter hereabouts as, tucked up in the Thermaic Gulf, the seas are not as clean as they might be. It is also worth noting that on Wednesday afternoons and from Saturday lunchtime at weekends the shops are closed and the city feels very dead.

No matter how you arrive, the easiest way of getting your bearings is to head for the **waterfront** (which would be attractive enough were it not for the water giving off an acidic smell that doesn't encourage one to sample the sea air for long). Those that brave the sparkle-less waves and murderous traffic that bedevil the promenade will find a good number of cafés defying the passing parade of cars. The collection of old buildings in the warren of small streets opposite the ferry terminal are even quite attractive, and emerging as a nightlife hub.

Most of the **sights** are to be found in the north and eastern sections of the city. The former (just to the north of the area on the map opposite) includes the well-preserved city walls and the only part of the pre-1917 town to survive the flames. Now known as the Kastra district, it is an atmospheric maze of tiny streets more reminiscent of a Turkish town and offers a considerable contrast with the bland, wide boulevards (albeit fairly leafy ones) running between the large squares of the rebuilt centre.

As befits a major city, bus links are good all year. However, Thessalonika is not well served by ferries, though island hoppers

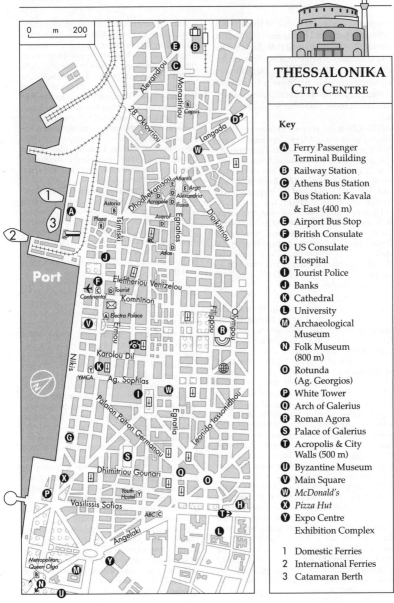

THESSALONIKA
CITY CENTRE

Key

- **A** Ferry Passenger Terminal Building
- **B** Railway Station
- **C** Athens Bus Station
- **D** Bus Station: Kavala & East (400 m)
- **E** Airport Bus Stop
- **F** British Consulate
- **G** US Consulate
- **H** Hospital
- **I** Tourist Police
- **J** Banks
- **K** Cathedral
- **L** University
- **M** Archaeological Museum
- **N** Folk Museum (800 m)
- **O** Rotunda (Ag. Georgios)
- **P** White Tower
- **Q** Arch of Galerius
- **R** Roman Agora
- **S** Palace of Galerius
- **T** Acropolis & City Walls (500 m)
- **U** Byzantine Museum
- **V** Main Square
- **W** *McDonald's*
- **X** *Pizza Hut*
- **Y** Expo Centre Exhibition Complex

- 1 Domestic Ferries
- 2 International Ferries
- 3 Catamaran Berth

can justify a visit by virtue of those boats (often booked solid by locals at the start of the local holiday season) that do run. The city is a little-known jumping-off point for the islands, and a preferable alternative to an uncomfortable night-train bound for Athens (high-speed trains make the journey in a much more palatable 4–5 hours).

⊨

As the nearest camping is 25 km away at Agia Triada, most budget travellers head for the hotels near the railway station. These usually fill up in August. Phone ahead if you can; best bets lie in the centre of town and include the D-class *Alexandria* (☎ 536185), *Ilissia* (☎ 528492) and *Atlas* (☎ 537046), and the E-class *Argo* (☎ 519770) and *Atlantis* (☎ 540131).

The area near the port is moving up-market, with existing hotels now being upgraded. There are also a few newer ones, notably the B-class *Plaza* (☎ 520120). A cheaper option is the C-class *Continental* (☎ 277563). To the east lies the expensive A-class *Electra Palace* (☎ 23 2221). There is also a *Youth Hostel* (☎ 225946) at 44 Alex. Svolou St.

👁👁

If you only have a short time in Thessalonika then you should head for the **Archaeological Museum** (②–⑦ 08.30–15.00; entrance fee: €3). It is in the middle of a massive refurbishment programme, and is partly closed, but the main exhibition is open. Entitled the **Gold of Macedon**, it is an impressive collection of gold artefacts (notably finely wrought wreaths). This area of Greece was part of ancient Macedon, a noted gold-producing region. Less valuable highlights include a stone sarcophagus with an interior painted to resemble a favourite room of the owner's house, and several iron toy carts, chairs and three-legged tables. The block next door is home to an icon-filled **Byzantine Museum** (②–⑦ 08.30–15.00; entrance fee: €3).

The city's main sights all lie to the south-east of the port/railway station area and can be divided into ancient and Byzantine/ medieval categories. Most impressive in the former category is the excellently preserved **Rotunda**: an intact Roman building dating back to 306 AD. Having served as everything from a museum to a mosque (the surviving abandoned minaret is very conspicuous), it is now the university church of Agios Georgios. Unfortunately it suffered major damage in an

earthquake in 1978. It has reopened after a long period of closure, but is still filled with a mass of scaffolding (hence the lack of an entry charge). There is not much inside, but in a few places fine ceiling mosaics remain to give just a hint of its previous sumptuous decoration.

Other ancient remains are fragmentary and less impressive. The much damaged **Arch of Galerius** (303 AD) is the best preserved, and was erected to celebrate the Roman Emperor's victory of the Persians at Armenia and Mesopotamia. It is decorated with very worn reliefs depicting the battles. Galerius also built a **Palace** but only foundations of this, the Roman **Agora** and **Hippodrome**, are extant and there is little on public display.

The great architectural jewels in Thessalonika's crown are the Byzantine churches dotted around the city and the medieval fortifications. Most famous of the churches is the rather plain-looking **St. Demetrius** standing near the Agora (it lies over the remains of the Roman city baths). Noted for its fine mosaics, it was badly damaged in the 1917 fire: the current building is a copy in all but name.

More substantive (and venerable) are the largely intact **City Walls** to the north of the downtown area. Originally they extended right around the town, the waterfront sections being demolished in the 19 c. Only one fragment remains in the form of the **White Tower**. Otherwise known as 'Lefkos Pirgos', this is a medieval construction built on older foundations, and now the nearest the city has to an identifiable emblem. Used for executions during Turkish rule, it was christened the 'Bloody Tower' by the locals after the sultan imprisoned and massacred his rebelling personal bodyguards here in 1826. The sultan took umbrage at the burghers' new name for his little home from home and painted the tower white by way of a response (note: it is no longer painted). It is now open to tourists (②–⑦ 08.30–15.00; entrance fee: €2), though bar a few photos of old Thessalonika, it has nothing of interest inside it. Views from the top are also a bit disappointing when you look away from the waterfront as most of the downtown buildings are as tall.

With your passport to hand you can also get into the home of the founder of modern Turkey, **Kemal Attaturk**, who was born in the city in 1881. Maintained by the Turkish government, and closed whenever Greco-Turkish tensions run high, the house lies east of the Kastra district, on Apostolou St.

Volos
ΒΟΛΟΣ; pop. 71,400.

CODE ☎ 24210
PORT POLICE ☎ 38888
NTOG OFFICE ☎ 23500

The number four city of Greece, Volos (often transcribed as 'Bolos') is set deep in a bay north of Evia, and is the mainland jumping-off point for the Northern Sporades island chain. Long an important port, the modern town lies atop the ancient city of Iolkos, home of Jason the Argonaut, from whence he set out in search of, and returned with, the mythical Golden Fleece.

Sadly, there is little to show of this pastoral ancestry these days — except the ugly appearance of a city that looks as if it ought to be the sort of place which manufactures sheep dip. As a result, most visitors just pass through, being either day-trippers from the islands or Athens-based

groups 'doing a Greek island' or using the town as a jumping-off point for the very attractive oak-wooded Mount Pelion peninsula rising up behind. This popular tourist attraction was home to the half-man, half-horse Centaurs that have long since hoofed it from the city-clad foothills to quieter parts, despite the existence of a good Archaeological Museum on Volos's bustling waterfront.

The means of getting away are very good, with a dozen buses a day to Athens as well as a rail link to Larissa (with high-speed links to Athens). Ferry connections with the Sporades are good all year, though other sea connections (including the uninspiring fishing-hamlet-clad islet of **Trikeri** to the south) are less consistent.

⊢

Both the D-class *Iasson* (☎ 26075) and E-class *Europa* (☎ 23624), just off the ferry quay, provide indifferent rooms that serve in a pinch. Private room availability is very poor.

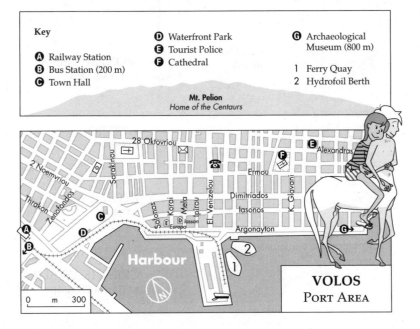

Key

Ⓐ Railway Station
Ⓑ Bus Station (200 m)
Ⓒ Town Hall
Ⓓ Waterfront Park
Ⓔ Tourist Police
Ⓕ Cathedral
Ⓖ Archaeological Museum (800 m)

1 Ferry Quay
2 Hydrofoil Berth

Mt. Pelion
Home of the Centaurs

VOLOS
PORT AREA

0   m   300

10
ARGO-SARONIC LINES

**AEGINA · ANGISTRI · ANTIKITHERA · GYTHIO · HYDRA
KITHERA · MONEMVASSIA · NEAPOLI · POROS · SPETSES**

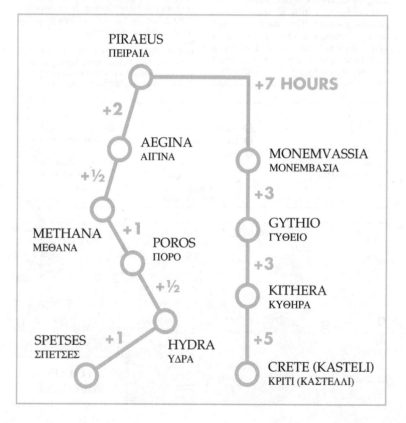

PIRAEUS
ΠΕΙΡΑΙΑ

+7 HOURS

+2

AEGINA
ΑΙΓΙΝΑ

MONEMVASSIA
ΜΟΝΕΜΒΑΣΙΑ

+½

+3

METHANA
ΜΕΘΑΝΑ

+1

POROS
ΠΟΡΟ

GYTHIO
ΓΥΘΕΙΟ

+3

+½

KITHERA
ΚΥΘΗΡΑ

SPETSES
ΣΠΕΤΣΕΣ

+1

HYDRA
ΥΔΡΑ

+5

CRETE (KASTELI)
ΚΡΙΤΙ (ΚΑΣΤΕΛΛΙ)

General Features

This 'Argo-Saronic' chapter encompasses ferry services to islands within the Saronic Gulf proper, as well as those running down the 'Argoid' or East Peloponnesian coast to Kithera and Crete. Ferries confine their runs within one of the two branches, the all-important linking services being provided by all too rare hydrofoils. The islands and ports also reflect this divide and range from among the most heavily touristed in Greece (within the Saronic Gulf, where the short distance to the capital provides a ready tourist and commuter market), to coastal hamlets further south that have fallen out of the ferry network and only see occasional hydrofoils.

Connections reach their nadir on Antikithera, the small island most poorly served by regular ferries in the Aegean. There is thus little middle ground between the two groups. Ports are either over-touristed with a veritable procession of landing-craft type ferries and hydrofoils running around (Aegina, Poros, Hydra and Spetses all qualify for this category thanks to their popularity as day-tripper and European package tour islands), or they can be almost too quiet for comfort (the Peloponnese and island of Kithera) relying on a couple of infrequent boats and an occasional long-range High Season hydrofoil. Aristotle and his golden mean clearly never found much favour in these parts.

If you like the idea of island hopping against a background of such extremes, then this route offers a happy mix of days when you can visit up to eight ports in 24 hours (if you feel mad enough to try it), and others when you have to wait as long for a ferry. One option definitely to be avoided are occasional tourist boats doing the 'three-island' day-cruise trips sometimes advertised in Athens tourist shops and travel agencies — taking in Aegina, Poros and Hydra. You can do these yourself over the course of a day for half the price (using hydrofoils and catamarans), and save even more using the local ferries.

1 Angistri
2 Methana
3 Souvala

4 Ag. Marina
5 Kosta
6 Porto Helio
7 Galatas

0   km   30

SARONIC GULF & EAST PELOPONNESE

Example Itinerary [2 Weeks]
The mix of over-touristed and relatively inaccessible ports of call offers an interesting holiday for those who like variety. Even so you will have to be prepared to compromise and adjust your schedule (particularly the latter part). Arrive on a favourable day and it is quite possible to get down the group (returning either via Crete and a direct boat back to Piraeus or by bus back up the Peloponnese). Otherwise you will have to skip a port.

Arrival/Departure Point
Athens is easily the best airport on offer. If you are offered a cheap flight to airports on either the Peloponnese or Crete, ignore the temptation; they are just too difficult to get back to in an emergency.

Season
If you are prepared to give it an extra week then this itinerary could be followed all year round or you could return via the Central Cyclades line. Otherwise the usual High Season advantages in terms of frequency of service apply.

1 Athens [2 Days]
An easy starting point and an easy first hop: all the boats start from the same quay at Piraeus and offer frequent starts for Aegina so you won't have to hang around for long.

2 Aegina [1 Day]
An interesting first port of call with enough to fill a day with sightseeing. But the inescapable evidence of mass tourism does little to nurture a get-away-from-it-all Greek island atmosphere. Accommodation can also be a problem in August, so if you are having real difficulty you could take an evening boat on down the line or alternatively, pick up an evening ferry to the neighbouring small beach island of Angistri.

3 Poros [1 Day]
The town itself can be done in a couple of hours but this does make a good base of operations if you prefer to 'do' the adjacent islands as

outings from one base. Mainland excursions to Mycenae and the famous theatre at Epidavros are possible from here too.

4 Spetses [2 Days]
The best beach island in the group and thus a good place to rest up for a couple of days. The mainland village of Kosta is also easily accessible, with buses to nearby tourist sites. Heading south from Spetses is the trickiest part of this itinerary. The most realistic options are either to hop to Kosta and use the mainland bus service to get to a southern Peloponnesian port, or to head back to Piraeus and pick up one of the rare ferries heading for Kithera.

5 Monemvassia [2 Days]
Monemvassia is visited by the rare hydrofoils heading for Kithera, but getting away again will be difficult unless you take a bus to Napoli and pick up the ferry from there.

6 Kithera [2 Days]
This quiet island offers a complete contrast with its northern Saronic sisters and is a worthy destination to aim for in its own right. That said, the first priority on arrival must be establishing when you can get off. If the wait for a boat on to Crete is too long you always have a boat to Gythio or Napoli on the Peloponnese (both offering bus links with Athens) as a safety option to fall back on. Alternatively, if you have tarried too long in the Saronic Gulf you can give the island a miss and head directly on to Crete.

7 Crete [2 Days]
Dumped on the eastern end of Crete you will have to get a bus from Kasteli to Chania and then another on to Iraklion. Here you can take time out to visit Knossos and the Archaeological Museum before taking the overnight boat back to Piraeus.

1 Athens [2 Days]
If you are planning to venture as far down this line as Crete you could do worse than skip a day in the capital at the beginning of your holiday to give you an extra day's safety at the end of your trip. Either way, as usual give yourself at least one clear day back in Athens before your return flight.

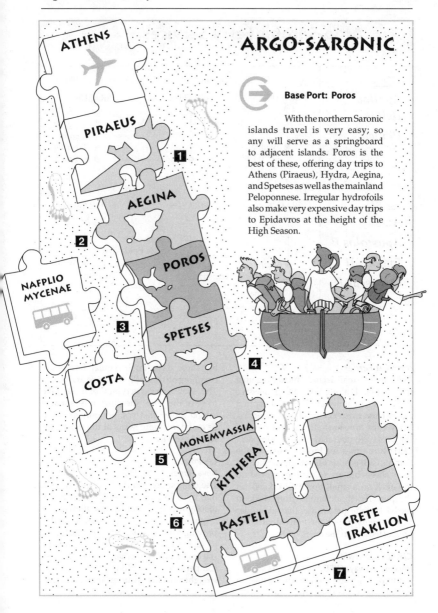

ARGO-SARONIC

Base Port: Poros

With the northern Saronic islands travel is very easy; so any will serve as a springboard to adjacent islands. Poros is the best of these, offering day trips to Athens (Piraeus), Hydra, Aegina, and Spetses as well as the mainland Peloponnese. Irregular hydrofoils also make very expensive day trips to Epidavros at the height of the High Season.

ATHENS

PIRAEUS

1

AEGINA

2

POROS

NAFPLIO MYCENAE

3

SPETSES

4

COSTA

MONEMVASSIA

5

KITHERA

6

KASTELI

CRETE IRAKLION

7

Argo-Saronic Ferry Services

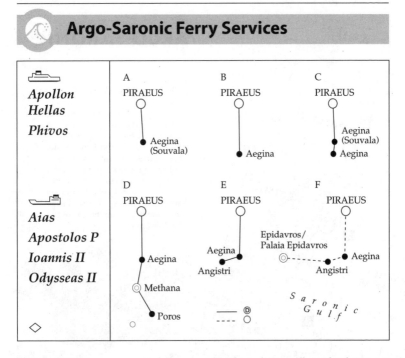

Main Car Ferries

The mix of small islands tucked against the mainland, along with either massive popularity or none at all, has conspired against the existence of large car ferries. Ferry runs are short affairs, and most of the boats are operated by one company. Departure times for Piraeus boats to the Saronic Gulf islands do not appear on EOT ferry sheets but are sometimes posted up in Greek on a small Port Police kiosk on the quay. Tickets are bought from kiosks at the back of the quay rather than at regular ticket agents (times for individual boats are posted up on these).

C/F *Apollon Hellas*

Hellenic Seaways / HFD; 1990; 1820 GRT.

Traditionally boats operating to the nearest islands have been landing-craft types, but these days small regular ferries are creaming off the traffic to Aegina and Paros. The *Apollon Hellas* is typical of these. Like most of the boats she offers a reasonable saloon (given that you are only going to be on board a few hours at the most) and reliable service.

C/F *Phivos*

Nova Ferries; 1989; 5287 GRT.

The biggest boat on the Piraeus—Aegina line by a long way, the *Phivos* is easily distinguished from the competition by her bright red hull. A speedy vessel, she is also proving to be very popular with the locals, to such an extent that other ferries have started to move elsewhere in search of less competitive waters. Most of her trips are straight runs to and from Aegina, though she can head on to Poros in Low Season.

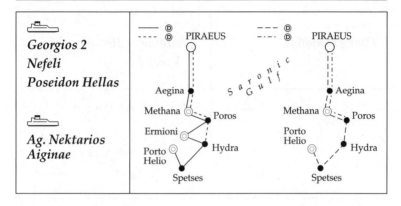

C/F *Aias* – C/F *Apostolos P*
C/F *Ioannis II* – C/F *Odysseas II*
Hellenic Seaways / HFD

These four landing-craft ferries operate in tandem. Each boat runs several times daily, with additional weekend sailings. The ferries are interchangeable, with little between them in terms of facilities — these are poor compared to larger ferries, but the journey time is short, so don't let this put you off. Most run a direct service to Aegina Town. Departures for Aegina (Souvala) are primarily for commercial vehicles. None of these boats heads further south than Poros.

In addition to landing-craft ferries, the Saronic Gulf is served by a number of small regular boats. Faster than the landing-craft types, they venture further down the line. At one time they competed against each other, but most now belong to one fleet and are frequently switched around.

C/F *Georgios 2*
Hellenic Seaways / HFD; 1990; 3438 GRT.

The largest of the small ferries on this route, the *Georgios 2* has been a mainstay here for over a decade. She is a pleasant enough craft and popular with the locals, in part because she operates all year round and has a larger saloon than her rivals. The only seriously chilling defect of note is her air conditioning, which is on the arctic side of cool.

C/F *Nefeli*
Hellenic Seaways / HFD; 1990; 2847 GRT.

Another long-standing stalwart on this route, this vessel is often deployed on a twice-daily Poros run. One of the mainstays of the northern Argo-Saronic line, she only ventures further south out of High Season.

C/F *Poseidon Hellas*
Hellenic Seaways / HFD; 1999; 2100 GRT.

A regular on the route for over a decade, this small ferry runs twice daily, to Aegina and Angistri, sometimes swapping itineraries with the *Apollon Hellas*. A boat that seems older than her years, she uses both bow and stern doors for embarkation.

C/F *Ag. Nektarios Aiginae*
Local; 1999; 1500 GRT.

Formerly the *Panagia Skiathou*, this small boat is a refugee from the Northern Sporades line, where she failed to compete successfully as a solo vessel. She has fared much better on the Aegina line. One of the newer boats running this service, her design (a sort of 'nautical Gothic') is a tad old-fashioned, and this could put some people off. Unusually for a ferry her bow name is in Greek rather than English.

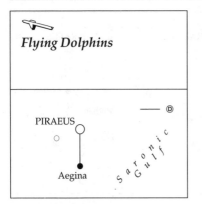

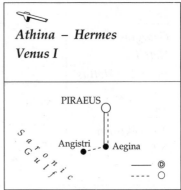

H/F *Flying Dolphin 10—20*
Hellenic Seaways / HFD

Because Aegina is close enough to be an off shore suburb of Athens, hydrofoils that call tend to be dedicated boats that just whizz back and forwards between the two destinations. These boats are very popular in the rush hours and at weekends, so it pays to book your return if it is going to coincide with these times.

H/Fs *Athina – Hermes – Venus I*
Aegean Flying Dolphins

A useful alternative to the Hellenic Seaways hydrofoils is offered by the three boats operated by Aegean Flying Dolphins. All run on the lucrative Aegina route, but some do continue on to Angistri in High Season half a dozen times a day. These boats make a good 'Plan B' if you find the more prominent alternatives booked up.

H/F *Dolphins I—IV*
Saronic Dolphins

The HFD hydrofoils have seen a number of competitors come and go on this route, with several operators trying their luck in recent years. The most recent is the Saronic Dolphins operation, running an hourly service to the resort of Agia Marina on Aegina. The limited popularity of the route has forced changes, with the addition of

Souvala, and latterly Poros and Hydra, to occasional itineraries. It is unclear if they will be around in 2012.

C/Ms *Saron Cat – Ydra Cat*

Long advertised at Piraeus, these two catamarans took years to appear and have been doing a 'now you see them, now you don't' act ever since. Their itineraries are equally problematic, with the advertised daily runs all the way down to Spetses often replaced with more mundane jaunts to Agia Marina on Aegina six or eight times daily. The net result of all this is that these are boats that are worth looking out for, but definitely not ones to build into the pre-planning stages of an island hopping holiday.

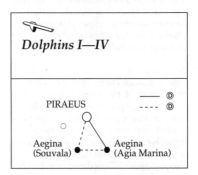

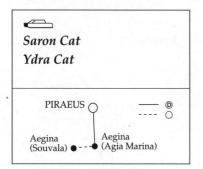

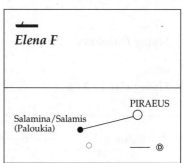

Small Passenger Boats

In addition to the regular ferries, hydrofoils and catamarans, a number of smaller passenger craft operate to the islands of Aegina, Angistri and Salamis. For the most part small vessels incapable of journeying far, they rely on commuters for their custom; each boat runs several times daily to its own set destination. Departures for the following 48 hours are usually posted up on the Saronic Gulf quay Port Police kiosk (they are listed separately at the end of the regular ferry departure times). Tickets for these boats are either bought on board or from mobile ticket 'desks' on the quayside. However, their popularity is on the wane—in part because of the economic slowdown, so some could well be missing in 2012. But they do offer a cheap way of visiting islands close to Athens.

Most likely to be of use is the **P/S Alexandros**, which provides a link with the resort of Agia Marina on Aegina. Note: these boats take at least double the hydrofoil journey time. Also of interest is the **P/S Elena F**, which is the biggest of the small boats running to Salamis.

A more popular and enjoyable means of venturing to Angistri is via a large caïque —the **T/B Angistri Express**—that runs four times daily in High Season from Aegina Town to the main Angistrian port at Skala and then Megalochorio (alias Milos). Decked out in a vivid sky blue with yellow trimmings, this caïque is pretty unmissable: she ties up on Aegina's waterfront near the marina and used to take on passengers here, but latterly she has chugged across the harbour to the ferry quay, and embarkation has proceeded there instead.

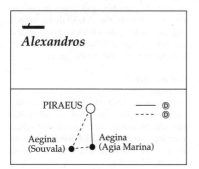

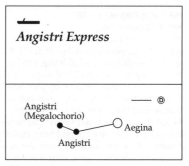

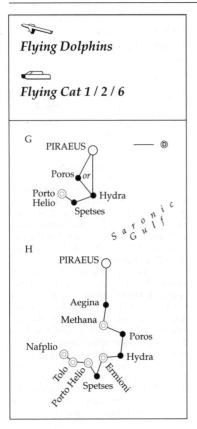

Flying Dolphins

Flying Cat 1 / 2 / 6

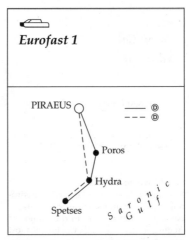

Eurofast 1

swim to nearby fishing boats. Despite this, it can pay to buy a return ticket: particularly for (1) the last hydrofoils from any given port, and (2) hydrofoils between Poros and Aegina, and Spetses and Poros, which are relatively few in number. Itinerary G is the most consistent of the routes run; most take in ports along H.

C/Ms *Flying Cat 1 / 2 / 6*
Hellenic Seaways / HFD

Operating alongside the hydrofoils are three popular catamarans, usually running itinerary G. Times are included in the hydrofoil timetable, and ticket prices are the same. This being so, take these boats if you can, as the ride is faster, smoother and quieter (though the *Flying Cat 2* is noisier than most cats) into the bargain.

C/M *Eurofast 1*
Euroseas

An occasional visitor hereabouts, this catamaran does the round-trip up and down the line mornings and afternoons when running — a useful addition to the options for those wanting to take a day trip from Athens to Spetses.

H/F *Flying Dolphin 1—30*
Hellenic Seaways / HFD

Hydrofoils are the most versatile and quickest way of hopping around the Saronic Gulf, so much so that some islands (e.g. Hydra) largely depend on them. They are popular and easy to use, and usually keep good time (the protected Saronic Gulf waters ensure that most of these services run reasonably to schedule). This is not to say that they haven't had their share of problems. In the summer of 2000 one caught fire off Aegina, forcing all on board to jump into the sea and

C/F *Vitsentzos Kornaros*
LANE Lines; 1976; 9735 GRT.

One of the few subsidized ferry routes left in Greece runs down the Peloponnese to Kithera and on to Crete. In its early years the boats on it called at all the small ports on the Peloponnesian coast. However, these have now been dropped from the schedules, and departures have fallen to one or two a week. The main vessel providing the link for the last two years has been the elderly *Vitsentzos Kornaros*. A passable enough boat, she was once a mainstay of the southern Dodecanese service between Rhodes and Crete. In 2011 this ferry restored the service to Monemvassia, which had been without ferry links for several years.

C/F *Porfyrousa*

This small ferry (with a distinctive superstructure at her bow) maintains a daily link between Kithera and the mainland port of Neapoli. Very much a lifeline service, she provides an occasional link to Antikithera, and has been known to venture to both Gythio and Crete (Kasteli) when the ferry running the *Vitsentzos Kornaros* route has had problems.

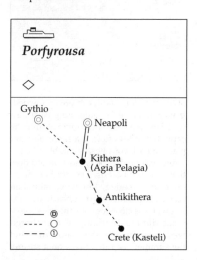

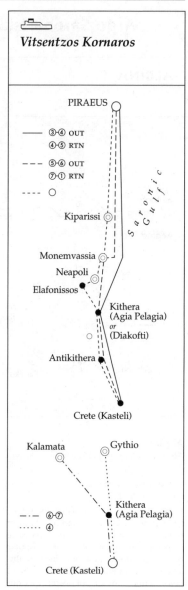

Argo-Saronic Islands & Ports

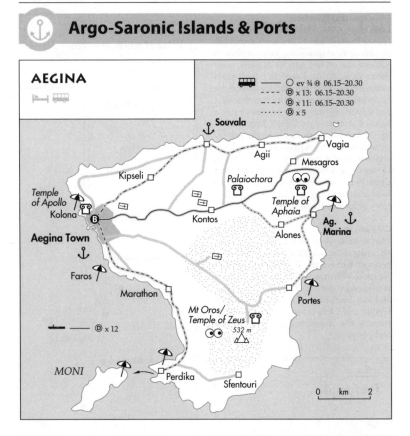

AEGINA

◯ ev ¾ ⊗ 06.15–20.30
---- Ⓓ x 13: 06.15–20.30
–·– Ⓓ x 11: 06.15–20.30
······ Ⓓ x 5

Souvala

Vagia

Agii

Mesagros

Kipseli

Palaiochora

Temple of Apollo
Kolona

Temple of Aphaia

Aegina Town

Kontos

Ag. Marina

Alones

Faros

Marathon

Portes

Mt Oros/
Temple of Zeus

532 m

Ⓓ x 12

MONI

Perdika

Sfentouri

0   km   2

Aegina

ΑΙΓΙΝΑ; 84 km²; pop. 10,000.

CODE ☎ 22970
TOURIST POLICE ☎ 23243
FIRST AID ☎ 22222

Lying a mere 20 km south of Piraeus, Aegina (pronounced 'Ee–genah') is among the most touristed of the Greek islands. Its close proximity to Athens makes it a popular day tripper destination (and incidentally, an ideal spot in which to fill a day in hand before a flight home), but despite this, out of August it is not noticeably overcrowded. If you don't mind commuting each day, the island is a viable base for exploring the capital, besides offering a more pleasant place to park your head at night.

Aegina's landscape is more varied than that of many islands. The northern third offers up wooded, low-lying mountain scenery and plenty of sandy beach coves for — given the closeness of Athens — somewhat dubious bathing. The sheltered west coast is particularly attractive, and the summer sea often takes on a steamy turquoise hue rarely seen elsewhere in the Aegean. Behind the shore the large west-coast plain is home to pistachio orchards by the score. Aegina is the pistachio nut capital of Greece, and it is difficult to forget it — given that the fronts of every tourist shop (and a good few others) are almost always hidden behind stacked bags of the little things. The southern part of the island is dominated by the impressive bulk of Mt. Oros and is something of a settle-ment-free zone.

The island's capital at **Aegina Town** was briefly more than just a nut capital; between 1826–28 it was actually the capital of the then only partially liberated Greece. Echoes of this heritage can be seen in the neo-clas-sical buildings that line a waterfront that is slightly marred by an often over-busy road. Remnants of the town's period as the ancient capital of Aegina are also visible in places, the most notable survival being the temple column standing on the lightly wooded headland — known as Kolona in consequence — just north of the port.

The town is the island's only settlement of any significant size, and is home to almost three-quarters of the population. Inevitably the waterfront is the focus for most of the visitor activity and it is lined with the usual collection of tavernas and tourist shops. The day tripper influence is very visible, with horses and carriages standing on the promenade awaiting a fare from the hordes disembarking onto the nearby ferry quay. The street running one block behind the waterfront has been pedestrianized and houses the souvenir shop overspill. But once you move further inland Aegina Town reveals itself to be surprisingly unspoilt, surrounded by nut orchards and pine trees.

To the south of the ferry quay, at the site of the ancient commercial harbour, you will find full-to-overflowing caïques selling fruit and vegetables, with a fresh fish market housed in a quayside alley opposite. To the north, just past a group of good — and therefore popular — waterfront tavernas

lies the sandy town beach. It runs inside the remains of the ancient city's trireme harbour. This was famous in the ancient world, though its name — it was known as the 'hidden harbour' — has caused more than one scholar to scratch their head because it isn't, well, exactly 'hidden', even after two and a half thousand years.

Along the beach road lie a bus ticket kiosk and several budget hotels. Ferry tickets are obtained from kiosks (often only staffed half an hour before the ferry is due to depart) next to the ferry quay. It is worth noting that if you are planning to return to Athens via a late afternoon/evening service — particularly at weekends — you should buy your ticket on arrival as boats tend to get booked solid by day-tripping Athenians who regularly flock to Aegina in search of a good 'local' beach.

Aegina's bus service is limited but good, running frequently along the northern coast and across the island to Agia Marina. Services heading south are far fewer, but this needn't be a handicap, for Aegina is ideally suited to gentle walking thanks to its relatively small size and the scenic landscape. Outside July and August, when temperatures are too high, a walk across the island taking in the Temple of Aphaia makes a great day trip. Given that Aegina has three ports, all with good links to Piraeus, it is quite feasible to arrive via one port and return to the captial from another.

Aegina's two other ports see at least four services a day running to and from Piraeus. The biggest after Aegina Town is at the island's second resort at **Agia Marina**. It is visited by both small passenger boats and hydrofoils (car ferry activity is now a thing of the past). This is because it is an unabashed package tour resort with all the trimmings (albeit one on a rather small scale). Even so, as far as disco-cities on the sand go it is better than most. Ironically, its main limitation is its beach: for most of its length it is without a beach road, so hotels have been built right up to the narrow strip of sand, leading to extremely overcrowded

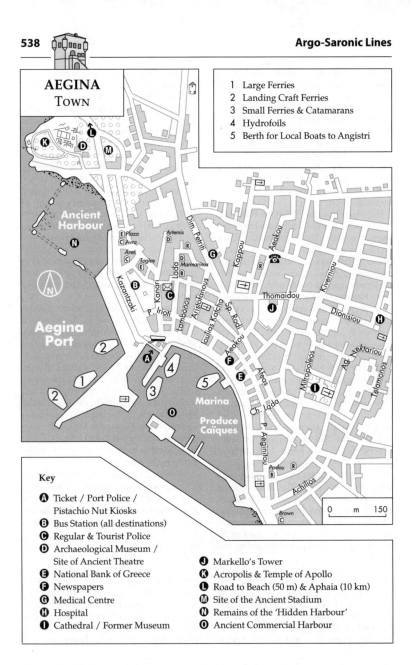

AEGINA
TOWN

1 Large Ferries
2 Landing Craft Ferries
3 Small Ferries & Catamarans
4 Hydrofoils
5 Berth for Local Boats to Angistri

Ancient Harbour

Aegina Port

Marina

Produce Caïques

Plaza
Avra
Artemis
Areti
Toglas
Marmarinos
Dim. Petriti
Aeakou
Kappou
Thomaidou
Dionisiou
Kazantzaki
P. Irioti
Kanari
Lada
Lambonos
Aristofanous
Ioulias Katcha
Sp. Rodi
Aeakou
Aleas
Ch. Lada
Mitropoleos
Ag. Nektariou
Kivemiou
Telamonos
P. Aeginitou
Achilios
Pavlou
Brown

0   m   150

Key

A Ticket / Port Police / Pistachio Nut Kiosks
B Bus Station (all destinations)
C Regular & Tourist Police
D Archaeological Museum / Site of Ancient Theatre
E National Bank of Greece
F Newspapers
G Medical Centre
H Hospital
I Cathedral / Former Museum
J Markello's Tower
K Acropolis & Temple of Apollo
L Road to Beach (50 m) & Aphaia (10 km)
M Site of the Ancient Stadium
N Remains of the 'Hidden Harbour'
O Ancient Commercial Harbour

and claustrophobic bathing. If nightlife is a priority then Agia Marina will appeal; otherwise the walk up the pine-forested hill to the Temple of Aphaia is likely to be of greater interest (the 2 km path looks to have been made by a runaway bulldozer).

The third of Aegina's ports, **Souvala**, is a tiny resort village with a reasonable beach and a large quay (adorned with landing-craft ferries that are used by lorries unwilling to negotiate the streets of Aegina Town). In truth it doesn't have much tourist appeal — though the taverna-lined waterfront is pretty enough — and most of the traffic at the port is commercial: Souvala is the gateway by which Aegina is resupplied by lorry. Foot passengers are usually conspicuous by their absence.

Other coastal villages are less developed, but gradually seeing a greater percentage of the tourist hordes, or failing this, have become villa-filled suburbs for the more affluent Athenians. The small fishing port of **Perdika** on the south-west coast is the most attractive, and surprisingly unspoilt, with some rooms on offer. The village straddles a small headland and offers both good tavernas and a very relaxed atmosphere. Just off shore is the uninhabited hilly pine-clad islet of **Moni**. As the name implies, the islet was once owned by one of Aegina's monasteries (though in fact the name means 'convent'). Today it is an official nature reserve and is home to a population of the rare kri-kri goat and some diminutive horses. There is also a cave favoured by turtles on the south coast. Moni can be visited by day-tripper boats from Perdika. Visitors are prohibited from staying overnight, though in times past the islet boasted a campsite.

Until just after 1800 Aegina's inhabitants were careful to live inland to protect themselves from all too frequent attacks. Given this, it is surprising that today the island has no major inland settlements. The biggest is the village of **Kontos**, which thrives on farming, olives and wine being the unsurprising products.

Not far from Kontos is the site of the island's now deserted medieval capital at **Palaiochora**. Cannily positioned on one of the few hillsides which cannot be seen from the sea, Palaiochora was the capital of Aegina for almost a millennium. When increasing pirate raids forced the islanders to move away from the coast they opted to resettle the site of an important ancient shrine known as Oie. After fortifying the top of the sanctuary mount they built a new town (using local stones that blended in with the hillside) around its slopes. Today only the main streets and the town's churches remain — all 36 of them. The result is a quaint church-speckled hillside that would make a fantastic excursion if they weren't all locked.

Most of Aegina's hotels are pre-booked by tour operators or inconveniently placed. In town there are plenty of mid-price-range options. The best of these are: the *Brown* (☎ 22271) at the south end of the town, along with the hotels north of the port: the *Marmarinos* (☎ 23510) just has the edge, though there is little between the *Plaza* (☎ 25600), *Avra* (☎ 22303), *Artemis* (☎ 25195) and the budget *Togias* (☎ 24242). Those looking for something a little different should try the *Pension Pavlou* (☎ 22795), which offers pricey, but atmospheric, rooms in an old town house. Being so close to Athens, Aegina sees regular rooms fill up very quickly in High Season, so arrive early.

Aegina has had a very up-and-down history, with occasional moments at the centre stage of Greek history interlaced with periods of total depopulation. Strategically placed at the top of the Saronic Gulf, Aegina was populated on and off from the Stone Age on. The first major incursion came with the Mycenaeans who took control c. 1400 BC. A gap in the archaeological record suggests the island was abandoned for several centuries during the Greek dark ages, but by 900 BC it had been repopulated. This was the start of a prolonged period of development that resulted in the island emerging as a serious maritime power in the 7 C. BC, also gaining a reputation for bronze working and pottery production. Growing wealth was reflected

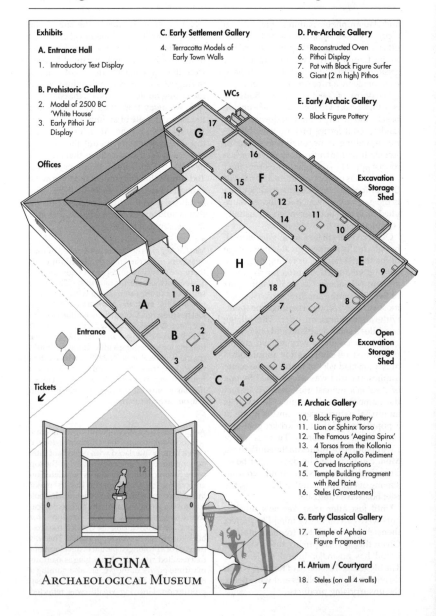

Exhibits

A. Entrance Hall

1. Introductory Text Display

B. Prehistoric Gallery

2. Model of 2500 BC 'White House'
3. Early Pithoi Jar Display

Offices

C. Early Settlement Gallery

4. Terracotta Models of Early Town Walls

WCs

D. Pre-Archaic Gallery

5. Reconstructed Oven
6. Pithoi Display
7. Pot with Black Figure Surfer
8. Giant (2 m high) Pithos

E. Early Archaic Gallery

9. Black Figure Pottery

Excavation Storage Shed

Open Excavation Storage Shed

Entrance

Tickets

F. Archaic Gallery

10. Black Figure Pottery
11. Lion or Sphinx Torso
12. The Famous 'Aegina Spinx'
13. 4 Torsos from the Kollonia Temple of Apollo Pediment
14. Carved Inscriptions
15. Temple Building Fragment with Red Paint
16. Steles (Gravestones)

G. Early Classical Gallery

17. Temple of Aphaia Figure Fragments

H. Atrium / Courtyard

18. Steles (on all 4 walls)

AEGINA
ARCHAEOLOGICAL MUSEUM

in the introduction of the first coinage in the Greek world. As Aegina's merchant fleet expanded so did her ability to fund and man a large trireme fleet: the island was the second largest contributor of ships after Athens at the Battle of Salamis in 480 BC.

However, the close proximity to Athens proved to be Aegina's downfall. Having such a powerful rival so close was too much for the Athenians to live with, and in a succession of conflicts Aegina's military power was gradually eroded. One of the opening moves of the Peloponnesian War saw Athens move in and expel the entire population. Following Athens' defeat in 404 BC, victorious Sparta allowed the survivors to return to Aegina, but thereafter the island was never a significant player.

From this point on Aegina's history was tied to that of Athens, only really parting company following the Latin takeover of the Aegean islands in 1204–07. The island was ruled by Catalan and Venetian families by turn, before being sacked — and the inhabitants enslaved — by the pirate Barbarossa in 1537. It was repopulated with Albanians before returning to Venetian control between 1654–1718. During the Greek independence struggle Aegina was the capital between 1826–28. This resulted in an influx of refugees from Psara and Chios, and saw the first coins of the new state minted in Aegina Town.

👀

Aegina offers up a busy day of sightseeing—so if you are day-tripping from Athens there is a lot to be said for arriving on a very early boat. There are three major attractions (listed in order of convenience rather than merit):

1. The Archaeological Museum
2. The Temple of Apollo
3. The Temple of Aphaia.

In addition there are a few 'smaller' sights that might grab your fancy. The first is easily accessible as it lies just a few blocks back from the waterfront: the oddly turreted **Markello's Tower** (also sometimes known as the 'Pink Tower' thanks to its pastel coloured stonework) is something of a mystery. The structure — complete with small circular corner turrets (known as 'bartizans') that have arrow slits angled to fire on unfortunates close to the walls — would appear to have been built c. 1400, during the period of Latin rule, but virtually nothing is known of its history. It presumably was abandoned when the population of

Aegina Town fled to safer Palaiochora some time after, only to be refurbished in 1802, when it became the office-cum-home of Greece's first governor. Sadly, this curiously cute structure is only open to visitors when it plays home to art exhibitions in its tiny ground-floor room.

In addition to the two temples already mentioned, Aegina also has a third major temple of interest — the **Temple of Zeus** on the peak of Mount Oros. Those making the donkey-path ascent will find that only the foundations survive, though the setting more than makes up for this. The final site of note is the monastery of **St. Catherine** on the road east of Aegina Town. It lies west of the abandoned former hill capital of **Palaiochora** on the site of a Temple of Aphrodite.

The Archaeological Museum

An easy walk from the ferry quay, Aegina's Archaeological Museum (open ⊛ ex ① 08.30–15.00) is one of the more successful in the Greek islands. Built in the form of a large Hellenistic house around a central atrium planted with orange trees, it stands at the entrance to the Kolona temple site (there is a joint entry charge of €3 — tickets from a kiosk at the site entrance just off the beach). The museum's exhibits are thoughtfully laid out, with the star attraction, the famous 6 c. BC 'Aegina Sphinx', carefully placed in a gallery directly opposite the main door. Stand in front of the museum entrance and you will spot it, framed through three sets of doorways.

Refurbished a few years ago, most of the museum's exhibits have explanatory texts in English and German (the latter because most of the 19 c. excavating on Aegina was undertaken by German archaeologists). Quite a lot of effort has gone into trying to explain the story of the Kolona settlement, though some exhibits aren't over-successful: a series of terracotta models of houses and walls at different periods are displayed so far apart from each other that comparison is impossible. Notable by their absence are displays of coins, metal objects or jewellery, but there is some good stuff here, notably a 2 m high pithos jar from c. 1900–1800 BC., and a pot sherd of similar vintage that appears to show a Rastafarian beach boy complete with surfboard.

The Temple of Apollo

Standing on a low headland just behind the Archaeological Museum is the crumbling lone column of a **Temple of Apollo**. It stands as a marker indicating the site of Aegina's ancient acropolis on the northern edge of the town. The walls were partially demolished by the Athenians. This, coupled with subsequent excavations aimed at exploring prehistoric settlement levels, has left the site a mass of jumbled foundations that aren't particularly intelligible, though they are still quite fun to walk around. Even the position of the temple and how the surviving column related to it would be ambiguous without the explanatory notice boards. It is certainly hard to believe that the structure once resembled the temple of Aphaia. The lone column is vaguely reminiscent of a withered finger, as severe weathering over the years has taken a heavy toll. Complete until 1765, when the upper half collapsed, it had a companion until 1802, when a second column alongside was toppled in a storm.

The Temple of Aphaia

Aegina's major tourist draw is the 5 c. BC **Temple of Aphaia** (⊕ 08.00–15.00/17.00: tickets €4). Named after a minor daughter goddess of Zeus, it is set atop a pine-tree-clad hill 10 km from Aegina Town, and is most easily visited by bus: the majority of services between Aegina Town and Agia Marina make the short detour to Aphaia. If you are starting from the town then you can buy both outward and return tickets from a kiosk at the bus station.

The temple is one of the best preserved in Greece, with a unique 2-storey inner colonnade (it is one of the few to retain any of its interior columns). Its appeal is enhanced by its relatively small size, being more approachable and less grandiose than the later temples that adorn Athens. Built around 490 BC, it reflects the transition between the Late Archaic and Classical traditions. The terrace setting with its views and lightning mast (one set of gable sculptures in Classical times and the western end seem to have been demolished by lightning strikes — the last in 1969) also helps to give the site a character all its own.

Given the high quality of preservation of the temple it won't come as a surprise to find that the pedimental sculptures are also well preserved. Too well preserved in fact: when the temple was excavated in 1811 by German archaeologists the sculpture uncovered excited so much attention that King Ludwig I of Bavaria, eager to acquire his own 'Elgin Marbles', had 17 figures shipped to Munich,

where they remain. Carved from the finest Parian marble, they were part of two scenes from the Trojan War. Figures from two earlier scenes that adorned the pediments were discovered in later excavations and these are now on display in Athens and Aegina (see below). It isn't clear why the figures were changed.

One rather disconcerting piece of information that will appeal to passing supernaturalists: Greece might be a long way from the Bermuda Triangle, but it does have an Aegean one. It is a faintly spooky fact that the Temple of Aphaia, the Parthenon in Athens and the Temple of Poseidon at Sounion sit at the points of a near perfect equilateral triangle. This is probably a coincidence given that all three buildings are sited on natural high points and it would be difficult to reposition any of them without damaging their settings, but is still a bit uncanny. The temple at Aphaia is the only one of the three from which it is possible to see the other two (at least you could in the good old days before Athenian smog and summer haze conspired to make this more an ambition than a practical reality). None the less, the views of the mainland from the temple precinct are still superb.

Down the hillside to the west of the temple precinct stands a small site museum grandly called the **Aphaia Archaeological Museum**. Considering that 80% of the pedimental sculptures are in Germany, with the bulk of the rest divided between the National Archaeological Museum in Athens and the island's Archaeological Museum at Kolona, it is a wonder that the site museum has anything in it at all. The exhibits are thinly spread, to be sure, but the building is worth exploring. There are three halls: the first has a display outlining the evolution of the site, backed up with a finely crafted wooden model of the temple precinct. The second hall has reconstructions of the pediments (complete with casts of the figures — only one on display is genuine). Its western end is open, revealing the floor below, and this double-storey area houses a pediment from the earlier (570 BC) Aphaia temple, and the reconstructed Archaic column that originally was topped by a sculptured sphinx and stood on the north-east corner of the terrace. The basement hall is devoted to fragments of the earlier temple and a model of it. The fragments were buried under the extended precinct when the later temple was built: many still retain traces of their paintwork.

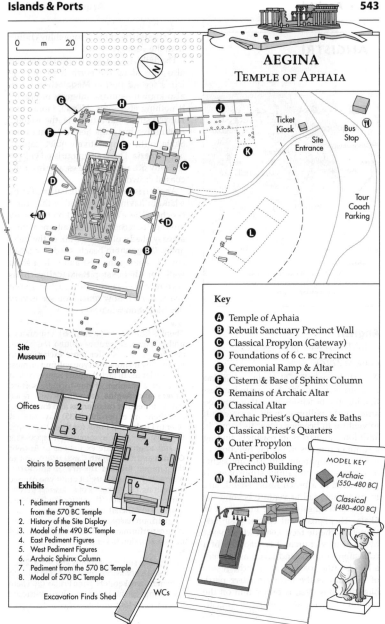

AEGINA
TEMPLE OF APHAIA

0 m 20

N

Ticket Kiosk

Bus Stop

Site Entrance

Tour Coach Parking

Site Museum

Entrance

Offices

Stairs to Basement Level

Exhibits

1. Pediment Fragments from the 570 BC Temple
2. History of the Site Display
3. Model of the 490 BC Temple
4. East Pediment Figures
5. West Pediment Figures
6. Archaic Sphinx Column
7. Pediment from the 570 BC Temple
8. Model of 570 BC Temple

Excavation Finds Shed

WCs

Key

Ⓐ Temple of Aphaia
Ⓑ Rebuilt Sanctuary Precinct Wall
Ⓒ Classical Propylon (Gateway)
Ⓓ Foundations of 6 C. BC Precinct
Ⓔ Ceremonial Ramp & Altar
Ⓕ Cistern & Base of Sphinx Column
Ⓖ Remains of Archaic Altar
Ⓗ Classical Altar
Ⓘ Archaic Priest's Quarters & Baths
Ⓙ Classical Priest's Quarters
Ⓚ Outer Propylon
Ⓛ Anti-peribolos (Precinct) Building
Ⓜ Mainland Views

MODEL KEY

Archaic (550–480 BC)

Classical (480–400 BC)

The P/S *Fourni Express*
Departs from Fourni
Village Beach

CHIOS
Town Waterfront

SAMOS
The Roman Catholic
Church on Vathi
Waterfront

Northern Coast east of
Karlovassi

Eastern Lines

FOURNI
Village Beach

Northern Aegean

SKOPELOS
Panagia ston Pirgho
at Skopelos Town

ALONISSOS
Alonissos' Beach Boats
in Patitiri Bay

THASSOS
View of Thassos Town
from the Acropolis

Ionian

KEFALONIA
Sami Beach & Tide Mill
Wheel

CORFU/KERKYRA
Old Town & Palace Wall
Staircase

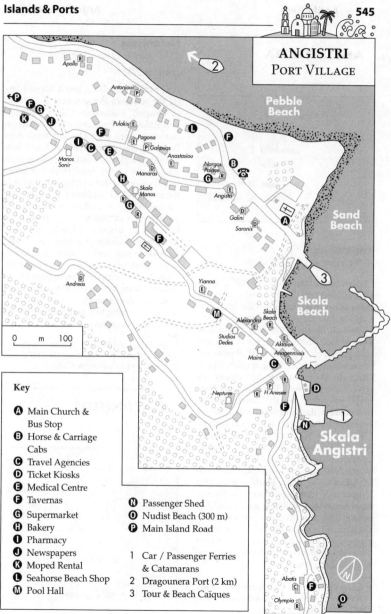

ANGISTRI
Port Village

Key

A Main Church & Bus Stop
B Horse & Carriage Cabs
C Travel Agencies
D Ticket Kiosks
E Medical Centre
F Tavernas
G Supermarket
H Bakery
I Pharmacy
J Newspapers
K Moped Rental
L Seahorse Beach Shop
M Pool Hall
N Passenger Shed
O Nudist Beach (300 m)
P Main Island Road

1 Car / Passenger Ferries & Catamarans
2 Dragounera Port (2 km)
3 Tour & Beach Caïques

ANTIKITHERA

Potamos

0   km   4

Galaniana

No bus service

No beach boat service

Antikithera

ΑΝΤΙΚΥΘΗΡΑ; 29 km²; pop. 115.

Occupying the straits between the Peloponnese and western Crete, this island is a dry mountain-top poking out of the sea that is likely to appeal only to extreme get-away-from-it-all fanatics. The tiny population lives in two dusty hamlets and sees few strangers. The oppressive air of isolation is encouraging the younger islanders to emigrate, so those that do remain see fewer friends as well. The only school has under ten pupils, and the island struggles to maintain the bare essentials (the vet hereabouts doubles up as the local doctor).

These days Antikithera is best known for its shipwrecks, one of which yielded up the bronze Ephebe of Antikithera now in the National Archaeological Museum in Athens. The Elgin Marbles were also temporarily sunk here en route to Britain. Most ferries steer well clear, and out of High Season links are reduced to one a week, so the island is inaccessible for all practicable purposes. If you want a quick look you can visit via a ferry en route to Crete, returning north 6 hours later.

It is not that much of an exaggeration to say 'Take a room here and you will double your host's annual income!'

Elafonissos

ΕΛΑΦΟΝΗΣΙ; 19 km²; pop. 270.

CODE ☎ 27340

An attractive, isolated beach island lying off the southern Peloponnese coast town of Neapoli, Elafonissos ('deer's island') was linked to the mainland by a narrow causeway until 1677. The only settlement lies at the site of this divide: a church now standing in glorious isolation (along with Elafonissos's only tree) from the other buildings on a spit of land tapering towards the mainland. Elafonissos town is a pretty fishing village that offers an ideal base if your notion of getting away from it all includes an absence of banks and other tourists. In addition, the island is blessed with clean seas and a superb sand beach 4 km south of the village (accessible via an irregular boat). Caïques augment ferry links, running to Neapoli (30 minutes east). There is also a landing-craft mainland service operating to a track running off the Neapoli—Peloponnese road.

Some rooms and 2 B-class pensions in the village: the *Asteri Tis Elafonissou* (☎ 61271) and the cheaper *Elafonissos* (☎ 61268).

ELAFONISSOS

Ⓓ x 2

0   km   4

Elafonissos

276 m

Sarakiniko

Levki Bay

No bus service

Ⓓ 10.00–16.00

Epidavros
ΕΠΙΔΑΥΡΟΣ

The name 'Epidavros' is applied to three closely related places. On ferry timetables (on the rare occasions that it appears) it refers to the small Peloponnesian port of **Palea Epidavros** — host to three campsites, a dozen hotels, a beach and the scanty remains of an ancient city. Some 6 km up the coast is the second destination to be graced by the name: **Nea Epidavros** — an attractive hamlet backed by orange groves. Finally, there is **Ancient Epidavros** — the famous sanctuary to the god of healing, Asklepios, and now one of Greece's premier archaeological sites thanks to its ancient theatre, easily the finest example ever built, and by marvellous good fortune also the best preserved. Buses run to the site daily from

EPIDAVROS
ANCIENT SANCTUARY

Key

- **Ⓐ** Theatre
- **Ⓑ** Gymnasium
- **Ⓒ** Temple of Asklepios
- **Ⓓ** Tholos
- **Ⓔ** Stadium
- **Ⓕ** Katagogion (160-room hotel)
- **Ⓖ** Portico of Kotys / Palaestra
- **Ⓗ** Abaton (dormitory for the sick)
- **Ⓘ** Temple of Artemis
- **Ⓙ** Temple of Themis
- **Ⓚ** Sanctuary of the Egyptian Gods
- **Ⓛ** Greek Baths
- **Ⓜ** Roman Baths
- **Ⓝ** Roman Houses
- **Ⓞ** Roman Odeon
- **Ⓟ** North Hall
- **Ⓠ** Fountain House
- **Ⓡ** Path to the Propylaea (gateway)

Main Path
Minor Path

ARISTOPHANES
THE BIRDS

ACT 3

ENTER
PEISTHETAIROS ...

Museum

Tickets

Coach Park

Road to
Palaia Epidavros

Modern productions of ancient plays at Epidavros are popular. However, don't come here expecting to see an accurate recreation. In Classical times the all-male cast donned terracotta masks, and in comedies such as The Birds, players wore tights with heavily padded buttocks and an over-long leather phallus that could be waved around to great comic effect. The bordering-on-crude nature of Old Attic Comedy accounts for the ambivalent attitude of the more conservative modern Greeks. As fine literature they laud the plays, but an excess of reality is rarely encouraged.

5 c. BC Comic Actor
in costume

0   m   75

Athens and from Palea Epidavros, 15 km away (taxis also run direct). Neighbouring Nafplio also has a bus service, and regular tours—some including performances at the theatre—are available from nearby islands such as Angistri, Aegina and Poros.

👀

Set among the attractive rolling wooded slopes of Mt. Kynortion, Ancient Epidavros (open ②–⑦ 08.30–15.00; tickets €3) was an important sanctuary to the healing god Asklepios (of staff and serpent fame). Although it didn't rank as highly as its counterpart on Kos, easier accessibility ensured that it became very affluent — a fact reflected in the quality of its buildings. By the end of the Ancient period it was just as rich as its rival, in part because the medical alternatives weren't up to much at the time.

The site was home to what was popularly considered the greatest **Theatre** in the Greek world thanks to its unrivalled symmetry, beauty and perfect acoustics, and by a remarkable stroke of luck it is almost perfectly preserved (though the stage buildings have gone). With seating for 14,000, the theatre was also one of the biggest in the Greek world and is a sightseeing must. In July and August it is home to the annual Epidavros festival, hosting performances of classical plays— *The Birds* of Aristophanes being a favourite. Tickets can be bought from various outlets in Athens so you don't need to come in advance to buy them. If you get the chance to go to a performance then take it as there is no guarantee that they will continue long into the future. Archaeologists are expressing worries over the damage being inflicted on the original stone seating by tourists attending performances, with high heels and chewing gum causing the most damage.

If hosting the best theatre wasn't enough, Epidavros was also the home of a **Tholos** (a circular pillared hall) that was deemed by many of its contemporaries to be simply the most beautiful Greek building ever erected — full stop. Sadly, the tholos (which housed a medicinal snake pit) is now nothing more than foundations and a few decorative fragments. Both these circular structures were built by the famed architect Polykleitos, c. 350 BC.

Contrasting vividly with the extant theatre are the other buildings on the site, which consist only of foundations. Only fragments

(now housed in the site **Museum**) survive of the famous, highly decorated, colonnaded tholos, but these (coupled with the description by Pausanias, who recorded that it was decorated with paintings by Pausias) are sufficient to give us a good idea of its form.

Other ghostly remnants of note are those of the **Stadium** (the sanctuary hosted its own games), a small **Temple of Asklepios** and an impressively large 4-quad **Katagogion** (a hotel that had 160 sleeping cells).

Gythio
ΓΥΘΕΙΟ; pop. 4,950.

CODE ☎ 27330
PORT POLICE ☎ 22262
TOURIST POLICE ☎ 27310 28701
POLICE ☎ 22271

The most important town strung along the south coast of the Peloponnese, Gythio offers an attractive Venetian house-fronted promenade, decked out with a number of reasonable fish restaurants and set close against the green foothills of Mount Laryssion. A good base for exploring the region, it is a pretty — if somewhat over-touristed — port with quite a history. Sparta's naval base during the Peloponnesian War, it was attacked and sacked by the Athenian navy in 455 BC (relations are now on a friendlier footing, with 4 buses running daily between the two — via Sparta). During the Roman era the town became an important production centre for murex — the imperial purple dye — extracted from sea molluscs by a method now lost. Most of ancient Gythio is now equally invisible: the only survival of note is a small theatre 400 m north of the current town. Ferry links are also rather poor as Gythio lies tucked 2–3 hours' steaming up the Gulf of Lakonia. Along with the odd tourist boat, they combine to provide an almost daily service to Kithera and its links with the outside world.

🛏

There are a dozen or more hotels in Gythio, but they tend to be comparatively expensive: this is up-market package tour country. The cheapest are the waterfront D-class *Akaion* (☎ 22294) and *Kranae* (☎ 22249). Fortunately rooms are on offer and well signposted around the harbour area of the town.

Å

Several olive-grove sites lie just off a good beach 5 km south of the town. Buses run hourly past the camping strip, though the sites rely on trailer-campers rather than backpackers.

GG

The main sight lies just to the south of the promenade: the small causeway-linked islet of **Marathonisi** (ancient Kranai). Famed in antiquity as the spot where Paris spent his first night with Helen (whose face launched the first thousand Greek ferries) while carrying her off to Troy, the islet attracted the curious from the first, prompting the erection of a Hellenistic temple of Aphrodite and a number of other shrines. As late as 1770, garbled tales of the Jolly Roger prompted the islet's Turkish masters in faraway İstanbul to sanction the building of a fortress tower (newly restored) to keep non-existent local brigands in hand. Apart from this construction, a couple of chapels, and a suitably phallic modern lighthouse, Marathonisi has no other buildings but is disappointingly covered in shrubby trees and hosts an annual summer pan-Hellenic mosquito convention so large that one wonders if any mortal has ever managed an untroubled night's sleep here.

Hydra

ΥΔΡΑ; 52 km²; pop. 3,000.

CODE ☎ 22980
PORT POLICE ☎ 52279
TOURIST POLICE ☎ 52205

A hilltop sticking out of the Aegean lacking roads or beaches, Hydra (pronounced '*EE-dra*') has overcome the disadvantages of a generally dour appearance to become one of the most touristed spots in Greece. This is due to a combination of a very attractive fortified harbour town and the close proximity of Athens (making it a perfect day-tripper island). Sadly, the numbers calling have turned the place into a tourist trap and the island is now arguably one of the least idyllic in the whole Aegean, with a constant procession of hydrofoils and tour-boats bringing in the crowds and encouraging the most expensive island prices in Greece.

Apart from the town, with its harbour walls adorned with cannon, Hydra has little to offer. Decked with steep hill paths and a scattering of monasteries, and with a car and motorbike ban, it is often touted as a

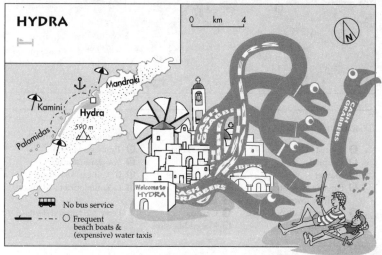

HYDRA

0   km   4

Mandraki

Kamini

Hydra

590 m

Palamidas

Welcome to HYDRA

🚌 No bus service

━━━ ┄┄┄ ○ Frequent beach boats & (expensive) water taxis

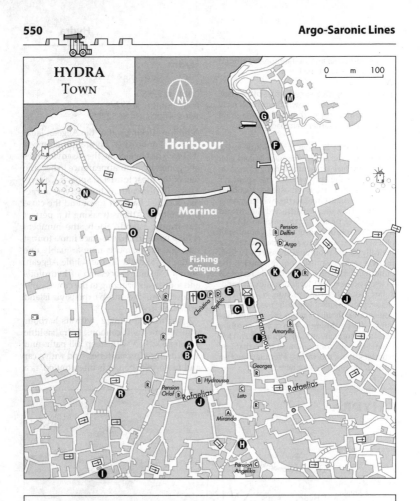

HYDRA TOWN

Harbour

Marina

Fishing Caïques

Pension Delfini

Argo

Christina
Sophia
Ekonomou
Amaryllis
Georges
Hydroussa
Pension Orlof
Rafaelias
Leto
Rafaelias
Miranda
Pension Angelika

1 Ferry / Hydrofoil Berth
2 Taxi Boats

Key

Ⓐ Tourist Police
Ⓑ Hospital
Ⓒ Market
Ⓓ Panagia Monastery / Clock Tower
Ⓔ National Bank of Greece
Ⓕ Museum
Ⓖ Old Arsenal / Port Police
Ⓗ Doctor
Ⓘ Supermarket
Ⓙ Pharmacy
Ⓚ Bakery
Ⓛ Cinema
Ⓜ Kriezis Mansion
Ⓝ Koundouriotis Mansion
Ⓞ Tombasis Mansion
Ⓟ Voulgaris Mansion
Ⓠ G. Voulgaris Mansion
Ⓡ L. Koundouriotis Mansion

1 Ferry / Hydrofoil Berth
2 Taxi Boats

hillwalking destination given the absence of anything else to do. Bathing areas are confined to three poor northerly beaches served by expensive taxi boats, and from rocks beneath the cannon-topped ramparts on the south promontory of the town.

📐

Pricey hotels and rooms. Book ahead if at all possible. The A-class *Miranda* (☎ 52230) and B-class *Hydroussa* (☎ 52217) are the premier hotels in town and with prices to match. Those on a tight budget will fare better at the C-class *Leto* (☎ 53385), the pension *Angelika* (☎ 53202) or the D-class *Argo* (☎ 52452). Also on the waterfront is the rather run-down D-class *Sophia* (☎ 52313). Right under the monastery belfry, certain disadvantages become all too apparent on the hour, every hour.

😵

Poor and insignificant in ancient times, Hydra's transformation into a gold and jewellery boutique has its origins in the 17th and 18th centuries, when, lying on the periphery of both Turkish and Venetian spheres of influence, the island bred a succession of autonomous buccaneer flash Harrys who successfully exploited the growth of Euro-Levantine trade. The town thrived and grew to support a population of 28,000 before post-independence decline reduced the numbers to around 3,000, eking out an existence by sponge fishing until tourism took off. Since then they have reverted to their piratical habits, practising on the hapless victims decanted by the tour boats.

👀

For most tourists **Hydra Town** is Hydra, as few venture beyond its boundaries. Very photogenic, it is snugly tucked into a fold in the barren hills and consists of neo-classical mansions, built during the years of prosperity, fanning up the hillsides behind the port. The bursting waterfront is distinguished by the 18 c. **Panagia Monastery**, built from the stones of the famous Temple of Poseidon on Poros.

The largely undamaged **harbour fortifications** are also impressive and do wonders for the feel of the town. Carefully restored (boutiques aside), they are worth stopping off for, before catching a hydrofoil to the next port of call when you feel a comparatively inexpensive drink coming on.

On the hillsides climbing up either side of the harbour are the 18 c. **mansions** built by the leading families of the day. Several of these

impressive buildings have been turned into museums. One of the best is the L. Koundouriotis Mansion: built in 1780 by a powerful shipowner, its three floors give a good impression of the money to be made by the islanders in the final decades of Ottoman rule.

Meantime, romantics will be disappointed to read that although sharing the same name as a mythical monster called the Hydra (a huge multi-headed water snake that grew two new heads each time one was cut off), the island has no connection with this wee beastie. This is not to say that monsters are unknown here: some have even rented accommodation in the summer months. Not least of these was the family of the late indicted war criminal Slobodan Milošević of Serbia.

Kalamata
ΚΑΛΑΜΑΤΑ; pop. 41,910.

CODE ☎ 27210
PORT POLICE ☎ 22218
TOURIST POLICE ☎ 23187

The second city of the Peloponnese (after Patras), Kalamata is a sprawling concrete conurbation well off the regular ferry trail. Tucked away in the deepest recess of the Messiniakos Gulf, it has a rail link with the rest of Greece and buses to Athens (8 daily) and Patras (2 daily). The bad news is that the bus station is 3 km from the port. To be honest, from any perspective Kalamata is a very ugly city. Badly damaged by a massive earthquake in 1986, it has yet to really recover from the event. A minor quake also struck in August 2000, bringing down a few ceilings and local spirits further.

📐

Limited number of budget hotels on or near the waterfront, including the *Plaza* (☎ 82590), the *Nevada* (☎ 82429) and the *Pension Avra* (☎ 82759). Offers of rooms are very rare.

🅰

Camping Patista (☎ 29525), 2 km east of the ferry quay, is an okayish beach site.

👀

With most of the Venetian and Turkish era buildings flattened by the earthquake, the only site of note that the city has left is a **Frankish Kastro** on a low acropolis just north of the bus station.

Kithera

KYΘHPA; 278 km²; pop. 2,600.

CODE ☎ 27350
PORT POLICE (AGIA PELAGIA) ☎ 33280
PORT POLICE (KAPSALI) ☎ 31222
POLICE ☎ 31206
FIRST AID ☎ 31243

Arguably deserving of the title of the last unspoilt large Greek island, Kithera (also frequently transcribed as 'Kythera' or 'Cythera') lies in glorious isolation from other island chains like a lump of rare meat falling off the Peloponnese fork. Unfortunately, there are few eaters; the remoteness of the place means that ferry connections are very limited indeed, and most visitors are not random island hoppers but dedicated travellers making the island their primary destination after journeying through the Peloponnese. The lack of an island chain to call its own has always left Kithera at something of a loose end.

Historically Kithera was administered as part of the Ionian group, but although sharing a similar history (of Venetian rather than Turkish rule), its appearance has more in common with the Cycladic islands. These days local schizophrenia is further enhanced by the additional complications of the island now being administered direct from Athens, and a largely migrant population. Like Kastelorizo in the Dodecanese, this is another Greek island where everyone seems to own an Australian passport. This results in Kithera being either appealingly full or uncomfortably empty as the number of town houses converted into holiday homes grows. However, bucking this trend, an increasing number of expatriates are choosing to retire on the island. While welcoming, they are not keen to see their dream island degenerate into yet another tourist resort.

A more serious handicap to enjoying the island is the limited nature of the public services (this is, in part, a consequence of the lack of tourists). Public transport is very poor: the school bus runs down the road bisecting the island twice daily in the summer, with frequent, but expensive, taxis making the most of this. If you want to make the most of Kithera then you need to bring or hire your own transport.

Most visitors arrive via the northern hamlet of **Agia Pelagia** (the destination for the local ferry link with the mainland). A dreamy — if rather unprepossessing — sort of place, Agia Pelagia took over from Kapsali as the island's main ferry port (including Piraeus traffic as well as any calling hydrofoils), only to see large ferry operators turn to Diakofti instead in the last few years.

On the back of the ferry traffic that still calls, Agia Pelagia has outlets offering rooms, but these are so spread out that they do little to encourage a cosy atmosphere. In this respect, the over-long quay hardly helps either. On the plus side, there are small coves either side of the port with quiet, sandy beaches. This is just as well as Agia Pelagia isn't really the best base from which to explore Kithera. If this is what you have come to do, then moving south opens up more options.

Tourists bent on sightseeing usually head straight for the scenic hilltop capital of **Chora** (home to a lovely, quiet, white-washed village with a notable number of oddly shaped chimneys) that meanders up the spine of a hill to an impressive but ruinous castle, or the resort port of **Kapsali** that lies below. Kapsali now sees no ferries — except when conditions prevent boats docking at Agia Pelagia. It has to rely on two pebble beaches in a bay divided by a small chapel-topped headland, plus its bar life, for its appeal. Other beaches are equally remote. The island's best sand beach lies beyond Kapsali on the south-east coast at **Fryiammos**, though without a moped it is a long dirt-track walk away.

The rest of Kithera is home to empty villages on rolling low hills with little vegetation; the best of these lies along the main island road at **Potamos**. Now slowly emerging as a convenient halfway-house between the settlements at each end of the island (though it lies well to the north), Potamos is home to the island's regular Sunday market and larger shops. Finally, the ferry dock in the middle of nowhere (no doubt built by the island's taxi drivers) at **Diakofti** deserves a mention. The quay isn't actually on Kithera at all, but is on the causeway-linked islet of Makrikithera.

⊨

Hotels are scattered thinly around the island, but the majority of beds are now to be found at **Agia Pelagia**. The D-class *Kytheria* (☎ 33321) and the B-class *Filoxenia* (☎ 33610), both close to the ferry quay, mop up evening arrivals, but you will find plenty of other offers of beds. Potamos also has some rooms and the *Pension Porfyra* (☎ 33329).

Chora meantime has the pricey, but lovely, B-class *Margarita* (☎ 31694) and a couple of cheaper pensions — notably *Pension Keti* (☎ 31318) — and some unsigned rooms.

Kapsali has the luxury B-class pension *Raikos* (☎ 31629), also rather pricey. Budget accommodation — notably the D-class *Aphrodite* (☎ 31328) and rare rooms along the beach — is usually snapped up in season.

Λ

Camping Kapsali (☎ 31580): a struggling pine-wood site on the outskirts of Kapsali, only open late June through to early September. It would be wise to check it is open before building it into your plans.

👀

The **Chora**, straddling a narrow 500 m ridge, and the Venetian **Kastro** (built in 1503) are the most accessible attractions that Kithera has to offer. The latter looks impressive from a distance but the remains are rather 'bitty'. The best reason to visit is the panoramic views of Kapsali and the coast. In Chora there is also a small town **Museum**. The most popular excursion is to the pretty village of **Milopotamos** with its fine **Cave of Agia Sophia**, and nearby, a Venetian castle.

Between Chora and Milopotamos lies the village of **Livadi**, complete with a bridge dating from the period of British rule (1814–1864). Looking incongruously out of place on a Greek island, it would happily pass as a railway viaduct anywhere in southern England. Kithera was noted in antiquity as the place where the goddess Aphrodite was born (or

KITHERA

Λ ⊨ ⚓ 🚌

0   km   7

✈ → Athens ⓓ x 4

🏛 **Agia Pelagia** ⚓

Potamos

🏛 **Paleochora**

✈ Diakofti ⚓

Cave 👀

506 m ⛰

Milopotamos

Paleopolis 👀

🏛 City & Temple of Aphrodite

🏛 Karvounades

Livadi 🏛

Kalamos

Chora 🏛

Cycladic 👀 **Kapsali** 🏛 Fryiammos
Style

Chora & Venetian ⚓⛵ Resort Village
Kastro

🚌 ····· ⓓ x 2: Ag. Pel: 09.00, 14.30
                   Kapsali: 11.00, 17.00

— No beach boat service

drawn) out of the sea (a claim also made by Cyprus). Kithera's claim was not disputed in antiquity and the centre (at **Paleopolis**) was home to a notable **Temple of Aphrodite** that the Roman-era travel writer Pausanias deemed to be the oldest, most beautiful, and most venerated in the world. A church constructed partly from the remaining temple stones now stands on the site.

The final site of note is the medieval town of **Paleochora** — abandoned after the island's entire population was sold into slavery by the pirate Kemal Reis in 1537.

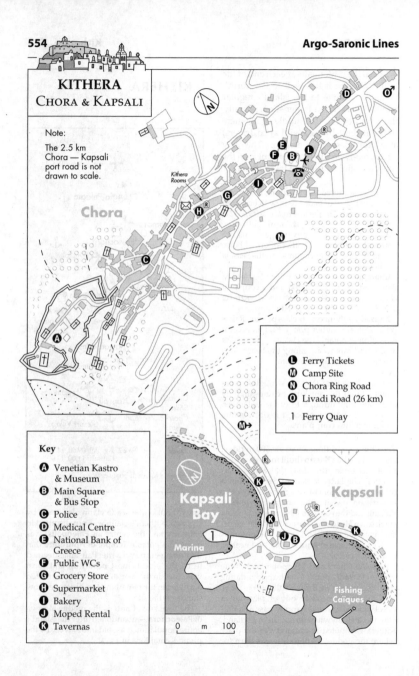

KITHERA
CHORA & KAPSALI

Note:

The 2.5 km
Chora — Kapsali
port road is not
drawn to scale.

Chora

Kithera
Rooms

Key

Ⓐ Venetian Kastro
& Museum

Ⓑ Main Square
& Bus Stop

Ⓒ Police

Ⓓ Medical Centre

Ⓔ National Bank of
Greece

Ⓕ Public WCs

Ⓖ Grocery Store

Ⓗ Supermarket

Ⓘ Bakery

Ⓙ Moped Rental

Ⓚ Tavernas

Ⓛ Ferry Tickets

Ⓜ Camp Site

Ⓝ Chora Ring Road

Ⓞ Livadi Road (26 km)

1 Ferry Quay

Kapsali
Bay

Marina

Kapsali

Fishing
Caïques

0   m   100

Methana

ΜΕΘΑΝΑ; pop. 998.

Methana is another of those Peloponnesian ports with poor bus links — this time on a peninsula jutting north from the Peloponnese into the Saronic Gulf. Occasional ferries as well as hydrofoils call, mostly one suspects because it is there and they are sailing past rather than any other reason. Most of the traffic is local rather than tourist for there is no beach or sightseeing reason to come here. As a result most visitors ship out on the same boat they arrive on.

Monemvassia

ΜΟΝΕΜΒΑΣΙΑ

CODE ☎ 27320
PORT POLICE ☎ 61266
POLICE ☎ 61210

A distinctive small town at the southern end of the Peloponnese, Monemvassia (or rather its adjacent mainland town of Gefira) lives off the tourism generated by the mini Gibraltar-cum-boulder offshore. From the sea both look a bit austere but this is deceptive: there are souvenir shops and tavernas aplenty on the mainland, while the boulder town lies on the southern flank out of view. They are linked by a causeway that also provides a quay for Kithera-bound ferries when they deign to call. Sadly that isn't often these days (though a weekly link did exist in the summer of 2011), so you will probably have to take in the rock via a mainland bus service: links are sufficiently infrequent that one leg of your journey is likely to be made this way.

⊨

Plenty of rooms are available as well as hotels. These include the E-class *Akroyali* (☎ 61306) and D-class *Aktaeon* (☎ 61234); both are near the causeway along with the C-class *Minoa* (☎ 61209). The A-class pension *Kastro* (☎ 61413) provides a more pricey alternative.

Λ

Camping Paradise (☎ 61123): a lovely and quiet site 3½ km south of the town.

MONEMVASSIA

Λ ⊨

🚌 → Athens Ⓓ x 3: 07.00 12.00 14.00
⟵ No beach boat service

Gefira   🔲 *Ag. Sophia*
         ⚓   300 m 🏠🏠 ♖♙
                                             ▢
         ◉◉   *Monemvassia*
      Causeway   ◉◉
      0   km   0.5   *Byzantine*
                                      Kastro & Town

👓
The 350 m '**Rock**' looks barren from the north, but once the ferry steams past the eastern side the remains of a fortress (dating back to Homeric times) and a medieval village dominate the rock. The main Byzantine centre on the Peloponnese, its (largely abandoned) upper and lower towns offer an interesting day's exploration, besides being the site of an important event in the struggle for Greek independence: an unjustifiable massacre of every man in the Turkish garrison in 1821.

Nafplio

ΝΑΥΠΛΙΟ; pop. 10,700.

CODE ☎ 27520
PORT POLICE ☎ 22974
POLICE ☎ 28131

Tucked into the Peloponnese coastline, stately Nafplio — also transcribed as 'Nauplion' — was briefly capital of the embryonic Greek state (1827–34) between Aegina and Athens and is visited by occasional hydrofoils. The tourist presence is high, thanks to the combination of a building programme which stalled when 'capital' status was lost, leaving the best preserved Venetian town in Greece, along with the daily influx from the nearby resort of **Tolo** (linked by bus and hydrofoil).

⊨

Rooms aren't thick on the ground, but there are plenty of budget hotels. The side streets near the ferry quay hide a number of them, including the musty D-class *Acropole* (☎ 27796). Best of the mid-range hotels is the *Agamemnon* (☎ 28021). Right at the top of the range, there is an A-class *Xenia* (☎ 28981) in the town.

Λ

Nearest is *Tolo Camping*, a usually crowded site 8 km to the east.

◯◯

The old town is worth a day's exploration, the highlights being three impressive castles (the most impressive is the islet of **Bourtzi** — a mini Alcatraz opposite the town waterfront; daily taxi boats make the 20-minute crossing 09.00–13.00, 16.00–19.00) and a small **Archaeological Museum** with an interesting display of Mycenaean artefacts.

Neapoli
ΝΕΑΠΟΛΗ

CODE ☎ 27340
PORT POLICE ☎ 22228
TOURIST POLICE ☎ 27310 28701

The most southerly port on the Peloponnese, Neapoli is tucked in the lip of the Gulf of Lakonia. Not that there is much to be laconic about, for there is nought here but a poorly connected and dusty town. The austere, 'end of the known world' feeling that pervades (that led to the ancients believing that the entrance to Hades — the underworld — lay at the southern tip of the Peloponnese) will do little for the tourist who likes their nightlife, though this is a resort town of sorts thanks to the long narrow beach bisected by the ferry quay. Most holidaymakers seem to be Greeks escaping the crowds elsewhere. If you are looking to get away from it all then Neapoli might have appeal — and nearby Elafonissos offers some attractive consolation.

⊨

Limited rooms, and three B-class pensions: the *Alivali* (☎ 22287), the *Arsenakos* (☎ 22991) and the *Limira Mare* (☎ 22208).

Peloponnese
ΠΕΛΟΠΟΝΝΗΣΟΣ

The Peloponnese is an important region of mainland Greece. As such it falls outside the remit of most Greek island guides, but is included here because many island hoppers visit — usually passing rapidly through en route from Patras to Athens, or, less commonly, because they take island-based excursions to sightseeing destinations within the region, or visit ports on the Peloponnesian coast (these are singled out as separate destinations within this chapter). The rest of the Peloponnese — an area with an impressively diverse landscape, so rich in history and sights that it would justify a guidebook in its own right — is also worth a brief mention.

In both an etymological and a literal sense the Peloponnese can claim honorary island status. The name literally means 'island of Pelops', and reflects the fact that even the ancients recognized that, but for the narrow Corinth isthmus which joins it to the rest of the Greek mainland, it was an island. On several occasions they attempted to turn this into reality by digging a canal (the Emperor Nero even set to with a solid gold shovel: a case of one clod getting to grips with another). For want of resources it remained stubbornly attached to the mainland until the 19 C., when the Corinth Canal turned the 'nissos' (island) in Peloponnissos into reality. Today rail and road bridges cross the canal — now a tourist destination in its own right. Sadly, it is so narrow that if you cross via the new Patras—Athens highway bridge you are unlikely to be aware that it exists at all.

The majority of visitors to the Peloponnese come via tour bus — though there is a reasonable coastal bus system and rail network. Unfortunately, like most transport in Greece, they are geared to moving the locals to and from Athens. This can make life difficult if you are trying to explore the region — as all roads and rails seem to lead to the Corinth Canal. This said, the bus system is robust enough to get you most

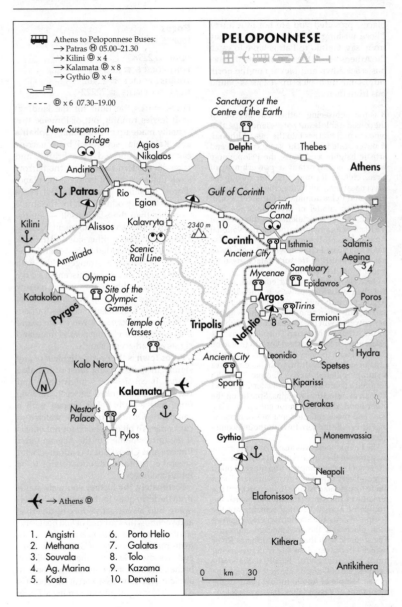

PELOPONNESE

Athens to Peloponnese Buses:
→ Patras Ⓗ 05.00–21.30
→ Kilini Ⓓ x 4
→ Kalamata Ⓓ x 8
→ Gythio Ⓓ x 4

---- Ⓓ x 6 07.30–19.00

Sanctuary at the
Centre of the Earth

Delphi   Thebes

Athens

New Suspension
Bridge

Agios
Nikolaos

Andirio

⚓ **Patras**   Rio   *Gulf of Corinth*
         Egion   Corinth
                                    Canal
Kilini   Alissos   Kalavryta   2340 m 10   **Corinth**   Isthmia   Salamis
⚓   *Ancient City*   Aegina
       Amaliada   *Scenic*   1   3 4
                       Rail Line   *Sanctuary*   2
   Olympia   Mycenae   Epidavros   Poros
           Site of the   **Argos**   Tirins   7
Katakolon   *Olympic*   8   Ermioni
           Games   6 5
Pyrgos   *Temple of*   **Tripolis**   **Nafplio**   Hydra
              Vasses   Leonidio   Spetses
Kalo Nero   *Ancient City*   Kiparissi

        Ⓝ   Sparta   Gerakas

Kalamata ✈
Nestor's   9
Palace   ⚓   Gythio
     Pylos   ⚓   Monemvassia

✈ → Athens Ⓓ   Neapoli

                              Elafonissos

1. Angistri	6. Porto Helio
2. Methana	7. Galatas
3. Souvala	8. Tolo
4. Ag. Marina	9. Kazama
5. Kosta	10. Derveni

Kithera

Antikithera

0   km   30

places, provided you are not in a hurry. Those wishing to make a rapid journey from, say, Gythio to Patras have to catch the Athens bus to the Corinth Canal (most buses set down and pick up on the north side), and then pick up a Patras-bound bus from there.
◦◦

It is the sightseeing, rather than beaches or the considerable beauty of the landscape, that tends to pull tourists into the area. Although it never scaled quite the same cultural and artistic heights as Athens, the Peloponnese was just as important a powerhouse of Greek culture. It came to the fore during the Mycenaean era, when the cities of Mycenae, Tirins and Pylos dominated the Greek world. The hilltop citadel of **Mycenae** is the best known, thanks to Schliemann's discovery of the Mask of Agamemnon (now in the National Archaeological Museum in Athens). **Tirins** also has a less visited citadel, while remote **Pylos** has the remains of **Nestor's Palace**, nestling under protective roofing.

Once the classical world emerged, so too did their successor powers in the cities of Argos, Corinth and Sparta. The latter two successfully overcame Athens at the height of her power to win the 30-year contest dubbed by the Athenian historian Thucydides as 'The Peloponnesian War'. **Ancient Corinth** (not to be confused with the very modern city nearby) is a major sightseeing draw, with the remains of a stumpy-pillared Archaic Temple of Apollo set amid a confused jumble of later Greek and Roman architectural remains. **Sparta**, on the other hand, didn't go in for culture in a big way, and this is reflected in a lack of remains that leaves the modern town without income-generating sights.

The Peloponnese was also host to the greatest games in the Greek world at **Olympia**. The site is not in island hopper's territory (though rare and very expensive excursions have been made from Ionian islands in the past), but the remains of the sanctuary are well worth the trouble of a visit. Leading remains are the Temple of Zeus, the Stadium where the games took place and the well-stocked museum. The scenery, with the nearby Alpheios River (which later covered the site with preserving mud), is also delightful. Finally, to the southeast lies one of Greece's greatest temples, the 420 BC **Temple of Apollo** tucked away in the mountains at **Vasses** (alias 'Basses/Bassae').

Poros
ΠΟΡΟΣ; 28 km²; pop. 4,500.

CODE ☎ 22980
PORT POLICE ☎ 22274
TOURIST POLICE ☎ 22462
HEALTH CENTRE ☎ 22222

Poros marks the limit for the landing-craft ferries running out of Piraeus. It is actually made up of two islands (**Sphalria** and **Kalaureia**) separated by a narrow canal and connected by a bridge, and takes its modern name from the narrow strait that separates it from the mainland, 'Poros' meaning 'passage'. In fact Poros is an extremely odd island; for the straits — rather than the island itself — are the focus of activity, with settlement running along the shores on either side and the bulk of the island relegated to hinterland. The 'island' sensation is strangely thin, with an atmosphere more reminiscent of a large coastal town ribboned around a narrow bay. Perhaps because of this and a lack of good beaches, Poros attracts less tourism than her neighbours. However, the island is a nice base for visiting nearby mainland sights and adjacent islands.

Poros Town is the only settlement of any significance, occupying most of Sphalria Island. It consists of whitewashed and red-tile houses banked between the long quay and a stubby hill topped with a campanile. On first arriving, the waterfront can come as a bit of a shock; for not only is it the third smelliest in the Aegean (after Piraeus and Chios) but it is adorned with several of the tackiest tourist shops to be found in Greece.

Fortunately, the further you walk south from the ferry quay the better it gets, developing into an attractive mix of tavernas and yachts, with a myriad of taxi boats and small car ferries scuttling across the straits to the mainland village of Galatas (the path ends at some rocks where the town children bathe). The backstreets are also reasonably attractive in a downbeat sort of way: but it is difficult to imagine anyone coming to Poros for the architecture. One suspects the main reason some tourists come back year after year is the low-key 'niceness' of the island, though if truth be told you don't have to go far to find better. Perhaps this is why cycle hire is so popular here — as it offers easy access to better mainland beaches.

Settlement on the wooded main island is largely confined to tourist developments along the straits (served by frequent buses). The coast south of the town is the busiest, with the bulk of the island's poor beaches (all pebble) and the now unused but pretty monastery of **Kalavrias** (alias Zoodochos Pigi). At the other end of the strait lies Russian Bay, home to an 1828 nautical conference in which Britain, France and Russia discussed the future of the independent Greek state. En route you will pass the beach at Neorio, arguably the best of the island's poor collection.

Walk inland, and Poros improves considerably, the abundance of trees being some compensation for the demolition of the WCs on the waterfront of Poros Town. **Galatas** is much more dowdy than Poros Town, though some efforts have been made to tart up the waterfront. Unless you are heading for the campsite there is no great reason to venture here.

Ⓗ

Poros Town offers the best chance of finding a room south of Aegina. There are also a number of easily located hotels along the waterfront. Closest to the ferry quay are the B-class *Latsi* (☎ 22392), the *Saron* (☎ 22279), and the C-class *Aktaion* (☎ 22281). More expensive hotels tend to be out of town on Kalavrias, the largest being the B-class *Poros* (☎ 22216).

There are also several waterfront hotels in **Galatas** if you draw a blank in Poros Town. These include the D-class *Saronis* (☎ 22356) and the C-class *Galatia* (☎ 22227) and *Papasotiriou* (☎ 22841).

Ⓐ

Camping Kirangelo (☎ 24520): small mainland site 1 km inland on the road north of Galatas. Avoid the tent village on the coast north of Galatas: this is a hospital resort run by the local health service for the elderly insane.

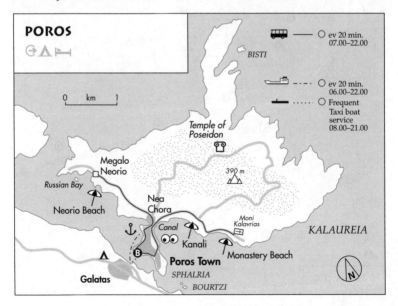

POROS

🚌 ——	○ ev 20 min. 07.00–22.00
🚢 - - -	○ ev 20 min. 06.00–22.00
⛴ ⋯⋯	○ Frequent Taxi boat service 08.00–21.00

0   km   1

BISTI

Temple of Poseidon

Megalo Neorio

Russian Bay

Neorio Beach

Nea Chora

390 m

Moni Kalavrias

KALAUREIA

Canal

Kanali

Monastery Beach

Poros Town

Galatas

SPHALRIA

BOURTZI

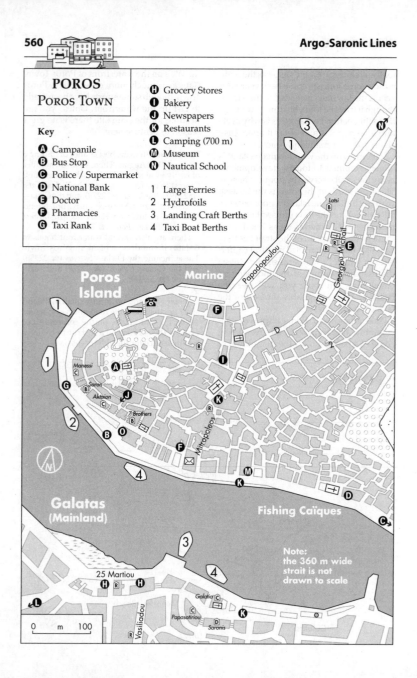

POROS
POROS TOWN

Key

- **Ⓐ** Campanile
- **Ⓑ** Bus Stop
- **Ⓒ** Police / Supermarket
- **Ⓓ** National Bank
- **Ⓔ** Doctor
- **Ⓕ** Pharmacies
- **Ⓖ** Taxi Rank
- **Ⓗ** Grocery Stores
- **Ⓘ** Bakery
- **Ⓙ** Newspapers
- **Ⓚ** Restaurants
- **Ⓛ** Camping (700 m)
- **Ⓜ** Museum
- **Ⓝ** Nautical School

- 1 Large Ferries
- 2 Hydrofoils
- 3 Landing Craft Berths
- 4 Taxi Boat Berths

Poros Island

Marina

Papadopoulou

Georgiou Michail

Latsi

Manessi
Saron
Aktaion
7 Brothers

Mitropoleos

Galatas
(Mainland)

Fishing Caïques

Note:
the 360 m wide
strait is not
drawn to scale

25 Martiou

Vasiliadou

Galatia

Papasatiriou

Saronis

0   m   100

∞

Poros Town has little of sightseeing interest beyond the waterfront itself and a small **Archaeological Museum** south-east of the ferry quay (the Venetians preferring to fortify one of the Bourtzi islets rather than build in the town). On the north side of Sphalria lies Greece's **Naval Cadet School** in the former home of the 19 c. Arsenal. As a result, the nearby ferry quay has played irregular host to odd ball vessels of the Greek navy. These have included the 1911-built heavy armoured cruiser *Georgios Averof* — which was laid up here between 1957–85 awaiting her future as a floating museum — and, in the 1980s, the replica Greek trireme (see p. 125) *Olympias*, which underwent her sea trials based here. If she ever puts to sea again the chances are that she will again include Poros on her itinerary.

Once out of the town, you will find Poros is all pine trees and hills, with an inland road around Kalaureia. This circuit offers a day's gentle strolling, taking in the views from the hills as well as the remains of the ancient city of Kalaureia. This settlement was home to one of ancient Greece's premier religious centres in the form of the 6 c. BC **Temple of Poseidon** (later demolished to furnish the masonry for Hydra Town's quayside monastery); here the great orator Demosthenes committed suicide in 322 BC (by nibbling on his poisoned pen while writing a farewell epistle — the original poison pen letter — to his family when his creditors seized him from the temple where he had sought sanctuary).

Porto Helio
ΠΟΡΤΟ ΧΕΛΙ

CODE ☎ 27540
PORT POLICE ☎ 51408

An extremely large tourist town that is better avoided. This resort has become the natural terminus for ferries and hydrofoils running down the islands in the gulf — so most depart northwards (up to ten daily). Irregular smaller craft do put in occasionally, but the local market is insufficient to generate much traffic.

⊨

Pre-booked hotels predominate, but some pricey rooms are available.

Spetses
ΣΠΕΤΣΕΣ; 22.5 km²; pop. 3,500.

CODE ☎ 22980
PORT POLICE ☎ 72245
TOURIST POLICE ☎ 73100
FIRST AID ☎ 72472

Sufficiently far from the capital to escape the worst of the day trippers, yet still close enough to be served by daily Piraeus ferries (just), Spetses is a gentle, small, pine-forested island particularly popular with English tourists (suburbia rather than the fish-and-chips brigade). This is in part due to the island's being the setting for John Fowles' novel *The Magus*, a popular tome that has ensured that many holidaymakers come to Spetses disposed to admire the place. The horses and traps that run along the waterfront of Spetses Town don't hurt either, though the paucity of good beaches results in a daily mass migration around the island that is not conducive to relaxed holiday-making.

Mansioned **Spetses Town** is apt to disappoint on first acquaintance: considering that it is the only settlement of any size on the island, the centre area is poorly laid out without the natural charm of most of the Cycladic island choras. It is also comparatively expensive. The tourist area is firmly focused around the streets near the new port. This is rather sad, as the too shallow old port is now reduced to a little-visited yacht marina. In fact, it is much the more attractive of the two, with the headland to the south graced with three windmills for good measure.

An island-wide ban on cars has served to increase the suburbs of Spetses Town while restricting the growth of other tourist centres. Movement around the island is thus greatly restricted. As a result, crowded buses run along the northern coast hotel strip as well as to the most popular beach on Spetses — at Ag. Anargiri. Better reached by beach boat (you don't have to fight for a place like you do on the afternoon buses heading back to Spetses Town), it offers the

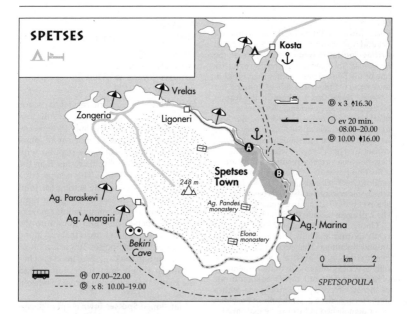

best sand beach on the island. Beach boats also run across the straits from Spetses Town to the adjacent beach near the quiet village of **Kosta**, supplementing the landing-craft ferry running to the village itself several times a day.

Tourist boats also make the crossing to Kosta and Porto Helio. Be very wary of some of these boats: they divide up into 'normal' multi-passenger beach boats and so-called sea 'taxis', individually hired and charging ludicrous 'tourist' fares.

Arrive early: block bookings by package tour operators mean that beds are scarce. Tourist agencies east of the ferry dock have lists, and one, *Takis Travel* (☎ 72888) — sited near the ferry quay — acts as an agent for most of the island hoteliers, the residue being covered by *Pine Island Tours* (☎ 72464). Close by the ferry quay are a number of hotels worth a try. These include the budget E-class *Alexandri* (☎ 73073), the D-class *Saronicos* (☎ 73741) and the C-class *Faros* (☎ 72613). Near the town beach are the D-class *Klimis* (☎ 73777) and *Stelios* (☎ 72364),

the latter complete with restaurant. Those with money to spend should try the A-class Edwardian *Posidonion* (☎ 72308).

▲
Camping Kosta (☎ 57571). Quiet mainland site 1 km west of Kosta village. A member of the *Harmonie* camping club scheme.

∞
Spetses, like Aegina and Hydra, played an important part in the struggle for Greek independence, furnishing the rebels with a cross between a Greek Boudicca and Lord Nelson in the form of a female admiral, Laskarina Bouboulina. Spetses Town has a **Museum** in one of the 18 c. mansions housing her bones and other independence material. The 8th of September also sees the commemoration of an 1822 naval victory when a Greek fireship forced an attacking Turkish fleet to withdraw from Spetses. This is re-enacted with the burning of a cast-adrift taxi boat each year.

Apart from the attractive **Bekiri Sea Cave** at **Ag. Anargiri** beach, Spetses lacks sights: agencies make a killing selling highly priced tours to worthy attractions on the Peloponnese such as Epidavros and Corinth.

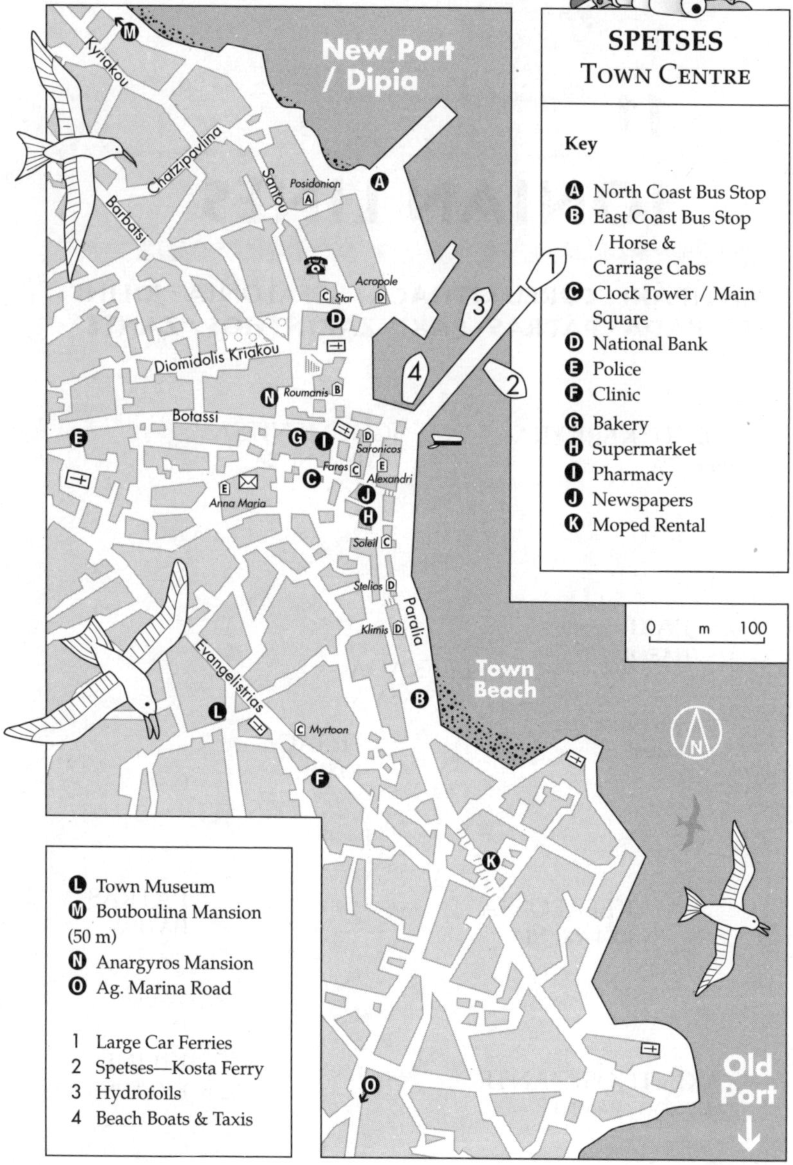

New Port / Dipia

Kyriakou

M

Chatzipavlina

Santou

Barbatsi

Posidonian

A

A

Acropole

C Star

D

D

Diomidolis Kriakou

N

Roumanis B

Botassi

G I

Saronicos D

C Faros C

E

Alexandri

J

E

Anna Maria

H

C Soleil

Stelios D

Klimis D

Paralia

B

Town Beach

C Myrtoon

F

L

Evangelistrias

K

O

Old Port ↓

E

1

3

4

2

N

SPETSES
TOWN CENTRE

Key

- **A** North Coast Bus Stop
- **B** East Coast Bus Stop / Horse & Carriage Cabs
- **C** Clock Tower / Main Square
- **D** National Bank
- **E** Police
- **F** Clinic
- **G** Bakery
- **H** Supermarket
- **I** Pharmacy
- **J** Newspapers
- **K** Moped Rental

0   m   100

- **L** Town Museum
- **M** Bouboulina Mansion (50 m)
- **N** Anargyros Mansion
- **O** Ag. Marina Road

1   Large Car Ferries
2   Spetses—Kosta Ferry
3   Hydrofoils
4   Beach Boats & Taxis

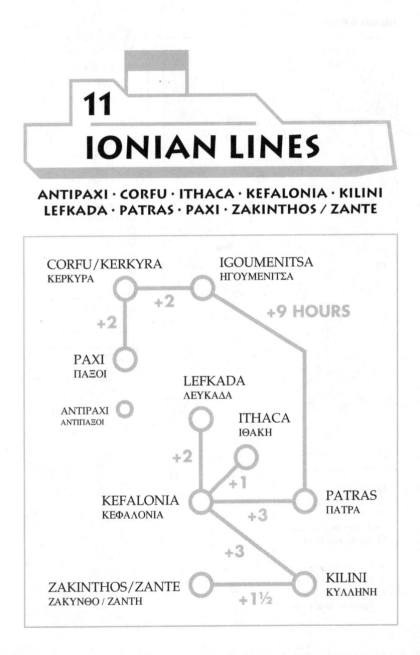

11
IONIAN LINES

**ANTIPAXI · CORFU · ITHACA · KEFALONIA · KILINI
LEFKADA · PATRAS · PAXI · ZAKINTHOS / ZANTE**

CORFU / KERKYRA
ΚΕΡΚΥΡΑ

IGOUMENITSA
ΗΓΟΥΜΕΝΙΤΣΑ

+2

+9 HOURS

+2

PAXI
ΠΑΞΟΙ

LEFKADA
ΛΕΥΚΑΔΑ

ANTIPAXI
ΑΝΤΙΠΑΞΟΙ

ITHACA
ΙΘΑΚΗ

+2

+1

KEFALONIA
ΚΕΦΑΛΟΝΙΑ

+3

PATRAS
ΠΑΤΡΑ

+3

ZAKINTHOS / ZANTE
ΖΑΚΥΝΘΟ / ΖΑΝΤΗ

+1½

KILINI
ΚΥΛΛΗΝΗ

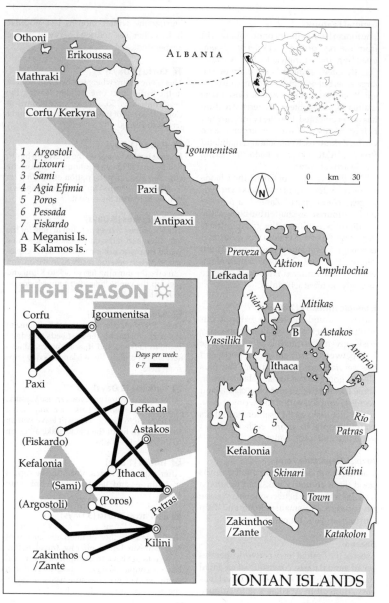

Othoni
Erikoussa
Mathraki
Corfu/Kerkyra

ALBANIA

Igoumenitsa

1 Argostoli
2 Lixouri
3 Sami
4 Agia Efimia
5 Poros
6 Pessada
7 Fiskardo
A Meganisi Is.
B Kalamos Is.

Paxi

Antipaxi

N

0   km   30

Preveza
Aktion   Amphilochia
Lefkada
Niari   Mitikas
A
B   Astakos
Vassiliki
7
Ithaca
Andirio

HIGH SEASON ☼

Corfu   Igoumenitsa

Days per week:
6-7

Paxi

Lefkada
Astakos

(Fiskardo)

Kefalonia

(Sami)   Ithaca

(Argostoli)   (Poros)

Zakinthos
/Zante

Kilini

Patras

4
2   3
1   5
6

Kefalonia

Skinari   Kilini

Town
Rio
Patras

Zakinthos
/Zante   Katakolon

IONIAN ISLANDS

General Features

The Ionian Islands lie uncomfortably adrift from the rest of the Greek ferry system, guarding the entrance to the Adriatic Sea. By Greek standards most are on the large side, but as they have comparatively small population ratios and lie close to the mainland, a fully integrated ferry structure has never emerged. Poor ferry links are not helped by the profusion of airports, with Corfu, Zakinthos, Kefalonia and mainland Preveza/Aktion near Lefkada all offering viable arrival points.

With the exception of Corfu, the islands see fewer independent travellers than their Aegean counterparts. Zante is a popular package tourist destination but being at the southern extremity of the group attracts very few ferries. Kefalonia is quiet and lacking a conveniently placed population centre. Ithaca (of Odysseus fame), along with Paxi and Antipaxi, is too small to figure strongly on ferry schedules.

Example Itinerary [2 Weeks]

Moving around the Ionian group is difficult but practicable on a one-hop-a-day basis, given that there is often only one boat between poorly connected ports, and bus services are equally poor. The plus side to going to the Ionian Islands lies in some lovely beaches and pine-clad island scenery, coupled with shimmeringly clean water that looks as if Poseidon has set his water-nymphs to giving each wavelet a good lick and a rub daily.

Arrival/Departure Point

Corfu is the obvious starting point given its good flight and ferry links, but Kefalonia and Zakinthos are better options if you are prepared to do a smaller circuit and drop Corfu from your itinerary.

Season

Most of the limited ferry network operates on an annual basis, consisting of essential mainland to island services. So travel is as easy/difficult in April as it is in August.

During the winter months less popular links either see reduced services or are suspended.

■ Corfu [2 Days]

This is one group where it is better to explore in the earlier part of a holiday, leaving the beach until later. So, after a couple of days on Corfu, take one of the international overnight ferries to Patras.

■ Patras [1 Day]

Having booked a seat on the afternoon bus to Kilini you will have a few hours to explore the city. You also have the option of heading on to Athens (3½ hours) for a couple of nights if you want to visit the capital.

■ Zakinthos [3 Days]

The Patras bus arrives at Kilini in time for the late afternoon ferry on to Zakinthos — one island that is worth a couple of days' exploration. When you are ready to move on you can take the morning ferry back to Kilini and pick up the connecting afternoon service on to Kefalonia (Argostoli).

■ Kefalonia [2 Days]

From Argostoli take a bus across Kefalonia to the port of Sami for the best beds and daily boats to Lefkada and Ithaca. You could also stay longer and do these islands as day trips from here.

■ Lefkada [2 Days]

Arriving on the first boat you can use Vassiliki as a base for exploring Lefkada before taking the ferry on to Ithaca. This will leave you on the northern tip of the island. Take a bus on to the capital — Vathi.

■ Ithaca [1 Day]

After exploring Ithaca, finish in the capital of Vathi — and its daily ferry link with Patras.

■ ■ Patras/Corfu [3 Days]

Returning to Patras you can pick up one of the limited number of international ferries (e.g. Minoan Lines) offering travel within Greece to get back to Corfu, where you will have a couple of days to take in Paxi and Antipaxi via Corfu pleasure boats, or lie on the beach before your flight home.

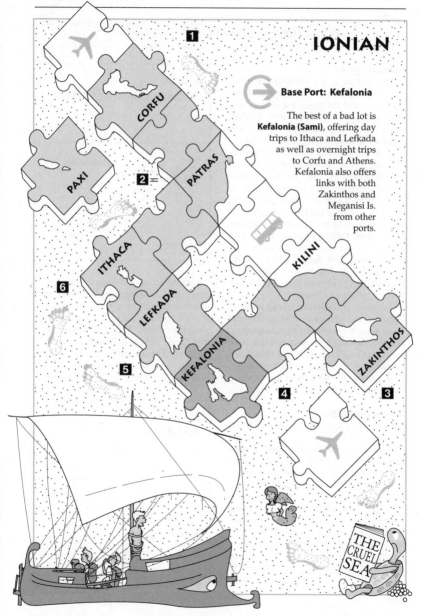

IONIAN

Base Port: Kefalonia

The best of a bad lot is **Kefalonia (Sami)**, offering day trips to Ithaca and Lefkada as well as overnight trips to Corfu and Athens. Kefalonia also offers links with both Zakinthos and Meganisi Is. from other ports.

CORFU

PAXI

PATRAS

ITHACA

KILINI

LEFKADA

KEFALONIA

ZAKINTHOS

THE CRUEL SEA

Ionian Ferry Services

Main Car Ferries

Given the lack of any obvious pattern of progression when travelling up or down the chain, and the over-long sailing time between the north and south Ionian Islands, it is not surprising that many ferry services are small boats operating out of a mainland port to an adjacent island, rather than running further afield. Moving between islands, therefore, often involves bouncing off the mainland by changing ferries at a mainland port or crossing an island to connect with a ferry operating out of a second port. Moreover, useful interconnecting ferries often run solo on routes, and you are pretty vulnerable should they not be operating. This doesn't happen often, but once every decade or so one or two disappear for a year, and then hopping can become quite a challenge.

The jokers in the Ionian Island pack are hydrofoil and catamaran services. Over the years several companies have started up and then failed after a season. Most have operated out of Patras or Corfu. None were operating in 2011, and at the time of this book's going to press there was nothing to suggest that this would change in 2012.

Minoan Lines & ANEK

The only ferry link between the north and south Ionian Islands is provided by the international ferries of the Greek-owned Minoan and ANEK Lines (landlubbers not in the know travel the complicated bus route from Igoumenitsa to Preveza/ Lefkada, and then continue island hopping from there). This situation reflects both the distances involved and the lack of island-hopping tourists in this part of the world. In theory any trans-Adriatic operator can provide domestic tickets, but it is only the main Greek operators that choose to promote them, so the simplest option is to go straight to them.

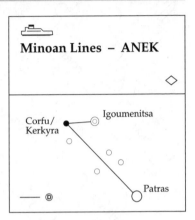

It is easy to use a domestic ticket on an international boat running between Patras or Kefalonia and Corfu; you just wave them around and are simply waved through passport control. The only downside is that 'deck' tickets do mean the outside deck— you've no entitlement to an inside seat on these boats and the crews aren't over-keen on seeing their lounges turned

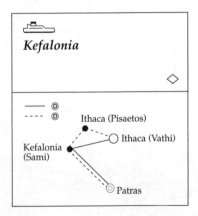

into backpackers' dormitories. Cabins or cheap aircraft-type seats can, however, be booked for overnight trips.

C/F *Kefalonia*
Strintzis Ferries; 1975; 3472 GRT.
Formerly the premier boat on the line, the *Kefalonia* appeared in the Ionian Sea in 1995. She has been on this route ever since, though in past years she has occasionally operated to Argostoli via Kilini out of High Season. A familiar friend to those who venture into this part of the world regularly, her 12.30 daily departure from Patras to Kefalonia is one of the few ferry times that never seems to change, though her livery occasionally does. To date she has operated under the banner of Strintzis Lines, Blue Ferries and now Strintzis Ferries. Overall, she is an appealing boat, and even if she isn't in the same class as the newest arrivals in Greece, her facilities are the best of any regular boat in the group, with escalators and an attractive open-plan saloon.

C/F *Eptanisos*
Strintzis Ferries; 1989; 3611 GRT.
The Kilini—Kefalonia service is the one

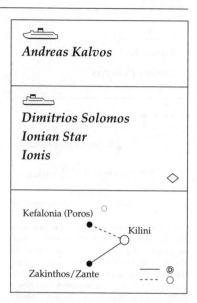

ferry route in the Ionian Islands that has consistently found it difficult to attract a ferry for more than one season or so. The service ought to be viable (particularly given the poor nature of public transport on Kefalonia), but a succession of ferries have tried it for a season and then moved on. After a couple of years when the service was maintained by the collection of ferries that normally run on the Kilini—Zakinthos route, the *Eptanisos* appeared in 2005, and hung around longer than her predecessors (though she shared the route with the *Andreas Kalvos* in 2008). As with all Strintzis boats, facilities are reasonable, and although she isn't among the premier boats in Greece you can travel on her with confidence.

C/F *Andreas Kalvos* – C/F *Dimitrios Solomos* C/F *Ionian Star* – C/F *Ionis*
Andreas Kalvos; 2004; 17340 GRT.
Dimitrios Solomos; 1990; 8844 GRT.
Ionian Star; 1992; 1930 GRT.
Ionis; 1977; 2963 GRT.

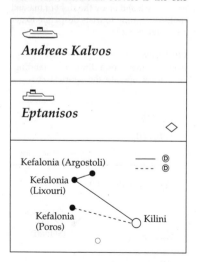

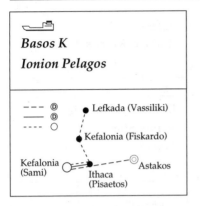

Four ferries provide the link between the mainland and Zakinthos, with a new high-speed boat — the *Andreas Kalvos* — dominating the scene when operating on the line. The remaining regular ferries run eight times daily in the summer, four times daily in Low Season. All independently operated under the Ionian Ferries banner, the boats run by rota, and you buy a ticket for a crossing rather than a boat (the *Andreas Kalvos* has her own high-price tickets). Of the regular ferries, the *Ionis* is arguably the best, followed by the smaller *Ionian Star*. The *Dimitrios Solomos* is a larger, chunkier affair and handles most of the container-lorry traffic.

C/F *Basos K* – C/F *Ionion Pelagos*

For over a decade useful small landing-craft-type car ferries have provided a morning and evening link between the port of Sami on Kefalonia and the isolated quay at Pisaetos on Ithaca. In past years this service was run as part of a twice-daily link to Vassiliki on Lefkada via Fiskardo. However, of late the boats on this line have been obliged to cover on the Kefalonia—Astakos route. This makes life difficult for travellers as the Fiskardo—Lefkada link is otherwise very awkward. Sadly, it would appear that this is unlikely to change in 2012: you might have to take a bus from Astakos to Lefkada.

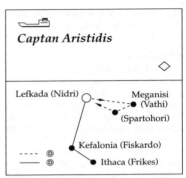

C/F *Captan Aristidis*

This landing-craft ferry runs a daily service from Lefkada to northern Kefalonia and Ithaca, as well as providing the small island of Meganisi with its main link with the outside world. The *Captan Aristidis* is usually on the route alone, but in past years has had support from other Lefkada-based ferries. In the summer the route is the preserve of Italian motorists pushing capacity well beyond its limits: arrive on the quayside early to secure a passage, then you can sit back and enjoy the sight of massed ranks of arguing tourists desperate to get a passage home.

C/F *Angela*

Each summer sees a diminutive landing-craft ferry operate the shortest crossing

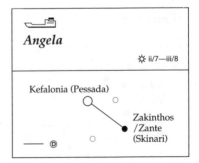

between Kefalonia and Zakinthos (Ski-nari, alias Agios Nikolaos). Services have remained unchanged in years, with the link only existing between mid-May and early October. However, unless you have your own transport, this is a poor link even when it is in operation, given the absence of bus services (out of the July—August High Season peak) to both ports of call.

C/F *Nireas* – P/S Local

Landing-craft-type ferries have provided the daily Corfu—Paxi island service for the last few years. For a long time threatened by the arrival of stiff competition from a catamaran and an advertised ferry that never appeared, they remain in service (though the name of the boat running the service does change from year to year). The only competition comes from tourist day-tripper boats which run irregularly to Corfu Town from Paxi.

C/F *Ioanna*

A small landing-craft ferry that is only of interest to motorists, the *Ioanna* runs a twice daily service between Ithaca and the mainland hamlet of Mitikas.

Large Corfu—Igoumenitsa Services

The Corfu—Igoumenitsa run is attracting a growing number of larger car ferries, vital during the winter months when the land-ing-craft ferries often can't operate.

C/F *Agia Theodora*

Kerkira Lines; 1989; 2336 GRT.
The new ferry on the block in 2004, this is an ex-Japanese boat. Now the best of the larger boats dedicated to this route, she seems to be creaming off quite a bit of the passenger traffic from landing-craft ferries.

C/F *Ekaterini P*

Fast Ferries; 1990; 2933 GRT.
This is an unmissable orange-hulled boat, seemingly trying to cash in on the success of Superfast by adopting a similar name. Popular with locals.

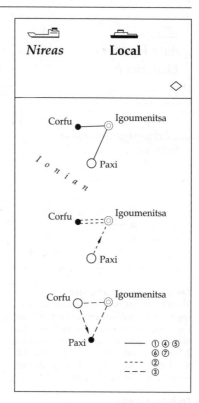

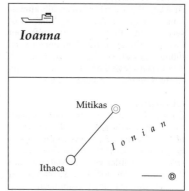

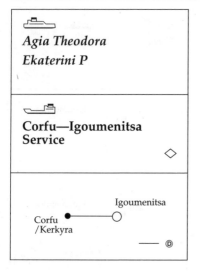

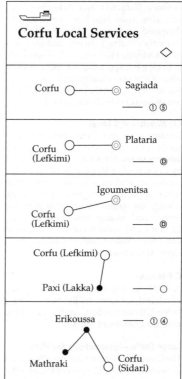

Corfu—Igoumenitsa Service

The 90-minute Corfu—Igoumenitsa crossing has some half-dozen landing-craft ferries operating an hourly service on a rota basis. The quay is 400 m north of Corfu Town's International ferry terminal building. Unchanging schedules are posted up on the quayside ticket office.

Corfu Local Ferries

An island the size of Corfu naturally attracts a number of mainland ferry links. Most services run to the port of Igoumenitsa, but there are others worth looking out for, even though they are of limited tourist appeal. The most useful is the 5 x ⑩ service between Corfu (Lefkimi) and Igoumenitsa.

C/F *Pegasus*

Corfu has a regular service to the three islets to the north of the island via the small port of Agios Stefanos. In past years the *Pegasus* has made the short journey several times a week. The regular visits to Mathraki and the Friday sailing to Erikoussa offer island hoppers day-tripping possibilities.

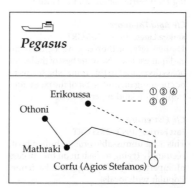

⚓ Ionian Islands & Ports

Astakos
ΑΣΤΑΚΟΣ

CODE ☎ 26460

A small village on the mainland west coast, Astakos was formerly the home port of a single ferry running daily to Ithaca and Kefalonia. It is still the departure point for the produce caïques that keep the small fishing community that struggles along on the isolated island of Kalamos (which lies to the north-west) supplied with essentials. However, erratic ferry connections aside, Astakos has little going for it. In truth, the beach aside, the most interesting thing in town is the bus stop.

⊨

Astakos has three hotels that cater for the few that get caught here. Top of the range is the B-class *Stratos* (☎ 41096). There are also two budget hotels in town: the D-class *Beach* (☎ 41135) and the *Byron* (☎ 41516).

Corfu / Kerkyra
KEPKYPA; 592 km²; pop. 89,600.

TOWN CODE ☎ 26610
NTOG/TOURIST POLICE ☎ 30265
EMERGENCY ☎ 100
PORT POLICE ☎ 34036
HOSPITAL ☎ 25400

Long considered one of the most beautiful of the Greek islands, Corfu is another of those islands that is known by two names: the touristy 'Corfu' — an imposed name of Byzantine origin, and the less familiar 'Kerkyra', the ancient name that is still preferred by most Greeks today. This double identity in a way neatly sums the place up. On the one hand it is now among the most package-tourist dominated parts of Greece (over 75% of visitors are Brits), but it is also large enough to enjoy the luxury of having dreamy backwaters still free of the excesses of mass tourism. This said, you do have to

venture quite far to escape the crowds, but on the plus side the island doesn't attract over half a million visitors each year without good reason: it is beautiful, people and all. Its location off the western seaboard of Greece, coupled with its relatively northerly latitude, means that it enjoys much more rainfall than most Greek islands: the result is a lush, green landscape regardless of the time of year.

Thanks to an impressive architectural legacy left by the colonizing Venetians (and to a lesser extent British), Corfu retains something of an 18th- or 19th-century colonial feel — an impression enhanced as you travel around by the large numbers of elderly foreigners living on the island: Corfu is a prime location for holiday homes in Greece. On occasions this has attracted less welcome visitors, and even in recent years the island has made the news because of attacks by Albanian pirates (particularly after a tourist was killed in 1996). Overlooking the Albanian coast, affluent Corfu proved too tempting a target; even the *Club Med* resort came under fire once. A 50-strong military unit is now in action to prevent further incidents. This has clearly worked, and invasions since have all been of the tourist kind.

As with most of the Ionian islands, the main settlement — **Corfu Town** — lies on the east coast facing the mainland. The centre is a sort of mini Venice without canals: a warren of tall shuttered Italianate buildings fronted with attractive shopping arcades, all looking slightly dilapidated in a picturesque sort of way. Add to this campanile-backed churches and some impressive fortress walls and you have a city that seems hardly Greek at all. The British got into the architecture act as well, adding most of the larger public buildings and park areas. The sum adds up to a very cosmopolitan mix, though in midsummer the reflected heat off the buildings and pavements can make Corfu Town oppressively hot. Sunsets, however, are spectacular, with flocks of birds taking wing, enjoying the cooler air.

Running north and south along the coast from Corfu Town are the worst of the island's package tour hotel-cum-beach strips. The strip **north of the town** is much the more depressing: it is all looking a bit tired. It isn't until you pass **Pirgi** that the hotels give out and the coast road scenery perks up, improving steadily until you reach the village of Kalami. A picturesque spot, **Kalami** was once the home of the Durrell brothers. Gerald Durrell is the best known, and did a major public relations job for Corfu via his idealized autobiography *My Family and Other Animals* describing their childhood upbringing here in the 1930s. Lawrence Durrell wrote *Prospero's Cell* at Kalami in 1945. Rising steeply up behind Kalami is Mt. Pantokrator: at 906 m it is the highest point on Corfu, and on a good day, it is claimed that those braving the ascent to the church at the top can see as far as the coast of Italy, eagle eyesight permitting.

South of Corfu Town, the tourist strip is less developed — thanks in part to the airport sandwiched between the town and a large lagoon. This provides something of a breakwater between the town and the southern tourist strip which erupts again at Benitses (one of the premier booze and snooze resorts of Greece) and the large resort of **Messoighi**. Thanks to a plethora of hotels facing onto family-friendly beaches **Benitses** is typical of the sort of resort that contrives to place Corfu close to the top of the 'expensive island' rankings. Plenty of young visitors with money to spend and a very vibrant beach and nightlife scene make this a good place if you are looking for glorious excess. This said, if nightlife and beach sports are not a priority, the overcrowding to be found here and the other east coast resorts will soon tempt you into venturing further afield.

The north and west sides of Corfu have the most to offer. **The north coast** is quite heavily touristed, but the main centres are not overwhelmed except at the High Season peak, and the area is generally more up-market. **Kassiopi** (the centre of Corfu in Roman times) is an attractive fishing village resort overlooked by the remains of a 12 c. castle built on the site of a Temple of Zeus. It occupies a wide bay skirted by wooded hills and headlands. Its facilities are stretched to the limit in August, but in June or September it is a very pleasant destination.

Much the same can be said for **Sidari**, another popular north coast resort town. Backed by rich farmland, it is a less picturesque — but equally lively — village offering excursion boats to the islets north of Corfu (see p. 578) as well as several notable beaches. Thanks to the easily eroded local sandstone, Sidari boasts several sea caves, tunnels and odd sea-filled channels. The best known of these rock-sided sea channels is the famous 'Canal d'Amour' which, despite its rather smutty-sounding name, is sufficiently attractive that local legend has it that amorous couples who swim through it will stay together for eternity (no doubt derived from an old folk memory of a couple of skinny-dipping local lovers washed out to sea by a passing sadistic deep water current).

A glance at an island map will quickly reveal — thanks to the obvious lack of high grade roads — that **the west coast** is significantly less developed. This is rather odd as this side of the island has the best of Corfu's beaches. The strands of good sand include Agios Georgios (both north and south), Glifada, Pelekas and **Mirtiotissa** (arguably Corfu's premier beach: its isolation ensures it gets the thumbs — among other things — up from nudists). In season all the beaches are busy none the less. Tour buses also process to the cliffs at **Paliokastritsa** which are another of the island's big draws — particularly at sunset. A mix of three small crescent sand bays

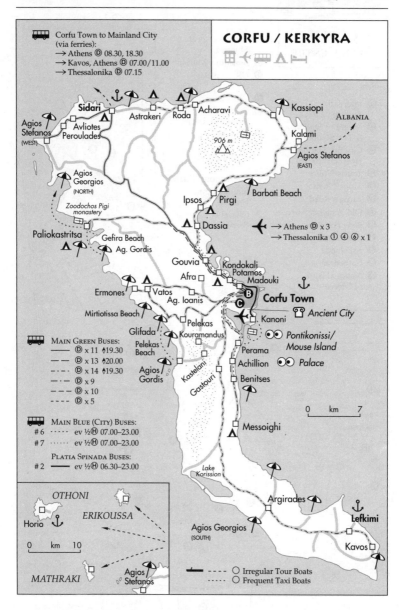

CORFU / KERKYRA

Corfu Town to Mainland City
(via ferries):
→ Athens Ⓓ 08.30, 18.30
→ Kavos, Athens Ⓓ 07.00/11.00
→ Thessalonika Ⓓ 07.15

Sidari
Agios Stefanos (WEST)
Avliotes
Peroulades
Astrakeri
Roda
Acharavi
Kassiopi
ALBANIA
Kalami
Agios Stefanos (EAST)
906 m
Agios Georgios (NORTH)
Zoodochos Pigi monastery
Ipsos
Pirgi
Barbati Beach
Paliokastritsa
Dassia
→ Athens Ⓓ x 3
→ Thessalonika ① ④ ⑥ x 1
Gefira Beach
Ag. Gordis
Gouvia
Kondokali
Potamos
Madouki
Ermones
Vatos
Afra
Ⓑ Corfu Town
Ancient City
Ag. Ioanis
Ⓒ
Mirtiotissa Beach
Kanoni
Pelekas
Glifada
Kouramandus
Pontikonissi/ Mouse Island
MAIN GREEN BUSES:
—— Ⓓ x 11 ☽19.30
— — Ⓓ x 13 ☽20.00
—·—· Ⓓ x 14 ☽19.30
—·— Ⓓ x 9
— — Ⓓ x 10
- - - - Ⓓ x 5
Pelekas Beach
Perama
Agios Gordis
Achillion
Palace
Kastelani
Benitses
Gastouri
MAIN BLUE (CITY) BUSES:
#6 ······ ev ½Ⓗ 07.00–23.00
#7 ······ ev ½Ⓗ 07.00–23.00
PLATIA SPINADA BUSES:
#2 —— ev ½Ⓗ 06.30–23.00
Messoighi
0   km   7
Lake Korission
OTHONI
ERIKOUSSA
Horio
Argirades
Lefkimi
0   km   10
Agios Georgios (SOUTH)
Kavos
MATHRAKI
Agios Stefanos
—— - - - ○ Irregular Tour Boats
······· ○ Frequent Taxi Boats

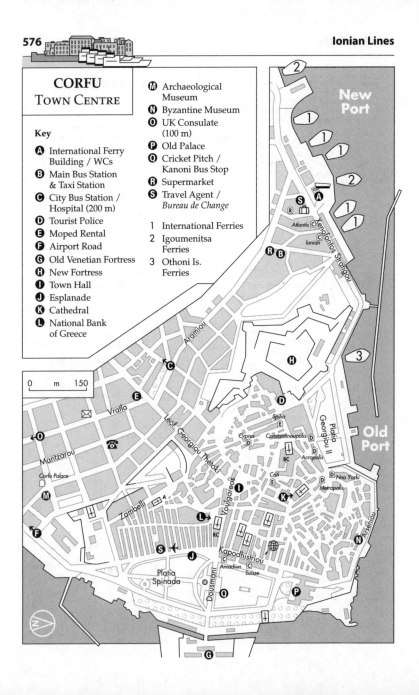

CORFU
TOWN CENTRE

Key

A International Ferry Building / WCs
B Main Bus Station & Taxi Station
C City Bus Station / Hospital (200 m)
D Tourist Police
E Moped Rental
F Airport Road
G Old Venetian Fortress
H New Fortress
I Town Hall
J Esplanade
K Cathedral
L National Bank of Greece
M Archaeological Museum
N Byzantine Museum
O UK Consulate (100 m)
P Old Palace
Q Cricket Pitch / Kanoni Bus Stop
R Supermarket
S Travel Agent / *Bureau de Change*

1 International Ferries
2 Igoumenitsa Ferries
3 Othoni Is. Ferries

New Port

Old Port

Platia Georgiou II

Xenofontas Stratigou

Atlantis
Ionian

Aramiou

Vrata

Leof. Georgiou Theotoki

Mantzarou

Corfu Palace

Zambelli

Platia Spinada

Dousmani

Kapodhistriou

Voulgareos

Spilia
Cyprus
Constantinoupolis
Acropolis
Criti
Nea Yorki
Metropolis
Arcadion
Suisse

Arseniou

0   m   150

draped around a thickly wooded headland, Paliokastritsa is very photogenic but often overwhelmed by the numbers visiting: the trick to any enjoyable visit is to forget the sunset and opt for an early morning visit instead, soaking up the scene before the crowds arrive.

The **southern limb of Corfu** is flatter and generally quieter than the rest of the island. The main road runs inland rather than along the coast (with feeder roads to the better beaches) and briefly skirts a freshwater lagoon — Lake Korission — which is home to some understandably shy wildlife. However, Corfu doesn't give up on tourist excess without a fight, and true to form the road runs to yet another resort town at the southern tip of the island. This one is the worst of the lot by a long way; the wildlife here are anything but shy. Youth-dominated **Kavos** is a beach and disco village where party types go to indulge. The best thing that can be said for this place is that it is a long way from anywhere else: it means that those looking for different types of holiday don't come into conflict. It shares a similar 'wild' party reputation with Faliraki on Rhodes and Laganas on Zakinthos, and suffers very similar problems.

Those looking to make a quick getaway will find that the nearby town of **Lefkimi** has a limited number of ferry services, though the bulk of these operate to Corfu Town. Most Corfu ferries are international, and the island sees an irritating stacking of services, with most departing in the same direction within a couple of hours of each other and then nothing for the rest of the day.

😮

Corfu started out life as a colony of Corinth, the first settlers traditionally arriving in 734 BC. But the island soon outgrew her mother city and the two clashed in the first known sea battle between Greek city states in 664 BC. Thereafter the island's history closely mirrors that of the other Ionian islands. Somewhat removed geographically from the threat of Persian invasion they took no significant part in the campaigns that saw Athens rise to power, though they did side with her during the Peloponnesian War. Following Athens' defeat Corfu saw a succession of oligarchic rulers, but was always on the fringes of the Hellenic world.

The island came under Roman rule in 229 BC, and was used by Octavian (later the emperor Augustus) for his base prior to the battle of Actium. Otherwise Corfu played no major role except as a stopping point for Roman notables heading east (Nero is said to have dropped in for a quick dance and a song in 67 AD). The years of quiet prosperity came to an end in 337 AD, when a period of insecure Byzantine rule began. Corfu's staging-post position left her an object of interest to various passing armies and ensured brief conquests by Goths, Normans and Angevins during the crusading years, before Venice took control in 1386. Thereafter Corfu was a vital bulwark against the Ottoman empire's expansion into Europe — this was one of the few Greek islands that never saw Turkish rule, though the island was raided and besieged in 1537 (when 20,000 inhabitants were carried off into slavery), 1571, 1573, and finally 1716. In this year Saint Spiridon — Corfu's patron saint — saved the day by bringing on a rainstorm in August, an event celebrated on the 11th of the month every year and by the naming of close on every fourth male born on the island after him.

The arrival of Napoleon in 1797 saw the end of Venetian rule on Corfu and ushered in a brief period of unstable French government (intermixed with periods of independence and Russian control). Stability only returned with the period of the British protectorate between 1815 and 1864, when control was ceded to the new Greek state.

🛏

The EOT (☎ 37520) and Tourist Police in Corfu Town offer free town as well as hotel and room information. Hotel space is more than adequate for most of the year, however there can be pressure on bed space in High Season, so booking ahead is a good idea if travelling then. Near the New Port are a few rooms and the elderly but just bearable *Ionian* (☎ 39915), which is adequate in a pinch. The Old Port has the over-popular budget *Constantinoupolis* (☎ 39826) and *Acropolis* (☎ 39569), and the very budget conscious will find that out of town there is a poor *IYHF Hostel* (☎ 91292) at Kondokali.

Prices rise as you move closer to the centre of Corfu Town. Nearer the top end of the market is the delightfully placed (if rather pricey) *Arcadion* (☎ 37670) overlooking the cricket pitch. Somewhat further out, is the excellent, but small, B-class *Dalia* (☎ 32341), in a renovated town house 500 m from the airport (at 9, Platia Ethnikou Stadiou). Not the cheapest hotel in town, but good value for money.

Λ

Camping mini-buses lay siege to the ferry terminal when the morning ferries come in and are thereafter absent. The best sites lie away from the tourist strip, and as usual in the Ionian islands are geared up to motor caravans rather than backpackers: *Vatos Camping* (☎ 94393) and *Paliokastritsa Camping* (☎ 26630 41204) on the west coast are arguably among the more attractive, along with the clutch of sites abutting the northern beaches — notably *Dolphin Camping* (☎ 26630 31552) near Sidari. Nightlife lovers usually stick to the sites on the tourist strip north of Corfu Town. These include Dassia's *Kada Beach Camping* (☎ 93595) and *Corfu Camping* (☎ 93246) at Ipsos.

⌀⌀

Corfu Town is the premier tourist attraction thanks to the delightful mix of Venetian, French and British Georgian buildings straddled by a couple of substantial Venetian fortresses partially demolished by the British when they left the islands in the 1860s. The focus of the town is park-like **Platia Spinada** or Esplanade, the site of the famous cricket pitch (the only one in Greece), and now used early Saturday mornings as a practice marching ground by the local high school band. Some gatherings here have been less happy: in WW2 the occupying German forces used the pitch as a collecting point for the island's Jewish population before they were transported to the concentration camps. The square is bounded on the western side by the **Liston**, a row of lovely tall arcaded houses-cum-cafés built during the brief period of French rule (1807–14), and on the east side by the impressively large moated **Old Fortress** — built on the Corfu ('two hills') promontory, and once the site of a Temple of Hera — though there is little sign of it today.

North of the cricket pitch lies the **Royal Palace**, looking like a Georgian English country house. It was built in 1819 to house a series of British high commissioners who considered themselves sufficiently high to require a throne room of the regal rather than the convenience variety. These days the recently refurbished

building is home to a somewhat eccentric and very un-Greek display of Chinese and Japanese porcelain and bronzes (the collection of a former Greek ambassador in the Far East).

Some 50 m south of the square lies Corfu's **Archaeological Museum**: home to the famous pedimental sculptures (dominated by a primitive figure of a Gorgon — considered to be among the greatest Archaic-period sculptures) from the Temple of Artemis (580 BC) in the ancient town. The museum is also home to an assorted collection of Classical and Roman sculpture recovered from various sites on the island. The best of these archaeological sites lies just south of Corfu Town: the ancient city of Kerkyra (now little more than foundations — including the Temple of Artemis). Beyond the ruins lies Kanoni, jumping-off point for a couple of monastery-topped islets. The first — **Vlakerani** — is linked to Corfu by a picture-postcard causeway, while **Pontikonissi** (or Mouse Island) is reached by regular caïque and is said to be the boat of Odysseus turned into stone by the wrathful Poseidon.

Further afield, Corfu has a disparate collection of other attractions which are worth a look if you are staying any length of time on the island. Nearest to Corfu Town is the 1891-built **Royal Palace** at Achillion; the summer home of Kaiser Wilhelm II from 1908–14, it was the birthplace of Prince Philip. It has recently hit the headlines as a potential fire sale property by the cash-strapped Greek government trying to raise funds as part of the ongoing EU-bailout saga. The locals aren't keen on losing their history to the highest bidder and are making a fuss. Far prettier, and most definitely not for sale, is the cliff and beauty spot of **Paliokastritsa**, home to a castle (c. 1200 AD) and monastery (1228) replete with icons (icon fans should also check out the **Byzantine Museum** in Corfu Town). This is home to one of the more important collections of icons in Greece.

To the north-east of Corfu lie three small islands also open to island hoppers. They see few tourists, but those that call usually end up raving about them. Regular ferries leave from Corfu Town, but given that each can be 'done' in a couple of hours it is better to visit by excursion boat from Corfu's north coast resorts. Arid and hilly **Othoni** is the largest, and the only one with a resident summer tourist population. Even so, it is very quiet with nothing to do except lounge on the beach and make the dusty walk to the inland chora. **Erikoussa** is the main objective for the Sidari excursion boats thanks to a good sand beach at the port village. **Mathraki**, the smallest, sees few tourists and her beaches are home to nesting loggerhead turtles each summer. Rooms are available on all three islets in High Season — though it is best to visit on an excursion first and if you want to come back and stay arrange the accommodation then. Erikoussa also has a small hotel.

Igoumenitsa
ΗΓΟΥΜΕΝΙΤΣΑ; pop. 6,500.

CODE ☎ 26650
WATERFRONT NTOG/EOT ☎ 22227
TOURIST POLICE ☎ 22222
POLICE ☎ 22100

Set within the inner recesses of a deep and steamy calm bay, largely unknown Igoumenitsa is one of those places which regularly prompts the question 'Where are we?' from puzzled ferry passengers looking down from passing sun decks. In fact, Igoumenitsa — despite being a surprisingly small place — is Greece's major western port north of the Gulf of Corinth and thus on the itineraries of a growing number of ferries. In spite of this, very few foot passengers choose to set down here (which in the circumstances is probably a very wise move — given the lack of a rail link and the very low number of bus departures to other parts of Greece). The port remains the preserve of container lorries looking for the fastest trans-Adriatic route to Athens.

Those island hoppers that do pass through have precious little incentive to linger, for Igoumenitsa does not inspire. Strung along the back of the bay, it is dominated by a long waterfront. The north end is fairly pleasant — given its commercial role — with a park of sorts filled with bushes and a rather fragrant public WC. Behind this lies a dusty collection of drab Greek streets, three or four blocks deep, of the kind that bedevils many a potentially attractive geographical location.

Efforts are being made to tart the place up a bit, with several of the main streets being pedestrianized, but it is a pretty thankless task given the quality of the street buildings. The EU has also put money in by funding the building of an excessively large new ferry terminal at the southern end of the town. It gleams, almost unused, at the half-dozen or so boats that briefly moor outside. Meantime, Corfu landing-craft ferries are still using the more conveniently placed old quays nearer the town centre.

Beyond seeking out one of the few tavernas (the best are scattered among the coffee bars lining the waterfront street on the road to the Medical Centre) Igoumenitsa offers nothing to do except catch the ferry to Corfu or Italy, or a bus out of town (if you can get a seat: they tend to get booked up, as the dilapidated bus station — that looks as if it would do one of the poorer regions of Albania proud — isn't a place where the locals want to linger). There are only four buses a day to Athens (◎ 08.30, 11.00, 14.30, 20.30), and one to Thessalonika (◎ 10.30). All the Athens-bound buses head south to the Gulf of Corinth and join the Patras—Athens road at the Rio suspension bridge.

⊨
Most folks head for Corfu Town rather than stay in the dozen-odd hotels in Igoumenitsa. However, there are advantages in staying here, not least because there is far less pressure on beds. In a pinch try the D-class *Egnatia* (☎ 23648) or, if you have the funds, the B-class (but dull) *Angelika Pallas*.

A
The very low number of backpackers visiting Igoumenitsa has resulted in a lack of suitable camping. There are several motorist-orientated sites on the coast south of the port, but they are inaccessible (thanks to the failure to provide camping buses) without your own transport.
◎◎
Igoumenitsa is home to a small, and hardly ever visited, Archaeological Museum.

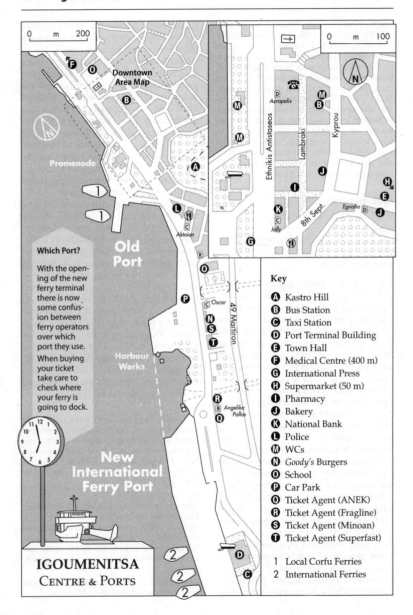

0 m 200

0 m 100

Downtown Area Map

Acropolis

Promenade

Ethnikis Antistaseos

Lambraki

Kyprou

Old Port

Aktaian

Egnatia

8th Sept.

Jolly

Which Port?

With the opening of the new ferry terminal there is now some confusion between ferry operators over which port they use.

When buying your ticket take care to check where your ferry is going to dock.

Harbour Works

Oscar

49 Martiron

Angelika Pallas

New International Ferry Port

IGOUMENITSA
Centre & Ports

Key

- **A** Kastro Hill
- **B** Bus Station
- **C** Taxi Station
- **D** Port Terminal Building
- **E** Town Hall
- **F** Medical Centre (400 m)
- **G** International Press
- **H** Supermarket (50 m)
- **I** Pharmacy
- **J** Bakery
- **K** National Bank
- **L** Police
- **M** WCs
- **N** *Goody's* Burgers
- **O** School
- **P** Car Park
- **Q** Ticket Agent (ANEK)
- **R** Ticket Agent (Fragline)
- **S** Ticket Agent (Minoan)
- **T** Ticket Agent (Superfast)

1 Local Corfu Ferries
2 International Ferries

Ithaca

ΙΘΑΚΗ; 96 km²; pop. 4,000.

CODE ☎ 26740
PORT POLICE ☎ 32209
POLICE ☎ 32205
HOSPITAL ☎ 32282

A small and very hilly island, Ithaca is literally two barely connected mountain peaks poking out of the sea. Ithaca lies steeped in the romance of myth rather than offering much in reality beyond a quiet tranquillity. The legendary home of Odysseus (alias Ulysses), hero of the *Odyssey* — and the siege of Troy, too, in a way (he was the devious hero who came up with the idea of the wooden horse) — there is little to do here except walk the hills, indulge in a little quiet romance and wonder why he spent ten years trying to get back. Indeed, there is little to show that he was ever here at all: no dead dogs on the beaches, no remains of a palace (home to his wife Penelope), and no sign of the suitors and attendant orgy girls — Ithaca has yielded little significant archaeological evidence to suggest it was a centre of power at the time.

The modern centre, such as it is, consists of the red-tiled house village of **Vathi** tucked deep into a bay in the middle of the island. Devastated in the 1953 earthquake that rocked all the southern Ionian Islands, it has been rebuilt sympathetically, and offers a taste of rural island life, spiced with the more tourist-orientated waterfront looking onto the prison islet of **Lanzareto** that graces the mouth of the bay.

Ferry links are better than might be expected considering the small population and the insignificance of Ithaca as a tourist island (thanks largely to poor pebble beaches and few obvious sights), with boats running to three island ports. Large ferries head for Vathi, with landing-craft ferries serving the small northern port of **Frikes** (from Lefkada) and **Pisaetos** (from Kefalonia). Pisaetos also sees occasional international boats that can't find the time to steam round to Vathi. This 'port' is no

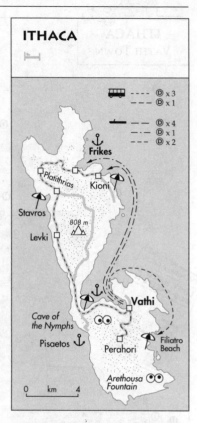

more than an isolated quay below a steep hillside decorated with a switchback dirt-track road, which defies the island bus and sees as few taxis.

Ithaca has a solitary bus that teeters along the precipitous hill roads to uninspiring **Stavros** (complete with several places offering rooms) and the hamlet villages on the northern half of the island, as well as to **Perahori**, the former centre in pirate-troubled days. High Season also sees taxi boats running from Vathi to the attractive pebble-beach villages of **Kioni** and Frikes. Formerly quiet fishing villages, they offer a gentle spot in which to spend a day or two.

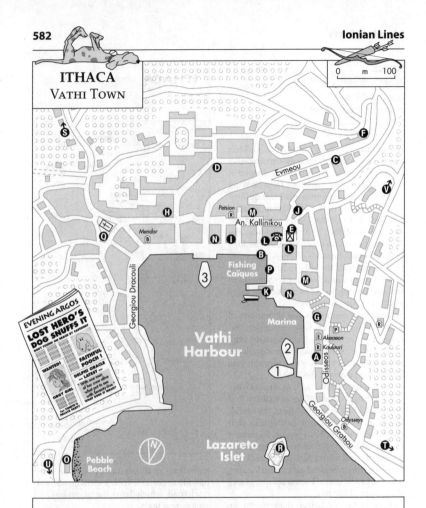

ITHACA
VATHI TOWN

Key

- **Ⓐ** Tourist Information
- **Ⓑ** Bus Stop & Taxi Rank
- **Ⓒ** Police
- **Ⓓ** Tourist Police
- **Ⓔ** National Bank of Greece
- **Ⓕ** Hospital
- **Ⓖ** Town Hall
- **Ⓗ** Archaeological Museum
- **Ⓘ** Pharmacy
- **Ⓙ** Bakery
- **Ⓚ** Public WCs
- **Ⓛ** Ticket Agent
- **Ⓜ** Moped Rental
- **Ⓝ** Tavernas
- **Ⓞ** Circe Club
- **Ⓟ** Pl. Elastathiou Dracouli
- **Ⓠ** Cathedral
- **Ⓡ** Former Prison
- **Ⓢ** Sarakiniko Bay Road
- **Ⓣ** North Ithaca Road
- **Ⓤ** Loutsa / Skinos Bay Road
- **Ⓥ** Perahori Road
- **1** Ferry Berth
- **2** Irregular Hydrofoils
- **3** Beach Boats

⊨

Accommodation on Ithaca is pretty limited, and what there is tends to be expensive. **Vathi** has some rooms and two B-class hotels: the *Mendor* (☎ 32433), on the waterfront near the caïque harbour, and at the western edge of town the hotel/pension *Odysseys* (☎ 32381) — also on the waterfront. There is also a C-class hotel in **Frikes**, the *Nostos* (☎ 31644), and a B-class hotel in Kioni: the *Kioni* (☎ 31362). A few rooms are also on offer at both.

ᛒᛒ

Vathi is host to a small **Archaeological Museum** which in truth has limited appeal. More interesting by far is the **Cave of the Nymphs** — a large cavern 1 km west of Vathi, said to have been used by Odysseus and the goddess Athena to hide the treasure the Phaeacians gave him immediately prior to his return from Troy. A second site with Homeric associations lies on the south-east corner of the island: the **Arethousian Fountain** offers a splendid excuse for some pleasant hill walking, but bring liquid with you as your objective is often drunk dry.

Katakolon
ΚΑΤΑΚΟΛΟ

CODE ☎ 26210

A sleepy little port on the west coast of the Peloponnese, Katakolon hovers on the fringe of the ferry system, appearing every other year or so on a new boat's itinerary before commercial realities set in and it returns to somnolent isolation. The reason for these calls by irregular ferries and cruise ships is the port's ready access to the site of ancient Olympia (27 km), home to the most important Temple of Zeus and the Olympic Games. Actually, the port is quite attractive itself, with an impressively long beach, several tavernas and hotels. Buses connect with the town of Pirgos (12 km away) and its links with Olympia, where you will find three campsites and a youth hostel if you are minded to stay.

⊨

Accommodation options in town are confined to three establishments: the A-class pension *Zefyros* (☎ 41170), the C-class hotel *Ionio* (☎ 41494), and the D-class *Delfini* (☎ 41214).

Kefalonia
ΚΕΦΑΛΛΩΝΙΑ; 781 km²; pop. 31,800.

ARGOSTOLI CODE ☎ 26710
SAMI CODE ☎ 26740
ARGOSTOLI NTOG OFFICE ☎ 22248
SAMI PORT POLICE ☎ 22031
POLICE ☎ 22200
HOSPITAL ☎ 22434

The second largest island in the Ionian group, mountainous Kefalonia is a quiet beach-holiday destination now enjoying a very high profile. This is in large part because the island is the setting for Louis de Bernières's best-selling novel *Captain Corelli's Mandolin*. But Kefalonia also hit the headlines in 1998 after the murder of a couple of its 3,000 British residents (allegedly by a pair of Albanian refugees), and thanks to the discovery of a British WW2 submarine off the south-east coast from which the one survivor of its sinking made a record-breaking deep-sea escape (though until the wreck was discovered — with its escape hatch open — his story wasn't believed).

This latest WW2 tale has simply added to Kefalonia's ability to promote itself on the back of the events of the last century rather than its previous 3,000 years of history. The most significant of these episodes were the Italian occupation of the island in WW2 and its bloody conclusion (when all but 33 of the Italian garrison of 9,000 were massacred by German forces during their takeover following the surrender of Italy in 1943), and the devastating earthquake that rocked the Ionian Islands in 1956, during which almost all the buildings on Kefalonia collapsed. These events provide the setting for (and are excellently described in) *Captain Corelli's Mandolin*.

Kefalonia is very much an island of visual contradictions. On the one hand it boasts some spectacular mountain scenery with a coastline of green pine-clad hills and sandy beach-lined coves, all bathed in a timeless light that makes one feel as if one is walking around in a polarized photograph; on

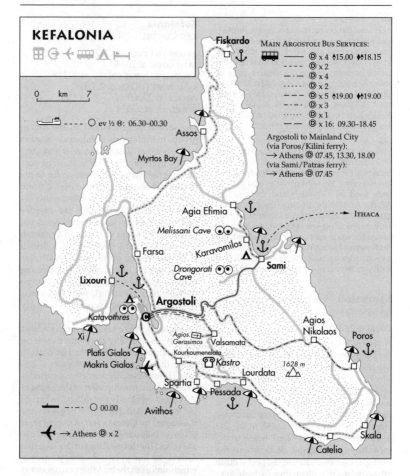

KEFALONIA

⊞ ⊖ ⊀ 🚌 ▲ ⊢

0   km   7

🛳 --- ○ ev ½ ⊕: 06.30–00.30

Fiskardo 🏴 ⚓

MAIN ARGOSTOLI BUS SERVICES:

🚌 ——— ⓓ x 4 ⬧15.00 ⬧⬧18.15
      ---- ⓓ x 2
      —·— ⓓ x 4
      ······ ⓓ x 2
      — — ⓓ x 5 ⬧19.00 ⬧⬧19.00
      —··— ⓓ x 3
      ······ ⓓ x 1
      — — ⓓ x 16: 09.30–18.45

Argostoli to Mainland City
(via Poros/Kilini ferry):
→ Athens ⓓ 07.45, 13.30, 18.00
(via Sami/Patras ferry):
→ Athens ⓓ 07.45

Assos 🏖

Myrtos Bay 🏖

Agia Efimia 🏖 ⚓

Melissani Cave ◉◉

Farsa 🏖

Drongorati Cave ◉◉

Karavomilos 🏖 ⚓
▲ **Sami**

- - → ITHACA

Lixouri 🏖 ⚓

▲
◉◉
Katavothres

Argostoli Ⓒ

Xi 🏖

Platis Gialos 🏖
Makris Gialos 🏖

Agios Gerasimos ⛪ Valsamata
Kourkoumenelata
⛪ *Kastro*

1628 m ▲▲

Agios Nikolaos 🏖

Poros 🏖 ⚓

Lourdata 🏖

Spartia 🏖
Pessada 🏖 ⚓

— —·— ○ 00.00

Avithos 🏖

Skala 🏖

Catelio 🏖

✈ → Athens ⓓ x 2

the other hand the island has been shorn of almost every attractive building that it once possessed. Unfortunately, the hurried rebuilding after the 1956 earthquake was more practical than poetic, leaving a result best summed up by Captain Corelli: 'Everything here used to be so pretty, and now everything is concrete.'

Don't, however, be put off by this lament: even without its old architecture Kefalonia

is a very attractive place, though you will encounter considerable difficulties in exploring the island if you are without your own transport. Kefalonia's fans tend to divide their time between a small hotel, a quiet beach, and a good book (an estimated one in five visitors now comes armed with *the* novel).

Size disparities are Kefalonia's great problem: the island is too big while the

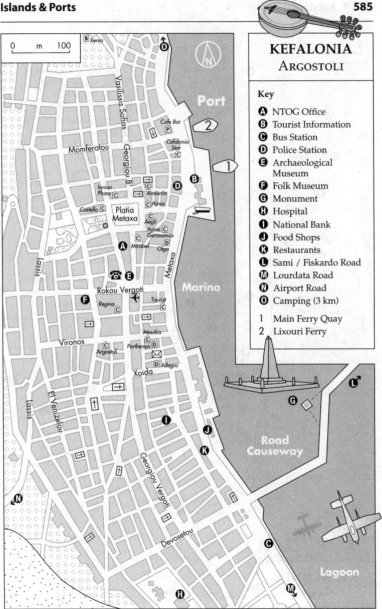

KEFALONIA
ARGOSTOLI

Key
Ⓐ NTOG Office
Ⓑ Tourist Information
Ⓒ Bus Station
Ⓓ Police Station
Ⓔ Archaeological Museum
Ⓕ Folk Museum
Ⓖ Monument
Ⓗ Hospital
Ⓘ National Bank
Ⓙ Food Shops
Ⓚ Restaurants
Ⓛ Sami / Fiskardo Road
Ⓜ Lourdata Road
Ⓝ Airport Road
Ⓞ Camping (3 km)

1 Main Ferry Quay
2 Lixouri Ferry

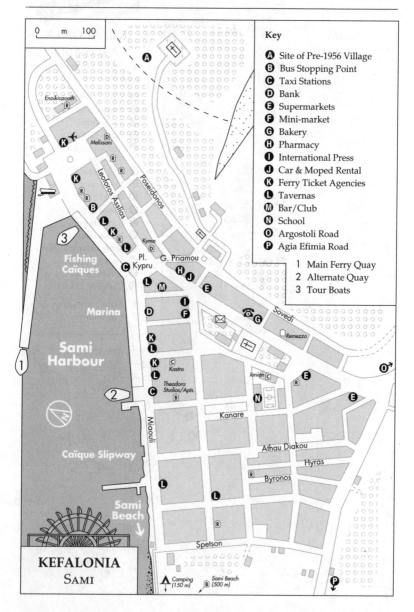

0   m   100

Key

- Ⓐ Site of Pre-1956 Village
- Ⓑ Bus Stopping Point
- Ⓒ Taxi Stations
- Ⓓ Bank
- Ⓔ Supermarkets
- Ⓕ Mini-market
- Ⓖ Bakery
- Ⓗ Pharmacy
- Ⓘ International Press
- Ⓙ Car & Moped Rental
- Ⓚ Ferry Ticket Agencies
- Ⓛ Tavernas
- Ⓜ Bar/Club
- Ⓝ School
- Ⓞ Argostoli Road
- Ⓟ Agia Efimia Road

1 Main Ferry Quay
2 Alternate Quay
3 Tour Boats

Enoikiazonth

Melissani

Leoforos Assilas

Poseidonos

Kyma

Pl. Kypru

G. Priamou

Fishing Caïques

Marina

Sami Harbour

Sovedi

Remezzo

Ionian

Kastro

Theodora Studios/Apts.

Caïque Slipway

Miaouli

Kanare

Athau Diakou

Hyras

Byronos

Sami Beach ↓

Spetson

▲ Camping (150 m)   Ⓑ Sami Beach (500 m)

KEFALONIA
SAMI

population centres are widely scattered and too small. As a result of both this — and the misfortune of the capital growing up on the far west side when all ferry links are either with the mainland or islands on the other three sides of the compass — an amazing seven ports have emerged offering ferry services. This wouldn't be a problem if there was an adequate bus service running between them but sadly there is not, and from midday on, you have to resort to the very expensive taxis.

Kefalonia's ports are a pretty disparate collection. **Argostoli**, the capital, is majestically sited in a picturesque bay beneath the mountains, and despite the lack of good ferry connections has managed to retain some sense of centre but very little else; it abjectly fails to do justice to its setting. From the air or the overlooking hillsides it looks fantastic, but once you arrive in town you will find yourself surrounded by very drab concrete structures: its buildings (many deliberately left with half-built top floors — so that the owners don't have to pay the local roof tax) would put Kefalonia very high in any 'Greek island with the ugliest capital' contest. Even the waterfront, complete with yachting marina, lacks sparkle. There is an EOT office just south of the ferry port, but otherwise there is nowhere to visit. Even the locals prefer to live on the western side of the bay at **Lixouri**, a port town almost as large as the capital, made up of nought but suburbs tarted up with the odd statue. A small landing-craft ferry runs between the two.

Of the other ports, the village of **Sami** has become the 'international' berth and the nearest thing Kefalonia has to a main ferry port and tourist resort (though these terms imply something far more grand). It was also used as the main location during the shooting of the film of *Captain Corelli's Mandolin* (if you visit Kefalonia and then view the film afterwards, it becomes an exercise in 'spot the location').

With a pleasant, taverna-lined waterfront that is atmospheric enough at night, and a fine pebble beach to the north of the port, Sami is the easiest place to stay if you are island hopping, though there isn't a great deal here beyond the hotels, promenade, and several supermarkets battling with each other for the very limited custom. Nightlife, such as it is (and to be honest, 'it' isn't much), is also centred here, but reflects the fact that few people come to Kefalonia to party.

The remaining ports/settlements on the island are poorly connected, but make pleasant places in which to stay; **Poros** is the most accessible thanks to the Kilini ferry. It consists of a large village with a long waterfront, which is more scruffy beach than promenade. It is connected to Argostoli by the same road that branches south to the small tourist resort village of **Skala**, with beaches (some of the best on the island) to the east a second home to the loggerhead turtle (see p. 600).

Fiskardo, perched on the northern finger, is the only village to retain most of its attractive, pre-earthquake Venetian buildings. These are clustered around a petite tree-lined bay, easily making it the most photogenic of the ports; the downside is that it is host to day trippers from the rest of the island (it is so isolated that it is an attractive day-trip destination) and Lefkada in consequence.

The village of **Agia Efimia**, 10 km north of Sami, is quietly attractive with a small pebble beach and the remains of a Roman villa crumbling nearby. The final port, at **Pessada**, is another very attractive village, but it has ferry schedules written by local taxi drivers and is to be avoided unless you have your own transport.

Kefalonia is primarily a beach island and has them in abundance. Finding one isn't difficult. Among the best known are those at **Makris Gialos** and **Platis Gialos**. These end at the small islet of **Tourkopodaro** (connected to Kefalonia by a beach).

Taverna-backed **Avithos** is also justifiably popular thanks to its fine red sand. Lixouri also has a notable red sand beach at **Xi**.

The beach at **Spartia** is more isolated and is backed by picturesque steep white cliffs.

◄┤

Bed supply is good on Kefalonia, despite the island being well off the backpacker trail and popular with Italian motorists hopping across the Adriatic (the tragic fate of the Italian WW2 garrison has left the islanders with a soft spot for the citizens of this occupying nation). However, beds on Kefalonia are pricey. The EOT office in Argostoli offers help in tracking spare beds down, along with free maps, bus timetables, and ferry information.

Argostoli has hotels aplenty; for a good budget hotel try the D-class *Allegro* (☎ 22268) or *Parthenon* (☎ 22246). More up-market are the C-class *Tourist* (☎ 22510), *Agios Gerasimos* (☎ 28697) and the *Mouikis* (☎ 23032). If you want to splash out, then there is a B-class *Xenia* (☎ 22233) at the north end of town.

Sami has several convenient hotels. Two, the C-class *Ionion* (☎ 22035) and D-class *Kyma* (☎ 22064), are both one block behind the promenade (the latter off the town square). Several blocks further back, with good bay views across to Ithaca, is the D-class *Melissani* (☎ 22464). There are also several houses offering rooms in the backstreets. **Poros** also has a good number of rooms advertised.

Λ

There are two reasonable sites on the island: most convenient is *Caravomilos Beach* (☎ 26740 22480) at **Sami**. A nice, mature tree-filled 'family' site behind a pebble beach, but (thanks to the large number of Italian motorists) very expensive. *Argostoli Beach* (☎ 26710 23487) is 2 km north of **Argostoli** and offers better value.

ᏀᏀ

Apart from a poor **Archaeological Museum**, the only 'sight' Argostoli has on offer is a small monument on the causeway across the neck of the bay south of the town — built to commemorate the glory of the British Empire (the British built most of the island's roads during 50 years of rule in the 19th century); it is now inscription-less but otherwise intact. During 1992, the mayor of Sami (a part-time archaeologist) discovered a major 14 c. BC Mycenaean beehive-shaped tomb on the outskirts of town, reopening speculation as to whether Kefalonia was the true 'Ithaca' of Odysseus — given the absence of finds there and the better topographical 'fit' of Kefalonia to the island described by Homer. This discovery will pre-sumably be open to the public at some point. Meantime, **island bus tours** out of Argostoli are very popular. These take in the **Venetian Kastro** of St. George, 9 km south of Argostoli, and the **Monastery of Agios Gerasimos** (home to the body of a monk who is now the island's little-known patron saint).

Fans of *Captain Corelli's Mandolin* are also visiting the island in increasing numbers with the express purpose of finding the Kefalonia described in the book. Needless to say the earthquake hasn't left much. The old village of **Farsa** is now a deserted ruin on a hillside above the Argostoli—Lixouri road, while Argostoli has lost the attractive tavernas that once lined Metaxa Square. As a result of this dearth of sites, many fans have to make do with visiting the beach beyond the village of **Spartia** from where Captain Corelli (and his mandolin strings) made his bid for freedom, and imbibing the odd beverage at the *Café Tselenti* (supposedly the model for Drosoula's taverna) in **Fiskardo**.

The most impressive sightseeing Kefalonia has to offer — beyond the island's lush mountain and coastal scenery — are its caves. These include the red-walled **Drongorati Cave** (entrance fee €5) 4 km south-west of Sami (which has such good acoustics that concerts are occasionally held in it), and the 100 m long **Melissani Cave** (entrance fee €5) on the Sami—Agia Efimia road (complete with a subterranean lake and tour boats).

En route you will find a **Tide-Mill Wheel** at **Karavomilos** — one of a number scattered around the Kefalonian coastline. The best known is at **Katavothres**, just north of Argostoli. For many years this (now over-touristed) site attracted interest thanks to the odd phenomenon of the sea seemingly flowing into the apparently inexhaustible sink hole found here. Attempts to track where the water went, with everything from dyes to petrol and sawdust, proved fruitless until 1963, when a party of Austrian geologists put 140 kg of a water-soluble green dye down the sink hole. Fourteen days later faint traces of the dye appeared 20 km away on the other side of the island at Karavomilos and Melissani cave.

Tour buses also combine with ferries to provide excursions to (1) **Zakinthos** (via Pessada), (2) the ruins of **Olympia** — home to the original Olympic Games and the famous Temple of Zeus (via Poros and Kilini) — and, (3) day trips to **Ithaca** and **Lefkada**.

Kilini
ΚΥΛΛΗΝΗ

CODE ☎ 26230

The major jumping-off point to the island of Zante, Kilini is a dusty little port with a beach on the west coast of the Peloponnese some 30 km south of Patras. Overland connections are poor; simply getting to this port is apt to be a pain. Two buses a day leave Patras during the week, with only the first running during the weekends. At Kilini they stop at the ticket office block behind the ferry quay, usually only skidding into town at breakneck speed a few minutes before ferries are due to depart. There is also a rail link between the ports — but no passenger trains.

┣┥

The Tourist Police office (☎ 92211) on the quay will point you in the direction of the limited (but rarely full) port rooms. The nearest hotels are 5 km to the south at **Kastro**.

Lefkada / Lefkas
ΛΕΥΚΑΔΑ; 303 km²; pop. 23,000.

CODE ☎ 26450
POLICE / TOURIST OFFICE ☎ 22346
HOSPITAL ☎ 22336

An island sufficiently close to the mainland to have a road link (via a bridge to the capital of Lefkada Town), Lefkada is barren and austere but spectacular thanks to its mountains and islet-littered coast. Tourist development has largely confined itself to the east and southern coasts, but is comparatively restrained, offering an appealing mix of taverna and tradition. Unusually for a Greek island, the capital — Lefkada Town — is not a ferry port. With the lagoon to the north now home to a yachting marina, and salt flats between it and the mainland, it doesn't feel like a coastal town. Tradition has it that Lefkada was joined to the mainland until a canal was dug in the 5 C. BC separating the town from the mainland. Earthquake damage is also all too evident here, but fortunately most of

the Venetian churches that make the town have survived, and the ad hoc rebuilding of houses (now limited to a maximum of two storeys high) has produced a charming tin-roof and plaster touch. This is one town that has actually been enhanced by earthquake 'repairs'. Unfortunately, accommodation is limited in the town and it is best visited as a day trip from one of Lefkada's ports.

Buses run frequently between the capital and main island towns, most passing through the resort port of **Nidri**, the starting point for boat tours circumnavigating a number of islets, including **Skorpios** — at one time owned by the Onassis family. A number of boats advertise swims *on* the island. Even if this was physically possible, in practice you are not allowed to venture beyond the beach if you are allowed to land, and usually swims are from the boat just offshore.

Despite this, these excursions offer value for money thanks to the visit to the sea cave on Meganisi. One boat even goes to Lefkada's best sand beach at **Porto Katsiki** — also visited by caïques from the port of **Vassiliki.** Home to the best windsurfing in Europe, off a poor pebble beach, this village gets very crowded, but is worth a look in the late afternoon when up to 100 windsurfers are skimming effortlessly up and down the bay. The best beaches on Lefkada are all on the remoter west side. In addition to Porto Katsiki there is an excellent sand beach behind the headland at **Ag. Nikitas**.

┣┥

High package-tourist presence (courtesy of the airport at Aktion: sometimes advertised as Lefkada airport) has driven up prices and reduced the available accommodation. **Lefkada** is the most likely town to have beds on offer. The E-class *Patrae* (☎ 22359) near the Agricultural Bank in the central square has a good reputation, as does the C-class *Santa Mavra* (☎ 22342) and the nearby E-class *Vyzantion* (☎ 22629). More up-market are the promenade B-class *Nircos* (☎ 24132) and *Lefkas* (☎ 23916). **Vassiliki** also has some budget hotels: the C-class *Lefkatas* (☎ 31229) and E-class *Paradissos* (☎ 31256), and a supply of B-class hotels full of package tourists.

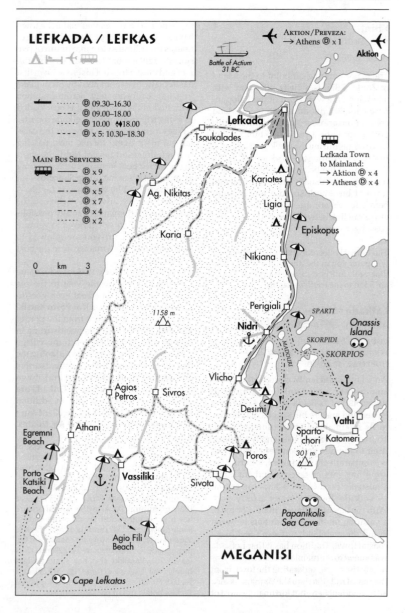

LEFKADA / LEFKAS

Battle of Actium
31 BC

Aktion/Preveza:
→ Athens Ⓓ x 1

Aktion

Ⓓ 09.30–16.30
Ⓓ 09.00–18.00
Ⓓ 10.00 ♦♦18.00
Ⓓ x 5: 10.30–18.30

Main Bus Services:
Ⓓ x 9
Ⓓ x 4
Ⓓ x 5
Ⓓ x 7
Ⓓ x 4
Ⓓ x 2

0   km   3

Lefkada

Tsoukalades

Lefkada Town
to Mainland:
→ Aktion Ⓓ x 4
→ Athens Ⓓ x 4

Kariotes

Ligia

Episkopus

Ag. Nikitas

Karia

Nikiana

Perigiali

SPARTI

Onassis
Island

1158 m

Nidri

SKORPIDI

SKORPIOS

MADOURI

Vlicho

Agios
Petros

Sivros

Desimi

Spartochori

Vathi

Katomeri

Athani

Egremni
Beach

Poros

301 m

Porto
Katsiki
Beach

Vassiliki

Sivota

Papanikolis
Sea Cave

Agio Fili
Beach

MEGANISI

Cape Lefkatas

LEFKADA TOWN

Key

A Main Square
B Bus Station
C Tourist Police
D Police
E National Bank of Greece
F Ionian Bank
G Hospital
H Taxi Station
I Supermarket
J Pharmacy
K Bakery
L Moped Rental
M Town Hall
N Cathedral
O Valaoritou Garden
P Chain Bridge & Causeway
Q Santa Maura Fort
R Line of Roman Aqueduct
S Town Park
T Nidri & Vassiliki Road

Λ

There are an impressive six camp sites on the island: *Camping Vassiliki Beach* (☎ 31308), usually full-to-bursting with windsurfers, is the most convenient; *Camping Desimi Beach* (☎ 95225), 3 km south of Nidri, is less so but offers more space. *Camping Kariotes Beach* (☎ 71103) is the nearest to Lefkada Town. The other sites — *Episkopos Beach* (☎ 92410), *Santa Mavra Camping* (☎ 95493) and *Poros Beach* (☎ 95452), running down the east coast — are geared to motorists.

∞

Lefkada's sights are more made up of places where things happened rather than things to see; over the years the island has become a veritable shrine to the sticky side of romance. Story has it that Aristotle, when a very old man, was asked if he regretted that his manly 'powers' had waned. He is said to have observed that it was the best thing that had ever happened to him, as it was 'like being unchained from a lunatic'.

Lefkada is, from top to tail, a testament to the acuteness of this observation. **Cape Lefkatas** became the Beachy Head of the ancient world after Sappho, the famous Lesbian poet (see p. 468), allegedly jumped off after experiencing a touch of unrequited love. The tip of this peninsula housed a **Temple of Apollo** (fragmentary remains extant) whose priests thought this action a terribly good idea and took to chucking sacrificial victims — with symbolic lover's dove wings tied to their limbs — over the edge in years thereafter (they were collected by boat after they hit the water).

Given the close proximity of this lover's leap, it is surprising that Antony and Cleopatra didn't take advantage of it in 31 BC after the disastrous naval **Battle of Actium** against Octavian, which took place just to the north of Lefkada just offshore from the airport of Preveza/Aktion. Instead, they winged it to Egypt and jumped into the next world from there. Romance struck again in the 19 c. when the German archaeologist Wilhelm Dörpfeld hit upon the idea that Lefkada was Homer's Ithaca and then spent futile years trying to prove it. Dying of old age before the total discrediting of his theory could prompt him to test the merits of Sappho's leap, he left some **Bronze Age Tomb** excavations south of Nidri — now little visited — and a bronze bust of himself on the town waterfront.

Meganisi

ΜΕΓΑΝΗΣΙ; 23 km²; pop. 250.

CODE ☎ 26450

A small island off the south-east coast of Lefkada, Meganisi is linked by a daily ferry from Nidri as well as several tour boats. If you are not planning to stay overnight then the latter are a better way of quickly seeing this gentle island. Most boats also call at the fishing village of **Vathi**, the largest settlement on the north coast, and occasionally at its tidier neighbour — **Spartochori** — as well.

⊨

A reasonable supply of rooms exist in all three villages. There is also a pricey A-class hotel in Katomeri: the *Meganissi* (☎ 51639).

∞

Nidri tourist boats run daily to the **Papanikolis Cave** on the west coast, said to be the second largest sea cave in Greece. The locals claim that they successfully hid a Greek submarine in it for much of the last war, but, appealing as this idea is, the more cynical will perceive that it must have been a very small submarine.

Patras

ΠΑΤΡΑ; pop. 141,530.

CODE ☎ 2610
TOURIST OFFICE ☎ 22 0902
NTOG OFFICE ☎ 65 3368
FIRST AID ☎ 150

The busiest international port in Greece after Piraeus, Patras is a popular destination for ferries running down the length of the Adriatic or south from Italy. However, the presence of thousands of holidaymakers passing through daily brings out some of the worst overpricing in Greece, the practical upshot being that if you want a top-class meal or bed you have to look pretty hard to find it. The city is also suffering from an influx of illegal immigrants, who, having broken into the EU via Greece, are now looking to cross over to richer Italy.

The third largest city in Greece, Patras's fate was sealed with the decision to rebuild the centre (following its destruction during the War of Independence) using an uninteresting grid pattern. The grime-laden buildings, relieved only by attractive park-like squares, offer little incentive to hang around, and few tourists do.

Fortunately, all facilities and means of escape are on or near the waterfront. The downside of this is that, alongside the various ferry terminals and the railway and bus stations, the quayside road is loaded with some very indifferent restaurants. Able to rely on a captive audience of travellers waiting for ferries (who are unlikely to ever return), they have little incentive to provide top-notch cuisine. Given this, the best advice has to be to feed before you arrive in the port area of town.

Most ticket agencies are only interested in selling international tickets, and all will accept credit cards—unless you are buying a ticket for a purely domestic boat. The latter are still usually sold on a cash basis. You will also find tickets for most domestic ferries and hydrofoils (if any) on sale from kiosks on the quay next to the boats.

A relatively recent change at Patras has been the introduction of signpost 'Gates' along the waterfront of the city centre port (known as the Northern Port). After many years in the building—courtesy of massive EU-funding — a new international ferry port (known as the Southern Port) finally opened in 2011, though it has yet to be completed. At present there isn't the space for ferries to berth for long periods, so you may find that your boat docks during the day at the city port and then moves to the Southern Port to embark passengers. Your ticket agent will indicate from which port your boat will depart, but all international travellers still have to clear passport control in the International Ferry Terminals to get their boarding pass and have it stamped (this is checked on boarding). Domestic ticket holders just show their tickets.

Patras is naturally a major destination for both trains and buses. The former depart from the Northern Port quayside station

every couple of hours and then crawl to Athens or the Peloponnese; the latter are based at a waterfront bus station (complete with a pricey, but popular, snack and drink shop) and offer a far wider variety of destinations. The most important of these are to: Athens (ⓑ 05.00–21.00), Thessalonika (ⓓ 08.30, 15.00) and Kilini (ⓓ 08.00, 14.45). Finally, the big Adriatic ferry lines run ultra-smooth air-conditioned buses to and from the centre of Athens. Seats can be booked along with your ticket. In many ways this is the best option if you are arriving in Greece as you can move straight from ferry to bus and thus manage to avoid Patras altogether.

H→

The friendly NTOG office (☎ 42 3866) located in the ferry terminal can point you in the direction of a room. The port area of town has the greatest concentration, with the waterfront D-class *Splendid* (☎ 27 6521) along with the C-class *Acropole* (☎ 27 9809) offering tolerable rooms at better than most prices. Near the bus station you will find the noisy C-class *Adonis* (☎ 22 4213) and the *Mediterranee* (☎ 27 9602) —located on Ag. Nikolaou, the main shopping street. The up-market *Rannia* (☎ 220114) lies on the next block east. Patras also has a couple of good pensions at the southern end of the port, the *Marie* (☎ 33 1302) and the *Nicos* (☎ 27 6183). There is also an IYHF *Youth Hostel* (☎ 42 7278) 2 km north at 68 Iroon Polytechniou.

A

There are several sites beyond the outer suburbs of Patras. The best is *Camping Rion* (☎ 99 1585): on the beach 7 km north.

◑◑

Patras has just enough sights to keep you occupied while you await your ferry. Greeks head for **St. Andrew's Cathedral**, a major shrine thanks to its role as the repository of the saint's head. Others make for the surprisingly impressive **Venetian Castle** on the site of the ancient **Acropolis**. Classical remains are confined to a restored **Odeon**. Patras also has a shiny new **Archaeological Museum** (open ②–⑦ 08.30–15.00). This is the best thing in town although it isn't conveniently placed. It is located on the main road out of town, some 1200 m from the Northern Port (move inland from the port terminal and turn left at the main road and it is on the right). It houses exhibits for most of the eastern Peloponnese region.

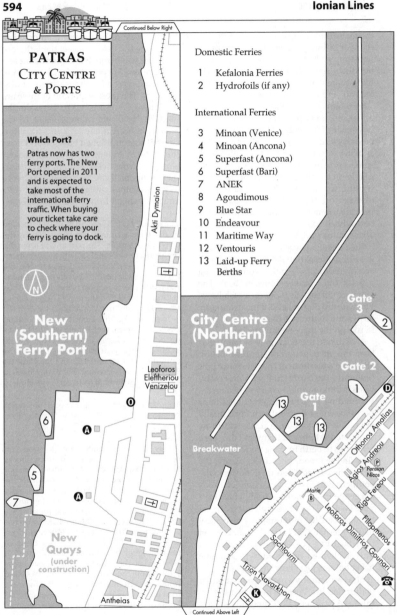

Continued Below Right

PATRAS
City Centre
& Ports

Which Port?

Patras now has two
ferry ports. The New
Port opened in 2011
and is expected to
take most of the
international ferry
traffic. When buying
your ticket take care
to check where your
ferry is going to dock.

Akti Dymaion

New
(Southern)
Ferry Port

Leoforos
Eleftheriou
Venizelou

New
Quays
(under
construction)

Antheias

Domestic Ferries

1   Kefalonia Ferries
2   Hydrofoils (if any)

International Ferries

3   Minoan (Venice)
4   Minoan (Ancona)
5   Superfast (Ancona)
6   Superfast (Bari)
7   ANEK
8   Agoudimous
9   Blue Star
10 Endeavour
11 Maritime Way
12 Ventouris
13 Laid-up Ferry
    Berths

City Centre
(Northern)
Port

Gate 3

Gate 2

Gate 1

Breakwater

Othonos Amalias

Agios Andreou

Pension
Nicos

Riga Fereou

Filopimenos

Marie

Leoforos Dimitrios Gounari

Sachtouri

Trion Navarkhon

Continued Above Left

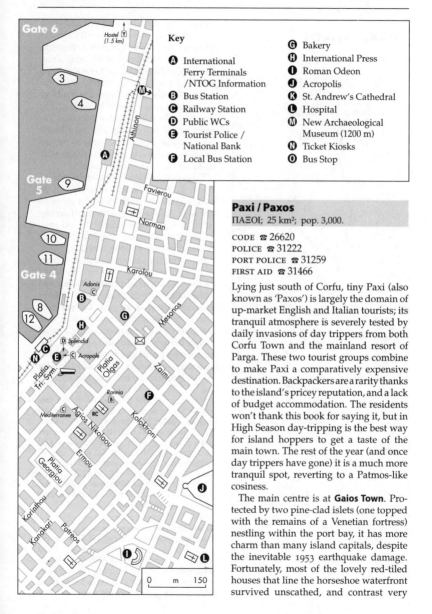

Key

Ⓐ International
Ferry Terminals
/NTOG Information
Ⓑ Bus Station
Ⓒ Railway Station
Ⓓ Public WCs
Ⓔ Tourist Police /
National Bank
Ⓕ Local Bus Station

Ⓖ Bakery
Ⓗ International Press
Ⓘ Roman Odeon
Ⓙ Acropolis
Ⓚ St. Andrew's Cathedral
Ⓛ Hospital
Ⓜ New Archaeological
Museum (1200 m)
Ⓝ Ticket Kiosks
Ⓞ Bus Stop

Paxi / Paxos

ΠΑΞΟΙ; 25 km²; pop. 3,000.

CODE ☎ 26620
POLICE ☎ 31222
PORT POLICE ☎ 31259
FIRST AID ☎ 31466

Lying just south of Corfu, tiny Paxi (also
known as 'Paxos') is largely the domain of
up-market English and Italian tourists; its
tranquil atmosphere is severely tested by
daily invasions of day trippers from both
Corfu Town and the mainland resort of
Parga. These two tourist groups combine
to make Paxi a comparatively expensive
destination. Backpackers are a rarity thanks
to the island's pricey reputation, and a lack
of budget accommodation. The residents
won't thank this book for saying it, but in
High Season day-tripping is the best way
for island hoppers to get a taste of the
main town. The rest of the year (and once
day trippers have gone) it is a much more
tranquil spot, reverting to a Patmos-like
cosiness.

The main centre is at **Gaios Town**. Protected by two pine-clad islets (one topped
with the remains of a Venetian fortress)
nestling within the port bay, it has more
charm than many island capitals, despite
the inevitable 1953 earthquake damage.
Fortunately, most of the lovely red-tiled
houses that line the horseshoe waterfront
survived unscathed, and contrast very

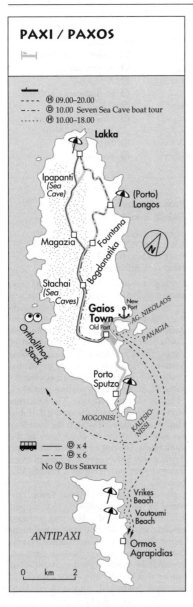

PAXI / PAXOS

⌂ 09.00–20.00
Ⓓ 10.00 Seven Sea Cave boat tour
⌂ 10.00–18.00

Lakka

Ipapanti
(Sea
Cave)

(Porto)
Longos

Magazia   Fountana
                 Bogdanatika

Stachai
(Sea
Caves)   Gaios   New
          Town   Port   AG. NIKOLAOS
Ortholithos Old Port
Stack   PANAGIA

Porto
Sputzo

MOGONISI   KALTSIO-
            NISSI

🚌 ──── Ⓓ x 4
   ──·── Ⓓ x 6
No ⑦ Bus Service

Vrikes
Beach

Voutoumi
Beach

ANTIPAXI   Ormos
                  Agrapidias

0   km   2

attractively with the sea canal and islets. Because of the narrowness of the channel the town now has an 'Old Port' harbouring caïques and tour boats, while ferries now dock at the 'New Port', a quay 600 m along the coast road. The waterfront aside, the town is little more than the main square with a couple of major streets behind, adding greatly to the village feel of the place. The town's only major weakness is the beach; a tiny pebble affair, it does little more than encourage visitors to opt for the caïques that head for two south-coast beaches.

The rest of Paxi (along with Antipaxi to the south) is characterized by low hills on the east side and dramatic cliffs and views on the west. Add to this the carpet of ancient olive groves — containing 200,000 trees — and Paxi's homely size, and the result is a near-perfect walking island.

Buses run regularly from a dusty square at the back of Gaios Town across the island to the small hamlet ports of Lakka and Longos (both of which have seen local ferry links with Corfu in the past). **Longos** is the more attractive settlement of the two, with a couple of tavernas overlooking a small caïque harbour. **Lakka** (also a popular destination for Corfu tour boats) is larger, but relies more on its narrow pine-lined bay for its not inconsiderable scenic appeal.

⌂

Hotels are few and pre-booked. If you can, phone ahead to reserve a room in July and August. **Gaios** has the bulk of the rooms. These include the *Vasilis* (☎ 32404), complete with a leafy garden, the *Spiros* (☎ 31172) and *Alexandros Studios* (☎ 32133) on the hill opposite the bus stop square, and the *Spiros* (☎ 32434) and *San Giorgio* (☎ 32223) on the Port Police headland. Elsewhere on the island **Lakka** has the D-class *Erida* hotel and a couple of tavernas offering rooms.

👓

Gaios has just enough sightseeing to keep the day trippers fully occupied. First among these is the town **Museum** housed in the old British Residency building. Although it is only a three-room affair, it is among the best of its kind and worth the €3 entrance fee. Exhibits include a rusty pistol that in its prime could

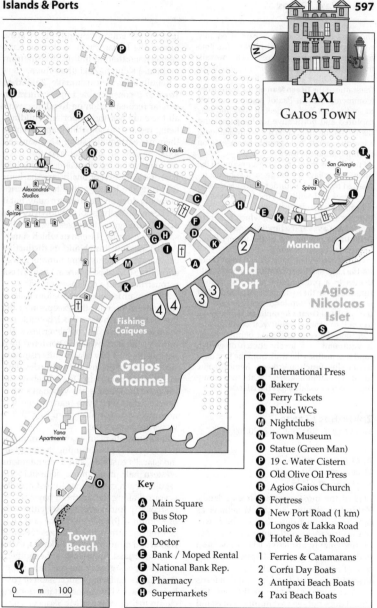

PAXI
GAIOS TOWN

Roula

Vasilis

Alexandros
Studios

Spiros

San Giorgio

Spiros

Marina

Old
Port

Agios
Nikolaos
Islet

Fishing
Caïques

Gaios
Channel

Yana
Apartments

Town
Beach

Key

- **A** Main Square
- **B** Bus Stop
- **C** Police
- **D** Doctor
- **E** Bank / Moped Rental
- **F** National Bank Rep.
- **G** Pharmacy
- **H** Supermarkets

- **I** International Press
- **J** Bakery
- **K** Ferry Tickets
- **L** Public WCs
- **M** Nightclubs
- **N** Town Museum
- **O** Statue (Green Man)
- **P** 19 c. Water Cistern
- **Q** Old Olive Oil Press
- **R** Agios Gaios Church
- **S** Fortress
- **T** New Port Road (1 km)
- **U** Longos & Lakka Road
- **V** Hotel & Beach Road

- 1 Ferries & Catamarans
- 2 Corfu Day Boats
- 3 Antipaxi Beach Boats
- 4 Paxi Beach Boats

0   m   100

shoot six bullets at once, a pair of equally rusty forceps and a five million drachma banknote. The museum also sells a town-walk map with notes on notables from churches to chimneys. Other sites worth hunting out are the statue of the **Green Man** on the waterfront (commemorating a Paxiot sailor who tried to set fire to a Turkish fleet in 1821 and was captured and burnt alive for his pains) and the intriguing 19 c. cistern — complete with a country-house-style grand staircase — on the hill behind the town.

From Gaios there are also excursions to the mainland village of **Parga**, a lovely white-washed town tucked under a hillside decked with trees and with a Crusader fortress on a headland beside the town. Caïques also visit the west coast of Paxi, which has three major **Sea Caves** and a limestone stack called **Ortholithos** poking out of the waters like a monstrous finger of stone.

Tourist boats also leave hourly from Gaios for the large satellite of **Antipaxi** to the south, thanks to a proliferation of sandy strands running down the east side of the island. Most boats call at the two large beaches north of the hamlet of **Ormos Agrapidias**, leaving you to walk to others should you covet greater seclusion. The best and most popular beach is **Voutoumi** — a lovely stretch of golden sand that justifies the walk from the first (and most visited beach) at **Vrikes** — home to some unofficial camping given the absence of any other accommodation on the island.

Zakinthos / Zante

ΖΑΚΥΝΘΟΣ; 402 km²; pop. 30,200.

CODE ☎ 26950
PORT POLICE ☎ 22417
POLICE ☎ 22550
HOSPITAL ☎ 22514

One of the most popular Greek islands, Zakinthos (known to the Venetians as 'Zante') was once described as 'the flower of the Orient'. Regrettably, what was once an undeniably attractive island has been badly scarred by the unhappy combination of a major earthquake (in 1953) and insensitive tourist development that leads some visitors wishing for another one. The island does not see vast numbers of island hoppers as it is inconveniently placed at the foot of the Ionian chain, with poor ferry connections: the only link of note runs from mainland Kilini to Zakinthos Town.

Rebuilt after the earthquake, **Zakinthos Town** is a considerable improvement on similar reconstruction on Kefalonia, with all the churches and important buildings being restored to something approaching their pre-earthquake state. That said, all look somewhat artificial and the town could never be described as cosy. This is in part due to the exceptionally large harbour that runs the length of the town. Ferries normally dock on the northern quay, but if the berths are full it is not unknown for new arrivals to disgorge their passengers on the southern quay (at the end of which stands Ag. Dionissiou church and its distinctive campanile — like its more famous model adorning St. Mark's Square in Venice, it is a reconstruction of a collapsed original).

All the main facilities are to be found along the waterfront, with the exception of the bus station which lies a block behind. The main focus of town life, however, lies to the north of the port, which is bordered by a reasonable EOT pay beach. Hills rise quite steeply behind the town, limiting development to the coastal strip. On a crest above the town are the remains of a Venetian kastro. Severely damaged by the earthquake, it is no longer a major attraction, though the views are impressive.

Zakinthos offers an enjoyable combination of a fertile plain running the length of the island's east side, and a mountainous western half, made more accessible via regular coach excursions. Tourist activity is spread along the southern bay and the east coast (popular with cyclists) either side of Zakinthos Town itself. To the north it is centred on the resortified villages of **Planos /Tsilivi** and more attractive **Alikanas**, to the south at **Argassi**. Argassi aside, the southern peninsula is arguably the prettiest part of the island — offering a succession of cove beaches backed by a wooded interior that climbs to the summit of Mt. Skopos, which

ZAKINTHOS / ZANTE

Blue Caves

Smuggler's Cove

Skinari

Volimes

Alikanas

Anafonitrias   Katastari   Drosia   Tsilivi

Apo Gerakari

Tragaki   Planos

756 m

Galarou   Macherado

Ag. Leontos   Laganas

Lithakia

Agalas

Caves   Keri

B Zakinthos Town

Argassi   Kalamaki   Vassilikos

BAN   PELUZO

SLOW   MARATHONISI

Laganas/Turtle (soup) Bay

⊕ 08.00–18.00
⊕ 10.00
O Speed Boats (now banned)
→ Athens ⊕ x 3

MAIN BUS SERVICES:
— ⊕ x 15
---- ⊕ x 8
— — ⊕ x 9
— — ⊕ x 3
--- ⊕ x 2
-·-· ⊕ x 9
····· ⊕ x 4

Zakinthos Town to Mainland City (via ferries):
→ Athens ⊕ 07.30, 12.30, 14.15, 17.30

0   km   3

rises up between **Kalamaki** and Argassi. The low peak is adorned with the scant remains of a temple of Artemis.

Marring all this, on the south coast lies the brash disco and beach resort of **Laganas**. The second largest settlement on Zakinthos, it takes the form of an otherwise lovely bay fringed with a ribbon of bars and clubs running the length of the beach. Every year it grows, with the authorities paying lip-service to the conservation needs of the rare loggerhead turtle nesting grounds on the resort's beaches (see overleaf), while doing little to improve the deteriorating situation. Of course it is perfectly possible to have a good holiday here by taking care to avoid the turtle beaches (there are plenty of conservationists willing to advise on which beaches are safe), but you also need to keep an eye open for yourselves. As with other holiday resorts, levels of all types of crime are higher than elsewhere in Greece (it is a sobering fact that the vast majority of tourist-related crime is perpetuated by tourists on tourists). If you've come here to party, keep this in mind and take care.

The local authorites are attempting to crack down on the problems, and the situation improved somewhat in 2010.

Moving around Zakinthos is easy as the island bus service is good, serving all the major tourist areas as well as running twice daily to all the other villages on the map overleaf — with the notable exception of the northern hamlet of **Skinari** from whence the ferry to Kefalonia departs. Zakinthos Town is also the starting point for popular tour boats to sights on the scenic north of the island. These include a day trip around the island (€30) and the beach at Smuggler's Cove (see below): this is one instance when forking out for an excursion is worth it.

⊨

The absence of large numbers of backpackers has limited the number of rooms on offer in the town. Hotels there are in profusion on the island. Most, however, are pre-booked solid by package tour operators. **Zakinthos Town** has the bulk of hotels likely to have empty beds. At the top end of the range is the waterfront B-class *Xenia* (☎ 22232), with the pricey new C-class *Palatino* (☎ 27780) 100 m behind. Nearby lies the *Diana* (☎ 28547). Cheaper options are the *Apollon* (☎ 22838) and *Aegli* (☎ 28317). Budget options are the D-class *Ionian* (☎ 22511) north of the Post Office and the *Omonia* (☎ 22113) in the southern suburbs.

Λ

The nearest site to Zakinthos Town is the good *Camping Zante* (☎ 44754) at Tsilivi Beach (reached via regular bus from the bus station). Further up the coast is *Camping Paradise* (☎ 61888), near the village of Mesogerakari and Drosia Beach. Laganas Bay is also home to a couple of sites: *Camping Laganas* (☎ 51585), in an olive grove 1 km west of the end of the town beach, and the better *Tartarouga Camping* (☎ 51417), down the road from Lithakia.

∞

All over Greece you will find postcards of a rusty wreck of a cargo ship set in a crescent beach of golden sand backed by towering cliffs: a beach boat runs daily to **Smuggler's Cove** (€30) as well as to the **Blue Caves** on the northern tip of the island — generally reckoned to be among the best sea caves in Greece. Coach tours are also popular as they enable tourists to take in the island sights without recourse to the main bus routes that tend to head direct to their destination. Most tours include a mountain monastery, cliff-edge sunset views and the salt-pans on the beach north of Alikanas (alias Alikes beach).

Laganas Bay (also known as **Turtle Bay**) offers you the dubious chance to try some turtle-spotting tourism. Blessed with a number of gently shelving beaches of a particularly fine sand, it has been the nesting area for some 80% of the Mediterranean's population of the shy **Loggerhead Turtle** for thousands of years, only to find the disco-city resort of **Laganas** develop on the main beach.

Unfortunately the tourist and turtle nesting seasons are the same, with dire consequences for the turtles. Coming ashore at night they lay eggs in the sand a mere 50 cm below the surface (when they can find a spot where the sand hasn't been packed hard by tourists). These hatch (assuming they haven't had a sun-umbrella pole rammed through the nest) at night, some eight weeks later, and the baby turtles then crawl towards the nearest bright light (in years past this was the moonlit sea: these days it is more likely to be the nearest disco). Meantime the female turtles, in between laying batches of eggs (or jettisoning them at sea rather than approach a neon-lit shore), bask in the bay, only to be regularly killed by, or lose limbs to, the tour boats' propellers.

The situation has deteriorated sharply since 2004 after the national park wardens protecting the turtles abandoned their jobs because they hadn't been paid in months. The tight zoning laws protecting the beaches went unregarded and developers moved in. A lack of funding for protection projects means that there is unlikely to be much change. This is a pity as Laganas, with the right development plan, could yet be reborn as a major eco-tourist destination.

Meantime, the only small shred of comfort is provided by the 'guaranteed' turtle-spotting tour boats. For although at worst you will see a turtle and be disturbing a very shy endangered reptile at a very vulnerable time in its reproduction cycle, at best you will pay a lot of money and won't see one at all, but something much more interesting. Happily for conservation fans, the prospect of having a boat load of turtle-spotters wanting refunds has on occasion prompted the odd operator to resort to underwater antics that would leave passing turtles shell-shocked with laughter — to say nothing if not grateful for being left alone.

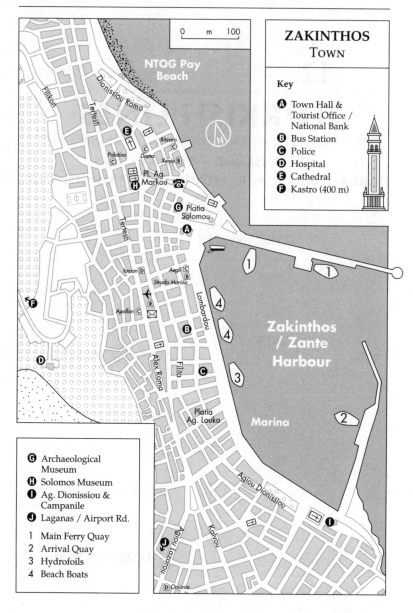

ZAKINTHOS
TOWN

Key

Ⓐ Town Hall &
Tourist Office /
National Bank
Ⓑ Bus Station
Ⓒ Police
Ⓓ Hospital
Ⓔ Cathedral
Ⓕ Kastro (400 m)

Ⓖ Archaeological
Museum
Ⓗ Solomos Museum
Ⓘ Ag. Dionissiou &
Campanile
Ⓙ Laganas / Airport Rd.

1 Main Ferry Quay
2 Arrival Quay
3 Hydrofoils
4 Beach Boats

12
TURKISH LINES

GREEK ISLAND — TURKEY LINKS
DARDANELLES · İSMİR · İSTANBUL · TURKISH ISLANDS

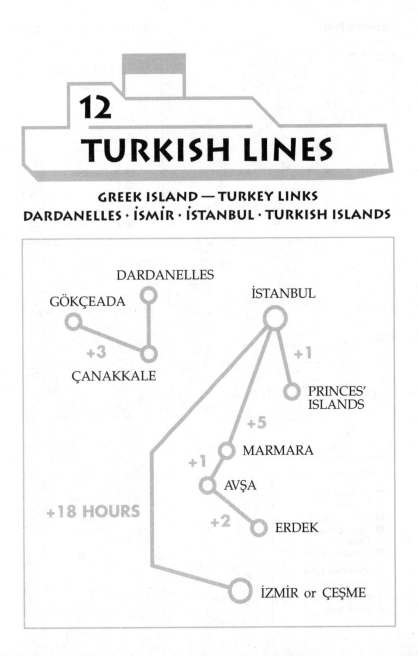

General Features

Given its size, Turkey is endowed with a remarkably limited ferry system. This is a historical accident born out of modern Turkey's failure to retain any of the large Aegean islands (apart from those guarding the entrance to the Dardanelles) once controlled by the Ottoman empire. As a result, ferries on the Turkish Aegean seaboard are — with the odd exception — confined to small international boats providing day-trip excursions to adjacent Greek islands: the ongoing political tension between Greece and Turkey, although less than in past years, prevents the emergence of more substantial links. Such islands where Turkey has sovereignty are tiny affairs that serve only to encourage local taxi boats bringing day trippers from nearby resorts, rather than acting as the necessary catalyst for the emergence of a ferry system. South of the Dardanelles, Turkey is the land of the local bus rather than the ferry. This absence of anything that could remotely be called an Aegean ferry system means that hopping in Turkish waters is, for most tourists, usually a day-trip option while following a Greek domestic route.

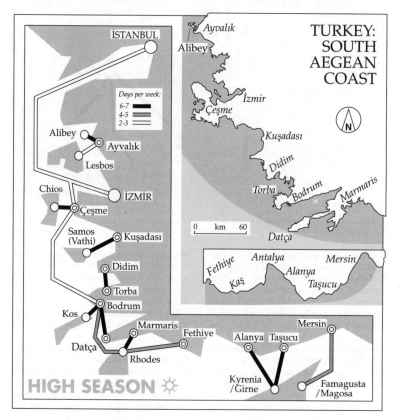

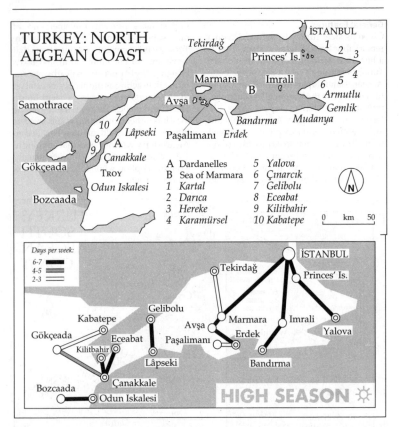

TURKEY: NORTH AEGEAN COAST

A Dardanelles
B Sea of Marmara
1 Kartal
2 Darıca
3 Hereke
4 Karamürsel
5 Yalova
6 Çınarcık
7 Gelibolu
8 Eceabat
9 Kilitbahir
10 Kabatepe

Days per week:
6-7
4-5
2-3

HIGH SEASON ☼

From the Aegean entrance of the Dardanelles through the Sea of Marmara to İstanbul, a very different state of affairs prevails, with a coherent ferry network in existence (backed up by short bus hops), courtesy of some dozen ex-'Greek' islands. In past years boats on most routes were provided by Turkish Maritime Lines — a company which successfully assumed the role of an unofficial state line. It is now defunct, and its absence has prompted a revolution in services, with new companies running high-speed catamarans now dominating the Dardanelles and Sea of

Marmara services, as well as the commuter boats operating along the Bosphorus. The result is a flowering of new services that does make description difficult as things are changing so much year on year.

The Turkish islands, meantime, are little visited (except by holidaying locals), and are very much a product of the messy aftermath of the border drawn up following the Greco-Turkish War of 1920–23. Home to almost exclusively ethnic Greek populations, the inhabitants found themselves on the 'wrong' side of the border, and though largely exempted from the painful forced population exchanges that occurred between the World Wars, most have subsequently left for Greece (thanks in part to cultural intimidation — something ethnic Turks 'stranded' in Greece also encountered). Home to new Turkish populations, they all have something of a 'someone's-sleeping-in-my-bed' air, with churches either abandoned or converted into mosques, and the old Greek place names replaced with suitably Turkish successors. You don't have to go far in Athens to find poignant books devoted to these 'lost' islands filled with photos of dilapidated churches and village buildings.

From a Greek perspective these are very much the 'unlucky Greek islands' — all 13 of them — and reflect the fact that the modern border between Greece and Turkey is historically and archaeologically a very artificial one, something akin to a cultural Berlin Wall enhanced by enforced population exchanges. For most of history the power that reigned supreme on one side of the Aegean also held sway on the other. The Turkish Aegean seaboard is thus littered with cities that to the ancients were as 'Greek' as Athens or Corinth are today.

Ironically, the archaeological remains tend to be better preserved than their Western Aegean counterparts, for deforestation of the mountains of Asia Minor caused extensive silting up of harbours on the Eastern Aegean seaboard leading to these cities being abandoned by the end of Roman rule, while prominent Greek cities elsewhere remained inhabited and grew into the built-over population centres of today. Hopping across to Turkey for a day for a spot of ancient 'Greek' city sightseeing combined with a Turkish coffee, and — it has to be said — a good whiff of the Orient besides, has thus become a popular feature of Greek island hopping holidays.

In the past the omnipresent threat of hostilities between Turkey and Greece — that reached its peak with the 1974 Turkish invasion of Cyprus after a military Cypriot regime sought union with Greece — has

severely limited ferry links. This uncomfortable situation has eased in recent years, but a number of reciprocal measures enforced after the invasion have had an impact on Greek island—Turkey services.

Decrees that passengers could only travel to the other country on the ship of the country they were departing from (producing two fleets at every crossing point) are no longer enforced (though the competing fleets remain). A second charter-flight ticket-issuing requirement that tourists who have entered Greece cannot spend a night in Turkey without losing their right to use the return half of their ticket is more serious and *remains in force*.

Fares

Turkey offers very good value for money, with the general cost of living about 25% cheaper than Greece. Ferry and catamaran ticket prices are similarly lower, though the number of useful sea travel options are also well down — given the limited nature of the Turkish ferry system. International travellers should also not forget that even small boats running between Greek islands and Turkey attract international port taxes.

Language

Modern Turkish is not the easiest of tongues to grapple with. Along the coast tourists can happily get by with a mix of English and German, but place names are often a bit of a mouthful. If you are planning to do more than a day trip or hop to İstanbul you should bring a language guide with you. Otherwise you can just about get by pronouncing:

Turkish	English
C	J
Ç	Ch
I	U
İ	E
J	S
Ö	Eu
Ş	Sh

Example Itineraries

Turkey has justly become a popular Greek-island-hopping day-excursion destination. If you find yourself on one of those islands offering excursions you should hop across; the contrast in culture and atmosphere is an experience well worth the cost of tickets. If you are on something longer than a two-week charter-flight return ticket, then Turkey offers some interesting island hopping possibilities too.

Arrival/Departure Point

The lack of anything other than local boats making the crossing to Turkey means that the islands of the Dodecanese and Eastern Aegean are the best starting points. Rhodes, Kos and Samos all have frequent charter flights.

A: Day Trips to Turkey

Day trips operate from Rhodes to Marmaris, Kos to Bodrum, Samos to Kuşadası, Chios to Çeşme and Lesbos to Ayvalık. Fares tend to be broadly similar regardless of which crossing you use, and reflect the fact that most of the 'ferries' are expensive day-tripper boats. You are usually left to your own devices in Turkey, but you can travel from Samos as part of a tour if so minded. Greek craft from Kos and Rhodes tend to be excursion boats, while their Turkish counterparts are closer to ferries. This distinction can become quite important, for if you travel by ferry you will be deemed an independent traveller and your passport will be stamped on entering and leaving the country.

Travellers on excursion boats, because they have a return ticket, are issued with a landing pass while passports (unstamped) are held by passport control. Ferries also have well-advertised return times. Excursion boats don't — so be careful to establish when they depart; they do NOT wait for late passengers. Miss the boat and you'll have to stay overnight, thereby jeopardizing your right to your charter flight home. Finally, it is hard to change

Turkish liras in Greek banks (best bet is to try branches of the National Bank). Turkish banks, after years of refusing to change drachmas, are now happy to accept euro notes. Traveller's cheques are no problem. If you do return from a day trip armed with wads of Turkish banknotes the best way of changing them is to offer them to day trippers boarding the next day's boat.

B: Turkish Excursion [10 Days]

Those with time to hand will find that a trip to Troy and Constantinople (both dear to Greek hearts) is easily achieved:

1 Lesbos

The closest crossing point to Troy, Lesbos offers irregular ferries to Ayvalık. Crossing points further south are more reliable options if you don't mind changing buses up the Turkish coast.

2 Ayvalık [1 Day]

Worth a day's exploration, with nearby Alibey to visit. Thereafter you can get a bus on to Çanakkale.

3 Çanakkale [3 Days]

Easily the best base for exploring the region, with plenty of accommodation and easy access to Troy and the battlefields of Gallipoli. Each offers a day of leisurely tourism, before heading on to Bandırma by bus.

4 5 Bandırma / Princes' Is. [1 Day]

From Bandırma you have several options. You can either take a regular ferry to İstanbul or break the journey with a visit to the Princes' Islands or travel via Erdek and Avşa.

6 İstanbul [3 Days]

Three days gives you time to do the sights and hop up the Bosphorus. Thereafter you can consider returning to Greece.

Return [2 Days]

Most direct route out of High Season is the weekly ferry from İstanbul to Piraeus. Otherwise the fastest return is via ferry to İzmir (though you can always return via ferry to Bandırma and then an İzmir train) and then bus to Çeşme and ferry to Chios.

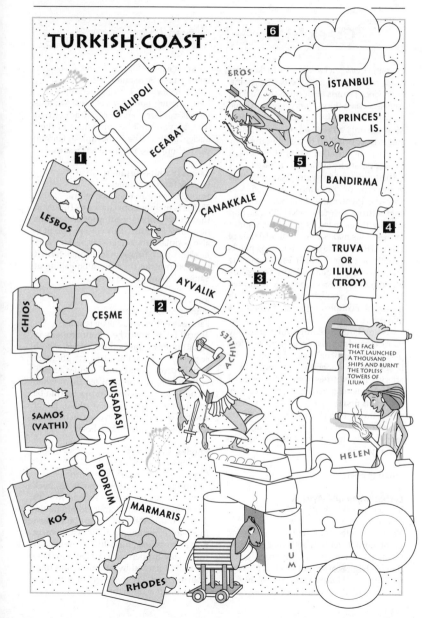

Greek Island — Turkey Links

Crossing between Greece and Turkey you must use a designated crossing point. Five Greek islands adjacent to the Turkish Aegean coast have ferry connections. However, the level of service varies greatly. Most are only advertised on a local basis, and exist courtesy of tourist day trippers. Services are curtailed out of High Season (most operate from May to October).

This tourist-driven regime is also reflected in the type of craft, and how much you pay: the greater the demand, the more competitive the fare. (NB. Prices and journey times listed here are for regular ferries.) This makes the popular islands of Kos and Rhodes the busiest crossing points as both have large Turkish resorts opposite them pushing up demand. The 'ferries' are little more than pleasure boats that can often take one or two cars driven aboard — with the aid of a couple of planks of wood as a makeshift ramp.

It is standard procedure at all ports to buy your ticket a day in advance. In practice, foot passengers can usually get on an afternoon boat (there are generally morning and late afternoon departures from both Greek and Turkish sides of a crossing), provided they get tickets first thing in the morning on the day of travel. Port taxes averaging €25 are levied on travellers staying overnight or longer. Day trippers don't usually have to pay anything.

Crossing points:

Lesbos (Mytilini)—Ayvalık
Journey time: 80 minutes.
Fare: €50 one way, €80 open return.
The most northerly and expensive crossing point, with fewer tourists than elsewhere. Small passenger ferries supposedly run daily in High Season, but services are now very erratic. Unless you have plenty of time to wait, don't consider crossing here.

Chios—Çeşme
Journey time: 90 minutes.
Fare: €40 one way, €70 open return.
Best crossing point for vehicles. Miniotis Ferries' car ferry service is well advertised (though you can't be sure which of their ancient boats will be on the run), and tickets can be bought as far afield as Piraeus.

Samos (Vathi)—Kuşadası
Journey time: 90 minutes.
Fare: €39 one way, €60 open return.
Traffic is mainly from Greece to Turkey in the form of tourists heading for the remains of nearby Ephesus. This crossing point is also popular with longer-stay backpackers heading into Turkey. Occasional tourist boats also make the run, often calling at Samos (Pithagorio) en route.

Kos—Bodrum
Journey time: 55 minutes.
Fare: €28 one way, €55 open return.
Tourist boats make the 1-hour crossing in equal numbers from both directions, as both centres are popular tourist resorts. There are both hydrofoils and small regular ferries, with little to choose between them when it comes to fares. Greek ferries tend to be small passenger-cruisers; Turkish, larger affairs. Cars and motorcycles can be taken across here on the Turkish boats.

Rhodes—Marmaris
Journey time: 110 minutes.
Fare: €30 one way, €55 open return.
The most southerly crossing point. As Greek boats find day excursions around Rhodes more profitable, hydrofoils dominate the Turkey traffic. All travel must be booked in advance: turning up at the last moment doesn't work here. Turkish boats are equally full of day trippers. In High Season there are tourist-packed hydrofoils to and from Bodrum and Fethiye (worth knowing about, but it is often difficult to get seats).

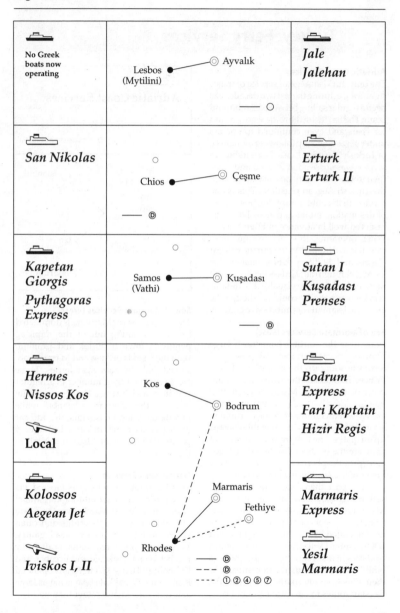

No Greek boats now operating

Lesbos (Mytilini) ● ── ◎ Ayvalık

── ○

Jale
Jalehan

San Nikolas

○

Chios ● ── ◎ Çeşme

── Ⓓ

Erturk
Erturk II

Kapetan Giorgis
Pythagoras Express

○

Samos (Vathi) ● ── ◎ Kuşadası

○

── Ⓓ

Sutan I
Kuşadası Prenses

Hermes
Nissos Kos

Local

○

Kos ● ── ◎ Bodrum

○

Bodrum Express
Fari Kaptain
Hizir Regis

Kolossos
Aegean Jet

Iviskos I, II

Marmaris ◎
Fethiye ◎

○

Rhodes ●

── Ⓓ
--- Ⓓ
---- ①②④⑤⑦

Marmaris Express

Yesil Marmaris

Turkey: Ferry Services

Adriatic Coast Services

The only Turkish Aegean service of major significance during the last two decades has been a regular sailing between İstanbul and İzmir. The ferries on the route were around for years and even continued to operate under new ownership following the demise of Turkish Maritime Lines. Regrettably the service was suspended in 2009 and since then there has been no service around the Turkish Aegean coastline. This is one service that could return for, regardless of destination, bunks and seats had to be reserved well in advance in High Season. When operating, this service sometimes saw İzmir dropped in favour of calls at Çeşme and Bodrum. Unfortunately, the journey through the Dardanelles occured at night on both legs, so visually this 18-hour service was not all it could be, though the arrival at İstanbul was impressive enough.

Sea of Marmara Services (East)

İstanbul is the starting point for a large number of catamarans and passenger ferries heading up the Bosphorus, to the Princes' Islands, and the towns on the south coast of the Sea of Marmara (including Bandırma and its rail link with İzmir). Most are crowded commuter services running several times daily, with timetables posted up on quays. The best from a tour point of view are the boats to the Princes' Islands and up the Bosphorus, which offer excellent views of the famous İstanbul skyline.

In the past there was little change to services as they were all run by Turkish Maritime Lines. Following their departure from the scene most of the major links are now operated by the catamaran-obsessed IDO (İstanbul Deniz Otobüsleri) Line which has brought in several *Highspeed*-type boats built by the same Australian company as their Greek counterparts. They run the flagship routes to Bandırma and Bursa.

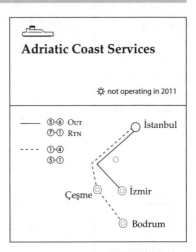

Adriatic Coast Services

☼ not operating in 2011

——— ⑤-⑥ Out
⑦-① Rtn

- - - - ①-④
⑤-①

İstanbul

Çeşme   İzmir

Bodrum

Sea of Marmara Services (West)

The western Sea of Marmara is dominated by boats running out of the Kapıdağ peninsula town of Erdek and İstanbul. Both the islands of Avşa and Marmara are served daily by passenger ferries. These are augmented by a number of irregular private craft: IDO run a High Season daily service to the islands from İstanbul, while private daily local boats take the odd car to the islands from Erdek and the Kapıdağ peninsula villages of Ilhan and Narli to the north.

Dardanelles Services

This important waterway is crossed via ro-ro ferries. These are odd-looking affairs with a large open car-deck, over the centre of which are the ship's bridge and cabin space sitting atop an overhead gantry. Very much sheltered-water craft, they run between Çanakkale and Eceabat, and Gelibolu and Lâpseki. The locally operated Kilitbahir—Çanakkale boat is not as large and runs on demand rather than hourly.

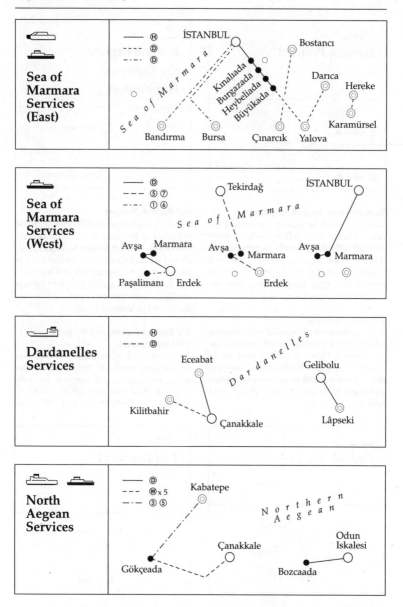

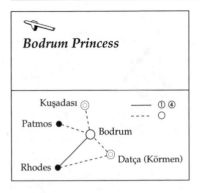

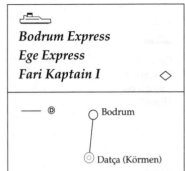

Turkish North Aegean Services

Gökçeada and Bozcaada are served by regular boats. Bozcaada has a twice-daily service, while Gökçeada is served five days a week from Çanakkale, and the remaining days from the small Gelibolu port of Kabatepe. Current timetables are available at Çanakkale.

T/B *Bodrum Queen*

Bodrum harbour is cluttered with wooden tourist boats offering pricey excursions. The *Bodrum Queen* is typical, running to assorted offshore islets. Most common are sailings to **Otok Is.** or two-island trips to **Korada Is.** (beach and hot springs) and **Ada Is.** (aquarium).

H/F *Bodrum Princess*

This frequently repainted Turkish hydrofoil runs out of Bodrum in the High Season, providing a direct service to Rhodes two days a week. During the remainder of her life she makes irregular excursions along the Turkish coast and day trips to Patmos and Kos. Note: you can't pick up this boat except at her starting point.

C/F *Bodrum Express* — C/F *Ege Express*
C/F *Fari Kaptain I*

The coast south of Bodrum is so indented that several small car ferries profit from this geography by offering a twice-daily crossing from Bodrum (09.00, 17.00) to the quay at **Körmen** (09.00, 17.00) some

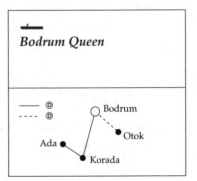

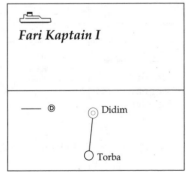

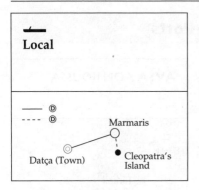

7 km north of Datça (bus service into town included in the price of the ferry ticket). A second summer service operates twice daily (09.00, 17.00) between Torba (again, ferry-ticket buses depart from Bodrum) and Didim (alias Didyma) to the north, home to a major temple of Apollo.

Marmaris Taxi Boats

Daily taxi boats run from Marmaris along the coast of the Datça peninsula to the town of Datça (some even continuing on to the ancient city of Knidos). In doing so they open up the possibility of doing a loop running Rhodes—Marmaris—Datça—Bodrum—Kos—Rhodes.

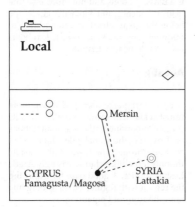

Turkey—North Cyprus Services:
Mersin—Famagusta

Turkish-occupied northern Cyprus is served by boats out of three south-coast ports. From the Turkish perspective these are full-blown international services. However, as Turkey is the only country which recognizes the so-called Turkish Republic of Northern Cyprus, these are de facto internal Turkish services.

Mersin (ancient Tarsus) — a large noisy seaport with nothing to recommend it beyond the ferry link — is the best of the ports, with the thrice-weekly service operating to the war-ruined derelict resort of Famagusta (now Turkish **Magosa**). Weekend sailing continues on to Syria (Lattakia).

Mainland—Kyrenia Links

Slightly closer to the Aegean is the resort town of Silifke and its port Taşucu. Again there is nothing of any interest in the place except the means of leaving it. Two small car ferries and a *Sea Bus* catamaran make the 7- and 3½-hour crossings respectively to the once attractive port of Kyrenia (now **Girne**) daily. The route is the most substantive link between Cyprus and the Turkish mainland. The small port of Alanya also has a catamaran service that runs daily during the High Season.

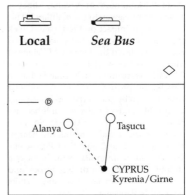

⚓ Turkish Islands & Ports

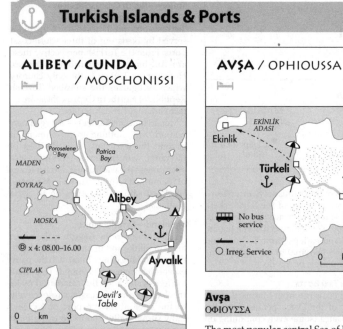

ALIBEY / CUNDA
/ MOSCHONISSI

AVŞA / OPHIOUSSA

Alibey / Cunda
ΜΟΣΧΟΝΙΣΣΙ

A small island north of Ayvalık, Alibey is linked by causeway to the mainland. This had a major impact on the former Greek population, who, unusually, were forced out and replaced by displaced Cretans of Turkish stock between the two world wars. This at least ensures that the island retains a Greek atmosphere, with a typical resortified town (linked by both ferry and hourly bus to Ayvalık), and several reasonable beaches (the best lying on the west coast). Northern Alibey is quiet and contains the nearest thing to the island 'sight' in Poroselene bay: famous in antiquity as the home of a dolphin who saved a drowning boy and did other party tricks for passing writers — notably Pausanias.

Avşa
ΟΦΙΟΥΣΣΑ

The most popular central Sea of Marmara island, Avşa has emerged in recent years as the getaway destination for the better off in İstanbul and its environs. The only town is a mass of hotels and not much else (the nearby beaches and vineyard landscape being the great attraction). In addition to frequent ferry links, occasional taxi boats head out to nearby Ekinlik.

Ayvalık

A new earthquake-damaged town, more ramshackle than scenic, Ayvalık owes its present importance to the nearby attractions of Troy and the Çanakkale—İzmir road running through the town. Alibey aside, the only ferry link is the increasingly erratic Lesbos service. A good base for exploring the region with regular buses to Bergama (and the ruins of Pergamum).

Bandırma

The main city on the Sea of Marmara south coast, Bandırma is a notable transportation hub, with buses to all the major Aegean and Marmarian towns, an important rail link to İzmir, and regular ferries to İstanbul. Home to both cement and sulphuric acid factories, the city is not likely to be in many visitors' lists of Turkish trip highlights in normal years. Unfortunately, times in these parts aren't normal. Between 1999 and 2002 all shops and cafés in the town were closed in a security clampdown over the captured Kurdish separatist leader Abdullah Ocalan (housed on nearby Imrali — see p. 619). The situation has eased, but this remains a destination that should be treated with caution.

Bodrum
ΑΛΙΚΑΡΝΑΣΣΟΣ

If you are planning to take a day trip from the Dodecanese to Turkey you will find that Bodrum is easily the most attractive of the ports on the Turkish seaboard that are accessible from the Greek islands. Now a major resort town, Bodrum has also, unfortunately, been targeted in the past by terrorists intent on disrupting Turkey's tourist industry, so some caution is necessary when visiting.

The mosque- and bazaar-filled town is one of the prettiest in the Aegean (the quayside girl selling drinks from inside a large plastic orange aside) and worth a day's visit in its own right. Those readers not constrained by the overnight limitations imposed on charter flight tickets who choose to stay in Bodrum should find the experience even more rewarding: the town is an attractive base from which to explore a coastline famed for beaches and beauty.

Only a very short ferry-ride from adjacent Kos Town, Bodrum is in many ways her Greek counterpart's twin sister. Both are modern package-tour resort towns with their centres built within the remains of notable ancient cities; both have a relaxed street plan, a scatter of minarets and palms gracing their skylines, and harbours dominated by impressive castles built by the same order of the Knights of St. John. However, Bodrum has two singular advantages that make it the more impressive of the two: the first is the Castle of St. Peter (which is much more substantial than the 'all curtain walls and no keep' affair on Kos); the second is the fact that the town is home to the remains of one of the Seven Wonders of the World: the Mausoleum — the famous tomb of the Hellenistic king of the city, Mausolus.

☠

Modern Bodrum stands atop ancient Halicarnassos. Founded c. 1200 BC, this Greek city rapidly prospered thanks to its good harbour and ideal position on the trade routes of the time. In Classical times it was also famed as the birthplace of the so-called 'Father of History' — the first recognized historian, Herodotus (c. 484–c. 429 BC), though these days his work is regarded as part faction, part travelogue, mostly good fun: filled with good tales, scandalous gossip and a large measure of historical detail about the war between Persia and the Greek states, his 'History' (literally 'enquiry' in the Greek) is one of the most readable of ancient books.

When the Persians advanced to the Aegean in 540 BC, Halicarnassos, which was in no position to resist, came under the overlordship of a succession of Carian kings, aiding the Persians at the Battle of Salamis (480 BC). The most famous of these rulers was Mausolus (377–353 BC), thanks to the tomb commissioned by his wife Artemisia II. The city was regained by the Greeks when Alexander the Great moved east in 334 BC, and came under Roman control in 129 BC. It was successfully attacked by pirates in 62 BC, after which it regained its prosperity under such figures as Cicero. In 1402 AD it was captured by the Knights of St. John, who surrendered it in 1523 without a fight (as part of the terms of withdrawal from the region following the surrender of Rhodes).

⊨

Although there are plenty of beds in town, rooms are hard to find in High Season: it is

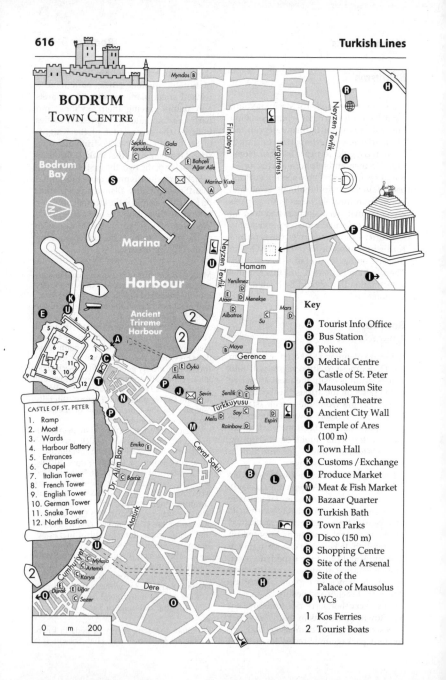

BODRUM
TOWN CENTRE

Bodrum Bay

Marina

Harbour

Ancient Trireme Harbour

Myndos [B]

Seçkin Konaklar [C]

Gala [C]

[E] Bahçeli Ağar Aile

Marina Vista [A]

Firkateyn

Turgutreis

Neyzen Tevfik

Neyzen Tevfik

Hamam

Yenilmez [E]

Ateş [E]   [D] Menekşe

Albatros [D]

[C] Su

Mars [C]

[E] Öykü

Alias [D]

Sevin [C]

Şenlik [E] [E]

Sedan [D]

Türkkuyusu

Maya [B]

Gerence

Melis [C]

Say [C]

Rainbow [D]

Espiri [D]

Emiko [E]

Cevat Şakir

Dr. Alim Bay

[C] Bartız

Atatürk

[C] Mylasa

[C] Artemis

[C] Karya

[E] Durak   [E] Uğar

[C] Sezer

Cumhuriyet

Dere

CASTLE OF ST. PETER

1. Ramp
2. Moat
3. Wards
4. Harbour Battery
5. Entrances
6. Chapel
7. Italian Tower
8. French Tower
9. English Tower
10. German Tower
11. Snake Tower
12. North Bastion

Key

- **A** Tourist Info Office
- **B** Bus Station
- **C** Police
- **D** Medical Centre
- **E** Castle of St. Peter
- **F** Mausoleum Site
- **G** Ancient Theatre
- **H** Ancient City Wall
- **I** Temple of Ares (100 m)
- **J** Town Hall
- **K** Customs / Exchange
- **L** Produce Market
- **M** Meat & Fish Market
- **N** Bazaar Quarter
- **O** Turkish Bath
- **P** Town Parks
- **Q** Disco (150 m)
- **R** Shopping Centre
- **S** Site of the Arsenal
- **T** Site of the Palace of Mausolus
- **U** WCs

1   Kos Ferries
2   Tourist Boats

0   m   200

essential to arrive on a morning boat. Best bets in the town centre are the good *Sedan* (☎ 252-316 0355), the *Su* (☎ 252-316 6906) and *Rainbow* (☎ 252-316 5170). Have money? — try *Marina Vista* (☎ 252-316 0356).

A
The town has a couple of indifferent sites. Best is *Uçar Camping* at Dere Sok, but it is only worth considering if you can't find a room.

≈☆
Bodrum has a well-merited reputation as a disco and bar hot-spot. This is in part due to the famous waterfront *Halikarnas Disco* with its deafening loudspeaker system. Other discos are to be found on the waterfront to the east of the castle and at the resort of Gümbet (which lies 5 km west of the old town).

ᏩᏩ
Sadly, the most famous structure in Bodrum — the **Mausoleum** (351 BC) — is all but invisible. After surviving intact until the 12 C. AD, it suffered earthquake damage, and was finally demolished by the Knights of St. John in 1522, when the stones were used to strengthen the castle against the cannons newly acquired by the Turks. Other fragments are now in the British Museum. The site is now home to a deep pit sporting a few blocks and foundations, along with a model of the monument in all its glory. The **Castle of St. Peter** is now the principal sight. Built between 1402–37 on the islet of Zephyrion, it is in very good condition. It is home to a good **Underwater Archaeology Exhibition** (based on ancient wrecks excavated during the 1970s) and a very sad performing monkey on a string.

Bozcaada
ΤΕΝΕΔΟΣ

A small Aegean island a few kilometres south-west of Troy, Bozcaada was known for over two millennia by the name recorded by Homer: Tenedos. Closed to tourists until the late 80s for military reasons (check with the tourist office in Çanakkale for the latest information regarding the need for possible visitor's permits), the island is one of the least spoilt and most attractive around. The only town lies on the north-east corner and is dominated by a well-preserved Genoese castle the equal of any in the Aegean. It lies

on the site of Justinian's warehouses, for the island was used as a granary storage base in the Byzantine era.

South of the town the shoreline is fringed by a succession of empty sand beaches, the best on the south coast proper, and it was to here that the Greek fleet retreated out of sight when they left the wooden horse outside the gates of Troy. The island economy continues to depend almost entirely on viticulture; mass tourism has yet to discover the delights of the — still very Greek — cobbled town, with its restaurant-fronted waterfront and dusty hotels in the streets behind.

Çanakkale

The largest port and best stopping-point on the Dardanelles (known to the Greeks as the Hellespont), Çanakkale is a pretty town offering plenty to do thanks to the combination of a well-preserved castle (home to a naval museum), a well-stocked archaeological museum, the Dardanelles ferry link, and the half-hourly buses from the town centre to Truva (the modern name for ancient Troy). The centre of town boasts a conspicuous clock tower, and in close proximity to this landmark you will find all the essentials—including the tourist office. Nearby tour operators offer day packages to both Troy and the Gallipoli battlefields across the Dardanelles (tours to this latter destination are the best way to visit given the absence of a good bus service).

Çeşme

A quaint little town with a pretty castle and interesting waterfront, marred by a terrorist bomb attack in 2005. Out on a limb at the end of the İzmir peninsula, it has become the main port for large international ferries along with the regular Chios boats — the pull of İzmir (a 90-minute bus ride away) being great. An appealing place to spend one's time with plenty of accommodation and camping to hand.

Datça

Deftly placed on one of the most attractive stretches of the Turkish coast, this quiet town, surrounding green pine forest and turquoise bay-lined Datça peninsula, is the real reason to hop from Rhodes to Marmaris. Taxi boats (and hourly buses) go to Datça from there. The town has plenty of rooms and a campsite, and is the jumping-off point (via tour boat or taxi) for Knidos, 34 km away on the tip of the peninsula. A major city in Classical times, it was home to the masterpiece of the sculptor Praxiteles — a (lost) statue of Aphrodite.

Eceabat

Main destination for Çanakkale ferries crossing to the Gelibolu peninsula. There isn't much here beyond the ferry terminal itself, Kilitbahir being the traditional landing point adjacent to Çanakkale.

Erdek

An attractive (courtesy of a lack of modern building) town on the Kapıdağ peninsula, Erdek is the main jumping-off point for the Sea of Marmara islands. The town has all the necessary tourist facilities (behind the tree- and restaurant-lined waterfront). Dolmuş taxis run frequently to nearby Bandırma, with its bus links to Çanakkale and other major centres.

Gelibolu

Known to most by its former name of Gallipoli, Gelibolu is the major port on the European side of the Dardanelles, giving its name to the whole peninsula (and of course, the disastrous WW1 Gallipoli campaign in which the Allies fought the Turks). Ferries dock on the outer quay, behind which lie two inner harbours bisected by a bridge. Pretty enough in a quiet sort of way, the town is home to a castle and also boasts a quayside statue of its most famous son, Piri Reis, a 16 c. cartographer and navigator. Hourly buses to İstanbul make Gelibolu more accessible than ferry links would suggest.

Gökçeada
ΙΜΒΡΟΣ; 597 km².

The only large Aegean island in Turkish hands, Gökçeada is still widely known by its former Greek name of Imbros (or Imroz). Heavily fortified thanks to its strategic position at the entrance of the Dardanelles, tourist access was prohibited until the late 80s when visitors with permits were admitted (information regarding any current requirements can be obtained from the tourist office in Çanakkale). Red tape has relaxed further since, but the number of tourists remains very small.

Visits to Gökçeada remain the preserve of the dedicated island hopper, intent on 'doing' every Greek or Aegean island,

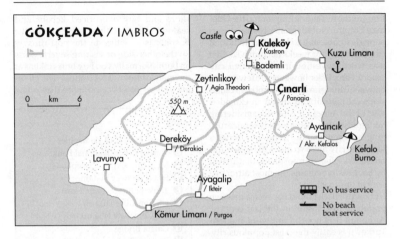

rather than the casual tourist. Green and very hilly, there is little disguising that of all the Turkish islands, this one more than any other feels — thanks to the heavy military presence — like an occupied zone. Although exempted from the 1920s population exchanges, the exclusively Greek inhabitants have been driven out over the last 30 years — unsung casualties of the Cyprus conflict. In the absence of a bus service, tourism is confined to the former chora (now Çınarli), and the town of Kaleköy — home to the island's best beach and an impressive castle. Both are linked by dolmuş taxi to the port at Kuzu Limanı.

Imrali
ΚΑΛΟΛΙΜΝΟ

The former Greek island of Kalolimno, Imrali is very much the unlucky 13th of the inhabited Turkish islands and definitely not on the tourist trail: if you end up landing here then something has gone very seriously wrong. At first sight it looks to be just another small barren island covered with a scattering of trees, and with a small port town, but in fact Imrali is Turkey's very own Alcatraz. Home to a high security prison

(from where the 'hero' of the film *Midnight Express* swam to freedom), the island has received considerable press attention of late as it is currently the home of the captured Kurdish separatist leader Abdullah Ocalan (now serving a life sentence). In 1999 the Turkish authorities removed the 250 prisoners normally housed here in order to hold a prisoner deemed so dangerous that naval boats constantly circle the island, while the neighbouring coastal towns of Bandırma and Mudanya have had all their shops and cafés closed.

Further captures of Kurdish separatists, and the huge devastation wrought by the massive 1999 earthquake (which left over 14,000 in the region dead), have ensured that Imrali and the south and east coastline of the Sea of Marmara is a region that has remained rather depressed and generally unattractive to tourists.

İstanbul
ΚΩΝΣΤΑΝΤΙΝΟΥΠΟΛΗ / ΒΥΖΑΝΤΙΟ

One of the great cities of the world, İstanbul is well worth almost any amount of effort involved in getting to it. Formerly known as Byzantium and then Constantinople, it was in turn the capital of the Eastern Roman

Empire, the Byzantine Empire and the Ottoman Empire. Not surprisingly, the city has enough sightseeing to keep the dedicated explorer busy for weeks (so much so, that it is worth investing in a dedicated city guide). Ferry links, however, are few and far between (though a goodly number of cruise ships call), but if you are on an extended tour of the Aegean it is worth considering taking advantage of the weekly service running between İstanbul and İzmir to pay a visit. The city owes so much to the sea and boasts a skyline so atmospheric that arrival by boat easily remains the most attractive way of approach.

Like Athens, İstanbul has seen a massive population explosion in the last century. Although it is not the capital of modern Turkey it is easily the most populous city, with a population now well in excess of 3 million. Similarities with the Greek capital do not end there, as the city has a good supply of cheap accommodation (some of it earthquake-proof) close to a historic centre surrounded by a sea of modern concrete. The same problems of pollution and traffic congestion that bedevil Athens are also to be found here.

İstanbul's principal port is located at Eminönü, adjacent to the Galata Bridge over the Golden Horn. All large ferries depart from here (a convenient quay as it backs onto the old part of the city that is home to all the major sights and the bulk of the budget accommodation). However, the İzmir ferry often lands its passengers at a quay 2 km to the north, on the far side of the Golden Horn.

Eminönü is also the departure point for cruises up the Bosphorus. These are just regular passenger ferries calling at all the European and Asian ports up to the entrance of the Black Sea (if you've ever fancied hopping a dozen or more times between Europe and Asia before dinner then this is your chance). Boats normally stop at the final Black Sea entrance port of **Anadolukavağı** for a couple of hours, so that passengers can get off on the Asian shore and buy overpriced kebabs and seafood dishes. Other ferries cross the Bosphorus — either to the port directly on the other side or visiting several ports on both. Normally you buy brass tokens at the quay or from street traders. The crossing will set you back no more than a few

---

Key

🅐 Tourist Office (Agia Sophia)
🅑 Tourist Office (National Bank)
🅒 Main Post Office / Telephones
🅓 Sikeci Railway Station
🅔 Topkapı Bus Station (2 km)
🅕 US Consulate (100 m)
    UK Consulate (400 m)
🅖 Galata Bridge
🅗 Atatürk Bridge
🅘 Ferry Ticket Office
🅙 Youth Hostel
🅚 Budget Hotel Area
🅛 Galata Tower
🅜 Agia Sophia Museum
🅝 Blue Mosque
🅞 Hippodrome
🅟 Topkapı Palace
🅠 Agia Irine
🅡 Beyaut Mosque
🅢 Süleymaniye Mosque
🅣 Yeni Cami Mosque
🅤 University
🅥 Egyptian Bazaar
🅦 Grand Bazaar
🅧 Atatürk Statue
🅨 Gülhane Park
🅩 Topkapı Palace Walls

1   International Ferry Port
2   Alternative Ferry Port (Arrivals)
3   Ferries to Princes' Islands & Boats
     running the length of the Bosphorus
4   Ferries to Kadiköy
5   Trans-Bosphorus Ferries
6   Karaköy Ferry Quay
7   Golden Horn Ferries

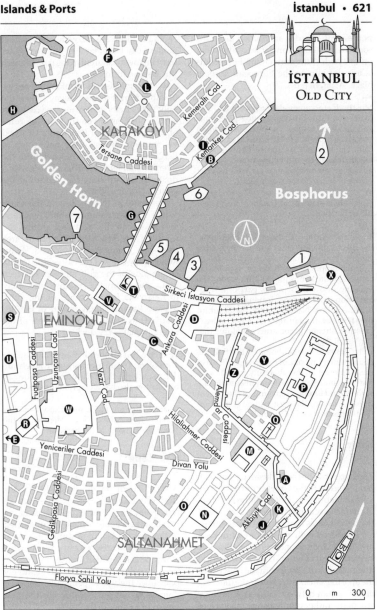

İSTANBUL
OLD CITY

pence/cents. Ferries are numerous on the southern crossings. Timetables can be found on quaysides (the convention hereabouts is to print info on the European ports in black, Asian in red).

🛏

Most budget accommodation is in the Old City in the small streets backing onto Agia Sophia and the Blue Mosque. The total of five youth hostels includes one IYHF hostel at 6 Caferige Cad. The helpful City Tourist Office is at 31 Divan Yolo on the old Hippodrome, and can advise on accommodation as well as offer plenty of blurb on the major sights.

Δ

Noisy short-stay site at *Londra Mocamp* near the city airport.

👁👁

Top of any touring hit list must be **Agia Sophia**, the great cathedral church of the Byzantine Empire, built in 532–37 AD. After the fall of Constantinople to the Turks in 1453 it was converted into a mosque. Atatürk turned the building into a museum as part of a secularization drive in 1935, leaving the Islamic ornamentation. Nearby stands the beautiful **Blue Mosque**. Built in 1609–16, it is a (failed?) Ottoman attempt to construct a building that surpassed Agia Sophia.

The **Topkapı Palace** (home of the Sultans, their harems, and one of the greatest displays of crown jewels) is the other truly great show in town—if one discounts the unmissable bustle of the **Grand Bazaar**. Remnants of the ancient city also survive: the most evident of these are the **Hippodrome** and **City Walls**.

İzmir
ΣΜΥΡΝΑ

The largest city on the Turkish Aegean coast, İzmir (formerly the Greek Smyrna) is now a major metropolis. Sadly, little architecture of character remains in what is now one of the ugliest cities (not many Aegean towns are lumbered with a 'Park of Culture') in one of the Mediterranean's most attractive bays: the Gulf of İzmir. The bulk of the old town was burnt down with the collapse of the abortive Greek attempt to take the coast of Asia Minor between 1919–22. The sheer size of the rather uninteresting (an ancient

agora and fortress aside) wide-boulevarded modern city has at least ensured a regular ferry link with İstanbul in the past (though this last ran in 2010).

Most foreign visitors are taking advantage of either ferries or the railway (this is the only Turkish city on the Aegean coast with such a link), or are en route to the ruins of the ancient city of Pergamum (reached via frequent buses to the new town of Bergama). İstanbul ferries leave from the international ferry berth (complete with a dusty locked-up duty-free centre) at the eastern corner of the gulf.

The centre of the city lies on the south side. The accompanying suburban sprawl spreads far to the west and around the northern side, hence the existence of three trans-bay commuter services: 1. From **Konak** quay (west of the city centre) to **Urla** (south side of the gulf midway between İzmir and Çeşme). 2. From Konak quay to **Karşıyaka** (on the north of the gulf). 3. From **Pasaport** quay (centre of the city seafront) to **Alsancak** (200 m west of the International Ferry dock).

🛏

Finding a bed for the night in İzmir is rarely a problem. Cheap pensions and hotels are densest around the railway station. The city bus station also has a helpful tourist office.

Δ

Nearest sites are at Çeşme. The village has several sites: notably *Fener Mocamp* on the promontory north of the harbour.

Kabatepe

A small town on the west side of the Gelibolu peninsula, Kabatepe has an infrequent ferry link with Gökçeada, an excellent beach and a museum dedicated to the 1915–16 Gallipoli campaign. Local taxis run to nearby ANZAC cove and the many cemeteries that house the 200,000 dead. Local public transport is relatively poor over the whole peninsula: buses or dolmuş taxis from Eceabat are the best means of getting to the town.

Kilitbahir

The narrowest crossing point on the Dardanelles runs between Kilitbahir and Çanakkale (1300 m) — hence the minor ferry link. Worth a visit thanks to the castle, built by Mehmet the Conqueror in 1452, that gives substance to the town's name, which means 'Key to the sea'.

Kuşadası

A rapidly growing tourist resort midway down Turkey's Aegean coast, Kuşadası is named 'Pigeon Island' — after a fortified islet linked to the town via a causeway. It draws the hordes thanks to its role as the jumping-off point to the nearby ruins of Ephesus, the best preserved of ancient Greek cities. A stream of cruise ships call, upping prices to Greek levels, but budget accommodation is still plentiful. The port used to figure more prominently on ferry schedules until the late 1990s. The city has also, unfortunately, been targeted by terrorists intent on disrupting Turkey's tourist industry: a number were killed in a bomb attack on a bus in July 2005.

Lâpseki

A small port that owes its existence to adjacent Gelibolu on the opposite side of the Dardanelles, Lâpseki is very much of an overspill town, relying on the ferry link between the two.

Marmara

The largest island in the Sea of Marmara, and from which it takes its medieval name, Marmara is a mountainous and rather inhospitable-looking place. The island was famous in the ancient world as one of the best sources of white marble: the whole northern half is composed of little else, leaving a windswept landscape with little vegetation and well scarred with three thousand years of quarrying. Southern Marmara has more going for it, with a fringe of pine trees and the best of the small population centres. Ferries stop at assorted points around the coast. Boats to Marmara town (home to two budget hotels and the island bank) often stop at Gundoğdu en route, and the former capital at Saraylar sees boats running north.

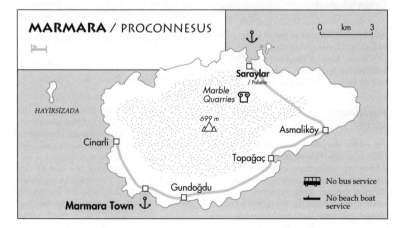

Marmaris

The most southerly Turkey—Greece crossing point, Marmaris has grown from a small fishing village to one of Turkey's leading tourist resorts. The town ribbons along the coast at the head of an islet-littered bay, against an attractive backdrop of mountains and pine trees, but lacking anything approaching a major 'sight', seeing is reduced to 'souking' up tourism with a Turkish flavour. There is enough going on to keep you happily occupied for a day but this is arguably the least interesting of Turkey's day-tripper ports. The ferries and hydrofoils to Rhodes are now the only regular services, though previous years have seen long-haul international ferries calling. Taxi boats run along the coast to Datça and to nearby **Cleopatra's Island** (sand imported from Egypt courtesy of one Marcus Antonius). Now sadly overrated and overcrowded.

⊨

Tourist Office opposite the ferry quay offers maps and a room-finding service.

⚠

Best site is *Camping Berch* west of the port.

Odun Iskalesi

Small mainland port adjacent to the island of Bozcaada. Also known as Yukyeri, there is nothing here of interest, excepting the twice-daily ferry link. Dolmuş taxis meet ferries and run to Çanakkale.

Paşalimanı
ΑΛΟΝΗ

An oddly shaped, low-lying island with little tourism. The economy is primarily driven by viticulture and shell-fishing. All settlements are very small and even 'hamlet' implies more than you will find on the ground. Most ferries run to the largest cluster of houses (and the island mosque)

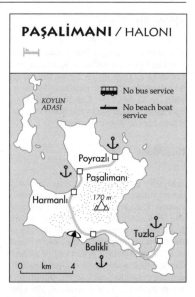

PAŞALİMANI / HALONI

No bus service

No beach boat service

KOYUN ADASI

Poyrazlı

Paşalimanı

Harmanlı   170 m

Tuzla

Balikli

0   km   4

at Paşalimanı, but you should be aware that boats (especially those operating out of the small village ports north of Erdek on the Kapıdağ peninsula often prefer to dock at other points—notably the wooded settlement of Balikli. Facilities ashore are all but non-existent, so bring provisions with you. Best way to visit is via a day trip, crossing by private boat on one of the days that a scheduled ferry offers a means of return.

Princes' Islands
10 km²; pop. 15,000.

A group 20 km to the south of the Bosphorus, these nine car-free islets (four accessible by ferry — though the express boats usually only call at the largest two) are a popular destination with tourists and locals alike, performing the role of city parks. The largely Armenian populations are now being displaced by increasing numbers of jet-setters building holiday homes. The islands gained their name as places of exile for Byzantine nobles and then members of the Sultan's family. Sadly, these days harems are few on the ground — though one island was briefly used as a rabbit farm. **Büyük** is the largest of the islands, and its Greek title (Prinkipo) gave the name to the group. Today it has a plethora of restaurants, hotels, horses and carriages, and gardens. **Heybeli** is a quieter version of the same, with a naval college and a Greek Orthodox school of theology. The interiors of both are wooded, as is smaller **Burgaz**, the only other island to boast a reasonably sized settlement.

Northern **Kınalı** is home to one tiny hamlet, and, along with **Sedef**, exists as a beach destination. The remaining islands are little more than rocks with only **Kaşik** readily accessible (via Heybeli beach boats). **Yassi** is now a prison and thus closed to tourists, while **Sivri** has an odd history as dumping ground for stray dogs rounded up from the streets of İstanbul, and **Tavsan** is uninhabited.

Tekirdağ

The only port of note on the northern Sea of Marmara coast, Tekirdağ is poorly connected with the rest of the Turkish ferry system, but offers good bus links with İstanbul. A growing resort town, outlying beaches are the main attraction.

Yalova

The destination of a number of İstanbul—Princes' Islands ferries, Yalova is a commuter town on the southern Sea of Marmara coast. Yalova also has daily links with **Darıca** and **Kartal** on the adjacent coast, as does **Çınarcık**, which also sees occasional Princes' Islands boats. These are the best of the local services (the service between the towns of **Hereke** and **Karamürsel** being the other link) between equally uninspiring towns off the tourist map.

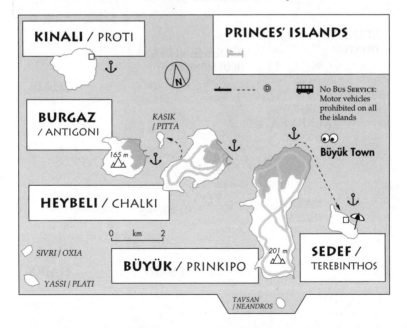

KINALI / PROTI

PRINCES' ISLANDS

No Bus Service: Motor vehicles prohibited on all the islands

BURGAZ / ANTIGONI

KASIK / PITTA

165 m

Büyük Town

HEYBELI / CHALKI

0   km   2

SIVRI / OXIA

YASSI / PLATI

BÜYÜK / PRINKIPO

201 m

SEDEF / TEREBINTHOS

TAVSAN / NEANDROS

13
INTERNATIONAL LINES

CYPRUS · EGYPT · GREECE · ISRAEL · ITALY (ANCONA
BARI · BRINDISI · VENICE) · LEBANON · TURKEY

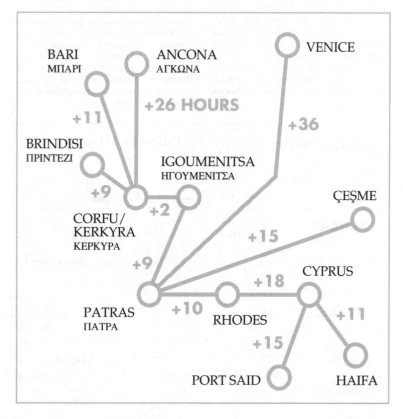

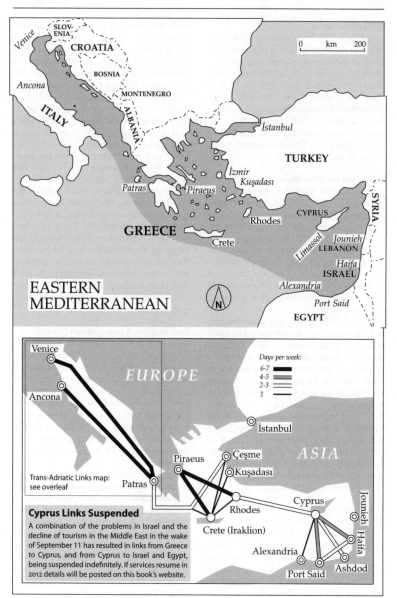

0 km 200

Venice
SLOV-
ENIA
CROATIA
BOSNIA
Ancona
MONTENEGRO
ALBANIA
ITALY
İstanbul
TURKEY
İzmir
Kuşadası
Patras
Piraeus
GREECE
Rhodes
CYPRUS
Crete
Limassol
Jounieh
LEBANON
Haifa
ISRAEL
EASTERN
MEDITERRANEAN
Alexandria
Port Said
EGYPT
SYRIA
N

Venice

Days per week:
6-7
4-5
2-3
1

EUROPE

Ancona

İstanbul

ASIA

Piraeus
Çeşme
Kuşadası

Trans-Adriatic Links map:
see overleaf
Patras

Rhodes
Cyprus
Jounieh

Cyprus Links Suspended

A combination of the problems in Israel and the
decline of tourism in the Middle East in the wake
of September 11 has resulted in links from Greece
to Cyprus, and from Cyprus to Israel and Egypt,
being suspended indefinitely. If services resume in
2012 details will be posted on this book's website.

Crete (Iraklion)
Alexandria
Haifa
Ashdod
Port Said

General Features

The Eastern Mediterranean is rather lop-sided in the distribution of ferry services. Beyond the extensive Greek and Croatian domestic systems there is little traffic other than international lines, and the bulk of these are confined to the Adriatic. Long-haul services across the Mediterranean are more constricted (when operating), with most services running along an Italy–Israel/Egypt axis. Operators ignore Syria, Lebanon and Libya.

1. Eastern Mediterranean

The number of 'true' long-haul ferries is very small — for, given the journey times and the subsequent level of fares, few routes can compete with the relative cheapness of air travel. Some of the ferries, thanks to six- to eight-hour stopovers in each port, are advertised as cruise ship operations. They are cheaper in all respects than true cruise liners but have the saving grace of allowing you more flexibility in planning your itinerary.

The lack of trans-Adriatic style competition on these longer routes also makes itself felt: many of the ferries are older ex-Greek domestic boats (this can be a problem considering the amount of time one has to spend aboard), banished to one last rusty Mediterranean run before being sold off to less safety-conscious SE Asia operators. Boats and routes also change frequently, in part as a result of this. Another factor that impacts on services is the Middle East political situation: the 'lifeline' ferry links that sometimes exist to Lebanon and Israel appear and disappear according to the current state of the land borders.

2. Adriatic

The Adriatic is very much part of Italy's backyard and treated as something akin to the English Channel, with the coastal resort towns of her rather bland east coast serving as jumping-off points. Almost all of the larger ferries run down the Adriatic to Greece, encouraged by the tourist hordes

who pass through each summer as well as the freight trade generated by Greece's membership of the EU (now enlarged thanks to the emergence of new trade routes following the wars that once blocked the land routes through former Yugoslavia).

This is a potent combination that produces the most competitive international ferry services in the Mediterranean: even deck-class passengers are treated with a modicum of respect. Ferries are much larger than those on other routes (with bigger or faster boats appearing every year), but you do have to be wary of maverick companies; the profits in this part of the world are such that the temptation to chuck on a clapped-out ferry to make a few easy Euros is often irresistible. Every year you will see at least one boat Nero would happily send his mother to sea in. Fortunately, they are easy enough to spot; a company producing a brochure without pictures of their boats is almost an admission that they are too clapped-out to survive a camera's critical eye.

Embarkation & Immigration Controls

As with much of Continental Europe the countries bordering the Adriatic have adopted a rather low-key approach to border controls. However, their 'abolition' within the EU has yet to have an appreciable effect in Greece (where you still have to show your passport and get an associated ferry boarding card). This said, it should be noted that all EU countries greet arriving passengers with the minimum of fuss anyway.

Passport control (when it happens at all) is now usually done on board ship in the self-service restaurant, so it pays to find out where it is before the arrival-at-port queue tells you. Customs procedures (where they exist) take place ashore. Embarking tends to be more complex; you are usually required to report for boarding 2–3 hours before departure so you have time to get your passport or boarding card stamped by immigration.

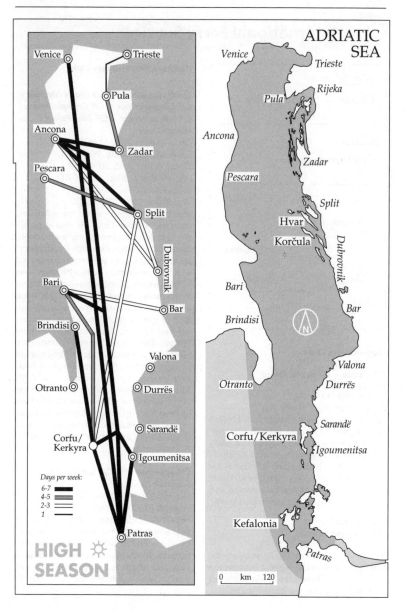

ADRIATIC
SEA

Venice
Trieste
Rijeka
Pula
Ancona
Zadar
Pescara
Split
Hvar
Korčula
Bari
Dubrovnik
Brindisi
Bar
Otranto
Valona
Durrës
Sarandë
Corfu/Kerkyra
Igoumenitsa
Kefalonia
Patras

Venice
Trieste
Pula
Ancona
Zadar
Pescara
Split
Dubrovnik
Bari
Bar
Brindisi
Valona
Otranto
Durrës
Sarandë
Corfu/
Kerkyra
Igoumenitsa
Patras

Days per week:
6-7
4-5
2-3
1

HIGH
SEASON

0   km   120

International Ferry Services

Cesme – Scotia Prince

Captain Zaman

```
                              ———  Ⓦ
                              - - -  Ⓦ
                              - - - -  ○
  ⊙ Ancona
     `-.
        `-.
           `-.
              `-.
                 ○ Çeşme
  Brindisi
  ○
                 Çeşme
                 ⊚
  Bari
  ○ - - - - - - -
```

Italy—Greece Links

C/F *Cesme* – C/F *Scotia Prince*
Marmara Lines
Cesme; 1974; 13336 GRT.
Scotia Prince; 1972; 11968 GRT.
Among the frequent changing of Eastern
Mediterranean services there is one con-
stant: Turkey's need to have links to Italy
to provide the large number of its nationals
in the EU with a homeland link. Boats are
elderly and change on a regular basis. Other
Turkish ports — Marmaris, Antalya and
İzmir — have seen services in past years.

C/F *Captain Zaman*
MedEuropean Seaways
Captain Zaman; 1972; 9562 GRT.
The newcomer to the scene in 2005, the
Captain Zaman is the biggest boat on the
Brindisi route. Other services out of Brindisi
and Bari are more rust-bucket affairs.

Northern Italy—Greece Links

C/F *Cruise Europa* – C/F *Cruise Olympia*
C/F *Europa Palace* – C/F *Olympia Palace*
C/F *Ikarus Palace* – C/F *Zeus Palace*
Minoan Lines
Cruise Europa; 2009; 53360 GRT.
Cruise Olympia; 2010; 53360 GRT.
Europa Palace; 2002; 30000 GRT.
Olympia Palace; 2001; 30000 GRT.
Ikarus Palace; 1997; 31000 GRT.
Zeus Palace; 2001; 27000 GRT.
The biggest name on the trans-Adriatic
crossing, Minoan Lines are also arguably
the best Adriatic line going, with a well-
merited reputation for a high-quality service. Even deck-class passengers are treated
as if they are human beings (though — as
with all international boats — you will find
your journey more comfortable if you book
an aircraft-type seat). With an impressive
fleet of newish high-speed boats running
up the Adriatic, Minoan provide more
options than any of the competition. They
offer a daily 23-hour service to Venice (route
C) in addition to their traditional 19-hour
Patras—Ancona run (routes A and B).
Minoan Lines are well placed to continue
at the top of the pile and are clearly bent
on re-enforcing their position thanks to the
arrival of two huge super-ferries (the new
Cruise Europa and *Cruise Olympia*) on the
Ancona route.

C/F *Superfast VI* – C/F *Superfast XI*
Superfast Ferries
Superfast VI; 2001; 23663 GRT.
Superfast XI; 2002; 30902 GRT.
Superfast Ferries arrived in the Adriatic in
1995 with two new ferries that took the route
by storm. The attraction of large and well-
promoted boats (thanks to their streamlined
look and bright red hulls) offering a fast
direct Patras—Ancona sailing (route B)
proved to be irresistible to many.

The arrival of the new high-speed Minoan Lines boats has prevented the company from capitalizing on this success by dominating the market. They have done their best to stay ahead by regularly moving their newest boats onto the Ancona route.

Thanks to an event totally out of keeping with their high reputation, Superfast also received some very negative publicity after the *Superfast III* suffered a major mishap in November 1999: an engine-room fire broke out in mid-Adriatic, forcing the ship to be abandoned (with Greek TV providing a running commentary by broadcasting the mobile-phone calls of panic-stricken passengers as they were herded into lifeboats). Ten Kurdish stowaways died.

The fact that a fire could take hold so quickly, and burn out the stern of the ship, does raise questions about modern ferry design. However, there have been no problems since and the Superfast Ferries fleet can be highly recommended.

C/F *Olympic Champion*
C/F *Hellenic Spirit*
C/F *Lefka Ori* – C/F *Sophocles Venizelos*
ANEK Lines

Olympic Champion; 2001; 30000 GRT.
Hellenic Spirit; 2002; 30000 GRT.
Lefka Ori; 1991; 29420 GRT.
Sophocles Venizelos; 1990; 13384 GRT.

The main rival of Minoan Lines on the Piraeus—Crete routes, ANEK (who share the same owners as Superfast Ferries) also provide an Adriatic service, though they have lost much of their competitive edge lately. ANEK have addressed this by introducing new, custom-built vessels: on the Patras—Ancona route they have two high-speed boats to match the competition with the *Olympic Champion* and *Hellenic Spirit*.

One reason ANEK have been weaker than their rivals has been their former preference for operating boats running north to out-of-the-way Trieste (route D), instead of the popular Venice favoured by their rivals. This changed in 2005 when all services were switched to Venice. ANEK

Cruise Europa
Cruise Olympia
Europa Palace
Olympia Palace
Ikarus Palace
Zeus Palace

◇

Superfast VI, XI

Olympic Champion
Hellenic Spirit

Lefka Ori
Sophocles Venizelos

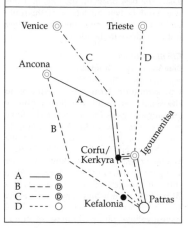

run a couple of regular ferries on the route. Both offer a comfortable trip and it can be argued that there is something to be said for travelling on smaller, less crowded boats. On the negative side, the smaller *Sophocles Venizelos* suffered an engine failure 100 km out of Bari in August 2004 which gave her passengers plenty of extra time to take in the balmy Adriatic sea and its views.

Bari—Greece Links

C/F *Superfast I* – C/F *Superfast II*
Superfast Ferries
Superfast I; 2008; 26000 GRT.
Superfast II; 2009; 26000 GRT.
Superfast Ferries dominated this route in the early noughties with two boats, only to move them on in 2005. Thereafter Blue Star (the companies share joint owners, so their boats are never placed in direct competition with each other) took over, only to see in 2010 Superfast return with two new boats. When their predecessors first appeared they had considerable impact, drastically curtailing the amount of competition from the far less attractive regular ferries. Both the Superfast boats (somewhat confusingly named after their predecessors) are likely to squeeze the competition again, being easily the best boats on the line, and this was certainly their impact in 2011: this route badly needs a major competitor to emerge if it is to thrive in the future.

C/F *Blue Horizon*
Blue Star Ferries / Strintzis
Blue Horizon; 1987; 16725 GRT.
On this route until 2010, this vessel moved to the Aegean but could yet return. Formerly running alongside the *Blue Star 1*, this ferry was not very successful running solo in the Adriatic. When she is operating she is adequate enough, but the *Blue Horizon* is a lesser beast, a fact recognized by her company livery. For she is adorned with a different smokestack colour: the new fast Blue Stars have a blue star on a yellow background; old boats like the *Blue Horizon* have a yellow star on a blue background.

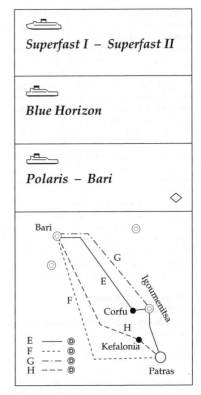

Superfast I – *Superfast II*

Blue Horizon

Polaris – *Bari*

C/F *Polaris* – C/F *Bari*
Ventouris Ferries
Polaris; 1975; 20326 GRT.
Bari; 1980; 7003 GRT.
In past years Ventouris Ferries managed to carve out a niche market by packing this route with their boats to discourage competition. This strategy failed with the arrival of fast, better equipped vessels, and they are now a very minor player, offering fewer boats almost every year. They subsist by offering the budget option for commercial vehicles, with hardly a tourist in sight. Any that do buy tickets tend to run when they see the boats. The weak *Polaris* is the worse of the two by a long way.

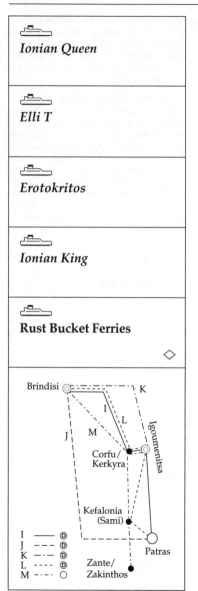

Ionian Queen

Elli T

Erotokritos

Ionian King

Rust Bucket Ferries

◇

I ——— Ⓓ
J – – – Ⓓ
K —·—· Ⓓ
L - - - - Ⓓ
M —··— ○

Brindisi · K · I · L · Igoumenitsa · J · M · Corfu/Kerkyra · Kefalonia (Sami) · Patras · Zante/Zakinthos

Brindisi—Greece Links

C/F *Ionian Queen*
Endeavour Lines
Ionian Queen; 1988; 19796 GRT.
The Brindisi—Greece route is the short and cheap Adriatic crossing. As a result it attracts a succession of smaller and older boats unable to make a go of it elsewhere. The comparatively low cost of the tickets has made the Brindisi run an unattractive option for the companies operating new high-speed ferries — to date. The *Ionian Queen* is a good example of the type of 'new' boat appearing on this low-profit route instead. She is just about the best ferry on the line, but this isn't saying a great deal, given the quality of the competition.

C/F *Elli T*
Endeavour Lines / HML
Elli T; 1976; 7020 GRT.
The *Elli T* has been rebranded twice since 2006, so don't be surprised to see her running in new colours this year. She operates at the lower end of the trans-Adriatic ferry league, most recently as surrogate vessel for the HML Ferries' oddball operation. Once one of the mainstays of the Brindisi—Patras route with four boats, HML Ferries have seen their profile sink considerably of late, and are now reduced to using independent older boats to implement their schedules. This is a great pity as their innovative itineraries take in islands otherwise inaccessible except by domestic ferries (notably Kefalonia, Paxos and Zakinthos). Worth looking out for, they are in need of some streamlined timetabling — their range of schedules is so great that it is impossible to say where their boats will be on any given day without much head-scratching over their near incomprehensible timetable.

C/F *Erotokritos*
Endeavour Lines
Erotokritos; 1974; 12888 GRT.
Once run by one of the other companies using older ferries on the route, the

Erotokritos was bought up from a failed operator. With a lick of new paint and some very aggressive advertising, this ferry is more visible than most. As with the *Ionian Queen*, she is a cut above the rest of the competition, but were these boats on any of the other routes they would be dismissed as okay for island hoppers and ferry fans on a nostalgia trip, but otherwise eminently avoidable.

C/F *Ionian King*
Agoudimos Lines
Ionian King; 1991; 19800 GRT.
The reasonably large *Ionian King* has been running solo since 2010 after being pushed off the Igoumenitsa—Bari route by the arrival of the two Superfast vessels. In 2011 she attempted an ambitious itinerary, running between Brindisi—Igoumenitsa—Kefalonia—Zakinthos. This was probably more out of desperation than any serious attempt to add variety to the options for Ionian Island hoppers. Hopefully she will persevere and run the service again in 2012. She is a ferry that can be used with confidence even if she is not in the top rank of trans-Adriatic vessels.

Rust Bucket Ferries
Most years see at least one elderly ferry chucked onto this route to make a quick euro or two during the High Season. They can usually be distinguished by the lack of photos of the ships in advertising. The rule of thumb is if the brochure or website hasn't got a picture then there is every reason to steer well clear.

AirSea Lines Seaplane Service
Odd ball operator AirSea Lines provided a seaplane service out of Corfu in the mid-noughties. After a couple of years of advertising, a seaplane flew on the Corfu—Brindisi route. It materialized in 2008, only to disappear when the company suspended all operations in 2010. The chances of this international service reappearing in 2012 must now be fairly slim, but if it is

operating then this is an 'interesting' way of making the crossing. Given the small number of seats on these planes (only 14), tickets are expensive, but the journey has real novelty value and is a must if you are travelling in style.

Local Corfu—Albania Services
Tour boats run from Corfu to Albanian Sarandë, doing the 90-minute run several days a week (these are apt to change each year). Several of them were formerly Royal Navy wooden-hulled minesweepers. These boats, if operating, will require you to buy your ticket a couple of days in advance (see p. 637 for details). Check different agents in Corfu: they rarely act for all the boats, so could offer different options for making the crossing.

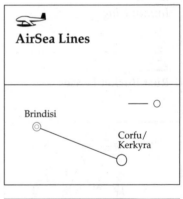

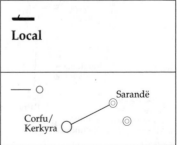

⚓ Trans-Adriatic Ports (Non-Greek)

Alexandria

Egypt is too far removed from the rest of the ferry network to figure widely on schedules. Services that do exist are rather irregular with most operating via the Cypriot port of Limassol. Alexandria is an attractive neocolonial city with good bus and rail links to the capital Cairo, some three hours' drive to the south. The port area is very extensive, though ferry traffic has declined with the reopening of the Suez Canal and Port Said. Ferry services have been suspended since 2003.

Ancona

The number one destination for north-bound Patras ferries, Ancona is a substantial — but thanks to its commercial activities not particularly attractive — city on the upper Italian Adriatic coast. The port is in many respects the best part of town thanks to Venetian-style fortifications that provide plenty of character. Ancona sees considerable ferry traffic thanks to good road connections north (and hence is a natural departure point for holidaying Italians from the northern cities) and trans-European rail links from the station conveniently sited up the hill behind the port (daily departures for Frankfurt and Munich). Nearby Rimini also has a daily overnight express train to Milan, Frankfurt and Amsterdam.

Ashdod

Very much Israel's second port, lying just north of the Gaza Strip, Ashdod very occasionally appears on cruise/ferry schedules. Links are very erratic. Given the troubled state of the Gaza Strip an increase in activity is unlikely.

Bari

An attractive — if unspectacular — city, Bari is too far south down the Italian boot to be an appealing port of call for travellers heading on to Northern Europe, nor is it sufficiently north to appeal to holidaying Italians either. As a result, it is very much the number three west-Adriatic ferry port. On the same rail line as Brindisi, but a longer journey by ferry, your chances of finding a train seat in summer are likely to be limited.

Brindisi

This pleasant city is the destination for the majority of the Patras—Italy ferries. This is due to the easy turn-around time (22 hours), thus allowing two ferries to combine and offer a daily service in each direction. This is the best arrival point if Rome or southern Italy is your next port of call. However, if you are passing through Italy you will still be faced with a long drive or rail journey north.

Cyprus

Offering an interesting mix of sun, sand and antiquities — to say nothing of Greek and British military cultural lifestyles coexisting — Cyprus is an 'interesting' variation on the Greek island experience. Now a full member of the EU, the island is ironically less accessible than in the past thanks to the suspension of East Mediterranean ferry services. Worse, it remains divided. Since the 1974 Turkish invasion the Cypriot Republic has been confined to the southern 60% of the island.

In the years since, the south of Cyprus has prospered, while the isolated Turkish-occupied north (set up as an unrecognized Turkish Cypriot republic) has stagnated and is now best known as a haven for those seeking to evade the law. At the time this book went to press, the north, although now technically part of the EU, remains inaccessible from the south: the UN-monitored Green Line between the two sides of the island cannot be crossed at any point (the only exceptions are rare day-exchanges between the two communities). However, change is in the air and talk of reunification is growing, so there is at least a small chance that cross-border visits by tourists might be possible in late 2012.

Given that northern Cyprus can only be accessed via Turkish ports, those services are covered in Chapter 12. You should note the potential pitfall of having a Turkish-Cypriot stamp in your passport. This can (though not always) cause severe difficulties when entering Greece, since you can be deemed to have inevitably been in receipt of 'stolen property' (e.g. by staying in a hotel owned by a displaced Greek Cypriot). Your new 'criminal' status will go down even less well if

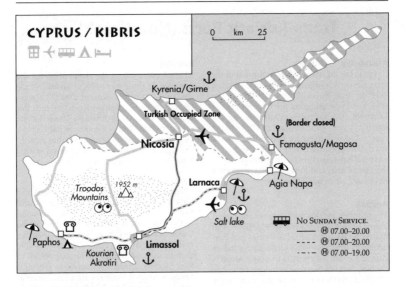

attempting to enter Greek Cyprus: you could well be denied entry.

With the division of the island has come a shift in the focus of Cypriot life, from the divided capital of Nicosia, to the south coast ports. **Limassol** (an unplanned concrete town) has became the de facto centre of Greek Cyprus as well as the ferry hub of the Eastern Mediterranean beyond Greece. The centre is quite pleasant in a garrison-town way, the British forces base at Akrotiri dominating the local economy. Helpful tourist offices at both ferry terminus building (linked to the centre by bus) and waterfront have free maps showing all hotels and guest houses. They also provide information on all the easily accessible sights from Limassol. First amongst these are the ruined cities at Kourion and Paphos and the Troodos Mountains: a cool retreat from the heat of the coast.

The island's second port is at **Larnaca**, a prosperous resort that has grown up since the invasion thanks to the new international airport and the need to replace lost Famagusta. The Costa del Sol atmosphere of the seafront (complete with a poor beach) contrasts greatly with the ghost-town ferry terminus 2 km east of the centre.

Durrës

The principal port of Albania and its nearby capital of Tirana, ugly Durrës is not a leading candidate for an increase in ferry activity in the near future. Until 2001 a thrice-monthly ferry link to Trieste was one of the principal means of entering the country, nowadays the primary link is a thrice-weekly ferry link with Bari.

Haifa

Haifa is a large and not particularly attractive port on the northern edge of Israel's Mediterranean seaboard. Conflict with her neighbours means that the country has no land route to Europe, and this has been (until ferry services were suspended) reflected in the relatively high level of ferry traffic linking Haifa with Limassol, Rhodes and Piraeus. This link operated three days a week in High Season and was maintained at twice-weekly level throughout the rest of the year. Since the peace treaty with Egypt irregular services to Alexandria and Port Said have also been on offer, but most were tourist/cruise ship vessels with prices to match. Most casual non-vehicle traffic on both these routes was gleaned from the ranks of the backpacker and kibbutz brigade. Security problems within the country are reflected on ferries that include Israel in their itineraries. This is tighter than on other boats and even if your destination is not Israel you can expect rigorous questioning and baggage searches on boarding.

Jounieh

This is a small port set safely in the Christian enclave of the Lebanon in a wide bay 20 km north of Beirut. A ferry link was established on the outbreak of the civil war that left Beirut port in ruins. For the bulk of the last 30 years it operated a 'rat run' to Larnaca on Cyprus. Services have been suspended for a number of years now and are unlikely to resume in 2012.

Otranto

Cornered on the heel of Italy, Otranto is too remote to attract ferry traffic bar the odd maverick boat, and even then only because it offers the shortest (a beguiling advertising point) Adriatic crossing from Corfu and Igoumenitsa. Poor road and rail connections with the rest of Italy.

Port Said

Lying on the north-eastern entrance to the Suez Canal, Port Said has regained its role among Egypt's premier commercial ports following the reopening of the waterway. Good bus links with Cairo, which is just as well since — canal excepted — there is little of interest here. Fortunately the Cairo road follows the bank of the canal (free sightseeing) so that arrival here has some advantages. That said, if you are arriving as an independent traveller outside a cruise/tour visit, you should allow 3–4 hours to negotiate the tortuous local immigration and customs processing operation. Ferry services with Cyprus remain suspended.

Sarandë

This growing town on Albania's southern coastline is visited by Corfu tour boats several days a week. Passengers pre-book two days in advance to enable visas to be prepared. When booking you are asked to provide your surname, forenames, father's name, place of birth, date of birth, nationality and occupation. As day trips go, the costs are quite high: expect to pay €70 return boat fare, plus a €9 port tax charge, with a tour excursion fee of

around €20 on top of that. Given the regular shortages in Albania, it is necessary to take anything out of the ordinary (e.g. medication) with you. Check with Corfu operators for info on the latest conditions.

Trieste

Argued over by Yugoslavia and Italy after WW2, Trieste voted to join the latter in a UN plebiscite. Despite this, it retains strong connections with the Slovenian Istrian peninsula and is awkwardly linked with the rest of Italy (though it is the terminus for several trans-Europe trains — notably to Budapest and Geneva). The northern gateway to Slovenia and Croatia, the city remains a ferry backwater — only ANEK Lines made a point of running services here. Even this connection ceased in 2005 when the line opted to run services out of Venice instead. Tucked away at the head of the Adriatic, it now looks as though the city may not see a resumption of ferry services.

Valona

Albania's third and most northerly port, it saw its first regular ferry service in 1993. A town with few facilities, it is unlikely to develop in the future. Conditions of passage as for Sarandë above.

Venice

Considering how great an impact Venice has had over the history and culture of the Mediterranean it is surprising how little it figures on ferry schedules (being confined to one or two daily boats to Greece in High Season, with irregular boats to Turkey some years). This is due to the same geographical difficulty that affects Trieste: being at the head of the Adriatic the city does not figure prominently on trans-European road or rail routes.

Since motoring in Venice is handicapped by the canal system, and the former Yugoslavia (a couple of hours away by road) is only very slowly returning to the fringes of the tourist map, it is inevitable that the *Stazione marittima* is underutilized. This is a pity, as arriving in Venice by boat is one of the best landfalls going, with ferries passing the Grand Canal and St Mark's Square. It is almost worth waiting for a Venice-bound ferry simply to enjoy this experience. In practice, however, Venice remains the preserve of long-distance travellers.

PORT TABLES

& REFERENCE:
FERRY COMPANIES · INTERNET · USEFUL GREEK · INDEX

STARTING PORT

HOPPING

OPTIONS

Note:

The following Port Tables show *typical* High Season ferry times. Islands and ports are listed alphabetically. Those islands that are known by two common names (eg. Santorini / Thira) are listed under the first (e.g. Santorini). Island ports are not listed separately by name but appear under their respective island's name. Minor ferry services already shown on island maps are not listed again here.

Aegina

Argo-Saronic p. 536

○ Typical daily departures:

06.10	*Aias*	Piraeus.
07.30	*Nefeli*	Piraeus.
08.40	*Poseidon Hellas*	Methana. Poros.
08.45	*Apostolos P*	Piraeus.
08.55	*Apollon Hellas*	Methana. Poros. Hydra. Spetses. Porto Helio.
09.00	*Phivos*	Poros.
09.10	*Georgios 2*	Methana. Poros. Spetses. Porto Helio.
09.30	*Angistri Express*	Angistri.
10.00	*Ag. Nektarios Aiginae*	Piraeus.
10.00	*Odysseas II*	Piraeus.
11.40	*Poseidon Hellas*	Piraeus.
12.15	*Angistri Express*	Angistri.
12.20	*Apollon Hellas*	Piraeus.
12.30	*Phivos*	Piraeus.
14.15	*Ag. Nektarios Aiginae*	Piraeus.
15.45	*Nefeli*	Piraeus.
15.50	*Angistri Express*	Angistri.
17.00	*Phivos*	Piraeus.
17.20	*Apollon Hellas*	Methana. Poros.
17.55	*Odysseas II*	Piraeus.
18.15	*Ag. Nektarios Aiginae*	Piraeus.
18.30	*Poseidon Hellas*	Piraeus.
19.00	*Angistri Express*	Angistri.
20.30	*Apollon Hellas*	Piraeus.

⑤ ⑥ ⑦
14.15	*Ioannis II*	Piraeus.
16.30	*Ioannis II*	Piraeus.
18.00	*Ioannis II*	Piraeus.
19.15	*Apostolos P*	Piraeus.

⑦
10.45	*Ioannis II*	Angistri.
21.00	*Ag. Nektarios Aiginae*	Piraeus.

〜 *Flying Dolphins* include:

Ⓗ 08.00–19.00   Piraeus (Great Harbour).
Ⓓ 09.45 17.15   Poros. Hydra. Spetses.

Aegina (Agia Marina)

Ⓓ
06.30	*Saron Cat*	Piraeus.
09.30	*Ydra Cat*	Piraeus.
13.00	*Saron Cat*	Piraeus.
17.00	*Ydra Cat*	Piraeus.
18.45	*Saron Cat*	Piraeus.

〜 Hydrofoils include:
Ⓓ 07.30 09.15 12.30 15.15
   17.15 19.15 21.00   Piraeus.

Aegina (Souvala)

Ⓓ
08.15	*Ioannis II*	Piraeus.
12.00	*Ioannis II*	Piraeus.

Ⓓ ex ⑥
17.30	*Apostolos P*	Piraeus.
19.30	*Aias*	Piraeus.

⑥
16.30	*Apostolos P*	Piraeus.

〜 Hydrofoils include:
Ⓓ 06.40 08.00 09.45 12.45
   14.15 16.15 18.15 21.15   Piraeus.

Days per week:
6-7 ▅▅▅
2-3 ══

PIRAEUS
Angistri
AEGINA
Epidavros
Nafplio   Moni   Poros
Porto Helio   Hydra
Tolo   Ermioni
Spetses

Agathonisi

Dodecanese p. 372

① ⑤
11.50   *Nissos Kalimnos*   Samos (Pithagorio).
14.45   *Nissos Kalimnos*   Samos (Pithagorio).
17.40   *Nissos Kalimnos*   Arki. Patmos. Lipsi.
                         Leros. Kalimnos.

⑥
13.45   *Dodekanisos Pride*   Lipsi. Leros (Agia Marina).
                         Kalimnos. Kos. Rhodes.

③ ⑦
12.50   *Nissos Kalimnos*   Samos (Pithagorio).
15.40   *Nissos Kalimnos*   Arki. Patmos. Lipsi.
                         Leros. Kalimnos.

Samos (Pithagorio)

AGATHONISI

Patmos

Lipsi

Leros

Kalimnos

Days per week:
2-3 ═══

Kos

Days per week:
2-3 ═══
Kavala
Limnos
AGIOS EFSTRATIOS
Rafina

Agios Efstratios

Northern Aegean
p. 490

①
00.10   *Aqua Maria*   Lavrio.

② ④
04.25   *Aqua Maria*   Limnos. Kavala.
22.40   *Aqua Maria*   Lavrio.

⑤
21.25   *Aqua Maria*   Limnos. Kavala.

⑥
14.10   *Aqua Maria*   Lavrio.

⑦
08.25   *Aqua Maria*   Limnos. Kavala.

○
00.00   *Aeolos*   Limnos.

Agios Konstantinos

Northern Aegean p. 490

Ⓓ
10.00   Hydrofoil   Skiathos. Skopelos (Glossa).
                     Skopelos. Alonissos.
14.00   Hydrofoil   Skiathos. Skopelos.
19.15   Hydrofoil   Skiathos. Skopelos (Glossa).
                     Skopelos. Alonissos.

Ⓓ
09.30   *Express Pegasus*   Skiathos.
                      Skopelos (Agnontas).
                      Alonissos.

①
11.00   *Panagia Parou*   Skiathos. Skopelos.

②
11.00   *Panagia Parou*   Skiathos. Skopelos.
                      Alonissos.

③
11.00   *Panagia Parou*   Skiathos. Skopelos.

④
11.00   *Panagia Parou*   Skiathos. Skopelos.

⑤
16.00   *Panagia Parou*   Skiathos. Skopelos.
                      Alonissos.

⑥
11.00   *Panagia Parou*   Skiathos. Skopelos.

⑦
11.00   *Panagia Parou*   Skiathos. Skopelos.
                      Alonissos.

Days per week:
6-7 ▬▬▬
Skiathos
Skopelos (Town)
(Glossa)
Alonissos
AGIOS KONSTANTINOS

Alexandroupolis

Northern Aegean p. 491

Alonissos

Northern Aegean
p. 493

Typical:

Ⓓ
| 08.00 | Hydrofoil | Samothrace. |
| 15.30 | Hydrofoil | Samothrace. |

① ②
| 10.00 | *Saos II* | Samothrace. |

③
| 16.00 | *Saos II* | Samothrace. |

④
| 17.00 | *Saos II* | Samothrace. |

⑤
| 10.00 | *Saos II* | Samothrace. |
| 17.00 | *Saos II* | Samothrace. |

⑥ ⑦
| 15.00 | *Saos II* | Samothrace. |

○
12.00	High Season Ferry	Limnos.
		Lesbos (Mytilini).
		Chios.
		Samos (Vathi).
		Kalimnos.
		Kos.
		Rhodes.

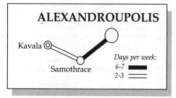

Ⓓ
06.30	Hydrofoil	Skopelos.
		Skopelos (Glossa).
		Skiathos.
		Volos.
14.00	Hydrofoil	Skopelos.
		Skopelos (Glossa).
14.45	*Express Pegasus*	Skopelos (Agnontas).
		Skiathos.
		Agios Konstantinos.
18.00	*Flying Cat 5/6*	Skopelos.
		Skopelos (Glossa).
		Skiathos.
		Volos.

②
12.40	*Achilleas*	Skopelos.
13.20	*Express Skiathos*	Skopelos.
		Skopelos (Glossa).
		Skiathos.
		Volos.
14.35	*Achilleas*	Evia (Kimi).
		Skyros.
15.20	*Panagia Parou*	Skopelos.
		Skiathos.
		Agios Konstantinos.

③
| 21.55 | *Express Skiathos* | Skiathos. |
| | | Volos. |

④
12.40	*Achilleas*	Skopelos.
14.35	*Achilleas*	Evia (Kimi).
		Skyros.
18.50	*Alikioni*	Skiathos.
		Volos.
21.55	*Express Skiathos*	Skiathos.
		Volos.

⑤
| 20.20 | *Panagia Parou* | Skiathos. |
| | | Agios Konstantinos. |

⑥
17.10	*Achilleas*	Skopelos.
18.50	*Achilleas*	Evia (Kimi).
		Skyros.

⑦
12.45	*Express Skiathos*	Skiathos.
		Volos.
15.20	*Panagia Parou*	Skopelos.
		Skiathos.
		Agios Konstantinos.

○
14.50	*Saos II*	Skiathos.
		Skopelos.
		Agios Konstantinos.

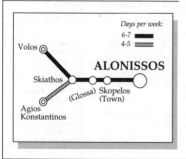

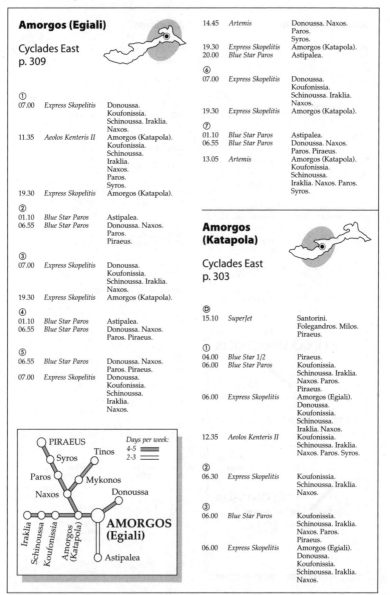

Amorgos (Egiali)

Cyclades East
p. 309

①

07.00	*Express Skopelitis*	Donoussa. Koufonissia. Schinoussa. Iraklia. Naxos.
11.35	*Aeolos Kenteris II*	Amorgos (Katapola). Koufonissia. Schinoussa. Iraklia. Naxos. Paros. Syros.
19.30	*Express Skopelitis*	Amorgos (Katapola).

②

| 01.10 | *Blue Star Paros* | Astipalea. |
| 06.55 | *Blue Star Paros* | Donoussa. Naxos. Paros. Piraeus. |

③

| 07.00 | *Express Skopelitis* | Donoussa. Koufonissia. Schinoussa. Iraklia. Naxos. |
| 19.30 | *Express Skopelitis* | Amorgos (Katapola). |

④

| 01.10 | *Blue Star Paros* | Astipalea. |
| 06.55 | *Blue Star Paros* | Donoussa. Naxos. Paros. Piraeus. |

⑤

| 06.55 | *Blue Star Paros* | Donoussa. Naxos. Paros. Piraeus. |
| 07.00 | *Express Skopelitis* | Donoussa. Koufonissia. Schinoussa. Iraklia. Naxos. |

14.45	*Artemis*	Donoussa. Naxos. Paros. Syros.
19.30	*Express Skopelitis*	Amorgos (Katapola).
20.00	*Blue Star Paros*	Astipalea.

⑥

| 07.00 | *Express Skopelitis* | Donoussa. Koufonissia. Schinoussa. Iraklia. Naxos. |
| 19.30 | *Express Skopelitis* | Amorgos (Katapola). |

⑦

01.10	*Blue Star Paros*	Astipalea.
06.55	*Blue Star Paros*	Donoussa. Naxos. Paros. Piraeus.
13.05	*Artemis*	Amorgos (Katapola). Koufonissia. Schinoussa. Iraklia. Naxos. Paros. Syros.

Amorgos (Katapola)

Cyclades East
p. 303

Ⓓ

| 15.10 | *SuperJet* | Santorini. Folegandros. Milos. Piraeus. |

①

04.00	*Blue Star 1/2*	Piraeus.
06.00	*Blue Star Paros*	Koufonissia. Schinoussa. Iraklia. Naxos. Paros. Piraeus.
06.00	*Express Skopelitis*	Amorgos (Egiali). Donoussa. Koufonissia. Schinoussa. Iraklia. Naxos.
12.35	*Aeolos Kenteris II*	Koufonissia. Schinoussa. Iraklia. Naxos. Paros. Syros.

②

| 06.30 | *Express Skopelitis* | Koufonissia. Schinoussa. Iraklia. Naxos. |

③

| 06.00 | *Blue Star Paros* | Koufonissia. Schinoussa. Iraklia. Naxos. Paros. Piraeus. |
| 06.00 | *Express Skopelitis* | Amorgos (Egiali). Donoussa. Koufonissia. Schinoussa. Iraklia. Naxos. |

```
           PIRAEUS          Days per week:
                            6-7  ▬▬▬
               Tinos        4-5  ▬▬▬
        Syros               2-3  ═══
    Paros        Mykonos
       Naxos              Donoussa
                        Amorgos
                        (Egiali)
         AMORGOS          Astipalea
         (Katapola)
   Iraklia
   Schinoussa
   Koufonissia
```

④
06.30   Express Skopelitis   Koufonissia.
                             Schinoussa. Iraklia.
                             Naxos.

⑤
06.00   Express Skopelitis   Amorgos (Egiali).
                             Donoussa. Koufonissia.
                             Schinoussa. Iraklia.
                             Naxos.
13.50   Artemis   Amorgos (Egiali).
                             Donoussa. Naxos.
                             Paros. Syros.

⑥
06.00   Blue Star Paros   Koufonissia.
                             Schinoussa. Iraklia.
                             Naxos. Paros. Piraeus.
06.00   Express Skopelitis   Amorgos (Egiali).
                             Donoussa. Koufonissia.
                             Schinoussa. Iraklia.
                             Naxos.

⑦
05.05   Blue Star 1/2   Patmos. Leros. Kos.
                             Rhodes.
08.15   Express Skopelitis   Koufonissia.
                             Santorini. Ios.
14.00   Artemis   Koufonissia.
                             Schinoussa. Iraklia.
                             Naxos. Paros. Syros.

Anafi

Cyclades East p. 311

②
16.00   Vitsentzos Kornaros   Santorini. Ios.
                              Sikinos.
                              Folegandros.
                              Milos.
                              Santorini.

③
07.00   Aeolos Kenteris II   Santorini. Thirasia.
                             Ios. Sikinos.
                             Folegandros.
                             Naxos.
                             Paros. Syros.

④
05.35   Prevelis   Kassos.
                             Karpathos.
                             Karpathos (Diafani).
                             Chalki.
                             Rhodes.
07.00   Artemis   Santorini. Thirasia.
                             Ios. Sikinos.
                             Folegandros. Naxos.
                             Paros. Syros.

⑥
10.45   Prevelis   Crete (Iraklion).
                             Crete (Sitia).
                             Kassos. Karpathos.
                             Rhodes.

⑦
07.00   Aeolos Kenteris II   Santorini. Thirasia.
                             Ios. Sikinos.
                             Folegandros.
                             Naxos.
                             Paros. Mykonos.
                             Syros.
20.00   Prevelis   Santorini. Piraeus.

○ * Not operating in 2011:

18.00   Arsinoe   Santorini.

Ancona

Italy p. 635

Ⓓ
13.30   Superfast VI/XI   Igoumenitsa.
                             Patras.

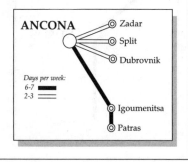

```
   ANCONA        ◎ Zadar
                 ◎ Split
                 ◎ Dubrovnik
   Days per week:
   6-7  ▬▬▬
   2-3  ═══
                 ◎ Igoumenitsa
                 ◎ Patras
```

16.00	ANEK Lines	Igoumenitsa. Patras.
17.00	*Cruise Europa/ Cruise Olympia*	Igoumenitsa. Patras.
19.00	*Superfast VI/XI*	Igoumenitsa. Patras.

Andros

Cyclades North
p. 215

①
09.45	*Penelope A*	Tinos. Mykonos.
09.55	*Superferry II*	Tinos. Mykonos.
10.00	*Theologos P*	Rafina.
16.05	*Penelope A*	Rafina.
16.30	*Superferry II*	Rafina.
19.40	*Theologos P*	Tinos. Mykonos.
21.15	*Penelope A*	Rafina.
21.45	*Superferry II*	Rafina.

②
09.45	*Penelope A*	Tinos. Mykonos.
09.55	*Superferry II*	Tinos. Mykonos. Naxos.
10.00	*Theologos P*	Rafina.
16.05	*Penelope A*	Rafina.
18.40	*Superferry II*	Rafina.
19.40	*Theologos P*	Tinos. Mykonos.
21.15	*Penelope A*	Rafina.

Days per week:
6-7 ▬▬▬
2-3 ═══

Rafina

ANDROS

Syros

Tinos

Mykonos

③
07.10	*Artemis*	Tinos. Syros.
09.45	*Penelope A*	Tinos. Mykonos.
09.55	*Superferry II*	Tinos. Mykonos. Naxos.
10.00	*Theologos P*	Rafina.
16.05	*Penelope A*	Rafina.
18.40	*Superferry II*	Rafina.
19.40	*Theologos P*	Tinos. Mykonos.

④
07.00	*Aqua Jewel*	Tinos. Syros.
09.45	*Penelope A*	Tinos. Mykonos.
09.55	*Superferry II*	Tinos. Mykonos. Naxos.
10.00	*Theologos P*	Rafina.
16.05	*Penelope A*	Rafina.
18.40	*Superferry II*	Rafina.
19.40	*Theologos P*	Tinos. Mykonos.
21.15	*Penelope A*	Rafina.
22.00	*Aeolos Kenteris II*	Tinos. Syros.

⑤
09.15	*Theologos P*	Tinos. Mykonos.
09.45	*Penelope A*	Tinos. Mykonos.
09.55	*Superferry II*	Tinos.
13.30	*Superferry II*	Rafina.
14.45	*Theologos P*	Rafina.
16.05	*Penelope A*	Rafina.
18.50	*Aeolos Kenteris II*	Tinos. Syros.
19.15	*Superferry II*	Tinos. Mykonos. Rafina.
20.10	*Theologos P*	Tinos. Mykonos. Rafina.
21.15	*Penelope A*	Rafina.

⑥
09.45	*Penelope A*	Tinos. Mykonos.
09.55	*Superferry II*	Tinos. Mykonos. Naxos.
14.45	*Theologos P*	Rafina.
18.00	*Penelope A*	Rafina.
18.40	*Superferry II*	Rafina.
19.40	*Theologos P*	Tinos. Mykonos.

⑦
09.45	*Penelope A*	Tinos. Mykonos.
09.55	*Superferry II*	Tinos. Mykonos.
14.45	*Theologos P*	Rafina.
16.05	*Penelope A*	Rafina.
16.30	*Superferry II*	Rafina.
20.00	*Theologos P*	Rafina.
21.15	*Penelope A*	Rafina.
21.45	*Superferry II*	Rafina.

Angistri

Argo-Saronic
p. 544

ⒹＤ
07.00	*Angistri Express*	Aegina.
10.00	*Angistri Express*	Aegina.
13.00	*Angistri Express*	Aegina.
15.00	*Angistri Express*	Aegina.
18.00	*Angistri Express*	Aegina.

①
05.55	*Manaras Express*	Piraeus.
07.10	*Kitsolakis Express*	Piraeus.
09.45	*Manaras Express*	Piraeus.
14.30	Hellenic Seaways	Aegina.
16.10	*Manaras Express*	Piraeus.
17.15	Hellenic Seaways	Aegina.
		Piraeus.

②
07.10	*Kitsolakis Express*	Piraeus.

② ③ ④
06.10	*Manaras Express*	Piraeus.
16.40	*Manaras Express*	Piraeus.

③
07.10	*Kitsolakis Express*	Piraeus.
14.30	Hellenic Seaways	Aegina.
17.15	Hellenic Seaways	Aegina. Piraeus.

④
07.10	*Kitsolakis Express*	Piraeus.

⑤
09.45	*Manaras Express*	Piraeus.
12.40	*Kitsolakis Express*	Piraeus.
14.30	Hellenic Seaways	Aegina.
15.30	*Manaras Express*	Piraeus.
17.15	Hellenic Seaways	Aegina.
		Piraeus.
20.15	*Manaras Express*	Piraeus.

⑥
06.15	*Kitsolakis Express*	Piraeus.
09.00	*Manaras Express*	Piraeus.
11.45	Hellenic Seaways	Aegina.
12.10	*Kitsolakis Express*	Piraeus.
15.45	Hellenic Seaways	Aegina.
		Piraeus.
17.00	*Manaras Express*	Piraeus.

⑦
12.00	Hellenic Seaways	Aegina.
15.00	*Manaras Express*	Piraeus.
16.00	*Kitsolakis Express*	Piraeus.
19.10	*Manaras Express*	Piraeus.
19.45	Hellenic Seaways	Aegina.
		Piraeus.

○
12.00	Hellenic Seaways	Epidavros.
14.30	Hellenic Seaways	Epidavros.

Antikithera

Argo-Saronic   p. 546

①
19.30	*Porfyrousa*	Kithera. Neapoli.

④
10.40	*Vitsentzos Kornaros*	Kithera.
		Gythio.
19.30	*Vitsentzos Kornaros*	Crete (Kasteli).

⑥
03.30	*Vitsentzos Kornaros*	Crete (Kasteli).
06.30	*Vitsentzos Kornaros*	Crete (Kasteli).

⑦
19.40	*Vitsentzos Kornaros*	Kithera.
		Monemvassia.
		Piraeus.

Antiparos

Cyclades Central
p. 139

Ⓓ Ⓗ
07.00–24.00;		
ev. 30 min		
10.30–20.30	*Agioi Anargiri*	Paros (Punta).

Ⓓ
x 10	*Antiparos Express/*	
	Kasos Express/	
	Panagia Parou	Paros.

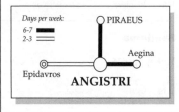

Days per week:
6-7
2-3
PIRAEUS
Aegina
Epidavros
ANGISTRI

Paros (Town)   *Days per week:*
6-7
Paros (Punta)
ANTIPAROS

Arki

Dodecanese
p. 372

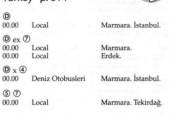

①
10.45	*Nissos Kalimnos*	Agathonisi.
		Samos (Pithagorio).
18.40	*Nissos Kalimnos*	Patmos. Lipsi.
		Leros.
		Kalimnos.

③ ⑦
11.40	*Nissos Kalimnos*	Agathonisi.
		Samos (Pithagorio).
16.50	*Nissos Kalimnos*	Patmos. Lipsi. Leros.
		Kalimnos.

⑤
| 18.40 | *Nissos Kalimnos* | Patmos. Lipsi. Leros. |
| | | Kalimnos. |

| 07.00 | *Nissos Kalimnos* | Kalimnos. |

⑦
05.15	*Blue Star Paros*	Amorgos (Egiali).
		Donoussa. Naxos.
		Paros. Piraeus.
09.35	*Diagoras*	Naxos. Paros.
		Piraeus.

Astakos

Ionian Line   p. 573

Ⓓ
| 13.00 | *Basos K/* | |
| | *Ionion Pelagos* | Kefalonia (Sami). |

Astipalea

Cyclades East
p. 314

②
05.15	*Blue Star Paros*	Amorgos (Egiali).
		Donoussa. Naxos.
		Paros. Piraeus.
07.00	*Nissos Kalimnos*	Kalimnos.

④
05.15	*Blue Star Paros*	Amorgos (Egiali).
		Donoussa. Naxos.
		Paros. Piraeus.
07.00	*Nissos Kalimnos*	Kalimnos.

⑤
05.15	*Blue Star Paros*	Amorgos (Egiali).
		Donoussa. Naxos.
		Paros. Piraeus.

⑥
02.55	*Diagoras*	Kalimnos. Kos. Nissiros.
		Tilos. Symi. Rhodes.
		Kastelorizo.

Avşa

Turkey p. 614

Ⓓ
| 00.00 | Local | Marmara. İstanbul. |

Ⓓ ex ⑦
| 00.00 | Local | Marmara. |
| 00.00 | Local | Erdek. |

Ⓓ x ④
| 00.00 | Deniz Otobusleri | Marmara. İstanbul. |

⑤ ⑦
| 00.00 | Local | Marmara. Tekirdağ. |

Ayvalık

Turkey p. 614

Ⓓ
| 08.00 | *Jale/Jalehan* | Lesbos (Mytilini). |
| 17.00 | *Jale/Jalehan* | Lesbos (Mytilini). |

Bandırma

Turkey p. 615

Ⓓ
| 01.15 | Local | İstanbul. |
| 14.30 | Local | İstanbul. |

Bari

Italy
p. 635

⒟		
18.00	Polaris/ Bari	Corfu. Igoumenitsa.
18.30	Endeavour Lines	Igoumenitsa. Patras.
20.00	Superfast I/ Superfast II	Igoumenitsa. Patras.

①		
20.00	Polaris/Bari	Corfu. Igoumenitsa.

○		
19.00	AK Ventouris	Patras.

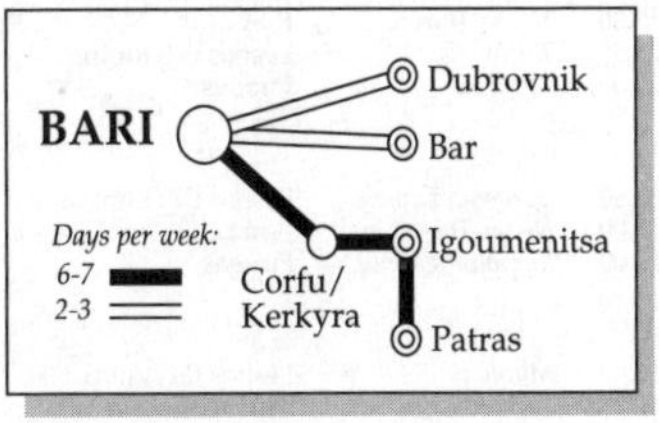

BARI — Dubrovnik, Bar, Igoumenitsa, Corfu/Kerkyra, Patras

Days per week:
6-7
2-3

Bodrum

Turkey
p. 615

⒟		
09.00	Bodrum Princess	Kos.
09.00	Fari Kaptain I	Kos.
09.30	Bodrum Express	Datça (Körmen).
11.00	Bodrum T/Bs	Orak Is.
11.00	Bodrum T/Bs	Korada Is. Ada Is.
16.00	Hermes	Kos.
17.00	Bodrum Express	Datça (Körmen).

Bozcaada

Turkey p. 617

⒟ x 2	Local	Odun Iskalesi.

Brindisi

Italy
p. 635

⒟		
19.00	Ionian Queen/ Erotokritos/ Elli T	Kefalonia (Sami). Patras.
20.30	Ionian Queen/ Erotokritos/ Elli T	Corfu. Igoumenitsa.

○		
16.00	Ionian King	Igoumentisa. Kefalonia (Sami). Zakinthos.

○		
20.00	Capatin Zaman	Çeşme.

○		
20.00	Poseidon	Çeşme.

ⓦ		
00.00	Cesme/ Scotia Prince	Çeşme.

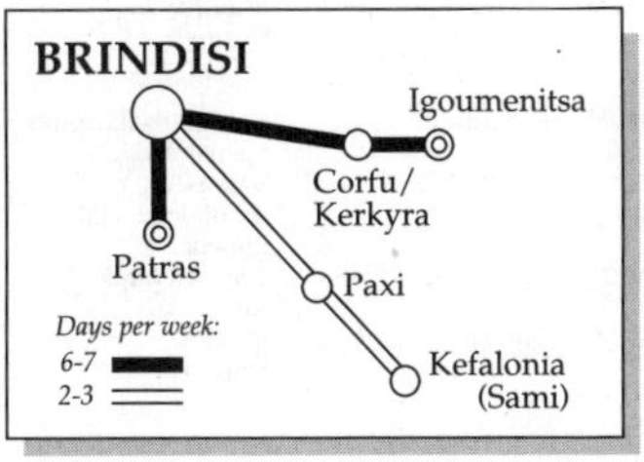

BRINDISI — Igoumenitsa, Corfu/Kerkyra, Patras, Paxi, Kefalonia (Sami)

Days per week:
6-7
2-3

Çeşme

Turkey
p. 618

⒟		
08.00	Erturk I	Chios.
18.00	Capetan Stamatis	Chios.

○		
20.00	Capatin Zaman	Brindisi.
20.00	Scotia Prince	Brindisi.

Chalki

Dodecanese
p. 373

Ⓓ ex ⑦
05.30	*Express Chalki/ Nikos Express*	Rhodes (Kamiros Skala).

②
12.30	*Prevelis*	Rhodes.
17.30	*Prevelis*	Karpathos. Kassos. Crete (Sitia). Crete (Iraklion). Santorini. Milos. Piraeus.

④
15.35	*Prevelis*	Rhodes. Karpathos. Kassos. Crete (Sitia). Crete (Iraklion). Santorini. Milos. Piraeus.

⑤
10.25	*Dodekanisos Express*	Tilos. Nissiros. Kos.
16.00	*Dodekanisos Express*	Rhodes. Symi.

⑦
10.00	*Prevelis*	Karpathos (Diafani). Karpathos. Kassos. Anafi. Santorini. Piraeus.
10.25	*Dodekanisos Express*	Tilos. Nissiros. Kos.
17.50	*Dodekanisos Express*	Rhodes. Symi.

Ⓞ PIRAEUS

Rhodes (Kamiros)

CHALKI Ⓞ Alimnia

Days per week: Karpathos

6-7
4-5
1

Kassos

Crete (Sitia)

Crete (Agios Nikolaos)

Chios

Eastern Line
p. 451

Ⓓ
08.00	Local	Çeşme.
14.00	*Oinoussai III*	Oinousses.

Ⓓ
00.40	*Nissos Chios*	Piraeus.
19.00	*Nissos Chios*	Lesbos (Mytilini).

①
04.00	*European Express*	Lesbos (Mytilini).
15.00	*Nissos Thira*	Psara.
22.00	*European Express*	Piraeus.

②
04.00	*Mytilene*	Lesbos (Mytilini).
13.05	*Taxiarchis*	Samos (Vathi).
15.00	*Nissos Thira*	Psara.
21.55	*Taxiarchis*	Lesbos (Mytilini).
22.00	*Mytilene*	Piraeus.

③
04.00	*European Express*	Lesbos (Mytilini).
15.00	*Nissos Thira*	Psara.
22.00	*European Express*	Piraeus.

④
04.00	*Mytilene*	Lesbos (Mytilini).
11.25	*Taxiarchis*	Samos (Karlovassi). Ikaria (Agios Kyrikos).
15.00	*Nissos Thira*	Psara.
22.00	*Mytilene*	Piraeus.
22.15	*Taxiarchis*	Lesbos (Mytilini).

⑤
04.00	*European Express*	Lesbos (Mytilini).
19.30	*Nissos Thira*	Psara.
22.00	*European Express*	Piraeus.

⑥
04.00	*Mytilene*	Lesbos (Mytilini).
11.25	*Taxiarchis*	Samos (Vathi).
15.00	*Nissos Thira*	Psara.

⑦
11.20	*Taxiarchis*	Lesbos (Mytilini).
19.30	*Nissos Thira*	Psara.
22.00	*Mytilene*	Piraeus.

Ⓞ * Not operating in 2011:

04.00	*Theofilos*	Lesbos (Mytilini).
10.50	*Samothraki*	Samos (Vathi).
17.25	*Samothraki*	Lesbos (Mytilini). Limnos. Thessalonika.
22.00	*Theofilos*	Piraeus.

07.00	Ventouris	Igoumenitsa.
07.30	*Ionian Queen/ Erotokritos/ Elli T*	Igoumenitsa.
09.15	*Ionian Queen/ Erotokritos/ Elli T*	Brindisi.
09.30	*Polaris/Bari*	Bari.
13.30	*Europa Palace/ Ikarus Palace/ Olympia Palace/ Zeus Palace*	Patras.
23.00	Ventouris	Bari.

①

16.30	*Lefka Ori*	Patras.

②

07.00	*Lefka Ori*	Igoumenitsa. Venice.
07.00	*Polaris/Bari*	Igoumenitsa.
22.30	*Sophocles Venizelos*	Patras.

③

22.30	*Lefka Ori*	Patras.

④

06.00	*Sophocles Venizelos*	Igoumenitsa. Venice.
23.00	*Lefka Ori*	Patras.

⑤

06.00	*Lefka Ori*	Igoumenitsa. Venice.

⑥

06.00	*Lefka Ori*	Igoumenitsa. Venice.
14.30	*Sophocles Venizelos*	Patras.

⑦

06.30	*Sophocles Venizelos*	Igoumenitsa. Venice.
14.30	*Lefka Ori*	Patras.
23.30	*Polaris/Bari*	Bari.

Thessalonika

Days per week:
6-7 ▬▬▬
2-3 ═══

Limnos

Lavrio

Lesbos (Mytilini)

Psara · Oinousses

Çeşme

CHIOS

PIRAEUS · Samos (Vathi)

Chios (Mesta)

Eastern Line
p. 453

②

14.30	*Panagia Thalassini*	Psara. Lavrio.

④

14.30	*Panagia Thalassini*	Psara. Lavrio.

⑦

09.00	*Nissos Thira*	Psara.
14.30	*Panagia Thalassini*	Psara. Lavrio.

Corfu / Kerkyra

Ionian Line
p. 573

Ⓓ

00.30	*Erotokritos/Elli T*	Brindisi.
05.00	*Polaris/Bari*	Igoumenitsa.
07.00	*Europa Palace/ Ikarus Palace/ Olympia Palace/ Zeus Palace*	Igoumenitsa. Venice.

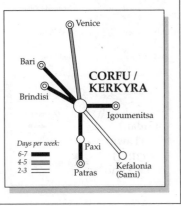

Venice

Bari

CORFU / KERKYRA

Brindisi

Igoumenitsa

Days per week:
6-7 ▬▬▬
4-5 ═══
2-3 ═══

Paxi

Patras

Kefalonia (Sami)

Domestic Services:

Ⓗ
06.00–22.00
Local C/F   Igoumenitsa.

Ⓓ
09.30   Ekaterini P   Igoumenitsa.
14.00   Ekaterini P   Igoumenitsa.
14.00   Pegasus T/B   Paxi (Old Port).
19.30   Ekaterini P   Igoumenitsa.

① ② ⑦
12.45   Local C/F   Igoumenitsa. Paxi.

③
07.30   Local C/F   Igoumenitsa. Paxi.

④ ⑤ ⑥
12.45   Local C/F   Igoumenitsa. Paxi.

○
00.00   Paxi. Preveza.
Amphilochia.

Corfu (Lefkimi)

Ionian Line
p. 577

Ⓓ
06.00 09.00 12.00
16.00 18.00
Local C/F   Igoumenitsa.

Corfu (Agios Stefanos)

① ③ ⑥
10.15   Local   Mathraki. Othoni.

③
08.15   Local   Erikoussa.

⑤
10.45   Local   Erikoussa.

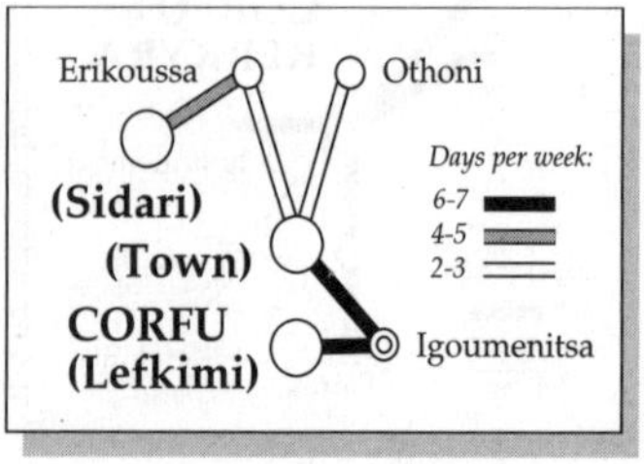

Erikoussa   Othoni

(Sidari)   Days per week:
(Town)   6-7 ▬▬▬
               4-5 ▬▬▬
CORFU   2-3 ═══
(Lefkimi)   Igoumenitsa

Crete
(Agia Roumeli)

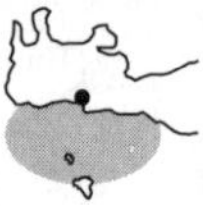

Crete
p. 351

Ⓓ
09.30   14.00 15.45 17.00
South Crete Line   Lutro.
Sfakia.

18.00   South Crete Line   Sfakia.
16.30   South Crete Line   Sougia.
Paleochora.

Crete
(Agios Nikolaos)

Crete
p. 336

Ⓓ
10.00   Tour Boats   Spinalonga.

○   * Not calling here in 2011:

10.00   Vitsentzos Kornaros/
Ierapetra L/Prevelis   Crete (Sitia).
Kassos.
Karpathos.
Karpathos (Diafani).
Chalki.
Rhodes.

17.15   Vitsentzos Kornaros/
Ierapetra L/Prevelis   Santorini.
Milos.
Piraeus.

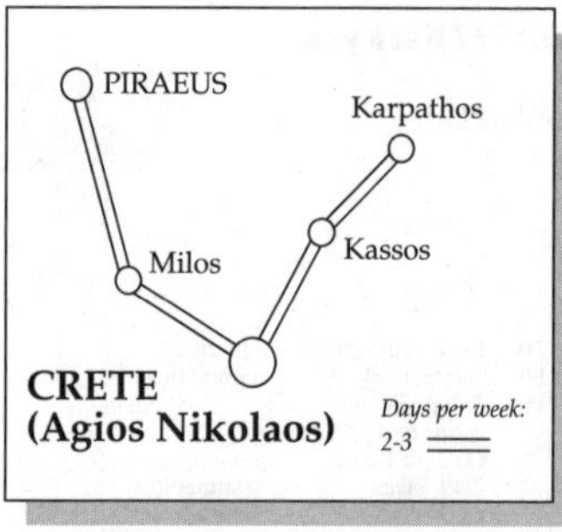

PIRAEUS
Karpathos
Milos   Kassos
CRETE
(Agios Nikolaos)   Days per week:
2-3 ═══

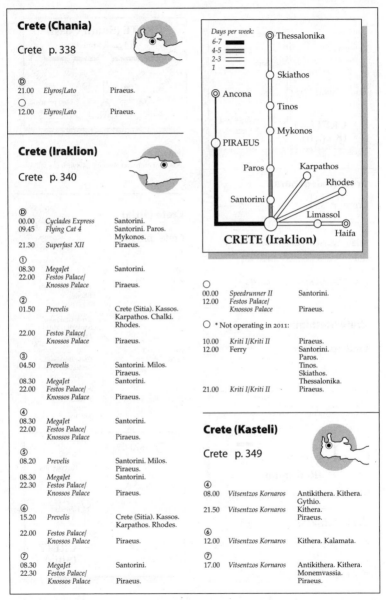

Crete (Chania)

Crete p. 338

Ⓓ
21.00   *Elyros/Lato*   Piraeus.
Ⓞ
12.00   *Elyros/Lato*   Piraeus.

Crete (Iraklion)

Crete p. 340

Ⓓ
00.00   *Cyclades Express*   Santorini.
09.45   *Flying Cat 4*   Santorini. Paros.
                              Mykonos.
21.30   *Superfast XII*   Piraeus.

①
08.30   *MegaJet*   Santorini.
22.00   *Festos Palace/*
         Knossos Palace   Piraeus.

②
01.50   *Prevelis*   Crete (Sitia). Kassos.
                              Karpathos. Chalki.
                              Rhodes.

22.00   *Festos Palace/*
         Knossos Palace   Piraeus.

③
04.50   *Prevelis*   Santorini. Milos.
                              Piraeus.
08.30   *MegaJet*   Santorini.
22.00   *Festos Palace/*
         Knossos Palace   Piraeus.

④
08.30   *MegaJet*   Santorini.
22.00   *Festos Palace/*
         Knossos Palace   Piraeus.

⑤
08.20   *Prevelis*   Santorini. Milos.
                              Piraeus.
08.30   *MegaJet*   Santorini.
22.30   *Festos Palace/*
         Knossos Palace   Piraeus.

⑥
15.20   *Prevelis*   Crete (Sitia). Kassos.
                              Karpathos. Rhodes.

22.00   *Festos Palace/*
         Knossos Palace   Piraeus.

⑦
08.30   *MegaJet*   Santorini.
22.30   *Festos Palace/*
         Knossos Palace   Piraeus.

Days per week:
6-7
4-5
2-3
1

Thessalonika
Skiathos
Ancona
Tinos
Mykonos
PIRAEUS
Paros   Karpathos
                     Rhodes
Santorini
               Limassol
CRETE (Iraklion)   Haifa

Ⓞ
00.00   *Speedrunner II*   Santorini.
12.00   *Festos Palace/*
         Knossos Palace   Piraeus.

Ⓞ * Not operating in 2011:

10.00   *Kriti I/Kriti II*   Piraeus.
12.00   *Ferry*   Santorini.
                              Paros.
                              Tinos.
                              Skiathos.
                              Thessalonika.
21.00   *Kriti I/Kriti II*   Piraeus.

Crete (Kasteli)

Crete p. 349

④
08.00   *Vitsentzos Kornaros*   Antikithera. Kithera.
                                  Gythio.
21.50   *Vitsentzos Kornaros*   Kithera.
                                  Piraeus.

⑥
12.00   *Vitsentzos Kornaros*   Kithera. Kalamata.

⑦
17.00   *Vitsentzos Kornaros*   Antikithera. Kithera.
                                  Monemvassia.
                                  Piraeus.

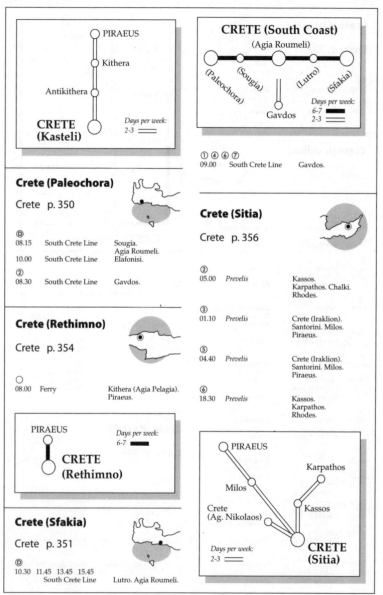

PIRAEUS
Kithera
Antikithera
CRETE (Kasteli)
Days per week: 2-3

CRETE (South Coast)
(Agia Roumeli)
(Paleochora) (Sougia) (Lutro) (Sfakia)
Gavdos
Days per week:
6-7
2-3

① ④ ⑥ ⑦
09.00   South Crete Line   Gavdos.

Crete (Paleochora)

Crete p. 350

ⓓ		
08.15	South Crete Line	Sougia. Agia Roumeli.
10.00	South Crete Line	Elafonisi.
②		
08.30	South Crete Line	Gavdos.

Crete (Rethimno)

Crete p. 354

○		
08.00	Ferry	Kithera (Agia Pelagia). Piraeus.

PIRAEUS
Days per week:
6-7
CRETE (Rethimno)

Crete (Sfakia)

Crete p. 351

ⓓ		
10.30 11.45 13.45 15.45 South Crete Line		Lutro. Agia Roumeli.

Crete (Sitia)

Crete p. 356

②		
05.00	*Prevelis*	Kassos. Karpathos. Chalki. Rhodes.
③		
01.10	*Prevelis*	Crete (Iraklion). Santorini. Milos. Piraeus.
⑤		
04.40	*Prevelis*	Crete (Iraklion). Santorini. Milos. Piraeus.
⑥		
18.30	*Prevelis*	Kassos. Karpathos. Rhodes.

PIRAEUS
Karpathos
Milos
Kassos
Crete (Ag. Nikolaos)
Days per week:
2-3
CRETE (Sitia)

○
12.40   *Vitsentzos Kornaros*   Kassos.
                                Karpathos.
                                Karpathos (Diafani).
                                Chalki.
                                Rhodes.

○
15.20   *Vitsentzos Kornaros*   Crete (Agios Nikolaos).
                                Santorini.
                                Milos.
                                Piraeus.

Cyprus (Limassol)

Cyprus p. 636

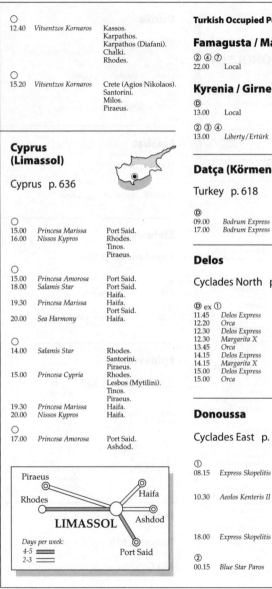

○
15.00   *Princesa Marissa*   Port Said.
16.00   *Nissos Kypros*   Rhodes.
                              Tinos.
                              Piraeus.

○
15.00   *Princesa Amorosa*   Port Said.
18.00   *Salamis Star*   Port Said.
                              Haifa.
19.30   *Princesa Marissa*   Haifa.
                              Port Said.
20.00   *Sea Harmony*   Haifa.

○
14.00   *Salamis Star*   Rhodes.
                              Santorini.
                              Piraeus.
15.00   *Princesa Cypria*   Rhodes.
                              Lesbos (Mytilini).
                              Tinos.
                              Piraeus.
19.30   *Princesa Marissa*   Haifa.
20.00   *Nissos Kypros*   Haifa.

○
17.00   *Princesa Amorosa*   Port Said.
                              Ashdod.

Piraeus
Rhodes
Haifa
LIMASSOL   Ashdod
Days per week:
4-5
2-3
Port Said

Turkish Occupied Ports:

Famagusta / Magosa

② ④ ⑦
22.00   Local   Mersin.

Kyrenia / Girne

Ⓓ
13.00   Local   Taşucu.

② ③ ④
13.00   *Liberty / Ertürk*   Taşucu.

Datça (Körmen)

Turkey p. 618

Ⓓ
09.00   *Bodrum Express*   Bodrum.
17.00   *Bodrum Express*   Bodrum.

Delos

Cyclades North p. 220

Ⓓ ex ①
11.45   *Delos Express*   Mykonos.
12.20   *Orca*   Mykonos.
12.30   *Delos Express*   Mykonos.
12.30   *Margarita X*   Mykonos.
13.45   *Orca*   Mykonos.
14.15   *Delos Express*   Mykonos.
14.15   *Margarita X*   Mykonos.
15.00   *Delos Express*   Mykonos.
15.00   *Orca*   Mykonos.

Donoussa

Cyclades East p. 318

①
08.15   *Express Skopelitis* Koufonissia.
                              Schinoussa. Iraklia.
                              Naxos.
10.30   *Aeolos Kenteris II* Amorgos (Egiali).
                              Amorgos (Katapola).
                              Koufonissia.
                              Schinoussa. Iraklia.
                              Naxos. Paros. Syros.
18.00   *Express Skopelitis* Amorgos (Egiali).
                              Amorgos (Katapola).

②
00.15   *Blue Star Paros*   Amorgos (Egiali).
                              Astipalea.

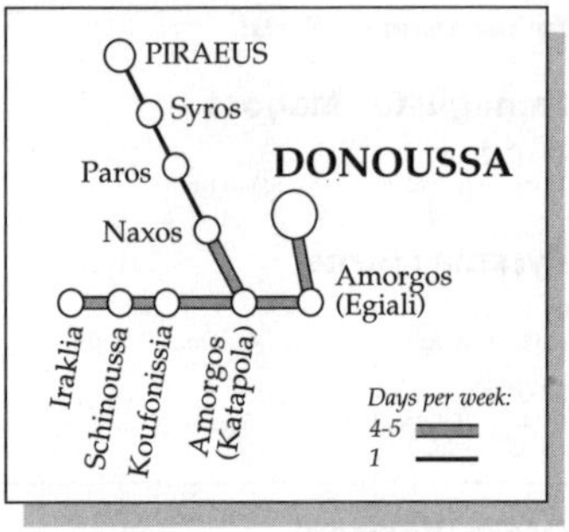

Days per week:
4-5
1

| 07.50 | *Blue Star Paros* | Naxos. Paros. Piraeus. |

③
| 08.15 | *Express Skopelitis* | Koufonissia. Schinoussa. Iraklia. Naxos. |
| 18.00 | *Express Skopelitis* | Amorgos (Egiali). Amorgos (Katapola). |

④
| 00.15 | *Blue Star Paros* | Amorgos (Egiali). Astipalea. |
| 07.50 | *Blue Star Paros* | Naxos. Paros. Piraeus. |

⑤
01.15	*Blue Star Paros*	Amorgos (Egiali). Astipalea.
07.50	*Blue Star Paros*	Naxos. Paros. Piraeus.
08.15	*Express Skopelitis*	Koufonissia. Schinoussa. Iraklia. Naxos.
15.55	*Artemis*	Naxos. Paros. Syros.
18.00	*Express Skopelitis*	Amorgos (Egiali). Amorgos (Katapola).

⑥
| 08.15 | *Express Skopelitis* | Koufonissia. Schinoussa. Iraklia. Naxos. |
| 18.00 | *Express Skopelitis* | Amorgos (Egiali). Amorgos (Katapola). |

⑦
00.15	*Blue Star Paros*	Amorgos (Egiali). Astipalea.
07.50	*Blue Star Paros*	Naxos. Paros. Piraeus.
11.15	*Artemis*	Amorgos (Egiali). Amorgos (Katapola). Koufonissia. Schinoussa. Iraklia. Naxos. Paros. Syros.

Durrës

Albania p. 636

○
| 12.00 | Adriatica | Bari. |
| 19.00 | Adriatica | Trieste. |

⑦
| 12.00 | Adriatica | Ancona. |

Eceabat

Turkey p. 618

Ⓓ ev 2Ⓗ 08.00–03.00   Çanakkale.

Elafonissos

Argo-Saronic p. 546

Ⓓ
| x 10 | | Neapoli. |

○
| 01.25 | | Kithera (Agia Pelagia). Crete (Kasteli). |

Epidavros

Argo-Saronic p. 547

○
09.50	*Flying Dolphin*	Aegina.
16.00	Local	Angistri. Aegina. Piraeus.
19.55	*Flying Dolphin*	Aegina.

○
| 17.15 | Local | Angistri. Aegina. Piraeus. |

Erdek

Turkey p. 618

Ⓓ ex ⑦
| 00.00 | Local | Avşa. Marmara. |

① ⑥
00.00   Local   Paşalimanı.

⑤ ⑦
00.00   Local   Avşa. Marmara. Tekirdağ.

Ermioni

Argo-Saronic

ⓓ
12.30   *Ioannis II*   Spetses.
14.30   *Ioannis II*   Hydra. Poros. Methana.
                         Aegina. Piraeus.

🚀 *Flying Dolphins* include:
ⓓ
x 6   Hydra. Piraeus.
x 4   Poros.

Evia (Kimi)

Cyclades North   p. 229

① ③
12.00   *Achilleas*   Skyros.
18.00   *Achilleas*   Skyros.

② ④
10.00   *Achilleas*   Alonissos. Skopelos.
18.30   *Achilleas*   Skyros.

⑤
12.00   *Achilleas*   Skyros.
20.00   *Achilleas*   Skyros.

⑥
10.00   *Achilleas*   Skyros.
14.30   *Achilleas*   Alonissos. Skopelos.
22.15   *Achilleas*   Skyros.

⑦
16.00   *Achilleas*   Skyros.
21.30   *Achilleas*   Skyros.

Volos
Skiathos
Skopelos
Alonissos
EVIA
(Kimi)   Skyros

Days per week:
6-7
2-3

Evia (Marmari)

Cyclades North
p. 229

ⓓ
06.00   *Artemisia*   Rafina.

① ② ③ ④
10.30   *Evia Star*   Rafina.
13.45   *Artemisia*   Rafina.
17.15   *Evia Star*   Rafina.
18.30   *Artemisia*   Rafina.

⑤
10.30   *Artemisia*   Rafina.
13.30   *Evia Star*   Rafina.
15.30   *Artemisia*   Rafina.
18.30   *Evia Star*   Rafina.

⑥
10.30   *Evia Star*   Rafina.
13.45   *Artemisia*   Rafina.
17.15   *Evia Star*   Rafina.

⑦
09.30   *Artemisia*   Rafina
14.00   *Artemisia*   Rafina.
17.15   *Artemisia*   Rafina.
20.45   *Evia Star*   Rafina.

Folegandros

Cyclades West
p. 260

ⓓ
10.50   *SuperJet*   Santorini.
                         Naxos.
                         Koufonissia.
                         Amorgos (Katapola).
17.45   *SuperJet*   Milos.
                         Piraeus.

①
20.00   *Artemis*   Kimolos. Milos.
22.20   *Speedrunner IV*   Sifnos.
                            Piraeus.

②
01.00   *Adamantis Korais*   Ios.
03.00   *Vitsentzos Kornaros* Sikinos. Ios.
                                 Santorini. Anafi.
09.50   *Artemis*   Sikinos.
                                 Santorini.
                                 Ios. Naxos.
                                 Syros.
10.55   *Adamantis Korais*   Kimolos. Milos.
                                 Sifnos. Serifos.
                                 Kythnos.
                                 Piraeus.

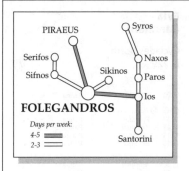

17.35	*Aeolos Kenteris II*	Sikinos. Ios. Thirasia. Santorini. Anafi.
21.45	*Vitsentzos Kornaros*	Milos. Santorini.

③
11.00	*Aeolos Kenteris II*	Naxos. Paros. Syros.
14.00	*Agios Georgios*	Sikinos. Ios. Santorini.
17.35	*Artemis*	Sikinos. Ios. Thirasia. Santorini. Anafi.
21.10	*Agios Georgios*	Sifnos. Piraeus.

④
12.15	*Artemis*	Naxos. Paros. Syros.
22.20	*Speedrunner IV*	Sifnos. Piraeus.

⑤
14.00	*Agios Georgios*	Sikinos. Ios. Santorini.
18.00	*Aqua Jewel*	Kimolos. Milos.
21.25	*Agios Georgios*	Kimolos. Sifnos. Piraeus.

⑥
09.40	*Aqua Jewel*	Sikinos. Ios. Naxos. Paros. Mykonos. Syros.
17.35	*Aeolos Kenteris II*	Sikinos. Ios. Thirasia. Santorini. Anafi.

⑦
11.50	*Aeolos Kenteris II*	Naxos. Paros. Mykonos. Syros.
14.35	*Adamantis Korais*	Kimolos. Sifnos. Serifos. Kythnos. Piraeus.

Fourni

Eastern Line p. 456

①
07.30	*Samos Sun*	Thimena. Samos (Karlovassi).

②
11.15	*Nissos Mykonos*	Ikaria (Agios Kyrikos). Mykonos. Syros. Piraeus.

③
05.20	*Nissos Mykonos*	Samos (Karlovassi). Samos (Vathi).
07.30	*Samos Sun*	Thimena. Samos (Karlovassi).

④
11.15	*Nissos Mykonos*	Ikaria (Agios Kyrikos). Mykonos. Syros. Piraeus.

⑤
05.15	*Nissos Mykonos*	Samos (Karlovassi). Samos (Vathi).
07.30	*Samos Sun*	Thimena. Samos (Karlovassi).

⑦
05.15	*Nissos Mykonos*	Samos (Karlovassi). Samos (Vathi).
15.20	*Nissos Mykonos*	Ikaria (Agios Kyrikos). Ikaria (Evdilos). Mykonos. Syros. Piraeus.

○
04.30	*Samos Spirit*	Thimena. Ikaria (Agios Kyrikos). Samos (Karlovassi).
00.00	*Panagia Theotokosos*	Samos (Karlovassi).

Gavdos

Crete p. 360

Ⓓ
16.00	*Gavdos Star*	Plakias.

②
15.30	South Crete Line	Sougia. Paleochora.

⑥ ⑦
16.00	South Crete Line	Sfakia.

Gökçeada

Turkey p. 618

Ⓦ x 5   Local   Çanakkale.

Gythio

Argo-Saronic p. 548

① ③
12.30   Local   Kithera (Agia Pelagia).
                           Neapoli.
④
15.00   Vitsentzos Kornaros   Kithera. Antikithera.
                              Crete (Kasteli).

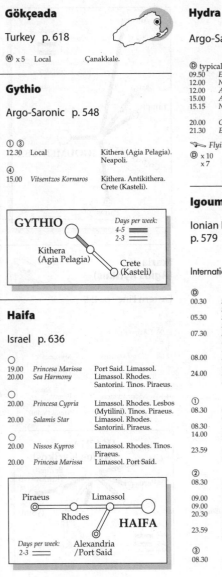

GYTHIO   Days per week:
                          4-5 ▰▰▰
                          2-3 ▭▭▭
Kithera
(Agia Pelagia)
                          Crete
                          (Kasteli)

Haifa

Israel p. 636

○
19.00   Princesa Marissa   Port Said. Limassol.
20.00   Sea Harmony   Limassol. Rhodes.
                           Santorini. Tinos. Piraeus.
○
20.00   Princesa Cypria   Limassol. Rhodes. Lesbos
                           (Mytilini). Tinos. Piraeus.
20.00   Salamis Star   Limassol. Rhodes.
                           Santorini. Piraeus.
○
20.00   Nissos Kypros   Limassol. Rhodes. Tinos.
                           Piraeus.
20.00   Princesa Marissa   Limassol. Port Said.

Piraeus   Limassol
        Rhodes
                        HAIFA
Days per week: Alexandria
2-3 ▭▭▭   /Port Said

Hydra

Argo-Saronic p. 549

Ⓓ typical:
09.50   Eurofast 1   Spetses.
12.00   Nefeli   Ermioni. Spetses.
12.00   Apollon Hellas   Spetses. Porto Helio.
15.00   Apollon Hellas   Aegina. Piraeus.
15.15   Nefeli   Poros. Methana.
                         Aegina. Piraeus.
20.00   Georgios 2   Piraeus.
21.30   Eurofast 1   Piraeus.

〜 Flying Dolphins include:
Ⓓ x 10   Piraeus.
   x 7   Poros. / Spetses. Porto Helio.

Igoumenitsa

Ionian Line
p. 579

International Services:

Ⓓ
00.30   Superfast V/
        Superfast VI   Ancona.
05.30   Superfast V/
        Superfast VI   Patras.
07.30   Ionian Queen/
        Erotokritos/
        Elli T   Corfu. Brindisi.
08.00   Polaris/
        Siren   Corfu. Bari.
24.00   Superfast I/
        Superfast II   Bari.

①
08.30   Cruise Europa/
        Cruise Olympia   Patras.
08.30   ANEK Lines   Venice.
14.00   Lefka Ori   Corfu.
                         Patras.
23.59   Cruise Europa/
        Cruise Olympia   Ancona.

②
08.30   Cruise Europa/
        Cruise Olympia   Patras.
09.00   Ionian King   Bari.
09.00   ANEK Lines   Venice.
20.30   Sophocles V   Corfu.
                         Patras.
23.59   Cruise Europa/
        Cruise Olympia   Ancona.

③
08.30   Cruise Europa/
        Cruise Olympia   Patras.

09.00	*Ionian King*	Patras.
20.30	*Lefka Ori*	Corfu.
		Patras.
23.30	*Ionian Queen*	Corfu.
		Brindisi.

④
08.30	*Cruise Europa/*	
	Cruise Olympia	Patras.
08.30	*Sophocles V*	Venice.
21.00	*Lefka Ori*	Corfu.
		Patras.
23.00	*Ionian King*	Bari.
23.00	*Cruise Europa/*	
	Cruise Olympia	Ancona.

⑤
08.30	*Cruise Europa/*	
	Cruise Olympia	Patras.
08.30	*Lefka Ori*	Venice.
23.00	*Cruise Europa/*	
	Cruise Olympia	Ancona.

⑥
08.30	*Cruise Europa/*	
	Cruise Olympia	Patras.
13.00	*Sophocles V*	Corfu.
		Patras.
23.00	*Ionian King*	Bari.
23.30	*Cruise Europa/*	
	Cruise Olympia	Ancona.

⑦
06.00	*Ionian King*	Patras.
08.30	*Cruise Europa/*	
	Cruise Olympia	Patras.
08.30	*Sophocles V*	Venice.
13.00	*Lefka Ori*	Corfu.
		Patras.
22.00	*Polaris/Bari*	Corfu.
		Bari.
23.30	*Cruise Europa/*	
	Cruise Olympia	Ancona.

○ * Not operating in 2011:

08.00	*Daliana/*	
	Milena	Patras.
22.00	*Daliana/*	
	Milena	Brindisi.
23.59	*Blue Star 1/*	
	Blue Horizon	Bari.

Domestic Services:

Ⓓ Ⓗ 05.00–22.00   Corfu.

Ⓓ
| 07.30 | 11.00 | 14.00 | |
| 16.00 | 19.30 | | Corfu (Lefkimi). |

| 05.45 | 11.30 | 16.15 | |
| | *Ekaterini P* | | Corfu. |

○
| 09.30 | Local C/F | Corfu. |
| 15.00 | Local C/F | Paxi. |

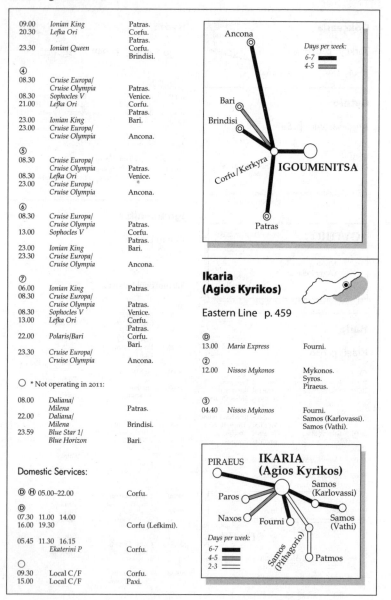

Ikaria
(Agios Kyrikos)

Eastern Line p. 459

Ⓓ
| 13.00 | *Maria Express* | Fourni. |

②
12.00	*Nissos Mykonos*	Mykonos.
		Syros.
		Piraeus.

③
04.40	*Nissos Mykonos*	Fourni.
		Samos (Karlovassi).
		Samos (Vathi).

④
12.00	*Nissos Mykonos*	Mykonos.
		Syros.
		Piraeus.
16.45	*Taxiarchis*	Samos (Karlovassi).
		Chios.
		Lesbos (Mytilini).

⑤
04.30	*Nissos Mykonos*	Fourni.
		Samos (Karlovassi).
		Samos (Vathi).

⑦
04.30	*Nissos Mykonos*	Fourni.
		Samos (Karlovassi).
		Samos (Vathi).
16.05	*Nissos Mykonos*	Ikaria (Evdilos).
		Mykonos.
		Syros.
		Piraeus.

○
05.45	*Samos Spirit*	Samos (Karlovassi).
15.10	*Samos Spirit*	Thimena.
		Fourni.

○ * Not operating in 2011:

11.20	Hydrofoil	Samos (Pithagorio).
15.30	Hydrofoil	Fourni. Patmos.
		Leros (Agia Marina).
		Kalimnos.
		Kos.

Ikaria
(Evdilos)

Eastern Line
p. 460

②
| 04.30 | *Nissos Mykonos* | Samos (Karlovassi). |
| | | Samos (Vathi). |

③
11.30	*Nissos Mykonos*	Mykonos.
		Syros.
		Piraeus.

④
| 04.30 | *Nissos Mykonos* | Samos (Karlovassi). |
| | | Samos (Vathi). |

⑤
| 11.30 | *Nissos Mykonos* | Mykonos. Syros. |
| | | Piraeus. |

⑥
04.30	*Nissos Mykonos*	Samos (Karlovassi).
		Samos (Vathi).
11.30	*Nissos Mykonos*	Mykonos. Syros.
		Piraeus.

Days per week:

**IKARIA
(Evdilos)**   6-7 ▬

PIRAEUS   Samos
                 (Vathi)

Samos
(Karlovassi)

⑦
17.10	*Nissos Mykonos*	Mykonos.
		Syros.
		Piraeus.

Ios

Cyclades Central
p. 148

①
10.35	*Highspeed 6*	Santorini.
11.40	*Flying Cat 3*	Santorini.
12.40	*Highspeed 6*	Piraeus.
15.50	*Artemis*	Santorini.
		Sikinos.
		Folegandros.
		Kimolos.
		Milos.
17.10	*Flying Cat 3*	Naxos. Mykonos.
		Tinos.
		Rafina.

②
04.50	*Vitsentzos Kornaros*	Santorini. Anafi.
09.45	*Adamantis Korais*	Folegandros.
		Kimolos. Milos.
		Sifnos. Serifos.
		Kythnos.
		Piraeus.
10.35	*Highspeed 6*	Santorini.
11.40	*Flying Cat 3*	Santorini.
12.40	*Highspeed 6*	Piraeus.
14.05	*Artemis*	Naxos. Syros.
17.10	*Flying Cat 3*	Naxos. Mykonos.
		Tinos.
		Rafina.
18.55	*Aeolos Kenteris II*	Thirasia.
		Santorini. Anafi.
19.50	*Vitsentzos Kornaros*	Sikinos.
		Folegandros.
		Milos.
		Santorini.

③
09.50	*Aeolos Kenteris II*	Sikinos.
		Folegandros.
		Naxos. Paros.
		Syros.

10.35	*Highspeed 6*	Santorini.
11.40	*Flying Cat 3*	Santorini.
12.40	*Highspeed 6*	Piraeus.
15.30	*Agios Georgios*	Santorini.
17.10	*Flying Cat 3*	Naxos. Mykonos.
		Tinos.
		Rafina.
19.10	*Artemis*	Thirasia.
		Santorini.
		Anafi.
19.50	*Agios Georgios*	Sikinos.
		Folegandros.
		Sifnos.
		Piraeus.

④

10.35	*Highspeed 6*	Santorini.
10.40	*Artemis*	Sikinos.
		Folegandros.
		Naxos. Paros.
		Syros.
11.40	*Flying Cat 3*	Santorini.
12.40	*Highspeed 6*	Piraeus.
17.10	*Flying Cat 3*	Naxos. Mykonos.
		Tinos.
		Rafina.

⑤

10.35	*Highspeed 6*	Santorini.
15.30	*Agios Georgios*	Santorini.
16.20	*Aqua Jewel*	Sikinos.
		Folegandros.
		Kimolos. Milos.
19.55	*Agios Georgios*	Sikinos.
		Folegandros.
		Kimolos. Sifnos.
		Piraeus.

⑥

10.35	*Highspeed 6*	Santorini.
11.05	*Aqua Jewel*	Naxos. Paros.
		Mykonos. Syros.
11.40	*Flying Cat 3*	Santorini.
12.40	*Highspeed 6*	Piraeus.

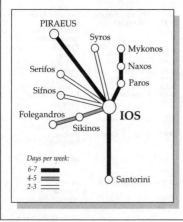

PIRAEUS
Syros
Mykonos
Serifos
Naxos
Sifnos
Paros
Folegandros
IOS
Sikinos
Santorini

Days per week:
6-7
4-5
2-3

17.10	*Flying Cat 3*	Naxos. Mykonos.
		Tinos.
		Rafina.
18.55	*Aeolos Kenteris II*	Thirasia.
		Santorini.
		Anafi.

⑦

10.10	*Aeolos Kenteris II*	Sikinos.
		Folegandros.
		Naxos. Paros.
		Mykonos.
		Syros.
10.35	*Highspeed 6*	Santorini.
12.40	*Highspeed 6*	Piraeus.
14.30	*Express Skopelitis*	Koufonissia.
		Amorgos (Katapola).

Iraklia

Cyclades East
p. 319

①

00.50	*Blue Star Paros*	Schinoussa.
		Koufonissia.
		Amorgos (Katapola).
08.00	*Blue Star Paros*	Naxos.
		Paros.
		Piraeus.
10.45	*Express Skopelitis*	Naxos.
14.20	*Aeolos Kenteris II*	Naxos.
		Paros.
		Syros.

②

09.45	*Express Skopelitis*	Naxos.
15.00	*Express Skopelitis*	Schinoussa.
		Koufonissia.
		Amorgos (Katapola).

③

00.50	*Blue Star Paros*	Schinoussa.
		Koufonissia.
		Amorgos (Katapola).
08.00	*Blue Star Paros*	Naxos.
		Paros.
		Piraeus.
10.45	*Express Skopelitis*	Naxos.

④

09.45	*Express Skopelitis*	Naxos.
15.00	*Express Skopelitis*	Schinoussa.
		Koufonissia.
		Amorgos (Katapola).

⑤

10.45	*Express Skopelitis*	Naxos.
11.35	*Artemis*	Schinoussa.
		Koufonissia.
		Amorgos (Katapola).
		Amorgos (Egiali).
		Donoussa.
		Naxos. Paros. Syros.

⑥
00.05	*Blue Star Paros*	Schinoussa. Koufonissia. Amorgos (Katapola).
08.00	*Blue Star Paros*	Naxos. Paros. Piraeus.
10.45	*Express Skopelitis*	Naxos.

⑦
| 16.05 | *Artemis* | Naxos. Paros. Syros. |

○
| 16.05 | *Express Skopelitis* | Schinoussa. Koufonissia. Amorgos (Katapola). |

İstanbul

Turkey
p. 619

Ⓓ Ⓗ
| 06.45–21.00 | Princes' Islands. [x 5 steaming on to Yalova or Çinarcik.] |

Ⓓ
08.00	Armutlu. Mudanya.
08.00	Marmara. Avşa.
09.30 20.00	Bandırma.
10.30 13.30	Bosphorus 'Tour'.

| x 4 | Deniz Otobusleri | Marmara. Avşa. |

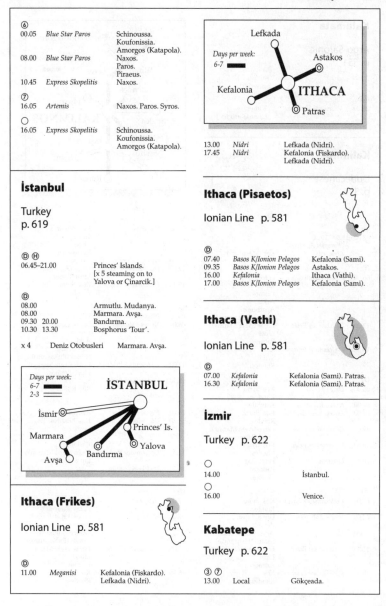

Days per week:
6-7
2-3

İSTANBUL

İsmir
Marmara
Avşa   Bandırma
Princes' Is.
Yalova

Ithaca (Frikes)

Ionian Line   p. 581

Ⓓ
| 11.00 | *Meganisi* | Kefalonia (Fiskardo). Lefkada (Nidri). |

Lefkada

Days per week:
6-7

Astakos

Kefalonia   **ITHACA**

Patras

| 13.00 | *Nidri* | Lefkada (Nidri). |
| 17.45 | *Nidri* | Kefalonia (Fiskardo). Lefkada (Nidri). |

Ithaca (Pisaetos)

Ionian Line   p. 581

Ⓓ
07.40	*Basos K/Ionion Pelagos*	Kefalonia (Sami).
09.35	*Basos K/Ionion Pelagos*	Astakos.
16.00	*Kefalonia*	Ithaca (Vathi).
17.00	*Basos K/Ionion Pelagos*	Kefalonia (Sami).

Ithaca (Vathi)

Ionian Line   p. 581

Ⓓ
| 07.00 | *Kefalonia* | Kefalonia (Sami). Patras. |
| 16.30 | *Kefalonia* | Kefalonia (Sami). Patras. |

İzmir

Turkey   p. 622

○
| 14.00 | | İstanbul. |
○
| 16.00 | | Venice. |

Kabatepe

Turkey   p. 622

③ ⑦
| 13.00 | Local | Gökçeada. |

Kalamata

Argo-Saronic
p. 551

Ⓖ
21.20　　*Vitsentzos Kornaros*　　Kithera.
　　　　　　　　　　　　　　　　Crete (Kasteli).

Kalimnos

Dodecanese
p. 376

Ⓓ
07.00　15.50　19.30
　　　Olympios Apollon/
　　　Atromitos　　　　　Kos (Mastihari).

①
06.00　　*Nissos Kalimnos*　　Leros.
　　　　　　　　　　　　　　　Lipsi.
　　　　　　　　　　　　　　　Patmos.
　　　　　　　　　　　　　　　Arki.
　　　　　　　　　　　　　　　Agathonisi.
　　　　　　　　　　　　　　　Samos (Pithagorio).
12.00　　*Dodekanisos Pride*　　Leros (Agia Marina).
　　　　　　　　　　　　　　　Lipsi.
　　　　　　　　　　　　　　　Patmos.
15.30　　*Dodekanisos Pride*　　Kos.
　　　　　　　　　　　　　　　Symi.
　　　　　　　　　　　　　　　Rhodes.

②
03.40　　*Diagoras*　　　　　Kos. Symi.
　　　　　　　　　　　　　　　Rhodes.
04.00　　*Nissos Kalimnos*　　Astipalea.
07.00　　*Dodekanisos Express*　Kos. Symi.
　　　　　　　　　　　　　　　Rhodes.
12.00　　*Dodekanisos Pride*　　Leros (Agia Marina).
　　　　　　　　　　　　　　　Lipsi. Patmos.
15.30　　*Dodekanisos Pride*　　Kos. Symi.
　　　　　　　　　　　　　　　Rhodes.
20.45　　*Diagoras*　　　　　Leros. Lipsi.
　　　　　　　　　　　　　　　Patmos.
　　　　　　　　　　　　　　　Piraeus.

③
07.00　　*Dodekanisos Express*　Kos. Symi.
　　　　　　　　　　　　　　　Rhodes.
07.00　　*Nissos Kalimnos*　　Leros. Lipsi.
　　　　　　　　　　　　　　　Patmos.
　　　　　　　　　　　　　　　Arki. Agathonisi.
　　　　　　　　　　　　　　　Samos (Pithagorio).
11.35　　*Dodekanisos Pride*　　Leros (Agia Marina).
　　　　　　　　　　　　　　　Lipsi.
　　　　　　　　　　　　　　　Patmos.
15.30　　*Dodekanisos Pride*　　Kos.
　　　　　　　　　　　　　　　Rhodes.

④
03.05　　*Diagoras*　　　　　Kos. Nissiros.
　　　　　　　　　　　　　　　Tilos.
　　　　　　　　　　　　　　　Rhodes.
　　　　　　　　　　　　　　　Kastelorizo.
04.00　　*Nissos Kalimnos*　　Astipalea.
12.00　　*Dodekanisos Pride*　　Leros (Agia Marina).
　　　　　　　　　　　　　　　Lipsi. Patmos.
15.30　　*Dodekanisos Pride*　　Kos. Symi.
　　　　　　　　　　　　　　　Rhodes.

⑤
03.10　　*Diagoras*　　　　　Piraeus.
06.00　　*Nissos Kalimnos*　　Leros. Lipsi.
　　　　　　　　　　　　　　　Patmos.
　　　　　　　　　　　　　　　Arki.
　　　　　　　　　　　　　　　Agathonisi.
　　　　　　　　　　　　　　　Samos (Pithagorio).
12.00　　*Dodekanisos Pride*　　Leros (Agia Marina).
　　　　　　　　　　　　　　　Lipsi. Patmos.
15.30　　*Dodekanisos Pride*　　Kos. Symi.
　　　　　　　　　　　　　　　Rhodes.

⑥
04.00　　*Nissos Kalimnos*　　Astipalea.
05.30　　*Diagoras*　　　　　Kos. Nissiros. Tilos.
　　　　　　　　　　　　　　　Symi.
　　　　　　　　　　　　　　　Rhodes.
　　　　　　　　　　　　　　　Kastelorizo.
11.35　　*Dodekanisos Pride*　　Leros (Agia Marina).
　　　　　　　　　　　　　　　Lipsi. Agathonisi.
15.50　　*Dodekanisos Pride*　　Kos.
　　　　　　　　　　　　　　　Rhodes.

⑦
07.00　　*Diagoras*　　　　　Astipalea. Naxos.
　　　　　　　　　　　　　　　Paros. Piraeus.
07.00　　*Nissos Kalimnos*　　Leros. Lipsi.
　　　　　　　　　　　　　　　Patmos.
　　　　　　　　　　　　　　　Arki. Agathonisi.
　　　　　　　　　　　　　　　Samos (Pithagorio).
12.00　　*Dodekanisos Pride*　　Leros (Agia Marina).
　　　　　　　　　　　　　　　Lipsi.
　　　　　　　　　　　　　　　Patmos.
15.30　　*Dodekanisos Pride*　　Kos.
　　　　　　　　　　　　　　　Rhodes.

○　* Not operating in 2011:

07.00	Hydrofoil	Kos.
		Leros (Agia Marina).
		Lipsi. Patmos.
08.15	Hydrofoil	Leros (Agia Marina).
		Patmos. Fourni.
		Ikaria (Agios Kyrikos).
		Samos (Pithagorio).
10.40	Hydrofoil	Kos.
		Samos (Pithagorio).
11.15	Hydrofoil	Kos.
11.30	Hydrofoil	Astipalea.
18.45	Hydrofoil	Kos.

Karpathos

Dodecanese
p. 383

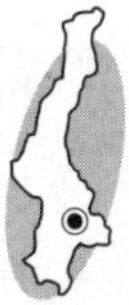

②
09.40	Prevelis	Chalki.
		Rhodes.
20.40	Prevelis	Kassos. Crete (Sitia).
		Crete (Iraklion). Santorini.
		Milos. Piraeus.

④
| 12.20 | Prevelis | Karpathos (Diafani). |
| | | Chalki. Rhodes. |

⑤
00.10	Prevelis	Kassos. Crete (Sitia).
		Crete (Iraklion). Santorini.
		Milos. Piraeus.

⑥
| 23.10 | Prevelis | Rhodes. |

⑦
| 13.35 | Prevelis | Kassos. Anafi. Santorini. |
| | | Piraeus. |

○
02.35	Ierapetra L	Kassos. Anafi.
		Santorini.
		Piraeus.
14.05	Ierapetra L	Karpathos (Diafani).
		Chalki.
		Rhodes.

Karpathos (Diafani)

Dodecanese
p. 384

④
| 13.25 | Prevelis | Chalki. Rhodes. |

⑦
12.15	Prevelis	Karpathos. Kassos.
		Anafi. Santorini.
		Piraeus.

○
01.20	Ierapetra L	Karpathos.
		Kassos.
		Anafi. Santorini.
		Piraeus.
08.45	Vitsentzos Kornaros	Karpathos.
		Kassos.
		Crete (Sitia).
		Crete (Agios Nikolaos).
		Santorini.
		Milos.
		Piraeus.
15.10	Ierapetra L	Chalki.
		Rhodes.

Kassos

Dodecanese　p. 386

②
07.50	Prevelis	Karpathos. Chalki.
		Rhodes.
22.20	Prevelis	Crete (Sitia).
		Crete (Iraklion).
		Santorini. Milos.
		Piraeus.

④
10.30	Prevelis	Karpathos.
		Karpathos (Diafani).
		Chalki. Rhodes.

⑤
| 01.50 | Prevelis | Crete (Sitia). Crete (Iraklion). |
| | | Santorini. Milos. Piraeus. |

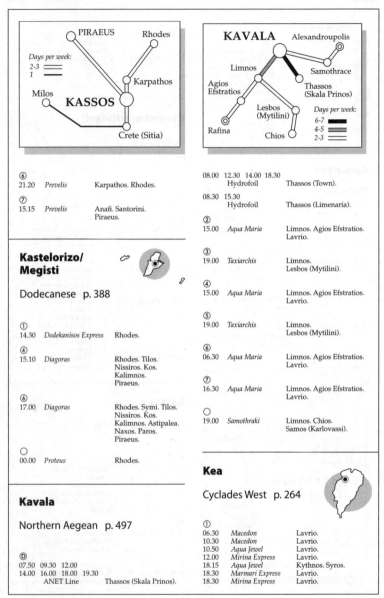

Dodecanese p. 388

⑥
21.20   *Prevelis*   Karpathos. Rhodes.

⑦
15.15   *Prevelis*   Anafi. Santorini.
                          Piraeus.

08.00 12.30 14.00 18.30
                  Hydrofoil   Thassos (Town).

08.30 15.30
                  Hydrofoil   Thassos (Limenaria).

②
15.00   *Aqua Maria*   Limnos. Agios Efstratios.
                          Lavrio.

③
19.00   *Taxiarchis*   Limnos.
                          Lesbos (Mytilini).

④
15.00   *Aqua Maria*   Limnos. Agios Efstratios.
                          Lavrio.

Kastelorizo/ Megisti

⑤
19.00   *Taxiarchis*   Limnos.
                          Lesbos (Mytilini).

⑥
06.30   *Aqua Maria*   Limnos. Agios Efstratios.
                          Lavrio.

Dodecanese p. 388

⑦
16.30   *Aqua Maria*   Limnos. Agios Efstratios.
                          Lavrio.

①
14.30   *Dodekanisos Express*   Rhodes.

○
19.00   *Samothraki*   Limnos. Chios.
                          Samos (Karlovassi).

④
15.10   *Diagoras*   Rhodes. Tilos.
                          Nissiros. Kos.
                          Kalimnos.
                          Piraeus.

⑥
17.00   *Diagoras*   Rhodes. Symi. Tilos.
                          Nissiros. Kos.
                          Kalimnos. Astipalea.
                          Naxos. Paros.
                          Piraeus.

Kea

Cyclades West p. 264

○
00.00   *Proteus*   Rhodes.

①
06.30   *Macedon*   Lavrio.
10.30   *Macedon*   Lavrio.
10.50   *Aqua Jewel*   Lavrio.
12.00   *Mirina Express* Lavrio.
18.15   *Aqua Jewel*   Kythnos. Syros.
18.30   *Marmari Express* Lavrio.
18.30   *Mirina Express* Lavrio.

Kavala

Northern Aegean p. 497

Ⓓ
07.50 09.30 12.00
14.00 16.00 18.00 19.30
                  ANET Line   Thassos (Skala Prinos).

②		
06.30	*Marmari Express*	Lavrio.
10.30	*Mirina Express*	Kythnos.
13.30	*Marmari Express*	Lavrio.
14.30	*Mirina Express*	Lavrio.
18.30	*Marmari Express*	Lavrio.

③		
06.30	*Macedon*	Lavrio.
13.30	*Macedon*	Lavrio.
21.15	*Aeolos Kenteris II*	Lavrio.

④		
06.30	*Marmari Express*	Lavrio.
07.00	*Mirina Express*	Lavrio.
12.00	*Mirina Express*	Lavrio.
13.00	*Marmari Express*	Lavrio.
13.30	*Aqua Jewel*	Lavrio.
16.00	*Aeolos Kenteris II*	Kythnos. Syros.
18.30	*Macedon*	Lavrio.

⑤		
06.30	*Macedon*	Lavrio.
08.00	*Aqua Jewel*	Kythnos. Syros. Paros. Naxos. Ios. Sikinos. Folegandros. Kimolos. Milos.
09.00	*Mirina Express*	Lavrio.
12.00	*Mirina Express*	Lavrio.
14.30	*Macedon*	Lavrio.
15.30	*Mirina Express*	Lavrio.
15.50	*Marmari Express*	Lavrio.
18.30	*Macedon*	Lavrio.
19.00	*Mirina Express*	Lavrio.
19.20	*Marmari Express*	Lavrio.

⑥		
06.00	*Mirina Express*	Lavrio.
09.20	*Marmari Express*	Lavrio.
10.20	*Mirina Express*	Lavrio.
10.30	*Macedon*	Lavrio.
12.00	*Artemis*	Lavrio.
16.00	*Macedon*	Lavrio.
19.30	*Mirina Express*	Lavrio.
20.00	*Macedon*	Lavrio.
20.25	*Artemis*	Kythnos. Syros.

⑦		
06.15	*Marmari Express*	Lavrio.
14.30	*Macedon*	Lavrio.
15.15	*Mirina Express*	Lavrio.
17.30	*Mirina Express*	Lavrio.
17.45	*Macedon*	Lavrio.
18.45	*Marmari Express*	Lavrio.
19.00	*Mirina Express*	Lavrio.
21.00	*Macedon*	Lavrio.
22.30	*Mirina Express*	Lavrio.

Days per week:
6-7 ▬

Kefalonia (Argostoli)

Ionian Line p. 587

Ⓗ	Local	Kefalonia (Lixouri).
Ⓓ		
07.30	*Ephanisos*	Kefalonia (Lixouri). Kilini.

Kefalonia (Fiskardo)

Ionian Line p. 587

Ⓓ		
10.30	*Meganisi*	Lefkada (Nidri).
12.00	*Nidri*	Ithaca (Frikes). Lefkada (Nidri).
17.00	*Meganisi*	Lefkada (Vathi).
19.00	*Nidri*	Lefkada (Nidri).

Kefalonia (Lixouri)

Ionian Line p. 587

Ⓗ	Local	Kefalonia (Argostoli).
Ⓓ		
07.35	*Ephanisos*	Kilini.
22.35	*Ephanisos*	Kefalonia (Argostoli).

Kefalonia (Pessada)

Ionian Line p. 587

Ⓓ		
07.45	*Angela*	Zakinthos (Skinaria).
17.30	*Angela*	Zakinthos (Skinaria).

KEFALONIA

Days per week:
6-7 ▬
2-3 ═

Kefalonia (Poros)

Ionian Line   p. 587

Ⓓ
13.45	*Ephanisos*	Kilini.
18.00	*Ephanisos*	Kilini.

Kefalonia (Sami)

Ionian Line
p. 587

International Services:

Ⓓ
06.30	*Ionian Queen/*	
	Erotokritos/	
	Elli T	Patmos.
20.45	*Ionian Queen/*	
	Erotokritos/	
	Elli T	Brindisi.

Domestic Services:

① ② ③ ④ ⑤
08.30	*Kefalonia*	Patras.
23.00	*Kefalonia*	Ithaca (Vathi).

⑥
08.30	*Kefalonia*	Patras.

⑦
23.00	*Kefalonia*	Ithaca (Vathi).

Keramoti

Northern Aegean   p. 498

Ⓓ
07.15	09.15	11.15	13.15	15.15	16.45
17.45	18.45	19.45	20.45	21.45	22.30
	ANET Line				Thassos (Town).

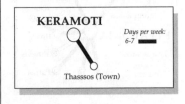

KERAMOTI

Days per week:
6-7 ▬

Thasssos (Town)

Kilini

Ionian Line   p. 589

Ⓓ
10.15	*Andreas Kalvos/*	
	Dionysios Solomos	Zakinthos.
11.30	*Ephanisos*	Kefalonia (Poros).
14.30	*Andreas Kalvos/*	
	Dionysios Solomos	Zakinthos.
15.45	*Ephanisos*	Kefalonia (Poros).
17.30	*Andreas Kalvos/*	
	Dionysios Solomos	Zakinthos.
20.15	*Ephanisos*	Kefalonia (Lixouri).
		Kefalonia (Argostoli).
20.15	*Andreas Kalvos/*	
	Dionysios Solomos	Zakinthos.

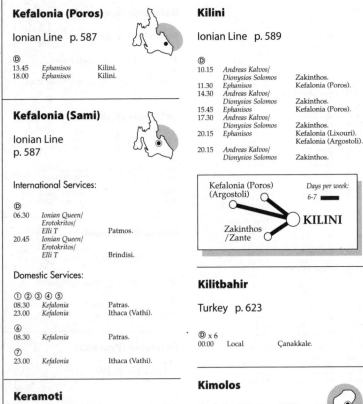

Kefalonia (Poros)
(Argostoli)

Days per week:
6-7 ▬

KILINI

Zakinthos
/Zante

Kilitbahir

Turkey   p. 623

Ⓓ x 6
00.00	Local	Çanakkale.

Kimolos

Cyclades West   p. 268

Ⓓ
07.15	10.40	13.00
16.00	19.45	
	Nissos Kimolos	Milos (Pollonia).

①
21.20	*Speedrunner IV*	Folegandros. Sifnos.
		Piraeus.
21.35	*Artemis*	Milos.
23.10	*Adamantis Korais*	Folegandros. Ios.

②
08.15	*Artemis*	Folegandros. Sikinos.
		Santorini. Ios. Naxos.
		Syros.
12.45	*Adamantis Korais*	Milos. Sifnos. Serifos.
		Kythnos. Piraeus.

13.55	*Agios Georgios*	Milos. Sifnos. Serifos. Kythnos. Piraeus.
14.35	*Aqua Jewel*	Milos.
17.05	*Aqua Jewel*	Sifnos. Serifos. Paros. Syros.

③
16.00	*Aqua Jewel*	Milos.
16.55	*Adamantis Korais*	Sifnos. Serifos. Kythnos. Piraeus.
18.25	*Aqua Jewel*	Sifnos. Serifos. Syros.

④
| 21.20 | *Speedrunner IV* | Folegandros. Sifnos. Piraeus. |
| 23.15 | *Adamantis Korais* | Sifnos. Serifos. Piraeus. |

⑤
16.55	*Adamantis Korais*	Sifnos. Serifos. Kythnos. Piraeus.
19.20	*Aqua Jewel*	Milos.
22.45	*Agios Georgios*	Sifnos. Piraeus.

⑥
| 08.15 | *Aqua Jewel* | Folegandros. Sikinos. Ios. Naxos. Paros. Mykonos. Syros. |

⑦
15.20	*Aqua Jewel*	Milos.
15.40	*Adamantis Korais*	Sifnos. Serifos. Kythnos. Piraeus.
16.35	*Agios Georgios*	Sifnos. Serifos. Kythnos. Piraeus.
17.40	*Aqua Jewel*	Sifnos. Serifos. Paros. Syros.

Kithera

Argo-Saronic p. 552

①
10.15	*Porfyrousa*	Neapoli.
15.15	*Porfyrousa*	Antikithera.
21.00	*Porfyrousa*	Neapoli.

②
| 11.45 | *Porfyrousa* | Neapoli. |
| 17.00 | *Porfyrousa* | Neapoli. |

③
11.45	*Porfyrousa*	Neapoli.
17.00	*Porfyrousa*	Neapoli.
22.00	*Vitsentzos Kornaros*	Crete (Kasteli).

④
11.45	*Porfyrousa*	Neapoli.
12.10	*Vitsentzos Kornaros*	Gythio.
17.00	*Porfyrousa*	Neapoli.
17.50	*Vitsentzos Kornaros*	Antikithera. Crete (Kasteli).

⑤
01.50	*Vitsentzos Kornaros*	Piraeus.
11.45	*Porfyrousa*	Neapoli.
17.00	*Porfyrousa*	Neapoli.

⑥
01.50	*Vitsentzos Kornaros*	Antikithera. Crete (Kasteli).
11.45	*Porfyrousa*	Neapoli.
16.00	*Vitsentzos Kornaros*	Kalamata.
17.00	*Porfyrousa*	Neapoli.

⑦
02.30	*Vitsentzos Kornaros*	Crete (Kasteli).
11.45	*Porfyrousa*	Neapoli.
17.00	*Porfyrousa*	Neapoli.
20.10	*Vitsentzos Kornaros*	Monemvassia. Piraeus.

Kos

Dodecanese
p. 392

Ⓓ
08.00	Hydrofoil	Rhodes.
08.00	Hydrofoil	Patmos.
10.00	Tour Boat	Kalimnos.
10.00	Tour Boat	Pserimos.
10.00	Tour Boat	Nissiros.
16.00	*Bodrum Princess*	Bodrum.
18.00	Hydrofoil	Rhodes.

①

06.10	*Blue Star 1/2*	Rhodes.
11.05	*Dodekanisos Pride*	Kalimnos.
		Leros (Agia Marina).
		Lipsi. Patmos.
16.20	*Dodekanisos Pride*	Symi.
		Rhodes.
20.35	*Blue Star 1/2*	Santorini.
		Piraeus.

②

05.10	*Diagoras*	Symi. Rhodes.
06.40	*Blue Star 1/2*	Rhodes.
07.45	*Dodekanisos Express*	Symi. Rhodes.
11.05	*Dodekanisos Pride*	Kalimnos.
		Leros (Agia Marina).
		Lipsi. Patmos.
16.20	*Dodekanisos Pride*	Symi. Rhodes.
17.35	*Dodekanisos Express*	Kalimnos.
19.25	*Diagoras*	Kalimnos. Leros.
		Lipsi.
		Patmos. Piraeus.
20.25	*Blue Star 1/2*	Santorini. Syros.
		Piraeus.

③

05.50	*Blue Star 1/2*	Rhodes.
07.45	*Dodekanisos Express*	Symi. Rhodes.
10.50	*Dodekanisos Pride*	Kalimnos.
		Leros (Agia Marina).
		Lipsi. Patmos.
16.30	*Dodekanisos Pride*	Rhodes.
20.05	*Blue Star 1/2*	Leros. Patmos.
		Piraeus.

④

04.25	*Diagoras*	Nissiros. Tilos.
		Rhodes.
		Kastelorizo.
06.00	*Blue Star 1/2*	Rhodes.
11.05	*Dodekanisos Pride*	Kalimnos.
		Leros (Agia Marina).
		Lipsi. Patmos.

13.30	*Blue Star 1/2*	Piraeus.
16.20	*Dodekanisos Pride*	Symi. Rhodes.
18.15	*Blue Star 1/2*	Rhodes.

⑤

01.50	*Diagoras*	Kalimnos.
		Piraeus.
03.00	*Blue Star 1/2*	Leros. Patmos.
		Piraeus.
09.35	*Blue Star 1/2*	Rhodes.
11.05	*Dodekanisos Pride*	Kalimnos.
		Leros (Agia Marina).
		Lipsi. Patmos.
13.15	*Dodekanisos Express*	Nissiros. Tilos.
		Chalki.
		Rhodes. Symi.
16.20	*Dodekanisos Pride*	Symi. Rhodes.
20.05	*Blue Star 1/2*	Santorini.
		Piraeus.

⑥

03.25	*Blue Star 1/2*	Rhodes.
06.50	*Diagoras*	Nissiros. Tilos.
		Symi.
		Rhodes.
		Kastelorizo.
10.50	*Dodekanisos Pride*	Kalimnos.
		Leros (Agia Marina).
		Lipsi. Agathonisi.
12.30	*Blue Star 1/2*	Piraeus.
16.30	*Dodekanisos Pride*	Rhodes.
18.35	*Blue Star 1/2*	Rhodes.

⑦

03.05	*Blue Star 1/2*	Piraeus.
05.40	*Diagoras*	Kalimnos.
		Astipalea.
		Naxos. Paros.
		Piraeus.
10.20	*Blue Star 1/2*	Rhodes.
11.05	*Dodekanisos Pride*	Kalimnos.
		Leros (Agia Marina).
		Lipsi. Patmos.
15.30	*Dodekanisos Express*	Nissiros. Tilos.
		Chalki.
		Rhodes.
		Symi.
16.20	*Dodekanisos Pride*	Rhodes.
20.35	*Blue Star 1/2*	Leros. Patmos.
		Amorgos (Katapola).
		Piraeus.

○ * Not operating in 2011:

07.30	Hydrofoil	Kalimnos.
		Leros (Agia Marina).
		Lipsi. Patmos.
		Agathonisi.
		Samos (Pithagorio).
14.00	Hydrofoil	Kalimnos.
		Leros (Agia Marina).
		Lipsi. Patmos.
		Samos (Pithagorio).
14.00	Hydrofoil	Symi. Rhodes.
16.00	Hydrofoil	Kalimnos.
		Leros (Agia Marina).
		Lipsi. Patmos.
		Ikaria (Agios Kyrikos).
		Fourni.
		Samos (Pithagorio).

PIRAEUS

Patmos

Days per week:
6-7
4-5
2-3

Lipsi

Leros

Kalimnos

Pserimos

KOS

Bodrum

Symi

Nissiros

Tilos

Rhodes

Kastelorizo

Kos (Kardamena)

Dodecanese
p. 396

Ⓓ
09.00   Nissiros Express   Nissiros.

Kos (Mastihari)

Dodecanese
p. 398

Ⓓ
09.00 16.30 22.00
           Olympios Apollon/
           Olympios Zeus   Kalimnos.

Kosta

Argo-Saronic p. 562

Ⓓ
10.30 13.30 17.00   Alexandros M   Spetses.

① ② ③ ④ ⑤
06.50 08.00 18.30   Alexandros M   Spetses.

Koufonissia

Cyclades East p. 323

Ⓓ
14.30   SuperJet   Amorgos (Katapola).
①
01.55   Blue Star Paros   Amorgos (Katapola).
06.55   Blue Star Paros   Schinoussa.
                              Iraklia.
                              Naxos.
                              Paros.
                              Piraeus.
09.30   Express Skopelitis   Schinoussa. Iraklia.
                              Naxos.
13.25   Aeolos Kenteris II   Schinoussa. Iraklia.
                              Naxos. Paros.
                              Syros.
16.45   Express Skopelitis   Donoussa.
                              Amorgos (Egiali).
                              Amorgos (Katapola).

②
08.45   Express Skopelitis   Schinoussa.
                              Iraklia.
                              Naxos.
16.15   Express Skopelitis   Amorgos (Katapola).

③
01.55   Blue Star Paros   Amorgos (Katapola).
06.55   Blue Star Paros   Schinoussa.
                              Iraklia.
                              Naxos. Paros.
                              Piraeus.
09.30   Express Skopelitis   Schinoussa. Iraklia.
                              Naxos.
16.45   Express Skopelitis   Donoussa.
                              Amorgos (Egiali).
                              Amorgos (Katapola).

④
08.45   Express Skopelitis   Schinoussa.
                              Iraklia.
                              Naxos.
16.15   Express Skopelitis   Amorgos (Katapola).
⑤
09.30   Express Skopelitis   Schinoussa. Iraklia.
                              Naxos.
12.45   Artemis   Amorgos (Katapola).
                              Amorgos (Egiali).
                              Donoussa.
                              Naxos.
                              Paros.
                              Syros.
16.45   Express Skopelitis   Donoussa.
                              Amorgos (Egiali).
                              Amorgos (Katapola).

⑥
01.05   Blue Star Paros   Amorgos (Katapola).
06.55   Blue Star Paros   Schinoussa. Iraklia.
                              Naxos.
                              Paros.
                              Piraeus.
09.30   Express Skopelitis   Schinoussa. Iraklia.
                              Naxos.
16.45   Express Skopelitis   Donoussa.
                              Amorgos (Egiali).
                              Amorgos (Katapola).

⑦
09.25   Express Skopelitis   Santorini. Ios.
14.55   Artemis   Schinoussa.
                              Iraklia.
                              Naxos.
                              Paros.
                              Syros.
16.45   Express Skopelitis   Amorgos (Katapola).

Kuşadası

Turkey p. 623

Ⓓ
08.00   Fari Kaptain/Sultan I   Samos (Vathi).
17.00   Kapetan Giorgis   Samos (Vathi).

Kythnos

Cyclades West   p. 272

①

09.15	*Marmari Express*	Lavrio.
09.30	*Aqua Jewel*	Kea. Lavrio.
10.30	*Agios Georgios*	Serifos. Sifnos. Milos.
17.50	*Adamantis Korais*	Serifos. Sifnos. Milos. Kimolos. Folegandros. Ios.
19.00	*Macedon*	Lavrio.
19.30	*Agios Georgios*	Piraeus.
19.40	*Aqua Jewel*	Syros.

②

10.30	*Agios Georgios*	Serifos. Sifnos. Kimolos. Milos.
12.15	*Mirina Express*	Kea. Lavrio.
17.40	*Macedon*	Lavrio.
18.20	*Adamantis Korais*	Piraeus.
19.30	*Agios Georgios*	Piraeus.

③

11.15	*Adamantis Korais*	Serifos. Sifnos. Milos. Kimolos.
17.00	*Marmari Express*	Lavrio.
20.15	*Aeolos Kenteris II*	Kea. Lavrio.
20.20	*Adamantis Korais*	Piraeus.

④

10.30	*Agios Georgios*	Serifos. Sifnos. Milos.
12.20	*Aqua Jewel*	Kea. Lavrio.
17.00	*Marmari Express*	Lavrio.
17.30	*Aeolos Kenteris II*	Syros.
17.50	*Adamantis Korais*	Serifos. Sifnos. Milos. Kimolos.
19.30	*Agios Georgios*	Piraeus.

⑤

09.25	*Aqua Jewel*	Syros. Paros. Naxos. Ios. Sikinos. Folegandros. Kimolos. Milos.
11.15	*Adamantis Korais*	Serifos. Sifnos. Milos. Kimolos.
20.00	*Macedon*	Lavrio.
20.20	*Adamantis Korais*	Piraeus.

⑥

10.30	*Agios Georgios*	Serifos. Sifnos. Milos.
10.30	*Artemis*	Kea. Lavrio.
11.50	*Adamantis Korais*	Serifos. Sifnos. Milos.
17.40	*Marmari Express*	Lavrio.
19.30	*Agios Georgios*	Piraeus.
21.50	*Artemis*	Syros.

⑦

10.30	*Agios Georgios*	Serifos. Sifnos. Milos. Kimolos.
13.00	*Mirina Express*	Kea. Lavrio.
15.00	*Marmari Express*	Lavrio.
19.00	*Adamantis Korais*	Piraeus.
20.20	*Agios Georgios*	Piraeus.

Lavrio

Athens & Piraeus   p. 120

①

07.00	*Marmari Express*	Kythnos.
08.30	*Macedon*	Kea.
09.00	*Mirina Express*	Kea.
15.30	*Mirina Express*	Kea.
16.30	*Marmari Express*	Kea.
17.00	*Aqua Jewel*	Kea. Kythnos. Syros.
17.00	*Panagia Thalassini*	Psara. Chios (Mesta).
20.00	*Aqua Maria*	Agios Efstratios. Limnos. Kavala.
20.00	*Marmari Express*	Kea.

②

08.30	*Macedon*	Kythnos.
08.30	*Marmari Express*	Kea.
09.00	*Mirina Express*	Kea. Kythnos.
15.30	*Marmari Express*	Kea.
16.30	*Mirina Express*	Kea.
20.00	*Macedon*	Kea.

③

08.30	*Macedon*	Kea.
08.30	*Marmari Express*	Kythnos.
15.30	*Macedon*	Kea.
17.00	*Panagia Thalassini*	Psara. Chios (Mesta).
19.30	*Mirina Express*	Kea.
20.00	*Aqua Maria*	Agios Efstratios. Limnos. Kavala.
20.00	*Marmari Express*	Kea.

④

08.30	*Marmari Express*	Kea.
10.00	*Mirina Express*	Kea.
14.30	*Macedon*	Kea.
14.45	*Marmari Express*	Kythnos.
15.00	*Aeolos Kenteris II*	Kea. Kythnos. Syros.
19.00	*Mirina Express*	Kea.
20.00	*Macedon*	Kea.

⑤

07.00	*Aqua Jewel*	Kea. Kythnos. Syros. Paros. Naxos. Ios. Sikinos. Folegandros. Kimolos. Milos.
08.30	*Macedon*	Kea.
10.00	*Mirina Express*	Kea.

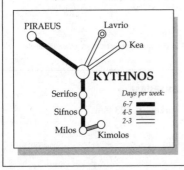

13.00	*Aqua Maria*	Agios Efstratios. Limnos. Kavala.
14.00	*Mirina Express*	Kea.
14.30	*Marmari Express*	Kea.
17.00	*Panagia Thalassini*	Psara. Chios (Mesta).
17.30	*Mirina Express*	Kea.
18.00	*Marmari Express*	Kea.
21.15	*Marmari Express*	Kea.
21.30	*Mirina Express*	Kea.

ⓖ

08.30	*Macedon*	Kythnos. Kea.
08.30	*Mirina Express*	Kea.
11.15	*Marmari Express*	Kythnos.
12.30	*Macedon*	Kea.
18.00	*Mirina Express*	Kea.
18.30	*Macedon*	Kea.
19.15	*Artemis*	Kea. Kythnos. Syros.
23.59	*Aqua Maria*	Agios Efstratios. Limnos. Kavala.

ⓖ

08.30	*Macedon*	Kea. Kythnos.
08.30	*Marmari Express*	Kythnos.
09.00	*Mirina Express*	Kythnos. Kea.
16.00	*Macedon*	Kea.
17.00	*Marmari Express*	Kea.
17.00	*Mirina Express*	Kea.
19.10	*Macedon*	Kea.
20.30	*Mirina Express*	Kea.

Lefkada (Nidri)

Ionian Line   p. 589

ⓓ
x 6: 07.20 11.45 13.15
17.00 18.30 20.00

	Meganisi	Meganisi (Vathi). Meganisi (Spartohori).
08.30	*Meganisi*	Kefalonia (Fiskardo).
10.00	*Nidri*	Kefalonia (Fiskardo). Ithaca (Frikes).
15.30	*Meganisi*	Kefalonia (Fiskardo).
16.30	*Nidri*	Ithaca (Frikes). Kefalonia (Fiskardo).

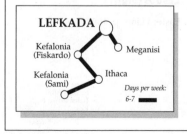

Lefkada (Vassiliki)

Ionian Line
p. 589

| ○ | | |
| 00.00 | *Basos K/ Ionion Pelagos* | Kefalonia (Fiskardo). Ithaca (Pisaetos). Kefalonia (Sami). |

Leros

Dodecanese   p. 406

①		
07.40	*Nissos Kalimnos*	Lipsi. Patmos. Arki. Agathonisi. Samos (Pithagorio).
21.50	*Nissos Kalimnos*	Kalimnos.
②		
01.55	*Diagoras*	Kalimnos. Kos. Symi. Rhodes.
22.45	*Diagoras*	Lipsi. Patmos. Piraeus.
③		
03.50	*Blue Star 1/2*	Kos. Rhodes.
08.40	*Nissos Kalimnos*	Lipsi. Patmos. Arki. Agathonisi. Samos (Pithagorio).
19.50	*Nissos Kalimnos*	Kalimnos.
21.50	*Blue Star 1/2*	Patmos. Piraeus.
④		
03.15	*Blue Star 1/2*	Kos. Rhodes.
16.30	*Blue Star 1/2*	Kos. Rhodes.

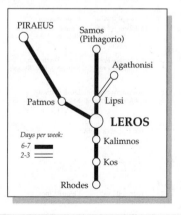

<table>
<tbody>
<tr><td>⑤</td><td></td><td></td></tr>
<tr><td>04.45</td><td>Blue Star 1/2</td><td>Patmos. Piraeus.</td></tr>
<tr><td>07.40</td><td>Nissos Kalimnos</td><td>Lipsi. Patmos. Arki.
Agathonisi.
Samos (Pithagorio).</td></tr>
<tr><td>21.50 ·</td><td>Nissos Kalimnos</td><td>Kalimnos.</td></tr>
</tbody>
</table>

⑦		
08.35	Blue Star 1/2	Kos. Rhodes.
08.40	Nissos Kalimnos	Lipsi. Patmos. Arki. Agathonisi. Samos (Pithagorio).
22.35	Blue Star 1/2	Patmos. Amorgos (Katapola). Piraeus.

Leros (Agia Marina)

Dodecanese
p. 408

①		
12.55	Dodekanisos Pride	Lipsi. Patmos.
14.30	Dodekanisos Pride	Kalimnos. Kos. Symi. Rhodes.

②		
12.55	Dodekanisos Pride	Lipsi. Patmos.
14.30	Dodekanisos Pride	Kalimnos. Kos. Symi. Rhodes.

③		
12.30	Dodekanisos Pride	Lipsi. Patmos.
14.30	Dodekanisos Pride	Kalimnos. Kos. Rhodes.

④		
12.55	Dodekanisos Pride	Lipsi. Patmos.
14.30	Dodekanisos Pride	Kalimnos. Kos. Symi. Rhodes.

⑤		
12.55	Dodekanisos Pride	Lipsi. Patmos.
14.30	Dodekanisos Pride	Kalimnos. Kos. Symi. Rhodes.

⑥		
12.30	Dodekanisos Pride	Lipsi. Agathonisi.
14.55	Dodekanisos Pride	Kalimnos. Kos. Rhodes.

⑦		
12.55	Dodekanisos Pride	Lipsi. Patmos.
14.30	Dodekanisos Pride	Kalimnos. Kos. Rhodes.

Flying Dolphins include:

① ② ④ ⑤		
09.10	Hydrofoil	Lipsi. Patmos.
17.00	Hydrofoil	Kalimnos. Kos.

⑥ ⑦		
09.20	Hydrofoil	Lipsi. Patmos.
16.00	Hydrofoil	Kalimnos. Kos.

Lesbos (Mytilini)

Eastern Line
p. 464

Ⓓ		
08.00	Jale/Jalehan	Ayvalık.

①		
18.00	European Express	Chios. Piraeus.
22.00	Nissos Chios	Chios. Piraeus.

②		
09.10	Taxiarchis	Chios. Samos (Vathi).
18.00	Mytilene	Chios. Piraeus.
22.00	Nissos Chios	Chios. Piraeus.

③		
02.20	Taxiarchis	Limnos. Kavala.
18.00	European Express	Chios. Piraeus.
22.00	Nissos Chios	Chios. Piraeus.

④		
07.00	Taxiarchis	Chios. Samos (Karlovassi). Ikaria (Agios Kyrikos).
18.00	Mytilene	Chios. Piraeus.
22.00	Nissos Chios	Chios. Piraeus.

⑤		
02.40	Taxiarchis	Limnos. Kavala.
18.00	European Express	Chios. Piraeus.
22.00	Nissos Chios	Chios. Piraeus.

⑥		
07.20	Taxiarchis	Chios. Samos (Vathi).
22.00	Nissos Chios	Chios. Piraeus.

⑦		
15.45	Taxiarchis	Limnos. Thessalonika.
18.00	Mytilene	Chios. Piraeus.
22.00	Nissos Chios	Chios. Piraeus.

○		
15.00	Theofilos	Limnos. Thessalonika.
18.00	Theofilos	Chios. Piraeus.

Lesbos (Sigri)

Eastern Line   p. 466

○		
08.30	Diagoras	Thessalonika.

○		
05.30	Diagoras	Chios. Samos (Vathi). Kalimnos. Kos. Rhodes.

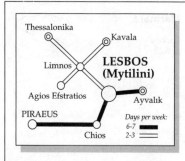

Thessalonika

Kavala

Limnos

LESBOS (Mytilini)

Agios Efstratios

Ayvalık

PIRAEUS

Days per week:
6-7
2-3

Chios

00.20	*Taxiarchis*	Lesbos (Mytilini).
12.30	*Aqua Maria*	Agios Efstratios.
		Lavrio.
⑦		
10.30	*Aqua Maria*	Kavala.
22.25	*Taxiarchis*	Thessalonika.
22.30	*Aqua Maria*	Agios Efstratios.
		Lavrio.

○ * Not operating in 2011:

05.00	*Saos II*	Agios Efstratios.
		Lavrio.
06.30	*Panagia Soumela*	Samothrace.
		Kavala.
08.30	*Saos II*	Evia (Kimi).
14.00	*Lissos*	Thessalonika.
22.15	*Panagia Soumela*	Agios Efstratios.
		Lavrio.
23.00	*Theofilos*	Thessalonika.

Limnos

Northern Aegean
p. 499

○		
05.00	*Aeolos*	Agios Efstratios.
②		
02.10	*Taxiarchis*	Lesbos (Mytilini).
07.30	*Aqua Maria*	Kavala.
21.00	*Aqua Maria*	Agios Efstratios.
		Lavrio.
③		
09.00	*Taxiarchis*	Kavala.
④		
00.20	*Taxiarchis*	Lesbos (Mytilini).
07.30	*Aqua Maria*	Kavala.
21.00	*Aqua Maria*	Agios Efstratios.
		Lavrio.
⑤		
09.20	*Taxiarchis*	Kavala.
⑥		
00.15	*Aqua Maria*	Kavala.

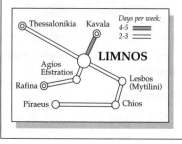

Thessalonikia   Kavala

Days per week:
4-5
2-3

LIMNOS

Agios Efstratios

Rafina

Lesbos (Mytilini)

Piraeus

Chios

Lipsi

Dodecanese
p. 408

Ⓓ		
08.00	*Captain Makis*	Leros.
16.00	*Patmos Star*	Patmos.
①		
08.50	*Nissos Kalimnos*	Patmos.
		Arki.
		Agathonisi.
		Samos (Pithagorio).
13.20	*Dodekanisos Pride*	Patmos.
		Leros (Agia Marina).
		Kalimnos.
		Kos. Symi.
		Rhodes.
20.40	*Nissos Kalimnos*	Leros.
		Kalimnos.
②		
00.45	*Diagoras*	Leros.
		Kalimnos.
		Kos. Symi.
		Rhodes.
13.20	*Dodekanisos Pride*	Patmos.
		Leros (Agia Marina).
		Kalimnos.
		Kos.
		Symi.
		Rhodes.
23.50	*Diagoras*	Patmos.
		Piraeus.
③		
09.50	*Nissos Kalimnos*	Patmos.
		Arki.
		Agathonisi.
		Samos (Pithagorio).
13.00	*Dodekanisos Pride*	Patmos.

| 14.00 | *Dodekanisos Pride* | Leros (Agia Marina). Kalimnos. Kos. Rhodes. |
| 18.40 | *Nissos Kalimnos* | Leros. Kalimnos. |

④
| 13.20 | *Dodekanisos Pride* | Patmos. Leros (Agia Marina). Kalimnos. Kos. Symi. Rhodes. |

⑤
08.50	*Nissos Kalimnos*	Patmos. Arki. Agathonisi. Samos (Pithagorio).
13.20	*Dodekanisos Pride*	Patmos. Leros (Agia Marina). Kalimnos. Kos. Symi. Rhodes.
20.40	*Nissos Kalimnos*	Leros. Kalimnos.

⑥
| 13.00 | *Dodekanisos Pride* | Agathonisi. |
| 14.30 | *Dodekanisos Pride* | Leros (Agia Marina). Kalimnos. Kos. Rhodes. |

⑦
09.50	*Nissos Kalimnos*	Patmos. Arki. Agathonisi. Samos (Pithagorio).
13.20	*Dodekanisos Pride*	Patmos. Leros (Agia Marina). Kalimnos. Kos. Rhodes.
18.40	*Nissos Kalimnos*	Leros. Kalimnos.

○ * Not operating in 2011:

09.25	Hydrofoil	Leros (Agia Marina). Kalimnos. Kos.
09.40	Hydrofoil	Patmos. Samos (Pithagorio). Kos. Rhodes.
16.00	Hydrofoil	Leros (Agia Marina). Kos. Kalimnos.
16.05	Hydrofoil	Patmos. Samos (Pithagorio).
16.30	Hydrofoil	Leros (Agia Marina). Kalimnos. Kos.

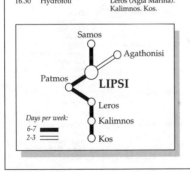

Samos
Agathonisi
Patmos
LIPSI
Leros
Kalimnos
Kos

Days per week:
6-7 ▬
2-3 ═══

Marmara

Turkey
p. 623

ⓓ x 4
| 00.00 | Deniz Otobusleri | Avşa. |
| 00.00 | Deniz Otobusleri | İstanbul. |

⑤ ⑦
| 00.00 | Local | Avşa. Erdek. |
| 00.00 | Local | Tekirdağ. |

Marmaris

Turkey
p. 624

ⓓ
| 09.00 | 16.00 | *Yesil Marmaris* | Rhodes. |

Meganisi (Spartochori)

Ionian Line
p. 592

ⓓ
| 08.00 | 14.00 | *Meganisi* | Lefkada (Nidri). |

Meganisi (Vathi)

Ionian Line   p. 592

ⓓ
07.45	*Meganisi*	Meganisi (Spartochori). Lefkada (Nidri).
13.45	*Meganisi*	Meganisi (Spartochori). Lefkada (Nidri).
17.00	*Meganisi*	Lefkada (Vathi).

Mersin

Turkey   p. 613

① ③ ⑤
| 22.00 | *Yeşilada* | Famagusta. |

Methana

Argo-Saronic
p. 555

ⓓ
06.30	*Ioannis II*	Aegina. Piraeus.
09.40	*Eftichia*	Poros.
09.55	*Apollon Hellas*	Poros. Hydra. Spetses. Porto Helio.
10.00	*Ioannis II*	Poros. Hydra. Ermioni. Spetses.
10.25	*Georgios 2*	Poros. Spetses. Porto Helio.
11.20	*Nefeli*	Aegina. Piraeus.
11.20	*Eftichia*	Aegina. Piraeus.
14.00	*Ioannis II*	Aegina. Piraeus.
16.45	*Apollon Hellas*	Aegina. Piraeus.
17.10	*Ioannis II*	Aegina. Piraeus.
17.25	*Georgios 2*	Aegina. Piraeus.
18.20	*Eftichia*	Poros.
19.30	*Apollon Hellas*	Aegina. Piraeus.

⑤
| 18.55 | *Ioannis II* | Aegina. Piraeus. |

⑦
| 18.00 | *Ioannis II* | Aegina. Piraeus. |

Milos

Cyclades West
p. 275

ⓓ
| 09.40 | *SuperJet* | Folegandros. Santorini. Naxos. Koufonissia. Amorgos (Katapola). |

①
11.25	*Speedrunner IV*	Sifnos. Serifos. Piraeus.
15.30	*Agios Georgios*	Sifnos. Serifos. Kythnos. Piraeus.
17.10	*Prevelis*	Santorini. Crete (Iraklion). Crete (Sitia). Kassos. Karpathos. Chalki. Rhodes.
19.00	*SuperJet*	Piraeus.
20.35	*Highspeed 5*	Sifnos. Serifos. Piraeus.
22.05	*Adamantis Korais*	Kimolos. Folegandros. Ios.

②
| 01.00 | *Vitsentzos Kornaros* | Folegandros. Sikinos. Ios. Santorini. Anafi. |

07.00	*Artemis*	Kimolos. Folegandros. Sikinos. Santorini. Ios. Naxos. Syros.
11.25	*Speedrunner IV*	Sifnos. Serifos. Piraeus.
14.00	*Adamantis Korais*	Sifnos. Serifos. Kythnos. Piraeus.
15.30	*Agios Georgios*	Sifnos. Serifos. Kythnos. Piraeus.
15.50	*Aqua Jewel*	Kimolos. Sifnos. Serifos. Paros. Syros.
19.00	*SuperJet*	Piraeus.
20.35	*Highspeed 5*	Sifnos. Serifos. Piraeus.
23.50	*Vitsentzos Kornaros*	Santorini.

③
11.25	*Speedrunner IV*	Sifnos. Serifos. Piraeus.
12.55	*Prevelis*	Piraeus.
15.45	*Adamantis Korais*	Kimolos. Sifnos. Serifos. Kythnos. Piraeus.
17.15	*Aqua Jewel*	Kimolos. Sifnos. Serifos. Syros.
19.00	*SuperJet*	Piraeus.
22.00	*Speedrunner IV*	Piraeus.

④
11.25	*Speedrunner IV*	Sifnos. Serifos. Piraeus.
15.30	*Agios Georgios*	Sifnos. Serifos. Kythnos. Piraeus.
19.00	*SuperJet*	Piraeus.
20.35	*Highspeed 5*	Sifnos. Serifos. Piraeus.

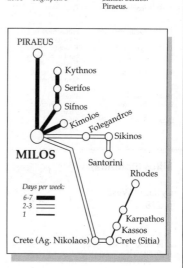

PIRAEUS

Kythnos

Serifos

Sifnos

Kimolos

Folegandros

Sikinos

MILOS

Santorini

Rhodes

Days per week:
6-7
2-3
1

Karpathos

Kassos

Crete (Ag. Nikolaos)   Crete (Sitia)

| 22.10 | *Adamantis Korais* | Kimolos. Sifnos. Serifos. Piraeus. |

⑤
11.25	*Speedrunner IV*	Sifnos. Serifos. Piraeus.
15.45	*Adamantis Korais*	Kimolos. Sifnos. Serifos. Kythnos. Piraeus.
16.35	*Prevelis*	Piraeus.
19.00	*SuperJet*	Piraeus.
20.35	*Highspeed 5*	Sifnos. Serifos. Piraeus.
22.00	*Speedrunner IV*	Piraeus.

⑥
05.10	*Prevelis*	Santorini. Anafi. Crete (Iraklion). Crete (Sitia). Kassos. Karpathos. Rhodes.
07.00	*Aqua Jewel*	Kimolos. Folegandros. Sikinos. Ios. Naxos. Paros. Mykonos. Syros.
11.25	*Speedrunner IV*	Sifnos. Serifos. Piraeus.
15.30	*Agios Georgios*	Sifnos. Serifos. Kythnos. Piraeus.
16.00	*Adamantis Korais*	Sifnos. Serifos. Piraeus.
19.00	*SuperJet*	Piraeus.
20.35	*Highspeed 5*	Sifnos. Serifos. Piraeus.
22.00	*Speedrunner IV*	Piraeus.

⑦
11.25	*Speedrunner IV*	Sifnos. Serifos. Piraeus.
15.30	*Agios Georgios*	Kimolos. Sifnos. Serifos. Kythnos. Piraeus.
16.30	*Aqua Jewel*	Kimolos. Sifnos. Serifos. Paros. Syros.
19.00	*SuperJet*	Piraeus.
20.35	*Highspeed 5*	Sifnos. Serifos. Piraeus.
22.00	*Speedrunner IV*	Sifnos. Piraeus.

Milos (Pollonia)

Cyclades West
p. 278

ⓓ
07.15 10.40 13.00
16.00 19.45
| | *Nissos Kimolos* | Kimolos. |

Monemvassia

Argo-Saronic p. 555

⑤
| 23.30 | *Vitsentzos Kornaros* | Kithera. Antikithera. Crete (Kasteli). |

⑦
| 23.30 | *Vitsentzos Kornaros* | Piraeus. |

Mykonos

Cyclades North
p. 233

ⓓ ex ①
08.30	*Delos Express*	Delos.
09.00	*Orca*	Delos.
09.30	*Margarita X*	Delos.
09.55	*Delos Express*	Delos.
10.15	*Orca*	Delos.
10.45	*Margarita X*	Delos.
11.00	*Delos Express*	Delos.
11.40	*Orca*	Delos.

ⓓ
09.40	*SeaJet 2*	Paros.
11.25	*Highspeed 5*	Syros. Piraeus.
11.45	*Speedrunner III*	Syros. Piraeus.
12.00	*SeaJet 2*	Tinos. Rafina.
14.15	*Blue Star Ithaki*	Tinos. Syros. Piraeus.
14.55	*Flying Cat 4*	Paros. Santorini. Crete (Iraklion).

①
07.25	*Theologos P*	Tinos. Andros. Rafina.
09.50	*Flying Cat 3*	Naxos. Ios. Santorini.
13.15	*Penelope A*	Tinos. Andros. Rafina.
13.40	*Superferry II*	Tinos. Andros. Rafina.
17.25	*SeaJet 2*	Paros.
19.00	*Flying Cat 3*	Tinos. Rafina.
19.20	*SeaJet 2*	Tinos. Rafina.
21.30	*Highspeed 6*	Tinos. Syros. Piraeus.

②
02.10	*Nissos Mykonos*	Ikaria (Evdilos). Samos (Karlovassi). Samos (Vathi).
07.25	*Theologos P*	Tinos. Andros. Rafina.
08.25	*Aqua Jewel*	Paros. Serifos. Sifnos. Kimolos. Milos.
09.50	*Flying Cat 3*	Naxos. Ios. Santorini.
12.15	*Superferry II*	Naxos.
13.15	*Aeolos Kenteris II*	Paros. Naxos. Folegandros. Sikinos. Ios. Thirasia. Santorini. Anafi.
13.15	*Penelope A*	Tinos. Andros. Rafina.
14.30	*Nissos Mykonos*	Syros. Piraeus.

16.00	Superferry II	Tinos. Andros. Rafina.
17.25	SeaJet 2	Paros.
19.00	Flying Cat 3	Tinos. Rafina.
19.20	SeaJet 2	Tinos. Rafina.
21.30	Highspeed 6	Tinos. Syros. Piraeus.

③

02.10	Nissos Mykonos	Ikaria (Agios Kyrikos). Fourni. Samos (Karlovassi). Samos (Vathi).
07.25	Theologos P	Tinos. Andros. Rafina.
09.50	Flying Cat 3	Naxos. Ios. Santorini.
12.15	Superferry II	Naxos.
13.15	Penelope A	Tinos. Andros. Rafina.
13.45	Nissos Mykonos	Syros. Piraeus.
16.00	Superferry II	Tinos. Andros. Rafina.
17.25	SeaJet 2	Paros.
19.00	Flying Cat 3	Tinos. Rafina.
19.20	SeaJet 2	Tinos. Rafina.

④

02.10	Nissos Mykonos	Ikaria (Evdilos). Samos (Karlovassi). Samos (Vathi).
07.25	Theologos P	Tinos. Andros. Rafina.
09.50	Flying Cat 3	Naxos. Ios. Santorini.
12.15	Superferry II	Naxos.
13.15	Penelope A	Tinos. Andros. Rafina.
14.30	Nissos Mykonos	Syros. Piraeus.
16.00	Superferry II	Tinos. Andros. Rafina.
17.25	SeaJet 2	Paros.
19.00	Flying Cat 3	Tinos. Rafina.
19.20	SeaJet 2	Tinos. Rafina.
21.30	Highspeed 6	Tinos. Syros. Piraeus.

⑤

02.10	Nissos Mykonos	Ikaria (Agios Kyrikos). Fourni. Samos (Karlovassi). Samos (Vathi).
12.00	Theologos P	Tinos. Andros. Rafina.
13.15	Penelope A	Tinos. Andros. Rafina.
13.40	Flying Cat 3	Tinos. Rafina.
13.45	Nissos Mykonos	Syros. Piraeus.
17.25	SeaJet 2	Tinos. Rafina.
18.50	Flying Cat 3	Tinos. Rafina.
21.30	Highspeed 6	Tinos. Syros. Piraeus.
21.50	Superferry II	Rafina.
22.35	SeaJet 2	Rafina.
23.00	Theologos P	Rafina.

⑥

02.10	Nissos Mykonos	Ikaria (Evdilos). Samos (Karlovassi). Samos (Vathi).
09.50	Flying Cat 3	Naxos. Ios. Santorini.
12.00	Theologos P	Tinos. Andros. Rafina.
12.15	Superferry II	Naxos.
13.15	Aeolos Kenteris II	Paros. Naxos. Folegandros. Sikinos. Ios. Thirasia. Santorini. Anafi.

Days per week:
6-7
4-5
2-3

13.45	Nissos Mykonos	Syros. Piraeus.
15.00	Penelope A	Tinos. Andros. Rafina.
16.00	Superferry II	Tinos. Andros. Rafina.
16.10	Aqua Jewel	Syros.
17.25	SeaJet 2	Paros.
19.00	Flying Cat 3	Tinos. Rafina.
19.20	SeaJet 2	Tinos. Rafina.
21.30	Highspeed 6	Tinos. Syros. Piraeus.

⑦

02.10	Nissos Mykonos	Ikaria (Agios Kyrikos). Fourni. Samos (Karlovassi). Samos (Vathi).
08.25	Aqua Jewel	Paros. Serifos. Sifnos. Kimolos. Milos.
12.00	Theologos P	Tinos. Andros. Rafina.
13.15	Penelope A	Tinos. Andros. Rafina.
13.40	Flying Cat 3	Tinos. Rafina.
13.40	Superferry II	Tinos. Andros. Rafina.
15.40	Aeolos Kenteris II	Syros.
16.55	SeaJet 2	Tinos. Rafina.
18.50	Flying Cat 3	Tinos. Rafina.
19.25	Nissos Mykonos	Syros. Piraeus.
21.30	Highspeed 6	Tinos. Syros. Piraeus.
21.45	SeaJet 2	Tinos. Rafina.

○ * Not operating in 2011:

| 12.00 | Ferry | Tinos. Syros. Alonissos. Skiathos. Thessalonika. |
| 17.40 | Ferry | Paros. Naxos. Ios. Santorini. Crete (Iraklion). |

Nafplio

Argo-Saronic p. 555

🐬 *Flying Dolphins*

○
08.00   Tolo. Porto Helio. Spetses. Ermioni.
          Hydra. Poros. Aegina. Piraeus.

Naxos

Cyclades Central
p. 154

①
09.15   *Aeolos Kenteris II*   Donoussa.
                                    Amorgos (Egiali).
                                    Amorgos (Katapola).
                                    Koufonissia.
                                    Schinoussa. Iraklia.
09.30   *Blue Star Paros*   Paros.
                                    Piraeus.
10.45   *Flying Cat 3*   Ios.
                                    Santorini.
11.20   *Highspeed 4*   Paros.
                                    Piraeus.
12.20   *Blue Star Naxos*   Santorini.
13.40   *SuperJet*   Koufonissia.
                                    Amorgos (Katapola).
14.00   *Artemis*   Ios. Santorini.
                                    Sikinos.
                                    Folegandros.
                                    Kimolos.
                                    Milos.
14.00   *Express Skopelitis*   Schinoussa.
                                    Koufonissia.
                                    Donoussa.
                                    Amorgos (Egiali).
                                    Amorgos (Katapola).
15.25   *Aeolos Kenteris II*   Paros.
                                    Syros.
18.05   *Flying Cat 3*   Mykonos. Tinos.
                                    Rafina.
18.45   *Blue Star Naxos*   Paros.
                                    Piraeus.
21.05   *Highspeed 4*   Paros.
                                    Piraeus.
22.45   *Blue Star Paros*   Donoussa.
                                    Amorgos (Egiali).
                                    Astipalea.

②
09.30   *Blue Star Paros*   Paros.
                                    Piraeus.
10.45   *Flying Cat 3*   Ios.
                                    Santorini.

11.20   *Highspeed 4*   Paros.
                                    Piraeus.
12.20   *Blue Star Naxos*   Santorini.
13.40   *SuperJet*   Koufonissia.
                                    Amorgos (Katapola).
14.00   *Express Skopelitis*   Iraklia. Schinoussa.
                                    Koufonissia.
                                    Amorgos (Katapola).
14.15   *Superferry II*   Mykonos. Tinos.
                                    Andros. Rafina.
15.55   *Aeolos Kenteris II*   Folegandros.
                                    Sikinos.
                                    Ios. Thirasia.
                                    Santorini.
                                    Anafi.
15.55   *Artemis*   Syros.
18.05   *Flying Cat 3*   Mykonos. Tinos.
                                    Rafina.
18.45   *Blue Star Naxos*   Paros.
                                    Piraeus.
21.05   *Highspeed 4*   Paros.
                                    Piraeus.
23.35   *Blue Star Paros*   Iraklia. Schinoussa.
                                    Koufonissia.
                                    Amorgos (Katapola).

③
09.30   *Blue Star Paros*   Paros.
                                    Piraeus.
10.45   *Flying Cat 3*   Ios.
                                    Santorini.
11.20   *Highspeed 4*   Paros.
                                    Piraeus.
12.20   *Blue Star Naxos*   Santorini.
12.35   *Aeolos Kenteris II*   Paros.
                                    Syros.
13.40   *SuperJet*   Koufonissia.
                                    Amorgos (Katapola).
14.00   *Express Skopelitis*   Schinoussa.
                                    Koufonissia.
                                    Donoussa.
                                    Amorgos (Egiali).
                                    Amorgos (Katapola).
14.15   *Superferry II*   Mykonos. Tinos.
                                    Andros. Rafina.
15.10   *Artemis*   Folegandros. Sikinos.
                                    Ios. Thirasia.
                                    Santorini. Anafi.
18.05   *Flying Cat 3*   Mykonos. Tinos.
                                    Rafina.
18.45   *Blue Star Naxos*   Paros.
                                    Piraeus.
21.05   *Speedrunner III*   Paros.
                                    Piraeus.
22.45   *Blue Star Paros*   Donoussa.
                                    Amorgos (Egiali).
                                    Astipalea.

④
09.30   *Blue Star Paros*   Paros.
                                    Piraeus.
10.45   *Flying Cat 3*   Ios.
                                    Santorini.
11.20   *Highspeed 4*   Paros.
                                    Piraeus.
12.20   *Blue Star Naxos*   Santorini.
13.40   *SuperJet*   Koufonissia.
                                    Amorgos (Katapola).
14.00   *Express Skopelitis*   Iraklia. Schinoussa.
                                    Koufonissia.
                                    Amorgos (Katapola).

14.15	*Superferry II*	Mykonos. Tinos. Andros. Rafina.
14.45	*Artemis*	Paros. Syros.
18.05	*Flying Cat 3*	Mykonos. Tinos. Rafina.
18.45	*Blue Star Naxos*	Paros. Piraeus.
21.05	*Highspeed 4*	Paros. Piraeus.
23.35	*Blue Star Paros*	Donoussa. Amorgos (Egiali). Astipalea.

⑤

09.30	*Blue Star Paros*	Paros. Piraeus.
10.10	*Artemis*	Iraklia. Schinoussa. Koufonissia. Amorgos (Katapola). Amorgos (Egiali). Donoussa.
11.20	*Highspeed 4*	Paros. Piraeus.
12.20	*Blue Star Naxos*	Santorini.
13.40	*SuperJet*	Koufonissia. Amorgos (Katapola).
14.00	*Express Skopelitis*	Schinoussa. Koufonissia. Donoussa. Amorgos (Egiali). Amorgos (Katapola).
14.50	*Aqua Jewel*	Ios. Sikinos. Folegandros. Kimolos. Milos.
17.45	*Artemis*	Paros. Syros.
18.45	*Blue Star Naxos*	Paros. Piraeus.
20.40	*Diagoras*	Santorini. Astipalea. Kalimnos. Kos. Nissiros. Tilos. Symi. Rhodes. Kastelorizo.
21.05	*Highspeed 4*	Paros. Piraeus.
22.45	*Blue Star Paros*	Iraklia. Schinoussa. Koufonissia. Amorgos (Katapola).

⑥

09.30	*Blue Star Paros*	Paros. Piraeus.
10.45	*Flying Cat 3*	Ios. Santorini.
11.20	*Highspeed 4*	Paros. Piraeus.
12.20	*Blue Star Naxos*	Santorini.
12.55	*Aqua Jewel*	Paros. Mykonos. Syros.
13.40	*SuperJet*	Koufonissia. Amorgos (Katapola).
14.00	*Express Skopelitis*	Schinoussa. Koufonissia. Donoussa. Amorgos (Egiali). Amorgos (Katapola).
14.15	*Superferry II*	Mykonos. Tinos. Andros. Rafina.
15.55	*Aeolos Kenteris II*	Folegandros. Sikinos. Ios. Thirasia. Santorini. Anafi.
18.05	*Flying Cat 3*	Mykonos. Tinos. Rafina.

Days per week:
6-7 ▬▬▬
2-3 ═══

18.45	*Blue Star Naxos*	Paros. Piraeus.
21.05	*Highspeed 4*	Paros. Piraeus.
22.45	*Blue Star Paros*	Donoussa. Amorgos (Egiali). Astipalea.

⑦

09.30	*Blue Star Paros*	Paros. Piraeus.
10.10	*Artemis*	Donoussa. Amorgos (Egiali). Amorgos (Katapola). Koufonissia. Schinoussa. Iraklia.
11.20	*Highspeed 4*	Paros. Piraeus.
12.20	*Blue Star Naxos*	Santorini.
13.10	*Aeolos Kenteris II*	Paros. Mykonos. Syros.
13.20	*Diagoras*	Paros. Piraeus.
13.40	*SuperJet*	Koufonissia. Amorgos (Katapola).
17.35	*Artemis*	Paros. Syros.
18.45	*Blue Star Naxos*	Paros. Piraeus.
21.05	*Highspeed 4*	Paros. Piraeus.
23.35	*Blue Star Paros*	Iraklia. Schinoussa. Koufonissia. Amorgos (Katapola).

○ * Not operating in 2011:

| 09.30 | Ferry | Paros. Mykonos. Tinos. Syros. Alonissos. Skiathos. Thessalonika. |
| 20.00 | Ferry | Ios. Santorini. Crete (Iraklion). |

Nea Moudania

Northern Aegean
p. 501

○
17.00   *Nona Mairy*   Limnos.
                         Alonissos.
                         Skopelos.
                         Skiathos.
                         Volos.

Nea Peramos

Northern Aegean
p. 501

Ⓓ 08.30 12.30 16.30 20.45
         ANET Line   Thassos (Skala Prinos).

Neapoli

Argo-Saronic
p. 556

Ⓓ
08.30 09.45 10.45 12.00
13.45 16.45 19.00
         Local   Elafonissos.

①
08.00   *Porfyrousa*   Kithera.
13.00   *Porfyrousa*   Kithera. Antikithera.

②
09.00   *Porfyrousa*   Kithera.
14.30   *Porfyrousa*   Kithera.

③
09.00   *Porfyrousa*   Kithera.
14.30   *Porfyrousa*   Kithera.

④ ⑤ ⑥ ⑦
09.05   *Porfyrousa*   Kithera.
14.30   *Porfyrousa*   Kithera.

Nissiros

Dodecanese
p. 412

Ⓓ
07.00   Taxi boat   Kos (Kardamena).

○
17.30   *SeaStar*   Tilos. Rhodes.

④
06.15   *Diagoras*   Tilos.
                       Rhodes.
                       Kastelorizo.

⑤
00.10   *Diagoras*   Kos. Kalimnos.
                       Piraeus.

12.10   *Dodekanisos Express*   Kos.
14.15   *Dodekanisos Express*   Tilos. Chalki.
                                  Rhodes. Symi.

⑥
08.30   *Diagoras*   Tilos. Symi.
                       Rhodes.
                       Kastelorizo.

⑦
04.00   *Diagoras*   Kos. Kalimnos.
                       Astipalea.
                       Naxos. Paros.
                       Piraeus.

12.10   *Dodekanisos Express*   Kos.
16.15   *Dodekanisos Express*   Tilos. Chalki.
                                  Rhodes.
                                  Symi.

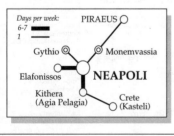

Days per week:
6-7
1

PIRAEUS
Gythio   Monemvassia
Elafonissos   **NEAPOLI**
Kithera
(Agia Pelagia)   Crete
(Kasteli)

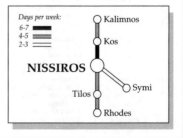

Days per week:
6-7
4-5
2-3

Kalimnos
Kos
NISSIROS
Tilos   Symi
Rhodes

Odun Iskalesi

Turkey p. 624

Ⓓ x ②
00.00   Local   Bozcaada.

Oinousses

Eastern Line
p. 469

Ⓓ
08.00   *Oinoussai III*   Chios.

Paros

Cyclades Central
p. 168

Ⓓ
09.45   10.30   11.30
12.30   13.30   14.30
16.00   17.30   19.00
         Antiparos Express
         Kasos Express
         Panagia Parou   Antiparos.

①
08.20   *Aeolos Kenteris II*   Naxos.
                                  Donoussa.
                                  Amorgos (Egiali).
                                  Amorgos (Katapola).
                                  Koufonissia.
                                  Schinoussa.
                                  Iraklia.
10.30   *Highspeed 4*   Naxos.
10.45   *Blue Star Paros*   Piraeus.
11.00   *SeaJet 2*   Mykonos.
                                  Tinos.
                                  Rafina.
11.15   *Blue Star Naxos*   Naxos.
                                  Santorini.
12.10   *Highspeed 4*   Piraeus.
13.55   *Flying Cat 4*   Mykonos.
15.55   *Flying Cat 4*   Santorini.
                                  Crete (Iraklion).
16.35   *Aeolos Kenteris II*   Syros.
18.25   *SeaJet 2*   Mykonos.
                                  Tinos.
                                  Rafina.

19.25	*Blue Star Naxos*	Piraeus.
20.10	*Highspeed 4*	Naxos.
20.30	*Speedrunner III*	Piraeus.
21.45	*Blue Star Paros*	Naxos.
		Donoussa.
		Amorgos (Egiali).
		Astipalea.
21.55	*Highspeed 4*	Piraeus.

②
10.25   *Aqua Jewel*   Serifos.
                                  Sifnos.
                                  Kimolos.
                                  Milos.
10.30   *Highspeed 4*   Naxos.
10.45   *Blue Star Paros*   Piraeus.
11.00   *SeaJet 2*   Mykonos.
                                  Tinos.
                                  Rafina.
11.15   *Blue Star Naxos*   Naxos.
                                  Santorini.
12.10   *Highspeed 4*   Piraeus.
13.55   *Flying Cat 4*   Mykonos.
15.00   *Aeolos Kenteris II*   Naxos.
                                  Folegandros.
                                  Sikinos.
                                  Ios.
                                  Thirasia.
                                  Santorini.
                                  Anafi.
15.55   *Flying Cat 4*   Santorini.
                                  Crete (Iraklion).
18.25   *SeaJet 2*   Mykonos.
                                  Tinos.
                                  Rafina.
19.25   *Blue Star Naxos*   Piraeus.
20.10   *Aqua Jewel*   Syros.
20.10   *Highspeed 4*   Naxos.
21.55   *Highspeed 4*   Piraeus.
22.30   *Blue Star Paros*   Naxos.
                                  Iraklia.
                                  Schinoussa.
                                  Koufonissia.
                                  Amorgos (Katapola).

③
10.30   *Highspeed 4*   Naxos.
10.45   *Blue Star Paros*   Piraeus.
11.00   *SeaJet 2*   Mykonos.
                                  Tinos.
                                  Rafina.
11.15   *Blue Star Naxos*   Naxos.
                                  Santorini.
12.10   *Highspeed 4*   Piraeus.
13.20   *Aeolos Kenteris II*   Syros.
13.50   *Artemis*   Naxos.
                                  Folegandros.
                                  Sikinos.
                                  Ios.
                                  Thirasia.
                                  Santorini.
                                  Anafi.
13.55   *Flying Cat 4*   Mykonos.
15.55   *Flying Cat 4*   Santorini.
                                  Crete (Iraklion).
18.25   *SeaJet 2*   Mykonos.
                                  Tinos.
                                  Rafina.
19.25   *Blue Star Naxos*   Piraeus.
20.15   *Speedrunner III*   Naxos.

21.45	*Blue Star Paros*	Naxos.
		Donoussa.
		Amorgos (Egiali).
		Astipalea.
21.50	*Speedrunner III*	Piraeus.

④

10.30	*Highspeed 4*	Naxos.
10.45	*Blue Star Paros*	Piraeus.
11.00	*SeaJet 2*	Mykonos.
		Tinos.
		Rafina.
11.15	*Blue Star Naxos*	Naxos.
		Santorini.
12.10	*Highspeed 4*	Piraeus.
13.55	*Flying Cat 4*	Mykonos.
15.55	*Flying Cat 4*	Santorini.
		Crete (Iraklion).
16.05	*Artemis*	Syros.
18.25	*SeaJet 2*	Mykonos.
		Tinos. Rafina.
19.25	*Blue Star Naxos*	Piraeus.
20.10	*Highspeed 4*	Naxos.
20.30	*Speedrunner III*	Piraeus.
21.55	*Highspeed 4*	Piraeus.
22.30	*Blue Star Paros*	Naxos. Donoussa.
		Amorgos (Egiali).
		Astipalea.

⑤

08.50	*Artemis*	Naxos.
		Iraklia.
		Schinoussa.
		Koufonissia.
		Amorgos (Katapola).
		Amorgos (Egiali).
		Donoussa.

PIRAEUS
Rafina
Tinos
Samos
Mykonos
Syros
Ikaria
Naxos
PAROS
Kou.
Don.
Antiparos
Amorgos
Milos
Sifnos
Ira.
Sikinos
Sch.
Astipalea
Ios
Folegandros
Santorini
Rhodes
Karpathos
Crete (Iraklion)

Days per week:
6-7
4-5
2-3

10.30	*Highspeed 4*	Naxos.
10.45	*Blue Star Paros*	Piraeus.
11.00	*SeaJet 2*	Mykonos.
		Tinos.
		Rafina.
11.15	*Blue Star Naxos*	Naxos.
		Santorini.
12.10	*Highspeed 4*	Piraeus.
13.55	*Aqua Jewel*	Naxos. Ios.
		Sikinos.
		Folegandros.
		Kimolos. Milos.
13.55	*Flying Cat 4*	Mykonos.
15.55	*Flying Cat 4*	Santorini.
		Crete (Iraklion).
19.05	*Artemis*	Syros.
19.25	*Blue Star Naxos*	Piraeus.
20.10	*Highspeed 4*	Naxos.
20.30	*Speedrunner III*	Piraeus.
21.45	*Blue Star Paros*	Naxos.
		Iraklia.
		Schinoussa.
		Koufonissia.
		Amorgos (Katapola).
21.55	*Highspeed 4*	Piraeus.

⑥

01.10	*Blue Star Ithaki*	Piraeus.
10.30	*Highspeed 4*	Naxos.
10.45	*Blue Star Paros*	Piraeus.
11.00	*SeaJet 2*	Mykonos.
		Tinos. Rafina.
11.15	*Blue Star Naxos*	Naxos.
		Santorini.
12.10	*Highspeed 4*	Piraeus.
13.55	*Flying Cat 4*	Mykonos.
14.10	*Aqua Jewel*	Mykonos.
		Syros.
15.00	*Aeolos Kenteris II*	Naxos.
		Folegandros.
		Sikinos. Ios.
		Thirasia.
		Santorini.
		Anafi.
15.55	*Flying Cat 4*	Santorini.
		Crete (Iraklion).
18.25	*SeaJet 2*	Mykonos.
		Tinos.
		Rafina.
19.25	*Blue Star Naxos*	Piraeus.
20.10	*Highspeed 4*	Naxos.
20.30	*Speedrunner III*	Piraeus.
21.45	*Blue Star Paros*	Naxos.
		Donoussa.
		Amorgos (Egiali).
		Astipalea.
21.55	*Highspeed 4*	Piraeus.

⑦

08.50	*Artemis*	Naxos.
		Donoussa.
		Amorgos (Egiali).
		Amorgos (Katapola).
		Koufonissia.
		Schinoussa.
		Iraklia.
09.50	*Aqua Jewel*	Serifos. Sifnos.
		Kimolos.
		Milos.
10.30	*Highspeed 4*	Naxos.
10.45	*Blue Star Paros*	Piraeus.

11.00	*SeaJet 2*	Mykonos. Tinos. Rafina.
11.15	*Blue Star Naxos*	Naxos. Santorini.
12.10	*Highspeed 4*	Piraeus.
13.55	*Flying Cat 4*	Mykonos.
14.00	*Aeolos Kenteris II*	Mykonos. Syros.
14.10	*Diagoras*	Piraeus.
15.55	*Flying Cat 4*	Santorini. Crete (Iraklion).
18.55	*Artemis*	Syros.
19.25	*Blue Star Naxos*	Piraeus.
20.10	*Highspeed 4*	Naxos.
20.30	*Speedrunner III*	Piraeus.
21.00	*Aqua Jewel*	Syros.
21.55	*Highspeed 4*	Piraeus.
22.30	*Blue Star Paros*	Naxos. Iraklia. Schinoussa. Koufonissia. Amorgos (Katapola).

○ * Not operating in 2011:

00.00	*Nissos Rodos*	Kos. Rhodes.
00.00	*Nissos Rodos*	Piraeus.
10.30	Ferry	Mykonos. Tinos. Syros. Alonissos. Skiathos. Thessalonika.
19.00	Ferry	Naxos. Ios. Santorini. Crete (Iraklion).

Paros (Piso Livadi)

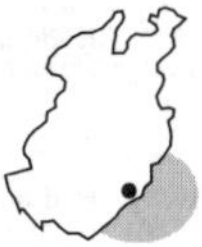

Cyclades
Central
p. 173

○
00.00	Beach Boat	Naxos.

○ * Not operating in 2011:

08.30	Hydrofoil	Ios. Santorini.
09.45	*Express Skopelitis*	Naxos.
13.00	*Flying Cat 4*	Naxos. Mykonos.
15.30	*Express Skopelitis*	Iraklia. Schinoussa. Koufonissia. Amorgos (Katapola).
16.00	*Flying Cat 4*	Ios. Santorini. Crete (Iraklion).

Paros (Punta)

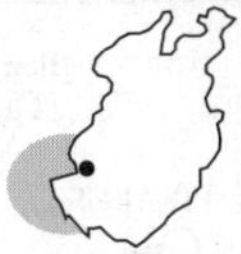

Cyclades
Central
p. 173

Ⓗ
07.00–10.00,
21.00–24.00;
ev. 30 min
10.30–20.30	*Agioi Anargiri*	Antiparos.

Paşalmanı

Turkey
p. 624

① ⑥
00.00	Local	Erdek.

Patmos

Dodecanese
p. 416

Ⓓ Tourist boats:
10.00	*Anna Express*	Lipsi. / Arki.
10.00	*Patmos Star*	Lipsi.
16.00	Local	Samos (Pithagorio).

①
09.45	*Nissos Kalimnos*	Arki. Agathonisi. Samos (Pithagorio).
13.45	*Dodekanisos Pride*	Leros (Agia Marina). Kalimnos. Kos. Symi. Rhodes.
19.30	*Nissos Kalimnos*	Lipsi. Leros. Kalimnos.
23.40	*Diagoras*	Lipsi. Leros. Kalimnos. Kos. Symi. Rhodes.

Days per week:
6-7 ▰▰▰
2-3 ═══

②

| 13.45 | *Dodekanisos Pride* | Leros (Agia Marina). Kalimnos. Kos. Symi. Rhodes. |

③

00.40	*Diagoras*	Piraeus.
02.30	*Blue Star 1/ Blue Star 2*	Leros. Kos. Rhodes.
10.50	*Nissos Kalimnos*	Arki. Agathonisi. Samos (Pithagorio).
13.30	*Dodekanisos Pride*	Lipsi. Leros (Agia Marina). Kalimnos. Kos. Rhodes.
17.45	*Nissos Kalimnos*	Lipsi. Leros. Kalimnos.
23.00	*Blue Star 1/ Blue Star 2*	Piraeus.

④

02.05	*Blue Star 1/ Blue Star 2*	Leros. Kos. Rhodes.
13.45	*Dodekanisos Pride*	Leros (Agia Marina). Kalimnos. Kos. Symi. Rhodes.
15.20	*Blue Star 1/ Blue Star 2*	Leros. Kos. Rhodes.

⑤

| 05.55 | *Blue Star 1/ Blue Star 2* | Piraeus. |

09.45	*Nissos Kalimnos*	Arki. Agathonisi. Samos (Pithagorio).
13.45	*Dodekanisos Pride*	Leros (Agia Marina). Kalimnos. Kos. Symi. Rhodes.
19.30	*Nissos Kalimnos*	Lipsi. Leros. Kalimnos.

⑦

07.25	*Blue Star 1/ Blue Star 2*	Leros. Kos. Rhodes.
10.50	*Nissos Kalimnos*	Arki. Agathonisi. Samos (Pithagorio).
13.45	*Dodekanisos Pride*	Leros (Agia Marina). Kalimnos. Kos. Rhodes.
17.45	*Nissos Kalimnos*	Lipsi. Leros. Kalimnos.
23.55	*Blue Star 1/ Blue Star 2*	Amorgos (Katapola). Piraeus.

○ * Not operating in 2011:

08.55	Hydrofoil	Leros (Agia Marina). Kalimnos. Kos.
10.00	Hydrofoil	Fourni. Ikaria (Agios Kyrikos). Samos (Pithagorio).
12.15	Hydrofoil	Samos (Pithagorio).
15.30	Hydrofoil	Lipsi. Leros (Agia Marina). Kos. Kalimnos. Rhodes.
16.00	Hydrofoil	Samos (Pithagorio).
16.30	Hydrofoil	Samos (Vathi).
17.00	Hydrofoil	Leros (Agia Marina). Kalimnos. Kos.

Patras

Ionian Line
p. 592

Domestic Services:

Ⓓ

| 12.30 | *Kefalonia* | Kefalonia (Sami). Ithaca (Pisaetos). Ithaca (Vathi). |

International Services:

Ⓓ
14.30	Superfast	Igoumenitsa. Ancona.
17.30	ANEK LInes	Igoumenitsa. Ancona.
17.30	Ionian Queen/	
	Erotokritos/Elli T	Kefalonia (Sami). Brindisi.
18.00	Cruise Europa/	
	Cruise Olympia	Igoumenitsa. Ancona.
18.00	Superfast I/	
	Superfast II	Igoumenitsa. Bari.
20.00	Superfast	Ancona.

①
16.00	Minoan	Igoumenitsa. Bari.
17.30	Ionian King	Brindisi.
23.59	Lefka Ori/	
	Sophocles V	Corfu. Igoumenitsa. Venice.

②
16.00	Minoan	Igoumenitsa. Bari.
19.00	AK Ventouris	Bari.
24.00	Minoan	Corfu. Igoumenitsa. Venice.

③
16.00	Minoan	Igoumenitsa. Bari.
17.30	Ionian King	Brindisi.
23.59	Lefka Ori/	
	Sophocles V	Corfu. Igoumenitsa. Venice.
24.00	Minoan	Corfu. Igoumenitsa. Venice.

④
16.00	Minoan	Igoumenitsa. Corfu. Bari.
19.00	AK Ventouris	Bari.
23.59	Lefka Ori/	
	Sophocles V	Corfu. Igoumenitsa. Venice.
24.00	Minoan	Corfu. Igoumenitsa. Venice.

⑤
16.00	Minoan	Igoumenitsa. Bari.
17.30	Ionian King	Brindisi.
23.59	Lefka Ori/	
	Sophocles V	Corfu. Igoumenitsa. Venice.
24.00	Minoan	Corfu. Igoumenitsa. Venice.

⑥
16.00	Minoan	Igoumenitsa. Corfu. Bari.
23.59	Lefka Ori/	
	Sophocles V	Corfu. Igoumenitsa. Venice.
24.00	Minoan	Corfu. Igoumenitsa. Venice.

⑦
16.00	Minoan	Igoumenitsa. Corfu. Bari.
19.00	AK Ventouris	Bari.
23.59	Lefka Ori/	
	Sophocles V	Corfu. Igoumenitsa. Venice.
24.00	Minoan	Corfu. Igoumenitsa. Venice.

Venice / Trieste / Ancona / Brindisi / Corfu/Kerkyra / Bari / Igoumenitsa / PATRAS / Ithaca / Kefalonia (Sami)

Days per week:
6-7
2-3

Paxi / Paxos

Ionian Line   p. 595

Ⓓ ex ③
| 07.15 | Local C/F | Igoumenitsa. Corfu. |

Ⓓ ex ⑦
| 07.30 | Tourist Boat | Corfu. |

③
| 12.00 | Local C/F | Igoumenitsa. Corfu. |

○
06.30	Ionian Queen/	
	Erotokritos/	
	Elli T	Igoumenitsa. Corfu. Brindisi.
07.30	Ionian Queen/	
	Erotokritos/	
	Elli T	Kefalonia (Sami). Patras.

Brindisi / Corfu/Kerkyra / PAXI / Patras

Days per week:
6-7
2-3

Piraeus

Athens & Piraeus   p. 116

Weekly updated
timetable for **Piraeus** at
greekislandhopping.com

Note:
Current weekly printed schedules are available from the central Athens and airport branches of the NTOG/
EOT. A 48-hour Saronic Gulf ferry schedule (in Greek) is sometimes posted up on the Port Police building
on the Saronic Gulf ferry quay. Otherwise Saronic Gulf ferry timetables are available from the quayside
ticket kiosks. International ferry information is obtained from respective agents.

International Services: (Suspended during 2011)

○
16.00	*Salamis Star*	Mykonos. Rhodes. Limassol. Port Said. Haifa.
19.00	*Sea Harmony*	Santorini. Patmos. Rhodes. Limassol. Haifa.
20.00	*Princesa Cypria*	Patmos. Limassol. Haifa.

Domestic Services:

1. Cyclades, Crete, Dodecanese, Eastern & Northern Aegean

①
07.00	*Highspeed 6*	Ios. Santorini.
07.00	*SuperJet*	Milos. Folegandros. Santorini. Naxos.
		Koufonissia. Amorgos (Katapola).
07.05	*Speedrunner IV*	Serifos. Sifnos. Milos.
07.15	*Highspeed 4*	Paros. Naxos.
07.25	*Blue Star Naxos*	Paros. Naxos. Santorini.
07.25	*Highspeed 5*	Syros. Tinos. Mykonos.
07.25	*Agios Georgios*	Kythnos. Serifos. Sifnos. Milos.
07.35	*Blue Star Ithaki*	Syros. Tinos. Mykonos.
07.35	*Speedrunner III*	Syros. Tinos. Mykonos.
12.00	*Prevelis*	Milos. Santorini. Crete (Iraklion). Crete (Sitia).
		Kassos. Karpathos. Chalki. Rhodes.
12.30	*Nissos Chios*	Chios. Lesbos (Mytilini).
14.30	*Adamantis Korais*	Kythnos. Serifos. Sifnos. Milos. Kimolos. Folegandros. Ios.
15.00	*Diagoras*	Patmos. Lipsi. Leros. Kalimnos. Kos. Symi. Rhodes.
16.30	*Highspeed 5*	Serifos. Sifnos. Milos.
16.55	*Highspeed 4*	Paros. Naxos.
17.05	*Speedrunner III*	Paros.
17.30	*Blue Star Paros*	Paros. Naxos. Donoussa. Amorgos (Egiali). Astipalea.
17.30	*Speedrunner IV*	Serifos. Sifnos. Kimolos. Folegandros.
17.45	*Highspeed 6*	Syros. Mykonos. Tinos.
19.00	*Blue Star 1/2*	Syros. Santorini. Kos. Rhodes.
19.00	*Mytilene*	Chios. Lesbos (Mytilini).
19.30	*Vitsentzos Kornaros*	Milos. Folegandros. Sikinos. Ios. Santorini. Anafi.
21.00	*Elyros/Lato*	Crete (Chania).
21.30	*Superfast XII*	Crete (Iraklion).
21.30	*Nissos Mykonos*	Syros. Mykonos. Ikaria (Evdilos). Samos (Karlovassi). Samos (Vathi).
22.00	*Festos Palace/*	
	Knossos Palace	Crete (Iraklion).

②
07.00	*Highspeed 6*	Ios. Santorini.
07.00	*SuperJet*	Milos. Folegandros. Santorini. Naxos. Koufonissia. Amorgos (Katapola).
07.05	*Speedrunner IV*	Serifos. Sifnos. Milos.
07.15	*Highspeed 4*	Paros. Naxos.
07.25	*Blue Star Naxos*	Paros. Naxos. Santorini.
07.25	*Highspeed 5*	Syros. Tinos. Mykonos.
07.25	*Agios Georgios*	Kythnos. Serifos. Sifnos. Kimolos. Milos.
07.35	*Blue Star Ithaki*	Syros. Tinos. Mykonos.
07.35	*Speedrunner III*	Syros. Tinos. Mykonos.
12.30	*Nissos Chios*	Chios. Lesbos (Mytilini).
16.30	*Highspeed 5*	Serifos. Sifnos. Milos.

16.55	Highspeed 4	Paros. Naxos.
17.30	Blue Star Paros	Syros. Paros. Naxos. Iraklia. Schinoussa. Koufonissia. Amorgos (Katapola).
17.45	Highspeed 6	Syros. Mykonos. Tinos.
19.00	Blue Star 1/2	Patmos. Leros. Kos. Rhodes.
19.00	European Express	Chios. Lesbos (Mytilini).
21.00	Elyros/Lato	Crete (Chania).
21.30	Superfast XII	Crete (Iraklion).
21.30	Nissos Mykonos	Syros. Mykonos. Ikaria (Agios Kyrikos). Fourni. Samos (Karlovassi). Samos (Vathi).
22.00	Festos Palace/ Knossos Palace	Crete (Iraklion).

③

07.00	Highspeed 6	Ios. Santorini.
07.00	SuperJet	Milos. Folegandros. Santorini. Naxos. Koufonissia. Amorgos (Katapola).
07.05	Speedrunner IV	Serifos. Sifnos. Milos.
07.15	Highspeed 4	Paros. Naxos.
07.25	Blue Star Naxos	Paros. Naxos. Santorini.
07.25	Highspeed 5	Syros. Tinos. Mykonos.
07.25	Agios Georgios	Serifos. Sifnos. Folegandros. Sikinos. Ios. Santorini.
07.35	Blue Star Ithaki	Syros. Tinos. Mykonos.
07.35	Speedrunner III	Syros. Tinos. Mykonos.
07.55	Adamantis Korais	Kythnos. Serifos. Sifnos. Milos. Kimolos.
12.30	Nissos Chios	Chios. Lesbos (Mytilini).
15.00	Diagoras	Santorini. Karpathos. Kos. Nissiros. Tilos. Rhodes. Kastelorizo.
15.00	Vitsentzos Kornaros	Kithera. Crete (Kasteli).
17.05	Speedrunner III	Paros. Naxos.
17.30	Blue Star Paros	Paros. Naxos. Donoussa. Amorgos (Egiali). Astipalea.
17.30	Speedrunner IV	Serifos. Sifnos. Milos.
19.00	Blue Star 1/2	Syros. Patmos. Leros. Kos. Rhodes.
19.00	Mytilene	Chios. Lesbos (Mytilini).
20.00	Prevelis	Santorini. Anafi. Kassos. Karpathos. Karpathos (Diafani). Chalki. Rhodes.
21.00	Elyros/Lato	Crete (Chania).
21.30	Superfast XII	Crete (Iraklion).
21.30	Nissos Mykonos	Syros. Mykonos. Ikaria (Evdilos). Samos (Karlovassi). Samos (Vathi).
22.00	Festos Palace/ Knossos Palace	Crete (Iraklion).

④

07.00	Highspeed 6	Ios. Santorini.
07.00	SuperJet	Milos. Folegandros. Santorini. Naxos. Koufonissia. Amorgos (Katapola).
07.05	Speedrunner IV	Serifos. Sifnos. Milos.
07.15	Highspeed 4	Paros. Naxos.
07.25	Blue Star Naxos	Paros. Naxos. Santorini.
07.25	Highspeed 5	Syros. Tinos. Mykonos.
07.25	Agios Georgios	Kythnos. Serifos. Sifnos. Milos.
07.35	Blue Star Ithaki	Syros. Tinos. Mykonos.
07.35	Speedrunner III	Syros. Tinos. Mykonos.
09.00	Blue Star 1/2	Patmos. Leros. Kos. Rhodes.
12.30	Nissos Chios	Chios. Lesbos (Mytilini).
14.30	Adamantis Korais	Kythnos. Serifos. Sifnos. Milos. Kimolos.
16.30	Highspeed 5	Serifos. Sifnos. Milos.
16.55	Highspeed 4	Paros. Naxos.
17.05	Speedrunner III	Paros.
17.30	Blue Star Paros	Syros. Paros. Naxos. Donoussa. Amorgos (Egiali). Astipalea.
17.30	Speedrunner IV	Serifos. Sifnos. Kimolos. Folegandros.
17.45	Highspeed 6	Syros. Mykonos. Tinos.
19.00	European Express	Chios. Lesbos (Mytilini).
21.00	Elyros/Lato	Crete (Chania).
21.30	Superfast XII	Crete (Iraklion).
21.30	Nissos Mykonos	Syros. Mykonos. Ikaria (Agios Kyrikos). Fourni. Samos (Karlovassi). Samos (Vathi).
22.00	Festos Palace/ Knossos Palace	Crete (Iraklion).
23.55	Blue Star 1/2	Santorini. Kos. Rhodes.

⑤

07.00	Highspeed 6	Ios. Santorini.
07.00	SuperJet	Milos. Folegandros. Santorini. Naxos. Koufonissia. Amorgos (Katapola).
07.05	Speedrunner IV	Serifos. Sifnos. Milos.
07.15	Highspeed 4	Paros. Naxos.

Piraeus:

07.25	*Blue Star Naxos*	Paros. Naxos. Santorini.
07.25	*Highspeed 5*	Syros. Tinos. Mykonos.
07.25	*Agios Georgios*	Serifos. Sifnos. Folegandros.
		Sikinos. Ios. Santorini.
07.35	*Blue Star Ithaki*	Syros. Tinos. Mykonos.
07.35	*Speedrunner III*	Syros. Tinos. Mykonos.
07.55	*Adamantis Korais*	Kythnos. Serifos. Sifnos. Milos. Kimolos.
12.30	*Nissos Chios*	Chios. Lesbos (Mytilini).
15.00	*Diagoras*	Naxos. Santorini. Astipalea. Kalimnos. Kos.
		Nissiros. Tilos. Symi. Rhodes. Kastelorizo.
16.30	*Highspeed 5*	Serifos. Sifnos. Milos.
16.55	*Highspeed 4*	Paros. Naxos.
17.05	*Speedrunner III*	Paros.
17.30	*Blue Star Paros*	Paros. Naxos. Iraklia. Schinoussa. Koufonissia. Amorgos (Katapola).
17.30	*Speedrunner IV*	Serifos. Sifnos. Milos.
17.45	*Highspeed 6*	Syros. Mykonos. Tinos.
18.00	*Vitsentzos Kornaros*	Monemvassia. Kithera. Antikithera. Crete (Kasteli).
19.00	*Blue Star 1/2*	Syros. Kos. Rhodes.
19.00	*Mytilene*	Chios. Lesbos (Mytilini).
21.00	*Blue Star Ithaki*	Paros.
21.00	*Elyros/Lato*	Crete (Chania).
21.30	*Superfast XII*	Crete (Iraklion).
21.30	*Nissos Mykonos*	Syros. Mykonos. Ikaria (Evdilos). Samos (Karlovassi). Samos (Vathi).
22.30	*Festos Palace/*	
	Knossos Palace	Crete (Iraklion).
23.59	*Prevelis*	Milos. Santorini. Anafi. Crete (Iraklion). Crete (Sitia).
		Kassos. Karpathos. Rhodes.

ⓖ

07.00	*Highspeed 6*	Ios. Santorini.
07.00	*SuperJet*	Milos. Folegandros. Santorini. Naxos. Koufonissia. Amorgos (Katapola).
07.05	*Speedrunner IV*	Serifos. Sifnos. Milos.
07.15	*Highspeed 4*	Paros. Naxos.
07.25	*Blue Star Naxos*	Paros. Naxos. Santorini.
07.25	*Highspeed 5*	Syros. Tinos. Mykonos.
07.25	*Agios Georgios*	Kythnos. Serifos. Sifnos. Milos.
08.30	*Adamantis Korais*	Kythnos. Serifos. Sifnos. Milos.
09.00	*Blue Star 1/2*	Santorini. Kos. Rhodes.
12.30	*Nissos Chios*	Chios. Lesbos (Mytilini).
16.30	*Highspeed 5*	Serifos. Sifnos. Milos.
16.55	*Highspeed 4*	Paros. Naxos.
17.05	*Speedrunner III*	Paros.
17.30	*Blue Star Paros*	Paros. Naxos. Donoussa. Amorgos (Egiali). Astipalea.
17.30	*Speedrunner IV*	Serifos. Sifnos. Milos.
17.45	*Highspeed 6*	Syros. Mykonos. Tinos.
21.00	*Elyros/Lato*	Crete (Chania).
21.30	*Superfast XII*	Crete (Iraklion).
21.30	*Nissos Mykonos*	Syros. Mykonos. Ikaria (Agios Kyrikos). Fourni.
		Samos (Karlovassi). Samos (Vathi).
22.00	*Festos Palace/*	
	Knossos Palace	Crete (Iraklion).
23.55	*Blue Star 1/2*	Amorgos (Katapola). Patmos. Leros. Kos. Rhodes.

ⓖ

07.00	*Highspeed 6*	Ios. Santorini.
07.00	*SuperJet*	Milos. Folegandros. Santorini. Naxos. Koufonissia.
		Amorgos (Katapola).
07.05	*Speedrunner IV*	Serifos. Sifnos. Milos.
07.15	*Highspeed 4*	Paros. Naxos.
07.25	*Blue Star Naxos*	Paros. Naxos. Santorini.
07.25	*Highspeed 5*	Syros. Tinos. Mykonos.
07.35	*Blue Star Ithaki*	Syros. Tinos. Mykonos.
07.35	*Speedrunner III*	Syros. Tinos. Mykonos.
07.35	*Agios Georgios*	Kythnos. Serifos. Sifnos. Milos. Kimolos.
07.55	*Adamantis Korais*	Sifnos. Folegandros. Kimolos.
12.30	*Nissos Chios*	Chios. Lesbos (Mytilini).
16.30	*Highspeed 5*	Serifos. Sifnos. Milos.

16.55	*Highspeed 4*	Paros. Naxos.
17.05	*Speedrunner III*	Paros.
17.30	*Blue Star Paros*	Syros. Paros. Naxos. Iraklia. Schinoussa. Koufonissia. Amorgos (Katapola).
17.30	*Speedrunner IV*	Serifos. Sifnos. Milos.
17.45	*Highspeed 6*	Syros. Mykonos. Tinos.
19.00	*Blue Star 1/2*	Santorini. Kos. Rhodes.
19.00	*European Express*	Chios. Lesbos (Mytilini).
21.00	*Elyros/Lato*	Crete (Chania).
21.30	*Superfast XII*	Crete (Iraklion).
22.00	*Festos Palace/*	
	Knossos Palace	Crete (Iraklion).

○
10.00	*Elyros/Lato*	Crete (Chania).
12.00	*Festos Palace/*	
	Knossos Palace	Crete (Iraklion).
21.00	*Kriti I/Kriti II*	Crete (Iraklion).

2. Saronic Gulf

(i). Regular Ferries & Catamarans

Ⓓ typical:
06.30	*Ioannis II*	Aegina (Souvala).
07.30	*Nefeli*	Aegina. Methana. Poros.
07.45	*Apollon Hellas*	Aegina. Methana. Poros. Hydra. Spetses.
		Porto Helio.
08.00	*Phivos*	Aegina. Poros.
08.00	*Saron Cat*	Aegina (Agia Marina).
08.00	*Eurofast 1*	Poros. Hydra. Spetses.
08.00	*Odysseas II*	Aegina. Angistri.
08.00	*Georgios 2*	Aegina. Methana. Poros. Spetses.
		Porto Helio.
08.30	*Flying Cat 1*	Poros. Hydra. Spetses. Porto Helio.
09.15	*Ioannis II*	Aegina (Souvala). Aegina.
10.30	*Poseidon Hellas*	Aegina. Methana. Poros.
13.20	*Eurofast 1*	Poros. Hydra. Spetses.
13.30	*Odysseas II*	Aegina. Angistri.
14.00	*Ydra Cat*	Aegina (Agia Marina).
14.00	*Ioannis II*	Aegina (Souvala). Aegina.
14.15	*Nefeli*	Aegina. Methana. Poros.
15.00	*Phivos*	Aegina. Poros.
15.30	*Ioannis II*	Aegina (Souvala).
18.00	*Ioannis II*	Aegina.
18.30	*Odysseas II*	Aegina. Angistri.
18.45	*Eurofast 1*	Hydra. Spetses.
18.45	*Eftichia*	Aegina. Methana. Poros. Hydra.
19.00	*Nefeli*	Aegina (Agia Marina).
20.00	*Poseidon Hellas*	Aegina.
20.30	*Flying Cat 1*	Poros. Hydra. Spetses. Porto Helio.
20.30	*Ioannis II*	Aegina.

(ii). Hydrofoils

Ⓓ Ⓗ
| 06.00–19.00 | | Aegina (Town). |
| 06.00–20.00 | | Aegina (Souvala). Aegina (Agia Marina). |

Ⓓ
x 12		Poros. Hydra. Ermioni. Spetses.
08.25		Hydra. Spetses. Porto Helio.
09.00		Aegina (Town). Methana. Poros. Hydra. Ermioni. Spetses. Porto Helio.
14.30		Hydra. Spetses. Porto Helio.
16.00		Aegina (Town). Methana. Poros. Hydra. Ermioni. Spetses.
		Porto Helio. Tolo.

Poros

Argo-Saronic p. 558

Ⓓ ev 20 min:
06.00–22.00	*Elpis I*	Galatas.

Ⓓ typical:
09.10	*Eurofast 1*	Hydra. Spetses.
10.00	*Flying Cat 1*	Piraeus.
10.30	*Poseidon Hellas*	Methana. Aegina. Piraeus.
10.30	*Ioannis II*	Hydra. Ermioni.
10.30	*Ag. Nektarios*	
	Aiginae	Hydra. Ermioni. Spetses.
10.45	*Nefeli*	Methana. Aegina. Piraeus.
10.50	*Apollon Hellas*	Methana. Aegina. Piraeus.
10.50	*Georgios 2*	Spetses. Porto Helio.
11.00	*Apollon Hellas*	Hydra. Spetses. Porto Helio.
11.50	*Eurofast 1*	Piraeus.
14.00	*Phivos*	Aegina. Piraeus.
14.30	*Eurofast 1*	Hydra. Spetses.
16.00	*Apollon Hellas*	Methana. Aegina. Piraeus.
17.00	*Eurofast 1*	Piraeus.
17.00	*Georgios 2*	Methana. Aegina. Piraeus.
17.20	*Poseidon Hellas*	Methana. Aegina. Piraeus. Aegina. Piraeus.
19.00	*Nefeli*	Methana. Aegina. Piraeus.

〜 *Flying Dolphins* include:

Ⓓ
x 6	Hydra.
x 7	Piraeus.
x 4	Spetses.

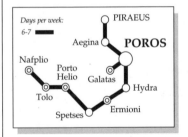

Days per week:
6-7 ▬▬

PIRAEUS
Aegina
POROS
Nafplio
Porto Helio
Galatas
Hydra
Tolo
Ermioni
Spetses

Port Said

Egypt p. 637

○
20.00	*Salamis Star*	Haifa. Limassol. Rhodes. Santorini. Piraeus.

Porto Helio

Argo-Saronic p. 561

Ⓓ
13.30	*Apollon Hellas*	Spetses. Hydra. Poros. Methana. Aegina. Piraeus.

〜 *Flying Dolphins* include:

Ⓓ x 10		Hydra. Spetses. Piraeus.

Princes' Islands

Turkey p. 624

Ⓓ x 6
06.45–21.00	Local	İstanbul.
00.00–00.00	Local	Yalova.

Psara

Eastern Line p. 470

①
07.00	*Nissos Thira*	Chios.
22.15	*Panagia Thalassini*	Chios (Mesta).

②
06.00	*Nissos Thira*	Chios.
16.00	*Panagia Thalassini*	Lavrio.

③
06.00	*Nissos Thira*	Chios.
22.15	*Panagia Thalassini*	Chios (Mesta).

④
07.00	*Nissos Thira*	Chios.
16.00	*Panagia Thalassini*	Lavrio.

⑤
07.00	*Nissos Thira*	Chios.
22.15	*Panagia Thalassini*	Chios (Mesta).

⑥
07.00	*Nissos Thira*	Chios.

⑦
07.00	*Nissos Thira*	Chios (Mesta).
16.00	*Panagia Thalassini*	Lavrio.
17.30	*Nissos Thira*	Chios.

○
00.00	*Panagia Soumela*	Agios Efstratios. Limnos. Kavala.

Rafina

Athens
& Piraeus
p. 122

Weekly updated
timetable for **Rafina** at
greekislandhopping.com

Ⓓ

07.30	Penelope A	Andros. Tinos. Mykonos.
07.30	SeaJet 2	Tinos. Mykonos. Paros.
08.30	Evia Star	Evia (Marmari).

①

07.30	Flying Cat 3	Tinos. Mykonos. Naxos. Ios. Santorini.
07.50	Superferry II	Andros. Tinos. Mykonos.
08.00	Artemisia	Evia (Karystos).
12.00	Evia Star	Evia (Marmari).
14.15	Artemisia	Evia (Karystos).
15.00	SeaJet 2	Tinos. Mykonos. Paros.
15.30	Evia Star	Evia (Marmari).
17.30	Theologos P	Andros. Tinos. Mykonos.
18.30	Artemisia	Evia (Karystos).
19.00	Evia Star	Evia (Marmari).
19.00	Penelope A	Andros.
19.20	Superferry II	Andros.

②

07.30	Flying Cat 3	Tinos. Mykonos. Naxos. Ios. Santorini.
07.50	Superferry II	Andros. Tinos. Mykonos. Naxos.
08.00	Artemisia	Evia (Karystos).
12.00	Evia Star	Evia (Marmari).

RAFINA

Kavala
Limnos
Ag. Efstratios
Evia (Marmari)
Evia (Karystos)
Syros
Andros
Paros
Tinos
Naxos
Mykonos
Little Cyclades
Amorgos

Days per week:
6-7 ▬▬▬
2-3 ═══

14.15 Artemisia — Evia (Karystos).
15.00 SeaJet 2 — Tinos. Mykonos. Paros.
15.30 Evia Star — Evia (Marmari).
17.30 Theologos P — Andros. Tinos. Mykonos.
18.30 Artemisia — Evia (Karystos).
19.00 Evia Star — Evia (Marmari).
19.00 Penelope A — Andros.

③

07.30	Flying Cat 3	Tinos. Mykonos. Naxos. Ios. Santorini.
07.50	Superferry II	Andros. Tinos. Mykonos. Naxos.
08.00	Artemisia	Evia (Karystos).
12.00	Evia Star	Evia (Marmari).
14.15	Artemisia	Evia (Karystos).
15.00	SeaJet 2	Tinos. Mykonos. Paros.
15.30	Evia Star	Evia (Marmari).
17.30	Theologos P	Andros. Tinos. Mykonos.
18.30	Artemisia	Evia (Karystos).
19.00	Evia Star	Evia (Marmari).

④

07.30	Flying Cat 3	Tinos. Mykonos. Naxos. Ios. Santorini.
07.50	Superferry II	Andros. Tinos. Mykonos. Naxos.
08.00	Artemisia	Evia (Karystos).
12.00	Evia Star	Evia (Marmari).
14.15	Artemisia	Evia (Karystos).
15.00	SeaJet 2	Tinos. Mykonos. Paros.
15.30	Evia Star	Evia (Marmari).
17.30	Theologos P	Andros. Tinos. Mykonos.
18.30	Artemisia	Evia (Karystos).
19.00	Evia Star	Evia (Marmari).
19.00	Penelope A	Andros.

⑤

07.05	Theologos P	Andros. Tinos. Mykonos.
07.30	Flying Cat 3	Tinos. Mykonos.
07.50	Superferry II	Andros. Tinos.
08.00	Artemisia	Evia (Karystos).
12.00	Artemisia	Evia (Marmari).
14.00	Evia Star	Evia (Marmari).
14.15	Artemisia	Evia (Karystos).
15.00	SeaJet 2	Tinos. Mykonos.
16.30	Flying Cat 3	Tinos. Mykonos.
17.00	Evia Star	Evia (Marmari).
17.00	Superferry II	Andros. Tinos. Mykonos.
18.00	Theologos P	Andros. Tinos. Mykonos.
19.00	Artemisia	Evia (Karystos).
19.00	Penelope A	Andros.
20.15	SeaJet 2	Tinos. Mykonos.
20.30	Evia Star	Evia (Marmari).

⑥

07.30	Flying Cat 3	Tinos. Mykonos. Naxos. Ios. Santorini.
07.50	Superferry II	Andros. Tinos. Mykonos. Naxos.
08.00	Artemisia	Evia (Marmari).
11.00	Artemisia	Evia (Karystos).

12.00	*Evia Star*	Evia (Marmari).
15.00	*SeaJet 2*	Tinos. Mykonos. Paros.
15.30	*Evia Star*	Evia (Marmari).
15.30	*Artemisia*	Evia (Marmari).
17.00	*Artemisia*	Evia (Marmari).
17.30	*Theologos P*	Andros. Tinos. Mykonos.
19.00	*Evia Star*	Evia (Marmari).
20.00	*Artemisia*	Evia (Karystos).
⑦		
07.30	*Flying Cat 3*	Tinos. Mykonos.
07.50	*Superferry II*	Andros. Tinos. Mykonos.
08.00	*Artemisia*	Evia (Karystos).
14.15	*Artemisia*	Evia (Karystos).
14.45	*SeaJet 2*	Mykonos. Tinos.
15.30	*Evia Star*	Evia (Marmari).
16.30	*Flying Cat 3*	Tinos. Mykonos.
17.30	*Theologos P*	Andros.
18.00	*Artemisia*	Evia (Karystos).
19.00	*Evia Star*	Evia (Marmari).
19.00	*Penelope A*	Andros.
19.20	*Superferry II*	Andros.
19.35	*SeaJet 2*	Mykonos. Tinos.
22.00	*Evia Star*	Evia (Marmari).
22.15	*Artemisia*	Evia (Karystos).
22.45	*Theologos P*	Tinos. Mykonos.

Rhodes

Dodecanese p. 419

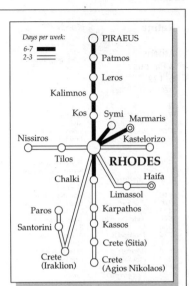

⑩		
08.00	Hydrofoil	Marmaris.
08.00	Hydrofoil	Kos.
17.00	Hydrofoil	Kos.
①		
08.00	*Dodekanisos Express*	Kastelorizo.
08.30	*Dodekanisos Pride*	Symi. Kos. Kalimnos. Leros (Agia Marina). Lipsi. Patmos.
09.00	*Symi II*	Symi (Panormitis). Symi.
10.00	*Proteus*	Symi. Symi (Panormitis).
17.00	*Blue Star 1/2*	Kos. Santorini. Piraeus.
17.00	*Dodekanisos Express*	Symi. Kos. Kalimnos.
②		
08.30	*Dodekanisos Pride*	Symi. Kos. Kalimnos. Leros (Agia Marina). Lipsi. Patmos.
09.00	*Proteus*	Symi (Panormitis). Symi.
09.00	*Symi II*	Symi (Panormitis). Symi.
15.00	*Diagoras*	Symi. Kos. Kalimnos. Leros. Lipsi. Patmos. Piraeus.
15.00	*Dodekanisos Express*	Symi. Kos. Kalimnos.

15.30	*Prevelis*	Chalki. Karpathos. Kassos. Crete (Sitia). Crete (Iraklion). Santorini. Milos. Piraeus.
17.00	*Blue Star 1/2*	Kos. Santorini. Syros. Piraeus.
18.30	*SeaStar*	Tilos.
③		
08.30	*Dodekanisos Pride*	Kos. Kalimnos. Leros (Agia Marina). Lipsi. Patmos.
09.00	*Symi II*	Symi (Panormitis). Symi.
10.00	*Proteus*	Symi. Symi (Panormitis).
10.30	*Dodekanisos Express*	Symi.
17.00	*Blue Star 1/2*	Kos. Leros. Patmos. Piraeus.
17.30	*Dodekanisos Express*	Symi.
18.30	*SeaStar*	Tilos.
④		
08.30	*Dodekanisos Pride*	Symi. Kos. Kalimnos. Leros (Agia Marina). Lipsi. Patmos.
09.00	*Symi II*	Symi (Panormitis). Symi.
09.10	*Dodekanisos Express*	Symi (Panormitis). Symi.
10.00	*Proteus*	Symi. Symi (Panormitis).
10.15	*Diagoras*	Kastelorizo.
10.30	*Blue Star 1/2*	Kos. Piraeus.

17.30	Dodekanisos Express	Symi.
19.00	Prevelis	Karpathos. Kassos.
		Crete (Sitia).
		Crete (Iraklion).
		Santorini. Milos.
		Piraeus.
20.00	Diagoras	Tilos. Nissiros. Kos.
		Kalimnos. Piraeus.
23.59	Blue Star 1/2	Kos. Leros. Patmos.
		Piraeus.

⑤

08.30	Dodekanisos Pride	Symi. Kos. Kalimnos.
		Leros (Agia Marina).
		Lipsi. Patmos.
09.00	Dodekanisos Express	Chalki. Tilos.
		Nissiros. Kos.
09.00	Symi II	Symi (Panormitis).
		Symi.
17.00	Blue Star 1/2	Kos. Santorini.
		Piraeus.
17.30	Dodekanisos Express	Symi.
18.30	SeaStar	Tilos.
18.30	Symi II	Symi.

⑥

08.30	Dodekanisos Pride	Kos. Kalimnos.
		Leros (Agia Marina).
		Lipsi. Agathonisi.
09.00	Dodekanisos Express	Symi.
		Turkey (Datça).
09.00	Symi II	Symi (Panormitis).
		Symi.
09.30	Blue Star 1/2	Kos. Piraeus.
10.00	Proteus	Symi.
		Symi (Panormitis).
13.25	Diagoras	Kastelorizo.
17.30	Dodekanisos Express	Symi.
23.00	Diagoras	Symi. Tilos. Nissiros.
		Kos. Kalimnos.
		Astipalea. Naxos.
		Paros. Piraeus.
23.59	Blue Star 1/2	Kos. Santorini.
		Piraeus.

⑦

08.00	Prevelis	Chalki.
		Karpathos (Diafani).
		Karpathos. Kassos.
		Anafi. Santorini.
		Piraeus.
08.30	Dodekanisos Pride	Symi. Kos. Kalimnos.
		Leros (Agia Marina).
		Lipsi. Patmos.
09.00	Dodekanisos Express	Chalki. Tilos.
		Nissiros. Kos.
09.00	Proteus	Symi (Panormitis).
		Symi.
09.00	Symi II	Symi (Panormitis).
		Symi.
17.00	Blue Star 1/2	Kos. Leros. Patmos.
		Amorgos (Katapola).
		Piraeus.
17.30	SeaStar	Tilos.
18.00	Proteus	Symi.
19.15	Dodekanisos Express	Symi.

○

00.00	Proteus	Kastelorizo.
08.45	SeaStar	Tilos. Nissiros.

Rhodes
(Kamiros Skala)

Dodecanese
p. 432

Ⓓ ex ⑦

14.30	Chalki/Nikos Express	Chalki.

③ ⑦

09.30	Chalki/Nikos Express	Chalki.

Salamina / Salamis
(Paloukia)

Athens & Piraeus
p. 123

Ⓓ Ⓗ

06.30–21.30	Taxi Boat	Piraeus.

Samos
(Karlovassi)

Eastern Line
p. 473

①

13.00	Samos Sun	Thimena.
		Fourni.

②

06.10	Nissos Mykonos	Samos (Vathi).
10.00	Nissos Mykonos	Fourni.
		Ikaria (Agios Kyrikos).
		Mykonos. Syros.
		Piraeus.
14.20	Panagia Theotokosos	Fourni (Chrisomilia).

③

06.45	Nissos Mykonos	Samos (Vathi).
10.00	Nissos Mykonos	Ikaria (Evdilos).
		Mykonos.
		Syros.
		Piraeus.
13.00	Samos Sun	Thimena.
		Fourni.
14.20	Panagia Theotokosos	Fourni (Chrisomilia).

④

06.10	Nissos Mykonos	Samos (Vathi).
10.00	Nissos Mykonos	Fourni.
		Ikaria (Agios Kyrikos).
		Mykonos.
		Syros.
		Piraeus.

14.50	*Taxiarchis*	Ikaria (Agios Kyrikos).
18.40	*Taxiarchis*	Chios.
		Lesbos (Mytilini).

Ⓢ
06.45	*Nissos Mykonos*	Samos (Vathi).
10.00	*Nissos Mykonos*	Ikaria (Evdilos).
		Mykonos. Syros.
		Piraeus.
13.00	*Samos Sun*	Thimena. Fourni.

⑥
06.10	*Nissos Mykonos*	Samos (Vathi).
10.00	*Nissos Mykonos*	Ikaria (Evdilos).
		Mykonos. Syros.
		Piraeus.

⑦
06.45	*Nissos Mykonos*	Samos (Vathi).
14.10	*Nissos Mykonos*	Fourni.
		Ikaria (Agios Kyrikos).
		Ikaria (Evdilos).
		Mykonos. Syros.
		Piraeus.

○
13.00	*Samos Spirit*	Ikaria (Agios Kyrikos).
		Thimena. Fourni.

○ * Not operating in 2011:

13.45	*Samothraki*	Ikaria (Agios Kyrikos).
17.00	*Samothraki*	Chios.
		Lesbos (Mytilini).
		Limnos. Kavala.

Samos (Pithagorio)

Eastern Line
p. 473

①
13.20	*Nissos Kalimnos*	Samos (Pithagorio).

16.15	*Nissos Kalimnos*	Agathonisi. Arki.
		Patmos. Lipsi.
		Leros.
		Kalimnos.

③
14.30	*Nissos Kalimnos*	Agathonisi. Arki.
		Patmos.
		Lipsi. Leros.
		Kalimnos.

⑤
13.20	*Nissos Kalimnos*	Samos (Pithagorio).
16.15	*Nissos Kalimnos*	Agathonisi. Arki.
		Patmos. Lipsi.
		Leros.
		Kalimnos.

⑦
14.30	*Nissos Kalimnos*	Agathonisi. Arki.
		Patmos. Lipsi.
		Leros.
		Kalimnos.

○ * Not operating in 2011:

07.50	Hydrofoil	Patmos.
		Leros (Agia Marina).
		Kalimnos. Kos.
07.50	Hydrofoil	Fourni.
		Ikaria (Agios Kyrikos).
		Patmos. Lipsi.
		Leros (Agia Marina).
		Kalimnos. Kos.
14.15	Hydrofoil	Patmos. Lipsi.
		Leros (Agia Marina).
		Kalimnos. Kos.

Samos (Vathi)

Eastern Line
p. 472

Ⓓ
08.00	*Kapetan Giorgis*	Kuşadası.
17.00	*Fari Kaptain/Sultan I*	Kuşadası.

②
09.00	*Nissos Mykonos*	Samos (Karlovassi).
		Fourni.
		Ikaria (Agios Kyrikos).
		Mykonos.
		Syros.
		Piraeus.
17.35	*Taxiarchis*	Chios.
		Lesbos (Mytilini).

③
09.00	*Nissos Mykonos*	Samos (Karlovassi).
		Ikaria (Evdilos).
		Mykonos.
		Syros.
		Piraeus.

08.00	*Theofilos*	Chios.
		Lesbos (Mytilini).
		Limnos.
		Thessalonika.
15.30	*Samothraki*	Chios.
		Lesbos (Mytilini).
		Limnos.
		Thessalonika.

Samothrace

Northern Aegean
p. 502

④

09.00	*Nissos Mykonos*	Samos (Karlovassi).
		Fourni.
		Ikaria (Agios Kyrikos).
		Mykonos. Syros.
		Piraeus.

⑤

09.00	*Nissos Mykonos*	Samos (Karlovassi).
		Ikaria (Evdilos).
		Mykonos.
		Syros.
		Piraeus.

⑥

09.00	*Nissos Mykonos*	Samos (Karlovassi).
		Ikaria (Evdilos).
		Mykonos.
		Syros.
		Piraeus.

⑦

07.00	*Taxiarchis*	Chios.
		Lesbos (Mytilini).
13.00	*Nissos Mykonos*	Samos (Karlovassi).
		Fourni.
		Ikaria (Agios Kyrikos).
		Ikaria (Evdilos).
		Mykonos.
		Syros. Piraeus.

○ * Not operating in 2011:

07.00	Hydrofoil	Samos (Pithagorio).
		Agathonisi.
		Patmos.
		Lipsi.
		Leros (Agia Marina).
		Kalimnos.
		Kos.
07.00	Hydrofoil	Samos (Pithagorio).
		Fourni.
		Ikaria (Agios Kyrikos).
		Patmos.
		Lipsi.
		Leros (Agia Marina).
		Kalimnos.
		Kos.
02.25	*Diagoras*	Chios. Lesbos (Sigri).
		Thessalonika.

①

17.00	*Saos II*	Alexandroupolis.

②

17.00	*Saos II*	Alexandroupolis.

③

17.00	*Saos II*	Alexandroupolis.

④

07.30	*Saos II*	Alexandroupolis.

⑤

13.15	*Saos II*	Alexandroupolis.

⑥

09.00	*Saos II*	Alexandroupolis.

⑦

11.30	*Saos II*	Alexandroupolis.
18.00	*Saos II*	Alexandroupolis.

○

08.30	Hydrofoil	Alexandroupolis.
14.15	Hydrofoil	Limnos.
18.00	Hydrofoil	Alexandroupolis.

○ * Not operating in 2011:

01.45	*Nona Mairy*	Limnos.
		Agios Efstratios.
		Lavrio.
09.30	*Panagia Soumela*	Kavala.
16.35	*Nona Mairy*	Kavala.
18.45	*Panagia Soumela*	Limnos.
		Agios Efstratios.
		Lavrio.

Santorini / Thira (Athinios)

Cyclades Central
p. 185

Ⓓ		
11.40	*Highspeed 6*	Ios. Piraeus.
11.40	*SuperJet*	Naxos. Koufonissia. Amorgos (Katapola).
12.00	*Flying Cat 4*	Paros. Mykonos.
15.30	*Blue Star Naxos*	Naxos. Paros. Piraeus.
16.45	*SuperJet*	Folegandros. Milos. Piraeus.
17.55	*Flying Cat 4*	Crete (Iraklion).

①		
00.45	*Blue Star 1/2*	Kos. Rhodes.
16.20	*Flying Cat 3*	Ios. Naxos. Mykonos. Tinos. Rafina.
17.30	*Artemis*	Sikinos. Folegandros. Kimolos. Milos.
18.15	*MegaJet*	Crete (Iraklion).
21.15	*Prevelis*	Crete (Iraklion). Crete (Sitia). Kassos. Karpathos. Chalki. Rhodes.

②		
02.00	*Blue Star 1/2*	Piraeus.
02.10	*Blue Star 1/2*	Kos. Rhodes.
06.00	*Vitsentzos Kornaros*	Anafi.
12.25	*Artemis*	Ios. Naxos. Syros.
16.20	*Flying Cat 3*	Ios. Naxos. Mykonos. Tinos. Rafina.
18.30	*Vitsentzos Kornaros*	Ios. Sikinos. Folegandros. Milos. Santorini.
20.25	*Aeolos Kenteris II*	Anafi.

③		
01.05	*Blue Star 1/2*	Syros. Piraeus.
08.15	*Aeolos Kenteris II*	Thirasia. Ios. Sikinos. Folegandros. Naxos. Paros. Syros.
09.10	*Prevelis*	Milos. Piraeus.
16.20	*Flying Cat 3*	Ios. Naxos. Mykonos. Tinos. Rafina.
18.15	*MegaJet*	Crete (Iraklion).
18.30	*Agios Georgios*	Ios. Sikinos. Folegandros. Sifnos. Piraeus.
21.05	*Artemis*	Anafi.
22.00	*Diagoras*	Karpathos. Kos. Nissiros. Tilos. Rhodes. Kastelorizo.

④		
04.05	*Prevelis*	Anafi. Kassos. Karpathos. Karpathos (Diafani). Chalki. Rhodes.

08.50	*Artemis*	Thirasia. Ios. Sikinos. Folegandros. Naxos. Paros. Syros.
16.20	*Flying Cat 3*	Ios. Naxos. Mykonos. Tinos. Rafina.
18.15	*MegaJet*	Crete (Iraklion).

⑤		
05.00	*Blue Star 1/2*	Kos. Rhodes.
12.40	*Prevelis*	Milos. Piraeus.
18.15	*MegaJet*	Crete (Iraklion).
18.30	*Agios Georgios*	Ios. Sikinos. Folegandros. Kimolos. Sifnos. Piraeus.
23.40	*Diagoras*	Astipalea. Kalimnos. Kos. Nissiros. Tilos. Symi. Rhodes. Kastelorizo.

⑥		
00.40	*Blue Star 1/2*	Piraeus.
09.15	*Prevelis*	Anafi. Crete (Iraklion). Crete (Sitia). Kassos. Karpathos. Rhodes.
14.00	*Blue Star 1/2*	Kos. Rhodes.
16.20	*Flying Cat 3*	Ios. Naxos. Mykonos. Tinos. Rafina.
20.25	*Aeolos Kenteris II*	Anafi.

⑦		
07.40	*Blue Star 1/2*	Piraeus.
08.25	*Aeolos Kenteris II*	Thirasia. Ios. Sikinos. Folegandros. Naxos. Paros. Mykonos. Syros.

Days per week:
6-7
4-5
2-3

12.00	*Express Skopelitis*	Ios. Koufonissia.
		Amorgos (Katapola).
18.15	*MegaJet*	Crete (Iraklion).
21.55	*Prevelis*	Piraeus.

○ * Not operating in 2011:

00.00	*Cyclades Express*	Crete (Iraklion).
00.00	*Speedrunner II*	Crete (Iraklion).
00.00	*Arsinoe*	Anafi.
00.00	*Theoskepasti*	Santorini (Old Port).
		Nea Kameni.
		Thirasia (Korfos).
		Thirasia.
		Santorini (Oia).
00.00	Hydrofoil	Ios.
		Naxos.
00.00	Ferry	Ios. Naxos.
		Paros.
		Mykonos.
		Tinos. Syros.
		Alonissos.
		Skiathos.
		Thessalonika.
00.00	Ferry	Crete (Iraklion).

Santorini (Fira / Old Port)

Cyclades Central p. 183

Ⓓ
09.15	Tour Boat	Nea Kameni.
10.30	*Nissos Thirassia*	Nea Kameni.
		Thirasia (Korfos).
		Thirasia (Riva).
		Santorini (Oia).
15.20	Tour Boat	Nea Kameni.
17.00	*Nissos Thirassia*	Santorini.

Schinoussa

Cyclades East   p. 326

①
01.10	*Blue Star Paros*	Koufonissia.
		Amorgos (Katapola).
07.40	*Blue Star Paros*	Iraklia. Naxos. Paros.
		Piraeus.
10.30	*Express Skopelitis*	Iraklia. Naxos.
14.05	*Aeolos Kenteris II*	Iraklia. Naxos. Paros.
		Syros.
16.00	*Express Skopelitis*	Koufonissia.
		Donoussa.
		Amorgos (Egiali).
		Amorgos (Katapola).

②
09.30	*Express Skopelitis*	Iraklia. Naxos.
15.30	*Express Skopelitis*	Koufonissia.
		Amorgos (Katapola).

③
01.10	*Blue Star Paros*	Koufonissia.
		Amorgos (Katapola).
07.40	*Blue Star Paros*	Iraklia. Naxos. Paros.
		Piraeus.
10.30	*Express Skopelitis*	Iraklia.
		Naxos.
16.00	*Express Skopelitis*	Koufonissia.
		Donoussa.
		Amorgos (Egiali).
		Amorgos (Katapola).

④
09.30	*Express Skopelitis*	Iraklia. Naxos.
15.30	*Express Skopelitis*	Koufonissia.
		Amorgos (Katapola).

⑤
10.30	*Express Skopelitis*	Iraklia. Naxos.
12.00	*Artemis*	Koufonissia.
		Amorgos (Katapola).
		Amorgos (Egiali).
		Donoussa.
		Naxos.
		Paros. Syros.
16.00	*Express Skopelitis*	Koufonissia.
		Donoussa.
		Amorgos (Egiali).
		Amorgos (Katapola).

⑥
00.25	*Blue Star Paros*	Koufonissia.
		Amorgos (Katapola).
07.40	*Blue Star Paros*	Iraklia. Naxos.
		Paros. Piraeus.
10.30	*Express Skopelitis*	Iraklia. Naxos.
16.00	*Express Skopelitis*	Koufonissia.
		Donoussa.
		Amorgos (Egiali).
		Amorgos (Katapola).

⑦
15.40	*Artemis*	Iraklia. Naxos.
		Paros. Syros.

Serifos

Cyclades West
p. 284

①
09.35	*Speedrunner IV*	Sifnos. Milos.
12.05	*Agios Georgios*	Sifnos. Milos.
13.05	*Speedrunner IV*	Piraeus.
17.55	*Agios Georgios*	Kythnos. Piraeus.
18.45	*Highspeed 5*	Sifnos. Milos.
19.30	*Adamantis Korais*	Sifnos. Milos. Kimolos. Folegandros. Ios.
20.05	*Speedrunner IV*	Sifnos. Kimolos. Folegandros.
22.20	*Highspeed 5*	Piraeus.

②
09.35	*Speedrunner IV*	Sifnos. Milos.
12.05	*Agios Georgios*	Sifnos. Kimolos. Milos.
12.15	*Aqua Jewel*	Sifnos. Kimolos. Milos.
13.05	*Speedrunner IV*	Piraeus.
16.40	*Adamantis Korais*	Kythnos. Piraeus.
17.55	*Agios Georgios*	Kythnos. Piraeus.
18.45	*Highspeed 5*	Sifnos. Milos.
19.15	*Aqua Jewel*	Paros. Syros.
22.20	*Highspeed 5*	Piraeus.

③
09.35	*Speedrunner IV*	Sifnos. Milos.
11.25	*Agios Georgios*	Sifnos. Folegandros. Sikinos. Ios. Santorini.
12.55	*Adamantis Korais*	Sifnos. Milos. Kimolos.
13.05	*Speedrunner IV*	Piraeus.
14.10	*Aqua Jewel*	Sifnos. Kimolos. Milos.
18.40	*Adamantis Korais*	Kythnos. Piraeus.
20.05	*Speedrunner IV*	Sifnos. Milos. Piraeus.
20.15	*Aqua Jewel*	Syros.

④
09.35	*Speedrunner IV*	Sifnos. Milos.
12.05	*Agios Georgios*	Sifnos. Milos.
13.05	*Speedrunner IV*	Piraeus.
17.55	*Agios Georgios*	Kythnos. Piraeus.
18.45	*Highspeed 5*	Sifnos. Milos.
19.30	*Adamantis Korais*	Sifnos. Milos. Kimolos.

④ (continued)
20.05	*Speedrunner IV*	Sifnos. Kimolos. Folegandros.
22.20	*Highspeed 5*	Piraeus.

⑤
01.00	*Adamantis Korais*	Piraeus.
09.35	*Speedrunner IV*	Sifnos. Milos.
11.25	*Agios Georgios*	Sifnos. Folegandros. Sikinos. Ios. Santorini.
12.55	*Adamantis Korais*	Sifnos. Milos. Kimolos.
13.05	*Speedrunner IV*	Piraeus.
18.40	*Adamantis Korais*	Kythnos. Piraeus.
18.45	*Highspeed 5*	Sifnos. Milos.
20.05	*Speedrunner IV*	Sifnos. Milos. Piraeus.
22.20	*Highspeed 5*	Piraeus.

⑥
09.35	*Speedrunner IV*	Sifnos. Milos.
12.05	*Agios Georgios*	Sifnos. Milos.
13.05	*Speedrunner IV*	Piraeus.
13.25	*Adamantis Korais*	Sifnos. Milos.
17.55	*Agios Georgios*	Kythnos. Piraeus.
18.20	*Adamantis Korais*	Piraeus.
18.45	*Highspeed 5*	Sifnos. Milos.
20.05	*Speedrunner IV*	Sifnos. Milos. Piraeus.
22.20	*Highspeed 5*	Piraeus.

⑦
09.35	*Speedrunner IV*	Sifnos. Milos.
11.40	*Aqua Jewel*	Sifnos. Kimolos. Milos.
12.05	*Agios Georgios*	Sifnos. Milos. Kimolos.
13.05	*Speedrunner IV*	Piraeus.
17.20	*Adamantis Korais*	Kythnos. Piraeus.
18.25	*Agios Georgios*	Kythnos. Piraeus.
18.45	*Highspeed 5*	Sifnos. Milos.
20.00	*Aqua Jewel*	Paros. Syros.
20.05	*Speedrunner IV*	Sifnos. Milos.
22.20	*Highspeed 5*	Piraeus.

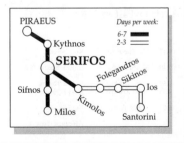

Sifnos

Cyclades West
p. 289

Ⓓ
| 10.10 | *Speedrunner IV* | Milos. |
| 12.30 | *Speedrunner IV* | Serifos. Piraeus. |

①
13.00	*Agios Georgios*	Milos.
17.00	*Agios Georgios*	Serifos. Kythnos. Piraeus.
19.25	*Highspeed 5*	Milos.
20.30	*Adamantis Korais*	Milos. Kimolos. Folegandros. Ios.
20.45	*Speedrunner IV*	Kimolos. Folegandros.
21.40	*Highspeed 5*	Serifos. Piraeus.
23.20	*Speedrunner IV*	Piraeus.

②
13.00	*Agios Georgios*	Kimolos. Milos.
13.20	*Aqua Jewel*	Kimolos. Milos.
15.40	*Adamantis Korais*	Serifos. Kythnos. Piraeus.
17.00	*Agios Georgios*	Serifos. Kythnos. Piraeus.
18.20	*Aqua Jewel*	Serifos. Paros. Syros.
19.25	*Highspeed 5*	Milos.
21.40	*Highspeed 5*	Serifos. Piraeus.

③
12.20	*Agios Georgios*	Folegandros. Sikinos. Ios. Santorini.
13.55	*Adamantis Korais*	Milos. Kimolos.
14.50	*Aqua Jewel*	Kimolos. Milos.
17.55	*Adamantis Korais*	Serifos. Kythnos. Piraeus.
19.35	*Aqua Jewel*	Serifos. Syros.
20.45	*Speedrunner IV*	Milos. Piraeus.

④
13.00	*Agios Georgios*	Milos.
17.00	*Agios Georgios*	Serifos. Kythnos. Piraeus.
19.25	*Highspeed 5*	Milos.
20.30	*Adamantis Korais*	Milos. Kimolos. Sifnos. Serifos. Piraeus.
20.45	*Speedrunner IV*	Kimolos. Folegandros.
21.40	*Highspeed 5*	Serifos. Piraeus.
23.20	*Speedrunner IV*	Piraeus.

⑤
00.15	*Adamantis Korais*	Serifos. Piraeus.
12.20	*Agios Georgios*	Folegandros. Sikinos. Ios. Santorini.
13.55	*Adamantis Korais*	Milos. Kimolos.
17.55	*Adamantis Korais*	Serifos. Kythnos. Piraeus.
19.25	*Highspeed 5*	Milos.
20.45	*Speedrunner IV*	Milos. Piraeus.
21.40	*Highspeed 5*	Serifos. Piraeus.
23.55	*Agios Georgios*	Piraeus.

⑥
13.00	*Agios Georgios*	Milos.
14.10	*Adamantis Korais*	Milos.
17.00	*Agios Georgios*	Serifos. Kythnos. Piraeus.
17.35	*Adamantis Korais*	Serifos. Piraeus.
19.25	*Highspeed 5*	Milos.
20.45	*Speedrunner IV*	Milos. Piraeus.
21.40	*Highspeed 5*	Serifos. Piraeus.

⑦
12.40	*Adamantis Korais*	Folegandros. Kimolos.
13.00	*Agios Georgios*	Milos. Kimolos.
14.20	*Aqua Jewel*	Kimolos. Milos.
16.30	*Adamantis Korais*	Serifos. Kythnos. Piraeus.
17.30	*Agios Georgios*	Serifos. Kythnos. Piraeus.
18.50	*Aqua Jewel*	Serifos. Paros. Syros.
19.25	*Highspeed 5*	Milos.
20.45	*Speedrunner IV*	Milos.
21.40	*Highspeed 5*	Serifos. Piraeus.
23.00	*Speedrunner IV*	Piraeus.

Sikinos

Cyclades West
p. 295

①
| 19.05 | *Artemis* | Folegandros. Kimolos. Milos. |

②
| 04.00 | *Vitsentzos Kornaros* | Ios. Santorini. Anafi. |

10.45	*Artemis*	Santorini. Ios. Naxos. Syros.
18.25	*Aeolos Kenteris II*	Ios. Thirasia. Santorini. Anafi.
21.15	*Vitsentzos Kornaros*	Folegandros. Milos. Santorini.

③
10.15	*Aeolos Kenteris II*	Folegandros. Naxos. Paros. Syros.
14.50	*Agios Georgios*	Ios. Santorini.
18.30	*Artemis*	Ios. Thirasia. Santorini. Anafi.
20.25	*Agios Georgios*	Folegandros. Sifnos. Piraeus.

④
| 11.20 | *Artemis* | Folegandros. Naxos. Paros. Syros. |

⑤
14.50	*Agios Georgios*	Ios. Santorini.
17.00	*Aqua Jewel*	Folegandros. Kimolos. Milos.
20.35	*Agios Georgios*	Folegandros. Kimolos. Sifnos. Piraeus.

⑥
| 10.25 | *Aqua Jewel* | Ios. Naxos. Paros. Mykonos. Syros. |
| 18.25 | *Aeolos Kenteris II* | Ios. Thirasia. Santorini. Anafi. |

⑦
| 10.40 | *Aeolos Kenteris II* | Folegandros. Naxos. Paros. Mykonos. Syros. |

Skiathos

Northern Aegean
p. 506

ⓓ
12.35	*Express Pegasus*	Skopelos (Agnontas). Alonissos.
14.20	*Flying Cat 5/6*	Skopelos (Glossa). Skopelos. Alonissos.
16.30	*Flying Cat 5/6*	Skopelos. Alonissos.
16.55	*Express Pegasus*	Agios Konstantinos.
19.45	*Flying Cat 5/6*	Volos.

①
10.35	*Express Skiathos*	Skopelos (Glossa).
12.30	*Express Skiathos*	Volos.
13.20	*Panagia Parou*	Skopelos.
16.00	*Alikioni*	Skopelos.
19.00	*Alikioni*	Volos.
19.35	*Express Skiathos*	Skopelos.
22.25	*Express Skiathos*	Volos.

②
10.35	*Express Skiathos*	Skopelos (Glossa). Skopelos. Alonissos.
13.20	*Panagia Parou*	Skopelos. Alonissos.
16.00	*Alikioni*	Skopelos. Thessalonika.
16.10	*Express Skiathos*	Volos.
17.20	*Panagia Parou*	Agios Konstantinos.

③
10.35	*Express Skiathos*	Skopelos (Glossa).
12.30	*Express Skiathos*	Volos.
13.20	*Panagia Parou*	Skopelos.
19.00	*Alikioni*	Volos.
19.35	*Express Skiathos*	Skopelos. Alonissos.
23.40	*Express Skiathos*	Volos.

④
10.35	*Express Skiathos*	Skopelos (Glossa).
12.30	*Express Skiathos*	Volos.
13.20	*Panagia Parou*	Skopelos.
16.00	*Alikioni*	Skopelos. Alonissos.
19.35	*Express Skiathos*	Skopelos. Alonissos.
20.20	*Alikioni*	Volos.
23.40	*Express Skiathos*	Volos.

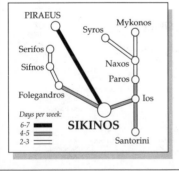

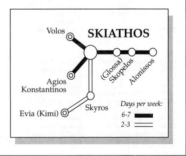

⑤
10.35	Express Skiathos	Skopelos (Glossa).
12.30	Express Skiathos	Volos.
16.00	Alikioni	Skopelos.
18.20	Panagia Parou	Skopelos. Alonissos.
19.00	Alikioni	Volos.
19.35	Express Skiathos	Skopelos.
21.40	Panagia Parou	Agios Konstantinos.
22.25	Express Skiathos	Volos.

⑥
10.35	Express Skiathos	Skopelos (Glossa).
12.30	Express Skiathos	Volos.
13.20	Panagia Parou	Skopelos.
16.00	Alikioni	Skopelos. Thessalonika.
19.35	Express Skiathos	Skopelos.
22.25	Express Skiathos	Volos.

⑦
10.35	Express Skiathos	Skopelos. Alonissos.
13.20	Panagia Parou	Skopelos. Alonissos.
14.30	Express Skiathos	Volos.
17.20	Panagia Parou	Agios Konstantinos.
19.00	Alikioni	Volos.
21.30	Express Skiathos	Skopelos (Glossa).
23.05	Express Skiathos	Volos.

🐬 *Flying Dolphins* include:

Ⓓ
07.55	Hydrofoil	Volos.
08.10	Hydrofoil	Agios Konstantinos.
10.20	Hydrofoil	Skopelos (Glossa). Skopelos. Alonissos.
12.10	Hydrofoil	Agios Konstantinos.
12.45	Hydrofoil	Volos. Skopelos. Alonissos.
16.50	Hydrofoil	Volos.
20.55	Hydrofoil	Skopelos (Glossa). Skopelos. Alonissos.

Skopelos

Northern Aegean
p. 510

Ⓓ
15.30	Flying Cat 5/6	Alonissos.
16.40	Flying Cat 5/6	Skiathos.
17.20	Flying Cat 5/6	Alonissos.
18.35	Flying Cat 5/6	Skopelos (Glossa). Skiathos. Volos.

①
16.00	Panagia Parou	Skiathos. Agios Konstantinos.
17.30	Alikioni	Skiathos. Volos.
21.05	Express Skiathos	Skiathos. Volos.

②
12.30	Express Skiathos	Alonissos.
13.45	Achilleas	Alonissos. Evia (Kimi). Skyros.
14.10	Express Skiathos	Skopelos (Glossa). Skiathos. Volos.
14.30	Panagia Parou	Alonissos.
16.10	Panagia Parou	Skiathos. Agios Konstantinos.
17.00	Alikioni	Thessalonika.

③
16.00	Panagia Parou	Skiathos. Agios Konstantinos.
17.30	Alikioni	Skiathos. Volos.
21.05	Express Skiathos	Alonissos.

④
13.45	Achilleas	Alonissos. Evia (Kimi). Skyros.
16.00	Panagia Parou	Skiathos. Agios Konstantinos.
17.30	Alikioni	Alonissos. Skiathos. Volos.
21.05	Express Skiathos	Alonissos.

⑤
17.30	Alikioni	Skiathos. Volos.
19.30	Panagia Parou	Alonissos. Skiathos. Agios Konstantinos.
21.05	Express Skiathos	Skiathos. Volos.

⑥
16.00	Panagia Parou	Skiathos. Agios Konstantinos.
17.00	Alikioni	Thessalonika.
18.00	Achilleas	Alonissos. Evia (Kimi). Skyros.
21.05	Express Skiathos	Skiathos. Volos.

⑦
12.00	Express Skiathos	Alonissos. Skiathos. Volos.
14.30	Panagia Parou	Alonissos.
16.10	Panagia Parou	Skiathos. Agios Konstantinos.
17.30	Alikioni	Skiathos. Volos.

Thessalonika

Days per week:
6-7
4-5

Volos

(Glossa)

Skiathos

Alonissos

SKOPELOS (Town)

Agios Konstantinos

Skyros

🐚 *Flying Dolphins* include:

Ⓓ

07.00	Hydrofoil	Skopelos (Glossa).
		Skiathos. Volos.
		Agios Konstantinos.
11.10	Hydrofoil	Alonissos.
12.10	Hydrofoil	Skiathos. Volos.
12.30	Hydrofoil	Alonissos.
14.30	Hydrofoil	Skopelos (Glossa).
		Skiathos. Volos.
15.30	Hydrofoil	Alonissos.
16.25	Hydrofoil	Skopelos (Glossa).
		Skiathos.
		Agios Konstantinos.
21.50	Hydrofoil	Alonissos.

Skopelos (Agnontas)

Northern Aegean p. 510

Ⓓ

13.45	*Express Pegasus*	Alonissos.
15.45	*Express Pegasus*	Skiathos.
		Agios Konstantinos.

Skopelos (Glossa)

Northern Aegean p. 512

Ⓓ

| 14.45 | *Flying Cat 5/6* | Skopelos. Alonissos. |
| 19.15 | *Flying Cat 5/6* | Skiathos. Volos. |

②

| 11.20 | *Express Skiathos* | Skopelos. Alonissos. |
| 15.20 | *Express Skiathos* | Skiathos. Volos. |

① ③ ④ ⑤ ⑥

| 11.05 | *Express Skiathos* | Skiathos. Volos. |

⑦

| 22.15 | *Express Skiathos* | Skiathos. Volos. |

🐚 *Flying Dolphins* include:

Ⓓ

07.30	Hydrofoil	Skiathos. Volos.
07.45	Hydrofoil	Skiathos.
		Agios Konstantinos.
11.55	Hydrofoil	Skopelos. Alonissos.
15.00	Hydrofoil	Skopelos. Alonissos.
15.00	Hydrofoil	Skiathos. Volos.
17.00	Hydrofoil	Skiathos.
21.10	Hydrofoil	Skopelos. Alonissos.

Skyros

Northern Aegean
p. 514

① ③

| 08.00 | *Achilleas* | Evia (Kimi). |
| 15.00 | *Achilleas* | Evia (Kimi). |

② ④

| 07.00 | *Achilleas* | Evia (Kimi). |
| | | Alonissos. Skopelos. |

⑤

| 08.00 | *Achilleas* | Evia (Kimi). |
| 17.00 | *Achilleas* | Evia (Kimi). |

⑥

| 07.00 | *Achilleas* | Evia (Kimi). |

⑦

| 13.00 | *Achilleas* | Evia (Kimi). |
| 19.30 | *Achilleas* | Evia (Kimi). |

Spetses

Argo-Saronic p. 561

Ⓓ

x6	*Alexandros M*	Kosta.
00.00	*Flying Cat 1*	Porto Helio.
10.10	*Flying Dolphin*	Porto Helio.
10.30	*Eurofast 1*	Hydra. Poros. Piraeus.
13.00	*Apollon Hellas*	Porto Helio.
14.00	*Apollon Hellas*	Hydra. Poros. Methana.
		Aegina. Piraeus.
14.45	*Georgios 2*	Poros. Methana.
		Aegina. Piraeus.
15.45	*Eurofast 1*	Hydra. Poros. Piraeus.
18.30	*Flying Cat 1*	Porto Helio.
19.20	*Flying Cat 1*	Hydra. Piraeus.

🐚 *Flying Dolphins:*

Ⓓ x 6   Poros. Piraeus.

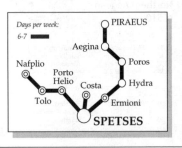

Days per week:
6-7 ▬▬
PIRAEUS
Aegina
Poros
Nafplio
Porto
Helio
Hydra
Costa
Tolo
Ermioni
SPETSES

Symi

Dodecanese
p. 433

Ⓓ		
16.00	*Symi / Symi II*	Rhodes.

①		
09.20	*Dodekanisos Pride*	Kos. Kalimnos. Leros (Agia Marina). Lipsi. Patmos.
15.00	*Proteus*	Symi (Panormitis). Rhodes.
17.45	*Dodekanisos Pride*	Rhodes.

②		
08.00	*Diagoras*	Rhodes.
09.20	*Dodekanisos Express*	Rhodes.
09.20	*Dodekanisos Pride*	Kos. Kalimnos. Leros (Agia Marina). Lipsi. Patmos.
16.00	*Dodekanisos Express*	Kos. Kalimnos.
16.00	*Proteus*	Rhodes.
16.50	*Diagoras*	Kos. Kalimnos. Leros. Lipsi. Patmos. Piraeus.
17.45	*Dodekanisos Pride*	Rhodes.

③		
09.20	*Dodekanisos Express*	Rhodes.
15.00	*Proteus*	Symi (Panormitis). Rhodes.
16.30	*Dodekanisos Express*	Rhodes.

④		
08.00	*Dodekanisos Express*	Rhodes.
09.20	*Dodekanisos Pride*	Kos. Kalimnos. Leros (Agia Marina). Lipsi. Patmos.
15.00	*Proteus*	Symi (Panormitis). Rhodes.
16.30	*Dodekanisos Express*	Rhodes.
17.45	*Dodekanisos Pride*	Rhodes.

⑤		
08.00	*Dodekanisos Express*	Rhodes. Chalki. Tilos. Nissiros. Kos.
09.20	*Dodekanisos Pride*	Kos. Kalimnos. Leros (Agia Marina). Lipsi. Patmos.

16.00	*Proteus*	Rhodes.
17.45	*Dodekanisos Pride*	Rhodes.

⑥		
06.30	*Symi II*	Rhodes.
08.00	*Dodekanisos Express*	Rhodes.
10.30	*Dodekanisos Express*	Turkey (Datça).
11.40	*Diagoras*	Rhodes. Kastelorizo.
15.00	*Proteus*	Symi (Panormitis). Rhodes.
16.30	*Dodekanisos Express*	Rhodes.

⑦		
00.40	*Diagoras*	Tilos. Nissiros. Kos. Kalimnos. Astipalea. Naxos. Paros. Piraeus.
08.00	*Dodekanisos Express*	Rhodes. Chalki. Tilos. Nissiros. Kos.
09.20	*Dodekanisos Pride*	Kos. Kalimnos. Leros (Agia Marina). Lipsi. Patmos.
16.00	*Proteus*	Rhodes.
17.30	*Symi II*	Rhodes.
21.00	*Dodekanisos Express*	Rhodes.

Symi (Panormitis)

① ③ ⑥		
12.00	*Symi II*	Symi.
17.00	*Proteus*	Rhodes.

② ⑤ ⑦		
12.00	*Proteus*	Symi.
12.00	*Symi II*	Symi.

④		
11.30	*Dodekanisos Express*	Symi.
12.00	*Symi II*	Symi.
17.00	*Proteus*	Rhodes.

Syros

Cyclades North
p. 242

Ⓓ		
10.00	*Highspeed 5*	Tinos. Mykonos.
10.35	*Speedrunner III*	Tinos. Mykonos.
11.30	*Blue Star Ithaki*	Tinos. Mykonos.
12.15	*Highspeed 5*	Piraeus.
12.35	*Speedrunner III*	Piraeus.
16.00	*Blue Star Ithaki*	Piraeus.

①		
07.00	*Aeolos Kenteris II*	Paros. Naxos. Donoussa. Amorgos (Egiali). Amorgos (Katapola). Koufonissia. Schinoussa. Iraklia.

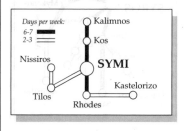

Days per week:
6-7 ▬▬
2-3 ═══

Kalimnos
Kos
Nissiros
SYMI
Kastelorizo
Tilos
Rhodes

Car & Passenger Ferry Liveries

International Line Only

Funnel Logo

Hull Logo

1 **AGOUDIMOS LINES**

2 **ALPHA FERRIES**

3 **ANEK LINES**

4 **ANEK SEA LINES**

5 **ANEN LINES**

6 **A. N. E. Θ.**
ANE THASSOS

7 **ANEZ LINES**

8 *Blue Ferries*
STRINTZIS LINES

9 *Blue Star Ferries*
STRINTZIS LINES

10 **C-LINK FERRIES**

11 **ENDEAVOR** LINES

12 **K. P. N. EUBOEA**

13 **FAST FERRIES**

14 **FEAX EXPRESS FERRIES**

15 **FIVE STARS LINES**

16 **GA FERRIES**

17 **GOUTOS LINES**

18 **HELLENIC SEAWAYS**
HELLAS FLYING DOLPHINS

19 **HML FERRIES**

20 JADROLINIJA

21 Kallisi ferries

22 KERKIRA LINES

23 L.A.N.E. LINES / λανε

24 LOUIS CRUISE LINES

25 MED LINK LINES

26 MINIOTIS LINES

27 MINOAN LINES highspeed

28 MINOAN LINES

29 NEL LINES

30 NEL LINES

31 NOVA FERRIES

32 POSEIDON LINES

33 SALAMIS LINES

34 SAOS FERRIES

35 SKYROS SHIPPING Co.

36 SMALL CYCLADES LINES

37 STRINTZIS FERRIES

38 SUPERFAST

39 TURKISH MARITIME LINES

40 TYROGALAS

41 VENTOURIS FERRIES

42 VENTOURIS SEA LINES

43 ZANTE FERRIES

Hydrofoil Liveries

44 A. N. E. THASSOS
Thission Dolphin

45 BODRUM EXPRESS LINES
Bodrum Princess

46 HELLAS FLYING DOL.
Flying / Mega Dolphin I-32

47 KIRIACOULIS MARITIME
Aristea M, Georgios M Gina I, II; Mazilena I, II Samos Flying Dolphins I-IV

48 LASUMZIS
Christos L Petros L

49 NEK AE
Marina II

50 SARONIC DOLPHINS
Dolphins I-V

Catamaran Liveries

51 AEGEAN SPEED LINES
SpeedRunner II, III, IV

52 DODEKANISOS SPEEDWAYS
Dodekanisos Express Dodekanisos Pride

53 EUROSEAS
Eurofast 1

54 HELLAS FLYING DOLPHINS
Highspeed 1, 2, 3, 4, 5, 6 Flying Cat I, 2, 3, 4, 5, 6

55 HELLENIC SEAWAYS / HELLAS FLYING DOL.
Express Skiathos

56 SEAJETS
MegaJet, SeaJet 2, SuperJet

57 SYMI ANE
Symi II Panormitis

58 TILOS ANE
SeaStar

07.00	*Aqua Jewel*	Mykonos. Paros. Serifos. Sifnos. Kimolos. Milos.
07.00	*Artemis*	Paros. Naxos. Donoussa. Amorgos (Egiali). Amorgos (Katapola). Koufonissia. Schinoussa. Iraklia.
20.25	*Nissos Mykonos*	Piraeus.
20.30	*Highspeed 6*	Mykonos. Tinos.
21.10	*Blue Star Paros*	Paros. Naxos. Iraklia. Schinoussa. Koufonissia. Amorgos (Katapola).
22.50	*Highspeed 6*	Piraeus.

Thessalonika

Northern Aegean
p. 521

| ① | | |
| 17.00 | *Taxiarchis* | Limnos. Lesbos (Mytilini). |

| ③ | | |
| 13.30 | *Alikioni* | Skopelos. Skiathos. Volos. |

| ⑦ | | |
| 13.30 | *Alikioni* | Skopelos. Skiathos. Volos. |

○ * Not operating in 2011:

08.00	*Theofilos*	Limnos. Lesbos (Mytilini). Chios. Samos (Vathi).
12.00	*Flying Cat 5/6*	Skiathos. Skopelos. Alonissos.
16.00	Ferry	Alonissos. Skiathos. Agios Konstantinos.
19.00	*Samothraki*	Limnos. Lesbos (Mytilini). Chios. Samos (Vathi).
20.00	*Diagoras*	Lesbos (Sigri). Chios. Samos (Vathi). Kalimnos. Kos.
23.59	Ferry	Skiathos. Alonissos. Syros. Tinos. Mykonos. Paros. Naxos. Ios. Santorini. Crete (Iraklion).

Thassos
(Skala Prinos)

Northern Aegean
p. 518

⑩		
06.00	07.20	12.00
14.15	16.00	18.00	19.00	Kavala.
10.30	14.30	19.00
	ANET Line	Nea Peramos.

Thassos
(Town)

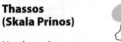

Northern Aegean
p. 518

⑩		
05.45	08.15	10.15	12.15
14.00	15.30	16.30	17.30
18.30	19.30	20.30	21.30
	ANET Line	Keramoti.
⑩ x 4	Hydrofoil	Kavala.
○		
00.00	Hydrofoil	Samothrace. Alexandroupolis.

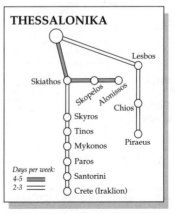

Thimena

Eastern Line   p. 458

① ③ ⑤
07.50   *Samos Sun*   Samos (Karlovassi).
14.50   *Samos Sun*   Fourni.

Days per week:
4-5
2-3

Kalimnos
Kos
Nissiros
Symi
Kastelorizo
TILOS   Rhodes

Thirasia

Cyclades Central   p. 202

②
19.55   *Aeolos Kenteris II*   Santorini. Anafi.

③
08.35   *Aeolos Kenteris II*   Ios. Sikinos.
Folegandros. Naxos.
Paros. Syros.
20.25   *Artemis*   Santorini. Anafi.

④
09.25   *Artemis*   Ios. Sikinos.
Folegandros. Naxos.
Paros. Syros.

⑥
19.55   *Aeolos Kenteris II*   Santorini. Anafi.

⑦
08.50   *Aeolos Kenteris II*   Ios. Sikinos.
Folegandros. Naxos.
Paros. Mykonos. Syros.

○ * Not operating in 2011:

13.00   *Theoskepasti*   Santorini (Oia).
Santorini (Old Port).
Santorini.
16.00   *Theoskepasti*   Santorini (Oia).
Santorini (Old Port).
Santorini.

Tilos

Dodecanese
p. 439

③
07.30   *SeaStar*   Rhodes.
21.00   *SeaStar*   Rhodes.

④
07.45   *Diagoras*   Rhodes. Kastelorizo.
22.30   *Diagoras*   Nissiros. Kos. Kalimnos.
Piraeus.

⑤
11.15   *Dodekanisos Express*   Nissiros.
Kos.
15.10   *Dodekanisos Express*   Chalki.
Rhodes.
Symi.

⑥
07.30   *SeaStar*   Rhodes.
09.50   *Diagoras*   Symi.
Rhodes.
Kastelorizo.

⑦
02.30   *Diagoras*   Nissiros.
Kos.
Kalimnos.
Astipalea.
Naxos.
Paros.
Piraeus.
11.15   *Dodekanisos Express*   Nissiros. Kos.
17.00   *Dodekanisos Express*   Chalki.
Rhodes.
Symi.
19.15   *SeaStar*   Rhodes.

○
00.00   *SeaStar*   Nissiros.
00.00   *SeaStar*   Rhodes.

Tinos

Cyclades North
p. 246

Ⓓ
09.25   *SeaJet 2*   Mykonos.
Paros.
10.40   *Highspeed 5*   Mykonos. Syros.
Piraeus.
11.10   *Speedrunner III*   Mykonos. Syros.
Piraeus.
11.30   *Penelope A*   Mykonos.
12.15   *Blue Star Ithaki*   Mykonos.
13.25   *SeaJet 2*   Rafina.
15.00   *Blue Star Ithaki*   Syros.
Piraeus.

① ①
01.55	Theologos P	Mykonos.
08.15	Theologos P	Andros. Rafina.
09.25	Flying Cat 3	Mykonos. Naxos.
		Ios. Santorini.
11.35	Superferry II	Mykonos.
14.10	Penelope A	Andros. Rafina.
14.30	Superferry II	Andros. Rafina.
16.55	SeaJet 2	Mykonos. Paros.
19.25	Flying Cat 3	Rafina.
19.50	SeaJet 2	Rafina.
21.30	Theologos P	Mykonos.
22.10	Highspeed 6	Syros.
		Piraeus.

②
08.15	Theologos P	Andros. Rafina.
09.25	Flying Cat 3	Mykonos. Naxos.
		Ios. Santorini.
11.35	Superferry II	Mykonos. Naxos.
14.10	Penelope A	Andros. Rafina.
16.50	Superferry II	Andros. Rafina.
16.55	SeaJet 2	Mykonos. Paros.
19.25	Flying Cat 3	Rafina.
19.50	SeaJet 2	Rafina.
21.30	Theologos P	Mykonos.
22.10	Highspeed 6	Syros.
		Piraeus.

③
05.20	Artemis	Andros.
08.15	Theologos P	Andros. Rafina.
09.15	Artemis	Syros.
09.25	Flying Cat 3	Mykonos.
		Naxos.
		Ios. Santorini.
11.35	Superferry II	Mykonos. Naxos.
14.10	Penelope A	Andros. Rafina.
16.50	Superferry II	Andros. Rafina.
16.55	SeaJet 2	Mykonos. Paros.
19.25	Flying Cat 3	Rafina.
19.50	SeaJet 2	Rafina.
21.30	Theologos P	Mykonos.
23.25	Aqua Jewel	Andros.

④
08.15	Theologos P	Andros. Rafina.
08.55	Aqua Jewel	Syros.
09.25	Flying Cat 3	Mykonos. Naxos.
		Ios. Santorini.
11.35	Superferry II	Mykonos.
		Naxos.
14.10	Penelope A	Andros. Rafina.
16.50	Superferry II	Andros. Rafina.
16.55	SeaJet 2	Mykonos. Paros.
19.25	Flying Cat 3	Rafina.
19.50	SeaJet 2	Rafina.
20.10	Aeolos Kenteris II	Andros.
21.30	Theologos P	Mykonos.
22.10	Highspeed 6	Syros. Piraeus.
22.50	Aeolos Kenteris II	Syros.

⑤
09.25	Flying Cat 3	Mykonos.
11.30	Theologos P	Mykonos.
11.45	Superferry II	Andros. Rafina.
12.45	Theologos P	Andros. Rafina.
14.05	Flying Cat 3	Rafina.
14.10	Penelope A	Andros. Rafina.
16.55	SeaJet 2	Mykonos.

17.00	Aeolos Kenteris II	Andros.
17.50	SeaJet 2	Rafina.
18.25	Flying Cat 3	Mykonos.
19.15	Flying Cat 3	Rafina.
20.40	Aeolos Kenteris II	Syros.
21.00	Superferry II	Mykonos. Rafina.
22.00	Theologos P	Mykonos. Rafina.
22.10	Highspeed 6	Syros. Piraeus.
22.10	SeaJet 2	Mykonos.
		Rafina.

⑥
09.25	Flying Cat 3	Mykonos. Naxos.
		Ios. Santorini.
11.35	Superferry II	Mykonos. Naxos.
12.45	Theologos P	Andros. Rafina.
16.00	Penelope A	Andros. Rafina.
16.50	Superferry II	Andros. Rafina.
16.55	SeaJet 2	Mykonos. Paros.
19.25	Flying Cat 3	Rafina.
19.50	SeaJet 2	Rafina.
21.30	Theologos P	Mykonos.
22.10	Highspeed 6	Syros.
		Piraeus.

⑦
09.25	Flying Cat 3	Mykonos.
11.35	Superferry II	Mykonos.
12.45	Theologos P	Andros. Rafina.
14.05	Flying Cat 3	Rafina.
14.10	Penelope A	Andros. Rafina.
14.30	Superferry II	Andros. Rafina.
17.20	SeaJet 2	Rafina.
18.25	Flying Cat 3	Mykonos.
19.15	Flying Cat 3	Rafina.
22.10	Highspeed 6	Syros. Piraeus.
22.10	SeaJet 2	Rafina.

Venice

Italy p. 637

ⓓ
14.00 Minoan Lines   Igoumenitsa. Corfu. Patras.

①
19.00 *Sophocles V*   Igoumenitsa. Corfu. Patras.

②
19.00 *Lefka Ori*   Igoumenitsa. Corfu. Patras.

③
18.00 *Lefka Ori*   Igoumenitsa. Corfu. Patras.

⑤
12.00 *Sophocles V*   Igoumenitsa. Corfu. Patras.

⑥
12.00 *Lefka Ori*   Igoumenitsa. Corfu. Patras.

⑦
12.00 *Lefka Ori*   Igoumenitsa. Corfu. Patras.

○
21.00   İzmir.

Volos

Northern Aegean p. 525

ⓓ
09.00 Hydrofoil   Skiathos. Skopelos (Glossa). Skopelos. Alonissos.
13.15 Hydrofoil   Skiathos. Skopelos (Glossa). Skopelos. Alonissos.
14.30 Hydrofoil   Skiathos. Skopelos.
19.30 Hydrofoil   Skiathos. Skopelos (Glossa). Skopelos. Alonissos.

①
07.45 *Express Skiathos*   Skiathos. Skopelos (Glossa).
13.30 *Alikioni*   Skiathos. Skopelos.
16.45 *Express Skiathos*   Skiathos. Skopelos.

②
07.45 *Express Skiathos*   Skiathos. Skopelos (Glossa). Skopelos. Alonissos.
13.30 *Alikioni*   Skiathos. Skopelos. Thessalonika.

③ ⑦
07.45 *Express Skiathos*   Skiathos.
16.45 *Express Skiathos*   Skiathos. Skopelos. Alonissos.

④ ⑤
07.45 *Express Skiathos*   Skiathos. Skopelos (Glossa).
13.30 *Alikioni*   Skiathos. Skopelos. Alonissos.
16.45 *Express Skiathos*   Skiathos. Skopelos. Alonissos.

⑥
07.45 *Express Skiathos*   Skiathos. Skopelos (Glossa).
13.30 *Alikioni*   Skiathos. Skopelos. Thessalonika.
16.45 *Express Skiathos*   Skiathos. Skopelos.

○
12.30 *Flying Cat 5/6*   Skiathos. Skopelos (Glossa). Skopelos. Alonissos.

Zakinthos / Zante (Town)

Ionian Line p. 598

ⓓ
05.30 08.00 09.00 10.45 13.00 14.30 18.00 19.45
   Andreas Kalvos/ Dimitrios Solomos/ Ionian Star/Ionis   Kilini.

○
12.00 *Ionian King*   Brindisi.

Zakinthos / Zante (Skinari)

Ionian Line p. 600

ⓓ
09.15 *Angela*   Kefalonia (Pessada).
19.30 *Angela*   Kefalonia (Pessada).

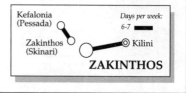

Kefalonia (Pessada)

Zakinthos (Skinari)

Kilini

ZAKINTHOS

Days per week:
6-7

ⓘ Online Updates

Updates to this book are now available online ...

The website attached to this book has pages updating the information contained in this edition. Check it out either before you go to Greece, or from cyber cafés in the islands, and get the latest information — both on the islands and the ever changing ferry situation.

ENTER

Guidebook Updates
Weekly Piraeus &
Rafina Timetables
Island Extras
Links

E-mail

GREEK ISLAND HOPPING *online*

The island hopper's web site

• Additional Information

There is a limit on what can be put into any printed guidebook, so the web offers us the chance to give you extra background material — for example: a weekly updated timetable for the Athenian ports of Piraeus and Rafina.

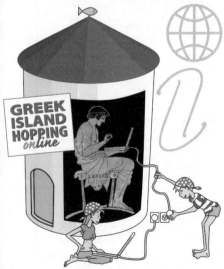

GREEK ISLAND HOPPING *online*

• Online in 2012 and beyond

The near future will see extra pages available online, expanding the information provided in this book. The list includes:

• **Amorgos**: a tour of Chozoviotissa Monastery.

• **Antiparos**: expanded coverage of the Kastro with 3D model views showing the building then and now.

• **Ios:** a write-up of the Archaeological Museum with 3D floor plan.

• **Kimolos:** a detailed look at the unique Kastro with 3D model views.

• **Kos:** a 3D tour of the Casa Romana.

• **Paros:** tours of (1) Ekatontapiliani Church and (2) the Archaeological Museum, both with 3D floor plans.

• **Piraeus:** tours of the pre-WW1 heavy armoured cruiser *Georgios Averof* and the Piraeus Archaeological Museum.

• **Naxos:** walking the Zeus Cave Trail.

• **Santorini:** a guide to the Thera Foundation Exhibition of the wall paintings from ancient Akrotiri.

• **Sifnos:** a 3D tour of the Mycenaean Acropolis at Agios Andreas.

Major Ferry Companies

Company	Livery No. (See Colour Liveries between pages 704–705)

AGOUDIMOS LINES   **1**
2 Kapodistriou
185 31
Piraeus, GREECE
☎ (210) 4133583
⊕ www.agoudimos-lines.com

Ionian King, Ionian Sky,
Kapetan Alexandros, Penelope A.

AEGEAN SPEED LINES   **51**
85 Vouliagmenis Ave.
16674
Athens, GREECE
☎ (210) 9690950
⊕ www.aegeanspeedlines.gr

SpeedRunner II, SpeedRunner III,
SpeedRunner IV.

ANEK LINES   **3**
N. Plastria-Apokoronou,
Chania, Crete,
GREECE
☎ (28210) 27600-10
FAX (28210) 27611
⊕ www.anek.gr

Aptera, Ariadne, Arkadi,
Artemis, El. Venizelos,
Hellenic Spirit, Hercules,
Kriti I, Kriti II,
Lato, Lefka Ori, Lissos,
Mount Olympos,
Olympic Champion,
Prevelis, Rethimno,
Sophocles V.

ANEN Lines   **5**
(20% owned by ANEK Lines)
32 Akti Possidonos
& 1 Leocharous Sts
185 31 Piraeus,
GREECE
☎ (210) 4197420

No ships operating in 2011.

BLUE STAR FERRIES /   **8, 9, 37**
BLUE FERRIES/
STRINTZIS
26 Akti Possidonos,
185 31 Piraeus,
GREECE
☎ (210) 4225000
⊕ www.strintzis.gr

Blue Star 1,
Blue Star 2,
Blue Star Delos,
Blue Star Ithaki,
Blue Star Naxos,
Blue Star Paros,
Blue Star Patmos,
Diagoras,
Eptanisos,
Kefalonia,
Superferry II.

G.A. FERRIES   **16**
(Currently in administration)
Akti Kondili & 2 Aitolikou,
Piraeus, GREECE
☎ (210) 4110007, 4110254
FAX (210) 4232383

Alkmini A,
Anthi Marina, Dimitra,
Dimitroula, JetFerry 1,
Marina, Milena,
Rodanthi, Romilda.

HELLENIC SEAWAYS   **18, 46, 54, 55**
(A subsiduary of
Hellas Flying Dolphins)
2 Defteras Merachias St.
185 35 Piraeus, GREECE
☎ (210) 4283555
⊕ www.dolphins.gr

Express Pegasus,
Express Skiathos,
Nissos Chios,
Nissos Mykonos,
Nissos Rodos.

Highspeed:
C/Ms *Highspeed 1,*
Highspeed 2, Highspeed 3,
Highspeed 4, Highspeed 5,
Highspeed 6,
Flying Cat 1–6,
H/Fs *Flying Dolphin 1–32.*

Saronic Gulf:
Aias, Apollon Hellas,
Apostolos P,
Georgios 2,
Ioannis II,
Nefeli, Odysseas II,
Poseidon Hellas.

LANE LINES   **23**
(50% owned by ANEK)
2 Loudovikou Street
185 31 Piraeus,
GREECE
☎ (210) 4274011

Ierapetra L,
Vitsentzos Kornaros.

LOUIS CRUISE LINES   **24**
54–58 Evagoras Avenue,
P.O. Box 1301 Nicosia, CYPRUS
☎ (02) 442114

Princesa Cypria,
Princesa Marissa.

MINOAN LINES S.A.   **27, 28**
17, 25th August St,
712 02, Iraklion, Crete, GREECE
☎ (2810) 330301
Passenger Office and Bus Terminal:
2 Vass. Kon/nou Avenue
116 35 Athens, GREECE
☎ (210) 7512356
Fax (210) 7520540
⊕ www.minoan.gr

Aretousa,
Cruise Europa, Cruise Olympia,
Daedalus,
Europa Palace, Festos Palace,
Ikarus Palace, Knossos Palace,
N. Kazantzakis,
Olympia Palace,
Prometheus, Zeus Palace.

NEL LINES /   **29, 30**
MARITIME Co. of LESVOS S.A.
(16.5% owned by ANEK)
47 Kountouriotou Street,
811 00 Mytilini, Lesbos,
GREECE
☎ (22510) 23097, 29087

Aeolos Kenteris I,
Aeolos Kenteris II,
Aqua Jewel,
Aqua Maria,
Cyclades Express,
European Express,
Mytilene,
Panagia Hozoviotissia,
Panagia Parou,
Panagia Thalassini,
Panagia Tinou,
Taxiarchis, Theofilos.

SAOS FERRIES   **34**
35–39 Akti Miaouli,
Piraeus, GREECE
☎ (210) 4293420   Fax (210) 4293423

Arsinoe, Nissos Limnos,
Nona Mairy, Panagia Soumela,
Samothraki, Saos II.

SEAJETS   **56**
2 Dimitriou Gounari Str.
185 31 Piraeus, GREECE
☎ (210) 4121001   Fax (210) 4121912

MegaJet, SeaJet 2, SuperJet.

SUPERFAST FERRIES   **38**
Amalias 30, 105 58 Athens, GREECE
☎ (210) 3313252
⊕ www.superfast.com

Superfast I–XII.

VENTOURIS FERRIES   **41**
91 Pireos Av. & Kithiron 2
185 41 Piraeus, GREECE
☎ (210) 4825815
⊕ www.ventouris.gr

Bari, Polaris.

ⓘ Useful Greek

The Greek Alphabet — Transliteration

Greek Capital	Small	English Equivalent	Name	Pronounced like
A	α	A	Alpha	cat
B	β	B/V	Beta	van
Γ	γ	G	Gamma	sugar/yes
Δ	δ	D	Delta	this
E	ε	E	Epsilon	egg
Z	ζ	Z	Zeta	zoo
H	η	E	Eta	feet
Θ	θ	TH	Theta	thick
I	ι	I	Iota	feet
K	κ	K	Kappa	king
Λ	λ	L	Lamtha	long
M	μ	M	Mu	man
N	ν	N	Nu	not
Ξ	ξ	TS/KS	Tsi/Xi	box
O	o	O	O-mikron	dot
Π	π	P	Pi	pick
P	ρ	R	Rho	red
Σ	σ, ς	S	Sigma	sit (ς only at the end of a word)
T	τ	T	Tau	tap
Y	υ	U	Upsilon	meet
Φ	φ	PH/F	Phi	fat
X	χ	CH/H	Chi	loch
Ψ	ψ	PS	Psi	lapse
Ω / Ω	ω	O	O-mega	dot

Combinations & Dipthongs

AI	αι	AI		egg
AY	αυ	AV/AF		have
EI	ει	I		seen
EY	ευ	EV/EF		ever/effort
OI	οι	I		seen
OY	ευ	OU		moon
ΓΓ	γγ	NG		go/ring
ΓΚ	γκ	G/NG		go/ring
ΜΠ	μπ	B		boat
NT	ντ	D/ND		dog/send
TZ	τζ	TS		deeds
ΤΣ	τσ	TS		deeds
YI	υι	I		seen

Greek   Pronunciation   English

Basics:

Ναι	Ne	Yes
Οχι	ochi	No
Παρακαλω	parakalo	Please
Ευχαριστω	efcharisto	Thank You
Με σογχωρειτε	me sinkhorite	Excuse Me
Φυγετε	fiyete	Hop It!
Βοηθεια	voithia	Help!
Γεια σας (pl.)	yassas (pl.)	Hello/
Γεια σου	yassoo (s.)	Goodbye
Καλημερα	Kalimera	Good morning
Καληνυχτα	Kalinihta	Good night
Συγνωμη	signomi	Sorry
Ποτε;	pote	When?
Ποσο;	posso	How much?
Που;	pu	Where?

Signs:

ΑΦΙΤΕΙΣ	Afitese	Arrivals
ΑΝΔΡΩΝ	Andron	Gentlemen
ΑΝΑΧΩΡΗΣΕΙΣ	Anachoresis	Departures
ΓΥΝΑΙΚΩΝ	Ginekon	Ladies
ΕΙΣΟΔΟΣ	Eisodos	Entrance
ΕΞΟΔΟΣ	Exodos	Exit
ΣΤΑΣΙΣ	Stasis	Bus Stop
ΤΟΥΑΛΕΤΕΣ	Toualetes	Toilets
ΦΑΡΜΑΚΕΙΟΝ	Farmakion	Pharmacy
ΞΕΝΟΔΟΧΕΙΟ	Zenodokhio	Hotel

Miscellaneous:

Αγια	Agia	Saint
Αστυνομια	Astinomia	Police Stn.
Εισιτηρια	Isitiria	Tickets
Λεωφορειο	Leoforio	Bus
Λιμανι	Limani	Port
Νησι / Νισι	Nissi	Island
Οδος	Odhos	Street
Πλατεια	Platia	Square
Πλοιο	Plio	Boat/Ferry
Σπηλαιο	Spileo	Cave
Τραινο	Treno	Train
Χωριο	Horio/Hora	Village

Numbers:

Ενας	enas	1
Δυο	deo	2
Τρεις /	Τρια	tris/tria
Τεσσερεις	tesseres	4
Πεντε	pende	5
Εξι	exi	6
Επτα	epta	7
Οκτω	okto	8
Εννεα	ennea	9
Δεκα	deka	10
Ενδεκα	andeka	11
Δωδεκα	dodeka	12
Δεκατρια	deka tria	13
Δεκατεσσερα	deka tessera	14
Εικοσι	ikosi	20
Πενηντα	peninda	50
Εκατο	ekato	100
Χιλια	chilia	1000

Days:

Δευτερα	deftera	Monday
Τριτη	triti	Tuesday
Τεταρτη	tetarti	Wednesday
Πεμπτη	pempti	Thursday
Παρασκευη	paraskevi	Friday
Ζαββατο	savato	Saturday
Κυριακη	kiriaki	Sunday
Σημερα	simera	Today
Αυριω	avrio	Tomorrow
Χθες	hthes	Yesterday

Accommodation:

Εχετε δωματια	ehete domatia	Do you have rooms?
Θελω ενα	thelo enna	I want a...
μονο	mono	single...
διπλο	thiplo	double...
δωματιο	domatio	room
για	yia	for...
δυο μερεζ	deo meres	two days
τρειζ μερεζ	tris meres	three days

USEFUL GREEK

i Index

Abbreviations:

Al — Albania, Cy — Cyprus, Eg — Egypt, Isr — Israel, It — Italy, Leb — Lebanon, N Cy — Northern Cyprus, Sy — Syria, Tk — Turkey.

C/F — Car Ferry, C/M — Catamaran, H/F — Hydrofoil, P/S — Passenger Ship, T/B — Tourist Boat or Taxi Boat.

Ferry Names are listed in *Italics*.

Ferry and Island Maps are indicated by **bold** page numbers; Street/Site Maps by <u>**underlined bold**</u> numbers.